ELEMENTS OF Literature

FIFTH COURSE

Literature of the United States *with* Literature of the Americas

For we must consider that
we shall be as a city
upon a hill . . .

— John Winthrop, 1630

HOLT, RINEHART AND WINSTON

A Harcourt Education Company

Austin • Orlando • Chicago • New York • Toronto • London • San Diego

CREDITS

EDITORIAL

Project Director: Kathleen Daniel
Managing Editor: Richard Sime
Senior Book Editors: Thomas F. Hirsch, Patricia McCambridge
Editorial Staff: Ian C. Lague, John Haffner Layden, Ron Ottaviano, Kathryn Rogers, Robert Hoyt, Christopher LeCluyse, Katie Vignery, Victoria Moreland, Marie Hoffman Price, Christy McBride, Michael Neibergall, Karen Kolar
Editorial Support: Laurie Muir, Dan Hunter, Ruth Hooker, Kelly Keeley, Margaret Sanchez
Editorial Permissions: Ann B. Farrar, Sacha Frey, Mark L. Hughs

Research and Development: Joan Burditt

Index: Robert Zolnerzak

PRODUCTION, DESIGN, AND PHOTO RESEARCH

Director: Athena Blackorby
Design Coordinator: Ruth Riley
Program Design: Kirchoff/Wohlberg, Inc.
Electronic Files: Banta Digital
Production: Dolores Keller
Photo Research: Kirchoff/Wohlberg, Inc., Omni Photo-Communications, Inc.
Photo Research Coordinator: Mary Monaco
Manufacturing: RR Donnelley & Sons Company, Willard, Ohio

COVER

Cover Artist: Greg Geisler
Photo Credits: Front cover: (New York), Raphael Macia/Photo Researchers, Inc.; (Boston), Walter Bibikow/FPG International; (Chicago), Nathan Benn/Woodfin Camp & Associates; (Dallas), Dan Budnik/Woodfin Camp & Associates; (Seattle), Porterfield/Chickering/Photo Researchers, Inc.; (Tampa), Ken Briggs/Tony Stone Images; (Providence), Joseph Sohm/Tony Stone Images; (San Francisco), David L. Brown/Nawrocki Stock Photo; (mountain forest), J. Robert Stottlemyer/International Stock; (mountain range), Toyohiro Yamada/FPG International; (sky), Zefa/Index Stock Imagery; (yellow foliage), Chad Ehlers/International Stock; (red foliage), H. Okamoto/Photonica. Back cover: (nautilus), Kathleen Campbell/Tony Stone Images.
Quotation on Cover: From a sermon delivered by John Winthrop, 1630. For a longer extract, see page 2.

Printed in the United States of America
ISBN 0-03-067283-X   6 048 03

PROGRAM AUTHORS

Kylene Beers wrote the Reading Matters section of the book and developed the accompanying *Reading Skills and Strategies* component. A former middle school teacher, Dr. Beers has turned her commitment to helping readers having difficulty into the major focus of her research, writing, speaking, and teaching. A clinical associate professor at the University of Houston, Dr. Beers is also currently the editor of the National Council of Teachers of English journal *Voices from the Middle*. She is the author of *When Kids Can't Read: The Reading Handbook for Teachers Grades 6–12* and co-editor of *Into Focus: Understanding and Creating Middle School Readers*. She has served on the review boards of the *English Journal* and *The ALAN Review*. Dr. Beers is a recipient of the NCTE Richard W. Halle Award. She currently serves on the board of directors of the International Reading Association's Special Interest Group on Adolescent Literature.

Robert E. Probst established the pedagogical framework for the 1997, 2000, and the current editions of *Elements of Literature*. Dr. Probst is Professor of English Education at Georgia State University. He has taught English in Maryland and been Supervisor of English for the Norfolk, Virginia, Public Schools. He is the author of *Response and Analysis: Teaching Literature in Junior and Senior High School* and has contributed chapters to such books as *Literature Instruction: A Focus on Student Response*; *Reader Response in the Classroom*; *Handbook of Research on Teaching the English Language Arts*; *Transactions with Literature*; and *For Louise M. Rosenblatt*. Dr. Probst has worked on the National Council of Teachers of English Committee on Research, the Commission on Reading, and the Commission on Curriculum. He has also served on the board of directors of the Adolescent Literature Assembly and is a member of the National Conference on Research in Language and Literacy.

Robert Anderson wrote the introductions to "Modern Drama" and "William Shakespeare." He also wrote the instructional materials for *The Miracle Worker* and *Romeo and Juliet*. Mr. Anderson is a playwright, novelist, screenwriter, and teacher. His plays include *Tea and Sympathy*; *Silent Night, Lonely Night*; *You Know I Can't Hear You When the Water's Running*; and *I Never Sang for My Father*. His screenplays include *The Nun's Story* and *The Sand Pebbles*. Mr. Anderson has taught at the Writers' Workshop at the University of Iowa, the American Theater Wing Professional Training Program, and the Salzburg Seminar in American Studies. He is a past president of the Dramatists' Guild, a past vice president of the Authors' League of America, and a member of the Theater Hall of Fame.

John Malcolm Brinnin wrote the Elements of Literature essays on poetry, biographies of the poets, and instructional materials on individual poems. Mr. Brinnin is the author of six volumes of poetry, which received many prizes and awards. He was a member of the American Academy and Institute of Arts and Letters. He was also a critic of poetry and a biographer of poets and was for a number of years director of New York's famous Poetry Center. His teaching career, begun at Vassar College, included long terms at the University of Connecticut and Boston University, where he succeeded Robert Lowell as Professor of Creative Writing and Contemporary Letters. Mr. Brinnin's books include *Dylan Thomas in America: An Intimate Journal* and *Sextet: T. S. Eliot & Truman Capote & Others*.

John Leggett wrote the Elements of Literature essays on the short story, biographies of the short-story writers, and instructional materials on individual short stories. Mr. Leggett is a novelist, a biographer, and a former teacher. He went to the Writers' Workshop at the University of Iowa in the spring of 1969, expecting to work there for a single semester. In 1970, he assumed temporary charge of the program, and for the next seventeen years he was its director. Mr. Leggett's novels include *Wilder Stone; The Gloucester Branch; Who Took the Gold Away?; Gulliver House;* and *Making Believe*. He also wrote the highly acclaimed biography *Ross and Tom: Two American Tragedies*.

SPECIAL CONTRIBUTORS

Gary Q. Arpin wrote the introductions to "Beginnings," "American Romanticism," "The American Renaissance," and "The Rise of Realism." He wrote the essays called "The American Language" and biographies of nonfiction writers in the early collections. Dr. Arpin received his doctorate from the University of Virginia, where he taught for several years before taking a position with Western Illinois University at Macomb. He has written articles on John Berryman and other American poets and has published a book, *John Berryman: A Reference Guide.*

Joseph Bruchac wrote the essay "The Sun Still Rises in the Same Sky: Native American Literatures." Mr. Bruchac is a professional storyteller and author inspired by his American Indian heritage and the Adirondack region where he lives. His work has appeared in more than five hundred publications, including the *American Poetry Review* and *National Geographic.* He has written more than sixty books for adults and children. His awards include the Cherokee Nation Prose Award, the Hope S. Dean Award for Notable Achievement in Children's Literature, and the Benjamin Franklin Award as "Person of the Year" by the Publishers' Marketing Association.

Thomas Hernacki co-authored the introduction to "Contemporary Literature" and wrote instructional material for some fiction and poetry. Dr. Hernacki is an educational writer specializing in modern and contemporary literature, particularly American poetry. A native of Chicago, he holds a doctorate in English from Columbia University. His dissertation explores "the poetics of place" in the works of Wallace Stevens. In the 1970s, he contributed to Northrop Frye's archetype-based literature series, *Uses of the Imagination.* Over the past two decades Dr. Hernacki has directed the editorial development of numerous literature and composition textbooks for secondary schools.

Susan Allen Toth co-authored the introduction to "Contemporary Literature" and wrote biographies and instructional material for contemporary nonfiction writers. Dr. Toth has written *Blooming: A Small-Town Girlhood,* about her childhood in Ames, Iowa; *Ivy Days: Making My Way Out East,* about her experiences at Smith College in Northampton, Massachusetts; and *How to Prepare for Your High-School Reunion and Other Mid-Life Musings.* She studied at the University of California at Berkeley and received her doctorate from the University of Minnesota. She is an adjunct professor and writer-in-residence at Macalester College in St. Paul, Minnesota. She contributes articles to many periodicals, including *Harper's, Redbook, McCall's,* and *The New York Times.*

WRITERS

The writers prepared instructional materials for the text under the supervision of Dr. Probst and the editorial staff.

Richard Cohen
Former Teacher
Novelist
Educational Writer and Editor
Austin, Texas

Jan Freeman
Poet
Educational Writer and Editor
Williamsburg, Massachusetts

Phyllis Goldenberg
Educational Writer and Editor
North Miami Beach, Florida

Lynn Hovland
Former Teacher
Educational Writer and Editor
Berkeley, California

Rose Sallberg Kam
Former Teacher
Educational Writer and Editor
Sacramento, California

Carroll Moulton
Former Teacher
Educational Writer and Editor
Southampton, New York

Susanna Nied
Former Teacher
Educational Writer and Editor
San Diego, California

Eileen Hillary Oshinsky
Educational Writer and Editor
Rhinebeck, New York

Mary Elizabeth Podhaizer
Former Teacher
Educational Writer and Editor
Colchester, Vermont

Gerry Tomlinson
Educational Writer and Editor
Lake Hopatcong, New Jersey

Joan Clark Tornow
Teacher
Austin, Texas

Sarah Wolbach
Educational Writer and Editor
Austin, Texas

REVIEWERS AND CONSULTANTS

The reviewers evaluated selections and/or instructional materials. Consultants provided advice on current pedagogy.

Elizabeth Aston-Sullivan
Crockett High School
Austin, Texas

Maura Casey
Skyline High School
Oakland, California

Eula Course
Scarborough High School
Houston, Texas

Joan M. Crimmins
Frank Scott Bunnell High School
Stratford, Connecticut

Barbara Freiberg
University Laboratory School,
 LSU
Baton Rouge, Louisiana

Glenda Johnson
Pine Tree Independent School
 District
Longview, Texas

Dan Leary
John Marshall High School
Cleveland, Ohio

Allison Madsen
Muncie Central High School
Muncie, Indiana

Elizabeth McGonigal
Round Rock High School
Round Rock, Texas

Maria Christina Reyna
Mission High School
Mission, Texas

Erma Richter
Port Neches-Groves High School
Port Neches, Texas

Marilyn Schroer
Fort Walton Beach High School
Fort Walton Beach, Florida

Carol Seacrist
Princess Anne High School
Virginia Beach, Virginia

Dr. Larry Stuber
Valparaiso High School
Valparaiso, Indiana

Anthony Ucciardo
Ford City High School
Ford City, Pennsylvania

Sarah Ann Wider
Colgate University
Hamilton, New York

John R. Williamson
Johnson Central Senior High
 School
Paintsville, Kentucky

Noretta M. Willig
Baldwin High School
Pittsburgh, Pennsylvania

Junko Yokota
National-Louis University
Evanston, Illinois

FIELD-TEST PARTICIPANTS

The following teachers participated in field-testing of prepublication materials for the series.

Janet Blackburn-Lewis
Western Guilford High
 School
Greensboro, North Carolina

Dana E. Bull
F. J. Turner High School
Beloit, Wisconsin

Maura Casey
Skyline High School
Oakland, California

Deborah N. Dean
Warner Robins Middle School
Warner Robins, Georgia

Gloria J. Dolesh
Friendly High School
Fort Washington, Maryland

Christina Donnelly
Parkdale High School
Riverdale, Maryland

Kay T. Dunlap
Norview High School
Norfolk, Virginia

Joseph Fitzgibbon
West Linn High School
West Linn, Oregon

Paul Garro
Taft High School
San Antonio, Texas

Suzanne Haffamier
Agoura High School
Agoura, California

Robert K. Jordan
Land O'Lakes High School
Land O'Lakes, Florida

Terry Juhl
Bella Vista High School
Fair Oaks, California

Elizabeth Keister
Blair Middle School
Norfolk, Virginia

Jane S. Kilgore
Warner Robins High School
Warner Robins, Georgia

Janet S. King
Reading High School
Reading, Pennsylvania

Cheryl L. Lambert
Milford Mill Academy
Baltimore, Maryland

Sarah A. Long
Robert Goddard Middle School
Seabrook, Maryland

Donna J. Magrum
Rogers High School
Toledo, Ohio

Nancy Maheras
Western High School
Las Vegas, Nevada

Mara Malone
Central High School
Baton Rouge, Louisiana

Margaret E. McKinnon
Roger L. Putnam Vocational-
Technical High School
Springfield, Massachusetts

Lourdes J. Medina
Pat Neff Middle School
San Antonio, Texas

Joan Mohon
Todd County Central High
 School
Elkton, Kentucky

Terrence R. Moore
John Muir High School
Pasadena, California

Gayle C. Morey
Countryside High School
Clearwater, Florida

Beverly Mudd
Western High School
Las Vegas, Nevada

Jan Nichols
Apollo High School
Glendale, Arizona

Jeffrey S. Norton
Lewis and Clark High
 School
Spokane, Washington

Barbara Powell
Todd County Central High
 School
Elkton, Kentucky

Gloria S. Pridmore
Morrow High School
Morrow, Georgia

Dee Richardson
Moore High School
Moore, Oklahoma

Carole A. Scala
Southwest Middle School
Orlando, Florida

Barbara A. Slaughter
Lewis and Clark High School
Spokane, Washington

Barbara B. Smith
Dr. Phillips 9th-Grade Center
Orlando, Florida

Sister Eileen Stephens, CSJ
Cathedral Preparatory Seminary
Elmhurst, New York

Sally Thompson
Andrew Jackson Middle School
Suitland, Maryland

Blanca M. Valledor
G. Holmes Braddock Senior
 High School
Miami, Florida

Charla J. Walton
John C. Fremont Junior High
 School
Las Vegas, Nevada

William Ward
Roger L. Putnam Vocational-
Technical High School
Springfield, Massachusetts

Lynn White
Tascosa High School
Amarillo, Texas

Noretta M. Willig
Baldwin High School
Pittsburgh, Pennsylvania

Deborah K. Woelflein
Merrimack High School
Merrimack, New Hampshire

CONTENTS IN BRIEF

Beginnings to 1800

Collection 1: Visions and Voyages

Collection 2: The Examined Life

Collection 3: The American Dream

COMMUNICATIONS WORKSHOPS
Writer's Workshop: Narrative: Autobiographical Incident
Language Workshop: Linking: Coordinating Conjunctions
Reading for Life: Monitoring Your Reading
Learning for Life: Researching the Immigrant Experience

American Romanticism

Collection 4: The Transforming Imagination

COMMUNICATIONS WORKSHOPS
Writer's Workshop: Exposition: Analyzing a Literary Work
Language Workshop: Smoothing It Out: Inserting Modifiers
Reading for Life: Reading Maps
Learning for Life: Environmental Concerns

The American Renaissance

Collection 5: The Life Worth Living

Collection 6: The Realms of Darkness

COMMUNICATIONS WORKSHOPS
Writer's Workshop: Persuasion: Controversial Issue
Language Workshop: Balance: Parallel Structure
Reading for Life: Evaluating Credibility of Sources
Learning for Life: A Model of Self-Reliance

A New American Poetry

Collection 7: The Large Hearts of Heroes

Collection 8: Tell It Slant

COMMUNICATIONS WORKSHOPS
Writer's Workshop: Exposition: Comparison-and-Contrast Essay
Language Workshop: Variety: Varying Sentence Beginnings
Reading for Life: Reading a Textbook
Learning for Life: The Changing World of Work

The Rise of Realism

Collection 9: Shackles

Collection 10: From Innocence to Experience

COMMUNICATIONS WORKSHOPS
Writer's Workshop: Exposition: Research Paper
Language Workshop: Appropriate Additions: Adverb and Adjective Clauses
Reading for Life: Reading a College Guide
Learning for Life: Monitoring the Media

The Moderns
1900–1950

Collection 11: Loss and Redemption

Collection 12: The Dream and the Reality

Collection 13: No Time for Heroes

COMMUNICATIONS WORKSHOPS
Writer's Workshop: Exposition: Analyzing Causes and Effects
Language Workshop: Relationships: Using Subordinating Conjunctions
Reading for Life: Interpreting and Constructing a Graphic Organizer

Collection 14: Shadows of the Past

Collection 15: I, Too, Sing America

Collection 16: Make It New!

COMMUNICATIONS WORKSHOPS
Writer's Workshop: Exposition: Interpretive Essay
Language Workshop: The Right Tense for Sense: Using the Literary Present
Reading for Life: Obtaining Information from an Internet Database
Learning for Life: Planning for the Future

American Drama

Collection 17: The Breaking of Charity

COMMUNICATIONS WORKSHOPS
Writer's Workshop: Persuasion: Problem-Solution Essay
Language Workshop: Fitting It All Together: Using Transitional Expressions
Reading for Life: Reading a Film Review
Learning for Life: Evaluating Play Choices

Contemporary Literature

Collection 18: The Wages of War

Collection 19: Discoveries and Awakenings

Collection 20: From Generation to Generation

Collection 21: The Created Self

COMMUNICATIONS WORKSHOPS
Writer's Workshop: Persuasion: Evaluation
Language Workshop: Words to the Wise: Using Effective Diction
Reading for Life: Reading Memoranda
Learning for Life: State of the Arts: Celebrating Cultural Diversity

Resource Center

Handbook of Literary Terms
Communications Handbook
Language Handbook
Glossary

CONTENTS

Reading Matters   xxxiv
Test Smarts   xlvi

■ **Maps**
   United States lvi–lvii
   United States Eastern Seaboard lviii
   Central and South America lvix

Beginnings to 1800

Beginnings *by* Gary Q. Arpin 2

Time Line 4

■ **A Closer Look**
   The Salem Witchcraft Trials 10

Collection 1
Visions and Voyages

The Journey *by* Mary Oliver . . . . POEM 19	

■ **Literature of the Americas** North America
The Sun Still Rises in the Same Sky:
   Native American Literature *by* Joseph Bruchac 20

Huron–Eastern
Woodland Traditional   **The Sky Tree** *retold by* Joseph Bruchac . . . . MYTH 22
Teton Sioux Traditional   **The Earth Only** *retold by* Used-As-A-Shield . . . . MYTH 23
Navajo Traditional   *from* **The House Made of Dawn** *translated by*
                     Washington Matthews . . . . CHANT 23
Nez Percé Traditional   **Coyote Finishes His Work** *retold by* Barry Lopez . . . MYTH 24

William Bradford 26   *from* **Of Plymouth Plantation** . . . . HISTORY 27

Anthony Lewis   **An American Story** / Connections . . . . NEWS FEATURE 34

                     ■ **Elements of Literature**   The Plain Style 35

                     ■ **Reading Skills and Strategies**
                     When a Dictionary Can Help. 37

Mary Rowlandson 38   *from* **A Narrative of the Captivity**. . . . . PERSONAL NARRATIVE . . 39
                     Literature and History / Captivity Narratives 42

                     The Southern Planters 48
William Byrd 49   *from* **The History of the Dividing Line** . . . . HISTORY 50

Olaudah Equiano 56 from **The Interesting Narrative of the Life of Olaudah Equiano** .... AUTOBIOGRAPHY 57

Africa *by* Doretha Williams / Student to Student ...... CONCRETE POEM 65

Collection 2

The Examined Life

from **Invisible Man** *by* Ralph Ellison 67

Anne Bradstreet 68 **Here Follow Some Verses upon the Burning of Our House, July 10, 1666** .... POEM 69

Edward Taylor 72 **Huswifery** .... POEM 73

■ **Elements of Literature   The Conceit** 74

■ **Literature of the Americas** Mexico

Sor Juana Inés de la Cruz 75 **World, in Hounding Me . . .** *translated from the Spanish by* Alan S. Trueblood .... POEM 76

En perseguirme, mundo . . . . POEMA 76

Jonathan Edwards 77 *from* **Sinners in the Hands of an Angry God** ... SERMON 79

Primary Sources / Sarah Pierrepont *and* My Sense of Divine Things *by* Jonathan Edwards .... JOURNALS 82

Benjamin Franklin 84 *from* **The Autobiography** .... AUTOBIOGRAPHY 85

Literature and Science / Time on His Side: Benjamin Banneker 90

Spotlight On / Sayings of Poor Richard *by* Benjamin Franklin 95

Robert Fulghum *from* **All I Really Need to Know I Learned in Kindergarten** / Connections .... ESSAY 96

Collection 3

The American Dream

Concord Hymn *by* Ralph Waldo Emerson .... POEM 99

Patrick Henry 100 **Speech to the Virginia Convention** .... POLITICAL SPEECH ... 101

Thomas Paine 106 *from* **The Crisis, No. 1** .... POLITICAL ESSAY 107

Spotlight On / Phillis Wheatley: A Revolutionary Woman 113

Thomas Jefferson 114 *from* **The Autobiography: The Declaration of Independence** .... AUTOBIOGRAPHY 115

Literature and Politics / Legacy of Peace and Unity: The Iroquois Constitution 120

Primary Sources / A Letter from Jefferson to
  His Daughter...................................LETTER...........124

Read On 126
The American Language "Revolutionary" English *by*
  Gary Q. Arpin 127

COMMUNICATIONS WORKSHOPS

Writer's Workshop Narrative Writing: Autobiographical Incident	130
Language Workshop Linking It Up: Coordinating Conjunctions	133
Reading for Life Monitoring Your Reading	134
Learning for Life Researching the Immigrant Experience	135

American Romanticism
1800–1860

American Romanticism *by* Gary Q. Arpin 138

Time Line 140

■ **A Closer Look**
  The City, Grim and Gray 142

Collection 4
The Transforming Imagination

	A Blessing *by* James Wright ....POEM..............151		
Washington Irving 152	**Rip Van Winkle** ....SHORT STORY.......153		
	Literature and Folklore / Enchanted Slumbers 162		
	■ **Reading Skills and Strategies**		
	Vocabulary: Using Context Clues 168		
William Cullen Bryant 169	**Thanatopsis** ....POEM..............170		
Derek Walcott	**Sea Canes** / Connections ....POEM..............173		
Henry Wadsworth Longfellow 175	**The Tide Rises, the Tide Falls** ....POEM..............176		
	The Cross of Snow ....POEM..............178		
	■ **Elements of Literature** **The Sonnet** 180		
John Greenleaf Whittier 181	*from* **Snow-Bound: A Winter Idyll** ....POEM..............182		

Oliver Wendell Holmes 187

The Chambered Nautilus . . . . POEM 188
Old Ironsides . . . . POEM 190
The Sea *by* Elizabeth Enloe / Student to Student . . . . POEM 192

Read On 194
The American Language "Noah's Ark": Webster's
   Dictionary *by* Gary Q. Arpin 195

COMMUNICATIONS WORKSHOPS

Writer's Workshop Expository Writing: Analyzing a Literary Work   198

Language Workshop Smoothing It Out: Inserting Modifiers   201

Reading for Life Reading Maps   202

Learning for Life Environmental Concerns   203

The American Renaissance
A Literary Coming of Age 1840–1860

The American Renaissance: A Literary Coming of Age *by* Gary Q. Arpin 206

■ **A Closer Look**
   That Was Then . . . 210

Collection 5
The Life Worth Living

from **Gift from the Sea** *by* Anne Morrow Lindbergh 215

Ralph Waldo Emerson 216   *from* **Nature** . . . . ESSAY 218

Spotlight On / Emerson's Aphorisms 222

Primary Sources / Hawthorne Talks About Emerson . . . ESSAY 223
from **Self-Reliance** . . . . ESSAY 224
Literature and Society / Onward to Utopia 226
Imagination *by* Shelby Pearl / Student to Student . . . . . . ESSAY 227

Henry David Thoreau 230   *from* **Walden, or Life in the Woods** . . . . AUTOBIOGRAPHY 232

Don Henley   *from* **Heaven Is Under Our Feet** / Connections . . . ESSAY 245

Henry David Thoreau   *from* **Resistance to Civil Government** . . . . ESSAY 248
Primary Sources / "A Healthy and Wholesome Man
   to Know" *by* Nathaniel Hawthorne *and*
   Sophia Peabody Hawthorne . . . . JOURNALS 255

Martin Luther King, Jr.   *from* **Letter from Birmingham City Jail** /
   Connections . . . . LETTER 256

Collection 6

The Realms of Darkness

from **The Night Country** *by* Loren Eiseley 259

Edgar Allan Poe 260 **The Fall of the House of Usher** . . . . SHORT STORY 262
Literature and Popular Culture / Poe the Pop Icon 261
Literature and Popular Culture / The Gothic Tradition 274

Reed Whittemore **The Fall of the House of Usher** / Connections . . . POEM 279

■ **Elements of Literature   Poe's Symbols** 280

Edgar Allan Poe **The Raven** . . . . POEM 282
Primary Sources / Poe's Process: Writing "The Raven"
by Edgar Allan Poe . . . . ESSAY 287

■ **Literature of the Americas** Argentina
Julio Cortázar 290 **House Taken Over** *translated from the Spanish by*
Paul Blackburn . . . . SHORT STORY 290

Nathaniel Hawthorne 296 **The Minister's Black Veil** . . . . SHORT STORY 298

■ **Reading Skills and Strategies**
Vocabulary: Tracing the Origins of Words 310

Herman Melville 311 *from* **Moby-Dick** . . . . NOVEL 313

Read On 330

COMMUNICATIONS WORKSHOPS

Writer's Workshop Persuasive Writing: Controversial Issue | 331

Language Workshop Keeping It in Balance: Parallel Structure | 337

Reading for Life Evaluating Credibility of Sources | 338

Learning for Life A Model of Self-Reliance | 339

A New American Poetry
Whitman and Dickinson

A New American Poetry: Whitman and Dickinson *by* John Malcolm Brinnin 342

Collection 7

The Large Hearts of Heroes

from **Song of Myself** *by* Walt Whitman . . . . POEM 347

Walt Whitman *348* **I Hear America Singing** . . . . POEM 351
from **Song of Myself**
   10. Alone far in the wilds . . . . POEM 353

■ **Elements of Literature   Free Verse** 355

from **33. I understand the large**
   hearts of heroes . . . . POEM 356
52. The spotted hawk swoops by . . . . POEM 359

Jimmy Santiago Baca **Who Understands Me but Me** / Connections . . . . POEM 360

Walt Whitman **A Sight in Camp in the Daybreak**
   Gray and Dim . . . . POEM 362
Primary Sources / *from* Specimen Days
   by Walt Whitman . . . . JOURNAL 363

■ **Literature of the Americas** Chile
Pablo Neruda *367* **Plenos Poderes** . . . . POEMA 368
Full Powers *translated from the Spanish by*
   Ben Belitt *and* Alastair Reid . . . . POEM 368

Collection 8

Tell It Slant

Emily Dickinson *by* Linda Pastan . . . . POEM 371

Emily Dickinson *372* **Heart! We will forget him!** . . . . POEM 374
If you were coming in the Fall . . . . POEM 376
Primary Sources / If you were coming in the Fall . . . . . . EDITED POEM 377
The Soul selects her own Society . . . . POEM 378

■ **Elements of Literature   Slant Rhyme** 380

The Mirror Girl—stares back at me *by* Brigid Spackman /
   Student to Student . . . . POEM 380
Some keep the Sabbath going to Church . . . . . POEM 381
I taste a liquor never brewed . . . . POEM 382

	Much Madness is divinest Sense . . . . POEM. 383
	Apparently with no surprise . . . . POEM. 385
	Tell all the Truth but tell it slant . . . . POEM. 386
	Success is counted sweetest . . . . POEM. 388

Anne Bernays **Emily Dickinson's Homestead** / Connections . . . MAGAZINE ARTICLE. . . 389

Emily Dickinson **Because I could not stop for Death** . . . . POEM. 391
I heard a Fly buzz—when I died . . . . POEM. 392
I died for Beauty—but was scarce . . . . POEM. 393

Primary Sources / "I sing . . . because I am afraid"
by Thomas Wentworth Higginson . . . . LETTER 394

Read On 397
The American Language A Period of Vocabulary
Growth *by* Gary Q. Arpin 398

COMMUNICATIONS WORKSHOPS

Writer's Workshop Expository Writing:
Comparison-and-Contrast Essay   401

Language Workshop Variety Is the Spice: Varying Sentence Beginnings   403

Reading for Life Reading a Textbook   404

Learning for Life The Changing World of Work   405

The Rise of Realism
The Civil War and Postwar Period 1850–1900

The Rise of Realism: The Civil War and Postwar Period *by* Gary Q. Arpin 408

Time Line 410

■ **A Closer Look**
  Eyes of an Era 414

Collection 9
Shackles

My Guilt *by* Maya Angelou. . . . . POEM. 423

Frederick Douglass 424 from **The Narrative of the Life of
    Frederick Douglass** . . . . AUTOBIOGRAPHY 425

Spotlight On / Spirituals and Code Songs *by* Frederick Douglass 432

Kate Chopin 435   **A Pair of Silk Stockings** . . . . SHORT STORY 437
Literature and History / Elegant Discomfort 440
Primary Sources / *Vogue Stories* by Emily Toth . . . . BIOGRAPHY 443

Pat Mora   **Now and Then, America** / Connections . . . . POEM 444

Spotlight On / American Indian Oratory
"For More Than a Hundred Winters . . ." *by* Black Hawk 446
"I Will Fight No More Forever" *by* Chief Joseph 448

Collection 10

From Innocence to Experience

Shiloh *by* Herman Melville . . . . POEM 449

Mark Twain 450   *from* **Life on the Mississippi** . . . . MEMOIR 452
Literature and Folklore / The Lure and Lore
of the Mississippi 458

Spotlight On / Mark Twain's Humor 465

Ambrose Bierce 466   **An Occurrence at Owl Creek Bridge** . . . . SHORT STORY 467

■ **Reading Skills and Strategies**
Vocabulary: Affixes—The Long and Short of It 475

Spotlight On / Voices from the Civil War *by* Theodore Upson,
Walt Whitman, Major Sullivan Ballou, Alexander Hunter,
Abraham Lincoln, Susie King Taylor, Frederick Douglass,
Mary Chesnut, *and* Seth M. Flint 476

Stephen Crane 484   **A Mystery of Heroism** . . . . SHORT STORY 487
What About Glory *by* Pindar VanArman /
Student to Student . . . . POEM 493
War Is Kind . . . . POEM 494

Jack London 495   **To Build a Fire** . . . . SHORT STORY 496

Paul G. Gill, Jr., M.D.   **Cold Kills: Hypothermia** / Connections . . . . MAGAZINE ARTICLE. . . 508

Read On 511
The American Language American Dialects
by Gary Q. Arpin 512

COMMUNICATIONS WORKSHOPS

Writer's Workshop Expository Writing: Research Paper   515

Language Workshop Appropriate Additions:
Adverb and Adjective Clauses   519

Reading for Life Reading a College Guide   520

Learning for Life Monitoring the Media   521

The Moderns 1900–1950

The Moderns by John Leggett *and* John Malcolm Brinnin 524

Time Line 526

■ **A Closer Look**
    The Best of Times, the Worst of Times 528

Collection 11

Loss and Redemption

	from **Knoxville: Summer 1915** *by* James Agee		537
Willa Cather 538	**A Wagner Matinée**	SHORT STORY	539
Thomas Wolfe 548	**His Father's Earth**	SHORT STORY	549
Robert Frost 558	Primary Sources / Frost on Frost's Diction	REMINISCENCE	559
	Design	POEM	560
	Nothing Gold Can Stay	POEM	562
Naomi Shihab Nye	**Trying to Name What Doesn't Change /**		
	Connections	POEM	563
Robert Frost	**Once by the Pacific**	POEM	564
	Neither Out Far Nor In Deep	POEM	565
	Birches	POEM	567
	The Death of the Hired Man	POEM	569
	Primary Sources / "I must have the pulse beat of rhythm. . . ." *by* Robert Frost	INTERVIEW	574

■ **Reading Skills and Strategies**
    Understanding Blank Verse 575

John Crowe Ransom 577	**Bells for John Whiteside's Daughter**	POEM	577
Robinson Jeffers 580	**Shine, Perishing Republic**	POEM	580

Collection 12

The Dream and the Reality

	from **Absolution** *by* F. Scott Fitzgerald		583
F. Scott Fitzgerald 584	**Winter Dreams**	SHORT STORY	586
	Primary Sources / A Letter to His Daughter *by* F. Scott Fitzgerald		603

John Steinbeck 606   **The Leader of the People** . . . . SHORT STORY 607
Literature and Film / The West and Its Mythmakers 616
Primary Sources / Nobel Prize Acceptance
    Speech, 1962 *by* John Steinbeck . . . . SPEECH 620

James Thurber 623   **The Secret Life of Walter Mitty** . . . . SHORT STORY 624
Primary Sources / *The New Yorker's* Farewell
    by E. B. White . . . . ESSAY 629

Charles M. Schulz   **Peanuts** / Connections . . . . CARTOON 630

Eudora Welty 633   **A Worn Path** . . . . SHORT STORY 634
Primary Sources / "Is Phoenix Jackson's Grandson
    Really Dead?" *by* Eudora Welty . . . . ESSAY 640

Collection 13

No Time for Heroes

The Explorer *by* Gwendolyn Brooks . . . . POEM 643

Edwin Arlington
Robinson 644   **Richard Cory** . . . . POEM 645
Miniver Cheevy . . . . POEM 646
Primary Sources / Robinson's Ruminations . . . . LETTERS 648

Ernest Hemingway 650   **Soldier's Home** . . . . SHORT STORY 652
Literature and Popular Culture / The Decade
    That Roared 656
Primary Sources / Nobel Prize Acceptance
    Speech, 1954 *by* Ernest Hemingway . . . . SPEECH 659

T. S. Eliot 661   **The Love Song of J. Alfred Prufrock** . . . . POEM 663
Critical Comment / The Oddest Love Song 667

John Malcolm Brinnin   from **Mr. Eliot, I Presume** / Connections . . . . BIOGRAPHY 668

Flannery O'Connor 672   **The Life You Save May Be Your Own** . . . . SHORT STORY 673
Primary Sources / The Adventures of Mr. Shiftlet
    by Flannery O'Connor . . . . LETTERS 682

■ **Elements of Literature   The Four "Modes" of Fiction** 683

COMMUNICATIONS WORKSHOPS

Writer's Workshop Expository Writing: Analyzing Causes and Effects   685

Language Workshop Showing Relationships: Using Subordinating
    Conjunctions   689

Reading for Life Interpreting and Constructing a Graphic Organizer   690

Collection 14

Shadows of the Past

Fall *by* Jimmy Santiago Baca . . . . POEM 691

Edgar Lee Masters 692   **Richard Bone** . . . . POEM 692
Primary Sources / The Genesis of Spoon River
     by Edgar Lee Masters . . . . AUTOBIOGRAPHY 693
"Butch" Weldy . . . . POEM 694
Fiddler Jones . . . . POEM 694
Petit, the Poet . . . . POEM 695
Mrs. George Reece . . . . POEM 695

Edna St. Vincent Millay 697   **Recuerdo** . . . . POEM 698
Primary Sources / "The brawny male sends his picture"
     by Edna St. Vincent Millay . . . . LETTER 700

Katherine Anne Porter 702   **The Jilting of Granny Weatherall** . . . . SHORT STORY 703

Conrad Aiken   *from* **Discordants** / Connections . . . . POEM 711

William Faulkner 713   **A Rose for Emily** . . . . SHORT STORY 715
Primary Sources / Nobel Prize Acceptance Speech, 1950
     by William Faulkner . . . . SPEECH 723

■ **Reading Skills and Strategies**
     Vocabulary: Semantic Features Analysis 726

■ **Literature of the Americas** Uruguay
Horacio Quiroga 727   **The Feather Pillow** *translated from the Spanish*
     by Margaret Sayers Peden . . . . SHORT STORY 728

Literature and Popular Culture / Reader Beware!
     Urban Legends We Hope Aren't True 732

Collection 15

I, Too, Sing America
The Harlem Renaissance

I, Too *by* Langston Hughes . . . . POEM 733

The Harlem Renaissance 734

James Weldon Johnson 736   **Go Down, Death** . . . . POEM 737
Primary Sources / God's Trombones
     by James Weldon Johnson . . . . PREFACE 740

Gwendolyn Brooks   **of De Witt Williams on his way to Lincoln
     Cemetery** / Connections . . . . POEM 741

Claude McKay 743   **America** . . . . POEM. 744

Countee Cullen 746   **Tableau** . . . . POEM. 747

Incident . . . . POEM. 748

Zora Neale Hurston 750   from **Dust Tracks on a Road** . . . . MEMOIR. 751

Primary Sources / In Search of a Story
by Zora Neale Hurston . . . . AUTOBIOGRAPHY 758

Langston Hughes 760   **The Weary Blues** . . . . POEM. 761

Literature and Music / Birth of the Blues. 763

Harlem . . . . POEM. 764

Primary Sources / Heyday in Harlem
by Langston Hughes . . . . ESSAY. 766

Collection 16

Make It New!

"Make it new! Art is a joyous thing." by Ezra Pound 769

Symbolism, Imagism, and Beyond by John Malcolm Brinnin 770

Ezra Pound 773   **The River-Merchant's Wife: A Letter** . . . . POEM. 774

Primary Sources / A Few Don'ts by an Imagiste
by Ezra Pound . . . . ARTICLE. 776

■ **Elements of Literature** **The Objective Correlative** 777

William Carlos Williams 778   **The Red Wheelbarrow** . . . . POEM. 779

Critical Comment / So Much Depends 779

The Great Figure . . . . POEM. 780

Primary Sources / Williams Talks About Poetry . . . . AUTOBIOGRAPHY 780

Spring and All . . . . POEM. 781

Wallace Stevens 783   **Anecdote of the Jar** . . . . POEM. 784

Disillusionment of Ten O'Clock . . . . POEM. 784

Critical Comment / Taking Dominion, Catching Tigers. 785

Primary Sources / Notebooks by Wallace Stevens 786

Marianne Moore 787   **Poetry**. . . . . POEM. 787

Archibald MacLeish   **Ars Poetica** / Connections . . . . POEM. 789

Wallace Stevens   **Of Modern Poetry** / Connections . . . . POEM. 790

Carl Sandburg 792   **Chicago** . . . . POEM. 792

E. E. Cummings 796   **what if a much of a which of a wind** . . . . POEM. 797

Primary Sources / "Miracles are to come"
by E. E. Cummings. . . . . PREFACE 797

somewhere i have never travelled,
gladly beyond . . . . POEM. 798

Read On 800

The American Language American Slang
   by Gary Q. Arpin 801

COMMUNICATIONS WORKSHOPS

Writer's Workshop Expository Writing: Interpretive Essay   804

Language Workshop The Right Tense for Sense:
  Using the Literary Present   807

Reading for Life Obtaining Information from an Internet Database   808

Learning for Life Planning for the Future   809

American Drama

American Drama *by* Robert Anderson 812

Collection 17

The Breaking of Charity

"In a sense I went naked to Salem. . . ."
   by Arthur Miller 825

Arthur Miller 826   **The Crucible** . . . . DRAMA 828
Why I Wrote *The Crucible* by Arthur Miller . . . . ESSAY 827

  ■ **Reading Skills and Strategies**
   Vocabulary: Doing Analogies 890

Read On 891

The American Language Euphemisms
   by Gary Q. Arpin 892

COMMUNICATIONS WORKSHOPS

Writer's Workshop Persuasive Writing: Problem-Solution Essay   895

Language Workshop Fitting It All Together:
  Using Transitional Expressions   899

Reading for Life Reading a Film Review   900

Learning for Life Evaluating Play Choices   901

Contemporary Literature 1950 to Present

Contemporary Literature *by* John Leggett, Susan Allen Toth,
John Malcolm Brinnin, *and* Thomas Hernacki 904

Time Line 906

■ **A Closer Look**
  Atomic Anxiety 908

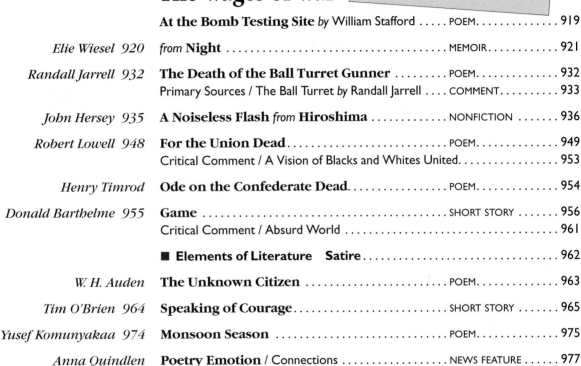

Collection 18

The Wages of War

	At the Bomb Testing Site *by* William Stafford ..... POEM 919
Elie Wiesel 920	*from* **Night** .... MEMOIR 921
Randall Jarrell 932	**The Death of the Ball Turret Gunner** .... POEM 932
	Primary Sources / The Ball Turret *by* Randall Jarrell .... COMMENT 933
John Hersey 935	**A Noiseless Flash** *from* **Hiroshima** .... NONFICTION 936
Robert Lowell 948	**For the Union Dead** .... POEM 949
	Critical Comment / A Vision of Blacks and Whites United 953
Henry Timrod	**Ode on the Confederate Dead** .... POEM 954
Donald Barthelme 955	**Game** .... SHORT STORY 956
	Critical Comment / Absurd World 961
	■ **Elements of Literature** **Satire** 962
W. H. Auden	**The Unknown Citizen** .... POEM 963
Tim O'Brien 964	**Speaking of Courage** .... SHORT STORY 965
Yusef Komunyakaa 974	**Monsoon Season** .... POEM 975
Anna Quindlen	**Poetry Emotion** / Connections .... NEWS FEATURE 977

Collection 19

Discoveries and Awakenings

Pine Tree Tops by Gary Snyder . . . . POEM 979

Bernard Malamud 980   **The Magic Barrel** . . . . SHORT STORY 981
Critical Comment / A Tale of Self-Discovery 993

■ **Literature of the Americas**   Colombia

Gabriel García Márquez 995   **The Handsomest Drowned Man in the World**
translated from the Spanish by Gregory Rabassa . . . . . . SHORT STORY 996

Theodore Roethke 1001   **Elegy for Jane** . . . . POEM 1002
Night Journey . . . . POEM 1003

Richard Wilbur 1005   **The Beautiful Changes** . . . . POEM 1006
Boy at the Window . . . . POEM 1007

Karl Shapiro 1009   **Auto Wreck** . . . . POEM 1010

Richard Wright 1012   *from* **Black Boy** . . . . AUTOBIOGRAPHY . . . 1013

Raymond Carver 1026   **Everything Stuck to Him** . . . . SHORT STORY 1027
Primary Sources / "Paddlewheel of Days"
by Raymond Carver . . . . INTERVIEW 1032

Elizabeth Bishop 1034   **The Fish** . . . . POEM 1035

Joy Harjo 1039   **Remember** . . . . POEM 1040

Maxine Hong Kingston 1043   **The Girl Who Wouldn't Talk** *from*
The Woman Warrior . . . . MEMOIR 1044
Literature and Society / The Chinese American Family 1050

William Least
Heat-Moon 1054   *from* **Blue Highways** . . . . TRAVEL WRITING . . . 1055

James Agee   *from* **Let Us Now Praise Famous Men** /
Connections . . . . ESSAY 1064

Collection 20

From Generation to Generation

Speaking by Simon J. Ortiz . . . . POEM 1067

John Updike 1068   **Son** . . . . SHORT STORY 1069

Anne Tyler   *from* **"Still Just Writing"** / Connections . . . . ESSAY 1074

Julia Alvarez 1076   **Daughter of Invention** . . . . SHORT STORY 1077
Literature and Technology / Patently American Inventions 1084

Anne Sexton 1088   **The Bells** . . . . POEM 1089
Young . . . . POEM 1090

N. Scott Momaday 1092   *from* **The Way to Rainy Mountain** . . . . MEMOIR 1093

Alice Walker 1101 *from* **In Search of Our Mothers' Gardens** ...... ESSAY 1102

Amy Tan 1109 *from* **Rules of the Game** *from* **The Joy Luck Club**... SHORT STORY...... 1110
Primary Sources / An Interview with Amy Tan....................... 1118

■ **Reading Skills and Strategies**
Vocabulary: Base Words, Roots, and Word Families................. 1120

Garrett
Hongo 1121 **What For** .... POEM 1122
Primary Sources / A Different Story *by*
Garrett Hongo.. ESSAY 1125

Collection 21

The Created Self

Autobiographia Literaria *by* Frank O'Hara ...... POEM 1127

Andrea Lee 1128 **New African** .... SHORT STORY...... 1129
James Baldwin 1141 **Autobiographical Notes**..................... AUTOBIOGRAPHY... 1142

Toni Morrison *from* **On James Baldwin** / Connections .... EULOGY 1146

Sylvia Plath 1148 **Mirror**..................................... POEM 1149
Mushrooms .... POEM 1150

■ **Literature of the Americas** Argentina
Jorge Luis Borges 1152 **Borges and Myself** *translated from the*
Spanish by Norman Thomas di Giovanni *and*
Jorge Luis Borges........................... FICTION 1152

James Dickey 1155 **The Lifeguard** .... POEM 1156
Sandra Cisneros 1158 **Straw into Gold**............................. ESSAY 1159
Judith Ortiz Cofer 1166 **The Latin Deli: An Ars Poetica**................ POEM 1167
Rita Dove 1170 **The Satisfaction Coal Company** .... POEM 1171
Literature and Culture / "And the Winner Is ...":
Major Literary Awards 1174
from An Interview with Rita Dove: Poet Laureate of
the United States *by* Moira Haney *and* Catherine
Nicholas / Student to Student 1175

Read On... 1177
The American Language High Tech's Influence
by Gary Q. Arpin.. 1178

COMMUNICATIONS WORKSHOPS

Writer's Workshop Persuasive Writing: Evaluation   1181

Language Workshop Words to the Wise: Using Effective Diction   1185

Reading for Life Reading Memoranda   1186

Learning for Life State of the Arts: Celebrating Cultural Diversity 1187

Resource Center

Handbook of Literary Terms   1189

Communications Handbook   1204

Active Reading Strategies   1204
Previewing and Setting a Purpose   1204
Reading Actively   1204
Dealing with Difficult Texts   1205
Making Sure You Understand a Text   1205

Study Skills   1205
Using a Dictionary   1205
Using a Thesaurus   1206
Using Study Guides   1206
Recognizing Logical Fallacies   1206

Research Strategies   1207
Using a Library or Media Center   1207
Using the Internet   1208

Evaluating and Citing Sources   1209
Taking Notes and Documenting
   Sources   1210
List of Sources Cited   1213

Writing for Life   1215
Writing Interoffice Memos   1215
Writing Effective Business Letters   1215

Writing a Personal Résumé   1217
College Admissions   1218
Proofreading   1218
Answering Essay Questions   1219

Language Handbook   1220
The Parts of Speech   1220
Agreement   1221
Using Verbs   1223
Using Pronouns   1225
Using Modifiers   1227
Phrases   1229
Clauses   1231
Sentence Structure   1232
Sentence Style   1235
Sentence Combining   1238
Capitalization   1238
Punctuation   1242, 1245
Spelling   1249
Glossary of Usage   1252

Glossary   1258

Acknowledgments   1264

Picture Credits   1269

Index of Skills   1271
Literary Terms   1271
Reading and Critical Thinking   1272
Language (Grammar,
   Usage, and Mechanics)   1274
Vocabulary and Spelling   1276
Writing   1276
Speaking, Listening, and Viewing   1277

Research and Study   1278
Crossing the Curriculum   1278
Critical Comments   1279
Creative Problem Solving   1279

Index of Art   1279
Fine Art   1279
Illustrations   1281
Cartoons and Cartoon Strips   1281
Maps   1281

Index of Authors and Titles   1282

SELECTIONS BY GENRE

Short Story

Rip Van Winkle. 153
The Fall of the House of Usher. 262
House Taken Over (Argentina). 290
The Minister's Black Veil 298
A Pair of Silk Stockings 437
An Occurrence at Owl Creek Bridge 467
A Mystery of Heroism. 487
To Build a Fire. 496
A Wagner Matinée. 539
His Father's Earth. 549
Winter Dreams 586
The Leader of the People 607
The Secret Life of Walter Mitty 624
Soldier's Home. 652
The Life You Save May Be Your Own 673
The Jilting of Granny Weatherall 703
A Rose for Emily 715
The Feather Pillow (Uruguay) 728
Game. 956
Speaking of Courage 965
The Magic Barrel 981
The Handsomest Drowned Man in the
  World 996
Everything Stuck to Him 1027
Son 1069
Daughter of Invention 1077
from Rules of the Game. 1110
New African. 1129
Borges and Myself (Argentina) 1152

Nonfiction

Article, Interview, and News Feature

An American Story 34
Emily Dickinson's Homestead. 389
Cold Kills: Hypothermia CONNECTIONS. 508
"I must have the pulse beat of rhythm. . . ." 574
A Few Don'ts by an Imagiste. 776
Poetry Emotion CONNECTIONS. 977

"Paddlewheel of Days" 1032
An Interview with Amy Tan 1118

Autobiography, Biography, Diary, and Letter

from The Interesting Narrative of the Life of
  Olaudah Equiano. 57
from The Autobiography 85
from The Autobiography: The Declaration
  of Independence 115
A Letter from Jefferson to His Daughter. 124
from Walden, or Life in the Woods 232
from Letter from Birmingham City Jail
  CONNECTIONS. 256
"I sing . . . because I am afraid" 394
from The Narrative of the Life of
  Frederick Douglass. 425
Vogue Stories. 443
Frost on Frost's Diction. 559
A Letter to His Daughter 603
Robinson's Ruminations 648
from Mr. Eliot, I Presume CONNECTIONS 668
The Adventures of Mr. Shiftlet 682
The Genesis of Spoon River 693
"The brawny male sends his picture" 700
In Search of a Story 758
Williams Talks About Poetry 780
from Black Boy 1013
Autobiographical Notes 1142

Essay

from All I Really Need to Know I
  Learned in Kindergarten CONNECTIONS. 96
from The Crisis, No. 1 107
from Gift from the Sea 215
from Nature 218
Hawthorne Talks About Emerson 223
from Self-Reliance. 224
from Heaven Is Under Our Feet
  CONNECTIONS. 245
from Resistance to Civil Government 248
Poe's Process: Writing "The Raven". 287
The New Yorker's Farewell 629

"Is Phoenix Jackson's Grandson
  Really Dead?" 640
Heyday in Harlem. 766
Why I Wrote *The Crucible* 827
from Let Us Now Praise Famous Men
  CONNECTIONS 1064
from "Still Just Writing" CONNECTIONS 1074
from In Search of Our Mothers' Gardens 1102
A Different Story 1125
Straw into Gold 1159

Journal

Sarah Pierrepont *and* My Sense of
  Divine Things 82
"A Healthy and Wholesome Man to Know" 255
from Specimen Days. 363

Literary Criticism

The Oddest Love Song 667
So Much Depends 779
Taking Dominion, Catching Tigers 785
A Vision of Blacks and Whites United 953
Absurd World 961
A Tale of Self-Discovery 993

Memoir

from Life on the Mississippi 452
from Dust Tracks on a Road 751
from Night. 921
The Girl Who Wouldn't Talk *from*
  The Woman Warrior 1044
from The Way to Rainy Mountain 1093

Nonfiction Novel

A Noiseless Flash *from* Hiroshima 936

Other Nonfiction

from Of Plymouth Plantation. 27
from A Narrative of the Captivity 39
from The History of the Dividing Line 50
from Sinners in the Hands of an Angry God 79
God's Trombones. 740
Notebooks 786
"Miracles are to come" 797
The Ball Turret. 933
from Blue Highways 1055
from On James Baldwin CONNECTIONS. 1146

Speech

Speech to the Virginia Convention. 101
Nobel Prize Acceptance Speech, 1962. 620
Nobel Prize Acceptance Speech, 1954. 659
Nobel Prize Acceptance Speech, 1950. 723

Poetry

The Journey 19
Here Follow Some Verses upon the
  Burning of Our House, July 10, 1666 69
Huswifery 73
World, in Hounding Me . . . (Mexico) 76
En perseguirme, mundo . . . (Mexico) 76
Concord Hymn 99
A Blessing 151
Thanatopsis 170
Sea Canes 173
The Tide Rises, the Tide Falls 176
The Cross of Snow 178
from Snow-Bound: A Winter Idyll. 182
The Chambered Nautilus 188
Old Ironsides 190
The Fall of the House of Usher. 279
The Raven. 282
from Song of Myself 347
I Hear America Singing 351
from Song of Myself
  10. Alone far in the wilds 353
  from 33. I understand the large hearts
    of heroes 356
  52. The spotted hawk swoops by 359
Who Understands Me but Me 360
A Sight in Camp in the Daybreak
  Gray and Dim 362
Plenos Poderes (Chile) 368
Full Powers (Chile). 368
Emily Dickinson 371
Heart! We will forget him! 374
If you were coming in the Fall 376
If you were coming in the Fall (edited) 377
The Soul selects her own Society. 378
Some keep the Sabbath going to Church 381
I taste a liquor never brewed 382
Much Madness is divinest Sense 383
Apparently with no surprise 385

Tell all the Truth but tell it slant 386
Success is counted sweetest 388
Because I could not stop for Death 391
I heard a Fly buzz—when I died 392
I died for Beauty—but was scarce 393
My Guilt 423
Now and Then, America 444
Shiloh 449
War Is Kind 494
Design 560
Nothing Gold Can Stay 562
Trying to Name What Doesn't Change
    CONNECTIONS 563
Once by the Pacific 564
Neither Out Far Nor In Deep 565
Birches 567
The Death of the Hired Man 569
Bells for John Whiteside's Daughter 577
Shine, Perishing Republic 580
The Explorer 643
Richard Cory 645
Miniver Cheevy 646
The Love Song of J. Alfred Prufrock 663
Fall 691
Richard Bone 692
"Butch" Weldy 694
Fiddler Jones 694
Petit, the Poet 695
Mrs. George Reece 695
Recuerdo 698
from Discordants CONNECTIONS 711
I, Too 733
Go Down, Death 737
of De Witt Williams on his way to
    Lincoln Cemetery CONNECTIONS 741
America 744
Tableau 747
Incident 748
The Weary Blues 761
Harlem 764
The River-Merchant's Wife: A Letter 774
The Red Wheelbarrow 779
The Great Figure 780
Spring and All 781
Anecdote of the Jar 784
Disillusionment of Ten O'Clock 784

Poetry 787
Ars Poetica CONNECTIONS 789
Of Modern Poetry CONNECTIONS 790
Chicago 792
what if a much of a which of a wind 797
somewhere I have never travelled,
    gladly beyond 798
At the Bomb Testing Site 919
The Death of the Ball Turret Gunner 932
For the Union Dead 949
Ode on the Confederate Dead 954
The Unknown Citizen 963
Monsoon Season 975
Pine Tree Tops 979
Elegy for Jane 1002
Night Journey 1003
The Beautiful Changes 1006
Boy at the Window 1007
Auto Wreck 1010
The Fish 1035
Remember 1040
Speaking 1067
The Bells 1089
Young 1090
What For 1122
Autobiographia Literaria 1127
Mirror 1149
Mushrooms 1150
The Lifeguard 1156
The Latin Deli: An Ars Poetica 1167
The Satisfaction Coal Company 1171

Chant and Myth

The Sky Tree 22
The Earth Only 23
from The House Made of Dawn 23
Coyote Finishes His Work 24

Drama

The Crucible 828

Novel

from Moby-Dick 313

FEATURES

Elements of Literature

The Plain Style 35
The Conceit 74
The Sonnet 180
Poe's Symbols 280
Free Verse 355
Slant Rhyme 380
The Four "Modes" of Fiction 683
The Objective Correlative 777
Satire 962

The American Language

"Revolutionary" English 127
"Noah's Ark": Webster's Dictionary 195
A Period of Vocabulary Growth 398
American Dialects 512
American Slang 801
Euphemisms 892
High Tech's Influence 1178

Primary Sources

Sarah Pierrepont *and* My Sense of
  Divine Things 82
A Letter from Jefferson to His Daughter 124
Hawthorne Talks About Emerson 223

"A Healthy and Wholesome Man to Know" 255
Poe's Process: Writing "The Raven" 287
from Specimen Days 363
If you were coming in the Fall 377
"I sing . . . because I am afraid" 394
Vogue Stories 443
Frost on Frost's Diction 559
"I must have the pulse beat of rhythm. . ." 574
A Letter to His Daughter 603
Nobel Prize Acceptance Speech, 1962 620
The New Yorker's Farewell 629
"Is Phoenix Jackson's Grandson Really Dead?" . . 640
Robinson's Ruminations 648
Nobel Prize Acceptance Speech, 1954 659
The Adventures of Mr. Shiftlet 682
The Genesis of Spoon River 693
"The brawny male sends his picture" 700
Nobel Prize Acceptance Speech, 1950 723
God's Trombones 740
In Search of a Story 758
Heyday in Harlem 766
A Few Don'ts by an Imagiste 776
Williams Talks About Poetry 780
Notebooks 786
"Miracles are to come" 797
The Ball Turret 933
"Paddlewheel of Days" 1032
An Interview with Amy Tan 1118
A Different Story 1125

Across the Curriculum

Literature and History: Captivity Narratives 42
Literature and Science: Benjamin Banneker 90
Literature and Politics: The Iroquois 120
Literature and Folklore: Enchanted Slumbers . . . 162
Literature and Society: Onward to Utopia 226
Literature and Popular Culture: Poe 261
Literature and Popular Culture: Gothic 274
Literature and History: Elegant Discomfort 440
Literature and Folklore: The Mississippi 458

Literature and Film: The West 616
Literature and Popular Culture: The Twenties . . 656
Literature and Popular Culture: Urban Legends . 732
Literature and Music: Birth of the Blues 763
Literature and Society: The Chinese American
    Family. 1050
Literature and Technology: American
    Inventions 1084
Literature and Culture: Literary Awards 1174

Student Models

Africa. 65
The Sea. 192
Imagination 227
The Mirror Girl—stares back at me. 380
What About Glory 493
from An Interview with Rita Dove: Poet
    Laureate of the United States 1175

Literature of the Americas

The Sky Tree (North America). 22
The Earth Only (North America). 23
from The House Made of Dawn
    (North America). 23
Coyote Finishes His Work (North America) 24
World, in Hounding Me . . . (Mexico). 76
En perseguirme, mundo . . . (Mexico) 76
House Taken Over (Argentina). 290
Plenos Poderes (Chile) 368
Full Powers (Chile). 368
The Feather Pillow (Uruguay). 728
Borges and Myself (Argentina) 1152

Writer's Workshops

Narrative Writing: Autobiographical Incident. . . 130
Expository Writing: Analyzing a Literary Work . 198
Persuasive Writing: Controversial Issue 331
Expository Writing:
    Comparison-and-Contrast Essay. 401
Expository Writing: Research Paper 515
Expository Writing: Causes and Effects. 685
Expository Writing: Interpretive Essay 804
Persuasive Writing: Problem-Solution Essay . . . 895
Persuasive Writing: Evaluation 1181

Reading for Life

Monitoring Your Reading. 134
Reading Maps 202
Evaluating Credibility of Sources 338
Reading a Textbook 404
Reading a College Guide 520
Graphic Organizer. 690
Internet Databases. 808
Reading a Film Review 900
Reading Memoranda 1186

Learning for Life

Researching the Immigrant Experience 135
Environmental Concerns. 203
A Model of Self-Reliance 339
The Changing World of Work 405
Monitoring the Media 521
Planning for the Future 809
Evaluating Play Choices 901
Celebrating Cultural Diversity 1187

SKILLS

Reading Skills and Strategies

Reading Matters xxxiv
Vocabulary: When a Dictionary
    Can Help 37
Vocabulary: Using Context Clues. 168
Vocabulary: Tracing the Origins
    of Words 310
Vocabulary: Affixes. 475
Understanding Blank Verse 575
Vocabulary: Semantic Features Analysis 726
Vocabulary: Doing Analogies. 890
Base Words, Roots, and
    Word Families. 1120

Language Workshops

Linking It Up: Coordinating Conjunctions 133
Smoothing It Out: Inserting Modifiers 201
Keeping It in Balance: Parallel Structure. 337
Varying Sentence Beginnings 403
Adverb and Adjective Clauses 519
Using Subordinating Conjunctions 689
Using the Literary Present 807
Using Transitional Expressions 899
Words to the Wise: Using Effective Diction . . . 1185

Assessment

Test Smarts xlvi
Answering Essay Questions 1219

Elements of Literature on the Internet

TO THE STUDENT

Discover more about the stories, poems, and essays in *Elements of Literature* by logging on to the Internet. At **go.hrw.com** we help you complete your homework assignments, learn more about your favorite writers, and find facts that support your ideas and inspire you with new ones. Here's how to log on:

1. Start your Web browser and enter **go.hrw.com** in the location field.

| Back | Forward | Reload | Home | Search |

Location: http://go.hrw.com

2. Note the keyword in your textbook.

 **go.hrw.com**
LE0 11-1

3. In your web browser, enter the keyword and click on GO.

http://go.hrw.com

LE0 11-1 go!
Enter keyword

Now that you've arrived, you can peek into the palaces and museums of the world, listen to stories of exploration and discovery, or view fires burning on the ocean floor. As you move through *Elements of Literature,* use the best online resources at **go.hrw.com.**

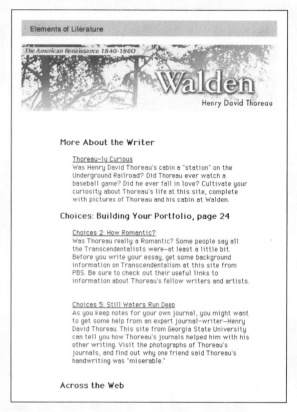

Elements of Literature

The American Renaissance 1840–1860

Walden
Henry David Thoreau

More About the Writer

Thoreau-ly Curious
Was Henry David Thoreau's cabin a "station" on the Underground Railroad? Did Thoreau ever watch a baseball game? Did he ever fall in love? Cultivate your curiosity about Thoreau's life at this site, complete with pictures of Thoreau and his cabin at Walden.

Choices: Building Your Portfolio, page 24

Choices 2: How Romantic?
Was Thoreau really a Romantic? Some people say all the Transcendentalists were—at least a little bit. Before you write your essay, get some background information on Transcendentalism at this site from PBS. Be sure to check out their useful links to information about Thoreau's fellow writers and artists.

Choices 5: Still Waters Run Deep
As you keep notes for your own journal, you might want to get some help from an expert journal-writer—Henry David Thoreau. This site from Georgia State University can tell you how Thoreau's journals helped him with his other writing. Visit the photographs of Thoreau's journals, and find out why one friend said Thoreau's handwriting was "miserable."

Across the Web

Enjoy the Internet, but be critical of the information you find there. Always evaluate your sources for credibility, accuracy, timeliness, and possible bias.

Web sites accessed through **go.hrw.com** are reviewed regularly. However, online materials change continually and without notice. Holt, Rinehart and Winston cannot ensure the accuracy or appropriateness of materials other than our own. Students, teachers, and guardians should assume responsibility for checking all online materials. A full description of Terms of Use can be found at **go.hrw.com.**

Building a Foundation for Success in Literature

A Foundation for Reading

Reading Matters *By Dr. Kylene Beers*

Improving Your Comprehension

Visualizing
Metacognition
Think-Aloud
Questioning the Text
Re-reading and Rewording
Summarizing Narrative Text
Summarizing Expository Text
Question Maps
Smart Words

Improving Your Reading Rate

Reading Rate and Homework
Figuring Out Your Reading Rate
Reading Rate Reminders

A Foundation for Test Taking

Test Smarts

Test Smarts Lesson 1: Understanding Analogy Questions

Test Smarts Lesson 2: Answering Questions About Rhetoric

Test Smarts Lesson 3: Answering Questions About Tone

Test Smarts Lesson 4: Evaluating Support

Test Smarts Lesson 5: Answering Open-Ended Essay Questions

Reading Matters

When the Text Is Tough

Remember the reading you did back in first, second, and third grades? Big print. Short texts. Easy words. Now in high school, however, the texts you read are often filled with small print, long chapters, and complicated plots or topics. Also, you now find yourself reading a variety of material—from your driver's ed handbook to college applications, from notes passed in the hall to graffiti printed on the wall, from job applications to income tax forms, from e-mail to e-zines, from classics to comics, from textbooks to checkbooks.

Doing something every day that you find difficult and tedious isn't much fun—and that includes reading. So, this section of this book is designed for you, to show you what to do when the text gets tough. Let's begin to look at some *reading* matters—because after all, reading *matters*.

READING UP CLOSE
◆ How to Use This Section

- **This section is for you.** Turn to it whenever you need to remind yourself about what to do when the text gets tough. Don't wait for your teacher to assign this section for you to read. It's your handbook. Use it.

- **Read the sections that you need.** You don't have to read every word. Skim the headings and find the information you need.

- **Use this information to help you with reading for other classes,** not just for the reading you do in this book.

- **Don't be afraid to *re-read* the information** you find in Reading Matters. The best readers constantly re-read information.

- **If you need more help, then check the index.** The index will direct you to other pages in this book with information on reading skills and strategies.

Effects of
The Quake

By Kenneth Howe

Improving Your Comprehension

Comprehension, your ability to understand what you read, is a critical part of the reading process. Your comprehension can be affected by many factors. Think about each of the following types of texts, and rate your comprehension of each from 1 (*never understand*) to 5 (*always understand*).

A) notes from your friends
B) e-mail messages from friends
C) college applications
D) job applications
E) magazines
F) computer manuals
G) Internet sites
H) school textbooks
I) novels you choose
J) novels your teachers choose for you

You probably didn't rate yourself the same for each type of text. Factors such as your interest level and the text's vocabulary level will cause your ratings to differ from text to text. Now, go back and look specifically at items H, I, and J. How did you rate there? If you think your comprehension of those materials is low, then you'll want to study the next few pages carefully. They are filled with tips to help you improve your comprehension.

READING UP CLOSE

◆ Monitoring Your Comprehension

Skilled readers often pay more attention to what they don't understand than what they do understand. Here are some symbols you could put on self-adhesive notes to put onto texts as you are reading so you can keep up with what's confusing you. Decide how you would use each symbol.

1)
2)
3)
4)
5)
6)
7)
8)
9)
10)

- **Visualizing.** The ability to visualize—or see in your mind—what you are reading is important for comprehension. To understand how visualizing makes a difference, try this quick test. When you get home, watch a television show you enjoy. Then, turn your back to the television set. How long will you keep "watching" the program that way? Probably not long. Why not? Because it would be boring if you couldn't see what was happening. The same is true with reading: If you can't "see" in your mind what is happening on the page, then you probably will tune out of reading quickly. You can improve your ability to visualize the text by practicing the following:

1. **Read a few sentences; then pause and describe what is happening on the page.** Forcing yourself to describe the scene will take some time at first, but will help in the long run.
2. **On a sheet of paper or a self-adhesive note, make a graphic representation of what is happening as you are reading.** For instance, if two characters are talking, draw two stick figures with arrows pointing between them to show yourself that they are talking.
3. **Discuss a scene or a part of a chapter with a buddy.** Talk about what you "saw" as you were reading.
4. **Read aloud.** If you are having troubling visualizing the text, it might be because you aren't really "hearing" it. Try reading a portion of your text aloud, using good expression and phrasing. As you hear the words, you may find it easier to see the scenes.

Metacognition. Your attention wanders for a moment as you are reading something, but your eyes don't quit moving from word to word. After a few minutes, you realize you are several pages beyond the last point where you can remember thinking about what you were reading. Then you know you need to back up and start over. This ability to think about your thinking— or in this case, lack of thinking—is called **metacognition.**

Metacognition refers to your ability to analyze what you are doing as you try to make sense of texts. Consequently, a critical part of metacognition is paying attention to what you are reading. It's normal to find that your attention *sometimes* wanders while reading. If it always wanders, though, then try either of the following: (1) Keep paper and pen close, and jot notes as you read; (2) read for a set amount of time (five minutes), and then stop and review what's happened since the last time you stopped. Lengthen this time as you find yourself able to focus longer. Take the quiz below to see what your metacognition level is. The lower the score, the more you need to focus on staying focused.

READING UP CLOSE

◆ Measuring Your Attention Quotient

Take the following survey to see what your Attention Quotient is. The lower the score, the less you pay attention to what you are reading. The higher the score, the more you pay attention.

When I read, I . . .

1. let my mind wander a lot.

1	(2)	3
most of the time	sometimes	almost never

2. forget what I'm reading.

1	(2)	3
most of the time	sometimes	almost never

3. get confused and stay confused or don't even realize I am confused.

1	(2)	3
most of the time	sometimes	almost never

4. discover I've turned lots of pages and don't have a clue as to what I read.

1	2	(3)
most of the time	sometimes	almost never

5. rarely finish whatever I'm supposed to be reading.

1	(2)	3
most of the time	sometimes	almost never

- **Think-Aloud.** Comprehension problems don't appear only after you *finish* reading. Confusion occurs *as* you read. Therefore, don't wait until you complete your reading assignment to try to understand the text; instead, work on comprehending while reading by becoming an active reader.

Active readers **predict, connect, clarify, question,** and **visualize** as they read. If you don't do those things, you need to pause while you read to

- make predictions,
- make connections,
- clarify in your own thoughts what you are reading,
- question what you don't understand, and
- visualize the text.

Here's José's think-aloud for "The Jilting of Granny Weatherall" (p. 704):

Page 704, 1st paragraph: "The doctor is visiting her at her house? This must be set long ago." **(Connection/Prediction)**

Page 706, top of the 2nd column: "Who are George and John? Maybe they are children that moved away? Or friends? Oh, maybe like old boyfriends?" **(Questioning/Prediction)**

Page 707, bottom of 1st column: "So John was her husband. But it says he'd be a child beside her, so…? Oh, he died, so now she's much older than he was when he died." **(Clarifying)**

Page 708: "See, George stood her up—see, that's who jilted her. And this part here, where it says she wants to tell him she forgot him—I don't think so! I think she'll be angry till she dies." **(Clarification/Prediction)**

Use the Think-Aloud strategy to practice your active-reading skills. Read a selection of text aloud to a partner. As you read, pause to make comments and ask questions. Your partner's job is to tally your comments and classify each according to the list above.

Questioning the Text. This scenario may be familiar: You've just finished reading one of the selections in this book. Then, you look at the questions that you'll be discussing tomorrow in class. You realize that you don't know the answers. In frustration, you decide to give up on the questions.

While giving up is one way to approach the problem, it's not the best approach. In fact, what you need to do is focus *more* on questions—and focus on them while reading. This doesn't mean memorizing study questions and looking for specific answers as you read. It means constantly asking yourself questions about characters, plot, point of view, setting, conflict, and even vocabulary while reading. This doesn't mean memorizing study questions and looking for specific answers as you read. It means constantly asking yourself questions about characters, plot, point of view, setting, conflict, and even vocabulary while reading. The more you question the text while reading, the better you'll be able to answer the questions at the end of the text after reading.

◆ Asking Questions During Reading

Here is a list of questions you can use as you read literary selections. You should recopy this list on note cards and keep it close as you read.

Character Questions

1. Who is the central character? Is this character the narrator? What are the greatest strengths and greatest weaknesses of this character?

2. Is the narrator telling the story as it is happening or upon looking back? Can you trust this narrator? What if the narrator were a different character? How would the story change? What point of view does the narrator have—first person, limited third person, omniscient—and how does that point of view impact the narrator's authority?

3. Who are the other characters? What makes them important to the central character? What do their actions reveal about their personalities? How do your thoughts about the characters change as you read the story? Can you find specific points in the text where your feelings about characters shift? Could any character have been omitted from the story?

4. Which character do you like the best? What would that character like about you?

Plot, Setting, and Conflict Questions

1. What are the major events in the plot? Which events are mandatory for the story to reach the conclusion it does? What prior knowledge is necessary for understanding this plot?

2. How does the setting impact the story? Could you change the location or the historical context and have the same story? How does the author situate the reader in the setting? Is the setting believable?

3. What event creates the conflict? How is the conflict resolved? How does the central character react to the conflict? How do other characters react?

Re-reading and Rewording. The best way to improve your comprehension is simply to **re-read.** The first time you read something, you get the basic idea of the text. The next time you read, you revise your understanding. Try thinking of your first reading as a draft—just like the first draft of an essay. As you revise your essay, you are improving your writing. As you revise your reading, you are improving your comprehension.

Sometimes, as you re-read, you find some specific sentences or even passages that you just don't understand. When that's the case, you need to spend some time closely studying those sentences. One effective way to tackle tough text is to **reword** the text:

1. On a piece of paper, write the sentences that are confusing you.
2. Leave a few blank lines between each line you write.
3. Then, choose the difficult words and reword them in the space above.

While you wouldn't want to reword every line of a long text—or even of a short one—this is a powerful way to help you understand key sentences.

READING UP CLOSE

◆ *One Student's Rewording*

Regina created this rewording for parts of *The Autobiography,* by Benjamin Franklin (p. 86). Notice how she does the third rewording a bit differently from the first two. You might like the sentence method better than the word method.

                  thought of the brave   difficult task   reaching
1. It was about this time I ~~conceived the bold~~ and ~~arduous project~~ of ~~arriving~~ at moral perfection (p. 92).

          reason, consequently arranged
2. For this ~~purpose,~~ I ~~therefore contrived~~ the following method (p. 92).

3. My intention being to acquire the *habitude* of all these virtues, I judged it would be well not to distract my attention by attempting the whole at once (p. 93): *Since I planned on making each of these a habit, I thought I'd do better by not trying to do all at one time.*

Summarizing Narrative Text. Understanding a long piece of text is easier if you can summarize chunks of it. If you are reading a **narrative,** or a story (including biography), then use a strategy called **Somebody Wanted But So (SWBS)** to help you write summaries of what you are reading.

SWBS is a powerful way to think about the characters in or subjects of a narrative and note what each did, what conflict each faced, and what the resolution was. As you write an SWBS statement for different characters or subjects within the same narrative, you are forcing yourself to rethink the narrative from different **points of view.**

Here are the steps for writing SWBS statements:
1. Write the words *Somebody, Wanted, But,* and *So* across four columns.
2. Under the *Somebody* column, write a character's name.
3. Then, under the *Wanted* column, write what that character wanted to do.
4. Next, under the *But* column, explain what happened that kept the character from doing what he or she wanted.
5. Finally, under the *So* column, explain the eventual outcome.
6. If you're making an SWBS chart for a long story or novel, you might need to write several statements at different points in the story.

Read this SWBS chart for the last paragraph of "Phillis Wheatley: A Revolutionary Woman" (p. 113), and then write your own for the first three paragraphs.

Somebody	Wanted	But	So
Phillis	wanted recognition for her work	but the white culture of her time refused to value her contribution	she died poor and alone.

Summarizing Expository Text. If summarizing the information in expository, or informational, texts is difficult, try a strategy called GIST.

Steps for GIST:

1. Choose three or four sections of text you want to summarize.
2. Read the first section of text.
3. Draw twenty blank lines on a sheet of paper.
4. Write a summary of the first section of text using exactly twenty words—one word for each blank.
5. Read the next section of text.
6. Now, in your next set of twenty blanks, write a new summary statement that combines your first summary with whatever you want to add from this second section of text. It's important to note that even though you've now read two sections, you still have only twenty blanks to fill, not forty.

Repeat this process one or two more times depending on how many more sections of text you have to read. When you are finished, you have a twenty-word statement that gives you the gist, or overall idea, of what the entire text was about.

After reading "Literature and Politics" (p. 120), Eric wrote the following GIST statements. Complete the third GIST statement yourself.

GIST #1 (for the first paragraph)

Jefferson and Franklin studied governments from the Bible, Greek and Roman times, and the Iroquois nation before writing the Constitution.

GIST #2 (adding the second paragraph of information)

Jefferson and Franklin studied the Bible, Greeks and Romans, and the Iroquois Confederacy, five groups united for peace and protection.

GIST #3 (adding the third paragraph of information)

_____ _____ _____ _____ _____ _____ _____ _____ _____ _____

_____ _____ _____ _____ _____ _____ _____ _____ _____ _____

- **Question Maps.** Most readers, at some point, will struggle with a text. Some readers find reading poetry a struggle, but they can breeze through computer magazines. Others find the technical language in computer magazines difficult but read poetry easily. It's not whether you struggle with texts that matters; instead, what matters is what you do when you struggle.

If you are an independent reader, then you know how to find the answers on your own—independently—to whatever causes you to struggle. If you are a dependent reader, you expect others to do the explaining for you. Dependent readers often say "I don't get it" and give up. Independent readers, by contrast, know what they don't get and then figure out how to get it.

If you think you are a dependent reader, then try using a Question Map like the one below. As you complete the chart, you'll be mapping your way toward independent reading.

1. In the first column, **list your questions** as you are reading.
2. In the second column, **make notes about each question** as you write the question. For instance, jot down what made you think about the question or what page you are on in the text.
3. In the third column, **list possibilities for finding answers.** Remember that re-reading the text is always a good idea. Other places to find answers include dictionaries (especially if you have questions about vocabulary), your own head (sometimes the text gives you part of the information, and you must figure out the rest), or other parts of the book (especially if you are reading a science, math, or history book).
4. In the final column, **jot down answers to your questions** only after you've made notes about them and thought out where to find answers to them. If you can't answer your question at this point, then it's time to see your teacher.

READING UP CLOSE

◆ One Student's Question Map

Here is Easton's Question Map for *Walden* (p. 233).

Questions	Notes	Places to find answers	Answers
1. What's a sojourner?	p. 234, 1st para.	dictionary	traveler
2. Who are poor students?	p. 234, bottom	in my head	could be money poor or not good in school
3. Did Thoreau really do this?	section break at p. 235	encyclopedia on Thoreau or biography	Yes! He did!

Smart Words. Sometimes you understand what you've read, but when it comes time to talk about or write about the selection, you can't find the words you want to help discuss the characters, theme, plot, or author's writing style. Here's a list of words that offer you springboards to discussion. They are beginning points—you still must be able to explain why you chose those words.

Words to Describe the Plot

Positive	Negative
realistic	unrealistic
good pace from scene to scene	plodding
suspenseful	predictable
satisfying	frustrating
conclusion	conclusion
subplots make sense	confusing subplots
well-developed ideas	sketchy ideas

Words to Describe Characters

Positive	Negative
original	stereotyped
believable	unbelievable
well-rounded	flat
dynamic—able to change	static—unable to change
well-developed	flawed

Words to Describe the Theme

Positive	Negative
important	trivial
subtle	overbearing
unique	overworked
powerful	ineffective
memorable	forgettable

Words to Describe the Author's Writing Style

Positive	Negative
descriptive, filled with figurative language	boring, no imagery
original	filled with clichés
lively, full of action	slow-moving
poetic or lyrical	plodding / jumpy

> **READING UP CLOSE**
> ◆ Using Smart Words
> Choose one of the selections you've read in *Elements of Literature* this semester and, using some of the words above, describe the plot, character, theme, and author's writing style. Remember to explain your word choices with examples from the story.

Improving Your Reading Rate

If your reading concerns are more about getting through the words than figuring out the meaning, then this part of Reading Matters is for you.

If you think you are a slow reader, then reading can seem overwhelming. But you can change your reading rate—the pace at which you read. All you have to do is practice. The point isn't to read so that you just rush over words—the I'mgoingto-readsofastthatallthewordsrunto-gether approach. Instead, the goal is to find a good pace that keeps you moving comfortably through the pages. Why is it important to establish a good reading rate? Let's do a little math to see why your silent reading rate counts. Try working out the math problem in the box above. Then compare your answers to the answers in the chart to the right.

> **MATH PROBLEM!**
> If you read 40 words per minute (WPM) and there are 400 words on a page, then how long will it take you to read 1 page? 5 pages? 10 pages? How long will it take if you read 80 WPM? 120 WPM? 200 WPM?

	1 page @400 words/page	5 pages @400 words/page	10 pages @400 words/page
40 WPM	10 minutes	50 minutes	100 minutes
80 WPM	5 minutes	25 minutes	50 minutes
120 WPM	3 minutes	17 minutes	34 minutes
200 WPM	2 minutes	10 minutes	20 minutes

Reading Rate and Homework

Now, assume that with literature homework, science homework, and social studies homework, in one night you have forty pages to read. If you are reading at 40 WPM, you are spending over six *hours* just reading the information; but at 120 WPM, you only spend about two hours. And at 200 WPM, you'd finish in one hour and twenty minutes.

> **READING UP CLOSE**
> ◆ **Tips on Varying Your Reading Rate**
> - Increasing your rate doesn't matter if your comprehension goes down.
>
> - Don't rush to read fast if that means understanding less. Plus, remember, your rate will vary as your purpose for reading varies.
>
> - You'll read more slowly when you are studying for a test than when you are skimming a text.

Figuring Out Your Reading Rate

To determine your silent-reading rate, you'll need three things: a watch with a second hand, a book, and someone who will watch the time for you. Then, do the following:

1. Have your friend time you as you begin reading to yourself.
2. Read at your normal rate. Don't speed just because you're being timed.
3. Stop when your friend tells you one minute is up.
4. Record the number of words you read in that minute.
5. Repeat this process several more times using different passages.
6. Then add the number of words together and divide by the number of times you timed yourself. That's your average number of words per minute.

Example

1st minute	180 words
2nd minute	215 words
3rd minute	190 words
	585 words ÷ 3 = 195 WPM

Reading Rate Reminders

1. **Make sure you aren't reading one word at a time with a pause between each word.** Practice phrasing words in your mind as you read. For instance, read the following rhyme. The first time you read it, pause between each word; but the second time, pause only where you see the slash marks. Hear the difference the phrasing makes?

   Mary had a little lamb. / Its fleece was white as snow. / Everywhere that Mary went / her lamb was sure to go. /

   Word-at-a-time reading is much slower than phrase reading. If you are reading a word at a time, you'll want to practice reading by phrases. You can hear good phrasing by listening to a book on tape.

2. **Make sure when you are reading silently that you really are silent.** As you read, avoid moving your lips or reading aloud softly. These habits slow you down!

3. **Don't use your finger to point to words as you read.** If you find that you always use your finger to point to words as you read, then you are probably reading one word at a time. Instead, use a bookmark to help yourself stay on the correct line while you practice your phrase reading.

4. **As you practice your fluency, remember that the single best way to improve your reading rate is simply to read more!** So, start reading more, and use the tips listed above. Soon, you'll find that reading too slowly isn't a problem anymore.

Test Smarts

LESSON 1 Understanding Analogy Questions

On standardized tests like the SAT, **analogy questions** ask you to identify a particular relationship between a pair of words, called the **stem word pair,** and then identify another pair of words that has the same relationship. Take a look at the analogy below:

> FINGER : HAND :: chapter : book

You would read this analogy this way: "*Finger* is to *hand* as *chapter* is to *book.*"

The analogy above expresses a **part-to-whole** relationship. Below are two other types of analogies commonly found on standardized tests.

- **Word to Synonym** (One word is paired with a similar, but usually not identical, word.)
    FOOD : NOURISHMENT :: fast : rapid
- **Agent to Acted Upon** (This type pairs something with another thing that is directly affected by it.)
    KEY : LOCK :: hammer : nail

On tests, analogy questions offer multiple-choice answers, as in the following example.

MECHANIC : MOTORCYCLE ::
A. laziness : exercise   **D.** physician : patient
B. irritation : salve   **E.** baker : cake
C. tapestry : weaving

Thinking It Through: Answering an Analogy Question

■ Follow the steps below to find the answer to an analogy question. The responses are based on the sample question above.

1. **Create a sentence explaining the relationship in the stem word pair.** A mechanic works on a motorcycle.

2. **Identify possible answers that contain the same relationship.** Laziness does *not* work on exercise, irritation does *not* work on a salve, and a tapestry does *not* work on a weaving, so **A, B,** and **C** can be eliminated.

3. **If you still have more than one possible answer, revise your sentence to describe more precisely the relationship in the stem word pair.** A mechanic keeps a motorcycle in working condition.

4. **Analyze the remaining possible answers to see if they fit your new sentence.** A physician (**D**) keeps a patient "in working condition," or healthy.

Practice

Directions. Read each stem word pair carefully, and choose the pair of words that has the same relationship. Then, on a separate sheet of paper, write a sentence explaining the relationship. For items 5 through 10, you should also identify the type of analogy.

1. BEG : BESEECH :: _____
  A. laugh : joke
  B. cry : weep
  C. think : act
  D. discover : camouflage
  E. plead : allow
  Type of analogy: *word to synonym*

2. PUNCTUATION : SENTENCE :: _____
  A. question : answer
  B. sock : shoe
  C. prison : cage
  D. signs : highway
  E. box : gift
  Type of analogy: *part to whole*

3. VETERINARIAN : CALF :: _____
  A. comb : brush
  B. gears : clock
  C. medicine : illness
  D. encouragement : conflict
  E. goals : success
  Type of analogy: *agent to acted upon*

4. LYRICS : SONG :: _____
  A. table : lamp
  B. dialogue : script
  C. poetry : prose
  D. trial : judgement
  E. plow : tractor
  Type of analogy: *part to whole*

5. PAINTER : CANVAS :: _____
  A. dentist : molars
  B. experiment : science
  C. concentration : distraction
  D. athlete : spine
  E. practice : skill
  Type of analogy:

6. EXERCISE : HEALTH :: _____
  A. running : marathon
  B. experience : decisions
  C. muscles : bones
  D. exhaustion : physique
  E. hunger : food
  Type of analogy:

7. BARBARIAN : SAVAGE :: _____
  A. gentleman : oaf
  B. athlete : coach
  C. collar : poodle
  D. nobleman : aristocrat
  E. manager : employee
  Type of analogy:

8. SHEEP : FLOCK :: _____
  A. milk : water
  B. street : road
  C. car : truck
  D. trees : orchard
  E. telephone : receiver
  Type of analogy:

9. LUMINOUS : GLOWING :: _____
  A. bright : pleasant
  B. murky : dim
  C. weathered : new
  D. upset : false
  E. foolish : wise
  Type of analogy:

10. SMITH : METAL :: _____
  A. potter : clay
  B. sergeant : troops
  C. merchant : glass
  D. teacher : students
  E. storyteller : listeners
  Type of analogy:

Test Smarts

LESSON 2 | Answering Questions About Rhetoric

Sophisticated writers of nonfiction do not simply list ideas. Whether their purpose is to persuade or inform, they craft their works by employing **rhetorical devices**—special techniques to make a point—such as **argument by analogy** (showing a parallel between two similar situations), **historical allusion** (referring to a famous historical figure or event), and **appeal to authority** (quoting an expert as support for an argument). On state or national tests you may encounter a question about the rhetoric rather than the content of a passage. For example, you might be asked why the author referred to a certain historical event or figure.

Read the following passage from an article about the aurora borealis; then, look at the question about its rhetoric that follows.

> For centuries, scientists attempted to understand the aurora borealis, or northern lights. Both Galileo and Descartes provided inaccurate explanations of the phenomenon.
>
> However, the light of understanding began to dawn in 1740, when Swedish scientists discovered that extensive magnetic disturbances occur on earth during large aurora borealis shows. Then, in 1859, while watching sunspots, a British astronomer saw a sudden, brief flare of sunlight. Shortly thereafter, spectacular auroras were observed from earth. The link between the northern lights and the sun was definitively established.

The writer mentions Galileo and Descartes to support the idea that the aurora borealis was—
A. unknown to famous scientists
B. difficult to explain
C. understood during the 1700s
D. easily analyzed by scientists

Thinking It Through: Answering Questions About Rhetoric

■ To determine the best possible answer:

1. **Determine the kind of question about rhetoric being asked.** The question refers to the author's allusion to two famous scientists.

2. **Consider each answer.** Answer **A** should be excluded because the passage states that the scientists were aware of the aurora borealis. **B** is a possible answer: For many years scientists attempted to understand the aurora borealis but failed. **C** is incorrect and should be excluded: The passage states that the aurora borealis was not understood until after the mid-1800s. **D** should also be excluded: The passage demonstrates that sophisticated scientific knowledge was needed to understand the phenomenon.

3. **Reevaluate your choice. B** is correct. The historical allusion shows even Galileo and Descartes were unable to explain the complex phenomenon.

Practice

Directions. Read the passage below. On a separate sheet of paper, list the numbers *1* through *5*. Then, for each numbered item, write the letter of the correct response.

During the 1870s, Americans across the nation began to be enthralled by the West in general and cowboys in particular. Craving an authentic taste of life on the range, they traveled west for "working" vacations on ranches.

These tourists sported spanking new Western fashions as eagerly as the ranch workers donned their usual worn, dusty garb. Ranch workers could not help but mock their wealthy imitators. No doubt, Buffalo Bill would have done the same. They called fake cowhands "dudes"; this derogatory label is believed to be derived from the German word for a lazy guy—<u>dudendop</u>.

In the 1870s, ranchers in Colorado became the first to charge dudes fees for the privilege of experiencing the Wild West. During the next decade, wealthy men from Great Britain began journeying to the American West to hunt wildlife. Excited by the prospect of luring such prosperous customers, one entrepreneur created a ranch for tourists only. The "dude ranch" was born.

Dude ranches eventually offered affordable vacations not only for the rich, but also for ordinary Americans. The ranches had a surge of success during World War I: Tourists couldn't travel to Europe, so they trekked west instead, surging in like the wagon trains of the 1800s. When cattle prices plummeted in the 1920s, visiting dudes became the only means of support for many ranches.

Still popular today, dude ranches offer tourists treats like television and air conditioning—amenities that an exhausted 1870s cowpoke would have relished.

1. The writer compares ranch workers with tourists in order to—
   A. create sympathy for the tourists
   B. point out their similarities
   C. explain the decline of ranching
   D. illustrate that the tourists were only pretending
   E. show that tourists hurt productivity

2. Why does the writer mention Buffalo Bill?
   A. to re-create the Western setting
   B. because Buffalo Bill worked on a dude ranch
   C. to provide an example of a German rancher
   D. to add the support of a famous cowhand to the ranchers' case
   E. to remind us that cowhands really did exist in those times

3. Why does the writer explain the probable source of the term *dude*?
   A. to point out discrimination against vacationers
   B. to support an explanation of the West's popularity

C. to emphasize the tourists' lack of experience with hard work
   D. to show that ranches were multiethnic
   E. to criticize cowhands' treatment of vacationers

4. The writer alludes to wagon trains to—
   A. make a comparison of means of transportation
   B. emphasize how difficult ranching was
   C. explain how tourists traveled west
   D. add support to the comparison of tourists and ranch workers
   E. emphasize the high volume of people visiting dude ranches during the war

5. The writer's point of view is that dude ranches were—
   A. a significant, if humorous, development in the history of the West
   B. a place for wealthy tourists only
   C. bad for the ranches and ranchers
   D. an embarrassing development that had no value and should never have happened
   E. successful because of wars

LESSON 3 Answering Questions About Tone

Standardized reading tests often ask you to identify the **tone** of a passage—the language that indicates the writer's attitude toward the subject and reader. Because tone is never stated outright, try to determine the implicit feelings, assumptions, and beliefs of the writer rather than focus on the argument given. Look for loaded or emotional words that convey the writer's attitude. For example, to say that a person is "narrow-minded" or that a book is "dull" reveals that the writer has a negative attitude—evident in the two adjectives *narrow-minded* and *dull*. Here is a typical reading passage and a question about its tone:

Residents who take pride in caring for their lawn need to be aware of some unpleasant truths. A lawn provides a soft open area where people can play and relax. However, keeping that lawn green can do serious harm to the environment.

Most lawns need to be watered frequently. This is unfortunate, because water is an increasingly precious resource. Lawns can also require fertilizer to nourish grass and discourage weeds. The majority of fertilizers contain phosphorus, which washes into storm sewers and eventually pollutes everything from streams to oceans. Many lawn owners use synthetic herbicides and pesticides to eliminate weeds and kill undesirable insects. These substances, most of which are toxic, are spread into the surrounding area by wind, sprinklers, and rain. Even lawn clippings have a harmful impact on the environment. Clippings clog landfills and end up in storm drains, where they carry the insidious residue of fertilizers, herbicides, and pesticides into our water.

> The writer's tone in this passage can best be described as
> **A.** intimidated
> **B.** neutral
> **C.** disapproving
> **D.** blindly hostile
> **E.** ironic

Thinking It Through: Answering Questions About Tone

■ Keep the following steps in mind when answering tone questions.

1. **Look for descriptive words that might reflect the writer's attitude.** In the passage, negative words such as *pollutes, toxic, harmful, clog,* and *insidious* indicate that the tone is not altogether neutral. Therefore, **B** is incorrect.

2. **Eliminate obviously incorrect answer choices.** Nothing in the text indicates an intimidated or ironic tone. Answers **A** and **E** are incorrect.

3. **Examine the remaining choices, and select the most appropriate answer.** **D** is an exaggeration, so the answer has to be **C**.

Practice

Directions. Read the passage below. On a separate sheet of paper, list the numbers *1* through *5*. Then, for each numbered item, write the letter of the correct response.

The next time you are outside at night, take a look at the sky. If you live in a city or suburb, you will probably see few, if any, stars. When we cannot see a deep black sky brilliant with stars, we lose a touchstone—a reminder of the mystery, enormity, and majesty of the cosmos.

The loss of our ability to see the stars is incalculable. However, the cause of this problem is readily apparent: too much light. Skyscrapers remain lit all night, poorly engineered street lighting creates needless glare, neon signs glow constantly, and everywhere excessively bright bulbs spill light into nearby areas. In some cities, the night sky is twenty-five to fifty times brighter than the sky over unpopulated areas. One solution is to replace fixtures that beam light indiscriminately into the sky with "shielded" fixtures—those that beam light toward the ground instead of horizontally or up into the sky.

Although it is true that replacing light-wasting fixtures in public areas with better-functioning designs will cost money, such lighting helps to conserve electricity. In fact, the expense of installing fixtures that reduce light pollution is sometimes regained through energy savings in as little as three years.

In addition, shielded lighting helps to reduce the glare caused by other wasteful lights. Decreased glare helps drivers to see other cars, pedestrians, and roadside objects more clearly, which could lead to a reduction in the number of nighttime traffic accidents.

Although light pollution may block your view of the Milky Way this evening, the solution to this problem is relatively simple and will benefit us all.

1. The writer's tone in this passage can best be described as—
   A. diplomatic
   B. uncaring
   C. exuberant
   D. malevolent
   E. humorous

2. Which of the following sentences from the passage best reveals the writer's attitude?
   A. the first sentence of the first paragraph
   B. the first sentence of the second paragraph
   C. the last sentence of the third paragraph
   D. the last sentence of the fourth paragraph
   E. the first sentence of the fourth paragraph

3. The writer's depiction of lighted skyscrapers and neon signs can best be described as—
   A. apologetic
   B. angry
   C. critical
   D. unreasonable
   E. admiring

4. What is the tone of the writer's description of a starry night sky?
   A. neutral
   B. sarcastic
   C. reverent
   D. fearful
   E. irritated

5. Which of the following phrases from the passage best indicates the writer's concern?
   A. light pollution
   B. the Milky Way
   C. neon signs
   D. traffic accidents
   E. overpopulation

Test Smarts

Whether it is a book review or a report on a scientific discovery, any article that you read will contain a main idea. The role of **support** (facts, details, examples) is also crucial, helping to establish the validity of the main idea. Some college entrance exams will ask you to judge the relevance of support within a written piece. Here is a typical reading passage and test question:

William Bryant Logan's book <u>Dirt: The Ecstatic Skin of the Earth</u> provides a valuable introduction to this fascinating but often neglected subject. The book is full of historical information that adds color and interest. For example, Logan, who writes a gardening column for <u>The New York Times</u>, marvels at the fact that everything on our planet is made from stardust—that is, dirt. The charming, and sometimes strange, stories throughout the text are the most appealing aspect of this book. Logan describes his childhood attempt to dig to China and his passion for prairie gullies, which often contain fossils. He also tells about a man who can accurately assess the acidity of soil by tasting it!

> Which of the following is least relevant to the reviewer's main idea?
> **A.** Logan describes his childhood attempt to dig to China.
> **B.** Logan works as a columnist for a major newspaper.
> **C.** Logan tells about a man who tests dirt by tasting it.
> **D.** The book states that everything on the planet is made from stardust, or dirt.

Thinking It Through: Evaluating Support

■ Use the following steps to answer a test question in which you are asked to evaluate support.

1. **Identify the author's *main idea*.** To find the main idea, look for repeated phrases and an emphasis on one particular subject. If the main idea is stated, it is usually found at the beginning of the passage. The reviewer's main idea is that this book is an interesting introduction to dirt.

2. **Apply each possible answer to this main idea.** Ask yourself: Does this answer choice *support* the main idea? By the process of elimination, you should end up with one answer that does not support the main idea. Answers **A, C,** and **D** are all interesting ideas related to the main idea— that the book is an interesting introduction to dirt. Answer **B** states a fact, but it does not support the author's main idea about the quality of the book. Therefore, it is the least relevant to the author's main idea.

3. **Review your choices.** If you have two answers left that seem irrelevant, apply them a second time to the main idea. Then, decide which one supplies the *least* amount of support.

Practice

Directions. Read the passage below. On a separate sheet of paper, list the numbers *1* through *5*. Then, for each numbered item, write the letter of the correct response.

Alberto Manguel's <u>A History of Reading</u> provides a fascinating and comprehensive overview of 6,000 years of reading. Manguel traces this mode of communication from ancient clay tablets to contemporary CD-ROMs.

Throughout his book, Manguel effectively mixes personal observations with analyses of reading in general. After describing the moment in early childhood when he realized that he could read a word on a billboard, Manguel moves seamlessly into an exploration of how varied reading can be. Reading, he explains, can include such things as parents reading the emotions on their baby's face. I've often misread my own infant's smiles as signs of happiness, when in fact they are signs of digestion.

Manguel also provides many enlivening details that demonstrate how important reading has been to people throughout history. He relates, for instance, how Japanese women created their own language and reading materials in the eleventh century. He tells about groups of people in history who learned how to read at the risk of severe punishment.

Manguel ends his book by noting that the history of reading has no conclusion.

1. Which of the following ideas is least relevant to the reviewer's main idea?
   A. Inferring another person's emotions can also be considered a form of reading.
   B. Manguel describes his realization that he could read a word on a billboard.
   C. Manguel relates how Japanese women created their own language and reading materials.
   D. The book contains many enlivening details.
   E. The reviewer misreads an infant's expression.

2. Which statement best supports the reviewer's opinion of *A History of Reading*?
   A. "Reading, he explains, can include such things as parents reading the emotions on their baby's face."
   B. "He tells about groups of people in history who learned how to read at the risk of severe punishment."
   C. "He relates, for instance, how Japanese women created their own language and reading materials in the eleventh century."
   D. "Manguel ends his book by noting that the history of reading has no conclusion."
   E. "Throughout his book, Manguel effectively mixes personal observations with analyses of reading in general."

3. The reviewer provides evidence that Manguel's book is—
   A. a detailed account with few original insights
   B. based primarily on his personal experiences
   C. both authoritative and interesting
   D. to be followed by a sequel
   E. long and uninteresting

4. What is the main idea of the third paragraph?
   A. Manguel shows that reading has always had a great impact on people.
   B. Reading is important to people worldwide.
   C. Manguel believes that there is no excuse for not learning to read.
   D. People have risked punishment to read.
   E. Reading is only for certain groups of people.

5. What explanation from the passage supports the reviewer's claim that the book is comprehensive?
   A. Reading has always been important.
   B. The book contains personal anecdotes.
   C. Eleventh-century Japanese women created their own language.
   D. The book traces the history of reading from clay tablets to CD-ROMs.
   E. The book contains many interesting details.

Test questions come in all shapes and sizes. Unlike a direct question about a particular selection, an **open-ended question** may ask you to develop your own thesis about a piece of literature and even let you decide which piece of literature to write about. Whether you are answering a question for your English final or for a national exam like the advanced placement test, it helps to have a strategy for composing your answer.

Look over the sample questions in the box to the right. It is important to note that both of these questions are asking two things:

- What does this work mean (thematically, not literally)?
- How does the author communicate that meaning (what devices or literary elements convey the meaning)?

If you learn to analyze writing prompts, you can easily turn your open-ended prompt into a clear, focused thesis sentence.

> - Discuss how the point of view from which a novel is told affects the reader's understanding of the theme or main idea.
> - Discuss a novel or play in which an early event foreshadows the main event or events that give the work meaning.

Thinking It Through: Developing a Thesis Statement

■ These steps will help you write a thesis statement for an open-ended question.

1. **Read the prompt carefully; underline the key phrases that identify the kind of work and the topic you should write about. Bracket the key phrases that tell you what your essay should accomplish.**

   Prompt: Choose <u>a novel or play that depicts a conflict between a character and a cultural or social attitude.</u> Write an essay in which you [Explain how the conflict contributes to the meaning of the work.]

2. **Choose a work that meets the requirements of prompt.**

3. **Use the underlined and bracketed material to create a thesis about the work you have chosen.** Be sure to include the **(a)** work's title; **(b)** author's name; **(c)** information on the work's theme or meaning; **(d)** information on the device or literary element you will address.

   In Nathaniel Hawthorne's <u>The Scarlet Letter</u>, the conflict between Hester Prynne and a cruel seventeenth-century Puritan community is used to dramatize the central theme of the novel—that a person can be redeemed through tireless, selfless work.

Practice

Directions. The graphic organizer below outlines five steps for developing a thesis statement for an open-ended essay question.

- Choose one of the writing prompts below.
- Copy the graphic organizer below onto a separate sheet of paper.
- Then, complete the graphic organizer to develop a thesis statement.

PROMPTS

- Discuss the ways in which setting reveals the theme of a particular novel.
- Discuss a novel in which symbolism is used to provide an added layer of meaning. Identify what the symbol or symbols represent and how they reveal the theme of the work.

- Discuss a novel in which an early event foreshadows the main event or events that give the work meaning.
- Discuss how the point of view from which a novel is told affects the reader's understanding of theme or main idea.

STEP 1
- Read the prompt carefully.
- Bracket words and phrases that tell you what type of work to write about.
- Underline words and phrases that tell the goal of your essay.

STEP 2 Choose a work (title and author) that suits the prompt:	

STEP 3 Write down the work's theme or meaning:	

STEP 4 Include specific information on the literary element through which you will address the work's theme:	

STEP 5
By combining the information from steps 2 through 4, write out your completed thesis statement.

Thesis statement: _____

_____

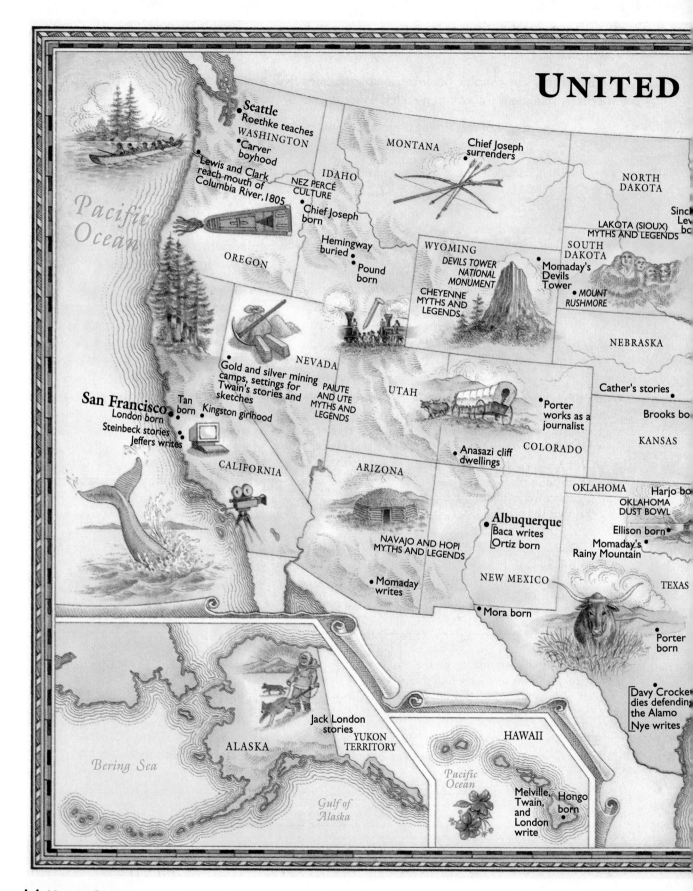

UNITED

Pacific Ocean

Seattle
Roethke teaches
WASHINGTON
Carver boyhood
Lewis and Clark reach mouth of Columbia River, 1805

OREGON

IDAHO
NEZ PERCÉ CULTURE
Chief Joseph born
Hemingway buried
Pound born

MONTANA
Chief Joseph surrenders

WYOMING
DEVILS TOWER NATIONAL MONUMENT
CHEYENNE MYTHS AND LEGENDS

NORTH DAKOTA
Sinc Lev bo

LAKOTA (SIOUX) MYTHS AND LEGENDS

SOUTH DAKOTA
Momaday's Devils Tower
MOUNT RUSHMORE

NEBRASKA

NEVADA
Gold and silver mining camps, settings for Twain's stories and sketches

PAIUTE AND UTE MYTHS AND LEGENDS

UTAH

San Francisco
London born
Steinbeck stories
Jeffers writes
Tan born
Kingston girlhood

CALIFORNIA

ARIZONA
NAVAJO AND HOPI MYTHS AND LEGENDS
Momaday writes

Porter works as a journalist

Anasazi cliff dwellings

COLORADO

Cather's stories
Brooks bo

KANSAS

OKLAHOMA
OKLAHOMA DUST BOWL
Harjo bo
Ellison born
Momaday's Rainy Mountain

Albuquerque
Baca writes
Ortiz born

NEW MEXICO
Mora born

TEXAS
Porter born

Davy Crocke dies defending the Alamo
Nye writes

ALASKA
Bering Sea

Jack London stories
YUKON TERRITORY

Gulf of Alaska

HAWAII
Pacific Ocean
Melville, Twain, and London write
Hongo born

STATES

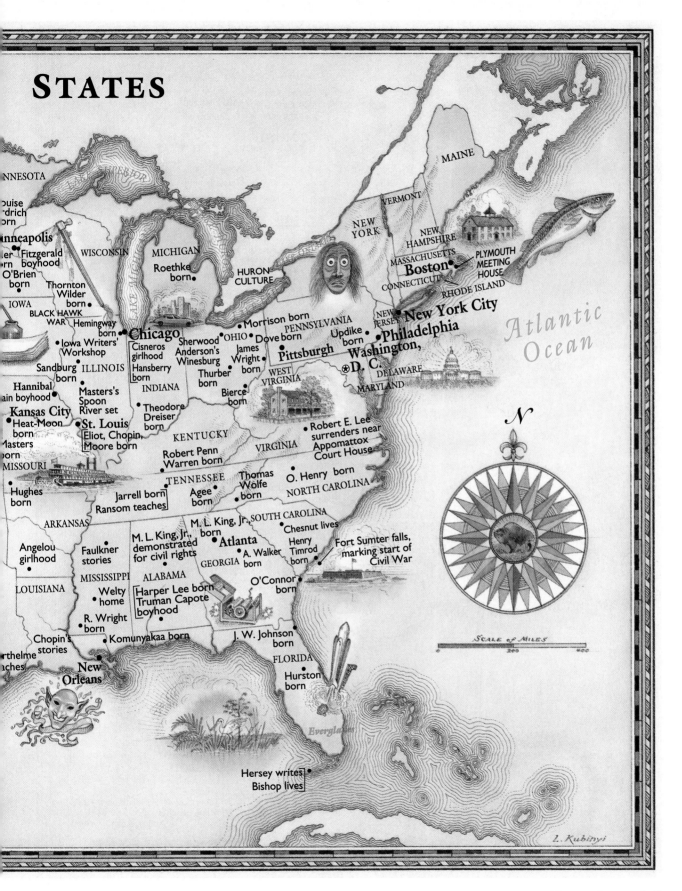

NNESOTA

ouise
rdrich
orn

nneapolis
er Fitzgerald
rn boyhood
O'Brien
born

Thornton
Wilder
born

IOWA
BLACK HAWK
WAR

Hemingway
born

Iowa Writers'
Workshop

Sandburg
born

ILLINOIS

Hannibal
ain boyhood

Kansas City
Heat-Moon
born

Masters
orn

MISSOURI

Hughes
born

ARKANSAS

Angelou
girlhood

LOUISIANA

Chopin's
stories
rthelme
aches

New
Orleans

WISCONSIN

MICHIGAN

Roethke
born

HURON
CULTURE

LAKE MICHIGAN
LAKE SUPERIOR

Chicago

Cisneros
girlhood
Hansberry
born

INDIANA

Masters's
Spoon
River set

Theodore
Dreiser
born

KENTUCKY

Robert Penn
Warren born

TENNESSEE

Jarrell born
Ransom teaches

Sherwood
Anderson's
Winesburg

Thurber
born

Morrison born
Dove born

OHIO

James
Wright
born

Bierce
born

WEST
VIRGINIA

Agee
born

Thomas
Wolfe
born

VIRGINIA

PENNSYLVANIA

Pittsburgh

MISSISSIPPI

Faulkner
stories

ALABAMA

Welty
home

R. Wright
born

Komunyakaa born

M. L. King, Jr.,
demonstrated
for civil rights

GEORGIA

Harper Lee born
Truman Capote
boyhood

M. L. King, Jr.,
born

Atlanta

A. Walker
born

J. W. Johnson
born

O'Connor
born

MAINE

VERMONT

NEW
YORK

NEW
HAMPSHIRE

MASSACHUSETTS

Boston

CONNECTICUT

RHODE ISLAND

PLYMOUTH
MEETING
HOUSE

NEW
JERSEY

New York City

Philadelphia

Updike
born

Washington,
D. C.

DELAWARE

MARYLAND

Robert E. Lee
surrenders near
Appomattox
Court House

O. Henry born

NORTH CAROLINA

SOUTH CAROLINA

Chesnut lives

Henry
Timrod
born

Fort Sumter falls,
marking start of
Civil War

Atlantic
Ocean

N

SCALE of MILES
0 200 400

FLORIDA

Hurston
born

Everglades

Hersey writes
Bishop lives

L. Kubinyi

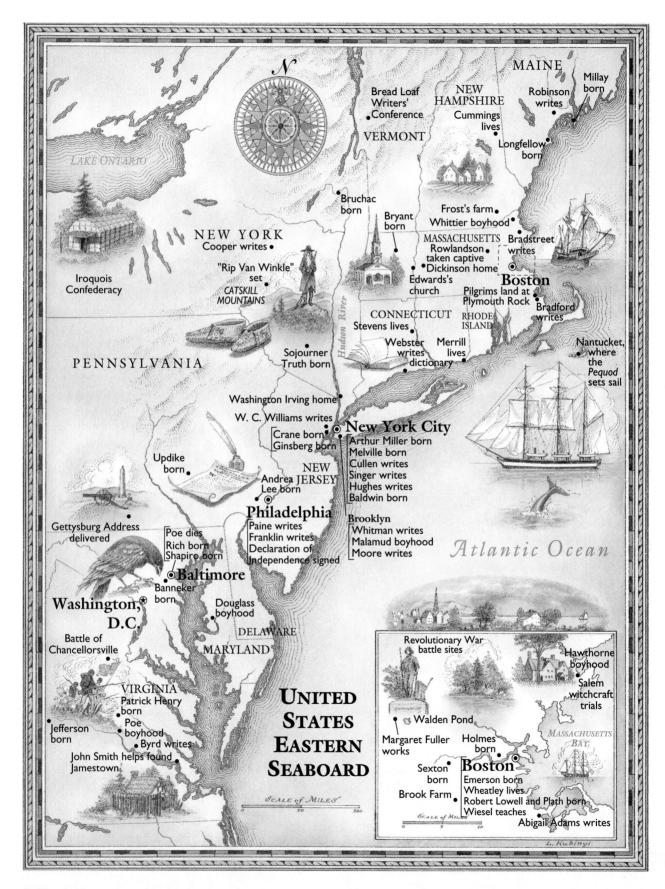

MAINE

Millay born

Robinson writes

NEW HAMPSHIRE
Cummings lives

Longfellow born

Bread Loaf Writers' Conference

VERMONT

Bruchac born

Bryant born

Frost's farm
Whittier boyhood

MASSACHUSETTS
Rowlandson taken captive
Dickinson home

Bradstreet writes

LAKE ONTARIO

NEW YORK
Cooper writes

"Rip Van Winkle" set
CATSKILL MOUNTAINS

Edwards's church

Boston
Pilgrims land at Plymouth Rock

Bradford writes

Iroquois Confederacy

CONNECTICUT
Stevens lives

RHODE ISLAND

Nantucket, where the *Pequod* sets sail

PENNSYLVANIA

Webster writes dictionary

Merrill lives

Sojourner Truth born

Hudson River

Washington Irving home
W. C. Williams writes

Crane born
Ginsberg born

New York City
Arthur Miller born
Melville born
Cullen writes
Singer writes
Hughes writes
Baldwin born

Updike born

NEW JERSEY
Andrea Lee born

Philadelphia
Paine writes
Franklin writes
Declaration of Independence signed

Brooklyn
Whitman writes
Malamud boyhood
Moore writes

Atlantic Ocean

Gettysburg Address delivered

Poe dies
Rich born
Shapiro born

Baltimore
Banneker born

Douglass boyhood

Washington, D.C.

DELAWARE

MARYLAND

Battle of Chancellorsville

VIRGINIA
Patrick Henry born

Poe boyhood

Byrd writes

Jefferson born

John Smith helps found Jamestown

UNITED STATES EASTERN SEABOARD

SCALE of MILES
0   50   100

Revolutionary War battle sites

Hawthorne boyhood

Salem witchcraft trials

Walden Pond

MASSACHUSETTS BAY

Margaret Fuller works

Holmes born

Sexton born

Brook Farm

Boston
Emerson born
Wheatley lives
Robert Lowell and Plath born
Wiesel teaches

Abigail Adams writes

SCALE of MILES
0   5   10

L. Kubinyi

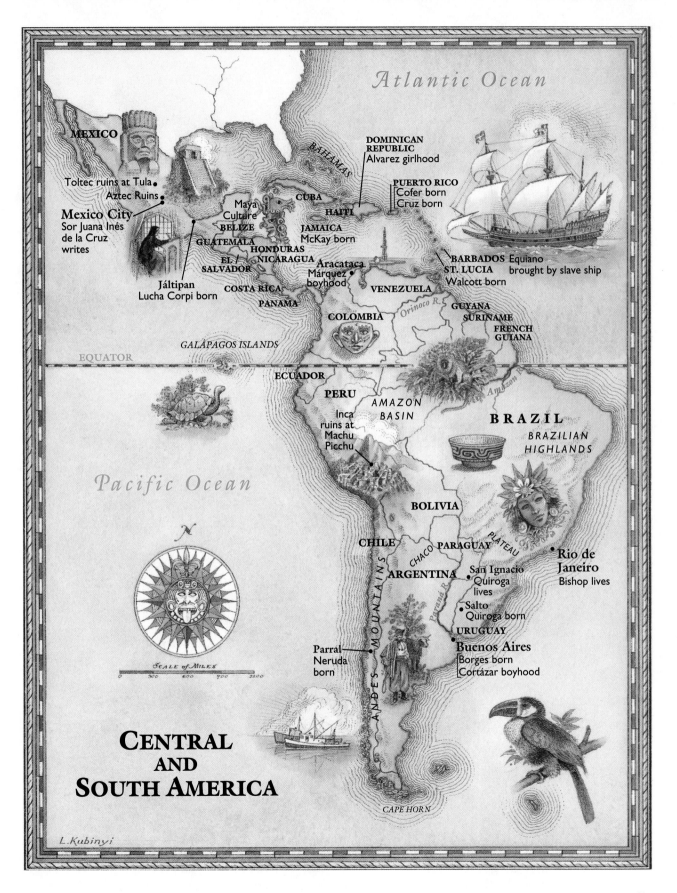

Atlantic Ocean

MEXICO

Toltec ruins at Tula
Aztec Ruins

Mexico City
Sor Juana Inés
de la Cruz
writes

Jáltipan
Lucha Corpi born

Maya
Culture

BELIZE
GUATEMALA
HONDURAS
EL / NICARAGUA
SALVADOR

COSTA RICA
PANAMA

CUBA

HAITI

JAMAICA
McKay born

BAHAMAS

DOMINICAN REPUBLIC
Alvarez girlhood

PUERTO RICO
Cofer born
Cruz born

BARBADOS
ST. LUCIA
Walcott born

Equiano
brought by slave ship

Aracataca
Márquez
boyhood

VENEZUELA

Orinoco R.

GUYANA
SURINAME
FRENCH GUIANA

COLOMBIA

GALÁPAGOS ISLANDS

EQUATOR

ECUADOR

PERU

Inca
ruins at
Machu
Picchu

AMAZON BASIN

Amazon

B R A Z I L

BRAZILIAN HIGHLANDS

Pacific Ocean

BOLIVIA

CHILE

ANDES MOUNTAINS

CHACO

PARAGUAY

PLATEAU

ARGENTINA

Paraná R.

San Ignacio
Quiroga
lives

Salto
Quiroga born

URUGUAY

Rio de Janeiro
Bishop lives

Buenos Aires
Borges born
Cortázar boyhood

Parral
Neruda
born

N

SCALE of MILES
0 300 600 700 1200

CENTRAL AND SOUTH AMERICA

CAPE HORN

L. Kubinyi

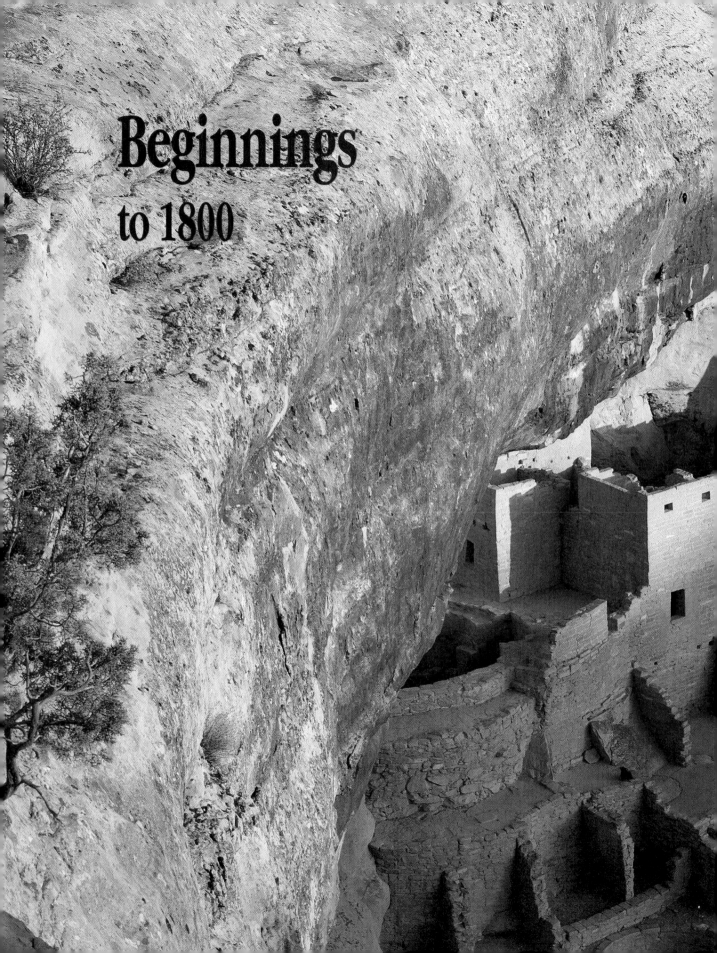

Beginnings
to 1800

This ancient city was built about A.D. 1100 by a pueblo people known as Anasazi ("the old ones"). By 1300, three hundred years before the Pilgrims landed on Plymouth Rock, this beautiful city had been mysteriously abandoned.

Cliff Palace at Mesa Verde National Park, Colorado. © David Muench

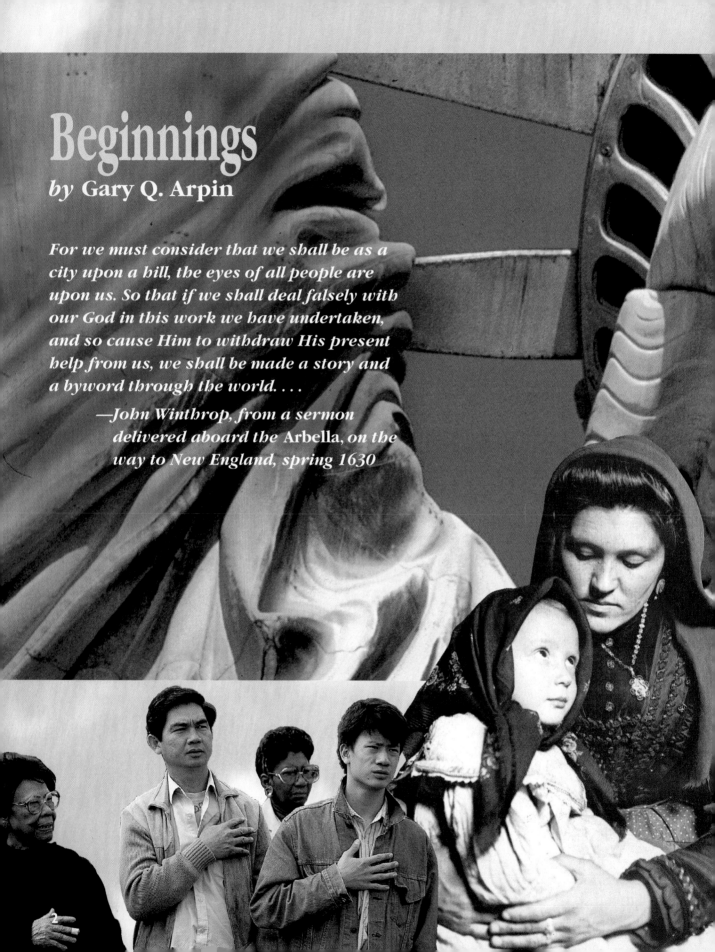

Beginnings

by Gary Q. Arpin

For we must consider that we shall be as a city upon a hill, the eyes of all people are upon us. So that if we shall deal falsely with our God in this work we have undertaken, and so cause Him to withdraw His present help from us, we shall be made a story and a byword through the world. . . .

—John Winthrop, from a sermon delivered aboard the Arbella, *on the way to New England, spring 1630*

The United States is a land of immigrants. The first people began entering North America on foot many thousands of years ago. Then came people in wooden sailing ships. Later, millions came against their will in the stifling holds of slave ships. Millions of others, lacking money for better accommodations, endured weeks of discomfort in cramped, uncomfortable steerage sections of ships. The latest immigrants probably are arriving by plane or even on flimsy rafts as you read these words. Most likely you, your relatives, or some of your classmates immigrated to this country.

The Granger Collection, New York.

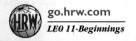

Beginnings to 1800

Reverend Jonathan Edwards (1750–1755) by Joseph Badger. Oil on canvas.

Yale University Art Gallery. Bequest of Eugene Phelps Edwards (1938.74).

LITERARY EVENTS

Spain's Miguel de Cervantes publishes his novel *Don Quixote,* in two parts, 1605, 1615

•

England's William Shakespeare writes *King Lear* and *Macbeth,* 1605–1606

Mary Rowlandson's captivity narrative is published, 1682

•

Anne Bradstreet's *The Tenth Muse Lately Sprung Up in America* is published in England, 1650

•

William Bradford writes *Of Plymouth Plantation,* 1630–1647

William Byrd writes *The History of the Dividing Line,* 1728

•

England's Jonathan Swift publishes the satiric novel *Gulliver's Travels,* 1726

•

England's Daniel Defoe publishes *Robinson Crusoe,* considered one of the first English novels, 1719

England's Henry Fielding publishes the novel *The History of Tom Jones,* 1749

•

Jonathan Edwards delivers his vivid sermon, "Sinners in the Hands of an Angry God," 1741

1450–1615	1615–1699	1700–1729	1730–1749

CULTURAL/HISTORICAL EVENTS

Christopher Columbus lands on an island in the Bahamas, 1492

•

Songhai Empire in West Africa reaches peak, c. 1493–1528

•

Protestant Reformation starts in Germany, 1517

•

Aztec Empire falls to Spanish army, 1521

•

Spanish explorer Álvar Núñez Cabeza de Vaca lands in Florida and spends eight years walking through Texas, New Mexico, and Arizona, 1528–1536

•

Settlement founded at Jamestown, Virginia, 1607

Mayflower Pilgrims land at Plymouth, 1620

•

Great Migration of Puritans to New England begins, c. 1630

•

Mughal emperor Shah Jahan builds Taj Mahal, in northern India, 1632–1638

•

Metacomet's war on Massachusetts Colonies begins, 1675

•

England's Isaac Newton explains laws of motion and gravity in *Principia Mathematica,* 1687

•

Slavery exists in all English colonies in North America, 1690

•

Twenty people executed in witch trials in Salem, Massachusetts, 1692

About 251,000 European settlers live in what is now the United States, 1700

•

Smallpox epidemic hits Boston, 1721

•

German composer Johann Sebastian Bach completes the oratorio *St. Matthew Passion,* 1729

The Great Awakening is touched off by a traveling English preacher, 1740–1745

•

George Frideric Handel's *Messiah* is first performed, in Dublin, Ireland, 1742

•

France's Charles de Montesquieu publishes *The Spirit of Laws,* a study of government later reflected in the U.S. Constitution, 1748

Arresting a witch in the streets of Salem.

The Granger Collection, New York.

Benjamin Franklin's sister-in-law Anne Franklin becomes first woman printer in New England, 1762

•

England's Samuel Johnson publishes his monumental *Dictionary of the English Language,* 1755

•

John Woolman publishes two antislavery essays, 1754, 1763

Thomas Paine publishes *Common Sense,* 1776

•

Patrick Henry demands liberty from British rule, at the Virginia Convention, 1775

•

Phillis Wheatley publishes *Poems on Various Subjects, Religious and Moral,* 1773

•

Benjamin Franklin begins to write his *Autobiography,* 1771

The Federalist, a series of essays by Alexander Hamilton, James Madison, and John Jay, urges voters to approve the U.S. Constitution, 1787–1788

•

Thomas Jefferson publishes *Notes on the State of Virginia,* 1785

•

France's Michel-Guillaume Jean de Crèvecoeur publishes *Letters from an American Farmer,* 1782

Phillis Wheatley.
The Granger Collection, New York.

England's Samuel Taylor Coleridge publishes *The Rime of the Ancient Mariner,* a long Romantic poem, 1798

1750–1769   1770–1779   1780–1789   1790–1800

Benjamin Franklin's experiments with a kite and a key prove that lightning is a manifestation of electricity, 1752

•

French and Indian War officially ends as British gain control of most French North American territory, 1763

•

American colonists hold Stamp Act Congress to protest a direct British tax, 1765; British repeal tax, 1766

Boston Tea Party occurs in Boston Harbor, 1773

•

First shots of American Revolution fired at Lexington and Concord, Massachusetts, April 19, 1775

•

Second Continental Congress adopts Declaration of Independence, July 4, 1776

Boston Tea Party.
Culver Pictures.

U.S. governed under Articles of Confederation, 1781–1788

•

American Revolutionary War ends as British surrender at Yorktown, Virginia, October 1781; peace treaty signed, 1783

•

Austrian composer Wolfgang Amadeus Mozart finishes the opera *Don Giovanni,* 1787

•

George Washington inaugurated as first president under U.S. Constitution, 1789

•

French Revolution begins, 1789

First census in America sets population at about 3.9 million, 1790

•

New York Stock Exchange organized, 1792

•

Invention of cotton gin leads to increase in slave labor, 1793

•

English physician Edward Jenner develops smallpox vaccine, 1796

•

Napoleon Bonaparte becomes dictator of France, 1799

•

Library of Congress established, 1800

•

Washington, D.C., named capital of U.S., 1800

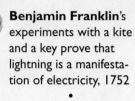

Stamp from Stamp Act, 1765.
© Collection of The New-York Historical Society.

Black Coat, a
Cherokee
chief (1836) by
George Catlin.
Oil on canvas.

The Granger
Collection, New
York.

Eskimo comb.

Breton Littlehales/
National Geographic
Image Collection.

The First Migration: Ice Age Travelers

Archaeological evidence tells us that anywhere from twenty
to over forty thousand years ago, Ice Age hunters traveling
with dogs crossed the Bering land bridge (now submerged
under the Bering Strait) from Siberia to what is now Alaska.
Slowly, these people and their descendants migrated south.
Over the centuries, other migrants followed
that route across the strait (some adventurers
possibly used other means to reach the
shores of North America). By the 1490s,
when the great wave of European exploration of the Americas started, numerous
groups of American Indians were living all over North
America. These societies were diverse, and each had its
own long history. (The Aztec Empire in present-day
Mexico was the largest Native American civilization in the
fifteenth century, with millions of people living within
its borders.)

> Columbus did not
> discover a new
> world; he estab-
> lished contact be-
> tween two worlds,
> both already old.
>
> —J. H. Parry,
> *The Spanish
> Seaborne Empire*
> (1966)

What's important to remember is that there were people
here when the Europeans arrived in the fifteenth century; descendants
of those people are still here, and their traditions remain. In 1994,
for example, the Pequots, whom the English met when they arrived
in what is now Connecticut, Rhode Island, and Massachusetts,
donated ten million dollars to the new National Museum of the
American Indian in Washington, D.C., to promote and save native
cultures.

**People first migrated to North America from twenty to
over forty thousand years ago. When the first Europeans
arrived in the fifteenth century, American Indians were
living in diverse societies spread across the continent.**

The Europeans Arrive: The Explorers

The first detailed European observations of life in this vast continent
were recorded in Spanish and French by explorers of the fifteenth and
sixteenth centuries. These writings open a window to a tumultuous
time when the so-called New World was the heady focus of the dreams
and desires of an entire era. Christopher Columbus
(1451–1506), Francisco Vásquez de Coronado
(1510–1554), and many others described the Americas
in a flurry of eagerly read letters, journals, and books.
Hoping to fund further expeditions, the explorers emphasized the Americas' abundant resources, the peace-
fulness and hospitality of the inhabitants, and the
promise of the unlimited wealth to be gained from
fantastic treasuries of gold.

Turtle and *Flamingo* (1585–1587) by John White. Watercolor.
Copyright British Museum, London. Courtesy of Lee Boltin.

Jacques Cartier's Discovery of the St. Lawrence River (1957) by Thomas H. Benton. Tempera on canvas (7′ × 6′).

In 1528, only thirty-six years after Columbus first sighted that flickering fire on the beach of San Salvador, a Spaniard named Álvar Núñez Cabeza de Vaca (c. 1490–1557) landed with an expedition (he was its treasurer) on the west coast of what is now Florida. Cabeza de Vaca and others left the ship and marched inland. They did not return. Their fleet waited an entire year for them, then departed for Mexico, giving up the explorers for dead. Lost in the Texas Gulf area, Cabeza de Vaca and his companions wandered for the next eight years in search of other Europeans who would help them to get home. Cabeza de Vaca's narrative of his journeys through what is now Texas is a gripping adventure story. It is also

Europeans did not find a wilderness here; rather, however involuntarily, they made one. Jamestown, Plymouth, Salem, Boston, Providence, New Amsterdam, Philadelphia—all grew upon sites previously occupied by Indian communities. So did Quebec and Montreal and Detroit and Chicago. The so-called settlement of America was a resettlement, a reoccupation of a land made waste by the diseases and demoralization introduced by the newcomers.

—Francis Jennings,
The Invasion of America (1975)

a firsthand account of the habits of some of the indigenous people in what is now the United States: what they ate (very little), how they housed themselves, and what their religious beliefs were. De Vaca also provides the first account of some animals and plants that the Europeans had never known existed.

Cabeza de Vaca and his shipmates were alternately captives or companions of the various Native American peoples they encountered on their long trek. Here is part of de Vaca's account of the expedition's experiences with a tribal group in the Gulf Coast area, struggling to survive a famine.

> The reason why the [Europeans] have killed and destroyed such infinite numbers of souls is solely because they have made gold their ultimate aim, seeking to load themselves with riches in the shortest time. . . . These lands, being so happy and so rich, and the people so humble, so patient, and so easily subjugated, they have . . . taken no more account of them . . . than—I will not say of animals, for would to God they had considered and treated them as animals—but as even less than the dung in the streets.
>
> —Bartolomé de Las Casas,
> *Very Brief Account of the
> Destruction of the Indies* (1542)

> Their support is principally roots, of two or three kinds, and they look for them over the face of all the country. The food is poor and gripes the persons who eat it. The roots require roasting two days: Many are very bitter, and withal difficult to be dug. They are sought the distance of two or three leagues, and so great is the want these people experience, that they cannot get through the year without them. Occasionally they kill deer, and at times take fish; but the quantity is so small and the famine so great, that they eat spiders and the eggs of ants, worms, lizards, salamanders, snakes, and vipers that kill whom they strike; and they eat earth and wood, and all that there is, the dung of deer, and other things that I omit to mention; and I honestly believe that were there stones in that land they would eat them. They save the bones of the fishes they consume, of snakes and other animals, that they may afterward beat them together and eat the powder.
>
> —Álvar Núñez Cabeza de Vaca

The first Europeans to visit the Americas were the explorers. Their enthusiastic accounts of the beauty and wealth of the Americas led to increased expeditions to what Renaissance Europeans saw as the New World.

The Puritan Legacy

Interesting and valuable as the explorers' writings are, they were not central to the development of the American literary tradition in the way the writings of the Puritans of New England were. In many respects, the American character has been shaped by the moral, ethical, and religious convictions of the Puritans.

The first and most famous group of these English Puritans landed, in 1620, on the tip of Cape Cod, just before Christmas. They were followed, ten years later, by seven hundred more Puritan settlers. By 1640, as many as twenty thousand English Puritans had sailed to what they called New England.

Although the real commerce of the Puritans was with heaven, they were competent in the business of the world as well: The founding of a new society in North America was a business venture as well as a spiritual one. For the Puritans, the everyday world and the spiritual world were closely intertwined.

Who Were These Puritans?

Puritan is a broad term, referring to a number of Protestant groups that, beginning about 1560, sought to "purify" the Church of England, which since the time of Henry VIII (who reigned from 1509 to 1547) had been virtually inseparable from the country's government. Like other Protestant reformers on the European continent, English Puritans wished to return to the simpler forms of worship and church organization described in the New Testament. For them, religion was first of all a personal, inner experience. They did not believe that the clergy or the government should or could act as an intermediary between the individual and God.

Many Puritans suffered persecution in England. Some were put in jail and whipped, their noses slit and their ears lopped off. Some fled England for Holland. But fearing that in Holland they would lose their identity as English Protestants, a small group led by William Bradford (page 26) and others set sail in 1620 for what was advertised as the New World. There they hoped to build a new society patterned after God's word.

The Puritans were single-minded visionaries convinced of the rightness of their beliefs, but they were also practical and businesslike. They felt that Christian worship and church organization should be simplified in order to more closely resemble Biblical models. Many Puritans were persecuted for their beliefs and fled England for Holland and, ultimately, for North America.

(Left) Page from *The Day of Doom* by Michael Wigglesworth.

Seal on meeting notice.

The Puritan Deacon Samuel Chapin (1899) by Augustus Saint-Gaudens. Bronze model.
James Graham & Sons, Inc., New York.

THE SALEM WITCHCRAFT TRIALS

The Trial for Witchcraft of George Jacobs, August 5, 1692 (1855) by T. H. Matteson. Oil on canvas.

Courtesy Peabody Essex Museum, Salem, Massachusetts.
Photograph by Mark Sexton.

During the cold, dreary winter of 1691–1692, the daughter and the niece of Samuel Parris, a minister in Salem Village, Massachusetts, began to dabble in magic. By February the two girls started having fits. Lesions appeared on their skin, and it seemed as though they were being choked by invisible hands. A doctor diagnosed the girls as being the victims of malicious witchcraft.

Urged to name those responsible for bewitching them, the girls accused Sarah Good and Sarah Osborne, two unpopular women from the village, and Tituba, a slave whom Samuel Parris had brought back from Barbados. During the subsequent trial, the girls writhed and moaned and behaved as though they were being choked. Based on this "evidence," Sarah Good was condemned. In an attempt to save her own life, Tituba confessed to being a witch. She claimed that there was a coven of witches in Massachusetts and testified that she had seen several names written in blood in the Devil's book. The witch hunt had begun.

> In Adam's Fall
> We sinned all.
>
> —*The New England Primer* (c. 1690)

Puritan Beliefs: Sinners All?

For a people who were so convinced they were right, the Puritans had to grapple with complex uncertainties. At the center of Puritan theology was an uneasy mixture of certainty and doubt. The certainty was that because of Adam and Eve's sin of disobedience, most of humanity would be damned for all eternity. But the Puritans were also certain that God in his mercy had sent his son Jesus Christ to earth to save particular people.

The doubt centered on whether a particular individual was one of the saved (the "elect") or one of the damned (the "unregenerate"). How did you know if you were saved or damned?

As it turns out, you did not know. A theology that was so clear-cut in its division of the world between saints and sinners was fuzzy when it came to determining which were which. There were two principal indications of the state of your soul, neither of them completely certain. You were saved by the grace of God, and you could *feel* this grace arriving, in an intensely emotional fashion. The inner arrival of God's grace was demonstrated by your outward

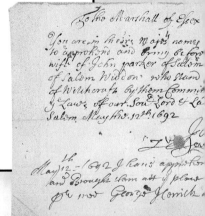

Warrant for the arrest of Ann Pudeator (1692).
Courtesy Peabody Essex Museum, Salem, Massachusetts.

Zealous ministers like Cotton Mather argued that the epidemic of witchcraft proved beyond a doubt that New England was a holy place, since the Devil was so interested in it. Mather and others demanded that all witches be rooted out and severely punished. Hundreds of people from Salem and other eastern Massachusetts towns came forward to testify that they were victims of witchcraft.

Before long the prisons were overcrowded, and a special court was established in Salem Village. Within the next ten months, about 150 people in this small community were accused of witchcraft. Neighbors, especially those with longstanding quarrels, turned on each other. Between June and September, nineteen people were hanged, and one man, Giles Corey, who had refused to plead either innocent or guilty, was crushed to death under a pile of stones.

What really happened at Salem? Many historians believe that Salem experienced a mass hysteria, a sort of shared delusion. Still others have suggested that a more restrictive form of government recently imposed on the Massachusetts Bay Colony, in addition to new economic pressures in the Colony's towns, may have led to bitterness, aggression, and outright paranoia. Perhaps the strict society of Puritan New England finally erupted under the strain of its repression. A recent theory proposes that fear of unusual or powerful "nonconformists"—particularly women—may have led to an attempt to constrain their behavior. Statistics show that the majority of the "witches" were unmarried women between the ages of forty and sixty: eccentric and independent loners with abrasive personalities. Some of them may have been "cunning folk," that is, midwives or people with unusual healing abilities and knowledge of herbal remedies. They were often women who could potentially come into their fathers' inheritances and therefore be seen as a threat to male power.

The Salem trials fascinate to this day. They are the subject of one of the great contemporary American plays, Arthur Miller's *The Crucible* (1953), which is printed in Collection 17 of this text (see page 829).

---

behavior. After receiving grace, you were "reborn" as a member of the community of saints, and you behaved like a saint. People hoping to be among the saved examined their inner lives closely for signs of grace, and they tried to live exemplary lives. So American Puritans came to value self-reliance, industriousness, temperance, and simplicity. These were, coincidentally, the ideal qualities needed to carve out a new society in a strange land.

> *Puritans believed that Adam and Eve's sin had damned most people for all eternity. They also believed that Jesus Christ had been sent to earth to save particular people, known as the "elect." It was difficult to know for certain if one was saved or damned, so the Puritans tried to behave in as exemplary a manner as possible.*

> God's altar needs not our polishing.
> —*The Bay Psalm Book* (1640)

Puritan Politics: Government by Contract

In the Puritan view, a covenant, or contract, existed between God and humanity. This spiritual covenant was a useful model for worldly social organization as well: Puritans believed that people should enter freely into agreements concerning their government. On the *Mayflower,* for example,

Pilgrims Signing the Compact Aboard the Mayflower, *November 11, 1620* (19th century). Colored mezzotint.

the Puritans composed and signed the Mayflower Compact, outlining how they would be governed once they landed. In this use of a contractual agreement, they prepared the ground for American constitutional democracy.

On the other hand, because the Puritans believed the saintly "elect" should exert great influence on government, their political views tended to be undemocratic. There was little room for compromise. The witchcraft hysteria in Salem, Massachusetts, in 1692 (pages 10–11), resulted in part from fear that the community's moral foundation was threatened, and therefore its political cohesion was also in danger.

The Bible in America

The Puritans read the Bible as the story of the creation, fall, wanderings, and rescue of the human race. Within this long and complex narrative, each Puritan could see connections to events in his or her own life or to events in the life of the community. Each Puritan was trained to see life as a pilgrimage, or journey, to salvation. Each Puritan learned to read his or her life the way a literary critic reads a book.

The Puritans believed that the Bible was the literal word of God. Reading the Bible was

---

Characteristics of Puritan Writing

- The Bible provided a model for Puritan writing: a conception of each individual life as a journey to salvation. Puritans saw direct connections between Biblical events and their own lives.

- Puritans used writing to explore their inner and outer lives for signs of the workings of God.

- Diaries and histories were the most common forms of expression in Puritan society; in them writers described the workings of God.

- Puritans favored a plain style, similar to that of the Geneva Bible. They stressed clarity of expression and avoided complicated figures of speech.

a necessity for all Puritans, as was the ability to understand theological debates. For these reasons, the Puritans placed great emphasis on education. Thus, Harvard College, originally intended to train Puritan ministers for the rapidly expanding Colony, was founded in 1636, only sixteen years after the first Pilgrims had landed. And, just three years later, the first printing press in the American Colonies was set up.

Their beliefs required the Puritans to keep a close watch on both the inner and outer events of their lives. This central aspect of the Puritan mind greatly affected their writings. Diaries and histories were important forms of Puritan literature, because they were used to record the workings of God.

> *Puritan belief in a spiritual compact between God and humanity paved the way for American constitutional democracy. The Puritans emphasized education so that people could read and understand the Bible and follow religious debates. Diaries and histories were important forms of Puritan literature.*

Title page of the *Bay Psalm Book* (1640).

The Granger Collection, New York.

The Age of Reason: Tinkerers and Experimenters

By the end of the seventeenth century, new ideas that had been fermenting in Europe began to present a challenge to the unshakable faith of the Puritans.

The Age of Reason, or the Enlightenment, began in Europe with the philosophers and scientists of the seventeenth and eighteenth centuries who called themselves rationalists. **Rationalism** is the belief that human beings can arrive at truth by using reason, rather than by relying on the authority of the past, on religious faith, or on intuition.

The Puritans saw God as actively and mysteriously involved in the workings of the universe; the rationalists saw God differently. The great English rationalist Sir Isaac Newton (1642–1727), who formulated the laws of gravity and motion, compared God to a clockmaker. Having created the perfect mechanism of this universe, God then left his creation to run on its own, like a clock. The rationalists believed that God's special gift to humanity was reason—the ability to think in an ordered, logical manner. This gift of reason enabled people to discover both scientific and spiritual truth. Everyone, then, had the capacity to regulate and improve his or her own life.

While the theoretical background for the Age of Reason took shape in Europe, a home-grown practicality and interest in scientific tinkering or experimenting already thrived in the American Colonies. From the earliest Colonial days, Americans had to be generalists and tinkerers; they had to make do with what they had, and they had to achieve results.

Sir Isaac Newton, President of the Royal Society (1802). Engraving, after a painting by Vanderbank.

The Granger Collection, New York.

Hornbook for children.
Rare Book Department, Free Library of Philadelphia.

The Smallpox Plague

The unlikely hero of America's first foray into scientific exploration was the strict Puritan minister Cotton Mather (1663–1728), who was interested in natural science and medicine.

In April 1721, a ship from the West Indies docked in Boston Harbor. This was not unusual, for trade with the West Indies was one of the foundations of New England economic life. This ship was different, though. For in addition to its cargo of sugar and molasses, this ship carried smallpox.

In the seventeenth and eighteenth centuries, smallpox was one of the scourges of life, as the AIDS virus is today. The disease spread rapidly, disfigured its victims, and was often fatal. The outbreak in Boston in 1721 was a major public-health problem. What was to be done?

Horrible outbreaks of smallpox had ravaged Native Americans ever since the white settlers first landed. Smallpox had been unknown in North America, and the native people had no immunity to the virus. Nearly a century before Boston's smallpox outbreak, Bradford described the horrors of the disease:

For want of bedding and linen and other helps . . . they fall into a lamentable condition as they lie on their hard mats, the pox breaking and mattering and running one into another, their skin cleaving by reason thereof to the mats they lie on. When they turn them, a whole side will flay off at once as it were, and they will be all of a gore blood, most fearful to behold. And then being very sore, what with cold and other distempers, they die like rotten sheep.

—William Bradford

Paul Revere's house, Boston.

At the time of the smallpox epidemic, Cotton Mather was working on what would be the first scholarly essay on medicine written in America. In his opening sentences he reveals his Puritan perspective: "Let us look upon sin as the cause of sickness." His religious point of view did not, however, prevent Mather from seeking cures for specific diseases. He had heard of a method for dealing with smallpox devised by a Turkish physician. The method seemed illogical, but it apparently worked. It was called inoculation. In June 1721, as the smallpox epidemic spread throughout Boston, Mather began a public campaign for inoculation.

Boston's medical community was violently opposed to such an experiment, especially one borrowed from the Muslims. The debate was vigorous, raging all the summer and into the fall. Controversy developed into violence: In November, Mather's house was bombed.

Despite such fierce opposition, Mather succeeded in inoculating nearly three hundred people. By the time the epidemic was over, in March of the following year, only six of these had died. Of the almost six thousand other people who contracted the disease (nearly half of Boston's population),

Cotton Mather (1727) by Peter Pelham. Mezzotint.

The Granger Collection, New York.

(Left) Paul Revere statue, Boston.
(Right) Old State House, Boston.

about eight hundred and fifty had died. The evidence, according to Mather's figures, was clear: Whether or not inoculation made much sense to scientists, it worked.

The smallpox controversy illustrates two interesting points about American life in the early eighteenth century. First, it shows that contradictory qualities of the American character often existed side by side. Puritan thinking was not limited to a rigid and narrow interpretation of the Bible; a devout Puritan like Mather could also be a practical scientist.

Mather's experiment also reveals that a practical approach to social change and scientific research was necessary in America. The frontier farmer with little access to tools shared a problem with the scientist who had few books and a whole new world of plants and animals to catalog. American thought had to be thought in action: an urge to improve the public welfare by being willing to experiment, to try things out, no matter what the authorities might say.

> What then is . . . this new man? . . . He is an American, who, leaving behind him all his ancient prejudices and manners, receives new ones from the new mode of life he has embraced, the new government he obeys, and the new rank he holds. . . . [In America] individuals of all nations are melted into a new race of men, whose labors . . . will one day cause great changes in the world.
>
> —Michel-Guillaume Jean de Crèvecoeur, *Letters from an American Farmer* (1782)

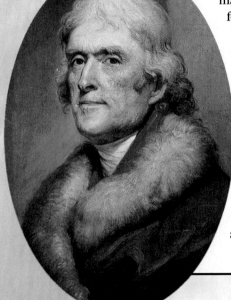

Thomas Jefferson (1805) by Rembrandt Peale. Oil on canvas. Accession number 1867.306.
© Collection of The New-York Historical Society.

Deism: Are People Basically Good?

Like the Puritans, the rationalists discovered God through the medium of the natural world, but in a different way. Rationalists thought it unlikely that God would choose to reveal himself only at particular times to particular people. It seemed much more reasonable to believe that God had made it possible for *all* people at *all* times to discover natural laws through their God-given power of reason.

This outlook, called **deism** (dē′iz′əm), was shared by many eighteenth-century thinkers, including many founders of the American nation. American deists came from different religious backgrounds. But the deists avoided supporting specific religious groups. They sought, instead, the principles that united all religions.

Deists believed that the universe was orderly and good. In contrast to the Puritans, deists stressed humanity's goodness. They believed in the perfectibility of every individual through the use of reason. God's objective, in the deist view, was the happiness of his creatures. Therefore, the best form of worship was to do good for others. There already existed in America an impulse to improve people's lives, as Cotton Mather's struggle to save Boston from small-

The Battle of Bunker Hill (detail) (1776) by Winthrop Chandler (1747–1790). United States. Oil on canvas (34½" × 53⅝").

Museum of Fine Arts, Boston/Gift of Mr. and Mrs. Gardner Richardson (1982.281).

pox illustrates. Deism elevated this impulse to one of the nation's highest goals. To this day, social welfare is still a political priority and still the subject of fierce debate.

The American struggle for independence was justified largely by appeals to rationalist principles. The Declaration of Independence bases its arguments on rationalist assumptions about the relations between people, God, and natural law.

> **In contrast to Puritans, deists believed that God was available to all people all of the time. Deists believed that people were inherently good, that every individual had the gift of reason and with that gift could perfect himself or herself and society.**

Reason and free inquiry . . . are the natural enemies of error, and of error only.

—Thomas Jefferson, *Notes on the State of Virginia* (1785)

Self-Made Americans

Most of the literature written in the American Colonies during the Age of Reason was, understandably, rooted in reality. This was an age of pamphlets, since most literature was intended to serve practical or political ends. Following the Revolutionary War (1775–1783), the problems of organizing and governing the new nation were of the highest importance.

The unquestioned masterpiece of the American Age of Reason is Benjamin Franklin's *Autobiography* (page 86). Franklin used the autobiographical narrative, a form common in Puritan writing, and took out its religious justification. Written in clear, witty prose, this account of the development of the self-made American provided the model for a story that would be told again and again. In the twentieth century, it appears in F. Scott Fitzgerald's novel *The Great Gatsby* (1925), as well as in the countless biographies and autobiographies of self-made men and women on the best-seller lists today.

E Pluribus Unum. Woodcarving.

Shelburne Museum, Shelburne, Vermont. Photograph by Ken Burris.

> **The masterpiece of the Revolutionary era is Franklin's Autobiography. Franklin took the Puritan impulse toward self-examination and molded it into the classic American rags-to-riches story—the triumph of the self-made person.**

Benjamin Franklin.

Drawing by David Levine. Reprinted with permission from *The New York Review of Books.* Copyright © 1967 NYREV, Inc.

The Rationalist Worldview

- People arrive at truth by using reason rather than by relying on the authority of the past, on religion, or on nonrational mental processes like intuition.
- God created the universe but does not interfere in its workings.
- The world operates according to God's rules, and through the use of reason we can discover those rules.
- People are basically good and perfectible.
- Since God wants people to be happy, they worship God best by helping other people.
- Human history is marked by progress toward a more perfect existence.

Quickwrite

Legacies of the Puritans and Rationalists

Do you see evidence of the worldviews of the Puritans and rationalists around you today? Think especially of debates about government, social welfare, and self-improvement. Write down a few of your observations about Puritanism and rationalism in American public life today. Give some examples.

Collection 1

VISIONS AND VOYAGES

Native American Literature
Bradford
Rowlandson
Byrd
Equiano

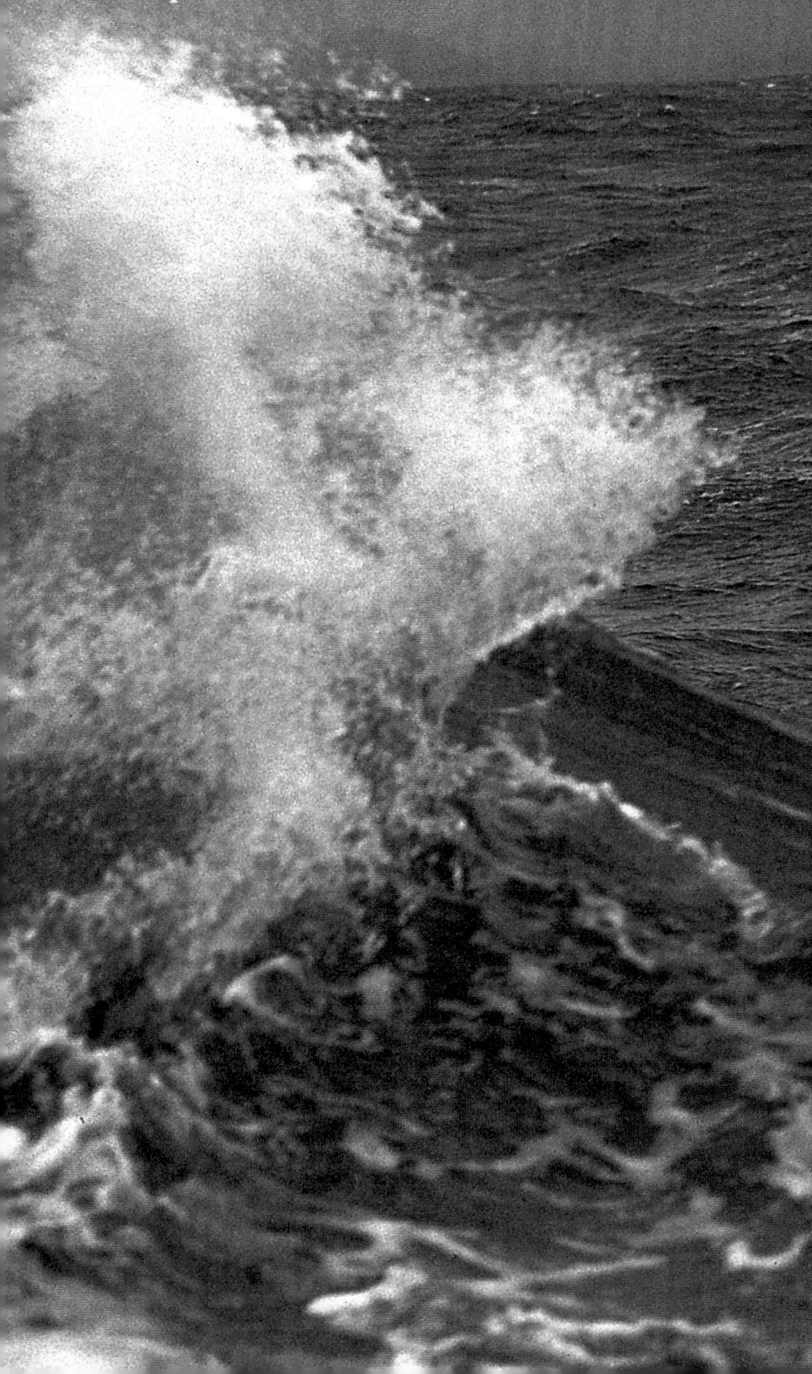

The Journey

One day you finally knew
what you had to do, and began,
though the voices around you
kept shouting
their bad advice—
though the whole house
began to tremble
and you felt the old tug
at your ankles.
"Mend my life!"
each voice cried.
But you didn't stop.
You knew what you had to do,
though the wind pried
with its stiff fingers
at the very foundations—
though their melancholy
was terrible.
It was already late
enough, and a wild night,
and the road full of fallen
branches and stones.
But little by little,
as you left their voices behind,
the stars began to burn
through the sheets of clouds,
and there was a new voice,
which you slowly
recognized as your own,
that kept you company
as you strode deeper and deeper
into the world,
determined to do
the only thing you could do—
determined to save
the only life you could save.

—Mary Oliver (1935–   )

The Sun Still Rises in the Same Sky: Native American Literature

by Joseph Bruchac

Background

Few peoples have been as appreciated and, at the same time, as misrepresented as the many different cultures today called "American Indian" or "Native American." Images of "Indians" are central to mainstream America, from Longfellow's misnamed epic poem *The Song of Hiawatha* (which actually tells the story of the Chippewa hero Manabozho, not the Iroquois Hiawatha) to the "cowboys and Indians" tradition of movies about the Old West. Yet it's only recently that the authentic literary voices of Native Americans have received serious attention. Native American literature has been a living oral tradition, but it was never treated with the same respect as European, or Western, literature. But Western literature itself has its roots firmly planted in the oral tradition—such ancient classics as the *Odyssey* and *Beowulf,* long before they were written down, were stories kept alive by word of mouth. The vast body of American Indian oral literature, encompassing dozens of epic narratives and countless thousands of stories, poems, songs, oratory, and chants, was not even recognized by Western scholars until the late 1800s. Until then, it was assumed that Native Americans had no literature.

Part of the problem scholars had in recognizing the rich traditions of American Indian literature was translating the texts from hundreds of different languages—a task often best done by Native Americans themselves. Over the decades, various American Indian writers—N. Scott Momaday, Louise Erdrich, Simon J. Ortiz, and Leslie Marmon Silko, among others—have revitalized Native American literature by combining their fluency in English with a deep understanding of their own languages and traditions.

We can make some important generalizations about American Indian oral traditions. First of all, Native American cultures use stories to teach moral lessons and convey practical information about the natural world. A story from the Abenaki people of Maine, for example, tells how Gluskabe catches all of the game animals. He is then told by

his grandmother to return the animals to the woods. They will die if they are kept in his bag, she tells him, and if they do die, there will be no game left for the people to come. In this one brief tale, important, life-sustaining lessons about greed, the wisdom of elders, and game management are conveyed in an entertaining and engaging way.

American Indian literature also reflects a view of the natural world that is more inclusive than the one typically seen in Western literature. The Native American universe is not dominated by human beings. Animals and humans are often interchangeable in myths and folk tales. Origin myths may even feature animals as the instruments of creation.

All American Indian cultures also show a keen awareness of the power of metaphor. Words are as powerful and alive as the human breath that carries them. Songs and chants can make things happen— call game animals, bring rain, cure the sick, or destroy an enemy. For Native Americans, speech, or oratory—often relying on striking similes drawn from nature—is a highly developed and respected literary form.

Passed on from generation to generation, oral traditions preserve historical continuity. But these traditions are also, like the Native American peoples themselves, tenacious, dynamic, and responsive to change. The American Indian worldview is not that of a progressive straight line, but of an endless circle. This cyclical nature of existence is reflected both in the natural world itself, with its changing seasons and cycles of birth, death, and rebirth, and in Native American ceremonies repeated year after year. Each summer, for example, the Lakota people have their Sun Dance. In pre-Columbian times, they went to the Sun Dance on foot; after the coming of the Spanish, they rode horses to the annual event. Today, the Lakota arrive by automobile. While a European eye might see the technology of transport as the important point of this anecdote, to a Lakota the issue of changing transportation is unimportant. It is, after all, only a different way of getting to the same place. The sun still rises in the same sky.

Quickwrite

Before you read these examples of Native American literature, make a KWL chart like the one below. Fill out the first two columns—what you already know about Native American literature and culture and what you'd like to learn about it. Leave the third column blank for now.

K What I Know	W What I Want to Know	L What I Learned

The Sky Tree

In the beginning, Earth was covered with water. In Sky Land, there were people living as they do now on Earth. In the middle of that land was the great Sky Tree. All of the food which the people in that Sky Land ate came from the great tree.

The old chief of that land lived with his wife, whose name was Aataentsic,[1] meaning "Ancient Woman," in their long house near the great tree. It came to be that the old chief became sick, and nothing could cure him. He grew weaker and weaker until it seemed he would die. Then a dream came to him, and he called Aataentsic to him.

"I have dreamed," he said, "and in my dream I saw how I can be healed. I must be given the fruit which grows at the very top of Sky Tree. You must cut it down and bring that fruit to me."

Aataentsic took her husband's stone ax and went to the great tree. As soon as she struck it, it split in half and toppled over. As it fell, a hole opened in Sky Land, and the tree fell through the hole. Aataentsic returned to the place where the old chief waited.

"My husband," she said, "when I cut the tree, it split in half and then fell through a great hole. Without the tree, there can be no life. I must follow it."

Then, leaving her husband, she went back to the hole in Sky Land and threw herself after the great tree.

As Aataentsic fell, Turtle looked up and saw her. Immediately Turtle called together all the water animals and told them what she had seen.

"What should be done?" Turtle said.

Beaver answered her. "You are the one who saw this happen. Tell us what to do."

"All of you must dive down," Turtle said. "Bring up soil from the bottom, and place it on my back."

Immediately all of the water animals began to dive down and bring up soil. Beaver, Mink, Muskrat, and Otter each brought up pawfuls of wet soil and placed the soil on Turtle's back until they had made an island of great size. When they were through, Aataentsic settled down gently on the new Earth, and the pieces of the great tree fell beside her and took root.

—*from* the Huron–Eastern Woodland tradition, *as retold by* Joseph Bruchac

Navajo sand painter at Hubbell Trading Post, Ganado, Arizona.

Jerry Jacka Photography.

---

1. Aataentsic (ä′tä·ent′sik).

The Earth Only

Wica'hcala kin	The old men
heya'pelo'	say
maka' kin	the earth
lece'la	only
tehan yunke'lo	endures
eha' pelo'	You spoke
ehan'kecon	truly
wica' yaka pelo'	You are right.

—*composed by* Used-As-A-Shield
  (Teton Sioux), *translated in* 1918

Storyteller figurine by Helen
Cordero. Pottery. Cochiti Pueblo,
New Mexico.

Courtesy of The Heard Museum, Phoenix,
Arizona/Jerry Jacka Photography.

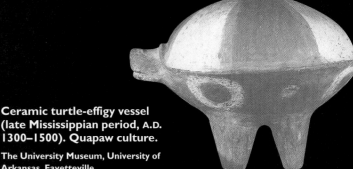

Ceramic turtle-effigy vessel
(late Mississippian period, A.D.
1300–1500). Quapaw culture.
The University Museum, University of
Arkansas, Fayetteville.

from The House Made of Dawn
from The Night Chant

In Tsegihi,
In the house made of dawn,
In the house made of evening twilight,
In the house made of dark cloud,
5 In the house made of male rain,
In the house made of dark mist,
In the house made of female rain,
In the house made of pollen,
In the house made of grasshoppers,
10 Where the dark mist curtains the doorway,
The path to which is on the rainbow,
Where the zigzag lightning stands on top,
Where the he-rain stands high on top,
Oh, male divinity!
15 With your moccasins of dark cloud, come to us. . . .

I have made your sacrifice.
I have prepared a smoke for you.
My feet restore for me.
My limbs restore for me.
20 My body restore for me.
My mind restore for me.
My voice restore for me. . . .

Happily I recover.
Happily my interior grows cool.
25 Happily my limbs regain their power.
Happily my head becomes cool.
Happily I hear again.
Happily I walk.
Impervious to pain, I walk.
30 Feeling light within, I walk.
With lively feelings, I walk. . . .

—*from* the Navajo tradition,
  translated by Washington Matthews

Coyote Finishes His Work

From the very beginning, Coyote was traveling around all over the earth. He did many wonderful things when he went along. He killed the monsters and the evil spirits that preyed on the people. He made the Indians, and put them out in tribes all over the world because Old Man Above wanted the earth to be inhabited all over, not just in one or two places.

He gave all the people different names and taught them different languages. This is why Indians live all over the country now and speak in different ways.

He taught the people how to eat and how to hunt the buffalo and catch eagles. He taught them what roots to eat and how to make a good lodge and what to wear. He taught them how to dance. Sometimes he made mistakes, and even though he was wise and powerful, he did many foolish things. But that was his way.

Coyote liked to play tricks. He thought about himself all the time, and told everyone he was a great warrior, but he was not. Sometimes he would go too far with some trick and get someone killed. Other times, he would have a trick played on himself by someone else. He got killed this way so many times that Fox and the birds got tired of bringing him back to life. Another way he got in trouble was trying to do what someone else did. This is how he came to be called Imitator.

Coyote was ugly too. The girls did not like him. But he was smart. He could change himself around and trick the women. Coyote got the girls when he wanted.

One time, Coyote had done everything he could think of and was traveling from one place to another place, looking for other things that needed to be done. Old Man saw him going along and said to himself, "Coyote has now done almost everything he is capable of doing. His work is almost done. It is time to bring him back to the place where he started."

So Great Spirit came down and traveled in the shape of an old man. He met Coyote.

Coyote said, "I am Coyote. Who are you?"

Old Man said, "I am Chief of the earth. It was I who sent you to set the world right."

"No," Coyote said, "you never sent me. I don't know you. If you are the Chief, take that lake over there and move it to the side of that mountain."

"No. If you are Coyote, let me see you do it."

Coyote did it.

"Now, move it back."

Coyote tried, but he could not do it. He thought this was strange. He tried again, but he could not do it.

Chief moved the lake back.

Coyote said, "Now I know you are the Chief."

Old Man said, "Your work is finished, Coyote. You have traveled far and done much good. Now you will go to where I have prepared a home for you."

Then Coyote disappeared. Now no one knows where he is anymore.

Old Man got ready to leave, too. He said to the Indians, "I will send messages to the earth by the spirits of the people who reach me but whose time to die has not yet come. They will carry messages to you from time to time. When their spirits come back into their bodies, they will revive and tell you their experiences.

"Coyote and myself, we will not be seen again until Earthwoman is very old. Then we shall return to earth, for it will require a change by that time. Coyote will come along first, and when you see him you will know I am coming. When I come along, all the spirits of the dead will be with me. There will be no more Other Side Camp. All the people will live together. Earthmother will go back to her first shape and live as a mother among her children. Then things will be made right."

Now they are waiting for Coyote.

—*from* the Nez Percé tradition,
retold by **Barry Lopez**

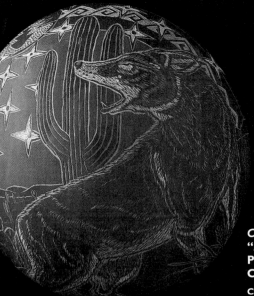

Sand painting, which represents storm, lightning, and the four seasons, by Michael Tsosie.

Courtesy of Fifth Generation Trading Company/Jerry Jacka Photography.

Coyote Crooner by Rosemary "Apple Blossom" Lonewolf. Pottery (3½″ × 4½″). Santa Clara Pueblo, New Mexico.

Courtesy Gallery 10, Scottsdale/Jerry Jacka Photography.

Coyote-Effigy Platform Pipe (Middle Woodland period, 200 B.C.–A.D. 100). Pipestone; Temper mound (6.4″ × 7″). Scioto County, Ohio. Ohio Hopewell culture.

Photograph © The Detroit Institute of Arts, 1995. Collection of Ohio Historical Society, Columbus. Photo courtesy © The Detroit Institute of Arts, Dirk Bakker, photographer (WL-117).

FINDING COMMON GROUND

Now that you've read these examples of Native American literature, meet in small groups to share your questions, comments, and discoveries.

- Each person in the group should review the KWL chart in his or her Quickwrite and fill in the third column, "What I Learned."

- As a group, discuss what members learned from reading these selections. Then go back to the "What I Want to Know" column, and decide if there are any other topics you'd like to discuss and learn more about. Be sure someone in the group records the suggested topics and any group responses.

- Choose some aspect of Native American culture you'd like to learn more about: storytelling, ceremonies, healing, symbols, dances, myths, historical figures, language, art, environmental issues, or whatever else you like. Choose something that grabs your interest, and, by yourself or with a partner, develop your own avenue of exploration. Share your newfound knowledge with the rest of the class.

William Bradford

(1590–1657)

William Bradford's life displayed a mixture of the commonplace and the extraordinary that was characteristic of the Puritan experience. Bradford was the son of a prosperous farmer in Yorkshire, England. He received no higher education but instead was taught the practical arts of farming. Despite his lack of formal training (or perhaps because of it), Bradford was to become a successful, longstanding Colonial governor in America, dealing out justice and settling disputes.

Growing up in England, Bradford took a radical step when he was twelve years old. Inspired by his reading of the Bible and by the sermons of a Puritan minister, Bradford began attending the meetings of a small group of Nonconformists, despite the vehement objections of his family and friends. It was illegal for Nonconformists to worship publicly, so the group met furtively in a private house in the nearby town of Scrooby. In 1606, when the group organized as a separate Congregational church, Bradford joined them. In 1608, under increasing pressure of persecution and fearful that they would be imprisoned, the Scrooby group crossed the North Sea to Holland. In 1620, after twelve years in Holland, the group was aided by London profiteers and merchants, who lent them a ship and crew as an investment. In September the Nonconformists sailed for America in order to found a community where they would be free to worship and live according to their beliefs.

For Bradford the hardships of the long ocean voyage did not end with the landing at Plymouth. In December, while the *Mayflower* was anchored in Provincetown Harbor, Bradford and other men took a small boat ashore to scout for a place to land and build shelter. When they returned, Bradford learned that his young wife had fallen or jumped from the ship. Perhaps Dorothy Bradford was in despair when land was finally sighted and she did not see the hoped-for green hills of an earthly paradise. Beyond the ship lay only the bleak sand dunes of Cape Cod. That bitter winter, half the settlers were to die of cold, disease, and malnutrition.

The following year, Bradford was elected governor of the plantation. "If he had not been a person of more than ordinary piety, wisdom, and courage," the Puritan preacher Cotton Mather later recorded, Bradford would "have sunk" under the difficulties of governing such a shaky settlement. Bradford proved to be an exemplary leader, and he went on to be elected governor of the Colony no fewer than thirty times.

As the Plymouth Colony prospered and grew, it also gradually disintegrated as a religious community, despite Bradford's efforts to hold it together. The ideal of the "city on the hill," the Pilgrims' dream of an ideal society founded on religious principles, gradually gave way to the realities of life in the new land. Bradford's record of this grand experiment ends in disappointment. When more fertile areas for settlement were found and when Boston became a more convenient port to England, Plymouth lost much of its population. "Thus was this poor church left," Bradford wrote in 1644, "like an ancient mother grown old and forsaken of her children. . . . Thus, she that had made many rich became herself poor."

Page from *Of Plimoth Plantation* by William Bradford.

Courtesy of the State Library of Massachusetts.

Before You Read

FROM OF PLYMOUTH PLANTATION

Make the Connection

Journey to Salvation

Every age has at least one figure or heroic type that seems to embody its ideals and aspirations. The Puritans who came to America identified so powerfully with one figure that they called themselves by that name: "Pilgrim." A pilgrim is someone who makes a pilgrimage, or a journey to a holy place. But for the Puritans, the word *pilgrimage* took on a wider meaning—it was a journey to salvation.

For the Pilgrims, the outward journey of their lives and the specific voyage to America were also inner, spiritual journeys. "A Christian is sailing through this world unto his heavenly country," the poet Anne Bradstreet (page 68) wrote some years after sailing across the Atlantic to America. "We must, therefore, be here as strangers and pilgrims, that we may plainly declare that we seek a city above."

Elements of Literature

The Plain Style

In their style of writing, as well as in their manner of worship, the Puritans favored the plain and unornamented. Though the style used by Puritan writers now seems hard to read, in the 1600s it was considered simple and direct. This **plain style** emphasized uncomplicated sentences and the use of everyday words from common speech, and it steered clear of elaborate figures of speech and imagery.

Reading Skills and Strategies

Using Study Strategies

When you encounter texts as challenging as Bradford's, two study strategies will help you: **note taking** and compiling a **time line of main events.**

As you read, jot down questions you have about the text, along with any of your personal responses to Bradford's ideas. For this text, be sure especially to note places where Bradford tries to link the Pilgrims' experience with God's plan for their salvation.

When you have finished reading, go back over the text and make a time line of the main events. You can include both main and subsidiary events by using a series-of-events chain like the one below. Put main events in the large boxes and subsidiary events in the smaller ones.

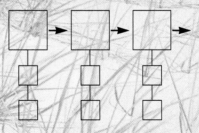

T he **plain style** is a way of writing that stresses simplicity and clarity of expression.

For more on the Plain Style, see page 35 and the Handbook of Literary Terms.

Background

In 1630, Bradford began to write this account of the Plymouth settlement, and he continued to write an annual account until 1647. Unlike many other early Colonial histories, it was not composed for immediate publication or to attract more colonists, but was intended to inspire future generations to carry on the Pilgrims' ideals. The first nine chapters of Bradford's history were copied into the Plymouth church records, but the entire manuscript was lost when British troops plundered the church during the Revolutionary War. Almost a century later, Governor Bradford's vellum-bound volume was discovered in the library of the bishop of London. *Of Plymouth Plantation* was first published in 1856 by the Massachusetts Historical Society. The manuscript was finally returned to the United States in 1897, and it can be seen today in Boston.

from Of Plymouth Plantation
William Bradford

They fell upon their knees and blessed

the God of Heaven who had brought them

over the vast and furious ocean . . .

Landing of the Pilgrims at Plymouth (1803) by Michel Felice Corné. Oil on canvas.

from Chapter 9

Of their Voyage, and how they Passed the Sea; and of their Safe Arrival at Cape Cod

September 6 [1620]. These troubles[1] being blown over, and now all being compact together in one ship, they put to sea again with a prosperous wind, which continued divers[2] days together, which was some encouragement unto them; yet, according to the usual manner, many were afflicted with seasickness. And I may not omit here a special work of God's providence. There was a proud and very profane young man, one of the seamen, of a lusty,[3] able body, which made him the more haughty; he would always be condemning the poor people in their sickness and cursing them daily with grievous execrations; and did not let to tell them that he hoped to help to cast half of them overboard before they came to their journey's end, and to make merry with what they had; and if he were by any gently reproved, he would curse and swear most bitterly. But it pleased God before they came half seas over, to smite this young man with a grievous disease, of which he died in a desperate manner, and so was himself the first that was thrown overboard. Thus his curses light on his own head, and it was an astonishment to all his fellows for they noted it to be the just hand of God upon him.

1. **troubles:** the return of the *Speedwell* to England and the transfer of her passengers to the *Mayflower*.
2. **divers** (dī′vərz): many.
3. **lusty:** energetic; robust.

WORDS TO OWN

profane (prō·fān′) *adj.*: irreverent.
haughty (hôt′ē) *adj.*: proud; disdainful of something or someone.
execrations (ek′si·krā′shənz) *n.*: angry words; curses.
reproved (ri·prōovd′) *v.*: reprimanded.

Ear of corn (1535), pages 29, 31, 32, 33.
The Granger Collection, New York.

After they had enjoyed fair winds and weather for a season, they were encountered many times with crosswinds and met with many fierce storms with which the ship was shroudly[4] shaken, and her upper works made very leaky; and one of the main beams in the midships was bowed and cracked, which put them in some fear that the ship could not be able to perform the voyage. So some of the chief of the company, perceiving the mariners to fear the sufficiency of the ship as appeared by their mutterings, they entered into serious consultation with the master and other officers of the ship, to consider in time of the danger, and rather to return than to cast themselves into a desperate and inevitable peril. And truly there was great distraction and difference of opinion amongst the mariners themselves; fain[5] would they do what could be done for their wages' sake (being now near half the seas over) and on the other hand they were loath[6] to hazard their lives too desperately. But in examining of all opinions, the master and others affirmed they knew the ship to be strong and firm underwater; and for the buckling of the main beam, there was a great iron screw the passengers brought out of Holland, which would raise the beam into his place; the which being done, the carpenter and master affirmed that with a post put under it, set firm in the lower deck and otherways bound, he would make it sufficient. And as for the decks and upper works, they would caulk them as well as they could, and though with the working of the ship they would not long keep staunch,[7] yet there would otherwise be no great danger, if they did not overpress her with sails. So they committed themselves to the will of God and resolved to proceed.

In sundry of these storms the winds were so fierce and the seas so high, as they could not bear a knot of sail, but were forced to hull[8] for divers days together. And in one of them, as they thus lay at hull in a mighty storm, a lusty young man called John Howland, coming upon some occasion above the gratings was, with a seele[9] of the ship, thrown into sea; but it pleased God that he caught hold of the topsail halyards[10] which hung overboard and ran out at length. Yet he held his hold (though he was sundry fathoms underwater) till he was hauled up by the same rope to the brim of the water, and then with a boathook and other means got into the ship again and his life saved. And though he was something ill with it, yet he lived many years after and became a profitable member both in church and commonwealth. In all this voyage there died but one of the passengers, which was William Butten, a youth, servant to Samuel Fuller, when they drew near the coast.

But to omit other things (that I may be brief) after long beating at sea they fell with that land which is called Cape Cod;[11] the which being made and certainly known to be it, they were not a little joyful. After some deliberation had amongst themselves and with the master of the ship, they tacked about and resolved to stand for the southward (the wind and weather being fair) to find some place about Hudson's River[12] for their habitation. But after they had sailed that course about half the day, they fell amongst dangerous shoals and roaring breakers, and they were so far entangled therewith as they conceived themselves in great danger; and the wind shrinking upon them withal, they resolved to bear up again for the Cape and thought themselves happy to get out of those dangers before night overtook them, as by God's good providence they did. And the next day they got into the Cape Harbor[13] where they rid in safety. . . .

Being thus arrived in a good harbor, and brought safe to land, they fell upon their knees and blessed the God of Heaven who had brought them over the vast and furious ocean, and

10. **halyards** (hal'yərdz): ropes for raising a sail.
11. **Cape Cod:** They sighted Cape Cod at daybreak on November 9, 1620.
12. **Hudson's River:** They were trying for Manhattan Island. Henry Hudson had made his voyage in 1609 and had claimed the area for the Dutch, but the English did not recognize the Dutch claim.
13. **Cape Harbor:** now called Provincetown Harbor. The sea voyage from England had taken sixty-five days.

WORDS TO OWN

consultation (kän'səl·tā'shən) *n.*: meeting to discuss or plan.

sundry (sun'drē) *adj.*: some.

---

4. **shroudly** (shrōōd'lē): shrewdly, used here in its archaic sense of "wickedly."
5. **fain** (fān): archaic for "gladly."
6. **loath** (lōth): reluctant.
7. **staunch** (stônch): watertight.
8. **hull:** to float without using the sails.
9. **seele:** sudden lurch to one side.

delivered them from all the perils and miseries thereof, again to set their feet on the firm and stable earth, their proper element. . . .

But here I cannot but stay and make a pause, and stand half amazed at this poor people's present condition; and so I think will the reader, too, when he well considers the same. Being thus passed the vast ocean, and a sea of troubles before in their preparation (as may be remembered by that which went before), they had now no friends to welcome them nor inns to entertain or refresh their weather-beaten bodies; no houses or much less towns to repair to, to seek for succor.[14] It is recorded in Scripture[15] as a mercy to the Apostle and his shipwrecked company, that the barbarians showed them no small kindness in refreshing them, but these savage barbarians, when they met with them (as after will appear) were readier to fill their sides full of arrows than otherwise. And for the season it was winter, and they that know the winters of that country know them to be sharp and violent, and subject to cruel and fierce storms, dangerous to travel to known places, much more to search an unknown coast. Besides, what could they see but a hideous and desolate wilderness, full of wild beasts and wild men—and what multitudes there might be of them they knew not. Neither could they, as it were, go up to the top of Pisgah[16] to view from this wilderness a more goodly country to feed their hopes; for which way soever they turned their eyes (save upward to the heavens) they could have little solace or content in respect of any outward objects. For summer being done, all things stand upon them with a weather-beaten face, and the whole country, full of woods and thickets, represented a wild and savage hue. If they looked behind them, there was the mighty ocean which they had passed and was now as a main bar and gulf to separate them from all the civil parts of the world. . . .

What could now sustain them but the Spirit of God and His grace? May not and ought not the children of these fathers rightly say: "Our fathers were Englishmen which came over this great ocean, and were ready to perish in this wilderness; but they cried unto the Lord, and He heard their voice and looked on their adversity,"[17] etc.? "Let them therefore praise the Lord, because He is good: And His mercies endure forever." "Yea, let them which have been redeemed of the Lord, show how He hath delivered them from the hand of the oppressor. When they wandered in the desert wilderness out of the way, and found no city to dwell in, both hungry and thirsty, their soul was overwhelmed in them. Let them confess before the Lord His lovingkindness and His wonderful works before the sons of men."[18]

from Chapter 11

The Starving Time

[1620–1621] But that which was most sad and lamentable was, that in two or three months' time half of their company died, especially in January and February, being the depth of winter, and wanting houses and other comforts; being infected with the scurvy and other diseases which this long voyage and their inaccommodate condition had brought upon them. So as there died sometimes two or three of a day in the foresaid time, that of 100 and odd persons, scarce fifty remained. And of these, in the time of most distress, there was but six or seven sound persons who to their great commendations, be it spoken, spared no pains night nor day, but with abundance of toil and hazard of their own health, fetched them wood, made them fires, dressed them meat, made their beds, washed their loathsome clothes, clothed and unclothed them. In a word, did all the homely and necessary offices for them which dainty and queasy stomachs cannot endure to hear named; and all this willingly and cheerfully, without any grudging in the least, showing herein their true love unto their friends and brethren; a rare example and worthy to be remembered. Two of these seven were Mr. William Brewster, their

---

14. **succor** (suk′ər): aid.
15. **Scripture:** In the Acts of the Apostles (Chapter 28), Paul tells how the shipwrecked Christians were helped by the "barbarous people" of Malta.
16. **Pisgah** (piz′gə): mountain from which Moses first viewed the Promised Land.

17. **they cried . . . their adversity:** paraphrase of Deuteronomy 26:7.
18. **Let them . . . the sons of men:** paraphrase of Psalm 107.

reverend Elder, and Myles Standish,[19] their Captain and military commander, unto whom myself and many others were much beholden in our low and sick condition. And yet the Lord so upheld these persons as in this general calamity they were not at all infected either with sickness or lameness. And what I have said of these I may say of many others who died in this general visitation, and others yet living; that whilst they had health, yea, or any strength continuing, they were not wanting to any that had need of them. And I doubt not but their recompense is with the Lord.

But I may not here pass by another remarkable passage not to be forgotten. As this calamity fell among the passengers that were to be left here to plant, and were hasted ashore and made to drink water that the seamen might have the more beer, and one[20] in his sickness desiring but a small can of beer, it was answered that if he were their own father he should have none. The disease began to fall amongst them also, so as almost half of their company died before they went away, and many of their officers and lustiest men, as the boatswain, gunner, three quartermasters, the cook and others. At which the Master was something strucken and sent to the sick ashore and told the Governor he should send for beer for them that had need of it, though he drunk water homeward bound.

But now amongst his company there was far another kind of carriage in this misery than amongst the passengers. For they that before had been boon companions in drinking and jollity in the time of their health and welfare, began now to desert one another in this calamity, saying they would not hazard their lives for them, they should be infected by coming to help them in their cabins; and so, after they came to lie by it, would do little or nothing for them but, "if they died, let them die." But such of the passengers as were yet aboard showed them what mercy they could, which made some of their hearts <u>relent</u>, as the boatswain (and some others) who was a proud young man and would often curse and scoff at the passengers. But when he grew weak, they had

compassion on him and helped him; then he confessed he did not deserve it at their hands, he had abused them in word and deed. "Oh!" (saith he) "you, I now see, show your love like Christians indeed one to another, but we let one another lie and die like dogs." Another lay cursing his wife, saying if it had not been for her he had never come this unlucky voyage, and anon cursing his fellows, saying he had done this and that for some of them; he had spent so much and so much amongst them, and they were now weary of him and did not help him, having need. Another gave his companion all he had, if he died, to help him in his weakness; he went and got a little spice and made him a mess of meat once or twice. And because he died not so soon as he expected, he went amongst his fellows and swore the rogue would cozen[21] him, he would see him choked before he made him any more meat; and yet the poor fellow died before morning.

Indian Relations

All this while the Indians came skulking about them, and would sometimes show themselves aloof off, but when any approached near them, they would run away; and once they stole away their tools where they had been at work and were gone to dinner. But about the 16th of March, a certain Indian came boldly amongst them and spoke to them in broken English, which they could well understand but marveled at it. At length they understood by <u>discourse</u> with him, that he was not of these parts, but belonged to the eastern parts where some English ships came to fish, with whom he was acquainted and could name sundry of them by their names, amongst whom he had got his language. He became profitable to them in acquainting them with many things concerning the state of the country in the east parts where he lived, which was afterward profitable unto them; as also of the people here, of their names, number

---

21. **cozen** (kuz′ən): cheat.

19. **Myles Standish** (c. 1584–1656): a soldier who had been hired to handle the colonists' military affairs. Not a member of the Puritan congregation, he still became a most steadfast ally.
20. **one:** Bradford himself.

Words to Own

relent (ri·lent′) v.: soften.
discourse (dis′kôrs′) n.: conversation.

and strength, of their situation and distance from this place, and who was chief amongst them. His name was Samoset.[22] He told them also of another Indian whose name was Squanto,[23] a native of this place, who had been in England and could speak better English than himself.

Being, after some time of entertainment and gifts dismissed, a while after he came again, and five more with him, and they brought again all the tools that were stolen away before, and made way for the coming of their great Sachem, called Massasoit.[24] Who, about four or five days after, came with the chief of his friends and other attendance, with the aforesaid Squanto. With whom, after friendly entertainment and some gifts given him, they made a peace with him (which hath now continued this 24 years)[25] in these terms:

1. That neither he nor any of his should injure or do hurt to any of their people.
2. That if any of his did hurt to any of theirs, he should send the offender, that they might punish him.
3. That if anything were taken away from any of theirs, he should cause it to be restored; and they should do the like to his.
4. If any did unjustly war against him, they would aid him; if any did war against them, he should aid them.
5. He should send to his neighbors confederates to certify them of this, that they might not wrong them, but might be likewise comprised in the conditions of peace.
6. That when their men came to them, they should leave their bows and arrows behind them.

After these things he returned to his place called Sowams, some 40 miles from this place, but Squanto continued with them and was their interpreter and was a special instrument sent of God for their good beyond their expectation. He directed them how to set their corn, where to take fish, and to procure other commodities, and was also their pilot to bring them to unknown places for their profit, and never left them till he died. He was a native of this place, and scarce any left alive besides himself. He was carried away with divers others by one Hunt, a master of a ship, who thought to sell them for slaves in Spain. But he got away for England and was entertained by a merchant in London, and employed to Newfoundland and other parts, and lastly brought hither into these parts by one Mr. Dermer, a gentleman employed by Sir Ferdinando Gorges and others for discovery and other designs in these parts. . . .

First Thanksgiving

They began now to gather in the small harvest they had, and to fit up their houses and dwellings against winter, being all well recovered in health and strength and had all things in good plenty. For as some were thus employed in affairs abroad, others were exercised in fishing, about cod and bass and other fish, of which they took good store, of which every family had their portion. All the summer there was no want; and now began to come in store of fowl, as winter approached, of which this place did abound when they came first (but afterward decreased by degrees). And besides waterfowl there was great store of wild turkeys, of which they took many, besides venison, etc. Besides they had about a peck of meal a week to a person, or now since harvest, Indian corn to that proportion. Which made many afterward write so largely of their plenty here to their friends in England, which were not feigned but true reports.[26]

---

22. Samoset (sam′ə·set′) (1590?–1655): a Pemaquid from Maine.
23. Squanto (skwän′tō) (1585?–1622): one of the few survivors of the Pawtuxet, an Algonquian people. He later joined Massasoit's Wampanoags.
24. Massasoit (mas′ə·soit′) (c. 1580–1661): sachem (chief) of the Wampanoags, who lived in the area which became Rhode Island and southern Massachusetts.
25. With whom . . . this 24 years: The treaty was kept faithfully until the reign of Massasoit's younger son, Metacomet (1639?–1676), also known to the colonists as King Philip. (See Mary Rowlandson's narrative on page 40.)

26. Which made . . . true reports: Although the specific day of the Plymouth colonists' first Thanksgiving is not known, it occurred in the fall of 1621. For three days, Massasoit and almost a hundred of his men joined the Pilgrims, feasting and playing games.

WORDS TO OWN

confederates (kən·fed′ər·its) n.: allies; persons who share a common purpose.
comprised (kəm·prīzd′) v.: included.

An American Story

ANTHONY LEWIS

Fifteen years ago this Thanksgiving weekend, a ten-year-old Vietnamese boy named Viet Dinh arrived in this country as a refugee. He was with his mother, four sisters, and a brother. They had two hundred dollars, which they spent on used winter coats.

They were boat people. They had left Vietnam on a small fishing boat, which lost its engine in a storm. They drifted for days until they made it to Malaysia—swimming in at night to avoid patrol boats that had fired at them. After months in a refugee camp, they were cleared for admission to the United States and flown to Portland, Oregon.

Two members of the family were left behind in Vietnam: Viet Dinh's father, Phong Dinh, and his older sister Van Dinh, who was twenty then. She stayed behind to help their father.

Phong Dinh had been a city councilman in Vung Tau during the Saigon regime. When the Communists took over in 1975, he was sent to a reeducation camp. He escaped from the camp on June 12, 1978, and was on the run when his wife and six children left.

Over the next five years, Phong Dinh tried unsuccessfully twenty-five times to get out of Vietnam by boat. He paid boatmen who never turned up or who were arrested. Finally, in 1983, he made it to the Philippines, and then to the United States.

That left the oldest child, Van Dinh. She had helped her father pay the boatmen. But it was six years before she managed to leave herself: on a boat that reached Hong Kong in August 1989.

The family here knew that she had left Vietnam because they got a message to that effect. But for a year they did not know she was in a Hong Kong refugee camp; indeed, they did not know whether she had landed anywhere or had gone down at sea, as many boat people had.

Van Dinh was kept in the locked Hong Kong camp for three years, waiting for clearance as a refugee. With her was her five-year-old son, Quan, who had a congenital heart condition. That made her desperate to reach the United States, but for years she could not even get an interview with those in charge of the refugee process in Hong Kong.

At the end of 1991, Viet Dinh, then twenty-three years old, sent me an essay he had written about his sister Van's plight in Hong Kong. I forwarded it to *The New York Times* Op-Ed page, and the editors published it in January 1992.

Last month I had another letter from Viet Dinh. It had good news about his sister. After his Op-Ed piece was published, other papers picked up the story. The Hong Kong authorities, feeling the pressure, finally interviewed Van Dinh—and found that she was entitled to refugee status. In September 1992, she made it to Portland. The family was reunited after fifteen years.

There is more to tell about the Dinh family, as I learned when I interviewed Viet. His parents are running a small grocery in Salem, Oregon. A sister, Anh, helps them. Another sister, Thu, is an accountant. Kathleen and Leanne are computer programmers. Viet's one brother, Bao, is an architect.

The child with the heart condition, Van's son Quan, has been treated in Portland. He is doing fine.

Van herself, after fourteen months in the United States, is

Vietnamese boat people rescued by the cargo ship *Medecins du Monde.*

Patrick Barvie/Gamma Liaison.

studying at a community college in Salem and working as an assembler in an electronics plant. "After she gets her English and cultural skills together," Viet said, "I think she'd like to open a business."

It is an American story, and one that I wish members of Congress and their constituents who are fulminating these days about "the immigrant threat" would think about. The Dinh family is doing exactly what immigrants on the Lower East Side and so many other places did in past years: struggling for themselves and making this country better.

There is no other country that has taken in so many people from so many places and cultures, and gained so much in the process. To turn away from that tradition now would do the United States great damage.

One more thing about Viet Dinh. His recent letter ended: "I graduated from the Harvard Law School in June and am now a law clerk for Judge Laurence H. Silberman of the U.S. Court of Appeals in Washington. Next year I clerk for Justice Sandra Day O'Connor at the Supreme Court."

—from The New York Times,
November 26, 1993

MAKING MEANINGS

First Thoughts

1. What qualities or beliefs of the Puritans do you think enabled them to deal with the hardships they faced both on their voyage and in America?

Reading Check

With several classmates, compare the **time lines** you compiled. Discuss any differences, and try to agree on a common set of main and subsidiary events.

Shaping Interpretations

2. At what points in his history does Bradford give inner, spiritual significance to outward events?

3. Consider the treaty drawn up with Massasoit (Chapter 11), and explain whether or not you feel its terms were equally favorable to both parties. What seems to be Bradford's attitude toward the Wampanoag?

4. One event that Bradford does not describe is the death of his wife, who either fell or jumped overboard in Provincetown Harbor. What reasons can you propose for his having omitted it? How would his history have been different if he had included this tragedy?

Extending the Text

5. In what ways might the Pilgrims' experiences be relevant to contemporary pioneers or refugees? In your response, take into account the experiences of the Dinh family in "An American Story" (see *Connections* on page 34).

ELEMENTS OF LITERATURE

The Plain Style

At the beginning of his history, Bradford says he will try to unfold his story "in a plain style, with singular regard unto the simple truth in all things." He means that he will not imitate the ornate "high style" that was in fashion in England at the time—a style that used classical allusions, Latin quotations, and elaborate figures of speech, as in this 1629 example from the poet and Anglican clergyman John Donne:

> First, for the incomprehensibleness of God, the understanding of man hath a limited, a determined latitude; it is an intelligence able to move that sphere which it is fixed to, but could not move a greater: I can comprehend *naturam naturatam,* created nature, but for that *natura naturans,* God himself, the understanding of man cannot comprehend.

In a sense, Bradford's stylistic preference reflected the division between the Puritans and the Anglicans in matters of worship. A plain writing style was in keeping with the Puritans' preference for plainness in all other things, especially in church ritual. They thought that a "plain style" was much more effective than an elevated or "high style" in revealing God's truth. The **plain style** imitated the style of the Bible the Puritans used: the Geneva Bible, published in 1560. (Other English Protestants of the time used the elegant King James translation, published in 1611.) Simple sentences, everyday language, and direct, unembellished statements—without such figures of speech as similes and metaphors—were the chief characteristics of the plain style.

Bradford's style may seem far from "plain" to a modern reader because it abounds in **Biblical quotations** and **allusions.** Also, his **syntax** and **vocabulary** are now **archaic,** or no longer in common use.

1. Identify and write down three of Bradford's sentences that contain elements of the plain style.

2. Recast the sentences into straightforward modern prose. In doing this, how has the "Biblical" sound been affected?

CHOICES: Building Your Portfolio

Comparing Writers' Purposes

2. Come to America!

Captain John Smith (c. 1580–1631) led the first permanent English settlement in America at Jamestown, Virginia, in 1607. He hoped to establish another colony in New England, and in order to attract settlers, he wrote a pamphlet. In the following excerpt, Smith, somewhat like a contemporary travel agent, attempts to persuade people to join him in the new land. Write a brief essay in which you contrast Smith's rosy promises with Bradford's actual experiences in America. Contrast the **purposes** of the two writers and their intended **audiences.** Note how each writer's **motivation** may affect his credibility.

> Here nature and liberty afford us that freely which in England we want, or it costs us dearly. What pleasure can be more than (being tired with any occasion ashore) in planting vines, fruits, or herbs, in contriving their own grounds to the pleasure of their own minds, their fields, gardens, orchards, buildings, ships, and other works, etc.; to re-create themselves before their own doors, in their own boats upon the sea, where man, woman, and child, with a small hook and line, by angling may take divers sorts of excellent fish at their pleasures? . . . He is a very bad fisher [who] cannot kill in one day with his hook and line one, two, or three hundred cods, which dressed and dried, if they be sold there for ten shillings the hundred [pounds], though in England they will give more than twenty, may not both the servant, the master, and merchant be well content with this gain? If a man work but three days in seven, he may get more than he can spend, unless he will be excessive. . . .
>
> For hunting, also, the woods, lakes, and rivers afford not only chase sufficient for any that delight in that kind of toil or pleasure, but such beasts to hunt that besides the delicacy of their bodies for food, their skins are so rich as may well recompense thy daily labor with a captain's pay.
>
> —John Smith,
> *from "A Description of New England," 1616*

Speaking and Listening

3. When Cultures Clash

As a class, divide into two groups, one representing the Pilgrims and the other the American Indians. Each of the two groups should further divide into smaller groups to discuss problems, conflicts, and grievances that have arisen, or may arise in the future, between the two cultures. Afterward, each small group should choose a person to represent the group's viewpoint in a panel discussion. Start with a brief statement by each panelist, followed by questions from all class members.

Reading Skills and Strategies

VOCABULARY: WHEN A DICTIONARY CAN HELP

English speakers from long ago used words that we no longer use or that have changed meaning over time. These obsolete words and meanings are called **archaisms.** No matter how carefully we read, we cannot always find the appropriate definition by using clues in the text. We need outside help—a dictionary.

Most of the time, when you want to look up a word you don't know, a collegiate or abridged dictionary will be all you need. However, when you are reading a work of early American literature, you may need to use an unabridged dictionary, such as *Webster's Third New International Dictionary* or the *Oxford English Dictionary* (called *OED* for short). These dictionaries define numerous archaisms.

Bradford uses the archaic word *fain* in his history (page 30). He uses it to describe the mariners' dilemma of whether to continue on in the damaged *Mayflower* or to return to England—"fain would they do what could be done for their wages' sake . . . and on the other hand they were loath to hazard their lives too desperately." *Fain* is a common archaism,

Of Plimoth Plantation by William Bradford. *Mayflower II,* a recreation of the *Mayflower.*

Ms. courtesy of the State Library of Massachusetts. Mayflower photo courtesy of Plimoth Plantation.

so an abridged dictionary ably covers its meaning, both as an adjective and an adverb:

> **fain** (fān) *adj.* [ME joyful, joyfully < OE *fægen*, glad, akin to ON *feginn* < IE base *pek-, to be satisfied > FAIR[1]] [Archaic] **1** glad; ready **2** reluctantly willing **3** eager —**adv.** [Archaic] with eagerness; gladly: used with *would* [he would *fain* stay]

Because you don't encounter archaisms that frequently, you'll probably want to keep a careful record of these words in a vocabulary notebook so that you can review them. You may want to make a chart like the one below.

Word _____	
Word's etymology	
Meaning in this context	
Is meaning still in use?	
Is word still in use?	
Other common meanings	
Does the word imply a value judgment? If so, what evidence supports it?	
Dictionary (or dictionaries) used	

Try It Out

Use a good dictionary—unabridged if necessary—to help you determine the meanings and parts of speech of the following underlined words as they are used in Bradford's history.

1. "These troubles being blown over, and now all being <u>compact</u> together in one ship . . ." (page 29)

2. ". . . and on the other hand they were loath to <u>hazard</u> their lives too desperately." (page 30)

3. ". . .they had now. . . no houses or much less towns to <u>repair</u> to, to seek for succor." (page 31)

Mary Rowlandson

(c. 1636–c. 1678)

From June 1675 to August 1676, the Wampanoag chief, Metacomet, called King Philip by the colonists, carried out a series of bloody raids on Colonial settlements in what is now called King Philip's War. The Puritans viewed the war as a sign of God's punishment for the sins of their young people (who had taken to dancing and wearing their hair long), but a conflict between colonists and American Indians was probably inevitable. It was the natural result of growing encroachments by the settlers on American Indian land. The native people of New England had been forced into ever more restricted areas, and, although they had sold the land, they rejected conditions stipulating that they could no longer hunt on it. To them, "selling" meant selling the right to share the land with the buyers, not selling its exclusive ownership.

Matters came to a head when Metacomet's former assistant, who had given information to the colonists, was killed by his own people. His killers were tried and hanged by the Puritans. This was too much for Metacomet to bear, and two weeks later the most severe war in the history of New England began. Its tragic result was the virtual extinction of the indigenous way of life in the region. Among the war's victims was Mary Rowlandson, the wife of the Congregational minister of Lancaster, a frontier town of about fifty families that was located thirty miles west of Boston. On a February morning, she and her three children were carried away by a Wampanoag raiding party that wanted to trade hostages for money. After eleven weeks and five days of captivity, Rowlandson's ransom was paid.

Courtesy of American Antiquarian Society.

She was to survive for only two more years.

Rowlandson's captors, it is important to realize, were only slightly better off than their prisoners. Virtually without food, they were chased from camp to camp by Colonial soldiers. Their captives, they thought, were the only currency with which to buy supplies and food. In a graphic passage, Rowlandson describes the lengths to which the Wampanoag were driven by their hunger, eating horses, dogs, frogs, skunks, rattlesnakes, and even tree bark. "They would pick up old bones," she wrote, "and cut them to pieces at the joints, and if they were full of worms and maggots, they would scald them over the fire to make the vermin come out, and then boil them, and drink up the liquor. . . . They would eat horse's guts, and ears, and all sorts of wild birds which they could catch. . . . I can but stand in admiration," she concluded, "to see the wonderful power of God in providing for such a vast number of our enemies in the wilderness, where there was nothing to be seen."

Rowlandson's narrative not only presents a terrifying and moving tale of frontier life but also provides insight into how the Puritans viewed their lives with a characteristic double vision. For Rowlandson, as for other Puritans, events had both a physical and a spiritual significance. She did not want merely to record her horrifying experience; she wished to demonstrate how it revealed God's purpose. The full title of her narrative (when first published in 1682) illustrates this intention: *The Sovereignty and Goodness of God, Together with the Faithfulness of His Promises Displayed: Being a Narrative of the Captivity and Restauration of Mrs. Mary Rowlandson.*

Make the Connection

Survival Skills

Who hasn't listened with rapt attention to stories of people enduring life-threatening circumstances—a flood, a plane crash on a snowy mountain, an earthquake, a wartime siege, or captivity as a hostage or prisoner of war? Perhaps our fascination with such stories comes from wondering how we would survive if we were put to the same test—instead of just sitting in safe surroundings reading about it.

Reading Skills and Strategies

Analyzing Text Structures: Chronological Order

As you read, keep track of events and how they affect Rowlandson by taking notes in three columns. Use the first column to list events in **chronological order** (also called time or sequential order). Use the second column to note where Rowlandson links her sufferings with those of people in the Bible. Use the third column to record her comments about her captors regarding some of the events. You will have more entries in the first column than in either of the other two.

Events in chronologi-cal order	References to Bible	Comments about captors

Portrait of Ninigret II, Chief of the Niantic Indians (c. 1681). Anonymous. American. Oil on canvas (33⅛″ × 30⅛″).

Elements of Literature

Allusions

The Puritans regarded Biblical captivity narratives, such as the enslavement of Moses and the Israelites by the Egyptians, as allegories representing the Christians' liberation from sin through the intervention of God's grace. Rowlandson views her experiences as a repetition of the same Biblical pattern and uses **allusions** to reflect her own situation. Through apt quotations from the Bible, Rowlandson places her experiences in the context of the ancient Biblical captivities.

> **A**n **allusion** is a reference to someone or something that is known from history, literature, religion, politics, sports, science, or some other branch of culture.
>
> *For more on Allusion, see the Handbook of Literary Terms.*

from A Narrative of the Captivity

Mary Rowlandson

The Move to an Indian Village on the Ware River, Near Braintree (February 12–27)

The morning being come, they prepared to go on their way. One of the Indians got up upon a horse, and they set me up behind him, with my poor sick babe in my lap. A very <u>wearisome</u> and <u>tedious</u> day I had of it; what with my own wound, and my child's being so exceeding sick, and in a <u>lamentable</u> condition with her wound. It may be easily judged what a poor feeble condition we were in, there being not the least crumb of refreshing that came within either of our mouths from Wednesday night to Saturday night, except only a little cold water. This day in the afternoon, about an hour by sun, we came to the place where they intended, *viz.*[1] an Indian town, called Wenimesset, norward of Quabaug. . . . I sat much alone with a poor wounded child in my lap, which moaned night and day, having nothing to revive the body, or cheer the spirits of her, but instead of that, sometimes one Indian would come and tell me one hour, that your master will knock your child in the head, and then a second, and then a third, your master will quickly knock your child in the head.

1. **viz.:** Latin for "namely."

WORDS TO OWN

wearisome (wir′i·səm) *adj.*: fatiguing; exhausting.
tedious (tē′dē·əs) *adj.*: tiring; dreary.
lamentable (lam′ən·tə·bəl) *adj.*: regrettable; distressing.

King Philip's sash, ornamented with glass beads (late 1600s). Wampanoag.

Peabody Museum, Harvard University. Photo by Hillel Burger.

This was the comfort I had from them, miserable comforters are ye all, as he said.[2] Thus nine days I sat upon my knees, with my babe in my lap, till my flesh was raw again; my child being even ready to depart this sorrowful world, they bade me carry it out to another wigwam (I suppose because they would not be troubled with such spectacles) whither I went with a very heavy heart, and down I sat with the picture of death in my lap. About two hours in the night, my sweet babe like a lamb departed this life, on February 18, 1675. It being about six years and five months old. It was nine days from the first wounding, in this miserable condition, without any refreshing of one nature or another, except a little cold water. I cannot but take notice, how at another time I could not bear to be in the room where any dead person was, but now the case is changed; I must and could lie down by my dead babe, side by side all the night after. I have thought since of the wonderful goodness of God to me, in preserving me in the use of my reason and senses, in that distressed time, that I did not use wicked and violent means to end my own miserable life. In the morning, when they understood that my child was dead they sent for me home to my master's wigwam: (by my master in this writing, must be understood Quanopin, who was a Sagamore,[3] and married King Philip's[4] wife's sister; not that he first took me, but I was sold to him by another Narragansett Indian, who took me when first I came out of the garrison). I went to take up my dead child in my arms to carry it with me, but they bid me let it alone: There was no resisting, but go I must and leave it. When I had been at my master's wigwam, I took the first opportunity I could get, to go look after my dead child: When I came I asked them what they had done with it. Then they told me it was upon the hill: Then they went and showed me where it was, where I saw the ground was newly digged, and there they told me they had buried it: There I left that child in the wilderness, and must commit it, and myself also in this wilderness condition, to him who is above all. God having taken away this dear child, I went to see my daughter Mary, who was at this same Indian town, at a wigwam not very far off, though we had little liberty or opportunity to see one another. She was about ten years old, and taken from the door at first by a Praying Ind.[5] and afterward sold for a gun. When I came in sight, she would fall aweeping; at which they were provoked, and would not let me come near her, but bade me be gone; which was a heart-cutting word to me. I had one child dead, another in the wilderness, I knew not where, the third they would not let me come near to: "Me (as he said) have ye bereaved of my Children, Joseph is not, and Simeon is not, and ye will take Benjamin also, all these things are against me."[6] I could not sit still in this condition, but kept walking from one place to another. And as I was going along, my heart was even overwhelmed with the thoughts of my condition, and that I should have children, and a nation which I knew not ruled over them. Whereupon I earnestly entreated the Lord, that He would consider my low estate, and show me a token for good, and if it were His blessed will, some sign and hope of some relief. And indeed quickly the Lord answered, in some measure, my poor prayers: For as I was going up and down mourning and lamenting my condition, my son came to me, and asked me how I did; I had not seen him before, since the destruction of the

---

2. he said: The Biblical allusion is to Job 16:2. In the passage cited, Job addresses those who try to console him in his afflictions. God had severely tested Job's faith by causing Job to lose his children and his money, and to break out in boils all over his body.
3. Sagamore (sag′ə·môr′): a secondary chief in the hierarchy of several Native American peoples.
4. King Philip's: Metacomet (1639?–1676), son of Massasoit (c. 1580–1661) and chief of the Wampanoag from 1661 to 1676, was called King Philip by the colonists. In 1675, Metacomet led the Wampanoag and other American Indians in an attempt to end settlements in New England. The colonists retaliated, and both sides sustained heavy losses of life in the resulting massacres, which came to be known as King Philip's War. Mary Rowlandson's captivity was part of this conflict. (See William Bradford's narrative *Of Plymouth Plantation*, page 33.)

5. Praying Ind.: Native Americans who converted to Christianity were known as "praying Indians." The Colonial assemblies allowed these converts to live in self-governing towns.
6. Me . . . against me: Rowlandson quotes Jacob's lament in Genesis 42:36. Jacob had only his youngest son, Benjamin, at home.

WORDS TO OWN

entreated (en·trēt′ed) v.: asked sincerely; prayed to.

Captivity Narratives

Mary Rowlandson's *A Narrative of the Captivity* was one of the most widely read prose works of the seventeenth century. It was especially popular in England, where people were eager for lurid tales of native inhabitants in the Americas. Rowlandson's story went through at least thirty editions, and it inspired a mass of imitations that were often partially faked or purely fictional. These "captivity" stories became one of the most widely produced forms of entertainment in America, but they had a tragic side effect: They contributed to the further deterioration of relations between American Indians and colonists.

Between the seventeenth and nineteenth centuries, as settlers moved westward and occupied American Indian lands, tensions between the two groups increased. American Indians, in retaliation for various injustices, raided settlements and took captives to ransom, to enslave, or to sell to the French or even to other native peoples. These captives didn't necessarily suffer

grim fates: Some captives actually chose to remain with their captors and were adopted by them; a few married American Indians and never expressed any desire to return to their original homes. Many of those who escaped or were ransomed recorded their experiences when they returned home. Eventually, thousands of captivity tales—of varying quality and accuracy—sprouted up all over the country. Scarcely any first editions of these books remain, as they were literally read and re-read to shreds by an eager public.

From Providence to propaganda. Because early captivity narratives were almost all told from the limited first-person point of view, they didn't provide much context for settlers' actions that may have provoked American Indian aggression. Typically, seventeenth-century captivity narratives begin with a brief description of a raid and the rounding up of hostages; they then focus on the gritty details of the day-to-day struggle for survival. The captives in these early narratives generally accept their condition as a

town, and I knew not where he was, till I was informed by himself, that he was amongst a smaller parcel of Indians, whose place was about six miles off; with tears in his eyes, he asked me whether his sister Sarah was dead; and told me he had seen his sister Mary; and prayed me, that I would not be troubled in reference to himself. . . . I cannot but take notice of the wonderful mercy of God to me in those afflictions, in sending me a Bible. One of the Indians that came from Medfield fight, had brought some <u>plunder</u>, came to me, and asked me, if I would have a Bible, he had got one in his basket. I was glad of it, and asked him, whether he thought the Indians would let me read. He answered, yes: So I took the Bible, and in that <u>melancholy</u> time, it came into my mind to

read first the 28th chapter of Deuteronomy,[7] which I did, and when I had read it, my dark heart wrought on this manner, that there was no mercy for me, that the blessings were gone, and the curses come in their room, and that I had lost my opportunity. But the Lord helped me still to go on reading till I came to Chapter 30 the seven first

7. 28th chapter of Deuteronomy: In Deuteronomy 28, Moses warns that God will bless those who obey Him and curse those who do not.

WORDS TO OWN
plunder (plun′dər) *n.*: goods seized, especially during wartime.
melancholy (mel′ən·käl′ē) *adj.*: sad; sorrowful.

punishment sent by God to test their faith, and any relief from their suffering is always evidence of Divine Providence, not sympathy from their captors. But by the eighteenth century, continuing animosity between settlers and American Indians, aggravated by the French and Indian War, led to a different kind of captivity narrative, one that was an undisguised expression of hatred toward Native Americans. No longer were captivity narratives instructive tales of physical and spiritual survival in the wilderness; now they were inflammatory propaganda, smugly asserting the superiority of Europeans.

Sensationalism and stereotypes. By the early nineteenth century, propaganda had turned into pure sensationalism. Journalists and authors of lurid fiction, gifted at manipulating the fantasies and prejudices of the reading public, revised the original narratives. They pulled out all the stops, using melodramatic plot devices and long passages of grisly detail. The public eagerly read these "penny dreadfuls" (the popular term for cheap magazines with tales of horror and crime), shuddering with mixed fascination and horror at fictional tales of American Indian atrocities and the suffering of innocent captives. The tawdriness of these publications didn't go unnoticed by more educated readers. Many actual nineteenth-century captives were reluctant to publish their stories, afraid that, by association with sleazy popular magazines, their experiences would not be taken seriously.

Some historians have argued that captivity narratives, by advancing the stereotype of the "savage Indian," made it easier for settlers to justify occupation of American Indian lands. By the late nineteenth century, with the "Indian threat" a thing of the past, captivity narratives gradually became less popular. But, unfortunately, stereotypes of the "bad" Indian and the "virtuous" European settler remained in the popular imagination well into the twentieth century, appearing in countless Western novels, Hollywood movies, and television programs.

verses, where I found, there was mercy promised again, if we would return to Him by repentance; and though we were scattered from one end of the earth to the other, yet the Lord would gather us together, and turn all those curses upon our enemies. I do not desire to live to forget this Scripture, and what comfort it was to me. . . .

The Fifth Remove

The occasion (as I thought) of their moving at this time, was, the English Army, it being near and following them: For they went, as if they had gone for their lives, for some considerable way, and then they made a stop, and chose some of their stoutest men, and sent them back to hold the English Army in play while the rest escaped: And then, like Jehu,[8] they marched on furiously, with their old, and with their young: Some carried their old <u>decrepit</u> mothers, some carried one, and some another. Four of them carried a great Indian upon a bier; but going through a thick wood with him, they were hindered, and could make no

8. Jehu (jē′hoo′): ninth century B.C. Israelite king. Jehu was said to be a "furious driver" (2 Kings 9:20), and Rowlandson's allusion here is to the speed and fury with which her captors moved away from the English Army.

WORDS TO OWN
decrepit (dē·krep′it) *adj.*: run down; worn out by age or use.

----

haste; whereupon they took him upon their backs, and carried him, one at a time, till they came to Bacquaug River. Upon a Friday, a little after noon we came to this river. When all the company was come up, and were gathered together, I thought to count the number of them, but they were so many, and being somewhat in motion, it was beyond my skill. In this travel, because of my wound, I was somewhat favored in my load; I carried only my knitting work and two quarts of parched meal: Being very faint I asked my mistress to give me one spoonful of the meal, but she would not give me a taste. They quickly fell to cutting dry trees, to make rafts to carry them over the river: and soon my turn came to go over: By the advantage of some brush which they had laid upon the raft to sit upon, I did not wet my foot (which many of themselves at the other end were mid-leg deep) which cannot but be acknowledged as a favor of God to my weakened body, it being a very cold time. I was not before acquainted with such kind of doings or dangers. "When thou passeth through the waters I will be with thee, and through the Rivers they shall not overflow thee," Isaiah, 43:2. A certain number of us got over the river that night, but it was the night after the Sabbath before all the company was got over. On the Saturday they boiled an old horse's leg which they had got, and so we drank of the broth, as soon as they thought it was ready, and when it was almost gone, they filled it up again.

The first week of my being among them, I hardly ate anything; the second week, I found my stomach grow very faint for want of something; and yet it was very hard to get down their filthy trash: but the third week, though I could think how formerly my stomach would turn against this or that, and I could starve and die before I could eat such things, yet they were sweet and <u>savory</u> to my taste. . . .

The Sixth Remove

We traveled on till night; and in the morning, we must go over the river to Philip's crew. When I was in the canoe, I could not but be amazed at the numerous crew of pagans that were on the bank on the other side. When I came ashore, they gathered all about me, I sitting alone in the midst: I observed they asked one another questions, and laughed, and rejoiced over their gains and victories. Then my heart began to fail: And I fell aweeping which was the first time to my remembrance, that I wept before them. Although I had met with so much <u>affliction</u>, and my heart was many times ready to break, yet could I not shed one tear in their sight: but rather had been all this while in a maze, and like one astonished: But now I may say as, Psalm 137:1, "By the rivers of Babylon, there we sat down: yea, we wept when we remembered Zion." There one of them asked me, why I wept, I could hardly tell what to say: Yet I answered, they would kill me: "No," said he, "none will hurt you." Then came one of them and gave me two spoonfuls of meal to comfort me, and another gave me half a pint of peas; which was more worth than many bushels at another time. Then I went to see King Philip, he bade me come in and sit down, and asked me whether I would smoke it (a usual compliment nowadays amongst saints and sinners) but this no way suited me. For though I had formerly used tobacco, yet I had left it ever since I was first taken. It seems to be a bait, the devil lays to make men lose their precious time: I remember with shame, how formerly, when I had taken two or three pipes, I was presently ready for another, such a <u>bewitching</u> thing it is: But I thank God, He has now given me power over it; surely there are many who may be better employed than to lie sucking a stinking tobacco pipe.

Now the Indians gather their forces to go against North Hampton: Overnight one went about yelling and hooting to give notice of the design. Whereupon they fell to boiling of groundnuts, and parching of corn (as many as had it) for their provision: And in the morning away they went. During my abode in this place, Philip spoke to me to make a shirt for his boy, which I did, for which he gave me a shilling: I offered the money to my master, but he bade me keep it: And with it I bought a piece of horseflesh. Afterward he

WORDS TO OWN

savory (sā′vər · ē) *adj*.: appetizing; agreeable.
affliction (ə · flik′shən) *n*.: pain; hardship.
bewitching (bē · wich′iŋ) *adj*.: enticing; irresistible.

Wampum belt. Iroquois.

Peabody Essex Museum, Salem, Massachusetts/Peabody Museum Collections. Photo by Mark Sexton.

asked me to make a cap for his boy, for which he invited me to dinner. I went, and he gave me a pancake, about as big as two fingers; it was made of parched wheat, beaten, and fried in bear's grease, but I thought I never tasted pleasanter meat in my life. There was a squaw who spoke to me to make a shirt for her *sannup,*[9] for which she gave me a piece of bear. Another asked me to knit a pair of stockings, for which she gave me a quart of peas: I boiled my peas and bear together, and invited my master and mistress to dinner, but the proud gossip, because I served them both in one dish, would eat nothing, except one bit that he gave her upon the point of his knife. . . .

The Move to the Ashuelot Valley, New Hampshire

But instead of going either to Albany or homeward, we must go five miles up the river, and then go over it. Here we abode[10] awhile. Here lived a sorry Indian, who spoke to me to make him a shirt. When I had done it, he would pay me nothing. But he living by the riverside, where I often went to fetch water, I would often be putting of him in mind, and calling for my pay: At last he told me if I would make another shirt, for a papoose not yet born, he would give me a knife, which he did when I had done it. I carried the knife in, and my master asked me to give it him, and I was not a little glad that I had anything that they would accept of, and be pleased with. When we were at this place, my master's maid came home, she had been gone three weeks into the Narragansett country, to fetch corn, where they had stored up some in the ground: She brought home about a

peck and half of corn. This was about the time that their great captain, Naananto,[11] was killed in the Narragansett country. My son being now about a mile from me, I asked liberty to go and see him, they bade me go, and away I went: but quickly lost myself, traveling over hills and through swamps, and could not find the way to him. And I cannot but admire at the wonderful power and goodness of God to me, in that, though I was gone from home, and met with all sorts of Indians, and those I had no knowledge of, and there being no Christian soul near me; yet not one of them offered the least imaginable miscarriage to me. I turned homeward again, and met with my master, he showed me the way to my son. . . .

But I was fain to go and look after something to satisfy my hunger, and going among the wigwams, I went into one, and there found a squaw who showed herself very kind to me, and gave me a piece of bear. I put it into my pocket, and came home, but could not find an opportunity to broil it, for fear they would get it from me, and there it lay all that day and night in my stinking pocket. In the morning I went to the same squaw, who had a kettle of groundnuts boiling; I asked her to let me boil my piece of bear in her kettle, which she did, and gave me some groundnuts to eat with it: And I cannot but think how pleasant it was to me. I have sometime seen bear baked very handsomely among the English, and some like it, but the thoughts that it was bear, made me tremble: But now that was savory to me that one would think was enough to turn the stomach of a brute creature.

One bitter cold day, I could find no room to sit down before the fire: I went out, and could not tell what to do, but I went in to another wigwam, where they were also sitting round the fire, but the squaw laid a skin for me, and bid me sit down, and gave me some groundnuts, and bade me come again: and told me they would buy me, if they were able, and yet these were strangers to me that I never saw before. . . .

9. *sannup* (san′up): husband.
10. abode (ə·bōd′): stayed.

11. **Naananto:** Naananto, or Canonchet (d. April 3, 1676), was a Narragansett leader who was the driving force behind the American Indians' wish to exterminate the New England colonists that resulted in King Philip's War. After his death, the conflict soon ended.

MAKING MEANINGS

First Thoughts

1. What do you think helped Mary Rowlandson survive and maintain her sanity?

Shaping Interpretations

2. What conflicting attitudes, if any, does Rowlandson reveal toward her captors? Do you think her attitude toward her captors changes as the narrative progresses? Explain.

3. The Puritans' habit of seeing specific meaning in their experiences helped them find significance in even very minor events. Describe at least two **allusions** to Biblical stories that Rowlandson makes during her captivity. In what specific ways does each of these Biblical stories resemble Rowlandson's?

4. Rowlandson's narrative was enormously popular in England. What reasons can you propose for its popularity? What aspects of Rowlandson's journal might have promoted stereotyped and hostile views toward American Indians?

Reading Check

a. List in **chronological order** the main events described in Rowlandson's *Narrative*.

b. What does Rowlandson tell us about how she was treated by her captors?

c. What jobs does Rowlandson do to earn her food? How does her attitude toward food change while she is a captive?

d. Find details that reveal that Rowlandson's captors themselves are desperate to find food.

5. In his classic work of psychology, *Man's Search for Meaning,* Dr. Viktor Frankl, a survivor of the Nazi concentration camps of World War II, tells how the best chance for survival in the camps was not physical endurance or general health but an internal sense that the experience, no matter how horrifying, had some ultimate meaning for the prisoner. Those who had strong religious faith, committed political views, or even just a strong love of family were far more likely to survive, both physically and mentally. In your view, what was Mary Rowlandson's ultimate source of meaning?

Challenging the Text

6. Despite her efforts to be accurate, Rowlandson's journal is full of **subjective reporting.** Instead of using neutral language (words with neither positive nor negative **connotations**), subjective reporting relies on "emotionally loaded" words—words with strongly positive or negative connotations. Select any extract from Rowlandson's journal, and find the emotionally loaded words or phrases that reveal her attitude toward her captors. What words or phrases does Rowlandson use that a detached, objective historian would *not* use?

Three American Indian baskets and a string of wampum.

Baskets: Peabody Museum, Harvard University, Cambridge, Massachusetts. Photo by Hillel Burger. Wampum: Peabody Essex Museum, Salem, Massachusetts/Peabody Museum Collections. Photo by Mark Sexton.

CHOICES: Building Your Portfolio

1. Collecting Ideas for an Autobiographical Incident

You've probably had the experience of changing your perception of someone or something. A negative viewpoint can soften over time and become more positive. But the reverse is also true: A good opinion or feeling can go sour. Write down your recollections of an instance in your life when your perception or opinion of something or someone changed as a result of a specific incident. Save your notes for possible use in the Writer's Workshop on page 130.

Comparing Texts

2. Sustained by Memories

On page 44, Mary Rowlandson makes an **allusion** to Psalm 137, which is a well-known "captivity" psalm. It was composed when the Israelites were held captive in Babylon by King Nebuchadnezzar. Read Psalm 137 below, and in a brief essay explain why Rowlandson thought of this psalm at a certain point in her sufferings. What parallel would she see between her experience and that of the psalmist? In her mind, what would "Babylon" be?

Creative Writing / Research

3. The Other Side of the Story

Write a journal entry from the point of view of a Wampanoag. Explain the position of your people, giving your reasons for the attack on the settlement and an explanation for the desperate conditions you have been enduring. Use history texts or encyclopedias as your sources. (You will find information under "King Philip's War" and "Metacomet.")

By the rivers of Babylon, there we sat down, yea, we wept, when we remembered Zion.

We hanged our harps upon the willows in the midst thereof.

For there they that carried us away captive required of us a song; and they that wasted us required of us mirth, saying, Sing us one of the songs of Zion.

How shall we sing the Lord's song in a strange land?

If I forget thee, O Jerusalem, let my right hand forget her cunning.

If I do not remember thee, let my tongue cleave to the roof of my mouth; if I prefer not Jerusalem above my chief joy.

Remember, O Lord, the children of Edom in the day of Jerusalem; who said, Raze it, raze it, even to the foundation thereof.

O daughter of Babylon, who art to be destroyed; happy shall he be, that rewardeth thee as thou hast served us.

Happy shall he be, that taketh and dasheth thy little ones against the stones.

—Psalm 137

The Southern Planters

In addition to the Puritan tradition of New England, there was another literary tradition in the American Colonies. This literature came from the Southern planters, also known as the Cavaliers, a group of people whose background and social views varied considerably from those of the Puritans.

There were many possible reasons for the differences. One factor may have been climate. The Southern climate was kind; it was warm and mild, and the land was enormously fertile. The Northern climate was harsher; springs and summers were brief, and winters were long and cold. Even the land in New England was hard. Its outcroppings of granite and bedrock broke plows and made farming difficult.

But economic and religious factors were even more important. The landholdings in New England were small for the most part; many colonists were small farmers or tradespeople who lived in villages and owned very little land. But the Southern planter was an aristocrat, the virtual ruler of a huge territory that was maintained by plentiful slave labor (though slavery was common in New England in those days, too).

Opposing Worldviews

Most Southerners belonged to the Church of England. In general, they were much more interested in the outside world—literature, music, art, politics, and the world of nature—than they were in the scrupulous examination of their own souls. Where the Puritan feared that the world's beauties were lures and sources of temptation, the Southerner saw the world as something to be conquered and enjoyed.

The Southern planters shared the worldview of the English Renaissance, with its emphasis on classical literature and scientific inquiry. Thus, when the Southerners wrote about life in America, they were apt to write about it in traditional ways. Even a work as original as *The Sot-Weed Factor* (1708), Ebenezer Cook's humorous tale of a tobacco merchant, was written in the bouncy couplets popular for satire in England.

A Renaissance Man

In many ways, William Byrd is a representative figure for the Southern writers of the Colonial period. He was truly a Renaissance man. He translated Greek and Latin works, composed original poetry (mostly satiric verse), and wrote about mathematics and medicine. Writing a generation before Thomas Jefferson (page 114), Byrd displayed the same intellectual curiosity that his fellow Virginian would so strongly exemplify later.

Byrd described the pleasures of the Southern planter's life: "I have a large family of my own, and my doors are open to everybody, yet I have no bills to pay. . . . I live in a kind of independence of everyone but Providence. . . . I must take care to keep all my people to their duty. . . . But then 'tis an amusement in this silent country."

William Byrd

(1674–1744)

It is worth remembering that Jamestown, Virginia, was named for James I, the king who vowed to harry the Puritans out of England. Virginia itself was named for Elizabeth I, the "Virgin Queen." These place names—and many others in the South—remind us of an important difference between Virginia and the Colonies of New England. New England was settled largely by those in conflict with British intellectual, theological, and social life; Virginia was settled by those in harmony with that life. By and large, the fervent, short-haired puritanical Round-heads went to New England; the aristocratic, long-haired, worldly Cavaliers went to Virginia.

William Byrd was a thorough Cavalier—worldly, sophisticated, and gentlemanly. Byrd was born in Virginia, the son of a wealthy landowner and merchant, but he was educated in England, where he spent half his life. In London, he acquired a passion for the theater, which the Puritans had once outlawed as immoral. Byrd had many scientific interests: He was even a member of the Royal Society, that pillar of the British scientific establishment.

Byrd alternated between living in England and living in Virginia. He preferred London, with its elegant homes, witty conversation, and gambling tables. During his visits to Westover, his 2,000-acre home in Virginia, he tried to keep alive both his social and intellectual life. Westover's gardens are still renowned, and its library of almost 4,000 volumes was rivaled in Byrd's time only by Cotton Mather's library in New England.

William Byrd (1704) by the Studio of Sir Godfrey Kneller. Oil on canvas.

Colonial Williamsburg Foundation, Williamsburg, Virginia (D583.1087).

Byrd had little in common with the New Englanders. He kept a diary, as many Puritans did. But the Puritans' diaries are primarily records of spiritual examination. Byrd's diary records the pleasures and practical concerns of a man of the world. Dinners, flirtations with women, literature, and natural science were of greater interest to him than matters of the spirit. In London in 1719, for example, he recorded a typical day:

> May 28. I rose about 7 o'clock and read a chapter in Hebrew and some Greek. I neglected my prayers, but had milk for breakfast. The weather was still warm and clear and very dry, the wind north. About eleven came Annie Wilkinson but I would not speak with her. I was disappointed in the [absence] of Mrs. B—s who wrote me word she would come and breakfast with me, so I read some English and ate some bread and butter because I was to dine late and about 3 o'clock went to dine with Sir Wilfred Lawson and ate some mutton. After dinner we talked a little and about 6 o'clock went to Kensington in Sir Wilfred's coach where there was a ball in the gardens and several ladies and among the rest Miss Perry whom I stuck most to and she complained I squeezed her hand. Here I stayed until 1 o'clock and then came home and neglected my prayers.

In 1728, Byrd joined a survey expedition of the disputed boundary line between Virginia and North Carolina. *The History of the Dividing Line* is far more than a simple record of that expedition. Witty and elegantly written, it is filled with philosophical observations and barbed comments on American Colonial life.

Make the Connection

The Observer's Eye
Byrd's *History of the Dividing Line*
is a record of personal experience, written while Byrd was
helping out on a survey expedition. Byrd must have realized
the value of his experience,
understanding that a journey of
any kind is an opportunity to
observe and learn. By paying
close attention—by seeing
clearly, not merely looking—any
traveler can learn about people,
places, and practices that are
different from those with which
he or she is familiar.

Reading Skills and Strategies

Identifying Tone
In the first extract from the *History*, Byrd ironically describes
the "modish frenzy" of early
travelers to America, a fashionable craze that he compares to
a "distemper" or illness. As you
read each section of Byrd's
journal, pay attention to Byrd's
tone. Jot down any words,
phrases, or expressions that
make Byrd seem very "mod-
ern"—and funny.

Elements of Literature

Satire
The ironic, barbed approach
Byrd takes in his *History* is in
sharp contrast to the straightforward style of a Puritan such
as William Bradford (page 26).
Like many British writers of his
time, Byrd excels at **satire,** the
use of ridicule to expose the
shortcomings of things he
observes.

> **S**atire is a type of writing
> that ridicules the short-
> comings of people or
> institutions, usually in an
> attempt to bring about
> some change.
>
> *For more on Satire, see the Handbook
> of Literary Terms.*

Background

William Byrd began his *History*
in 1728. By then, more than a
century had passed since the
first English settlers reached
Virginia. Byrd's journal was
found among his personal papers after his death and wasn't
published until 1841.

from
The History of the Dividing Line
William Byrd

Early Virginia Colonies

As it happened some ages before to be the
fashion to saunter to the Holy Land and go
upon other Quixote adventures,[1] so it was now
grown the humor to take a trip to America. The
Spaniards had lately discovered rich mines in their
part of the West Indies, which made their maritime
neighbors eager to do so too. This modish frenzy,
being still more inflamed by the charming account
given of Virginia by the first adventurers, made
many fond of removing to such a Paradise.

Happy was he, and still happier she, that could

---

1. **Quixote** (kē·hōt′ē) **adventures:** foolish adventures,
like those taken by the mad hero of Miguel de Cervantes's
novel *The Ingenious Gentleman Don Quixote de la
Mancha.*

get themselves transported, fondly expecting their coarsest utensils in that happy place would be of massy[2] silver.

This made it easy for the Company to <u>procure</u> as many volunteers as they wanted for their new colony, but, like most other undertakers who have no assistance from the public, they starved the design by too much frugality; for, unwilling to launch out at first into too much expense, they shipped off but few people at a time, and those but scantily provided. The adventurers were, besides, idle and extravagant and expected they might live without work in so plentiful a country.

These wretches were set ashore not far from Roanoke Inlet, but by some fatal disagreement or laziness were either starved or cut to pieces by the Indians.

Several repeated misadventures of this kind did for some time <u>allay</u> the itch of sailing to this

new world, but the distemper broke out again about the year 1606. Then it happened that the Earl of Southampton and several other persons <u>eminent</u> for their quality and estates were invited into the Company, who applied themselves once more to people the then almost abandoned colony. For this purpose they embarked about an hundred men, most of them <u>reprobates</u> of good families and related to some of the Company who were men of quality and fortune.

The ships that carried them made a shift to find a more direct way to Virginia and ventured

2. **massy:** weighty.

WORDS TO OWN

procure (prō·kyoor′) *v.:* to gain; obtain; acquire.
allay (a·lā′) *v.:* lessen; relieve.
eminent (em′ə·nənt) *adj.:* well known for excellence; important; outstanding.
reprobates (rep′rə·bāts′) *n. pl.:* people without any sense of duty or decency.

The Plantation (c. 1825). Unknown American artist. Oil on wood (19⅛″ × 29½″).

The Metropolitan Museum of Art, Gift of Edgar William and Bernice Chrysler Garbisch, 1963 (63.201.3). Photograph © 1984 The Metropolitan Museum of Art.

through the capes into the Bay of Chesapeake. The same night they came to an anchor at the mouth of Powhatan, the same as James River, where they built a small fort at a place called Point Comfort.

This settlement stood its ground from that time forward, in spite of all the blunders and disagreement of the first adventurers and the many calamities that befell the colony afterward. The six gentlemen who were first named of the Company by the Crown and who were empowered to choose an annual president from among themselves were always engaged in factions and quarrels, while the rest detested work more than famine. At this rate the colony must have come to nothing had it not been for the vigilance and bravery of Captain Smith,[3] who struck a terror into all the Indians round about. This gentleman took some pains to persuade the men to plant Indian corn, but they looked upon all labor as a curse. They chose rather to depend upon the musty provisions that were sent from England; and when they failed they were forced to take more pains to seek for wild fruits in the woods than they would have taken in tilling the ground. Besides, this exposed them to be knocked in the head by the Indians and gave them fluxes[4] into the bargain, which thinned the plantation very much. To supply this mortality, they were reinforced the year following with a greater number of people, amongst which were fewer gentlemen and more laborers, who, however, took care not to kill themselves with work. These found the first adventurers in a very starving condition but relieved their wants with the fresh supply they brought with them. From Kecoughtan[5] they extended themselves as far as Jamestown, where, like true Englishmen, they built a church that cost no more than fifty pounds and a tavern that cost five hundred.

3. **Captain Smith:** John Smith (c. 1580–1631) helped found Jamestown, Virginia, the first permanent English settlement in America.
4. **fluxes** (fluks′iz): dysentery; severe diarrhea.
5. **Kecoughtan** (kē′kō′tan): present-day site of Hampton, Virginia.

As the Colony grew, violence frequently erupted between the settlers and the American Indians. Byrd offers his solution to the conflicts between the two cultures.

Intermarriage

They had now made peace with the Indians, but there was one thing wanting to make that peace lasting. The natives could by no means persuade themselves that the English were heartily their friends so long as they disdained to intermarry with them. And, in earnest, had the English consulted their own security and the good of the colony, had they intended either to civilize or convert these gentiles,[6] they would have brought their stomachs to embrace this prudent alliance.

The Indians are generally tall and well proportioned, which may make full amends for the darkness of their complexions. Add to this that they are healthy and strong, with constitutions untainted by lewdness and not enfeebled by luxury. Besides, morals and all considered, I cannot think the Indians were much greater heathens than the first adventurers, who, had they been good Christians, would have had the charity to take this only method of converting the natives to Christianity. For, after all that can

6. **gentiles** (jen′tīlz′): here, nonbelievers. Historically, among Christians, *gentile* meant a pagan or nonbeliever. (*Gentile* comes from a Latin word meaning "foreigner.") The term is more commonly used by Jews to refer to those who are not Jewish.

WORDS TO OWN
disdained (dis·dānd′) v.: refused; disapproved; scorned.
prudent (prōōd′′nt) adj.: well thought out; cautious.

----

be said, a sprightly lover is the most prevailing[7] missionary that can be sent amongst these or any other infidels.

Besides, the poor Indians would have had less reason to complain that the English took away their land if they had received it by way of a portion with their daughters. Had such affinities been contracted in the beginning, how much bloodshed had been prevented and how populous would the country have been, and, consequently, how considerable! Nor would the shade of the skin have been any reproach at this day, for if a Moor may be washed white in three generations, surely an Indian might have been blanched in two.

The French, for their parts, have not been so squeamish in Canada, who upon trial find abundance of attraction in the Indians. Their late grand monarch thought it not below even the dignity of a Frenchman to become one flesh with this people and therefore ordered 100 livres[8] for any of his subjects, man or woman, that would intermarry with a native.

By this piece of policy we find the French interest very much strengthened amongst the savages and their religion, such as it is, propagated just as far as their love. And I heartily wish this well-concerted scheme don't hereafter give the French an advantage over His Majesty's good subjects on the northern continent of America.

Byrd's surveying party is guided by an American Indian named Bearskin. Here, Byrd records Bearskin's religious beliefs.

7. **prevailing** (prē·vāl′iŋ): convincing.
8. **livres** (lē′vərz): former French monetary unit worth about a pound of silver each.

The Native Religion

In the evening we examined our friend Bearskin concerning the religion of his country, and he explained it to us without any of that reserve to which his nation is subject. He told us he believed there was one supreme god, who had several subaltern[9] deities under him. And that this master god made the world a long time ago. That he told the sun, the moon, and stars their business in the beginning, which they, with good looking-after, have faithfully performed ever since. That the same power that made all things at first has taken care to keep them in the same method and motion ever since. He believed that God had formed many worlds before he formed this, but that those worlds either grew old and ruinous or were destroyed for the dishonesty of the inhabitants. That God is very just and very good, ever well pleased with those men who possess those godlike qualities. That he takes good people into his safe protection, makes them very rich, fills their bellies plentifully, preserves them from sickness and from being surprised or overcome by their enemies. But all such as tell lies and cheat those they have dealings with he never fails to punish with sickness, poverty, and hunger and, after all that, suffers them to be knocked on the head and scalped by those that fight against them.

He believed that after death both good and bad people are conducted by a strong guard into a great road, in which departed souls travel together for some time till at a certain distance this road forks into two paths, the one extremely level and the other stony and mountainous. Here the good are parted from the bad

9. **subaltern** (səb·ôl′tərn): subordinate; of inferior rank or position.

WORDS TO OWN

populous (päp′yо̄о·ləs) *adj.*: crowded with people.
squeamish (skwēm′ish) *adj.*: easily offended.
propagated (präp′ə·gāt′id) *v.*: transmitted or spread.

by a flash of lightning, the first being hurried away to the right, the other to the left. The right-hand road leads to a charming, warm country, where the spring is everlasting and every month is May; and as the year is always in its youth, so are the people, and particularly the women are bright as stars and never scold. That in this happy climate there are deer, turkeys, elks, and buffaloes innumerable, perpetually fat and gentle, while the trees are loaded with delicious fruit quite throughout the four seasons. That the soil brings forth corn spontaneously, without the curse of labor, and so very wholesome that none who have the happiness to eat of it are ever sick, grow old, or die. Near the entrance into this blessed land sits a <u>venerable</u> old man on a mat richly woven, who examines strictly all that are brought before him, and if they have behaved well, the guards are ordered to open the crystal gate and let them enter into the land of delight.

The left-hand path is very rugged and uneven, leading to a dark and barren country where it is always winter. The ground is the whole year round covered with snow, and nothing is to be seen upon the trees but icicles. All the people are hungry yet have not a morsel of anything to eat except a bitter kind of potato, that gives them the dry gripes[10] and fills their whole body with loathsome ulcers that stink and are insupportably painful. Here all the women are old and ugly, having claws like a panther with which they fly upon the men that slight their passion. For it seems these haggard old furies[11] are intolerably fond and expect a vast deal of cherishing. They talk much and exceedingly shrill, giving exquisite pain to the drum of the ear, which in that place of the torment is so tender that every sharp note wounds it to the quick. At the end of this path sits a dreadful old woman on a monstrous toadstool, whose head is covered with rattlesnakes instead of tresses, with glaring white eyes that strike a terror un-

10. **dry gripes:** stomach cramps.
11. **furies** (fyoor′ēz): violent, vengeful women. In Greek and Roman mythology, the Furies are fierce avenging spirits.

speakable into all that behold her. This hag pronounces sentence of woe upon all the miserable wretches that hold up their hands at her tribunal. After this they are delivered over to huge turkey buzzards, like harpies,[12] that fly away with them to the place above mentioned. Here, after they have been tormented a certain number of years according to their several degrees of guilt, they are again driven back into this world to try if they will mend their manners and merit a place the next time in the regions of bliss.

This was the substance of Bearskin's religion and was as much to the purpose as could be expected from a mere state of nature, without one glimpse of revelation or philosophy. It contained, however, the three great articles of natural religion: the belief of a god, the moral distinction between good and evil, and the expectation of rewards and punishments in another world.

12. **harpies** (här′pēz): evil mythological creatures with women's heads and birds' wings and legs.

WORDS TO OWN
venerable (ven′ər·ə·bəl) *adj*.: respected; esteemed for age or distinguished character.

MAKING MEANINGS

First Thoughts

1. Did you find Byrd more or less interesting than the other Colonial writers you've read? What passages did you record in your reading notes because they struck you as funny or "modern"?

Shaping Interpretations

2. Describe Byrd's **tone**—his attitude toward his subject, the people he mentions, and his intended audience. Does the tone remain consistent throughout, or does it change? Cite passages to support your analysis.

3. What examples of **satire** did you find in Byrd's account of the early settlers of Virginia? Based on this scathing portrait, what personal qualities do you think Byrd admired?

4. Why might Byrd's observations on the first settlements in Virginia be less reliable than Bradford's on the Plymouth Colony (page 28)?

5. According to his description of Bearskin's religious beliefs, what "articles," or elements, of religion does Byrd consider most important? How closely do his views agree with those expressed by Mary Rowlandson (page 40)?

Extending the Text

6. What issues, events, or attitudes in American society today would be good topics for **satire?**

Reading Check

a. What reasons does Byrd suggest for the failure of the first Virginia settlements?

b. Explain Byrd's point of view about the first colonists and their expectations of life in North America.

c. Why does Byrd favor intermarriage with American Indians?

d. What, according to Byrd, are the three basic religious beliefs of Bearskin, the American Indian guide?

CHOICES: Building Your Portfolio

Writer's Notebook

1. Collecting Ideas for an Autobiographical Incident

Byrd's keen perceptions and mastery of the language resulted in phrases such as this: ". . . their coarsest utensils . . . would be of massy silver" (page 51). Make a list of phrases that describe vividly an experience you have had that was significant in some way. Keep your notes; you may find them useful in the Writer's Workshop on page 130.

Comparing Texts

2. Different as Night and Day

In a brief essay, compare and contrast the excerpts from Byrd's *History* with William Bradford's account of the Puritan landing at Plymouth (pages 28–33). Consider specifically how the two accounts differ in **purpose, tone,** and **style.**

Creative Writing

3. Puritans and Planters

Imagine that you are a Puritan who has just returned from a visit to Jamestown. In a journal entry, describe the Southern planters, their approach to life, their physical appearance, and their interests, contrasting them with members of your own Puritan society.

Olaudah Equiano

(c. 1745–1797)

Olaudah Equiano (ō·lōō′dä ek′wē·än′o) was the first African writer to reach a sizable audience of American readers. A member of the Ibo people, Equiano was born in a part of West Africa that is now Nigeria. When he was only eleven years old, Equiano, along with his sister, was kidnapped from his home by African raiders involved in the slave trade. Over a period of six or seven months, during which he and his sister were separated, the slave traders took Equiano to a series of way stations. When he reached the coast, Equiano was put aboard one of the infamous slave ships bound for Barbados, an island in the West Indies, in the Caribbean. Slave labor was in demand to work on the sugar plantations in the Caribbean. In his narrative, Equiano vividly describes this cruel and horrifying part of the slave route, which was known as "the Middle Passage."

After a short stay in Barbados, Equiano was sold to a British military officer, who gave him the name Gustavus Vassa, after a Swedish king. Equiano served with this officer during the Seven Years' War between England and France and gained great skill as a seaman. In time, a Quaker merchant from Philadelphia purchased Equiano. From his own profitable business ventures while managing his master's business, Equiano saved enough money to purchase his freedom in 1766, after having been enslaved for almost ten years. He was about twenty-one years old.

After buying his freedom, Equiano worked as a sailor and led an exciting and adventurous life, sailing on exploratory expeditions to the Arctic and Central America. He finally settled in England, where he made his living as a free servant, a musician, and a barber. He also became active in the antislavery movement. In 1781, the captain of the *Zong*, which was transporting more than four hundred Africans to Jamaica, threw overboard a third of the shackled captives in order to collect the insurance. In 1783, Equiano

Portrait of a Negro Man, Olaudah Equiano in 1780s, by English School (eighteenth century), previously attributed to Joshua Reynolds. Oil on canvas.

Royal Albert Memorial Museum, Exeter/Bridgeman Art Library, London/New York.

was instrumental in bringing this atrocity to the attention of the public and the British naval authorities. When the abolition of the slave trade became a hotly debated issue in the English Parliament, Equiano actively campaigned against slavery, writing letters to officials and newspapers and visiting abolitionist leaders.

Equiano's autobiography, published in England in 1789, was titled *The Interesting Narrative of the Life of Olaudah Equiano, or Gustavus Vassa, the African.* Reprinted in New York in 1791, the book—considered the first great black autobiography—proved popular with readers in the United States as well as abroad. The author's account of the horrors he suffered struck a responsive chord with northern abolitionists, but by then Equiano had settled in London. In 1792, he married an Englishwoman, Susanna Cullen.

Though Equiano traveled widely, he never returned to the United States. Nor did he ever again see his native Africa, to which he dreamed of returning. He defined himself, to the end of his life, simply as "the African."

Before You Read

FROM THE INTERESTING NARRATIVE OF THE LIFE OF OLAUDAH EQUIANO

Make the Connection

Against Their Will

The first Africans in the Americas were unwilling immigrants who arrived on slave ships before 1600. Between the seventeenth and nineteenth centuries, about ten million people were captured in Africa and shipped to North and South America and the islands of the West Indies, where they were enslaved. People were literally seized from their homes and sold as commodities, with no thought for their human rights.

Quickwrite

Before you read Equiano's account, make a KWL chart like the one below. Fill out the first two columns—what you already know about slavery and the slave trade in the eighteenth century and what you'd like to learn about it. Leave the third column blank.

K What I Know	W What I Want to Know	L What I Learned

Elements of Literature

Autobiography

Equiano's **autobiography** is one of the first slave narratives by a black African to be published. Many accounts of the horrors of slavery were firsthand accounts used by abolitionists in the nineteenth century to fuel the crusade against slavery.

> An **autobiography** is a firsthand account of a writer's own life.
>
> *For more on Autobiography, see the Handbook of Literary Terms.*

from The Interesting Narrative of the Life of Olaudah Equiano

Olaudah Equiano

Kidnapped

My father, besides many slaves, had a numerous family of which seven lived to grow up, including myself and a sister who was the only daughter. As I was the youngest of the sons I became, of course, the greatest favorite with my mother and was always with her; and she used to take particular pains to form my mind. I was trained up from my earliest years in the art of war, my daily exercise was shooting and throwing javelins, and my mother adorned me with emblems after the manner of our greatest warriors. In this way I grew up till I was turned the age of 11, when an end was put to my happiness in the following manner. Generally when the grown people in the neighborhood were gone far in the fields to labor, the children assembled together in some of the neighbors' premises to play, and commonly some of us used to get up a tree to look for any <u>assailant</u> or kidnapper that might come upon us, for they sometimes took those opportunities of our parents' absence to attack and carry off as many as they could seize. One day, as I was watching at the top of a tree in our yard, I saw one of those people come into the yard of our next neighbor but one to kidnap, there being many stout young people in it. Immediately on this I gave the alarm of the rogue and he was surrounded by the stoutest of them, who entangled him with cords so that he could not escape till some of the grown people came and secured him.

But alas! ere long it was my fate to be thus attacked and to be carried off when none of the grown people were nigh. One day, when all our people were gone out to their works as usual and only I and my dear sister were left to mind the house, two men and a woman got over our walls, and in a moment seized us both, and without giving us time to cry out or make resistance they stopped our mouths and ran off with us into the nearest wood. Here they tied our hands and continued to carry us as far as they could till night came on, when we reached a small house where the robbers halted for refreshment and spent the night. We were then unbound but were unable to take any food, and being quite overpowered by fatigue and grief, our only relief was some sleep, which allayed our misfortune for a short time. The next morning we left the house and continued traveling all the day. For a long time we had kept to the woods, but at last we came into a road which I believed I knew. I had now some hopes of being delivered, for we had advanced but a little way before I discovered some people at a distance,

Slave Deck of the Albanoz (1843–1847) by Lt. Francis Meynell. Watercolor on paper.
National Maritime Museum, Greenwich, England.

on which I began to cry out for assistance: But my cries had no other effect than to make them tie me faster and stop my mouth, and then they put me into a large sack. They also stopped my sister's mouth and tied her hands, and in this manner we proceeded till we were out of the sight of these people.

When we went to rest the following night they offered us some victuals, but we refused it, and the only comfort we had was in being in one another's arms all that night and bathing each other with our tears. But alas! we were soon deprived of even the small comfort of weeping together. The next day proved a day of greater sorrow than I had yet experienced, for my sister and I were then separated while we lay clasped in each other's arms. It was in vain that we besought them not to part us; she was torn from me and immediately carried away, while I was left in a state of distraction not to be described. I cried and grieved continually, and for several days I did not eat anything but what they forced into my mouth. At length, after many days' traveling, during which I had often changed masters, I got into the hands of a chieftain in a very pleasant country. This man had two wives and some children, and they all used me extremely well and did all they could to comfort me, particularly the first wife, who was something like my mother. Although I was a great many days' journey from my father's house, yet these people spoke exactly the same language with us. This first master of mine, as I may call him, was a smith, and my principal employment was working his bellows, which were the same kind as I had seen in my vicinity. They were in some respects not unlike the stoves here in gentlemen's kitchens, and were covered over with leather; and in the middle of that leather a stick was fixed, and a person stood up and worked it in the same manner as is done to pump water out of a cask with a hand pump. I believe it was gold he worked, for it was of a lovely bright yellow color and was worn by the women on their wrists and ankles. . . .

Soon after this my master's only daughter and child by his first wife sickened and died, which affected him so much that for some time he was almost frantic, and really would have killed himself had he not been watched and prevented. However, in a small time afterward he recovered and I was again sold. I was now carried to the left of the sun's rising, through many different countries and a number of large woods. The people I was sold to used to carry me very often when I was tired either on their shoulders or on their backs. I saw many convenient well-built sheds along the roads at proper distances, to accommodate the merchants and travelers who lay in those buildings along with their wives, who often accompany them; and they always go well armed.

From the time I left my own nation I always found somebody that understood me till I came to the seacoast. The languages of different nations did not totally differ, nor were they so copious as those of the Europeans, particularly the English. They were therefore easily learned, and while I was journeying thus through Africa I acquired two or three different tongues. In this manner I had been traveling for a considerable time, when one evening, to my great surprise, whom should I see brought to the house where I was but my dear sister! As soon as she saw me she gave a loud shriek and ran into my arms—I was quite overpowered: Neither of us could speak, but for a considerable time clung to each other in mutual embraces, unable to do anything but weep. Our meeting affected all who saw us, and indeed I must acknowledge, in honor of those sable destroyers of human rights, that I never met with any ill-treatment or saw any offered to their slaves except tying them, when necessary, to keep them from running away.

When these people knew we were brother and sister they indulged us to be together, and the man to whom I supposed we belonged lay with us, he in the middle while she and I held one another by the hands across his breast all night; and thus for a while we forgot our misfortunes in the joy of being together: But even this small comfort was soon to have an end, for scarcely had the fatal morning appeared when she was again torn from me forever! I was now more miserable, if possible, than before. The small relief which her presence gave me from pain was gone, and the wretchedness of my situation was redoubled by my anxiety after her fate and my apprehensions

WORDS TO OWN

distraction (di·strak′shən) *n.*: mental disturbance or distress.

lest her sufferings should be greater than mine, when I could not be with her to alleviate them. . . .

I did not long remain after my sister. I was again sold and carried through a number of places till, after traveling a considerable time, I came to a town called Tinmah in the most beautiful country I had yet seen in Africa. It was extremely rich, and there were many rivulets which flowed through it and supplied a large pond in the center of town, where the people washed. Here I first saw and tasted coconuts, which I thought superior to any nuts I had ever tasted before; and the trees, which were loaded, were also interspersed amongst the houses, which had commodious shades adjoining and were in the same manner as ours, the insides being neatly plastered and whitewashed. Here I also saw and tasted for the first time sugar cane. Their money consisted of little white shells the size of the fingernail. I was sold here for 172 of them by a merchant who lived and brought me there. I had been about two or three days at his house when a wealthy widow, a neighbor of his, came there one evening, and brought with her an only son, a young gentleman about my own age and size. Here they saw me; and, having taken a fancy to me, I was bought of the merchant, and went home with them. Her house and premises were situated close to one of those rivulets I have mentioned, and were the finest I ever saw in Africa: They were very extensive, and she had a number of slaves to attend her. The next day I was washed and perfumed, and when mealtime came I was led into the presence of my mistress, and ate and drank before her with her son. This filled me with astonishment; and I could scarce help expressing my surprise that the young gentleman should suffer me, who was bound, to eat with him who was free; and not only so, but that he would not at any time either eat or drink till I had taken first, because I was the eldest, which was agreeable to our custom. Indeed everything here, and all their treatment of me, made me forget that I was a slave. The language of these people resembled ours so nearly that we understood each other perfectly. They had also the very same customs as we. There were likewise slaves daily to attend us, while my young master and I with other boys sported with our darts and bows and arrows, as I had been used to do at home. In this resemblance to my former happy state I passed about two months; and I now began to think I was to be adopted into the family, and was beginning to be reconciled to my situation, and to forget by degrees my misfortunes, when all at once the delusion vanished; for without the least previous knowledge, one morning early, while my dear master and companion was still asleep, I was wakened out of my reverie to fresh sorrow, and hurried away even amongst the uncircumcised.

Thus at the very moment I dreamed of the greatest happiness, I found myself most miserable; and it seemed as if fortune wished to give me this taste of joy only to render the reverse more poignant. The change I now experienced was as painful as it was sudden and unexpected. It was a change indeed from a state of bliss to a scene which is inexpressible by me, as it discovered to me an element I had never before beheld and till then had no idea of, and wherein such instances of hardship and cruelty continually occurred as I can never reflect on but with horror. . . .

The Slave Ship

The first object which saluted[1] my eyes when I arrived on the coast was the sea, and a slave ship which was then riding at anchor and waiting for its cargo. These filled me with astonishment, which was soon converted into terror when I was carried on board. I was immediately handled and tossed up to see if I were sound by some of the crew, and I was now persuaded that I had gotten into a world of bad spirits and that they were going to kill me. Their complexions too differing so much from ours, their long hair and the language they spoke (which was very different from any I had ever heard) united to confirm me in this belief. Indeed such were the horrors of my views and fears at the moment that, if ten thousand worlds had been my own, I would have freely parted with them all to have exchanged my condition with that of the meanest[2] slave in my own

1. **saluted:** met.
2. **meanest:** lowest.

WORDS TO OWN

alleviate (ə·lē′vē·āt′) v.: to relieve; reduce.
interspersed (in′tər·spʉrsd′) v.: placed at intervals.
commodious (kə·mō′dē·əs) adj.: spacious.

---

country. When I looked round the ship too and saw a large furnace or copper boiling and a multitude of black people of every description chained together, every one of their <u>countenances</u> expressing <u>dejection</u> and sorrow, I no longer doubted of my fate; and quite overpowered with horror and anguish, I fell motionless on the deck and fainted. When I recovered a little I found some black people about me, who I believed were some of those who had brought me on board and had been receiving their pay; they talked to me in order to cheer me, but all in vain. I asked them if we were not to be eaten by those white men with horrible looks, red faces, and loose hair. They told me I was not, and one of the crew brought me a small portion of spirituous liquor in a wineglass, but being afraid of him I would not take it out of his hand. One of the blacks therefore took it from him and gave it to me, and I took a little down my palate, which instead of reviving me, as they thought it would, threw me into the greatest consternation at the strange feeling it

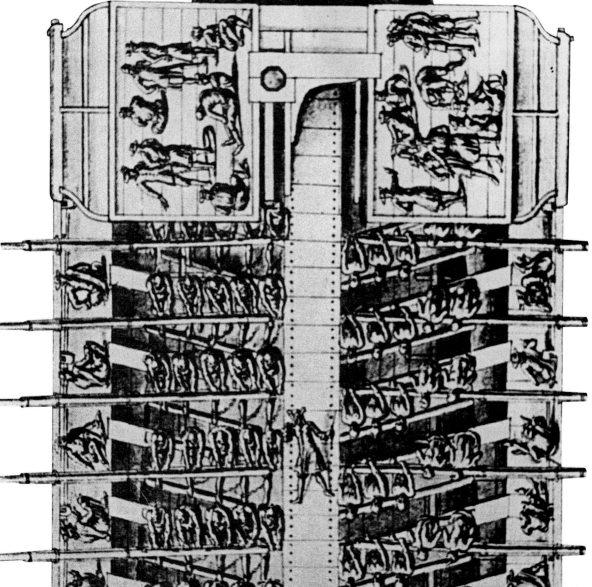

A galley manned by slaves.

WORDS TO OWN

countenances (koun′tə·nəns·əz) *n. pl.:* faces.
dejection (dē·jek′shən) *n.:* discouragement.

---

produced, having never tasted such any liquor before. Soon after this the blacks who brought me on board went off, and left me abandoned to despair.

I now saw myself deprived of all chance of returning to my native country or even the least glimpse of hope of gaining the shore, which I now considered as friendly; and I even wished for my former slavery in preference to my present situation, which was filled with horrors of every kind, still heightened by my ignorance of what I was to undergo. I was not long suffered to indulge my grief; I was soon put down under the decks, and there I received such a salutation in my nostrils as I had never experienced in my life: So that with the loathsomeness of the stench and crying together, I became so sick and low that I was not able to eat, nor had I the least desire to taste anything. I now wished for the last friend, death, to relieve me; but soon, to my grief, two of the white men offered me eatables, and on my refusing to eat, one of them held me fast by the hands and laid me across, I think, the windlass,[3] and tied my feet while the other flogged me severely. I had never experienced anything of this kind before, and although, not being used to the water, I naturally feared that element the first time I saw it, yet nevertheless could I have got over the nettings I would have jumped over the side, but I could not; and besides, the crew used to watch us very closely who were not chained down to the decks, lest we should leap into the water: And I have seen some of these poor African prisoners most severely cut for attempting to do so, and hourly whipped for not eating. This indeed was often the case with myself. In a little time after, amongst the poor chained men I found some of my own nation, which in a small degree gave ease to my mind. I inquired of these what was to be done with us; they gave me to understand we were to be carried to these white people's country to work for them. I then was a little revived, and thought if it were no worse than working, my situation was not so desperate: But

3. **windlass** (wind'ləs): device used to raise and lower heavy objects, like a ship's anchor.

still I feared I should be put to death, the white people looked and acted, as I thought, in so savage a manner; for I had never seen among my people such instances of brutal cruelty, and this not only shown toward us blacks but also to some of the whites themselves. One white man in particular I saw, when we were permitted to be on deck, flogged so unmercifully with a large rope near the foremast that he died in consequence of it; and they tossed him over the side as they would have done a brute. This made me fear these people the more, and I expected nothing less than to be treated in the same manner. I could not help ex-

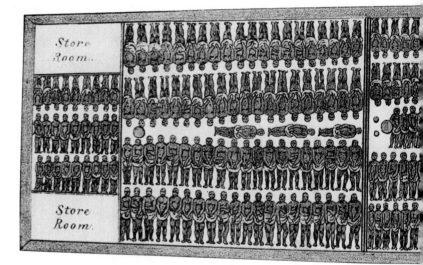

Drawing showing people squeezed together on the lower deck of a slave ship.

pressing my fears and apprehensions to some of my countrymen: I asked them if these people had no country but lived in this hollow place (the ship): They told me they did not, but came from a distant one. "Then," said I, "how comes it in all our country we never heard of them?" They told me because they lived so very far off. I then asked where were their women? Had they any like themselves? I was told they had: "And why," said I, "do we not see them?" They answered, because they were left behind. I asked how the vessel could go? They told me they could not tell, but that there were cloths put upon the masts by the help of the ropes I saw, and then the vessel went on; and the white men had some spell or magic they put in the water when they liked in order to stop the vessel. I was exceedingly amazed at this account and really thought they were spirits. I therefore wished much to be from amongst them for I expected they would sacrifice me: But my wishes were vain, for we were so quartered that it was impossible for any of us to make our escape.

While we stayed on the coast I was mostly on deck, and one day, to my great astonishment, I saw one of these vessels coming in with the sails up. As soon as the whites saw it they gave a great shout, at which we were amazed; and the more so as the vessel appeared larger by approaching nearer. At last she came to an anchor in my sight, and when the anchor was let go I and my countrymen who saw it were lost in astonishment to ob-

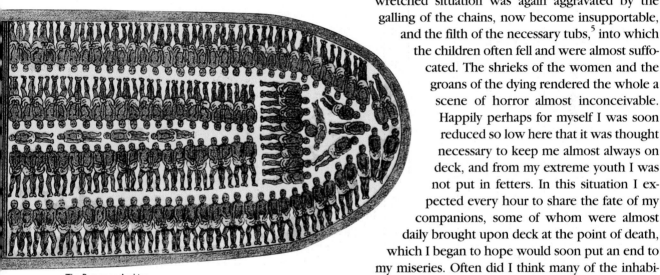

The Bettmann Archive.

serve the vessel stop, and were now convinced it was done by magic. Soon after this the other ship got her boats out, and they came on board of us, and the people of both ships seemed very glad to see each other. Several of the strangers also shook hands with us black people, and made motions with their hands, signifying I suppose we were to go to their country; but we did not understand them. At last, when the ship we were in had got in all her cargo, they made ready with many fearful noises, and we were all put under deck so that we could not see how they managed the vessel.

But this disappointment was the least of my sorrow. The stench of the hold[4] while we were on the coast was so intolerably loathsome that it was dan-

4. **hold:** enclosed area below a ship's deck, where cargo is usually stored.

gerous to remain there for any time, and some of us had been permitted to stay on the deck for the fresh air; but now that the whole ship's cargo were confined together it became absolutely pestilential. The closeness of the place and the heat of the climate, added to the number in the ship, which was so crowded that each had scarcely room to turn himself, almost suffocated us. This produced <u>copious</u> perspirations, so that the air soon became unfit for respiration from a variety of loathsome smells, and brought on a sickness among the slaves, of which many died, thus falling victims to the <u>improvident</u> avarice, as I may call it, of their purchasers. This wretched situation was again aggravated by the galling of the chains, now become insupportable, and the filth of the necessary tubs,[5] into which the children often fell and were almost suffocated. The shrieks of the women and the groans of the dying rendered the whole a scene of horror almost inconceivable. Happily perhaps for myself I was soon reduced so low here that it was thought necessary to keep me almost always on deck, and from my extreme youth I was not put in fetters. In this situation I expected every hour to share the fate of my companions, some of whom were almost daily brought upon deck at the point of death, which I began to hope would soon put an end to my miseries. Often did I think many of the inhabitants of the deep much more happy than myself. I envied them the freedom they enjoyed, and as often wished I could change my condition for theirs. Every circumstance I met with served only to render my state more painful, and heighten my apprehensions and my opinion of the cruelty of the whites. One day they had taken a number of fishes, and when they had killed and satisfied themselves with as many as they thought fit, to our astonishment who were on the deck, rather than give any of them to us to eat as we expected, they tossed the remaining fish into the sea again, although we

5. **necessary tubs:** toilets.

- -

WORDS TO OWN

copious (kō′pē·əs) *adj.*: great amounts of.
improvident (im·präv′ə·dənt) *adj.*: careless; not providing for the future.

- -

begged and prayed for some as well as we could, but in vain; and some of my countrymen, being pressed by hunger, took an opportunity when they thought no one saw them of trying to get a little privately; but they were discovered, and the attempt procured them some very severe floggings.

One day, when we had a smooth sea and moderate wind, two of my wearied countrymen who were chained together (I was near them at the time), preferring death to such a life of misery, somehow made through the nettings and jumped into the sea: Immediately another quite dejected fellow, who on account of his illness was suffered to be out of irons, also followed their example; and I believe many more would very soon have done the same if they had not been prevented by the ship's crew, who were instantly alarmed. Those of us that were the most active were in a moment put down under the deck, and there was such a noise and confusion amongst the people of the ship as I never heard before, to stop her and get the boat out to go after the slaves. However two of the wretches were drowned, but they got the other and afterward flogged him unmercifully for thus attempting to prefer death to slavery. In this manner we continued to undergo more hardships than I can now relate, hardships which are inseparable from this accursed trade. Many a time we were near suffocation from the want of fresh air, which we were often without for whole days together. This and the stench of the necessary tubs carried off many.

During our passage I first saw flying fishes, which surprised me very much: They used frequently to fly across the ship and many of them fell on the deck. I also now first saw the use of the quadrant; I had often with astonishment seen the mariners make observations with it, and I could not think what it meant. They at last took notice of my surprise, and one of them, willing to increase it as well as to gratify my curiosity, made me one day look through it. The clouds appeared to me to be land, which disappeared as they passed along. This heightened my wonder, and I was now more persuaded than ever that I was in another world and that everything about me was magic. At last we came in sight of the island of Barbados, at which the whites on board gave a great shout and made many signs of joy to us. We did not know what to think of this, but as the vessel drew nearer we plainly saw the harbor and other ships of different kinds and

sizes, and we soon anchored amongst them off Bridgetown. Many merchants and planters now came on board, though it was in the evening. They put us in separate parcels and examined us attentively. They also made us jump, and pointed to the land, signifying we were to go there. We thought by this we should be eaten by these ugly men, as they appeared to us; and when soon after we were all put down under the deck again, there was much dread and trembling among us, and nothing but bitter cries to be heard all the night from these apprehensions, insomuch that at last the white people got some old slaves from the land to pacify us. They told us we were not to be eaten but to work, and were soon to go on land where we should see many of our countrypeople. This report eased us much; and sure enough soon after we were landed there came to us Africans of all languages.

We were conducted immediately to the merchant's yard, where we were all pent up together like so many sheep in a fold without regard to sex or age. As every object was new to me everything I saw filled me with surprise. What struck me first was that the houses were built with stories, and in every other respect different from those in Africa: But I was still more astonished on seeing people on horseback. I did not know what this could mean, and indeed I thought these people were full of nothing but magical arts. While I was in this astonishment one of my fellow prisoners spoke to a countryman of his about the horses, who said they were the same kind they had in their country. I understood them though they were from a distant part of Africa, and I thought it odd I had not seen any horses there; but afterward when I came to converse with different Africans I found they had many horses amongst them, and much larger than those I then saw.

We were not many days in the merchant's custody before we were sold after their usual manner, which is this: On a signal given (as the beat of a drum) the buyers rush at once into the yard where the slaves are confined, and make choice of that parcel they like best. The noise and clamor with which this is attended and the eagerness visible in the countenances of the buyers serve not a little to

---

WORDS TO OWN

moderate (mäd′ər·it) *adj.*: gentle.

increase the apprehensions of the terrified Africans, who may well be supposed to consider them as the ministers of that destruction to which they think themselves devoted. In this manner, without scruple, are relations and friends separated, most of them never to see each other again. I remember in the vessel in which I was brought over, in the men's apartment there were several brothers who, in the sale, were sold in different lots; and it was very moving on this occasion to see and hear their cries at parting. O, ye nominal Christians! might not an African ask you, Learned you this from your God who says unto you, Do unto all men as you would men should do unto you? Is it not enough that we are torn from our country and friends to toil for your luxury and lust of gain? Must every tender feeling be likewise sacrificed to your avarice? Are the dearest friends and relations, now rendered more dear by their separation from their kindred, still to be parted from each other and thus prevented from cheering the gloom of slavery with the small comfort of being together and mingling their sufferings and sorrows? Why are parents to lose their children, brothers their sisters, or husbands their wives? Surely this is a new refinement in cruelty which, while it has no advantage to atone for it, thus aggravates distress and adds fresh horrors even to the wretchedness of slavery.

Africa

I am a descendant of Kings, Queens.
In my ear rings the faint tum-tum
of the African drum, whispering its rich
rhythms, echoing throughout the motherland. My
coarse hair captured the African breeze; braided
itself into the locks; twisting, winding, causing it
to stand on end. My quick tongue once knew the melodies
of Egypt; notes bouncing off of each other in chaos, yet
combining to make beautiful music. My feet covered with
the African earth from which my trunk was torn, but roots still
cling. My hips swing to and fro to the sound of the tum-tum
as once did my mother's mother,
and her mother before her.
The hands that molded me
have carefully molded
the generation before;
pouring life, love, and
heritage into my veins
to pass to my own
so they will be
descendants of
Kings, Queens.

—Doretha Williams
Topeka West High School
Topeka, Kansas

MAKING MEANINGS

First Thoughts

1. What **images** from Equiano's account are most memorable or horrifying to you?

Shaping Interpretations

2. Fill in the third column in the KWL chart you made in your Quickwrite. Did your understanding of slavery and the slave trade change? Explain.

3. What was Equiano's life like before he was taken captive? How does his description of his life affect your feelings about his enslavement?

4. Equiano is "handled and tossed up" by some of the crew as soon as he is taken on board the ship. Why? What do you think would have happened to him if the crew had found him unsatisfactory?

5. Why does Equiano include the flogging of a crew member in his account?

6. What is the basic contradiction between the crew's main goal and the treatment of its captives?

Extending the Text

7. How do you account for the depth of human cruelty described in parts of this autobiography? What current events reveal a similar capacity for brutishness in human nature?

Challenging the Text

8. How reliable do you think **autobiographies** are? On the other hand, what can autobiographies, such as Equiano's, tell you that other historical documents cannot?

Reading Check

a. How is Equiano treated by his captors and owners while he is still enslaved in West Africa?

b. Under what circumstances is Equiano twice parted from his sister?

c. How do some Africans on board the ship try to escape life in bondage?

d. Why does the ship's crew keep Equiano on deck most of the time?

CHOICES:
Building Your Portfolio

Writer's Notebook

1. Collecting Ideas for an Autobiographical Incident

Write down your memories of an incident in your life when you felt that one of your rights was being restricted or otherwise jeopardized. What kind of action, if any, were you able to take to protect that right? What did you learn about yourself as a result of the incident? Keep your notes for possible use in the Writer's Workshop on page 130.

Comparing Texts

2. Immigration Experiences

Equiano's journey to the Americas was quite different from that of the Pilgrims. In a brief essay, compare and contrast his experience with that of the voyagers on the *Mayflower* (see page 28). To generate ideas, you might want to use a Venn diagram like the one below:

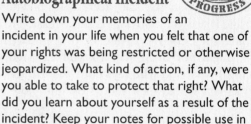

Creative Writing / Art

3. Teach Your Children Well

Create a picture book for children that will teach them about some aspect of African American heritage—perhaps something that you've just learned from Equiano's account. Research your topic, and report your findings in clear, easy-to-read language for children. You might even want to write in poetic form, as the student writer on page 65 did. Illustrate your children's book.

Collection 2

THE EXAMINED LIFE

Bradstreet
Taylor
Sor Juana
Edwards
Franklin

All my life I had been looking for something, and everywhere I turned someone tried to tell me what it was. I accepted their answers too, though they were often in contradiction and even self-contradictory. I was naïve. I was looking for myself and asking everyone except myself questions which I, and only I, could answer. It took me a long time and much painful boomeranging of my expectations to achieve a realization everyone else appears to have been born with: That I am nobody but myself.

—Ralph Ellison,
from *Invisible Man*

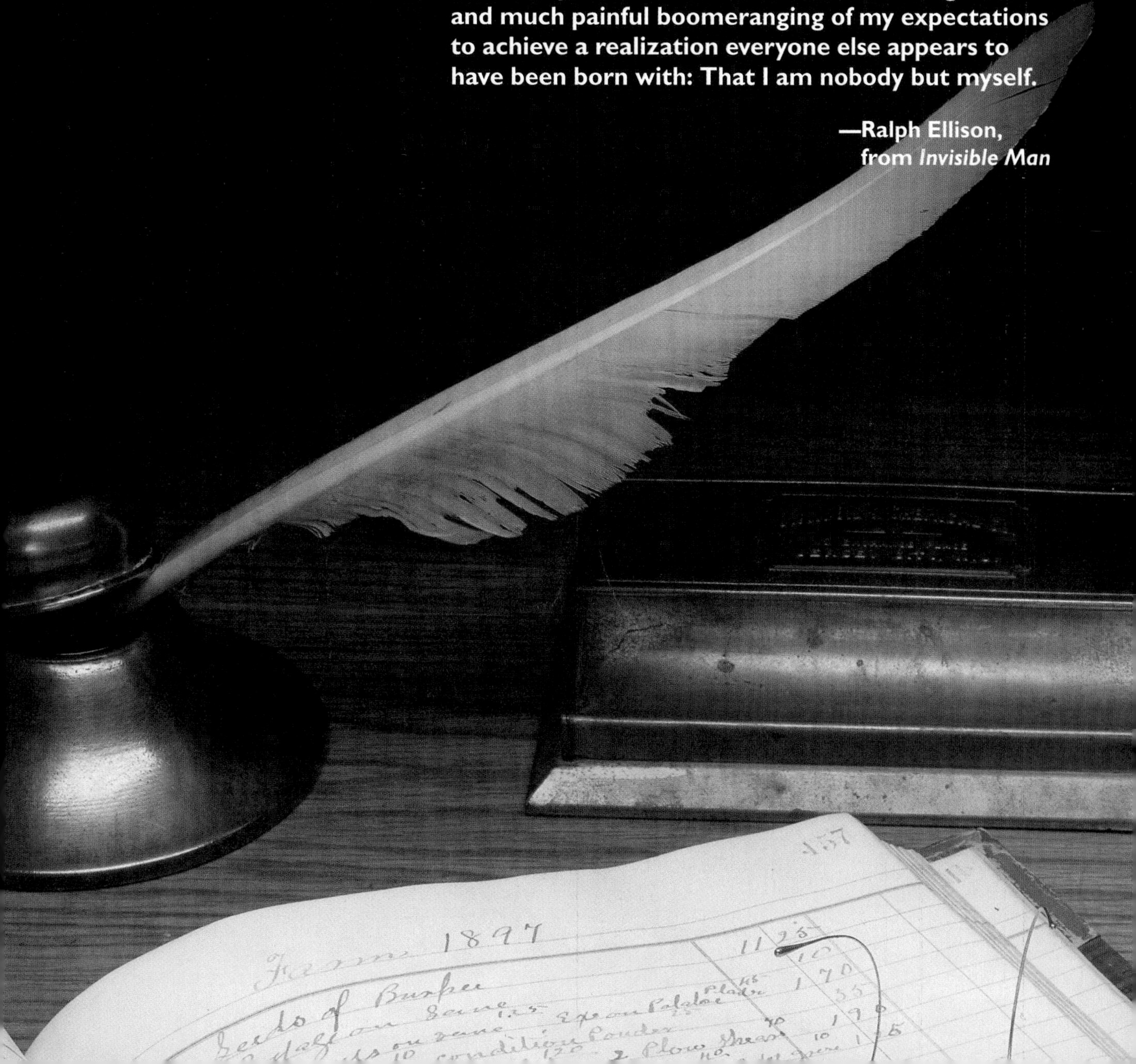

Anne Bradstreet

(1612–1672)

Who could have guessed that the writer who would begin the history of American poetry would be an immigrant, teenage bride? This fact seems less far-fetched when we know something about the life of the young woman who came from England to America when the Colonies were no more than a few villages precariously perched between the ocean and the wilderness.

Shakespeare was still alive when Anne Bradstreet was born, and like many budding poets, she found in Shake-speare, and in other great English poets, sources of inspiration and technique that would one day run like threads of gold through the fabric of her own work. However, what most determined the course of Anne Bradstreet's life was not a poetic influence but a religious one.

Anne Bradstreet was born into a family of Puritans. She accepted their reformist views as naturally as most children accept the religious teachings of a parent. When she was about sixteen, she married a well-educated and zealous young Puritan by the name of Simon Bradstreet. Two years later, in 1630, Simon, Anne, and Anne's father journeyed across the Atlantic to the part of New England around Salem that would become known as the Massachusetts Bay Colony. There her father and then her husband rose to prominence, each serving as governor of the colony, while Anne kept house first in Cambridge, then Ipswich, and finally in Andover. She raised four boys and four

Anne Bradstreet (detail) (1948) by Harry Grylls. Stained glass.

Reproduced by kind permission of the vicar and church wardens of St. Botolph's Church, Boston, England.

girls and, without seeking an audience or publication, found time to write poems.

Bradstreet's poems might never have come to light had it not been for John Woodbridge, her brother-in-law and a minister in Andover. In 1648, he went to England and, in 1650, without consulting the author herself, published Bradstreet's poems in London under the title *The Tenth Muse Lately Sprung Up in America . . . By a Gentlewoman in those Parts.*

In one stroke, an obscure wife and mother from the meadows of New England was placed among the nine Muses of art and learning sacred to the ancient Greeks. In itself, this was embarrassing enough. But in the middle of the seventeenth century, the real arrogance was that a woman would aspire to a place among the august company of established male poets. *The Tenth Muse* fared better with critics and the public than Anne expected (later, even the learned Puritan minister Cotton Mather praised her work), and she felt encouraged to write for the rest of her life.

Today, Anne Bradstreet is remembered not for her elaborate earlier poems that focus on public events, but for a few simple, personal lyrics about such things as the birth of children, the death of grandchildren, her love for her husband, her son's departure for England, and her own illnesses and adversities. In a letter to her children just before she died, she wrote: "Among all my experiences of God's gracious dealings with me I have constantly observed this, that He hath never suffered me long to sit loose from Him, but by one affliction or other hath made me look home, and search what was amiss."

HERE FOLLOW SOME VERSES UPON THE BURNING OF OUR HOUSE, JULY 10, 1666

Make the Connection
Tests of Strength

How we deal with losses in life is perhaps the greatest test of our inner strength. Some losses are so enormous that they shake us to our core and challenge our very sense of self. Response to such a loss is the topic of this poem: It portrays an internal debate, a kind of dialogue between self and soul.

Reading Skills and Strategies

Analyzing Text Structures: Inversion

Anne Bradstreet's poem is filled with **inversions.** In an inversion, the words of a sentence or phrase are wrenched out of our normal English syntax, or word order: "In silent night when rest I took," instead of "In silent night when I took rest." In English poetry of the previous centuries, poets used inversion frequently to accommodate the demands of **meter** or **rhyme.** As you read Bradstreet's poem, pay close attention to her use of inversion. Then, go through the poem line by line, and rewrite it so that these words appear in normal order. Read the new poem aloud. Jot down some notes on how this "noninverted version" changes the meter and emphases of the poem.

Here Follow Some Verses upon the Burning of Our House, July 10, 1666

Anne Bradstreet

In silent night when rest I took
For sorrow near I did not look
I wakened was with thund'ring noise
And piteous shrieks of dreadful voice.
5 That fearful sound of "Fire!" and "Fire!"
Let no man know is my desire.
I, starting up, the light did spy,
And to my God my heart did cry
To strengthen me in my distress
10 And not to leave me succorless.°
Then, coming out, beheld a space
The flame consume my dwelling place.
And when I could no longer look,
I blest His name that gave and took,°
15 That laid my goods now in the dust.
Yea, so it was, and so 'twas just.
It was His own, it was not mine,
Far be it that I should repine;
He might of all justly bereft

10. **succorless** (suk'ər·lis): without aid or assistance; helpless.
14. **that gave and took:** allusion to Job 1:21, "The Lord gave, and the Lord hath taken away; blessed be the name of the Lord."

20 But yet sufficient for us left.
When by the ruins oft I past
My sorrowing eyes aside did cast,
And here and there the places spy
Where oft I sat and long did lie:
25 Here stood that trunk, and there that chest,
There lay that store I counted best.
My pleasant things in ashes lie,
And them behold no more shall I.
Under thy roof no guest shall sit,
30 Nor at thy table eat a bit.
No pleasant tale shall e'er be told,
Nor things recounted done of old.
No candle e'er shall shine in thee,
Nor bridegroom's voice e'er heard shall be.
35 In silence ever shall thou lie,
Adieu, Adieu,° all's vanity.
Then straight I 'gin my heart to chide,

And did thy wealth on earth abide?
Didst fix thy hope on mold'ring dust?
40 The arm of flesh didst make thy trust?
Raise up thy thoughts above the sky
That dunghill mists away may fly.
Thou hast an house on high erect,
Framed by that mighty Architect,
45 With glory richly furnished,
Stands permanent though this be fled.
It's purchased and paid for too
By Him who hath enough to do.
A price so vast as is unknown
50 Yet by His gift is made thine own;
There's wealth enough, I need no more,
Farewell, my pelf,° farewell my store.
The world no longer let me love,
My hope and treasure lies above.

36. Adieu (à·dyö′): French for "goodbye."

52. pelf: wealth or worldly goods. Sometimes used as a term of contempt.

Embroidered chair seat cover (1725–1750) by the Bradstreet family. American, New England, Boston area. Colored wool embroidered on cotton and linen twill (44 cm × 54 cm).

MAKING MEANINGS

First Thoughts

1. Sometimes bad things happen to good people. Do you think any good can come from difficulties in life? Explain.

Shaping Interpretations

2. What are some of the specific losses that Bradstreet dwells on in the first half of the poem?

3. Bradstreet speaks of another "house" in an **extended metaphor** at the end of the poem. What is this house, who is its architect, and how is it better than the house she has lost? (For more information about extended metaphor, see page 188.)

4. *Pelf*—a word designating riches or worldly goods—is usually used only when the riches or goods are considered to be slightly tainted, ill-gotten, or stolen. Why do you suppose Bradstreet uses such a bitter word in line 52 to describe her own cherished treasures?

5. Using your "noninverted" version of the poem as a starting point, write a paraphrase of the entire poem. A **paraphrase** is a restatement of a text in your own words. Paraphrasing a text can help you clarify and interpret difficult or ambiguous passages.

Challenging the Text

6. Some readers have felt that, by so lovingly enumerating her losses, Bradstreet is "crying out to heaven" in a way that unconsciously reveals more attachment to her earthly possessions than she would admit to. On the other hand, what Bradstreet does *not* reveal in this poem is significant: Hundreds of books, as well as her papers and all her unpublished poems, were also lost in the fire. Using specific examples from the text, explain whether or not, by the end of the poem, you are convinced that the speaker means what she says.

Cradle of Peregrine White, first English child born in New England.

Courtesy of the Pilgrim Society, Plymouth, Massachusetts.

CHOICES:
Building Your Portfolio

Writer's Notebook

1. Collecting Ideas for an Autobiographical Incident

Write a few sentences about a time in your own life that seemed to you like a "baptism of fire"—a time when you were tested by challenges, such as peer pressure. Keep your notes for possible use in the Writer's Workshop on page 130.

Interpreting a Poem

2. Trials and Tribulations

In the Book of Job in the Bible, Job endures great misery, yet he is still able to say, "The Lord gave, and the Lord hath taken away; blessed be the name of the Lord" (Job 1:21). Bradstreet expresses a similar attitude in her poem; twice she checks herself from mourning over the loss of her beloved possessions. The first instance is in lines 14–20; the second begins with line 37. In a brief essay, discuss Bradstreet's attitude toward earthly suffering and the providence of God.

Creative Writing

3. The Taste of Adversity

An **aphorism** is a brief, cleverly worded statement that makes a wise observation about life. In Anne Bradstreet's book of aphorisms, *Meditations Divine and Moral*, she writes: "If we had no winter, the spring would not be so pleasant; if we did not sometimes taste of adversity, prosperity would not be so welcome." Using this observation and Bradstreet's poem as starting points, compose your own aphorism about adversity in life.

Edward Taylor

(1642?–1729)

To Puritans, the universe of God's Creation was sublime and magnificent. But to Edward Taylor, the universe could also be—*a bowling alley,* with God the bowler and the sun his bowling ball. This is the kind of imaginative surprise that made Taylor unique among American Puritan writers.

The publication in 1939 of *The Poetical Works of Edward Taylor* was the third important instance in American literature when buried poetic treasure was discovered. The first discovery occurred when Anne Bradstreet's brother-in-law carried her "private" poems to England and had them printed without her consent. The second occurred in 1890, when the heirs of Emily Dickinson (page 372) ignored her wishes and published the poems she had saved carefully in little packets that were to be destroyed after her death.

Headstone on Reverend Silas Bigelow's grave in Paxton, Massachusetts (1769). Carved by William Young.

Of these discoveries, the case of Edward Taylor is perhaps the most remarkable. Taylor wrote an enormous amount of poetry, but he allowed only a portion of one poem to be published during his lifetime. For many years, his brilliant poems moldered in the archives of Yale Library, to which Taylor's grandson had donated them. Then, once again, a body of work that an author had expected to remain unpublished came to light—in this case, with such compelling force as to cause the history of early poetry in America to be rewritten.

Edward Taylor was born in Leicestershire, England, near the town of Coventry. Like Anne Bradstreet, he was raised in a family that held dissenting views about many of the practices of the Church of England. Taylor lost a teaching position in England because he refused to take an oath—required by the royal Act of Uniformity—that conflicted with his religious beliefs. Feeling more and more uncomfortable in the religious climate of his country, where the Act of Uniformity was contributing to the persecution of Puritans, he determined to seek the freedom that other Nonconformists had found in Colonial America. In 1668, Taylor sailed for Boston.

Friends had equipped Taylor with letters of introduction to some of the established Colonial leaders, among them the great Puritan minister Increase Mather (1639–1723). Impressed with the young man's credentials and charmed by his personality, Mather and other influential people eased Taylor's way into Harvard College.

After training for the ministry, Taylor accepted a call in 1671 to become pastor of a church in Westfield, Massachusetts. Taylor stayed in Westfield for the rest of his life. During his fifty-eight years in this frontier town, he faithfully tended the spiritual needs of his flock. Taylor himself increased the flock by fourteen members—he had eight children by his first wife and six by his second. By the time he died in 1729, Taylor had outlived a number of his children.

After Taylor's death, only one book of poetry was found in his personal library—Anne Bradstreet's *The Tenth Muse Lately Sprung Up in America.* Like Bradstreet, Taylor could have had little notion that his poems, which he had scrupulously put away, would outlive him with a radiance bright enough to penetrate the darkness of two centuries of obscurity.

HRW go.hrw.com

LE0 11-2

Before You Read

HUSWIFERY

Make the Connection

By the Grace of God

Today many people believe that individual identity is shaped by numerous factors, such as family, friends, education, geography, and personal beliefs. The Puritans believed that each aspect of their identity was shaped by God and that all their emotions, thoughts, desires, and behavior should be directed toward God's service and glorification. The Puritans endlessly examined their lives for evidence of God's grace.

Reading Skills and Strategies

Analyzing Text Structures: Extended Metaphors

This poem contains a startling **extended metaphor**—a comparison between two very different things: making cloth and experiencing God's grace. This unusual type of comparison is known as a **conceit** (see page 74). As you read the poem, keep a double-entry journal. In the first column, list the implements and materials used in spinning cloth. In the second column, next to each item, list the spiritual experience that Taylor compares to the act of spinning.

Background

Huswifery (huz′wif′ər·ē) is an archaic spelling of *housewifery*, which means "the care and management of a household." It suggests the whole range of domestic responsibilities, as well as the qualities of thrift and orderliness. A *housewife* (huz′if) also came to be the name for a small sewing kit.

Huswifery

Edward Taylor

Make me, O Lord, thy Spinning Wheel complete.
    Thy Holy Word my Distaff° make for me.
Make mine Affections thy Swift Flyers neat
    And make my Soul thy holy Spool to be.
5   My Conversation make to be thy Reel
    And reel the yarn thereon spun of thy Wheel.

Make me thy Loom then, knit therein this Twine:
    And make thy Holy Spirit, Lord, wind quills:°
Then weave the Web thyself. The yarn is fine.
10   Thine Ordinances° make my Fulling Mills.°
    Then dye the same in Heavenly Colors Choice,
    All pinked° with Varnished° Flowers of Paradise.

Then clothe therewith mine Understanding, Will,
    Affections, Judgment, Conscience, Memory,
15 My Words, and Actions, that their shine may fill
    My ways with glory and thee glorify.
    Then mine apparel shall display before ye
    That I am Clothed in Holy robes for glory.

2. distaff (dis′taf′): On spinning wheels, the distaff is a stick around which fibers are wound before they are spun into thread. Flyers help govern the rate of spinning. The finished thread is wound upon a reel, or spool.

8. quills: a loom's spools or bobbins, on which thread is wound before weaving.

10. ordinances: religious rules and laws.
Fulling Mills: Fulling, or milling, is the term used for the processing of raw wool cloth through a combination of washing, heating, and compressing. The cloth is processed in fulling mills to preshrink and treat the individual fibers, thereby enhancing its appearance in finished fabrics.
12. pinked: decorated. **varnished:** embellished.

MAKING MEANINGS

First Thoughts

1. Did you respond emotionally or intellectually to Taylor's extended comparison? Did you feel involved with the poem or distant from it? Why?

Shaping Interpretations

2. The poet states his main **metaphor** in the first line. What does he ask the Lord to make him?

3. Using your reading notes to help you review the poem, describe the specific ways that Taylor extends this central comparison.

4. Describe the relationship between this speaker and God. What does the speaker say will make him a complete and fulfilled person?

5. What transformation does the poet describe in the last two lines?

6. *Huswifery* can mean "thrift," or making the most of what one has. Who is practicing the art of huswifery in this poem?

ELEMENTS OF LITERATURE

The Conceit

In poetry, the term **conceit** refers to a startling **extended metaphor** or other **figure of speech** that makes a surprising, even shocking, connection between two different things. The connection may be witty, strange, exaggerated, or cleverly elaborate. When Emily Dickinson (page 372) compared the setting sun to a housewife sweeping up the sky with multicolored brooms and carelessly dropping shreds behind her, she created more than a metaphor: She created a conceit.

Conceits, then, are startling figures of speech that are extended as far as the poet wants to take them. They are exercises of imagination, devices for making us see sometimes profound connections between vastly different things in the world.

Making up a conceit. Devise your own original conceit. Begin by thinking of ordinary comparisons. Then try to match one half of a comparison with something no one is likely to have thought of before. Begin your conceit: _____ is like _____.

CHOICES: Building Your Portfolio

Writer's Notebook

1. Collecting Ideas for an Autobiographical Incident

Write down two or three incidents in your own life that helped define your identity. Keep your notes for possible use in the Writer's Workshop on page 130.

Comparing Extended Metaphors

2. Special Fabrics

In the excerpt below from the Reverend Jesse Jackson's speech to the Democratic National Convention in 1988, Jackson develops an interesting **extended metaphor.** Although Jackson and Taylor are comparing different things, look for similarities in their metaphors. In a brief essay, examine these questions: Does each speaker conclude the metaphor with a kind of transformation? How is each metaphor visual—what does each help you see? In general, how effective do you find each extended metaphor to be?

> America's not a blanket, woven from one thread, one color, one cloth. When I was a child growing up in Greenville, South Carolina, and Grandmother could not afford a blanket, she didn't complain, and we did not freeze. Instead she took pieces of old cloth—patches, wool, silk, gabardine, crockersack on the patches—barely good enough to wipe off your shoes with.
>
> But they didn't stay that way very long. With sturdy hands and a strong cord, she sewed them together into a quilt, a thing of beauty and power and culture.
>
> Now . . . we must build such a quilt.
>
> —Jesse Jackson

Sor Juana Inés de la Cruz
(1648–1695)

Juana Ramírez de Asbaje was born in a village located between two volcanoes southeast of Mexico City. A solitary child with unusual intellectual curiosity, Juana learned to read and write by the age of six or seven. At age six, she heard of the university in Mexico City and pleaded with her mother to send her there dressed like a man. Her request denied, she threw herself into reading and study in her grandfather's library—a world of books and learning that, in the seventeenth century, was still a man's world. As a child she continued to learn Latin after taking only twenty lessons. She was a harsh taskmaster, cutting off her hair if she failed to learn her Latin grammar according to the schedule she had set for herself. "It didn't seem right to me," she wrote, "that a head so naked of knowledge should be dressed up with hair." She also stopped eating cheese, one of her favorite foods, because she had heard that it dulled the mind.

At sixteen, Juana was presented at the court of the Spanish viceroy in Mexico City, where she charmed everyone with her wit, beauty, and brilliance. She served as a lady-in-waiting for four years, then abruptly decided to enter a convent at the age of twenty, taking the name Sor (Sister) Juana Inés de la Cruz. For the next twenty-five years, she lived in a small apartment where she studied and wrote, amassing a huge library of about four thousand volumes and collecting musical and scientific instruments. She also proved to be a shrewd businesswoman, accruing a fortune, making investments, and serving as the convent's bookkeeper and archivist.

Sor Juana Inés de la Cruz (1750) by Miguel Cabrera (1695–1768). Oil on canvas.

Courtesy of Schalkwijk/Art Resource, New York.

Sor Juana's superiors in the Catholic Church continually criticized her for her intellectual pursuits and justifications of secular learning. Most controversial was her long autobiographical letter to a Catholic bishop, in which she defended the rights of women to be educated and intellectually independent—even to undertake public careers. For reasons that are unclear, Sor Juana suddenly abandoned her studies and sold her library, giving the money to the poor and devoting herself exclusively to her religious duties. She wrote nothing during the last two years of her life. In 1695, while nursing her sisters who had been stricken with the plague, Sor Juana became ill and died.

Before You Read

WORLD, IN HOUNDING ME . . .

Background

At about the same time the Puritan poets Anne Bradstreet and Edward Taylor were in New England writing poems in praise of God, the brilliant Catholic nun Sor Juana Inés de la Cruz was writing poems, plays, songs, and essays in a convent in New Spain (in present-day Mexico). The contemporary Mexican poet Octavio Paz (1914–1998) considered Sor Juana's poems to be among "the most elegant and refined in Spanish. Few poets in our language equal her, and those who surpass her can be counted on the fingers of one hand." In her own time, Sor Juana was called "the tenth muse from Mexico," and her visitors spent evenings in an atmosphere similar to one of Europe's most cultivated salons, discussing ideas and reciting poems over biscuits, fruit, and cups of chocolate.

Reading Skills and Strategies

Responding to a Poem

As you read the following poem by Sor Juana, write down your thoughts, feelings, and questions. In particular, note the similarities or differences between this poem and those you have read by Bradstreet and Taylor.

World, in Hounding Me . . .

Sor Juana Inés de la Cruz

translated from the Spanish
by **Alan S. Trueblood**

    World, in hounding me, what do you gain?
How can it harm you if I choose, astutely,
rather to stock my mind with things of beauty,
than waste its stock on every beauty's claim?
5   Costliness and wealth bring me no pleasure;
the only happiness I care to find
derives from setting treasure in my mind,
and not from mind that's set on winning treasure.
    I prize no comeliness.° All fair things pay
10 to time, the victor, their appointed fee
and treasure cheats even the practiced eye.
    Mine is the better and the truer way:
to leave the vanities of life aside,
not throw my life away on vanity.

9. **comeliness:** beauty.

En perseguirme, mundo . . .

Sor Juana Inés de la Cruz

    En perseguirme, mundo, ¿qué interesas?
¿En qué te ofendo, cuando sólo intento
poner bellezas en mi entendimiento
y no mi entendimiento en las bellezas?
5   Yo no estimo tesoros ni riquezas;
y así, siempre me causa más contento
poner riquezas en mi pensamiento
que no mi pensamiento en las riquezas.
    Y no estimo hermosura que, vencida,
10 es despojo civil de las edades,
ni riqueza me agrada fementida,
    teniendo por mejor, en mis verdades,
consumir vanidades de la vida
que consumir la vida en vanidades.

FINDING COMMON GROUND

Using the notes you wrote while reading, meet in small groups to hold your own "salon," in which you discuss your questions about and responses to this poem.

As a group, agree on the topics you want to talk about that are suggested by this poem: how you feel about Sor Juana's message, how the poem is similar to or different from the poetry of the Puritan writers you have read, or whatever else you want to discuss.

Jonathan Edwards

(1703–1758)

Despite his fire-and-brimstone imagery, Jonathan Edwards was not merely a stern, zealous preacher. He was a brilliant, thoughtful, and complicated man. Science, reason, and observation of the physical world confirmed Edwards's deeply spiritual vision of a universe filled with the presence of God.

Edwards's abilities were recognized early. Groomed to succeed his grandfather as pastor of the Congregational Church in Northampton, Massachusetts, Edwards entered Yale when he was only thirteen. When his grandfather died in 1729, Edwards mounted the pulpit and quickly established himself as a strong-willed and charismatic pastor.

Edwards's formidable presence and vivid sermons helped to bring about the religious revival known as the Great Awakening. This revival began in Northampton in the 1730s and during the next fifteen years spread throughout the eastern seaboard. The Great Awakening was marked by waves of conversions that were so intensely emotional as to amount at times to mass hysteria.

The Great Awakening began at a time when enthusiasm for the old Puritan religion was declining. To offset the losses in their congregations, churches had been accepting growing numbers of "unregenerate" Christians—people who accepted church doctrine and lived upright lives but who had not confessed to being born again in God's grace, and so were not considered to be saved.

Edwards became known for his extremism as a pastor. In his sermons he didn't hesitate to accuse prominent church members, by name, of relapsing into sin. Edwards's strictness eventually proved to be too much for his congregation, and in 1750 he was dismissed from his prestigious position as pastor of Northampton. After rejecting a number of pastorships offered to him, Edwards relocated to the raw and remote Mohican community of Stockbridge,

Reverend Jonathan Edwards (1750–1755) by Joseph Badger (1708–1765). Oil on canvas (28½″ × 22″).

Massachusetts. After eight years of missionary work in virtual exile, shared with his wife Sarah, Edwards was named president of the College of New Jersey (later called Princeton University). Three months after assuming this position, he died of a smallpox inoculation—a modern medical procedure that, ironically, had been promoted by the fierce Puritan minister Cotton Mather.

Intellectually, Edwards straddled two ages: the modern, secular world exemplified by such men as Benjamin Franklin (page 84), and the religious world of his zealous Puritan ancestors. He believed (like Franklin) in reason and learning, the value of independent intellect, and the power of the human will. On the other hand, he believed (like Mather) in the lowliness of human beings in relation to God's majesty and the ultimate futility of merely human efforts to achieve salvation. Edwards, as "the last Puritan," stood between Puritan America and modern America. Tragically, he fit into neither world.

Yale University Art Gallery, Bequest of Eugene Phelps Edwards (1938.74).

Before You Read

FROM SINNERS IN THE HANDS OF AN ANGRY GOD

Make the Connection

The Great Motivator

Ralph Waldo Emerson (page 216) wrote that "Fear is an instructor of great sagacity and the herald of all revolutions." Many people would agree that fear is one of the most powerful motivators of human behavior. Fear of injury makes us buckle our seat belts. Fear of failure makes some of us study or work harder. Edwards and other pastors used harsh warnings in their sermons to make "sinners" understand the precariousness of their situation by actually *feeling* the fear and horror of their sinful state.

Reading Skills and Strategies

Analyzing Literary Language

As you read Edwards's sermon, write down the phrases or details that you find particularly vivid or frightening. Make special note of the three central **figures of speech** in paragraphs 4–7 on pages 80–81.

Elements of Literature

Figures of Speech

Figures of speech describe one thing in terms of another, very different thing. Although Edwards's belief in eternal damnation is literal, he uses figures of speech to compare God's wrath to ordinary, everyday things that his listeners could relate to and understand.

Background

This is Edwards's most famous sermon, which he delivered on a visit to the congregation at Enfield, Connecticut, in 1741. The "natural men" he is trying to awaken and persuade are those people in the congregation who have not been "born again," meaning they have not accepted Christ as their savior. Edwards's methods in the sermon were influenced by the work of the English philosopher John Locke (1632–1704). Locke believed that everything we know comes from experience, and he emphasized that understanding and feeling were two distinct kinds of knowledge. (To Edwards, the difference between these two kinds of knowledge was like the difference between reading the word *fire* and actually being burned.) Edwards's sermon had a powerful effect on the congregation; several times he had to ask his shrieking and swooning audience for quiet.

> **F**igures of speech are words or phrases that compare one thing to another, unlike thing.
>
> *For more on Figures of Speech, see the Handbook of Literary Terms.*

The Progress of Sin (detail) (1744) by Benjamin Keach. Woodcut.

Sinclair Hamilton Collection no. 21. Graphic Arts Collections. Visual Materials Division. Department of Rare Books and Special Collections. Princeton University Libraries.

from Sinners in the Hands of an Angry God

Jonathan Edwards

So that, thus it is that natural men are held in the hand of God, over the pit of hell; they have deserved the fiery pit, and are already sentenced to it; and God is dreadfully <u>provoked</u>, His anger is as great toward them as to those that are actually suffering the executions of the fierceness of His wrath in hell, and they have done nothing in the least to <u>appease</u> or abate that anger, neither is God in the least bound by any promise to hold them up one moment: The devil is waiting for them, hell is gaping for them, the flames gather and flash about them, and would fain lay hold on them, and swallow them up; the fire pent up in their own hearts is struggling to break out: And they have no interest in any Mediator, there are no means within reach that can be any security to them.

WORDS TO OWN
provoked (prō·vōkt′) *adj.*: enraged; angered.
appease (ə·pēz′) *v.*: to calm; satisfy.

In short, they have no refuge, nothing to take hold of; all that preserves them every moment is the mere arbitrary will, and uncovenanted, unobliged forbearance of an incensed God.

The use of this awful subject may be for awakening unconverted persons in this congregation. This that you have heard is the case of every one of you that are out of Christ. That world of misery, that lake of burning brimstone, is extended abroad under you. There is the dreadful pit of the glowing flames of the wrath of God; there is hell's wide gaping mouth open; and you have nothing to stand upon, nor anything to take hold of; there is nothing between you and hell but the air; it is only the power and mere pleasure of God that holds you up.

You probably are not sensible of this; you find you are kept out of hell, but do not see the hand of God in it; but look at other things, as the good state of your bodily constitution, your care of your own life, and the means you use for your own preservation. But indeed these things are nothing; if God should withdraw His hand, they would avail no more to keep you from falling, than the thin air to hold up a person that is suspended in it.

Your wickedness makes you as it were heavy as lead, and to tend downward with great weight and pressure toward hell; and if God should let you go, you would immediately sink and swiftly descend and plunge into the bottomless gulf, and your healthy constitution, and your own care and prudence, and best contrivance, and all your righteousness, would have no more influence to uphold you and keep you out of hell, than a spider's web would have to stop a fallen rock. . . .

The wrath of God is like great waters that are dammed for the present; they increase more and more, and rise higher and higher, till an outlet is given; and the longer the stream is stopped, the more rapid and mighty is its course, when once it is let loose. It is true, that judgment against your evil works has not been executed hitherto; the floods of God's vengeance have been withheld; but your guilt in the meantime is constantly increasing, and you are every day treasuring up more wrath; the waters are constantly rising, and waxing more and more mighty; and there is nothing but the mere pleasure of God that holds the waters back, that are unwilling to be stopped, and press hard to go forward. If God should only withdraw His hand from the floodgate, it would immediately fly open, and the fiery floods of the fierceness and wrath of God, would rush forth with inconceivable fury, and would come upon you with omnipotent power; and if your strength were ten thousand times greater than it is, yea, ten thousand times greater than the strength of the stoutest, sturdiest devil in hell, it would be nothing to withstand or endure it.

The bow of God's wrath is bent, and the arrow made ready on the string, and justice bends the arrow at your heart, and strains the bow, and it is nothing but the mere pleasure of God, and that of an angry God, without any promise or obligation at all, that keeps

Words to Own

constitution (kän'stə·tōō'shən) *n.*: physical condition.
contrivance (kən·trī'vəns) *n.*: scheme; plan.
inconceivable (in'kən·sēv'ə·bəl) *adj.*: unimaginable; beyond understanding.
omnipotent (äm·nip'ə·tənt) *adj.*: all-powerful.

the arrow one moment from being made drunk with your blood. Thus all you that never passed under a great change of heart, by the mighty power of the Spirit of God upon your souls; all you that were never born again, and made new creatures, and raised from being dead in sin, to a state of new, and before altogether unexperienced light and life, are in the hands of an angry God. However you may have reformed your life in many things, and may have had religious affections,[1] and may keep up a form of religion in your families and closets,[2] and in the house of God, it is nothing but His mere pleasure that keeps you from being this moment swallowed up in everlasting destruction. However unconvinced you may now be of the truth of what you hear, by and by you will be fully convinced of it. Those that are gone from being in the like circumstances with you, see that it was so with them; for destruction came suddenly upon most of them; when they expected nothing of it, and while they were saying, peace and safety: Now they see, that those things on which they depended for peace and safety, were nothing but thin air and empty shadows.

The God that holds you over the pit of hell, much as one holds a spider, or some loathsome insect over the fire, abhors you, and is dreadfully provoked: His wrath toward you burns like fire; He looks upon you as worthy of nothing else but to be cast into the fire; He is of purer eyes than to bear to have you in His sight; you are ten thousand times more abominable in His eyes than the most hateful venomous serpent is in ours. You have offended Him infinitely more than ever a stub-

1. **affections:** feelings.
2. **closets:** rooms for prayer and meditation.

born rebel did his prince; and yet it is nothing but His hand that holds you from falling into the fire every moment. It is to be ascribed to nothing else, that you did not go to hell the last night; that you was suffered to awake again in this world, after you closed your eyes to sleep. And there is no other reason to be given, why you have not dropped into hell since you arose in the morning, but that God's hand has held you up. There is no other reason to be given why you have not gone to hell, since you have sat here in the house of God, provoking His pure eyes by your sinful wicked manner of attending His solemn worship. Yea, there is nothing else that is to be given as a reason why you do not this very moment drop down into hell.

O sinner! Consider the fearful danger you are in: It is a great furnace of wrath, a wide and bottomless pit, full of the fire of wrath, that you are held over in the hand of that God, whose wrath is provoked and incensed as much against you, as against many of the damned in hell. You hang by a slender thread, with the flames of divine wrath flashing about it, and ready every moment to singe it, and burn it asunder; and you have no interest in any Mediator, and nothing to lay hold of to save yourself, nothing to keep off the flames of wrath, nothing of your own, nothing that you ever have done, nothing that you can do, to induce God to spare you one moment. . . .

WORDS TO OWN

abhors (ab·hôrz′) v.: scorns; hates.
abominable (ə·bäm′ə·nə·bəl) adj: disgusting; loathsome.
ascribed (ə·skrībd′) v.: attributed to a certain cause.
induce (in·do͞os′) v.: to persuade; force; cause.

When Jonathan Edwards was twenty years old, he wrote a journal entry describing thirteen-year-old Sarah Pierrepont of New Haven. Edwards idealized Sarah and viewed her as a source of great spiritual strength. He wrote this tribute before he had even seen her. They were married four years later. In the second entry, from his unfinished autobiography, Edwards records a spiritual experience.

Sarah Pierrepont

They say there is a young lady in [New Haven] who is beloved of that Great Being who made and rules the world, and that there are certain seasons in which this Great Being, in some way or another invisible, comes to her and fills her mind with exceeding sweet delight, and that she hardly cares for anything, except to meditate on Him—that she expects after a while to be received up where He is, to be raised up out of the world and caught up into heaven; being assured that He loves her too well to let her remain at a distance from Him always. There she is to dwell with Him, and to be ravished with His love and delight forever. Therefore, if you present all the world before her, with the richest of its treasures, she disregards it and cares not for it, and is unmindful of any pain or affliction. She has a strange sweetness in her mind, and singular purity in her affections; is most just and conscientious in all her conduct; and you could not persuade her to do anything wrong or sinful, if you would give her all the world, lest she should offend this Great Being. She is of a wonderful sweetness, calmness, and universal benevolence of mind; especially after this Great God had manifested Himself to her mind. She will sometimes go about from place to place, singing sweetly; and seems to be always full of joy and pleasure; and no one knows for what. She loves to be alone, walking in the fields and groves, and seems to have someone invisible always conversing with her.

—Jonathan Edwards

My Sense of Divine Things

. . . And as I was walking there, and looking up on the sky and clouds, there came into my mind so sweet a sense of the glorious *majesty* and *grace* of God, that I know not how to express. I seemed to see them both in a sweet conjunction; majesty and meekness joined together; it was a sweet, and gentle, and holy majesty; and also a majestic meekness; an awful sweetness; a high, and great, and holy gentleness.

After this my sense of divine things gradually increased, and became more and more lively, and had more of that inward sweetness. The appearance of everything was altered; there seemed to be, as it were, a calm, sweet cast, or appearance of divine glory, in almost everything. God's excellency, his wisdom, his purity, and love, seemed to appear in everything; in the sun, and moon, and stars; in the clouds and blue sky; in the grass, flowers, trees; in the water, and all nature; which used greatly to fix my mind. I often used to sit and view the moon for continuance; and in the day spent much time in viewing the clouds and sky, to behold the sweet glory of God in these things; in the meantime, singing forth, with a low voice, my contemplations of the Creator and Redeemer. And scarce anything, among all the works of nature, was so sweet to me as thunder and lightning; formerly, nothing had been so terrible to me. Before, I used to be uncommonly terrified with thunder, and to be struck with terror when I saw a thunderstorm rising; but now, on the contrary, it rejoiced me. I felt God, so to speak, at the first appearance of a thunderstorm; and used to take the opportunity, at such times, to fix myself in order to view the clouds and see the lightning's play, and hear the majestic and awful voice of God's thunder, which oftentimes was exceedingly entertaining, leading me to sweet contemplations of my great and glorious God.

—Jonathan Edwards

MAKING MEANINGS

First Thoughts

1. If you had been a member of the congregation listening to Edwards's sermon, what do you think your reaction would have been?

Reading Check

Identify the three famous **figures of speech** that Edwards develops in paragraphs 4–7 of the sermon. What things is he comparing in each one? How does Edwards extend each figure of speech?

Shaping Interpretations

2. What references in the sermon might be interpreted as **allusions** to divine mercy?

3. Edwards is directing his sermon to what he calls "natural men," those members  of his congregation who have not been "reborn." Review your reading notes. What **images** and **figures of speech** do you think helped Edwards's listeners to *feel* the peril of their sinful condition?

4. Edwards strikes fear into the hearts of his listeners in order to persuade them to act to avoid everlasting torment. Which specific **metaphors** and **similes** in the sermon do you think were probably the most persuasive?

Challenging the Text

5. If you had a chance to respond to Edwards, what would you say?

CHOICES: Building Your Portfolio

Writer's Notebook

1. Collecting Ideas for an Autobiographical Incident

The former middleweight boxing champion Sugar Ray Leonard once wrote of his success, "What helped me develop my quickness was fear. I think the rougher the

opponent, the quicker I am." Freewrite about an incident in your own life when fear or anxiety motivated you to take action, make a change, or try harder at something. Save your notes for possible use in the Writer's Workshop on page 130.

Comparing Texts

2. The Other Edwards

In a brief essay, compare the ideas about God that Edwards expresses in his sermon with those he expresses in Primary Sources (page 82). How do you explain the apparent differences between the "two" Edwardses?

Speaking and Listening

3. Fire and Fervor

Today's fiery religious orators are successors to Jonathan Edwards and other preachers of the Great Awakening. With four or five other students, form a panel to discuss the following questions in class: (a) Are "fire-and-brimstone" sermons still effective today, or are other methods used to motivate congregations? (b) What aspects of Edwards's sermon would be effective today? (c) Would modern telecommunications enhance or detract from Edwards's sermon?

Creative Writing

4. What the Parishioners Said

You and your family have just returned to your home in Enfield after listening to Pastor Edwards's sermon. Write a script of a conversation between the members of your family, including the reactions of both adults and children.

Mrs. Jonathan Edwards (1750–1755) by Joseph Badger (1708–1765). Oil on canvas (30⅜" × 25½").

Yale University Art Gallery. Bequest of Eugene Phelps Edwards (1938.75).

Benjamin Franklin

(1706–1790)

Few people have been so energetically devoted to improvement—both self-improvement and the improvement of society—as Benjamin Franklin. Franklin's many accomplishments can only be summarized. Born in Boston, one of seventeen children, he rose from poverty to eminence even though he had to leave school early in order to work. By the time he was twenty-four, he was a prosperous merchant, owner of a successful print shop, and publisher of *The Pennsylvania Gazette*. He helped found the Academy of Philadelphia (which became the University of Pennsylvania), the American Philosophical Society, and the first public library in America. He promoted numerous municipal projects in Philadelphia: paved streets, sewer lines, improved street lighting, and a fire brigade. He was a scientist and an important inventor: His research, especially on electricity, resulted in his election to England's Royal Society. In addition, he invented an open heating stove (called a Franklin stove), bifocal eyeglasses, a type of harmonica, and a rocking chair that could swat flies. Like Thomas Jefferson (page 114), Franklin was a tinkerer, constantly looking for ways to make things work a little better or more efficiently.

Scientist, Socialite, and "Snake"

At forty-one, Franklin had made enough money to retire from business. He hoped to devote the rest of his life to study and scientific research, but this was not to be. Franklin possessed uncommon talents as a diplomat and negotiator, and for the rest of his life he used these skills in the service of his state and his country. Franklin lived in London in the 1750s and '60s, representing the interests of Pennsylvania as an agent of the Pennsylvania Assembly. A decade later he was back in London lobbying for the Colonies in their dispute with Britain, hoping to bring about a reconciliation that would prevent war. Franklin's wit and charm made him enormously popular in London for

Benjamin Franklin (1777) after Jean-Baptiste Greuze. Oil on canvas (28⅝″ × 22⅝″).

many years; he once said that he was invited out to dinner there six nights a week. But by 1774, when he was sixty-eight, the stress between Britain and the Colonies had become too great for even this shrewd diplomat to control. The King's Privy Council publicly attacked him for his policies; the British press called him an "old snake." Franklin finally relinquished his hopes for peace and sailed for America in 1775.

When Franklin arrived home, he was greeted with news that the first battles of the Revolutionary War had been fought at Lexington and Concord, Massachusetts. The "shot heard round the world" had been fired. After helping to draft the Declaration of Independence in 1776, Franklin left for Paris to negotiate the treaty that brought the French into the war on America's side. When Franklin landed in France, Lord Stormont, the British ambassador, caustically remarked: "I look upon him as a dangerous engine, and am very sorry that some English frigate did not meet with him by the way."

The Jack of All Trades

In Paris, Franklin was even more popular than he had once been in England. Playing the role of the sophisticated but homespun American, Franklin described himself as "an old man, with gray hair appearing under a marten fur cap, among the powdered heads of Paris." When the Revolution was over, he helped negotiate the peace, and he was a member of the Constitutional Convention in 1787. His death three years later was cause for international mourning.

Franklin's practicality, like the success story of his life, is typically American, but it has not been universally admired throughout the nation's history. The American novelist Herman Melville (page 311) gave this picture of Franklin: "Jack of all trades, master of each and mastered by none—the type and genius of his land. Franklin was everything but a poet." Franklin did lack a poet's depth of imagination and emotion, but his literary talents and accomplishments were substantial. He was especially gifted as a wit, as the lightly ironic tone of his *Autobiography* testifies.

> **Franklin's practicality is typically American.**

Franklin's talents were so great that he could have left his mark on many areas of intellectual accomplishment. As the biographer Carl Van Doren wrote of him, "Mind and will, talent and art, strength and ease, wit and grace met in him as if nature had been lavish and happy when he was shaped."

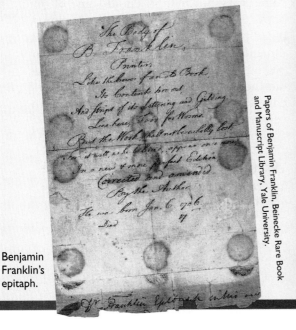

Benjamin Franklin's epitaph.

Papers of Benjamin Franklin, Beinecke Rare Book and Manuscript Library, Yale University.

Make the Connection

The Road to Success

"Rags-to-riches" is the Cinderella-like success story at the core of American life and culture. The slew of once-popular novels by Horatio Alger (1832–1899) chronicle just such success stories—the meteoric rise from humble beginnings to wealth. Rags-to-riches is the story of many Hollywood movie stars and producers (such as Charles Chaplin) and of this country's early business and industrial giants (such as Andrew Carnegie), some of whom were immigrants from other lands. It is still the story of numerous people today, from well-known athletes, performers, and other celebrities to unsung people you might even know yourself.

Quickwrite

Using a chart like the one below, make a list of qualities that you think are necessary for success. Can these qualities be acquired, or do people have to be born with them? Do you think that the same basic qualities are required to be successful at anything?

A Successful Person		
IS decisive	HAS goals	PLANS ahead

Background

Franklin began his *Autobiography* when he was sixty-five and continued it intermittently for years, although he never finished it and it was not published during his lifetime. When Franklin was a teenager, he was apprenticed to his older brother James, who printed a Boston newspaper. As an apprentice, Franklin felt he was treated harshly, and disputes arose between the brothers. This selection begins with Franklin's escape from a second, secret "indenture," or contract of service, that his brother had forced him to sign.

from The Autobiography

Benjamin Franklin

Leaving Boston

At length, a fresh difference arising between my brother and me, I took upon me to assert my freedom, presuming that he would not venture to produce the new indentures. It was not fair in me to take this advantage, and this I therefore reckon one of the first errata[1] of my life; but the unfairness of it weighed little with me, when under the impressions of resentment for the blows his passion too often urged him to be-

Benjamin Franklin.
Drawing by David Levine. Reprinted with permission from *The New York Review of Books*. Copyright © 1973 NYREV, Inc.

stow upon me, though he was otherwise not an ill-natured man: Perhaps I was too saucy and provoking.

When he found I would leave him, he took care to prevent my getting employment in any other printing house of the town, by going round and speaking to every master, who accordingly refused to give me work. I then thought of going to New York, as the nearest place where there was a printer; and I was rather inclined to leave Boston when I reflected that I had already made myself a little obnoxious to the governing party, and, from the arbitrary proceedings of the Assem-

bly in my brother's case, it was likely I might, if I stayed, soon bring myself into scrapes; and farther, that my indiscreet disputations about religion began to make me pointed at with horror by good people as an infidel or atheist. I determined on the point, but my father now siding with my brother, I was sensible that, if I attempted to go openly, means would be used to prevent me. My friend Collins, therefore, undertook to manage a little for me. He agreed with the captain of a New York sloop for my passage, under the notion of my being a young acquaintance of his, that had got a naughty girl with child, whose friends would compel me to marry

I wished to live without committing any fault at any time.

her, and therefore I could not appear or come away publicly. So I sold some of my books to raise a little money, was taken on board privately, and as we had a fair wind, in three days I found myself in New York, near 300 miles from home, a boy of but 17, without the least recommendation to, or knowledge of any person in the place, and with very little money in my pocket.

WORDS TO OWN

assert (ə·sʉrt′) *v*.: to declare; claim.
arbitrary (är′bə·trer′ē) *adj*.: based on whims or individual preferences.
indiscreet (in′di·skrēt′) *adj*.: careless in speech or action.

---

1. **errata** (er·rät′ə): Latin for "errors"; a printer's term.

Benjamin Franklin Drawing Electricity from the Sky (c. 1805) by Benjamin West (1738–1820). Oil on paper on canvas (13¼″ × 10″).

My inclinations for the sea were by this time worn out, or I might now have gratified them. But, having a trade, and supposing myself a pretty good workman, I offered my service to the printer in the place, old Mr. William Bradford,[2] who had been the first printer in Pennsylvania, but removed from thence upon the quarrel of George Keith. He could give me no employment, having little to do, and help enough already; but says he, "My son at Philadelphia has lately lost his principal hand,[3] Aquila Rose, by death; if you go thither, I believe he may employ you." Philadelphia was 100 miles further; I set out, however, in a boat for Amboy,[4] leaving my chest and things to follow me round by sea.

In crossing the bay, we met with a squall that tore our rotten sails to pieces, prevented our getting into the Kill,[5] and drove us upon Long Island. In our way, a drunken Dutchman, who was a passenger too, fell overboard; when he was sinking, I reached through the water to his shock pate,[6] and drew him up, so that we got him in again. His ducking sobered him a little, and he went to sleep, taking first out of his pocket a book, which he desired I would dry for him. It proved to be my old favorite author, Bunyan's *Pilgrim's Progress*,[7] in Dutch, finely printed on good paper, with copper cuts,[8] a

2. **William Bradford:** one of the first American printers; not to be confused with *Of Plymouth Plantation* author William Bradford (page 26). Bradford (1663–1752) set up the first printing presses in Philadelphia (1685) and New York (1693).
3. **principal hand:** best employee.
4. **Amboy:** Perth Amboy, New Jersey.
5. **Kill:** channel (from the Dutch *kil*). Based on the explorations of Henry Hudson in 1609, the Dutch claimed land in the Middle Colonies and gave Dutch names to some of its geographic features.
6. **shock pate** (pāt): shaggy head.
7. *Pilgrim's Progress*: religious allegory by the Puritan writer John Bunyan (1628–1688), first published in 1678. It tells how the hero, Christian, makes his journey to salvation. Notice that Franklin admires the book for literary and historical, rather than religious, reasons.
8. **copper cuts:** engravings.

dress better than I had ever seen it wear in its own language. I have since found that it has been translated into most of the languages of Europe, and suppose it has been more generally read than any other book, except perhaps the Bible. Honest John was the first that I know of who mixed narration and dialogue; a method of writing very engaging to the reader, who in the most interesting parts finds himself, as it were, brought into the company and present at the discourse. . . .

When we drew near the island, we found it was at a place where there could be no landing, there being a great surf on the stony beach. So we dropped anchor, and swung round toward the shore. Some people came down to the water edge and hallooed to us, as we did to them; but the wind was so high, and the surf so loud, that we could not hear so as to understand each other. There were canoes on the shore, and we made signs, and hallooed that they should fetch us; but they either did not understand us, or thought it impracticable, so they went away, and night coming on, we had no remedy but to wait till the wind should abate; and, in the meantime, the boatman and I concluded to sleep, if we could; and so crowded into the scuttle,[9] with the Dutchman, who was still wet, and the spray beating over the head of our boat, leaked through to us, so that we were soon almost as wet as he. In this manner we lay all night, with very little rest; but, the wind abating the next day, we made a shift to reach Amboy before night, having been thirty hours on the water, without victuals,[10] or any drink but a bottle of filthy rum, and the water we sailed on being salt.

9. **scuttle:** covered opening in hull or deck of a ship.
10. **victuals** (vit′′lz): food; sometimes spelled "vittles."

WORDS TO OWN
abate (ə·bāt′) *v.*: lessen.

In the evening I found myself very fever-ish, and went in to bed; but, having read somewhere that cold water drank plentifully was good for a fever, I followed the prescrip-tion, sweat plentiful most of the night, my fever left me, and in the morning, crossing the ferry, I proceeded on my journey on foot, having fifty miles to Burlington,[11] where I was told I should find boats that would carry me the rest of the way to Philadelphia.

It rained very hard all the day; I was thor-oughly soaked, and by noon a good deal tired; so I stopped at a poor inn, where I stayed all night, beginning now to wish that I had never left home. I cut so miserable a figure, too, that I found, by the questions asked me, I was suspected to be some run-away servant, and in danger of being taken up on that suspicion. However, I proceeded the next day, and got in the evening to an

Speak not but what may benefit others or yourself; avoid trifling conversation.

Drawing by David Levine. Reprinted with permission from *The New York Review of Books*. Copyright © 1973 NYREV, Inc.

inn, within eight or ten miles of Burlington, kept by one Dr. Brown. He entered into con-versation with me while I took some refresh-ment, and, finding I had read a little, became very sociable and friendly. Our acquaintance continued as long as he lived. He had been, I imagine, an <u>itinerant</u> doctor, for there was no town in England, or country in Europe, of which he could not give a very particular account. He had some letters,[12] and was in-genious, but much of an unbeliever, and wickedly undertook, some years after, to travesty the Bible in doggerel verse, as Cot-

11. Burlington: Burlington, New Jersey; about eighteen miles from Philadelphia.
12. letters: education.

ton had done Virgil.[13] By this means he set many of the facts in a very ridiculous light, and might have hurt weak minds if his work had been published; but it never was.

At his house I lay that night, and the next morning reached Burlington, but had the mortification to find that the regular boats were gone a little before my coming, and no other expected to go before Tuesday, this being Saturday; wherefore I returned to an old woman in the town, of whom I had bought gingerbread to eat on the water, and asked her advice. She invited me to lodge at her house till a passage by water should offer; and being tired with my foot traveling, I accepted the invitation. She understanding I was a printer, would have had me stay at that town and follow my business, being ig-norant of the stock necessary to begin with. She was very hospitable, gave me a dinner of oxcheek with great goodwill, accepting only of a pot of ale in return; and I thought myself fixed till Tuesday should come. How-ever, walking in the evening by the side of the river, a boat came by, which I found was going toward Philadelphia, with several people in her. They took me in, and, as there was no wind, we rowed all the way; and about midnight, not having yet seen the city, some of the com-pany were confident we must have passed it, and would row no farther; the others knew not where we were; so we put toward the shore, got into a creek, landed near an old fence, with the rails of which we made a fire, the night being cold, in October, and

13. doggerel . . . Virgil: Doggerel is irregularly constructed comical verse, often used for satirical purposes. In 1664, Charles Cotton (1630-1687) published a doggerel version, or a parody, of the *Aeneid*, an epic poem by the Roman poet Virgil (70-19 B.C.).

WORDS TO OWN
itinerant (ī·tin′ər·ənt) *adj.*: traveling.

Time on His Side: Benjamin Banneker

Poor Richard's Almanack (page 95) was a best-seller in its time, but Benjamin Franklin is not the only important figure in the history of the American almanac. Between 1792 and 1797, six remarkable almanacs were published by Benjamin Banneker (1731–1806), a Maryland farmer, astronomer, mathematician, and the first African American to have calculated almanacs. Banneker's almanacs, published in twenty-eight editions, were among the most successful almanacs of his era.

Self-taught scientist . . . Benjamin Banneker was the son of free African Americans. His grandmother was an Englishwoman, and his grandfather, who claimed to be an African prince, had the name Bannke or Bannaka. His grandmother taught him to read and write, and for a while he attended a one-room, interracial school where, recalled an African American classmate, "all his delight was to dive into his books." Banneker was mostly self-taught, and throughout his life he acquired considerable computational skill. For enjoyment he devised mathematical puzzles, some of them in verse. At twenty-two, using only a borrowed pocket watch and a picture of a clock as models, Banneker built a functioning wooden clock, each gear carved by hand, which struck the hours for over fifty years. Later in life, Banneker developed a passionate interest in the stars, and, in 1788, he calculated a solar eclipse using nothing but books as a guide.

---

there we remained till daylight. Then one of the company knew the place to be Cooper's Creek, a little above Philadelphia, which we saw as soon as we got out of the creek, and arrived there about eight or nine o'clock on the Sunday morning, and landed at the Market Street wharf.

Arrival in Philadelphia

I have been the more particular in this description of my journey, and shall be so of my first entry into that city, that you may in your mind compare such unlikely beginnings with the figure I have since made there. I was in my working dress, my best clothes being to come round by sea. I was dirty from my journey; my pockets were stuffed out with shirts and stockings, and I knew no soul nor where to look for lodging. I was fatigued with traveling, rowing, and want of rest, I was very hungry; and my whole stock of cash consisted of a Dutch dollar, and about a shilling in copper. The latter I gave the people of the boat for my passage, who at first refused it, on account of my rowing; but I insisted on their taking it. A man being sometimes more generous when he has but a little money than when he has plenty, perhaps through fear of being thought to have but little.

Then I walked up the street, gazing about till near the market house I met a boy with bread. I had made many a meal on bread, and, inquiring where he got it, I went immediately to the baker's he directed me to, in Second Street, and asked for biscuit, intending such as we had in Boston; but they, it seems, were not made in Philadelphia. Then I asked for a three-penny loaf, and was told

Banneker published his almanacs to advance not only the cause of science, but also the cause of African Americans. In 1791, Banneker sent a manuscript copy of his first almanac to Secretary of State Thomas Jefferson, along with a famous letter in which he urges Jefferson to recognize the equality of all people and calls for the abolition of slavery. Jefferson in turn sent the almanac to the Academy of Sciences in Paris, the foremost body of scientific learning in France. Thus, Banneker achieved transatlantic fame through his almanacs, as Franklin did through his writings and diplomatic career.

Benjamin Banneker, from one of his almanacs, c. 1795, by an unknown artist. Woodcut.

Maryland Historical Society.

. . . and star-gazing sage. Banneker was described by those who knew him as having the thoughtful demeanor of a sage as he leaned on the long staff that he always carried with him. Toward the end of his life, living alone in a small log house on his farm, Banneker continued to watch the stars, putter in his garden, study bees and locusts, play the violin and flute, and record his observations in a journal that became a unique record of an eighteenth-century almanac maker's method. His lifelong preoccupation with the measurement of time assured him a prominent place in the early history of science in America. Appropriately, the wooden clock Banneker had constructed kept excellent time until two days after his death: As Banneker's body was being lowered into his grave, his house a few yards away caught fire, destroying the clock he had made more than fifty years before.

---

they had none such. So not considering or knowing the difference of money, and the greater cheapness nor the names of his bread, I bade him give me three-penny worth of any sort. He gave me, accordingly, three great puffy rolls. I was surprised at the quantity, but took it, and,

Tolerate no uncleanliness in body, clothes, or habitation.

Drawing by David Levine. Reprinted with permission from *The New York Review of Books*. Copyright © 1973 NYREV, Inc.

having no room in my pockets, walked off with a roll under each arm, and eating the other. Thus I went up Market Street as far as Fourth Street, passing by the door of Mr. Read, my future wife's father; when she, standing at the door, saw me, and thought I made, as I certainly did, a most awkward, ridiculous appearance. Then I turned and went down Chestnut Street and part of Walnut Street, eating my roll all the way, and, coming round, found myself again at Market Street wharf, near the boat I came in, to which I went for a draft of the river water; and, being filled with one of my rolls, gave the other two to a woman and her child that came down the river in the boat with us, and were waiting to go farther.

Thus refreshed, I walked again up the street, which by this time had many clean-dressed people in it, who were all walking the same way. I joined them, and thereby was led into the great meetinghouse of the

Quakers near the market. I sat down among them, and, after looking round awhile and hearing nothing said, being very drowsy through labor and want of rest the preceding night, I fell fast asleep, and continued so till the meeting broke up, when one was kind enough to rouse me. This was, therefore, the first house I was in, or slept in, in Philadelphia. . . .

Arriving at Moral Perfection

It was about this time I conceived the bold and arduous project of arriving at moral perfection. I wished to live without committing any fault at any time; I would conquer all that either natural inclination, custom, or company might lead me into. As I knew, or thought I knew, what was right and wrong, I did not see why I might not always do the one and avoid the other. But I soon found I had undertaken a task of more difficulty than I had imagined. While my care was employed in guarding against one fault, I was often surprised by another; habit took the advantage of inattention; inclination was sometimes too strong for reason. I concluded, at length, that the mere speculative conviction that it was our interest to be completely virtuous, was not sufficient to prevent our slipping; and that the contrary habits must be broken, and good ones acquired and established, before we can have any dependence on a steady, uniform rectitude of conduct. For this purpose I therefore contrived the following method.

WORDS TO OWN
arduous (är′jōō·əs) *adj.*: difficult.
rectitude (rek′tə·tōōd′) *n.*: correctness.

Second Street, North from Market Street, with Christ Church, Philadelphia (1799) by W. Birch & Son. Colored line engraving.

In the various enumerations of the moral virtues I had met with in my reading, I found the catalog more or less numerous, as different writers included more or fewer ideas under the same name. Temperance, for example, was by some confined to eating and drinking, while by others it was extended to mean the moderating every other pleasure, appetite, inclination, or passion, bodily or mental, even to our avarice and ambition. I proposed to myself, for the sake of clearness, to use rather more names, with fewer ideas annexed to each, than a few names with more ideas; and I included under thirteen names of virtues all that at that time occurred to me as necessary or desirable, and annexed to each a short precept, which fully expressed the extent I gave to its meaning.

These names of virtues, with their precepts, were:

1. *Temperance.* Eat not to dullness; drink not to elevation.

2. *Silence.* Speak not but what may benefit others or yourself; avoid trifling conversation.

3. *Order.* Let all your things have their places; let each part of your business have its time.

4. *Resolution.* Resolve to perform what you ought; perform without fail what you resolve.

5. *Frugality.* Make no expense but to do good to others or yourself; i.e., waste nothing.

6. *Industry.* Lose no time; be always employed in something useful; cut off all unnecessary actions.

7. *Sincerity.* Use no hurtful deceit; think innocently and justly, and, if you speak, speak accordingly.

8. *Justice.* Wrong none by doing injuries, or omitting the benefits that are your duty.

9. *Moderation.* Avoid extremes; forbear resenting injuries so much as you think they deserve.

10. *Cleanliness.* Tolerate no uncleanliness in body, clothes, or habitation.

11. *Tranquility.* Be not disturbed at trifles, or at accidents common or unavoidable.

12. *Chastity.* Rarely use venery[14] but for health or offspring, never to dullness, weakness, or the injury of your own or another's peace or reputation.

13. *Humility.* Imitate Jesus and Socrates.[15]

My intention being to acquire the *habitude* of all these virtues, I judged it would be well not to distract my attention by attempting the whole at once, but to fix it on one of them at a time; and, when I should be master of that, then to proceed to another, and so on, till I should have gone through the thirteen; and, as the previous acquisition of some might facilitate the acquisition of certain others, I arranged them with that view, as they stand above. *Temperance* first, as it tends to procure that coolness and clearness of head, which is so necessary where constant vigilance was to be kept up, and guard maintained against the unremitting attraction of ancient habits, and the force of perpetual temptations. This being acquired and established, *silence* would be more easy; and my desire being to gain knowledge at the same time that I improved in virtue, and considering that in conversation it was obtained rather by the use of the ears than of the tongue, and therefore wishing to break a habit I was getting into of prattling, punning, and joking, which only made me acceptable to trifling company, I gave *silence*

14. **venery** (ven′ər·ē): sex.
15. **Socrates** (säk′rə·tēz′) (470–399 B.C.): Greek philosopher. He is said to have lived a simple, virtuous life.

WORDS TO OWN
facilitate (fə·sil′ə·tāt′) *v.:* make easier.

----

the second place. This and the next, *order,* I expected would allow me more time for attending to my project and my studies. *Resolution,* once become habitual, would keep me firm in my endeavors to obtain all the subsequent virtues; *frugality* and *industry* freeing me from my remaining debt, and producing affluence and independence, would make more easy the practice of *sincerity* and *justice,* etc., etc. Conceiving then, that, agreeably to the advice of Pythagoras[16] in his Golden Verses, daily examination would be necessary, I contrived the following method for conducting that examination.

I made a little book, in which I allotted a page for each of the virtues. I ruled each page with red ink, so as to have seven columns, one for each day of the week, marking each column with a letter for the day. I crossed these columns with thirteen red lines, marking the beginning of each line with the first letter of one of the virtues, on which line, and in its proper column, I might mark, by a little black spot, every fault I found upon examination to have been committed respecting that virtue upon that day.

I determined to give a week's strict attention to each of the virtues successively. Thus, in the first week, my great guard was to avoid every[17] the least offense against *temperance,* leaving the other virtues to their ordinary chance, only marking every evening the faults of the day. Thus, if in the first week I could keep my first line, marked T, clear of spots, I supposed the habit of that virtue so much strengthened, and its opposite weakened, that I might venture extending my attention to include the next, and for the following week keep both lines clear of spots. Proceeding thus to the last, I could go through a course complete in thirteen weeks, and four courses in a year. And like him who, having a garden to weed, does not attempt to eradicate all the bad herbs at

16. **Pythagoras** (pi·thag′ə·rəs): Greek philosopher and mathematician of the sixth century B.C.
17. **every:** archaic for "even."

Form of the Pages

		S	M	T	W	T	F	S
Temperance								
Eat not to dullness. *Drink not to elevation.*								
T								
S								
O								
R								
F								
I								
S								
J								
M								
Cl								
T								
Ch								
H								

once, which would exceed his reach and his strength, but works on one of the beds at a time, and, having accomplished the first, proceeds to a second, so I should have, I hoped, the encouraging pleasure of seeing on my pages the progress I made in virtue, by clearing successively my lines of their spots, till in the end, by a number of courses, I should be happy in viewing a clean book, after a thirteen weeks' daily examination. . . .

WORDS TO OWN
subsequent (sub′si·kwənt) *adj.*: following.
eradicate (i·rad′i·kāt′) *v.*: to eliminate.

Panel from an engraving for Benjamin
Franklin's *Poor Richard Illustrated* (c. 1800).

SPOTLIGHT ON

Sayings of Poor Richard

Poor Richard's Almanack was Franklin's biggest publishing success, and it continued to appear for over twenty-five years. Every house had an almanac. Almanacs calculated the tides and the phases of the moon, claimed to forecast the weather for the next year, and even provided astrological advice for those who believed in it. Many almanacs also supplied recipes, jokes, and **aphorisms.** "Poor Richard" was an imaginary astrologer, who had a critical wife named Bridget. One year Bridget wrote the maxims, to answer those her husband had written the year before on female idleness. Once, Bridget included "better" weather forecasts so that women would know the good days for drying their clothes.

Franklin took Poor Richard's wit and wisdom where he found it—from old sayings in other languages, from other writers, and from popular adages. He never hesitated to rework the texts to suit his own purposes. For example, for the 1758 almanac, Franklin skimmed all his previous editions to compose a single speech on economy. This speech, called "The Way to Wealth," has become one of the best known of Franklin's works. It has been mistakenly believed to be representative of Poor Richard's wisdom. Poor Richard often called for prudence and thrift, but he just as often favored extravagance.

1. Love your neighbor; yet don't pull down your hedge.

2. If a man empties his purse into his head, no man can take it away from him. An investment in knowledge always pays the best interest.

3. Three may keep a secret if two of them are dead.

4. Tart words make no friends; a spoonful of honey will catch more flies than a gallon of vinegar.

5. Glass, china, and reputation are easily cracked and never well mended.

6. Fish and visitors smell in three days.

7. He that lieth down with dogs shall rise up with fleas.

8. One today is worth two to-morrows.

9. A truly great man will neither trample on a worm nor sneak to an emperor.

10. A little neglect may breed mischief; for want of a nail the shoe was lost; for want of a shoe the horse was lost; for want of a horse the rider was lost; for want of the rider the battle was lost.

11. If you would know the value of money, go and try to borrow some; he that goes a-borrowing goes a-sorrowing.

12. He that composes himself is wiser than he that composes books.

13. He that is of the opinion that money will do everything may well be suspected of doing everything for money.

14. If a man could have half his wishes, he would double his troubles.

15. 'Tis hard for an empty bag to stand upright.

16. A small leak will sink a great ship.

17. A plowman on his legs is higher than a gentleman on his knees.

18. Keep your eyes wide open before marriage, half shut afterward.

19. Nothing brings more pain than too much pleasure; nothing more bondage than too much liberty.

Behind Ben Franklin's project for achieving moral perfection lies what seems to be a common human impulse—the need to simplify life, to get at the root of what's fundamental to us. In 1986, Robert Fulghum (fool'jum) published some thoughts of his own about how to live a full and happy life, in a best-selling book called *All I Really Need to Know I Learned in Kindergarten.*

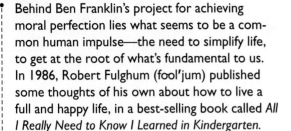

from All I Really Need to Know I Learned in Kindergarten

Robert Fulghum

Each spring, for many years, I have set myself the task of writing a personal statement of belief: a Credo. When I was younger, the statement ran for many pages, trying to cover every base, with no loose ends. It sounded like a Supreme Court brief, as if words could resolve all conflicts about the meaning of existence.

The Credo has grown shorter in recent years—sometimes cynical, sometimes comical, sometimes bland—but I keep working at it. Recently I set out to get the statement of personal belief down to one page in simple terms, fully understanding the naïve idealism that implied. . . .

I realized then that I already know most of what's necessary to live a meaningful life—that it isn't all that complicated. *I know it.* And have known it for a long, long time. Living it—well, that's another matter, yes? Here's my Credo:

All I really need to know about how to live and what to do and how to be I learned in kindergarten. Wisdom was not at the top of the graduate-school mountain, but there in the sandpile at Sunday School. These are the things I learned:

Share everything.
Play fair.
Don't hit people.
Put things back where you found them.
Clean up your own mess.
Don't take things that aren't yours.
Say you're sorry when you hurt somebody.
Wash your hands before you eat.
Flush.
Warm cookies and cold milk are good for you.
Live a balanced life—learn some and think some and draw and paint and sing and dance and play and work every day some.
Take a nap every afternoon.
When you go out into the world, watch out for traffic, hold hands, and stick together.
Be aware of wonder. Remember the little seed in the Styrofoam cup: The roots go down and the plant goes up and nobody really knows how or why, but we are all like that.
Goldfish and hamsters and white mice and even the little seed in the Styrofoam cup—they all die. So do we.
And then remember the Dick-and-Jane books and the first word you learned—the biggest word of all—LOOK.

. . . Think what a better world it would be if we all—the whole world—had cookies and milk about three o'clock every afternoon and then lay down with our blankies for a nap. Or if all governments had as a basic policy to always put things back where they found them and to clean up their own mess.

And it is still true, no matter how old you are—when you go out into the world, it is best to hold hands and stick together.

MAKING MEANINGS

First Thoughts

1. If you had to name one character trait that you think made Franklin a success, what would it be? Review the chart you made in your Quickwrite to help you decide.

Shaping Interpretations

2. Franklin examines his actions and motives, discussing them at length throughout *The Autobiography*. Yet many of his personality traits are revealed through his actions, not through direct statements. What does the difficult journey from Boston to Philadelphia reveal about the **character** of young Franklin?

3. What does Franklin's project for moral perfection reveal about his views of human nature and his attitudes toward education? Do you agree or disagree with his views?

4. Franklin ends his list of virtues with "humility." Did you find evidence of pride—the opposite of humility—in his history? If so, where?

5. Which virtue on Franklin's list do you think is most important? least important? Why?

Connecting with the Text

6. Franklin resolves to acquire certain virtues through which he believes he will improve himself. Think of one of your own past resolutions, perhaps one you made on a New Year's Eve.

Reading Check

a. Why did Franklin decide to leave Boston secretly? How did he raise money for the journey from Boston to New York?

b. Today the trip from Boston to Philadelphia on a comfortable train takes five hours. On a map, trace the stages of Franklin's journey to Philadelphia.

c. What was Franklin's condition in life when he arrived in Philadelphia?

d. What virtue does Franklin place first on his list for achieving moral perfection? Why?

Were you able to keep it? Do you think making a resolution, as Franklin did, is a productive way of improving oneself? Explain.

Extending the Text

7. Compare Robert Fulghum's list of things learned in kindergarten (see *Connections,* page 96) to Franklin's list of virtues. Which list do you think would apply more broadly to people today? In general, how does Franklin's scheme for arriving at moral perfection compare with self-help books available today?

Challenging the Text

8. Reactions to Franklin's *Autobiography* have sometimes been negative. Read the following comment by Mark Twain. Based on Twain's **tone,** how does Twain feel about Franklin? Do you agree or disagree with Twain's assessment? Why?

> [Franklin had] a malevolence which is without parallel in history; he would work all day and then sit up nights and let on to be studying algebra by the light of a smoldering fire, so that all the boys might have to do that also, or else have Benjamin Franklin thrown upon them. Not satisfied with these proceedings, he had a fashion of living wholly on bread and water, and studying astronomy at mealtime—a thing which has brought affliction to millions of boys since, whose fathers had read Franklin's pernicious biography.
>
> —Mark Twain

9. As we read any **autobiography,** we have to ask ourselves if the writer is creating a character called "Myself," the same way that a novelist creates a fictional character. Has Franklin, the great inventor, invented an idealized version of himself in his autobiography? In other words, is he trying to make himself look good? Or do you think he is presenting himself just as he really was, warts and all? Explain and justify your opinion. (You might want to read a good **biography** of Franklin, such as the one by Ronald W. Clark [1989].)

Writer's Notebook

1. Collecting Ideas for an Autobiographical Incident

WORK IN PROGRESS

A favorite question of job interviewers and college admissions officers is "What do you regard as your greatest strength?" Identify the character trait in yourself that you consider the most important or most valuable, and freewrite about an incident that demonstrated this trait in action. Did this aspect of your personality contribute to your success at something? Keep your notes for possible use in the Writer's Workshop on page 130.

Comparing Texts

2. Monuments of the American Tradition

Reread the selection by Jonathan Edwards (page 79), and write a brief essay in which you compare and contrast the Puritan preacher with Ben Franklin. When writing your essay, consider the following: (a) each man's goals in life; (b) his reasons for having these goals; and (c) the means by which he achieves his goals. Be sure to cite at least one way in which these two Americans are alike.

Creative Writing

3. Becoming Virtuous

Develop your own list of virtues and accompanying precepts. (You don't need as many as Franklin outlined, but you should have at least seven.) Then create your own "book of virtues," patterned after Franklin's (page 94). For one week, keep daily track of your "progress in virtue." (Unlike Franklin, you'll be keeping track of all the virtues simultaneously, not successively.) At the end of a week, write a brief report on how well the "book of virtues" worked for you. What did you learn? Is this a habit you'd like to continue?

Crossing the Curriculum: Science

4. Scientific Minds

Research either Benjamin Franklin's or Benjamin Banneker's (page 90) contributions to science and invention. What were their greatest accomplishments? What was the most surprising discovery each man made? Present your findings about either man's scientific interests, methods, and discoveries in one of the following forms: a written or oral report; a comic strip; a script for a documentary; or a story for children.

Applying Ideas

5. Franklin Today

Write a proposal to the editor-in-chief of a publishing company, suggesting that Franklin's *Autobiography* be published in a special new edition marketed as a self-help book. Using quotes from *The Autobiography*, give specific reasons why people today can still learn from Franklin.

Creative Writing

6. Our Almanac

As a class, create an almanac that covers a one-month period. Include weather forecasts, upcoming school and community events, and your own original maxims, jokes, and recipes.

Research / Art

7. Words from the Wise

Research **aphorisms** from Franklin and other sources (you might find some on bumper stickers and on the Internet) to find ones that you think would be especially helpful to high school students. Then, collect them in the form of a small booklet called "Words to Live By." You may use calligraphy, illustrations, or computer graphics to decorate your booklet.

Drawing by David Levine. Reprinted with permission from *The New York Review of Books.* Copyright © 1973 NYREV, Inc.

Justice

Resolution

Tranquility

Frugality

Cleanliness

Order

Collection 3

THE AMERICAN DREAM

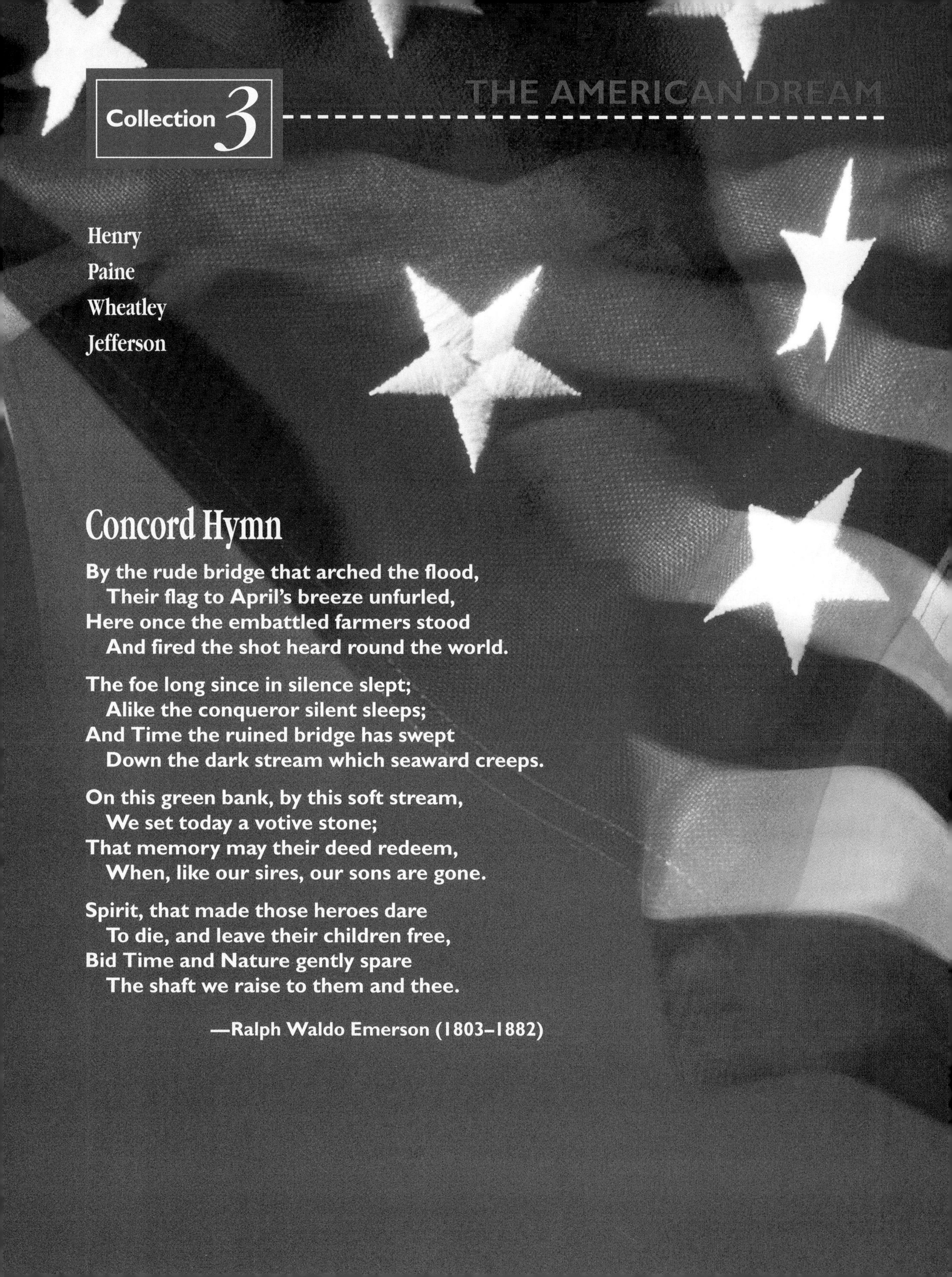

Henry

Paine

Wheatley

Jefferson

Concord Hymn

By the rude bridge that arched the flood,
   Their flag to April's breeze unfurled,
Here once the embattled farmers stood
   And fired the shot heard round the world.

The foe long since in silence slept;
   Alike the conqueror silent sleeps;
And Time the ruined bridge has swept
   Down the dark stream which seaward creeps.

On this green bank, by this soft stream,
   We set today a votive stone;
That memory may their deed redeem,
   When, like our sires, our sons are gone.

Spirit, that made those heroes dare
   To die, and leave their children free,
Bid Time and Nature gently spare
   The shaft we raise to them and thee.

—Ralph Waldo Emerson (1803–1882)

Patrick Henry

(1736–1799)

One fiery act can catapult someone from obscurity to fame. That is what happened to Patrick Henry, a young representative who stood up in the Virginia House of Burgesses one day in 1765. He delivered a dynamic, thundering speech against the hated Stamp Act, with which the British Parliament instituted taxes on all newspapers and public documents. For the ten years following his declaration of resistance, Henry—a tall, lank, somber-looking man who favored the kind of clothing a preacher might wear—was recognized as one of the most persuasive figures in Virginia politics.

Henry had not always been so successful. Born in a frontier region of Virginia, he was raised in a cultured but modest environment. During his youth the country was undergoing the religious revival known as the Great Awakening, and young Patrick often accompanied his mother to hear the sermons of the traveling preachers. Later, as a young man, he made several unsuccessful stabs at farming and merchant life before discovering his love of oratory and his true calling: the law.

In 1765, the twenty-nine-year-old lawyer was chosen to represent his region in the Virginia House of Burgesses. Henry's speech against the Stamp Act was the first of the two most famous speeches in American Colonial history. The second, his famous "liberty or death" speech, came ten years later in 1775 as the Colonies were nearing the breaking point with England. Following the Boston Tea Party in December 1773, the British had closed the port of Boston and inaugurated other harsh measures referred to by the colonists as the "Intolerable Acts." When the First Continental Congress protested these acts, the British Crown relieved the Colonies of taxation on a number of conditions. One condition was that the colonists fully support British rule and contribute toward the maintenance of British

Patrick Henry (1820–1830). Anonymous. Oil on canvas.
Shelburne Museum, Shelburne, Vermont. Photograph by Ken Burris.

troops in America, whose numbers were increasing greatly. On March 20, 1775, the Virginia House of Burgesses held a convention in St. John's Episcopal Church in Richmond to decide how to respond to the growing British military threat. George Washington and Thomas Jefferson (page 114) were both present.

On March 23, after several speeches in favor of compromise with the British, Patrick Henry rose to defend his resolution to take up arms. Later, a clergyman who was present recalled that during Henry's speech he felt "sick with excitement." As the speech reached its climax, Henry is said to have grabbed an ivory letter opener and plunged it toward his chest at the final word *death*.

Henry persuaded the delegation. The Virginia Convention voted to arm its people against England. On April 19, 1775, the Battle of Lexington, Massachusetts, ignited the Revolutionary War.

Make the Connection

Words into Actions

Words—acts of both thought and feeling—shape us; they are tools of self-making. We know now how much blood and suffering resulted from Henry's words "Give me liberty or give me death!" and what pride his impassioned cry continues to generate years after it was spoken. The "American dream," as we loosely call our aspirations toward freedom, self-reliance, and self-creation, is defined in large part by the words of the men and women who helped to shape America in its early years.

Elements of Literature

Persuasion

Persuasion is a form of speaking or writing that aims to move an audience to take a specific action. A good persuasive speaker or writer uses both head and heart—reasons and feelings, or logic and emotion—to win over an audience. To be successful, a writer or speaker must provide reasons to support a particular opinion or course of action. In the final analysis, though, audiences are often won over not only by the force of the speaker's arguments but also by the power of his or her personality.

> **P**ersuasion is a form of discourse that uses reason and emotional appeals to convince another person to think or act in a certain way.
>
> *For more on Persuasion, see the Handbook of Literary Terms.*

Reading Skills and Strategies

Recognizing Modes of Persuasion

Patrick Henry uses two modes of **persuasion**: appeals to **logic** and appeals to **emotions** or values. As you read, track these two methods in a double-column chart. In the left column, list Henry's logical reasons for wanting war. In the right column, write down his emotional appeals. As you take notes, star (✶) those appeals that you find most effective. Place an "x" next to appeals that strike you as deceptive or faulty.

Background

The historian Garry Wills described Patrick Henry in this way: ". . . he had the actor's trick, in his oratory, of lifting his whole body up toward climaxes, along with his voice, as if he *could* add cubits by wanting to. . . . No one who beheld him incandescent with a Cause ever forgot the experience. . . ."

Although Henry's 1775 speech is one of the most famous in all American oratory, no manuscript of it exists. Henry's biographer, William Wirt, pieced together the traditionally accepted text forty years after it was delivered, using notes of people who were present at the speech. As you read Henry's speech, try to envision the physical surroundings of its delivery: a church in eighteenth-century Richmond, Virginia, on an early spring day. Try, also, to imagine the manner in which Henry delivered his speech.

Speech to the Virginia Convention

Patrick Henry

Mr. President: No man thinks more highly than I do of the patriotism, as well as abilities, of the very worthy gentlemen who have just addressed the House. But different men often see the same subject in different lights; and, therefore, I hope that it will not be thought disrespectful to those gentlemen, if, entertaining as I do, opinions of a character very opposite to theirs, I shall speak forth my sentiments freely and without reserve. This is no time for ceremony. The question before the House is one of awful moment[1] to this country. For my own part I consider it as nothing less than a question of freedom or slavery; and in proportion to the magnitude of the subject ought to be the freedom of the debate. It is only in this way that we can hope to arrive at truth, and fulfill the great responsibility which we hold to God and our country. Should I keep back my opinions at such a time, through fear of giving offense, I should consider myself as guilty of treason toward my country, and of an act of disloyalty toward the majesty of heaven, which I revere above all earthly kings.

Mr. President, it is natural to man to indulge in the illusions of hope. We are apt to shut our eyes against a painful truth, and listen to the song of that siren, till she transforms us into beasts.[2] Is this the part of wise men, engaged in a great and arduous struggle for liberty? Are we disposed to be of the number of those who, having eyes, see not, and having ears, hear not, the things which so nearly concern their temporal salvation? For my part, whatever anguish of spirit it may cost, I am willing to know the whole truth; to know the worst and to provide for it.

I have but one lamp by which my feet are guided; and that is the lamp of experience. I know of no way of judging of the future but by the past. And judging by the past, I wish to know what there has been in the conduct of the British ministry for the last ten years, to justify those hopes with which gentlemen have been pleased to solace themselves and the House? Is it that insidious smile with which our petition[3] has been lately received? Trust it not, sir; it will prove a snare to your feet. Suffer not yourselves to be betrayed with a kiss. Ask yourselves how this gracious reception of our petition comports[4] with these warlike preparations which cover our waters and darken our land. Are fleets and armies necessary to a work of love and reconciliation? Have we shown ourselves so unwilling to be reconciled, that force must be called in to win back our love? Let us not deceive ourselves, sir. These are the implements of war and subjugation; the last arguments to which kings resort.

---

1. awful moment: great importance.
2. listen . . . beasts: In Greek mythology, the sirens are sea-maidens whose seductive singing lures men to wreck their boats on coastal rocks. In the *Odyssey*, an epic by the Greek poet Homer (c. eighth century B.C.), Circe, an enchanter, transforms Odysseus' men into swine after they arrive at her island home. Henry's allusion combines these two stories.

3. our petition: The First Continental Congress had recently protested against new tax laws. King George III had withdrawn the laws conditionally, but the colonists were unwilling to accept his conditions.
4. comports: agrees.

WORDS TO OWN

solace (säl′is) *v.*: to comfort.
insidious (in·sid′ē·əs) *adj.*: sly; sneaky.

Patrick Henry Arguing the Parson's Cause (c. 1830),
attributed to George Cooke. Oil on canvas.

Virginia Historical Society, Richmond, Virginia.

I ask gentlemen, sir, what means this martial array, if its purpose be not to force us to submission? Can gentlemen assign any other possible motives for it? Has Great Britain any enemy, in this quarter of the world, to call for all this accumulation of navies and armies? No, sir, she has none. They are meant for us; they can be meant for no other. They are sent over to bind and rivet upon us those chains which the British ministry have been so long forging. And what have we to oppose to them? Shall we try argument? Sir, we have been trying that for the last ten years. Have we anything new to offer on the subject? Nothing. We have held the subject up in every light of which it is capable; but it has been all in vain. Shall we resort to entreaty and humble supplication? What terms shall we find which have not been already exhausted? Let us not, I beseech you, sir, deceive ourselves longer. Sir, we have done everything that could be done, to avert the storm which is now coming on. We have petitioned; we have remonstrated; we have supplicated; we have prostrated ourselves before the throne, and have implored its interposition[5] to arrest the tyrannical hands of the ministry and Parliament. Our petitions have been slighted; our remonstrances have produced additional violence and insult; our supplications have been disregarded; and we have been spurned, with contempt, from the foot of the throne. In vain, after these things, may we indulge the fond[6] hope of peace and reconciliation. There is no longer any room for hope. If we wish to be free—if we mean to preserve inviolate those inestimable privileges for which we have been so long contending—if we mean not basely to abandon the noble struggle in which we have been so long engaged, and which we have pledged ourselves never to abandon until the glorious object of our contest shall be obtained, we must fight! I repeat it, sir, we must fight! An appeal to arms and to the God of Hosts is all that is left us!

They tell us, sir, that we are weak; unable to cope with so formidable an adversary. But when shall we be stronger? Will it be the next week, or the next year? Will it be when we are totally disarmed, and when a British guard shall be stationed in every house? Shall we gather strength by irresolution and inaction? Shall we acquire the means of effectual resistance, by lying supinely on our backs, and hugging the delusive phantom of hope, until our enemies shall have bound us hand and foot? Sir, we are not weak, if we make a proper use of the means which the God of nature hath placed in our power. Three millions of people, armed in the holy cause of liberty, and in such a country as that which we possess, are invincible by any force which our enemy can send against us. Besides, sir, we shall not fight our battles alone. There is a just God who presides over the destinies of nations; and who will raise up friends to fight our battles for us. The battle, sir, is not to the strong alone; it is to the vigilant, the active, the brave. Besides, sir, we have no election.[7] If we were base enough to desire it, it is now too late to retire from the contest. There is no retreat, but in submission and slavery! Our chains are forged! Their clanking may be heard on the plains of Boston! The war is inevitable—and let it come! I repeat it, sir, let it come!

It is in vain, sir, to extenuate the matter. Gentlemen may cry peace, peace—but there is no peace. The war is actually begun! The next gale that sweeps from the north will bring to our ears the clash of resounding arms! Our brethren are already in the field! Why stand we here idle? What is it that gentlemen wish? What would they have? Is life so dear, or peace so sweet, as to be purchased at the price of chains and slavery? Forbid it, Almighty God! I know not what course others may take; but as for me, give me liberty, or give me death!

7. **election:** choice.

WORDS TO OWN

martial (mär′shəl) *adj.:* warlike.
supplication (sup′lə·kā′shən) *n.:* earnest plea.
avert (ə·vʉrt′) *v.:* to prevent; turn away.
spurned (spʉrnd) *v.:* rejected.
inviolate (in·vī′ə·lit) *adj.:* uncorrupted.
adversary (ad′vər·ser′ē) *n.:* opponent.
vigilant (vij′ə·lənt) *adj.* used as *n.:* watchful.
inevitable (in·ev′i·tə·bəl) *adj.:* not avoidable.

----

5. **interposition:** intervention; stepping in to try to solve the problem.
6. **fond:** foolishly optimistic.

MAKING MEANINGS

First Thoughts

1. How did Henry's speech affect you?

Reading Check

What is the **main idea** of Henry's speech?

Shaping Interpretations

2. Review your double-column chart, noting especially the arguments you starred (★) and those you marked with an "x." What made these arguments powerful or weak? Were you more convinced by Henry's appeals to **logic** or by his appeals to **emotion**? What conclusions can you draw about the art of persuasion?

3. In paragraph four, what **metaphors** does Henry use to describe the coming war?

4. Henry makes use of the **rhetorical question**— a question that is asked for effect. Rhetorical questions, which are often used in **persuasion,** presume the audience agrees with the speaker on the answers, and so no answer is expected or required. Find a series of rhetorical questions in the fifth paragraph of this speech. Why do you think Henry uses this device, rather than straightforward statements of fact, to make his points? How does this technique make his speech more persuasive?

Extending the Text

5. Because Henry's audience knew the Bible, as well as classical mythology, the orator knew he could count on certain **allusions** producing emotional effects. Look up the classical or Biblical passages Henry alludes to in each of the following statements from his speech. How would each allusion relate to the conflict in Virginia in 1775? Could any of them relate to life today? Explain.

   a. "We are apt to . . . listen to the song of that siren, till she transforms us into beasts." (*Odyssey,* Books 10 and 12)

   b. "Are we disposed to be of the number of those who, having eyes, see not, and having ears, hear not the things which so nearly concern their temporal salvation?" (Ezekiel 12:2)

   c. "Suffer not yourselves to be betrayed with a kiss." (Luke 22:47–48)

CHOICES: Building Your Portfolio

Writer's Notebook

1. Collecting Ideas for an Autobiographical Incident

Write about an action you took or a particular time in your life that seems like a turning point—a decisive period that helped define the person you are today. Save your notes for possible use in the Writer's Workshop on page 130.

Comparing Orations

2. Politician and Preacher

In a brief essay, compare and contrast Henry's speech with Jonathan Edwards's sermon "Sinners in the Hands of an Angry God" (page 79). Consider the specific ways in which the speeches are alike and how they are different. Use the following chart to help organize your material.

Elements of the Oration	Edwards	Henry
Speaker's purpose and audience		
Main idea		
Appeals to reason and emotion		
Use of rhetorical questions and other literary devices		
Overall effectiveness		

Speaking and Listening

3. A Call to Action

Recast part or all of Henry's speech to pertain to some issue today that calls for action— poverty, drugs, crime, or military intervention to help end violent oppression in another country. Deliver the recast speech to the class.

Thomas Paine

(1737–1809)

The most persuasive writer of the American Revolution came from an unlikely background. Thomas Paine, the poorly educated son of a corset maker, was born in England and spent his first thirty-seven years drifting through occupations— corset maker, grocer, tobacconist, schoolteacher, tax collector. In 1774, Paine was dismissed from his job as a tax collector for attempting to organize the employees in a demand for higher wages (an unusual activity in those days). Like many others at that time and since, he came to America to make a new start.

With a letter of introduction from Benjamin Franklin (page 84), whom he had met in London, Paine went to Philadelphia, where he worked as a journalist. In the conflict between England and the Colonies, he quickly identified with the underdog. In January 1776, he published the most important written work in support of American independence: *Common Sense,* a forty-seven-page pamphlet that denounced King George III as a "royal brute" and asserted that a continent should not remain tied to an island. The pamphlet sold a half million copies—in a country whose total population was roughly two and a quarter million.

After the Revolution, Paine lived peacefully in New York and New Jersey until 1787, when he returned to Europe. There he became involved once more in radical revolutionary politics, supporting the French Revolution. In 1791, he composed *The Rights of Man,* a reply to the English

Thomas Paine (1806–1807) by John Wesley Jarvis. Oil on canvas.

© 1998 Board of Trustees, National Gallery of Art, Washington, D.C. Gift of Marion B. Maurice.

statesman Edmund Burke's condemnation of the French revolt. *The Rights of Man* was an impassioned defense of republican government and a call to the English people to overthrow their king. Although he was not living in England at the time, Paine was tried for treason there and banned from the country. Safe in France from English law, he was briefly celebrated as a hero of the French Revolution but was soon imprisoned in France for being a citizen of an enemy nation (England). James Monroe, the American minister to France at the time, gained his release in 1794 by insisting that Paine was an American citizen.

Paine's final notable work, *The Age of Reason,* was published in two parts, the first in 1794 and the second in 1796. Expounding the principles of deism (page 16), the book was controversial in America. Americans did not fully understand the book and thought Paine was an atheist— that he did not believe in God. When Paine returned to America in 1802, he was a virtual outcast, scorned as a dangerous radical and nonbeliever. He was stripped of his right to vote, had no money, and was continually harassed. When he died in New York in 1809, he was denied burial in consecrated ground. His body was buried on his farm in New Rochelle.

Even in death, though, Thomas Paine was not allowed to rest. In 1819, an English sympathizer dug up Paine's body and removed it and the coffin to England, intending to erect a memorial to the author of *The Rights of Man.* But no monument was ever built. The last record of Paine's remains shows that the coffin and the bones were acquired by a furniture dealer in England in 1844.

Before You Read

FROM THE CRISIS, NO. 1

Reenactment of a redcoat musket firing, Trenton, New Jersey.

Make the Connection

A Common Cause

At various times in life, we have to put aside personal feelings and make sacrifices for a common cause or team effort. The early American colonists had to do just that, for much was being asked of them. At the time Thomas Paine wrote *The Crisis, No. 1*, the colonists had to make a crucial decision: Should they kneel as English subjects, or stand as Americans? As Benjamin Franklin (page 84) said, "We must all hang together, or assuredly we shall all hang separately."

Reading Skills and Strategies

Recognizing Modes of Persuasion

A good writer of **persuasion** like Thomas Paine uses a variety of literary techniques that appeal to both **logic** and **emotions**. In

The Crisis, watch especially for these two—an **analogy** that compares the king with a thief, and an **anecdote** about a tavern keeper and his child. As you read, write down the extent to which each appeals to logic and to emotions.

Elements of Literature

Style

A writer's **style** is principally determined by sentence length, **diction,** and use of **figurative language** and **imagery.** Thomas Paine uses a combination of styles: Direct, common speech is mixed with heightened, impassioned expressions sharpened by dramatic rhetorical techniques. Paine says that he speaks "in language as plain as A, B, C," yet he also includes such lofty declarations as "What we obtain too cheap, we esteem too lightly."

> **S**tyle is the distinctive way in which a writer uses language.
>
> *For more on Style, see the Handbook of Literary Terms.*

Background

In 1776, Paine joined the Continental army as it retreated across New Jersey to Philadelphia. During the journey, he began writing a series of sixteen pamphlets called *The American Crisis,* commenting on the war and urging Americans not to give up the fight. The first of these pamphlets was read to Washington's troops in December 1776, a few days before the army recrossed the Delaware River to attack the British-held city of Trenton, New Jersey.

from The Crisis, No. 1

Thomas Paine

These are the times that try men's souls. The summer soldier and the sunshine patriot will, in this crisis, shrink from the service of his country; but he that stands it NOW, deserves the love and thanks of man and woman. Tyranny, like hell, is not easily conquered; yet we have this consolation with us, that the harder the conflict, the more glorious the triumph. What we obtain too cheap, we esteem too lightly; 'tis dearness only that gives everything its value. Heaven knows how to put a proper price upon its goods; and it would be strange indeed, if so celestial an article as FREEDOM should not be highly rated. Britain, with an army to enforce her tyranny, has declared that she has a right (*not only to* TAX) but "to BIND *us in* ALL CASES WHATSOEVER,"[1] and if being *bound in that manner,* is not slavery, then is there not such a thing as slavery upon earth. Even the expression is impious, for so unlimited a power can belong only to God.

Whether the independence of the continent was declared too soon, or delayed too long, I will not now enter into as an argument; my own simple opinion is, that had it been eight months earlier, it would have been much better. We did not make a proper use of last winter, neither could we, while we were in a dependent state. However, the fault, if it were one, was all our own; we have none to blame but ourselves. But no great deal is lost yet; all that Howe[2] has been doing for this month past, is rather a ravage than a conquest, which the spirit of the Jerseys[3] a year ago would have quickly repulsed, and which time and a little resolution will soon recover.

I have as little superstition in me as any man living, but my secret opinion has ever been, and still is, that God Almighty will not give up a people to military destruction, or leave them unsupportedly to perish, who have so earnestly and so repeatedly sought to avoid the calamities of war, by every decent method which wisdom could invent. Neither have I so much of the infidel in me, as to suppose that he has relinquished the government of the world, and given us up to the care of devils; and as I do not, I cannot see on what grounds the king of Britain can look up to heaven for help against us: A common murderer, a highwayman,[4] or a housebreaker, has as good a pretense as he....

I once felt all that kind of anger, which a man ought to feel, against the mean[5] principles that are held by the Tories:[6] A noted one, who kept a tavern at Amboy,[7] was standing at his door, with as pretty a child in his hand, about eight or nine years old, as I ever saw, and after speaking his mind as freely as he thought was prudent, finished with this unfatherly expression, *"Well! Give me peace in my day."* Not a man lives on the continent but fully believes that a separation must sometime or other

---

4. **highwayman:** thief who patrols the roads frequented by travelers, with the intent of stealing their valuables.
5. **mean:** low.
6. **Tories:** those who supported British rule in the American Colonies.
7. **Amboy:** Perth Amboy, New Jersey.

1. **to bind . . . whatsoever:** In response to Colonial protests over the Stamp Act (which taxed all commercial and legal documents in the Colonies), Parliament repealed the act on March 17, 1766. On the same day, it passed the Declaratory Act, which stated that Parliament had the right "to make laws . . . to bind the colonies and people of America . . . in all cases whatsoever."
2. **Howe:** Sir William Howe (1729-1814), commander in chief (1775-1778) of the British forces in America during the Revolution.
3. **Jerseys:** New Jersey was at this time divided into East Jersey and West Jersey.

- -

WORDS TO OWN

tyranny (tir′ə·nē) *n*.: oppression.
consolation (kän′sə·lā′shən) *n*.: comfort.
celestial (sə·les′chəl) *adj*.: divine; perfect.
impious (im′pē·əs) *adj*.: irreverent.
ravage (rav′ij) *n*.: act of violent destruction.
relinquished (ri·liŋ′kwisht) *v*.: given up.
pretense (prē·tens′) *n*.: false claim.

- -

The Granger Collection, New York (pewter button, pages 108 and 110).

finally take place, and a generous parent should have said, *"If there must be trouble let it be in my day, that my child may have peace";* and this single reflection, well applied, is sufficient to awaken every man to duty. Not a place upon earth might be so happy as America. Her situation is remote from all the wrangling world, and she has nothing to do but to trade with them. A man can distinguish himself between temper and principle, and I am as confident, as I am that God governs the world, that America will never be happy till she gets clear of foreign dominion. Wars, without ceasing, will break out till that period arrives, and the continent must in the end be conqueror; for though the flame of liberty may sometimes cease to shine, the coal can never expire.

America did not, nor does not want[8] force; but she wanted a proper application of that force. Wisdom is not the purchase of a day, and it is no wonder that we should err at the first setting off. From an excess of tenderness, we were unwilling to raise an army, and trusted our cause to the temporary de-

8. **want:** lack.

fense of a well-meaning militia. A summer's experience has now taught us better; yet with those troops, while they were collected, we were able to set bounds to the progress of the enemy, and—thank God!—they are again assembling. I always consider militia as the best troops in the world for a sudden exertion, but they will not do for a long campaign. Howe, it is probable, will make an attempt on this city;[9] should he fail on this side the Delaware, he is ruined: If he succeeds, our cause is not ruined. He stakes all on his side against a part on ours; admitting he succeeds, the consequence will be, that armies from both ends of the continent will march to assist their suffering friends in the middle

9. **this city:** Philadelphia.

- -
WORDS TO OWN
dominion (də·min′yən) *n*.: rule.
- -

Colonial campfire reenactment, Valley Forge, Pennsylvania.

states; for he cannot go everywhere; it is impossible. I consider Howe the greatest enemy the Tories have; he is bringing a war into their country, which, had it not been for him and partly for themselves, they had been clear of. Should he now be expelled, I wish with all the devotion of a *Christian,* that the names of Whig[10] and Tory may never more be mentioned; but should the Tories give him encouragement to come, or assistance if he come, I as sincerely wish that our next year's arms may expel them from the continent, and that congress appropriate their possessions to the relief of those who have suffered in well doing. A single successful battle next year will settle the whole. America could carry on a two years' war by the confiscation of the property of disaffected[11] persons; and be made happy by their expulsion. Say not that this is revenge, call it rather the soft resentment of a suffering people, who, having no object in view but the *good* of *all,* have staked their *own all* upon a seemingly doubtful event. Yet it is folly to argue against determined hardness; <u>eloquence</u> may strike the ear, and the language of sorrow draw forth the tear of compassion, but nothing can reach the heart that is steeled with prejudice.

Quitting this class of men, I turn with the warm ardor of a friend to those who have nobly stood, and are yet determined to stand the matter out: I call not upon a few, but upon all; not on *this* state or *that* state, but on *every* state; up and help us; lay your shoulders to the wheel; better have too much force than too little, when so great an object is at stake. Let it be told to the future world, that in the depth of winter, when nothing but hope and virtue could survive, that the city and the country, alarmed at one common danger, came forth to meet and to repulse it. Say not that thousands are gone, turn out your tens of thousands;[12] throw not the burden of the day upon Providence, but *"show your faith by your works,"*[13] that God may bless

Sentry and cannon reenactment, Valley Forge, Pennsylvania.

you. It matters not where you live, or what rank of life you hold, the evil or the blessing will reach you all. The far and the near, the home counties and the back, the rich and the poor, will suffer or rejoice alike. The heart that feels not now, is dead: The blood of his children will curse his cowardice, who shrinks back at a time when a little might have saved the whole, and made *them* happy. (I love the man that can smile at trouble; that can gather strength from distress; and grow brave by reflection.) 'Tis the business of little minds to shrink; but he whose heart is firm, and whose conscience approves his conduct, will pursue his principles unto death. My own line of reasoning is to myself as straight and clear as a ray of light. Not all the treasures of the world, so far as I believe, could have induced me to support an offensive war, for I think it murder; but if a thief breaks into my house, burns and destroys my property, and kills or threatens to kill me, or those that are in it, and to *"bind me in all cases whatsoever,"* to his absolute will, am I to suffer it? What signifies it to me, whether he who does it is a king or a common man; my countryman, or not my countryman; whether it be done by an individual villain or an army of them? If we reason to the root of things we shall find no difference; neither can any just

---

10. **Whig:** The Whigs were colonists who supported the Revolution.
11. **disaffected:** disloyal, especially toward the government.
12. **thousands:** "Saul hath slain his thousands, and David his ten thousands" (1 Samuel 18:7).
13. **show . . . works:** "Show me thy faith without thy works, and I will show thee my faith by my works" (James 2:18).

WORDS TO OWN

eloquence (el′ə·kwəns) *n.:* well-articulated, persuasive speech.

cause be assigned why we should punish in the one case and pardon in the other. Let them call me rebel, and welcome, I feel no concern from it; but I should suffer the misery of devils, were I to make a whore of my soul by swearing allegiance to one whose character is that of a sottish,[14] stupid, stubborn, worthless, brutish man. I conceive likewise a horrid idea in receiving mercy from a being, who at the last day shall be shrieking to the rocks and mountains to cover him, and fleeing with terror from the orphan, the widow, and the slain of America.

There are cases which cannot be overdone by language, and this is one. There are persons too who see not the full extent of the evil which threatens them; they solace themselves with hopes that the enemy, if he succeeds, will be merciful. Is this the madness of folly, to expect mercy from those who have refused to do justice; and even mercy, where conquest is the object, is only a trick of war; the cunning of the fox is as murderous as the violence of the wolf; and we ought to guard equally against both. Howe's first object is partly by threats and partly by promises, to terrify or seduce the people to deliver up their arms and to receive mercy. The ministry recommended the same plan to Gage,[15] and this is what the Tories call making their peace, *"a peace which passeth all understanding,"*[16] *indeed!* A peace which would be the immediate forerunner of a worse ruin than any we have yet thought of. Ye men of Pennsylvania, do reason upon these things! Were the back counties to give up their arms, they would fall an easy prey to the Indians, who are all armed; this perhaps is what some Tories would not be sorry for. Were the home counties to deliver up their arms, they would be exposed to the resentment of the back counties, who would then have it in their power to chastise their defection at pleasure. And were any one state to give up its arms, *that* state must be garrisoned by Howe's army of Britains and Hessians[17] to preserve it from the anger of the rest. Mutual fear is the principal link in the chain of mutual love, and woe be to that state that breaks the compact. Howe is mercifully inviting you to barbarous destruction, and men must be either rogues or fools that will not see it. I dwell not upon the powers of imagination; I bring reason to your ears; and in language as plain as A, B, C, hold up truth to your eyes.

I thank God that I fear not. I see no real cause for fear. I know our situation well and can see the way out of it. While our army was collected, Howe dared not risk a battle, and it is no credit to him that he decamped from the White Plains, and waited a mean opportunity to ravage the defenseless Jerseys;[18] but it is great credit to us, that, with a handful of men, we sustained an orderly retreat for near an hundred miles, brought off our ammunition, all our field pieces, the greatest part of our stores, and had four rivers to pass. None can say that our retreat was precipitate,[19] for we were near three weeks in performing it, that the country[20] might have time to come in. Twice we marched back to meet the enemy, and remained out till dark. The sign of fear was not seen in our camp, and had not some of the cowardly and disaffected inhabitants spread false alarms through the country, the Jerseys had never been ravaged. Once more we are again collected and collecting, our new army at both ends of the continent is recruiting fast, and we shall be able to open the next campaign with sixty thousand men, well armed and clothed. This is our situation, and who will may know it. By perseverance and fortitude we have the prospect of a glorious issue; by cowardice and submission, the sad choice of a variety of evils—a ravaged country—a depopulated city—habitations without safety, and slavery without hope—our homes turned into barracks and bawdy-houses for Hessians, and a future race to provide for, whose fathers we shall doubt of. Look on this picture and weep over it! And if there yet remains one thoughtless wretch who believes it not, let him suffer it unlamented.

14. sottish (sät′ish): stupid or foolish from too much drinking.
15. Gage: General Thomas Gage (1721–1787), head of the British forces in America (1763–1775) before General Howe.
16. a peace . . . understanding: ironic echo of Paul's epistle to the Philippians (4:7).
17. Hessians (hesh′ənz): German troops, mostly from the region of Hesse, hired to fight on the British side.

18. White Plains . . . Jerseys: Howe had defeated Washington at White Plains, New York, in 1776 but had failed to press his advantage.
19. precipitate (prē·sip′ə·tit): sudden; unexpected.
20. country: the local people. Paine uses the term to refer to local volunteers.

WORDS TO OWN

perseverance (pʉr′sə·vir′əns) n.: persistence.

MAKING MEANINGS

First Thoughts

1. Which passages in this excerpt were especially stirring?

Shaping Interpretations

2. The pamphlet opens with two famous **images** (page 108). What kinds of people does Paine identify with summer and sunshine? Why are these images appropriate?

3. Explain the meaning of Paine's **metaphor** "Mutual fear is the principal link in the chain of mutual love" (page 111). Do you agree or disagree with this idea, and why?

4. An **analogy** is a comparison between two things that are alike in certain respects.  Analogies are used often in **argument** and **persuasion** to demonstrate the logic of one idea by showing how it is similar to another, accepted idea. Analogies can be tricky, though, because few ideas or situations are completely alike in all aspects. What analogy does Paine draw when he talks about the thief (page 110)? What point is he making, and how might an opponent answer?

Extending the Text

5. How do you think Ralph Waldo Emerson, author of "Concord Hymn" (page 99), would respond to Paine's arguments and his writing **style**? How would people today react?

Reading Check

a. What reasons does Paine give for his confidence that God will favor the Americans?

b. Explain Paine's point in telling the **anecdote** about the Tory tavern keeper. Is he appealing more to reason or to emotions?

c. What powerful emotional appeal does Paine make at the end of his essay?

d. What is Paine's **main idea**? What details support it?

CHOICES: Building Your Portfolio

Writer's Notebook

1. Collecting Ideas for an Autobiographical Incident

WORK IN PROGRESS

Have you ever joined with others in a team effort for a common cause? Briefly describe the experience: What was the purpose of banding together? Did taking part in group action involve personal sacrifices on your part? Save your notes for possible use in the Writer's Workshop on page 130.

Evaluating Ideas

2. A Paine Prescription

"Not a place upon earth might be so happy as America. Her situation is remote from all the wrangling world, and she has nothing to do but to trade with them. . . . I am . . . confident . . . that America will never be happy till she gets clear of foreign dominion" (page 109). In a brief essay, evaluate these words from Paine's pamphlet. Considering the world as it is today, how would you reply to Paine?

Creative Writing

3. Crisis Zone

Imagine you are one of the volunteers who listened to this pamphlet being read a few days before Christmas, in 1776, just before you were to cross the Delaware River and attack General Howe and his troops in Trenton. In a paragraph, poem, or song lyrics, express how you felt while the pamphlet was being read, and describe the responses of the people around you.

Sir William Howe (1729–1814), British commander-in-chief in America during Revolutionary War.

The Granger Collection, New York.

Phillis Wheatley: A Revolutionary Woman

Phillis Wheatley (1773). Frontispiece of *Poems* by Phillis Wheatley. Engraving.

The Granger Collection, New York.

All the odds were stacked against her—she was an enslaved African, young, and female. But Phillis Wheatley (c. 1753–1784) published her first poem when she was barely thirteen, and by the time she was twenty years old she had developed a reputation as a poet whose work was praised by George Washington and Thomas Jefferson (page 114).

When Phillis Wheatley was about seven or eight years old, she, like Olaudah Equiano (page 56), was stolen from her home in West Africa. She arrived in America on board a slave ship in 1761. At first, of course, she spoke no English. But she was purchased by the Wheatley family of Boston to assist Mrs. Susanna Wheatley and was treated kindly. Pleased to find this young woman intelligent and eager to learn, the Wheatleys provided her with an excellent education, equal to that of any free person in Boston at the time.

Susanna Wheatley arranged the London publication of a volume of Phillis's poems in 1773; the book received generally encouraging reviews, and it was read widely in England, France, and the American Colonies. Around this time, Phillis was given her freedom, though she chose to remain with the Wheatleys. When they died, she married John Peters, a freeman, in 1778.

Wheatley's poems imitate the style popular in the poetry of her time: She uses a Latinate vocabulary, inversions, and elevated diction. The following stanza is from her poem to the earl of Dartmouth, who had just been appointed secretary of state in charge of the American Colonies (1772). Dartmouth, she hopes, will be open to the colonists' grievances.

from **To the Right Honorable William, Earl of Dartmouth, His Majesty's Principal Secretary of State for North America, etc.**

Should you, my lord, while you peruse my song,
Wonder from whence my love of *Freedom* sprung,
Whence flow these wishes for the common good,
By feeling hearts alone best understood,
I, young in life, by seeming cruel fate
Was snatch'd from *Afric's* fancy'd happy seat:
What pangs excruciating must molest,
What sorrows labor in my parent's breast?
Steel'd was that soul and by no misery mov'd
That from a father seiz'd his babe belov'd:
Such, such my case. And can I then but pray
Others may never feel tyrannic sway?

—Phillis Wheatley

Wheatley's life ended on a tragic note. Her married life was filled with personal, financial, and familial hardships. Wheatley bore three children, but none of them survived. When she herself was sick and poor, the same society that lavished attention on her as a kind of "sideshow attraction"—an enslaved woman who could write lofty poetry—abandoned her to a position of powerlessness and anonymity. She died in her early thirties, destitute and grieving, without having published another book of poems. Since her death, however, her poems have been reprinted and, in the twentieth century, have again attracted lavish attention. Today Phillis Wheatley is praised as a true pioneer—the first African American poet in North America.

Thomas Jefferson

(1743–1826)

At a White House dinner in 1962 honoring forty-nine Nobel Prize winners, President John F. Kennedy hailed his guests as "the most extraordinary collection of talent, of human knowledge, that has ever been gathered together at the White House, with the possible exception of when Thomas Jefferson dined alone." President Kennedy was exaggerating only slightly.

Thomas Jefferson, the brilliant and versatile third president of the United States, was an accomplished statesman, architect, botanist, paleontologist, linguist, and musician. He displayed the range of interests that we associate with the eighteenth-century mind at its best.

Jefferson was born in the red-clay country of what is now Albemarle County, Virginia. Jefferson's father, a surveyor and magistrate, died when Thomas was fourteen, but he had provided his son with an excellent classical education and a 5,000-acre estate. After attending the College of William and Mary, Jefferson became a lawyer, a member of the Virginia House of Burgesses, and a spokesperson for the rights of personal liberty and religious freedom. In 1774, he wrote a pamphlet called *A Summary View of the Rights of British America,* a call for the rejection of parliamentary authority. This pamphlet established his reputation, and two years later, the Second Continental Congress chose him to help draft the Declaration of Independence.

During the Revolution, Jefferson served for a time as governor of Virginia. When the British invaded Virginia, he retired to Monticello, the home he had designed, and devoted himself to his family and to scientific research. During this time he also composed most of his *Notes on the State of Virginia.* Shortly after Jefferson's beloved wife Martha died in 1782, he returned to public life, in part as an escape from his private grief. He served as minister to France, secretary of state, vice president, and president from 1801–1809.

A determined opponent of federal power, Jefferson embodied the principles of what would

Thomas Jefferson (1791) by Charles Willson Peale. Oil on canvas.

Independence National Historical Park, Philadelphia, Pennsylvania.

come to be called Jeffersonian democracy. He believed in the rights of individuals and states to govern themselves as much as possible. Politically and personally, he strove to keep power vested in the agrarian backbone of the country. He also expanded the country enormously in 1803: The Louisiana Purchase doubled the size of the United States, adding land that would later be divided into part or all of fifteen states. And as for Jefferson's presidential style, he avoided public displays and wore simple clothes: A president, he thought, should neither act nor look like a king. At state dinners, he eliminated seating by rank.

After his presidency, Jefferson retired once again to Monticello. He devoted his energy to establishing the University of Virginia, planning its courses of study and designing many of its buildings. In 1826, both Jefferson (at eighty-three) and the former president John Adams (at ninety) became gravely ill. Both hoped to live to see the fiftieth anniversary of the independence they had done so much to ensure. Jefferson died on the morning of July 4, several hours before Adams, whose last words were "Thomas Jefferson still survives."

Make the Connection

The Burden of Freedom

Without a doubt, the corner-stone of the "American dream" is the ideal of freedom. The words of the Declaration of Independence are a ringing affirmation of freedom. Yet Jefferson knew well that freedom's twin is responsibility—every kind of liberty we enjoy has to be balanced by an equal amount of personal responsibility.

Reading Skills and Strategies

Identifying the Main Idea

Read the entire Declaration of Independence, and then write its **main idea** in your own words. Next, reread the text and locate the main arguments that support the idea you noted. Note also the details that underpin each argument. Arrange your notes in outline form or in a diagram like this:

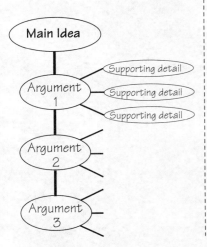

Elements of Literature

Parallelism

Parallelism is the repeated use of sentences, clauses, or phrases with identical or similar structures. For example, when Jefferson cites the truths that are "self-evident," he begins each clause with *that*. He also begins a long series of paragraphs with the words "He has. ..." Jefferson's use of parallelism emphasizes his view that all the truths he presents are of equal importance. The parallel structure also creates a stately **rhythm** or cadence in the Declaration. Listen for this cadence as you read passages aloud.

> **P**arallelism, or parallel structure, is the repetition of grammatically similar words, phrases, clauses, or sentences to emphasize a point or stir the emotions of a reader or listener.
>
> *For more on Parallelism, see the Handbook of Literary Terms.*

Background

Four other writers worked with Jefferson on the draft of the Declaration that was submitted to Congress: John Adams of Massachusetts, Roger Sherman of Connecticut, Robert Livingston of New York, and Benjamin Franklin of Pennsylvania (page 84). Few changes were made by these other writers, but Congress insisted on several major alterations. Jefferson was upset by what he called "mutilations" of his document.

In this excerpt from his *Autobiography,* Jefferson offers a fascinating glimpse of how the most celebrated document in American history was put together. The underlined passages in the Declaration show the parts omitted by Congress from the original. The words added by Congress appear in the margins. Think about why Congress may have made the changes it did to the original draft.

Declaration of Independence.

National Archives.

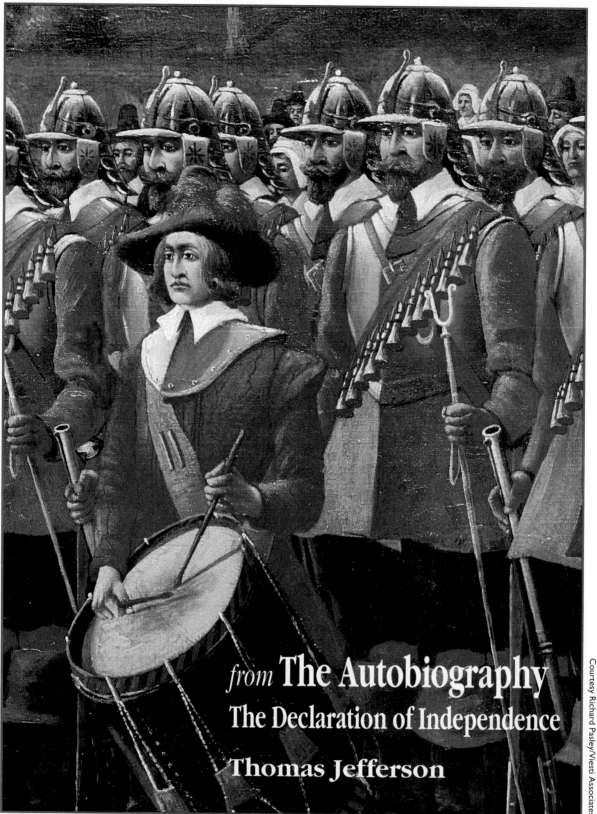

from **The Autobiography**
The Declaration of Independence

Thomas Jefferson

The First Muster of the Ancient and Honorable Artillery Company (detail) (1902) by F. Russell Bates.
Oil on canvas (48" x 30"). Ancient and Honorable Artillery Company, Faneuil Hall, Boston.

Congress proceeded the same day to consider the Declaration of Independence, which had been reported and lain on the table the Friday preceding, and on Monday referred to a committee of the whole. The pusillanimous[1] idea that we had friends in England worth keeping terms with, still haunted the minds of many. For this reason, those passages which conveyed <u>censures</u> on the people of England were struck out, lest they should give them offense. The clause too, reprobating the enslaving the inhabitants of Africa, was struck out in complaisance to South Carolina and Georgia, who had never attempted to restrain the importation of slaves, and who, on the contrary, still wished to continue it. Our northern brethren also, I believe, felt a little tender under those censures; for though their people had very few slaves themselves, yet they had been pretty considerable carriers of them to others. The debates, having taken up the greater parts of the 2d, 3d, and 4th days of July, were, on the evening of the last, closed; the Declaration was reported by the committee, agreed to by the House, and signed by every member present, except Mr. Dickinson.[2] As the sentiments of men are known not only by what they receive, but what they reject also, I will state the form of the Declaration as originally reported. The parts struck out by Congress shall be distinguished by a black line drawn under them; and those inserted by them shall be placed in the margin, or in a concurrent column.

1. **pusillanimous** (pyo͞o′si·lan′ə·məs): cowardly; lacking courage.

2. **Mr. Dickinson:** John Dickinson (1732–1808), one of Pennsylvania's representatives to the Second Continental Congress, led the conservative opposition to the Declaration and refused to sign the document.

A Declaration by the Representatives of the United States of America, in General Congress Assembled

When, in the course of human events, it becomes necessary for one people to dissolve the political bands which have connected them with another, and to assume among the powers of the earth the separate and equal station to which the laws of nature and of nature's God entitle them, a decent respect to the opinions of mankind requires that they should declare the causes which impel them to the separation.

We hold these truths to be self-evident: that all men are created equal; that they are endowed by their creator with <u>inherent and inalienable rights;</u>[3] that among these are life, liberty, and the pursuit of happiness; that to secure these rights, governments are instituted among men, deriving their just powers from the consent of the governed; that whenever any form of government becomes destructive of these ends, it is the right of the people to alter or to abolish it, and to institute new government, laying its foundation on such principles, and organizing its powers in such form, as to them shall seem most likely to effect their safety and happiness. Prudence, indeed, will dictate that governments long established should not be

certain

3. **inalienable** (in·āl′yən·ə·bəl) **rights:** rights that cannot be taken away.

Thomas Jefferson (date and artist unknown). Fragment of white marble.
Maryland Historical Society.

changed for light and transient causes; and accordingly all experience hath shown that mankind are more disposed to suffer while evils are sufferable, than to right themselves by abolishing the forms to which they are accustomed. But when a long train of abuses and usurpations,[4] begun at a distinguished[5] period and pursuing invariably the same object, evinces a design to reduce them under absolute despotism, it is their right, it is their duty to throw off such government, and to provide new guards for their future security. Such has been the patient sufferance of these colonies; and such is now the necessity which constrains them to expunge their   alter
former systems of government. The history of the present king of Great Britain is a history of unremitting injuries and usurpations,   repeated
among which appears no solitary fact to contradict the uniform tenor of the rest, but all have in direct object the establishment of   all having
an absolute tyranny over these states. To prove this, let facts be submitted to a candid world for the truth of which we pledge a faith yet unsullied by falsehood.

He has refused his assent to laws the most wholesome and necessary for the public good.

He has forbidden his governors to pass laws of immediate and pressing importance, unless suspended in their operation till his assent should be obtained; and, when so suspended, he has utterly neglected to attend to them.

He has refused to pass other laws for the accommodation of large districts of people, unless those people would relinquish the right of representation in the legislature, a right inestimable to them, and formidable to tyrants only.[6]

He has called together legislative bodies at places unusual, uncomfortable, and distant from the depository of their public records, for the sole purpose of fatiguing them into compliance with his measures.

He has dissolved representative houses repeatedly and continually for opposing with manly firmness his invasions on the rights of the people.

He has refused for a long time after such dissolutions to cause others to be elected, whereby the legislative powers, incapable of annihilation, have returned to the people at large for their exercise, the state remaining, in the meantime, exposed to all the dangers of invasion from without and convulsions within.

4. **usurpations** (yo͞o'zər·pā'shənz): acts of unlawful or forceful seizure of property, power, rights, and the like.
5. **distinguished** (di·stiŋ'gwisht): clearly defined.
6. **formidable . . . only:** causing fear only to tyrants.

WORDS TO OWN
transient (tran'shənt) *adj.*: temporary; passing.
constrains (kən·strānz') *v.*: forces.
expunge (ek·spunj') *v.*: erase; remove.
candid (kan'did) *adj.*: unbiased; fair.

He has endeavored to prevent the population of these states; for that purpose obstructing the laws for naturalization of foreigners, refusing to pass others to encourage their migrations hither, and raising the conditions of new appropriations of lands.

He has suffered the administration of justice totally to cease in some of these states refusing his assent to laws for establishing judiciary powers.

obstructed / by

He has made our judges dependent on his will alone for the tenure of their offices, and the amount and payment of their salaries.

He has erected a multitude of new offices, by a self-assumed power and sent hither swarms of new officers to harass our people and eat out their substance.

He has kept among us in times of peace standing armies and ships of war without the consent of our legislatures.

He has affected to render the military independent of, and superior to, the civil power.

He has combined with others[7] to subject us to a jurisdiction foreign to our constitutions and unacknowledged by our laws, giving

7. **others:** members of British Parliament and their supporters and agents.

The Declaration of Independence, July 4, 1776 by John Trumbull (1756–1843). Oil on canvas.

Yale University Art Gallery, Trumbull Collection.

Legacy of Peace and Unity: The Iroquois Constitution

Before Revolutionary patriots put pen to paper to draft the U.S. Constitution in 1787, Colonial leaders such as Thomas Jefferson and Benjamin Franklin studied examples of government from Greek and Roman times, examples from the Bible, and an example flourishing closer to home: the Iroquois Confederacy.

The Iroquois Confederacy, also known as the League of Five Nations, was a union of the Senecas, Cayugas, Onondagas, Oneidas, and Mohawks (the Tuscaroras joined later). Around 1500, so the legend goes, a Mohawk visionary named Dekanawidah convinced the nations to unite in order to establish peace and to protect "life, property and liberty." Thanks to the constitution they created, called the Law of the Great Peace, the confederacy became a formidable power; by 1750, it numbered about fifteen thousand people, and Iroquois hunters and warriors ranged over one million square miles.

The oldest living constitution. The Iroquois Constitution, which still governs the Iroquois today, is regarded as the world's oldest living constitution. It gives member tribes equal voice in the nation's affairs, spells out a system of checks and balances, and guarantees political and religious freedom. Most amazing by European standards of the time, the Iroquois Constitution grants extensive political power to women, who hold the right to nominate and impeach chiefs. The constitution specifies that "Women shall be considered the progenitors of the Nation. They shall own the land and the soil. Men and women shall follow the status of the mother."

The Iroquois Confederacy had what Jefferson and Franklin were searching for: a constitution infused with basic principles of democracy and federalism. Franklin

his assent to their acts of pretended legislation for quartering large bodies of armed troops among us; for protecting them by a mock trial from punishment for any murders which they should commit on the inhabitants of these states; for cutting off our trade with all parts of the world; for imposing taxes on us without our consent; for depriving us [ ] of the benefits of trial by jury; for transporting us beyond seas to be tried for pretended offenses; for abolishing the free system of English laws in a neighboring province,[8] establishing therein an arbitrary government, and enlarging its boundaries, so as to render it at once an example and fit instrument for introducing the same absolute rule into these <u>states</u>; for taking away our charters, abolishing our most valuable laws, and altering fundamentally the forms of our governments; for suspending our own legislatures, and declaring themselves invested with power to legislate for us in all cases whatsoever.

in many cases

colonies

8. **neighboring province:** Québec in Canada.

championed the Iroquois example after meeting confederacy representatives at the Albany Congress in 1754, which was held to recruit the Iroquois as allies against the French. The result was Franklin's Albany Plan of Union between the Colonies, and, though the plan failed, it helped shape the Articles of Confederation and the U.S. Constitution.

The strength of five arrows. The Iroquois Constitution survives as a brilliant American political and literary work, filled with rich symbolism. Dekanawidah had envisioned a huge evergreen "Tree of Peace" whose spreading roots represented the five nations of the Haudenosaunee (Iroquois). After unification, a symbolic tree was planted. According to the constitution, "We place at the top of the Tree of the Long Leaves an Eagle who is able to see afar. If he sees in the distance any evil approaching or any danger threatening, he will at once warn the people of the Confederacy." An eagle atop the tree of peace, clutching five arrows bound together by a deer sinew (much harder to break than one arrow alone), symbolizes the Iroquois Confederacy—and it is this image we see pictured on the back of the U.S. quarter.

In 1988, to mark the bicentennial of the U.S. Constitution, Congress passed a joint resolution stating that "the confederation of the original Thirteen Colonies into one republic was influenced by the political system developed by the Iroquois Confederacy, as were many of the democratic principles which were incorporated into the Constitution itself." Like the five arrows bound together, the Iroquois political and literary legacy is entwined forever with ideals that continue to shape American life.

He has <u>abdicated</u> government here <u>withdrawing his governors, and declaring us out of his allegiance and protection.</u>

by declaring us out of his protection, and waging war against us.

He has plundered our seas, ravaged our coasts, burnt our towns, and destroyed the lives of our people.

He is at this time transporting large armies of foreign mercenaries to complete the works of death, desolation, and tyranny already begun with circumstances of cruelty and perfidy [ ] unworthy the head of a civilized nation.

scarcely paralleled in the most barbarous ages, and totally

He has constrained our fellow citizens taken captive on the high seas, to bear arms against their country, to become the executioners of their friends and brethren, or to fall themselves by their hands.

He has [ ] endeavored to bring on the inhabitants of our frontiers, the merciless Indian savages, whose known rule of warfare is

excited domestic insurrection among us, and has

WORDS TO OWN
abdicated (ab′di·kāt′id) v.: given up responsibility for.

---

an undistinguished destruction of all ages, sexes, and conditions of existence.

He has incited treasonable insurrections of our fellow citizens, with the allurements of forfeiture and confiscation of our property.

He has waged cruel war against human nature itself, violating its most sacred rights of life and liberty in the persons of a distant people who never offended him, captivating and carrying them into slavery in another hemisphere, or to incur miserable death in their transportation thither. This piratical warfare, the opprobrium[9] of INFIDEL powers, is the warfare of the CHRISTIAN king of Great Britain. Determined to keep open a market where MEN should be bought and sold, he has prostituted his negative[10] for suppressing every legislative attempt to prohibit or to restrain this execrable commerce. And that this assemblage of horrors might want no fact of distinguished die,[11] he is now exciting those very people to rise in arms among us, and to purchase that liberty of which he has deprived them, by murdering the people on whom he also obtruded them: thus paying off former crimes committed against the LIBERTIES of one people, with crimes which he urges them to commit against the LIVES of another.

In every stage of these oppressions we have petitioned for redress in the most humble terms: Our repeated petitions have been answered only by repeated injuries.

A prince whose character is thus marked by every act which may define a tyrant is unfit to be the ruler of a [ ] people who mean to be free. Future ages will scarcely believe that the hardiness of one man adventured, within the short compass of twelve years only, to lay a foundation so broad and so undisguised for tyranny over a people fostered and fixed in principles of freedom.

Nor have we been wanting in attentions to our British brethren. We have warned them from time to time of attempts by their legislature to extend a jurisdiction over these our states. We have reminded them of the circumstances of our emigration and settlement here, no one of which could warrant so strange a pretension: that these were effected at the expense of our own blood and treasure, unassisted by the wealth or the strength of Great Britain: that in constituting indeed our several forms of government, we had adopted one common king, thereby laying a foundation for perpetual league and amity with them: but that submission to their parliament was no part of our constitution, nor ever in idea, if history may be credited: and, we [ ] appealed to their native justice and magnanimity as well as to the ties of our

free

an unwarrantable / us

have

and we have conjured[12] them by

9. **opprobrium** (ə·prō′brē·əm): shameful conduct.
10. **negative:** veto.
11. **fact of distinguished die:** clear stamp or mark of distinction. Jefferson is being sarcastic here.
12. **conjured** (kən·jŏŏrd′): solemnly called upon.

WORDS TO OWN

confiscation (kän′fis·kā′shən) *n.*: seizure of property by authority.
magnanimity (mag′nə·nim′ə·tē) *n.*: nobility of spirit.

----

common kindred to disavow these usurpations which were likely to interrupt our connection and correspondence. They too have been deaf to the voice of justice and of consanguinity,[13] and when occasions have been given them, by the regular course of their laws, of removing from their councils the disturbers of our harmony, they have, by their free election, re-established them in power. At this very time too, they are permitting their chief magistrate to send over not only soldiers of our common blood, but Scotch and foreign mercenaries to invade and destroy us. These facts have given the last stab to agonizing affection, and manly spirit bids us to renounce forever these unfeeling brethren. We must endeavor to forget our former love for them, and hold them as we hold the rest of mankind, enemies in war, in peace friends. We might have been a free and a great people together; but a communication of grandeur and of freedom, it seems, is below their dignity. Be it so, since they will have it. The road to happiness and to glory is open to us too. We will tread it apart from them and acquiesce in the necessity which denounces[14] our eternal separation [ ]!

We, therefore, the representatives of the United States of America in General Congress assembled, [ ] do in the name, and by the authority of the good people of these states reject and renounce all allegiance and subjection to the kings of Great Britain and all others who may hereafter claim by, through or under them; we utterly dissolve all political connection which may heretofore have subsisted between us and the people or parliament of Great Britain: And finally we do assert and declare these colonies to be free and independent states, and that as free and independent states, they have full power to levy war, conclude peace, contract alliances, establish commerce, and to do all other acts and things which independent states may of right do.

And for the support of this declaration, [ ] we mutually pledge to each other our lives, our fortunes, and our sacred honor.

The Declaration thus signed on the 4th, on paper, was engrossed on parchment, and signed again on the 2d of August.

Marginal annotations:

would inevitably

We must therefore

and hold them as we hold the rest of mankind, enemies in war, in peace friends.

appealing to the supreme judge of the world for the rectitude of our intentions,

colonies, solemnly publish and declare, that these united colonies are, and of right ought to be free and independent states; that they are absolved from all allegiance to the British crown, and that all political connection between them and the state of Great Britain is, and ought to be, totally dissolved;

with a firm reliance on the protection of divine providence,

---

13. consanguinity (kän′saŋ·gwin′ə·tē): kinship; family relationship.
14. denounces (dē·nɑuns′iz): archaic for "announces, proclaims."

Words to Own

renounce (ri·nɑuns′) *v.:* to give up.
acquiesce (ak′wē·es′) *v.:* agree or accept quietly.

Syng silver used at the signing of the Declaration of Independence, Independence Hall, Philadelphia, Pennsylvania.

Joe Viesti/Viesti Associates.

A Letter from Jefferson to His Daughter

In 1784, Jefferson was sent to Paris to work out the treaty ending the Revolutionary War. Jefferson stayed in France for five years. His daughter Patsy was in a Catholic convent school in Paris when Jefferson wrote this letter from the south of France. The wrist Jefferson complains of in the letter had been injured a few months earlier.

Aix-en-Provence, March 28, 1787

I was happy, my dear Patsy, to receive, on my arrival here, your letter informing me of your health and occupations. I have not written to you sooner because I have been almost constantly on the road. My journey hitherto has been a very pleasing one. It was undertaken with the hope that the mineral waters of this place might restore strength to my wrist. Other considerations also concurred. Instruction, amusement, and abstraction from business, of which I had too much at Paris. I am glad to learn that you are employed in things new and good in your music and drawing. You know what have been my fears for some time past; that you do not employ yourself so closely as I could wish. You have promised me a more assiduous attention, and I have great confidence in what you promise. It is your future happiness which interests me, and nothing can contribute more to it (moral rectitude always excepted) than the contracting a habit of industry and activity. Of all the cankers of human happiness, none corrodes it with so silent, yet so baneful a tooth, as indolence. . . . It is while we are young that the habit of industry is formed. If not then, it never is afterward. The fortune of our lives therefore depends on employing well the short period of youth. If at any moment, my dear, you catch yourself in idleness, start from it as you would from the precipice of a gulf. You are not, however, to consider yourself as unemployed while taking exercise. That is necessary for your health, and health is the first of all objects. For this reason if you leave your dancing master for the summer, you must increase your other exercise. I do not like your saying that you are unable to read the ancient print of your Livy,[1] but with the aid of your master. We are always equal to what we undertake with resolution. A little degree of this will enable you to decipher your Livy. If you always lean on your master, you will never be able to proceed without him. It is a part of the American character to consider nothing as desperate; to surmount every difficulty by resolution and contrivance. In Europe there are shops for every want. Its inhabitants therefore have no idea that their wants can be furnished otherwise. Remote from all other aid, we are obliged to invent and to execute; to find means within ourselves, and not to lean on others. Consider therefore the conquering your Livy as an exercise in the habit of surmounting difficulties, a habit which will be necessary to you in the country where you are to live, and without which you will be thought a very helpless animal, and less esteemed. . . .

You ask me to write you long letters. I will do it, my dear, on condition you will read them from time to time, and practice what they will inculcate. Their precepts will be dictated by experience, by a perfect knowledge of the situation in which you will be placed, and by the fondest love for you. This it is which makes me wish to see you more qualified than common. My expectations from you are high: yet not higher than you may attain. Industry and resolution are all that are wanting. Nobody in this world can make me so happy, or so miserable, as you. Retirement from public life will ere long become necessary for me. To your sister and yourself I look to render the evening of my life serene and contented. Its morning has been clouded by loss after loss till I have nothing left but you. I do not doubt either your affection or dispositions. But great exertions are necessary, and you have little time left to make them. Be industrious then, my dear child. Think nothing unsurmountable by resolution and application, and you will be all that I wish you to be. . . .

Continue to love me with all the warmth with which you are beloved by, my dear Patsy, yours affectionately,

TH: JEFFERSON

1. **Livy:** Roman historian (59 B.C.–A.D. 17).

MAKING MEANINGS

First Thoughts

1. What word, phrase, or **image** struck you as most important? Why?

Shaping Interpretations

2. What changes show a desire not to make an absolute break with the English people? Why do you think it would be important that the new nation maintain its "consanguinity," or close kinship, with the English people?

3. Which changes seem to have been adopted primarily for stylistic reasons, such as clarity or greater impact, and which for political reasons?

4. Find at least two passages in the Declaration that use **parallelism.** What is the effect of the parallel structure on the *idea* of the passage?

Reading Check

a. What is the **main idea**  of the Declaration of Independence?

b. List the truths that Jefferson considers self-evident.

c. List the offenses charged to the king of England.

d. What are some of the powers of the independent countries?

CHOICES: Building Your Portfolio

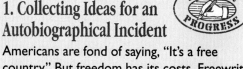

Writer's Notebook

1. Collecting Ideas for an Autobiographical Incident

WORK IN PROGRESS

Americans are fond of saying, "It's a free country." But freedom has its costs. Freewrite about an experience you've had that showed that freedom can bring both benefits and burdens, gains and losses. Keep your notes; you may use them later in the Writer's Workshop on page 130.

Summarizing a Document

2. In the Course of Human Events

Review your reading notes on the **main idea** and supporting arguments of the Declaration of Independence. Then, write a one- or two-paragraph summary of the central **theme** of the document. Include some of the supporting arguments with relevant details.

Responding to a Text

3. A Voice for Women

On March 31, 1776, Abigail Adams (1744–1818) wrote to her husband John Adams, who was on the committee preparing the Declaration of Independence. In a brief essay, respond to this excerpt from her letter.

> … in the new Code of Laws which I suppose it will be necessary for you to make, I desire you would remember the ladies, and be more generous and favorable to them than your ancestors. Do not put such unlimited power into the hands of the husbands. Remember all men would be tyrants if they could. If particular care and attention is not paid to the ladies, we are determined to foment a rebellion, and will not hold ourselves bound by any laws in which we have no voice, or representation.
>
> —Abigail Adams

Speaking and Listening

4. Unequal Signs

In "Harrison Bergeron," a famous short story by Kurt Vonnegut, Jr. (1922–   ), Vonnegut imagines a future America in which "everybody was finally equal": "Nobody was smarter than anybody else. Nobody was better-looking than anybody else. Nobody was stronger or quicker than anybody else." In a panel discussion, explore what you and your classmates think the framers of the Declaration meant by the statement "all men are created equal." Then, discuss why some people believe that all Americans, in fact, are not yet equal.

READ ON

Coming to America

"It was 1906. I was six years old and we were on a train with some other immigrants. . . . When people on the train spoke to me in Russian, I said, 'Speak only English. I'm an Americanka now.'" Thus recalls Sonia Walinsky, just one of dozens of immigrants whose testimonials Joan Morrison and Charlotte Fox Zabusky gathered in *American Mosaic* (E. P. Dutton), a collection of vivid remembrances by Americans from many lands.

For a Captive Audience

In 1704, as part of the fighting during the War of the Spanish Succession, or Queen Anne's War, a French and American Indian raiding party captured a family of British Puritans in Deerfield, Massachusetts. Though the rest of the family was released, young Eunice Williams remained with the Mohawks, refusing to return home even when she could. The prize-winning historian John Demos tells Eunice's gripping story in *The Unredeemed Captive* (Alfred A. Knopf).

Puritan Principles

Puritan culture has had a profound impact on the American character. In *The Puritan Experiment* (St. Martin's), the historian Francis J. Bremer explores this culture, from its origins in sixteenth-century England to its role in colonial America.

A famous fictional account of the Puritan era is Nathaniel Hawthorne's powerful novel *The Scarlet Letter*, which examines the consequences of private sin and public penance. It touches on many familiar conflicts in literature— emotion vs. reason, love vs. hate, and the individual vs. society. It has also inspired several film adaptations. This title is available in the HRW Library.

Another Passage

In 1830, African American Rutherford Calhoun, newly freed from slavery, stows away on a ship without realizing it is bound for Africa and the slave trade. His trip is chronicled in Charles Johnson's National Book Award– winning novel *Middle Passage* (Atheneum).

Revolutionary Tales

What was it like to be there when "the shot heard round the world" was fired? In *April Morning* (Crown), Howard Fast describes the first battle of the Revolution from the viewpoint of young Adam Cooper of the Lexington militia. For another view of the time, try Fast's historical novel, *Citizen Tom Paine* (Grove Press), the story of the famous patriot from his early days in poverty to his last days in infamy.

The American Language

"Revolutionary" English

by Gary Q. Arpin

As American English began to develop in the years following the settlement of North America by Europeans, differences between British and American usage became more and more apparent. British travelers noticed that Americans spoke with a nasality that was disagreeable to their British ears. The visitors also noticed what they thought of as corruptions of the language: Words were being used in "barbarous" ways, and brand-new words were being coined at an alarming rate.

Effects of Physical Separation

The simple fact of physical separation caused some of the differences between British and American English. Differences in pronunciation, for example, became marked as the accents of speakers on both sides of the ocean gradually changed. Such differences are apparent even today; for example, British speakers omit the vowel before the second r in words like *secretary* and *laboratory,* but most Americans pronounce all the syllables in such words.

Physical separation also resulted in differences in usage. In the Colonies, for example, and especially in New England, it was common to hear someone speak of throwing a *rock*. In Britain, however, *rock* continued to refer only to a massive stone, such as Plymouth Rock. Throwing a rock would have seemed as odd to a British person as tossing a boulder would be to an American.

Sometimes the meaning or usage of a word would change in England while Americans retained its older meaning. The American usage of *guess* to mean "suppose" is an example of this. In the eighteenth and nineteenth centuries, "I guess" in this sense sounded odd to British visitors, who would have said, "I suppose." But these visitors were unaware that "I guess" had been common in England until the eighteenth century. (It even appears in the writings of Chaucer and Shakespeare.) The British also criticized Americans for saying *fall* instead of *autumn,* apparently unaware that *fall* had been used in England until around 1750.

Ugly Americanisms

The word *Americanism* came into use to describe a word or expression that originated in the United States or that was peculiar to the States. The word was first used in print in 1781 by the Reverend John Witherspoon, a Scottish clergyman who had come to this country in 1768 to become president of the College of New Jersey (now Princeton University). Witherspoon traveled a good deal and recorded words and phrases that were peculiar to the United States. Many of these words are so common today that it's hard to imagine a time when they might have been considered unusual. Among the Americanisms recorded by Witherspoon were *to notify,* meaning "to inform"; *mad,* in the sense of "angry"; *chunks,* to describe big pieces of wood; *spell,* meaning "a period of time" (as in "a spell of bad weather"); *once in a while,* meaning "occasionally"; and *tote,* meaning "to carry."

Some critics considered English to be a complete language that had evolved through the centuries to a state of perfection in the eighteenth century. Any change was horrendous to them, especially any change brought about by people thought to be unrefined. As one writer put it around 1800, "A language, arrived at its zenith, requires no introduction of new words."

Some years later, the same point was made by a British purist in response to a question posed by the American language expert Noah Webster (page 195). Webster had asked, "If a word becomes universally current in America . . . why should it not take its station in the language?" The British purist, a certain Captain Basil Hall, replied, "Because there are words enough already."

> If, as many people thought, literature was an authority for usage, then there was little authority supporting American usage.

Reinforcing the purist's position was the fact that until the early nineteenth century, there was little distinctly *American* literature. There was not much demonstration of the *power* of the American idiom, and little indication that American speech could lead to anything of lasting worth. If, as many people thought, literature was an authority for usage, then there was little authority supporting American usage.

Many people on both sides of the question expected, or feared, that the two forms of English would eventually grow separate until the two groups would no longer understand each other. They predicted that Americans, completely cut off from their past, would have to read the works of Shakespeare and Milton in translation.

"What Language Should Americans Speak?"

The conflict between purists and advocates of change was especially heated in America in the eighteenth and nineteenth centuries. On the American side, the rejection of English authority in language was for some an aspect of America's rejection of English political authority. In 1788, a march in New York supporting the ratification of the U.S. Constitution contained a language contingent. This group carried a scroll advocating the use of something called "Federal English." A Federal English would establish the independence of American English and, at the same time, preserve the purity of the language in its new home.

The most radical political position on language argued for the establishment in America of a completely new language. At various times French, Greek, and Hebrew were suggested as alternatives. Each had as its principal virtue, apparently, the fact that it was not English. Nor was it Spanish, the other main Colonial language, or one of the many Native American languages. (Though words like *raccoon* from Virginia Algonquian and *totem* from Ojibwa have been with us since the eighteenth century, English was only minimally influenced by the languages of American Indians, largely because political dominance was held by English-speaking settlers.)

Democratic Language

Some proponents of American English pointed to the humble, democratic character of the language as its greatest virtue: Class distinctions were not marked by accents in America, as they were in Britain, and geographical differences in speech were not nearly as important.

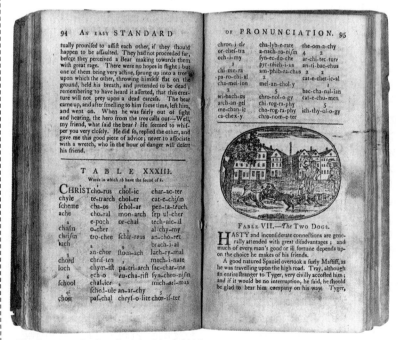

The American Spelling Book by Noah Webster.

Because of this, an American would (in theory, at least) be immediately understood and accepted wherever he or she went in the country, which was not the case in England. Of course, there were still some regional differences in language. One writer's observation that "America has no dialects" was surely overstated.

John Adams (1735–1826) argued for the establishment of an American academy that would try to govern the usage of English in America and protect it against whatever changes might originate in England in the future. Having established its democratic purpose and its independence from the British, American English would thereafter remain stable or at least change only in approved ways.

Language Resists Rules

Language changes primarily according to the way it is used, not the way authorities say it should be used. Thomas Jefferson (page 114), perhaps the best American linguist of the Revolutionary period, took the most reasonable view. Speaking of the foundations of an American academy, he wrote:

> If, like the French Academicians, it were proposed to *fix* our language, it would be fortunate that the step was not taken in the days of our Saxon ancestors, whose vocabulary would ill express the science of this day.

Thus, Jefferson found himself at odds with both British and American purists. And he was right. The move for an academy finally died, and the American language continued to develop in its own unpredictable and exuberant ways.

Try It Out

1. **Researching word origins.** Eighteenth-century British purists complained about the ways Americans adapted words to suit life in the Colonies. Their criticism was based on an assumption that words should develop historically from their roots, not in response to need and usage. Explain how the histories of the following words, all in common English usage, puncture the purists' argument. A good dictionary will give you the information you need.

clue	precocious
companion	steward
daughter	town
expedite	

2. **Contrasting pronunciations.** Look up the following items in an American dictionary that includes British pronunciations (such as *Webster's New World Dictionary*) or in a British dictionary (like the *Oxford English Dictionary*). How is each pronounced in Great Britain? in the United States?

ate	schedule
been	lieutenant
clerk	the letter *z*

3. **Analyzing Americanisms.** The following expressions are all Americanisms—they originated in America or have a usage peculiar to American speech. What do the words reveal about features and customs that were uniquely American? What other Americanisms can you add to the list?

cold snap	potpie
dude	ranch
everglade	salt lick
Indian summer	snowshoe

4. **Debating language regulation.** In France and in Québec province in Canada, official or semiofficial organizations try to regulate the usage of language. Such organizations decide on proper spelling and whether a foreign word should be accepted into the language, among other things. Should such an organization oversee American English as John Adams suggested? Together with four or five other students, discuss this issue. The discussion should (1) begin by stating why the question is of interest to Americans; (2) present some reasons why an American-language regulatory commission would be a good idea; (3) offer some reasons why language regulation would *not* be a good idea; and (4) conclude by stating whether such an organization to regulate American English should or should not be established.

Writer's Workshop

**Technology
HELP**

See Writer's Workshop 2
CD-ROM. *Assignment: Autobiographical Incident.*

ASSIGNMENT
**Write a narrative
about a significant
incident in your life
that helped you to
learn more about
yourself.**

AIM
**To express yourself;
to inform.**

AUDIENCE
**Your classmates,
family, or general
readers.**

NARRATIVE WRITING

AUTOBIOGRAPHICAL INCIDENT

The ancient Greeks followed an important maxim: "Know thyself." The Greek philosopher Plato went even further and said, "The life which is unexamined is not worth living." Many of the early American writers you have studied in these collections struggled to make sense of themselves and their experiences. From the Puritan tendency to examine oneself for signs of salvation to Benjamin Franklin's inventory of methods for attaining moral perfection to the latest biographies, memoirs, and self-help books on the best-seller lists, self-examination has been an important feature of the American character. You can do a little of your own self-examination by writing about an **autobiographical incident:** an event from your life that taught you something, that contributed to your self-knowledge.

Prewriting

1. **Choosing an incident.** An incident is a specific occurrence—usually one that takes place over a short period of time. The incident you choose to narrate might be a moment of crisis or danger, but it might just as likely be a quiet, seemingly ordinary event that nevertheless had significance for you. If you've kept your Writer's Notebook notes from these collections, you may already have some ideas for an autobiographical incident you want to recount.

   If you still haven't decided what to write about, it might help to draw a "road map" of your life, an **overview** that starts at birth and extends to the present. As you draw the map, locate significant events with brief **headings.** At points where you think the course of your life changed in an important way, draw a turn in the road. Look over your road map, and select the topic that draws your interest the most and isn't too private to comfortably share with others.

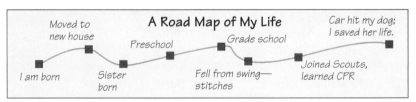

2. **Freewriting to remember details.** To recall specific details about your incident, freewrite your memories of it. Pay special attention to

details that involve the senses: What smells, sounds, sights, tastes, and textures characterized your experience? If you have difficulty recalling details of the incident, here are some memory-prompting techniques you can try:

- **Visualizing.** Close your eyes and see the scene in your mind. Sketch the images as they occur to you.

- **Visiting.** If you can, go back to the location where the event took place. Note details, and give your memories time to emerge.

- **Interviewing.** Talk to people who were involved—family members, friends, neighbors, and teachers. Ask how they remember the incident.

- **Using memory "souvenirs."** Find objects and other artifacts you associate with the incident—a photo, a scarf, a song, a diary entry, even a smell—and focus on the memories they bring back.

3. **Discovering your meaning.** Most likely, the meaning of your incident will emerge in the process of writing. You might, however, want to write a brief, private statement of what the incident meant to you. Or, you may want to discuss it with a friend or relative. These steps can help you focus your ideas when you're shaping your initial draft.

Drafting

1. **Establishing the context.** Your readers may need some background, or context, in order to understand how and why the incident is significant in your life. Select necessary details about people, places, relationships, and prior events that put the incident in context.

2. **Conveying a tone.** Depending on the incident, its effects, and your own personality, your attitude toward the subject might be lighthearted, satirical, nostalgic, angry, rueful, or solemn. As you write, and as you re-read your first draft, make sure that this attitude, or **tone,** is deliberately chosen and is the one you wish to communicate to your readers.

3. **Ordering events.** Most narratives move forward chronologically, from the first event in a sequence to the last. To give yourself a basic framework for your narrative during this initial draft stage, try following the pattern of organization shown on the right. In revision stages, you can experiment with the order, perhaps beginning with the climax of the action and then using flashbacks to show what led up to the central incident.

4. **Using narrative devices:**

- **Be specific: Show, don't simply tell.** Use specific names of people, places, and objects. Instead of "dog," write "Bobbi, my black Labrador

Strategies for Elaboration

Here are some effective ways to open an autobiographical incident.

1. **Use intriguing dialogue:** "Any reason there's a fish in the bathtub?" Janine asked me casually.

2. **Hint at things to come:** A box of old, musty books changed my life.

3. **Join events in progress:** This was it—my first vocal solo. So I opened my mouth and— squeaked.

Try It Out

Fill out the following to generate a framework for your essay.

Introduction

_____

Order of events

1. _____

2. _____

3. _____

Conclusion

_____

**Communications
Handbook
H E L P**

See Proofreading.

**Language
Handbook
H E L P**

*Quotation Marks,
page 1246.*

retriever." Record specific gestures, movements, body language: "My heart pumped wildly as I ran from the front porch to the horrible scene." Describe sounds, smells, tastes, and physical sensations.

- **Use dramatic techniques.**   Use flashbacks or foreshadowing if they increase suspense and help your pacing. Play on the element of surprise by withholding some important information from your readers until the crucial moment. Add tension and suspense.

- **Use realistic dialogue.**   Record as accurately as you can what you and others said. Dialogue can effectively reveal character and move the events of your narrative forward.

5. **Writing a satisfying conclusion.**   Your conclusion may simply reveal the final outcome of events, or it may be the place where you make clear how the incident you reported was significant for you. For example, your clearheaded response to an incident in which your dog was hit by a car might have been central to the development of your self-confidence.

Model: A Conclusion

All through my childhood I had felt a bit uncertain of myself. Anything new, even if it was something as simple as learning a new craft at camp or going to a party where I didn't know many people, always filled me with dread. What if I wasn't good enough? What if I failed? Those feelings of inadequacy were never quite as strong after the incident with my dog Bobbi. I had kept my head during a crisis and saved my dog's life. My love for my dog had made me brave, and my moment of bravery made me believe in myself to a degree I never had before.

Evaluating and Revising

1. **Peer review.**   With a group of students, read and discuss one another's autobiographical narratives. Here are some focal points for discussion:

   - Did the writer describe the experience in sufficient detail?

   - Were any details out of place or unnecessary?

   - What areas could the writer improve? Does the narrative need more details, better pacing, more dialogue, or more effective organization?

   - How effective was the writer in getting you to care about the incident and the effect it had on his or her life? Did the writing seem honest and personal? Was the tone appropriate to the content?

   - Did the narrative come to a satisfying conclusion? Could you understand why the incident was significant for the writer?

2. **Self-evaluation.**   After you've listened to your peers' comments, look over the Evaluation Criteria, and see if your essay contains everything on the list. Identify three areas for improvement in your essay, and make appropriate revisions.

Language Workshop

LINKING IT UP: COORDINATING CONJUNCTIONS

Here's one way to describe Benjamin Franklin's plight when he first arrived in Philadelphia:

> Benjamin Franklin was practically penniless when he arrived in Philadelphia. He was able to buy some bread.

Here's a better way to express the same information:

> Benjamin Franklin was practically penniless when he arrived in Philadelphia, *yet* he was able to buy some bread.

In the second sentence, the writer combined two related thoughts into a single sentence by using a connective word—in this case, the **coordinating conjunction** *yet*. Separating two thoughts into two sentences is not incorrect; there are times when short, simple sentences sound best. However, using **coordinating conjunctions** to combine two thoughts into one sentence can result in more graceful **syntax,** or sentence structure.

| Some Connective Words and What They Indicate ||
Conjunction	Indicates
and	similarity, addition
but	opposition, contrast
yet	opposition, contrast
or	choice
nor	negation
so	cause and effect, result
for	explanation

All the words in the chart above function as coordinating conjunctions, but some can also function as other parts of speech. For example, *for* is a preposition in this sentence: "We went to the store *for* apples." However, the word *for* is a conjunction in this sentence: "We went to a store downtown, *for* the store on our block was closed." To combine two related sentences into a single sentence, you will need to select an appropriate conjunction.

Writer's Workshop Follow-Up: Revising

Reread the autobiographical narrative you wrote for the Writer's Workshop (page 130). Are there any short, choppy sentences that have a clear relationship to one another? Where appropriate, use conjunctions to combine such sentences and make your writing flow more gracefully.

Technology HELP

See Language Workshop CD-ROM. *Key word entry: connective words and phrases.*

Language Handbook HELP

Combining by Coordinating Ideas, page 1238.

Try It Out

Combine each pair of sentences into one sentence, using the most appropriate conjunction from the chart. Make necessary revisions so that the resulting sentence reads smoothly.

1. Franklin wished to achieve moral perfection. He devised a book in which he could record his transgressions and his progress.

2. It is not easy to achieve moral perfection. One can still try.

Reading for Life

Monitoring Your Reading

Situation

Suppose a U.S. government document has been published in a newspaper or on the Internet and you have to evaluate it — either because it's part of your job or because the document is important to you as a voter. The strategies that follow will help you read such a document.

Strategies

Do background research.

- Use a textbook, an encyclopedia, or the Internet to review the historical or political context of the document.

Monitor and adjust your reading.

- Be aware of any difficulty you are having in understanding the document.
- Read more slowly if the material is complex.
- If necessary, adjust your purpose for reading the document. (Major purposes for reading include *enjoying, understanding, interpreting,* and *solving problems.*) As you read an official document, you may decide that you must interpret it as well as merely understand it on a literal level.

Break down difficult texts.

- Break down complicated sentences into shorter sentences; identify modifiers and the sentence elements they modify.

Address http://www.whitehouse.gov

BY THE PRESIDENT OF THE UNITED STATES OF AMERICA
A PROCLAMATION
        Whereas it appears that a state of war exists between Austria, Prussia, Sardinia, Great Britain, and the United Netherlands on the one part and France on the other, and the duty and interest of the United States require that they should with sincerity and good faith adopt and pursue a conduct friendly and impartial toward the belligerent powers:
        I have therefore thought fit by these presents to declare the disposition of the United States to observe the conduct aforesaid toward those powers respectively, and to exhort and warn the citizens of the United States carefully to avoid all acts and proceeding whatsoever which may in any manner tend to contravene such disposition.
        And I do hereby also make known that whosoever of the citizens of the United States shall render himself liable to punishment or forfeiture under the law of nations by committing, aiding, or abetting hostilities against any of the said powers, or by carrying to any of them those articles which are deemed contraband by the modern usage of nations, will not receive the protection of the United States against such punishment or forfeiture . . .
        Philadelphia, the 22d of April, 1793
        Geo. WASHINGTON

Use context clues or a dictionary to define unfamiliar words.

- If you are unsure of meaning, reread sentences. See if context clues help you understand the sentence. If not, consult a reference book or speak with a knowledgeable person.
- Ask yourself questions based on what you *do* understand. Ask, for example, "Does this familiar word mean something different in this context?"

Find the main idea, or key passage, of the document.

Using the Strategies

1. What is the date of the document reprinted on this page?
2. Who issued the document? What is its title?

3. What is the world situation described in the first paragraph?
4. Use context clues to see if you can define *aforesaid, exhort, contravene, forfeiture,* and *contraband.* Be sure to check your guesses in a dictionary.
5. What is the main idea of this document?

Extending the Strategies

In a library or on the Internet, find a law recently enacted by the U.S. government or your state government. Make a copy of the law. Then, apply these strategies to your reading and evaluation of the legislation. Be sure to share your understanding of the legislation with other readers.

Learning for Life

Researching the Immigrant Experience

Problem

The three collections you've studied thus far tell the stories of some of the earliest immigrants to America. The experiences of each early immigrant group were unique.

Project

Use library and community resources to research the experiences of one or more immigrant groups, past or present.

Preparation

Form a small research team. Agree on responsibilities for each team member. Decide which aspect, or aspects, of the immigrant experience each member will focus on.

Procedure

1. Research the experiences of one or more of the following groups on their journeys to America:
   - Africans brought to the United States to be enslaved
   - Irish who immigrated as a result of the potato famine in the 1840s
   - Jews who fled persecution in Europe and Russia
   - Cubans who fled from the Communist revolution
   - Vietnamese who came after the Vietnam War ended in 1975

   - other groups currently immigrating to the United States in large numbers from countries in the Caribbean, the Middle East, Latin America, East Asia, Africa, Europe, and other parts of the world

2. Supplement library research by interviewing people in your own community who are recent immigrants or who remember stories about grandparents, parents, or other relatives who immigrated to the United States.

3. Keep a record of all your sources. Evaluate and organize your information. Then prepare your presentation. You may want to focus on the following topics for the group or groups you are researching:
   - how the circumstances of the immigration affected the subsequent adjustment of the group in the United States
   - particular obstacles encountered in this country
   - important achievements and accomplishments
   - contributions to U.S. society
   - noteworthy individuals

Presentation

Present your research in one of the following formats (or another format that your teacher approves):

1. **Original Play**
   Write and present a play in which your team presents the story of an immigrant group or groups in the United States. Use props, costumes, food, music, and other audio and visual support.

2. **Time Line**
   As a class, collaborate on a wall-sized time line that includes names of immigrant groups, dates of significant events in the history of U.S. immigration, quotations, illustrations and photographs, and other data.

3. **Multimedia Presentation**
   Write a script based on your findings, and read it to the class, supplementing it with audio and visual aids: recorded music, photos, slides, overhead transparencies, posters, video or audio interviews, and props (clothing, food, art objects).

   No matter which format you choose, consider sharing your presentation with an audience outside the class: school, library, newspaper, TV station, or a cultural or ethnic club or association.

Processing

What did you learn about the immigrant experience by doing this project? For your portfolio, write your reflections on this statement: "Every American is descended from immigrants."

American
Romanticism

1800–1860

The Grand Canyon of the Yellowstone (1872) by Thomas Moran
(1837–1926). Oil on canvas (84″ × 144¼″).

American Romanticism

by Gary Q. Arpin

*. . . a glorification of yearning,
striving, and becoming . . .*
—David Perkins

The Pattern of the Journey

The journey—there is probably no pattern so common in all of
narrative literature, from the Bible, to the Greek epic the *Odyssey,* to
modern films like *The Wizard of Oz* and *Forrest Gump.* Very early in

Emigrants Crossing the Plains (detail) (1867) by Albert Bierstadt. Oil on canvas (67″ x 102″).

National Cowboy Hall of Fame and Western Heritage Center, Oklahoma City, Oklahoma.

his *Autobiography* (page 86), Benjamin Franklin describes in great detail an important American journey: a personal quest in which the young Ben leaves his home in Boston and travels to Philadelphia. The significance of Franklin's journey is clear: It is a declaration of independence, a move away from the constraints of his family and toward a city where he might prosper. It is, in other words, a quest for opportunity. Without stretching the metaphor too greatly, we can see in Franklin's journey an expression of both his personal goals and the goals of eighteenth-century America: a reaching out for independence, prosperity, commerce, and urbane civilization.

Franklin wrote about his journey to Philadelphia in 1771. In 1799, the American writer Charles Brockden Brown described a very different journey to Philadelphia in his Romantic novel *Arthur Mervyn.* In this tale a young farmboy hero leaves his home in the country for Philadelphia. Instead of finding a place of promise where he can make his dreams come true, however, the boy is plunged into a plague-ridden urban world of decay, corruption, and evil. The Philadelphia of this novel is no city of promise; it is an industrial hell that devours all hope and ambition.

The journeys described in Franklin's *Autobiography* and Brown's *Arthur Mervyn* make clear the differences between

The long-distance journey is part of our history, both real and fictional: Lewis and Clark, the pioneers in their Conestogas, the Joads in their overloaded jalopy. Something about the nation— its breadth, its variety, its vastness—beckons the adventurer, the eccentric, the fame seeker. Balloonists, glider pilots, joggers, and bladers. People on pogo sticks and unicycles.

—*The New York Times*
April 24, 1995

American Romanticism 1800–1860

James Fenimore Cooper. English. Engraving (4″ x 6″). The Granger Collection, New York.

William Wordsworth and Samuel Taylor Coleridge publish *Lyrical Ballads,* a landmark of English Romanticism, 1798

•

England's Mary Wollstonecraft publishes *A Vindication of the Rights of Woman,* 1792

William Cullen Bryant publishes "Thanatopsis," 1817

Noah Webster publishes a landmark dictionary of American English, 1828

•

James Fenimore Cooper publishes *The Pioneers,* 1823

•

Washington Irving publishes *The Sketch Book of Geoffrey Crayon, Gent.,* 1820

France's Alexis de Tocqueville publishes *Democracy in America,* a noted study of U.S. political and social institutions, 1835

•

John Greenleaf Whittier publishes *Justice and Expediency,* in which he calls for the abolition of slavery, 1833

•

Oliver Wendell Holmes publishes "Old Ironsides," 1830

1790–1809	1810–1819	1820–1829	1830–1839

First ten amendments, Bill of Rights, added to U.S. Constitution, 1791

•

Eli Whitney's improved cotton gin increases U.S. cotton cultivation and expands demand for slave labor, 1794

Smithsonian Institution.

•

U.S. population is 5.3 million, 1800

•

Washington, D.C., becomes U.S. capital, 1800

•

President Thomas Jefferson negotiates Louisiana Purchase from France, more than doubling U.S. territory, 1803

Miguel Hidalgo y Costilla launches the Mexican war of independence from Spain, 1810

•

In War of 1812, British burn much of Washington, D.C., 1814

•

Francis Scott Key, commemorating the War of 1812, writes "The Star-Spangled Banner," 1814

•

Napoleon I of France is defeated at Waterloo and subsequently exiled, 1815

•

Simón Bolívar, South American independence leader, becomes Greater Colombia's first president, 1819

Missouri admitted as a slave state, Maine as a free state, in Missouri Compromise, 1820–1821

•

Liberia founded on west coast of Africa as a settlement for freed U.S. slaves, 1822

•

Peru assures its independence by defeating Spain at Ayacucho, 1824

•

Erie Canal opens, connecting Great Lakes and Atlantic Ocean, 1825

•

Thomas Jefferson and John Adams die on same day, July 4, 1826

Underground Railroad, a secret system for helping fugitive slaves reach safety, is organized, c. 1830

•

Thomas Cole completes *The Oxbow,* an early Hudson River School Romantic landscape painting, 1836

•

Queen Victoria of England is crowned, 1837

•

U.S. Army forces Cherokees out of Georgia on long Trail of Tears to Oklahoma, 1838

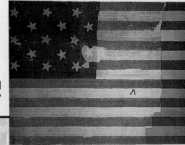

(Right) The flag that flew over Fort McHenry and inspired "The Star-Spangled Banner."

Margaret Fuller publishes *Woman in the Nineteenth Century,* the first full-length study of women's position in American society, 1845

•

Edgar Allan Poe publishes *The Raven and Other Poems,* 1845

•

Ralph Waldo Emerson publishes his first collection, *Essays,* including "Self-Reliance" and "The Over-Soul," 1841

Margaret Fuller. After a painting (c. 1872) by Alonzo Chappel.
The Granger Collection, New York.

James Russell Lowell publishes *The Biglow Papers,* satirical poems opposing the Mexican War and written in a Yankee dialect, 1848

Emily Dickinson begins to copy her poems into bound booklets, 1858

•

Henry David Thoreau publishes *Walden,* 1854

•

Herman Melville publishes *Moby-Dick; or, The Whale,* 1851

•

Nathaniel Hawthorne publishes *The Scarlet Letter,* 1850

Henry Wadsworth Longfellow (1871) by Theodore Wust. Watercolor on ivory.

Henry Wadsworth Longfellow publishes *The Courtship of Miles Standish,* 1858

•

Walt Whitman publishes the first edition of his book of poems, *Leaves of Grass,* 1855

1840–1849

1850–1859

U.S. population is 17.1 million, 1840

•

Brook Farm undertakes experiment in cooperative living, 1841–1847

•

By Treaty of Nanking, China cedes Hong Kong to Great Britain and opens five ports to foreign trade, 1842

•

First baseball game under rules resembling the modern sport played at Hoboken, N.J.; the New York Club defeats the Knickerbockers 23 to 1, 1846

•

U.S. annexes Texas, 1845; leads to war with Mexico, 1846–1848

Famine in Ireland due to potato crop failure causes increased emigration from Ireland to U.S., 1846

•

Lucretia Mott and Elizabeth Cady Stanton organize first women's rights convention in the U.S. at Seneca Falls, N.Y., 1848

•

California gold rush begins as thousands of gold miners travel to Sacramento area, 1849

Oberlin College established as one of first coeducational colleges in the U.S., 1837

•

The New York Times founded, 1851

•

Modern Republican Party organized to oppose the extension of slavery, 1854

•

After Indian revolt against British East India Company rule, British government takes over administration of India, 1858

Commodore Matthew Perry opens two Japanese ports to U.S. trade, 1854

•

U.S. Supreme Court's *Dred Scott* decision antagonizes antislavery forces, 1857

•

Abraham Lincoln and Stephen A. Douglas stage a noted series of seven debates as candidates for the Illinois seat in the U.S. Senate, 1858

The Granger Collection, New York.

Broadway at Spring Street (1855) by Hyppolite Sebron
(1801–1879). Oil on canvas (29$\frac{1}{4}$" × 42$\frac{1}{2}$").

THE CITY, GRIM
AND GRAY

In the first half of the nineteenth century, the largest American cities were Boston, Philadelphia, Baltimore, Charleston, and, largest of all, New York. The Romantic writers represented in this collection would have been very familiar with New York; some of them, like Washington Irving and William Cullen Bryant, even lived there. What was life like in the largest American city of the early 1800s?

Between 1820 and 1840, the population of New York more than doubled, from 124,000 to 312,000 people. In the 1830s, the first official tenements were built—buildings where a bathtub might be shared with four hundred people, where eight or more people might live in a single room without furniture, and where tenants might be ragpickers who kept their smelly stashes inside their homes. The soundtrack to the squalor and dinginess of life in one of these buildings might be provided by the bloodcurdling screeches of chickens being slaughtered indoors for the night's meal.

The city streets were fouled with droppings from the main source of transportation: horses. When a horse was injured in a collision or had collapsed from malnutrition or overwork, it was left to die on the curbside. Its body might remain on the street for days or weeks at a time. Given

the views of the rationalists and those of the Romantics. To Franklin and other rationalists, the city was a place to find success and self-realization. To the Romantic writers who came after Franklin, though, the city, far from being the seat of civilization, was often a place of moral ambiguity and, worse, of corruption and death.

The characteristic Romantic journey is to the countryside, which Romantics associated with independence, moral clarity, and healthful living. Sometimes, though, as in the works of Gothic-influenced writers like Edgar Allan Poe (page 260), the Romantic journey was a voyage to the country of the imagination. But whatever the destination of the Romantic journey, it was a flight both *from* something and *to* something. In fact, America's first truly popular professional writer is today known principally for an immortal story about an escape from civilization and responsibility. The writer was Washington Irving, and the escape was made by Rip Van Winkle (page 154).

American Romanticism can best be described as a journey away from the corruption of civilization and the limits of rational thought and toward the integrity of nature and the freedom of the imagination.

such conditions, it's no surprise that disease was rampant. In Manhattan in the summer of 1832, one third of the city's population—those who could afford to leave—left the city to escape a cholera epidemic that killed an average of one hundred people a day.

There were 20,000 homeless children on the streets of New York. Some worked in sweatshops, some sold toothpicks or newspapers, others turned to petty crime. If they lived to be twenty, they were lucky; disease, accidents, exposure, violence, and starvation took most of them long before that time.

Crime and violence were no strangers to the city. Waterfront gangs often included "pirates" who would kill for next to nothing. On the infamous Cherry Street, 15,000 sailors were robbed in a single year. Throughout the city, buildings sometimes burned to the ground while various competing fire companies fought with each other over who had the right to put out the fire. There were even riots on the streets: In 1834, men opposed to the abolition of slavery burned down homes, churches, and a school, trying to destroy free African Americans and their supporters.

There was one bright spot in the picture of squalor and degradation, though: talk in the 1840s of constructing a huge and expensive city park, to be built for "health and recreation." It was the poet William Cullen Bryant's idea—a dream of bringing a taste of the blessed countryside to a city wracked with poverty, illness, and crime. But New Yorkers would have to wait until after the Civil War for their oasis: Central Park would not become a completed reality until 1876.

Culver Pictures.

A tenement-house alley gang.

The Romantic Sensibility: Celebrating the Imagination

In general, **Romanticism** is the name given to those schools of thought that value feeling and intuition over reason. The first rumblings of Romanticism were felt in Germany in the second half of the eighteenth century. Romanticism had a strong influence on literature, music, and painting in Europe and England well into the nineteenth century. But Romanticism came relatively late to America, and, as you will see in this collection and in the collections that follow, it took different forms.

Romanticism, especially in Europe, developed in part as a reaction against **rationalism.** In the sooty wake of the Industrial Revolution, with its squalid cities and wretched working conditions, people had come to realize the limits of reason. The Romantics came to believe that the imagination was able to apprehend truths that the rational mind could not reach. These truths were usually accompanied by powerful emotion and associated with natural, unspoiled beauty. To the Romantic sensibility the imagination, spontaneity, individual feelings, and wild nature were of greater value than reason, logic, planning, and cultivation. The Romantics did not flatly reject

> The question of common sense is always "What is it good for?"—a question which would abolish the rose and be answered triumphantly by the cabbage.
>
> —James Russell Lowell

logical thought as invalid for all purposes. But for the purpose of art, they placed a new premium on intuitive, "felt" experience.

To the Romantic mind, poetry was the highest and most sublime embodiment of the imagination. Romantic artists often contrasted poetry with science, which they saw as destroying the very truth it claimed to seek. Edgar Allan Poe, for example, called science a "vulture" with wings of "dull realities," preying on the hearts of poets.

Romanticism, originally a European movement, emphasized feeling and intuition over reason, sought wisdom in natural beauty, and valued poetry above all other works of the imagination.

Romantic Escapism: From Dull Realities to Higher Realms

The Romantics wanted to rise above "dull realities" to a realm of higher truth. They did this in two principal ways. First, the Romantics searched for exotic settings in the more "natural" past or in a world far removed from the grimy and noisy industrial age. Sometimes they found this world in the supernatural realm, or in old legends and folklore. Second, the Romantics tried to contemplate the natural world until dull reality fell away to reveal underlying beauty and truth.

We can most easily see the first Romantic approach in the development of the Gothic novel, with its wild, haunted landscapes, supernatural events, and mysterious medieval castles.

> ## Characteristics of American Romanticism
>
> - Values feeling and intuition over reason
> - Places faith in inner experience and the power of the imagination
> - Shuns the artificiality of civilization and seeks unspoiled nature
> - Prefers youthful innocence to educated sophistication
> - Champions individual freedom and the worth of the individual
> - Contemplates nature's beauty as a path to spiritual and moral development
> - Looks backward to the wisdom of the past and distrusts progress
> - Finds beauty and truth in exotic locales, the supernatural realm, and the inner world of the imagination
> - Sees poetry as the highest expression of the imagination
> - Finds inspiration in myth, legend, and folk culture

F Street, Washington, D.C. (1821) by Baroness Hyde de Neuville (c. 1749–1849). Watercolor and pencil ($7^1/_2$" × $9^7/_8$").
© Collection of the New-York Historical Society.

Illustration by Wilfred Satty for Edgar Allan Poe's "The Fall of the House of Usher."

The Gothic, with its roots in French, German, and English literature, seemed an unlikely transplant to the new nation of America, where there were seemingly no places old enough to have accumulated a contingent of ghosts or to reek of the decay of ages. But even writers in America, notably Edgar Allan Poe, were attracted to the exotic, otherworldly trappings of the Gothic. In America, particularly in the works of Poe, the Gothic took a turn toward the psychological exploration of the human mind.

The second Romantic approach, the contemplation of the natural world, is evident in many lyric poems. In a typical Romantic poem, the speaker sees a commonplace object or event. A flower found by a stream or a waterfowl flying overhead brings the speaker to some important, deeply felt insight, which is then recorded in the poem. This contemplative process is similar to the way the Puritans drew moral lessons from nature. The difference is one of emphasis and goal. The Puritans' lessons were defined by their religion. In nature they found the God they knew from the Bible. The Romantics, on the other hand, found a far less clearly defined divinity in nature. Their contemplation of the natural world led to a more generalized emotional and intellectual awakening.

> They who dream by day are cognizant of many things which escape those who dream only by night.
>
> —Edgar Allan Poe

American Romanticism took two roads on the journey to understanding higher truths. One road led to the exploration of the past and of exotic, even supernatural, realms; the other road led to the contemplation of the natural world.

The American Novel and the Wilderness Experience

During the Romantic period, the big question about American literature was: Would American writers continue to imitate the English and European models, or would they finally develop a distinctive literature of their own? While the Romantic poets of the period were still staying close to traditional forms, American novelists were discovering that the subject matter available to them was very different from the subjects available to European writers. America provided a sense of limitless frontiers that Europe, so long settled, simply did not possess. Thus, the development of the American novel coincided with westward expansion, with the growth of a nationalist spirit, and with the rapid spread of cities. All these factors tended to reinforce the idealization of frontier life. A "geography of the imagination" developed, in which town, country, and frontier would play a powerful role in American life and literature—as they continue to do today.

> You steal Englishmen's books and think Englishmen's thoughts,
> With their salt on her tail your wild eagle is caught;
> Your literature suits its each whisper and motion
> To what will be thought of it over the ocean.
>
> —James Russell Lowell, *from A Fable for Critics*

We can see how the novel developed in America by looking at the early career of James Fenimore Cooper (1789–1851). Cooper's first novel, *Precaution* (1820), describes life in an English country vicarage. His second novel, *The Spy* (1821), was influenced by the romances of the Scottish novelist Sir Walter Scott, though it is set during the American Revolution. It was in his third novel, *The Pioneers* (1823), that Cooper finally broke free of European constraints. In this novel, Cooper explored uniquely American settings and characters: frontier communities, American Indians, backwoodsmen, and the wilderness of western New York and Pennsylvania. Most of all, he created the first American heroic figure: Natty Bumppo (also known variously as Hawkeye, Deerslayer, and Leatherstocking), a heroic, virtuous, skillful frontiersman whose simple morality, love of nature, distrust of town life, and almost superhuman resourcefulness mark him as a true Romantic hero. It was this character who appeared in the rest of the Leatherstocking tales—a highly popular series of sequels that Cooper wrote over the next eighteen years.

Title page of *The Deerslayer* (1925) illustrated by N. C. Wyeth (1882–1945).

American novelists looked to westward expansion and the development of the frontier for inspiration, creating subject matter that broke with European tradition.

Hurd-La Rinconada Gallery, San Patricio, New Mexico.

The Deerslayer (detail) (1925) illustrated by N. C. Wyeth (1882–1945).

A New Kind of Hero

Most Europeans had an image of the American as unsophisticated and uncivilized. This was a stereotype that Ben Franklin, when he lived in France, took great pains to demonstrate was unfair and untrue. But Cooper and other Romantic novelists who followed him took no such pains. Instead, by creating such heroes as Natty Bumppo, they turned the insult on its head. Virtue, they implied, was in American innocence, not in European sophistication. Eternal truths were waiting to be discovered not in dusty libraries or crowded cities or glittering court life, but in the American wilderness that was unknown and unavailable to Europeans.

It has been a matter of marvel to my European readers, that a man from the wilds of America should express himself in tolerable English. I was looked upon as something new and strange in American literature. . . .

—Washington Irving

Cooper's Natty Bumppo is a triumph of American innocence and an example of one of the most important outgrowths of the early American novel: the American Romantic hero. Here at last was a new kind of heroic figure, one quite different from the hero of the Age of Reason. The rationalist hero—exemplified by a real-life figure such as Ben Franklin—was worldly, educated, sophisticated, and bent on making a place for himself in civilization. The typical hero of American Romantic fiction, on the other hand, was youthful, innocent, intuitive, and close to nature. He was also, by today's standards, hopelessly uneasy with women, who were usually seen (by male writers, at least) to represent civilization and the impulse to "domesticate."

Today, Americans still create Romantic heroes; the twentieth-century descendants of Natty Bumppo are all around us. They can be found in the guise of dozens of pop culture heroes: the Lone Ranger, Superman, Luke Skywalker, Indiana Jones, and any number of Western, detective, and fantasy heroes.

His face would have had little to recommend it except youth, were it not for an expression that seldom failed to win upon those who had leisure to examine it, and to yield to the feeling of confidence it created. This expression was simply that of guileless truth, sustained by an earnestness of purpose, and a sincerity of feeling, that rendered it remarkable.

—James Fenimore Cooper, describing Natty Bumppo, from *The Deerslayer*

20th Century Fox (Courtesy Kobal).

Daniel Day-Lewis as Natty Bumppo in the movie *The Last of the Mohicans* (1992).

Harrison Ford in the movie *Raiders of the Lost Ark* (1981).

Photofest.

The American Romantic hero possesses qualities of youthfulness, innocence, intuitiveness, and closeness to the natural world that set him solidly apart from the hero of the Age of Reason.

American Romantic Poetry: Read at Every Fireside

The American Romantic novelists looked for new subject matter and innovative themes, but the opposite tendency appears in the works of the Romantic poets represented in this collection. Like Franklin, these Romantic poets wanted to prove that Americans were not unsophisticated hicks, and they attempted to prove this by working solidly within European literary traditions rather than by crafting a different and unique American voice. Even when they constructed poems with American settings and subject matter, the American Romantic poets used typically English themes, meter, and imagery. In a sense, they wrote in a style that a cultivated person from England who had recently immigrated to America might be expected to use.

In many respects the American poets in this collection looked backward—over their shoulders, as it were—at established European literary models. Their poetry was limited by this slavish devotion to tradition and by their own allegiance to standard meter and diction, which resulted in poems with skillful but predictable "dum-de-dum" rhythms. Yet, for generations, many of their poems were staples of home and school reading.

In fact, the Fireside Poets, as the Boston group of Henry Wadsworth Longfellow (page 175), John Greenleaf Whittier (page 181), Oliver Wendell Holmes (page 187), and James Russell Lowell (1819–1891) was called, were, in their own time and for many decades afterward, the most popular poets America had ever produced. In many ways their popularity has never been matched. They were called "Fireside Poets" because their poems were so often read aloud at the fireside as family entertainment. They were also sometimes called "Schoolroom Poets" because their poems were, for many years, memorized and recited in American classrooms.

Although the Fireside Poets' attempts to create a new American literature relied too reverently on the literature of the past, we should not view them only as backward-looking traditionalists. Certainly, they were not great innovators. Their choice of subject matter—love, patriotism, nature, family, God, and religion—was, for the most part, comforting rather than challenging to their audience. Their poetry could be preachy and didactic, their symbolism could be heavy and obvious, and they often wrote in a "pretty" or pleasing style that took the edge off their messages. (A well-

Characteristics of the American Romantic Hero

- Is young, or possesses youthful qualities
- Is innocent and pure of purpose
- Has a sense of honor based not on society's rules but on some higher principle
- Has a knowledge of people and of life based on deep, intuitive understanding, not on formal learning
- Loves nature and avoids town life
- Quests for some higher truth in the natural world

loved inspirational "Fireside" poem is on the right.) However, Whittier, for one, wrote powerful anti-slavery poems, and all of the Fireside Poets furthered the evolution of American poetry by introducing uniquely American subject matter in their choices of topics: American folk themes, descriptions of the American landscape, abolitionist issues, American Indian culture, and celebrations of American people, places, and events.

Limited by their essential literary conservatism, the Fireside Poets were unable to recognize the poetry of the future, which was being written right under their noses. Whittier's response in 1855 to reading the first volume of a certain poet's work was to throw the book into the fire. Ralph Waldo Emerson's response was much more far-sighted. "I greet you," Emerson wrote to this maverick new poet, Walt Whitman, "at the beginning of a great career."

The Fireside Poets, immensely popular in their time, created some poems of lasting merit, but their essential literary conservatism prevented them from being truly innovative. The first uniquely American poetry was yet to be created.

Quickwrite
Rationalist or Romantic?

If you had to classify yourself as either a rationalist or a Romantic, which would you be? Would you be a practical, ambitious, worldly Benjamin Franklin or an intuitive, close-to-nature Romantic? Which traits—of either school of thought—do you truly value and think you would like to encourage in your own life? Freewrite an exploration of your thoughts on this issue.

A Psalm of Life

Tell me not, in mournful numbers,
    Life is but an empty dream!
For the soul is dead that slumbers,
    And things are not what they seem.

Life is real—life is earnest—
    And the grave is not its goal:
Dust thou art, to dust returnest,
    Was not spoken of the soul.

Not enjoyment, and not sorrow,
    Is our destined end or way;
But to *act*, that each tomorrow
    Find us farther than today.

Art is long, and time is fleeting,
    And our hearts, though stout and brave,
Still, like muffled drums, are beating
    Funeral marches to the grave.

In the world's broad field of battle,
    In the bivouac of Life,
Be not like dumb, driven cattle!
    Be a hero in the strife!

Trust no Future, howe'er pleasant!
    Let the dead Past bury its dead!
Act—act in the glorious Present!
    Heart within, and God o'erhead!

Lives of great men all remind us
    We can make *our* lives sublime,
And, departing, leave behind us
    Footsteps on the sands of time.

Footsteps, that, perhaps another,
    Sailing o'er life's solemn main,
A forlorn and shipwrecked brother,
    Seeing, shall take heart again.

Let us then be up and doing,
    With a heart for any fate;
Still achieving, still pursuing,
    Learn to labor and to wait.

—Henry Wadsworth Longfellow

THE TRANSFORMING IMAGINATION

Collection 4

Irving
Bryant
Longfellow
Whittier
Holmes

A Blessing

Just off the highway to Rochester, Minnesota,
Twilight bounds softly forth on the grass,
And the eyes of those two Indian ponies
Darken with kindness.
They have come gladly out of the willows
To welcome my friend and me.
We step over the barbed wire into the pasture
Where they have been grazing all day, alone.
They ripple tensely, they can hardly contain their happiness
That we have come.
They bow shyly as wet swans. They love each other.
There is no loneliness like theirs.
At home once more,
They begin munching the young tufts of spring in the darkness.
I would like to hold the slenderer one in my arms,
For she has walked over to me
And nuzzled my left hand.
She is black and white,
Her mane falls wild on her forehead,
And the light breeze moves me to caress her long ear
That is delicate as the skin over a girl's wrist.
Suddenly I realize
That if I stepped out of my body I would break
Into blossom.

—James Wright (1927–1980)

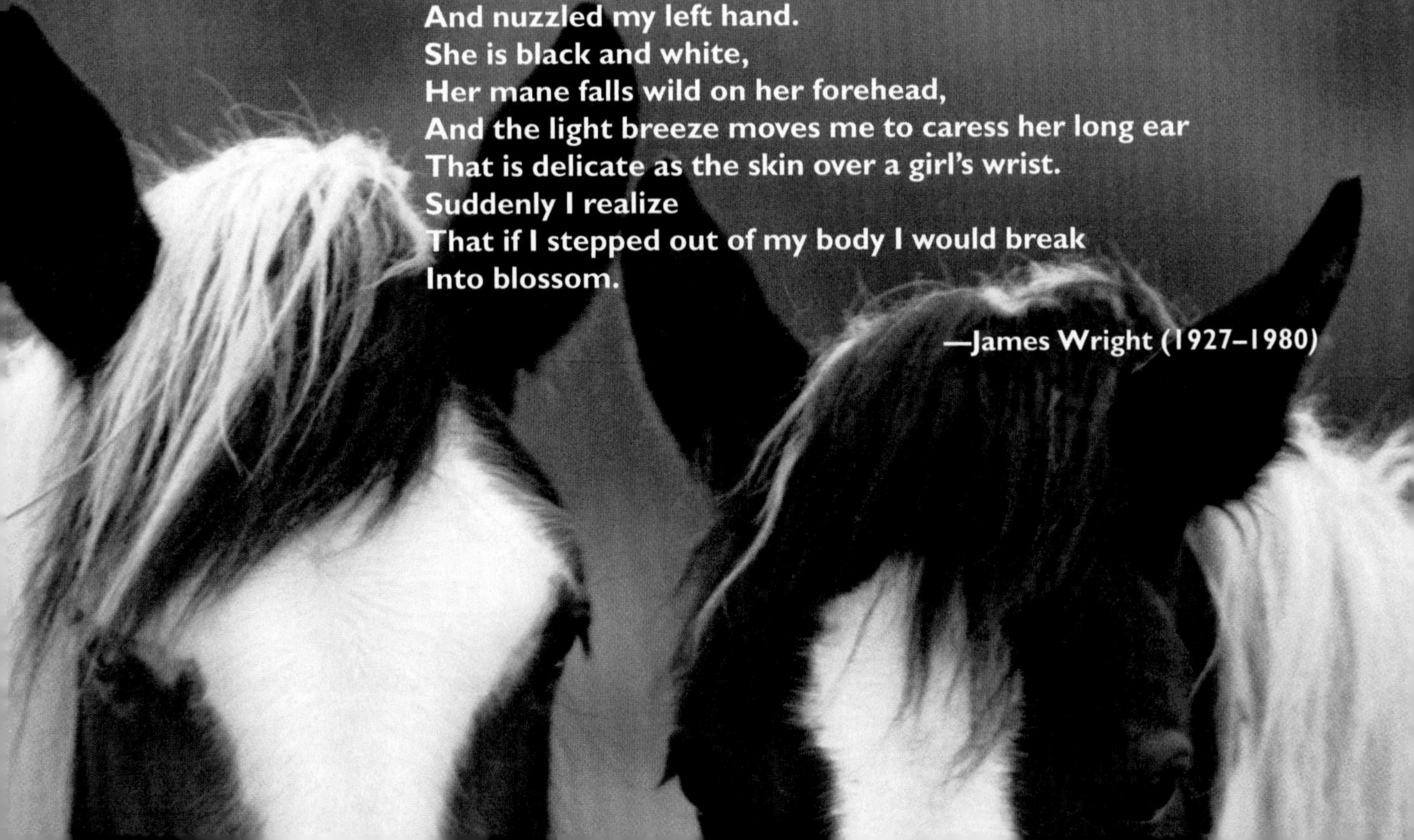

Washington Irving

(1783–1859)

Many people in Europe and England felt that America would never develop a literary voice of its own. But then came Washington Irving, the youngest and not-too-well-educated son of a pious hardware importer and his amiable wife. Irving, who was from New York City, had a genius for inventing comic fictional narrators. (In fact, he did not sign his real name to his work until he was over fifty.) The first of these narrators Irving called Jonathan Oldstyle, Gent.—a caricature of those British writers who could not accept the simple values of the new nation.

Irving's second invented narrator was called Diedrich Knickerbocker. Irving pretended that Knickerbocker was the author of a book called *A History of New York, from the Beginning of the World to the End of the Dutch Dynasty.* The mysterious Knickerbocker is supposed to have left the manuscript to his landlord in payment of back rent. This fake and comical history, in which the entire American past is ridiculed, established Washington Irving as the foremost New York satirist.

All this time Irving was enjoying the literary societies that were popular then in New York. His interest in law, which he practiced half-heartedly, was lukewarm. In 1815, he was sent off by his father to Liverpool, England, to look after the failing overseas branch of the family business. Irving found the business beyond repair, but he loved the British literary scene and stayed abroad for seventeen years. He was particularly attracted to the works of the Romantic novelist Sir Walter Scott (1771–1832), who gave Irving advice that was to make his reputation. Scott told the younger writer to read the German Romantics and find inspiration in folklore and legends.

Now Irving made the decision he had previously lacked the courage to make. He decided against putting further energy into business and its "sordid, dusty, soul-killing way of life." He would now give himself entirely to writing. In 1817, Irving began to write the first drafts of stories based on German folk tales. These were narrated by yet another of Irving's comic voices, Geoffrey Crayon, and the stories were collected under the title *The Sketch Book* (1819–1820). This book carried Irving to the summit of international success.

Washington Irving (1809) by John Wesley Jarvis (1780–1840). Oil on wood panel (33″ × 26″).

Something about Irving's comic narrators touched a responsive chord in the American public. Even though Irving borrowed openly from a European past, he brought to his material a droll new voice, as inflated as a preacher's or politician's at one moment, self-mocking the next. It was a voice the new nation recognized as its own.

Irving gave his country its first international literary celebrity. This was a role Irving enjoyed exploiting to the fullest. He had always loved parties and people and praise. Now he had access to the literary circles of the world. It was a remarkable achievement for the unpromising child of a middle-class American family.

Irving never again wrote anything that matched the success of the two great comic tales in *The Sketch Book.* Today we remember Irving for Rip Van Winkle who slept through the American Revolution, and the Headless Horseman who plagued the lovelorn Yankee schoolteacher Ichabod Crane in the dreamy glen of Sleepy Hollow, in New York's lush Hudson Valley.

Historic Hudson Valley, Tarrytown, New York.

Before You Read

RIP VAN WINKLE

Make the Connection

What if, instead of moving along with the rest of the world, you were placed in suspended animation for twenty years? When you woke from your "nap," your expectations and views would be the same as they were when you fell "asleep." The world, however, would be very different.

Reading Skills and Strategies

Drawing Inferences and Making Predictions

An **inference** is an educated guess based on clues in the text and your own knowledge and experience. A **prediction** is a special type of inference—an educated guess about what will happen later. Some predictions may not turn out to be accurate, and adjusting them is an essential part of active reading. As you read "Rip Van Winkle," take notes in chart form. First, identify a clue that suggests or **foreshadows** what might happen further into the story. (Pictures that illustrate the story can be the basis of your predictions too.) Make a prediction based on the clue. Later, note what actually happens. Repeat this process as you read.

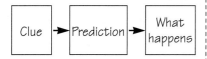

A good writer always surprises you. That is the pleasure of actively participating in a story—you are engaged with the writer in a game of wits.

Elements of Literature

Setting

Misty mountaintops, a mysterious forest, an old-fashioned village, a distant era—these are some details of **setting** that Irving uses in "Rip Van Winkle." Like many Romantic writers, Irving was fascinated by times past and by wild, natural landscapes. In this story it is setting that effects a magical change in the hero and sets the **plot** in motion.

> **S**etting is the physical, geographical, and historical environment in which a story takes place.
>
> *For more on Setting, see the Handbook of Literary Terms.*

Background

Even for its first readers in 1819, "Rip Van Winkle" was a story about times past. The story begins just before the Revolutionary War, which started in 1775—before Irving was even born. Irving draws on the history of the America he knew during his childhood, when George Washington was everyone's hero and the Democrats and Federalists were the young nation's two political parties.

"It was with some difficulty that he found the way to his own house." From *Rip Van Winkle* (New York: David McKay, 1921) illustrated by N. C. Wyeth (1882–1945). Oil on canvas (48″ × 38″).

Millport Conservancy and Museum.

Rip Van Winkle

A Posthumous Writing of Diedrich Knickerbocker

Washington Irving

The following tale was found among the papers of the late Diedrich Knickerbocker, an old gentleman of New York, who was very curious in the Dutch history of the province, and the manners of the descendants from its primitive settlers. His historical researches, however, did not lie so much among books, as among men; for the former are lamentably scanty on his favorite topics; whereas he found the old burghers,[1] and still more, their wives, rich in that legendary lore so invaluable to true history. Whenever, therefore, he happened upon a genuine Dutch family, snugly shut up in its low roofed farmhouse, under a spreading sycamore, he looked upon it as a little clasped volume of black letter,[2] and studied it with the zeal of a bookworm.

The result of all these researches was a history of the province, during the reign of the Dutch governors, which he published some years since. There have been various opinions as to the literary character of his work and, to tell the truth, it is not a whit better than it should be. Its chief merit is its <u>scrupulous</u> accuracy, which indeed was a little <u>questioned</u> on its first appearance, but has since been completely established; and it is now admitted into all historical collections as a book of unquestionable authority.

The old gentleman died shortly after the publication of his work, and now that he is dead and gone, it cannot do much harm to his memory to say that his time might have been much better employed in weightier labors. He, however, was apt to ride his hobby his own way; and though it did now and then kick up the dust a little in the eyes of his neighbors, and grieve the spirit of some friends for whom he felt the truest deference and affection; yet his errors and follies are remembered "more in sorrow than in anger," and it begins to be suspected that he never intended to injure or offend. But however his memory may be appreciated by critics, it is still held dear by many folk whose good opinion is well worth having; particularly by certain biscuit bakers, who have gone so far as to imprint his likeness on their New Year cakes, and have thus given him a chance for immortality, almost equal to being stamped on a Waterloo[3] medal, or a Queen Anne's farthing.[4]

---

1. **burghers:** citizens.
2. **black letter:** ornamental printing font, now called Old English or Gothic.

3. **Waterloo:** Belgian town where the British and their allies finally defeated Napoleon I, emperor of France, on June 18, 1815.
4. **farthing:** former British coin worth one fourth of a British penny.

WORDS TO OWN

scrupulous (skrōō′pyə·ləs) *adj.*: careful; painstaking.

Whoever has made a voyage up the Hudson must remember the Kaatskill[5] Mountains. They are a dismembered branch of the great Appalachian family, and are seen away to the west of the river swelling up to noble height and lording it over the surrounding country. Every change of season, every change of weather, indeed every hour of the day, produces some change in the magical hues and shapes of these mountains, and they are regarded by all the good wives far and near as perfect barometers. When the weather is fair and settled they are clothed in blue and purple, and print their bold outlines on the clear evening sky; but sometimes, when the rest of the landscape is cloudless, they will gather a hood of gray vapors about their summits, which, in the last rays of the setting sun, will glow and light up like a crown of glory.

Title page of *Rip Van Winkle* (1921) illustrated by N. C. Wyeth. Lithograph.

At the foot of these fairy mountains the voyager may have descried the light smoke curling up from a village, whose shingle roofs gleam among the trees, just where the blue tints of the upland melt away into the fresh green of the nearer landscape. It is a little village of great antiquity, having been founded by some of the Dutch colonists in the early times of the province, just about the beginning of the government of the good Peter Stuyvesant[6] (may he rest in peace!), and there were some of the houses of the original settlers standing within a few years; built of small yellow bricks brought from Holland, having latticed windows and gable fronts, surmounted with weathercocks.

In that same village, and in one of these very houses (which to tell the precise truth was sadly timeworn and weather-beaten) there lived many years since, while the country was yet a province of Great Britain, a simple good-natured fellow of the name of Rip Van Winkle. He was a descendant of the Van Winkles who figured so gallantly in the chivalrous days of Peter Stuyvesant, and accompanied him to the siege of Fort Christina.[7] He inherited, however, but little of the martial character of his ancestors. I have observed that he was a simple good-natured man; he was moreover a kind neighbor, and an obedient, henpecked husband. Indeed to the latter circumstance might be owing that meekness of spirit which gained him such universal popularity; for those men are most apt to be obsequious and conciliating abroad, who are under the discipline of shrews at home. Their tempers doubtless are rendered pliant and malleable in the fiery furnace of domestic tribulation, and a curtain lecture[8] is worth all the sermons in the world for teaching the virtues of patience and long-suffering. A termagant[9] wife may therefore in some respects be considered a tolerable blessing—and if so, Rip Van Winkle was thrice blessed.

Certain it is that he was a great favorite among all the good wives of the village, who as usual with the amiable sex, took his part in all family squabbles, and never failed, whenever they talked those matters over in their evening gossipings, to lay all the blame on Dame[10] Van Winkle. The

7. Fort Christina: Delaware's first permanent settlement; founded by Swedish colonists on the Delaware River and captured by Stuyvesant from the Swedes in 1655. Present-day site of Wilmington, Delaware.
8. curtain lecture: scolding delivered by a wife to her husband, from behind the curtains of an old-fashioned bed.
9. termagant (tur′mə·gənt): abusive; scolding.
10. Dame: title formerly used for the woman in charge of a household.

5. Kaatskill: original Dutch spelling of *Catskill*.
6. Peter Stuyvesant (stī′və·sənt): last Dutch governor of New Netherland (1647–1664), a Dutch colony in America. Irving is being ironic here. Stuyvesant was unpopular with the Dutch colonists, who considered him intolerant and harsh.

WORDS TO OWN

obsequious (əb·sē′kwē·əs) *adj.*: overly obedient; submissive.
malleable (mal′ē·ə·bəl) *adj.*: capable of being shaped.
amiable (ā′mē·ə·bəl) *adj.*: agreeable; likable.

children of the village too would shout with joy whenever he approached. He assisted at their sports, made their playthings, taught them to fly kites and shoot marbles, and told them long stories of ghosts, witches, and Indians. Whenever he went dodging about the village he was surrounded by a troop of them hanging on his skirts, clambering on his back and playing a thousand tricks on him with impunity; and not a dog would bark at him throughout the neighborhood.

The great error in Rip's composition was an insuperable aversion to all kinds of profitable labor. It could not be from the want of assiduity[11] or perseverance; for he would sit on a wet rock, with a rod as long and heavy as a Tartar's lance,[12] and fish all day without a murmur, even though he should not be encouraged by a single nibble. He would carry a fowling piece[13] on his shoulder for hours together, trudging through woods, and swamps and up hill and down dale, to shoot a few squirrels or wild pigeons; he would never refuse to assist a neighbor even in the roughest toil, and was a foremost man at all country frolics for husking Indian corn, or building stone fences; the women of the village too used to employ him to run their errands and to do such little odd jobs as their less obliging husbands would not do for them—in a word Rip was ready to attend to anybody's business but his own; but as to doing family duty, and keeping his farm in order, he found it impossible.

In fact he declared it was of no use to work on his farm; it was the most pestilent little piece of ground in the whole country; everything about it went wrong and would go wrong in spite of him. His fences were continually falling to pieces; his cow would either go astray or get among the cabbages; weeds were sure to grow quicker in his fields than anywhere else; the rain always made a point of setting in just as he had some outdoor work to do. So that though his patrimonial estate had dwindled away under his management, acre by acre until there was little more left than a mere

patch of Indian corn and potatoes, yet it was the worst-conditioned farm in the neighborhood.

His children too were as ragged and wild as if they belonged to nobody. His son Rip, an urchin begotten in his own likeness, promised to inherit the habits with the old clothes of his father. He was generally seen trooping like a colt at his mother's heels, equipped in a pair of his father's castoff galligaskins,[14] which he had much ado to hold up with one hand, as a fine lady does her train in bad weather.

Rip Van Winkle, however, was one of those happy mortals of foolish, well-oiled dispositions, who take the world easy, eat white bread or brown, whichever can be got with least thought or trouble, and would rather starve on a penny than work for a pound. If left to himself, he would have whistled life away in perfect contentment, but his wife kept continually dinning in his ears about his idleness, his carelessness, and the ruin he was bringing on his family. Morning, noon, and night, her tongue was incessantly going, and everything he said or did was sure to produce a torrent of household eloquence. Rip had but one way of replying to all lectures of the kind, and that by frequent use had grown into a habit. He shrugged his shoulders, shook his head, cast up his eyes, but said nothing. This, however, always provoked a fresh volley from his wife, so that he was fain to draw off his forces and take to the outside of the house—the only side which in truth belongs to a henpecked husband.

Rip's sole domestic adherent was his dog Wolf who was as much henpecked as his master, for Dame Van Winkle regarded them as companions in idleness, and even looked upon Wolf with an evil eye as the cause of his master's going so often astray. True it is, in all points of spirit befitting an honorable dog, he was as courageous an animal as ever scoured the woods—but what courage can withstand the ever-during and all-besetting[15] terrors of a woman's tongue? The moment Wolf entered the house his crest fell, his tail drooped to the ground or curled between his legs, he sneaked about with a gallows air,[16] casting many a

---

11. assiduity (as′ə·dyoo′ə·tē): close and continuous application of effort.

12. Tartar's lance: Tartars, now usually spelled Tatars, are a Turkic-speaking people of Europe and Asia. When they invaded China and eastern Europe in the thirteenth century, each Tatar cavalryman carried a battle-ax, a sword, and a twelve-foot lance.

13. fowling piece: shotgun used in hunting wild birds.

14. galligaskins (gal′i·gas′kinz): loose, baggy pants.

15. ever-during and all-besetting: everlasting and continually attacking.

16. with a gallows air: like someone condemned to be hanged.

sidelong glance at Dame Van Winkle, and at the least flourish of a broomstick or ladle he would fly to the door with yelping precipitation.[17]

Times grew worse and worse with Rip Van Winkle as years of matrimony rolled on; a tart temper never mellows with age, and a sharp tongue is the only edged tool that grows keener with constant use. For a long while he used to console himself when driven from home, by frequenting a kind of perpetual club of the sages, philosophers, and other idle personages of the village which held its sessions on a bench before a small inn, designated by a rubicund portrait of his majesty George the Third. Here they used to sit in the shade, through a long lazy summer's day, talking listlessly over village gossip, or telling endless sleepy stories about nothing. But it would have been worth any statesman's money to have heard the profound discussions that sometimes took place, when by chance an old newspaper fell into their hands from some passing traveler. How solemnly they would listen to the contents as drawled out by Derrick Van Bummel the schoolmaster, a dapper, learned little man, who was not to be daunted by the most gigantic word in the dictionary; and how sagely they would deliberate upon public events some months after they had taken place.

The opinions of this junto[18] were completely controlled by Nicholaus Vedder, a patriarch of the village, and landlord of the inn, at the door of which he took his seat from morning till night, just moving sufficiently to avoid the sun and keep in the shade of a large tree; so that the neighbors could tell the hour by his movements as accurately as by a sundial. It is true he was rarely heard to speak, but smoked his pipe incessantly. His adherents, however (for every great man has his adherents), perfectly understood him and knew how to gather his opinions. When anything that was read or related displeased him, he was observed to smoke his pipe <u>vehemently</u>, and to send forth short, frequent, and angry puffs; but when pleased he would inhale the smoke slowly and tranquilly and emit it in light and <u>placid</u> clouds, and sometimes taking the pipe from his mouth

and letting the fragrant vapor curl about his nose, would gravely nod his head in token of perfect approbation.

From even this stronghold the unlucky Rip was at length routed by his termagant wife who would suddenly break in upon the tranquility of the assemblage and call the members all to naught; nor was that august personage Nicholaus Vedder himself sacred from the daring tongue of this terrible virago,[19] who charged him outright with encouraging her husband in habits of idleness.

Poor Rip was at last reduced almost to despair; and his only alternative to escape from the labor of the farm and the clamor of his wife, was to take gun in hand and stroll away into the woods. Here he would sometimes seat himself at the foot of a tree and share the contents of his wallet[20] with Wolf, with whom he sympathized as a fellow sufferer in persecution. "Poor Wolf," he would say, "thy mistress leads thee a dog's life of it, but never mind my lad, whilst I live thou shalt never want a friend to stand by thee!" Wolf would wag his tail, look wistfully in his master's face, and if dogs can feel pity I verily believe he reciprocated the sentiment with all his heart.

In a long ramble of the kind on a fine autumnal day, Rip had unconsciously scrambled to one of the highest parts of the Kaatskill Mountains. He was after his favorite sport of squirrel shooting and the still solitudes had echoed and reechoed with the reports of his gun. Panting and fatigued he threw himself, late in the afternoon, on a green knoll, covered with mountain herbage, that crowned the brow of a precipice. From an opening between the trees he could overlook all the lower country for many a mile of rich woodland. He saw at a distance the lordly Hudson, far, far below him, moving on its silent but majestic course, with the reflection of a purple cloud, or the sail of a lagging bark[21] here and there sleeping on its glassy bosom, and at last losing itself in the blue highlands.

19. virago (vi·rā′gō): quarrelsome, scolding woman.
20. wallet: knapsack.
21. lagging bark: slow-moving boat.

- -

WORDS TO OWN

vehemently (vē′ə·mənt·lē) *adv.*: emphatically.
placid (plas′id) *adj.*: calm; quiet.

- -

17. precipitation: haste; suddenness.
18. junto (jun′tō): council; group with a common purpose.

Rip Chased from Home by His Wife (detail) (1880) by Albertus Del Orient Browere
(1814–1887). Oil on canvas (36″ × 50″).

On the other side he looked down into a deep mountain glen, wild, lonely, and shagged, the bottom filled with fragments from the impending cliffs and scarcely lighted by the reflected rays of the setting sun. For some time Rip lay musing on this scene, evening was gradually advancing, the mountains began to throw their long blue shadows over the valleys, he saw that it would be dark, long before he could reach the village, and he heaved a heavy sigh when he thought of encountering the terrors of Dame Van Winkle.

As he was about to descend he heard a voice from a distance hallooing "Rip Van Winkle! Rip Van Winkle!" He looked around, but could see nothing but a crow winging its solitary flight across the mountain. He thought his fancy must have deceived him and turned again to descend, when he heard the same cry ring through the still evening air: "Rip Van Winkle! Rip Van Winkle!"— at the same time Wolf bristled up his back and giving a low growl, skulked to his master's side, looking fearfully down into the glen. Rip now felt a vague apprehension stealing over him; he looked anxiously in the same direction and perceived a strange figure slowly toiling up the rocks and bending under the weight of something he carried on his back. He was surprised to see any human being in this lonely and unfrequented place, but supposing it to be someone of the neighborhood in need of his assistance he hastened down to yield it.

On nearer approach he was still more surprised at the singularity of the stranger's appearance. He was a short, square-built old fellow, with thick bushy hair and a grizzled beard. His dress was of the antique Dutch fashion, a cloth jerkin[22] strapped round the waist, several pair of breeches, the outer one of ample volume decorated with rows of buttons down the sides and bunches at the knees. He bore on his shoulder a stout keg that seemed full of liquor, and made signs for Rip to approach and assist him with the load. Though rather shy and distrustful of this new acquaintance Rip complied with his usual alacrity, and mutually relieving each other they clambered up a narrow gully apparently the dry

22. **jerkin** (jʉr′kin): sleeveless jacket.

bed of a mountain torrent. As they ascended, Rip every now and then heard long rolling peals like distant thunder, that seemed to issue out of a deep ravine or rather cleft between lofty rocks, toward which their rugged path conducted. He paused for an instant, but supposing it to be the muttering of one of those transient thundershowers which often take place in mountain heights, he proceeded. Passing through the ravine they came to a hollow like a small amphitheater, surrounded by perpendicular precipices, over the brinks of which impending trees shot their branches, so that you only caught glimpses of the azure sky and the bright evening cloud. During the whole time Rip and his companion had labored on in silence, for though the former marveled greatly what could be the object of carrying a keg of liquor up this wild mountain, yet there was something strange and incomprehensible about the unknown, that inspired awe and checked familiarity.

On entering the amphitheater new objects of wonder presented themselves. On a level spot in the center was a company of odd-looking personages playing at ninepins.[23] They were dressed in a quaint, outlandish fashion—some wore short doublets,[24] others jerkins with long knives in their belts and most of them had enormous breeches of similar style with that of the guide's. Their visages too were peculiar. One had a large head, broad face, and small piggish eyes. The face of another seemed to consist entirely of nose, and was surmounted by a white sugarloaf hat, set off with a little red cock's tail. They all had beards of various shapes and colors. There was one who seemed to be the commander. He was a stout old gentleman, with a weather-beaten countenance. He wore a laced doublet, broad belt and hanger,[25] high-crowned hat and feather, red stockings, and high-heeled shoes with roses[26] in them. The whole group reminded Rip of the figures in an old Flemish painting, in the parlor of Dominie Van Schaick the village parson, and which had been brought over from Holland at the time of the settlement.

What seemed particularly odd to Rip was, that though these folks were evidently amusing themselves, yet they maintained the gravest faces, the most mysterious silence, and were, withal, the most melancholy party of pleasure he had ever witnessed. Nothing interrupted the stillness of the scene, but the noise of the balls, which, whenever they were rolled, echoed along the mountains like rumbling peals of thunder.

As Rip and his companion approached them they suddenly desisted from their play and stared at him with such fixed statuelike gaze, and such strange uncouth, lackluster countenances, that his heart turned within him, and his knees smote together. His companion now emptied the contents of the keg into large flagons[27] and made signs to him to wait upon the company. He obeyed with fear and trembling; they quaffed the liquor in profound silence and then returned to their game.

By degrees Rip's awe and apprehension subsided. He even ventured, when no eye was fixed upon him, to taste the beverage, which he found had much of the flavor of excellent Hollands.[28] He was naturally a thirsty soul and was soon tempted to repeat the draft. One taste provoked another, and he reiterated his visits to the flagon so often that at length his senses were overpowered, his eyes swam in his head—his head gradually declined and he fell into a deep sleep.

On awaking he found himself on the green knoll from whence he had first seen the old man of the glen. He rubbed his eyes—it was a bright, sunny morning. The birds were hopping and twittering among the bushes, and the eagle was wheeling aloft and breasting the pure mountain breeze. "Surely," thought Rip, "I have not slept here all night." He recalled the occurrences before he fell asleep. The strange man with a keg of liquor—the mountain ravine—the wild retreat among the rocks—the woebegone party at ninepins—the flagon—"ah! that flagon! that wicked flagon!" thought Rip—"what excuse shall I make to Dame Van Winkle?"

He looked round for his gun, but in place of the clean well-oiled fowling piece he found an old

23. **ninepins:** a bowling game.
24. **doublets:** closefitting jackets.
25. **hanger:** short, curved sword hung from the belt.
26. **roses:** ornaments shaped like roses; often called rosettes.

27. **flagons:** bottlelike containers for liquids.
28. **Hollands:** Dutch gin.

- -

WORDS TO OWN

reiterated (rē·it′ə·rāt′id) v.: repeated.

- -

firelock[29] lying by him, the barrel encrusted with rust; the lock falling off and the stock[30] worm-eaten. He now suspected that the grave roysters of the mountain had put a trick upon him, and having dosed him with liquor, had robbed him of his gun. Wolf too had disappeared, but he might have strayed away after a squirrel or partridge. He whistled after him and shouted his name—but all in vain; the echoes repeated his whistle and shout, but no dog was to be seen.

He determined to revisit the scene of the last evening's gambol, and if he met with any of the party, to demand his dog and gun. As he arose to walk he found himself stiff in the joints and wanting in his usual activity. "These mountain beds do not agree with me," thought Rip, "and if this frolic should lay me up with a fit of the rheumatism, I shall have a blessed time with Dame Van Winkle." With some difficulty he got down into the glen; he found the gully up which he and his companion had ascended the preceding evening, but to his astonishment a mountain stream was now foaming down it; leaping from rock to rock, and filling the glen with babbling murmurs. He, however, made shift to scramble up its sides working his toilsome way through thickets of birch, sassafras, and witch hazel, and sometimes tripped up or entangled by the wild grapevines that twisted their coils and tendrils from tree to tree, and spread a kind of network in his path.

At length he reached to where the ravine had opened through the cliffs, to the amphitheater—but no traces of such opening remained. The rocks presented a high impenetrable wall over which the torrent came tumbling in a sheet of feathery foam, and fell into a broad deep basin black from the shadows of the surrounding forest. Here then poor Rip was brought to a stand. He again called and whistled after his dog—he was only answered by the cawing of a flock of idle crows, sporting high in air about a dry tree that overhung a sunny precipice; and who, secure in their elevation seemed to look down and scoff at the poor man's perplexities.

What was to be done? The morning was passing away and Rip felt famished for want of his breakfast. He grieved to give up his dog and gun; he dreaded to meet his wife; but it would not do to starve among the mountains. He shook his head, shouldered the rusty firelock, and with a heart full of trouble and anxiety, turned his steps homeward.

As he approached the village he met a number of people, but none whom he knew, which somewhat surprised him, for he had thought himself acquainted with everyone in the country round. Their dress too was of a different fashion from that to which he was accustomed. They all stared at him with equal marks of surprise, and whenever they cast their eyes upon him, invariably stroked their chins. The constant recurrence of this gesture induced Rip involuntarily to do the same, when to his astonishment he found his beard had grown a foot long!

He had now entered the skirts of the village. A troop of strange children ran at his heels, hooting after him and pointing at his gray beard. The dogs too, not one of which he recognized for an old acquaintance, barked at him as he passed. The very village was altered—it was larger and more populous. There were rows of houses which he had never seen before, and those which had been his familiar haunts had disappeared. Strange names were over the doors—strange faces at the windows—everything was strange. His mind now misgave him; he began to doubt whether both he and the world around him were not bewitched. Surely this was his native village which he had left but the day before. There stood the Kaatskill Mountains—there ran the silver Hudson at a distance—there was every hill and dale precisely as it had always been—Rip was sorely perplexed— "That flagon last night," thought he, "has addled my poor head sadly!"

It was with some difficulty that he found the way to his own house, which he approached with silent awe, expecting every moment to hear the

---

29. firelock: early type of gun.
30. stock: wooden handle attached to metal gun barrel.

Rip Van Winkle Asleep (detail) (1880) by Albertus Del Orient Browere (1814–1887). Oil on canvas.

shrill voice of Dame Van Winkle. He found the house gone to decay—the roof fallen in, the windows shattered, and the doors off the hinges. A half-starved dog that looked like Wolf was skulking about it. Rip called him by name but the cur snarled, showed his teeth, and passed on. This was an unkind cut indeed—"My very dog," sighed poor Rip, "has forgotten me!"

He entered the house, which, to tell the truth, Dame Van Winkle had always kept in neat order. It was empty, forlorn, and apparently abandoned. This desolateness overcame all his connubial[31] fears—he called loudly for his wife and children—the lonely chambers rung for a moment with his voice, and then all again was silence.

He now hurried forth and hastened to his old resort, the village inn—but it too was gone. A large, rickety wooden building stood in its place, with great gaping windows, some of them broken, and mended with old hats and petticoats, and over the door was printed "The Union Hotel, by Jonathan Doolittle." Instead of the great tree, that used to shelter the quiet little Dutch inn of yore, there now was reared a tall naked pole with something on top that looked like a red nightcap,[32] and from it was fluttering a flag on which was a singular assemblage of stars and stripes—all this was strange and incomprehensible. He recognized on the sign, however, the ruby face of King George under which he had smoked so many a peaceful pipe, but even this was singularly metamorphosed.[33] The red coat was changed for one of blue and buff; a sword was held in the hand instead of a scepter; the head was decorated with a cocked hat, and underneath was printed in large characters[34] GENERAL WASHINGTON.

There was as usual a crowd of folk about the door; but none that Rip recollected. The very character of people seemed changed. There was a busy, bustling disputatious tone about it, instead of the accustomed phlegm and drowsy tranquility.

31. connubial (kə·nōō′bē·əl): related to marriage.

32. red nightcap: "liberty cap"; worn as a symbol of independence during the French and American Revolutions.
33. metamorphosed (met′ə·môr′fōzd′): transformed.
34. characters: letters.

He looked in vain for the sage Nicholaus Vedder with his broad face, double chin, and fair long pipe, uttering clouds of tobacco smoke instead of idle speeches. Or Van Bummel the schoolmaster doling forth the contents of an ancient newspaper. In place of these a lean bilious-looking fellow with his pockets full of handbills, was haranguing vehemently about rights of citizens —elections—members of Congress—liberty— Bunker's hill—heroes of Seventy-six—and other

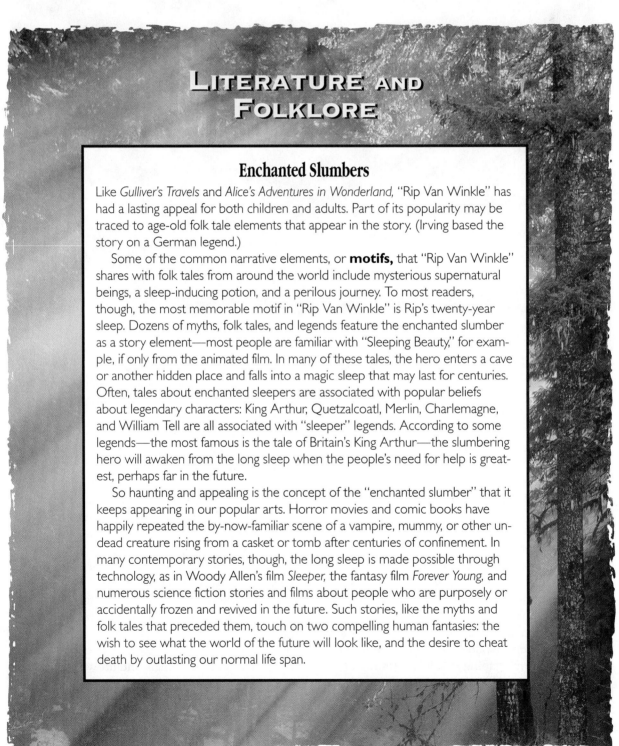

LITERATURE AND FOLKLORE

Enchanted Slumbers

Like *Gulliver's Travels* and *Alice's Adventures in Wonderland,* "Rip Van Winkle" has had a lasting appeal for both children and adults. Part of its popularity may be traced to age-old folk tale elements that appear in the story. (Irving based the story on a German legend.)

Some of the common narrative elements, or **motifs,** that "Rip Van Winkle" shares with folk tales from around the world include mysterious supernatural beings, a sleep-inducing potion, and a perilous journey. To most readers, though, the most memorable motif in "Rip Van Winkle" is Rip's twenty-year sleep. Dozens of myths, folk tales, and legends feature the enchanted slumber as a story element—most people are familiar with "Sleeping Beauty," for example, if only from the animated film. In many of these tales, the hero enters a cave or another hidden place and falls into a magic sleep that may last for centuries. Often, tales about enchanted sleepers are associated with popular beliefs about legendary characters: King Arthur, Quetzalcoatl, Merlin, Charlemagne, and William Tell are all associated with "sleeper" legends. According to some legends—the most famous is the tale of Britain's King Arthur—the slumbering hero will awaken from the long sleep when the people's need for help is greatest, perhaps far in the future.

So haunting and appealing is the concept of the "enchanted slumber" that it keeps appearing in our popular arts. Horror movies and comic books have happily repeated the by-now-familiar scene of a vampire, mummy, or other un-dead creature rising from a casket or tomb after centuries of confinement. In many contemporary stories, though, the long sleep is made possible through technology, as in Woody Allen's film *Sleeper,* the fantasy film *Forever Young,* and numerous science fiction stories and films about people who are purposely or accidentally frozen and revived in the future. Such stories, like the myths and folk tales that preceded them, touch on two compelling human fantasies: the wish to see what the world of the future will look like, and the desire to cheat death by outlasting our normal life span.

words which were a perfect Babylonish jargon[35] to the bewildered Van Winkle.

The appearance of Rip with his long grizzled beard, his rusty fowling piece, his uncouth dress, and an army of women and children at his heels soon attracted the attention of the tavern politicians. They crowded around him eyeing him from head to foot, with great curiosity. The orator bustled up to him, and drawing him partly aside, inquired "on which side he voted?"—Rip stared in vacant stupidity. Another short but busy little fellow, pulled him by the arm and rising on tiptoe, inquired in his ear "whether he was Federal or Democrat?"[36]—Rip was equally at a loss to comprehend the question—when a knowing, self-important old gentleman, in a sharp cocked hat, made his way through the crowd, putting them to the right and left with his elbows as he passed, and planting himself before Van Winkle, with one arm akimbo, the other resting on his cane, his keen eyes and sharp hat penetrating as it were into his very soul, demanded in an austere tone— "what brought him to the election with a gun on his shoulder and a mob at his heels, and whether he meant to breed a riot in the village?"—"Alas gentlemen," cried Rip, somewhat dismayed, "I am a poor quiet man, a native of the place, and a loyal subject of the King—God bless him!"

Here a general shout burst from the bystanders—"A Tory![37] a Tory! a spy! a Refugee![38] hustle him! away with him!"—It was with great difficulty that the self-important man in the cocked hat restored order; and having assumed a tenfold austerity of brow demanded again of the unknown culprit, what he came there for and whom he was seeking. The poor man humbly assured him that he meant no harm; but merely came there in search of some of his neighbors, who used to keep about the tavern.

"—Well—who are they?—name them."

Rip bethought himself a moment and inquired, "Where's Nicholaus Vedder?"

There was a silence for a little while, when an old man replied, in a thin, piping voice, "Nicholaus Vedder? Why he is dead and gone these eighteen years! There was a wooden tombstone in the churchyard that used to tell all about him, but that's rotted and gone too."

"Where's Brom Dutcher?"

"Oh he went off to the army in the beginning of the war; some say he was killed at the storming of Stoney Point—others say he was drowned in a squall at the foot of Antony's Nose[39]—I don't know—he never came back again."

"Where's Van Bummel the schoolmaster?"

"He went off to the wars too—was a great militia general, and is now in Congress."

Rip's heart died away at hearing of these sad changes in his home and friends, and finding himself thus alone in the world—every answer puzzled him too by treating of such enormous lapses of time and of matters which he could not understand—war—Congress, Stoney Point—he had no courage to ask after any more friends, but cried out in despair, "Does nobody here know Rip Van Winkle?"

"Oh. Rip Van Winkle?" exclaimed two or three—"oh to be sure!—that's Rip Van Winkle—yonder—leaning against the tree."

Rip looked and beheld a precise counterpart of himself, as he went up the mountain: apparently as lazy and certainly as ragged! The poor fellow was now completely confounded. He doubted his own identity, and whether he was himself or another man. In the midst of his bewilderment the man in the cocked hat demanded who he was—what was his name?

"God knows," exclaimed he, at his wit's end, "I'm not myself.—I'm somebody else—that's me yonder—no—that's somebody else got into my shoes—I was myself last night; but I fell asleep on the mountain—and they've changed my gun—and everything's changed—and I'm changed—and I can't tell what's my name, or who I am!"

---

35. Babylonish jargon: confusing language. According to Genesis 11:1-9, when the people of the earth tried to build a tower high enough to reach heaven, God caused the people to speak many different languages. Because they could no longer communicate, they abandoned the project, which is now known as the Tower of Babel.

36. Federal or Democrat: American political parties after the Revolution. Federals favored a strong centralized government; Democrats favored states' rights.

37. Tory: one who supported British rule in the American Colonies.

38. Refugee: member of a group of British sympathizers, especially in New York State, who attacked supporters of the American cause, during the Revolutionary period.

39. Antony's Nose: mountain near West Point in New York.

The bystanders began now to look at each other, nod, wink significantly, and tap their fingers against their foreheads. There was a whisper also about securing the gun, and keeping the old fellow from doing mischief—at the very suggestion of which, the self-important man in the cocked hat retired with some precipitation. At this critical moment a fresh likely looking woman pressed through the throng to get a peep at the gray-bearded man. She had a chubby child in her arms, which frightened at his looks began to cry. "Hush Rip," cried she, "hush you little fool, the old man won't hurt you." The name of the child, the air of the mother, the tone of her voice all awakened a train of recollections in his mind. "What is your name my good woman?" asked he.

"Judith Gardenier."

"And your father's name?"

"Ah, poor man, Rip Van Winkle was his name, but it's twenty years since he went away from home with his gun and never has been heard of since—his dog came home without him—but whether he shot himself, or was carried away by the Indians nobody can tell. I was then but a little girl."

Rip had but one question more to ask, but he put it with a faltering voice—

"Where's your mother?"—

Oh she too had died but a short time since— 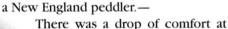 she broke a blood vessel in a fit of passion at a New England peddler.—

There was a drop of comfort at least in this intelligence. The honest man could contain himself no longer—he caught his daughter and her child in his arms.— "I am your father!" cried he—"Young Rip Van Winkle once—old Rip Van Winkle now!— does nobody know poor Rip Van Winkle!"

All stood amazed, until an old woman tottering out from among the crowd put her hand to her brow and peering under it in his face for a moment

exclaimed—"Sure enough!—it is Rip Van Winkle —it is himself—welcome home again old neighbor—why, where have you been these twenty long years?"

Rip's story was soon told, for the whole twenty years had been to him but as one night. The neighbors stared when they heard it; some were seen to wink at each other and put their tongues in their cheeks, and the self-important man in the cocked hat, who when the alarm was over had returned to the field, screwed down the corners of his mouth and shook his head—upon which there was a general shaking of the head throughout the assemblage.

It was determined, however, to take the opinion of old Peter Vanderdonk, who was seen slowly advancing up the road. He was a descendant of the historian of that name, who wrote one of the earliest accounts of the province. Peter was the most ancient inhabitant of the village and well versed in all the wonderful events and traditions of the neighborhood. He recollected Rip at once, and corroborated his story in the most satisfactory manner. He assured the company that it was a fact handed down from his ancestor the historian, that the Kaatskill Mountains had always been haunted by strange beings. That it was affirmed that the great Hendrick Hudson,[40] the first discoverer of the river and country, kept a kind of vigil there every twenty years, with his crew of the *Half Moon*—being permitted in this way to revisit the scenes of his enterprise and keep a guardian eye upon the river and the great city called by his name.[41] That his father had once seen them in their old Dutch dresses playing at ninepins in a hollow of the mountain; and that he himself had heard one summer afternoon the sound of their balls, like distant peals of thunder.

To make a long story short—the company broke up, and returned to the more important concerns of the election. Rip's daughter took him home to live with her; she had a snug well-furnished house, and a stout cheery farmer for a husband whom Rip recollected for one of the

40. Hendrick Hudson: Henry Hudson (?–1611), an English navigator hired by the Dutch, explored the river later named for him, in his ship, the *Half Moon*. Hudson's explorations were the basis for early Dutch claims in North America.

41. great . . . name: Hudson, New York.

urchins that used to climb upon his back. As to Rip's son and heir, who was the ditto of himself seen leaning against the tree; he was employed to work on the farm; but evinced an hereditary disposition to attend to anything else but his business.

Rip now resumed his old walks and habits; he soon found many of his former cronies, though all rather the worse for the wear and tear of time; and preferred making friends among the rising generation, with whom he soon grew into great favor. Having nothing to do at home, and being arrived at that happy age when a man can be idle, with impunity, he took his place once more on the bench at the inn door and was reverenced as one of the patriarchs of the village and a chronicle of the old times "before the war." It was some time before he could get into the regular track of gossip, or could be made to comprehend the strange events that had taken place during his torpor. How that there had been a revolutionary war—that the country had thrown off the yoke of Old England and that instead of being a subject of his majesty George the Third, he was now a free citizen of the United States. Rip in fact was no politician; the changes of states and empires made but little impression on him; but there was one species of despotism under which he had long groaned and that was petticoat government. Happily that was at an end—he had got his neck out of the yoke of matrimony, and could go in and out whenever he pleased without dreading the tyranny of Dame Van Winkle. Whenever her name was mentioned, however, he shook his head, shrugged his shoulders, and cast up his eyes; which might pass either for an expression of resignation to his fate or joy at his deliverance.

He used to tell his story to every stranger that arrived at Mr. Doolittle's Hotel. He was observed at first to vary on some points, every time he told it, which was doubtless owing to his having so recently awaked. It at last settled down precisely to the tale I have related and not a man, woman, or child in the neighborhood but knew it by heart. Some always pretended to doubt the reality of it, and insisted that Rip had been out of his head, and that this was one point on which he always remained flighty. The old Dutch inhabitants, however, almost universally gave it full credit—Even to this day they never hear a thunderstorm of a summer afternoon about the Kaatskill, but they say Hendrick Hudson and his crew are at their game of ninepins; and it is a common wish of all henpecked husbands in the neighborhood, when life hangs heavy on their hands, that they might have a quieting draft out of Rip Van Winkle's flagon.

Note

The foregoing tale one would suspect had been suggested to Mr. Knickerbocker by a little German superstition about the emperor Frederick *der Rothbart* and the Kypphäuser Mountain;[42] the subjoined note, however, which he had appended to the tale, shows that it is an absolute fact, narrated with his usual fidelity.—

"The story of Rip Van Winkle may seem incredible to many, but nevertheless I give it my full belief, for I know the vicinity of our old Dutch settlements to have been very subject to marvelous events and appearances. Indeed I have heard many stranger stories than this, in the villages along the Hudson; all of which were too well authenticated to admit of a doubt. I have even talked with Rip Van Winkle myself, who when last I saw him was a very venerable old man and so perfectly rational and consistent on every other point, that I think no conscientious person could refuse to take this into the bargain—nay I have seen a certificate on the subject taken before a country justice and signed with a cross in the justice's own handwriting. The story therefore is beyond the possibility of doubt.

D. K."

---

42. emperor . . . Mountain: Frederick I, emperor of the Holy Roman Empire (1152–1190); also called der Rothbart (German for "red beard") or Barbarossa. Although he died near the Mediterranean during the Crusades, according to folk legend he sleeps on Kypphäuser (now called Kyffhäuser) Mountain in Germany.

WORDS TO OWN

torpor (tôr′pər) *n*.: inactive period.
fidelity (fə·del′ə·tē) *n*.: accuracy.
conscientious (kän′shē·en′shəs) *adj*.: careful and honest.

MAKING MEANINGS

First Thoughts

1. In what ways is this a classic story of wish fulfillment?

> **Reading Check**
>
> Make a before-and-after chart of what happened in the story before Rip's sleep and what happened after he woke up.

Shaping Interpretations

2. In his introductory note, the narrator (who is Geoffrey Crayon) explains that the manuscript of "Rip Van Winkle" was written by Diedrich Knickerbocker, the narrator of Irving's earlier *History of New York*. How does Irving use his two narrators—Geoffrey Crayon and Diedrich Knickerbocker—to defend the tale's credibility? How would you describe Irving's **tone** in these introductory passages?

3. What details in "Rip Van Winkle" do you think reveal a Romantic fascination with the past and nature? Find some descriptions of the **setting** that you think reflect a Romantic's point of view.

4. Irving was a Romantic, but he was also a satirist. What elements of this story—including the narrator's commentaries—are **satirical**? Who or what are Irving's targets?

5. How would you state the **theme** of this story?

Connecting with the Text

6. Do you find "Rip" humorous, or do you think it's too outdated to be funny to us today? Explain your response with examples from the story.

Extending the Text

7. How does the fictional **character** of Rip Van Winkle contrast with the historical character of Benjamin Franklin, the self-made man (page 84)? Where do you still see both character types in American life today?

Challenging the Text

8. Dame Van Winkle and Rip are **stereotyped characters** that have been found in literature throughout the ages—the nagging wife and the henpecked husband. Can you identify these character types in current literature and in popular movies and TV shows? What is your response to Irving's characterization of Dame Van Winkle?

9. Review the prediction chart you made while reading. Did Irving succeed in surprising you, or did you find his story predictable? Explain.

READING SKILLS AND STRATEGIES

Reading Inflated Diction

One of the hallmarks of Irving's humor is his use of **inflated diction** (pompous, high-flown language) to describe commonplace things. For example, rather than simply saying that Rip is "lazy," or that he "hates work," Irving states that Rip has "an insuperable aversion to all kinds of profitable labor."

1. Skim the story to find at least two other comically inflated descriptions of Rip's family life.

2. Rephrase each inflated description in plain English.

3. How did Irving's inflated diction affect your reading of the story?

Washington Irving.

Drawing by David Levine.
Reprinted with permission from
The New York Review of Books.
Copyright ©1976 NYREV, Inc.

CHOICES: Building Your Portfolio

1. Collecting Ideas for a Literary Analysis

When you analyze a literary work, you might want to investigate the ways it follows or deviates from a conventional **plot** pattern. You can show how "Rip Van Winkle," for example, relates to the archetypal plot of a classic work like the *Odyssey*. Use a chart like the one below to track Irving's use of this particular plot line. You'll probably note very quickly how Irving alters this traditional pattern. Keep your notes for possible use in the Writer's Workshop on page 198.

Hero	Plot
Perilous journey	
Use of supernatural	
Disguises	
Recognition scene	
Wife	

Explaining an Analogy

2. Parallel Awakenings

Rip's awakening has been seen by many critics as an analogy to the awakening of the new American nation. In a short essay, cite the specific details that support the idea that Rip's emancipation from his wife is like America's emancipation from Great Britain. In your essay, discuss how each "story" is about winning independence from a tyrant.

Analyzing Conflict

3. The Battle of the Sexes

This story reflects a **conflict** that has been used by hundreds of other writers of comedy, before and after Irving. The conflict might be described as the battle of the sexes. In a brief essay, tell how Irving's story reflects this conflict; name other comedies (in books, on TV, and in the movies) that use the same conflict; and explain your own response to its continued use and popularity.

©Touchstone Pictures and Television, Inc.

Sparring partners. The TV show *Home Improvement* with Patricia Richardson and Tim Allen.

Creative Writing

4. Dame Van Winkle Has Her Say

Write an epilogue to this story called "Dame Van Winkle." Describe her response to Rip's disappearance. Was she also emancipated? Will you have Dame Van Winkle tell her own story or let Diedrich Knickerbocker continue?

Creative Writing

5. After Twenty Years

The world is always changing, often in unexpected and amazing ways. Think about the future: What will the world be like in twenty years? Then, write an article that could appear in a newspaper twenty years from today. Your article can be about a current event of the time; it can also be an editorial or even an advice column.

Creative Writing / Art

6. Missing Person

You're a private investigator trying to discover the whereabouts of the missing Rip Van Winkle. First, compile a profile or dossier on Rip: a list of his character traits, a list of possible motives he may have had for wanting to escape, and brief interviews with people who knew him. Include a "missing person" sketch of Rip as you visualize him.

Reading Skills and Strategies

VOCABULARY: USING CONTEXT CLUES

Using **context clues**—clues to meaning that are in the text—is the best way to figure out the meaning of a word without interrupting yourself to check the dictionary. A word's context includes the words and sentences that surround it. Washington Irving's "Rip Van Winkle" provides examples of six kinds of context clues (there are more) that you will commonly encounter in your reading.

1. Example

". . . they *quaffed* the liquor in profound silence. . . ." (page 159)

Liquor is an example of something you can *quaff*. You can infer that *quaff* means "to drink."

2. Restatement

"He even ventured . . . to taste the beverage . . . and was soon tempted to repeat the **draft**." (page 159)

"Repeat the *draft*" seems to restate "taste the beverage," so you can infer that *draft* means "drinking."

3. Summary

". . . he was observed to smoke his pipe **vehemently,** and to send forth short, frequent, and angry puffs. . . ." (page 157)

The clause after the comma tells you the meaning of *vehemently*.

4. Contrast

". . . he was rarely heard to speak, but smoked his pipe **incessantly**." (page 157)

The conjunction *but* sets up an opposition—it helps you know that *incessantly* is the opposite of "rarely." *Incessantly* means "without stopping."

5. Items in a Series

"They were dressed in a **quaint,** outlandish fashion. . . ." (page 159)

The comma between *quaint* and *outlandish* lets you know they may be close in meaning.

6. Cause and Effect

". . . Rip felt **famished** for want of his breakfast." (page 160)

"For want of" indicates that being *famished* is a result of not having eaten breakfast. *Famished* means "extremely hungry."

Try It Out

Mapping unfamiliar words. A word map like the one below can help you use context clues to figure out words or phrases you may not know. It can also help you to make further associations with the new word that will enable you to "own" the word—to make it an active part of your vocabulary.

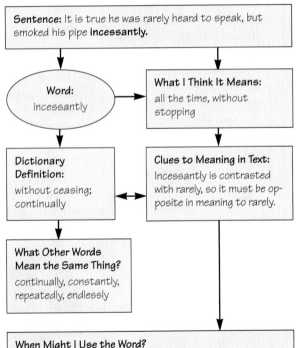

Sentence: It is true he was rarely heard to speak, but smoked his pipe **incessantly.**

Word: incessantly

What I Think It Means: all the time, without stopping

Dictionary Definition: without ceasing; continually

Clues to Meaning in Text: Incessantly is contrasted with rarely, so it must be opposite in meaning to rarely.

What Other Words Mean the Same Thing? continually, constantly, repeatedly, endlessly

When Might I Use the Word? It seems like a word I'd use when I wanted to exaggerate something, like an action. If someone talked a lot and it bothered me, I might say he or she talked incessantly.

William Cullen Bryant

(1794–1878)

Poetry is a lonely occupation, but not a solitary one. Poets of any consequence rarely write in isolation from the influence of their predecessors or from the influence of other poets of their own time. When William Cullen Bryant was still an adolescent, he read a book of poems that would change his life: *Lyrical Ballads,* published in 1798 by his great English contemporaries William Wordsworth and Samuel Taylor Coleridge. This volume of poetry and theory focused the expression and much of the philosophy of the Romantic era. The book was a powerful source of inspiration for poets who wanted to replace conventional poetic diction with the common speech of their own time. Bryant was one of these poets—the first mature American Romantic, the country boy who translated the messages of English Romanticism into his native tongue.

Two other important factors supported the influence of English Romanticism on Bryant's poetry. One factor was Bryant's own growing attraction to the philosophy of deism (page 16), which held that divinity could be found in nature. The other factor was the geography of his surroundings, which placed Bryant in immediate contact with everything that supported this philosophy.

By the time of Bryant's birth, western Massachusetts was no longer a Colonial frontier, but a widely settled countryside. Over the next hundred years and more, its farms, steepled towns, and mountain forests would be the homes of many poets. These writers would find in their surroundings metaphors to express their sense of correspondence between human life and the life of nature. After Bryant, the same New England seasons would turn for Herman Melville and Emily Dickinson, and later for Robert Frost and Richard Wilbur. All these poets were intimate with the shadows and whispers of the Berkshires and the adjacent Green Mountains. All would make their own small plot of ground part of the permanent landscape of American poetry.

Bryant was born in Cummington, Massachusetts. His father was a physician, and his mother came from a family of clergy. Bryant's literary gifts were evident from an early age: By the age of nine he was already writing poetry and had earned a reputation as a prodigy.

Bryant was tutored for a career as a lawyer, but with the publication of "Thanatopsis" his literary future was assured. In his late twenties he moved to New York City and for many years played the triple role of editor, critic, and poet.

Bryant became not only a famous literary figure, but also an influential voice in religion and politics. An outspoken liberal, Bryant supported social reform, free speech, and the growing movement for the abolition of slavery. He was also one of the founders of the Republican Party, which, in his lifetime, would produce one of America's great presidents, Abraham Lincoln. When Bryant died at the age of eighty-three, he was a millionaire and so widely honored at home and abroad that he had become a kind of national monument, the widely acknowledged "father of American poetry."

Today Bryant's poems are not read as the spiritual counsels they were meant to be; instead, they are read as period pieces that authentically reflect their time. Yet even when Bryant's poems seem more like moral fables than free expressions of the imagination, they ring with an air of piety and sincerity no one can doubt.

William Cullen Bryant (1833) by James Frothingham (1786–1864). American. Oil on canvas (21″ × 17½″).

Courtesy Museum of Fine Arts, Boston. Gift of Maxim Karolik for the M. & M. Karolik Collection of American Paintings, 1815–1865 (62.271).

Fawn's Leap, Catskill, New York (detail) (1868) by John W. Hill
(1812–1879). Oil on canvas (30″ × 38″).

Before You Read

THANATOPSIS

Make the Connection

The Endless Cycle

Romantic poets looked to nature for lessons—lessons that we too can see all around us. One of the ever-present lessons of nature is the organic cycle of birth, growth, death, and rebirth. Think of some of the ways that nature reminds us of this endless cycle of life, death, and rebirth. Do you find this aspect of nature disturbing or comforting?

Reading Skills and Strategies

Tracking Your Responses

As you read the poem, you may wish to keep a double-entry journal. In the left column, record a passage from the poem that particularly interests you. (It may remind you of something in your own experience or strike you with its vivid imagery; or it may be something you disagree with or don't quite understand.) In the right column, jot down your response to the passage. Pay special attention to Nature's "lesson," starting with line 17 and ending with line 72.

Background

Bryant composed the first version of this poem when he was only sixteen, during solitary rambles in the woods. In the poem, he draws moral lessons from nature, which was typical of the popular poetry of his time. *Thanatopsis* is a word Bryant coined by joining two Greek words, *thanatos* (death) and *opsis* (seeing). The word is defined by the poem: a way of looking at death and a way of thinking about it.

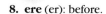

Thanatopsis

William Cullen Bryant

To him who in the love of Nature holds
Communion with her visible forms, she speaks
A various language; for his gayer hours
She has a voice of gladness, and a smile
5   And eloquence of beauty, and she glides
Into his darker musings, with a mild
And healing sympathy, that steals away
Their sharpness, ere° he is aware. When thoughts
Of the last bitter hour come like a blight
10 Over thy spirit, and sad images
Of the stern agony, and shroud, and pall,°
And breathless darkness, and the narrow house,°
Make thee to shudder, and grow sick at heart;—
Go forth, under the open sky, and list°
15 To Nature's teachings, while from all around—
Earth and her waters, and the depths of air—
Comes a still voice.—

            Yet° a few days, and thee
The all-beholding sun shall see no more
In all his course; nor yet in the cold ground,
20 Where thy pale form was laid, with many tears,
Nor in the embrace of ocean, shall exist
Thy image. Earth, that nourished thee, shall claim
Thy growth, to be resolved to earth again,
And, lost each human trace, surrendering up
25 Thine individual being, shalt thou go
To mix forever with the elements,
To be a brother to the insensible rock
And to the sluggish clod, which the rude swain°
Turns with his share,° and treads upon. The oak
30 Shall send his roots abroad, and pierce thy mold.

    Yet not to thine eternal resting place
Shalt thou retire alone, nor couldst thou wish
Couch more magnificent. Thou shalt lie down
With patriarchs of the infant world—with kings,
35 The powerful of the earth—the wise, the good,
Fair forms, and hoary seers° of ages past,
All in one mighty sepulcher.° The hills
Rock-ribbed and ancient as the sun,—the vales
Stretching in pensive quietness between;
40 The venerable woods—rivers that move
In majesty, and the complaining brooks
That make the meadows green; and, poured round all,
Old Ocean's gray and melancholy waste,—

8. ere (er): before.

11. pall (pôl): coffin cover.
12. narrow house: grave.

14. list: listen.

17. Yet . . . : Here, the voice of Nature begins to speak.

28. rude swain: uneducated country youth.
29. share: short for "plowshare."

36. hoary seers: white-haired prophets.
37. sepulcher (sep′əl·kər): burial place.

Are but the solemn decorations all
45 Of the great tomb of man. The golden sun,
The planets, all the infinite host of heaven,
Are shining on the sad abodes of death,
Through the still lapse of ages. All that tread
The globe are but a handful to the tribes
50 That slumber in its bosom.—Take the wings
Of morning,° pierce the Barcan wilderness,°
Or lose thyself in the continuous woods
Where rolls the Oregon,° and hears no sound,
Save his own dashings—yet the dead are there:
55 And millions in those solitudes, since first
The flight of years began, have laid them down
In their last sleep—the dead reign there alone.
So shalt thou rest, and what if thou withdraw
In silence from the living, and no friend
60 Take note of thy departure? All that breathe
Will share thy destiny. The gay will laugh
When thou art gone, the solemn brood of care
Plod on, and each one as before will chase
His favorite phantom; yet all these shall leave
65 Their mirth and their employments, and shall come
And make their bed with thee. As the long train
Of ages glides away, the sons of men,
The youth in life's fresh spring, and he who goes
In the full strength of years, matron and maid,
70 The speechless babe, and the gray-headed man—
Shall one by one be gathered to thy side,
By those, who in their turn shall follow them.

    So° live, that when thy summons comes to join
The innumerable caravan, which moves
75 To that mysterious realm, where each shall take
His chamber in the silent halls of death,
Thou go not, like the quarry slave at night,
Scourged to his dungeon, but, sustained and soothed
By an unfaltering trust, approach thy grave,
80 Like one who wraps the drapery of his couch
About him, and lies down to pleasant dreams.

51. Take . . . morning: allusion to Psalm 139:9: "If I take the wings of the morning . . ." **Barcan wilderness:** desert near Barca (now al-Marj), Libya, in North Africa.
53. Oregon: early name for the Columbia River, which flows between Washington and Oregon.

73. So . . . : The speaker's voice resumes here.

Derek Walcott, who was born in 1930 on the island of St. Lucia in the Caribbean, won the 1992 Nobel Prize in literature. In "Sea Canes," Walcott, like Bryant, reflects on nature as he tries to come to his own understanding of loss and death. "Sea Canes" refers to wild canes—tall, slender, bamboo-like plants that grow near water.

Sea Canes

Derek Walcott

Half my friends are dead.
I will make you new ones, said earth.
No, give me them back, as they were, instead,
with faults and all, I cried.

5 Tonight I can snatch their talk
from the faint surf's drone
through the canes, but I cannot walk

on the moonlit leaves of ocean
down that white road alone,
10 or float with the dreaming motion

of owls leaving earth's load.
O earth, the number of friends you keep
exceeds those left to be loved.

The sea canes by the cliff flash green and silver;
15 they were the seraph lances of my faith,
but out of what is lost grows something
    stronger

that has the rational radiance of stone,
enduring moonlight, further than despair,
strong as the wind, that through dividing canes

20 brings those we love before us, as they were,
with faults and all, not nobler, just there.

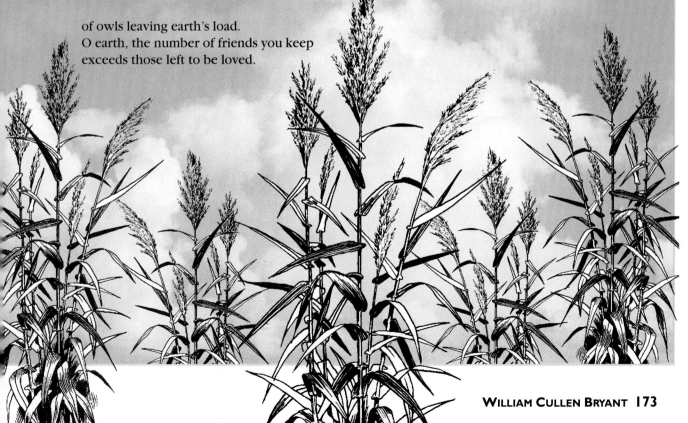

MAKING MEANINGS

First Thoughts

1. What thoughts or feelings expressed in "Thanatopsis" strike you as especially important or puzzling or controversial? Be sure to check your double-entry journal.

Shaping Interpretations

2. How does this poem reveal the Romantic conviction that the universe, far from operating like a machine, is really a living organism that undergoes constant cyclical changes? How is this "organic" view of the universe comforting to the speaker?

3. In line 31, what shift in the **tone** of the poem occurs? What comfort is offered in this section of the poem?

4. At the conclusion of the speech of the "still voice" (line 72), the speaker's voice resumes for the concluding section, or summing up. In your own words, state the main thrust of his advice. Do you find his advice wise and consoling, or disturbing? Or do you have some other reaction? Explain.

5. Some readers think this poem expresses a traditional notion of an afterlife in heaven, while others find in it a very untraditional view of an afterlife in which people rejoin the great chain of Nature instead of ascending to a heavenly realm. Which **images** in the poem support each of these interpretations?

6. Is this poem about death or about life? Explain.

Extending the Text

7. Read "A Blessing" by James Wright on page 151. Then, compare the ways in which Wright's and Bryant's imaginations work when they look at nature.

Challenging the Text

8. Many readers today read a poem like "Thanatopsis" simply as a period piece that has only historical interest, yet Bryant's intention was that his poem be taken seriously as spiritual counsel. In what ways does Bryant's poem still speak to us today, if at all?

READING SKILLS AND STRATEGIES

Reading Inverted Sentences

In order to maintain his meter and to create certain sound effects, Bryant often uses **inversion**—a reversal of the usual English word order. For example, "Yet not to thine eternal resting place / Shalt thou retire alone" is an inversion of "Yet thou shalt not retire alone to thine eternal resting place."

1. Find three examples of inversion in the first thirty lines of "Thanatopsis."

2. Revise each example to conform to usual English word order. How do your revisions change the meter and affect the clarity of the lines?

CHOICES: Building Your Portfolio

Writer's Notebook

1. Collecting Ideas for a Literary Analysis

If you were to write an analysis of "Thanatopsis," you might want to focus on its **theme.** Try now to state the poem's theme as precisely as you can. Then, jot down several passages of the poem that support this theme. Keep your notes for possible use in the Writer's Workshop on page 198.

Comparing Ideas

2. A Puritan Writes to a Romantic

How might Anne Bradstreet (page 68) or Jonathan Edwards (page 77) have reacted to Bryant's meditation on death? Write a letter from Bradstreet or Edwards to Bryant that conveys Puritan reactions to the poem.

Art

3. Picture This

You have been commissioned to provide illustrations for two poems: Bryant's "Thanatopsis" and Walcott's "Sea Canes" (see *Connections,* page 173). Create an image for each poem that communicates each poet's insights.

Henry Wadsworth Longfellow

(1807–1882)

National Portrait Gallery, Smithsonian Institution, Washington, D.C./Art Resource, NY.

Longfellow was and still is the most popular poet America has ever produced. With the possible exception of Robert Frost (page 558), no twentieth-century poet has ever reached "household name" status, let alone achieved the kind of recognition suggested by the word *popular*.

Longfellow's immense popularity was based largely on his appeal to an audience hungry for sermons and lessons. That audience wanted assurances that their cherished values would prevail over the new forces of history—such as industrialization—that were threatening to destroy them. In themselves, the values Longfellow endorsed were positive forces in the making of the American character. But his tendency to leave these values unexamined led to poetry that often offered easy comfort at the expense of illumination.

Born in Portland, Maine, Longfellow was never far from the rocks and splashing waves of the Atlantic Coast, or from the cultural and religious influences of the well-to-do families who lived "north of Boston." Longfellow's early interest in foreign languages and literature led him naturally to an academic career. After attending Portland Academy, he continued his education at nearby Bowdoin College (where Nathaniel Hawthorne was one of his classmates), and then pursued three additional years of study in France, Spain, Italy, and Germany. When he returned, he joined the Bowdoin faculty, married, and began to write a series of prose sketches drawn from his experiences abroad.

During a second European trip in 1835, Longfellow's young wife died of a miscarriage. When he returned to America, still dealing with a "sorrow and a grief that almost killed," the young widower became a professor of French and Spanish at Harvard; seven years later he married Frances Appleton, whom he had met in Europe after his first wife's death. He settled into eighteen years of happily married life, living

Henry Wadsworth Longfellow (1871) by Theodore Wust (active 1860–1901). Watercolor on ivory (3½″ × 2¾″).

in the Cambridge mansion Craigie House (a gift from his new father-in-law), fathering six children, and producing some of his most celebrated poetry, much of it based on American legends: *Evangeline* (1847) and *The Song of Hiawatha* (1855).

By 1854, Longfellow had resigned from Harvard and devoted himself to writing full time. But seven years later a second tragedy struck: His wife Frances died in a fiery accident at home, when a lighted match or hot sealing wax she was using on a letter ignited her summer dress. Longfellow tried to save her, smothering the flames with a rug, and was badly burned himself.

Longfellow now devoted himself to his work with a religious and literary zeal. By the end of his long and productive life, he had become for Americans the symbolic figure of The Poet: wise, gray-bearded, haloed with goodness, and living in a world of still-untold romance. He was given honorary degrees by Cambridge and Oxford Universities in England and was received by Queen Victoria. Two years after his death, Longfellow's marble image was unveiled in the Poets' Corner in Westminster Abbey. He was the first American to be so honored.

Before You Read

THE TIDE RISES, THE TIDE FALLS

Make the Connection

Finite and Infinite

Nature repeats its cycles without foreseeable end. Summer turns to winter, day follows night, the tide rises and falls. In comparison, a person's lifetime is limited. There are no repeated cycles, just one journey from life's beginning to its end. Is there a lesson to be learned from the contrast between what we observe in the natural world and what we observe in our own existence?

Quickwrite

Write a few lines on how you see yourself in relation to nature. Are you an integral part of the natural world around you, or do you live in it without being part of it? Is nature your friend or your enemy?

Elements of Literature

Meter: A Pattern of Sounds

Meter is a pattern of stressed and unstressed syllables in poetry. **Scanning** a poem means marking the stressed syllables with the symbol (´) and the unstressed syllables with the symbol (˘).

A metrical unit of poetry is called a **foot,** which always contains at least one stressed syllable and usually one or more unstressed syllables. A common type of foot is the **iamb**—an unstressed syllable followed by a stressed syllable. The meter of "The Tide Rises, the Tide Falls"

Meditation by the Sea,
Anonymous, n.d. Oil on canvas
(13¹/₂″ × 19¹/₂″; 34.3 cm x 49.5 cm).

Gift of Maxim Karolik for the M. and M. Karolik
Collection of American Paintings, 1815–1865.
Courtesy Museum of Fine Arts, Boston.

is essentially iambic. Read this line aloud giving special stress to syllables marked (ˊ).

Ă·lóng / thĕ séa- / sánds dámp / ănd brówn

Poets usually include variations within a metrical pattern in order to avoid a mechanical, singsong effect. In the poem's first line, notice how Longfellow avoids a purely iambic meter by pairing two stressed syllables, which is a metrical foot called a **spondee.**

Read the entire poem aloud to feel the rise and fall of its rhythm, just like the rise and fall of the tide.

Meter is a pattern of stressed and unstressed syllables in poetry.

For more on Meter, see the Handbook of Literary Terms.

The Tide Rises, the Tide Falls

Henry Wadsworth Longfellow

The tide rises, the tide falls,
The twilight darkens, the curlew° calls;
Along the sea-sands damp and brown
The traveller hastens toward the town,
5   And the tide rises, the tide falls.

Darkness settles on roofs and walls,
But the sea, the sea in the darkness calls;
The little waves, with their soft, white hands,
Efface° the footprints in the sands,
10   And the tide rises, the tide falls.

The morning breaks; the steeds in their stalls
Stamp and neigh, as the hostler° calls;
The day returns, but nevermore
Returns the traveller to the shore,
15   And the tide rises, the tide falls.

2. **curlew** (kur′lōō′): large, brownish shorebird with long legs.
9. **Efface** (ə·fās′): wipe out; erase.
12. **hostler** (häs′lər): person who takes care of horses.

Before You Read

THE CROSS OF SNOW

Make the Connection

A Meaningful Image

Romantic poets often used aspects of nature to mirror or express emotions that might be too painful or personal to express directly. In this poem the poet has taken a dramatic sight from nature and transformed it through words into a powerful **image** that conveys several layers of intensely personal meaning.

Quickwrite

Of all human emotions, grief is one of the most difficult to express adequately. Think of an image from nature that could be used to describe a feeling of great sorrow. Set up your comparison like a **metaphor:** "Grief is _____." Then, explore in a few sentences some of the ways grief is like this image you have chosen.

Background

"I shall win this lady, or I shall die," Longfellow had written of Fanny Appleton, his second wife, who kept him waiting seven years before she agreed to marry him. Longfellow wrote this poem eighteen years after Fanny died in a fire. Three years later, Longfellow died without having shown it to anyone. Discovered among his papers, it was published four years later and immediately became one of his most famous poems. With a large audience waiting to read everything he wrote, why do you think Longfellow put this lyric aside?

Mount of the Holy Cross–Colorado (1873) by William Henry Jackson. Tinted photograph.
Historical Society of Colorado.

The Cross of Snow

Henry Wadsworth Longfellow

In the long, sleepless watches of the night,
    A gentle face—the face of one long dead—
    Looks at me from the wall, where round its head
    The night lamp casts a halo of pale light.
5 Here in this room she died; and soul more white
    Never through martyrdom of fire was led
    To its repose; nor can in books be read
    The legend of a life more benedight.°
There is a mountain in the distant West
10   That, sun-defying, in its deep ravines
    Displays a cross of snow upon its side.
Such is the cross I wear upon my breast
    These eighteen years, through all the changing scenes
    And seasons, changeless since the day she died.

8. benedight (ben′ə·dīt′) *adj.*: archaic for "blessed."

MAKING MEANINGS

The Tide Rises, the Tide Falls

First Thoughts

1. "Footprints on the sands of time" is a common expression referring to mortality and the passing of time. In the second stanza, what do you think is implied about the fate of the traveler when his footprints are washed away?

Shaping Interpretations

2. How does the division into stanzas reflect the passage of time in the poem?

3. What feeling is suggested by the stamping and neighing of the horses when morning comes? What contrasting feeling is suggested by what we are told about the traveler in this stanza?

4. **Onomatopoeia** is a poetic technique in which the sounds of words are used to echo their sense. If you have ever heard the call of a curlew, you know that the words "curlew calls" in line 2 echo the sound this shore bird itself makes. (Its cry is particularly mournful at dusk.) What sound do you think dominates this poem? What atmosphere does it suggest?

5. How does the **meter** of the poem reflect the movement of the tides?

6. Do you think this is a poem about one specific traveler? Or could it be seen as a "drama" about everyone's life? What do you think is suggested by the tide's continuing to rise and fall, despite the fact that the human traveler is gone?

Extending the Text

7. In your Quickwrite notes, how did you view yourself in relation to the natural world? Do you connect with the sentiments in this poem?

Challenging the Text

8. The waves are **personified** in stanza 2 as having "soft, white hands." This is an example of Longfellow's poetic style, which some readers think is too cute, or too sentimental, to be effective. Do you think the personification is justified here? Why or why not?

The Cross of Snow

First Thoughts

1. How did you respond to the strong personal emotion expressed in the poem? Were any of Longfellow's **images** of grief similar to the **metaphor** you explored in your Quickwrite? Explain.

Shaping Interpretations

2. The phrase "martyrdom of fire" in line 6 might confuse readers who did not know that Longfellow's wife had died in a fire. What is Longfellow suggesting about his wife's character when he uses such a powerful word to describe her death?

3. The phrase "watches of the night" usually refers to the rounds made by a watchman as he guards a house or a neighborhood. At certain hours the watch would call "All is well." What are Longfellow's figurative "watches of the night" (line 1)?

4. Explain how the phrase "sun-defying" (line 10) suggests conditions of weather and geology that might actually produce a permanent cross of snow on the side of a mountain. How does the poet relate the idea of a "sun-defying" formation of snow to his own feelings?

Extending the Text

5. What do you think about public expressions of personal grief? (Remember that Longfellow did not show "The Cross of Snow" to anyone during his lifetime.) How does the mass media—TV, radio, magazines, newspapers—affect our views of what's private and what's not? (Think of examples from news programs, talk shows, magazines, and documentaries.)

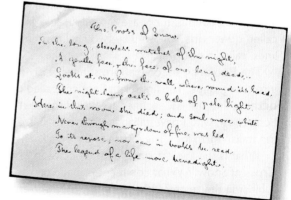

Portion of the original manuscript of "The Cross of Snow" by Henry Wadsworth Longfellow.
By permission of the Houghton Library, Harvard University.

ELEMENTS OF LITERATURE

The Sonnet

"The Cross of Snow" is a **sonnet,** a rhymed fourteen-line poem, usually written in **iambic pentameter.** *Iambic pentameter* describes verse in which each line is composed of five iambs. An **iamb** is a pair of syllables, an unstressed followed by a stressed syllable (ˇ´).

The sonnet is one of the oldest and most enduring poetic forms in world literature. Two of its early masters were the Italian poet Petrarch (1304–1374) and the English playwright William Shakespeare (1564–1616). In later periods, the sonnet was taken up by writers such as John Milton, William Wordsworth, John Keats, Elizabeth Barrett Browning, Edna St. Vincent Millay, John Berryman, Robert Frost, and Robert Lowell.

Two principal forms of the sonnet have been used in English. In the **Elizabethan,** or **Shakespearean,** sonnet, there are three four-line groups, called **quatrains,** followed by two final rhyming lines, called a **couplet.**

The **Petrarchan,** or **Italian,** sonnet, is divided into two groups: The first eight lines are called the **octave,** and the last six lines are called the **sestet.** Longfellow, who knew Italian literature well, used the Italian form for "The Cross of Snow."

What is the subject stated in the octave in "The Cross of Snow"? What comment is made on the subject in the sestet? What is the **rhyme scheme**?

What Is a Sonnet?

1. A sonnet has fourteen lines arranged in a specific pattern. It uses a set rhyme scheme.

2. The typical rhyme scheme in a Petrarchan, or Italian, sonnet is *abba, abba, cde, cde.*

3. The usual rhyme scheme in a Shakespearean sonnet is *abab, cdcd, efef, gg.*

4. The first part of a sonnet usually introduces a subject. The last group of lines makes a comment on the subject. When you read a sonnet, look for the subject and the comment on the subject.

CHOICES:
Building Your Portfolio

Writer's Notebook

1. Collecting Ideas for a Literary Analysis

When you write an analysis of a poem, you might concentrate on the **melodies of language**—on how the poem's language (sound) reinforces its meaning (sense). Read the Longfellow poems aloud to hear their music (or listen to them read aloud on audiotape). Then, jot down examples of the devices the poet uses to create his music—**meter, rhyme, refrain, onomatopoeia, alliteration.** Save your notes for possible use in the Writer's Workshop on page 198.

Comparing Poems

2. Complete and Incomplete

In a short essay, contrast the attitude toward death in "The Tide Rises, the Tide Falls" with that in "The Cross of Snow." Consider this question: Is it important that one poem is about an unnamed traveler while the other is about a specific person?

Evaluating Visuals

3. Visual and Verbal

In a brief essay, evaluate the fine art that accompanies "The Tide Rises, the Tide Falls." Is the image appropriate to the **mood** and **message** of the poem? Cite details from both the poem and the painting to support your position.

Music / Performance

4. A Traveler's Song

Compose and then perform for classmates a musical setting for "The Tide Rises, the Tide Falls." The setting should approximate the **tone** and **atmosphere** of the poem. Alternatively, choose an existing musical recording, an instrumental piece suitable in mood and tempo, and read or recite the poem while the music plays in the background.

John Greenleaf Whittier

(1807–1892)

John Greenleaf Whittier sent five dollars and this advice to a young man who had asked for help with his schooling: "I am sorry for the circumstance of thy condition for I have known what it is to be without money, and to live by hard labor. But, as to education, use thy leisure in educating thyself. Read and study a little every day, and before thee art twenty years of age, thee will find that a school is not needed."

Unlike the other Fireside Poets—Longfellow, Holmes, and Lowell—who were raised in privilege and enjoyed a distinguished education, Whittier was born into a poor Quaker family and had little formal schooling. Whittier started to write poetry when he was about fourteen years old, after his schoolmaster lent him a book by the popular Scottish poet Robert Burns (1759–1796), who had revived the Scottish literary heritage and written memorably of rural life.

At nineteen Whittier met the man whose influence would change the course of his life: the abolitionist William Lloyd Garrison (1805–1879). Garrison, then the editor of the local newspaper, had published a poem by the unknown young poet, and out of curiosity he journeyed out to the family farm to meet Whittier. He urged Whittier's father to give his son more schooling. "Poetry will not give him *bread*," was the father's terse reply.

With Garrison's help, the young Whittier found work in Boston as a newspaper editor. He soon immersed himself in current affairs, working side by side with Garrison, one of the most influential leaders in the antislavery movement. Whittier believed, as Garrison did, that slavery was not only unconstitutional, but also a sin against humanity—a conviction supported by his Quaker beliefs. At twenty-five Whittier paid for the publication of his own pamphlet, *Justice and Expediency* (1833), in which he called for an immediate end to slavery. As a result of

John Greenleaf Whittier (1833) by Robert Peckham (1785–1877). Oil on canvas (27″ × 21½″).

his stand against slavery, Whittier faced stone-throwing mobs, and magazines refused to print his poems.

In 1835, Whittier was elected to the Massachusetts state legislature. For the next quarter century, until the outbreak of the Civil War, Whittier worked tirelessly for the abolition of slavery. He contributed poems and articles to the *National Era,* which he also edited from 1847 to 1860. (It was this weekly newspaper that published Harriet Beecher Stowe's powerful antislavery novel, *Uncle Tom's Cabin,* in installments during 1851–1852.)

After the Civil War, Whittier retired to Amesbury, Massachusetts, where he wrote *Snow-Bound* (1866), a long poem of 759 lines that many critics consider his masterpiece. The poem made Whittier famous and, for the first time, financially comfortable.

Until he was well into his eighties, Whittier continued to publish poetry on homey incidents from rural life, episodes from Colonial history, and the humanitarian ideals of justice, religious faith, and tolerance. As much as his poetry, Whittier's humane convictions and moral example left a permanent mark on his era.

Make the Connection

United We Stand

Sometimes hard times hold a blessing in disguise—they can draw us closer to other people. A warm bond of intimacy can develop even between total strangers who find themselves stranded, in trouble, or sharing unexpected pressures and hardships.

Quickwrite

Write a few sentences about a time when you experienced an un-expected sense of intimacy and even joy while sharing a difficult experience with other people. The experience could be a citywide blackout, a storm, or even a rush to meet a last-minute deadline on a proj-ect. What do you remember about the experience?

Background

An **idyll** is a nostalgic work describing a pleasant rural scene or homey setting. In *Snow-Bound,* Whittier looks back fondly on the life he spent as a boy in the farm-house in Haverhill, Massachusetts, where his family had lived since 1688. Whittier remembers what we would call "an ex-tended family," a gathering under one roof of eight or nine related people of varying ages, along with the male boarder who taught school nearby. Imprisoned by the storm, these people had to live for days without news of the outside world. Their rooms were dimly lighted by candles or perhaps by oil lamps. Their food, stored in crocks, barrels, and briny vats, was kept in the cellar. Water came from a pump in the kitchen or a well in the yard. A bathroom as we know it today did not exist. For heat and cooking, they burned wood. Life, in a word, was hard. But, like many peo-ple, Whittier found in his past a kind of benediction, or blessing.

from Snow-Bound: A Winter Idyll

John Greenleaf Whittier

To the memory of the household it describes,
this poem is dedicated by the author

> The sun that brief December day
> Rose cheerless over hills of gray,
> And, darkly circled, gave at noon
> A sadder light than waning moon.
> 5 Slow tracing down the thickening sky
> Its mute and ominous prophecy,
> A portent seeming less than threat,
> It sank from sight before it set.
> A chill no coat, however stout,
> 10 Of homespun stuff could quite shut out,
> A hard, dull bitterness of cold,
> That checked, mid-vein, the circling race
> Of lifeblood in the sharpened face,
> The coming of the snowstorm told.
> 15 The wind blew east; we heard the roar
> Of Ocean on his wintry shore,
> And felt the strong pulse throbbing there
> Beat with low rhythm our inland air.
>
> Meanwhile we did our nightly chores,—
> 20 Brought in the wood from out of doors,
> Littered° the stalls, and from the mows°
> Raked down the herd's-grass for the cows:
> Heard the horse whinnying for his corn;
> And, sharply clashing horn on horn,
> 25 Impatient down the stanchion° rows
> The cattle shake their walnut bows;°
> While, peering from his early perch
> Upon the scaffold's pole° of birch,
> The cock his crested helmet bent
> 30 And down his querulous challenge sent.

21. littered: scattered straw for beds. **mows:** haylofts where feed is stored.
25. stanchion (stanʹchən): device placed around a cow's neck to keep the cow in its stall.
26. walnut bows: wooden yokes for harnessing cattle.
28. scaffold's pole: pole in the loft of a barn.

The Cotters Saturday Night (detail) (c. 1815) by Eunice Pinney (1770–1849).
Pen and watercolor on paper.

Unwarmed by any sunset light
The gray day darkened into night,
A night made hoary° with the swarm
And whirl-dance of the blinding storm,
35 As zigzag, wavering to and fro,
Crossed and recrossed the wingëd snow:
And ere the early bedtime came
The white drift piled the window frame,
And through the glass the clothesline posts
40 Looked in like tall and sheeted ghosts.

So all night long the storm roared on:
The morning broke without a sun;
In tiny spherule° traced with lines
Of Nature's geometric signs,
45 In starry flake, and pellicle,°
All day the hoary meteor fell;
And, when the second morning shone,
We looked upon a world unknown,
On nothing we could call our own.

50 Around the glistening wonder bent
The blue walls of the firmament,
No cloud above, no earth below,—
A universe of sky and snow!
The old familiar sights of ours
55 Took marvelous shapes; strange domes and towers
Rose up where sty or corncrib stood,
Or garden wall, or belt of wood;
A smooth white mound the brush pile showed,
A fenceless drift what once was road;
60 The bridle post an old man sat
With loose-flung coat and high cocked hat;
The well curb° had a Chinese roof;
And even the long sweep,° high aloof,
In its slant splendor, seemed to tell
65 Of Pisa's leaning miracle.°

62. well curb: frame over a well.
63. sweep: long pole with a bucket attached, used for getting water from a well.
65. Pisa's leaning miracle: Leaning Tower of Pisa in Italy. Whittier refers to it as a miracle because it looks as if it should fall over.

33. hoary (hôr′ē): white, as with age or frost.
43. spherule (sfer′ool): sphere.
45. pellicle (pel′i·kəl): thin film. Whittier is describing different kinds of falling snow.

JOHN GREENLEAF WHITTIER 183

A prompt, decisive man, no breath
Our father wasted: "Boys, a path!"
Well pleased, (for when did farmer boy
Count such a summons less than joy?)
70 Our buskins° on our feet we drew;
With mittened hands, and caps drawn low,
To guard our necks and ears from snow,
We cut the solid whiteness through.
And, where the drift was deepest, made
75 A tunnel walled and overlaid
With dazzling crystal: We had read
Of rare Aladdin's° wondrous cave,
And to our own his name we gave,
With many a wish the luck were ours
80 To test his lamp's supernal powers.
We reached the barn with merry din,
And roused the prisoned brutes within.
The old horse thrust his long head out,
And grave with wonder gazed about;
85 The cock his lusty greeting said,
And forth his speckled harem led;
The oxen lashed their tails, and hooked,
And mild reproach of hunger looked;
The hornëd patriarch of the sheep,
90 Like Egypt's Amun° roused from sleep,
Shook his sage head with gesture mute,
And emphasized with stamp of foot.

All day the gusty north wind bore
The loosening drift its breath before;
95 Low circling round its southern zone,
The sun through dazzling snow mist shone.
No church bell lent its Christian tone
To the savage air, no social smoke
Curled over woods of snow-hung oak.
100 A solitude made more intense
By dreary-voicëd elements,
The shrieking of the mindless wind,
The moaning tree boughs swaying blind,
And on the glass the unmeaning beat
105 Of ghostly fingertips of sleet.
Beyond the circle of our hearth
No welcome sound of toil or mirth

70. buskins (bus′kinz): calf- or knee-high leather
boots.
77. Aladdin's: Aladdin is a young man in *The Arabian Nights* who finds a treasure in a cave.
90. Amun: god of ancient Egypt (also spelled Amon
or Ammon). He is sometimes represented as a
human with a ram's head.

Winter in the Country: A Cold Morning (1862)
by George Henry Durrie (1820–1863). Oil on canvas (26″ × 36″).

Unbound the spell, and testified
Of human life and thought outside.
110 We minded° that the sharpest ear
The buried brooklet could not hear,
The music of whose liquid lip
Had been to us companionship,
And, in our lonely life, had grown
115 To have an almost human tone.

As night drew on, and, from the crest
Of wooded knolls that ridged the west,
The sun, a snow-blown traveler, sank
From sight beneath the smothering bank,

110. minded: realized.

135 Our own warm hearth seemed blazing free.
The crane and pendent trammels° showed,
The Turks' heads° on the andirons° glowed;
While childish fancy, prompt to tell
The meaning of the miracle,
140 Whispered the old rhyme: *"Under the tree,*
When fire outdoors burns merrily,
There the witches are making tea."

The moon above the eastern wood
Shone at its full; the hill range stood
145 Transfigured in the silver flood,
Its blown snows flashing cold and keen,
Dead white, save where some sharp ravine
Took shadow, or the somber green
Of hemlocks turned to pitchy black
150 Against the whiteness at their back.
For such a world and such a night
Most fitting that unwarming light,
Which only seemed where'er it fell
To make the coldness visible.

155 Shut in from all the world without,
We sat the clean-winged° hearth about,
Content to let the north wind roar
In baffled rage at pane and door,
While the red logs before us beat
160 The frost line back with tropic heat;
And ever, when a louder blast
Shook beam and rafter as it passed,
The merrier up its roaring draft
The great throat of the chimney laughed;
165 The house dog on his paws outspread
Laid to the fire his drowsy head,
The cat's dark silhouette on the wall
A couchant° tiger's seemed to fall;
And, for the winter fireside meet,
170 Between the andirons' straddling feet,
The mug of cider simmered slow,
The apples sputtered in a row,
And, close at hand, the basket stood
With nuts from brown October's wood.

120 We piled, with care, our nightly stack
Of wood against the chimney back,—
The oaken log, green, huge, and thick,
And on its top the stout backstick;
The knotty forestick laid apart,
125 And filled between with curious art
The ragged brush; then, hovering near,
We watched the first red blaze appear,
Heard the sharp crackle, caught the gleam
On whitewashed wall and sagging beam,
130 Until the old, rude-furnished room
Burst, flowerlike, into rosy bloom;
While radiant with a mimic flame
Outside the sparkling drift became,
And through the bare-boughed lilac tree

136. crane . . . trammels: swinging arm (crane) attached to the fireplace, with iron hooks (trammels) from which cooking pots are hung.
137. Turks' heads: ornamental shapes resembling turbans. **andirons:** metal supports used to hold wood in a fireplace.
156. clean-winged: Turkey wings were used to brush ashes from the hearth.
168. couchant (kou′chənt): crouching.

MAKING MEANINGS

First Thoughts

1. What did you see as you read this part of *Snow-Bound*?

Shaping Interpretations

2. The first eighteen lines of the poem create a **mood** of foreboding and expectation. List the **images** that help build this mood.

3. The poet emphasizes the fabulous nature of the snowbound world. What specific **imagery** helps us see his farmyard as if it's an exotic sight from another world?

4. Another reference to folklore and the fabulous occurs in the lines describing the crystal cave. In line 80, what do the boys wish they could do? What other details in the poem connect the fabulous or the imaginary with the snowbound farmhouse?

Connecting with the Text

5. A few days spent locked up with family or friends would have some effect on your mood. How do you think you would feel if you were snowbound or otherwise confined with other people? Refer to your Quickwrite notes for ideas.

READING SKILLS AND STRATEGIES

Recognizing Allusions

Snow-Bound was an enormously popular poem, and until a few generations ago, parts of it could be recited by almost every schoolchild in America. However, the poem is not necessarily "easy"; what makes it difficult for some readers are its many **allusions**—references to people and events from history, literature, the arts, or other aspects of culture.

Skim the poem and find allusions to (1) architecture, (2) literature, and (3) history. Which of the references did you recognize? (Did you have to refer to the footnotes?) What do these allusions tell you about the kind of education Whittier assumed his readers would have?

CHOICES: Building Your Portfolio

Writer's Notebook

1. Collecting Ideas for a Literary Analysis

Review the extract from *Snow-Bound,* and take notes on its most powerful **images.** Look for images that evoke sensations of sight, hearing, taste, smell, and even touch. What comparisons help to make the images particularly vivid? Save your notes for possible use in the Writer's Workshop on page 198.

Analyzing a Poem's Appeal

2. The Pull of the Past

When *Snow-Bound* was published, it was an immediate best-seller, and it continued to be reprinted well into the twentieth century. By then, the kind of life it pictures had all but vanished. In one paragraph or more, explain how you would account for the continuing appeal of this poem. Include in your analysis any similar appeals to the romantic past that you find 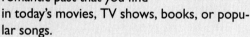 in today's movies, TV shows, books, or popular songs.

Speaking and Listening / Analyzing Poetry's Persuasive Power

3. End Slavery!

In his own time Whittier considered himself an abolitionist first and a poet second. Find several of Whittier's antislavery poems—"The Hunters of Men" or "The Farewell," for example—and read them aloud to the class. Then, as a class, discuss the effectiveness of these poems as antislavery messages.

Oliver Wendell Holmes

(1809–1894)

"Everybody wants to have a hand in a great discovery," Oliver Wendell Holmes wrote in 1846, when, for the first time, an American surgeon used gas to make a patient unconscious during surgery. Holmes, a physician himself, suggested the word *anesthesia* (without feeling), and the name stuck.

A descendant of Anne Bradstreet (page 68), Holmes was born into an already distinguished family in Cambridge, Massachusetts, and he graduated from Harvard College—just a short distance from home. Before turning to medicine, Holmes had studied law, a subject he found "cold and cheerless." He was a twenty-one-year-old law student when the United States government's plan to destroy the warship USS *Constitution* inspired him to write "Old Ironsides," a poem that aroused public sentiment to save the ship and made him famous.

In spite of this early taste of literary glory, Holmes became a physician, because he felt it could teach him about humanity. He was twenty-seven when he published his first book of poetry and, almost at the same time, was awarded a medical degree from Harvard. Combining poetry and medicine did not seem unusual to Dr. Holmes, who was said to hear poetic meter in the rhythm of the human heart.

One of the founders of *The Atlantic Monthly* magazine in 1857 (he also named it), Holmes gained a national reputation from a series of chatty, urbane, and sometimes irreverently witty essays that were eventually collected under the title *The Autocrat of the Breakfast Table* (1858). The leading character, recognizable as Holmes himself, presided over the lively table talk at an imaginary Boston boardinghouse.

Holmes's poetry is, for the most part, light and even comic. It comments on the social and intellectual shortcomings of his contemporaries, particularly those who aspired to higher forms of verse than he himself dared to write. But, on the evidence of his serious poems, such

Oliver Wendell Holmes (1858) by Thomas Hicks (1823–1890). Oil on canvas (53.4 cm × 43.1 cm).

as "The Chambered Nautilus," Holmes had earned the right to judge, not from an envious spirit but in the confidence of an equal talent.

Today, Holmes is perhaps remembered more as a phenomenon—an aristocrat with the common touch, an artist with a passion for science—than as a poet. The famous wit that made his books best-sellers in their day has long become outdated, but the benign figure of Oliver Wendell Holmes remains. It is impossible to forget the gentleness and humor of a man who, beginning his practice as a young physician, hung out a sign saying GRATEFUL FOR SMALL FEVERS.

Before You Read

THE CHAMBERED NAUTILUS

Make the Connection

Things Change

Throughout our lives we outgrow old things and move on to new ones: clothes, attitudes, interests, jobs, types of entertainment—even friendships. As we learn more about ourselves and the world, we're often challenged to widen our perspectives and rethink our assumptions—and the process is not always comfortable.

Quickwrite

Read the Background that follows, and then look at the picture of the nautilus shell, at right. Write a few sentences reflecting on the shell and the creature that once lived in it. If the shell were "human," what would you say to it?

Elements of Literature

Extended Metaphor

A **metaphor** is a figure of speech that makes a comparison between two very unlike things. Sometimes writers extend a metaphor—that is, they take it as far it can logically be developed. An **extended metaphor** may continue for several lines, or it may be developed throughout an entire work.

> **A**n **extended metaphor** is a figure of speech developed throughout several lines or an entire work.
>
> *For more on Metaphor, see the Handbook of Literary Terms.*

Background

A nautilus is a sea creature that lives in a shell, one of those mollusks that grow year by year from the size of a tiny bead to the size of a pumpkin. In Holmes's own description the nautilus shell is composed of a "series of enlarging compartments successively dwelt in by the animal that inhabits the shell, which is built in a widening spiral." The word *nautilus* comes from the Greek word for "sailor," reminding us that the Greeks thought this shell could actually move on the surface of the water, using a membrane as its sail. The nautilus is not only one of the most beautiful objects in nature; it is also one of the most fragile life-containing vessels.

The first three stanzas of this poem are a meditation upon the life and death of the nautilus. In the next-to-last stanza, the poet begins an **apostrophe** (a direct address to an object or to someone who is not present). The visual description here is like the scene in Shakespeare's *Hamlet* (Act V), in which a gravedigger unearths the skull of a man Hamlet knew. Hamlet holds the skull up to the light and speaks words about life and destiny that the skull evokes for him. We might picture the speaker in "The Chambered Nautilus" holding the shell before him and speaking.

The Chambered Nautilus

Oliver Wendell Holmes

This is the ship of pearl, which, poets feign,°
   Sails the unshadowed main,—
   The venturous bark that flings
On the sweet summer wind its purpled wings
5 In gulfs enchanted, where the siren° sings,
   And coral reefs lie bare,
Where the cold sea maids° rise to sun their streaming hair.

Its webs of living gauze no more unfurl;
   Wrecked is the ship of pearl!
10   And every chambered cell,
Where its dim dreaming life was wont to dwell,
As the frail tenant shaped his growing shell,
   Before thee lies revealed,—
Its irised° ceiling rent,° its sunless crypt unsealed!

15 Year after year beheld the silent toil
   That spread his lustrous coil;
   Still, as the spiral grew,
He left the past year's dwelling for the new,
Stole with soft step its shining archway through,
20   Built up its idle door,
Stretched in his last-found home, and knew the old no more.

Thanks for the heavenly message brought by thee,
   Child of the wandering sea,
   Cast from her lap, forlorn!
25 From thy dead lips a clearer note is born
Than ever Triton blew from wreathèd horn!°
   While on mine ear it rings,
Through the deep caves of thought I hear a voice that sings:—

Build thee more stately mansions, O my soul,
30   As the swift seasons roll!
   Leave thy low-vaulted past!
Let each new temple, nobler than the last,
Shut thee from heaven with a dome more vast,
   Till thou at length art free,
35 Leaving thine outgrown shell by life's unresting sea!

1. feign (fān): archaic for "imagine."

5. siren (sī′rən): in Greek mythology, one of a group of sea maidens whose seductive singing lures sailors to wreck their ships on coastal rocks.
7. sea maids: mermaids or sea nymphs.

14. irised (ī′risd): iridescent; rainbowlike. Iris is the Greek goddess of the rainbow. **rent:** torn.

26. than . . . wreathèd (rēth′id) **horn:** echoes a line from "The World Is Too Much with Us," a sonnet by English poet William Wordsworth (1770–1850): "Or hear old Triton blow his wreathèd horn." In Greek mythology, Triton is a sea god, often represented as blowing a trumpet made from a conch shell. *Wreathèd* means "coiled" or "spiral-shaped."

Make the Connection

Word Power

As the old saying tells us, "The pen is mightier than the sword." Words can be powerful tools for resolving conflicts, righting wrongs, or otherwise influencing human actions and emotions. Words can preserve or destroy, praise or protest. They can change the world. The words in this poem saved an American legacy: a historic ship.

Quickwrite

Think of some historical object or place in your own state, city, town, or neighborhood that is being threatened with destruction—or could be one day. Jot down as many reasons as you can think of for why this piece of history should be preserved.

Background

In 1830, the forty-four-gun American warship USS *Constitution,* which had defeated the British warship *Guerrière* in the War of 1812, was scheduled to be scrapped. Holmes sent this poem to the Boston *Daily Advertiser* in protest. The poem aroused public sentiment and saved the ship, which you can still visit in Boston Harbor today.

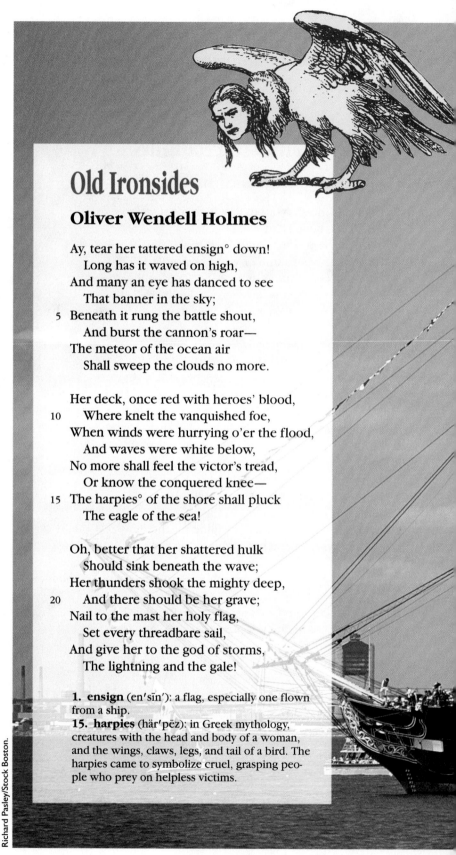

Old Ironsides

Oliver Wendell Holmes

Ay, tear her tattered ensign° down!
    Long has it waved on high,
And many an eye has danced to see
    That banner in the sky;
5 Beneath it rung the battle shout,
    And burst the cannon's roar—
The meteor of the ocean air
    Shall sweep the clouds no more.

Her deck, once red with heroes' blood,
10   Where knelt the vanquished foe,
When winds were hurrying o'er the flood,
    And waves were white below,
No more shall feel the victor's tread,
    Or know the conquered knee—
15 The harpies° of the shore shall pluck
    The eagle of the sea!

Oh, better that her shattered hulk
    Should sink beneath the wave;
Her thunders shook the mighty deep,
20   And there should be her grave;
Nail to the mast her holy flag,
    Set every threadbare sail,
And give her to the god of storms,
    The lightning and the gale!

1. ensign (en′sīn′): a flag, especially one flown from a ship.
15. harpies (här′pēz): in Greek mythology, creatures with the head and body of a woman, and the wings, claws, legs, and tail of a bird. The harpies came to symbolize cruel, grasping people who prey on helpless victims.

Richard Pasley/Stock Boston.

USS *Constitution* in Boston Harbor.

The Sea

Shells and pebbles roll in
the mist of gentle waves.
    A mother cries, a daughter
    mourns.
    The ship went down in the
    storm.
Timber is tossed by the
mountains of the violent sea,
which churns against the cliffs.
    The captain's cry, the
    shipmate's tears.
As the angry waves scatter
their hope like sea spray
    against the wind.

—Elizabeth Enloe
Shades Valley Resource
Learning Center
Birmingham, Alabama

MAKING MEANINGS

The Chambered Nautilus

First Thoughts

1. Review
your
Quickwrite
notes.
Compare
your thoughts
with what the
speaker of the
poem thinks
as *he* looks at
the nautilus.

Reading Check

a. What **metaphor** describes the nautilus in line 1?

b. What **images** in the first stanza help you picture where the nautilus first sailed?

c. According to the second stanza, what has happened to the nautilus?

d. Why does the speaker thank the nautilus in the fourth stanza?

Shaping Interpretations

2. Stanza 3 describes the ways the nautilus grows. The poet uses a **metaphor** comparing the nautilus to a person who changes homes. What details describe how this happens year after year?

3. Step by step, describe the **extended metaphor.** What are the "stately mansions" (line 29), the "low-vaulted past" (line 31), "each new temple" (line 32), the "outgrown shell" (line 35), and the "unresting sea" (line 35)?

Extending the Text

4. "The Chambered Nautilus" is one of the most enduring poems in American literature. (Abraham Lincoln is said to have known it by heart.) Why do you think this poem has endured? Do you think it will still be read one hundred years from now? Be sure to give your reasons.

Challenging the Text

5. Did you find this poem more optimistic than Bryant's "Thanatopsis" (page 171)? Why or why not?

Old Ironsides

First Thoughts

1. Do you think that historical relics like *Old Ironsides* should be preserved? If, very soon, *Old Ironsides* were found to be in danger of sinking at its dock in Boston, do you think most Americans would let it go? Give reasons why or why not.

Shaping Interpretations

2. In simple terms, what message does the first stanza present? What is **ironic** about the way Holmes states his message?

3. When a ship is broken up in the dockyards, it is said to be *scrapped*—that is, stripped of everything valuable or reusable. Is Holmes comparing

the directors of the scrapping business to harpies in stanza 2, or is his scorn directed at someone else? Explain.

4. What do you think the poet wants the ship to **symbolize**?

5. Why do you think this poem was successful in getting the public to save the ship? Point out specific words and phrases that you found particularly persuasive.

Extending the Text

6. Think about specific issues in today's world that have inspired public movements for preservation. Do you think a poem like "Old Ironsides" would be able to sway public opinion today? Why or why not?

CHOICES: Building Your Portfolio

Writer's Notebook

1. Collecting Ideas for a Literary Analysis

Think about the **extended metaphor** in "The Chambered Nautilus" and the ship as **symbol** in "Old Ironsides." Sum up as clearly as you can what the metaphor is and what the ship symbolizes. Then, freewrite on how the metaphor and symbol are used in each poem. Save your notes for possible use in the Writer's Workshop on page 198.

Analyzing a Poem's Message

2. A Heavenly Message

In a brief essay, discuss the message of Holmes's poem "The Chambered Nautilus." First, discuss in what part of the poem the "heavenly message" of the shell is revealed. Then **paraphrase** this mes-

sage—that is, state in your own words what the "voice that sings" says to the speaker. Finally, discuss whether you feel the poet has been successful in developing and leading up to the poem's message. Does the message seem tacked on to give the poem a moral, or is it a natural outgrowth of the poem? How can you relate the message of the poem to your own life?

Crossing the Curriculum: Technical Writing

3. A Scientific Stance

How would Holmes the scientist have described the chambered nautilus? Gather scientific data about the nautilus from other sources, and write an objective, accurate, scientific description of the creature. Include specific data on its vital statistics. What questions might a scientist ask of the nautilus? Present your findings in class. Include a scientific illustration, if you wish.

Creative Writing / Research / Art

4. The Story of a Ship

Research the history of the USS *Constitution,* from its days as a warship to its current use as a tourist attraction in Boston Harbor. Write a short story for children in which you describe the ship and tell its life story. Provide your own colorful illustrations.

Creative Writing

5. A Meditation

We might imagine that Holmes was inspired to write "The Chambered Nautilus" while he was looking at the beautiful nautilus shell. The student poem on page 192 might have been written while the writer was looking at or thinking about the sea. Write a meditation of your own, imitating one of these poems. (Check your Quickwrite notes.) Focus on some object or scene that brings memories, lessons, events, or stories to mind. Open with a line that tells what you are looking at.

Women of Wonder

If "Rip Van Winkle" whetted your appetite for folk tales, consider *The Maid of the North* (Holt, Rinehart and Winston) by Ethel Johnston Phelps. The author collects and retells a variety of traditional folk tales with one thing in common—the heroes are all enterprising females! The twenty-one tales come from many parts of the world, including Africa, Japan, Scandinavia, and North America.

Past, Present, and Future

"If Albert Einstein is right once again . . . then hard as it may be to comprehend, the summer of 1894 *still exists*." Modern-day magazine photographer Si Morley proves Einstein's theory when he travels back to nineteenth-century New York City in Jack Finney's best-selling science fiction classic *Time and Again* (Simon and Schuster). Further time-travel adventures appear in Finney's recent sequel, *From Time to Time* (Simon and Schuster).

The Face of One Long Dead

"The Cross of Snow" is a poem of mourning for a lost love whose absence haunts the speaker years after her death. For an epic treatment of this theme, try reading Emily Brontë's classic *Wuthering Heights*. Inspired by many of the same Romantic poets that influenced Longfellow, Brontë's novel chronicles a tragic love of such intensity that it transcends even death. The novel has been adapted into several films, the most famous starring Laurence Olivier and Merle Oberon. This title is available in the HRW Library.

By the Seashore

"One never knows what chance treasures these easy unconscious rollers may toss up, on the smooth white sand of the conscious mind; what perfectly rounded stone, what rare shell from the ocean floor." In her acclaimed book *Gift from the Sea* (Random House), Anne Morrow Lindbergh describes a seaside vacation in which the shells she discovers on the beach prompt valuable inner discoveries about life.

The Rockets' Red Glare

If you liked Oliver Wendell Holmes's "Old Ironsides," then answers to questions like these might really interest you: Why was the Battle of New Orleans fought after the War of 1812 was officially over? Which battle scenes inspired "The Star-Spangled Banner"? Popular historian Walter Lord answers these and other questions in *The Dawn's Early Light* (W. W. Norton), a lively account of the conflict known in its day as the Second War of Independence.

The American Language

"Noah's Ark": Webster's Dictionary

by Gary Q. Arpin

By the nineteenth century, many Americans felt the need for some kind of authority to govern matters of usage. In England, the ultimate linguistic authority was royal—the King's English. In America, matters were very different.

In a relatively stable social structure, people of a particular class will speak the way their friends and associates speak, and questions of right and wrong speech patterns won't even be raised. In societies where social structure is fluid, though, the matter becomes more complex.

In eighteenth-century England, for instance, the rigid social structure began to give way as the middle class grew. People of humble origins had started to become successful in business. These newly well-to-do sent their children to recently founded schools that, among other things, taught the language habits of the aristocracy the middle class wanted to imitate. Written grammars dictating English usage became popular, and schoolmasters began to take over authority in matters of English language usage. *A New Guide to the English Tongue* (1747) by Thomas Dilworth was a popular grammar book in England.

In America the teaching of English arose for similar reasons. Before the Revolution it would have been difficult to find an "English School" in the Colonies—that is, a school that emphasized English grammar over Latin grammar. After the Revolution, though, regular instruction in English grammar became common in the public schools, as the Colonial social structure gave way to a more fluid and democratic society. However, the only available textbooks came from England. This was clearly an awkward situation for a new nation that wanted to establish linguistic independence.

An American Spelling Book

Enter Noah Webster (1758–1843), a schoolmaster from Connecticut. Webster was looking for a way to finance his legal education, and he was also passionately dedicated to the cause of American English. To help advance these two causes, Webster published a spelling book in 1783, when he was twenty-five. Even though it was based in important respects on English models—Dilworth's grammar and Samuel Johnson's great *Dictionary of the English Language* (1755)—the spelling book turned out to be a major force in the drive for American linguistic independence. Over the generations, *The American Spelling Book* (also known as the "Blue-Backed Speller") was issued in numerous editions, and more than sixty million copies were sold.

Webster prepared his speller and his later textbooks for a purpose:

> . . . to reform the abuses and corruption which . . . tincture the conversation of the polite part of Americans . . . and especially to render the pronunciation . . . accurate and uniform by demolishing those obvious distinctions of provincial dialects.

Webster reasoned that accurate and uniform American spelling would lead to uniform American speech, and that uniformity in speech would "reconcile the people of America to each other."

Consistency in Spelling

The whole idea of consistency in spelling was fairly new in Webster's time and was directly related to the increasing use of the printing press. Until the 1700s, people followed rather flexible rules of spelling. In fact, some letters of the alphabet were not completely fixed: *i, j, y, u, v,* and *w* were not yet distinct letters. Sometimes a word would be written with an *e* at the end and sometimes not. Thus, *join* might be written *ioyn* or *joyne* or *ioyne*. The word *the* was frequently written *ye,* the *y* in this case being a form of an obsolete Middle English letter that stood for the sound *th.*

Early editions of Webster's American speller were quite conservative—that is, most of the spellings were consistent with Samuel Johnson's English spellings. The main exception was Webster's omission of *k* in words ending in *–ck.* Where Dr. Johnson's dictionary had *publick* and *musick,* Webster's speller had *public* and *music.* By 1789, though, Webster offered more radical ideas regarding spelling, and they aroused a great deal of mocking resistance, even in his own country.

Webster's first principle was the "omission of all superfluous or silent letters"—such as the *k* in *musick* and all silent vowels and consonants. *Bread, give, friend, programme, travelled,* and *built* thus became *bred, giv, frend, program, traveled,* and *bilt.*

Webster's second principle was to regularize spelling and sound. For example, *grieve* and *mean* contain the same vowel sounds spelled differently. Webster used *ee* for both as well as anywhere that sound oc- curred—*greev* and *meen,* and also *pleez* and *bleet.* Similarly, *laugh* and *draught* became *laf* and *draft, plough* became *plow,* and *women* became *wimmin.*

Webster gradually yielded to public pressure and modified his more radical spellings. Still, vir- tually all of the present differ- ences between British and American spelling were advo- cated by Webster.

Webster's First Dictionary (1806)

Readers were no doubt very surprised when they came across words spelled *tung, fether, soop,* and *definit* in Webster's first dictionary, *A Compendious Dictio- nary of the English Language,* pub- lished in 1806.

Many of Webster's recom- mended pronunci- ations must have been surprising as well. Webster dis- liked fashionable and urban peo- ple and manners almost as much as he disliked British ways. He hated any pronunciation that smacked of being affected or too fashionable. Webster re- jected the *yu* sound in words such as *lecture, nature, figure,* and *tenure* as affectations. He rec- ommended that they be pro- nounced *lecter, nater, figger,* and *tenor.*

Webster laid down stern rules regarding spelling and pro- nunciation, but he was often willing to bow to the practice of common people in matters of grammar and usage. The single thread running through these two contradictory attitudes was

Webster's democratic desire for a common, regular American language.

Many of Webster's spelling reforms and odd pronounce- ments make him appear to be a crackpot, and there is no ques- tion that there was something of the crackpot about him. He had a degree from Yale, but as a linguist he was self-taught. Like many self-taught people, he had odd gaps in his learning. As a re- sult, his etymologies, or word histories, were frequently incorrect.

> Many of Webster's spelling reforms and odd pronouncements make him appear to be a crackpot, and there is no question that there was something of the crackpot about him.

Webster's Amer- ican Dictionary (1828)

Even though his enthusiasms and spotty knowledge led him astray, Webster was no fool, and he was enormously energetic. His 1806 dictionary defined 37,000 words and indicated their pronuncia- tion. The 1828 *American Dictionary of the English Language* was an incredible accomplish- ment for one person. It defined 70,000 words and provided etymologies as well as pronunci- ations. More than 12,000 defini- tions were published for the first time. Webster was the first lexicographer to include Ameri- canisms such as *lot* ("a piece of land"), *to spell* ("to relieve some- one at work"), and *clever* ("good-natured"). "Such local terms exist," Webster had writ- ten some years before, "in spite of lexicographers and critics. Is this *my* fault? And if local terms exist, why not explain them? . . . How are such words to be understood without the aid of a dictionary?"

The *American Dictionary* also included the new American meanings of older English words and settled for all time the changes in word endings that distinguish American from modern British usage: *–er* for *–re* (*center* rather than *centre*); *–or* for *–our* (*favor* rather than *favour*); *–c* for *–ck* (*music* rather than *musick*); *–ck* for *–que* (*check* rather than *cheque*); *–ize* for *–ise* (*legalize* rather than *legalise*); and *–ler* for *–ller* (*traveler* rather than *traveller*). We say *skedule* rather than *shedule* because Webster thought the pronunciation of *schedule* should follow the example of *school*.

Webster's Legacy

English purists shuddered to learn of Webster's determination to include American words and usages, and one critic suggested that the resulting volume of "foul and unclean" things be dubbed "Noah's Ark."

But Webster's pronouncements, even when they had little sound linguistic reasoning behind them, settled the uncertainties about authority in American English. Generations of Americans decided on the correctness of a word or a usage or a spelling by "looking it up in Webster's," and every household had to have a copy of Webster's dictionary next to the Bible.

By 1828, Webster's radical view of the development of American English had moder-

ated, though his patriotism had not diminished. "The body of the language is the same as in England," he wrote in the Preface to the *American Dictionary*, "and it is desirable to perpetuate that sameness." In the same Preface, though, he pointed proudly at the burgeoning American literature as a source of richness and at the growth of the language as a source of pride.

Over the years many of Noah Webster's etymologies have been corrected, and spelling has been regularized further. Old words have taken on new meanings, and thousands of new words have been added to American English. Yet Webster was a central figure in the evolution of American English, and his name continues to signify excellence in dictionaries. Two of the United States' biggest sellers, *Webster's New World Dictionary* and *Merriam-Webster's Collegiate Dictionary,* still proudly display his name in their titles. Webster would have been pleased to have seen the fruits of his labors.

Try It Out

1. **Using consistent spelling.** Consider this sentence written by Webster in his reformed spelling. "Every possible reezon that could ever be offered for altering the spelling of wurds, stil exists in full force; and if a gradual reform should not be made in our language, it wil proov that we are less under the influence of reezon than our ancestors." What incon-

sistencies do you see in Webster's reformed spelling? Find a brief prose passage of your choice and write it in your own simplified—but consistent—spelling. Accompany your passage with a brief explanation of the rules for your reformed spelling.

2. **Spelling sounds.** Make a list of words that are spelled in similar ways but are pronounced differently (such as *tough* and *bough*). Then, make a list of pairs of words that are spelled differently but have similar pronunciations (such as *dead* and *bed*). How would a consistent spelling rule help, for example, students for whom English is a second language? Would there be any drawbacks to consistent spelling?

3. **Inventing alternate spellings.** Nonstandard forms of simplified spellings have flourished in product names ("Tastee Treetz"); road signs ("Thruway North"); and even pop music groups ("Boyz II Men"). List five other examples of nonstandard spellings from your everyday experience. Then try inventing five original product or business names that use nonstandard spellings.

Writer's Workshop

Technology
HELP

See Writer's Workshop 2
CD-ROM. *Assignment:*
Interpretation.

ASSIGNMENT

Write an essay in
which you analyze
the key elements
of a literary work,
paying special atten-
tion to their purpose,
effect, and relation
to the work's overall
meaning.

AIM

To analyze; to
inform; to explain.

AUDIENCE

Your teacher, class-
mates, family, or
a school literary
magazine.

A Tip for an Analysis

In writing a critical
analysis, there is often
an urge to summarize
a text in great detail.
Do not give in to this
temptation. In a liter-
ary analysis, your job is
to analyze, not summa-
rize. You may need to
add a brief summary in
your introduction, but
it should be *very* brief.

EXPOSITORY WRITING

ANALYZING A LITERARY WORK

When you read a literary work, your first response is often a strong feeling:
"This poem really moved me," or "I thought this story was upsetting!" In a literary analysis, you go beyond this first response, to understand how and why
the work produces these effects. Writing an analysis gives you a chance to take
a work apart and explain how it creates meaning. You do this by looking at the
literary elements that form its structure.

Prewriting

1. **Choose a literary work.** If you haven't been assigned a
   specific literary work to analyze, your first step will be
   to choose a work that you're interested in. Look over the
   notes you took for the Work in Progress assignments in this
   collection. Which selections caught your attention? What key literary
   elements make these works effective? Do your notes suggest a topic that
   would give you material for a sustained analysis?

2. **Focus your analysis.** You can discuss a wide range of literary elements in
   the work you choose, but your analysis will be stronger if you narrow your
   focus to one or two. Try to isolate the most prominent elements—those
   that distinguish the work, that contribute to its overall effect, and that help
   communicate its central theme or message. Here are some possible topics
   for a focused analysis:

   • The role of setting in "Rip Van Winkle"
   • Symbolism in "The Tide Rises, the Tide Falls"
   • Natural imagery in "Snow-Bound: A Winter Idyll"
   • The function of metaphor in "The Chambered Nautilus"

3. **Write a thesis statement.** Your thesis statement will be the controlling idea of your analysis. It will state a generalization about the work. A
   thesis statement is important because it will also determine the organizational structure of your essay. Experiment with a variety of thesis statements until you have crystallized your thoughts in a single strong sentence.
   Make sure your thesis statement isn't so broad that it could be the subject
   of an entire book, or so narrow that it can't be developed to much more
   than a paragraph.

   Example thesis statement: In "The Chambered Nautilus," the speaker
   uses an extended metaphor to compare the growth of the nautilus in its
   shell to the growth of a human soul.

4. **Gather Evidence.** Reread the text at least twice as you negotiate your interpretation of the material. Then, list all the evidence you can find to support your thesis statement. While most of your evidence should come from the text itself (your **primary source**), you may also want to use citations from **secondary sources** if they are relevant to your main ideas. (Secondary sources are critical reviews, biographies, encyclopedia entries, and similar works.) Cite specific lines from your primary source; then, paraphrase their meaning in your own words. You may want to group your evidence into a **graphic organizer** like this:

Element	Examples	Support for Thesis
Metaphor	"ship of pearl," 1 "venturous bark," 3 "frail tenant," 12 "crypt unsealed," 14 "the silent toil," 15	In these first three stanzas, the speaker describes the life and death of a nautilus in human terms— comparing its shell to a variety of human dwellings: a ship, a building for a tenant, a tomb. These metaphors also suggest aspects of the human spirit: its dreamy thirst for adventure, its frailty, its experience of death.
	"heavenly message brought by thee," 22 "Build thee more stately mansions, O my soul," 29 "each new temple, nobler than the last," 32	In the last two stanzas, the speaker celebrates the growth and movement of the nautilus as a metaphor for the growth of his own soul, which expands into bigger and more noble dwellings until it is at last released from the body.

5. **Organize your ideas.** Before you begin to write your first draft, decide how you will present your ideas and then make an outline. Look at your graphic organizer to see how you grouped your main ideas and supporting details. You may want to organize your points in **chronological order,** the order in which the elements occur in the text. If your main ideas and supporting evidence focus on a particular theme, purpose, or effect, you might consider organizing your ideas in **order of importance:** emphasize your most powerful point first (*or* build up to it and place it at the end). As you make your outline, be sure that your main ideas and supporting details follow a logical progression. Be sure also to include in each paragraph details that directly support your thesis.

Strategies for Elaboration

To make the opening of your essay more interesting:

1. **Hook your reader's interest.** Open your introductory paragraph with an intriguing question, an anecdote, or a personal comment that relates to your thesis statement.

2. **Try for drama.** Open your essay with a dramatic quote from the piece, one that relates particularly well to your main idea.

3. **Make connections to theme.** Briefly refer to the theme of the text and describe how the elements you are analyzing relate to the theme.

Language Handbook H E L P

See Using Modifiers, pages 1227-1228; Quotation Marks and Ellipsis Points, page 1247.

**Communications
Handbook
H E L P**

See Proofreading.

**Revision
S T R A T E G I E S**

*Because a literary analysis
can be subjective, you
should aim for precise word
choice, or diction. Replace
vague words with specific
ones; if necessary, refer to a
thesaurus.*

▌ *Evaluation Criteria*

A good literary analysis
*1. opens with a striking
quotation, anecdote,
question, or personal
comment*
*2. provides necessary back-
ground information on
the work being studied*
*3. states the thesis concisely
and directly, with main
ideas presented in the
order in which they will
be discussed*
*4. provides ample support-
ing evidence from the text
for each main idea*
*5. follows a clear and
consistent pattern of
organization*
*6. quotes accurately from
primary and secondary
sources, citing page and
line numbers*
*7. closes with a summary
that restates the main
idea*

Drafting

1. **Introducing your ideas.**   The main purpose of your introductory paragraph is to state your thesis, or main idea. Your thesis statement should be
clear, concise, and direct. Avoid vagueness, ambiguity, and overstatement
(claiming more than you can actually demonstrate). Your introductory
paragraph should also identify the work you are writing about (by title and
author) and provide whatever background information you think the
reader will need (for example, dates, information on the author, literary
history, and historical context).

2. **Analyzing and supporting.**   Your outline and your graphic organizer
will come in handy as you write the body of your essay. Follow the organization of your main ideas and supporting details set up in your outline.
Use the entries on your graphic organizer to direct your analyses of the
meaning, the purpose, and the effects of each element.

    While the main source of support for your argument will be citations
and paraphrases from your primary source, you may want to bolster your
claims with additional support. Here are some strategies to reinforce
your analysis:

    • Make appeals to common sense and everyday experience.

    • Include references to other literary works. (Do other writers or
    works use literary elements in a similar way?)

    • Present relevant facts or details from the author's life. (Does the work
    reflect personal events in the writer's life or historical events that oc-
    curred during his or her lifetime?)

    • Use quotations from experts. (Have critics written about the work
    and said something interesting about these particular elements?)

    • Offer personal responses. (Do the responses have the potential to add
    authenticity and originality to your analysis?)

3. **Closing the essay.**   Think of a way to summarize or restate your thesis
at the end so that you pull all the threads of your analysis together. As you
wrap up, you may want to note any questions you still have about the
work. (Don't hesitate to admit that you don't have all the answers.)

Evaluating and Revising

1. **Peer review.**   As a peer reviewer, comment on the following questions:

    • Is the thesis statement clear, concise, and direct?

    • Does the writer supply good supporting details from the text itself?

    • Is the essay organized clearly—in chronological order, in order of
    importance, or in some other logical order?

    • Does each paragraph make a clear point that supports the thesis?

    • Is the essay brought to a satisfying conclusion?

2. **Self-evaluation.**   Read your peers' comments, be objective, and respond
to them honestly. Try to reread your own essay as if you were not the author. Do you see places where you can improve the essay's organization,
or make it clearer or stronger?

Language Workshop

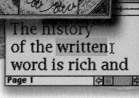
SMOOTHING IT OUT: INSERTING MODIFIERS

Imagine that Washington Irving had described Rip Van Winkle in this way:

> Rip Van Winkle was a simple fellow. He was also good-natured and helpful.

The description above is passable, but it's choppy and bland. (Try reading it aloud to catch its dull sound.) Here is a more vivid and readable description:

> Rip Van Winkle was a simple, good-natured, helpful fellow.

The following example provides information about where Rip Van Winkle lived. Once again, however, the sentences are short and choppy:

> Rip Van Winkle lived at the foot of the Kaatskill Mountains. He lived in a small house. It was timeworn and weather-beaten.

If the information were combined into one sentence, it would read much more smoothly:

> Rip Van Winkle lived in a small, timeworn, weather-beaten house at the foot of the Kaatskill Mountains.

Guidelines for Inserting Modifiers into Sentences

1. If your description is made up of several short, choppy sentences, look for the one that is your **base sentence**—the sentence that expresses the central idea. In the first example above, "Rip Van Winkle was a simple fellow" is the base sentence.
2. Look for modifiers in the other descriptive sentences. A modifier may be an adjective, adverb, prepositional phrase, or some other word or phrase that helps describe another word in the sentence.
3. Insert modifiers from the other sentences into the base sentence. Where necessary, change the word order and punctuation. For example, you might need to change a period to a comma.
4. When you transfer a modifier from one sentence to another, make sure it modifies the same word it used to.

Writer's Workshop Follow-Up: Revising

Reread the analysis you wrote for the Writer's Workshop (page 198). Does it contain any bland or choppy sentences that you could combine by using modifiers? Don't be overly eager to combine sentences; sometimes a short, unembellished sentence is exactly right for your purposes.

Technology HELP

See Language Workshop CD-ROM. *Key word entry: inserting modifiers.*

Language Handbook HELP

See Using Modifiers, pages 1227–1228.

Try It Out

Turn each of the following sentence pairs into a single sentence by inserting modifiers from the second sentence into the base sentence.

1. The children of the village shouted whenever Rip Van Winkle approached. They shouted with joy and expectancy.
2. Rip's daughter took him to her home. Her home was snug and well furnished.

Situation

Meriwether Lewis and William Clark's exploration of the American West (1804–1806) was a key event in the westward expansion of the United States and helped fuel the romantic imagination. Suppose you are planning a vacation in which you will retrace part of the route taken by these famous explorers.

Strategies

Select the right kind of map for your purposes.

- A U.S. road map shows the system of roadways currently linking cities, states, and geographical features. Most road maps also indicate campsites, parks, airports, and places of interest.

- A political map can show government divisions such as counties, congressional districts, and judicial jurisdictions.

- A physical or topographical map shows landforms, often with their elevation.

- A historical map shows the locations of important historical events, routes, and settlements.

- A special-purpose map may show such things as population density, agricultural products, and industrial zones.

Use map features.

- Map features include the map title, the compass rose, the

Central South Dakota

- ⋯⋯ Lewis and Clark Route, 1804
- ▲ State Park
- ■ Point of Interest
- ✪ State Capital
- ● Cities and Towns
- — Highways

0   25 miles

distance scale (or scale bar), and the legend or key (explaining symbols used on the map).

Using the Strategies

1. Let's examine Lewis and Clark's route in present-day South Dakota, shown on the map above. What waterway did the expedition follow?

2. Approximately how many miles did Lewis and Clark travel between Chamberlain and Mobridge?

3. Traveling today by road, which of the two main routes from Chamberlain to Pierre is likely to be faster? In which two compass directions would you travel?

4. What three places of special interest could you visit in or near Pierre?

Extending the Strategies

- Use a historical map and a current road map to plan a sightseeing trip of New York's Lower Hudson Valley, made famous by Washington Irving.

- Use appropriate maps to plan a 10-mile bicycle ride or a 5-mile hike near where you live.

NOTE: Many maps are available on the Internet.

Problem

American Romantic writers shared the belief that human beings can learn lessons from nature and that human activities should be conducted in harmony with the natural world. What are we doing today to ensure a better harmony with nature? What more can we do?

Project

Increase public consciousness of an important environmental issue. Explore specific ways that you, your family, your school, or your community can move toward a lifestyle that is in greater harmony with nature.

Preparation

1. Brainstorm with other students to identify various environmental groups in your community, and arrange to interview representatives from several of these groups. Consider as possible interviewees city planners, soil conservationists, organic farmers, wildlife biologists, and waste-disposal experts.

2. Contact environmental organizations, and request brochures, mission statements, and articles. Organizations to contact include the Sierra Club, the National Audubon Society, the World Wildlife Fund, and the U.S. Environmental Protection Agency.

3. Research some aspect of the history of the environmental movement. Look up information on key figures, such as John Muir, John James Audubon, Rachel Carson, and David Brower. Also consider writers and artists who have made the environment a central topic in their works— for example, Wendell Berry and Edward Abbey.

Procedure

1. If you are interviewing individuals, prepare a list of questions beforehand, but think of these questions as only a general guide. The person, or persons, being interviewed may introduce some interesting angle or a different topic.

2. Examine and evaluate your research, narrowing it down to a manageable topic that truly interests you.

3. If you are researching the history of the environmental movement, go beyond the library to other sources of information: city parks, environmental organizations, museums, and galleries.

Presentation

Present your information in one of the following formats (or another that your teacher approves):

1. **An Ecologically Sound Business**

   Write up a proposal for a business that would be environment-friendly. Include with your proposal a statement of your business philosophy, as well as a scrapbook that includes published materials (articles, brochures) that lend credibility to your idea for a business. You may also include quotations from environmental groups, transcripts of your interviews with people who work with the environment, and any visuals (artwork, photographs, diagrams, graphs) that support your proposal.

2. **An Advertising Campaign**

   With one or more other students, plan and develop an advertising campaign to make your school and community more environmentally aware. Make posters, design and create brochures and fliers, and come up with catchy slogans and logos that will get your message across.

3. **A Video Documentary**

   Make a short video documentary on some aspect of the environmental movement. Show the video to your class.

Processing

What did you learn about contemporary environmentalism by doing this project? What are some beliefs and policies you discovered that you agree with? Are there any ideas you disagree with? Write a reflection for your portfolio.

The American Renaissance

A Literary Coming of Age
1840–1860

A Philosopher's Camp in the Adirondacks (1858) by William James Stillman. Oil on canvas.

Concord Free Public Library, Concord, Massachusetts.

Girls' Evening School (c. 1840). American. Anonymous. Pencil and watercolor (13 ½" × 18 ⅛").

The American Renaissance

A Literary Coming of Age   *by* **Gary Q. Arpin**

Literature the Americans have none. . . . In the four quarters of the globe, who reads an American book?

> *—Sydney Smith, English critic, 1818*

We have listened too long to the courtly muses of Europe. . . . The mind of this country, taught to aim at low objects, eats upon itself. . . . We will walk on our own feet; we will work with our own hands; we will speak our own minds. . . . A nation of men will for the first time exist, because each believes himself inspired by the Divine Soul which also inspires all men.

> *—Ralph Waldo Emerson*
> *from "The American Scholar," 1837*

go.hrw.com
LEO 11-American Renaissance

A remarkable party took place on August 5, 1850, in Stockbridge, Massachusetts. Among those attending were a Boston publisher and two of his authors, Oliver Wendell Holmes (page 187) and Nathaniel Hawthorne (page 296), and a New York editor and two of *his* authors, Cornelius Mathews and Herman Melville (page 311). The party began in the morning with a climb in the Berkshire Mountains. The group was in good humor—in part, perhaps, because of a champagne picnic lunch. During the climb, Melville leaned out over the steep cliffs to demonstrate how sailors took in sail. Hawthorne, usually very restrained, loosened up enough to look wildly about for the great carbuncle (a deep-red gem), the subject of a tale, based on a local legend, that he had written many years before.

The hike in the Berkshires was followed in the evening by a long dinner. The table conversation turned to American literature. In response to a statement made by Holmes praising English writers, Melville vigorously defended American writers.

Would there ever be an American writer as great as England's William Shakespeare? This question started a heated discussion, with Melville again firmly supporting the American side. Hawthorne found himself agreeing with Melville, whom he had never met before.

> It is that blackness in Hawthorne that . . . fixes and fascinates me.
> —Herman Melville

By the mid–nineteenth century, learned people still debated whether America would ever produce great writing. At a celebrated gathering in 1850, Nathaniel Hawthorne and Herman Melville firmly agreed that it would.

Bandbox depicting Erie Canal. About 1830.

Cooper-Hewitt National Design Museum, Smithsonian Institution/Art Resource, NY. Gift of Sarah and Eleanor Hewitt (1918–19-12a, b).

Hawthorne and Melville: Opposites Attract

It seemed highly unlikely that these two writers would become friends. Herman Melville was an ex-sailor with little formal education. He had lived in the South Seas and had written a remarkable first novel, *Typee* (1846), about his adventures. At the time of the party, Melville was hard at work on his fifth novel, which, it appeared, would be very long.

Nathaniel Hawthorne, who was fifteen years older than Melville, was well educated, reserved, and a bit of a loner. He had written many short stories and had recently published *The Scarlet Letter* (1850), a novel about sin and hypocrisy in Puritan New England.

Despite their different backgrounds, a friendship sprang up between the two writers. "I met Melville the other day," Hawthorne wrote to a friend, "and liked him so much that I have asked him to spend a few days with me before leaving these parts." This was the beginning of an association that came at a critical point in Melville's life, when he was hard at work on his masterpiece, *Moby-Dick*.

After the meeting, Melville sat down and read Hawthorne's works—and was exposed for the first time to what he called the "power of blackness" in Hawthorne's writing.

Nathaniel Hawthorne and Herman Melville discovered a common bond: They both saw a dark side to human existence, and they sought to record this aspect of human nature in their works.

> Think of it. To go down to posterity as a "man who lived among the cannibals."
>
> —Herman Melville, writing about himself to Hawthorne

Puritan neighbors avoiding Hester Prynne. From *The Scarlet Letter* by Nathaniel Hawthorne. Lithograph after a painting by George H. Boughton.

The Granger Collection, New York.

MOBY-DICK;

OR,

THE WHALE.

BY

HERMAN MELVILLE,

AUTHOR OF
"TYPEE," "OMOO," "REDBURN," "MARDI," "WHITE-JACKET."

NEW YORK:
ROTHERS, PUBLISHERS.
HARD BENTLEY.

Peabody Essex Museum, Salem, Massachusetts.

First Flowering: A Declaration of Literary Independence

The immediate result of Melville's meeting with Hawthorne was a magazine essay in which Melville passionately defended American literature. Stating that England was in many ways "alien to us," Melville urged American readers to "prize and cherish" their own writers. In a burst of literary patriotism, Melville claimed that, in Hawthorne, America was very close to producing its own Shakespeare.

Melville's horn blowing for American writing coincided with a vital period in American literature. It was a time when the American landscape and American culture would finally find their place in a literature distinct from European models. Writers were aware of this, and they sometimes used the word *renaissance* (ren'ə·säns'), meaning "rebirth," to describe this extraordinary explosion of American literary genius. When Americans referred to themselves as living in a renaissance, they were comparing their times to the European Renaissance, a period of extraordinary cultural vitality that lasted from about the fourteenth to the sixteenth century. A better term, however, for what happened in the still-raw America of the mid-1800s might be "coming of age." From 1849 to 1855, American writers produced a remarkable body of work, enough masterpieces for a national literature.

> Nothing is at last sacred but the integrity of your own mind.
> —Ralph Waldo Emerson

In the mid–nineteenth century, writers such as Nathaniel Hawthorne, Ralph Waldo Emerson, Henry David Thoreau, and Herman Melville produced some of the early masterpieces of American literature.

Intellectual and Social Life in New England

This burst of American literature can be traced in large measure to the intellectual and social ferment in New England. New England had long been known for its interest in self-improvement and intellectual inquiry. This interest found expression in the Lyceum (lī·sē'əm) movement, begun in 1826 in Millbury, Massachusetts. Lyceum organizations, soon established in many communities, had a number of goals, including educating adults, training teachers, establishing museums, and instituting social reforms. A typical part of a Lyceum program was a course of lectures in winter. These became immensely popular in New England and the Midwest. One of the most popular speakers was Ralph Waldo Emerson (page 216).

This was a time of social improvement in other ways too. New England was a center of many reform movements. Horace Mann dedicated

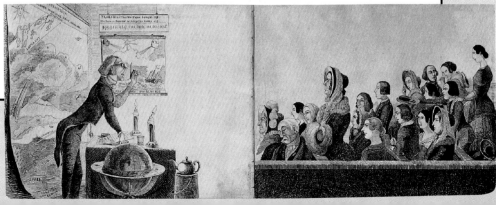

Lyceum Lecture by James Pollard Espy at Clinton Hall (1841) by an unknown artist. Pen and ink.

Museum of the City of New York.

THAT WAS THEN...

What would your life be like if you lived in the 1840s?

For one thing, it probably would be shorter. On average, you could expect to live only about forty years. A quarter of your friends would die relatively young, many of them victims of tuberculosis, the nineteenth-century plague.

Your world would be far less crowded than it is now. In 1840, there were about 17 million people living in the United States. (In contrast, by 1995 there were about 260 million Americans.) Some 3 million of them were of African heritage, and of those, only about half a million were not enslaved.

Back of the State House in Philadelphia by **William Birch.**

Library of Congress.

---

himself to improving public education; Dorothea Dix sought to relieve the horrible conditions in institutions for the mentally ill; William Lloyd Garrison and other abolitionists struggled to put an end to slavery; feminists like Elizabeth Peabody, Margaret Fuller, and Emma Willard campaigned to increase women's rights.

Social causes, both reasonable and crackpot, abounded during this time. Numerous utopian (yoo·tō′pē·ən) projects—plans for creating a more perfect society—were developed. In 1840, Emerson wryly remarked that every man who could read had plans in his pocket for a new community. Emerson was speaking from personal experience, for he was a member of one of the most influential of these utopian groups.

> *Ralph Waldo Emerson was a primary force behind the flowering of American culture. He helped inspire numerous reform movements that aimed to improve public education, end slavery, elevate the status of women, and generally smooth the edges off the rough social conditions of the time. Various utopian groups drew up comprehensive plans for a better society.*

The Transcendentalists: True Reality Is Spiritual

Emerson's utopian group quickly became known as "The Transcendental Club." The term *transcendental* comes from the eighteenth-century

Cities were rapidly expanding in the 1840s. The five largest were Boston, New York City, Philadelphia, Baltimore, and Charleston. Visitors to New York were stunned by the filth there. There was no citywide garbage collection, and pigs moved freely about the streets.

Chances are you'd live in the country, though, in a house heated by wood or coal fires and lit by oil lamps. Your father most likely would be a farmer, and your mother probably would concentrate on taking care of the home but would help out with the farm. You would probably have several brothers or sisters. If you went to school (many young people didn't), you'd likely walk to a one-room schoolhouse. There, side-by-side with students of varying ages, you'd be taught reading, writing, arithmetic, and proper behavior. It's possible

you'd already be married at your age. Both rich and poor married quite young—as early as thirteen or fourteen in the South.

What would you do for fun? In rural areas, you'd probably go dancing on weekend nights or attend cornhusking contests or quilting bees. You might start learning about a new pastime called baseball—the first game closely resembling the modern sport took place in 1846. You might read for entertainment. But wherever you lived, your main form of entertainment would probably be visiting friends and neighbors.

Who would be your heroes? Probably not athletes or entertainers. The main heroes were politicians, especially those with military backgrounds. Just about everyone's favorite hero was George Washington.

German philosopher Immanuel Kant. The word refers to the idea that in determining the ultimate reality of God, the universe, the self, and other important matters, one must transcend, or go beyond, everyday human experience in the physical world. Intuition is an important tool for discovering truth.

For Emerson, **Transcendentalism** was not a new philosophy but "the very oldest of thoughts cast into the mold of these new times." That "oldest of thoughts" was Idealism, which had already been articulated by the Greek philosopher Plato in the fourth century B.C. Idealists said that true reality involved ideas rather than the world as perceived by the senses. Idealists sought the permanent reality that underlay physical appearances. The Americans who called themselves Transcendentalists were idealists, but in a broader, more practical sense. Like many Americans today, they believed in human perfectibility, and they worked to achieve this goal.

To recall these village lyceums, these rude country halls, evening meetings in odd churches, barns, schools, and banquet rooms, tents spread in preparation for the idyllic summer's opening of the college year . . . is to imagine a time when people still looked to literary men for guidance. . . . Emerson made a thousand appearances, crossed the Mississippi on ice in dead winter to deliver a lecture in Iowa, was bumped, jostled, frozen in wagons, carriages, flatboats, steamboats, trains (where he felt so solitary that he vowed he would go over to any man reading a book and hug him).

—Alfred Kazin,
    from An American Procession

Emerson and Transcendentalism: The American Roots

Though Emerson was skeptical of many of the Transcendentalists' ideas and projects, he was the most influential and best-known member of the group, largely because of his lectures and books. His writing and that of his friend Henry David Thoreau (page 230) clearly and forcefully expressed Transcendental ideas. As developed by Emerson, Transcendentalism grafted ideas from Europe and Asia onto a home-grown American philosophical stem. Its American roots included Puritan thought, the beliefs of the eighteenth-century religious revivalist Jonathan Edwards (page 77), and the Romantic tradition exemplified by William Cullen Bryant (page 169).

> I was simmering, simmering, simmering; Emerson brought me to a boil.
>
> —Walt Whitman

The Puritans believed that God revealed himself to people through the Bible and through the physical world. William Bradford (page 26), for example, saw the death of an abusive sailor on the *Mayflower* as the direct action of God in the human world. Anne Bradstreet (page 68) saw evidence of God in the grandeur of nature. Jonathan Edwards found God's wisdom, purity, and love in the sun, moon, and stars—in fact, in all of nature. This native mysticism—also typical of **Romanticism**—reappears in Emerson's thought. "Every natural fact," Emerson wrote, "is a symbol of some spiritual fact."

Transcendentalism was based partly on the philosophy of Idealism, which dated back to ancient Greece. It was based also on the ideas of American thinkers ranging from the Puritans to the nineteenth-century Romantics. Transcendentalists viewed nature as a doorway to a mystical world holding important truths.

Ralph Waldo Emerson.
Drawing by David Levine. Reprinted with permission from *The New York Review of Books.* Copyright ©1968 NYREV, Inc.

Emerson's Optimistic Outlook

Emerson's mystical view of the world sprang not from logic but from intuition. Intuition is our capacity to know things spontaneously and immediately through our emotions rather than through our reasoning abilities. Intuitive thought—the kind Emerson believed in—contrasts with the rational thinking of someone like Benjamin Franklin (page 84). Franklin did not gaze on nature and feel the presence of a Divine Soul; Franklin looked at nature and saw something to be examined scientifically and used to help humanity.

An intense feeling of optimism was one product of Emerson's belief that we can find God directly in nature. God is good, and God works through nature, Emerson believed. Therefore, even the natural events that seem most tragic— disease, death, disaster—can be explained on a spiritual level. Death is simply a part of the cycle of life. We are capable of evil because we are separated from a direct, intuitive knowledge of God, according to Emerson. But if we simply trust ourselves—that is, trust in the power each of us has to know God directly—then we will realize that each of us is also part of the Divine Soul, the source of all good.

Emerson's sense of optimism and hope appealed to audiences who lived in a period of economic downturns, regional strife, and conflict over slavery. Your condition today, Emerson seemed to tell his readers and listeners, may seem dull and disheartening, but it need not be. If you discover the God within you, he suggested, your lives will partake of the grandeur of the universe.

"What do you think of the world to come?" an admirer asked the philosopher.

"One world at a time," Thoreau replied.

Old Manse in Concord, where first Emerson and then Hawthorne lived.

Steve Solum/ Bruce Coleman, Inc.

Emerson believed in the power of intuition, our ability to learn directly without conscious use of reasoning. He emphasized the importance of each individual, and his outlook was optimistic.

Melville, Hawthorne, and Poe: A Challenge to the Transcendentalists

Emerson's idealism was exciting for his audiences, but not all the writers and thinkers of the time agreed with Transcendentalist thought. "To one who has weathered Cape Horn as a common sailor," Herman Melville wrote of Emerson's ideas, "what stuff all this is."

Some people think of Nathaniel Hawthorne, Herman Melville, and Edgar Allan Poe (page 260) as anti-Transcendentalists, because their view of the world seems so profoundly opposed to the optimistic view of Emerson and his followers. But these Dark Romantics, as they are

known, had much in common with the Transcendentalists. Both groups valued intuition over logic and reason. Both groups, like the Puritans before them, saw signs and symbols in human events—as Anne Bradstreet found spiritual significance in the fire that destroyed her house (page 69). (Not surprisingly, the Dark Romantics used the literary technique of **symbolism** to great effect in their works.)

The Dark Romantics didn't disagree with Emerson's belief that spiritual facts lie behind the appearances of nature; they disagreed with the premise that those facts are necessarily good, or harmless. Emerson, they felt, had taken the ecstatic, mystical elements of Puritan thought and ignored its dark side— its emphasis on Original Sin, its sense of the innate depravity of human beings, and its Calvinistic notions of predestination. The Dark Romantics

came along to redress the balance. Their view of existence developed from both the mystical and the melancholy aspects of Puritan thought. In their works, they explored the conflict between good and evil, the psychological effects of guilt and sin, and even madness and derangement in the human psyche. Behind the pasteboard masks of social respectability, the Dark Romantics saw the blankness and the horror of evil. From this imaginative, unflinching vision they shaped a uniquely American literature.

Portrait of Edgar Allan Poe (1985) by Rick McCollum. Oil on linen board with oil pencil.

Courtesy Rick McCollum.

The works of writers such as Hawthorne, Melville, and Poe acknowledged the existence of sin, pain, and evil in human life and formed a counterpoint to the optimism of the Transcendentalists.

Quickwrite
How Do You See Yourself?

Do you agree with the Transcendentalists' optimistic views of human perfectibility? Or are you more like the Dark Romantics, believing that the world has a dark, irrational side that can't be ignored? Write down your own opinions about the ideas of the Transcendentalists and the Dark Romantics. How do you see yourself in relation to them?

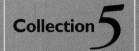

Emerson

Thoreau

I find I live quite happily without those things I think necessary in winter in the North. And as I write these words, I remember, with some shock at the disparity in our lives, a similar statement made by a friend of mine in France who spent three years in a German prison camp. Of course, he said, qualifying his remark, they did not get enough to eat, they were sometimes atrociously treated, they had little physical freedom. And yet, prison life taught him how little one can get along with, and what extraordinary spiritual freedom and peace such simplification can bring. I remember again, ironically, that today more of us in America than anywhere else in the world have the luxury of choice between simplicity and complication of life. And for the most part, we, who could choose simplicity, choose complication. War, prison, survival periods, enforce a form of simplicity on man. The monk and the nun choose it of their own free will. But if one accidentally finds it, as I have for a few days, one finds also the serenity it brings.

—Anne Morrow Lindbergh,
from Gift from the Sea

Ralph Waldo Emerson

(1803–1882)

Shortly before the poet Walt Whitman died, he honored a man whose ideas had influenced him profoundly throughout his own long and controversial career. "America in the future," he wrote, "in her long train of poets and writers, while knowing more vehement and luxurious ones, will, I think, acknowledge nothing nearer [than] this man, the actual beginner of the whole procession."

"This man" was Ralph Waldo Emerson. Emerson expressed, better than anyone before him, the advantages of a young land—its freedom from the old, corrupt, and dying thought and customs of Europe; its access to higher laws directly through nature rather than indirectly through books and the teachings of the past; its energy; and its opportunity to reform the world.

Emerson was one of those rare writers who appealed both to intellectuals and to the general public. His influence on the popular mind—thanks to the thousands of lectures he gave throughout the United States—was strong. Although Emerson had something of a reputation for being hard to understand, his lectures were usually quite accessible. "I had heard of him as full of transcendentalisms, myths, and oracular gibberish," Herman Melville wrote a friend after hearing Emerson lecture. "To my surprise, I found him quite intelligible." Melville added wryly, "To say truth, they told me that that night he was unusually plain."

Despite his great influence, it is difficult even to classify what kind of writer Emerson was. *Essayist* is too limited, and *philosopher* is too broad. The best term, perhaps, is *poet*—a poet whose best work was not always in verse.

"I am born a poet," Emerson wrote to his fiancée, Lydia Jackson, in 1835, "of a low class without doubt, yet a poet. That is my nature and vocation. My singing, be sure, is very 'husky,' and is for the most part in prose. Still am I a poet in the sense of a perceiver and dear lover of the harmonies that are in the soul and in matter. . . ."

Ralph Waldo Emerson (c. 1867) by William Henry Furness, Jr. (1828–1867). Oil on canvas (45¾″ × 36³/₁₆″).

The Burden of Expectation

Emerson was born in Boston in 1803 to a family that was cultured but poor. When he was only eight years old, his father, a Unitarian minister, died of tuberculosis. His mother, left with six growing children to care for, opened a boardinghouse.

The father's place in the lives of the Emerson children was taken by their aunt. Mary Moody Emerson was a strict Calvinist who emphasized self-sacrifice and whose enormous energy drove the Emerson boys to achievement. "She had the misfortune," Emerson later wrote, "of spinning with a greater velocity than any of the other tops."

Every step of Emerson's life had been laid out for him from an early age. He was to go to Harvard and become a minister like his father and the seven generations of Emersons before him. Emerson uncomfortably obeyed. His life was a series of attempts to establish his own identity against this background of expectation.

Young Rebel

Emerson entered Harvard at fourteen. He was an indifferent student, although he read widely in philosophy and theology. Upon graduation, Emerson took a job at a school run by his uncle and prepared himself, with many doubts, for the Unitarian ministry. In 1829, at the age of

go.hrw.com
LEO 11-5

twenty-five, he accepted a post at Boston's Second Church; that same year, he married Ellen Tucker, a beautiful but fragile seventeen-year-old already in the early stages of tuberculosis. Seventeen months later, Ellen died.

Emerson's grief coincided with a growing disbelief in some of the central doctrines of his religion. In June 1832, he shocked his congregation by resigning the ministry and setting off on an extended tour of Europe. There he met and conversed with the Romantic poets William Wordsworth and Samuel Taylor Coleridge, as well as other influential writers.

Emerson's New Pulpit

Returning to the United States in late 1833, Emerson settled in Concord, Massachusetts, and soon married Lydia Jackson. He began to supplement his meager income by giving lectures and found in that occupation "a new pulpit," as he once wrote. Emerson's view was distinctively American in that he denied the importance of the past: "Let us unfetter ourselves of our historical associations and find a pure standard in the idea of man."

> "Let us . . . find a pure standard in the idea of man."

The last phrase points to Emerson's focus on humanity. Individual men and women were part of this "idea of man" in the same way that individual souls were part of a larger entity, which Emerson later called the "Over-Soul." The idea of nature also corresponded to the idea of man—both were part of a universal whole in which people could see their souls reflected.

Over the years, Emerson's influence grew. In 1837, he excited the student audience at Harvard with the lecture now known as "The American Scholar." In the speech, Emerson demanded that American scholars free themselves from the shackles of the past. "Our day of dependence," he declared, "our long apprenticeship to the learning of other lands, draws to a close."

A year later, Emerson was invited back to Harvard to speak to a group of divinity students. His speech, "The Divinity School Address," called for a rejection of institutional religion in favor of a personal relation with God. Religious truth, Emerson said, was "an intuition. It cannot be received at second hand." The lecture so outraged Harvard authorities (who heard in it a denial of the divinity of Christ) that three decades passed before Emerson was allowed to speak there again.

Twilight of an Idol

With the author's growing fame, Concord increasingly became a destination for truth-seeking young people who looked to Emerson as their guru. The young responded to Emerson's predictions that they were on the verge of a new age; intellectuals responded to his philosophical ideas about the relations among humanity, nature, and God; and society as a whole responded to his optimism.

That optimism was dealt a severe blow in 1842 when Emerson's son Waldo died of scarlet fever at the age of five. By nature a rather reserved man, Emerson had found in Waldo someone to whom he could show his love spontaneously. At the child's death, he shrank into an emotional shell from which he never emerged. "How can I hope for a friend," he wrote in his journal, "who have never been one?"

In later years, Emerson suffered from a severe loss of memory and had difficulty recalling the most ordinary words. This affliction resulted in his increasing public silence, and when he did appear in public, he read from notes.

In the autumn of 1881, Walt Whitman paid Emerson a visit of respect and was asked to dinner. Whitman wrote that Emerson "though a listener and apparently an alert one, remained silent through the whole talk and discussion. A lady friend [Louisa May Alcott] quietly took a seat next to him, to give special attention. A good color in his face, eyes clear, with the well-known expression of sweetness, and the old clear-peering aspect quite the same." Six months later, Emerson was dead.

Before You Read

FROM NATURE

"Standing on the bare ground, — my head bathed by the blithe air, & uplifted into infinite space, — all mean egotism vanishes. I become a transparent Eyeball." Nature, p. 13.

Caricature of Emerson by Christopher Pearce Cranch from *Illustrations of the New Philosophy.*

Make the Connection

Nature Nurtures

Exhilarated by nature's beauty and tranquility, Emerson felt he was in tune with his better self, in harmony with eternal things. If today we commune with nature in order to find ourselves, we may be taking up Emerson's search for "an original relation to the universe."

Reading Skills and Strategies

Monitoring Your Reading

As you study these essays, look for key passages that seem to state the **main idea** of a section. **Paraphrase** statements that seem difficult or puzzling to you. Check the footnotes, and use the glossary at the back of the book for definitions of difficult words. Above all, be sure to ask questions of the text.

Elements of Literature

Imagery

Emerson the poet helps out Emerson the philosopher in this essay, *showing* us scenes of nature that he loves rather than just *telling* us about his feelings in general. As you read, look for the **imagery**—descriptive language that appeals to one or more of our five senses—that Emerson uses.

> **I**magery is the use of language to evoke a picture or concrete sensation of a person, thing, place, or an experience.
>
> *For more on Imagery, see the Handbook of Literary Terms.*

Background

In his introduction to the book *Nature,* from which the following chapter is taken, Emerson offers a clue to the underlying purpose of his work when he encourages his contemporaries to look directly at nature:

"Our age is retrospective. It builds the sepulchers of the fathers. It writes biographies, histories, and criticism. The foregoing generations beheld God and nature face to face; we, through their eyes. Why should we not also enjoy an original relation to the universe? Why should we not have a poetry and philosophy of insight and not of tradition, and a religion by revelation to us, and not the history of theirs?"

Dover Plains, Dutchess County, New York (1848) by Asher Brown Durand.
Oil on canvas (42½″ × 60½″).

from Nature

Ralph Waldo Emerson

To go into solitude, a man needs to retire as much from his chamber[1] as from society. I am not solitary while I read and write, though nobody is with me. But if a man would be alone, let him look at the stars. The rays that come from those heavenly worlds, will separate between him and vulgar things. One might think the atmosphere was made transparent with this design, to give man, in the heavenly bodies, the <u>perpetual</u> presence of the <u>sublime</u>. Seen in the streets of cities, how great they are! If the stars should appear one night in a thousand years, how would men believe and adore; and preserve for many generations the remembrance of the city of God which had been shown! But every night come out these envoys of beauty, and light the universe with their <u>admonishing</u> smile.

1. **chamber:** room.

WORDS TO OWN
perpetual (pər·pech′o͞o·əl) *adj.*: constant; unchanging.
sublime (sə·blīm′) *adj.* used as *n.*: that which inspires awe.
admonishing (ad·män′ish·iŋ) *v.* used as *adj.*: mildly warning.

The stars awaken a certain reverence, because though always present, they are always inaccessible; but all natural objects make a kindred impression, when the mind is open to their influence. Nature never wears a mean appearance. Neither does the wisest man extort all her secret, and lose his curiosity by finding out all her perfection. Nature never became a toy to a wise spirit. The flowers, the animals, the mountains, reflected all the wisdom of his best hour, as much as they had delighted the simplicity of his childhood.

When we speak of nature in this manner, we have a distinct but most poetical sense in the mind. We mean the integrity of impression made by manifold natural objects. It is this which distinguishes the stick of timber of the woodcutter, from the tree of the poet. The charming landscape which I saw this morning, is indubitably made up of some twenty or thirty farms. Miller owns this field, Locke that, and Manning the woodland beyond. But none of them owns the landscape. There is a property in the horizon which no man has but he whose eye can integrate all the parts, that is, the poet. This is the best part of these men's farms, yet to this their warranty deeds[2] give no title.

To speak truly, few adult persons can see nature. Most persons do not see the sun. At least they have a very superficial seeing. The sun illuminates only the eye of the man, but shines into the eye and the heart of the child. The lover of nature is he whose inward and outward senses are still truly adjusted to each other; who has retained the spirit of infancy even into the era of manhood. His intercourse with heaven and earth, becomes part of his daily food. In the presence of nature, a wild delight runs through the man, in spite of real sorrows. Nature says—he is my creature, and maugre[3] all his impertinent griefs, he shall be glad with me. Not the sun or the summer alone, but every hour and season yields its tribute of delight; for every hour and change corresponds to and authorizes a different state of the mind, from breathless noon to grimmest midnight. Nature is a setting that fits equally well a comic or a mourning piece. In good health, the air is a cordial[4] of incredible virtue. Crossing a bare common, in snow puddles, at twilight, under a clouded sky, without having in my thoughts any occurrence of special good fortune, I have enjoyed a perfect exhilaration. Almost I fear to think how glad I am. In the woods too, a man casts off his years,

2. **warranty deeds:** legal documents showing ownership of property.
3. **maugre** (mô′gər): archaic for "in spite of" or "despite."
4. **cordial** (kôr′jəl): a liquor that stimulates the heart.

- -

WORDS TO OWN

manifold (man′ə·fōld′) *adj.:* many different.
indubitably (in·dōō′bi·tə·blē) *adv.:* without a doubt.
integrate (in′tə·grāt′) *v.:* unify.

- -

as the snake his slough, and at what period soever of life, is always a child. In the woods, is perpetual youth. Within these plantations of God, a decorum and sanctity reign, a perennial festival is dressed, and the guest sees not how he should tire of them in a thousand years. In the woods, we return to reason and faith. There I feel that nothing can befall me in life—no disgrace, no calamity (leaving me my eyes), which nature cannot repair. Standing on the bare ground—my head bathed by the blithe air, and uplifted into infinite space—all mean egotism vanishes. I become a transparent eyeball. I am nothing. I see all. The currents of the Universal Being circulate through me; I am part or particle of God. The name of the nearest friend sounds then foreign and accidental. To be brothers, to be acquaintances—master or servant, is then a trifle and a disturbance. I am the lover of uncontained and immortal beauty. In the wilderness, I find something more dear and connate[5] than in streets or villages. In the tranquil landscape, and especially in the distant line of the horizon, man beholds somewhat[6] as beautiful as his own nature.

The greatest delight which the fields and woods minister, is the suggestion of an occult relation between man and the vegetable. I am not alone and unacknowledged. They nod to me and I to them. The waving of the boughs in the storm, is new to me and old. It takes me by surprise, and yet is not unknown. Its effect is like that of a higher thought or a better emotion coming over me, when I deemed I was thinking justly or doing right.

Yet it is certain that the power to produce this delight, does not reside in nature, but in man, or in a harmony of both. It is necessary to use these pleasures with great temperance. For, nature is not always tricked[7] in holiday attire, but the same scene which yesterday breathed perfume and glittered as for the frolic of the nymphs, is overspread with melancholy today. Nature always wears the colors of the spirit. To a man laboring under calamity, the heat of his own fire hath sadness in it. Then, there is a kind of contempt of the landscape felt by him who has just lost by death a dear friend. The sky is less grand as it shuts down over less worth in the population.

5. **connate:** inborn.
6. **somewhat:** something.
7. **tricked:** dressed up.

WORDS TO OWN

slough (sluf) *n.*: outer layer of a snake's skin, which is shed periodically.
perennial (pər·en′ē·əl) *adj.*: recurring yearly.
blithe (blīth) *adj.*: carefree.
occult (ə·kult′) *adj.*: hidden.

SPOTLIGHT ON
Emerson's Aphorisms

A Study Table (1882) by William Harnett. Oil on canvas (39⅞″ × 51⅜″).

Munson-Williams-Proctor Institute Museum of Art, Utica, New York.

Studded throughout Emerson's work are quotable, memorable sayings on broad topics. These are **aphorisms**—short statements that express wise or clever observations about life. (Aphorisms are also called "maxims" or "adages.") Try paraphrasing Emerson's aphorisms in your own words: You'll see how much meaning the writer has packed into a few words. That is what makes an aphorism memorable.

Many of Emerson's aphorisms originated in the journal he began keeping when he was a junior in college; by the end of his life, it filled many volumes.

For more aphorisms, see those by the poet Wallace Stevens, page 786.

I confess I am a little cynical on some topics, and when a whole nation is roaring Patriotism at the top of its voice, I am fain[1] to explore the cleanness of its hands and purity of its heart. I have generally found the gravest and most useful citizens are not the easiest provoked to swell the noise, though they may be punctual at the polls.

—*Journals,* 1824

Don't trust children with edge tools. Don't trust man, great God, with more power than he has, until he has learned to use that little better. What a hell should we make of the world if we could do what we would! Put a button on the foil[2] till the young fencers have learned not to put each other's eyes out.

—*Journals,* 1832

The maker of a sentence, like the other artist, launches out into the infinite and builds a road into Chaos and old Night, and is followed by those who hear him with something of wild, creative delight.

—*Journals,* 1834

Poetry must be as new as foam and as old as the rock.

—*Journals,* 1844

The invariable mark of wisdom is to see the miraculous in the common.

—*Nature*

A man is a god in ruins.

—*Nature*

Nothing can bring you peace but yourself. Nothing can bring you peace but the triumph of principles.

—*"Self-Reliance"*

Prayer as a means to effect a private end is meanness and theft. It supposes dualism and not a unity in nature and consciousness. As soon as the man is at one with God, he will not beg. He will then see prayer in all action.

—*"Self-Reliance"*

This time, like all times, is a very good one, if we but know what to do with it.

—*"The American Scholar"*

Books are the best of things, well used; abused, among the worst.

—*"The American Scholar"*

Public and private avarice make the air we breathe thick and fat.

—*"The American Scholar"*

1. fain: reluctantly willing.   **2. foil:** sword.

Hawthorne Talks About Emerson

Emerson, who thought of sin as merely a child's case of measles on the world, and Nathaniel Hawthorne, who plumbed the nature of evil, could never talk together. For a time, Hawthorne lived at Brook Farm, a self-governing, experimental community of Transcendentalists, founded by the minister George Ripley. But he left after a few months, finding the high-minded discussions stifling. Hawthorne then lived for a time in a house called the Old Manse in Concord, the same house where Emerson had written his first book, *Nature*. Here, in a passage from his essay called "The Old Manse," Hawthorne talks about Emerson and the "hobgoblins" who came to Concord seeking answers to the riddle of the world.

These hobgoblins of flesh and blood were attracted thither by the widespreading influence of a great original thinker, who had his earthly abode at the opposite extremity of our village. His mind acted upon other minds of a certain constitution with wonderful magnetism, and drew many men upon long pilgrimages to speak with him face to face. Young visionaries—to whom just so much of insight had been imparted as to make life all a labyrinth[1] around them—came to seek the clue that should guide them out of their self-involved bewilderment. Gray-headed theorists—whose systems, at first air, had finally imprisoned them in an iron framework—traveled painfully to his door, not to ask deliverance, but to invite the free spirit into their own thralldom.[2] People that had lighted on a new thought, or a thought that they fancied new, came to Emerson, as the finder of a glittering gem hastens to a lapidary,[3] to ascertain its quality and value. Uncertain,

1. **labyrinth:** maze.
2. **thralldom:** servitude.
3. **lapidary:** gem dealer.

troubled, earnest wanderers through the midnight of the moral world beheld his intellectual fire as a beacon burning on a hilltop, and, climbing the difficult ascent, looked forth into the surrounding obscurity more hopefully than hitherto. The light revealed objects unseen before—mountains, gleaming lakes, glimpses of a creation among the chaos; but also, as was unavoidable, it attracted bats and owls and the whole host of night birds, which flapped their dusky wings against the gazer's eyes, and sometimes were mistaken for fowls of angelic feather. Such delusions always hover nigh whenever a beacon-fire of truth is kindled.

For myself, there had been epochs of my life when I, too, might have asked of this prophet the master word that should solve me the riddle of the universe; but now, being happy, I felt as if there were no question to be put, and therefore admired Emerson as a poet of deep beauty and austere tenderness, but sought nothing from him as a philosopher. It was good, nevertheless, to meet him in the wood paths, or sometimes in our avenue, with that pure, intellectual gleam diffused about his presence like the garment of a shining one; and he so quiet, so simple, so without pretension, encountering each man alive as if expecting to receive more than he could impart. And, in truth, the heart of many an ordinary man had, perchance, inscriptions which he could not read. But it was impossible to dwell in his vicinity without inhaling more or less the mountain atmosphere of his lofty thought, which, in the brains of some people, wrought a singular giddiness—new truth being as heady as new wine. Never was a poor little country village infested with such a variety of queer, strangely dressed, oddly behaved mortals, most of whom took upon themselves to be important agents of the world's destiny, yet were simply bores of a very intense water. . . .

—Nathaniel Hawthorne,
from "The Old Manse"

FROM **SELF-RELIANCE**

Make the Connection

Rugged Individualism

For Americans in the early years of the country's history, belonging to a bold, young nation was a tremendous source of group pride. Perhaps the greatest source of that pride was the high value the group placed on individual liberty. In 1841, Emerson nourished this creed of individualism with his essay "Self-Reliance."

Quickwrite

Write down the associations you make with the word *self-reliance*: definitions, examples, and synonyms. How does self-reliance differ from selfishness or self-centeredness?

Elements of Literature

Figures of Speech

Emerson makes many of his points through a series of **figures of speech** that compare abstract ideas with ordinary things or events, such as "Society is a joint-stock company." Some of his figures of speech are difficult and require rereading before you can fully understand Emerson's point.

A **figure of speech** is a word or phrase that describes one thing in terms of another and that is not meant to be taken literally.

For more on Figures of Speech, see page 78 and the Handbook of Literary Terms.

Long Island Farmer Husking Corn (1833–1834) by William Sidney Mount. Oil on canvas mounted on panel (20⅞″ × 16⅞″).

The Museums at Stony Brook, Stony Brook, New York. Gift of Mr. & Mrs. Ward Melville.

from Self-Reliance

Ralph Waldo Emerson

There is a time in every man's education . . . when he arrives at the <u>conviction</u> that envy is ignorance; that imitation is <u>suicide</u>; that he must take himself for better, for worse, as his portion; that though the wide universe is full of good, no kernel of nourishing corn can come to him but through his toil bestowed on that plot of ground which is given to him to till. The power which resides in him is new in nature, and none but he knows what that is which he can do, nor does he know until he has tried. Not for nothing one face, one character, one fact makes much impression on him, and another none. This sculpture in the memory is not without preestablished harmony. The eye was placed where one ray should fall, that it might testify of that particular ray. We but half express ourselves, and are ashamed of that divine idea which each of us represents. It may be safely trusted as <u>proportionate</u> and of good issues, so it be faithfully <u>imparted</u>, but God will not have his work made <u>manifest</u> by cowards. A man is relieved and gay when he has put his heart into his work and done his best; but what he has said or done otherwise, shall give him no peace. It is a deliverance which does not deliver. In the attempt his genius deserts him; no muse befriends; no invention, no hope.

Trust thyself: Every heart vibrates to that iron string. Accept the place the divine Providence has found for you; the society of your contemporaries, the connection of events. Great men have always done so and confided themselves childlike to the genius of their age, betraying their perception that the absolutely trustworthy was seated at their heart, working through their hands, <u>predominating</u> in all their being. And we are now men, and must accept in the highest mind the same <u>transcendent</u> destiny; and not minors and invalids in a protected corner, not cowards fleeing before a revolution, but guides, redeemers, and <u>benefactors</u>, obeying the Almighty effort, and advancing on Chaos and the Dark. . . .

These are the voices which we hear in solitude, but they grow faint and inaudible as we enter into the world. Society everywhere is in <u>conspiracy</u> against the manhood of every one of its members. Society is a joint-stock company in which the members agree for the better securing of his bread to each shareholder, to surrender the liberty and culture of the eater. The virtue in most request is conformity. Self-reliance is its <u>aversion</u>. It loves not realities and creators, but names and customs.

Whoso would be a man must be a nonconformist. He who would gather immortal palms[1] must not be hindered by the name of goodness, but must explore if it be goodness. Nothing is at last sacred but the <u>integrity</u> of your own mind. Absolve you to yourself, and you shall have the suffrage of the world. . . .

A foolish consistency is the hobgoblin of little minds, adored by little statesmen and philosophers and divines. With consistency a great soul has simply nothing to do. He may as well concern himself with his shadow on the wall. Speak what you think now in hard words, and tomorrow speak what tomorrow thinks in hard words again, though it contradict everything you said today— "Ah, so you shall be sure to be misunderstood"— Is it so bad then to be misunderstood? Pythagoras was misunderstood, and Socrates, and Jesus, and Luther, and Copernicus, and Galileo, and Newton,[2] and every pure and wise spirit that ever took flesh. To be great is to be misunderstood. . . .

---

1. he who . . . immortal palms: he who would win fame. In ancient times, palm leaves were carried as a symbol of victory or triumph.
2. Pythagoras . . . Newton: people whose contributions to scientific, philosophical, and religious thought were ignored or suppressed during their lifetimes.

- -

WORDS TO OWN

conviction (kən·vik′shən) *n.*: belief.
proportionate (prō·pôr′shən·it) *adj.*: having a correct relationship between parts; balanced.
imparted (im·pärt′əd) *v.*: revealed.
manifest (man′ə·fest′) *adj.*: plain; clear.
predominating (prē·däm′ə·nāt′iŋ) *v.* used as *adj.*: having influence.
transcendent (tran·sen′dənt) *adj.*: excelling; surpassing.
benefactors (ben′ə·fak′tərz) *n. pl.*: people who help others.
conspiracy (kən·spir′ə·sē) *n.*: secret plot with a harmful or illegal purpose.
aversion (ə·vur′zhən) *n.*: intense dislike.
integrity (in·teg′rə·tē) *n.*: sound moral principles; honesty.

- -

Onward to Utopia

For thousands of years people have tried to create utopias—communities that reflect a particular philosophy of how to live. The word *utopia,* based on a Greek word meaning both "no place" and "good place," originated during the Renaissance. From Pythagoras and Plato in ancient Greece to Thomas More in sixteenth-century England to the commune experiments of late twentieth-century America, men and women have experimented with utopian communities.

Emerson was in the thick of 1830s utopian reform. The utopian group that met in each other's homes starting in 1836 became known as "The Transcendental Club" and included a wide range of members and beliefs. Besides Emerson, there was George Ripley, founder of Brook Farm in Massachusetts, a self-governing experimental community that survived for six years and was home briefly to Nathaniel Hawthorne. There was Bronson Alcott, a radical educator who co-founded the community Fruitlands and was the father of Louisa May Alcott (author of *Little Women*). And there was Margaret Fuller, an influential feminist and critic, who edited the Transcendentalist publication *The Dial.*

Why did utopian communities flourish in the United States during the mid-nineteenth century? For one thing, it was a time of great uncertainty and change as citizens struggled with slavery, the unequal status of women, the cruel treatment of American Indians, and some grim effects of industrialization. Rebelling against the status quo, utopian communities tried to create prosperous and harmonious environments. Many were religious communities founded on ideals of nonviolence and communal ownership, and some were transplants from Europe: The Shaker communities, founded by Ann Lee, got their start in England about 1772. In many utopian communities, African Americans and women could find more equality than in society at large.

Community members often had to abide by rules that were quite restrictive. At Fruitlands, the short-lived vegetarian community established by Bronson Alcott, residents were permitted to eat only vegetables that grew up toward heaven—no root vegetables such as carrots and potatoes were allowed! They also did not take milk from cows or wool from sheep, nor would they use animals to pull plows.

Most utopian ventures failed within a few years; as the Transcendentalists of Brook Farm discovered, innovative thinkers aren't necessarily willing or successful farmers. But several utopian communities did endure for decades. Some—like the Shakers, the Oneida Community, and the Amana Church Society—lasted well into the twentieth century and are widely known for excellent products, from furniture to flatware to appliances. In all, more than 100,000 Americans participated in utopian communities in the nineteenth century.

Imagination

A personal response to
Ralph Waldo Emerson's essay,
"Self-Reliance"

Imagine a flower growing in a garden. Create the surroundings—perhaps a brook or a tree, possibly a butterfly nearby. Picture the tranquility of the scene. Now color the sky and the grasses. What color will your flower be? Red? White? Yellow? Did you choose that color because it was that of a flower you had seen somewhere in nature or in a painting? Did you color your flower according to accepted values—a red rose, a yellow daffodil, a white lily—laid down years ago by other artists or nature itself? Now close your eyes for a moment and visualize a brilliant purple rose in your garden. What do you think? Is that flower wrong? Many people would think a purple rose silly, the product of an ignorant child, perhaps. They would tell you that roses can't possibly be purple—everybody knows that! And yet, who can say that an idea is wrong? A purple rose. Think: If the world accepted only "normal" visions, nothing new would ever be created. No one would dare stray from the "luster of the firmaments laid down by bards and sages." There would be no imagination, no fantasy, no chimerical creatures.

Imagine a great arch, soaring into the heavens—a "firmament," if you will, of "bards and sages." People of long ago built this arch, strengthening it with their ideas, extending the graceful curve until it once again touched the ground. They cherished their arch and nurtured it with fancy and imagination. The keystone proclaimed in scripted letters: "Imagine! From a gleam in the darkness can a new world be created!" The arch shone in the sunlight, ethereal and majestic. Then, the imagination stopped—people condemned fanciful inventions and the people who imagined them. People closed their minds, determined to preserve the old way of thinking as the only correct way. Relinquishing their creativity, they discarded their visions in favor of "normality," the way things "should be." Slowly, the arch crumbled. With no imagination to sustain its graceful form, it grew weaker and weaker, eventually vanishing altogether. As it faded into people's memories, their universe, too, shrank quietly, until they realized that they had nothing left; every object had its "normal" shape, size, and color.

And so they sit, clutching their red roses, amidst the remains of their imagination.

—Shelby Pearl, James Madison High School, Vienna, Virginia

MAKING MEANINGS

from Nature

First Thoughts

1. Look back over your reading notes, and discuss passages that struck you as difficult or puzzling. What reading strategies could you apply to figure out the meaning of each?

> **Reading Check**
>
> What three or four sentences from the essay do you think express Emerson's **main ideas**? Paraphrase each of the sentences you choose.

Shaping Interpretations

2. How would our attitude toward the stars change if they appeared only once every thousand years? What point is Emerson making about nature with this attention-getting example?

3. What do you think Emerson means by a "poetical sense" of looking at nature? What **images** illustrate the distinction between nature used for practical benefits and nature viewed in this poetic way?

4. Emerson's **image** of a "transparent eyeball" in the fourth paragraph is one of the most famous passages in all of his works. How is this image a description of a visionary experience of God?

5. Describe the relation presented, starting in the fourth paragraph, between people, nature, and God. According to Emerson, is God to be found only in nature, only in people, or in some elements they share?

Connecting with the Text

6. "To speak truly," Emerson says, "few adult persons can see nature." Emerson sees children as having the advantage over adults when it comes to having a direct experience of nature. Do you agree with Emerson? What do people seem to lose as they grow older?

from Self-Reliance

First Thoughts

1. Look at the associations you made with self-reliance before reading Emerson. How does your understanding of the term compare with Emerson's?

> **Reading Check**
>
> a. According to the second paragraph, what is the destiny of every human being?
> b. What is the opposite of self-reliance?

Shaping Interpretations

2. What do you think Emerson means by "that divine idea which each of us represents" (paragraph 1)?

3. What does Emerson think of people who call for consistency in thought and action and who fear being misunderstood?

Connecting with the Text

4. Do you think there's too little, too much, or just the right amount of emphasis on individualism in our society today? What might Emerson have thought about our focus on the individual?

5. If this essay were to be delivered as a political address during a presidential campaign today, how do you think people would respond?

READING SKILLS AND STRATEGIES

Understanding Figures of Speech

In "Self-Reliance," Emerson makes many of his points through a series of **figures of speech**—comparisons between two things that are basically unlike each other. **Context** can sometimes help you understand difficult figures of speech.

1. Describe what Emerson compares with these things and events: planting corn, an iron string, a joint-stock company, a shadow on the wall.

2. Explain what Emerson means by the famous **metaphor** that opens the final paragraph. What exactly is meant by a "hobgoblin," a "little mind," a "foolish consistency"? What do you think Emerson would consider a "wise" consistency?

CHOICES: Building Your Portfolio

Writer's Notebook

1. Collecting Ideas for Writing About a Controversial Issue

Brainstorm a list of controversial issues that people debate and disagree about. Write down as many topics as you can possibly think of. Keep your notes; you may use them later in the Writer's Workshop on page 331.

Evaluating Ideas / Creative Writing

2. Trick or Truth?

On page 227, you'll find a student response to this statement from another portion of Emerson's "Self-Reliance": "A man should learn to detect and watch that gleam of light which flashes across his mind from within, more than the luster of the firmament of bards and sages." Write your own response in the form of an essay, fable, or poem (about one page long) to one of the following statements from Emerson:

a. "Envy is ignorance."

b. "Trust thyself: Every heart vibrates to that iron string."

c. "To be great is to be misunderstood."

d. "A foolish consistency is the hobgoblin of little minds."

Analyzing Paradoxes

3. Not Contradictory

Emerson was fond of using **paradox,** the linking of seemingly contradictory elements (as in the line from *Romeo and Juliet:* "Parting is such sweet sorrow"). Read the following sentences from *Nature,* and write a brief explanation of the meaning of each paradox. End your explanation with an expression of each statement in your own words.

a. "I am not solitary while I read and write, though nobody is with me."

b. "But every night come out these envoys of beauty, and light the universe with their admonishing smile."

c. "Most persons do not see the sun."

d. "Almost I fear to think how glad I am."

Developing an Idea

4. A Personal Definition

"Self-Reliance" is one long definition. But Emerson's definition of self-reliance is fuller, more thought-provoking, more poetic, more personal, and less exact than a dictionary definition. Write a one- or two-paragraph **extended definition** of a human quality that you feel is valuable or important. Like Emerson, you might want to begin with a hook, an attention-grabbing introduction.

Identifying Aphorisms / Speaking and Listening

5. Sage Sayings

With a small group of classmates, brainstorm a list of modern **aphorisms:** lines from popular songs or political speeches, things you've read, things you've heard in conversation, things you yourself have said or thought—even sayings from bumper stickers or T-shirts. Have one member of the group write down the sayings. As a group, interpret and briefly discuss each entry. What do these sayings tell you about the values of modern society? Compare and contrast them with Emerson's values.

Crossing the Curriculum: Social Studies

6. Inventing Utopia

With one or more partners, make a plan for a community based on the ideals you've found in Emerson. Give the community a name, and decide on a geographical setting for it. What kind of government would the community have? What would be its economic base? What would be the attractions of life in this community? What would be the population be? What problems would the community face? Finally, draw a map of your fictional community, and write a description of its goals.

Henry David Thoreau

(1817–1862)

On July 4, 1845 (the date was apparently accidental), a young man ended a three-year stay at the house of a friend and moved to a cabin on the shores of Walden Pond in Massachusetts. He was almost twenty-eight years old and, to all appearances, a failure. He had lasted only two weeks as a schoolteacher (he refused to whip a child, then a mandatory form of punishment); his public lectures had been un-inspiring; the woman to whom he had proposed marriage had turned him down; and he had little in-terest in the family busi-ness. Despite his impres-sive Harvard education, he had not realized his lit-erary ambitions.

If ever a person looked like a self-*un*made man, a man who had squandered the advantages of intelli-gence, education, and the friendship of brilliant and successful people, it was Henry David Thoreau. On top of all his other problems, Thoreau was difficult to get along with. Three days before Thoreau went to Walden, Nathaniel Hawthorne (page 296) wrote to a New York publisher that Thoreau was "te-dious, tiresome, and intolerable. And yet," Hawthorne added, "he has great qualities of in-tellect and character."

Even his closest friends had doubts about Thoreau. "He seemed born for great enter-prise and for command," Emerson said years later at Thoreau's funeral, "and I so much regret the loss of his rare powers of action, that I can-not help counting it a fault in him that he had no ambition. Wanting this, instead of engineer-ing for all America, he was the captain of a huckleberry party."

Henry David Thoreau (1856) by Benjamin D. Maxham. Photograph.

National Portrait Gallery/Smithsonian Institution/Art Resource, NY.

What Emerson failed to see, and what Thoreau knew (or hoped) all along, was that by leading a berry-picking party on a jaunt in the woods he could "engineer for all America" in the most profound way. This paradox is at the center of Thoreau's life and work.

The Student Who Wouldn't Wear Black

Thoreau was born in Concord, Massachusetts, in 1817. His father was a moderately successful manu-facturer of pencils. His mother took in boarders, among them the sister of Emerson's wife, thus estab-lishing the relationship be-tween the two families. As a boy, Thoreau tramped the woods and fields around Concord, often with a fishing rod and seldom with a gun.

Thoreau entered Harvard in 1833 and gradu-ated four years later. Inde-pendent and eccentric even then, he attended chapel in a green coat, "because," he wrote, "the rules required black." He never ranked higher than the middle of his class, but he was extremely well read. He became thoroughly familiar with English litera-ture and with the German philosophers who provided many of the underpinnings of Tran-scendentalism.

After returning to Concord and teaching school, Thoreau went to New York in 1843, but he pined for his hometown. After six months of struggling, he gave up and returned to Concord. A friend proposed that Henry and he sail to Europe and work their way across the Continent, but Henry turned him down. He appeared to be floundering, but in fact he knew what he was doing; Thoreau's voyage would be inward, and it would depart from Walden Pond, where Emerson had offered him the use of some land.

Walden: Life in Its Essence

The experiment at Walden Pond was an attempt to rediscover the grandeur of a simple life led close to nature. Though only two miles from town, Walden offered a focus for Thoreau's contemplative urge. "I wish to meet the facts of life," he wrote in his journal, "the vital facts, which are the phenomena or actuality the gods meant to show us . . . and so I came down here."

This private confrontation was to Thoreau's mind the truly heroic enterprise of his time. "I am glad to remember tonight as I sit by my door," he wrote on the evening of July 7, "that I too am at least a remote descendant of that heroic race of men of whom there is a tradition. I too sit here on the shore of my Ithaca, a fellow wanderer and survivor of Ulysses."

When he looked toward town, Thoreau saw his fellow citizens so caught up in making a living that they had become one-dimensional. "The mass of men," as one of the most famous sentences in *Walden* puts it, "lead lives of quiet desperation." He hoped to wake them up and show them that the heroic enterprise of confronting the "vital facts of life" lay literally in their own back yards.

Walden—one of the most well-known works ever produced in America—owes much of its artistic success to Thoreau's blending of style and content. He looked to nature, rather than to the stylists of the past, for a model. To Thoreau, a style that imitated nature would speak fundamental spiritual truths. Thoreau wished to build sentences "which lie like boulders on the page, up and down or across; which contain the seed of other sentences, not mere repetition, but creation; which a man might sell his grounds and castles to build."

> **T**horeau's voyage would be inward, and it would depart from Walden Pond.

Thoreau the Protester

It was while he was at Walden that Thoreau's other famous act took place. As a protest against the Mexican War, which he and many others saw as an attempt to extend American slaveholding territory, Thoreau refused to pay his poll tax, and spent a night in jail as a result. While at Walden, and again in 1851 (after the Fugitive Slave Act had been passed), Thoreau helped fugitives escaping slavery make their way to Canada. In 1859, he was one of the first defenders of John Brown, the radical abolitionist who staged a famous raid on the Federal arsenal at Harpers Ferry in Virginia.

Thoreau remained at Walden for a little more than two years. In 1847, he left the cabin and moved back into the Emersons' house, in exchange for a few hours a day of odd jobs and gardening. During the next few years, he worked on *Walden* (which was published in 1854) and essays such as "Resistance to Civil Government." The latter, delivered as a lecture in 1848 and published as an essay in 1849, had little immediate influence, but few essays have had such an overwhelming, long-term effect on human history. It was especially important in helping to inspire the passive resistance used by Mohandas K. Gandhi in India and, later, by Martin Luther King, Jr., in the United States.

Thoreau moved back into his parents' house in 1848 and lived there the rest of his life. He supported himself by making pencils, taking odd jobs—he was an excellent carpenter, mason, and gardener—and doing survey work on the land around Concord. He became a kind of local recordkeeper, a fount of knowledge about the amount of rainfall and snowfall and the first days of frost. He could predict to the day when each wildflower in the area would bloom.

In 1860, Thoreau caught a cold, and it soon became clear that beneath the cold lay incurable tuberculosis. He faced his coming death with great calm. The town constable, Sam Staples (who had jailed Thoreau for refusing to pay his poll tax), told Emerson that he "never saw a man dying with so much pleasure and peace."

"Henry, have you made your peace with God?" his aunt is said to have asked him toward the end. "Why, Aunt," he replied, "I didn't know we had ever quarreled."

Before You Read

FROM WALDEN, OR LIFE IN THE WOODS

Make the Connection

What's Necessary

Thoreau went to Walden Pond to find out what was necessary in life and what could be done without. He discovered that the key to making his life more fulfilling was to make it simpler.

Few people go off to the woods for a couple of years to find out how they really want to live. Every thinking person, however, stops at times to ask, "How do I really want to live? What do I need in order to feel fulfilled—and what am I doing now that's unnecessary?" Thoreau can be an inspiration for anyone who asks these questions.

Reading Skills and Strategies

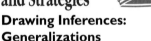

Drawing Inferences: Generalizations

Active readers make generalizations based on information they get from their reading and on their own experiences. Such a **generalization** is a specific type of **inference**—a conclusion that extends the ideas in a text to a broader situation. Like all inferences, generalizations are reasonable guesses. For example, after reading Thoreau's call for "simplicity, simplicity!" you might reasonably guess that he believed people should lead lives focused on what matters most to them, while eliminating unnecessary complexity. You need not agree with the generalization; you are simply extending the implications of an idea into new territory. (You would probably need to do additional research before stating that Thoreau in fact agreed with your generalization.)

As you read *Walden*, take notes in the form of a double-entry journal. In the left column, list Thoreau's ideas. In the right column, examine some of the interesting generalizations that logically follow from his views.

Elements of Literature

Point of View

In the second paragraph of this excerpt, Thoreau justifies using the **first-person point of view** to narrate his experiences at Walden Pond. "[I]t is, after all, always the first person that is speaking," he writes. Think about what Thoreau might mean. As you read, look for passages in which you think the use of the first person makes a difference.

> In the **first-person point of view,** the narrative is told by a particular person who uses the personal pronoun *I* or *we* to describe experiences.
>
> *For more on Point of View, see the Handbook of Literary Terms.*

Thoreau's journals and a writing box.

The Pierpont Morgan Library / Art Resource, NY.

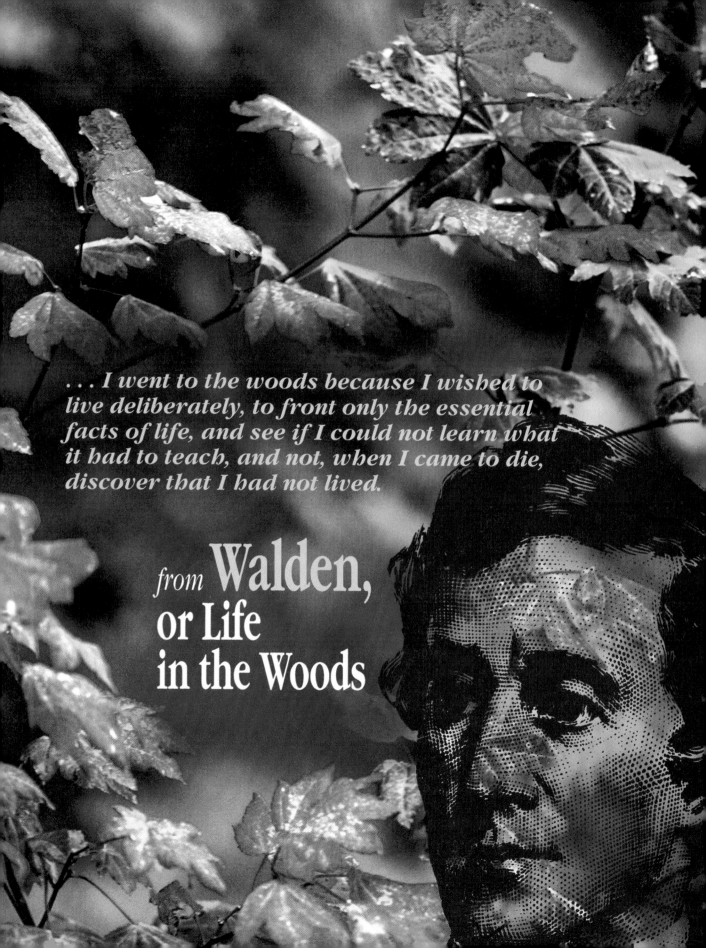

. . . I went to the woods because I wished to live deliberately, to front only the essential facts of life, and see if I could not learn what it had to teach, and not, when I came to die, discover that I had not lived.

from **Walden, or Life in the Woods**

from **Economy**

When I wrote the following pages, or rather the bulk of them, I lived alone, in the woods, a mile from any neighbor, in a house which I had built myself, on the shore of Walden Pond, in Concord, Massachusetts, and earned my living by the labor of my hands only. I lived there two years and two months. At present I am a sojourner in civilized life again.

I should not obtrude my affairs so much on the notice of my readers if very particular inquiries had not been made by my townsmen concerning my mode of life, which some would call impertinent, though they do not appear to me at all impertinent, but, considering the circumstances, very natural and pertinent. Some have asked what I got to eat; if I did not feel lonesome; if I was not afraid; and the like. Others have been curious to learn what portion of my income I devoted to charitable purposes; and some, who have large families, how many poor children I maintained. I will therefore ask those of my readers who feel no particular interest in me to pardon me if I undertake to answer some of these questions in this book. In most books, the *I*, or first person, is omitted; in this it will be retained; that, in respect to egotism, is the main difference. We commonly do not remember that it is, after all, always the first person that is speaking. I should not talk so much about myself if there were anybody else whom I knew as well. Unfortunately, I am confined to this theme by the narrowness of my experience. Moreover, I, on my side, require of every writer, first or last, a simple and sincere account of his own life, and not merely what he has heard of other men's lives; some such account as he would send to his kindred from a distant land; for if he has lived sincerely, it must have been in a distant land to me. Perhaps these pages are more particularly addressed to poor students. As for the rest of my readers, they will accept such portions as apply to them. I trust that none will stretch the seams in putting on the coat, for it may do good service to him whom it fits. . . .

By the middle of April, for I made no haste in my work, but rather made the most of it, my house was framed and ready for the raising. I had already bought the shanty of James Collins, an Irishman who worked on the Fitchburg Railroad, for boards. James Collins's shanty was considered an uncommonly fine one. When I called to see it he was not at home. I walked about the outside, at first unobserved from within, the window was so deep and high. It was of small dimensions, with a peaked cottage roof, and not much else to be seen, the dirt being raised five feet all around as if it were a compost heap. The roof was the soundest part, though a good deal warped and made brittle by the sun. Doorsill there was none, but a perennial passage for the hens under the door board. Mrs. C. came to the door and asked me to view it from the inside. The hens were driven in by my approach. It was dark, and had a dirt floor for the most part, dank, clammy, and aguish,¹ only here a board and there a board which would not bear removal. She lighted a lamp to show me the inside of the roof and the walls, and also that the board floor extended under the bed, warning me not to step into the cellar, a sort of dust hole two feet deep. In her own words, they were "good boards overhead, good boards all around, and a good window"—of two whole squares originally, only the cat had passed out that way lately. There was a stove, a bed, and a place to sit, an infant in the house where it was born, a silk parasol, gilt-framed looking glass, and a patent new coffee mill nailed to an oak sapling, all told. The bargain was soon concluded, for James had in the meanwhile returned. I to pay four dollars and twenty-five cents tonight, he to vacate at five tomorrow morning, selling to nobody else meanwhile: I to take possession at six. It were well, he said, to be there early, and anticipate certain indistinct but wholly unjust claims on the score of ground rent and fuel. This he assured me was the only encumbrance. At six I passed him and his family on the

---

1. **aguish** (āʹgyōo·ish): likely to cause ague, or fever and chills.

- -

WORDS TO OWN

pertinent (purʹtə·nənt) *adj.*: to the point; applying to the situation.
encumbrance (en·kumʹbrəns) *n.*: burden; hindrance.

- -

road. One large bundle held their all—bed, coffee mill, looking glass, hens—all but the cat; she took to the woods and became a wild cat, and, as I learned afterward, trod in a trap set for woodchucks, and so became a dead cat at last.

I took down this dwelling the same morning, drawing the nails, and removed it to the pond side by small cartloads, spreading the boards on the grass there to bleach and warp back again in the sun. One early thrush gave me a note or two as I drove along the woodland path. I was informed treacherously by a young Patrick that neighbor Seeley, an Irishman, in the intervals of the carting, transferred the still tolerable, straight, and drivable nails, staples, and spikes to his pocket, and then stood when I came back to pass the time of day, and look freshly up, unconcerned, with spring thoughts, at the devastation; there being a dearth of work, as he said. He was there to represent spectatordom, and help make this seemingly insignificant event one with the removal of the gods of Troy.[2]

I dug my cellar in the side of a hill sloping to the south, where a woodchuck had formerly dug his burrow, down through sumac and blackberry roots, and the lowest stain of vegetation, six feet square by seven deep, to a fine sand where potatoes would not freeze in any winter. The sides were left shelving, and not stoned; but the sun having never shone on them, the sand still keeps its place. It was but two hours' work. I took particular pleasure in this breaking of ground, for in almost all latitudes men dig into the earth for an equable temperature. Under the most splendid house in the city is still to be found the cellar where they store their roots as of old, and long after the superstructure has disappeared posterity remark its dent in the earth. The house is still but a sort of porch at the entrance of a burrow.

At length, in the beginning of May, with the help of some of my acquaintances, rather to improve so good an occasion for neighborliness than from any necessity, I set up the frame of my house. No man was ever more honored in the character of his raisers[3] than I. They are destined, I trust, to assist at the raising of loftier structures one day. I began to occupy my house on the 4th of July, as soon as it was boarded and roofed, for the boards were carefully featheredged and lapped,[4] so that it was perfectly <u>impervious</u> to rain, but before boarding I laid the foundation of a chimney at one end, bringing two cartloads of stones up the hill from the pond in my arms. I built the chimney after my hoeing in the fall, before a fire became necessary for warmth, doing my cooking in the meanwhile out of doors on the ground, early in the morning: which mode I still think is in some respects more convenient and agreeable than the usual one. When it stormed before my bread was baked, I fixed a few boards over the fire, and sat under them to watch my loaf, and passed some pleasant hours in that way. In those days, when my hands were much employed, I read but little, but the least scraps of paper which lay on the ground, my holder, or tablecloth, afforded me as much entertainment, in fact answered the same purpose as the *Iliad*.[5]

It would be worth the while to build still more deliberately than I did, considering, for instance, what foundation a door, a window, a cellar, a garret, have in the nature of man, and perchance never raising any superstructure until we found a better reason for it than our <u>temporal</u> necessities even. There is some of the same fitness in a man's building his own house that there is in a bird's building its own nest. Who knows but if men constructed their dwellings with their own hands, and provided food for themselves and families simply and honestly enough, the poetic faculty would be universally developed, as birds univer-

2. **the gods of Troy:** Thoreau loved classical allusions. Here, he humorously compares taking down a little cabin with the destruction of the great ancient city of Troy. In the *Aeneid*, by Virgil (70–19 B.C.), the conquering Greeks carry off the images of the Trojan gods after the fall of Troy.

3. **raisers:** Thoreau's helpers included the Transcendentalist writers Ralph Waldo Emerson (page 216), Bronson Alcott (1799–1888), and William Ellery Channing (1780–1842), hence the reference in the next sentence to raising loftier structures one day.

4. **featheredged and lapped:** The edges were cut at an angle and overlapped.

5. **the *Iliad*:** Homer's epic about the Greek siege of Troy.

WORDS TO OWN

impervious (im·pur′vē·əs) *adj.*: resistant; impenetrable.

temporal (tem′pə·rəl) *adj.*: worldly.

sally sing when they are so engaged? But alas! we do like cowbirds and cuckoos, which lay their eggs in nests which other birds have built, and cheer no traveler with their chattering and unmusical notes. Shall we forever resign the pleasure of construction to the carpenter? What does architecture amount to in the experience of the mass of men? I never in all my walks came across a man engaged in so simple and natural an occupation as building his house. . . .

Before winter I built a chimney, and shingled the sides of my house, which were already impervious to rain, with imperfect and sappy shingles made of the first slice of the log, whose edges I was obliged to straighten with a plane.

I have thus a tight shingled and plastered house, ten feet wide by fifteen long, and eight-foot posts, with a garret and a closet, a large window on each side, two trapdoors, one door at the end, and a brick fireplace opposite. The exact cost of my house, paying the usual price for such materials as I used, but not counting the work, all of which was done by myself, was as follows; and I give the details because very few are able to tell exactly what their houses cost, and fewer still, if any, the separate cost of the various materials which compose them—

Boards,	$ 8 03 ½	mostly shanty boards
Refuse shingles for roof and sides,	4 00	
Laths,	1 25	
Two secondhand windows with glass,	2 43	
One thousand old brick,	4 00	
Two casks of lime,	2 40	That was high
Hair,	0 31	More than I needed
Mantle-tree iron,	0 15	
Nails,	3 90	
Hinges and screws,	0 14	
Latch,	0 10	
Chalk,	0 01	
Transportation,	1 40	I carried a good
In all,	$28 12 ½	part on my back

. . . Before I finished my house, wishing to earn ten or twelve dollars by some honest and agreeable method, in order to meet my unusual expenses, I planted about two acres and a half of light and sandy soil near it chiefly with beans, but also a small part with potatoes, corn, peas, and turnips. The whole lot contains eleven acres, mostly growing up to pines and hickories, and was sold the preceding season for eight dollars and eight cents an acre. One farmer said that it was "good for nothing but to raise cheeping squirrels on." I put no manure whatever on this land, not being the owner, but merely a squatter, and not expecting to cultivate so much again, and I did not quite hoe it all once. I got out several cords of stumps in plowing, which supplied me with fuel for a long time, and left small circles of virgin mold, easily distinguishable through the summer by the greater luxuriance of the beans there. The dead and for the most part unmerchantable wood behind my house, and the driftwood from the pond, have supplied the remainder of my fuel. I was obliged to hire a team and a man for the plowing, though I held the plow myself. My farm outgoes for the first season were, for implements, seed, work, etc., $14.72 ½. The seed corn was given me. This never costs anything to speak of, unless you plant more than enough. I got twelve bushels of beans, and eighteen bushels of potatoes, beside some peas and sweet corn. The yellow corn and turnips were too late to come to anything. My whole income from the farm was

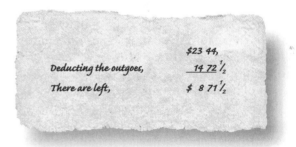

	$23 44,
Deducting the outgoes,	14 72 ½
There are left,	$ 8 71 ½

beside produce consumed and on hand at the time this estimate was made of the value of $4.50—the amount on hand much more than balancing a little grass which I did not raise. All things considered, that is, considering the importance of a man's soul and of today, notwithstanding the short time occupied by my experiment, nay, partly even because of its transient character, I believe that that was doing better than any farmer in Concord did that year. . . .

from Where I Lived, and What I Lived For

. . . I went to the woods because I wished to live deliberately, to front only the essential facts of life, and see if I could not learn what it had to teach, and not, when I came to die, discover that I had not lived. I did not wish to live what was not life, living is so dear; nor did I wish to practice resignation, unless it was quite necessary. I wanted to live deep and suck out all the marrow of life, to live so sturdily and Spartan-like[6] as to put to rout all that was not life, to cut a broad swath and shave close, to drive life into a corner, and reduce it to its lowest terms, and, if it proved to be mean, why then to get the whole and genuine meanness of it, and publish its meanness to the world; or if it were sublime, to know it by experience, and be able to give a true account of it in my next excursion. For most men, it appears to me, are in a strange uncertainty about it, whether it is of the devil or of God, and have *somewhat hastily* concluded that it is the chief end of man here to "glorify God and enjoy him forever."[7]

Still we live meanly, like ants; though the fable tells us that we were long ago changed into men; like pygmies we fight with cranes;[8] it is error upon error, and clout upon clout, and our best virtue has for its occasion a superfluous and evitable wretchedness. Our life is frittered away by detail. An honest man has hardly need to count more than his ten fingers, or in extreme cases he may add his ten toes, and lump the rest. Simplicity, simplicity, simplicity! I say, let your affairs be as two or three, and not a hundred or a thousand; instead of a million count half a dozen, and keep your accounts on your thumbnail. In the midst of this chopping sea of civilized life, such are the clouds and storms and quicksands and thousand-and-one items to be allowed for, that a man has to live, if he would not founder and go to the bottom and not make his port at all, by dead reckoning, and he must be a great calculator indeed who succeeds. Simplify, simplify. Instead of three meals a day, if it be necessary eat but one; instead of a hundred dishes, five; and reduce other things in proportion. Our life is like a German Confederacy,[9] made up of petty states with its boundary forever fluctuating, so that even a German cannot tell you how it is bounded at any moment. The nation itself, with all its so-called internal improvements, which, by the way are all external and superficial, is just such an unwieldy and overgrown establishment, cluttered with furniture and tripped up by its own traps, ruined by luxury and heedless expense, by want of calculation and a worthy aim, as the million households in the land; and the only cure for it, as for them, is in a rigid economy, a stern and more than Spartan simplicity of life and elevation of purpose. It lives too fast. Men think that it is essential that the *Nation* have commerce, and export ice, and talk through a telegraph, and ride thirty miles an hour, without a doubt, whether *they* do or not; but whether we should live like baboons or like men, is a little uncertain. If we do not get out sleepers,[10] and forge rails, and devote days and nights to the work, but go to tinkering upon our *lives* to improve *them,* who will build railroads? And if railroads are not built, how shall we get to heaven in season? But if we stay at home and mind our business, who will want railroads? We do not ride on the railroad; it rides upon us. Did you ever think what those sleepers are that underlie the railroad? Each one is

---

6. **Spartan-like:** like the Spartans, the hardy, frugal, and highly disciplined citizens of the ancient Greek city-state Sparta.
7. **glorify . . . forever:** answer to catechism question, "What is the chief end of man?"
8. **the fable . . . cranes:** In a Greek fable, Zeus changes ants into men. In the *Iliad,* Homer compares the Trojans to cranes fighting with pygmies.

9. **German Confederacy:** At the time Thoreau was writing, Germany was not yet a unified nation.
10. **sleepers:** British usage for "railroad ties"; so called because they lie flat.

WORDS TO OWN

superfluous (sə·pʉr′flo͞o·əs) *adj.*: unnecessary.

---

a man, an Irishman, or a Yankee man. The rails are laid on them, and they are covered with sand, and the cars run smoothly over them. They are sound sleepers, I assure you. And every few years a new lot is laid down and run over; so that, if some have the pleasure of riding on a rail, others have the misfortune to be ridden upon. And when they run over a man that is walking in his sleep, a supernumerary[11] sleeper in the wrong position, and wake him up, they suddenly stop the cars, and make a hue and cry about it, as if this were an exception. I am glad to know that it takes a gang of men for every five miles to keep the sleepers down and level in their beds as it is, for this is a sign that they may sometime get up again. . . .

from Solitude

. . . Some of my pleasantest hours were during the long rainstorms in the spring or fall, which confined me to the house for the afternoon as well as the forenoon, soothed by their ceaseless roar and pelting; when an early twilight ushered in a long evening in which many thoughts had time to take root and unfold themselves. In those driving northeast rains which tried the village houses so, when the maids stood ready with mop and pail in front entries to keep the deluge out, I sat behind my door in my little house, which was all entry, and thoroughly enjoyed its protection. In one heavy thundershower the lightning struck a large pitch pine across the pond, making a very conspicuous and perfectly regular spiral groove from top to bottom, an inch or more deep, and four or five inches wide, as you would groove a walking stick. I passed it again the other day, and was struck with awe on looking up and beholding that mark, now more distinct than ever, where a terrific and resistless bolt came down out of the harmless sky eight years ago. Men frequently say to me, "I should think you would feel lonesome down there, and want to be nearer to folks, rainy

and snowy days and nights especially." I am tempted to reply to such—This whole earth which we inhabit is but a point in space. How far apart, think you, dwell the two most distant inhabitants of yonder star, the breadth of whose disk cannot be appreciated by our instruments? Why should I feel lonely? Is not our planet in the Milky Way? This which you put seems to me not to be the most important question. What sort of space is that which separates a man from his fellows and makes him solitary? I have found that no exertion of the legs can bring two minds much nearer to one another. What do we want most to dwell near to? Not to many men surely, the depot, the post office, the barroom, the meetinghouse, the schoolhouse, the grocery, Beacon Hill, or the Five Points, where men most congregate, but to the perennial source of our life, whence in all our experience we have found that to issue, as the willow stands near the water and sends out its roots in that direction. This will vary with different natures, but this is the place where a wise man will dig his cellar. . . .

from The Bean Field

Meanwhile my beans, the length of whose rows, added together, was seven miles already planted, were impatient to be hoed, for the earliest had grown considerably before the latest were in the ground; indeed they were not easily to be put off. What was the meaning of this so steady and self-respecting, this small Herculean labor, I knew not. I came to love my rows, my beans, though so many more than I wanted. They attached me to the earth, and so I got strength like Antaeus.[12] But why should I raise them? Only Heaven knows. This was my curious labor all summer—to make this portion of the earth's surface, which had yielded only cinquefoil, blackberries, johnswort, and the like, before, sweet wild fruits and pleasant

---

11. **supernumerary** (soo′pər·noo′mə·rer′ē): additional; unnecessary.

12. **Antaeus** (an·tē′əs): in Greek mythology, the giant who draws strength from the earth, his mother.

Quaker Ladies (1956) by Andrew Wyeth. Watercolor and drypoint.

flowers, produce instead this pulse.[13] What shall I learn of beans or beans of me? I cherish them, I hoe them, early and late I have an eye to them; and this is my day's work. It is a fine broad leaf to look on. My auxiliaries are the dews and rains which water this dry soil, and what fertility is in the soil itself, which for the most part is lean and effete. My enemies are worms, cool days, and most of all woodchucks. The last have nibbled for me a quarter of an acre clean. But what right had I to oust johnswort and the rest, and break up their ancient herb garden? Soon, however, the remaining beans will be too tough for them, and go forward to meet new foes. . . .

It was a singular experience that long acquaintance which I cultivated with beans, what with planting, and hoeing, and harvesting, and threshing, and picking over and selling them—the last was the hardest of all—I might add eating, for I did taste. I was determined to know beans. When they were growing, I used to hoe from five

o'clock in the morning till noon, and commonly spent the rest of the day about other affairs. Consider the intimate and curious acquaintance one makes with various kinds of weeds—it will bear some iteration in the account, for there was no little iteration in the labor—disturbing their delicate organizations so ruthlessly, and making such invidious distinctions with his hoe, leveling whole ranks of one species, and sedulously cultivating another. That's Roman wormwood—that's pigweed—that's sorrel—that's pipergrass—have at him, chop him up, turn his roots upward to the sun, don't let him have a fiber in the shade, if you do he'll turn himself t'other side up and be as green as a leek in two days. A long war, not with cranes, but with weeds, those Trojans who had sun and rain and dews on their side. Daily the beans saw me come to their rescue armed with a hoe, and thin the ranks of their enemies, filling up the trenches with weedy dead. Many a lusty

---

13. pulse: beans, peas, and other edible seeds of plants having pods.

WORDS TO OWN

effete (e·fēt′) *adj.:* sterile; unproductive.

---

crest-waving Hector,[14] that towered a whole foot above his crowding comrades, fell before my weapon and rolled in the dust. . . .

from Brute Neighbors

. . . One day when I went out to my woodpile, or rather my pile of stumps, I observed two large ants, the one red, the other much larger, nearly half an inch long, and black, fiercely contending with one another. Having once got hold they never let go, but struggled and wrestled and rolled on the chips <u>inces-</u>santly. Looking farther, I was surprised to find that the chips were covered with such combatants, that it was not a *duellum,* but a *bellum,*[15] a war between two races of ants, the red always pitted against the black, and frequently two red ones to one black. The legions of these Myrmidons[16] covered all the hills and vales in my wood yard, and the ground was already strewn with the dead and dying, both red and black. It was the only battle which I have ever witnessed, the only battlefield I ever trod while the battle was raging; internecine[17] war; the red republicans on the one hand, and the black imperialists on the other. On every side they were engaged in deadly combat, yet without any noise that I could hear, and human soldiers never fought so resolutely. I watched a couple that were fast locked in each other's embraces, in a little sunny valley amid the chips, now at noonday prepared to fight till the sun went down, or life went out. The smaller red champion had fastened himself like a vise to his adversary's front, and through all the tumblings on that field never for an instant ceased to gnaw at one of his feelers near the root, having already caused the other to go by the board; while the stronger black one dashed him from side to side, and, as I saw on looking nearer, had already divested him of several of his members. They fought with more pertinacity than bulldogs. Neither manifested the least disposition to retreat. It was evident that their battle cry was "Conquer or die." In the meanwhile there came along a single red ant on the hillside of this valley, evidently full of excitement, who either had dispatched his foe, or had not yet taken part in the battle; probably the latter, for he had lost none of his limbs; whose mother had charged him to return with his shield or upon it.[18] Or perchance he was some Achilles, who had nourished his wrath apart, and had now come to avenge or rescue his Patroclus.[19] He saw this unequal combat from afar—for the blacks were nearly twice the size of the red—he drew near with rapid pace till he stood on his guard within half an inch of the combatants; then, watching his opportunity, he sprang upon the black warrior, and commenced his operations near the root of his right foreleg, leaving the foe to select among his own members; and so there were three united for life, as if a new kind of attraction had been invented which put all other locks and cements to shame. I should not have wondered by this time to find that they had their respective musical bands stationed on some eminent chip, and playing their national airs the while, to excite the slow and cheer the dying combatants. I was myself excited somewhat even as if they had been men. The more you think of it, the less the difference. And certainly there is not the fight recorded in Concord history, at least, if in the history of America, that will bear a moment's comparison with this, whether for the numbers engaged in it, or for the patriotism and heroism displayed. For numbers and for carnage it was an Austerlitz or Dresden.[20]

---

18. return . . . upon it: echoes the traditional charge of Spartan mothers to their warrior sons: return victorious or dead.
19. Achilles . . . Patroclus (pə·trō′kləs): In the *Iliad,* Achilles withdraws from the battle at Troy but rejoins the fight after his friend Patroclus is killed.
20. Austerlitz or Dresden: major battles of the Napoleonic Wars.

- -

WORDS TO OWN

incessantly (in·ses′ənt·lē) *adv.*: without stopping.

- -

---

14. Hector: In the *Iliad,* Hector is the Trojan prince killed by the Greek hero Achilles.
15. not a *duellum,* but a *bellum:* not a duel, but a war.
16. Myrmidons: Achilles' soldiers in the *Iliad. Myrmex* is Greek for "ant."
17. internecine (in′tər·nē′sin): harmful to both sides of the group.

Concord Fight! Two killed on the patriots' side, and Luther Blanchard wounded! Why here every ant was a Buttrick—"Fire! for God's sake fire!"— and thousands shared the fate of Davis and Hosmer.[21] There was not one hireling there. I have no doubt that it was a principle they fought for, as much as our ancestors, and not to avoid a three-penny tax on their tea; and the results of this battle will be as important and memorable to those whom it concerns as those of the Battle of Bunker Hill, at least.

I took up the chip on which the three I have particularly described were struggling, carried it into my house, and placed it under a tumbler on my windowsill, in order to see the issue. Holding a microscope to the first-mentioned red ant, I saw that, though he was assiduously gnawing at the near foreleg of his enemy, having severed his remaining feeler, his own breast was all torn away, exposing what vitals he had there to the jaws of the black warrior, whose breastplate was apparently too thick for him to pierce; and the dark carbuncles of the sufferer's eyes shone with ferocity such as war only could excite. They struggled half an hour longer under the tumbler, and when I looked again the black soldier had severed the heads of his foes from their bodies, and the still living heads were hanging on either side of him like ghastly trophies at his saddlebow, still apparently as firmly fastened as ever, and he was endeavoring with feeble struggles, being without feelers and with only the remnant of a leg, and I know not how many other wounds, to divest himself of them; which at length, after half an hour more, he accomplished. I raised the glass, and he went off over the windowsill in that crippled state. Whether he finally survived that combat, and spent the remainder of his days in some Hôtel des Invalides,[22] I do not know; but I thought that his industry would not be worth much thereafter. I never learned which party was victorious, nor the cause of the war; but I felt for the rest of that day as if I had had my feelings excited and harrowed by witnessing the struggle, the ferocity and carnage, of a human battle before my door. . . .

In the fall the loon (*Colymbus glacialis*) came, as usual, to molt and bathe in the pond, making the woods ring with his wild laughter before I had risen. At rumor of his arrival all the Mill-dam sportsmen are on the alert, in gigs and on foot, two by two and three by three, with patent rifles and conical balls and spyglasses. They come rustling through the woods like autumn leaves, at least ten men to one loon. Some station themselves on this side of the pond, some on that, for the poor bird cannot be omnipresent; if he dive here he must come up there. But now the kind October wind rises, rustling the leaves and rippling the surface of the water, so that no loon can be heard or seen, though his foes sweep the pond with spyglasses, and make the woods resound with their discharges. The waves generously rise and dash angrily, taking sides with all waterfowl, and our sportsmen must beat a retreat to town and shop and unfinished jobs. But they were too often successful. When I went to get a pail of water early in the morning I frequently saw this stately bird sailing out of my cove within a few rods.[23] If I endeavored to overtake him in a boat, in order to see how he would maneuver, he would dive and be completely lost, so that I did not discover him again, sometimes, till the latter part of the day. But I was more than a match for him on the surface. He commonly went off in a rain.

As I was paddling along the north shore one very calm October afternoon, for such days especially they settle onto the lakes, like the milkweed down, having looked in vain over the pond for a loon, suddenly one, sailing out from the shore toward the middle a few rods in front of me, set up his wild laugh and betrayed himself. I pursued with a paddle and he dived, but when he came up I was nearer than before. He dived again, but I miscalculated the direction he would take, and we were fifty rods apart when he came to the surface this time, for I had helped to widen the interval; and again he laughed long and loud, and with more reason than before. He maneuvered so cunningly that I could not get within half a dozen

21. Luther . . . Hosmer: All these men fought at the Battle of Concord, the first battle of the Revolutionary War. Major John Buttrick led the minutemen who defeated the British. Isaac Davis and Abner Hosmer were the two colonists killed.
22. Hôtel des Invalides (ō·tel′ dez ēn′vä·lēd′): Home for Disabled Soldiers, a veterans' hospital in Paris, France. Napoleon I (1769–1821) is buried there.

23. rods: One rod measures 16½ feet.

Common Loon (1833) by John James Audubon. Watercolor, graphite, gouache, pastel.

rods of him. Each time, when he came to the surface, turning his head this way and that, he coolly surveyed the water and the land, and apparently chose his course so that he might come up where there was the widest expanse of water and at the greatest distance from the boat. It was surprising how quickly he made up his mind and put his resolve into execution. He led me at once to the widest part of the pond, and could not be driven from it. While he was thinking one thing in his brain, I was endeavoring to divine his thought in mine. It was a pretty game, played on the smooth surface of the pond, a man against a loon. Suddenly your adversary's checker disappears beneath the board, and the problem is to place yours nearest to where his will appear again. Sometimes he would come up unexpectedly on the opposite side of me, having apparently passed directly under the boat. So long-winded was he and so unweariable, that when he had swum farthest he would immediately plunge again, nevertheless; and then no wit could divine where in the deep pond, beneath the smooth surface, he might be speeding his way like a fish, for he had time and ability to visit the bottom of the pond in its deepest part. It is said that loons have been caught in the New York lakes eighty feet beneath the surface, with hooks set for trout—though Walden is deeper than that. How surprised must the fishes be to see this ungainly visitor from another sphere speeding his way amid their schools! Yet he appeared to know his course as surely underwater as on the surface, and swam much faster there. Once or twice I saw a ripple where he approached the surface, just put his head out to reconnoiter, and instantly dived again. I found that it was as well for me to rest on my oars and wait his reappearing as to endeavor to calculate where he would rise; for again and again, when I was straining my eyes over the surface one way, I would suddenly be startled by his unearthly laugh behind me. But why, after displaying so much cunning, did he invariably betray himself the moment he came up by that loud laugh? Did not his white breast enough betray him? He was indeed a silly loon, I thought. I could commonly hear the plash of the water when he came up, and so also detected him. But after an hour he seemed as fresh as ever, dived as willingly, and swam yet farther than at first. It was surprising to see how serenely he sailed off with unruffled breast when he came to the surface, doing all the work with his webbed feet beneath. His usual note was this demoniac laughter, yet somewhat like that of a waterfowl; but occasionally, when he had balked me most successfully and come up a long way off, he uttered a long-drawn unearthly howl, probably more like that of a wolf than any bird; as when a beast puts his muzzle to the ground and deliberately howls. This was his looning—perhaps the wildest sound that is ever heard here, making the woods ring far and wide. I concluded that he laughed in <u>derision</u> of my efforts confident of his own resources. Though the sky was by this time overcast, the pond was so smooth that I could see where he broke the surface when I did not hear him. His white breast, the stillness of the air, and the smoothness of the water were all against him. At length, having come up fifty rods off, he uttered one of those prolonged howls, as if calling on the god of loons to aid him, and immediately there came a wind from the east and rippled the surface, and filled the whole air with misty rain, and I was impressed as if it were the prayer of the loon answered, and his god was angry with me; and so I left him disappearing far away on the <u>tumultuous</u> surface. . . .

from Conclusion

. . . I left the woods for as good a reason as I went there. Perhaps it seemed to me that I had several more lives to live, and could not spare any more time for that one. It is remarkable how easily and insensibly we fall into a particular route, and make a beaten track for ourselves. I had not lived there a week before my feet wore a path from my door to the pond side; and though it is five or six years since I trod it, it is still quite distinct. It is true, I fear, that others may have fallen into it, and so helped to keep it open. The surface of the earth is soft and impressible by the feet of men; and so with the paths which the mind travels. How worn and dusty, then, must be the highways of the world, how deep the ruts of tradition and conformity! I did not wish to take a cabin passage, but rather to go before the mast and on the deck of the world, for there I could best see the moonlight amid the mountains. I do not wish to go below now.

I learned this, at least, by my experiment: That if one advances confidently in the direction of his dreams, and endeavors to live the life which he has imagined, he will meet with a success unexpected in common hours. He will put some things behind, will pass an invisible boundary; new, universal, and more liberal laws will begin to establish themselves around and within him; or the old laws be expanded, and interpreted in his favor in a more liberal sense, and he will live with the license of a higher order of beings. In proportion as he simplifies his life, the laws of the universe will appear less complex, and solitude will not be solitude, nor poverty poverty, nor weakness weakness. If you have built castles in the air, your work need not be lost; that is where they should be. Now put the foundations under them. . . .

Some are dinning in our ears that we Americans, and moderns generally, are intellectual dwarfs compared with the ancients, or even the Elizabethan men. But what is that to the purpose? A living dog is better than a dead lion.[24] Shall a man go and hang himself because he belongs to the race of pygmies, and not be the biggest pygmy that he can? Let everyone mind his own business, and endeavor to be what he was made.

Why should we be in such desperate haste to succeed and in such desperate enterprises? If a man does not keep pace with his companions, perhaps it is because he hears a different drum-

24. A living dog . . . lion: Ecclesiastes 9:4.

WORDS TO OWN
derision (di·rizh′ən) *n.*: ridicule; contempt.
tumultuous (tōō·mul′chōō·əs) *adj.*: stormy; turbulent.

mer. Let him step to the music which he hears, however measured or far away. It is not important that he should mature as soon as an apple tree or an oak. Shall he turn his spring into summer? If the condition of things which we were made for is not yet, what were any reality which we can substitute? We will not be shipwrecked on a vain reality. Shall we with pains erect a heaven of blue glass over ourselves, though when it is done we shall be sure to gaze still at the true <u>ethereal</u> heaven far above, as if the former were not? . . .

The life in us is like the water in the river. It may rise this year higher than man has ever known it, and flood the parched uplands; even this may be the eventful year, which will drown out all our muskrats. It was not always dry land where we dwell. I see far inland the banks which the stream anciently washed, before science began to record its freshets. Everyone has heard the story which has gone the rounds of New England, of a strong and beautiful bug which came out of the dry leaf of an old table of apple-tree wood, which had stood in a farmer's kitchen for sixty years, first in Connecticut, and afterward in Massachusetts—from an egg deposited in the living tree many years earlier still, as appeared by counting the annual layers beyond it; which was heard gnawing out for several weeks, hatched perchance by the heat of an urn. Who does not feel his faith in a resurrection and immortality strengthened by hearing of this? Who knows what beautiful and winged life, whose egg has been buried for ages under many concentric layers of woodenness in the dead dry life of society, deposited at first in the alburnum[25] of the green and living tree, which has been gradually converted into the semblance of its well-seasoned tomb—heard perchance gnawing out now for years by the astonished family of man, as they sat round the festive board—may unexpectedly come forth from amidst society's most trivial and handselled[26] furniture, to enjoy its perfect summer life at last!

I do not say that John or Jonathan[27] will realize all this; but such is the character of that morrow which mere lapse of time can never make to dawn. The light which puts out our eyes is darkness to us. Only that day dawns to which we are awake. There is more day to dawn. The sun is but a morning star.

25. alburnum: sapwood; soft wood between the inner bark and the hard core of a tree.
26. handselled: given as a mere token of good wishes; therefore, of no great value in itself.
27. John or Jonathan: John Bull and Brother Jonathan were traditional personifications of England and the United States respectively.

WORDS TO OWN

ethereal (ē·thir′ē·əl) *adj.:* not earthly; spiritual.

A journal page (1845) by Henry David Thoreau.

The Pierpont Morgan Library/ Art Resource, NY.

244

In 1990, the popular musician and songwriter Don Henley (of the rock group the Eagles) founded the Walden Woods Project to protect a part of Walden Woods under threat of real-estate development. Here Henley talks about how Thoreau and Emerson contributed to his "spiritual awakening" and his commitment to the preservation of Walden Woods.

from Heaven Is Under Our Feet

Don Henley

I honestly don't remember when I was first introduced to the works of Henry David Thoreau or by whom. It may have been my venerable high school English teacher, Margaret Lovelace, or it may have been one of my university professors. I was lucky enough to have a few exceptional ones and that is sometimes all a kid needs—just one or two really good teachers can make all the difference in the world. It can inspire and change a life. . . .

Thoreau's writing struck me like a thunderbolt. Like all great literature, it articulated something that I knew intuitively, but could not quite bring into focus for myself. I loved Emerson, too, and his essay, "Self-Reliance," was instrumental in giving me the courage to become a songwriter. The works of both men were part of a spiritual awakening in which I rediscovered my hometown and the beauty of the surrounding landscape, and, through that, some evidence of a "Higher Power," or God, if you like. This epiphany brought great comfort and relief. . . .

. . . [T]here has been a great deal of curiosity, speculation, and, in some quarters, skepticism bordering on cynicism, as to how and why I came to be involved in the movement to preserve the stomping grounds of Henry David Thoreau and his friend and mentor, Ralph Waldo Emerson. What, in other words, is California rock and roll trash doing meddling around in something as seemingly esoteric and high-minded as literature (pronounced "LIT-tra-chure"), philosophy, and history—the American Transcendentalist Movement and all its ascetic practitioners. Seems perfectly natural to me. American Literature, like the air we breathe, belongs—or should belong—to everybody. . . . The great halls of learning may keep Thoreau's literature and principles alive, but they will be of little help in fortifying the well from whence they sprang.

. . . Unfortunately, the focus of preservation efforts has come to rest on the pond and its immediate surroundings. That is all well and good, except that there remain approximately two thousand six hundred acres that are inside the historic boundaries of Walden Woods and deserve protection as well. Thoreau did not live *in* Walden Pond; he lived beside it. The man did not walk on water, he walked several miles a day through the woods, and his musings and writings therein figure at least as prominently in his literature as Walden Pond does. In other words, the width and breadth of his inspiration, the scope of his legacy is not limited to one sixty-two-acre pond, and it is absurd to think so. Walden Woods is not a pristine, grand tract of wilderness, but it is still, for the most part, exceedingly beautiful and inspiring. It is, for all intents and purposes, the cradle of the American environmental movement and should be preserved for its intrinsic, symbolic value or, as Ed Schofield, Thoreau Society president, so succinctly put it, "When Walden goes, all the issues radiating out from Walden go, too. If the prime place can be disposed of, how much easier to dispose of the issues it represents." Otherwise, we might just as well turn all our national parks, our monuments to freedom and independence, into theme parks and shopping malls.

MAKING MEANINGS

First Thoughts

1. What do you think of Thoreau — as a writer and as a personality? Is his message still valid, or do you find it dated and irrelevant?

Shaping Interpretations

2. What does Thoreau mean when he says, "Simplify, simplify" (page 237)? Do you think he has a valid point here? Explain.

Reading Check

a. According to the second paragraph in "Economy," why has Thoreau decided to write about his life?

b. How does Thoreau answer the questions implied in the title "Where I Lived, and What I Lived For"?

c. What arguments does Thoreau present in "Solitude" to demonstrate that he is not lonely in his isolated situation?

d. What satisfactions does Thoreau find in the labor of raising beans in "The Bean Field"?

3. How would you summarize Thoreau's ideas on technological progress, judging from what he says about railroads and other inventions of his era? Do you agree with him? Why or why not?

4. What do you think Thoreau means in his final paragraph by the words "Only that day dawns to which we are awake"?

5. What do you think is the lesson of the **parable** involving the insect in the wood table at the conclusion of *Walden*?

Connecting with the Text

6. Review your double-entry journal. What **generalizations** did you make based on Thoreau's ideas? Did you find that some of his ideas, if extended, would prove to be unworkable? Did you disagree with any of these thoughts? Be sure to discuss your journal entries in class.

7. If it were possible, would you like to spend a day or two with Thoreau? What would you most like to discuss with him?

Extending the Text

8. In *Connections* on page 245, the rock star Don Henley declares that Walden Woods is "the cradle of the American environmental movement and should be preserved for its intrinsic, symbolic value." In what ways do you think Thoreau's *Walden* has influenced the environmental movement in the United States? Do you agree with Henley that Walden Woods should be preserved because it has symbolic value to our society? Explain.

Challenging the Text

9. The Pulitzer Prize–winning author Wallace Stegner (1909–1993), who admired much of Thoreau's thought, once made this observation about Thoreau's message in *Walden:* "At times he sounds perilously like his spiritual descendants of the 1960s, who trusted no one over thirty and believed that they existed outside of, and were exempt from, the society they were protesting." Do you agree or disagree with Stegner's statement? Support or refute it with examples from *Walden.*

READING SKILLS AND STRATEGIES

Unlocking Meaning in Metaphors

Thoreau's **metaphors** are highly visual. Though they're clever and original, they aren't far-fetched. Thoreau takes his comparisons from nature and from other things he and his audience are familiar with, such as clothes and sailing. To be sure you understand Thoreau's figures of speech, **paraphrase** the following metaphors.

1. "As for the rest of my readers, they will accept such portions as apply to them. I trust that none will stretch the seams in putting on the coat, for it may do good service to him whom it fits." (page 234)

2. "I wanted to live deep and suck out all the marrow of life. . . ." (page 237)

3. "If a man does not keep pace with his companions, perhaps it is because he hears a different drummer. Let him step to the music which he hears, however measured or far away." (page 243)

Writer's Notebook

1. Collecting Ideas for Writing About a Controversial Issue

In the Writer's Notebook on page 229, you drew up a list of controversial issues. By now you might have added to your list—especially after reading Thoreau. Review your topics. Under each, write questions that you would like to explore. For example, if one of your topics is preserving wilderness areas, you might pose the question "Should wilderness areas be preserved at the cost of new housing?" Save your notes for possible use in the Writer's Workshop on page 331.

Analyzing *Walden*

2. How Romantic?

In a brief essay, evaluate evidence of the Romantic point of view in *Walden*—for instance, the emphasis on intuition, the power of nature, and the importance of human emotion. Is Thoreau a Romantic, in your opinion? Or, can you identify strong anti-Romantic strains in his thinking? (Review the characteristics of Romanticism on page 144.) Be sure to quote details from *Walden* to support your evaluation.

Supporting a Topic Sentence

3. Everyday Miracles

"The invariable mark of wisdom," Emerson wrote, "is to find the miraculous in the common." Using Emerson's statement as your topic sentence, choose a scene from *Walden,* and in a brief essay use details from *Walden* to show how Thoreau finds "the miraculous in the common."

Creative Writing

4. Thoreau on Our Times

Thoreau would undoubtedly have strong, and probably controversial, opinions on many aspects of present-day technology and society. Write a paragraph or two as if you are Thoreau, expressing your opinion on an aspect of modern life. Use the **first-person point of view.** Find support in *Walden* for your position.

Creative Writing

5. Still Waters Run Deep

Walden does not record monumental events; it describes the ordinary events that most people would let pass unnoticed. Do the same for a day in your life. Take a few minutes at intervals throughout the day to write down your impressions of what is going on around you. At the end of the day, record in a journal what you saw, what you heard, and what you thought. Did any-thing remind you of Thoreau's experiences? Did anything convey a lesson or seem to hold a message?

Creative Writing / Performance

6. In My Solitude

Suppose that a Puritan like Mary Rowlandson (page 38) or a rationalist like Benjamin Franklin (page 84) had done the "Walden experiment." Write a journal entry from the point of view of the Puritan or rationalist of your choice, recording the experience of solitude at Walden Pond. What lessons or morals does the person draw from the experience? How is the perspective different from Thoreau's? Read the journal entry aloud to the class, speaking like the person who might have written it.

Crossing the Curriculum: Science

7. Further Into Nature

Thoreau is remembered not only as a philosophical writer but as a keen observer of nature. Choose an aspect of nature that Thoreau mentions—an ant war, a loon, a bean field, or something less obvious—and do some research in a library or on the Internet. Find at least three facts about the subject that go beyond the information Thoreau provides. Report your findings to the class.

Make the Connection

Civil Disobedience

The idea of civil disobedience is probably familiar to you if you know anything about the U.S. civil rights struggles of the 1960s or the struggle of Mohandas K. ("Mahatma") Gandhi and his followers to achieve independence for India in the first half of the twentieth century. Both movements were inspired by the essay that follows.

Some readers have concluded that this essay shows that Thoreau merely wanted to withdraw from life and all its difficult questions. Others see Thoreau's action as the logical outcome of his convictions. Decide for yourself if Thoreau's position is admirable or not.

Quickwrite

Under what circumstances would you be willing to go to jail for a moral or political principle? Write a brief description of the principle and of your feelings about it. Alternatively, explain why you wouldn't be willing to commit civil disobedience under any circumstances.

Elements of Literature

Paradox

A **paradox** is a statement that expresses the complexity of life by showing how opposing ideas can be both contradictory and

Gandhi during the last months of his life in Birla House, New Delhi, India. He was assassinated in January 1948, shortly after India achieved independence.

Henri Cartier-Bresson/Magnum.

true, as in Emily Dickinson's famous line "Tell all the Truth but tell it slant—" (page 386). Paradox was one of Thoreau's favorite literary devices. The idea that a contradiction can contain a truth is in itself paradoxical—and truthful.

> A **paradox** is a statement that appears self-contradictory but that reveals a kind of truth.
>
> *For more on Paradox, see the Handbook of Literary Terms.*

Background

In July 1846, Thoreau's stay at Walden Pond was interrupted by a night in jail. Thoreau was arrested because he refused to pay a tax to the state—primarily because he was opposed to the government's support of slavery. The Concord police offered to pay the tax for Thoreau, but he refused that also. He was forced, therefore, to spend the night in jail, and he might have spent more time there, except that someone, probably his aunt, paid the tax for him. This night in jail inspired the essay known as "Resistance to Civil Government" or "Civil Disobedience."

from Resistance to Civil Government

Henry David Thoreau

I heartily accept the motto—"That government is best which governs least";[1] and I should like to see it acted up to more rapidly and systematically. Carried out, it finally amounts to this, which also I believe—"That government is best which governs not at all"; and when men are prepared for it, that will be the kind of government which they will have. Government is at best but an <u>expedient</u>; but most governments are usually, and all governments are sometimes, inexpedient. The objections which have been brought against a standing army, and they are many and weighty, and deserve to prevail, may also at last be brought against a standing government. The standing army is only an arm of the standing government. The government itself, which is only the mode which the people have chosen to execute their will, is equally liable to be abused and <u>perverted</u> before the people can act through it. Witness the present Mexican war, the work of comparatively a few individuals using the standing government as their tool; for, in the outset, the people would not have consented to this measure.[2]

1. **That . . . least:** This statement, attributed to Thomas Jefferson, was the motto of the New York *Democratic Review,* which had published two of Thoreau's essays.
2. **this measure:** On May 9, 1846, President James K. Polk (1795–1849) received word that Mexico had attacked United States troops. He then asked Congress to declare war, which they did on May 13. Some Americans, including Thoreau, thought the war was unjustified. Because Thoreau would not support the war with his taxes, he went to jail.

WORDS TO OWN
expedient (ek·spē′dē·ənt) *n.:* convenience; means to an end.
perverted (pər·vurt′id) *v.:* misdirected; corrupted.

This American government—what is it but a tradition, though a recent one, endeavoring to transmit itself unimpaired to <u>posterity</u>, but each instant losing some of its integrity? It has not the vitality and force of a single living man; for a single man can bend it to his will. It is a sort of wooden gun to the people themselves; and, if ever they should use it in earnest as a real one against each other, it will surely split. But it is not the less necessary for this; for the people must have some complicated machinery or other, and hear its din, to satisfy that idea of government which they have. Governments show thus how successfully men can be imposed on, even impose on themselves, for their own advantage. It is excellent, we must all allow; yet this government never of itself furthered any enterprise, but by the <u>alacrity</u> with which it got out of its way. *It* does not keep the country free. *It* does not settle the West. *It* does not educate. The character <u>inherent</u> in the American people has done all that has been accomplished; and it would have done somewhat more, if the government had not sometimes got in its way. For government is an expedient by which men would fain[3] succeed in letting one another alone; and, as has been said, when it is most expedient, the governed are most let alone by it. Trade and commerce, if they were not made of India rubber, would never manage to bounce over the obstacles which legislators are continually putting in their way; and, if one were to judge these men wholly by the effects of their actions, and not partly by their intentions, they would deserve to be classed and punished with those mischievous persons who put obstructions on the railroads.

But, to speak practically and as a citizen, unlike those who call themselves no-government men, I ask for, not at once no government, but *at once* a better government. Let every man make known what kind of government would command his respect, and that will be one step toward obtaining it.

After all, the practical reason why, when the power is once in the hands of the people, a majority are permitted, and for a long period continue, to rule, is not because they are most likely to be in the right, nor because this seems fairest to the minority, but because they are physically the strongest. But a government in which the majority rule in all cases cannot be based on justice, even as far as men understand it. Can there not be a government in which majorities do not virtually decide right and wrong, but conscience?—in which majorities decide only those questions to which the rule of expediency is applicable? Must the citizen ever for a moment, or in the least degree, resign his conscience to the legislator? Why has every man a conscience, then? I think that we should be men first, and subjects afterward. It is not desirable to cultivate a respect for the law, so much as for the right. The only obligation which I have a right to assume, is to do at any time what I think right. . . .

It is not a man's duty, as a matter of course, to devote himself to the eradication of any, even the most enormous wrong; he may still properly have other concerns to engage him; but it is his duty, at least, to wash his hands of it, and, if he gives it no thought longer, not to give it practically his support. If I devote myself to other pursuits and contemplations, I must first see, at least, that I do not pursue them sitting upon another man's shoulders. I must get off him first, that he may pursue his contemplations too. See what gross inconsistency is tolerated. I have heard some of my townsmen say, "I should like to have them order me out to help put down an <u>insurrection</u> of the slaves, or to march to Mexico—see if I would go"; and yet these very men have each, directly by their allegiance, and so indirectly, at least, by their money, furnished a substitute. The soldier is applauded who refuses to serve in an unjust war by those who do not refuse to sustain the unjust government which makes the war; is applauded by those whose own act and authority he disregards and sets at nought; as if the State were <u>penitent</u> to that degree that it hired one to scourge it while it sinned, but not to that degree that it left off sinning for a moment. Thus, under the name of order

---

3. **fain:** archaic for "gladly" or "willingly."

WORDS TO OWN

posterity (päs·ter′ə·tē) *n*.: generations to come.
alacrity (ə·lak′rə·tē) *n*.: promptness in responding; eagerness.
inherent (in·hir′ənt) *adj*.: inborn.
insurrection (in′sə·rek′shən) *n*.: rebellion; revolt.
penitent (pen′i·tənt) *adj*.: sorry for doing wrong.

and civil government, we are all made at last to pay homage to and support our own meanness. After the first blush of sin, comes its indifference and from immoral it becomes, as it were, *un-moral*, and not quite unnecessary to that life which we have made. . . .

I meet this American government, or its representative the State government, directly, and face to face, once a year, no more, in the person of its tax-gatherer; this is the only mode in which a man situated as I am necessarily meets it; and it then says distinctly, Recognize me; and the simplest, the most <u>effectual</u>, and, in the present posture of affairs, the indispensablest mode of treating with it on this head, of expressing your little satisfaction with and love for it, is to deny it then. My civil neighbor, the tax-gatherer, is the very man I have to deal with—for it is, after all, with men and not with parchment that I quarrel—and he has voluntarily chosen to be an agent of the government. How shall he ever know well what he is and does as an officer of the government, or as a man, until he is obliged to consider whether he shall treat me, his neighbor, for whom he has respect, as a neighbor and well-disposed man, or as a maniac and disturber of the peace, and see if he can get over this <u>obstruction</u> to his neighborliness without a ruder and more <u>impetuous</u> thought or speech corresponding with his action? I know this well, that if one thousand, if one hundred, if ten men whom I could name—if ten *honest* men only—aye, if *one* HONEST man, in this State of Massachusetts, *ceasing to hold slaves,* were actually to withdraw from this copartnership, and be locked up in the county jail therefor, it would be the abolition of slavery in America. For it matters not how small the beginning may seem to be: What is once well done is done forever. . . .

I have paid no poll tax[4] for six years. I was put into a jail once on this account, for one night; and, as I stood considering the walls of solid stone,

two or three feet thick, the door of wood and iron, a foot thick, and the iron grating which strained the light, I could not help being struck with the foolishness of that institution which treated me as if I were mere flesh and blood and bones, to be locked up. I wondered that it should have concluded at length that this was the best use it could put me to, and had never thought to avail itself of my services in some way. I saw that, if there was a wall of stone between me and my townsmen, there was a still more difficult one to climb or break through, before they could get to be as free as I was. I did not for a moment feel confined, and the walls seemed a great waste of stone and mortar. I felt as if I alone of all my townsmen had paid my tax. They plainly did not know how to treat me, but behaved like persons who are underbred. In every threat and in every compliment there was a blunder; for they thought that my chief desire was to stand the other side of that stone wall. I could not but smile to see how industriously they locked the door on my meditations, which followed them out again without let or hindrance, and *they* were really all that was dangerous. As they could not reach me, they had resolved to punish my body; just as boys, if they cannot come at some person against whom they have a spite, will abuse his dog. I saw that the State was half-witted, that it was timid as a lone woman with her silver spoons, and that it did not know its friends from its foes, and I lost all my remaining respect for it, and pitied it. . . .

The night in prison was novel and interesting enough. The prisoners in their shirt sleeves were enjoying a chat and the evening air in the doorway, when I entered. But the jailer said, "Come, boys, it is time to lock up"; and so they dispersed, and I heard the sound of their steps returning into the hollow apartments. My roommate was

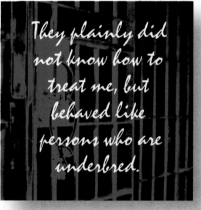

They plainly did not know how to treat me, but behaved like persons who are underbred.

---

4. **poll tax:** fee some states and localities required from each citizen as a qualification for voting. It is now considered unconstitutional in the United States to charge such a tax.

WORDS TO OWN
effectual (e·fek′chōō·əl) *adj.:* productive; efficient.
obstruction (əb·struk′shən) *n.:* blockage; hindrance.
impetuous (im·pech′ōō·əs) *adj.:* impulsive.

John Brown Going to His Hanging (1942) by Horace Pippin. Oil on canvas (24 ⅛″ × 30 ¼″).

introduced to me by the jailer, as "a first-rate fellow and a clever man." When the door was locked, he showed me where to hang my hat, and how he managed matters there. The rooms were whitewashed once a month; and this one, at least, was the whitest, most simply furnished, and probably the neatest apartment in the town. He naturally wanted to know where I came from, and what brought me there; and, when I had told him, I asked him in my turn how he came there, presuming him to be an honest man, of course; and, as the world goes, I believe he was. "Why," said he, "they accuse me of burning a barn; but I never did it." As near as I could discover, he had probably gone to bed in a barn when drunk, and smoked his pipe there; and so a barn was burnt. He had the reputation of being a clever man, had been there some three months waiting for his trial to come on, and would have to wait as much longer; but he was quite domesticated and contented, since he got his board for nothing, and thought that he was well treated.

He occupied one window, and I the other; and I saw, that, if one stayed there long, his principal business would be to look out the window. I had soon read all the tracts that were left there, and examined where former prisoners had broken out, and where a grate had been sawed off, and heard the history of the various occupants of that room; for I found that even here there was a history and a gossip which never circulated beyond the walls of the jail. Probably this is the only house in the town where verses are composed, which are afterward printed in a circular form, but not published. I was shown quite a long list of verses which were composed by some young men who had been detected in an attempt to escape, who avenged themselves by singing them.

I pumped my fellow prisoner as dry as I could, for fear I should never see him again; but at length he showed me which was my bed, and left me to blow out the lamp.

It was like traveling into a far country, such as I had never expected to behold, to lie there for one night. It seemed to me that I never had heard the town-clock strike before, nor the evening sounds of the village; for we slept with the windows open, which were inside the grating. It was to see my native village in the light of the middle ages, and our Concord was turned into a Rhine stream, and visions of knights and castles passed before me. They were the voices of old burghers that I heard in the streets. I was an involuntary spectator and auditor of whatever was done and said in the kitchen of the adjacent village inn—a wholly new and rare experience to me. It was a closer view of my native town. I was fairly inside of it. I never had seen its institutions before. This is one of its peculiar institutions; for it is a shire town.[5] I began to comprehend what its inhabitants were about.

5. **shire town:** town where a court sits, like a county seat.

In the morning, our breakfasts were put through the hole in the door, in small oblong-square tin pans, made to fit, and holding a pint of chocolate, with brown bread, and an iron spoon. When they called for the vessels again, I was green enough to return what bread I had left; but my comrade seized it, and said that I should lay that up for lunch or dinner. Soon after, he was let out to work at haying in a neighboring field, whither he went every day, and would not be back till noon; so he bade me good day, saying that he doubted if he should see me again.

When I came out of prison—for someone interfered, and paid the tax—I did not perceive that great changes had taken place on the common, such as he observed who went in a youth, and emerged a tottering and gray-headed man; and yet a change had to my eyes come over the scene—the town, and State, and country—greater than any that mere time could effect. I saw yet more distinctly the State in which I lived. I saw to what extent the people among whom I lived could be trusted as good neighbors and friends; that their friendship was for summer weather only; that they did not greatly purpose to do right; that they were a distinct race from me by their prejudices and superstitions, as the Chinamen and Malays are; that, in their sacrifices to humanity, they ran no risks, not even to their property; that, after all, they were not so noble but they treated the thief as he had treated them, and hoped, by a certain outward observance and a few prayers, and by walking in a particular straight though useless path from time to time, to save their souls. This may be to judge my neighbors harshly; for I believe that most of them are not aware that they have such an institution as the jail in their village.

It was formerly the custom in our village, when a poor debtor came out of jail, for his acquaintances to salute him, looking through their fingers, which were crossed to represent the grating of a jail window, "How do ye do?" My neighbors did not thus salute me, but first looked at me, and then at one another, as if I had returned from a long journey. I was put into jail as I was going to the shoemaker's to get a shoe which was mended. When I was let out the next morning, I proceeded to finish my errand, and, having put on my mended shoe, joined a huckleberry party, who were impatient to put themselves under my conduct; and in half an hour—for the horse was soon tackled[6]—was in the midst of a huckleberry field, on one of our highest hills, two miles off; and then the State was nowhere to be seen.

This is the whole history of "My Prisons." . . .

The authority of government, even such as I am willing to submit to—for I will cheerfully obey those who know and can do better than I, and in many things even those who neither know nor can do so well—is still an impure one: To be strictly just, it must have the sanction and consent of the governed. It can have no pure right over my person and property but what I concede to it. The progress from an absolute to a limited monarchy, from a limited monarchy to a democracy, is a progress toward a true respect for the individual. Is a democracy, such as we know it, the last improvement possible in government? Is it not possible to take a step further toward recognizing and organizing the rights of man? There will never be a really free and enlightened State, until the State comes to recognize the individual as a higher and independent power, from which all its own power and authority are derived, and treats him accordingly. I please myself with imagining a State at last which can afford to be just to all men, and to treat the individual with respect as a neighbor; which even would not think it inconsistent with its own repose, if a few were to live aloof from it, not meddling with it, nor embraced by it, who fulfilled all the duties of neighbors and fellow men. A State which bore this kind of fruit, and suffered it to drop off as fast as it ripened, would prepare the way for a still more perfect and glorious State, which also I have imagined, but not yet anywhere seen.

I please myself with imagining a State at last which can afford to be just to all men, and to treat the individual with respect as a neighbor...

6. **tackled:** harnessed.

"A Healthy and Wholesome Man to Know"

• On August 31, 1842, the young Thoreau had dinner with Nathaniel Hawthorne (page 296). In his notebooks, Hawthorne gave this description of his guest (whose name he spells "Thorow").

Henry David Thoreau in his traveling outfit, at age 37 (c. 1854). Sketch.

The Bettmann Archive.

Mr. Thorow dined with us yesterday. He is a singular character—a young man with much of wild original nature still remaining in him; and so far as he is sophisticated, it is in a way and method of his own. He is as ugly as sin, long-nosed, queer-mouthed, and with uncouth and somewhat rustic, although courteous manners, corresponding very well with such an exterior. But his ugliness is of an honest and agreeable fashion, and becomes him much better than beauty. He was educated, I believe, at Cambridge, and formerly kept school in this town; but for two or three years back, he has repudiated all regular modes of getting a living, and seems inclined to lead a sort of Indian life. . . . He has been for some time an inmate of Mr. Emerson's family; and, in requital, he labors in the garden, and performs such other offices as may suit him—being entertained by Mr. Emerson for the sake of what true manhood there is in him. Mr. Thorow is a keen and delicate observer of nature—a genuine observer, which, I suspect, is almost as rare a character as even an original poet; and Nature, in return for his love, seems to adopt him as her especial child, and shows him secrets which few others are allowed to witness. He is familiar with beast, fish, fowl, and reptile, and has strange stories to tell of adventures, and friendly passages with these lower brethren of mortality. . . . With all this he has more than a tincture of literature—a deep and true taste for poetry, especially the elder poets. . . . On the whole, I find him a healthy and wholesome man to know.

—Nathaniel Hawthorne

• • • • •

• Hawthorne's wife, Sophia, described a skating trio on the Concord River: Emerson, Thoreau, and Hawthorne are on the ice. (In ancient Greece, a *dithyramb* was a wild, emotional hymn. In Greek and Roman myth, Bacchus is the god of wine and merrymaking.)

One afternoon, Mr. Emerson and Mr. Thoreau went with him [Hawthorne] down the river. Henry Thoreau is an experienced skater, and was figuring dithyrambic dances and Bacchic leaps on the ice—very remarkable, but very ugly, methought. Next him followed Mr. Hawthorne who, wrapped in his cloak, moved like a self-impelled Greek statue, stately and grave. Mr. Emerson closed the line, evidently too weary to hold himself erect, pitching head-foremost, half lying on the air.

—Sophia Peabody Hawthorne

Connections

The Reverend Dr. Martin Luther King, Jr., was a leader of the U.S. civil rights movement in the 1960s. He wrote this open letter on April 16, 1963, while serving a sentence for participating in a civil rights demonstration.

from Letter from Birmingham City Jail

Martin Luther King, Jr.

You express a great deal of anxiety over our willingness to break laws. This is certainly a legitimate concern. Since we so diligently urge people to obey the Supreme Court's decision of 1954 outlawing segregation in the public schools, it is rather strange and paradoxical to find us consciously breaking laws. One may well ask, "How can you advocate breaking some laws and obeying others?" The answer is found in the fact that there are two types of laws: there are *just* and there are *unjust* laws. I would agree with Saint Augustine that "An unjust law is no law at all."

Now what is the difference between the two? How does one determine when a law is just or unjust? A just law is a man-made code that squares with the moral law or the law of God. An unjust law is a code that is out of harmony with the moral law. . . .

An unjust law is a code inflicted upon a minority which that minority had no part in enacting or creating because they did not have the unhampered right to vote. Who can say that the legislature of Alabama which set up the segregation laws was democratically elected? Throughout the state of Alabama all types of conniving methods are used to prevent Negroes from becoming registered voters and there are some counties without a single Negro registered to vote despite the fact that the Negro constitutes a majority of the population. Can any law set up in such a state be considered democratically structured?

These are just a few examples of unjust and just laws. There are some instances when a law is just on its face and unjust in its application. For instance, I was arrested Friday on a charge of parading without a permit. Now there is nothing wrong with an ordinance which requires a permit for a parade, but when the ordinance is used to preserve segregation and to deny citizens the First Amendment privilege of peaceful assembly and peaceful protest, then it becomes unjust.

I hope you can see the distinction I am trying to point out. In no sense do I advocate evading or defying the law as the rabid segregationist would do. This would lead to anarchy. One who breaks an unjust law must do it *openly, lovingly* (not hatefully as the white mothers did in New Orleans when they were seen on television screaming, "nigger, nigger, nigger"), and with a willingness to accept the penalty. I submit that an individual who breaks a law that conscience tells him is unjust, and willingly accepts the penalty by staying in jail to arouse the conscience of the community over its injustice, is in reality expressing the very highest respect for law.

Martin Luther King, Jr., being booked at a police station.
Charles Moore/Black Star.

MAKING MEANINGS

First Thoughts

1. Would you have spent the night in jail as Thoreau did? Explain.

Shaping Interpretations

2. Explain the truth in each of these **paradoxes.**
   a. "I saw that, if there was a wall of stone between me and my townsmen, there was a still more difficult one to climb or break through, before they could get to be as free as I was." (page 251)
   b. "I felt as if I alone of all my townsmen had paid my tax." (page 251)

3. How are Thoreau's perceptions of his fellow citizens changed by his night in jail?

4. What idea is Thoreau stressing in telling us about getting his shoe fixed and leading the huckleberry party on the day he was released?

5. From what you know about American Romanticism (pages 138–150), would you say that Thoreau's assumptions and points in this essay are fundamentally Romantic? Explain.

6. What influences of Emerson's thought can you find in "Resistance to Civil Government"?

Connecting with the Text

7. Review your Quickwrite notes about civil disobedience. Which of Thoreau's arguments did you find convincing, and

Reading Check

a. Explain what Thoreau thinks is wrong with majority rule. What does he say is the only obligation he has a right to assume?

b. What does Thoreau predict about slavery in America?

c. Explain why Thoreau was put in jail. What were his feelings about the government when he was in jail?

d. At the end of the essay, what qualities does Thoreau envision in an ideal "perfect and glorious State"?

which did you disagree with? Could there be civil order if each person always followed his or her own conscience? Explain.

Extending the Text

8. Comment on how Thoreau's main points in this essay relate to the points Martin Luther King, Jr., makes in **Connections** on page 256. How do Thoreau's and Dr. King's views relate to American life today?

Challenging the Text

9. Imagine that someone has made the following observation: "When Thoreau let someone pay the tax for him, he betrayed his own principles. He became just like the people he criticized, who opposed the Mexican War but supported it with their tax money. If he had wanted to make a truly courageous and effective protest, he should have insisted on staying in jail." Do you agree with this statement? Why or why not?

READING SKILLS AND STRATEGIES

Determining the Precise Meanings of Words

1. "After the first blush of sin," writes Thoreau on page 251, "comes its indifference and from immoral it becomes, as it were, *unmoral* . . ."
   a. The word *indifference* can mean "neutrality" or "apathy." What is the difference between the two meanings? Which meaning does the word have here?
   b. How is *unmoral* different from *immoral*?

2. Thoreau was arrested because he did not pay "poll tax."
   a. The word *poll* comes from a Middle English word for "top of the head." Usage has added other meanings, including the sense of "individual" ("one head"). What do you think a "poll tax" is?
   b. What do the words *poll, pollster,* and *poll booth* mean today? How are they related to the sense of "head"?

CHOICES: Building Your Portfolio

Nelson Mandela, who became president of South Africa in 1994 after spending many years imprisoned for his political views.

AP/Wide World Photos.

Poe

Cortázar

Hawthorne

Melville

If you cannot bear the silence and the darkness, do not go there; if you dislike black night and yawning chasms, never make them your profession. If you fear the sound of water hurrying through crevices toward unknown and mysterious destinations, do not consider it. Seek out the sunshine. It is a simple prescription. Avoid the darkness.

It is a simple prescription, but you will not follow it. You will turn immediately to the darkness. You will be drawn to it by cords of fear and of longing. You will imagine that you are tired of the sunlight; the waters that unnerve you will tug in the ancient recesses of your mind; the midnight will seem restful—you will end by going down.

—Loren Eiseley,
from The Night Country

Edgar Allan Poe
(1809–1849)

"The want of parental affection," wrote Poe, "has been the heaviest of my trials." Edgar Poe was, indeed, most unfortunate in his parents. His father, David Poe, was a mediocre traveling actor who drank heavily. His mother, Elizabeth Arnold, was a talented actress who was deserted by her husband when Edgar was still a baby. She died on tour in Richmond, Virginia, leaving Edgar virtually an orphan before his third birthday.

The boy was taken in by John and Frances Allan, a charitable and childless couple in Richmond. John Allan, an ambitious and self-righteous merchant, became Edgar's guardian (and the source of the writer's middle name). He provided generously for Edgar's early education, but he never formally adopted the boy.

Although Frances Allan was kind to Edgar, the boy grew up feeling both the lack of a natural father and the disapproval of his foster father. John Allan made no secret of his disappointment in Edgar—in his idleness, in his indifference to business life, and in his literary ambitions. Surely Allan's criticism added to Edgar's growing moodiness.

Edgar Allan Poe.

The Bettmann Archive.

Breaking Away

At seventeen, Edgar entered the University of Virginia. He did well in his studies but was resentful of the meager allowance Allan gave him. When he tried to earn extra money by gambling, he went deep into debt. On discovering this, Allan refused to help his foster son and instead withdrew him from college.

After an especially bitter quarrel with Allan, Poe ran off to Boston to make his own way in the world. There, in 1827, he published a small volume of poems, *Tamerlane*. The book did not attract much attention, and Poe could find no other work. In despair, he joined the army. He was promoted to the rank of sergeant major, but he disliked the enlisted man's life and appealed to Allan for help. At the request of his wife, who was dying, Allan interceded for Edgar (for the last time) and agreed to help him enter the U.S. Military Academy at West Point. Poe's motive in going to the Academy was probably to please his foster father.

While waiting to get into the Academy, Poe published a second book of poems, *El Aaraaf,* in 1829 and received his first real recognition as a writer. The next year, while at West Point, Poe learned that Allan (now a widower) had remarried and that the woman was young enough to have children. Since this appeared to end all hope of becoming Allan's heir, Poe had himself dismissed from West Point.

Exploring the Darkness and the Depths

Poe moved in with an aunt, Maria Poe Clemm, in Baltimore, Maryland. In 1835, he married her thirteen-year-old daughter, Virginia. The difference in their ages and Virginia's poor health resulted in a very odd marriage. But need and a strong sense of family drew the three housemates together.

Poe supported his family by working as an editor at various magazines. He wrote when he could find the time, completing his only full-length novel, *The Narrative of Arthur Gordon Pym,* several years after his marriage. But it was his short stories that had the greatest effect on other writers.

HRW

go.hrw.com

LEO 11-6

In "The Gold Bug," and in the tales built around the intuitive sleuth C. Auguste Dupin, "The Purloined Letter" and "The Murders in the Rue Morgue," Poe laid the foundations for the modern detective story. In fact, he inspired Sir Arthur Conan Doyle to create Sherlock Holmes. In tales such as "The Tell-Tale Heart" and "The Cask of Amontillado," Poe inspired the Russian novelist Feodor Dostoevski (1821–1881) to explore the criminal mind.

Poe was a master of the psychological thriller. His tales of the ghastly and the grotesque are peopled with distraught narrators, deranged heroes, and doomed heroines. Yet his purpose in creating such characters was not to present readers with convincing likenesses of human beings—nor merely to shock and frighten. Instead, Poe wanted to take us behind the curtain that separates the everyday from the incredible. He wanted to leave behind the sunlit, tangible, rational world and discover the unsettling truth that lies in the dark, irrational depths of the human mind.

Small Triumphs and Great Tragedy

Poe produced a considerable body of work in spite of humiliating poverty and a serious drinking problem. The slightest amount of alcohol made him senseless; yet he drank to escape a reality he found agonizing. Publication of his poem "The Raven" in 1845 brought him some fame at last, but financial security still eluded him.

When Virginia died of tuberculosis in 1847, Poe and "Muddy" (Virginia's mother) were left alone. Poe grew more unstable and contracted illnesses, including a brain lesion that would leave him little time to live. But he pursued romance relentlessly, always looking for someone to "adopt" him. In 1849, during a visit to Virginia to a woman he hoped to marry, Poe disappeared. A week later, he was found in a Baltimore tavern—delirious, his clothing torn and wet from a raging storm. He regained enough consciousness to pray "Lord help my poor soul" before he died four days later. It was a tragic yet strangely appropriate end to the tortured life of a man obsessed by loss and death.

LITERATURE AND POPULAR CULTURE

Poe the Pop Icon

Can you guess what Edgar Allan Poe has in common with Elvis Presley, Marilyn Monroe, the Beatles, Michael Jordan, and the cast of *Star Trek*? Like all of the above, Poe is a legend of popular culture. Consider these facts:

- Poe's works have been translated into virtually every language.
- Such popular writers as Stephen King and Ray Bradbury point to Poe as their literary forefather.
- The Mystery Writers of America annually honors great achievements in mystery writing with the "Edgar"—the equivalent of an Oscar or an Emmy.
- Poe has been immortalized in the popular arts, on everything from posters, buttons, and coffee mugs to bumper stickers and T-shirts.
- Poe has been "ushered" into twentieth-century pop culture through dozens of film adaptations, including *The Masque of the Red Death, The Black Cat, The Tomb of Ligeia,* and *The Pit and the Pendulum.*

Keep your eye out for Poe. He may be closer than you think.

Vincent Price in *The Masque of the Red Death.*

Movie Still Archives.

Make the Connection

The Furnishings of Our Nightmares

Why do we watch movies like *Dracula, Psycho,* and *Jurassic Park*? Why do we make best-sellers of books by authors like Stephen King and Anne Rice?

In everyday life, we all feel fright from time to time: We tremble, sweat, get tense. Maybe those responses are designed to send us flying from danger to a less threatening place. Perhaps it's the need to periodically rehearse those feelings in a safe place that draws us to those scary movies and terrifying tales. Although we each have different furnishings for our nightmares, we all respond in similar ways to images of crumbling houses, reeking swamps, lonely moors, and characters who are sick in mind and body, who speak little and never hum or whistle.

Reading Skills and Strategies

Using Resources

Poe's story, perhaps the most famous horror story in American literature, is written in the ornate style favored in the 1800s. If you have difficulty reading the story, you can use various strategies and resources:

- If a sentence is very complicated, look for its **main subject and verb.** Then, look for words that the phrases modify.
- If you don't understand Poe's **allusions,** use the footnotes.
- If an unfamiliar word is not defined in a footnote, try the

glossary at the back of the book. Or use **context clues** to guess at the word's meaning and so continue with the story.

- Use the **question boxes** in the margins of the story. These questions will help you sum up important sections or note the **main ideas** of key passages.
- Make **predictions** and modify them as you read. It is the nature of a horror story to make you intensely anxious about what will happen next.

Elements of Literature

Atmosphere

A rotting mansion, mysterious illnesses, strange sounds at night, a person buried alive: Poe uses all of these Gothic details—and more (a list would stretch to the bottom of the page)—to create a single effect, a mood, or **atmosphere,** of dread and menace. Notice how Poe begins to build his mood in the very first paragraph of this story, with its hissing s sounds and powerful sensory images. It's a good paragraph to read aloud—listen to its sounds and feel its effects. Which words and phrases in this paragraph make you aware that the narrator is leaving one region and entering another, uncertain one?

> **A**tmosphere is the mood or feeling created in a piece of writing.
>
> *For more on Atmosphere, see the Handbook of Literary Terms.*

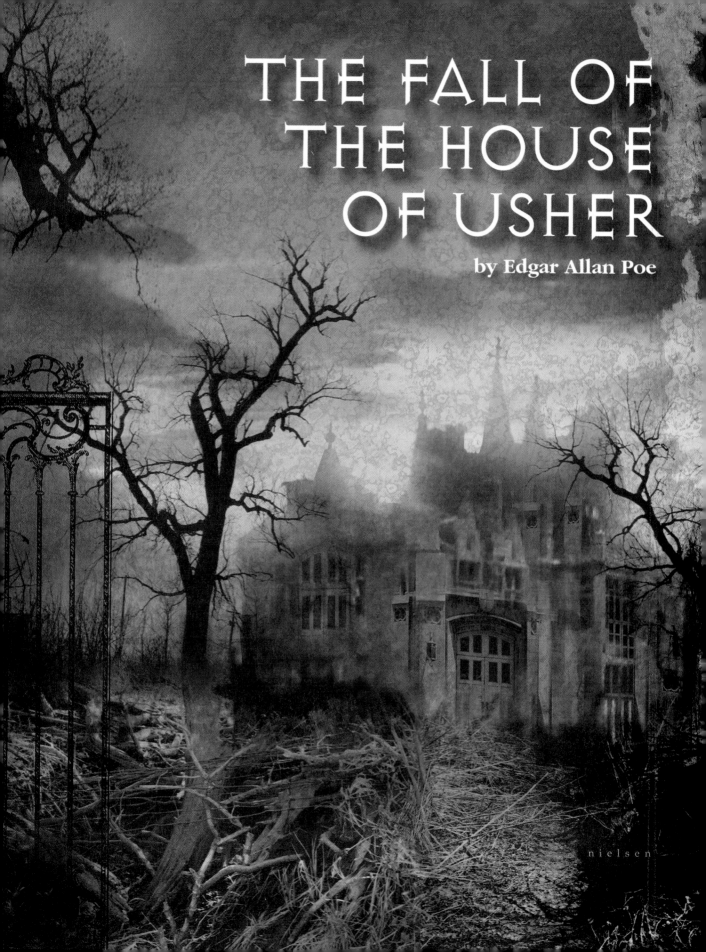

THE FALL OF THE HOUSE OF USHER

by Edgar Allan Poe

nielsen

Son cœur est un luth suspendu;
Sitôt qu'on le touche il résonne.[1]

—*De Béranger*

During the whole of a dull, dark, and soundless day in the autumn of the year, when the clouds hung oppressively low in the heavens, I had been passing alone, on horseback, through a singularly dreary tract of country; and at length found myself, as the shades of the evening drew on, within view of the melancholy House of Usher. I know not how it was—but, with the first glimpse of the building, a sense of insufferable gloom <u>pervaded</u> my spirit. I say insufferable; for the feeling was unrelieved by any of that half-pleasurable, because poetic, sentiment, with which the mind usually receives even the sternest natural images of the desolate or terrible. I looked upon the scene before me—upon the mere[2] house, and the simple landscape features of the domain—upon the bleak walls—upon the vacant eyelike windows—upon a few rank sedges[3]—and upon a few white trunks of decayed trees—with an utter depression of soul which I can compare to no earthly sensation more properly than to the afterdream of the reveler upon opium—the bitter lapse into everyday life—the hideous dropping off of the veil. There was an iciness, a sinking, a sickening of the heart—an unredeemed dreariness of thought which no goading of the imagination could torture into aught[4] of the sublime. What was it—I paused to think—what was it that so unnerved me in the contemplation of the House of Usher? It was a mystery all insoluble; nor could I grapple with the shadowy fancies that crowded upon me as I pondered. I was forced to fall back upon the unsatisfactory conclusion, that while, beyond doubt, there *are* combinations of very simple natural objects which have the power of thus affecting us, still the analysis of this power lies among considerations beyond our depth. It was possible, I reflected, that a mere different arrangement of the particulars of the scene, of the details of the picture, would be sufficient to modify, or perhaps to annihilate its capacity for sorrowful impression; and, acting upon this idea, I reined my horse to the precipitous brink of a black and lurid tarn[5] that lay in unruffled luster by the dwelling, and gazed down—but with a shudder even more thrilling than before—upon the remodeled and inverted images of the gray sedge, and the ghastly tree stems, and the vacant and eyelike windows.

> The narrator is riding on horseback to visit the House of Usher.
>
> **?** *What are the narrator's first impressions as he draws near to the House of Usher?*

Nevertheless, in this mansion of gloom I now proposed to myself a <u>sojourn</u> of some weeks. Its proprietor, Roderick Usher, had been one of my boon companions in boyhood; but many years had elapsed since our last meeting. A letter, however, had lately reached me in a distant part of the country—a letter from him—which, in its wildly importunate nature, had admitted of no other than a personal reply. The MS.[6] gave evidence of nervous agitation. The writer spoke of acute bodily illness—of a mental disorder which oppressed him—and of an earnest desire to see me, as his best, and indeed his only personal friend, with a view of attempting, by the cheerfulness of my society, some alleviation of his malady. It was the manner in which all this, and much more, was said—it was the apparent *heart* that went with his request—which allowed me no room for hesitation; and I accordingly obeyed forthwith what I still considered a very singular summons.

Although, as boys, we had been even intimate associates, yet I really knew little of my friend. His reserve had been always excessive and habitual. I was aware, however, that his very ancient family had been noted, time out of mind, for a peculiar sensibility of temperament, displaying itself,

---

1. *Son cœur . . . il résonne:* "His heart is a suspended lute; / Whenever one touches it, it resounds." From "Le Refus" ("The Refusal") by Pierre-Jean de Béranger (1780–1857).
2. **mere** (mir): lake.
3. **sedges:** grasslike plants that grow in watery ground.
4. **aught** (ôt): anything.

5. **tarn:** small but deep mountain lake. Its waters are dark from the decomposition of vegetation and because there is no circulation.
6. **MS.:** abbreviation for "manuscript."

WORDS TO OWN

pervaded (pər·vād′id) *v.*: spread throughout.
sojourn (sō′jurn) *n.*: short stay.

through long ages, in many works of exalted art, and manifested, of late, in repeated deeds of munificent yet unobtrusive charity, as well as in a passionate devotion to the intricacies, perhaps even more than to the orthodox and easily recognizable beauties, of musical science. I had learned, too, the very remarkable fact, that the stem of the Usher race, all time-honored as it was, had put forth, at no period, any enduring branch; in other words, that the entire family lay in the direct line of descent, and had always, with very trifling and very temporary variation, so lain. It was this deficiency, I considered, while running over in thought the perfect keeping of the character of the premises with the accredited character of the people, and while speculating upon the possible influence which the one, in the long lapse of centuries, might have exercised upon the other—it was this deficiency, perhaps, of collateral issue,[7] and the consequent undeviating transmission, from sire to son, of the patrimony with the name, which had, at length, so identified the two as to merge the original title of the estate in the quaint and equivocal appellation of the "House of Usher"—an appellation which seemed to include, in the minds of the peasantry who used it, both the family and the family mansion.

I have said that the sole effect of my somewhat childish experiment—that of looking down within the tarn—had been to deepen the first singular impression. There can be no doubt that the consciousness of the rapid increase of my superstition—for why should I not so term it?—served mainly to accelerate the increase itself. Such, I have long known, is the paradoxical law of all sentiments having terror as a basis. And it might have been for this reason only, that, when I again uplifted my eyes to the house itself, from its image in the pool, there grew in my mind a strange fancy—a fancy so ridiculous, indeed, that I but mention it to show the vivid force of the sensations which oppressed me. I had so worked upon my imagination as really to believe that about the whole mansion and domain there hung an atmosphere peculiar to themselves and their immediate vicinity—an atmosphere which had no affinity with the air

of heaven, but which had reeked up from the decayed trees, and the gray wall and the silent tarn—a pestilent and mystic vapor, dull, sluggish, faintly discernible, and leaden-hued.

Shaking off from my spirit what *must* have been a dream, I scanned more narrowly the real aspect of the building. Its principal feature seemed to be that of an excessive antiquity. The discoloration of ages had been great. Minute fungi overspread the whole exterior, hanging in a fine tangled webwork from the eaves. Yet all this was apart from any extraordinary dilapidation. No portion of the masonry had fallen; and there appeared to be a wild inconsistency between its still perfect adaptation of parts, and the crumbling condition of the individual stones. In this there was much that reminded me of the specious totality of old woodwork which has rotted for long years in some neglected vault, with no disturbance from the breath of the external air. Beyond this indication of extensive decay, however, the fabric gave little token of instability. Perhaps the eye of a scrutinizing observer might have discovered a barely perceptible fissure, which, extending from the roof of the building in front, made its way down the wall in a zigzag direction, until it became lost in the sullen waters of the tarn.

? *What details in this description of the house seem most significant?*

Noticing these things, I rode over a short causeway to the house. A servant-in-waiting took my horse, and I entered the Gothic archway of the

---

7. **collateral issue:** relatives, such as cousins, who share the same ancestors but who are not in a direct line of descent.

WORDS TO OWN

equivocal (ē·kwiv′ə·kəl) *adj.*: having more than one meaning.

discernible (di·surn′ə·bəl) *adj.*: noticeable.

specious (spē′shəs) *adj.*: seemingly sound, but not really so.

scrutinizing (skro̅o̅t′′n·īz′in) *v.* used as *adj.*: carefully observant.

hall.[8] A valet, of stealthy step, thence conducted me, in silence, through many dark and intricate passages in my progress to the *studio* of his master. Much that I encountered on the way contributed, I know not how, to heighten the vague sentiments of which I have already spoken. While the objects around me—while the carvings of the ceilings, the somber tapestries of the walls, the ebon blackness of the floors, and the phantasmagoric[9] armorial trophies which rattled as I strode, were but matters to which, or to such as which, I had been accustomed from my infancy—while I hesitated not to acknowledge how familiar was all this—I still wondered to find how unfamiliar were the fancies which ordinary images were stirring up. On one of the staircases, I met the physician of the family. His countenance, I thought, wore a mingled expression of low cunning and perplexity. He accosted me with trepidation and passed on. The valet now threw open a door and ushered me into the presence of his master.

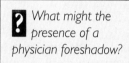
? What might the presence of a physician foreshadow?

The room in which I found myself was very large and lofty. The windows were long, narrow, and pointed, and at so vast a distance from the black oaken floor as to be altogether inaccessible from within. Feeble gleams of encrimsoned light made their way through the trellised panes, and served to render sufficiently distinct the more prominent objects around; the eye, however, struggled in vain to reach the remoter angles of the chamber, or the recesses of the vaulted and fretted[10] ceiling. Dark draperies hung upon the walls. The general furniture was profuse, comfortless, antique, and tattered. Many books and musical instruments lay scattered about, but failed to give any vitality to the scene. I felt that I breathed an atmosphere of sorrow. An air of stern, deep, and irredeemable gloom hung over and pervaded all.

Upon my entrance, Usher arose from a sofa on which he had been lying at full length, and greeted me with a vivacious warmth which had

much in it, I at first thought, of an overdone cordiality—of the constrained effort of the *ennuyé*[11] man of the world. A glance, however, at his countenance, convinced me of his perfect sincerity. We sat down; and for some moments, while he spoke not, I gazed upon him with a feeling half of pity, half of awe. Surely, man had never before so terribly altered, in so brief a period, as had Roderick Usher! It was with difficulty that I could bring myself to admit the identity of the wan being before me with the companion of my early boyhood. Yet the character of his face had been at all times remarkable. A cadaverousness[12] of complexion; an eye large, liquid, and luminous beyond comparison; lips somewhat thin and very pallid, but of a surpassingly beautiful curve; a nose of a delicate Hebrew model, but with a breadth of nostril unusual in similar formations; a finely molded chin, speaking, in its want of prominence, of a want of moral energy; hair of a more than weblike softness and tenuity;[13] these features, with an inordinate expansion above the regions of the temple, made up altogether a countenance not easily to be forgotten. And now in the mere exaggeration of the prevailing character of these features, and of the expression they were wont to convey, lay so much of change that I doubted to whom I spoke. The now ghastly pallor of the skin, and the now miraculous luster of the eye, above all things startled and even awed me. The silken hair, too, had been suffered to grow all unheeded, and as, in its wild gossamer texture, it floated rather than fell about the face, I could not, even with effort, connect its arabesque[14] expression with any idea of simple humanity.

In the manner of my friend I was at once struck with an incoherence—an inconsistency; and I soon found this to arise from a series of feeble and futile struggles to overcome an habitual trepi-

11. **ennuyé** (än·*n*wē·ā′): French for "bored" or "jaded."
12. **cadaverousness:** paleness or gauntness, as a corpse.
13. **tenuity:** fineness; lack of substance.
14. **arabesque:** strangely mixed; fantastic.

8. **Gothic . . . hall:** The hallway looked like a Gothic arch—high, pointed, and elaborately carved.
9. **phantasmagoric** (fan·taz′mə·gôr′ik): images appearing to change rapidly, like the events in a dream.
10. **fretted:** carved in an ornamental architectural design.

WORDS TO OWN
profuse (prō·fyōōs′) *adj*.: abundant.
vivacious (vī·vā′shəs) *adj*.: cheerful; lively.
pallid (pal′id) *adj*.: pale.
inordinate (in·ôr′də·nit) *adj*.: excessive.

dancy—an excessive nervous agitation. For something of this nature I had indeed been prepared, no less by his letter, than by reminiscences of certain boyish traits, and by conclusions deduced from his peculiar physical conformation and temperament. His action was alternately vivacious and sullen. His voice varied rapidly from a tremulous indecision (when the animal spirits seemed utterly in abeyance) to that species of energetic concision—that abrupt, weighty, unhurried, and hollow-sounding enunciation—that leaden, self-balanced and perfectly modulated guttural utterance, which may be observed in the lost drunkard, or the irreclaimable eater of opium, during the periods of his most intense excitement.

> The narrator is shocked by how much Roderick Usher has changed over the years.
>
> ❓ *What details in the description of Roderick Usher give you a vivid picture of his physical appearance and mannerisms?*

It was thus that he spoke of the object of my visit, of his earnest desire to see me, and of the solace he expected me to afford him. He entered, at some length, into what he conceived to be the nature of his malady. It was, he said, a constitutional and a family evil, and one for which he despaired to find a remedy—a mere nervous affection,[15] he immediately added, which would undoubtedly soon pass. It displayed itself in a host of unnatural sensations. Some of these, as he detailed them, interested and bewildered me; although, perhaps, the terms, and the general manner of the narration had their weight. He suffered much from a morbid acuteness of the senses; the most insipid food was alone endurable; he could wear only garments of certain texture; the odors of all flowers were oppressive; his eyes were tortured by even a faint light; and there were but peculiar sounds, and these from stringed instruments, which did not inspire him with horror.

To an anomalous[16] species of terror I found him a bounden slave. "I shall perish," said he, "I *must* perish in this deplorable folly. Thus, thus, and not otherwise, shall I be lost. I dread the events of the future, not in themselves, but in their results. I shudder at the thought of any, even the most trivial, incident, which may operate upon this intolerable agitation of soul. I have, indeed, no abhorrence of danger, except in its absolute effect—in terror. In this unnerved—in this pitiable condition—I feel that the period will sooner or later arrive when I must abandon life and reason together, in some struggle with the grim phantasm, FEAR."

I learned, moreover, at intervals, and through broken and equivocal hints, another singular feature of his mental condition. He was enchained by certain superstitious impressions in regard to the dwelling which he tenanted, and whence, for many years, he had never ventured forth—in regard to an influence whose supposititious[17] force was conveyed in terms too shadowy here to be restated—an influence which some peculiarities in the mere form and substance of his family mansion, had, by dint of long sufferance, he said, obtained over his spirit—an effect which the *physique* of the gray walls and turrets, and of the dim tarn into which they all looked down, had, at length, brought about upon the *morale* of his existence.

> The narrator learns that Usher suffers from a nervous disorder that heightens all his senses.
>
> ❓ *What "singular feature" of Usher's mental condition does the narrator discover?*

He admitted, however, although with hesitation, that much of the peculiar gloom which thus afflicted him could be traced to a more natural and far more palpable origin—to the severe and long-continued illness—indeed to the evidently approaching dissolution—of a tenderly beloved sister—his sole companion for long years—his last and only relative on earth. "Her decease," he said, with a bitterness which I can never forget, "would leave him (him the hopeless and the frail) the last of the ancient race of the Ushers." While

15. **affection:** ailment; disorder.
16. **anomalous:** abnormal.

17. **supposititious** (sə·päz′ə·tish′əs): supposed; assumed; hypothetical.

WORDS TO OWN

insipid (in·sip′id) *adj.*: bland; without flavor.
palpable (pal′pə·bəl) *adj.*: obvious; perceivable.

---

he spoke, the lady Madeline (for so was she called) passed slowly through a remote portion of the apartment, and, without having noticed my presence, disappeared. I regarded her with an utter astonishment not unmingled with dread—and yet I found it impossible to account for such feelings. A sensation of <u>stupor</u> oppressed me, as my eyes followed her retreating steps. When a door, at length, closed upon her, my glance sought instinctively and eagerly the countenance of the brother—but he had buried his face in his hands, and I could only perceive that a far more than ordinary wanness had overspread the emaciated fingers through which trickled many passionate tears.

The disease of the lady Madeline had long baffled the skill of her physicians. A settled apathy, a gradual wasting away of the person, and frequent although transient affections of a partially cataleptical[18] character, were the unusual diagnosis. Hitherto she had steadily borne up against the pressure of her malady, and had not betaken herself finally to bed; but, on the closing in of the evening of my arrival at the house, she succumbed (as her brother told me at night with inexpressible agitation) to the prostrating power of the destroyer; and I learned that the glimpse I had obtained of her person would thus probably be the last I should obtain—that the lady, at least while living, would be seen by me no more.

> Usher, who has not left his mansion in years, discloses a natural reason for his gloom: the strange illness of his sister Madeline.

For several days ensuing, her name was unmentioned by either Usher or myself: And during this period I was busied in earnest endeavors to alleviate the melancholy of my friend. We painted and read together; or I listened, as if in a dream, to the wild improvisations of his speaking guitar. And thus, as a closer and still closer intimacy admitted me more unreservedly into the recesses of his spirit, the more bitterly did I perceive the futility of all attempt at cheering a mind from which darkness, as if an inherent positive quality, poured forth upon all objects of the moral and physical universe, in one unceasing radiation of gloom.

I shall ever bear about me a memory of the many solemn hours I thus spent alone with the master of the House of Usher. Yet I should fail in any attempt to convey an idea of the exact character of the studies, or of the occupations, in which he involved me, or led me the way. An excited and highly distempered ideality[19] threw a sulfureous[20] luster over all. His long improvised dirges will ring forever in my ears. Among other things, I hold painfully in mind a certain singular perversion and amplification of the wild air of the last waltz of Von Weber.[21] From the paintings over which his elaborate fancy brooded, and which grew, touch by touch, into vaguenesses at which I shuddered the more thrillingly, because I shuddered knowing not why—from these paintings (vivid as their images now are before me) I would in vain endeavor to educe more than a small portion which should lie within the compass of merely written words. By the utter simplicity, by the nakedness of his designs, he arrested and overawed attention. If ever mortal painted an idea, that mortal was Roderick Usher. For me at least—in the circumstances then surrounding me—there arose out of the pure abstractions which the hypochondriac contrived to throw upon his canvas, an intensity of intolerable awe, no shadow of which felt I ever yet in the contemplation of the certainly glowing yet too concrete reveries of Fuseli.[22]

> The narrator tries to cheer Usher by painting and reading with him and listening to him play the guitar.

19. **distempered ideality:** mental derangement.
20. **sulfureous** (sul·fyoor'ē·əs): hellish; infernal. Poe's description probably comes from the yellowish color of sulfur, which is associated with the fires of hell.
21. **Von Weber:** Carl Maria von Weber (1786–1826), German Romantic composer.
22. **Fuseli:** Johann Heinrich Füssli (1741–1825), Swiss painter who lived in England and is known for scenes of horror and the supernatural.

18. **cataleptical** (kat'ə·lep'tik·əl): Catalepsy is an emotional condition, associated with disorders such as epilepsy and schizophrenia, which may cause the victim to lose sensation and the ability to move the limbs, or even the entire body. In a cataleptic attack, Madeline could be as stiff as a corpse.

WORDS TO OWN

stupor (stoo'pər) n.: state of mental dullness; loss of the senses.

One of the phantasmagoric conceptions of my friend, partaking not so rigidly of the spirit of abstraction, may be shadowed forth, although feebly, in words. A small picture presented the interior of an immensely long and rectangular vault or tunnel, with low walls, smooth, white, and without interruption or device. Certain accessory points of the design served well to convey the idea that this excavation lay at an exceeding depth below the surface of the earth. No outlet was observed in any portion of its vast extent, and no torch, or other artificial source of light was discernible; yet a flood of intense rays rolled throughout, and bathed the whole in a ghastly and inappropriate splendor.

I have just spoken of that <u>morbid</u> condition of the auditory nerve which rendered all music intolerable to the sufferer with the exception of certain effects of stringed instruments. It was, perhaps, the narrow limits to which he thus confined himself upon the guitar, which gave birth, in great measure, to the fantastic character of his performances. But the fervid *facility* of his *impromptus*[23] could not be so accounted for. They must have been, and were, in the notes, as well as in the words of his wild fantasias (for he not unfrequently accompanied himself with rhymed verbal improvisations), the result of that intense mental collectedness and concentration to which I have previously alluded as observable only in the moments of the highest artificial excitement. The words of one of these rhapsodies I have easily remembered. I was, perhaps, the more forcibly impressed with it, as he gave it, because, in the under or mystic current of its meaning, I fancied

> **?** Do you think the narrator is a reliable source of information about the Ushers and their house? Do the narrator's interpretations of Roderick's personality make sense to you? Would you analyze Roderick differently?

that I perceived, and for the first time, a full consciousness on the part of Usher, of the tottering of his lofty reason upon her throne. The verses, which were entitled "The Haunted Palace," ran very nearly, if not accurately, thus:

> **?** What are some of the characteristics of the works of art and musical compositions that Roderick produces? As you read the lyric "The Haunted Palace," ask yourself what it reveals about Roderick's frame of mind.

I

In the greenest of our valleys,
    By good angels tenanted,
Once a fair and stately palace—
    Radiant palace—reared its head.
In the monarch Thought's dominion—
    It stood there!
Never seraph[24] spread a pinion[25]
    Over fabric half so fair.

II

Banners yellow, glorious, golden,
    On its roof did float and flow;
(This—all this—was in the olden
    Time long ago)
And every gentle air that dallied,
    In that sweet day,
Along the ramparts plumed and pallid,
    A winged odor went away.

III

Wanderers in that happy valley
    Through two luminous windows saw
Spirits moving musically
    To a lute's well-tunéd law,
Round about a throne, where sitting
    (Porphyrogene!)[26]
In state his glory well befitting,
    The ruler of the realm was seen.

24. **seraph:** angel.
25. **pinion** (pin′yən): wing.
26. **porphyrogene** (pôr·fir′ə·jēn′): Poe coined this word from "porphyry," a purple dye reserved for royalty, to mean "one born to the purple," or "one of royal blood."

WORDS TO OWN
morbid (môr′bid) *adj.*: diseased; unhealthy.

23. **impromptus** (im·prämp′tōōz′): spontaneous performances.

IV

And all with pearl and ruby glowing
    Was the fair palace door,
Through which came flowing, flowing, flowing,
    And sparkling evermore,
A troop of Echoes whose sweet duty
    Was but to sing,
In voices of surpassing beauty,
    The wit and wisdom of their king.

V

But evil things, in robes of sorrow,
    Assailed the monarch's high estate;
(Ah, let us mourn, for never morrow
    Shall dawn upon him, desolate!)
And, round about his home, the glory
    That blushed and bloomed
Is but a dim-remembered story
    Of the old time entombed.

VI

And travelers now within that valley,
    Through the red-litten[27] windows, see
Vast forms that move fantastically
    To a discordant melody;
While, like a rapid ghastly river,
    Through the pale door,
A hideous throng rush out forever,
    And laugh—but smile no more.

I well remember that suggestions arising from this ballad led us into a train of thought wherein there became manifest an opinion of Usher's which I mention not so much on account of its novelty (for other men have thought thus), as on account of the pertinacity with which he maintained it. This opinion, in its general form, was that of the sentience[28] of all vegetable things. But, in his disordered fancy, the idea had assumed a more daring character, and trespassed, under certain conditions, upon the kingdom of inorganization.[29] I lack words to express the full extent, or the earnest *abandon* of his persuasion. The be-

lief, however, was connected (as I have previously hinted) with the gray stones of the home of his forefathers. The conditions of the sentience had been here, he imagined, fulfilled in the method of collocation of these stones—in the order of their arrangement, as well as in that of the many *fungi* which overspread them, and of the decayed trees which stood around—above all, in the long undisturbed endurance of this arrangement, and in its reduplication in the still waters of the tarn. Its evidence—the evidence of the sentience—was to be seen, he said (and I here started as he spoke), in the gradual yet certain condensation of an atmosphere of their own about the waters and the walls. The result was discoverable, he added, in that silent, yet importunate and terrible influence which for centuries had molded the destinies of his family, and which made *him* what I now saw him—what he was. Such opinions need no comment, and I will make none.

> Usher expresses his belief that not only all living things but also all nonliving things are sentient, or conscious.
>
> **?** *What specific details in the story thus far suggest that Usher's belief is reflected by his surroundings?*

Our books—the books which, for years, had formed no small portion of the mental existence of the invalid—were, as might be supposed, in strict keeping with this character of phantasm. We pored together over such works as the *Ververt et Chartreuse* of Gresset; the *Belphegor* of Machiavelli; the *Heaven and Hell* of Swedenborg; *The Subterranean Voyage of Nicholas Klimm* by Holberg; the Chiromancy of Robert Flud, of Jean D'Indaginé, and of De la Chambre; the *Journey into the Blue Distance* of Tieck; and *The City of the Sun* of Campanella. One favorite volume was a small octavo edition of the *Directorium Inquisitorum*, by the Dominican Eymeric de Gironne; and there were passages in Pomponius Mela, about the old African Satyrs and Ægipans,[30] over which Usher would sit dreaming for hours. His

---

27. red-litten: red-lighted; Poe coined this archaic-sounding term.
28. sentience (sen′shəns): consciousness.
29. kingdom of inorganization: world of inorganic objects.

30. *Ververt et Chartreuse . . . Satyrs and Ægipans:* The books, authors, and subjects listed have to do with mysticism, magic, and horror.

chief delight, however, was found in the perusal of an exceedingly rare and curious book in quarto Gothic—the manual of a forgotten church—the *Vigiliae Mortuorum*[31] *secundum Chorum Ecclesiae Maguntinae.*

I could not help thinking of the wild ritual of this work, and of its probable influence upon the hypochondriac, when, one evening, having informed me abruptly that the lady Madeline was no more, he stated his intention of preserving her corpse for a fortnight (previously to its final interment), in one of the numerous vaults within the main walls of the building. The worldly reason, however, assigned for this singular proceeding, was one which I did not feel at liberty to dispute. The brother had been led to his resolution (so he told me) by consideration of the unusual character of the malady of the deceased, of certain obtrusive and eager inquiries on the part of her medical men, and of the remote and exposed situation of the burial ground of the family. I will not deny that when I called to mind the sinister countenance of the person whom I met upon the staircase,[32] on the day of my arrival at the house, I had no desire to oppose what I regarded as at best but a harmless, and by no means an unnatural, precaution.[33]

> Usher suddenly announces that his sister Madeline has died. Before her final burial, Usher plans to inter Madeline temporarily in a vault within the house, to prevent doctors from stealing her body for an autopsy.

At the request of Usher, I personally aided him in the arrangements for the temporary entombment. The body having been encoffined, we two alone bore it to its rest. The vault in which we placed it (and which had been so long unopened that our torches, half smothered in its oppressive atmosphere, gave us little opportunity for investigation) was small, damp, and entirely without means of admission for light; lying, at great depth, immediately beneath that portion of the building in which was my own sleeping apartment. It had been used, apparently, in remote feudal times, for the worst purposes of a dungeon-keep,[34] and, in later days, as a place of deposit for powder, or some other highly combustible substance, as a portion of its floor, and the whole interior of a long archway through which we reached it, were carefully sheathed with copper. The door, of massive iron, had been, also, similarly protected. Its immense weight caused an unusually sharp grating sound, as it moved upon its hinges.

> **?** In what area of the world might the house be located?

Having deposited our mournful burden upon tressels within this region of horror, we partially turned aside the yet unscrewed lid of the coffin, and looked upon the face of the tenant. A striking similitude between the brother and sister now first arrested my attention; and Usher, divining, perhaps, my thoughts, murmured out some few words from which I learned that the deceased and himself had been twins, and that sympathies of a scarcely intelligible nature had always existed between them. Our glances, however, rested not long upon the dead—for we could not regard her unawed. The disease which had thus entombed the lady in the maturity of youth, had left, as usual in all maladies of a strictly cataleptical character, the mockery of a faint blush upon the bosom and the face, and that suspiciously lingering smile upon the lip which is so terrible in death. We replaced and screwed down the lid, and, having secured the door of iron, made our way, with toil, into the scarcely less gloomy apartments of the upper portion of the house.

> **?** What does the narrator notice about Madeline's appearance and condition after looking at her corpse?

And now, some days of bitter grief having elapsed, an observable change came over the

---

31. *Vigiliae Mortuorum:* Latin for "vigil of the dead."
32. **person . . . staircase:** the physician.
33. **precaution:** Usher wishes to be sure his sister's body will not be dissected by doctors. At the time, bodies were sometimes stolen and sold to medical students for dissection and study.

34. **dungeon-keep:** underground prison.

- -

WORDS TO OWN

similitude (sə·mil′ə·tōōd′) *n.:* likeness.

- -

LITERATURE AND POPULAR CULTURE

The Gothic Tradition

What is Gothic? The word *Gothic* comes from an architectural style of the late Middle Ages in Europe. People later used the term *Gothic* to describe a kind of romantic, scary novel that sprang up in Germany in the late 1700s and early 1800s. These eerie Gothic novels summoned up the mysterious atmosphere suggested by all those old castles and cathedrals, whose dank dungeons and secret passageways might have witnessed any number of sinister or even supernatural events.

Real page-turners. One of the earliest and most successful Gothic novels in English was written by a woman. Ann Radcliffe's *The Mysteries of Udolpho* (1794) was only the first of many Gothics penned by women, who took up writing Gothic novels as a way to make a living. The public eagerly devoured these sensational stories, which sold the way Stephen King best-sellers do today. Gothic novels so saturated the popular culture of the time that, in 1818, *Northanger Abbey* was published—a novel by the English writer Jane Austen that parodies the Gothic. By the nineteenth century, several novels of high literary merit by women writers fell solidly within the Gothic framework: Mary Shelley's *Frankenstein, or the Modern Prometheus,* Charlotte Brontë's *Jane Eyre,* and Emily Brontë's *Wuthering Heights.* In our time, women writers such as Shirley Jackson, Daphne du Maurier, Barbara Michaels, and Anne Rice have kept the Gothic tradition alive and well.

features of the mental disorder of my friend. His ordinary manner had vanished. His ordinary occupations were neglected or forgotten. He roamed from chamber to chamber with hurried, unequal, and objectless step. The pallor of his countenance had assumed, if possible, a more ghastly hue—but the luminousness of his eye had utterly gone out. The once occasional huskiness of his tone was heard no more; and a tremulous quaver, as if of extreme terror, habitually characterized his utterance. There were times, indeed, when I thought his unceasingly agitated mind was laboring with some oppressive secret, to divulge which he struggled for the necessary courage. At times, again, I was obliged to resolve all into the mere inexplicable vagaries[35] of madness, for I beheld him gazing upon vacancy for long hours, in an attitude of the profoundest attention, as if listening to some imaginary sound. It was no wonder that his condition terrified—that it infected me. I felt creeping upon me, by slow yet certain degrees, the wild influences of his own fantastic yet impressive superstitions.

It was, especially, upon retiring to bed late in the night of the seventh or eighth day after the placing of the lady Madeline within the dungeon, that I experienced the full power of such feelings. Sleep came not near my couch—while the hours waned and waned away. I struggled to reason off the nervousness which had dominion over me. I endeavored to believe that much, if not all of what I felt, was due to the bewildering influence of the gloomy furniture of the room—of the dark and tattered draperies, which, tortured into mo-

35. **vagaries** (vā′gər·ēz): whims.

tion by the breath of a rising tempest, swayed fitfully to and fro upon the walls, and rustled uneasily about the decorations of the bed. But my efforts were fruitless. An irrepressible tremor gradually pervaded my frame; and, at length, there sat upon my very heart an incubus[36] of utterly causeless alarm. Shaking this off with a gasp and a struggle, I uplifted myself upon the pillows, and, peering earnestly within the intense darkness of the chamber, harkened—I know not why, except that an instinctive spirit prompted me—to certain low and indefinite sounds which came, through the pauses of the storm, at long intervals, I knew not whence. Overpowered by an intense sentiment of horror, unaccountable yet unendurable, I threw on my clothes with haste (for I felt that I should sleep no more during the night), and endeavored to arouse myself from the pitiable condition into which I had fallen, by pacing rapidly to and fro through the apartment.

I had taken but few turns in this manner, when a light step on an adjoining staircase arrested my attention. I presently recognized it as that of Usher. In an instant afterward he rapped, with a gentle touch, at my door, and entered, bearing a lamp. His countenance was, as usual, cadaverously wan—but, moreover, there was a species of mad hilarity in his eyes—an evidently restrained *hysteria* in his whole demeanor. His air appalled me—but anything was preferable to the solitude which I had so long endured, and I even welcomed his presence as a relief.

> About a week after Madeline's death, an agitated Usher wanders through the house. The narrator, unable to sleep, is overcome by the atmosphere of dread around him.
>
> **?** *Describe the emotional states of the narrator and Roderick. In what ways are their reactions similar?*

"And you have not seen it?" he said abruptly, after having stared about him for some moments in silence—"you have not then seen it?—but, stay! you shall." Thus speaking, and having carefully shaded his lamp, he hurried to one of the casements, and threw it freely open to the storm.

The impetuous fury of the entering gust nearly lifted us from our feet. It was, indeed, a tempestuous yet sternly beautiful night, and one wildly singular in its terror and its beauty. A whirlwind had apparently collected its force in our vicinity; for there were frequent and violent alterations in the direction of the wind; and the exceeding density of the clouds (which hung so low as to press upon the turrets of the house) did not prevent our perceiving the lifelike velocity with which they flew careering from all points against each other, without passing away into the distance. I say that even their exceeding density did not prevent our perceiving this—yet we had no glimpse of the moon or stars—nor was there any flashing forth of the lightning. But the under surfaces of the huge masses of agitated vapor, as well as all terrestrial objects immediately around us, were glowing in the unnatural light of a faintly luminous and distinctly visible gaseous exhalation which hung about and enshrouded the mansion.

"You must not—you shall not behold this!" said I, shudderingly, to Usher, as I led him, with a gentle violence, from the window to a seat. "These appearances, which bewilder you, are merely electrical phenomena not uncommon—or it may be that they have their ghastly origin in the rank miasma of the tarn.[37] Let us close this casement—the air is chilling and dangerous to your frame. Here is one of your favorite romances. I will read, and you shall listen;—and so we will pass away this terrible night together."

The antique volume which I had taken up was the *Mad Trist* of Sir Launcelot Canning;[38] but I had called it a favorite of Usher's more in sad jest than in earnest; for, in truth, there is little in its uncouth and unimaginative prolixity[39] which could have had interest for the lofty and spiritual ideality of my friend. It was, however, the only book

---

37. **rank miasma** (mī·az′mə) **. . . tarn:** The decomposing matter of the tarn could have given rise to swamp gas or electrical discharges, resulting in frightening optical illusions.
38. ***Mad Trist* of Sir Launcelot Canning:** a book invented by Poe for this story.
39. **prolixity** (prō·lik′sə·tē): wordiness.

- -

WORDS TO OWN
demeanor (di·mēn′ər) *n.:* behavior; conduct.

- -

---

36. **incubus** (in′kyōo·bəs): nightmare. In medieval times, it was believed that nightmares were caused by demons (incubi) who tormented the sleeping.

immediately at hand; and I indulged a vague hope that the excitement which now agitated the hypochondriac, might find relief (for the history of mental disorder is full of similar anomalies) even in the extremeness of the folly which I should read. Could I have judged, indeed, by the wild overstrained air of vivacity with which he harkened, or apparently harkened, to the words of the tale, I might well have congratulated myself upon the success of my design.

> **?** What does the narrator do to try to calm Usher?

I had arrived at that well-known portion of the story where Ethelred, the hero of the *Trist,* having sought in vain for peaceable admission into the dwelling of the hermit, proceeds to make good an entrance by force. Here, it will be remembered, the words of the narrative run thus:

"And Ethelred, who was by nature of a doughty[40] heart, and who was now mighty withal, on account of the powerfulness of the wine which he had drunken, waited no longer to hold parley with the hermit, who, in sooth, was of an obstinate and maliceful turn, but, feeling the rain upon his shoulders, and fearing the rising of the tempest, uplifted his mace outright, and, with blows, made quickly room in the plankings of the door for his gauntleted hand; and now pulling therewith sturdily, he so cracked, and ripped, and tore all asunder, that the noise of the dry and hollow-sounding wood alarumed and reverberated throughout the forest."

At the termination of this sentence I started, and for a moment, paused; for it appeared to me (although I at once concluded that my excited fancy had deceived me)—it appeared to me that, from some very remote portion of the mansion, there came, indistinctly, to my ears, what might have been, in its exact similarity of character, the echo (but a stifled and dull one certainly) of the very cracking and ripping sound which Sir Launcelot had so particularly described. It was, beyond doubt, the coincidence alone which had arrested my attention; for, amid the rattling of the sashes of the casements, and the ordinary commingled noises of the still increasing storm, the sound, in itself, had nothing, surely, which should

have interested or disturbed me. I continued the story:

"But the good champion Ethelred, now entering within the door, was sore enraged and amazed to perceive no signal of the maliceful hermit; but, in the stead thereof, a dragon of a scaly and prodigious demeanor, and of a fiery tongue, which sate in guard before a palace of gold, with a floor of silver; and upon the wall there hung a shield of shining brass with this legend enwritten—

Who entereth herein, a conqueror hath bin;
Who slayeth the dragon, the shield he shall win;

And Ethelred uplifted his mace, and struck upon the head of the dragon, which fell before him, and gave up his pesty breath, with a shriek so horrid and harsh, and withal so piercing, that Ethelred had fain to close his ears with his hands against the dreadful noise of it, the like whereof was never before heard."

> The narrator continues reading aloud from the book about a medieval knight.
>
> **?** How does the story-within-a-story about Ethelred relate to the main story about the narrator and Usher?

Here again I paused abruptly, and now with a feeling of wild amazement—for there could be no doubt whatever that, in this instance, I did actually hear (although from what direction it proceeded I found it impossible to say) a low and apparently distant, but harsh, protracted, and most unusual screaming or grating sound—the exact counterpart of what my fancy had already conjured up for the dragon's unnatural shriek as described by the romancer.

Oppressed, as I certainly was, upon the occurrence of this second and most extraordinary coincidence, by a thousand conflicting sensations, in which wonder and extreme terror were predominant, I still retained sufficient presence of mind to avoid exciting, by any observation, the sensitive nervousness of my companion. I was by

---

40. **doughty** (dout'ē): courageous.

WORDS TO OWN

obstinate (äb'stə·nət) *adj.*: stubborn.
prodigious (prō·dij'əs) *adj.*: of great size and power.

no means certain that he had noticed the sounds in question; although, assuredly, a strange alteration had, during the last few minutes, taken place in his demeanor. From a position fronting my own, he had gradually brought round his chair, so as to sit with his face to the door of the chamber; and thus I could but partially perceive his features, although I saw that his lips trembled as if he were murmuring inaudibly. His head had dropped upon his breast—yet I knew that he was not asleep, from the wide and rigid opening of the eye as I caught a glance of it in profile. The motion of his body, too, was at variance with this idea—for he rocked from side to side with a gentle yet constant and uniform sway. Having rapidly taken notice of all this, I resumed the narrative of Sir Launcelot, which thus proceeded:

"And now, the champion, having escaped from the terrible fury of the dragon, bethinking himself of the brazen shield, and of the breaking up of the enchantment which was upon it, removed the carcass from out of the way before him, and approached valorously over the silver pavement of the castle to where the shield was upon the wall; which in sooth tarried not for his full coming, but fell down at his feet upon the silver floor, with a mighty great and terrible ringing sound."

No sooner had these syllables passed my lips, than—as if a shield of brass had indeed, at the moment, fallen heavily upon a floor of silver—I became aware of a distinct, hollow, metallic, and clangorous, yet apparently muffled reverberation. Completely unnerved, I leaped to my feet; but the measured rocking movement of Usher was undisturbed. I rushed to the chair in which he sat. His eyes were bent fixedly before him, and throughout his whole countenance there reigned a stony rigidity. But, as I placed my hand upon his shoulder, there came a strong shudder over his whole person; a sickly smile quivered about his lips; and I saw that he spoke in a low, hurried, and gibbering murmur, as if unconscious of my presence. Bending closely over him, I at length drank in the hideous import of his words.

? What coincidences unnerve the narrator during his reading of the book? How would you describe the atmosphere of the story at this point?

"Not hear it?—yes, I hear it, and *have* heard it. Long—long—long—many minutes, many hours, many days, have I heard it—yet I dared not—oh, pity me, miserable wretch that I am!—I dared not—I *dared* not speak! *We have put her living in the tomb!* Said I not that my senses were acute? I *now* tell you that I heard her first feeble movements in the hollow coffin. I heard them—many, many days ago—yet I dared not—*I dared not speak!* And now—tonight—Ethelred—ha! ha!—the breaking of the hermit's door, and the death cry of the dragon, and the clangor of the shield!—say, rather, the rending of her coffin, and the grating of the iron hinges of her prison, and her struggles within the coppered archway of the vault! Oh whither shall I fly? Will she not be here anon? Is she not hurrying to upbraid me for my haste? Have I not heard her footstep on the stair? Do I not distinguish that heavy and horrible beating of her heart? *Madman!*"—here he sprang furiously to his feet, and shrieked out his syllables, as if in the effort he were giving up his soul—*"Madman! I tell you that she now stands without the door!"*

Hearing the noises in the house, Usher has become increasingly distraught.

? What horrible conjecture has Usher not dared to express until now? Locate the sentence that explains the exact connection between the three noises in the story of Ethelred and the three noises in the house of Usher.

As if in the superhuman energy of his utterance there had been found the potency of a spell—the huge antique panels to which the speaker pointed, threw slowly back, upon the instant, their ponderous and ebony jaws. It was the work of the rushing gust—but then without those doors there *did* stand the lofty and enshrouded figure of the lady Madeline of Usher. There was blood upon her white robes, and the evidence of some bitter struggle upon every portion of her

---

WORDS TO OWN

potency (pōt″n·sē) *n.*: strength; power.

emaciated frame. For a moment she remained trembling and reeling to and fro upon the threshold—then, with a low moaning cry, fell heavily inward upon the person of her brother, and in her violent and now final death agonies, bore him to the floor a corpse, and a victim to the terrors he had anticipated.

From that chamber, and from that mansion, I fled aghast. The storm was still abroad in all its wrath as I found myself crossing the old causeway. Suddenly there shot along the path a wild light, and I turned to see whence a gleam so unusual could have issued; for the vast house and its shadows were alone behind me. The radiance

WORDS TO OWN

emaciated (ē·mā′shē·āt′id) *v.* used as *adj.*: unusually thin.

was that of the full, setting, and blood-red moon, which now shone vividly through that once barely discernible fissure, of which I have before spoken as extending from the roof of the building, in a zigzag direction, to the base. While I gazed, this fissure rapidly widened—there came a fierce breath of the whirlwind—the entire orb of the satellite burst at once upon my sight—my brain reeled as I saw the mighty walls rushing asunder—there was a long tumultuous shouting sound like the voice of a thousand waters—and the deep and dank tarn at my feet closed sullenly and silently over the fragments of the *"House of Usher."*

? What happens to Roderick Usher? to the house of Usher? to the narrator? What image are you left with at the end of the story?

Connections ----- A POEM

The Fall of the House of Usher

Reed Whittemore

It was a big boxy wreck of a house
Owned by a classmate of mine named Rod Usher,
Who lived in the thing with his twin sister.
He was a louse and she was a souse.

5 While I was visiting them one wet summer, she died.
We buried her,
Or rather we stuck her in a back room for a bit, meaning to bury her
When the graveyard dried.

But the weather got wetter.
10 One night we were both waked by a twister,
Plus a screeching and howling outside that turned out to be sister
Up and dying again, making it hard for Rod to forget her.
He didn't. He and she died in a heap, and I left quick,
Which was lucky since the house fell in right after,
                              Like a ton of brick.

MAKING MEANINGS

First Thoughts

1. Did you like "Usher"? How successful was Poe's use of Gothic devices in creating an **atmosphere** of dread?

Reading Check

Imagine that you are telling a friend about the story. List the **main events** in **chronological order.**

Shaping Interpretations

2. What do Roderick's artistic efforts—his guitar solo, his painting, and his poem "The Haunted Palace"—reveal about his state of mind?

3. Why do you think Poe made Roderick and Madeline *twins*—not just brother and sister?

4. The story is presented from the **point of view** of a typical Poe narrator—a character who claims to provide an objective view, but whose rationality becomes suspect during the course of the tale. What evidence can you find that the narrator's state of mind may be deteriorating? How does this uncertainty about the narrator's objectivity affect your response to the story?

5. What do you infer was basically wrong with the Ushers? What evidence do you find to support this **inference**?

6. What do you think is happening at the end of the story, when Madeline Usher appears? (Is she a hallucination, a ghost, or a real person who has been buried alive?) Support your response with evidence from the story.

7. Poe said that the poem "The Haunted Palace" is meant to suggest a disordered brain. How might the whole story be read as an allegory of a journey into the human mind? (An **allegory** is a story or poem that can be read on one level for its literal meaning and on a second level for its symbolic meaning.) What could the final *fall* of the house represent?

Challenging the Text

8. Which details in this story fail to make sense to you? For example, how could the narrator not have known his old friend had a *twin*? (Be sure to refer to your reading notes.) Discuss your challenges with other readers.

ELEMENTS OF LITERATURE

Poe's Symbols

What do these symbols mean to you?

The images above are sometimes called conventional, or public, symbols. This means that they are well known, at least in a particular culture, and that their meaning is agreed upon.

Writers and artists often create their own unique **symbols.** In this story, for example, Poe has Roderick mention his strange theory of the "sentience," or consciousness, of the mansion's stones. It could be that Poe is suggesting a relationship between the house and Roderick's mind. As we think about this, we might decide that the decaying house symbolizes Roderick's decaying sanity.

With a group, list details from Poe's story that might be symbolic. Next to each item, write your guess as to what it symbolizes.

Guidelines for Recognizing Symbols

1. A symbol is a concrete object, a person, a place, or an action that works on at least two levels: It functions as itself and suggests a wider meaning.

2. Symbols are often visual.

3. The symbol is identified with something that is very different from it, yet the two things share a similar quality.

4. The writer gives the symbol a great deal of emphasis.

5. The symbol usually relates to the story's theme.

Sensing Connotations: Creating Atmosphere

All words have particular **denotations,** or specific dictionary definitions. Some words also have **connotations**—associations and emotional overtones that people have come to attach to them. For example, the word *puzzling* suggests that something is mildly confusing or confounding. The word *bewildering* goes a step further, suggesting that something is so puzzling as to be hopelessly confusing.

Words that have especially strong positive or negative connotations are called **loaded,** or **suggestive, words.** Poe felt that a story's mood, or **atmosphere,** was of paramount importance, so it's no surprise that he often used suggestive words to manipulate our emotional responses.

1. Reread the famous first paragraph of Poe's story. Which words suggest decay, sterility, finality, and emptiness? List them.

2. Rewrite the first few sentences of the first paragraph. Change the time of day, the time of year, and the weather conditions to paint a cheerful or cozy picture of the house of Usher. How does your choice of words change the atmosphere of the paragraph?

CHOICES: Building Your Portfolio

Writer's Notebook

1. Collecting Ideas for a Controversial Issue

Using the topic you explored in an earlier Writer's Notebook (page 258), or another controversial topic of your choice, write down two or three emotional appeals. Use words with strong **connotative** meanings to persuade readers to accept your position on the issue. Save your notes for possible use in the Writer's Workshop on page 331.

WORK IN PROGRESS

Interpreting a Story

2. What's It All About?

Select one of these interpretations of "The Fall of the House of Usher"—or develop a position of your own—and defend it in a brief essay.

- The house personifies the diseased, dying Usher family.
- The narrator is insane or dreaming. The entire story is a projection of his mind.
- The story is an **allegory** about an artist who is drawn on a journey through the dark side of the human mind.

Creative Writing

3. Changing Genres

Tell the story of the house of Usher in another genre: a poem, a newspaper article, a magazine interview, a script, a picture book, a comic strip—even a drawing or song. For inspiration, see Reed Whittemore's poem "The Fall of the House of Usher" (*Connections,* page 279).

Music

4. A Little Night Music

Search for music—classical, jazz, contemporary instrumental, rock, movie soundtracks—that to you evokes the **atmosphere** and events of the story. Play the music for the class and explain why you chose it.

Art

5. House of Horrors

What does the house of Usher *look* like? Draw, paint, or even build your vision of this ghastly Gothic structure.

Monitoring Your Reading

6. Talk It Over

With a group, discuss the reading problems posed by Poe's story and share the strategies you used to work them out.

Before You Read

THE RAVEN

Make the Connection

Exploring the Dark Side
"The Raven" has the sound of a lyric, but, actually, it is a narrative poem with a plot that leads the reader from curiosity to horror. The poem explores one aspect of the dark side of human nature: what Poe himself called "that species of despair which delights in self-torture." In the jargon of psychology, the narrator "projects" onto the bird whatever his own wild imagination dredges up.

Reading Skills and Strategies

Analyzing the Melodies of Language
You'll enjoy "The Raven" more if you read it aloud. After you have read the poem aloud once, write down some lines and passages that strike you as being especially musical, clever, or memorable.

Elements of Literature

Sound Effects
One of the reasons "The Raven" became so popular was that it was catchy in the way a song can be. Like many songs, the poem uses evocative rhythms, clever rhymes,

alliteration, and other sound effects. These elements make the poem cry out for oral interpretation. (For more on Sound Effects, see page 288 and the Handbook of Literary Terms.)

Background

It may be hard to imagine today, but when Poe's "The Raven" was first published in 1845, it was a hit—a popular success with the same kind of impact that the Beatles' first single had in 1962. It seemed as though everyone read "The Raven," recited it, and talked about it. Poe became a household name with this poem, but he received only about ten dollars for it.

The Raven

Edgar Allan Poe

Once upon a midnight dreary, while I pondered, weak and weary,
Over many a quaint and curious volume of forgotten lore—
While I nodded, nearly napping, suddenly there came a tapping,
As of someone gently rapping, rapping at my chamber door—
5 " 'Tis some visitor," I muttered, "tapping at my chamber door—
     Only this and nothing more."

Ah, distinctly I remember it was in the bleak December;
And each separate dying ember wrought its ghost upon the floor.
Eagerly I wished the morrow;—vainly I had sought to borrow
10 From my books surcease° of sorrow—sorrow for the lost Lenore—
For the rare and radiant maiden whom the angels name Lenore—
     Nameless *here* for evermore.

10. **surcease:** an end.

And the silken, sad, uncertain rustling of each purple curtain
Thrilled me—filled me with fantastic terrors never felt before;
15 So that now, to still the beating of my heart, I stood repeating
" 'Tis some visitor entreating entrance at my chamber door—
Some late visitor entreating entrance at my chamber door;—
     This it is and nothing more."

Presently my soul grew stronger; hesitating then no longer,
20 "Sir," said I, "or Madam, truly your forgiveness I implore;
But the fact is I was napping, and so gently you came rapping,
And so faintly you came tapping, tapping at my chamber door,
That I scarce was sure I heard you"—here I opened wide the door;——
     Darkness there and nothing more.

25 Deep into that darkness peering, long I stood there wondering, fearing,
Doubting, dreaming dreams no mortal ever dared to dream before;
But the silence was unbroken, and the stillness gave no token,
And the only word there spoken was the whispered word, "Lenore?"
This I whispered, and an echo murmured back the word, "Lenore!"
30   Merely this and nothing more.

Back into the chamber turning, all my soul within me burning,
Soon again I heard a tapping somewhat louder than before.
"Surely," said I, "surely that is something at my window lattice;
Let me see, then, what thereat is, and this mystery explore—
35 Let my heart be still a moment and this mystery explore;—
     'Tis the wind and nothing more!"

Open here I flung the shutter, when, with many a flirt and flutter,
In there stepped a stately Raven of the saintly days of yore;°
Not the least obeisance° made he; not a minute stopped or stayed he;
40 But, with mien of lord or lady, perched above my chamber door—
Perched upon a bust of Pallas° just above my chamber door—
     Perched, and sat, and nothing more.

Then this ebony bird beguiling my sad fancy into smiling,
By the grave and stern decorum of the countenance it wore,
45 "Though thy crest be shorn and shaven, thou," I said, "art sure no craven,
Ghastly grim and ancient Raven wandering from the Nightly shore—
Tell me what thy lordly name is on the Night's Plutonian shore!"°
     Quoth the Raven "Nevermore."

38. Raven . . . of yore: "Of yore" is an obsolete way of saying "of time long past." Poe's
allusion is to 1 Kings 17:1–6, which tells of the prophet Elijah being fed by ravens in
the wilderness.
39. obeisance (ō·bā′səns): gesture of respect or subservience.
41. Pallas: Pallas Athena, the Greek goddess of wisdom.
47. Plutonian shore: Pluto is the Greek god of the underworld—the land of
darkness—called Hades (hā′dēz′). Hades is separated from the world of the living by
several rivers, hence the mention of a shore.

Much I marveled this ungainly fowl to hear discourse so plainly,
50 Though its answer little meaning—little relevancy bore;
For we cannot help agreeing that no living human being
Ever yet was blessed with seeing bird above his chamber door—
Bird or beast upon the sculptured bust above his chamber door,
      With such name as "Nevermore."

55 But the Raven, sitting lonely on the placid bust, spoke only
That one word, as if his soul in that one word he did outpour.
Nothing farther then he uttered—not a feather then he fluttered—
Till I scarcely more than muttered "Other friends have flown before—
On the morrow *he* will leave me, as my Hopes have flown before."
60   Then the bird said "Nevermore."

Startled at the stillness broken by reply so aptly spoken,
"Doubtless," said I, "what it utters is its only stock and store
Caught from some unhappy master whom unmerciful Disaster
Followed fast and followed faster till his songs one burden bore—
65 Till the dirges of his Hope that melancholy burden bore
     Of 'Never—nevermore.' "

But the Raven still beguiling my sad fancy into smiling,
Straight I wheeled a cushioned seat in front of bird, and bust and door;
Then, upon the velvet sinking, I betook myself to linking
70 Fancy unto fancy, thinking what this ominous bird of yore—
What this grim, ungainly, ghastly, gaunt, and ominous bird of yore
     Meant in croaking "Nevermore."

This I sat engaged in guessing, but no syllable expressing
To the fowl whose fiery eyes now burned into my bosom's core;
75 This and more I sat divining, with my head at ease reclining
On the cushion's velvet lining that the lamplight gloated o'er,
But whose velvet-violet lining with the lamplight gloating o'er,
     She shall press, ah, nevermore!

Then, methought, the air grew denser, perfumed from an unseen censer
80 Swung by seraphim° whose footfalls tinkled on the tufted floor.
"Wretch," I cried, "thy God hath lent thee—by these angels he hath sent thee
Respite—respite and nepenthe° from thy memories of Lenore;
Quaff, oh quaff this kind nepenthe and forget this lost Lenore!"
           Quoth the Raven "Nevermore."

85 "Prophet!" said I, "thing of evil!—prophet still, if bird or devil!—
      Whether Tempter sent, or whether tempest tossed thee here ashore,
Desolate yet all undaunted, on this desert land enchanted—
On this home by Horror haunted—tell me truly, I implore—
Is there—*is* there balm in Gilead?°—tell me—tell me, I implore!"
90   Quoth the Raven "Nevermore."

"Prophet!" said I, "thing of evil!—prophet still, if bird or devil!
By that Heaven that bends above us—by that God we both adore—
Tell this soul with sorrow laden if, within the distant Aidenn,°
It shall clasp a sainted maiden whom the angels name Lenore—
95 Clasp a rare and radiant maiden whom the angels name Lenore."
           Quoth the Raven "Nevermore."

"Be that word our sign of parting, bird or fiend!" I shrieked, upstarting—
"Get thee back into the tempest and the Night's Plutonian shore!
Leave no black plume as a token of that lie thy soul hath spoken!
100 Leave my loneliness unbroken!—quit the bust above my door!
Take thy beak from out my heart, and take thy form from off my door!"
           Quoth the Raven "Nevermore."

And the Raven, never flitting, still is sitting, *still* is sitting
On the pallid bust of Pallas just above my chamber door;
105 And his eyes have all the seeming of a demon's that is dreaming,
      And the lamplight o'er him streaming throws his shadow on the floor;
And my soul from out that shadow that lies floating on the floor
           Shall be lifted—nevermore!

80. seraphim: the highest of the nine ranks of angels; often pictured as
having three sets of wings.
82. nepenthe (nē·pen'thē): a sleeping potion that people once believed would
relieve pain and sorrow. Eventually it came to stand for anything that brought
such relief.
89. Is . . . Gilead: literally, "Is there any relief from my sorrow?" Poe
paraphrases a line from Jeremiah 8:22: "Is there no balm in Gilead?" Gilead was
a region in ancient Palestine known for its healing herbs, such as balm. Balm
has come to mean any healing ointment.
93. Aidenn: Arabic for "Eden" or "Heaven."

Poe's Process: Writing "The Raven"

Several years after the hugely successful publication of "The Raven," Poe wrote an essay describing how he composed the poem. He described the writing of the poem as though he were solving a mathematical puzzle. Here are the first stages of Poe's writing process:

1. He decided he wanted to write a poem with a melancholy effect.

2. Then he decided that the melancholy would be reinforced by the refrain "Nevermore" (he liked its sound) and that a raven would utter the refrain. (Before he settled on a raven, though, he considered an owl and even a parrot.)

3. Finally, he decided his subject would be what he thought was the most melancholy subject in the world: a lover's mourning for a beautiful woman who has died.

Now Poe was ready to write. The first stanza he wrote, he claimed, was the climactic one, lines 85–90. From there he set about choosing his details: the interior space in which the lover, who is a student, and the Raven are brought together; the tapping that introduces the Raven; the fact that the night is stormy rather than calm; and the action of the Raven alighting on the bust of Pallas.

Then Poe goes on to describe his writing process:

> . . . The raven addressed, answers with its customary word, "Nevermore"—a word which finds immediate echo in the melancholy heart of the student, who, giving utterance aloud to certain thoughts suggested by the occasion, is again startled by the fowl's repetition of "Nevermore." The student now guesses the state of the case, but is impelled, as I have before explained, by the human thirst for self-torture, and in part by superstition, to propound such queries to the bird as will bring him, the lover, the most of the luxury of sorrow, through the anticipated answer "Nevermore.". . .

> It will be observed that the words "from out my heart," involve the first metaphorical expression in the poem. They, with the answer, "Nevermore," dispose the mind to seek a moral in all that has been previously narrated. The reader begins now to regard the Raven as emblematical [symbolic]—but it is not until the very last line of the very last stanza, that the intention of making him emblematical of *Mournful and never ending Remembrance* is permitted distinctly to be seen. . . .

—Edgar Allan Poe

Illustration by Wilfred Satty for "The Fall of the House of Usher."

MAKING MEANINGS

First Thoughts

1. Do you think there really *was* a raven in the speaker's chambers? Why or why not? If not, what is your explanation for what happened on that "midnight dreary" in the speaker's room?

Shaping Interpretations

2. How would you describe the **atmosphere** created by the setting? Which **images** in the beginning of the poem create this atmosphere?

3. In line 101, what do you think the speaker might mean when he begs the bird, "Take thy beak from out my heart"?

4. The speaker's **tone** changes as the Raven gradually turns from a comic figure into a demonic figure. Trace these changes in tone. Is there evidence in the last stanza that the speaker goes mad? Explain.

5. How did the poem's **sound effects** affect your response to the poem? Go back to the text and the notes you made after reading the poem aloud. Then, cite passages that you'd especially like to read aloud.

6. By the end of the poem, what do you think it means that the Raven "*still* is sitting" in the speaker's chamber?

7. Many readers take the Raven as a **symbol**—it functions as a real raven in the poem, but it also has a broader, figurative meaning. What, in your opinion, does the Raven symbolize? Why do you suppose Poe chose a raven to carry this meaning rather than a chicken, hawk, sparrow, or other bird? (For more on symbols, see page 280. For Poe's thoughts on the Raven, see Primary Sources, page 287.)

Connecting with the Text

8. What do you make of the poem's speaker? Freewrite some thoughts that you imagine might be running through his head during or after the events of the poem. Then get together with a small group of other students, and take turns being the speaker, who has been put on the "hot seat" to answer questions.

Extending the Text

9. Compare "The Raven" with any other stories you know of in which a person is deeply moved by the loss of someone he or she loves. One such story is "The Jilting of Granny Weatherall" (page 704) by Katherine Anne Porter.

Challenging the Text

10. Suppose someone said to you that "The Raven" is not worth reading because it's unbelievable. How would you answer this challenge?

READING SKILLS AND STRATEGIES

Hearing Sound Effects

"The Raven" is a virtuoso performance in the use of **internal rhyme**—rhyme that occurs within the lines, or repetition of an end rhyme within a line. "Dreary" and "weary" in line 1 prepare us for a pattern of internal rhyming sounds. "Napping," "tapping," and "rapping" in lines 3 and 4 make us expect more. Some of Poe's rhymes are ingenious. Not many writers would think of rhyming "window lattice" with "what thereat is" (lines 33–34).

Skillful use of repetition occurs with the **refrain** "Nevermore"; it is also an important element in the **rhyme scheme** of the poem. Poe keeps the sound of the word echoing in our ears through repetition combined with changes in tone.

Throughout the poem, Poe uses the technique of **alliteration** (the repetition of a consonant sound) to create **onomatopoeia**—the use of words with sounds that actually echo their sense. A good example of alliteration is in line 71, where the hard *g* is repeated four times, almost resulting in a tongue twister: "this grim, ungainly, ghastly, gaunt, and ominous bird of yore."

1. Locate the internal rhymes in lines 79–84 and 91–96. What other internal rhymes can you find?

2. What other word are you reminded of when you hear the refrain "Nevermore"? How does this echo affect you?

3. Where in lines 13–18 and 37–42 is alliteration used to create onomatopoeia?

CHOICES: Building Your Portfolio

"One more time."

Julio Cortázar

(1914–1984)

Julio Cortázar was born in Brussels, Belgium, to Argentine parents. The family returned to Argentina when Cortázar was six, and he was educated there. As an adult, he first supported his writing career by teaching high school and university courses, then by managing a publishing association, and finally by working as a translator. A change in Argentina's political regime caused him to move to France in 1951. In Paris, he worked as a translator for the United Nations. He eventually became a French citizen, but he retained his Argentine citizenship, and he always thought of himself as both South American and European.

Because Cortázar believed that sober, objective reality masks a hidden dimension of the fantastic, he used his stories to awaken readers to that dimension. Like nightmares that begin with ordinary scenes that are distorted into something bizarre, his stories move seamlessly from reality to fantasy. As the critic Alexander Coleman observed, "Cortázar's stories start in a disarmingly conversational way, with plenty of local touches. . . . But something always seems to go awry just when we least expect it."

One of Cortázar's short stories was the basis for Michelangelo Antonioni's classic film *Blow Up* (1966).

Julio Cortázar.

Diego Goldberg/Sygma.

Before You Read

Background

Julio Cortázar once explained the effects of first reading Edgar Allan Poe at the age of nine: "I stole the book . . . because my mother didn't want me to read it; she thought I was too young and she was right. The book scared me and I was ill for three months, because I believed in it."

Cortázar's fascination with Poe continued into his adult life. As a translator, he rendered four books of Poe into Spanish. As a writer, he echoed Poe in producing novels and stories in which nightmare intrudes into ordinary reality.

Cortázar's link with Poe is especially noticeable in "House Taken Over." As in Poe's "The Fall of the House of Usher," a house is occupied by the last members of a family line. In Cortázar's house, a brother and a sister experience a gradual, mysterious takeover of their ancestral home. They accept the takeover calmly . . . or do they?

Reading Skills and Strategies

Using Questions to Understand a Text
As you read "House Taken Over," write down notes in response to these questions:

- What humdrum routines mark the daily life of the narrator and his sister?

- At what point do you begin to think there is something strange about their house?

- How does the behavior of the brother and sister during sleep differ from their behavior during waking hours?

- Who—or what—do you think the narrator and his sister mean by "they"?

- How is this story similar to and different from Poe's "The Fall of the House of Usher"?

When you finish, sketch the layout of the interior of the house.

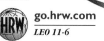

go.hrw.com
LEO 11-6

House Taken Over

Julio Cortázar

translated from the Spanish
by **Paul Blackburn**

We liked the house because, apart from its being old and spacious (in a day when old houses go down for a profitable auction of their construction materials), it kept the memories of great-grandparents, our paternal grandfather, our parents, and the whole of childhood.

Irene and I got used to staying in the house by ourselves, which was crazy, eight people could have lived in that place and not have gotten in each other's way. We rose at seven in the morning and got the cleaning done, and about eleven I left Irene to finish off whatever rooms and went to the kitchen. We lunched at noon precisely; then there was nothing left to do but a few dirty plates. It was pleasant to take lunch and commune with the great hollow, silent house, and it was enough for us just to keep it clean. We ended up thinking, at times, that that was what had kept us from marrying. Irene turned down two suitors for no particular reason, and María Esther went and died on me before we could manage to get engaged. We were easing into our forties with the unvoiced concept that the quiet, simple marriage of sister and brother was the indispensable end to a line established in this house by our grandparents. We would die here someday, obscure and distant cousins would inherit the place, have it torn down, sell the bricks, and get rich on the building plot; or more justly and better yet, we would topple it ourselves before it was too late.

The Empire of Light (1954) by René Magritte. Oil on canvas (146 cm × 114 cm).

Irene never bothered anyone. Once the morning housework was finished, she spent the rest of the day on the sofa in her bedroom, knitting. I couldn't tell you why she knitted so much; I think women knit when they discover that it's a fat excuse to do nothing at all. But Irene was not like that, she always knitted necessities, sweaters for winter, socks for me, handy morning robes and bedjackets for herself. Sometimes she would do a jacket, then unravel it the next moment because there was something that didn't please her; it was pleasant to see a pile of tangled wool in her knitting basket fighting a losing battle for a few hours to retain its shape. Saturdays I went downtown to buy wool; Irene had faith in my good taste, was pleased with the colors and never a skein[1] had to be returned. I took advantage of these trips to make the rounds of the bookstores, uselessly asking if they had anything new in French literature. Nothing worthwhile had arrived in Argentina since 1939.

But it's the house I want to talk about, the house and Irene, I'm not very important. I wonder what Irene would have done without her knitting. One can reread a book, but once a pullover is finished you can't do it over again, it's some kind of disgrace. One day I found that the drawer at the bottom of the chiffonier, replete with mothballs, was filled with shawls, white, green, lilac. Stacked amid a great smell of camphor[2]—it was like a shop; I didn't have the nerve to ask her what she planned to do with them. We didn't have to earn our living, there was plenty coming in from the farms each month, even piling up. But Irene was only interested in the knitting and showed a wonderful dexterity, and for me the hours slipped away watching her, her hands like silver sea urchins, needles flashing, and one or two knitting baskets on the floor, the balls of yarn jumping about. It was lovely.

How not to remember the layout of that house. The dining room, a living room with tapestries, the library, and three large bedrooms in the section most recessed, the one that faced toward Rodríguez Peña.[3] Only a corridor with its massive oak door separated that part from the front wing, where there was a bath, the kitchen, our bedrooms, and the hall. One entered the house through a vestibule[4] with enameled tiles, and a wrought-iron grated door opened onto the living room. You had to come in through the vestibule and open the gate to go into the living room; the doors to our bedrooms were on either side of this, and opposite it was the corridor leading to the back section; going down the passage, one swung open the oak door beyond which was the other part of the house; or just before the door, one could turn to the left and go down a narrower passageway which led to the kitchen and the bath. When the door was open, you became aware of the size of the house; when it was closed, you had the impression of an apartment, like the ones they build today, with barely enough room to move around in. Irene and I always lived in this part of the house and hardly ever went beyond the oak door except to do the cleaning. Incredible how much dust collected on the furniture. It may be Buenos Aires is a clean city, but she owes it to her population and nothing else. There's too much dust in the air, the slightest breeze and it's back on the marble console tops and in the diamond patterns of the tooled-leather desk set. It's a lot of work to get it off with a feather duster; the motes rise and hang in the air, and settle again a minute later on the pianos and the furniture.

I'll always have a clear memory of it because it happened so simply and without fuss. Irene was knitting in her bedroom, it was eight at night, and I suddenly decided to put the water up for *maté*.[5] I went down the corridor as far as the oak door, which was ajar, then turned into the hall toward the kitchen, when I heard something in the library or the dining room. The sound came through muted

1. **skein** (skān): coiled length of thread or yarn.
2. **camphor:** chemical used as an insect repellent.
3. **Rodríguez Peña:** street in Buenos Aires, Argentina.
4. **vestibule:** small entrance hall.
5. **maté** (mä′tā′): tealike beverage made from dried leaves of a South American evergreen tree.

and indistinct, a chair being knocked over onto the carpet or the muffled buzzing of a conversation. At the same time or a second later, I heard it at the end of the passage which led from those two rooms toward the door. I hurled myself against the door before it was too late and shut it, leaned on it with the weight of my body; luckily, the key was on our side; moreover, I ran the great bolt into place, just to be safe.

I went down to the kitchen, heated the kettle, and when I got back with the tray of *maté*, I told Irene:

"I had to shut the door to the passage. They've taken over the back part."

She let her knitting fall and looked at me with her tired, serious eyes.

"You're sure?"

I nodded.

"In that case," she said, picking up her needles again, "we'll have to live on this side."

I sipped at the *maté* very carefully, but she took her time starting her work again. I remember it was a gray vest she was knitting. I liked that vest.

The first few days were painful, since we'd both left so many things in the part that had been taken over. My collection of French literature, for example, was still in the library. Irene had left several folios of stationery and a pair of slippers that she used a lot in the winter. I missed my briar pipe, and Irene, I think, regretted the loss of an ancient bottle of Hesperidin.[6] It happened repeatedly (but only in the first few days) that we would close some drawer or cabinet and look at one another sadly.

"It's not here."

One thing more among the many lost on the other side of the house.

But there were advantages, too. The cleaning was so much simplified that, even when we got up late, nine-thirty for instance, by eleven we were sitting around with our arms folded. Irene got into the habit of coming to the kitchen with me to help get lunch. We thought about it and decided on this: while I prepared the lunch, Irene would cook up dishes that could be eaten cold in the evening. We were happy with the arrangement because it was always such a bother to have to leave our bedrooms in the evening and start to cook. Now we made do with the table in Irene's room and platters of cold supper.

Since it left her more time for knitting, Irene was content. I was a little lost without my books, but so as not to inflict myself on my sister, I set about reordering papa's stamp collection; that killed some time. We amused ourselves sufficiently, each with his own thing, almost always getting together in Irene's bedroom, which was the more comfortable. Every once in a while, Irene might say:

"Look at this pattern I just figured out, doesn't it look like clover?"

After a bit it was I, pushing a small square of paper in front of her so that she could see the excellence of some stamp or another from Eupen-et-Malmédy.[7] We were fine, and little by little we stopped thinking. You can live without thinking.

(Whenever Irene talked in her sleep, I woke up immediately and stayed awake. I never could get used to this voice from a statue or a parrot, a voice that came out of the dreams, not from a throat. Irene said that in my sleep I flailed about enormously and shook the blankets off. We had the living room between us, but at night you could hear everything in the house. We heard each other breathing, coughing, could even feel each other reaching for the light switch when, as happened frequently, neither of us could fall asleep.

Aside from our nocturnal rumblings, everything was quiet in the house. During the day there were the household sounds, the metallic click of knitting needles, the rustle of stamp-album pages turning. The oak door was massive, I think I said that. In the kitchen or

---

6. **Hesperidin** (hes·per′i·din): liquid made from the rind of citrus fruits and used for various medicinal purposes.

7. **Eupen-et-Malmédy** (ə·pen′ā·mäl′mā·dē′): district in eastern Belgium.

the bath, which adjoined the part that was taken over, we managed to talk loudly, or Irene sang lullabies. In a kitchen there's always too much noise, the plates and glasses, for there to be interruptions from other sounds. We seldom allowed ourselves silence there, but when we went back to our rooms or to the living room, then the house grew quiet, half-lit, we ended by stepping around more slowly so as not to disturb one another. I think it was because of this that I woke up irremediably and at once when Irene began to talk in her sleep.)

Except for the consequences, it's nearly a matter of repeating the same scene over again. I was thirsty that night, and before we went to sleep, I told Irene that I was going to the kitchen for a glass of water. From the door of the bedroom (she was knitting) I heard the noise in the kitchen; if not the kitchen, then the bath, the passage off at that angle dulled the sound. Irene noticed how brusquely I had paused, and came up beside me without a word. We stood listening to the noises, growing more and more sure that they were on our side of the oak door, if not the kitchen then the bath, or in the hall itself at the turn, almost next to us.

We didn't wait to look at one another. I took Irene's arm and forced her to run with me to the wrought-iron door, not waiting to look back. You could hear the noises, still muffled but louder, just behind us. I slammed the grating and we stopped in the vestibule. Now there was nothing to be heard.

"They've taken over our section," Irene said. The knitting had reeled off from her hands and the yarn ran back toward the door and disappeared under it. When she saw that the balls of yarn were on the other side, she dropped the knitting without looking at it.

"Did you have time to bring anything?" I asked hopelessly.

"No, nothing."

We had what we had on. I remembered fifteen thousand pesos in the wardrobe in my bedroom. Too late now.

I still had my wristwatch on and saw that it was 11 P.M. I took Irene around the waist (I think she was crying) and that was how we went into the street. Before we left, I felt terrible; I locked the front door up tight and tossed the key down the sewer. It wouldn't do to have some poor devil decide to go in and rob the house, at that hour and with the house taken over.

FINDING COMMON GROUND

Meet in a small group to discuss your notes on the story. Have one member of the group record conclusions the group agrees upon.

• Take turns sharing what you wrote in response to the questions on page 290.

• Focus especially on Cortázar's huge omission—the identity of "they." What conclusion does the group reach about who "they" are? What evidence supports this conclusion?

• After you have compared Cortázar's story with Poe's "The Fall of the House of Usher," decide whether the main point of Cortázar's story is the end of a family line or something else. What evidence supports your conclusions?

• Agree on a sketch of the layout of the house's interior. Is the story unclear on any areas?

• Reconvene as a class, and listen to reports from all of the groups. Has class discussion changed your initial interpretation of the story?

Nathaniel Hawthorne (1840) by Charles Osgood. Oil on canvas.

Peabody Essex Museum, Salem, Massachusetts. Photo by Mark Sexton (121.459).

Nathaniel Hawthorne

(1804–1864)

Nathaniel Hawthorne was an unusually handsome man, with a loving and beloved wife. By midlife he had earned recognition as a writer and won the admiration of his contemporaries. Nevertheless, he became increasingly dissatisfied, remote, and disappointing to his friends. It was as if his dark insights into the human heart had cast gloom into his own. His fiction, which has survived the changing tastes of many generations and is more admired today than when it was written, is fueled by an awareness of the guilt that accompanies a Puritan conscience. This shadow of guilt appears to have darkened Hawthorne's life.

The source of darkness is thought to lie in Hawthorne's illustrious ancestors. William Hathorne, a serious soldier and judge, came to the Massachusetts Colony in 1630. Hawthorne describes him in the preamble to *The Scarlet Letter* as the "bearded, sable-cloaked, and steeple-crowned progenitor." William Hathorne's son, John, was also a judge. During the Salem witch trials of 1692, he played a minor role in sentencing nineteen of the accused to death.

By 1804, however, the year of Hawthorne's birth in Salem, the family had lost its wealth and renown. His own father, a sea captain, died during a voyage and left his grief-stricken wife with three young children to raise and few resources beyond the charity of relatives.

Prisoner of the Dismal Chamber

Hawthorne (who added the *w* to the family name to ensure a broad *a* in its pronunciation) attended schools in Salem and college at Bowdoin in Maine. Here, by his own judgment, he was an idle student, "rather choosing to nurse my own fancies than to dig into Greek roots." He chewed tobacco, played cards, drank wine at the taverns, and avoided intellectual company in favor of pleasure. After graduation, Hawthorne wrote to his sister Elizabeth, "I shall never make a distinguished figure in the world, and all I hope or wish is to plod along with the multitude." There is good reason to believe that this was an ironic statement, concealing an ambition that burned intensely.

Returning to Salem, Hawthorne set himself up in what he called the "dismal chamber," a room on the third floor of the family house. He kept himself a virtual prisoner there for the next twelve years, until he had learned the craft of fiction. In 1837, Hawthorne emerged to publish a collection of stories, *Twice-Told Tales*. They offered a vision of the human heart as a lurking place for the secrets of past sins. The book won Hawthorne just enough success to encourage further work.

Over the next few years Hawthorne courted and became engaged to Sophia Peabody, and he briefly joined the utopian experiment in communal living at Brook Farm. Neither the shoveling of manure nor the endless, lofty discussions of the Transcendentalists appealed to him. After their marriage in 1842, the Hawthornes

go.hrw.com
LEO 11-6

moved into the Old Manse in Concord, where Emerson had lived before them. Hawthorne often walked with Thoreau and Emerson, but neither creativity nor warm friendship resulted.

A Novel with No "Cheering Light"

Making only the barest living from his stories, Hawthorne had to accept a political appointment as surveyor to the Salem customhouse in 1846. The job freed him from financial worry, but he hated the work. In 1849, he lost the job. Despite this loss and the simultaneous death of his mother, he somehow found the energies for his masterwork, *The Scarlet Letter.* It was, he said, "positively a hell-fired story, into which I found it almost impossible to throw any cheering light."

The novel is set in Puritan Boston during the mid–seventeenth century. The title refers to a cloth letter *A* that the narrator finds in a customhouse, along with documents outlining the tragic story of Hester Prynne, who bore an illegitimate child. Refusing to name the baby's father, she was sentenced to wear the scarlet *A* (for adultery) on her breast. The tale is one of sin and redemption, and the tragic consequences of hypocrisy and concealed guilt.

The novel's publication in 1850 brought Hawthorne wide acclaim, some money, and the admiration and friendship of Herman Melville. Another great novel, *The House of the Seven Gables,* appeared the following year.

Out of Harmony with His Times

In 1853, President Franklin Pierce—Hawthorne's old friend from his days at Bowdoin—offered Hawthorne the post of United States consul at Liverpool. Hawthorne and his family lived in Europe for seven years. As an expatriate, however, he found his creativity dwindling, and he had become inexplicably dejected. Even his return to America in 1860 was oddly cheerless. After his years abroad, he was disenchanted with both the Europe where he had been and the America from which he now felt estranged. His old friend Pierce, for whom he had written a campaign biography in 1852, had been defeated for reelection. Abraham Lincoln was in the White House, and with the onset of the Civil War, Hawthorne felt out of harmony with his times.

Back in Concord, Hawthorne found himself unable to complete the several fiction projects he had promised his publisher. His health declined. On the night of May 18, 1864, while on a trip with Pierce, Hawthorne died in a New Hampshire hotel room.

Emerson felt that Hawthorne, no longer able to endure his solitude, "died of it." Emerson also noted in his journal, after attending Hawthorne's funeral, that he was sorry he hadn't known Hawthorne better. And he recorded this sadly ironic anecdote: "One day, when I found him on the top of his hill, in the woods, he paced back the path to his house, and said, 'This path is the only remembrance of me that will remain.'"

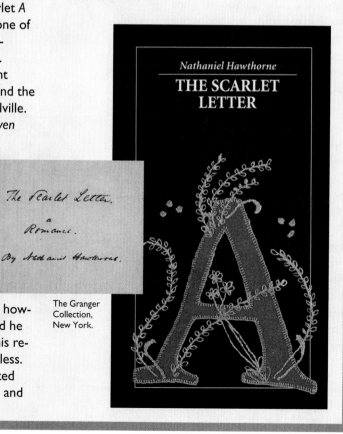

The Granger Collection, New York.

Before You Read

THE MINISTER'S BLACK VEIL

Make the Connection

Secret Sin

The narrator of this story remarks that the "saddest of all prisons" is a person's "own heart." Hawthorne expertly imagined the sometimes fantastic ways in which people suffer guilt for secret sins they have committed in the past. He shows us that guilty secrets serve to isolate people from the world and from their relationships with others.

Reading Skills and Strategies

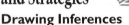

Drawing Inferences

When you come to Goodman Gray's line "Our parson has gone mad!" (page 300), stop and write down three possible reasons why the minister has draped his face with the black material ordinarily used by mourners.

Elements of Literature

Symbol

A **symbol** is something that has meaning in itself but also stands for something more than itself. Hawthorne—indeed, all the Dark Romantics—used symbolism as a technical strategy in his writing. As the title suggests, Hawthorne's central symbol in this story is a "horrible black veil," a "dismal shade" that separates its wearer from the world.

As you read, be aware of the ways this symbol directs your thoughts to the story's central **theme**.

> **A symbol** is a person, place, thing, or event that has meaning in itself and also stands for something more than itself.
>
> *For more on Symbol, see page 280 and the Handbook of Literary Terms.*

Background

This story, like much of Hawthorne's best work, is set in the times of his Puritan ancestors, an era he viewed as "characterized by . . . gloom and piety."

Hawthorne added the following note to the story: "Another clergyman in New England, Mr. Joseph Moody, of York, Maine, who died about eighty years since, made himself remarkable by the same eccentricity that is here related of the Reverend Mr. Hooper. In this case, however, the symbol had a different import. In early life he had accidentally killed a beloved friend; and from that day till the hour of his own death, he hid his face from men."

Illustration by Elenore Plaisted Abbott for "The Minister's Black Veil," from the 1900 edition of *Twice-Told Tales.*

Houghton Mifflin Company.

> "He has changed himself into something awful, only by hiding his face."

The Minister's Black Veil

A Parable

Nathaniel Hawthorne

The sexton[1] stood in the porch of Milford meetinghouse, pulling lustily at the bell rope. The old people of the village came stooping along the street. Children, with bright faces, tripped merrily beside their parents, or mimicked a graver gait, in the conscious dignity of their Sunday clothes. Spruce bachelors looked sidelong at the pretty maidens, and fancied that the Sabbath sunshine made them prettier than on weekdays. When the throng had mostly streamed into the porch, the sexton began to toll the bell, keeping his eye on the Reverend Mr. Hooper's door. The first glimpse of the clergyman's figure was the signal for the bell to cease its summons.

1. **sexton:** church officer or employee whose duties may include maintenance, ringing the bells, and digging graves.

"But what has good Parson Hooper got upon his face?" cried the sexton in astonishment.

All within hearing immediately turned about, and beheld the semblance of Mr. Hooper, pacing slowly his meditative way toward the meetinghouse. With one accord they started, expressing more wonder than if some strange minister were coming to dust the cushions of Mr. Hooper's pulpit.

"Are you sure it is our parson?" inquired Goodman[2] Gray of the sexton.

"Of a certainty it is good Mr. Hooper," replied the sexton. "He was to have exchanged pulpits with Parson Shute of Westbury; but Parson Shute sent to excuse himself yesterday, being to preach a funeral sermon."

The cause of so much amazement may appear sufficiently slight. Mr. Hooper, a gentlemanly person of about thirty, though still a bachelor, was dressed with due clerical neatness, as if a careful wife had starched his band, and brushed the weekly dust from his Sunday's garb. There was but one thing remarkable in his appearance. Swathed about his forehead, and hanging down over his face, so low as to be shaken by his breath, Mr. Hooper had on a black veil. On a nearer view, it seemed to consist of two folds of crape,[3] which entirely concealed his features, except the mouth and chin, but probably did not intercept his sight, farther than to give a darkened aspect to all living and inanimate things. With this gloomy shade before him, good Mr. Hooper walked onward, at a slow and quiet pace, stooping somewhat and looking on the ground, as is customary with abstracted men, yet nodding kindly to those of his parishioners who still waited on the meetinghouse steps. But so wonder-struck were they, that his greeting hardly met with a return.

"I can't really feel as if good Mr. Hooper's face was behind that piece of crape," said the sexton.

"I don't like it," muttered an old woman, as she hobbled into the meetinghouse. "He has changed himself into something awful, only by hiding his face."

"Our parson has gone mad!" cried Goodman Gray, following him across the threshold.

A rumor of some unaccountable phenomenon had preceded Mr. Hooper into the meetinghouse, and set all the congregation astir. Few could refrain from twisting their heads toward the door; many stood upright, and turned directly about; while several little boys clambered upon the seats, and came down again with a terrible racket. There was a general bustle, a rustling of the women's gowns and shuffling of the men's feet, greatly at variance with that hushed repose which should attend the entrance of the minister. But Mr. Hooper appeared not to notice the perturbation of his people. He entered with an almost noiseless step, bent his head mildly to the pews on each side, and bowed as he passed his oldest parishioner, a white-haired great-grandsire, who occupied an armchair in the center of the aisle. It was strange to observe, how slowly this venerable man became conscious of something singular in the appearance of his pastor. He seemed not fully to partake of the prevailing wonder, till Mr. Hooper had ascended the stairs, and showed himself in the pulpit, face to face with his congregation, except for the black veil. That mysterious emblem was never once withdrawn. It shook with his measured breath as he gave out the psalm; it threw its obscurity between him and the holy page, as he read the Scriptures; and while he prayed, the veil lay heavily on his uplifted countenance. Did he seek to hide it from the dread Being whom he was addressing?

Such was the effect of this simple piece of crape, that more than one woman of delicate nerves was forced to leave the meetinghouse. Yet perhaps the pale-faced congregation was almost as fearful a sight to the minister, as his black veil to them.

Mr. Hooper had the reputation of a good preacher, but not an energetic one: He strove to win his people heavenward, by mild persuasive influences, rather than to drive them thither, by the thunders of the Word. The sermon which he now delivered, was marked by the same characteristics of style and manner, as the general series of his pulpit oratory. But there was something, either in the sentiment of the discourse itself, or in

---

2. **Goodman:** form of polite address similar to *mister.*
3. **crape:** kind of black cloth worn as a sign of mourning; from the French word *crêpe.*

the imagination of the auditors, which made it greatly the most powerful effort that they had ever heard from their pastor's lips. It was tinged, rather more darkly than usual, with the gentle gloom of Mr. Hooper's temperament. The subject had reference to secret sin, and those sad mysteries which we hide from our nearest and dearest, and would fain conceal from our own consciousness, even forgetting that the Omniscient[4] can detect them. A subtle power was breathed into his words. Each member of the congregation, the most innocent girl, and the man of hardened breast, felt as if the preacher had crept upon them, behind his awful veil, and discovered their hoarded iniquity of deed or thought. Many spread their clasped hands on their bosoms. There was nothing terrible in what Mr. Hooper said; at least, no violence; and yet, with every tremor of his melancholy voice, the hearers quaked. An unsought pathos came hand in hand with awe. So sensible were the audience of some unwonted attribute in their minister, that they longed for a breath of wind to blow aside the veil, almost believing that a stranger's visage would be discovered, though the form, gesture, and voice were those of Mr. Hooper.

At the close of the services, the people hurried out with indecorous confusion, eager to communicate their pent-up amazement, and conscious of lighter spirits, the moment they lost sight of the black veil. Some gathered in little circles, huddled closely together, with their mouths all whispering in the center; some went homeward alone, wrapped in silent meditation; some talked loudly, and profaned the Sabbath day with ostentatious laughter. A few shook their sagacious heads, intimating that they could penetrate the mystery; while one or two affirmed that there was no mystery at all, but only that Mr. Hooper's eyes were so weakened by the midnight lamp, as to require a shade. After a brief interval, forth came good Mr. Hooper also, in the rear of his flock. Turning his veiled face from one group to another, he paid due reverence to the hoary heads, saluted the middle-aged with kind dignity, as their friend and spiritual guide, greeted the young with mingled authority and love, and laid his hands on the little children's heads to bless them. Such was always

his custom on the Sabbath day. Strange and bewildered looks repaid him for his courtesy. None, as on former occasions, aspired to the honor of walking by their pastor's side. Old Squire Saunders, doubtless by an accidental lapse of memory, neglected to invite Mr. Hooper to his table, where the good clergyman had been wont to bless the food, almost every Sunday since his settlement. He returned, therefore, to the parsonage, and, at the moment of closing the door, was observed to look back upon the people, all of whom had their eyes fixed upon the minister. A sad smile gleamed faintly from beneath the black veil, and flickered about his mouth, glimmering as he disappeared.

"How strange," said a lady, "that a simple black veil, such as any woman might wear on her bonnet, should become such a terrible thing on Mr. Hooper's face!"

"Something must surely be amiss with Mr. Hooper's intellects," observed her husband, the physician of the village. "But the strangest part of the affair is the effect of this vagary, even on a sober-minded man like myself. The black veil, though it covers only our pastor's face, throws its influence over his whole person, and makes him ghostlike from head to foot. Do you not feel it so?"

"Truly do I," replied the lady; "and I would not be alone with him for the world. I wonder he is not afraid to be alone with himself!"

"Men sometimes are so," said her husband.

The afternoon service was attended with similar circumstances. At its conclusion, the bell tolled for the funeral of a young lady. The relatives and friends were assembled in the house, and the more distant acquaintances stood about the door, speaking of the good qualities of the deceased, when their talk was interrupted by the appearance of Mr. Hooper, still covered with his black veil. It was now an appropriate emblem. The clergyman stepped into the room where the corpse was laid, and bent over the coffin, to take a last farewell of his deceased parishioner. As he stooped, the veil hung straight down from his forehead, so that, if her eyelids had not been

4. **the Omniscient:** the all-knowing God.

WORDS TO OWN

iniquity (i·nik′wi·tē): *n.:* wickedness.
ostentatious (äs′tən·tā′shəs) *adj.:* conspicuous.
sagacious (sə·gā′shəs) *adj.:* wise; keenly perceptive.

The Sermon (1886) by Julius Gari Melchers. Oil on canvas.

National Museum of American Art, Bequest of Henry Ward Ranger through The National Academy of Design. Courtesy Art Resource.

closed forever, the dead maiden might have seen his face. Could Mr. Hooper be fearful of her glance, that he so hastily caught back the black veil? A person, who watched the interview between the dead and living, scrupled[5] not to affirm, that, at the instant when the clergyman's features were disclosed, the corpse had slightly shuddered, rustling the shroud and muslin cap, though the countenance retained the composure of death. A superstitious old woman was the only witness of this prodigy.[6] From the coffin, Mr.

5. **scrupled:** hesitated.
6. **prodigy:** extraordinary act that foretells the future.

Hooper passed into the chamber of the mourners, and thence to the head of the staircase, to make the funeral prayer. It was a tender and heart-dissolving prayer, full of sorrow, yet so imbued with celestial hopes, that the music of a heavenly harp, swept by the fingers of the dead, seemed faintly to be heard among the saddest accents of the minister. The people trembled, though they but darkly understood him, when he prayed that they, and himself, and all of mortal race, might be ready, as he trusted this young maiden had been, for the dreadful hour that should snatch the veil from their faces. The bearers went heavily forth, and the mourners followed, saddening all the street, with the dead before them, and Mr. Hooper in his black veil behind.

"Why do you look back?" said one in the procession to his partner.

"I had a fancy," replied she, "that the minister and the maiden's spirit were walking hand in hand."

"And so had I, at the same moment," said the other.

That night, the handsomest couple in Milford village were to be joined in wedlock. Though reckoned a melancholy man, Mr. Hooper had a placid cheerfulness for such occasions, which often excited a sympathetic smile, where livelier merriment would have been thrown away. There was no quality of his disposition which made him more beloved than this. The company at the wedding awaited his arrival with impatience, trusting that the strange awe, which had gathered over him throughout the day, would now be dispelled. But such was not the result. When Mr. Hooper came, the first thing that their eyes rested on was the same horrible black veil, which had added deeper gloom to the funeral, and could portend nothing but evil to the wedding. Such was its immediate effect on the guests, that a cloud seemed to have rolled duskily from beneath the black crape, and dimmed the light of the candles. The bridal pair stood up before the minister. But the bride's cold fingers quivered in the tremulous hand of the bridegroom, and her deathlike paleness caused a whisper, that the maiden who had been buried a few hours before, was come from her grave to be married. If ever another wedding were so dismal, it was that famous one, where they tolled the wedding knell.[7] After performing the ceremony, Mr. Hooper raised a glass of wine to his lips, wishing happiness to the new-married couple, in a strain of mild pleasantry that ought to have brightened the features of the guests, like a cheerful gleam from the hearth. At that instant, catching a glimpse of his figure in the looking glass, the black veil involved his own spirit in the horror with which it overwhelmed all others. His frame shuddered—his lips grew white—he spilt the untasted wine upon the carpet—and rushed forth into the darkness. For the Earth, too, had on her Black Veil.

The next day, the whole village of Milford talked of little else than Parson Hooper's black veil. That, and the mystery concealed behind it, supplied a topic for discussion between acquaintances meeting in the street, and good women gossiping at their open windows. It was the first item of news that the tavern keeper told to his guests. The children babbled of it on their way to school. One imitative little imp covered his face with an old black handkerchief, thereby so affrighting his playmates, that the panic seized himself, and he well nigh lost his wits by his own waggery.[8]

It was remarkable, that, of all the busybodies and impertinent people in the parish, not one ventured to put the plain question to Mr. Hooper, wherefore he did this thing. Hitherto, whenever there appeared the slightest call for such interference, he had never lacked advisers, nor shown himself averse to be guided by their judgment. If he erred at all, it was by so painful a degree of self-distrust, that even the mildest censure would lead him to consider an indifferent action as a crime. Yet, though so well acquainted with this amiable weakness, no individual among his parishioners chose to make the black veil a subject of friendly remonstrance. There was a feeling of dread, neither plainly confessed nor carefully concealed, which caused each to shift the responsibility upon another, till at length it was found expedient to send a deputation of the church, in order to deal with Mr. Hooper about the mystery, before it should grow into a scandal. Never did an embassy so ill discharge its duties. The minister received them with friendly courtesy, but became silent, after they were seated, leaving to his visitors the whole burden of introducing their important business. The topic, it might be supposed, was obvious enough. There was the black veil, swathed round Mr. Hooper's forehead, and concealing every feature above his placid mouth, on which, at times, they could perceive the glimmering of a melancholy smile. But that piece of crape, to their

8. **waggery:** joke.

7. **If . . . wedding knell:** reference to Hawthorne's story "The Wedding Knell." A knell is the ringing of a bell.

WORDS TO OWN

portend (pôr·tend′) v.: signify.

> **Her eyes were fixed insensibly on the black veil, when, like a sudden twilight in the air, its terrors fell around her.**

imagination, seemed to hang down before his heart, the symbol of a fearful secret between him and them. Were the veil but cast aside, they might speak freely of it, but not till then. Thus they sat a considerable time, speechless, confused, and shrinking uneasily from Mr. Hooper's eye, which they felt to be fixed upon them with an invisible glance. Finally, the deputies returned abashed to their constituents, pronouncing the matter too weighty to be handled, except by a council of the churches, if, indeed, it might not require a general synod.[9]

But there was one person in the village, unappalled by the awe with which the black veil had impressed all beside herself. When the deputies returned without an explanation, or even venturing to demand one, she, with the calm energy of her character, determined to chase away the strange cloud that appeared to be settling round Mr. Hooper, every moment more darkly than before. As his plighted[10] wife, it should be her privilege to know what the black veil concealed. At the minister's first visit, therefore, she entered upon the subject, with a direct simplicity, which made the task easier both for him and her. After he had seated himself, she fixed her eyes steadfastly upon the veil, but could discern nothing of the dreadful gloom that had so overawed the multitude: It was but a double fold of crape, hanging down from his forehead to his mouth, and slightly stirring with his breath.

9. synod (sin′əd): governing body of a group of churches.
10. plighted: promised.

"No," said she aloud, and smiling, "there is nothing terrible in this piece of crape, except that it hides a face which I am always glad to look upon. Come, good sir, let the sun shine from behind the cloud. First lay aside your black veil: Then tell me why you put it on."

Mr. Hooper's smile glimmered faintly.

"There is an hour to come," said he, "when all of us shall cast aside our veils. Take it not amiss, beloved friend, if I wear this piece of crape till then."

"Your words are a mystery too," returned the young lady. "Take away the veil from them, at least."

"Elizabeth, I will," said he, "so far as my vow may suffer me. Know, then, this veil is a type and a symbol, and I am bound to wear it ever, both in light and darkness, in solitude and before the gaze of multitudes, and as with strangers, so with my familiar friends. No mortal eye will see it withdrawn. This dismal shade must separate me from the world: Even you, Elizabeth, can never come behind it!"

"What grievous affliction hath befallen you," she earnestly inquired, "that you should thus darken your eyes forever?"

"If it be a sign of mourning," replied Mr. Hooper, "I, perhaps, like most other mortals, have sorrows dark enough to be typified by a black veil."

"But what if the world will not believe that it is the type of an innocent sorrow?" urged Elizabeth. "Beloved and respected as you are, there may be whispers, that you hide your face under the consciousness of secret sin. For the sake of your holy office, do away this scandal!"

The color rose into her cheeks, as she intimated the nature of the rumors that were already abroad in the village. But Mr. Hooper's mildness did not forsake him. He even smiled again—that same sad smile, which always appeared like a faint glimmering of light, proceeding from the obscurity beneath the veil.

"If I hide my face for sorrow, there is cause enough," he merely replied; "and if I cover it for secret sin, what mortal might not do the same?"

And with this gentle, but unconquerable obstinacy, did he resist all her entreaties. At length Elizabeth sat silent. For a few moments she appeared lost in thought, considering, probably, what new methods might be tried, to withdraw her lover from so dark a fantasy, which, if it had no other meaning, was perhaps a symptom of mental disease. Though of a firmer character than his own, the tears rolled down her cheeks. But, in an instant, as it were, a new feeling took the place of sorrow: Her eyes were fixed insensibly on the black veil, when, like a sudden twilight in the air, its terrors fell around her. She arose, and stood trembling before him.

"And do you feel it then at last?" said he mournfully.

She made no reply, but covered her eyes with her hand, and turned to leave the room. He rushed forward and caught her arm.

"Have patience with me, Elizabeth!" cried he passionately. "Do not desert me, though this veil must be between us here on earth. Be mine, and hereafter there shall be no veil over my face, no darkness between our souls! It is but a mortal veil—it is not for eternity! Oh! you know not how lonely I am, and how frightened to be alone behind my black veil. Do not leave me in this miserable obscurity forever!"

"Lift the veil but once, and look me in the face," said she.

"Never! It cannot be!" replied Mr. Hooper.

"Then, farewell!" said Elizabeth.

She withdrew her arm from his grasp, and slowly departed, pausing at the door, to give one long, shuddering gaze, that seemed almost to penetrate the mystery of the black veil. But, even amid his grief, Mr. Hooper smiled to think that only a material emblem had separated him from happiness, though the horrors which it shadowed forth, must be drawn darkly between the fondest of lovers.

From that time no attempts were made to re-move Mr. Hooper's black veil, or, by a direct appeal, to discover the secret which it was supposed to hide. By persons who claimed a superiority to popular prejudice, it was reckoned merely an eccentric whim, such as often mingles with the sober actions of men otherwise rational, and tinges them all with its own semblance of insanity. But with the multitude, good Mr. Hooper was irreparably a bugbear.[11] He could not walk the streets with any peace of mind, so conscious was he that the gentle and timid would turn aside to avoid him, and that others would make it a point of hardihood to throw themselves in his way. The impertinence of the latter class compelled him to give up his customary walk, at sunset, to the burial ground; for when he leaned pensively over the gate, there would always be faces behind the gravestones, peeping at his black veil. A fable went the rounds, that the stare of the dead people drove him thence. It grieved him, to the very depth of his kind heart, to observe how the children fled from his approach, breaking up their merriest sports, while his melancholy figure was yet afar off. Their instinctive dread caused him to feel, more strongly than aught else, that a preternatural[12] horror was interwoven with the threads of the black crape. In truth, his own antipathy to the veil was known to be so great, that he never willingly passed before a mirror, nor stooped to drink at a still fountain, lest, in its peaceful bosom, he should be affrighted by himself. This was what gave plausibility to the whispers, that Mr. Hooper's conscience tortured him for some great crime, too horrible to be entirely concealed, or otherwise than so obscurely intimated. Thus, from beneath the black veil, there rolled a cloud into the sunshine, an ambiguity of sin or sorrow, which enveloped the poor minister, so that love or sympathy could never reach him. It

11. **bugbear:** source of irrational fears.
12. **preternatural:** abnormal; supernatural.

WORDS TO OWN

obscurity (əb·skyoor′ə·tē) *n.:* something hidden or concealed.

pensively (pen′siv·lē) *adv.:* thinking deeply or seriously.

antipathy (an·tip′ə·thē) *n.:* strong dislike.

plausibility (plô′zə·bil′i·tē) *n.:* believability.

was said, that ghost and fiend consorted with him there. With self-shudderings and outward terrors, he walked continually in its shadow, groping darkly within his own soul, or gazing through a medium that saddened the whole world. Even the lawless wind, it was believed, respected his dreadful secret, and never blew aside the veil. But still good Mr. Hooper sadly smiled, at the pale visages of the worldly throng as he passed by.

Among all its bad influences, the black veil had the one desirable effect, of making its wearer a very efficient clergyman. By the aid of his mysterious emblem—for there was no other apparent cause—he became a man of awful power, over souls that were in agony for sin. His converts always regarded him with a dread peculiar to themselves, affirming, though but figuratively, that, before he brought them to celestial light, they had been with him behind the black veil. Its gloom, indeed, enabled him to sympathize with all dark affections. Dying sinners cried aloud for Mr. Hooper, and would not yield their breath till he appeared; though ever, as he stooped to whisper consolation, they shuddered at the veiled face so near their own. Such were the terrors of the black veil, even when Death had bared his visage! Strangers came long distances to attend service at his church, with the mere idle purpose of gazing at his figure, because it was forbidden them to behold his face. But many were made to quake ere they departed! Once, during Governor Belcher's[13] administration, Mr. Hooper was appointed to preach the election sermon. Covered with his black veil, he stood before the chief magistrate, the council, and the representatives, and wrought so deep an impression, that the legislative measures of that year, were characterized by all the gloom and piety of our earliest ancestral sway.

In this manner Mr. Hooper spent a long life, irreproachable in outward act, yet shrouded in dismal suspicions; kind and loving, though unloved, and dimly feared; a man apart from men, shunned in their health and joy, but ever summoned to their aid in mortal anguish. As years wore on, shedding their snows above his sable veil, he acquired a name throughout the New England

churches, and they called him Father Hooper. Nearly all his parishioners, who were of mature age when he was settled, had been borne away by many a funeral: He had one congregation in the church, and a more crowded one in the churchyard; and having wrought so late into the evening, and done his work so well, it was now good Father Hooper's turn to rest.

Several persons were visible by the shaded candlelight, in the death chamber of the old clergyman. Natural connections he had none. But there was the decorously grave, though unmoved physician, seeking only to mitigate the last pangs of the patient whom he could not save. There were the deacons, and other eminently pious members of his church. There, also, was the Reverend Mr. Clark, of Westbury, a young and zealous divine, who had ridden in haste to pray by the bedside of the expiring minister. There was the nurse, no hired handmaiden of death, but one whose calm affection had endured thus long, in secrecy, in solitude, amid the chill of age, and would not perish, even at the dying hour. Who, but Elizabeth! And there lay the hoary head of good Father Hooper upon the death-pillow, with the black veil still swathed about his brow and reaching down over his face, so that each more difficult gasp of his faint breath caused it to stir. All through life that piece of crape had hung between him and the world: It had separated him from cheerful brotherhood and woman's love, and kept him in that saddest of all prisons, his own heart; and still it lay upon his face, as if to deepen the gloom of his darksome chamber, and shade him from the sunshine of eternity.

For some time previous, his mind had been confused, wavering doubtfully between the past and the present, and hovering forward, as it were, at intervals, into the indistinctness of the world to come. There had been feverish turns, which tossed him from side to side, and wore away what little strength he had. But in his most convulsive struggles, and in the wildest vagaries of his intellect, when no other thought retained its sober influence, he still showed an awful solicitude lest the black veil should slip aside. Even if his bewildered soul could have forgotten, there was a faithful woman at his pillow, who, with averted eyes, would have covered that aged face, which she had last beheld in the comeliness of manhood. At

13. **Governor Belcher's:** Jonathan Belcher (1682–1757) was governor of the Massachusetts Bay Colony from 1730 to 1741.

... there he sat, shivering with the arms of death around him, while the black veil hung down ...

length the death-stricken old man lay quietly in the torpor of mental and bodily exhaustion, with an imperceptible pulse, and breath that grew fainter and fainter, except when a long, deep, and irregular inspiration seemed to prelude the flight of his spirit.

The minister of Westbury approached the bedside.

"Venerable Father Hooper," said he, "the moment of your release is at hand. Are you ready for the lifting of the veil, that shuts in time from eternity?"

Father Hooper at first replied merely by a feeble motion of his head; then, apprehensive, perhaps, that his meaning might be doubtful, he exerted himself to speak.

"Yea," said he, in faint accents, "my soul hath a patient weariness until that veil be lifted."

"And is it fitting," resumed the Reverend Mr. Clark, "that a man so given to prayer, of such a blameless example, holy in deed and thought, so far as mortal judgment may pronounce; is it fitting that a father in the church should leave a shadow on his memory, that may seem to blacken a life so pure? I pray you, my venerable brother, let not this thing be! Suffer us to be gladdened by your triumphant aspect, as you go to your reward. Before the veil of eternity be lifted, let me cast aside this black veil from your face!"

And thus speaking, the Reverend Mr. Clark bent forward to reveal the mystery of so many years. But, exerting a sudden energy, that made all the beholders stand aghast, Father Hooper snatched both his hands from beneath the bedclothes, and pressed them strongly on the black veil, resolute to struggle, if the minister of Westbury would contend with a dying man.

"Never!" cried the veiled clergyman. "On earth, never!"

"Dark old man!" exclaimed the affrighted minister, "with what horrible crime upon your soul are you now passing to the judgment?"

Father Hooper's breath heaved; it rattled in his throat; but, with a mighty effort, grasping forward with his hands, he caught hold of life, and held it back till he should speak. He even raised himself in bed; and there he sat, shivering with the arms of death around him, while the black veil hung down, awful, at that last moment, in the gathered terrors of a lifetime. And yet the faint, sad smile, so often there, now seemed to glimmer from its obscurity, and linger on Father Hooper's lips.

"Why do you tremble at me alone?" cried he, turning his veiled face round the circle of pale spectators. "Tremble also at each other! Have men avoided me, and women shown no pity, and children screamed and fled, only for my black veil? What, but the mystery which it obscurely typifies, has made this piece of crape so awful? When the friend shows his inmost heart to his friend; the lover to his best-beloved; when man does not vainly shrink from the eye of his Creator, loathsomely treasuring up the secret of his sin; then deem me a monster, for the symbol beneath which I have lived, and die! I look around me, and, lo! on every visage a Black Veil!"

While his auditors shrank from one another, in mutual affright, Father Hooper fell back upon his pillow, a veiled corpse, with a faint smile lingering on the lips. Still veiled, they laid him in his coffin, and a veiled corpse they bore him to the grave. The grass of many years has sprung up and withered on that grave, the burial-stone is mossgrown, and good Mr. Hooper's face is dust; but awful is still the thought, that it moldered beneath the Black Veil!

WORDS TO OWN

resolute (rez′ə·lōōt′) adj.: determined.

MAKING MEANINGS

First Thoughts

1. What did you predict was the reason for the minister's veil? Why do you think your prediction was, or was not, correct?

Shaping Interpretations

2. Trace the progression of Elizabeth's response to the veil. How do you explain her changing attitudes?

3. Explain the narrator's remark on page 306 about the human heart being the "saddest of all prisons." Do you agree or disagree? Do you think this observation refers only to Hooper, or is it true of everyone in the story?

4. Would you describe the narrator's **tone** as neutral or emotional? (Think particularly of the words the narrator uses in referring to the veil.) Make a list of specific **connotative** words and phrases that contribute to the story's tone. How do the words the narrator uses affect the story's tone and **atmosphere**?

5. On his deathbed, Hooper says, "I look around me, and, lo! on every visage a Black Veil!" Explain that statement. In what ways is Hooper's veil a **symbol**? What do you think it symbolizes?

Reading Check

a. How does the congregation respond at first to Mr. Hooper's black veil? Why?

b. Briefly describe Hooper's **character** as revealed in the story's opening paragraphs. What does the congregation's attitude toward him seem to have been up to this point?

c. In a single afternoon, Hooper presides at both a funeral and a wedding. How do people react to the presence of the veil at each event?

d. What explanation does Hooper give to Elizabeth, his fiancée, of why he wears the veil? What arguments against wearing the veil does she make?

6. Does Hooper's veil have any positive effects during his long life? Explain.

7. Hawthorne added the subtitle "A Parable" to this story, indicating the importance moral themes had for him. A **parable** is a short, simple story from which a moral or religious lesson can be drawn. Unlike many of the world's parables, which come from religious scriptures such as the Bible, this story is a literary parable with meanings that may be ambiguous and elusive rather than clear-cut. What would you say is the moral lesson of this story—its **theme,** or main idea? In what sense *is* it a parable?

8. Why do you think the villagers bury Hooper without removing the veil?

Connecting with the Text

9. Almost all people, at some point in life, have done things that made them feel guilty and that they have concealed from others. What do you think is useful and beneficial about having a sense of guilt, and what is harmful about it? In what ways can guilt isolate people, and in what ways can it bring people together?

READING SKILLS AND STRATEGIES

Understanding Archaisms

If modern readers have trouble with Hawthorne, it is with his **archaic,** or old-fashioned, language (see page 37). **Context clues** (page 168) should help you figure out any language that is strange. Which word or words in each of the following passages from the story are rarely used today? Rephrase each passage in a modern idiom. Are any of these words used today in different senses?

1. "So sensible were the audience of some unwonted attribute in their minister. . . ." (page 301)

2. "A superstitious old woman was the only witness of this prodigy." (page 302)

3. ". . . he well nigh lost his wits by his own waggery." (page 303)

4. ". . . having wrought so late into the evening. . . ." (page 306)

Choices: Building Your Portfolio

Writer's Notebook

1. Collecting Ideas for a Controversial Issue

You can find topics for persuasive essays in the literature you read. For example, you might find a specific passage in Hawthorne's famous story that you would like to support or argue with. Or, you might find an issue here that people disagree on—perhaps something on the nature of guilt or the psychological effects of isolation. Or, you might want to take a controversial stand on interpreting this story. Take notes on possible topics, jot down details to support your position, and save your work for possible use in the Writer's Workshop on page 331.

Comparing Ideas

2. On Human Nature

In *Nature,* on page 219, Emerson says that we are "part or particle of God," and that in the beauties of nature we can behold something "as beautiful as [our] own nature." In a brief essay, explain how Emerson's views of human nature compare or contrast with Hawthorne's. Cite specific passages from both writers to support what you say. Do you agree with either writer? Why or why not?

Comparing Religious Beliefs

3. Hawthorne and Puritanism

In a brief essay, compare and contrast the attitudes revealed in Hawthorne's story to attitudes held by Puritans such as Jonathan Edwards (see Edwards's sermon "Sinners in the Hands of an Angry God" on page 79). Consider especially attitudes toward sin, guilt, and the conditions necessary for salvation. How do you think Hawthorne felt about the tenets of Puritanism?

Creative Writing

4. Behind the Veil

Write a brief autobiographical sketch of Mr. Hooper, using the **first-person point of view.** Using clues from the text, and your own imagination, have Hooper explain the significance of the veil and how he first thought of wearing it. Let him describe how he feels wearing it all the time.

Critical Thinking/ Speaking and Listening

5. Rating the Prose

In a group of three or more students, discuss similarities and differences between Hawthorne and Poe, based on your reading of their works. Compare and contrast their literary styles, their choices of subject matter, their **themes,** and their use of **symbolism.** Discuss which author's work you prefer and why. Present your group's "verdict" to the rest of the class.

Creative Writing/ Performance

6. Theatrical Version

With one or more partners, write a condensed version of the story, to be spoken aloud. You'll need to create some dialogue on the basis of narrated scenes. The major characters will be Hooper, Elizabeth, and the narrator, who will summarize events and describe characters. Perform your reader's theater for the class.

Interpreting a Story

7. A Crime of Dark Dye

Edgar Allan Poe said that Hooper wore the veil because ". . . a crime of dark dye (having reference to the 'young lady') has been committed. . . ." What do you think Poe is referring to? Does this interpretation make sense to you, or do you think it is too literal? (Think about whether the story would have been more effective had Hawthorne revealed why Hooper wears the veil.) Write a brief essay expressing your views.

Reading Skills and Strategies

VOCABULARY: TRACING THE ORIGINS OF WORDS

While some languages have few imported words, English is a language full of borrowings. Many English words come originally from Latin by way of Germanic languages or Old English. Other words have Greek, French, Native American, or Spanish origins. And this is just the tip of the iceberg.

Since Latin words make up such a large part of our language, learning the meaning of an English word that comes from Latin may help you understand the meanings of other English words derived from Latin. Such words are considered members of the same word family. You can learn about word families by consulting a dictionary to discover a word's **etymology**—the history of its origins and development.

Hanging tales on words.
Learning the etymology of a word can help you to quickly recognize related words. It can also help you to remember a new word by giving you interesting and perhaps surprising information. For example, the noun *volcano*

Vulcan making a new armor for Achilles.

The Granger Collection, New York.

is derived from *Vulcan*, the Roman god of fire and forges. If you can use a word's etymology to "hang a tale" on a word—that is, associate an interesting fact or anecdote with it—you're more likely to remember the word.

Here are some words that come from Latin. All of them appear in Hawthorne's story. See if the etymologies help you to remember and use these words.

averted from *a-*, "from" + *vertere*, "to turn"
Meaning: turned away from; kept from happening

celestial from *caelestis*, "heaven"
Meaning: of the heavens

discern from *dis-*, "apart" + *cernere*, "to separate"
Meaning: to separate (a thing) mentally from another or others; to recognize as separate or different

obscurity from *obscurus*, "covered over"
Meaning: the condition of being unclear or indistinct; not easily understood

placid from *placidus*, "to please"
Meaning: undisturbed; tranquil; calm; quiet

preclude from *pre-*, "before" + *claudere*, "to close"
Meaning: to make impossible, especially in advance; to shut out; to prevent

sagacious from *sagax*, "wise; foreseeing"
Meaning: having or showing keen perception or discernment; having or showing sound judgment

Try It Out

Charting etymologies. When you find an unfamiliar word, looking it up in a dictionary and recording its etymology along with its meaning can both help you remember it *and* make it a permanent part of your vocabulary. Try using a chart like the one below to record etymologies for the following words from Hawthorne and for any other new words you want to own and use.

iniquity (page 301)   ambiguity (page 305)

superstitious (page 302)   vagaries (page 306)

portend (page 303)   prelude (page 307)

Word	
Etymology	
Meanings	
Where Found	

Herman Melville

(1819–1891)

It is the central irony of Herman Melville's career that his triumphant achievement, now widely recognized as one of the greatest American novels, was almost wholly ignored while its author was alive. Melville's contemporaries—so absorbed with success; so eager to discover it, bestow it, reward it, celebrate it—passed by *Moby-Dick* without the barest recognition.

As a result, Melville spent the last third of his life in poverty and despair, thinking himself a failure. His disappointment was even more painful because he had known easy, early success with his adventure stories. With ambitious, serious work, he met only failure and humiliation.

It is a further irony that Melville became resigned to the contempt of the world; that in spite of the painfulness of the world's judgment, he deliberately decided in the world's favor. In a remark that was to be echoed by the twentieth-century novelist William Faulkner, Melville once remarked that "failure is the true test of greatness."

A Whale Ship Was His College

Herman Melville was born into a distinguished family—wealthy Boston merchants on his father's side, early New York landowners on his mother's, Revolutionary War heroes on both. But his father went bankrupt in 1830, suffered an emotional breakdown, and died when Melville was twelve. Melville's mother, an austere, God-fearing woman, moved with her eight children from New York City to Albany. Under the pressures of poverty, she became even more remote from her children.

The teenage Melville clerked in his brother's hat store and in his uncle's bank, taught school in Pittsfield, Massachusetts, and tried writing articles and stories. However, faced with a grim life in his family's house, he took to the sea in 1839 as cabin boy on a merchant ship.

A whaling expedition to the South Seas followed in 1841. A year and a half later, Melville

Herman Melville (1870) by Joseph Eaton. Oil on canvas.
By permission of the Houghton Library, Harvard University, Cambridge, Massachusetts (H585).

jumped ship at the Marquesas Islands and stumbled upon the valley of the Typees, who were reputed to be cannibals but turned out to be gentle and hospitable. After a month, Melville signed on to an Australian ship, which he deserted in a semimutiny at Papeete. He roamed the islands of Tahiti and Moorea, working in the fields and studying island life, before joining a whaler to Honolulu, and then enlisting as a seaman on a U.S. Navy frigate. When his ship docked at Boston in October 1844, a career's worth of seagoing adventure had ended. Ishmael, the young narrator of *Moby-Dick,* surely voices Melville's own sentiments when he says, "A whale ship was my Yale College and my Harvard."

The Road to Success

In less than two years, Melville produced a book of slightly fictionalized travel memoirs, *Typee,* that became an immediate success. With the publication of four other semiautobiographical sea tales between 1847 and 1850, Melville became one of the most popular authors of the

day. He was now married to the former Eliza-beth Shaw, daughter of an old family friend. In the course of their long and often troubled marriage, she bore four children and was never more loyal and devoted than at times of crisis.

In the fall of 1850, Melville bought a farm near Pittsfield, Massachusetts. Nathaniel Hawthorne, who lived in nearby Lenox, re-sponded to Melville's admiration, and they saw much of each other. Hawthorne's example en-couraged Melville, who was writing a book that would both exploit his whaling experience and, on a far more ambitious plane, seek the ulti-mate truth of human existence. That truth, and the mystery of whether it is benign or evil in na-ture, is embodied in Moby-Dick, the great white whale that gives the book its title and central symbol.

Melville found the perfect narrator for his whale story in a young character named Ishmael, who has a keen eye and a questioning voice. Moreover, Melville saw his other main character clearly: Captain Ahab, standing on the *Pequod*'s quarter-deck with his peg leg, his heart full of brooding vengeance. In Ahab, Melville created an obsessed, tragic, larger-than-life figure with few equals in American literature.

> "I have written a wicked book. . . ."

When he finished *Moby-Dick* in July 1851, Melville sensed that he had taken a great risk and won. He dedicated his great novel to Hawthorne and wrote him, "I have written a wicked book, and feel spotless as the lamb."

To Risk All—and Lose

Yet for all Melville's bright expectations, *Moby-Dick* was a failure. Critics and readers alike were either puzzled or indifferent, and Melville finally had to admit that his literary career had foundered. He wrote Hawthorne:

> The calm, the coolness, the silent grass-growing mood in which a man *ought* always to compose—that, I fear, can seldom be

mine. Dollars damn me; and the malicious Devil is forever grinning in upon me, holding the door ajar. My dear Sir, a presentiment [feeling of fear about the future] is on me —I shall at last be worn out and perish. . . . What I feel most moved to write, that is banned—it will not pay. Yet, altogether, write the *other* way I cannot. So the product is a final hash, and all my books are botches.

Melville was in debt, unable to meet the needs of his family, and in ill health. However, he continued to hope for a change in his fortunes. In the next six years, he published three poorly received novels.

In 1856, Melville scraped together enough money for a trip to Europe and the Middle East. He returned home with his emotions restored, but his literary and financial fortunes still low.

In 1866, Melville found a job, much as Hawthorne had, with the customhouse. But if the work gave him the financial security he yearned for, the "grass-growing" peace of mind was still denied him. A different kind of tragedy hit the following year when his son Malcolm took to his room and killed himself with a pistol.

True to the Dreams of Youth

Although Melville never stopped writing during this dark period, almost none of his work found a publisher, and he was obliged to bring it out in private editions of only a few copies. To end this period in Melville's life, there was further tragedy. In 1886, his son Stanwix, always an un-stable wanderer, died in San Francisco.

At about the same time, Elizabeth, Melville's wife, came into a small inheritance which allowed her husband to retire from the custom-house and begin work on a book that would become another masterpiece. This was *Billy Budd*. When Melville died on September 28, 1891, the novella lay unwanted in his desk drawer. In 1924, thirty-three years later, it was published and acclaimed. Near the desk where Melville had composed it, a note was found. It read, "Keep true to the dreams of thy youth."

Before You Read

FROM **MOBY-DICK**

Make the Connection

**The Meaning of
a White Whale**

Moby-Dick is both a thrilling sea story about men who hunt whales in wooden boats and a search for the truth of human existence. The mystery of whether existence is benign, indifferent, or evil is embodied in Moby-Dick, the great white whale.

Elements of Literature

Characterization

To create the larger-than-life **characterization** of Captain Ahab, Melville uses all the tools at a writer's command: He tells us directly (through the narrator, Ishmael) what Ahab is like, he describes Ahab's appearance and clothing, he lets us overhear Ahab speaking and thinking, he shows Ahab in action, and he shows us how other characters feel about and behave toward Ahab.

> **C**haracterization is the process by which a writer reveals a character's personality.
>
> *For more on Characterization, see the Handbook of Literary Terms.*

Reading Skills and Strategies

Drawing Inferences about Character

By combining clues in the text with what experience has taught us about people, we can draw **inferences,** or conclusions, about the kind of people we meet in literature.

As you read these episodes from *Moby-Dick,* watch especially for clues to the characters of Captain Ahab and the first mate, Starbuck.

To take notes on these men as you read, divide a sheet of paper into two columns. In the left column, list details in the text that tell you something significant about each man. After you complete your reading, review the clues you've noted. Then, in the right column, write the inferences you can make about the characters of Ahab and Starbuck. What kind of people are they? What drives each man?

from Moby-Dick

Herman Melville

Two chapters from Melville's great novel will give you only a taste of its characters, setting, plot, and themes. The novel opens with the famous line, "Call me Ishmael." The narrator who adopts this pseudonym is a moody young New Yorker who takes to sea to escape the "damp, drizzly November in my soul." First traveling to the Massachusetts seaport of New Bedford, he shares a room with a South Sea Islander named Queequeg. Becoming friends, the two go to the island of Nantucket, where they sign on for a three-year voyage on the whaling ship Pequod, *under the command of the mysterious Captain Ahab. While still ashore, Ishmael receives warnings of disaster; but he ships out anyway, and the* Pequod, *weirdly decorated with whale*

bones, sets sail on an icy Christmas Day. The officers and crew are an assortment of men from all over the world: South Pacific islanders, Massachusetts Gay-Head Indians, inhabitants of the Isle of Man off the coast of Ireland, and more. The harpooners are Queequeg, Tashtego, and Daggoo; the first, second, and third mates are Starbuck, Stubb, and Flask, respectively.

Shortly before the chapter "The Quarter-Deck," Stubb and Ahab have quarreled violently, and an ominous dream has suggested to Stubb that he beware of his captain's anger. In this chapter, Ahab calls the men to assemble on the deck, where he will reveal the true nature of his quest.

Background illustration by Rockwell Kent from *Moby-Dick.*
Rockwell Kent Collection, Rare Book and Manuscript Library, Columbia University.

HERMAN MELVILLE 313

The Quarter-Deck

(Enter Ahab: Then all.)

It was not a great while after the affair of the pipe,[1] that one morning shortly after breakfast, Ahab, as was his wont, ascended the cabin gangway to the deck. There most sea captains usually walk at that hour, as country gentlemen, after the same meal, take a few turns in the garden.

Soon his steady, ivory stride was heard, as to and fro he paced his old rounds, upon planks so familiar to his tread, that they were all over dented, like geological stones, with the peculiar mark of his walk. Did you fixedly gaze, too, upon that ribbed and dented brow; there also, you would see still stranger footprints—the footprints of his one unsleeping, ever-pacing thought.

But on the occasion in question, those dents looked deeper, even as his nervous step that morning left a deeper mark. And, so full of his thought was Ahab, that at every uniform turn that he made, now at the mainmast and now at the binnacle,[2] you could almost see that thought turn in him as he turned, and pace in him as he paced; so completely possessing him, indeed, that it all but seemed the inward mold of every outer movement.

"D'ye mark him, Flask?" whispered Stubb; "the chick that's in him pecks the shell. 'Twill soon be out."

The hours wore on—Ahab now shut up within

---

1. **affair of the pipe:** Ahab had thrown his pipe overboard one evening when he realized that he had no business with "this thing that is meant for sereneness."

2. **binnacle:** upright stand holding the ship's compass.

his cabin; anon, pacing the deck, with the same intense bigotry of purpose in his aspect.

It drew near the close of day. Suddenly he came to a halt by the bulwarks,[3] and inserting his bone leg into the auger hole there, and with one hand grasping a shroud, he ordered Starbuck to send everybody aft.

"Sir!" said the mate, astonished at an order seldom or never given on shipboard except in some extraordinary case.

"Send everybody aft," repeated Ahab. "Mastheads, there! Come down!"

When the entire ship's company were assembled, and with curious and not wholly unapprehensive faces were eyeing him, for he looked not unlike the weather horizon when a storm is coming up, Ahab, after rapidly glancing over the bulwarks, and then darting his eyes among the crew, started from his standpoint; and as though not a soul were nigh him resumed his heavy turns upon the deck. With bent head and half-slouched hat he continued to pace; unmindful of the wondering whispering among the men; till Stubb cautiously whispered to Flask, that Ahab must have summoned them there for the purpose of witnessing a pedestrian feat. But this did not last long. Vehemently pausing, he cried—

"What do ye do when ye see a whale, men?"

"Sing out for him!" was the impulsive rejoinder from a score of clubbed[4] voices.

3. **bulwarks** (bul′wərks): above-deck part of a ship's side.

4. **clubbed**: united.

WORDS TO OWN
rejoinder (ri·join′dər) *n.*: answer.

"Good!" cried Ahab, with a wild approval in his tones; observing the hearty animation into which his unexpected question had so magnetically thrown them.

"And what do ye next, men?"

"Lower away, and after him!"

"And what tune is it ye pull to, men?"

"A dead whale or a stove[5] boat!"

More and more strangely and fiercely glad and approving grew the countenance of the old man at every shout; while the mariners began to gaze curiously at each other, as if marveling how it was that they themselves became so excited at such seemingly purposeless questions.

But, they were all eagerness again, as Ahab, now half-revolving in his pivot hole, with one hand reaching high up a shroud, and tightly, almost convulsively grasping it, addressed them thus—

"All ye mastheaders have before now heard me give orders about a white whale. Look ye! d'ye see this Spanish ounce of gold?"—holding up a broad bright coin to the sun—"it is a sixteen-dollar piece, men. D'ye see it? Mr. Starbuck, hand me yon top-maul."[6]

While the mate was getting the hammer, Ahab, without speaking, was slowly rubbing the gold piece against the skirts of his jacket, as if to heighten its luster, and without using any words was meanwhile lowly humming to himself, producing a sound so strangely muffled and inarticulate that it seemed the mechanical humming of the wheels of his vitality in him.

Receiving the top-maul from Starbuck, he advanced toward the mainmast with the hammer uplifted in one hand, exhibiting the gold with the other, and with a high raised voice exclaiming: "Whosoever of ye raises me a white-headed whale with a wrinkled brow and a crooked jaw; whosoever of ye raises me that white-headed whale, with three holes punctured in his starboard fluke[7]—look ye, whosoever of ye raises me that same white whale, he shall have this gold ounce, my boys!"

"Huzza! huzza!" cried the seamen, as with swinging tarpaulins they hailed the act of nailing the gold to the mast.

"It's a white whale, I say," resumed Ahab, as he threw down the top-maul; "a white whale. Skin your eyes for him, men; look sharp for white water; if ye see but a bubble, sing out."

All this while Tashtego, Daggoo, and Queequeg had looked on with even more intense interest and surprise than the rest, and at the mention of the wrinkled brow and crooked jaw they had started as if each was separately touched by some specific recollection.

"Captain Ahab," said Tashtego, "that white whale must be the same that some call Moby-Dick."

"Moby-Dick?" shouted Ahab. "Do ye know the white whale then, Tash?"

"Does he fantail[8] a little curious, sir, before he goes down?" said the Gay-Header deliberately.

"And has he a curious spout, too," said Daggoo, "very bushy, even for a parmacety,[9] and mighty quick, Captain Ahab?"

"And he have one, two, tree—oh! good many iron in him hide, too, Captain," cried Queequeg disjointedly, "all twiske-tee be-twisk, like him—him——" faltering hard for a word, and screwing his hand round and round as though uncorking a bottle—"like him—him——"

"Corkscrew!" cried Ahab, "aye, Queequeg, the harpoons lie all twisted and wrenched in him; aye, Daggoo, his spout is a big one, like a whole shock of wheat, and white as a pile of our Nantucket wool after the great annual sheepshearing; aye, Tashtego, and he fantails like a split jib in a squall. Death and devils! men, it is Moby-Dick ye have seen—Moby-Dick—Moby-Dick!"

"Captain Ahab," said Starbuck, who, with Stubb and Flask, had thus far been eyeing his superior with increasing surprise, but at last seemed struck with a thought which somewhat explained all the wonder. "Captain Ahab, I have heard of Moby-Dick—but it was not Moby-Dick that took off thy leg?"

"Who told thee that?" cried Ahab; then pausing, "Aye, Starbuck; aye, my hearties all round; it was Moby-Dick that dismasted me; Moby-Dick that brought me to this dead stump I stand on now. Aye, Aye," he shouted, with a terrific, loud, animal

---

5. **stove:** with a hole smashed in it.
6. **top-maul:** heavy wooden hammer.
7. **starboard fluke:** right-hand side of the whale's tail.

8. **fantail:** spread the tail like a fan.
9. **parmacety** (pär′mə·sed′ē): slang for "spermaceti" (a sperm whale).

sob, like that of a heart-stricken moose; "Aye, aye! it was that accursed white whale that razeed[10] me; made a poor pegging lubber[11] of me for ever and a day!" Then tossing both arms, with measureless <u>imprecations</u> he shouted out: "Aye, aye! and I'll chase him round Good Hope and round the Horn, and round the Norway Maelstrom, and round perdition's flames before I give him up. And this is what ye have shipped for, men! to chase that white whale on both sides of land, and over all sides of earth, till he spouts black blood and rolls fin out. What say ye, men, will ye splice[12] hands on it, now? I think ye do look brave."

"Aye, aye!" shouted the harpooners and seamen, running closer to the excited old man: "a sharp eye for the White Whale; a sharp lance for Moby-Dick!"

"God bless ye," he seemed to half sob and half shout. "God bless ye, men. Steward! Go draw the great measure of grog.[13] But what's this long face about, Mr. Starbuck; wilt thou not chase the White Whale? Art not game for Moby-Dick?"

"I am game for his crooked jaw, and for the jaws of Death too, Captain Ahab, if it fairly comes in the way of the business we follow; but I came here to hunt whales, not my commander's vengeance. How many barrels will thy vengeance yield thee even if thou gettest it, Captain Ahab? It will not fetch thee much in our Nantucket market."

"Nantucket market! Hoot! But come closer, Starbuck; thou requirest a little lower layer. If money's to be the measurer, man, and the accountants have computed their great countinghouse the globe, by girdling it with guineas, one to every three parts of an inch; then, let me tell thee, that my vengeance will fetch a great premium *here*!"

"He smites his chest," whispered Stubb, "what's that for? Methinks it rings most vast, but hollow."

"Vengeance on a dumb brute!" cried Starbuck, "that simply smote thee from blindest instinct! Madness! To be enraged with a dumb thing, Captain Ahab, seems blasphemous."

"Hark ye yet again—the little lower layer. All visible objects, man, are but as pasteboard masks.

But in each event—in the living act, the undoubted deed—there, some unknown but still reasoning thing puts forth the moldings of its features from behind the unreasoning mask. If man will strike, strike through the mask! How can the prisoner reach outside except by thrusting through the wall? To me, the White Whale is that wall, shoved near to me. Sometimes I think there's naught beyond. But 'tis enough. He tasks me; he heaps me; I see in him outrageous strength, with an <u>inscrutable</u> malice sinewing it. That inscrutable thing is chiefly what I hate; and be the White Whale agent, or be the White Whale principal, I will wreak that hate upon him. Talk not to me of blasphemy, man; I'd strike the sun if it insulted me. For could the sun do that, then could I do the other; since there is ever a sort of fair play herein, jealousy presiding over all creations. But not my master, man, is even that fair play. Who's over me? Truth hath no confines. Take off thine eye! More intolerable than fiends' glarings is a doltish stare! So, so; thou reddenest and palest; my heat has melted thee to anger-glow. But look ye, Starbuck, what is said in heat, that thing unsays itself. There are men from whom warm words are small indignity. I meant not to incense thee. Let it go. Look! see yonder Turkish cheeks of spotted tawn—living, breathing pictures painted by the sun. The pagan leopards—the unrecking and unworshipping things, that live; and seek, and give no reasons for the torrid life they feel! The crew, man, the crew! Are they not one and all with Ahab, in this matter of the whale? See Stubb! he laughs! See yonder Chilean! he snorts to think of it. Stand up amid the general hurricane, thy one tossed sapling cannot, Starbuck! And what is it? Reckon it. 'Tis but to help strike a fin; no wondrous feat for Starbuck. What is it more? From this one poor hunt, then, the best lance out of all Nantucket, surely he will not hang back, when every foremast-hand has clutched a whetstone? Ah! constrainings seize thee; I see! the billow lifts thee! Speak, but speak!—Aye, aye! thy silence, then, *that* voices thee. (*Aside*) Something shot from my dilated nostrils, he has inhaled it in his lungs.

---

10. **razeed** (rā·zēd′): to *razee* is to make a wooden warship lower by removing the upper deck.
11. **lubber:** big, slow, clumsy person.
12. **splice:** join.
13. **grog:** watered-down liquor drunk by sailors.

WORDS TO OWN

imprecations (im′pri·kā′shənz) *n. pl.*: curses.
inscrutable (in·skrōōt′ə·bəl) *adj.*: mysterious.

Starbuck now is mine; cannot oppose me now, without rebellion."

"God keep me!—keep us all!" murmured Starbuck lowly.

But in his joy at the enchanted, tacit acquiescence of the mate, Ahab did not hear his foreboding invocation; nor yet the low laugh from the hold; nor yet the presaging vibrations of the winds in the cordage; nor yet the hollow flap of the sails against the masts, as for a moment their hearts sank in. For again Starbuck's downcast eyes lighted up with the stubbornness of life; the subterranean laugh died away; the winds blew on; the sails filled out; the ship heaved and rolled as before. Ah, ye admonitions and warnings! Why stay ye not when ye come? But rather are ye predictions than warnings, ye shadows! Yet not so much predictions from without, as verifications of the foregoing things within. For with little external to constrain us, the innermost necessities in our being, these still drive us on.

"The measure! the measure!" cried Ahab.

Receiving the brimming pewter, and turning to the harpooneers, he ordered them to produce their weapons. Then ranging them before him near the capstan,[14] with their harpoons in their hands, while his three mates stood at his side with their lances, and the rest of the ship's company formed a circle round the group; he stood for an instant searchingly eyeing every man of his crew. But those wild eyes met his, as the bloodshot eyes of the prairie wolves meet the eye of their leader, ere he rushes on at their head in the trail of the bison; but, alas! only to fall into the hidden snare of the Indian.

"Drink and pass!" he cried, handing the heavy charged flagon to the nearest seaman. "The crew alone now drink. Round with it, round! Short drafts—long swallows, men; 'tis hot as Satan's hoof. So, so; it goes round excellently. It spiralizes in ye; forks out at the serpent-snapping eye. Well done; almost drained. That way it went, this way it comes. Hand it me—here's a hollow! Men, ye seem the years; so brimming life is gulped and gone. Steward, refill!

"Attend now, my braves. I have mustered ye all round this capstan; and ye, mates, flank me with your lances; and ye, harpooneers, stand there with your irons; and ye, stout mariners, ring me in, that I may in some sort revive a noble custom of my fisherman fathers before me. O men, you will yet see that—— Ha! boy, come back? bad pennies come not sooner. Hand it me. Why, now, this pewter had run brimming again, wert not thou St. Vitus's imp[15]—away, thou ague!

"Advance, ye mates! Cross your lances full before me. Well done! Let me touch the axis." So saying, with extended arm, he grasped the three level, radiating lances at their crossed center; while so doing, suddenly and nervously twitched them; meanwhile, glancing intently from Starbuck to Stubb, from Stubb to Flask. It seemed as though, by some nameless, interior volition, he would fain have shocked into them the same fiery emotion accumulated within the Leyden jar[16] of his own magnetic life. The three mates quailed before his strong, sustained, and mystic aspect. Stubb and Flask looked sideways from him; the honest eye of Starbuck fell downright.

"In vain!" cried Ahab; "but, maybe, 'tis well. For did ye three but once take the full-forced shock, then mine own electric thing, *that* had perhaps expired from out me. Perchance, too, it would have dropped ye dead. Perchance ye need it not. Down lances! And now, ye mates, I do appoint ye three cupbearers to my three pagan kinsmen there—yon three most honorable gentlemen and noblemen, my valiant harpooneers. Disdain the task? What, when the great Pope washes the feet of beggars, using his tiara for ewer?[17] Oh, my sweet cardinals! your own condescension, *that* shall bend ye to it. I do not order ye; ye will it. Cut

---

15. St. Vitus's imp: Saint Vitus is the patron saint of people ill with chorea, a nervous disorder characterized by irregular, jerking movements. An imp is a mischievous child or young demon. Ahab is complaining that the steward's clumsiness caused the pitcher of grog to be spilled.

16. Leyden jar: device for storing electrical charges.

17. tiara for ewer: literally, "crown for a pitcher"; a reference to the practice of the pope washing the feet of the poor on Holy Thursday, in imitation of Jesus' washing the feet of his disciples.

WORDS TO OWN

tacit (tas′it) *adj.*: implied but not expressed openly.

volition (vō·lish′ən) *n.*: will.

---

14. capstan: similar to a winch; a large cylinder, usually on a ship's deck, around which cables are wound to lift heavy objects such as anchors and weights.

Sailors—Companion to the Tailors (detail) (mid–19th century). Unsigned, attributed to John Cranch.
Oil on wood panel.

your seizings and draw the poles, ye harpooneers!"

Silently obeying the order, the three harpooneers now stood with the detached iron part of their harpoons, some three feet long, held, barbs up, before him.

"Stab me not with that keen steel! Cant[18] them; cant them over! know ye not the goblet end? Turn up the socket! So, so; now, ye cupbearers, advance. The irons! take them; hold them while I fill!" Forthwith, slowly going from one officer to the other, he brimmed the harpoon sockets with the fiery waters from the pewter.

"Now, three to three, ye stand. Commend the murderous chalices! Bestow them, ye who are now made parties to this indissoluble league. Ha! Starbuck! but the deed is done! Yon ratifying sun now waits to sit upon it. Drink, ye harpooneers! drink and swear, ye men that man the deathful whaleboat's bow—Death to Moby-Dick! God hunt us all, if we do not hunt Moby-Dick to his death!" The long, barbed steel goblets were lifted; and to cries and maledictions[19] against the White Whale, the spirits were simultaneously quaffed down with a hiss. Starbuck paled, and turned, and shivered. Once more, and finally, the replenished pewter went the rounds among the frantic crew; when, waving his free hand to them, they all dispersed; and Ahab retired within his cabin.

18. **cant:** overturn or tilt.

19. **maledictions** (mal′ə·dik′shənz): curses.

MAKING MEANINGS

First Thoughts

1. What words would you use to describe Captain Ahab? Do you pity him, fear him, or feel something else?

Shaping Interpretations

2. What are Starbuck's misgivings about Ahab's pursuit of the great white whale? What does this help us infer about Starbuck's **character?**

3. Why do you think Starbuck gives in to Ahab?

Reading Check

a. After his obsessive pacing of the deck, what command does Ahab issue to the crew? Why does Ahab meet with his crew?

b. What do you learn about Moby-Dick's appearance from Ahab's dialogue with his crew?

c. Toward the end of the chapter, what does Ahab order the mates to do with their lances?

d. Where does the narrative shift from Ishmael's **point of view** to an **omniscient** point of view? What details in this chapter could only be known by an omniscient narrator?

4. Explain the idea Ahab expresses in his famous **metaphor** comparing visible objects to "pasteboard masks" (page 317). What do you think he means when he says "strike through the mask"?

5. What **symbolic** meaning might the white whale have? (Recall Ahab's comment that the white whale "is that wall. . . . Sometimes I think there's naught beyond.")

6. What might the ship and crew **symbolize?** Do they form a microcosm—a world in miniature? If you see them as symbols, do you read the text differently? Explain.

7. What details in the drinking scene suggest a **parody** or mockery of a religious ritual? What might the scene signify about Ahab's quest?

8. What inferences can you draw about Ahab's **character** when he says "Talk not to me of blasphemy, man; I'd strike the sun if it insulted me" (page 317)? What did he say prior to this that sounded like blasphemy—that is, mockery of God?

9. Identify the details in this chapter that **foreshadow** disaster for the Pequod and its crew. What do you think will happen next?

Extending the Text

10. Who are Ahab and Ishmael in the Bible? Look up Ahab's story in 1 Kings 16:29–22:40 and Ishmael's story in Genesis 21:9–21. Why do you think Melville chose these names?

Following the ritual on the quarter-deck, in which Ahab fills the harpoon-tips with liquor and reveals the object of his chase, we hear three characters privately reflect on their journey's goal. Ahab recognizes himself as a driven man; Starbuck reflects on what he sees as the captain's insanity; and Stubb fatalistically resigns himself to whatever destiny may bring. That night a squall threatens to strike the ship, and the crew become tense. At last we are about to meet the object of Ahab's obsession—the white whale, Moby-Dick.

from Moby-Dick

I, Ishmael, was one of that crew; my shouts had gone up with the rest; my oath had been welded with theirs; and stronger I shouted, and more did I hammer and clinch my oath, because of the dread in my soul. A wild, mystical, sympathetical feeling was in me; Ahab's quenchless feud seemed mine. With greedy ears I learned the history of that murderous monster against whom I and all the others had taken our oaths of violence and revenge.

For some time past, though at intervals only, the unaccompanied, secluded White Whale had haunted those uncivilized seas mostly frequented by the sperm whale fishermen. But not all of them knew of his existence; only a few of them, comparatively, had knowingly seen him; while the number who as yet had actually and knowingly given battle to him, was small indeed. For, owing to the large number of whale-cruisers; the disorderly way they were sprinkled over the entire watery circumference, many of them adventurously pushing their quest along solitary latitudes, so as seldom or never for a whole twelvemonth or more on a stretch, to encounter a single news-telling sail of any sort; the inordinate length of each separate voyage; the irregularity of the times of sailing from home; all these, with other circumstances, direct and indirect, long obstructed the spread through the whole worldwide whaling fleet of the special individualizing tidings concerning Moby-Dick. It was hardly to be doubted, that several vessels reported to have encountered, at such or such a time, or on such or such a meridian, a sperm whale of uncommon magnitude and malignity,[1] which whale, after doing great mischief to his assailants, had completely escaped them; to some minds it was not an unfair presumption, I say, that the whale in question must have been no other than Moby-Dick. Yet as of late

---

1. malignity (mə·lig′nə·tē): intense ill will.

the sperm whale fishery had been marked by various and not unfrequent instances of great ferocity, cunning, and malice in the monster attacked; therefore it was, that those who by accident ignorantly gave battle to Moby-Dick; such hunters, perhaps, for the most part, were content to ascribe the peculiar terror he bred, more, as it were, to the perils of the sperm whale fishery at large, than to the individual cause. In that way, mostly, the disastrous encounter between Ahab and the whale had hitherto been popularly regarded.

And as for those who, previously hearing of the White Whale, by chance caught sight of him; in the beginning of the thing they had every one of them, almost, as boldly and fearlessly lowered for him, as for any other whale of that species. But at length, such calamities did ensue in these assaults—not restricted to sprained wrists and ankles, broken limbs, or devouring amputations—but fatal to the last degree of fatality; those repeated disastrous repulses, all accumulating and piling their terrors upon Moby-Dick; those things had gone far to shake the fortitude of many brave hunters, to whom the story of the White Whale had eventually come.

Nor did wild rumors of all sorts fail to exaggerate, and still the more horrify the true histories of these deadly encounters. For not only do fabulous rumors naturally grow out of the very body of all surprising terrible events—as the smitten tree gives birth to its fungi; but, in maritime life, far more than in that of terra firma, wild rumors abound, wherever there is any adequate reality for them to cling to. And as the sea surpasses the land in this matter, so the whale-fishery surpasses every other sort of maritime life, in the wonderfulness and fearfulness of the rumors which sometimes circulate there. For not only are whalemen as a body unexempt from that ignorance and superstitiousness hereditary to all sailors; but of all sailors, they are by all odds the most directly brought into contact with whatever is appallingly astonishing in the sea; face to face they not only eye its greatest marvels, but, hand to jaw, give battle to them. Alone, in such remotest waters, that though you sailed a thousand miles, and passed a thousand shores, you would not come to any chiseled hearthstone, or aught hospitable beneath that part of the sun; in such latitudes and longitudes, pursuing too such a calling as he does, the whaleman is wrapped by influences all tending to make his fancy pregnant with many a mighty birth.

No wonder, then, that ever gathering volume from the mere transit over the wildest watery spaces, the outblown rumors of the White Whale did in the end incorporate with themselves all manner of morbid hints, and half-formed fetal suggestions of supernatural agencies, which eventually invested Moby-Dick with new terrors unborrowed from anything that visibly appears. So that in many cases such a panic did he finally strike, that few who by those rumors, at least, had heard of the White Whale, few of those hunters were willing to encounter the perils of his jaw.

But there were still other and more vital practical influences at work. Not even at the present day has the original prestige of the sperm whale, as fearfully distinguished from all other species of the leviathan,[2] died out of the minds of the whalemen as a body. There are those this day among them, who, though intelligent and courageous enough in offering battle to the Greenland or right whale, would perhaps, either from professional inexperience, or incompetency, or timidity, decline a contest with the sperm whale; at any rate, there are plenty of whalemen, especially among those whaling nations not sailing under the American flag, who have never hostilely encountered the sperm whale, but whose sole knowledge of the leviathan is restricted to the ignoble monster primitively pursued in the North; seated on their hatches, these men will hearken with a childish fireside interest and awe, to the wild, strange tales of Southern whaling. Nor is the preeminent tremendousness of the great sperm whale anywhere more feelingly comprehended, than on board of those prows which stem him. . . .

So that overawed by the rumors and portents concerning him, not a few of the fishermen recalled, in reference to Moby-Dick, the earlier days of the sperm whale fishery, when it was

2. **leviathan** (lə·vī′ə·thən): huge sea monster.

WORDS TO OWN
ferocity (fə·räs′ə·tē) n.: fierce cruelty.

Painted sternboard from the ship *Mary and Susan*.

oftentimes hard to induce long-practiced right whalemen to embark in the perils of this new and daring warfare; such men protesting that although other leviathans might be hopefully pursued, yet to chase and point lance at such an apparition as the sperm whale was not for mortal man. That to attempt it, would be inevitably to be torn into a quick eternity. On this head, there are some remarkable documents that may be consulted.

Nevertheless, some there were, who even in the face of these things were ready to give chase to Moby-Dick; and a still greater number who, chancing only to hear of him distantly and vaguely, without the specific details of any certain calamity, and without superstitious accompaniments, were sufficiently hardy not to flee from the battle it offered.

One of the wild suggestings referred to, as at last coming to be linked with the White Whale in the minds of the superstitiously inclined, was the unearthly conceit that Moby-Dick was ubiquitous; that he had actually been encountered in opposite latitudes at one and the same instant of time.

Nor, credulous as such minds must have been, was this conceit altogether without some faint show of superstitious probability. For as the secrets of the currents in the seas have never yet been divulged, even to the most erudite research; so the hidden ways of the sperm whale when beneath the surface remain, in great part, unaccountable to his pursuers; and from time to time have originated the most curious and contradictory speculations regarding them, especially concerning the mystic modes whereby, after sounding to a great depth, he transports himself with such vast swiftness to the most widely distant points.

It is a thing well known to both American and English whale-ships, and as well a thing placed upon authoritative record years ago by Scoresby, that some whales have been captured far north in

WORDS TO OWN

apparition (ap'ə·rish'ən) *n.*: unexpected sight or ghostlike figure that appears suddenly.

ubiquitous (yo͞o·bik'wə·təs) *adj.*: everywhere at the same time.

erudite (er'yo͞o·dīt') *adj.*: scholarly; well informed.

the Pacific, in whose bodies have been found the barbs of harpoons darted in the Greenland seas. Nor is it to be gainsaid, that in some of these instances it has been declared that the interval of time between the two assaults could not have exceeded very many days. Hence, by inference, it has been believed by some whalemen, that the Nor'west Passage,[3] so long a problem to man, was never a problem to the whale. . . .

Forced into familiarity, then, with such prodigies as these; and knowing that after repeated, intrepid assaults, the White Whale had escaped alive; it cannot be much matter of surprise that some whalemen should go still further in their superstitions; declaring Moby-Dick not only ubiquitous, but immortal (for immortality is but ubiquity in time); that though groves of spears should be planted in his flanks, he would still swim away unharmed; or if indeed he should ever be made to spout thick blood, such a sight would be but a ghastly deception; for again in unensanguined[4] billows hundreds of leagues away, his unsullied jet would once more be seen.

But even stripped of these supernatural surmisings, there was enough in the earthly make and incontestable character of the monster to strike the imagination with unwonted power. For, it was not so much his uncommon bulk that so much distinguished him from other sperm whales, but, as was elsewhere thrown out—a peculiar snow-white wrinkled forehead, and a high, pyramidical white hump. These were his prominent features; the tokens whereby, even in the limitless, uncharted seas, he revealed his identity, at a long distance, to those who knew him.

The rest of his body was so streaked, and spotted, and marbled with the same shrouded hue, that, in the end, he had gained his distinctive appellation of the White Whale; a name, indeed, literally justified by his vivid aspect, when seen gliding at high noon through a dark blue sea, leaving a milky-way wake of creamy foam, all spangled with golden gleamings.

Nor was it his unwonted magnitude, nor his remarkable hue, nor yet his deformed lower jaw,

3. **Nor'west Passage:** waterways that connect the Atlantic and Pacific Oceans, discovered in the mid-1800s.
4. **unensanguined** (un·en·saŋ′gwind): unbloodied.

A Whaling Scene (mid–19th century). Unsigned. Oil on canvas.

that so much invested the whale with natural terror, as that unexampled, intelligent malignity which, according to specific accounts, he had over and over again evinced in his assaults. More than all, his treacherous retreats struck more of dismay than perhaps aught else. For, when swimming before his exulting pursuers, with every apparent symptom of alarm, he had several times

bruited[6] ashore, were by no means unusual in the fishery; yet, in most instances, such seemed the White Whale's infernal aforethought of ferocity, that every dismembering or death that he caused, was not wholly regarded as having been inflicted by an unintelligent agent.

Judge, then, to what pitches of inflamed, distracted fury the minds of his more desperate hunters were impelled, when amid the chips of chewed boats, and the sinking limbs of torn comrades, they swam out of the white curds of the whale's direful wrath into the serene, exasperating sunlight, that smiled on, as if at a birth or a bridal.

His three boats stove around him, and oars and men both whirling in the eddies, one captain, seizing the line-knife from his broken prow, had dashed at the whale, as an Arkansas duelist at his foe, blindly seeking with a six-inch blade to reach the fathom-deep life of the whale. That captain was Ahab. And then it was, that suddenly sweeping his sickle-shaped lower jaw beneath him, Moby-Dick had reaped away Ahab's leg, as a mower a blade of grass in the field. No turbaned Turk, no hired Venetian or Malay, could have smote him with more seeming malice. Small reason was there to doubt, then, that ever since that almost fatal encounter, Ahab had cherished a wild vindictiveness against the whale, all the more fell for that in his frantic morbidness he at last came to identify with him, not only all his bodily woes, but all his intellectual and spiritual exasperations. The White Whale swam before him as the monomaniac incarnation of all those malicious agencies which some deep men feel eating in them, till they are left living on with half a heart and half a lung. That intangible malignity which has been from the beginning; to whose dominion even the modern Christians ascribe one-half of the worlds; which the ancient Ophites of the East reverenced in their statue devil—Ahab did not fall down and worship it like them; but deliriously transferring its idea to the abhorred White Whale, he pitted himself, all mutilated, against it. All that most maddens and torments; all that stirs up the lees of things; all truth with malice in it; all that cracks the sinews and cakes the brain; all the subtle

Peabody Essex Museum, Salem, Massachusetts. Photo by Mark Sexton (M171/09).

been known to turn round suddenly, and, bearing down upon them, either stave[5] their boats to splinters, or drive them back in consternation to their ship.

Already several fatalities had attended his chase. But though similar disasters, however little

5. **stave:** smash.

6. **bruited** (brōōt′id): reported; rumored.

demonisms of life and thought; all evil, to crazy Ahab, were visibly personified, and made practically assailable in Moby-Dick. He piled upon the whale's white hump the sum of all the general rage and hate felt by his whole race from Adam down; and then, as if his chest had been a mortar, he burst his hot heart's shell upon it.

It is not probable that this monomania in him took its instant rise at the precise time of his bodily dismemberment. Then, in darting at the monster, knife in hand, he had but given loose to a sudden, passionate, corporal animosity; and when he received the stroke that tore him, he probably but felt the agonizing bodily laceration, but nothing more. Yet, when by this collision forced to turn toward home, and for long months of days and weeks, Ahab and anguish lay stretched together in one hammock, rounding in midwinter that dreary, howling Patagonian Cape; then it was, that his torn body and gashed soul bled into one another; and so interfusing, made him mad. That it was only then, on the homeward voyage, after the encounter, that the final monomania seized him, seems all but certain from the fact that, at intervals during the passage, he was a raving lunatic; and, though unlimbed of a leg, yet such vital strength yet lurked in his Egyptian chest, and was moreover intensified by his delirium, that his mates were forced to lace him fast, even there, as he sailed, raving in his hammock. In a straitjacket, he swung to the mad rockings of the gales. And, when running into more sufferable latitudes, the ship, with mild stunsails spread, floated across the tranquil tropics, and, to all appearances, the old man's delirium seemed left behind him with the Cape Horn swells, and he came forth from his dark den into the blessed light and air; even then, when he bore that firm, collected front, however pale, and issued his calm orders once again; and his mates thanked God the direful madness was now gone; even then, Ahab, in his hidden self, raved on. Human madness is oftentimes a cunning and most feline thing. When you think it fled, it may have but become transfigured into some still subtler form. Ahab's full lunacy subsided not, but deepeningly contracted; like the unabated Hudson, when that noble Northman flows narrowly, but unfathomably through the Highland gorge. But, as in his narrow-flowing monomania, not one jot of Ahab's broad madness had been left behind;

so in that broad madness, not one jot of his great natural intellect had perished. That before living agent, now became the living instrument. If such a furious trope[7] may stand, his special lunacy stormed his general sanity, and carried it, and turned all its concentrated cannon upon its own mad mark; so that far from having lost his strength, Ahab, to that one end, did now possess a thousandfold more potency than ever he had sanely brought to bear upon any one reasonable object. . . .

Now, in his heart, Ahab had some glimpse of this, namely: all my means are sane, my motive and my object mad. Yet without power to kill, or change, or shun the fact, he likewise knew that to mankind he did long dissemble; in some sort, did still. But that thing of his dissembling was only subject to his perceptibility, not to his will determinate. Nevertheless, so well did he succeed in that dissembling, that when with ivory leg he stepped ashore at last, no Nantucketer thought him otherwise than but naturally grieved, and that to the quick, with the terrible casualty which had overtaken him.

The report of his undeniable delirium at sea was likewise popularly ascribed to a kindred cause. And so too, all the added moodiness which always afterward, to the very day of sailing in the *Pequod* on the present voyage, sat brooding on his brow. Nor is it so very unlikely, that far from distrusting his fitness for another whaling voyage, on account of such dark symptoms, the calculating people of that prudent isle were inclined to harbor the conceit, that for those very reasons he was all the better qualified and set on edge, for a pursuit so full of rage and wildness as the bloody hunt of whales. Gnawed within and scorched without, with the unfixed, unrelenting fangs of some incurable idea; such an one, could he be found, would seem the very man to dart his iron and lift his lance against the most appalling of all brutes. Or, if for any reason thought to be corporeally <u>incapacitated</u> for that, yet such an one would seem superlatively competent to cheer and howl on his underlings to the attack. But be all this as it may, certain it is, that with the mad secret of his unabated rage bolted up and keyed in him, Ahab had purposely sailed upon the present voyage with the one only and all-engrossing object of hunting the White Whale. Had any one of his old acquaintances on shore but half dreamed of what was lurking in him then, how soon would their aghast and righteous souls have wrenched the ship from such a fiendish man! They were bent on profitable cruises, the profit to be counted down in dollars from the mint. He was intent on an audacious, immitigable, and supernatural revenge.

Here, then, was this gray-headed, ungodly old man, chasing with curses a Job's whale[8] round the world, at the head of a crew, too, chiefly made up of mongrel renegades, and castaways, and cannibals—morally enfeebled, also, by the incompetence of mere unaided virtue or right-mindedness in Starbuck, the invulnerable jollity of indifference and recklessness in Stubb, and the pervading mediocrity in Flask. Such a crew, so officered, seemed specially picked and packed by some infernal fatality to help him to his monomaniac revenge. How it was that they so aboundingly responded to the old man's ire—by what evil magic their souls were possessed, that at times his hate seemed almost theirs; the White Whale as much their insufferable foe as his; how all this came to be—what the White Whale was to them, or how to their unconscious understandings, also, in some dim, unsuspected way, he might have seemed the gliding great demon of the seas of life—all this to explain, would be to dive deeper than Ishmael can go. The subterranean miner that works in us all, how can one tell whither leads his shaft by the ever shifting, muffled sound of his pick? Who does not feel the irresistible arm drag? What skiff in tow of a seventy-four[9] can stand still? For one, I gave myself up to the abandonment of the time and the place; but while yet all a-rush to encounter the whale, could see naught in that brute but the deadliest ill.

8. Job's whale: curse or affliction. In the Bible, Job was visited with grievous afflictions as a test of his faith in God.
9. skiff . . . seventy-four: small boat being pulled by a larger one.

7. trope (trōp): figure of speech.

WORDS TO OWN

incapacitated (in′kə·pas′ə·tāt′id) *adj.*: disabled.

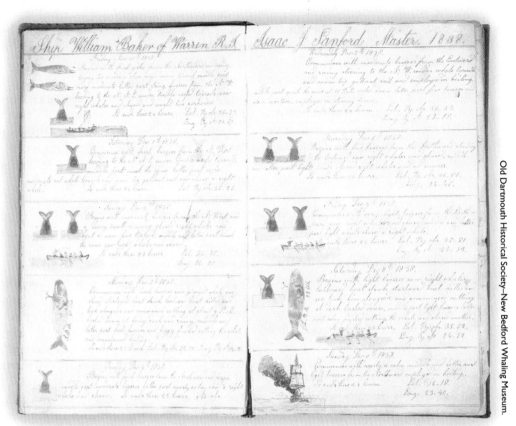

Page from whaling logbook.

MAKING MEANINGS

First Thoughts

1. What idea or statement in this chapter did you respond to most strongly? Explain.

Reading Check

With a partner or two, chart the **major events** in the development of Ahab's obsession with the white whale.

Shaping Interpretations

2. After Moby-Dick's attack, how is Ahab's rational behavior deceptive—but how does it also help him toward his goal? What does this tell you about Ahab's personality?

3. What supernatural qualities do the sailors attribute to Moby-Dick? What is the effect of turning Moby-Dick into a mythical monster?

4. The final paragraph draws a picture of the *Pequod*'s crew as they travel the world's oceans on Ahab's quest. What is the narrator's attitude here toward the ship's captain, the crew, and the quest?

Extending the Text

5. What **images** used to describe Moby-Dick in this chapter suggest beauty as well as horror? Can you think of any other instances (from life or literature) where these two qualities are combined in one person or event or thing?

6. An **epic** is a long narrative, written in heightened language, which recounts a quest undertaken by a heroic character who embodies the values of a particular society. (Homer's *Odyssey*, for example, is a famous epic of ancient Greece.) In what ways does *Moby-Dick* resemble an epic? What mid-nineteenth-century American values might Ahab embody?

CHOICES: Building Your Portfolio

Writer's Notebook

1. Collecting Ideas for a Controversial Issue

Melville's novel is full of ideas that you could use as the focus of a persuasive essay. Pick a passage that contains such an idea. How does the passage connect to life today? What do you think it means? Do you disagree with the passage? Save your notes for the Writer's Workshop on page 331.

Interpreting a Symbol

2. Who Knows, Exactly?

The British novelist and poet D. H. Lawrence wrote this about *Moby-Dick*:

> A hunt. The last great hunt.
> For what?
> For Moby-Dick, the huge white sperm whale: who is old, hoary, monstrous, and swims alone; who is unspeakably terrible in his wrath, having so often been attacked; and snow-white.
> Of course he is a symbol.
> Of what?
> I doubt that even Melville knew exactly. That's the best of it.
>
> —D. H. Lawrence

In a brief essay, explain what you think Moby-Dick **symbolizes**—insofar as you can tell from what you've read. Cite passages to support your interpretation.

Critical Thinking / Speaking and Listening

3. Analyzing Ahab

In a panel discussion with two or three classmates, analyze the **character** of Captain Ahab. To prepare your analysis, refer to your reading notes and gather your data in a chart like the following:

What we know about Ahab:	
From his speech	
From his actions	
From his appearance	
From his thoughts	

Comparing Ideas

4. Ahab and Transcendentalism

Write a brief essay comparing Ahab's **monologue** in "The Quarter-Deck" (beginning on page 317 with "Hark ye yet again . . .") to Transcendentalist ideas (see pages 210–212). In what ways does the speech reflect Transcendentalist thought, and in what ways does it reject it? In your essay, you might want to include quotations from Emerson or Thoreau.

Creative Writing

5. The Voice of Ahab

We hear most of the events of *Moby-Dick* from Ishmael's **point of view.** Now let Captain Ahab speak. In two or three paragraphs, write his thoughts on the night after the ritual on the quarter-deck. What does Ahab want? What does he fear? How does he feel about the crew?

Crossing the Curriculum: Science

6. Whales Today

Research and deliver a brief oral report to your class on some aspect of whales or whaling that interests you: for example, what the major types of whales are, how the whale population has changed since the 1850s, what whaling activities continue today, and what efforts have been made to preserve whales from extinction. Accompany your report with graphs, maps, or photographs. (The Internet should be a good source of information.)

READ ON

Time Is But a Stream

In *The Survival of the Bark Canoe* (Farrar, Straus & Giroux), John McPhee explores the New England wilderness on a no-frills paddling trip in a hand-made birch-bark canoe, much as Henry David Thoreau once did. Thoreau's own journey is chronicled in *A Week on the Concord and Merrimack Rivers* (Ticknor and Fields).

Civil Disobedience

In the struggle for India's independence, Mohandas K. (Mahatma) Gandhi successfully put Thoreau's ideas on nonviolent resistance into action to effect change. Gandhi's successes helped inspire Martin Luther King, Jr., in the United States. Find out more about Gandhi's achievements in *An Autobiography: The Story of My Experiments with Truth* (Greenleaf Books) and in the award-winning film *Gandhi* (1982), directed by Richard Attenborough and featuring Ben Kingsley in the title role.

More Unwholesome Houses

Shirley Jackson's eerie fiction often focuses on houses that are not quite . . . normal. In *We Have Always Lived in the Castle* (Viking Press), two odd sisters live in the strangest house in town. In *The Haunting of Hill House* (Viking Penguin), a group of psychics tries to discover if Hill House really *is* haunted. The latter book was adapted into a classic horror film, *The Haunting* (1963), directed by Robert Wise and starring Julie Harris.

A Smorgasbord of Scares

The critic Alberto Manguel defines "fantastic literature"—including horror, fantasy, and magic realism—as "the impossible seeping into the possible." *Black Water* and *Black Water 2* (Clarkson N. Potter), edited by Manguel, are anthologies of short "fantastic literature" by an international list of authors including Edgar Allan Poe, Nathaniel Hawthorne, Julio Cortázar, Ursula K. Le Guin, and Ryunosuke Akutagawa.

Save the Whales

As a result of so much whaling, several species of whale are now endangered. The Canadian environmentalist Farley Mowat pleads for the preservation of these intelligent creatures in *A Whale for the Killing* (Little, Brown), his real-life account of a tormented whale trapped in a Newfoundland tide pool.

Writer's Workshop

PERSUASIVE WRITING

CONTROVERSIAL ISSUE

In "Resistance to Civil Government," Thoreau tries to persuade people to look at government in a new way—a way that certainly not everyone would agree with. Disagreement is the essence of controversy, and a controversial issue is one that reasonable people can argue convincingly from two or more vantage points. Many current local, national, and world events qualify as controversial issues, since people may take sides on them. When you take up a controversial issue in writing, your primary goals are to communicate your views on the issue and to persuade your readers to take your position seriously—even to change their minds. To achieve these goals, you will draw on an arsenal of persuasive techniques to present and defend your point of view.

Prewriting

1. **Finding out what you care about.**   If you've kept any of the Writer's Notebook activities from these collections, you might already have ideas for a controversial issue you'd like to write about. If not, one way to generate ideas for an issue worth writing about is to list topics. On a sheet of paper, draw a vertical line down the center. In the left-hand column, brainstorm a list of controversial topics. Your possible topics could relate to your town, your city, your state, or the nation, or they might be suggested by subjects you've been studying in school. (Controversy can even stem from a literary work: Did Madeline Usher really come back from the dead? Was there really a raven in the young scholar's room?) In the right-hand column, write ideas for possible issues connected with these topics. List the ideas in question form. For example, your list might include the topic "drinking among young people." A question suggested by this topic might be, "Should the drinking age be raised to twenty-three?" If you want to explore a controversial literary issue, your list could include relevant quotations from a story or poem you want to work with. Think of issues that have not only captured your intellectual interest but also stirred your emotions.

   Another way to discover current controversial issues is to read the editorial page in your local newspaper and to closely watch television news programs. Should your city have a teen curfew? Should your state require helmets for bicycle riders? Should the federal government set aside land to protect an endangered species? In each case, the issue is a matter of dispute about which reasonable people disagree.

Technology HELP

See Writer's Workshop 2 CD-ROM. *Assignment: Controversial Issue.*

ASSIGNMENT
   Write an essay in which you take a stand on a controversial issue that you feel strongly about.

AIM
   To shape your audience's opinions and feelings; to persuade them to take your position seriously; to urge an audience to take an action or change a stance on an issue.

AUDIENCE
   Individuals or a group interested in your issue; your teacher; your classmates.

Strategies for Elaboration: Finding a Topic

- Read the Letters to the Editor sections in your school and local newspapers.
- Watch local and national news programs on television.
- Discuss current controversial issues with family and friends.
- Go over your reading notes and other class notes to find a controversial literary issue you might want to argue.
- Consider both sides of the issues that interest you, and develop a point of view for each issue.

2. **Selecting and defining one issue.**   Put an asterisk next to the issues about which you have the strongest feelings and have the most to say. Share these preferred issues with one or two classmates, explaining your positions. (Listen to the ideas of your peers, too, to help them clarify their thinking.) Use these questions to help you choose an issue:

- Is the issue important to you?
- Can the issue be argued, and can the arguments be supported with evidence? (For example, whether life in the city is better than life in the country is a matter of personal preference; it can't be supported with evidence.)
- Is there an audience that is interested in this topic and that you would like to convince?

3. **Trying out a position statement.**   Write a brief, direct statement of where you stand on the issue. This is your **position statement,** or **proposition**—the thesis statement of your persuasive essay. If, for example, your question is "Should there be a teen curfew to curtail juvenile crime?" then your position statement might read, "The most effective way to cut down on juvenile crime in our city is to implement a teen curfew." Your position statement might be one, two, or three sentences long. In many cases, a position statement indicates one or two broad, fundamental reasons for a writer's position.

4. **Setting up a pro-con table.**   It's important that you understand and anticipate all the arguments and counterarguments that your issue gives rise to. Make a two-column chart headed "Pro" on the left-hand side and "Con" on the right-hand side. In the Pro column, jot down all the reasons you can think of for the "in favor" side of the issue; in the Con column, list all the reasons you can think of for the "against" side. (See page 333 for an example.)

5. **Listing arguments and counterarguments.**   Using your pro-con table as a basis, write a more extensive list of possible arguments to support your side and a list of possible objections, or counterarguments, for the other side. Once again, share your prewriting with a group of classmates. They might provide for your position support that you have overlooked, and they can comment upon the validity of your arguments.

What happens if, as you collect arguments for and against the issue, you come across an opposing argument that you can't refute? In fairness, you can't just ignore such an argument; you must acknowledge it and affirm its validity. This is called **conceding a point.** It's not a weakness to give the opposing side a nod; in fact, it's a sign of strength that shows you have thoroughly considered all sides and are being fair.

Model

Topic: Should there be a citywide teen curfew?

Pro	Con
controls gang violence	prohibits legitimate activities
minimizes auto accidents	requires expanded police force
reduces underage drinking	further overloads justice system with people who may have broken no other law
minimizes vandalism	takes away liberties from those not involved in criminal activities

6. **Searching for evidence.**   You should do some research to find objective and reliable support for your position. This may include library research to find irrefutable facts—such as statistics, examples, and anecdotes. It may also include interviews with people who, as authorities on the issue, can offer expert opinions. Brainstorm a list of possible research sources you can consult for evidence in support of your issue. Then begin your search.

Drafting

1. **Your credibility is at stake.**   To be truly effective, your essay will have to be well reasoned and feature plenty of support that no one could argue with (examples, expert opinions, quotations, statistics), that is, any sound evidence that makes a good case for your position. Be sure to deal thoroughly and fairly with possible arguments against your stance.

2. **Crafting an effective introduction.**   In persuasive writing, it's important to make your readers care about the issue from the outset. Convince them that the issue affects them—even if they're on the other side. Begin with an attention-getting anecdote or example, a surprising statistic, or a rhetorical question. (A rhetorical question is a question asked to make people think; it is not a "real" question that actually requires an answer. See page 105.) Then, clearly identify the issue, and state your position on it.

3. **Organizing your work.**   There are three major ways to organize a controversial-issue essay:

   • **Order of importance.**   You can develop your argument according to order of importance, beginning with either the most important or the least important reason for supporting your position. If, for example, you

begin with the most important reason, then you would move methodically through your other reasons, ending with the least important. It can
also be effective to save the heaviest ammunition for last, leading from the
least to the most important reason.

- **Chronological order.**   The order in which events occur in time is
  chronological order. Presenting your points in this order is especially
  helpful in making cause-and-effect relationships clear.
- **Logical order.**   In logical order, you present your opponents' positions
  or arguments and then present your refutations of them through comparison and contrast. You may present all the objections first, followed by all
  your rebuttals; or you may move back and forth from each objection to
  its respective rebuttal.

4. **Using logical appeals.**   Rather than merely listing abstract arguments to
   support your position, make your arguments concrete. Whenever possible,
   use your library research to add documented facts, anecdotes, quotations,
   and expert opinions. Provide real-life examples of the causes and effects of
   adopting the position you are arguing for or against. An extended example,
   or case study, can sometimes be sustained throughout an essay or even
   be used as an organizational device. Well-reasoned hypothetical cases, or
   scenarios, can sometimes be used for support as well, especially if you make
   the scenario believable. All of these are **logical appeals**—appeals that are
   made to the audience's reason. Logical appeals include both reasons and
   evidence, and they make your arguments more appealing to the audience
   because they engender trust. They also make it harder for the other side
   to challenge you and for your audience to reject your reasoning. But watch
   out for *overgeneralization* (broad statements that lack sufficient support),
   oversimplification (concentrating on only one or a few aspects of a complex
   issue), and other lapses in logic. Signs of sloppy thinking and a lack of
   objectivity can diminish your audience's trust in you.

5. **Appealing to emotions.**   The power of persuasive writing resides not
   just in logical argument, but also in emotional appeals. To develop emotional
   appeals, think about the evidence you've collected that will speak to your
   readers' hearts: Examples, vivid details, anecdotes, and personal experiences can all be used effectively.

6. **The power of loaded words.**   You are also using emotional appeals
   when you take advantage of the power of **connotative language.** Every
   word has a **denotative meaning**—its dictionary definition—as well as its
   connotative meaning—the feelings or attitudes the word suggests.
   Words like *integrity, honor,* and *steadfastness* have positive associations, or
   connotations, and if you used them in describing a political candidate, you
   would be giving him or her excellent "press." Words like *rigidity, self-interest,*
   and *stubbornness,* on the other hand, have negative connotations, and your
   candidate would appear less desirable if described with those words.
   Connotative words are "loaded" words that pack a punch. Used sparingly
   and carefully, they will cause readers to become not only intellectually involved, but emotionally involved as well. Consider the following example
   from Thoreau's "Resistance to Civil Government."

> I saw that, if there was a *wall of stone* between me and my towns-men, there was a still more *difficult* one to climb or *break through*, before they could get to be as free as I was. I did not for a moment feel *confined*, and the walls seemed a great waste of *stone and mortar*. I felt as if I alone of all my townsmen had paid my tax. They plainly did not know how to treat me, but behaved like persons who are *underbred*. In every *threat* and in every compliment there was a *blunder*; for they thought that my chief desire was to stand the other side of that *stone wall*.
>
> —Henry David Thoreau

Language Handbook HELP

See Combining Sentences for Variety, page 1238.

The italicized words and phrases have strong connotative meanings. In choosing these particular words, Thoreau is able to evoke an emotional response that extends beyond the literal meaning of the passage. His feelings about the restrictive nature of society come through loud and clear.

7. **Audience.** When writing about a controversial issue, it's crucial to consider your audience's response, since affecting their opinions is your primary goal. Think about how much your audience already knows about your issue, and provide background information accordingly. Also, think about whether they are likely to agree or disagree with your position. If they are inclined to disagree, put yourself in their shoes: What counterarguments will be the most compelling? What points might you have to concede?

8. **Closing your essay.** The conclusion of your essay should leave the audience feeling that an issue has been adequately and fairly explored. You might repeat your position statement at the end but in different words than those used at the beginning. Or, you might make a strong statement about what might happen if the course of action you recommend is not followed.

Evaluating and Revising

1. **Peer review.** Exchange essays with a classmate. As you read each other's essays, consider the following questions:
   - Is the issue well defined and interesting to you?
   - Is the writer's position clearly stated at the beginning of the essay?
   - Does the writer use both logical and emotional appeals effectively?
   - Which reasons are most persuasive? least persuasive? Which should be developed further?
   - Is the order in which reasons are presented effective? If not, what changes should the writer make?
   - Is the evidence relevant and credible?
   - Does the writer convincingly rebut arguments against his or her position?
   - Does the writer seem to have considered the intended audience?

■ *Evaluation Criteria*

A good controversial issue essay
1. defines the issue and the writer's stand on it
2. includes a strong and credible position statement (thesis)
3. develops a position clearly, in convincing and well-developed arguments
4. includes and answers important counterarguments, showing consideration of the audience's point of view
5. is organized logically
6. has a conclusion that shows that the writer is clear about the outcome he or she desires

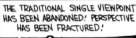

Revision
STRATEGIES

Review your essay or speech for unclear writing. Make abstract ideas concrete. Use straightforward diction and clear syntax. If any sentences are convoluted, rewrite them.

Communications
Handbook
HELP

See Proofreading.

2. **Self-evaluation.** Pay especially close attention to the response you get from peers or others who read your draft and who disagree with your position. They can provide you with especially useful feedback as to the persuasive power of your essay. If you can win their respect with your arguments, then you may be able to influence their opinions, too. Have you listened to constructive criticism with an open mind?

Underline passages that seemed to make your readers puzzled, impatient, or bored, and revise them so that they are stronger, both in terms of logic and language. Varying your sentence structure can also help you retain your readers' interest. However, don't assume that disagreement on your audience's part means ineffectiveness on your part. People can disagree with even the most powerful persuasive writing.

Language Workshop

KEEPING IT IN BALANCE: PARALLEL STRUCTURE

When you link ideas within a sentence, be aware of balance in your writing. You can make your writing smoother and more balanced by using **parallel structure,** placing equivalent ideas in the same grammatical form.

In the following sentence, the boldface structures are *not* parallel:

> The professor said that **to read Emerson** is more useful than **watching television.**

"To read" is an infinitive form, but "watching" is a gerund. You can make the structures parallel by changing the sentence so that both forms are equivalent, as in the following example:

> The professor said that **reading Emerson** is more useful than **watching television.** [gerunds in both cases]

The key to parallel structure is balance: You use the same grammatical form to express equal, or parallel, ideas. If you use a gerund to express one idea, use another gerund to express the idea to which it is linked. Pair an infinitive with an infinitive, a clause with a clause, a noun with a noun, and so on.

Here are some situations when you would want to be certain that your sentences have parallel structure.

1. Use parallel structure when you link coordinate ideas.

> Emerson believed **that people must be true to their unique capabilities** and **that they must practice self-reliance.** [noun clause paired with noun clause]

2. Use parallel structure to compare or contrast ideas.

> Emerson's **lectures** were often more accessible than his **essays.** [noun contrasted with a noun]

3. Use parallel structure to link ideas when you are using **correlative conjunctions**—pairs of conjunctions such as *both . . . and, either . . . or, neither . . . nor,* or *not only . . . but also.*

> Emerson was *not only* **a great lecturer** *but also* **a gifted poet.**

Writer's Workshop Follow-Up: Revising

Parallel structures are important in persuasive writing because they clearly organize ideas in a sentence and create a smooth, authoritative rhythm. Reread the persuasive essay you wrote on a controversial issue for the Writer's Workshop (page 331), and correct any lapses in parallelism.

Technology HELP

See Language Workshop CD-ROM. *Key word entry: parallel structure.*

Language Handbook HELP

See Using Parallel Structure, pages 1235-1236.

Try It Out

Rewrite the following sentences, making them parallel in structure.

1. To Emerson, it was important that people be nonconformists, true to themselves, and listen to their intuition.

2. Thoreau's writing style involves the use of paradox, imagery, and he also used many figures of speech.

3. Many students find it easier to read Thoreau's *Walden* than reading anything by Emerson.

Reading for Life

Evaluating Credibility of Sources

Situation

Suppose you share Herman Melville's interest in nineteenth-century American whaling and want to write a book for children about this subject. You should begin by identifying various sources of information that will help you plan your book. Then, evaluate the credibility of these sources.

Strategies

Evaluate the author's or director's credentials.

- Does the author have any special training in the field?
- Is the author associated with a respected organization, such as a university, museum, scientific institute, or professional organization?
- Has he or she produced other books, articles, or video material on the same or on a similar subject? If so, read a few reviews to get a sense of the person's reliability.
- Does the author have any ulterior motives or conflicts of interest that might affect his or her credibility?

For Internet sources, evaluate the quality of the Web site.

- Is the Web site well-planned and well-edited, without spelling and other errors?
- Does the Web site offer a comprehensive overview, or

is it just bare-bones with few necessary details?

For video sources, evaluate the accuracy of the images.

- Are the images well researched and faithful to the facts? Is there distortion through clever editing?

Evaluate the timeliness.

- Has the information been eclipsed by more recent research?

Using the Strategies

Examine the material in the box on this page.

1. Which print authors would probably provide the most reliable and most relevant information? Why?

2. Which Internet sources would you use? Why?

3. Which sources would you not use? Why?

Extending the Strategies

- Think of another subject you would like to learn more about. Jot down questions you want answered. Then, do research in a library and on the Internet and make a list of three print and electronic sources you could refer to with confidence. If you like, write up your research findings. You might also suggest additional aspects of the subject that need to be investigated.

Sources on Nineteenth-Century American Whaling:

Books

Creighton, Margaret S. *Rites & Passages: The Experience of American Whaling, 1830–1870.* Cambridge: Cambridge University Press, 1995.

——.*Dogwatch and Liberty Days: Seafaring Life in the 19th Century.* Salem, MA: Peabody Museum Press, 1982.

Gourley, Catherine. *Hunting Neptune's Giants: True Stories of American Whaling.* Brookfield, Conn.: Millbrook Publishers, 1995.

Murphy, Jim. *Gone a Whaling: The Lure of the Sea & the Hunt for the Great Whale.* New York: Houghton Mifflin Company, 1998.

Films

Moby Dick (1956), directed by John Huston.

Free Willy 2: The Adventure Home (1995), directed by Dwight H. Little.

Internet

New Bedford Whaling Museum History and Mission, http://www.whalingmuseum.org/about.htm

History of Whaling, http://curry.edschool.virginia.edu/go/Whales/HisWhaling.HTML

Whales on the Net, http://whales.magna.com.au/HISTORY/index.html

Eden's Killer Whale Museum, http://www.acr.net.au/whales/history.html

Note: URLs for illustrative purposes only; may not be current.

Learning for Life

A Model of Self-Reliance

Problem

Emerson's self-reliant individual is a nonconformist who finds strength and fulfillment in solitude and in being true to his or her unique nature. "Nothing is at last sacred but the integrity of your own mind," Emerson tells us. In *Walden,* Thoreau makes a similar observation: "If a man does not keep pace with his companions, perhaps it is because he hears a different drummer." Who is the self-reliant individual? What can we learn from the person who "hears a different drummer"?

Project

Research a living or dead person who you think fulfills Emerson's ideal of the self-reliant individual—someone who stands apart from the multitude and exemplifies integrity, nonconformity, and uniqueness. Demonstrate how that person can be a role model for us all.

Preparation

1. Reread the excerpt from Emerson's essay "Self-Reliance," and make notes on what qualities he identifies as being central to the self-reliant individual. If you disagree with any of his points, make note of your disagreements. Add any qualities that you think are necessary for a self-reliant person to possess.

2. You may already have some ideas about people, living or dead, who strike you as being models of self-reliance. If you don't, brainstorm with your teacher, family, or classmates. Look through magazines, newspapers, encyclopedias, and books for ideas. Perhaps someone you know fits your definition of a self-reliant person.

Procedure

1. List the criteria you've come up with for a truly self-reliant person. Your criteria may be based solely on Emerson's ideas, or you may introduce some of your own criteria.

2. Research and take notes on the person you have chosen as an example of a self-reliant person. If the person is someone in your community or someone you know well, tape-record an interview with him or her.

Presentation

Present what you have learned in one of the following formats (or another format your teacher approves):

1. **Encyclopedia Entry**
   Write an encyclopedia entry about the person. Instead of simply presenting a narrative of the events of the person's life, focus on his or her accomplishments and philosophy. Demonstrate how this person is, or was, truly self-reliant. Include visual images.

2. **Short Story**
   Write a short story about the self-reliant person you researched. Describe the person's daily life, thoughts and feelings, and the reactions of others to his or her individuality and accomplishments. Publish your story in your school newspaper, or read it to your class.

3. **School for Self-Reliance**
   Prepare a brochure advertising a private school founded by the person you researched. The school should be dedicated to building self-reliant individuals, and it should emphasize the virtues and knowledge considered most important by the founder. Include a statement of the school's philosophy and an outline of the course of study—what subjects will be taught, what extracurricular activities will be encouraged, how classes will be run, and so on. Illustrate your brochure.

Processing

What did you learn about Emerson's principles of self-reliance by completing this project? Is it really possible to live a self-reliant life? Is it desirable to be a nonconformist? Are there any drawbacks to being self-reliant? Write your reflections for your portfolio.

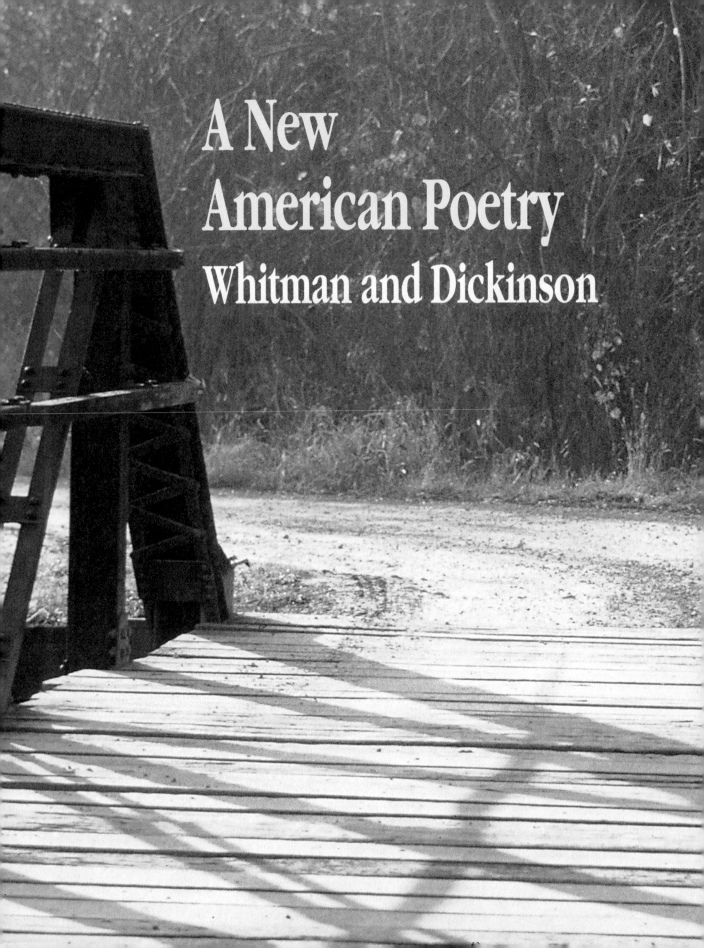

A New American Poetry
Whitman and Dickinson

A New American Poetry
Whitman and Dickinson

by **John Malcolm Brinnin**

If you want me again look for me under your boot-soles.

—Walt Whitman

This is my letter to the World
That never wrote to me—

—Emily Dickinson

The two greatest American poets of the nineteenth century were so different from one another, both as artists and as personalities, that only a nation as varied in character as the United States could possibly contain them.

Walt Whitman worked with bold strokes on a broad canvas; Emily Dickinson worked with the delicacy of a miniaturist. Whitman was sociable and gregarious, a traveler; Dickinson was private and shy, content to remain in one secluded spot through all of her lifetime.

While both poets were close observers of people and of life's daily activities, the emphasis they gave to what impressed them was so distinct as to make them opposites. Whitman was the public spokesman of the masses and the prophet of progress. "I hear America singing," he said, and he joined his eloquent voice to that chorus. Dickinson was the obscure homebody, peering through the curtains of her house in a country village, who found in nature metaphors for the spirit and recorded them with no thought of an audience. Whitman expected that his celebration of universal brotherhood and the bright destiny of democracy would be carried like a message into the future. Dickinson expected nothing but oblivion for the poetry that was her "letter to the World."

Whitman and Dickinson were true innovators who expressed themselves in poetic voices that broke with the established literary traditions of their time.

Two Seams in the Fabric

Whitman's career might be regarded as another American success story—the story of an amiable young man who drifted into his thirties, working at one job after another, never "finding himself" until, at his own expense, he boldly published *Leaves of Grass* (1855). The book made him famous around the world. Dickinson's career as a poet began after her death. It is one of those ironies of history in which a writer dies unknown, only to have fame thrust upon her by succeeding generations.

Walt Whitman.

Drawing by David Levine. Reprinted with permission from *The New York Review of Books.* Copyright © 1970 NYREV, Inc.

> A great poem is for ages and ages in common and for all degrees and complexions and all departments and sects and for a woman as much as a man and a man as much as a woman. A great poem is no finish to a man or a woman but rather a beginning.
>
> —Walt Whitman,
> *Leaves of Grass*

(12.)

Introduction to the London Edition.

Leaves of Grass 1881

America - That new world in so many respects besides its geography - has perhaps afforded nothing even in the astonishing products of the fields of its politics, its mechanical invention, material growth, & the like, more original, more autochthonic, than its late contribution in the field of literature; the Poem, or poetic writings, named *Leaves of Grass*, which in the following pages, we present sent to the British public.

"Introduction" to the London edition of *Leaves of Grass,* 1861. Autograph manuscript.

The Pierpont Morgan Library/Art Resource, NY.

Whitman and Dickinson represent two distinct seams in the fabric of American poetry, one slightly uneven and the other carefully measured and stitched tight. Whitman was as extravagant with words as he was careless with repetition and self-contradiction. Aiming for the large, overall impression, he filled his pages with long lists as he strained to catalog everything in sight. His technique is based on **cadence**—the long, easy sweep of sound that echoes the Bible and the speeches of orators and preachers. This cadence is the basis for his **free verse:** poetry without rhyme or meter.

Manuscript for "I died for Beauty" by Emily Dickinson.

By permission of the Houghton Library, Harvard University, Cambridge, Massachusetts.

> The proof of a poet is that his country absorbs him as affectionately as he has absorbed it.
>
> — Walt Whitman, *Leaves of Grass*

Revisions made by Walt Whitman to his poem "O Captain! My Captain!"

Library of Congress.

O the bleeding drops of red

O CAPTAIN! MY CAPTAIN!

BY WALT WHITMAN.

I.

O CAPTAIN! my captain! our fearful trip is done;
The ship has weathered every rack, the prize we sought is won;
The port is near, the bells I hear, the people all exulting,
While follow eyes the steady keel, the vessel grim and daring.
But O heart! heart! heart!
Leave you not the little spot,
Where on the deck my captain lies,
Fallen cold and dead.

II.

O captain! my captain! rise up and hear the bells;
Rise up! for you the flag is flung, for you the bugle trills;
For you bouquets and ribboned wreaths, for you the shores a-crowd-
ing:
For you they call, the swaying mass, their eager faces turning.
O captain! dear father!
This arm beneath your head
It is some dream that on the deck
You 've fallen cold and dead.

III.

My captain does not answer, his lips are pale and still;
My father does not feel my arm, he has no pulse nor will.
But the ship, the ship is anchored safe, its voyage closed and done;
From fearful trip the victor ship comes in with object won!
Exult, O shores! and ring, O bells!
But I, with silent tread,
Walk the spot my captain lies
Fallen cold and dead.

beneath your head and sound.

Emily Dickinson's bedroom.

Dress that belonged to Emily Dickinson.

Dickinson, on the other hand, wrote with the precision of a diamond cutter. Meticulous in her choice of words, she aimed to evoke the feelings of things rather than simply to name them. She was always searching for the one right phrase that would fix a thought in the mind. Her technique is economical, and her neat stanzas are controlled by the demands of rhyme and the meters she found in her hymn book.

Dickinson used precise language and unique poetic forms to simultaneously reveal and conceal her private thoughts and feelings. Whitman, on the other hand, let loose his passion, philosophy, and observations in a torrent of language shaped by cadence rather than traditional meter.

Models for Future Poets

As the history of our poetry shows, both modes of expression have continued to be used by American writers. Both poets have served as models for twentieth-century poets who have been drawn to the visions they fulfilled and the techniques they mastered. Poetry as public speech written in the cadences of free verse remains a part of our literature; poetry as private observation, carefully crafted in rhyme and meter, still attracts young writers who tend to regard poems as experiences rather than as statements.

Walt Whitman
August 3 1884

Leaves

of

Grass.

Brooklyn, New York:
1855.

Emily Dickinson

Like you, I belong to yesterday,
to the bays where
day is anchored to
wait for its hour.

Like me, you belong to today,
the progression of that hour
when what is unborn
begins to throb.

We are cultivators of
the unsayable, weavers
of singulars, migrant
workers in search of
floating gardens as yet
unsown, as yet unharvested.

—Lucha Corpi,
translated from the Spanish by
Catherine Rodríguez-Nieto

The coequal importance of the two poetic methods has never been more clearly affirmed than in the following words by Ezra Pound (see page 773). Pound speaks for himself here as a poet more attuned to the abbreviations of Dickinson than to the expansiveness of Whitman. Nevertheless, he offers in this poem a benediction that represents the feeling of every poet who has envied the gemlike artistry of Dickinson and the all-embracing power of Whitman:

A Damascus blade gleaming and glancing in the sun was her wit. Her swift poetic rapture was like the long glistening note of a bird one hears in the June woods at high noon, but can never see. Like a magician she caught the shadowy apparitions of her brain and tossed them in startling picturesqueness to her friends, who, charmed with their simplicity and homeliness as well as profundity, fretted that she had so easily made palpable the tantalizing fancies forever eluding their bungling, fettered grasp.

—*from* Susan Dickinson's obituary for Emily Dickinson, published in the *Springfield Republican,* May 18, 1886

A Pact

I make a pact with you, Walt Whitman—
I have detested you long enough.
I come to you as a grown child
Who has had a pig-headed father;
I am old enough now to make friends.
It was you that broke the new wood,
Now is a time for carving.
We have one sap and one root—
Let there be commerce between us.

—Ezra Pound

Quickwrite

Whitman was a public poet; Dickinson, a private one. Yet both have had a lasting influence on American poets who have followed them. Write your thoughts and feelings about poetry. What do you think is the value of poetry? What roles can poets and poetry serve in contemporary life?

Whitman
Neruda

from Song of Myself

1.

I celebrate myself, and sing myself,
And what I assume you shall assume,
For every atom belonging to me as good belongs to you.

I loaf and invite my soul,
I lean and loaf at my ease observing a spear of summer grass.

My tongue, every atom of my blood, form'd from this soil, this air,
Born here of parents born here from parents the same, and their
    parents the same,
I, now thirty-seven years old in perfect health begin,
Hoping to cease not till death.

Creeds and schools in abeyance,
Retiring back a while sufficed at what they are, but never forgotten,
I harbor for good or bad, I permit to speak at every hazard,
Nature without check with original energy.

—Walt Whitman, *from Leaves of Grass*

Walt Whitman

(1819–1892)

Less than a hundred years after the United States was founded, the new nation found its voice in a poet who spoke to all the world. His name was Walt Whitman, and he struck a note in literature that was as forthright, as original, and as deeply charged with democracy's energies as the land that produced him.

Student of the World

Whitman was born on May 31, 1819, to parents of Dutch and English descent. They kept a farm in West Hills, Long Island, in what is today the town of Huntington. His father's ancestors had come from England only twenty years after the landing of the *Mayflower* and had settled in Connecticut. On his mother's side, his ancestors were among the early immigrants from Holland who settled on Manhattan Island and along the Hudson River. Whitman and his seven brothers and sisters were able to assume their essential American-ness with an uncommon confidence. They knew their American grandparents, and they grew up in circumstances that allowed them both the communal experience of country life and the experience of Brooklyn, a new city on its way to becoming a metropolis.

Here young Walter went to school until he was eleven. He then worked as an office clerk and printer's assistant, and for a time he taught school. On weekends spent along the beaches and in the woods of Long Island, Whitman read Sir Walter Scott, the Bible, Shakespeare, Homer, Dante, and ancient Hindu poetry. He never became a scholar; he never went to college.

Before Whitman was twenty, his feeling for the written word and his fascination with the boomtown atmosphere of Brooklyn led him into journalism. After ten years of this, he took a kind of working vacation—a difficult overland trip by train, horse-drawn coach, and riverboat to New Orleans. There he put his journalistic talent to work for the *Crescent* and his own talent for observation to work for himself. After a few months, he returned to New York by way of the Great Lakes and a side trip to Niagara Falls. By this time Whitman had added to his limited sense of America the experience of a wilderness surrendering its vastness to civilization. He also had become acquainted with the entirely alien culture that French Catholic New Orleans represented to him.

Back in Brooklyn, Whitman accepted an offer to become editor of the *Brooklyn Freeman*. For the next six or seven years, he supplemented his income as a part-time carpenter and building contractor. All this while, he was keeping notebooks and quietly putting together the sprawling collection of poems that would transform his life and change the course of American literature.

The Making of a Masterpiece

In 1855, Whitman published his collection at his own expense under the title *Leaves of Grass*. Since the book was too boldly new and strange to win the attention of reviewers or readers who had fixed ideas about poetry, its publication went all but unnoticed. To stir up interest in the book, he sent samples to people whose endorsement he thought might be useful. One of these samples reached Ralph Waldo Emerson, who at once wrote to Whitman the most important letter Whitman would ever receive:

Concord, Massachusetts, 21 July, 1855

Dear Sir—I am not blind to the worth of the wonderful gift of *Leaves of Grass*. I find it the most extraordinary piece of wit and wisdom that America has yet contributed. I am very happy in reading it, as great power makes us happy. It meets the demand I am always making of what seemed the sterile and stingy Nature, as if too much handiwork, or too much lymph in the temperament, were making our Western wits fat and mean.

I give you joy of your free and brave thought. I have great joy in it. I find incomparable things said incomparably well, as they must be. I find the courage of treatment

go.hrw.com

LEO 11-7

which so delights us, and which large perception only can inspire.

I greet you at the beginning of a great career, which yet must have had a long foreground somewhere, for such a start. I rubbed my eyes a little, to see if this sunbeam were no illusion; but the solid sense of the book is a sober certainty. It has the best merits, namely, of fortifying and encouraging.

I did not know until I last night saw the book advertised in a newspaper that I could trust the name as real and available for a post-office. I wish to see my benefactor, and have felt much like striking my tasks and visiting New York to pay you my respects.

R. W. Emerson

The "long foreground" of which Emerson wrote had not been the careful, confident period of preparation to which many poets devote themselves before they are ready to publish. Instead, it had been a precarious existence. Journalism had kept Whitman going financially, but not even the editorials he wrote for the *Brooklyn Eagle* had brought him distinction. On the surface, at least, his "long foreground" of preparation had been a mixture of hack work and jack-of-all-trades ingenuity.

By the time he was ready to declare himself a poet and to publish the first version of his book, Walt Whitman was unique. *Leaves of Grass* is a masterpiece that Whitman was to expand and revise through many editions. Its process of growth did not end until the ninth, "deathbed" edition was published in 1891, thirty-six years after its first appearance. It is a spiritual autobiography that tells the story of an enchanted observer who says who he is at every opportunity and claims what he loves by naming it. "Camerado," he wrote, "this is no book / Who touches this touches a man."

In the Crowd, but Not of It

The figure we know today as Walt Whitman was conceived and created by the poet himself. Whitman endorsed his "image" and sold it to the public with a promoter's skill worthy of P. T. Barnum, the great show manager of the nineteenth century. At first glance that figure is a bundle of contradictions. Whitman seems to have had the theatrical flair of a con artist and the selfless dignity of a saint; the sensibility of an artist and the carefree spirit of a hobo; the blustery egotism of a braggart and the demure shyness of a shrinking violet. On second glance these contradictions disappear: Walt Whitman was everything he seemed to be. The figure he so carefully crafted and put on display was not a surrogate, but the man himself.

Walt Whitman.

Courtesy of Ohio Wesleyan University, Bayley-Whitman Collection, Delaware, Ohio.

"One would see him afar off," wrote the great naturalist John Burroughs, "in the crowd but not of it—a large, slow-moving figure, clad in gray, with broad-brimmed hat and gray beard—or, quite as frequently, on the front platform of the street horse-cars with the driver. . . . Whitman was of large mold in every way, and of bold, far-reaching schemes, and is very sure to fare better at the hands of large men than of small. The first and last impression which his personal presence always made upon one was of a nature wonderfully gentle, tender, and benignant. . . . I was impressed by the fine grain and clean, fresh quality of the man. . . . He always had the look of a man who had just taken a bath."

If there is a side of Whitman that today we would associate with "image building," or self-promotion, there is nothing in his poetry to suggest that it was anything but the product of the kind of genius that permanently changes the history of art. He modified standard, "King's English" diction and abandoned traditional rhyme schemes and formal meters in favor of the rhythms and speech patterns of free verse.

Everything Under the Sun

The result was poetry that could sing and speak of everything under the sun. Its sweep was easy and its range was broad. Suddenly, poetry was no longer a matter of organized word structures that neatly clicked shut at the last line; instead, it was a series of open-ended units of rhythm that flowed one into the other and demanded to be read in their totality.

> **T**he result was poetry that could sing and speak of everything under the sun.

"Whitman throws his chunky language at the reader," writes the critic Paul Zweig. "He cajoles and thunders; he chants, celebrates, chuckles, and caresses. He spills from his capacious American soul every dreg of un-Englishness, every street sound thumbing its nose at traditional subject matter and tone. Here is Samson pulling the house of literature down around his ears, yet singing in the ruins."

Walt Whitman had invented a way of writing poetry that perfectly accommodated his way of seeing. His form is loose enough to allow for long lists and catalogs abundant in detail; it is also flexible enough to include delicate moments of lyricism as well as stretches of blustering oratory. This form served Whitman as observer and prophet—as a private man tending the wounded in the hospital wards of the Civil War, and as the public man who gave voice to the grief of a nation in his great elegy for the slain Abraham Lincoln, "When Lilacs Last in the Dooryard Bloom'd."

An American Epic

When Whitman died in 1892, he had met a great personal goal. He had enlarged the possibilities of American poetry to include the lyricism of simple speech and the grand design of the epic.

How is *Leaves of Grass* like an epic? Who is its hero? What is its action? The hero is the poet, and he is a hero not of the ancient past but of the future. As in all epics, the action takes the form of a journey. In *Leaves of Grass,* the journey is the one the speaker takes as he becomes a poet:

> I am the poet of the Body and I am the poet of
> the Soul . . .
> I am the poet of the woman the same as the
> man . . .
> I am not the poet of goodness only, I do not
> decline to be the poet of wickedness
> also. . . .

By the end of his epic journey, which even takes him down into a kind of hell, the poet has also been transformed. The "I" has become identified with every element in the universe and has been reborn as something divine. The poet has become the saving force that Whitman believed was the true role of the American poet.

Nothing quite like it had ever been done in America before.

Before You Read

I HEAR AMERICA SINGING

Make the Connection

Work of Their Own

This famous lyric appears in *Leaves of Grass* and serves to introduce one of the poet's major themes: America's cultural diversity. In this poem, Whitman celebrates work through the "varied carols" of men and women who take pride in their occupations.

Quickwrite

Why do you think a poet who celebrates American culture would focus on work songs rather than on love songs or some other kind of song? Write down the sorts of jobs you would expect to be celebrated in a truly American epic written today.

Elements of Literature

Catalog

One of the most obvious characteristics of Whitman's poetry is his frequent use of **catalogs**—long lists of related things, people, or events. Keep an eye out for catalogs in this poem and others by Whitman.

I Hear America Singing

Walt Whitman

I hear America singing, the varied carols I hear,
Those of mechanics, each one singing his as it should be blithe and
    strong,
The carpenter singing his as he measures his plank or beam,
The mason singing his as he makes ready for work, or leaves off
    work,
5 The boatman singing what belongs to him in his boat, the deckhand
    singing on the steamboat deck,
The shoemaker singing as he sits on his bench, the hatter singing as
    he stands,
The wood-cutter's song, the plowboy's on his way in the
    morning, or at noon intermission or at sundown,
The delicious singing of the mother, or of the young wife at work, or
    of the girl sewing or washing,
Each singing what belongs to him or her and to none else,
The day what belongs to the day—at night the party of young
10 fellows, robust, friendly,
Singing with open mouths their strong melodious songs.

Construction of the Dam (1937) by
William Gropper. Mural study,
Department of the Interior,
National Park Service.

National Museum of American Art,
Washington, D.C./Courtesy Art Resource, NY.

MAKING MEANINGS

First Thoughts

1. Imagine what kinds of singing Whitman might hear if he were alive today. In what ways might these "songs" be different from those he heard in his own time? In what ways would they be the same as what he heard? Before you answer, review your Quickwrite notes.

Shaping Interpretations

2. Perhaps what Whitman has in mind here are not the actual work songs associated with various trades, but something more subtle. What would you say this poem is really about?

3. A feeling of acceptance, even of contentment, runs throughout the sounds of these many voices. Considering the long hours and small pay of laborers in the nineteenth century, would you say Whitman is romanticizing or idealizing their lot? Or would you say the songs he hears are expressions of independence and joy in life? Support your response with specific references to the poem.

Make the Connection

The Poet as Director

Here the speaker both ob-
serves and participates in the
diversity of American experience. Whitman carefully juxtaposes different scenes and
emotions in these movielike
glimpses into the broad
American scene. The speaker
presents himself as though
he were not only the cinema-
tographer who shoots the
pictures but also the director
behind each scene who
arranges just what each frame
will look like.

Reading Skills and Strategies

Summarizing a Text

As you read this poem, pay attention to the arrangement of
details and images. Then, as an
aid in understanding the text,
briefly summarize the scene
presented in each stanza.

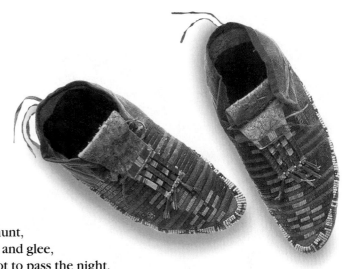

from Song of Myself

Walt Whitman

10.

Alone far in the wilds and mountains I hunt,
Wandering amazed at my own lightness and glee,
In the late afternoon choosing a safe spot to pass the night,
Kindling a fire and broiling the fresh-kill'd game,
5 Falling asleep on the gather'd leaves with my dog and gun by my side.

The Yankee clipper is under her sky-sails,° she cuts the sparkle and scud,°
My eyes settle the land, I bend at her prow or shout joyously from the deck.

The boatmen and clam-diggers arose early and stopt for me,
I tuck'd my trowser-ends in my boots and went and had a good time;
10 You should have been with us that day round the chowder-kettle.

I saw the marriage of the trapper in the open air in the far west, the bride was a red girl,
Her father and his friends sat near cross-legged and dumbly smoking, they had moccasins to
    their feet and large thick blankets hanging from their shoulders,
On a bank lounged the trapper, he was drest mostly in skins, his luxuriant beard and curls
    protected his neck, he held his bride by the hand,
She had long eyelashes, her head was bare, her coarse straight locks descended upon her
    voluptuous limbs and reach'd to her feet.

6. sky-sails: small sails atop a square-rigged mast. **scud:** windblown sea spray or foam.

15 The runaway slave came to my house and stopt outside,
    I heard his motions crackling the twigs of the woodpile,
    Through the swung half-door of the kitchen I saw him limpsy° and weak,
    And went where he sat on a log and led him in and assured him,
    And brought water and fill'd a tub for his sweated body and bruis'd feet,
    And gave him a room that enter'd from my own, and gave him some coarse clean
20   clothes,
    And remember perfectly well his revolving eyes and his awkwardness,
    And remember putting plasters on the galls° of his neck and ankles;
    He stayed with me a week before he was recuperated and pass'd north,
    I had him sit next me at table, my fire-lock lean'd in the corner.

    17. limpsy: limp; exhausted.
    22. galls: sores.

Lost on the Prairie (1837) by Alfred Jacob Miller. Watercolor on paper (9¼″ × 13½″).
Stark Museum of Art, Orange, Texas.

MAKING MEANINGS

First Thoughts

1. What **images** of sight, touch, and sound in this poem are most vivid to you?

Shaping Interpretations

2. In the five stanzas of this poem, the speaker observes and participates in five American scenes. Look at the summaries you made while reading, and describe the scene in each stanza. What feelings did each scene evoke?

3. Whitman changes the **tone** of this poem when he describes the fourth and fifth scenes. Identify the tone of the first three scenes. What is the tone of the last two scenes? What effect do you think the poet hoped to create by changing the tone?

4. When you read the poem aloud, what repetitions of sentence patterns help to create a **cadence**—a rhythmic rise and fall of your voice as the lines are spoken aloud? What feelings does the cadence create?

5. In the last scene, the "runaway slave" is one of thousands who entrusted their lives to those who would help them escape. What do you think the stanza—especially the last line—shows about the speaker's relationship with his guest?

Connecting with the Text

6. If you could drop yourself into one particular American setting today, which would you choose? Explain your response.

ELEMENTS OF LITERATURE

Free Verse

Today we are so used to poetry written in free verse that we take it for granted. But in Whitman's time, Americans preferred poetry that was like the poetry being written in England; they expected a poem to show the very strictest concern for **meter** and **rhyme.** Thus, Whitman's sprawling lines were revolutionary, as was his daring use of American slang, foreign words, and words he occasionally made up to suit his purpose.

Free verse is poetry that is written without concern for regular rhyme schemes and meter. But free verse is not really free at all. Whitman abandoned meter and regular rhyme schemes, but he made full use of these other literary elements:

- **Alliteration:** the repetition of similar consonant sounds
- **Assonance:** the repetition of similar vowel sounds
- **Imagery:** the use of language to evoke visual pictures, as well as sensations of smell, hearing, taste, and touch
- **Onomatopoeia:** the use of words whose sounds echo their meaning (such as *buzz*)
- **Parallel structure:** the repetition of the same or similar words, phrases, clauses, or sentences

When you read Whitman's lines aloud, you hear **cadence,** the run of words that rise and fall in emphasis when he has a particular point to make and measures his lines to emphasize it. As you can see from Whitman's poems, cadence does not depend on any strict count of stressed syllables.

Poets who, like Whitman, choose to write in cadence have nothing but their own sense of balance and proportion to tell them when a line should end and when it should continue. They must rely completely on their own sense of spacing and timing, and on their own feelings about what sounds right to them.

In the twentieth century, many poets have accepted the challenge of writing in free verse, trusting their own sense of balance and measure. A poem written in regular meter might be compared to a metronome, which keeps a predictable, mechanical beat. Free verse, on the other hand, might be compared to the style of a jazz drummer, who may vary the beat throughout a performance.

Reading aloud. To best hear Whitman's cadences, you should read his poems aloud. In the collection opener, "Song of Myself," Number 1 (page 347), you should hear no fewer than thirty-three occurrences of the same consonant sound. What sound do you hear? What other examples of **repetition** help create the **rhythms** and music in Whitman's supposedly "free" verse?

Make the Connection

"All these I feel or am"

Much of Whitman's work is distinguished by his attempt to erase the line between observer and object. The poet does this in order to—imaginatively speaking—*become* the thing or person he is talking about. Whitman is capable not only of sympathy, but also of *empathy*—the ability to share in another's thoughts or feelings. This excerpt from the thirty-third section of "Song of Myself" includes one of Whitman's most famous lines: "I am the man, I suffer'd, I was there." Through empathy, Whitman explores the greatness of heart that characterizes some unlikely heroes.

Reading Skills and Strategies

Supporting Inferences with Text Evidence

Throughout "Song of Myself," Whitman honors individuals whose hardships and courageous acts make them true heroes. As you read, write down words and phrases that reveal Whitman's ability to feel empathy for those quite different from himself.

from **Song of Myself**

Walt Whitman

from **33.**

I understand the large hearts of heroes,
The courage of present times and all times,
How the skipper saw the crowded and rudderless wreck of
    the steam-ship, and Death chasing it up and down the
    storm,
How he knuckled tight and gave not back an inch, and was
    faithful of days and faithful of nights,
And chalk'd in large letters on a board, *Be of good cheer, we*
5   *will not desert you;*
How he follow'd with them and tack'd with them three days
    and would not give it up,
How he saved the drifting company at last,
How the lank loose-gown'd women look'd when boated from
    the side of their prepared graves,
How the silent old-faced infants and the lifted sick, and the
    sharp-lipp'd unshaved men;
10 All this I swallow, it tastes good, I like it well, it becomes mine,
I am the man, I suffer'd, I was there.°

The disdain and calmness of martyrs,
The mother of old, condemn'd for a witch, burnt with dry
    wood, her children gazing on,
The hounded slave that flags in the race, leans by the fence,
    blowing, cover'd with sweat,
The twinges that sting like needles his legs and neck, the
15   murderous buckshot and the bullets,
All these I feel or am.

1–11. I understand . . . I was there: This stanza was inspired by an actual incident that occurred in 1853. According to reports in the New York *Weekly Tribune* of January 21, 1854, the ship *San Francisco* sailed from New York City on December 22, 1853, destined for South America. A violent storm hit the ship several hundred miles out of port, washing many passengers overboard. The captain of another ship helped rescue the survivors. A copy of the newspaper story was found among Whitman's papers after his death.

A Ride for Liberty—The Fugitive Slaves (c. 1862) by Eastman Johnson. Oil on board
(22″ × 26¼″).

I am the hounded slave, I wince at the bite of the dogs,
Hell and despair are upon me, crack and again crack the
    marksmen,
I clutch the rails of the fence, my gore dribs,° thinn'd with the   **19. dribs:** dribbles.
    ooze of my skin,
20 I fall on the weeds and stones,
The riders spur their unwilling horses, haul close,
Taunt my dizzy ears and beat me violently over the head with
    whip-stocks.

Agonies are one of my changes of garments,
I do not ask the wounded person how he feels, I myself
    become the wounded person,
25 My hurts turn livid upon me as I lean on a cane and observe.

I am the mash'd fireman with breast-bone broken,
Tumbling walls buried me in their debris,
Heat and smoke I inspired,° I heard the yelling shouts of my   **28. inspired:** breathed in.
    comrades,
I heard the distant click of their picks and shovels,
30 They have clear'd the beams away, they tenderly lift me forth.

I lie in the night air in my red shirt, the pervading hush is for
    my sake,
Painless after all I lie exhausted but not so unhappy,
White and beautiful are the faces around me, the heads are
    bared of their fire-caps,
The kneeling crowd fades with the light of the torches.

35 Distant and dead resuscitate,
They show as the dial or move as the hands of me, I am the
    clock myself.

I am an old artillerist, I tell of my fort's bombardment,
I am there again.

Again the long roll of the drummers,
40 Again the attacking cannon, mortars,
Again to my listening ears the cannon responsive.

I take part, I see and hear the whole,
The cries, curses, roar, the plaudits for well-aim'd shots,
The ambulanza° slowly passing trailing its red drip,
Workmen searching after damages, making indispensable
45   repairs,
The fall of grenades through the rent roof, the fan-shaped
    explosion,
The whizz of limbs, heads, stone, wood, iron, high in the air.

Again gurgles the mouth of my dying general, he furiously
    waves with his hand,
He gasps through the clot *Mind not me—mind—the*
    entrenchments.

44. ambulanza (äm·bo͞o·länt′sə):
Italian for "ambulance."

MAKING MEANINGS

First Thoughts

1. How did you respond to Whitman's **catalog** of heroic individuals? Which details packed the strongest emotional punch?

Shaping Interpretations

2. Look back at your reading notes. What words and phrases indicate Whitman's empathy with heroic people? What **images** of sight and sound help us feel we also are there?

3. At what moments does the speaker restate the point that "I am the man, I suffer'd, I was there"? What is the effect of these restatements?

4. How would you describe the speaker's **tone**? What are his feelings for these heroes?

5. Notice the way Whitman alternates between groups of very long lines and groups of very short lines. What is the reason for each short line? How would you use your voice in reading each short line aloud?

6. What do the heroes Whitman describes suggest about the poet's concept of heroism?

Connecting with the Text

7. Whitman empathizes with people by using the pronoun *I*. How does his use of the **first-person point of view** affect you as you read this poem?

Extending the Text

8. If you could add a contemporary hero to this poem, whom would you choose, and why?

Highly Personal

In this final song, Whitman restates some of the **themes** that have run throughout "Song of Myself." The poet weaves these themes in and out of this final verse like a composer filling a song with familiar refrains. Since the most insistently present element throughout "Song of Myself" is the mind and spirit of the speaker himself, this passage is highly personal. True to his nature, Whitman mocks his own egotism. But, true to his confidence in himself, he also proclaims his importance—and his inescapability.

Reading Skills and Strategies

Comparing Themes Across Texts

The final section of "Song of Myself" is a coda—a summing up and restatement of the entire poem's themes. As you read this concluding section of the poem, write down your observations about how particular lines and phrases echo themes and concepts you've already encountered in the Whitman poems you've read.

from Song of Myself

Walt Whitman

52.

The spotted hawk swoops by and accuses me, he complains
    of my gab and my loitering.

I too am not a bit tamed, I too am untranslatable,
I sound my barbaric yawp over the roofs of the world.

The last scud° of day holds back for me,
It flings my likeness after the rest and true as any on the
    shadow'd wilds,
5 It coaxes me to the vapor and the dusk.

I depart as air, I shake my white locks at the runaway sun,
I effuse° my flesh in eddies, and drift it in lacy jags.

I bequeath myself to the dirt to grow from the grass I love,
10 If you want me again look for me under your boot-soles.

You will hardly know who I am or what I mean,
But I shall be good health to you nevertheless,
And filter and fiber your blood.

Failing to fetch me at first keep encouraged,
15 Missing me one place search another,
I stop somewhere waiting for you.

4. **scud:** windblown mist and low clouds.
8. **effuse:** spread out.

Michael O'Shaughnessy/Red Crane Books.

Jimmy Santiago Baca.

Who Understands Me but Me

Jimmy Santiago Baca

They turn the water off, so I live without water,
they build walls higher, so I live without treetops,
they paint the windows black, so I live without sunshine,
they lock my cage, so I live without going anywhere,
5 they take each last tear I have, I live without tears,
they take my heart and rip it open, I live without heart,
they take my life and crush it, so I live without a future,
they say I am beastly and fiendish, so I have no friends,
they stop up each hope, so I have no passage out of hell,
10 they give me pain, so I live with pain,
they give me hate, so I live with my hate,
they have changed me, and I am not the same man,
they give me no shower, so I live with my smell,
they separate me from my brothers, so I live without brothers,
15 who understands me when I say this is beautiful?
who understands me when I say I have found other freedoms?

I cannot fly or make something appear in my hand,
I cannot make the heavens open or the earth tremble,
I can live with myself, and I am amazed at myself, my love, my beauty,
20 I am taken by my failures, astounded by my fears,
I am stubborn and childish,
in the midst of this wreckage of life they incurred,

> I practice being myself,
> and I have found parts of myself never dreamed of by me,
> 25 they were goaded out from under rocks in my heart
> when the walls were built higher,
> when the water was turned off and the windows painted black.
> I followed these signs
> like an old tracker and followed the tracks deep into myself,
> 30 followed the blood-spotted path,
> deeper into dangerous regions, and found so many parts of my-
>   self,
> who taught me water is not everything,
> and gave me new eyes to see through walls,
> and when they spoke, sunlight came out of their mouths,
> 35 and I was laughing at me with them,
> we laughed like children and made pacts to always be loyal,
> who understands me when I say this is beautiful?

MAKING MEANINGS

First Thoughts

1. What, in your opinion, is the most important—or most interesting, or most puzzling—line in Whitman's poem?

Shaping Interpretations

2. How does Whitman show his connection to the natural world in this poem? For example, what qualities does he say he shares with the spotted hawk?

3. What verb tense does Whitman use in this poem and other selections from "Song of Myself"? How would the effect have been different if the speaker had spoken in a different tense?

4. What might Whitman mean by line 10: "If you want me again look for me under your boot-soles"?

5. The first line of "Song of Myself" is "I celebrate myself, and sing myself"; the last line is "I stop somewhere waiting for you." Taking into account all that you have learned of the poet's character and the range of his poetry, tell what you think the last words of poem Number 52 reveal about Whitman's purpose in writing "Song of Myself."

6. Reread the Whitman poems, including the collection opener (page 347), and review your reading notes. Then, sum up the **themes** restated in the coda to "Song of Myself."

7. Suppose you had to select a line or word from Whitman's works to characterize him. Which line(s) or word(s) from these excerpts from "Song of Myself" would you select, and why?

Extending the Text

8. What ties do you see between Baca's poem (**Connections,** page 360) and Whitman's poems? Consider each poet's **style** and **message.**

9. You've already studied some of the American poets who preceded Whitman—Poe (page 260), Longfellow (page 175), Bryant (page 169), and other Romantics. Based on what you know about the work of these earlier poets, what do you think Whitman means when he describes his own poetry as his "barbaric yawp" (line 3)?

10. Some readers of this poem have further taken the meaning of "barbaric yawp" to refer to the way Europeans might have viewed the "American experiment" of democracy. What do you think?

Before You Read

A SIGHT IN CAMP IN THE DAYBREAK GRAY AND DIM

Make the Connection

The Suffering of Thousands

In December 1862, Whitman traveled to Virginia to care for his brother George, who was wounded at the first battle of Fredericksburg. Though he discovered that George's injuries were minor, Whitman witnessed the terrible suffering of hundreds of other young men. Whitman volunteered to assist the staffs of several medical field units and hospitals. Comforting and feeding the injured and dying, bringing them treats, dressing their wounds, reading to them, and writing letters home to their families, Whitman helped to care for close to a hundred thousand soldiers by the end of the war. His experiences brought a wider dimension of tragedy into his poetry.

Reading Skills and Strategies

Identifying Sources

When Whitman was visiting his wounded brother in Virginia, he took these notes:

"*Sight at daybreak*—in camp in front of the hospital tent on a stretcher (three dead men lying), each with a blanket spread over him—I lift up one and look at the young man's face, calm and yellow—'tis strange!

(Young man: I think this face of yours the face of my dead Christ!)"

As you read the following poem, write down the **images** that Whitman has drawn from his wartime notes.

Wounded Drummer Boy (c. 1862–1865) by William Morris Hunt (1824–1879). American. Oil on canvas (14″ × 19¼″).

Museum of Fine Arts, Boston/Gift from the Isaac Fenno Collection (18.393).

A Sight in Camp in the Daybreak Gray and Dim

Walt Whitman

A sight in camp in the daybreak gray and dim,
As from my tent I emerge so early sleepless,
As slow I walk in the cool fresh air the path near by the hospital tent,
Three forms I see on stretchers lying, brought out there untended lying,
5 Over each the blanket spread, ample brownish woolen blanket,
Gray and heavy blanket, folding, covering all.

Curious I halt and silent stand,
Then with light fingers I from the face of the nearest the first just lift the blanket;
Who are you elderly man so gaunt and grim, with well-gray'd hair, and flesh all sunken
    about the eyes?
10 Who are you my dear comrade?

Then to the second I step—and who are you my child and darling?
Who are you sweet boy with cheeks yet blooming?

Then to the third—a face nor child nor old, very calm, as of beautiful yellow-white ivory;
Young man I think I know you—I think this face is the face of the Christ himself,
15 Dead and divine and brother of all, and here again he lies.

from Specimen Days

The following extracts are from Whitman's "memoranda book," which he called *Specimen Days*.

The Inauguration

March 4, 1865—The President[1] very quietly rode down to the Capitol in his own carriage, by himself, on a sharp trot, about noon, either because he wished to be on hand to sign bills, or to get rid of marching in line with the absurd procession, the muslin temple of liberty, and pasteboard monitor. I saw him on his return, at three o'clock, after the performance was over. He was in his plain two-horse barouche,[2] and looked very much worn and tired; the lines, indeed, of vast responsibilities, intricate questions, and demands of life and death, cut deeper than ever upon his dark brown face; yet all the old goodness, tenderness, sadness, and canny shrewdness, underneath the furrows. (I never see that man without feeling that he is one to become personally attached to, for his combination of purest, heartiest tenderness, and native western form of manliness.) By his side sat his little boy, of ten years. There were no soldiers, only a lot of civilians on horseback, with huge yellow scarves over their shoulders, riding around the carriage. (At the inauguration four years ago, he rode down and back again surrounded by a dense mass of armed cavalrymen eight deep, with drawn sabers; and there were sharpshooters stationed at every corner on the route.) I ought to make mention of the closing levee[3] of Saturday night last. Never before was such a compact jam in front of the White House—all the grounds filled, and away out to the spacious sidewalks. I was there, as I took a notion to go—was in the rush inside with the crowd—surged along the passageways, the Blue and other rooms, and through the great East Room. Crowds of country people, some very funny. Fine music from the Marine band, off in a side place. I saw Mr. Lincoln, dressed all in black, with white kid gloves and a claw-hammer coat, receiving, as in duty bound, shaking hands, looking very disconsolate, and as if he would give anything to be somewhere else.

The Real War Will Never Get in the Books

And so goodbye to the war. I know not how it may have been, or may be, to others—to me the main interest I found (and still, on recollection, find) in the rank and file of the armies, both sides, and in those specimens amid the hospitals, and even the dead on the field. To me the points illustrating the latent personal character and eligibilities of these States, in the two or three millions of American young and middle-aged men, North and South, embodied in those armies—and especially the one-third or one-fourth of their number, stricken by wounds or disease at some time in the course of the contest—were of more significance even than the political interests involved. (As so much of a race depends on how it faces death, and how it stands personal anguish and sickness. As, in the glints of emotions under emergencies, and the indirect traits and asides in Plutarch, we get far profounder clues to the antique world than all its more formal history.)

Future years will never know the seething hell and the black infernal background of countless minor scenes and interiors, (not the

---

1. **The President:** Abraham Lincoln. He would be assassinated in April, just a month after Whitman wrote this.
2. **barouche** (bə·rōōsh′): four-wheeled, horse-drawn carriage.
3. **levee:** reception.

official surface courteousness of the generals, not the few great battles) of the Secession war; and it is best they should not—the real war will never get in the books. In the mushy influences of current times, too, the fervid atmosphere and typical events of those years are in danger of being totally forgotten. I have at night watched by the side of a sick man in the hospital, one who could not live many hours. I have seen his eyes flash and burn as he raised himself and recurred to the cruelties on his surrendered brother, and mutilations of the corpse afterward. (See, in the preceding pages, the incident at Upperville—the seventeen killed as in the description, were left there on the ground. After they dropped dead, no one touched them—all were made sure of, however. The carcasses were left for the citizens to bury or not, as they chose.)

Such was the war. It was not a quadrille[4] in a ballroom. Its interior history will not only never be written—its practicality, minutiae of deeds and passions, will never be even suggested. The actual soldier of 1862–1865, North and South, with all his ways, his incredible dauntlessness, habits, practices, tastes, language, his fierce friendship, his appetite, rankness, his superb strength and animality, lawless gait, and a hundred unnamed lights and shades

4. **quadrille** (kwə·dril′): French dance for four couples.

of camp, I say, will never be written—perhaps must not and should not be.

The preceding notes may furnish a few stray glimpses into that life, and into those lurid interiors, never to be fully conveyed to the future. The hospital part of the drama from 1861 to 1865, deserves indeed to be recorded. Of that many-threaded drama, with its sudden and strange surprises, its confounding of prophecies, its moments of despair, the dread of foreign interference, the interminable campaigns, the bloody battles, the mighty and cumbrous and green armies, the drafts and bounties—the immense money expenditure, like a heavy-pouring constant rain—with, over the whole land, the last three years of the struggle, an unending, universal mourning wail of women, parents, orphans—the marrow of the tragedy concentrated in those Army Hospitals—(it seemed sometimes as if the whole interest of the land, North and South, was one vast central hospital, and all the rest of the affair but flanges)—those forming the untold and unwritten history of the war—infinitely greater (like life's) than the few scraps and distortions that are ever told or written. Think how much, and of importance, will be—how much, civic and military, has already been—buried in the grave, in eternal darkness.

—Walt Whitman

MAKING MEANINGS

First Thoughts

1. What was your emotional response to "A Sight in Camp"? What specific words or **images** affected your response?

Shaping Interpretations

2. Look back at the notes you took while reading. How did Whitman develop the **setting** from the notes that inspired the poem?

Which **images** in the poem spring directly from Whitman's own experiences?

3. Why, given the circumstances of the Civil War, might the poet have seen the face of Christ on one of the dead soldiers? What might be the significance of the fact that the "forms" are a trio?

4. In Whitman's poems, we seem to be overhearing a man's conversation with himself. How would you describe the **tone** of this poem? What main elements support your description?

5. The point of the poem is never openly stated. What do you think is the **message** behind the poem?

6. Paul Zweig, one of Whitman's biographers, says that Whitman had a genius for the single line, "the verbal snapshot." Do you agree with this observation? Which **images** in this poem make particularly unusual and evocative "verbal snapshots"?

Extending the Text

7. Think of movies or television series you have seen set during the Civil War. Based on what you know about the Civil War, which media depictions strike you as best capturing the "real war" that Whitman describes in *Specimen Days* (page 363)?

CHOICES: Building Your Portfolio

Writer's Notebook

1. Collecting Ideas for a Comparison-Contrast Essay

In the Writer's Workshop on page 401, you'll write an essay comparing and contrasting two pieces of litera- ture. You might find an interesting topic for your essay in comparing and con- trasting Whitman with one or two of the Fireside Poets (see pages 149–150). Before you start taking notes, read this statement of Whitman's: "For grounds for Leaves of Grass, as a poem, I abandoned conven- tional themes, which do not appear in it: none of the stock ornamentation or choice plots of love or war, or high, exceptional person- ages of Old World song . . . no legend, or myth, or ro- mance, nor euphemism, nor rhyme." Jot down notes now on the ways in which Whitman's poems differ from the poems of the

Fireside Poets. Focus on the poetic features mentioned by Whitman. Save your notes.

Performance

2. Barbaric Yawp

Prepare a public reading of Whitman's poems. You will have to decide when you will use solo readers and when you will use a chorus. For some poems, you might want to use musical accompaniment. Be sure to ask your audience to evaluate your performance.

Creative Writing / Speaking and Listening

3. My Walt Whitman

Write a free-verse poem in the tradition of Walt Whit- man, using one of the poems in this collection as a model. (You could even begin your poem with one of Whitman's openers, such as "I hear America singing" or "I cele- brate myself.") Before you start, make notes on the fol- lowing to help you decide on subject matter:

- How would Whitman cele- brate diversity today?

- Who would be his over- looked heroes?
- What landscapes would he cherish?
- With whom would he empathize?
- What "songs," or lives, would he pay tribute to?

When you write in free verse (see page 355), you are freeing yourself from the demands of a rhyme scheme and meter. However, you will want to use **imagery** and **sound effects** (alliteration, repetition, parallel structure), as well as one or more of Whitman's techniques: catalogs, rolling cadences, and modulations of voice that result in a specific tone.

When you finish your poem, organize a class poetry reading. As you and other students read your poems aloud, identify the images and tone that seem the most like those Whitman used.

Comparing Ideas

4. Reading Nature

You have seen that it was a habit of the Puritans to "read" nature for signs of divinity. You have also seen how the Tran- scendentalists "read" nature.

In a brief essay, compare and contrast Whitman's "reading" of nature with that of the Puritan William Bradford (page 26) and the Transcendentalist Ralph Waldo Emerson (page 216).

Comparing Diction and Style

5. Whitman's Prose and Poetry

Read the sample of Whitman's prose writing in Primary Sources on page 363. In a brief essay, compare the **diction** and **style** of his prose with that of his poems. Before you write, collect your data in a chart like the following:

	Prose	Poetry
Tone		
Democratic feelings		
Use of lists and catalogs		
Use of vigorous language		

Analyzing Poetry

6. A Close Look

In an essay, analyze the poems by Whitman presented here (including the one on page 347). Focus on analyzing an aspect of his poems that interests you: perhaps his everyday American diction, his use of catalogs, his application of elements of free verse, his commonplace subject matter, his celebration of the ordinary person as hero, or his themes of identification with nature and with all of human existence. Open your essay with a thesis statement that clearly states the main idea of your analysis. Be sure to use evidence from the poems to support your main points.

Music

7. Whitman's Music

Music, singing, melody—Whitman's poetry resonates with references to music and sound. Find a recording of vocal or instrumental music that expresses the spirit of Walt Whitman's poetry, and play it for the class. Or, if you wish, compose and play your own musical tribute to Whitman.

Art

8. Design a Book Cover

In the first edition of *Leaves of Grass,* Whitman selected a green, pebbled cloth for the cover of his book. He stamped the title *Leaves of Grass* in gold paint, using simple letters with roots descending from the letters and leaves shooting up above them. The book was roughly the size of a piece of typewriter paper, about eight by eleven-and-a-quarter inches.

Design a new cover for Whitman's *Leaves of Grass.* Try to reflect the feeling or content of the poems in your design, but also reflect your personal response to Whitman's poetry. Hold an art show, and display your cover design with the designs of other students.

Crossing the Curriculum: History

9. Eyewitness to War

At your school or local library, find a book of pictures by a Civil War photographer (page 414). Make a chart comparing photographic depictions of soldiers with Whitman's poetic depiction in "A Sight in Camp in the Daybreak Gray and Dim." Set up a museum display using reproductions of Civil War photographs accompanied by captions written in Whitmanesque style.

Maria Stenzel/National Geographic Image Collection, Courtesy Walt Whitman House, Camden, New Jersey.

Pablo Neruda.

Pablo Neruda

(1904–1973)

Pablo Neruda was born and educated in Chile. Neruda wrote that he went out "hunting poems" as a child, and he received his first acclaim as a poet at the age of sixteen when he won first prize in a poetry competition. By the age of twenty he was already regarded as a young poet with great promise. In addition to enjoying an enormously full and diverse life as a writer, Neruda served as a diplomat and a member of the Chilean Senate for several years. He also lived in exile from his homeland when the Chilean right-wing government outlawed his socialistic political party and terminated his senatorial position. Before resettling on Isla Negra, in Chile, in 1953, Neruda lived in many countries around the world, including Burma (now called Myanmar), Italy, Spain, France, Mexico, Russia, and China. In 1971, he was awarded the Nobel Prize in literature. Known for his diverse range of poetic styles and voices, Neruda is celebrated for his humanism, his call for peace and equality, and his love and respect for the natural elements of the world. His poems are questions, riddles, political shouts, observations, homages, and introspective movements toward truth. Like Whitman, he has influenced and inspired many of the great poets of the twentieth century.

Before You Read
FULL POWERS

Background

Like many great writers the world over, the Chilean poet Pablo Neruda was deeply inspired by Walt Whitman's *Leaves of Grass*. In fact, this Nobel laureate declared that Whitman was his most important literary influence. Neruda made the following remarks to a New York City audience a year before his death:

"I was barely fifteen when I discovered Walt Whitman, my primary creditor. I stand here among you today still owing this marvelous debt that has helped me live.

"To renegotiate this debt is to begin by making it public, by proclaiming myself the humble servant of the poet who measured the earth with long, slow strides, pausing everywhere to love and to examine, to learn, to teach, and to admire. . . . Clearly, he feared neither morality nor immorality, nor did he attempt to define the boundaries between pure and impure poetry. He is the first absolute poet, and it was his intention not only to sing but to impart his vast vision of the relationships of men and of nations. In this sense, his obvious nationalism is part of an organic universality. He considers himself indebted to happiness and sorrow, to advanced cultures and primitive societies.

"Greatness has many faces, but I, a poet who writes in Spanish, learned more from Walt Whitman than from Cervantes [Spain's premier Renaissance novelist, poet, and playwright]. In Whitman's poetry the ignorant are never humbled, and the human condition is never derided.

"We are still living in a Whitmanesque epoch. . . . The bard complained of the all-powerful European influence that continued to dominate the literature of his time. In fact, it was he, Walt Whitman, in the persona of a specific geography, who for the first time in history brought honor to an American name."

Reading Skills and Strategies

Recognizing Shared Characteristics of Cultures
In many ways, Whitman and Neruda are two poets cut from the same cloth, even though they emerged from different cultures, years apart. As you read Neruda's poem, write down **images** and feelings that remind you of parts of "Song of Myself." Be especially aware of lines that seem actually to refer to Whitman's poetry.

Plenos Poderes

Pablo Neruda

A puro sol escribo, a plena calle,
a pleno mar, en donde puedo canto,
sólo la noche errante me detiene
pero en su interrupción recojo espacio,
5   recojo sombra para mucho tiempo.

El trigo negro de la noche crece
mientras mis ojos miden la pradera
y así de sol a sol hago las llaves:
busco en la oscuridad las cerraduras
10   y voy abriendo al mar las puertas rotas
hasta llenar armarios con espuma.

Y no me canso de ir y de volver,
no me para la muerte con su piedra,
no me canso de ser y de no ser.

15   A veces me pregunto si de donde
si de padre o de madre o cordillera
heredé los deberes minerales,

los hilos de un océano encendido
y sé que sigo y sigo porque sigo
20   y canto porque canto y porque canto.

Full Powers

Pablo Neruda

translated from the Spanish by
Ben Belitt and Alastair Reid

I write in the clear sun, in the teeming street,
at full sea-tide, in a place where I can sing;
only the wayward night inhibits me,
but, interrupted by it, I recover space,
5   I gather shadows to last me a long time.

The black crop of the night is growing
while my eyes meanwhile take measure of the meadows.
So, from one sun to the next, I forge the keys.
In the darkness, I look for the locks
10   and keep on opening broken doors to the sea,
for it to fill the wardrobes with its foam.

And I do not weary of going and returning.
Death, in its stone aspect, does not halt me.
I am weary neither of being nor of non-being.

15   Sometimes I puzzle over origins—
was it from my father, my mother, or the mountains
that I inherited debts to minerality,

the fine threads spreading from a sea on fire?
And I know that I keep on going for the going's sake,
20   and I sing because I sing and because I sing.

No tiene explicación lo que acontece
cuando cierro los ojos y circulo
como entre dos canales submarinos,
uno a morir me lleva en su ramaje
25 y el otro canta para que yo cante.

Así pues de no ser estoy compuesto
y como el mar asalta el arrecife
con cápsulas saladas de blancura
y retrata le piedra con la ola,
30 así lo que en la muerte me rodea
abre en mí la ventana de la vida
y en pleno paroxismo estoy durmiendo.
A plena luz camino por la sombra.

There is no way of explaining what does happen
when I close my eyes and waver
as between two lost channels under water.
One lifts me in its branches toward my dying,
25 and the other sings in order that I may sing.

And so I am made up of a non-being,
and, as the sea goes battering at a reef
in wave on wave of salty white-tops
and drags back stones in its retreating wash,
30 so what there is in death surrounding me
opens in me a window out to living,
and, in the spasm of being, I go on sleeping.
In the full light of day, I walk in the shade.

FINDING COMMON GROUND

Now that you've read Neruda's poem, meet in a small group, and share the comments you recorded while reading.

Read your notes aloud, and discuss each other's observations and thoughts.

- Identify the **images** and feelings that different members of your group jotted down.
- Discuss the elements in the poem that seem to refer directly to Whitman's "Song of Myself."

- List the qualities that Whitman and Neruda seem to share. For instance, how do they view themselves in relation to others? How do they view the natural world in relation to the world of people and industry?
- If possible, have a Spanish-speaker read «Plenos Poderes» to the class, followed by a reading of "Full Powers." Then, compare and contrast the sound and meter of the two poems. Was the translator faithful to the original?
- Share your observations and thoughts with the rest of the class.

Emily Dickinson

We think of her hidden in a white dress
among the folded linens and sachets
of well-kept cupboards, or just out of sight
sending jellies and notes with no address
to all the wondering Amherst neighbors.
Eccentric as New England weather
the stiff wind of her mind, stinging or gentle,
blew two half-imagined lovers off.
Yet legend won't explain the sheer sanity
of vision, the serious mischief
of language, the economy of pain.

—Linda Pastan (1932–   )

Emily Dickinson

(1830–1886)

A brief outline of Emily Dickinson's life reads like the plot of a story destined to become a legend. Once upon a time there was born to a religious and well-to-do New England family a daughter, whom they named Emily. As a child, she was lively, well behaved, and obedient; she took pleasure in the busy household of which she was a part and in the seasonal games, parties, and outings of a village snowy cold in winter and brilliantly green and flowering in the summer.

At home she learned to cook and sew. When she was old enough, she was sent to a school where strict rules did not keep Emily and the other girls from displaying their high spirits as they enjoyed the entertainments of boarding school life. Emily took part in these, but not always with as much enthusiasm as she might have. As she said many years later, something sad and reserved in her nature made her "a mourner among the children."

Culver Pictures.

To her family and friends, everything about the young Dickinson seemed normal. No one doubted that she would grow gracefully into womanhood, make a good marriage, and settle into a village life of churchgoing, holiday gatherings, and neighborly harmony. But something happened in her life that has been the subject of speculation for decades.

When Dickinson was twenty-four years old, her father, who had become a U.S. congressman, took her with him to Washington, D.C., and then on to Philadelphia. The journey seems to have marked the start of a turning point in her life. Her father may have taken her with him because she had fallen in love with someone she could never marry. This person might have been a married lawyer, older than Emily, a man who would die that year of tuberculosis.

Whatever happened, it seems likely that in the course of the journey, Emily fell in love with someone else: Charles Wadsworth, who was also married and who was pastor of the Arch Street Presbyterian Church in Philadelphia. Letters to Wadsworth show that Dickinson saw him as a "muse," someone who could inspire her, someone she could love passionately in her imagination.

But, in 1862, Wadsworth took up a new assignment in San Francisco. His leaving seems to have caused a great crisis in Dickinson's life: "I sing," she wrote around this time, "as the boy does by the burying ground, because I am afraid."

The Recluse of Amherst

The young woman quietly and abruptly withdrew from all social life except that involving her immediate family. Within a few years, dressed always in white—like the bride she would never become—she had gone into a state of seclusion. Her only activities were household tasks and the writing of poems that she either kept to herself or sent out as valentines, birthday greetings, or notes to go with the gift of a cherry pie or a batch of cookies.

Around the time that Wadsworth was preparing to move to California, Dickinson sent a few of her poems to Thomas Wentworth Higginson (page 394). As editor of the *Atlantic Monthly,* Higginson had been encouraging the work of younger poets. Higginson never became a substitute for Wadsworth, but he did serve as a kindly, distant "teacher" and "mentor." Eventually, Dickinson gave up hope of ever finding a wider audience than her few friends and relatives. About 1861, she wrote "I'm Nobody! Who are you? / Are you—Nobody—too?"

During her lifetime, Emily Dickinson published no more than a handful of her typically

brief poems. She seemed to lack all concern for an audience, and she went so far as to instruct her family to destroy any poems she might leave behind after her death. Still, she saw to it that bundles of handwritten poems were carefully wrapped and put away in places where, after her death, friendly, appreciative, and, finally, astonished eyes would find them. The poems were assembled and edited by different family members and friends; they were then published in installments so frequent that readers began to wonder when they would ever end.

Then, in 1955, a collection called *The Poems of Emily Dickinson* was finally made available. This was the devoted work of Thomas H. Johnson, a scholar who, unlike Dickinson's earlier editors, refrained from making "presentable" entities of poems whose punctuation, rhyme schemes, syntax, and word choice were frequently baffling. Instead, he attempted to remain faithful to the original manuscript.

As a result of Johnson's research, whole generations of readers who had grown up on Dickinson poems were faced with new versions of those poems, versions that sometimes rescued Dickinson's originals from the tamperings of her first editors. Sometimes these originals made emphases, which, in the interest of "smoothness," those editors had overlooked.

Here is an example of how one stanza was changed by the original editors. Johnson's version is first:

> We passed the School, where Children strove
> At Recess—in the Ring—
> We passed the Fields of Gazing Grain—
> We passed the Setting Sun—

And this is how the early editor changed it:

> We passed the school where children played
> Their lessons scarcely done;
> We passed the fields of gazing grain,
> We passed the setting sun.

The Secret of Genius

When Dickinson died at the age of fifty-five, hardly anyone knew that the strange, shy woman in their midst was a poet whose sharp and delicate voice would echo for generations to come. Some seventy years after her death, when the quarrels among her relatives who had inherited her manuscripts had died down and all her poems were finally published, she was recognized as one of the greatest poets America, and perhaps the world, had produced.

The self-imposed restrictions of Dickinson's actual life were more than matched by her ability to see the universal in the particular, and vice versa. She perceived the relationship between a drop of dew and a flood, between a grain of sand and a desert. These perceptions helped her make metaphors that embraced experiences far beyond the limited compass of Amherst village life.

> She perceived the relationship between a drop of dew and a flood.

Yet, no matter how far her imagination ranged, Dickinson never denied those experiences their truth as aspects of a cycle of existence important in itself. When an Amherst neighbor's barn caught fire and lit up the sky, it was a real barn at the edge of a real pasture, and its loss became a matter of local anguish. But these local actualities did not prevent Dickinson from regarding the incident as a reminder of ultimate doom, of the Biblical prophecies of destruction of the earth by fire.

Behind the now famous legend of Emily Dickinson, and the plays and novels that have romanticized and sentimentalized her life, is a woman whose genius made its own rules, followed its own commands, and found its own fulfillment. Emily Dickinson's life as a recluse may have been richer, more varied, and—in the satisfactions that come with the exercise of natural talent—even happier than the lives of those around her. In the prospect of history, we can see that the untold secret of Emily Dickinson's emotional life is secondary to the great secret of her genius, the secret that destiny would not let her keep.

Make the Connection

The Head and the Heart

Here we have Dickinson's version of the old story of unrequited love—or of love that is impossible because of the circumstances of the lovers. The substance of this poem is conflict—between will and emotion, between the thinking mind and the feeling heart.

Quickwrite

Are most people persuaded more by the promptings of intellect or of feeling? On a separate sheet, write examples from real life, literature, or films.

Heart! We will forget him!

Emily Dickinson

Heart! We will forget him!
You and I—tonight!
You may forget the warmth he gave—
I will forget the light!

When you have done, pray tell me
That I may straight begin!
Haste! lest while you're lagging
I remember him!

Original manuscript of Emily Dickinson's "I keep my pledge" and "Heart! We will forget him!"

Reprinted by permission of the publishers and the Trustees of Amherst College from *The Poems of Emily Dickinson*, Thomas H. Johnson, ed., Cambridge, Mass.: The Belknap Press of Harvard University Press, Copyright © 1951, 1955, 1979, 1983 by the President and Fellows of Harvard College. Manuscript image courtesy of the Amherst College Library.

Memories (1885–1886) by William M. Chase. Oil on canvas (50½″ × 37″).

Make the Connection

From the Ordinary, the Extraordinary

Poetry becomes metaphysical when its **imagery** and **figures of speech** are intellectual and sometimes far-fetched and fantastic. In metaphysical poetry, ordinary things are often seen in relation to the universal. Private emotions, such as unfulfilled love, take on the importance of great and profound events. See if you think this poem meets these requirements.

Quickwrite

Think of a story, movie, or song that deals with the hope of romantic fulfillment—a hope so profound that it can be maintained almost forever. Jot down some notes on this question: Why do you think this topic interests so many people?

Pastoral Scene by George Inness (1825–1894). Oil on canvas (51 cm × 76 cm).
R. C. Love Gallery, Chicago. Courtesy Rosenthal Art Slides, Worcester, Massachusetts.

If you were coming in the Fall

Emily Dickinson

If you were coming in the Fall,
I'd brush the Summer by
With half a smile, and half a spurn,
As Housewives do, a Fly.

5 If I could see you in a year,
I'd wind the months in balls—
And put them each in separate Drawers,
For fear the numbers fuse—

If only Centuries, delayed,
10 I'd count them on my Hand,
Subtracting, till my fingers dropped
Into Van Dieman's Land,°

If certain, when this life was out—
That yours and mine, should be
15 I'd toss it yonder, like a Rind,
And take Eternity—

But, now, uncertain of the length
Of this, that is between,
It goads me, like the Goblin Bee—
20 That will not state—its sting.

12. Van Dieman's (dē′mənz) **Land:** former name of Tasmania, an island that is a state of Australia.

The editors of Dickinson's poems, feeling that the poet's original works needed improvements, frequently altered them. Usually the editors' goal was to make Dickinson's poems more traditionally "poetic"—that is, to provide conventional rhymes and rhythms and to get rid of what they thought were awkward phrasings and punctuation. Here is a copy of "If you were coming in the Fall" with the alterations Dickinson's original editors made. Describe the kinds of changes the editors made, and evaluate them. Why do you think each change was made? How do the changes affect the poem? Why did Dickinson write the poem the way she did?

> If you were coming in the Fall,
> I'd brush the Summer by
> With half a smile, and half a spurn,
> As Housewives do, a Fly.
>
> 5   If I could see you in a year,
> I'd wind the months in balls—
> And put them each in separate Drawers,
> *Until their time befalls.*
> For fear the numbers fuse—
>
> If only Centuries, delayed,
> 10   I'd count them on my Hand,
> Subtracting, till my fingers dropped
> Into Van Dieman's Land.
>
> If certain, when this life was out—
> That your's and mine, should be
> 15   I'd toss it yonder, like a Rind,
>   *taste*
> And take Eternity—
>   *all ignorant*
> But, now, uncertain of the length
>   *time's uncertain wing*
> Of this, that is between,
> It goads me, like the Goblin Bee—
> 20   That will not state—it's sting.

THE SOUL SELECTS HER OWN SOCIETY

Make the Connection

Choices of the Soul

This poem is about choices and the mysterious instinct that leads each one of us to prefer certain things and cherish certain people above all others. In Dickinson's view, this instinct has less to do with the discriminations of the mind than with the yearnings of that spiritual part of us that some call the soul.

Quickwrite

How do you think most people select their friends, with their minds (thoughts), with their souls (feelings), or with a combination of the two? Write your responses to this question on a separate sheet. If you like, cite examples to support your viewpoint.

Woman with Parasol—Turned to Left (1886) by Claude Monet. Oil on canvas.

The Soul selects her own Society

Emily Dickinson

The Soul selects her own Society—
Then—shuts the Door—
To her divine Majority—
Present no more—

5 Unmoved—she notes the Chariots—pausing—
At her low Gate—
Unmoved—an Emperor be kneeling
Upon her Mat—

I've known her—from an ample nation—
10 Choose One—
Then—close the Valves of her attention—
Like Stone—

MAKING MEANINGS

Heart! We will forget him!

First Thoughts

1. Review your Quickwrite notes. Whom do you identify with in this poem—the head or the heart? Why?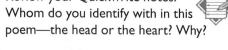

Shaping Interpretations

2. Why do you think the heart is asked to take the lead in this situation?

3. What do you think the speaker means by "warmth" and "light"? If you were trying to forget someone, which would you try to forget first?

4. Exclamation points punctuate this little poem, as if the speaker were saying, "Hurry up! We must get this over with!" Why do you suppose the speaker is in such a hurry?

5. Read the feature on **slant rhyme** on page 380. Then, describe the **rhyme scheme** of the poem, noting the instance of slant rhyme. What is the function of the end rhymes?

6. Some would say this poem is **ironic** to the core: The speaker doesn't really expect to—doesn't want to—forget the man. Do you agree? Why or why not?

If you were coming in the Fall

First Thoughts

1. Look over your Quickwrite notes. Do you think the hopes expressed in the poem are fairly common, or are they far-fetched? Explain.

Shaping Interpretations

2. How would you describe the speaker's situation? How does she feel about it?

3. What two things are being compared in the **simile** in the first stanza?

4. In the second stanza, what domestic articles are the months compared to? Why does the speaker put them in separate drawers?

5. Van Dieman's Land has come to mean places on the globe farthest away from us. Given this information, how would you paraphrase the third stanza?

6. How would you describe the speaker's **tone** in the first four stanzas? How does it change in the fifth stanza, where her exaggerations disappear? What goads, or pushes, her against her will?

7. In folklore, a goblin is a tormenting creature. What do you think Dickinson is suggesting when she says that the bee is a goblin and will not "state" its sting?

Challenging the Text

8. What changes, if any, would you suggest in capitalization and punctuation in this poem? Why?

The Soul selects her own Society

First Thoughts

1. What advantages and disadvantages may lie in a selection as strict as this soul makes? Do most people make choices like this? (Check your Quickwrite notes.)

Shaping Interpretations

2. *Majority* has at least two meanings: "having reached full legal age" (or "having come into one's own") and "the greater part of something." It could also mean "superiority" (an obsolete usage). What do you think it means in this poem? What kind of person does the adjective "divine" suggest?

3. Do you think the phrase "Valves of her attention" is derived from organic things (valves of a clamshell) or mechanical ones (valves of a faucet)? What do you picture happening here?

4. Dickinson's early editors changed the word *valves* to *lids*. How does this change the **metaphor**? How does it change what you *see*?

5. Look at the **meter** of lines 10 and 12. How does their rhythmical pattern differ from the corresponding lines in the first and second stanzas? What is the effect of this difference?

Challenging the Text

6. Dickinson did not give her poems titles. (The titles in this text are the first lines of the poems.) Her early editors called this poem "Exclusion." In what ways does this title apply? In what ways is it limiting?

ELEMENTS OF LITERATURE

Slant Rhyme

Not long ago, **exact rhyme**—two or more words whose syllables share identical sounds, as in the words *free* and *bee*—was part of every poet's craft. Today it is still the most familiar aspect of sound in poetry. But rhyme has, over the years, fallen out of favor with many poets. One reason is that these poets feel almost all the exact rhymes in English have been used over and over again. Another reason is that imposed rhymes can act as a constraint and can limit expression. Some poets, as a solution, have abandoned rhyme altogether. Other poets, like Dickinson, use slant rhyme.

Slant rhyme is a close, but not exact, rhyming sound. (It is also called **off rhyme, half rhyme,** or **approximate rhyme.**) Word pairs like *society/majority* or *nerve/love* are examples of slant rhymes—"not quite, but almost" rhyming sounds. Part of the shock value of Dickinson's poems comes from her use of slant rhyme. Slant rhyme makes many readers uncomfortable—in the way that a sharp or flat note on a piano would disturb a listener who wasn't expecting it.

Analyzing slant rhyme. Slant rhyme is a subtle use of sound. It is often used to force our attention onto particular words. For example, the last word in "The Soul selects her own Society," *stone,* stands out because it doesn't match exactly in sound with the word *one.* Why is it important that the word *stone* be emphasized? To hear and understand the difference, imagine that Dickinson had ended her poem with the words, "And be done."

1. How many exact rhymes do you find in "The Soul selects her own Society"? How many slant rhymes can you find? What rhyming sounds were you expecting to hear in each case?

2. Look through Dickinson's other poems for slant rhymes. Read them aloud, and see if you can identify the purpose and effect of each rhyme.

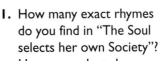

First printing of *Poems* by Emily Dickinson.
Amherst College Library, Amherst, Massachusetts.

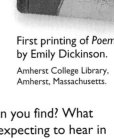

The Mirror Girl—stares back at me
(In the Style of Emily Dickinson)

The Mirror Girl—stares back at me—
With a Look that knows too much—
And a Skin that's never felt the Burn
Of a soft—caressing—Touch

She speaks with Lips that smile—and laugh—
But never have been—kissed—
And cries with careful—Countenance—
That never has been missed

The Mirror Girl is cold and crystal—
Hard enough to feel—
But who is to say, on the other Side,
She's not the One who's real?

The Mirror Girl is a stoic Thing—
That does not pain or ache—
But while I suffer and endure—
The Mirror Girl merely—breaks

—Brigid Spackman
James E. Taylor Senior High School
Katy, Texas

First appeared in *Merlyn's Pen: The National Magazines of Student Writing*

SOME KEEP THE SABBATH GOING TO CHURCH

Make the Connection

Transcendence

Although she rejected the teachings of her family's Congregationalist church, Dickinson was a deeply spiritual poet who constantly reflected on the divine. The fifth of seven poems published in her lifetime appeared on March 12, 1864. It was titled "My Sabbath," and unlike this version, it used the word "going" instead of "getting" in line 11. Later called "A Service of Song," it was included in a collection published in 1890, after Dickinson's death.

Quickwrite

Does a church—or any place of worship—have to be a human-built construction made expressly for worship, or can there be a broader understanding of what a church is? Record your thoughts on a separate sheet of paper.

©Collection of The New-York Historical Society.

Bobolink (1822) by John J. Audubon. Watercolor, graphite, pastel, gouache, selective glazing.

Some keep the Sabbath going to Church

Emily Dickinson

Some keep the Sabbath going to Church—
I keep it, staying at Home—
With a Bobolink° for a Chorister°—
And an Orchard, for a Dome—

5 Some keep the Sabbath in Surplice°—
I just wear my Wings—
And instead of tolling the Bell, for Church,
Our little Sexton°—sings.

God preaches, a noted Clergyman—
10 And the sermon is never long,
So instead of getting to Heaven, at last—
I'm going, all along.

---

3. bobolink: small bird. **chorister:** choir member.
5. surplice (sur′plis): loose white vestment worn by clergy or choir members on top of longer robes.
8. sexton: church officer or employee whose various duties may include maintenance and ringing the bells.

Before You Read

I TASTE A LIQUOR NEVER BREWED

Make the Connection

Intoxicating Inspiration
Some critics believe that Dickinson is making fun of Emerson (page 216) in the following poem. Like Emerson's poem "Bacchus," this poem compares a poet's feeling of inspiration to the feeling of intoxication some get when drinking liquor. However, in contrast to Emerson's serious tone, Dickinson's is humorous.

Quickwrite

Record some of your own remembrances of what it feels like to be inspired, or describe some of the qualities you associate with inspiration or even with complete absorption in doing something you love.

Passion Flowers and Hummingbirds (c. 1865) by Martin Johnson Heade. Oil on canvas (15 ¼″ × 21½″).

Gift of Mrs. Maxim Karolik for the M. and M. Karolik Collection of American Paintings, 1815–1865. Courtesy of Museum of Fine Arts, Boston.

I taste a liquor never brewed

Emily Dickinson

I taste a liquor never brewed—
From Tankards scooped in Pearl—
Not all the Vats upon the Rhine°
Yield such an Alcohol!

5 Inebriate° of Air—am I—
And Debauchee° of Dew—
Reeling—thro endless summer days—
From inns of Molten Blue—

When "Landlords" turn the drunken Bee
10 Out of the Foxglove's° door—
When Butterflies—renounce their "drams"—
I shall but drink the more!

Till Seraphs° swing their snowy Hats—
And Saints—to windows run—
15 To see the little Tippler°
Leaning against the—Sun—

3. Rhine: an allusion to the Rhine River in Germany, an area that is noted for fine wine and beer.

5. inebriate: (in·ē′brē·it′): drunk.

6. debauchee (deb′ô·shē′): person who overindulges in pleasures.

10. foxglove's: A foxglove is a kind of plant with cuplike flowers.

13. seraphs: angels of the highest order.

15. tippler: drinker.

Before You Read

MUCH MADNESS IS DIVINEST SENSE

Make the Connection

The Solace of Solitude
Since her death, Dickinson has often been portrayed as the mad recluse of Amherst. In fact, Dickinson lived as many other great poets (and quite a few "ordinary" people) have lived —deliberately choosing solitude for contemplation, reading, and writing.

Quickwrite

Write down what you think the unusual title of this poem means.

Much Madness is divinest Sense

Emily Dickinson

Much Madness is divinest Sense—
To a discerning Eye—
Much Sense—the starkest Madness—
'Tis the Majority
In this, as All, prevail—
Assent—and you are sane—
Demur—you're straightway dangerous—
And handled with a Chain—

Garden at Emily Dickinson's house.

MAKING MEANINGS

Some keep the Sabbath going to Church

First Thoughts

1. Review your Quickwrite notes. What is your response to the speaker's "Church"?

Shaping Interpretations

2. In what ways does the speaker keep the Sabbath? How might keeping the Sabbath as others do affect her worship?

3. What is the speaker's relationship to nature? How is this revealed in the **metaphors** the speaker chooses?

4. What do you think the speaker means in the last line by saying "I'm going, all along"?

Extending the Text

5. What kinds of people might share the speaker's preference? Who would disagree with this way of keeping the Sabbath?

Challenging the Text

6. Which **title** do you feel better suits the poem: "My Sabbath" or "A Service of Song"? Or do you have a better title? Explain your answer.

I taste a liquor never brewed

First Thoughts

1. Review your Quickwrite notes, and explain whether you have ever felt what this speaker is feeling. Do you think the **analogy,** or comparison, of inspiration to intoxication works? Why or why not?

Shaping Interpretations

2. What is the speaker drinking in the poem? Why doesn't he or she want to stop?

3. Who would the "Landlords" in stanza 3 be? What details in the poem suggest a **tone** of defiance?

4. Where is the little "Tippler," or drinker, in the last stanza? Can you see any significance in the last word of the poem?

Extending the Text

5. Many readers see this poem, at least in part, as a description of the inspiration that drives artists to create. What other human activities or emotions could it pertain to?

Much Madness is divinest Sense

First Thoughts

1. What kinds of people might take this poem as a personal "anthem"? Does anything in this poem reflect ideas you have had about yourself?

Shaping Interpretations

2. What is the meaning of the two **paradoxes,** or apparent contradictions, in the first three lines? How do they affect the poem's meaning?

3. What do you think is the poem's **theme**? What does the speaker think about the individual's proper relationship to society?

4. Dickinson liked to use dashes—a mark of punctuation her first editors usually removed. How do dashes help emphasize certain ideas in this poem?

5. What would you say is Dickinson's **tone** in this poem? What similarities do you notice to other poems in this collection?

Extending the Text

6. The public has often said of creative and independent thinkers that they are "crazy." Name at least three people—writers, artists, inventors, or other creative types (besides Dickinson)—who are or have been considered "mad." In what ways is their "madness" a kind of "sense," at least in terms of their work? Are they really mad at all? (Did you mention these ideas in your Quickwrite?)

Make the Connection

Metaphor Metamorphosis

Dickinson had only to look out her window to see the ordinary—and extraordinary—powers of nature at work. In using **metaphors** built on images of birds, flies, and flowers, her deceptively innocent observations reveal deep and sometimes disturbing ideas.

Quickwrite

Do you think nature is essentially benign, or threatening and hostile? Create a double-column chart in which you write evidence of nature's benevolence in one column and evidence of nature's destructiveness in the other.

Jim Zipp/Photo Researchers.

Apparently with no surprise

Emily Dickinson

Apparently with no surprise
To any happy Flower
The Frost beheads it at its play—
In accidental power—
The blonde Assassin passes on—
The Sun proceeds unmoved
To measure off another Day
For an Approving God.

Make the Connection
Forms of Truth
Dickinson's famous line "Tell all the Truth but tell it slant" may reveal her method of survival as well as the essence of her own poetry.

Quickwrite
What do you think it would mean to tell the truth "slant"? Write some examples of the truth "told slant."

Tell all the Truth but tell it slant

Emily Dickinson

Tell all the Truth but tell it slant—
Success in Circuit° lies
Too bright for our infirm Delight
The Truth's superb surprise
As Lightning to the Children eased
With explanation kind
The Truth must dazzle gradually
Or every man be blind—

2. **circuit:** an indirect path.

Rooms by the Sea (1951) by Edward Hopper. Oil on canvas.

Before You Read

SUCCESS IS COUNTED SWEETEST

Make the Connection

The Taste of Fame

In 1862, Dickinson sent this poem along with three others to Thomas Wentworth Higginson, editor of the *Atlantic Monthly*, to ask his advice about the quality of her poems. It is one of several poems that show Dickinson's feelings about success and her struggles with the world.

Quickwrite

Write down some of your own thoughts about success. How do people feel who always encounter failure?

Background

Literary scholars debate Dickinson's lack of interest in publishing and recognition. This poem, included in *A Masque of Poets,* is one of the poems that Dickinson did publish during her lifetime. Ironically, many readers thought it was written by Ralph Waldo Emerson (page 216).

Taps (c. 1907–1909) by Gilbert Gaul. Oil on canvas (32¾″ × 43″).
Collection of the Birmingham Museum of Art, Birmingham, Alabama. Gift of John Meyer.

Success is counted sweetest

Emily Dickinson

Success is counted sweetest
By those who ne'er succeed.
To comprehend a nectar°
Requires sorest° need.

5 Not one of all the purple Host°
Who took the Flag today
Can tell the definition
So clear of Victory

As he defeated—dying—
10 On whose forbidden ear
The distant strains of triumph
Burst agonized and clear!

3. nectar: a name for the drink of the Greek and Roman gods; also, a term applied to any delicious beverage.
4. sorest: deepest; most extreme.
5. purple host: royal army.

The following excerpts describe a visit to the Dickinson house—called the Homestead—in Amherst, Massachusetts. (See photos on pages 345 and 383.)

Emily Dickinson's Homestead

The place today is decidedly light, airy, underfurnished. Even so, Emily Dickinson's singular presence is felt almost from the moment you step inside the front door and your guide begins to talk about "Emily" as if the two of them had recently had a tête-à-tête about fresh flowers or what sort of cake to bake for Sunday dinner. . . .

At the Homestead, as in a good many other "restored" writers' houses, most of the furniture, curtains, toys, saucepans, and God-knows-what-else have been gathered together decades after its owners have removed to a far less stressful existence. Very little of the actual stuff is there; most of it has been gathered by buying or begging from folks who happen to own pieces that fit the particular decorating bill. While the outside walls are intact, the domestic apparatus inside them is only an approximation of what was there when the famous writer lived in its midst. Yet we go out of our way to visit these temples to the Word, if only for a whiff of the Great One who once prowled the premises seeking the mot juste[1] or staring out the window, waiting for a nudge from the muse. . . .

Emily's bedroom contains the few things that almost certainly belonged to her: a Franklin stove, a sleigh bed adorned with a paisley shawl I was dying to touch but was not quick enough. The family cradle is here, too, an odd touch in a spinster's room. In the middle of the room, one of her dresses (it looks like a size eight) is draped on a headless dummy inside a Plexiglas case. The display destroys the illusion that she might return from her beloved garden at any moment. But the dress is irresistible— made of heavy white cotton with twelve nickel-sized buttons down the front, long sleeves, a custom-ordered patch pocket (to tuck scraps of paper into), and the trim look of a head nurse's uniform. On the windowsill is a basket with a cord attached to it, which she filled with cookies she baked and then lowered out the window to nephews and nieces.

We were told by our guide . . . that Emily was "lucky in a way—she never had to go out to work" and that she was "witty and funny." Pointing to pictures of three men in Emily's life, [the guide] said that the poet "only liked intellectual men. My pick [for Emily's true love] is Bowles," meaning Samuel Bowles, editor of the *Springfield Daily Republican,* who may have been the "Master" to whom Emily addressed a series of letters. Bowles was married. Personally, I think Emily tended to pick her men for their unavailability—what she didn't need was a husband.

—Anne Bernays, *from* "A Poet's Safe Haven in Amherst," *The New York Times Magazine,* October 1, 1989

---

1. **mot juste** (mō zhüst′): French for "right word."

MAKING MEANINGS

Apparently with no surprise

First Thoughts

1. What is the message of this poem? Do you feel it is shocking, reassuring, or something else?

Shaping Interpretations

2. What is the "blonde Assassin"?

3. How are the flower, the frost, and the sun **personified** in this poem? What kind of person does each seem to be compared to?

4. A **pun** is a play on words based on multiple meanings of a single word or words that sound alike but mean different things. What pun is in line 6? How would you explain it?

5. According to the speaker, how does God feel about the flower's beheading? How do you think the speaker feels?

Extending the Text

6. How does the speaker's attitude toward nature differ from Emerson's attitude in the excerpt from his essay *Nature* (page 219)? Is either point of view supported by the chart you made before reading the poem? Explain.

Tell all the Truth but tell it slant

First Thoughts

1. Look back over your Quickwrite notes. How would you define the word *slant* as it is used in the poem? Is telling something "slant" different from lying?

Shaping Interpretations

2. Explain the meaning of "Circuit" (line 2) in the context of the poem. What is "Too bright for our infirm Delight" (line 3)?

3. Lines 5 and 6 provide an example to illustrate the poet's point about truth. As is typical of Dickinson's technique, she omits several words

in these lines. How would you rephrase the lines to make a full sentence?

4. According to the last two lines, why must the truth be told "slant"? How would you define *dazzle* and *blind* here?

5. What **metaphor** is implied in line 7? What is "Truth" being compared with?

Challenging the Text

6. Do you agree with the poet's message? In what way can this lyric be seen as a reference to the way poetry "works"?

Success is counted sweetest

First Thoughts

1. According to the speaker, who is likely to count success as sweetest? Review your Quickwrite notes. Do you think the poet is on target in describing the feelings of people who fail?

Shaping Interpretations

2. Purple is a color associated with blood shed in battle (the Purple Heart medal is given to those killed or wounded in battle). Purple is also a color associated with royalty or nobility. What is the "purple Host" in line 5?

3. Whose ear is mentioned in line 10? What is the ear "forbidden" to hear?

4. Describe the **image** you see in the last stanza.

Connecting with the Text

5. Do you agree with the idea expressed in lines 3–4? Why or why not? How would you **paraphrase** these lines?

6. Have you ever been like the soldier in the last stanza—in agony because someone else is being proclaimed winner? What other circumstances in life (other than a wartime battle) could this situation be applied to? Could it describe the feelings of a poet who could not publish her work?

BECAUSE I COULD NOT STOP FOR DEATH

Make the Connection

Drawn by Death

Like many other **metaphors** in Dickinson's poetry, the one in this poem imaginatively captures the most awesome and inevitable of human experiences—death—and does so with playfulness and wit. The literal elements of the metaphor are simple: Dying is compared to an unexpected ride in a horse-drawn carriage. But these are just about the only simple elements in a poem that depends for its effect on **irony,** on gradual comprehension, and on a blithe **tone** that is much at odds with the subject of the story being told.

Reading Skills and Strategies

Summarizing a Text

Dickinson uses time in an unusual way. As you read, sum up what is happening in each stanza, and note when the events occur.

Because I could not stop for Death

Emily Dickinson

Because I could not stop for Death—
He kindly stopped for me—
The Carriage held but just Ourselves—
And Immortality.

5 We slowly drove—He knew no haste
And I had put away
My labor and my leisure too,
For His Civility—

We passed the School, where Children strove
10 At Recess—in the Ring—
We passed the Fields of Gazing Grain—
We passed the Setting Sun—

Or rather—He passed Us—
The Dews drew quivering and chill—
15 For only Gossamer,° my Gown—
My Tippet—only Tulle°—

We paused before a House that seemed
A Swelling of the Ground—
The Roof was scarcely visible—
20 The Cornice°—in the Ground—

Since then—'tis Centuries—and yet
Feels shorter than the Day
I first surmised the Horses Heads
Were toward Eternity—

15. **gossamer:** thin, soft material.
16. **tippet . . . tulle:** shawl made of fine netting.
20. **cornice:** projecting horizontal molding at the top of a building.

Make the Connection

Death Be Not Proud

This poem begins with such boldness and continues with such quick shifts of attention that we may not stop to think about what we are hearing—a voice from the dead.

Quickwrite

Write down what you would expect someone to sense at the time of death—that ultimate moment when we cannot "see to see."

I heard a Fly buzz—when I died

Emily Dickinson

I heard a Fly buzz—when I died—
The Stillness in the Room
Was like the Stillness in the Air—
Between the Heaves of Storm—

5   The Eyes around—had wrung them dry—
And Breaths were gathering firm
For that last Onset—when the King
Be witnessed—in the Room—

I willed my Keepsakes—Signed away
10 What portion of me be
Assignable—and then it was
There interposed a Fly—

With Blue—uncertain stumbling Buzz—
Between the light—and me—
15 And then the Windows failed—and then
I could not see to see—

Wind from the Sea (1947) by Andrew Wyeth. Tempera (18½″ × 27½″).

Mead Art Museum, Amherst College. Gift of Charles and Janet Morgan.

Before You Read

I DIED FOR BEAUTY—BUT WAS SCARCE

Make the Connection

Beauty and Truth

The following lines, which conclude John Keats's "Ode on a Grecian Urn," are among the most famous lines in English poetry:

> "Beauty is truth, truth
>   beauty"—that is all
> Ye know on earth, and all ye
>   need to know.

Emily Dickinson knew these lines, and in this poem she presents her own version of the theme suggested by Keats.

Quickwrite

Beauty and Truth are two concepts that have been defined and debated for centuries. Write your own definitions of Beauty and Truth.

Michael Cornish.

I died for Beauty—but was scarce

Emily Dickinson

I died for Beauty—but was scarce
Adjusted in the Tomb
When One who died for Truth, was lain
In an adjoining Room—

5 He questioned softly "Why I failed"?
"For Beauty," I replied—
"And I—for Truth—Themself are One—
We Bretheren, are," He said—

And so, as Kinsmen, met a Night—
10 We talked between the Rooms—
Until the Moss had reached our lips—
And covered up—our names—

"I sing ... because I am afraid"

In 1862, Emily Dickinson sent the critic Thomas Wentworth Higginson a letter and four poems, asking for critical help. Dickinson saw him as a mentor, and they corresponded for several years. Four years after Dickinson's death, Higginson assisted Mabel Loomis Todd in editing Dickinson's poems. The following year, Higginson wrote an article in *The Atlantic Monthly* about his experiences with Emily Dickinson.

I remember to have ventured on some criticism which she afterwards called "surgery," and on some questions, part of which she evaded, as will be seen, with a naive skill such as the most experienced and worldly coquette might envy. Her second letter (received April 26, 1862) was as follows:

Mr. Higginson,—Your kindness claimed earlier gratitude, but I was ill, and write today from my pillow.

Thank you for the surgery; it was not so painful as I supposed. I bring you others, as you ask. . . .

You asked how old I was? I made no verse, but one or two, until this winter, sir.

I had a terror since September, I could tell to none; and so I sing, as the boy does of the burying ground, because I am afraid.

You inquire my books. For poets, I have Keats, and Mr. and Mrs. Browning. For prose, Mr. Ruskin, Sir Thomas Browne, and the Revelations. I went to school, but in your manner of the phrase had no education. When a little girl, I had a friend who taught me Immortality; but venturing too near, himself, he never returned. Soon after my tutor died, and for several years my lexicon was my only companion. Then I found one more, but he was not contented I be his scholar, so he left the land.

You ask of my companions. Hills, sir, and the sundown, and a dog large as myself, that my father bought me. They are better than beings because they know, but do not tell; and the noise in the pool at noon excels my piano.

I have a brother and sister; my mother does not care for thought, and father, too busy with his briefs to notice what we do. He buys me many books, but begs me not to read them, because he fears they joggle the mind. They are religious, except me. . . .

But I fear my story fatigues you. I would like to learn. Could you tell me how to grow, or is it unconveyed, like melody or witchcraft?

You speak of Mr. Whitman. I never read his book, but was told that it was disgraceful. . . .

. . . I must soon have written to ask her for her picture, that I might form some impression of my enigmatical correspondent. To this came the following reply, in July 1862:

Could you believe me without? I had no portrait, now, but am small, like the wren; and my hair is bold, like the chestnut bur; and my eyes, like the sherry in the glass, that the guest leaves. Would this do just as well?

It often alarms father. He says death might occur, and he has molds [photographs] of all the rest, but has no mold of me. . . .

—Thomas Wentworth Higginson,
from "Emily Dickinson's Letters"

MAKING MEANINGS

Because I could not stop for Death

First Thoughts

1. If you were going to **personify** Death, would Death be like the person described in this poem? Why or why not?

Shaping Interpretations

2. Can you paraphrase the first two lines in a way that emphasizes their **irony**? What word in line 2 tells you that the tone is ironic?

3. In stanza 2, *civility* means "politeness." How does this kind of behavior on the part of Death and the speaker extend the **irony** of the first stanza?

4. What three things do the riders pass in stanza 3? What is significant about the fact that the sun passes the carriage in stanzas 4–5, and about the nature of the change in temperature? Be sure to review your reading notes.

5. Stanza 5 is a riddle in itself. What is the nearly buried house?

6. Do you think the concluding stanza introduces a **tone** of terror, because the speaker has suddenly realized she will ride on forever, conscious of being dead? Or is the poem really an expression of trust and even triumph? Explain your response.

Challenging the Text

7. The critic Alfred Kazin said of the last stanza of this poem: "What that famous Eternity is, we cannot say." Do you agree with Kazin? What do *you* think Dickinson meant by the "Eternity" the horses were going toward?

I heard a Fly buzz—when I died

First Thoughts

1. Do you find this poem grotesque, moving, humorous, or something else? Look back over your Quickwrite notes, and explain whether or not you were surprised by the poem's conclusion.

Shaping Interpretations

2. According to the second and third stanzas, how had the speaker and those around her prepared for death?

3. What are the dying person and those around her expecting to find in the room? What appears instead, and why is this **ironic**?

4. In line 4, Dickinson used the word "Heaves" to refer to the behavior of storms. Why is "Heaves" an appropriate word to describe what is happening in the poem?

5. How does the poet use pauses and specific words in lines 12–13 to make the appearance of the fly dramatic and lively?

6. In the third stanza, what portion of the speaker is "assignable"? What portion, by implication, is *not* assignable?

7. Who is the "King" (line 7)? What does the phrase "the Windows failed" (line 15) mean?

8. What **tone** do you hear in this poem? What feeling do you think the poet expresses by inserting the fly into this deathbed scene?

I died for Beauty—but was scarce

First Thoughts

1. What thoughts and feelings would you say are expressed in this poem? Are they similar to or different from those you recorded in your Quickwrite notes? Explain.

Shaping Interpretations

2. What is the situation described in the first stanza? What do the two speakers have in common that allows one of them to claim they are "Bretheren," or brothers?

3. In the third stanza the "Moss" is real, but it is also a **metaphor**. What do you think it represents? What is significant in the fact that it covers up the speakers' names?

4. **Slant rhyme** makes the last word stand out. Do you think this is an important word? Why or why not?

5. What do you think Dickinson's **message** is? Would you say it is optimistic or pessimistic?

CHOICES: Building Your Portfolio

Writer's Notebook

1. Collecting Ideas for a Comparison-Contrast Essay

One interesting topic for a comparison-contrast essay would be an examination of how one of Emily Dickinson's poems compares with a poem by an earlier poet—perhaps "Huswifery" by Edward Taylor (page 73), "Upon the Burning of Our House" by Anne Bradstreet (page 69), or "Thanatopsis" by William Cullen Bryant (page 171). Take notes now on how one of these poems compares with one of Dickinson's poems. You might collect your notes in a chart like the one below.

	Dickinson Poem	Other Poem
Subject matter		
Theme		
Tone		
Figures of Speech		

Save your notes for the Writer's Workshop on page 401.

Creative Writing

2. Echoes of Dickinson

Write a poem that treats one of the themes that engaged Emily Dickinson: love and loss, the spiritual life, death and immortality, nature, or the power of the imagination. You might even use one of Dickinson's lines as your opener. Experiment with **metaphors, similes,** and **slant rhymes.** Try out Dickinson's style of punctuation and capitalization, or invent your own unique style. For inspiration, read the student poem on page 380.

Analyzing Meter / Music

3. Hymn to Her

Dickinson let the strict **meters** she found in her hymn-book provide the basic beat for her poems, but the variations she introduced gave her poems subtlety and prevented monotony. In a brief essay, analyze at least two of her poems to show how she uses this traditional hymn meter:

> 8 syllables in line 1
> 8 syllables in line 3
>
> 6 syllables in line 2
> 6 syllables in line 4

Then show how she also uses a short hymn meter of 6, 6, 8, and 6 syllables. To see how closely some of the poems conform to a hymn meter, you might try singing "If you were coming in the Fall" to the tune of "O God, Our Help in Ages Past."

Performance / Research

4. Dickinson Onstage

With a partner or a small group, prepare a script for a performance called "An Evening with Emily Dickinson." In the script, let Dickinson tell about her life, her views of poetry and language, and her feelings about nature, faith, and eternity. Include in your performance readings of selected poems. You might want to include Linda Pastan's poem "Emily Dickinson" (page 371). Present your performance for the class.

Art

5. Book of Poems

Dickinson sewed the final copies of her poems into the form of small booklets. To make your own small book, fold four pages of white paper in half. Then, gather them at the fold, which will give you sixteen pages. Select poems you would like to reproduce—either your own, or some favorite poems by Dickinson or by other poets. On the first page, design a book cover including a title. Then, copy one poem onto each of the remaining pages. Try to match your penmanship or calligraphy with the feelings conveyed in the poems. (You might also use a computer, choosing fonts appropriate to the poems.) Finally, sew your book along the fold.

READ ON

Song of Himself

Around the turn of the twelfth century, the Persian scientist Omar Khayyám produced several well-known works in mathematics and astronomy, as well as a series of quatrains, or four-line poems, for which he is now even more famous. The brilliant 1850s English translation by Edward FitzGerald of *The Rubáiyát of Omar Khayyám* made Khayyám the rage of the Victorian era. This powerful expression of the Persian poet's personal vision and philosophy of life has remained in print for over a century.

Legacy in Latin America

Who's the most popular U.S. poet in Latin America? The answer is probably Walt Whitman. One of his greatest admirers was the Cuban poet José Martí, who introduced Whitman's work to Spanish-speaking audiences at the turn of the century. Whitman's influence on Martí's own verse is evident in *José Martí: Major Poems* (Holmes and Meier), a bilingual edition with English translation by Elinor Randall, edited by Philip Foner.

Beholder of Mysteries

"I am no scientist," Annie Dillard says of herself. "I am a wanderer with a background in theology and a penchant for quirky facts." In *Pilgrim at Tinker Creek* (Harper and Row), Dillard draws on her experiences in an isolated Virginia valley to create a memorable reflection on life, death, and the mysteries of nature.

The Country Way

Maxine Kumin has always drawn from nature in producing her vivid poetry. *In Deep* (Viking) is the Pulitzer Prize–winning poet's collection of essays on country living. Of special interest is the last essay, "A Sense of Place," which examines nature's role in inspiring the poetic imagination.

Before and After Dickinson

Did you know that the world's first known poet was a woman? Her name was Enheduanna, and she was born around 2300 B.C. She was the daughter of a king and served as a Sumerian moon priestess. She is just one of many women poets whose works appear in *A Book of Women Poets from Antiquity to Now* (Schocken Books), a collection edited by Aliki and Willis Barnstone.

The American Language

A Period of Vocabulary Growth

by Gary Q. Arpin

Languages are always changing and growing, adding new words and expressions and shading the meaning of terms that already exist. American English enjoyed a remarkable period of growth in the first half of the nineteenth century as a variety of sources contributed to its expanding vocabulary.

Backwoods English

The word *backwoods* was first recorded in 1709. Some sixty-five years later, the word *backwoodsman* appeared. John Pickering, a linguist in the nineteenth century, wrote that the word was applied "by the people of the commercial towns in the United States, to those who inhabit the territory westward of the Allegheny Mountains." Backwoodsmen themselves used more colorful terms. They called themselves *ring-tailed roarers* or *mollagausaugers* (courageous men). The exploits of the backwoodsmen during the War of 1812 made them famous, and when Davy Crockett came to Washington, D.C., in 1827 as a congressman from Tennessee, people stared at him in the street. The following year, another backwoodsman, Andrew Jackson, was elected president.

Backwoods English teems with exaggeration and exuberant bragging—language equal to the awesome task of surviving on a new frontier. Crockett almanacs, collections of speeches by Davy Crockett that were popular from the 1830s to the 1850s, brought this backwoods language into Eastern homes. Here's an example:

> Hosses, I am with you! and while the stars of Uncle Sam, and the stripes of his country wave triumphantly in the breeze, whar, whar, whar is the craven, low-lived, chicken-bred, toad-hoppin', red-mounted, bristle-headed mother's son of ye who will not raise the beacon light of triumph, smouse the citadel of the aggressor, and squeeze ahead for Liberty and Glory! Whoop! h-u-rah, hosses, come along—Crockett's with you—show us the enemy!

Woodcut from *Davy Crockett Almanac* (1835).

Courtesy American Antiquarian Society.

Most backwoods slang had a short life, though some words and phrases have survived. Phrases like *fly off the handle, pull up stakes, a knock-down-drag-out fight, up a tree,* and *doing a land-office business* all date from this period.

The American Vernacular in Literature

The first half of the nineteenth century resounded with calls to establish an independent national literature describing the American landscape and dealing with American manners and interests, and by midcentury American literature was in full flower. To describe American phenomena, writers began to turn to the **vernacular**—the common spoken language of a region. The Crockett almanacs were a kind of subliterature, but by the 1870s, Mark Twain (page 450) was recording the language of the American West in substantial books like *Adventures of Huckleberry Finn, Roughing It,* and *Life on the Mississippi.*

Walt Whitman (page 348) also used American vernacular to create literature of a high order. In *Leaves of Grass,* he proclaims the virtues of American English:

> The English language befriends the grand American expression. . . . It is the powerful language of resistance—it is the dialect of common sense. It is the speech of the proud and melancholy races and of all who aspire. It is the chosen tongue to express growth, faith, self-esteem, freedom, justice, equality, friendliness, amplitude, prudence, decision, and courage. It is the medium that shall well nigh express the inexpressible.

Whitman frequently tapped American vernacular in his verse. For instance, he quite pointedly employed an Americanism (*to loaf*) in the first lines of "Song of Myself" (page 347):

> I loaf and invite my soul,
> I lean and loaf . . . observing a spear of summer grass.

In *Two Years Before the Mast* (1840), Richard Henry Dana, Jr., called *loafer* "the newly invented Yankee word." Four years later, in *Martin Chuzzlewit,* part of which is set in America, the British novelist Charles Dickens put *loaf* in quotation marks to show that it was a peculiarly American term. Whitman's use of the verb *loaf* eleven years later proclaimed his Americanness just as surely as if he had called himself a ring-tailed roarer.

The Language of the Stump: Political Coinage

The American vernacular did not appear only in literature. It was also spoken on the political platform, or "stump." (Candidates for office would stand on tree stumps to deliver their speeches.) Here is part of a speech by a candidate for office in Oregon in 1858:

> Fellow-citizens, you might as well try to dry up the Atlantic Ocean with a broomstraw, or draw this 'ere stump from under my feet with a harnessed gad-fly, as to convince me that I ain't gwine to be elected this heat [race]. My opponent don't stand a chance; not a sniff. Why, he ain't as intellectual as a common sized shad. . . . If thar's anybody this side of whar the sun begins to blister the yea'th [heath] that can wallop me, let him show himself—I'm ready. Boys, I go in for the American Eagle, claws, stars, stripes, and all; and may I bust my everlastin' buttonholes ef I don't knock down, drag out, and gouge everybody as denies me!

This so-called stump style is long gone, but many phrases coined by politicians of the period are still used. For instance, the word *gerrymander* was

> Whitman's use of the verb *loaf* proclaimed his Americanness just as surely as if he had called himself a ring-tailed roarer.

coined in 1812 after Massachusetts Governor Elbridge Gerry reorganized the state election districts in order to maintain control of the state senate. One of the resulting districts was absurdly long and serpentine. The artist Gilbert Stuart saw a map of the districts in the office of a local newspaper editor. Noting its resemblance to a salamander, Stuart gave the district a head, wings, and claws. The editor proclaimed it a "gerrymander," and thus the word was born.

From the Art Collection of Nations Bank.

Stump Speaker (1853–1854). Drawing from *Stump Speaking* by George Caleb Bingham. Brush, black ink, and wash over pencil (11½" × 9½").

The Language of the Press

Newspapers began to flourish in America in the late 1830s, thanks to improved printing methods that made penny newspapers profitable. Papers tried to attract readers with colorful language. One of the ways they did this was to invent whimsical abbreviations. The most famous Americanism of them all—*OK*—originated as a witty abbreviation. *OK* was first used to mean "oll korrect" (a deliberate misspelling of "all correct") in a Boston newspaper in 1839. *OK* might never have survived as an expression had the New York Democratic Club not dubbed itself "The OK Club" during the 1840 presidential election. The Democrats intended *OK* to stand for "Old Kinderhook," a nickname for their candidate, President Martin Van Buren, a native of the town of Kinderhook, New York. Their opponents, however, claimed that *OK* stood for "oll korrect" and that the expression had been coined by former president Andrew Jackson, who had misspelled "all correct." (This was to remind voters that Van Buren was Jackson's personal choice as successor and to make fun of Jackson's limited education.) "OK!" became a Democratic rallying cry during that boisterous election year and remained in widespread popular use.

The Influence of Immigrants

The late 1840s saw a tremendous increase in the number of immigrants to the United States. In 1845, about 100,000 immigrants arrived; by 1854, the number had grown to 500,000. A large number of immigrants during the mid-nineteenth century were Germans, many of whom sought haven from political disorder. The German influence on American English was strong, especially in words for food (*sauerkraut, frankfurter, hamburger, noodle*). German also gave us *kindergarten* (children's garden); *bum* (probably from *bummler*, meaning "loafer"); *dumb,* in the sense of "stupid" (from *dumm*); and *fresh,* meaning "saucy" or "impertinent" (from *frech,* "impudent").

However, the greatest source of **loanwords**—words borrowed from other languages—in the nineteenth century was Spanish. As Americans moved westward into territory originally settled by the Spanish, they came upon a host of items that are still known by their Spanish names. *Mustang, lasso, ranch, fiesta, plaza, bronco, canyon,* and *patio* are just a few commonly used English words of Spanish origin.

Try It Out

1. **Using suffixes to change parts of speech.** Americans frequently change nouns into verbs or adjectives, and verbs into nouns or adjectives, often through the addition of a suffix. The first suffix popularly used in the United States to make new nouns was *–ery. Printery* was coined in 1638. Other common suffixes used to change a word's function are *–logy, –ism, –ize,* and *–ish.* Make a list of five words that have been formed by the addition of each of these suffixes. What information is given in the dictionary about each word's origin?

2. **Compiling specialized vocabulary.** Nearly every occupation coins its own special vocabulary, which may then find its way into general usage. Compile a brief dictionary of the special vocabulary of people in a business or industry you are familiar with (stockbrokers, doctors, lawyers, politicians, advertisers, news reporters, weather forecasters, restaurant workers, computer programmers, athletes, musicians, and so on). Explain the meaning of each word or phrase, and, if you can, explain its derivation. Which of these words or phrases have been picked up and used by people outside the occupation? How many have been added to American English in the last twenty years or less? (Think of terms like *compact disc, virtual reality,* and *fax.*)

3. **Identifying loanwords.** With a partner or small group, make a "Loanword Lexicon"—a dictionary of words used in American English that were originally borrowed from other languages. You might try making a dictionary of loanwords from a particular language— Spanish or Japanese, for example—or a dictionary of specialized words (names of animals, foods, or inventions, for example) that are actually loanwords.

Writer's Workshop

The history
of the written
word is rich a
Page 1

EXPOSITORY WRITING

COMPARISON-AND-CONTRAST ESSAY

Life is a continual series of decisions. Which movie will you see tonight—a drama starring your favorite actor, or a comedy with a cast of newcomers? By thinking in this way, you apply the strategy of comparison and contrast to everyday decisions. When you write a comparison-and-contrast essay, you examine the similarities and differences of two subjects. As a result, you understand the subjects better, and your evaluations and decisions become easier.

Prewriting

1. **Choosing topics.**   Sometimes subjects to compare or contrast will be assigned to you—two novels, for example. When you need to choose two subjects on your own, be sure they have something obviously in common or have some significant differences. You might, for example, *compare* William Cullen Bryant and Emily Dickinson because they are both American poets; you might also *contrast* their poetic styles. Choose topics on which you know you can access relevant information, drawn from your own experience or from research.

2. **Developing a thesis statement.**   As you explore your two subjects, you need to decide to what extent you will stress their similarities and to what extent you will stress their differences. Your thesis statement—the main idea of the essay—should reflect that decision and should be clear and straightforward: "William Cullen Bryant and Emily Dickinson both saw death as a solemn event, but their tones and images reveal profoundly different attitudes toward death."

3. **Organizing your essay.**   You can help your readers understand the relationships between your subjects by using either the block method or the point-by-point method of organization. In the **block method,** you first discuss all the relevant elements of one subject and then all the relevant elements of the second subject. In the **point-by-point method,** you discuss one element at a time, as it relates to both subjects; then you go on to the next element. On the next page is a chart that shows how the two methods work.

WORK IN PROGRESS

ASSIGNMENT
  Write an essay comparing and contrasting two poems, focusing on such elements as subject matter, theme, tone, and figures of speech.

AIM
  To inform; to explain; to analyze.

AUDIENCE
  Your classmates, family, and general readers.

Try It Out

Fill out an organization chart like this one to generate a possible framework for the body of your essay.

Subject 1 _____
Elements

1. _____
2. _____
3. _____

Subject 2 _____
Elements

1. _____
2. _____
3. _____

Language Handbook H E L P

See Comparison of Modifiers, pages 1227–1228; Using Parallel Structure, pages 1235–1236.

Communications Handbook H E L P

See Proofreading.

■ *Evaluation Criteria*

A good comparison-and-contrast essay
1. *opens with an attention-getting statement*
2. *makes a clear thesis statement*
3. *uses the block method or the point-by-point method to present an argument*
4. *uses specific details to support the comparison-contrast*
5. *handles the features in the same order for both topics*
6. *closes with a summary*

Model

BLOCK METHOD	POINT-BY-POINT METHOD
Subject 1: "Because I could not stop for Death" 　Element 1: theme 　Element 2: tone 　Element 3: figures of speech Subject 2: "Thanatopsis" 　Element 1: theme 　Element 2: tone 　Element 3: figures of speech	Element 1: theme 　Subject 1: "Because I could not stop for Death" 　Subject 2: "Thanatopsis" Element 2: tone 　Subject 1: "Because I could not stop for Death" 　Subject 2: "Thanatopsis" Element 3: figures of speech 　Subject 1: "Because I could not stop for Death" 　Subject 2: "Thanatopsis"

Drafting

1. **Introduction.** Get your readers' attention with an amusing or dramatic anecdote, a surprising question, a powerful quotation, or a pointed detail. Then, clearly and carefully state your thesis.

   Remember that comparing two subjects does not mean that you must completely ignore their differences. Essays that explore similarities often begin by citing one or two differences and *then* focusing primarily on the similarities. The reverse is also true: Essays that contrast two subjects often begin by citing one or two similarities. You can build your introduction around such statements. By acknowledging both similarities and differences, you show your audience that you are aware of various aspects of your topic and that your perspective is not one-sided or simplistic.

2. **Body.** Use the block method or the point-by-point method to present the information you've gathered. Use facts, quotations, examples, and other kinds of information to elaborate the elements of each poem. Remain consistent throughout, maintaining your method of organization.

   Remember that your main goal is to understand or explain your subjects, the two poems you've selected; comparing and contrasting are simply methods to achieve that end. What light do the similarities and differences throw on your subjects? Ask yourself what new insights you have gained about the poems now that you have compared and contrasted them.

   To draw special attention to the comparisons and contrasts you make, you might want to use **parallel structure** in your sentences. Parallel structure is a natural way to express both similarities and differences. For example, you might say "While Bryant's tone is grand and romantic, Dickinson's tone is blithe and ironic."

3. **Conclusion.** Bring the essay to a satisfying close by summarizing or restating the main idea. You may wish to leave the reader with a final question or comment, perhaps indicating other topics or other features for comparison and contrast.

Language Workshop

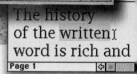

The history
of the written
word is rich and

Page 1

VARIETY IS THE SPICE: VARYING SENTENCE BEGINNINGS

The basic, no-frills English sentence begins with a subject that is closely followed by a verb: *Emily Dickinson wrote poems.* If every sentence followed that same pattern, however, readers would be unbearably bored. By using a variety of sentence beginnings, you can improve your style and hold your readers' interest. To vary sentences, you can use introductory words, phrases, or clauses.

1. Start a sentence with a modifier or modifiers.
   Private and *reclusive,* Emily Dickinson rarely tried to publish her poetry.

2. Start a sentence with a transitional word or phrase.
   Therefore, Dickinson's choice of subjects was bold and adventurous.

3. Start a sentence with a prepositional phrase.
   Throughout his writing career, Walt Whitman publicized himself frequently and enthusiastically.

4. Start a sentence with a verbal phrase.
   To understand a poem, read it at least twice.

5. Start a sentence with a dependent clause.
   After they died, Whitman and Dickinson took their places among the greatest nineteenth-century poets.

Writer's Workshop Follow-Up: Revising

Reread the comparison-and-contrast essay you wrote for the Writer's Workshop (page 401). Do too many of your sentences begin the same way? If so, revise them using strategies you've learned in this lesson. Remember to reword sentences for clarity, being careful to place phrase modifiers close to the words they modify. Don't feel that every sentence has to begin with a phrase or clause, however; sometimes a simple sentence will give you exactly the tone and emphasis you need.

Technology HELP

See Language Workshop CD-ROM. *Key word entry: sentences—beginnings.*

Language Handbook HELP

See Revising for Variety, page 1237.

Try It Out

With a partner, revise each of the following sentences by altering its beginning according to the strategy indicated in parentheses.

1. Walt Whitman never went to college, but he read widely. (transition)

2. Emily Dickinson was a reclusive person whose inner life was remarkably rich. (modifier)

3. Whitman's long poems are, in the opinion of many academics, as laboriously crafted as Dickinson's short poems. (dependent clause)

4. It is beside the point to attempt to rank Dickinson and Whitman in order of greatness. (verbal phrase)

Reading for Life

Reading a Textbook

Situation

Suppose that you wish to do a special project on Emily Dickinson. Your first stop (before throwing yourself into extensive research in a library or on the Internet) might be to explore information available in this literature textbook. Here are strategies you can use to evaluate and read almost any textbook.

Strategies

Examine basic parts of the textbook.

- These basic parts include the book's Table of Contents, the author pages, the unit chapter overviews, and parts of the backmatter, including various indices.

Identify special features of the textbook.

- These might include time lines, statistical tables, unique images related to the book's content, firsthand sources, various types of commentary, lists of books for further reading, and special material in the back matter, such as the Glossary and, in this textbook, the Language Handbook.

Examine the book to see if it contains information relevant to your research needs.

- List questions you'd like answered. Then, examine the book to confirm that it contains information you're seeking.

Take notes on important passages.

- Take precise and complete notes on passages that focus on issues relevant to your topic.

- Outline key passages. You can use either of the following standard outline approaches.

  I. Main idea
    A. Supporting point
      I. Detail
        a. Information or further detail

  Main idea
  - Supporting detail
  - Supporting detail
  - Supporting detail

Using the Strategies

Answer the following questions by examining this textbook:

1. Which author of this textbook wrote the introductory material on Whitman and Dickinson? What are the writer's qualifications?

2. According to the Table of Contents, what special features are included with the poems by Dickinson?

3. How does this textbook "place" Dickinson—in what historical context and under what thematic grouping?

4. Flip through the section on Dickinson. What other special features do you find?

5. Where in the textbook will you find an overview of Dickinson and her place as an American poet?

6. Suppose you are especially interested in Dickinson's poetic techniques. Which features in this book will help you to examine the structure of her poems?

7. If you wanted to travel to Amherst, Massachusetts, to visit the Dickinson house, which features might interest you? (Remember to look at pictures too.)

8. Find Dickinson's biography. Outline the main ideas and supporting details in this biography. What questions do you have that you want to do further research on?

9. Draw up a list of all the questions you have about Dickinson, based on information in this text. What further research would you like to undertake?

Extending the Strategies

Test Your Skill

Identify a topic or aspect of your everyday life about which you might want to consult a reference book or textbook. (Think of questions you might have about sports, automobile repair, or health.)

You might also use the strategies on this page to examine another textbook you use in school—in history, science, modern language, or math.

Learning for Life

The Changing World of Work

Problem

In "I Hear America Singing," Walt Whitman presents a catalog of occupations that would have been familiar in his time. Since Whitman's time, however, the world of work has changed drastically, and it continues to change at a rapid rate. How will the world of work change for the average American in the next decade?

Project

Research one career field to discover how it may change over the next decade, what skills a person will need in order to work in that field, and what new occupations may emerge in that field.

Preparation

1. Decide what aspect of the broad topic *occupations* you'll focus on. Choose a field that you think you might be interested in pursuing one day. If you're interested in health care, for instance, you might want to research developing trends in health-care careers.

2. Use the *5W-How?* questions (*Who? What? When? Where? Why? How?*) to help you find the information you need. *How* will health care change? *Who* will be most affected by the changes? *When* are changes likely to occur?

3. Brainstorm a list of possible resources for your research.

Procedure

1. Start by getting an overview of your chosen occupation by consulting the government publications *Dictionary of Occupational Titles* and *Occupational Outlook Handbook.*

2. Cast your net wide for research information, but be sure you're using reliable and current sources.

   • Contact trade and professional organizations, and request publications from them.

   • Check with special-interest newsgroups on the Internet.

   • Consult local college or university career services offices.

   • Interview someone currently working in the field you're interested in.

3. Analyze your findings. Can you make some educated guesses about how the occupation you have researched will change in the next decade or so? How can people interested in that occupation prepare themselves for it?

Presentation

To present your findings, use one of the following formats (or another that your teacher approves):

1. **Radio Spot**
   Tape-record for possible broadcast a radio program in which you share your findings about coming changes in the occupation you researched.

2. **Brochure**
   Create a brochure that could be used by a student career-services office or a vocational-technical center ten years from now. The brochure should give specific information about education, training, and job skills necessary for the career you have researched. Make your brochure look as professional as possible; use desktop publishing, if you can, and provide illustrations.

3. **A Mock Interview**
   With another student, write and act out a scenario in which a person ten years from now is interviewing for a job in the field you researched. The dialogue of the interview should reveal what tasks and responsibilities the job will entail, what kind of education and skills are necessary, and what kind of career path the person being interviewed can expect.

Processing

What challenges await the American worker, and how do you think you and other students can better prepare yourselves for the future world of work? Write a reflection for your portfolio.

Prisoners from the Front (detail) by Winslow Homer (1836–1910).
Oil on canvas (24˝ x 38˝).

The Rise of Realism
The Civil War and Postwar Period
1850–1900

The Rise of Realism
The Civil War and Postwar Period

by **Gary Q. Arpin**

A man said to the universe:
"Sir, I exist!"
"However," replied the universe,
"The fact has not created in me
A sense of obligation."
—Stephen Crane

Evening Gun Fort Sumter (detail) by John Gadsby Chapman. (Painted in Rome, 1864, after a sketch made by his son Conrad Wise Chapman). Oil on board.

On the evening of April 12, 1861, Walt Whitman attended the opera at the Academy of Music in Manhattan. After the opera, he was walking down Broadway toward Brooklyn when, as he later wrote, "I heard in the distance the loud cries of the newsboys, who came presently tearing and yelling up the street, rushing from side to side even more furiously than usual. I bought an extra and crossed to the Metropolitan Hotel . . . where the great lamps were still brightly blazing, and, with a crowd of others, who gathered impromptu, read the news, which was evidently authentic."

The news that Whitman and the others read so avidly was of the Confederate attack on Fort Sumter, the opening shots of the Civil War. Thus solemnly

War is at best barbarism. . . . Its glory is all moonshine. . . . War is hell.

—Union General William Tecumseh Sherman

Quilt by Varina Davis.
The Museum of the Confederacy, Richmond, Virginia. Photograph by Katherine Wetzel.

LITERARY EVENTS

Sojourner Truth (1864) by an unidentified photographer.

National Portrait Gallery, Smithsonian Institution, Washington, D.C.

Sojourner Truth, abolitionist and women's rights advocate, dictates *Narrative of Sojourner Truth*, c. 1850

France's Gustave Flaubert publishes a classic realistic novel, *Madame Bovary*, 1856

•

Herman Melville publishes *The Piazza Tales*, short stories including "Bartleby the Scrivener," 1856

•

Harriet Beecher Stowe publishes an influential novel about slavery, *Uncle Tom's Cabin*, 1851–1852

Harriet Beecher Stowe (c. 1852). Daguerreotype.

The Granger Collection, New York.

Bret Harte publishes the short story "The Outcasts of Poker Flat," 1869

Russian author Leo Tolstoy completes his panoramic novel *War and Peace*, 1869

•

Louisa May Alcott publishes a popular novel about growing up, *Little Women*, 1868–1869

Louisa May Alcott. Oil over a photograph.

The Granger Collection, New York.

1850–1859   1860–1869

CULTURAL/HISTORICAL EVENTS

Fugitive Slave Act imposes stiff penalties on anyone helping a person escape enslavement, 1850

•

Susan B. Anthony and Elizabeth Cady Stanton become co-leaders of U.S. women's rights movement, early 1850s

The Sepoy Rebellion, a large-scale uprising against British rule in India, ends, 1858

•

England's Charles Darwin explains his groundbreaking theory of evolution in *Origin of Species*, 1859

Susan B. Anthony and Elizabeth Cady Stanton.

Julia Ward Howe by John Elliott (c. 1910) and William H. Cotton (c. 1925). Oil on canvas.

National Portrait Gallery, Gift of Mrs. John Elliott 1933. Courtesy Art Resource.

First shots of Civil War fired, April 1861

•

Confederate troops defeat Union forces at Bull Run in Virginia, in the first major battle of the Civil War, July 1861

•

Julia Ward Howe publishes the song "The Battle Hymn of the Republic," 1862

•

President Abraham Lincoln delivers the Gettysburg Address at the dedication of a Civil War cemetery, November 1863

•

Confederate surrender at Appomattox Court House in Virginia ends Civil War, April 1865

President Lincoln is assassinated in Ford's Theater, Washington, D.C., April 14, 1865

•

The Thirteenth Amendment to the U.S. Constitution, outlawing slavery, is ratified, 1865

•

U.S. purchases Alaska from Russia, 1867

•

Restoration of Meiji emperor opens a period of modernization in Japan, 1867

Abraham Lincoln (1863). Photograph by Alexander Gardner.

Library of Congress.

Henry James.
Archive Photos.

William Dean Howells.
The Granger Collection, New York.

Henry James publishes the novel *Daisy Miller,* a study of European and American manners, 1879

•

Mark Twain publishes the popular novel *The Adventures of Tom Sawyer* and begins work on a famous sequel, *Adventures of Huckleberry Finn,* 1876

William Dean Howells publishes the realistic novel *The Rise of Silas Lapham,* 1885

•

José Martí, Cuban writer and independence leader, publishes his poetry collection *Ismaelillo,* 1882

•

Russian novelist Fyodor Dostoyevsky publishes *The Brothers Karamazov,* 1879–1880

Stephen Crane publishes *The Red Badge of Courage,* about a soldier's response to the Civil War, 1895

•

Kate Chopin publishes *Bayou Folk,* short stories about life in Louisiana, 1894

Russia's Anton Chekhov writes the realistic drama *Uncle Vanya,* 1899

•

African American writer Paul Laurence Dunbar publishes his poetry collection *Lyrics of Lowly Life,* 1896

•

Sarah Orne Jewett publishes *The Country of the Pointed Firs,* about life in a Maine seaport, 1896

1870–1879   1880–1889   1890–1900

John D. Rockefeller founds the Standard Oil Company of Ohio, 1870

•

Sioux soldiers defeat U.S. forces under Gen. George A. Custer on the Little Bighorn in Dakota Territory, 1876

•

Alexander Graham Bell patents the first telephone, 1876

•

Thomas Edison patents the first phonograph, 1878

Clara Barton organizes the American Red Cross, 1881

•

Booker T. Washington founds Tuskegee Institute, 1881

•

Statue of Liberty is dedicated, 1886

James Naismith invents game of basketball, at Springfield, Massachusetts, 1891

•

Naturalist John Muir publishes *The Mountains of California,* 1894

•

German physicist Wilhelm Roentgen discovers X-rays, 1895

Athens, Greece, is the site of the first modern Olympic Games, 1896

•

U.S. annexes Hawaii and wins Spanish-American War (gaining Puerto Rico, Guam, and the Philippines), 1898

•

U.S. population is about 76 million, 1900

•

Austrian physician Sigmund Freud advances the field of psychiatry by publishing *The Interpretation of Dreams,* 1900

Prisoners from the Front by Winslow Homer (1836–1910). Oil on canvas (24″ x 38″).

The Metropolitan Museum of Art. Gift of Mrs. Frank B. Porter, 1922 (22.207). Photograph © 1995 The Metropolitan Museum of Art.

Young Soldier: Separate Study of a Soldier Giving Water to a Wounded Companion (1861) by Winslow Homer (1836–1910). Oil, gouache, black crayon on canvas (36 cm × 17.5 cm).

Cooper-Hewitt, National Design Museum, Smithsonian Institution; Gift of Charles Savage Homer, Jr./Courtesy Art Resource, NY.

began, for one of the few American poets or novelists who would witness it firsthand, the greatest cataclysm in United States history.

Responses to the War: Idealism . . .

In Concord, Massachusetts, home of Ralph Waldo Emerson, Henry David Thoreau, Nathaniel Hawthorne, and many other intellectual leaders of the nation, army volunteers met in 1861 at the bridge that Emerson had immortalized in "Concord Hymn" (page 99), his famous poem about the beginning of the American Revolution. Emerson had for decades warned that this day would come if slavery were not abolished. Now that the day had arrived, he was filled with patriotic fervor. He watched the Concord volunteers march to Boston, and he visited a navy yard, declaring that "sometimes gunpowder smells good."

Emerson had great respect for the Southern will to fight, however, and he suspected, quite rightly, that the war would not be over in a few months as some people had predicted. When the Concord volunteers returned a few months later from the First Battle of Bull Run (July 1861), defeated and disillusioned, many of them unwilling to reenlist, Emerson maintained his conviction that the war must be pursued.

Still, Northern disillusionment after the early defeat at Bull Run was strong. With a keen eye for the sad details, Whitman recorded the sense of gloomy defeat in Washington in late July when Northern troops returned from the disaster of Bull Run:

> The defeated troops commenced pouring into Washington over the Long Bridge at daylight on Monday, 22nd— day drizzling all through with rain. The Saturday and Sunday of the battle

> The war with its defeats and uncertainties is immensely better than what we lately called the integrity of the Republic, as amputation is better than cancer.
>
> —Ralph Waldo Emerson

(20th, 21st) had been parched and hot to an extreme—the dust, the grime and smoke, in layers, sweated in followed by other layers again sweated in, absorbed by those excited souls—their clothes all saturated with the clay-powder filling the air— stirred up everywhere on the dry roads and trodden fields by the regiments, swarming wagons, artillery, etc.—all the men with this coating of murk and sweat and rain, now recoiling back, pouring over the Long Bridge—a horrible march of twenty miles, returning to Washington baffled, humiliated, panic-struck. Where are the vaunts, and the proud boasts with which you went forth? Where are your banners, and your bands of music, and your ropes to bring back your prisoners? Well, there isn't a band playing—and there isn't a flag but clings ashamed and lank to its staff.

—Walt Whitman

Civil War ambulance.

Culver Pictures.

Future years will never know the seething hell and the black infernal background of the countless minor scenes and interiors . . . and it is best they should not—the real war will never get in the books.

—Walt Whitman

A patient in Armory Square Hospital, Washington, D.C., during the Civil War. Photograph (detail).

© Collection of The New-York Historical Society.

Late in 1862, Whitman traveled to Virginia to find his brother George, who had been wounded in battle. After George was nursed back to health, Whitman remained in Washington off and on, working part time and serving as a volunteer hospital visitor, comforting the wounded and writing to their loved ones. The condition of the wounded was appalling. Many of the injured had to remain on the battlefield for two or three days until the camp hospitals had room for them. Antiseptics were primitive, as were operating-room techniques. Anesthesia was virtually unknown. A major wound meant amputation or even death.

Whitman estimated that in three years as a camp hospital volunteer, he visited tens of thousands of wounded men. "I am the man," he had written in "Song of Myself," "I suffer'd, I was there," and now he *was* there, in the real heart of

EYES OF AN ERA

Television's close-up coverage of modern warfare has made the thick of battle a common sight on the nightly news. But during the American Civil War, photographs were the closest thing to newscasts. By the latter part of the 1800s, technical advances began to allow for truly mobile photographers. As a result, the Civil War became the first war to be fully documented in pictures. Cameras went on the march, up in observation balloons, and to sea on battleships. More than three hundred civilian photographers covered the Union's Army of the Potomac alone. But newspapers could not yet reproduce photos, so photographers did brisk business selling "war views" and portraits of soldiers directly to the public.

Cameras of the time could not capture motion; charging troops and thrusting bayonets came out as hazy blurs. But cameras richly recorded the preparations and the aftermath of war. After battles, photographers roamed the killing fields, shooting pictures while wearing handkerchiefs across their faces to block the stench of death. They captured the war's still lifes—fields and forests filled with dead soldiers, blasted cities and landscapes, and scenes taken inside prisons, hospitals, and camps.

Many of the pioneering Civil War photojournalists were probably motivated more by profit than by a sense of history. The most famous of these war photographers was Mathew Brady (c. 1823–1896). Brady was among the first photographers to think of moving mini-darkrooms into combat areas; usually, these darkrooms were customized delivery wagons, which soldiers nicknamed "what-is-it" wagons. Though Brady helped inspire Civil War photography with his views of the First Battle of Bull Run in 1861, more often he employed courageous photographers, such as Alexander Gardner and Timothy O'Sullivan, to take their cameras onto the battlefields. Brady helped guarantee the war's rich visual record, but

America. In his poems, he had presented a panoramic vision of America; now America passed through the hospital tents in the form of wounded men from every state in the Union and the Confederacy. Nevertheless, out of the horror that he viewed, Whitman was able to derive an optimistic vision of the American character, of "the actual soldier of 1862-65 . . . with all his ways, his incredible dauntlessness, habits, practices, tastes, language, his fierce friendship, his appetite, rankness, his superb strength—and a hundred unnamed lights and shades."

. . . and Disillusionment

The war that strengthened Whitman's optimism served at the same time to justify Herman Melville's pessimism. Melville's poems about the war, collected in *Battle-Pieces and Aspects of the War* (1866), were often dark and foreboding. Of the elation following the firing on Fort Sumter, Melville wrote:

Woman freed from slavery learning to read. Leib Image Archives, York, Pennsylvania.

it was the skill and heroism of Gardner, O'Sullivan, and nameless others that actually produced the legacy of Civil War pictures.

Gardner came closer than anyone else to capturing an actual battle scene when he set his camera on a ridge overlooking the Battle of Antietam in Maryland in 1862. Gardner's genius at film processing and composition helped raise photographic coverage of the war to the level of art. He recognized that "verbal representations" of the war "may or may not have the merit of accuracy; but photographic presentments of them will be accepted by posterity with an undoubting faith."

O'Sullivan was one of the bravest and most brilliant of Brady's assistants. When bridge builders whom O'Sullivan was photographing were targeted by enemy sharpshooters, he calmly continued taking pictures while men screamed and fell. One of O'Sullivan's post-battle pictures shows corpses littering the quiet Gettysburg Cemetery; a sign hanging by the cemetery gatepost proclaims, with grim irony, that there is a five-dollar fine for discharging a firearm within cemetery limits.

Photographers fought heavy equipment, stray bullets, rain, mud, insects, foliage, wandering livestock, and frozen hands. Processing photographs in the field was complicated and messy: Many pictures were ruined when they were washed in streams where debris could stick to the gummy image.

Though about a million photos were taken, the photographic record of the war is incomplete. Neither Brady, Gardner, nor O'Sullivan arrived in time to capture the surrender at Appomattox in 1865. And lack of supplies made Confederate field photography virtually nonexistent after 1861.

Sadly, most Civil War photographers and their work fell into obscurity after the war. Hundreds of glass negatives were sold to gardeners for greenhouse windows, and, decades later, many of the glass plates ended up as eyepieces in gas masks worn by soldiers in World War I.

O, the rising of the People
    Came with the springing of the grass,
They rebounded from dejection
    After Easter came to pass.
And the young were all elation
    Hearing Sumter's cannon roar. . . .
But the elders with foreboding
    Mourned the days forever o'er,
And recalled the forest proverb,
    The Iroquois' old saw:
Grief to every graybeard
    When young Indians lead the war.

—Herman Melville

Artist sketching the battlefield of Gettysburg, July, 1863. Photograph by T. H. O'Sullivan.

Melville was fascinated by the war, but he never wrote a novel about it. The poems in *Battle-Pieces,* based on newspaper accounts of the battles as well as visits to battlefields, record the heroism and futility of the fighting on both sides and demonstrate respect for Southern soldiers as well as Northern troops. But in some of the best poems, there is a sense of human nature being stripped bare, revealing not the heroism and strength that Whitman found, but, rather, humanity's basic evil.

The American Civil War (1861–1865) resulted in terrible blood-shed as the national government sought to preserve the Union by ending the secession of Southern states. Despite his firsthand experience of the aftermath of battle, Walt Whitman retained an optimistic view of the American character. But the horrors of war merely reinforced the pessimism of Herman Melville.

The War in Literature

There was enough atrocity and heroism in the war to feed the views of both Melville and Whitman. What is odd, though, is that Melville's *Battle-Pieces* (which was ignored until the twentieth century) and Whitman's *Drum-Taps* (1865) and *Specimen Days and Collect* (1882) comprise the bulk of the war's immediate legacy of poetry and fiction. Although there were many works of historical interest—soldiers' letters and diaries, as well as journalistic writings—works of literary significance were rare, prompting the question: Why did an event of such magnitude result in such a scant literary output?

> With malice toward none; with charity for all; with firmness in the right, as God gives us to see the right, let us strive on to finish the work we are in; to bind up the nation's wounds; to care for him who shall have borne the battle, and for his widow, and his orphan—to do all which may achieve and cherish a just and lasting peace, among ourselves, and with all nations.
>
> —President Abraham Lincoln, Second Inaugural Address, March 4, 1865

Modern readers think that one byproduct of a war is a literary account of it, largely in the form of novels and poems by people who participated in the war. Modern writers like Ernest Hemingway went to war intending to return with the material for novels. This was not the case with the Civil War. Few major American writers saw the Civil War firsthand. Emerson was in Concord during most of the war, "knitting socks and mittens for soldiers," as he wrote to his son, and "writing patriotic lectures." Thoreau, who had been a fervent abolitionist, died in 1862, and Hawthorne died two years later. Emily Dickinson remained in Amherst, Massachusetts, but the country's grief with the war seems to have informed her poetry. Of the younger generation of writers, William Dean Howells, Henry James, and Henry Adams were abroad. Perhaps most important, though, traditional literary forms of the time were inadequate to express the horrifying details of the Civil War. The literary form most appropriate for handling such strong material—the realistic novel—had not yet been fully developed in the United States. Thus, the great novel of the war, *The Red Badge of Courage,* had to wait to be written by a man who was not born until six years after the war had ended: Stephen Crane.

Detail from original manuscript of Stephen Crane's *The Red Badge of Courage.*
University of Virginia Library.

Harriet Tubman Series No. 9 (1939–40) by Jacob Lawrence.

Hampton University Museum, Hampton, Virginia. Courtesy of the artist and
the Francine Seders Gallery, Seattle, WA.

Very little important poetry and fiction issued directly from the Civil War, largely because few major American writers experienced the war firsthand. Direct accounts of the war found their way into other types of literature, however, including poignant letters and diaries. The "real war" would not find a place in American fiction until the development of the realistic novel.

The Rise of Realism

One of the most enduring subjects for prose fiction has always been the exploits of larger-than-life heroes. Born of the chivalric romance, the **romantic novel** presents readers with lives lived idealistically—beyond the level of everyday life. The heroes and heroines of the novels of James Fenimore Cooper, for example, engage in romantic adventures

Look at me! Look at my arm! I have plowed and planted, and gathered into barns, and no man could head me! And ain't I a woman? I could work as much and eat as much as a man—when I could get it—and bear the lash as well! And ain't I a woman? I have borne thirteen children, and seen most sold off to slavery, and when I cried out with my mother's grief, none but Jesus heard me! And ain't I a woman?

—Sojourner Truth
(born in slavery in Ulster County, New York, c. 1797)

filled with courageous acts, daring chases, and exciting escapes. Cooper's Leatherstocking, or Hawkeye, like his modern-day heirs James Bond and Indiana Jones, has uncommon abilities that enable him to survive and prevail. His adventures are a far cry from the ordinary lives led by most of Cooper's readers. Such exciting exploits have always been a staple of prose fiction—and, before that, of epic poetry.

In America, the great fiction writers of the mid–nineteenth century, Edgar Allan Poe, Nathaniel Hawthorne, and Herman Melville, shared an aversion to simple realism. These writers used romance not simply to entertain readers, but to reveal truths that would be hidden in a realistic story that limited itself to what actually could happen.

After the Civil War, however, a new generation of writers came of age. They were known as **realists,** writers who aimed at a "very minute fidelity" to the common course of ordinary life. Their subjects were drawn from the slums of the rapidly growing cities, from the factories that were rapidly replacing farmlands, and from the lives of far from idealized characters: poor factory workers, corrupt politicians, even prostitutes.

Children in Mullen's Alley, off Cherry Street, New York City (c. 1888). Photograph by Jacob Riis.

Realism Takes Root in Europe

Realism was well entrenched in Europe by the time it began to flower in the United States. It developed in the work of such writers as Daniel Defoe, George Eliot, Anthony Trollope, Honoré de Balzac, Stendhal, Gustave Flaubert, and Leo Tolstoy. These writers tried to represent faithfully the environment and the manners of everyday life: the way ordinary people lived and dressed, and what they thought and felt and talked about.

But realism was not simply concerned with recording wallpaper patterns, hairstyles, or the subjects of conversations. It sought also to explain *why* ordinary people behave the way they do. Realistic novelists often relied on the emerging sciences of human and animal behavior—biology, psychology, and sociology—as well as on their own insights and observations.

> Language grows out of life, out of its needs and experiences. . . . Good work in language presupposes and depends on a real knowledge of things.
>
> —Annie Sullivan

> The only reason for the existence of a novel is that it does attempt to represent life.
>
> —Henry James

The literary movement known as realism dominated American fiction from the late nineteenth century to the middle of the twentieth. Realists sought to accurately portray real life, without filtering it through personal feelings, romanticism, or idealism.

American Regionalism: Brush Strokes of Local Color

In America, realism had its roots in **regionalism,** literature that emphasizes a specific geographic setting and that makes use of the speech and manners of the people who live in that region. Sarah Orne Jewett, Kate Chopin, Harriet Beecher Stowe, Bret Harte, and Charles W. Chesnutt are noted early regionalists who recorded the peculiarities of speech and temperament in their parts of a rapidly expanding nation. (Regionalism flourished again in the 1920s and 1930s, especially in the South, and is still today an important aspect of American literature.)

While regional writers strove to be realistic in their depiction of speech patterns and manners, they were often unrealistic—even sentimental—in their depiction of character and social environment. For example, the Southern writer Thomas Nelson Page, who wrote popular post–Civil War novels about the South before the war, stressed the romantic "moonlight and magnolia" environment at the expense of the realities of a social world that relied on slavery. Realism as a literary movement in the United States went far beyond regionalism in its concern for accuracy in portraying social conditions and human motivation.

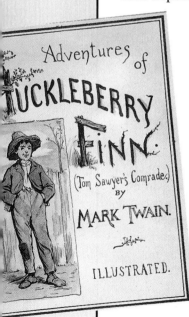

Original edition of Mark Twain's *Adventures of Huckleberry Finn* (1885). The Granger Collection, New York.

Coming and Going of the Pony Express (1900) by Frederic Remington.
Oil on canvas (26″ × 39″).

The Thomas Gilcrease Institute of American History and Art, Tulsa, Oklahoma.

> All modern American literature comes from one book by Mark Twain called *Huckleberry Finn*.
>
> —Ernest Hemingway

Mark Twain is the best-known example of a regional writer whose realism far surpassed local bounds. Although he first established his reputation as a regional humorist, Twain evolved into a writer whose comic view of society became increasingly satiric. His best novel, *Adventures of Huckleberry Finn* (1884), describes the moral growth of a comic character in an environment that is at the same time physically beautiful and morally repugnant. *Huckleberry Finn* combines a biting picture of some of the injustices inherent in pre–Civil War life with a lyrical portrait of the American landscape.

American realism had its roots in regionalism, literature that focuses on a relatively small geographical area and attempts to accurately reproduce the speech and manners of that region.

Realism and Naturalism: A Lens on Everyday Life

The most active proponent of realism in American fiction was William Dean Howells, editor of the influential magazine *The Atlantic Monthly.* In both his fiction and his critical writings, Howells insisted that realism should deal with the lives of ordinary people, be faithful to the development of character even at the expense of action, and discuss the social questions perplexing Americans. Howells's "smiling realism" portrayed an America where people may act foolishly but where their good qualities eventually win out. "Ah! poor Real Life, which I love," Howells wrote in one of his many essays, "can I make others share the delight I find in thy foolish and insipid face?" For Howells, life *was,* even at its worst, merely "foolish and insipid," and this proved to be his greatest limitation as a novelist.

Other realistic novelists viewed life as a much rougher clash of contrary forces. The Californian Frank Norris, for example, agreed with Howells that the proper subject for fiction was the ordinary person, but he found Howells's fiction too strait-laced and narrow. It was, Norris said, "as respectable as a church and proper as a deacon." Norris was an earthier writer, interested in the impact of large social forces on individuals. His best-known novel, *The Octopus* (1901), is about the struggles between wheat farmers and the railroad monopoly in California. Norris was not the first to use the novel to examine social institutions with the aim of reforming them; Harriet Beecher Stowe's novel *Uncle Tom's Cabin* (1852) had been published before the Civil War and, according to Lincoln (and many historians), played a large part in helping to cause the war. But *Uncle Tom's Cabin* was more melodrama than realistic fiction.

Norris is generally considered to be a **naturalist.** Following the lead of the French novelist Emile Zola, naturalists relied heavily on the growing scientific disciplines of psychology and sociology. In their fiction, they attempted to dissect human behavior with as much objectivity as a scientist would dissect a frog or a cadaver. For naturalists, human behavior was determined by forces beyond the individual's power, especially by biology and environment. The naturalists tended to look at human life as a grim losing battle. Their characters often had only limited choices and motivations. In the eyes of some naturalist writers, human beings were totally subject to the natural laws of the universe; like animals, they lived crudely, by instinct, unable to control their own destinies.

Advertisement for Harriet Beecher Stowe's *Uncle Tom's Cabin* (1852).

Culver Pictures.

135,000 SETS, 270,000 VOLUMES SOLD.

UNCLE TOM'S CABIN

FOR SALE HERE.

AN EDITION FOR THE MILLION, COMPLETE IN 1 Vol., PRICE 37 1-2 CENTS.
"   "   IN GERMAN, IN 1 Vol., PRICE 50 CENTS.
"   "   IN 2 Vols., CLOTH, 6 PLATES, PRICE $1.50.
SUPERB ILLUSTRATED EDITION, IN 1 Vol., WITH 153 ENGRAVINGS,
PRICES FROM $2.50 TO $5.00.

The Greatest Book of the Age.

Psychological Fiction: Inside the Human Mind

On the other hand, the New York–born Henry James, considered America's greatest writer of the **psychological novel,** concentrated principally on fine distinctions in character motivation. James was a realist, but no realist could be further from the blunt, naturalistic view that people were driven by animal-like instincts. In his finely tuned studies of human motivation, James opened the inner mind to the techniques of fiction. He was mainly interested in complex social and psychological situations. Many of his novels, including *Daisy Miller* (1879) and *The Portrait of a Lady* (1881), take place in Europe, because James considered European society to be both more complex and more sinister than American society. He frequently contrasts innocent, eager Americans with sophisticated, more reserved Europeans. In a typically "Jamesian" fiction, a straightforward American confronts the complexities of European society and either defeats or is defeated by them.

Stephen Crane was as profound a psychologist as James, but his principal interest was the human character at moments of stress. For James, the proper setting for an examination of human behavior under pressure was the drawing room; for Crane, it was the battlefield, the streets of a slum, or a lifeboat lost at sea. Although Crane is sometimes referred to as a naturalist, he is probably best thought of as an **ironist;** he was the first of many modern American writers—later including Ernest Hemingway and Kurt Vonnegut, Jr.—to juxtapose human pretensions with the indifference of the universe. Of all the nineteenth-century realists, only Crane could describe a stabbing death (in his story "The Blue Hotel") in this coolly cynical manner: "[The blade] shot forward, and a human body, this citadel of virtue, wisdom, power, was pierced as easily as if it had been a melon." It would take this sensibility to get the "real war" in the books at last.

> [Crane's] importance lies not only in those few works of his which completely come off, like "The Open Boat," but in his constantly seeking the primitive facts, the forbidden places, the dangerous people.
>
> —Alfred Kazin

Realism in American literature branched out in several directions, from the "smiling realism" of William Dean Howells to the gritty naturalism of Frank Norris, and from the psychological realism of Henry James to the ironic stance of Stephen Crane.

Reading Skills and Strategies
Establishing a Purpose for Reading

Think about what you already know about such topics as the Civil War, slavery, Reconstruction, the expansion and settlement of the frontier, and the rise of cities after the Civil War. Make a KWL chart (see page 431) in which you write down what you know about this period of American history and literature and what you want to know. Fill out what you have learned as you read the collections that follow.

Douglass

Spirituals and Code Songs

Chopin

American Indian Oratory

My Guilt

My guilt is "slavery's chains," too long
the clang of iron falls down the years.
This brother's sold. This sister's gone
is bitter wax, lining my ears.
My guilt made music with the tears.

My crime is "heroes, dead and gone"
dead Vesey, Turner, Gabriel,
dead Malcolm, Marcus, Martin King.
They fought too hard, they loved too well.
My crime is I'm alive to tell.

My sin is "hanging from a tree"
I do not scream, it makes me proud.
I take to dying like a man.
I do it to impress the crowd.
My sin lies in not screaming loud.

—Maya Angelou (1928–   )

Slave Hunt, Dismal Swamp, Virginia (detail) (1862) by Thomas Moran
(American, 1837–1926). Oil on canvas.
The Philbrook Museum of Art, 1947.8.44.

Frederick Douglass

(1817?–1895)

Frederick Douglass was born into slavery in Talbot County, on the Eastern Shore of Maryland, and was separated from his mother soon after his birth. "The practice of separating children from their mothers," wrote Douglass years later, "and hiring the latter out at distances too great to admit of their meeting, except at long intervals, is a marked feature of the cruelty and barbarity of the slave system. But it is in harmony with the grand aim of slavery, which, always and everywhere, is to reduce man to a level with the brute. It is a successful method of obliterating from the mind and heart of the slave all just ideas of the sacredness of the family. . . ."

Since records were not kept of the birth of children born into slavery, Douglass was never sure of his exact age: "Genealogical trees do not flourish among slaves," he was to remark ironically later. Although Douglass received no formal education, he did teach himself to read with the help, at first, of members of the household he served. Later, these same people became furious when they saw Douglass reading a book or a newspaper; education, they decided, was incompatible with being enslaved.

When Douglass was about twenty-one, he satisfied his hunger for freedom by escaping to Massachusetts, where he married and soon started to make public speeches in support of the abolitionist cause. He changed his last name from Bailey to Douglass, after the hero of the romantic novel *The Lady of the Lake* by Sir Walter Scott.

In 1845, Douglass went to England, largely because of the danger he faced as a fugitive, especially after the publication that same year of his autobiography, *The Narrative of the Life of Frederick Douglass, an American Slave.* In England, he mobilized antislavery sentiment and became independent when British friends collected around $700 to purchase his freedom.

When he returned to the United States in 1847, Douglass founded a newspaper, the *North Star.* (The name was chosen because escapees used this star as a guide north.) In his newspaper, Douglass championed the abolition of slavery. In 1855, he published a revised version of his life's story, titled *My Bondage and My Freedom.* These "escape" narratives, like earlier "captivity" stories (page 40), were enormously popular, and Douglass's were widely read and very influential in the abolitionist cause.

When the Civil War began, Douglass worked ardently for the Underground Railroad, the secret network of abolitionists and their sympathizers that helped many people held in slavery escape to the North. He also energetically helped to recruit African American soldiers for the Union armies.

Continuing to write and lecture after the war, Douglass argued that the surest way to rehabilitate his tragically scarred people was through education. In 1881, he published yet another version of his autobiography, titled *The Life and Times of Frederick Douglass.* Today, Douglass is revered for the courage with which he insistently proclaimed his profoundly humane values, and admired for the quiet eloquence of his writing style.

Make the Connection

Fighting Back

While he was still enslaved, Frederick Douglass fought against society's shackles to assert his human rights and defend his dignity against a brutal, dehumanizing institution. His courageous action became a remarkable turning point in his life. Perhaps his actions will remind you of other heroic men and women who have taken stands against oppression.

Reading Skills and Strategies

Dialogue with the Text

As you read, fill out an event-prediction-outcome chart like the one below. Each time Douglass acts to assert his human rights, write down your prediction—or fear—about what might happen to him as a result. As you continue reading, write down what actually happens. Do any of the outcomes surprise you?

Event in Story	Prediction About Outcome	Actual Outcome

Background

Douglass has been compared with Benjamin Franklin (page 84), another self-made man who struggled against tremendous odds to achieve distinction at a critical time in his nation's history. But Douglass's story, of course, is different from Franklin's. Franklin was never enslaved. He was never "owned" by another human being and considered to be of no more significance than a piece of personal property.

In the following selection from *The Narrative of the Life of Frederick Douglass*, Douglass provides a graphic account of a critical incident that occurred when he was sixteen years old. Earlier in his narrative, he explained to his readers "how a man was made a slave"; now he sets out to explain "how a slave was made a man." At the time, Douglass was owned by a man named Thomas who had rented Douglass for a year to a man named Covey.

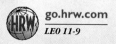

from The Narrative of the Life of Frederick Douglass

Frederick Douglass

The Battle with Mr. Covey

I have already intimated that my condition was much worse, during the first six months of my stay at Mr. Covey's, than in the last six. The circumstances leading to the change in Mr. Covey's course toward me form an epoch in my humble history. You have seen how a man was made a slave; you shall see how a slave was made a man. On one of the hottest days of the month of August, 1833, Bill Smith, William Hughes, a slave named Eli, and myself, were engaged in fanning wheat.[1] Hughes was clearing the fanned wheat from before the fan, Eli was turning, Smith was feeding, and I was carrying wheat to the fan. The work was simple, requiring strength rather than intellect; yet, to one entirely unused to such work, it came very hard.

About three o'clock of that day, I broke down; my strength failed me; I was seized with a violent aching of the head, attended with extreme dizziness; I trembled in every limb. Finding what was coming, I nerved myself up, feeling it would never do to stop work. I stood as long as I could stagger to the hopper with grain. When I could stand no longer, I fell, and felt as if held down by an immense weight. The fan of course stopped; everyone had his own work to do; and no one could do the work of the other, and have his own go on at the same time.

Mr. Covey was at the house, about one hundred yards from the treading yard where we were fanning. On hearing the fan stop, he left immediately, and came to the spot where we were. He hastily inquired what the matter was. Bill answered that I was sick, and there was no one to bring wheat to the fan. I had by this time crawled away under the side of the post-and-rail fence by which the yard was enclosed, hoping to find relief by getting out of the sun. He then asked where I was. He was told by one of the hands.

He came to the spot, and, after looking at me awhile, asked me what was the matter. I told him as

1. **fanning wheat:** separating usable grain.

well as I could, for I scarce had strength to speak. He then gave me a savage kick in the side, and told me to get up. I tried to do so, but fell back in the attempt. He gave me another kick, and again told me to rise. I again tried, and succeeded in gaining my feet; but, stooping to get the tub with which I was feeding the fan, I again staggered and fell. While down in this situation, Mr. Covey took up the hickory slat with which Hughes had been striking off the half-bushel measure, and with it gave me a heavy blow upon the head, making a large wound, and the blood ran freely; and with this again told me to get up. I made no effort to comply, having now made up my mind to let him do his worst. In a short time after receiving this blow, my head grew better. Mr. Covey had now left me to my fate.

At this moment I resolved, for the first time, to go to my master, enter a complaint, and ask his protection. In order to [do] this, I must that afternoon walk seven miles; and this, under the circumstances, was truly a severe undertaking. I was exceedingly feeble; made so as much by the kicks and blows which I received, as by the severe fit of sickness to which I had been subjected. I, however, watched my chance, while Covey was looking in an opposite direction, and started for St. Michael's. I succeeded in getting a considerable distance on my way to the woods, when Covey discovered me, and called after me to come back, threatening what he would do if I did not come. I disregarded both his calls and his threats, and made my way to the woods as fast as my feeble state would allow; and thinking I might be overhauled by him if I kept the road, I walked through the woods, keeping far enough from the road to

---

WORDS TO OWN

intimated (in′tə·māt′əd) v.: stated indirectly; hinted.
comply (kəm·plī′) v.: to obey; to agree to a request.

Frederick Douglass Series No. 10 (1938–1939) by Jacob Lawrence. Casein tempera on gessoed hardboard (17 7/8″ × 12″).

Frederick Douglass Series No. 9 (1938–1939) by Jacob Lawrence. Casein tempera on gessoed hardboard (12" × 17⅞"). Hampton University Museum, Hampton, Virginia. Courtesy of the artist and the Francine Seders Gallery, Seattle, WA.

avoid detection, and near enough to prevent losing my way.

I had not gone far before my little strength again failed me. I could go no farther. I fell down, and lay for a considerable time. The blood was yet oozing from the wound on my head. For a time I thought I should bleed to death; and think now that I should have done so, but that the blood so matted my hair as to stop the wound. After lying there about three quarters of an hour, I nerved myself up again, and started on my way, through bogs and briers, barefooted and bareheaded, tearing my feet sometimes at nearly every step; and after a journey of about seven miles, occupying some five hours to perform it, I arrived at master's store. I then presented an appearance enough to affect any but a heart of iron. From the crown of my head to my feet, I was covered with blood. My hair was all clotted with dust and blood; my shirt was stiff with blood. My legs and feet were torn in sundry places with briers and thorns, and were also covered with blood. I suppose I looked like a man who had escaped a den of wild beasts, and barely escaped them.

In this state I appeared before my master, humbly entreating him to <u>interpose</u> his authority for my protection. I told him all the circumstances as well as I could, and it seemed, as I spoke, at times to affect him. He would then walk the floor, and seek to justify Covey by saying he expected I deserved it. He asked me what I wanted. I told

him, to let me get a new home; that as sure as I lived with Mr. Covey again, I should live with but to die with him; that Covey would surely kill me; he was in a fair way for it. Master Thomas ridiculed the idea that there was any danger of Mr. Covey's killing me, and said that he knew Mr. Covey; that he was a good man, and that he could not think of taking me from him; that, should he do so, he would lose the whole year's wages; that I belonged to Mr. Covey for one year, and that I must go back to him, come what might; and that I must not trouble him with any more stories, or that he would himself *get hold of me*. After threatening me thus, he gave me a very large dose of salts, telling me that I might remain in St. Michael's that night (it being quite late), but that I must be off back to Mr. Covey's early in the morning; and that if I did not, he would *get hold of me,* which meant that he would whip me.

I remained all night, and, according to his orders, I started off to Covey's in the morning (Saturday morning), wearied in body and broken in spirit. I got no supper that night, or breakfast that morning. I reached Covey's about nine o'clock; and just as I was getting over the fence that divided Mrs. Kemp's fields from ours, out ran Covey

WORDS TO OWN

interpose (in′tər·pōz′) v.: to put forth in order to intervene.

with his cowskin, to give me another whipping. Before he could reach me, I succeeded in getting to the cornfield; and as the corn was very high, it afforded me the means of hiding. He seemed very angry, and searched for me a long time. My behavior was altogether unaccountable. He finally gave up the chase, thinking, I suppose, that I must come home for something to eat; he would give himself no further trouble in looking for me. I spent that day mostly in the woods, having the alternative before me—to go home and be whipped to death, or stay in the woods and be starved to death.

That night, I fell in with Sandy Jenkins, a slave with whom I was somewhat acquainted. Sandy had a free wife who lived about four miles from Mr. Covey's; and it being Saturday, he was on his way to see her. I told him my circumstances, and he very kindly invited me to go home with him. I went home with him, and talked this whole matter over, and got his advice as to what course it was best for me to pursue. I found Sandy an old advisor.[2] He told me, with great solemnity, I must go back to Covey; but that before I went, I must go with him into another part of the woods, where there was a certain *root,* which, if I would take some of it with me, carrying it *always on my right side,* would render it impossible for Mr. Covey, or any other white man, to whip me. He said he had carried it for years; and since he had done so, he had never received a blow, and never expected to while he carried it. I at first rejected the idea, that the simple carrying of a root in my pocket would have any such effect as he had said, and was not disposed to take it; but Sandy impressed the necessity with much earnestness, telling me it could do no harm, if it did no good. To please him, I at length took the root, and, according to his direction, carried it upon my right side. This was Sunday morning.

I immediately started for home; and upon entering the yard gate, out came Mr. Covey on his way to meeting. He spoke to me very kindly, made me drive the pigs from a lot near by, and passed on toward the church. Now, this singular conduct of Mr. Covey really made me begin to think that there was something in the *root* which Sandy had given me; and had it been on any other

2. **an old advisor:** someone who can offer good advice.

day than Sunday, I could have attributed the conduct to no other cause than the influence of that root; and as it was, I was half inclined to think the *root* to be something more than I at first had taken it to be. All went well till Monday morning. On this morning, the virtue of the *root* was fully tested.

Long before daylight, I was called to go and rub, curry, and feed the horses. I obeyed, and was glad to obey. But while thus engaged, while in the act of throwing down some blades from the loft, Mr. Covey entered the stable with a long rope; and just as I was half out of the loft, he caught hold of my legs, and was about tying me. As soon as I found what he was up to, I gave a sudden spring, and as I did so, he holding to my legs, I was brought sprawling on the stable floor. Mr. Covey seemed now to think he had me, and could do what he pleased; but at this moment—from whence came the spirit I don't know—I resolved to fight; and, suiting my action to the resolution, I seized Covey hard by the throat; and as I did so, I rose. He held on to me, and I to him. My resistance was so entirely unexpected, that Covey seemed taken all aback. He trembled like a leaf. This gave me assurance, and I held him uneasy, causing the blood to run where I touched him with the ends of my fingers. Mr. Covey soon called out to Hughes for help. Hughes came, and, while Covey held me, attempted to tie my right hand. While he was in the act of doing so, I watched my chance, and gave him a heavy kick close under the ribs. This kick fairly sickened Hughes, so that he left me in the hands of Mr. Covey.

This kick had the effect of not only weakening Hughes, but Covey also. When he saw Hughes bending over with pain, his courage quailed.[3] He asked me if I meant to persist in my resistance. I told him I did, come what might; that he had used me like a brute for six months, and that I was determined to be used so no longer. With that, he

3. **quailed:** faltered.

WORDS TO OWN

solemnity (sə·lem′nə·tē) *n.:* seriousness.
render (ren′dər) *v.:* make.
singular (siŋ′gyə·lər) *adj.:* remarkable.
attributed (ə·trib′yōōt·id) *v.:* believed to result from.
curry (kʉr′ē) *v.:* to groom.

---

strove to drag me to a stick that was lying just out of the stable door. He meant to knock me down. But just as he was leaning over to get the stick, I seized him with both hands by his collar, and brought him by a sudden snatch to the ground. By this time, Bill came. Covey called upon him for assistance. Bill wanted to know what he could do. Covey said, "Take hold of him, take hold of him!" Bill said his master hired him out to work, and not to help to whip me; so he left Covey and myself to fight our own battle out. We were at it for nearly two hours. Covey at length let me go, puffing and blowing at a great rate, saying that if I had not resisted, he would not have whipped me half so much. The truth was, that he had not whipped me at all. I considered him as getting entirely the worst end of the bargain; for he had drawn no blood from me, but I had from him. The whole six months afterward, that I spent with Mr. Covey, he never laid the weight of his finger upon me in anger. He would occasionally say, he didn't want to get hold of me again. "No," thought I, "you need not; for you will come off worse than you did before."

This battle with Mr. Covey was the turning point in my career as a slave. It rekindled the few expiring embers of freedom, and revived within me a sense of my own manhood. It recalled the departed self-confidence, and inspired me again with a determination to be free. The gratification afforded by the triumph was a full compensation for whatever else might follow, even death itself. He only can understand the deep satisfaction which I experienced, who has himself repelled by force the bloody arm of slavery. I felt as I never felt before. It was a glorious resurrection, from the tomb of slavery, to the heaven of freedom. My long-crushed spirit rose, cowardice departed, bold defiance took its place; and I now resolved that, however long I might remain a slave in form, the day had passed forever when I could be a slave in fact.

- -

WORDS TO OWN

expiring (ek·spīr'iŋ) v. used as *adj.*: dying.
afforded (ə·fôrd'əd) v. used as *adj.*: given; provided.

- -

MAKING MEANINGS

First Thoughts

1. Review the event-prediction-outcome chart you made as you read. Which details, events, or aspects of Douglass's account surprised you?

Shaping Interpretations

2. The root Sandy Jenkins gives to Douglass is a *talisman*, an object believed to possess supernatural powers. What does Douglass discover is even more powerful than the root?

3. What elements of humor do you find in the part of the story involving Sandy Jenkins? Explain.

4. Based on this account, how would you **characterize** the young Frederick Douglass?

5. What does the entire incident reveal about Covey's **character**?

6. At the end of the selection, Douglass distinguishes between being "a slave in form" and "a slave in fact." Explain the meaning of this distinction.

Extending the Text

7. "He only can understand the deep satisfaction which I experienced, who has himself repelled by force the bloody arm of slavery" (page 430). In what ways is Douglass's statement true? In what ways might it not be true? Discuss how Douglass's feelings might apply to the problems of racism today.

Reading Check

a. What action does Douglass take after Covey strikes him? What does Thomas order Douglass to do?

b. What is Covey's reaction when Douglass returns from his visit to Thomas?

c. Explain how Sandy Jenkins helps Douglass.

d. Describe what Douglass calls the turning point in his life as a slave.

ELEMENTS OF LITERATURE

Douglass's Metaphors

At the end of the selection, Douglass uses **metaphors** that suggest resurrection and rebirth.

1. Explain the comparison implied in this line: "It [the battle] rekindled the few expiring embers of freedom." How are these **images** related to the idea of rebirth?

2. What is Douglass implicitly comparing slavery to when he refers to "the bloody arm of slavery"?

3. Find the passage that specifically compares Douglass's experience to a rebirth. In this comparison, what is being compared to what?

CHOICES: Building Your Portfolio

Writer's Notebook

1. Collecting Ideas for a Research Paper

Douglass's narrative is a rich source of information, perspectives, and imagery on topics such as slavery, human rights, self-esteem, racism, and freedom. In a KWL chart like the one below, explore a topic suggested by Douglass's narrative that you would be interested in gathering more information about. Save your notes for possible use in the Writer's Workshop on page 515.

K What I Know	W What I Want to Know	L What I Learned

Comparing and Contrasting Ideas

2. Emerson Applied

Reread Emerson's essay "Self-Reliance" (page 224). Then, write a brief essay in which you (a) explain which of Emerson's ideas relate to Douglass's experience and (b) identify any of Emerson's ideas that seem to be contradicted by Douglass's narrative.

Creative Writing

3. Responding to Other Voices

You have already read the work of other writers who have championed principles of freedom, such as Bradford, Jefferson, Paine, Franklin, Emerson, Thoreau, and Whitman. Write a letter or a journal entry in which Douglass responds to one of these writers, expressing his views of their writings, beliefs, actions, or achievements.

Crossing the Curriculum: History

4. Freedom Fighters

With two other students, research the lives of three people who have opposed racial discrimination. Among the people you might consider are the South African leaders Nelson Mandela, Helen Suzman, and Desmond Tutu; the American civil rights leaders W.E.B. Du Bois, Roy Wilkins, Malcolm X, and Martin Luther King, Jr.; Senator Daniel K. Inouye and others who have protested the internment of Japanese Americans in the United States during World War II; and Raoul Wallenberg, Janus Korczak, and Oskar Schindler, who worked to save Jewish lives during the Nazi Holocaust in Europe. Present a panel discussion in which each group member summarizes the life and career of a freedom fighter and explains how that person helped advance the cause of human rights.

Desmond Tutu.
UPI/Bettmann.

SPOTLIGHT ON
Spirituals and Code Songs

Frederick Douglass (detail) (c. 1844), attributed to Elisha Hammond. Oil on canvas (27½″ × 22½″).

National Portrait Gallery, Smithsonian Institution. Courtesy Art Resource, NY.

The moving and intensely emotional songs known as spirituals largely developed from the oral traditions of Africans held in slavery in the South before the Civil War. Spirituals, like other kinds of folk literature and music, were composed by anonymous artists and passed on orally. They were inevitably altered and re-fined, so numerous versions of a particular spiritual might exist. Many spirituals combine African melodies and rhythms with elements of white Southern religious music.

In this passage from *My Bondage and My Freedom*, Frederick Douglass writes eloquently about songs of slavery—called sorrow songs by the later African American writer W.E.B. Du Bois.

Slaves are generally expected to sing as well as to work. A silent slave is not liked by masters or overseers. *"Make a noise, make a noise,"* and *"bear a hand"* are the words usually addressed to the slaves when there is silence amongst them. This may account for the almost constant singing heard in the southern states. . . . On allowance day, those who visited the great house farm were peculiarly excited and noisy. While on their way, they would make the dense old woods, for miles around, reverberate with their wild notes. These were not always merry because they were wild. On the contrary, they were mostly of a plaintive cast, and told a tale of grief and sorrow. In the most boisterous outbursts of rapturous senti-ment, there was ever a tinge of deep melancholy. I have never heard any songs like those any-where since I left slavery, ex-cept when in Ireland. There I heard the same *wailing notes,* and was much affected by them. It was during the famine of 1845–1846. In all the songs of the slaves, there was ever some expression in praise of the great house farm; something which would flatter the pride of

the owner, and, possibly, draw a favorable glance from him.

. . . I cannot better express my sense of them now, than ten years ago, when, in sketching my life, I thus spoke of this feature of my plantation experience:

. . . The hearing of those wild notes always depressed my spirits, and filled my heart with ineffable sadness. The mere recurrence, even now, afflicts my spirit, and while I am writing these lines, my tears are falling. To those songs I trace my first glimmering conceptions of the dehumanizing character of slavery. I can never get rid of that conception. Those songs still follow me, to deepen my hatred of slavery, and quicken my sympathies for my brethren in bonds. If any one wishes to be impressed with a sense of the soul-killing power of slavery, let him go to Colonel Lloyd's plantation, and, on allowance day, place himself in the deep, pine woods, and there let him, in silence, thoughtfully analyze the sounds that shall pass through the chambers of his soul, and if he is not thus impressed, it will only be because "there is no flesh in his obdurate heart."

—Frederick Douglass

Harriet Tubman and the Freedom Train (detail) (1989) by Barbara Olsen. Gouache, collage (22½" × 30").

© Barbara Olsen. Collection of Dr. and Mrs. J. S. Kahn.

Spirituals were concerned above all with issues of freedom: spiritual freedom in the form of salvation and literal freedom from the shackles of slavery. Many people during the time of slavery were called Moses by those looking for a deliverer to loose their chains. Harriet Tubman, for example, used Moses as her code name in her work with the Underground Railroad. A Methodist minister named Francis Asbury was also known as Moses, and according to some scholars, the spiritual "Go Down, Moses" really is a plea for Asbury's help. Ultimately, of course, the name Moses refers to the man who, according to the Book of Exodus in the Bible, delivered the ancient Israelites from slavery in Egypt.

Some of the songs were code songs, or signal songs— that is, details in the songs provided runaways with directions, times, and meeting places for their escape. For example, the drinking gourd in "Follow the Drinking Gourd" is the Big Dipper, a group of stars; two stars in the bowl of the Big Dipper point to the North Star. A drinking gourd is actually the shell of a vegetable related to the squash or melon, dried and hollowed out for drinking.

The Old Plantation (c. 1795) by an unknown artist (South Carolina). Watercolor on laid paper (11¹¹/₁₆″ × 17⅞″).

Abby Aldrich Rockefeller Folk Art Center, Williamsburg, Virginia.

Go Down, Moses

Go down, Moses,
Way down in Egypt land
Tell old Pharaoh
To let my people go.

5　When Israel was in Egypt land
Let my people go
Oppressed so hard they could not
　stand
Let my people go.

Go down, Moses,
10　Way down in Egypt land
Tell old Pharaoh,
"Let my people go."

"Thus saith the Lord," bold Moses
　said,
"Let my people go;
15　If not I'll smite your firstborn dead
Let my people go."

Go down, Moses,
Way down in Egypt land,
Tell old Pharaoh,
20　"Let my people go!"

Follow the Drinking Gourd

When the sun comes back and the first quail
　calls,
　Follow the drinking gourd,
For the old man is a-waiting for to carry you
　to freedom
　If you follow the drinking gourd.

[Refrain]
5　Follow the drinking gourd,
　Follow the drinking gourd,
For the old man is a-waiting for to carry you
　to freedom
　If you follow the drinking gourd.

The river bank will make a very good road,
10　　The dead trees show you the way,
Left foot, peg foot traveling on
　Follow the drinking gourd. [Refrain]

The river ends between two hills,
　Follow the drinking gourd.
15　There's another river on the other side,
　Following the drinking gourd. [Refrain]

Where the little river meets the great big
　river,
　Follow the drinking gourd.
The old man is a-waiting for to carry you to
　freedom,
20　　If you follow the drinking gourd. [Refrain]

Kate Chopin

(1851–1904)

Kate Chopin's work went unrecognized, and was even scorned, during her lifetime. Along with many other literary pioneers, Chopin never lived to see her work vindicated.

Kate Chopin was born Katherine O'Flaherty in St. Louis, Missouri, to an Irish immigrant father and a mother descended from French Creole aristocrats. (Creoles are people of French or Spanish descent who are born in the states bordering the Gulf of Mexico but who retain their European culture.) Kate's prosperous parents encouraged her early interest in music and reading; her mother invited such a flurry of stimulating visitors to their house that Kate sometimes escaped to the attic to read. She was given lessons in French and piano for a time by her worldly great-grandmother, who stirred the child's imagination with vivid tales of old St. Louis. Kate became a witty and popular young woman with a notably independent turn of mind.

At nineteen, Kate married Oscar Chopin, a French Creole from New Orleans, and they enjoyed a long European honeymoon, visiting art galleries and attending operas. The Chopins settled in Louisiana and reared a family of six children, but, when Kate was thirty-two, Oscar died suddenly from swamp fever. Kate returned to St. Louis, and it was then that she began to write. She published a poem when she was thirty-eight, followed by some short stories. In 1890, she published her first novel.

Chopin's short stories concern the life of French Creoles in Louisiana. Published in national magazines and collected in two volumes called *Bayou Folk* (1894) and *A Night in Acadie* (1897), the stories were praised for their accurate portrayal of the French Creole strand in American culture. Chopin's theme, however, was a much more controversial matter: the repression of women in Victorian America.

This theme was presented most dramatically in her novel *The Awakening* (1899). The novel portrays a dissatisfied New Orleans wife who breaks from the confines of her marriage and, in her quest for freedom, flagrantly defies the Victorian ideals of motherhood and domesticity. The novel was greeted with hostility by American critics, who condemned it as sordid and vulgar. Victorians, who looked to literature for moral lessons, saw only an immoral lesson in *The Awakening*. The novel was removed from circulation in St. Louis libraries, some of Chopin's friends shunned her, and the local arts club denied her membership. Chopin was disheartened enough by this rejection to allow her writing to languish, and she produced little more before her death in 1904. After her death, her work fell into obscurity, and often copies of her books couldn't even be obtained.

The Awakening and many of Chopin's other works were rediscovered decades after her death. With the help of discerning critics and the women's movement of the 1960s and 1970s, Kate Chopin is now recognized as a novelist of skill and perception, whose work appeared half a century before its time.

Before You Read

A PAIR OF SILK STOCKINGS

Make the Connection

Escaping the Humdrum

From time to time, everyone feels trapped by the humdrum duties of daily life. All of us—probably even rock stars and world travelers—fantasize about escape from routines that come to feel boring or confining. For a nineteenth-century woman of limited means trying to satisfy the needs of her family, even a brief reprieve from the demands of domestic life could be a life-changing bid for freedom and a temporary escape from day-to-day duties.

Reading Skills and Strategies

Dialogue with the Text

Read the story's first two paragraphs, and then stop. Write down your predictions of what Mrs. Sommers will do with her unexpected possession of money—a sum equivalent to a generous weekly salary in the 1890s.

Background

As you read, be aware that nylon had not yet been invented in the 1890s; most women wore long, thick, cotton stockings. Silk stockings ranked as pure luxury. Also, as you'll see in this story, fifteen dollars in the 1890s could buy far more than two meals at a fast-food restaurant.

The Cup of Tea (1879) by Mary Cassatt (1844–1926). Oil on canvas (36⅜″ × 25¾″).

The Metropolitan Museum of Art, New York. From the Collection of James Stillman. Gift of Dr. Ernest G. Stillman, 1922 (22.16.17). Photograph ©1983 The Metropolitan Museum of Art.

A Pair of Silk Stockings

Kate Chopin

Little Mrs. Sommers one day found herself the unexpected possessor of fifteen dollars. It seemed to her a very large amount of money, and the way in which it stuffed and bulged her worn old *porte-monnaie*[1] gave her a feeling of importance such as she had not enjoyed for years.

The question of investment was one that occupied her greatly. For a day or two she walked about apparently in a dreamy state, but really absorbed in speculation and calculation. She did not wish to act hastily, to do anything she might afterward regret. But it was during the still hours of the night when she lay awake revolving plans in her mind that she seemed to see her way clearly toward a proper and judicious use of the money.

A dollar or two should be added to the price usually paid for Janie's shoes, which would ensure their lasting an appreciable time longer than they usually did. She would buy so-and-so many yards of percale[2] for new shirtwaists for the boys and Janie and Mag. She had intended to make the old ones do by skillful patching. Mag should have another gown. She had seen some beautiful patterns, veritable bargains in the shop windows. And still there would be left enough for new stockings—two pairs apiece—and what darning that would save for a while!

1. *porte-monnaie* (pôrt·mô·nā′): French for "purse."

2. **percale:** finely woven cotton cloth.

WORDS TO OWN

judicious (jo͞o·dish′əs) *adj.*: cautious; wise.
appreciable (ə·prē′shə·bəl) *adj.*: measurable.
veritable (ver′i·tə·bəl) *adj.*: genuine; true.

She would get caps for the boys and sailor hats for the girls. The vision of her little brood looking fresh and dainty and new for once in their lives excited her and made her restless and wakeful with anticipation.

The neighbors sometimes talked of certain "better days" that little Mrs. Sommers had known before she had ever thought of being Mrs. Sommers. She herself indulged in no such morbid retrospection.[3] She had no time—no second of time to devote to the past. The needs of the present absorbed her every faculty. A vision of the future like some dim, gaunt monster sometimes appalled her, but luckily tomorrow never comes.

Mrs. Sommers was one who knew the value of bargains; who could stand for hours making her way inch by inch toward the desired object that was selling below cost. She could elbow her way if need be; she had learned to clutch a piece of goods and hold it and stick to it with persistence and determination till her turn came to be served, no matter when it came.

But that day she was a little faint and tired. She had swallowed a light luncheon—no! when she came to think of it, between getting the children fed and the place righted, and preparing herself for the shopping bout, she had actually forgotten to eat any luncheon at all!

She sat herself upon a revolving stool before a counter that was comparatively deserted, trying to gather strength and courage to charge through an eager multitude that was besieging breastworks[4] of shirting and figured lawn. An all-gone limp feeling had come over her and she rested her hand aimlessly upon the counter. She wore no gloves. By degrees she grew aware that her hand had encountered something very soothing, very pleasant to touch. She looked down to see that her hand lay upon a pile of silk stockings. A placard nearby announced that they had been reduced in price from two dollars and fifty cents to one dollar and ninety-eight cents; and a young girl who stood behind the counter asked her if she wished to examine their line of silk hosiery. She smiled, just as if she had been asked to inspect a tiara of diamonds with the ultimate view of purchasing it. But she went on feeling the soft, sheeny luxurious things—with both hands now, holding them up to see them glisten, and to feel them glide serpentlike through her fingers.

Two hectic blotches came suddenly into her pale cheeks. She looked up at the girl.

"Do you think there are any eights-and-a-half among these?"

There were any number of eights-and-a-half. In fact, there were more of that size than any other. Here was a light blue pair; there were some lavender, some all black, and various shades of tan and gray. Mrs. Sommers selected a black pair and looked at them very long and closely. She pretended to be examining their texture, which the clerk assured her was excellent.

"A dollar and ninety-eight cents," she mused aloud. "Well, I'll take this pair." She handed the girl a five-dollar bill and waited for her change and for her parcel. What a very small parcel it was! It seemed lost in the depths of her shabby old shopping bag.

Mrs. Sommers after that did not move in the direction of the bargain counter. She took the elevator, which carried her to an upper floor into the region of the ladies' waiting rooms. Here, in a retired corner, she exchanged her cotton stockings for the new silk ones which she had just bought. She was not going through any acute mental process or reasoning with herself, nor was she

3. **morbid retrospection:** brooding on things in the past.
4. **breastworks:** low walls put up as barricades. The bolts of shirting material and fine patterned cotton, or "figured lawn," are compared to barricades being stormed by shoppers.

WORDS TO OWN

acute (ə·kyōot′) *adj*.: keen; sharp.

The Fitting (1891) by Mary Cassatt (1844–1926).
Color print with drypoint, softground, and aquatint (14¾″ × 10⅛″).

Elegant Discomfort

In the 1890s, clothing was layered, hot, heavy, and expensive. Rows of buttons fastened everything from men's pants to women's long gloves. Styles followed those of London and Paris. City shops carried, at a range of prices, everything from boots to ribbons, but women's dresses were still custom-made. By today's standards, people did not own much clothing, and they often had old garments remodeled instead of buying expensive new ones. The natural fabrics—wool, silk, cotton—could be spoiled by the harsh soaps of the day, so clothes were brushed more often than they were cleaned. Men and women alike used perfumes and scents to conceal odor.

Stepping out in style. A well-turned-out man in the 1890s wore a derby hat and a lined suit. His shirt had a long tail and a detachable collar. His coat was buttoned so high that it sometimes concealed his cravat (tie)—the one item declaring his personal taste. His underclothes might be knitted from wool. For outerwear, he might own an Inverness cape (a loose overcoat with an arm-length cape) or an Ulster (a long, belted coat). Men generally kept their hair trimmed above the collar, and many wore full moustaches or neat beards.

The fashionable woman of the time wore a large, brimmed hat and a full-length suit or dress. For clerical work or the new crazes of tennis and bicycling,

---

striving to explain to her satisfaction the motive of her action. She was not thinking at all. She seemed for the time to be taking a rest from that <u>laborious</u> and fatiguing function and to have abandoned herself to some mechanical impulse that directed her actions and freed her of responsibility.

How good was the touch of the raw silk to her flesh! She felt like lying back in the cushioned chair and <u>reveling</u> for a while in the luxury of it. She did for a little while. Then she replaced her shoes, rolled the cotton stockings together, and thrust them into her bag. After doing this she crossed straight over to the shoe department and took her seat to be fitted.

She was <u>fastidious</u>. The clerk could not make her out; he could not reconcile her shoes with her stockings, and she was not too easily pleased. She held back her skirts and turned her feet one way and her head another way as she glanced down at the polished, pointed-tipped boots. Her foot and ankle looked very pretty. She could not realize that they belonged to her and were a part of herself. She wanted an excellent and stylish fit, she

WORDS TO OWN

laborious (lə·bôr′ē·əs) *adj.*: difficult; involving much hard work.
reveling (rev′əl·iŋ) *v.*: taking pleasure.
fastidious (fas·tid′ē·əs) *adj.*: difficult to please; critical.

she tucked a shirtwaist (a blouse tailored like a man's shirt) into a full skirt. At home, she could receive guests in a loosefitting tea gown adorned with pleats and lace. But on formal occasions she had to strap herself into a painful corset—a tightly fitting, upper-body undergarment often stiffened with bone—and wear a dress that emphasized her bosom in front and hips behind. Although not so extreme as the bustles and front lifts of earlier decades, the resulting corseted shape, seen from the side, was that of a slightly tilted hourglass. Her cotton or silk underwear might be trimmed with lace, embroidery, or ribbon. For outerwear, she donned a shaped cape. She usually wore her hair swept up into a chignon (a knot of hair worn at the nape of the neck), with the sides rolled to frame her face. She finished everything off with ribbons, lace, and jewelry.

Dressing for success. The point of fashion, then as now, was to make a statement. The gloves Mrs. Sommers tries on, for example, would have been an expensive item and so tightfitting as to be useless for work, marking the wearer as a "lady of leisure." Women also needed to dress to attract social invitations and a good marriage. This point was clear to Lily Bart, the protagonist of *The House of Mirth,* a turn-of-the-century novel by the American writer Edith Wharton (1862–1937). As Lily puts it, "If I were shabby no one would have me: A woman is asked out as much for her clothes as for herself. The clothes are the background, the frame, if you like: They don't make success, but they are a part of it."

told the young fellow who served her, and she did not mind the difference of a dollar or two more in the price so long as she got what she desired.

It was a long time since Mrs. Sommers had been fitted with gloves. On rare occasions when she had bought a pair they were always "bargains," so cheap that it would have been preposterous and unreasonable to have expected them to be fitted to the hand.

Now she rested her elbow on the cushion of the glove counter, and a pretty, pleasant young creature, delicate and deft of touch, drew a long-wristed "kid" over Mrs. Sommers's hand. She smoothed it down over the wrist and buttoned it neatly, and both lost themselves for a second or two in admiring contemplation of the little symmetrical gloved hand. But there were other places where money might be spent.

There were books and magazines piled up in the window of a stall a few paces down the street. Mrs. Sommers bought two high-priced magazines such as she had been accustomed to read in the days when she had been accustomed to other pleasant things. She carried them without wrapping. As well as she could she lifted her skirts at the crossings. Her stockings and boots and well-fitting gloves had worked marvels in her bearing—had given her

WORDS TO OWN
preposterous (prē·päs′tər·əs) *adj.*: ridiculous.

Trade card of a glove manufacturer (c. 1890).

feared it might. She seated herself at a small table alone, and an attentive waiter at once approached to take her order. She did not want a profusion; she craved a nice and tasty bite—a half dozen bluepoints,[5] a plump chop with cress, a something sweet—a crème-frappé,[6] for instance; a glass of Rhine wine, and after all a small cup of black coffee.

While waiting to be served she removed her gloves very leisurely and laid them beside her. Then she picked up a magazine and glanced through it, cutting the pages with a blunt edge of her knife.[7] It was all very agreeable. The damask was even more spotless than it had seemed through the window, and the crystal more sparkling. There were quiet ladies and gentlemen, who did not notice her, lunching at the small tables like her own. A soft, pleasing strain of music could be heard, and a gentle breeze was blowing through the window. She tasted a bite, and she read a word or two, and she sipped the amber wine and wiggled her toes in the silk stockings. The price of it made no difference. She counted the money out to the waiter and left an extra coin on his tray, whereupon he bowed before her as before a princess of royal blood.

There was still money in her purse, and her next temptation presented itself in the shape of a matinée poster.

It was a little later when she entered the theater, the play had begun, and the house seemed to her to be packed. But there were vacant seats here and there, and into one of them she was ushered, between brilliantly dressed women who had gone there to kill time and eat candy and display their gaudy attire. There were many others who were there solely for the play and acting. It is safe to say there was

5. **bluepoints:** small oysters.
6. **crème-frappé** (krĕm·frā·pā′): dessert similar to ice cream.
7. **cutting . . . knife:** At one time, magazines and books were often sold with folded, untrimmed pages. These outer edges had to be cut apart before one could read them.

WORDS TO OWN

gaudy (gôd′ē) *adj.*: showy, but lacking in good taste.

a feeling of assurance, a sense of belonging to the well-dressed multitude.

She was very hungry. Another time she would have stilled the cravings for food until reaching her own home, where she would have brewed herself a cup of tea and taken a snack of anything that was available. But the impulse that was guiding her would not suffer her to entertain any such thought.

There was a restaurant at the corner. She had never entered its doors; from the outside she had sometimes caught glimpses of spotless damask and shining crystal, and soft-stepping waiters serving people of fashion.

When she entered, her appearance created no surprise, no consternation, as she had half no one present who bore quite the attitude which Mrs. Sommers did to her surroundings. She gathered in the whole—stage and players and people in one wide impression, and absorbed it and enjoyed it. She laughed at the comedy and wept—she and the gaudy woman next to her wept over the tragedy. And they talked a little together over it. And the gaudy woman wiped her eyes and sniffled on a tiny square of filmy, perfumed lace and passed little Mrs. Sommers her box of candy.

The play was over, the music ceased, the crowd filed out. It was like a dream ended. People scattered in all directions. Mrs. Sommers went to the corner and waited for the cable car.

A man with keen eyes, who sat opposite her, seemed to like the study of her small, pale face. It puzzled him to decipher what he saw there. In truth, he saw nothing—unless he were wizard enough to detect a poignant wish, a powerful longing that the cable car would never stop anywhere, but go on and on with her forever.

WORDS TO OWN

poignant (poin′yənt) *adj.:* emotionally moving.

PRIMARY Sources — A BIOGRAPHY

Vogue Stories

Kate Chopin had trouble selling her stories. *Vogue* magazine, however, whose readership consisted mainly of young women from wealthy families, agreed to publish much of her work.

The title of Chopin's last *Vogue* story of the 1890s, "A Pair of Silk Stockings," suggests a tale for the rich—but it is really a message to *Vogue* readers about how the other half lives. Its central character, a struggling mother who once had "certain better days," must now scrimp to buy necessities for her children. But when Mrs. Sommers suddenly finds herself with fifteen dollars, she yields to temptation and spends all the money on herself: silk stockings, new boots, kid gloves, a tasty lunch, and a matinée. On the streetcar home, she feels "a poignant wish, a powerful longing that the cable car would never stop anywhere, but go on and on with her forever."

Mrs. Sommers was the kind of woman that *Vogue* readers might pass by on the street without noticing—but by the late 1890s, living frugally in St. Louis, Kate Chopin had seen the effects of poverty and urban strife on

The Bettmann Archive.

women. *Vogue,* unlike other magazines, did not expect her to write for "the young person" about domesticity and womanly self-sacrifice. *Vogue* allowed her to describe what she had seen, honestly and fearlessly.

Vogue moved with her; other magazines refused.

—Emily Toth, *from Kate Chopin*

Now and Then, America

Pat Mora

Who wants to rot
beneath dry, winter grass
in a numbered grave
in a numbered row
5 in a section labeled Eternal Peace
with neighbors plagued
by limp, plastic roses
springing from their toes?
Grant me a little life now and then, America.

10 Who wants to rot
as she marches through life
in a pinstriped suit
neck chained in a soft, silk bow
in step, in style, insane.
15 Let me in
to boardrooms wearing hot
colors, my hair long and free,
maybe speaking Spanish.
Risk my difference, my surprises.
20 Grant me a little life, America.

And when I die, plant *zempasúchitl*,°
flowers of the dead, and at my head
plant organ cactus, green fleshy
fingers sprouting, like in Oaxaca.°
25 Let desert creatures hide
in the orange blooms.
Let birds nest in the cactus stems.
Let me go knowing life
flower and song
30 will continue right above my bones.

21. ***zempasúchitl*** (sem·pä·sōō′chē·t′l).
24. **Oaxaca** (wə·häk′ə).

Pat Mora.

Arte Publico Press.

MAKING MEANINGS

First Thoughts

1. What is Mrs. Sommers feeling as we leave her on the streetcar? Are you surprised or shocked by her "poignant wish"?

Reading Check

a. List the uses Mrs. Sommers plans to make of the fifteen dollars.

b. List the items on which Mrs. Sommers actually spends the money.

Shaping Interpretations

2. The author describes her as "little Mrs. Sommers," and we learn that she has several children, lacks the time to recall "better days," and regards the future as a "dim, gaunt monster." No mention is made of her husband or source of income. How would you describe the **character** of Mrs. Sommers? How do you feel about what she does with the fifteen dollars?

3. Review the predictions you made after reading the first two paragraphs of the story. Can you explain why they were—or were not—on target? What details about Mrs. Sommers's earlier life might help explain the **motivation** for her shopping spree?

4. When Mrs. Sommers first feels the silk stockings, they "glide serpentlike through her fingers." What does a serpent often **symbolize** in Western culture? Explain whether or not you think Chopin's use of the word here is significant.

Extending the Text

5. This story is over a hundred years old. Do you think it is an old-fashioned story that could not happen today, or is the story still relevant? Could you see Mrs. Sommers in a TV sitcom? Could her conflict also be experienced by a man?

Challenging the Text

6. A feminist critic might say that this story is about a woman who strikes out to gain personal freedom and identity. A Marxist critic might say it is about the class struggle. The critic Barbara C. Ewell writes, "The power of money to enhance self-esteem and confidence is the core of this poignant tale." Which critic, if any, do you agree with? Why?

CHOICES: Building Your Portfolio

Writer's Notebook

1. Collecting Ideas for a Research Paper

Brainstorm a list of topics suggested by Chopin's story that you would be interested in researching and reporting on, such as women's issues, the evolution of clothing, or city life in the 1890s. For each topic, list some effective ways to present the information that you gather for your report: interviews, descriptions, drawings, and tables or charts. Save your notes for possible use in the Writer's Workshop on page 515.

Comparing and Contrasting Themes

2. Breaking Bonds

Both Chopin and Pat Mora, in the **Connection** on page 444, write about escape, freedom, identity, and individuality. In a brief essay, compare and contrast the two writers' attitudes toward these **themes**. What kinds of images do they each use to convey their messages?

Creative Writing

3. The Untold Story

At the end of the story, Mrs. Sommers wishes the cable car would "go on and on" without ever stopping. What do you think the rest of Mrs. Sommers's life will be like? Will this day of indulgence mark a turning point in her life? Write one or more paragraphs telling the rest of Mrs. Sommers's story. Try to keep your version consistent with the character created in the story.

American Indian Oratory

In the nineteenth century, American Indians felt keenly the shackles placed on them by the United States government. As the westward migration of European settlers increased, due in part to the California gold rush (1849) and the Civil War (1861–1865), Native Americans were forced to defend their land; more than two hundred fierce battles were fought between 1869 and 1878 alone.

For centuries, most American Indians have relied on spoken language for diplomacy, decision making, and preservation of their history and culture. In Native American cultures, spoken language mystically links the natural and spiritual worlds and has the power to shape and control events. Thus, American Indians have often chosen their leaders in part for their eloquence. Important speeches are even memorized exactly as spoken and passed on orally to future generations.

Faced with the destruction of their traditional way of life, Native Americans hoped that eloquent words might succeed where other weapons had failed. Their hopes were misplaced.

Black Hawk

Black Hawk (1767–1838) was born in what today is Illinois. He was leader of the Sauk—a group of Algonquian people native to present-day Michigan, Wisconsin, and Illinois. A proven warrior from his teens, Black Hawk earned renown for bravery and for oratory that roused his listeners to action. He spent much of his life battling the spread of European settlement. In the following excerpt from a speech he made in 1832, Black Hawk inspires his people to defend their land. However, in the ensuing conflict, the Black Hawk War, the Sauk were soundly defeated by U.S. forces.

"For More Than a Hundred Winters Our Nation Was a Powerful, Happy, and United People"

Headmen, Chiefs, Braves, and Warriors of the Sauks: For more than a hundred winters our nation was a powerful, happy, and united people. The Great Spirit gave to us a territory, seven hundred miles in length, along the Mississippi, reaching from Prairie du Chien[1] to the mouth of the Illinois River. This vast territory was composed of some of the finest and best land for the home and use of the Indian ever found in this country. The woods and prairies teemed with buffalo, moose, elk, bear, and deer, with other game suitable to our enjoyment, while its lakes, rivers, creeks, and ponds were alive with the very best kinds of fish, for our food. The islands in the Mississippi were our gardens, where the Great Spirit caused berries, plums, and other fruits to grow in great abundance, while the soil, when cultivated, produced corn, beans, pumpkins, and squash of the finest quality and largest quantities. Our children were never known to cry of hunger, and no stranger, red or white, was permitted to enter our lodges without finding food and rest. Our nation was respected by all who came in contact with it, for we had the ability as well as the courage to defend and maintain our rights of territory, person, and property against the world. Then, indeed, was it an honor to be called a Sauk, for that name was a passport to our people traveling in other territories and among other nations. But an evil day befell us when we became a divided nation, and with that division our glory deserted us, leaving us with the hearts and heels of the rabbit in place of the courage and strength of the bear.

All this was brought about by the long guns, who now claim all our territory east of the

1. **Prairie du Chien** (prer′ēd·ə·shēn): trading town at the junction of the Wisconsin and Mississippi Rivers; now a city in Wisconsin.

Black Hawk and Five Other Saukie Prisoners (1861–1869) by George Catlin. Oil on paperboard mounted on heavier paperboard (18⅝" × 24¹⁵/₁₆").

Paul Mellon Collection, ©1998 Board of Trustees, National Gallery of Art, Washington, D.C.

Black Hawk, Prominent Sauk Chief (detail) (1832) by George Catlin. Oil on canvas (29" × 24").

National Museum of American Art, Washington, D.C. Gift of Mrs. Joseph Harrison, Jr. Courtesy Art Resource, NY.

Mississippi, including Saukenuk,[2] our ancient village, where all of us were born, raised, lived, hunted, fished, and loved, and near which are our corn lands, which have yielded abundant harvests for a hundred winters, and where sleep the bones of our sacred dead, and around which cluster our fondest recollections of heroism and noble deeds of charity done by our fathers, who were Sauks, not only in name, but in courage and action. I thank the Great Spirit for making me a Sauk, and the son of a great Sauk chief, and a lineal descendant of Nanamakee, the founder of our nation.

The Great Spirit is the friend and protector of the Sauks, and has accompanied me as your War Chief upon the warpath against our enemies, and has given me skill to direct and you the courage to achieve a hundred victories over our enemies upon the warpath. . . . The Great Spirit created this country for the use and benefit of his red children, and placed them in full possession of it, and we were happy and contented. Why did he send the palefaces across the great ocean to take it from us? When they landed on our territory they were received as long-absent brothers whom the Great Spirit had returned to us. Food and rest were freely given them by our fathers, who treated them all the more kindly on account of their weak and helpless condition. Had our fathers the desire, they could have crushed the intruders out of existence with the same ease we kill the bloodsucking mosquitoes. Little did our fathers then think they were taking to their bosoms, and warming them to life, a lot of torpid, half-frozen, and starving vipers, which in a few winters would fix their deadly fangs upon the very bosoms that had nursed and cared for them when they needed help.

—Black Hawk

2. Saukenuk: a village of the Sauk, located where the Rock River joins the Mississippi; present-day site of Rock Island, Illinois.

Chief Joseph

Born in what is now Oregon, Chief Joseph (c.1840–1904) has become a symbol of the heroic fighting spirit of his people, the Nez Percé. In battles during 1877, he fought thirteen different U.S. military commands, defeating almost all of them. He then made a masterful one-thousand–mile retreat toward Canada through the mountainous country of the Pacific Northwest. His caravan, which included women and children, made it to within thirty miles of the border before exhaustion and near starvation forced them to surrender after eleven weeks of flight. Chief Joseph delivered the following speech upon his surrender to the U.S. Army in October 1877. He spent most of the rest of his life on a reservation in the present-day state of Washington.

"I Will Fight No More Forever"

Tell General Howard[1] I know his heart. What he told me before, I have in my heart. I am tired of fighting. Our chiefs are killed. Looking Glass[2] is dead. Toohoolhoolzote[3] is dead. The old men are all dead. It is the young men who say yes and no. He who led on the young men is dead. It is cold and we have no blankets. The little children are freezing to death. My people, some of them, have run away to the hills and have no blankets, no food; no one knows where they are—perhaps freezing to death. I want to have time to look for my children and see how many I can find. Maybe I shall find them among the dead. Hear me, my chiefs. I am tired; my heart is sick and sad. From where the sun now stands I will fight no more forever.

—Chief Joseph

1. **General Howard:** Oliver Otis Howard (1830–1909), Civil War general and founder of Howard University in Washington, D.C. (1867). Howard was the military commander who presented the Nez Percé with an ultimatum to give up their land in Idaho and move to a reservation.
2. **Looking Glass** (c. 1823–1877): ally of Chief Joseph. Looking Glass was killed in battle on the day this speech was delivered.
3. **Toohoolhoolzote** (c. 1810–1877): Nez Percé shaman and chief who argued against giving up Nez Percé lands.

Collection 10

FROM INNOCENCE TO EXPERIENCE

Twain

Bierce

Voices from the Civil War

Crane

London

Shiloh

A Requiem

(April, 1862)

Skimming lightly, wheeling still,
   The swallows fly low
Over the field in clouded days,
   The forest-field of Shiloh—
Over the field where April rain
Solaced the parched ones stretched in pain
Through the pause of night
That followed the Sunday fight
   Around the church of Shiloh—
The church so lone, the log-built one,
That echoed to many a parting groan
      And natural prayer
   Of dying foemen mingled there—
Foemen at morn, but friends at eve—
   Fame or country least their care:
(What like a bullet can undeceive!)
   But now they lie low,
While over them the swallows skim,
   And all is hushed at Shiloh.

—Herman Melville (1819–1891)

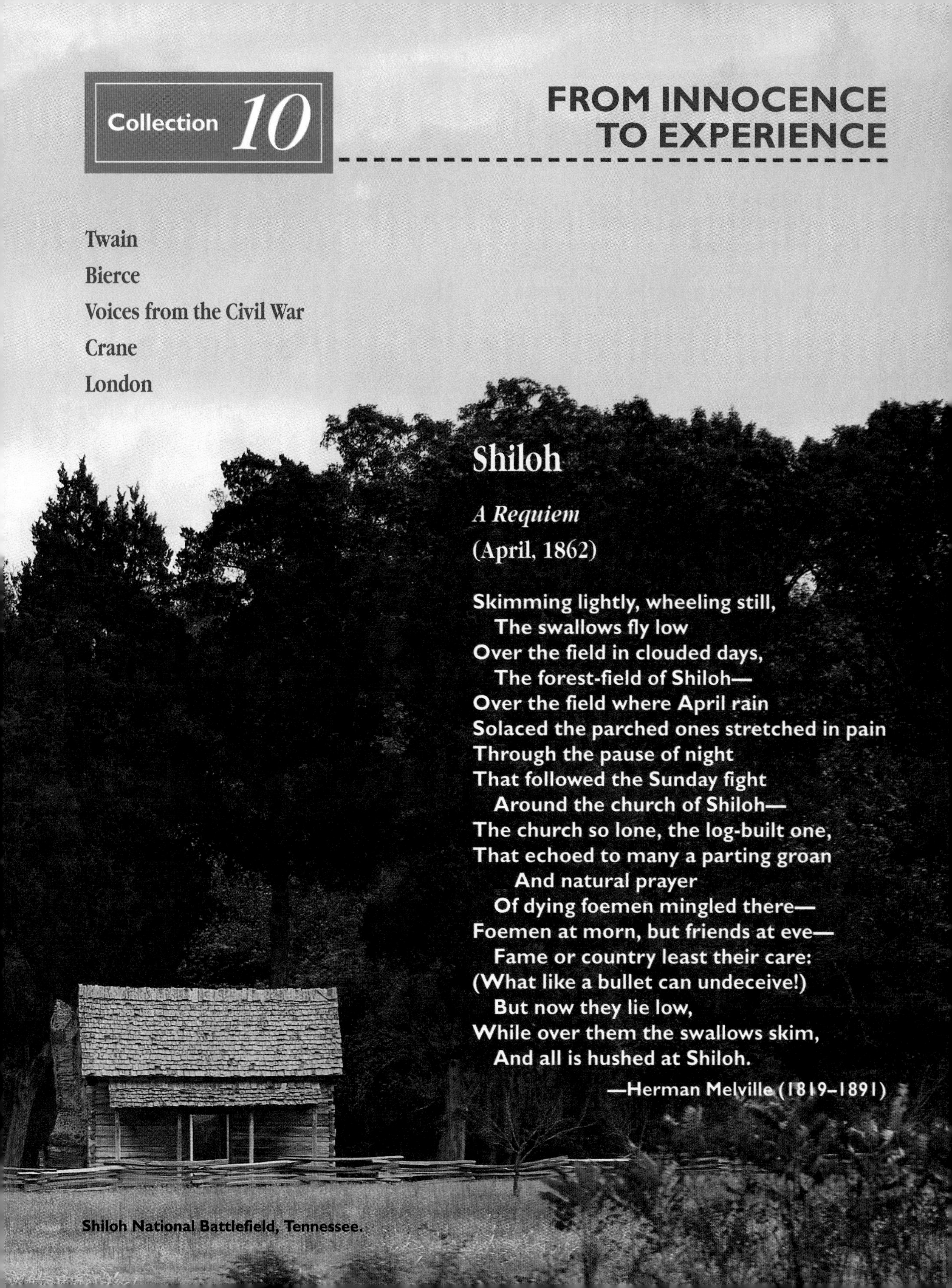

Shiloh National Battlefield, Tennessee.

Mark Twain

(1835–1910)

Mark Twain is the most celebrated humorist in American history. His ability to make us laugh has contributed to the singular popularity of his books, not just in Twain's own time but in following generations. Since humor is by nature very difficult to translate from language to language, it is even more surprising to find that Twain's appeal has traveled throughout the world.

The great humorist is also, ironically, our great realist. Behind the backwoods humor—especially in his novel *Adventures of Huckleberry Finn*—is a revelation of the illusions that exist in American life. Huck's journey on a raft with the escaped slave Jim is not a "hymn to boyhood." It is a dramatization of the grim realities of a slaveholding society.

Although Twain became remarkably successful, his later life was shadowed by disappointment and tragedy, and as he grew older he turned into a bitter man. He once told his friend William Dean Howells, the influential novelist and editor of *The Atlantic Monthly,* "Everyone is a moon and has a dark side which he never shows to anybody."

"Mark Twain!"

Twain was born Samuel Langhorne Clemens in the backwoods of Missouri. His father, John Clemens, a bright, ambitious, but impractical Virginian, had married Jane Lampton, a witty, dynamic woman who was also a great beauty. When John's store failed in 1839, he moved his hopes and his family to Hannibal, Missouri—the Mississippi River town that Sam, writing as Mark Twain, would later fashion into the setting of the most renowned boyhood in American literature, that of Tom Sawyer.

Sam's own carefree boyhood ended at twelve when his father died. Helping to support his mother and sister, he went to work setting type and editing copy for the newspaper started by his older brother Orion. At eighteen, Sam set

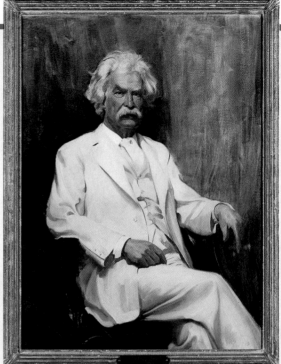

Mark Twain (1935) by Frank Edwin Larson (1895–1991). Oil on canvas (48″ × 36″).

out on his own. Over the next fifteen years, he worked as a printer in various towns from Missouri to the East Coast. Smitten by a love for the magical steamboats that plied the Mississippi, he even apprenticed himself for a time to the greatest of the steamboat pilots, Horace Bixby. From Bixby, Sam Clemens learned the bends and shallows of the great river from Minnesota to the Louisiana delta. It was the leadsman's cry of "Mark twain!"—announcing a water depth of two fathoms (twelve feet)—that provided him with his celebrated pen name.

A Gold Mine of Humor

For a short time during the Civil War, Twain was a soldier with a company of Confederate irregulars. (He said he learned more about retreating than fighting.) But he soon abandoned the military life for that of a gold prospector in Nevada. While he found little gold there, he did discover the rich mine of storytelling within himself. With his Missouri drawl and relaxed manner, Twain captivated audiences. His secret lay in his deft use of a faintly pompous platform manner: In pretending not to recognize the coarseness or absurdity of his material, Twain's deadpan attitude added to his material's hilarity.

Twain soon turned his comic voice to prose, working as a journalist between 1862 and 1871. In 1865, he achieved wide recognition as a humorist with the publication of his hilarious version of an old tall tale, "The Celebrated Jumping Frog of Calaveras County." Four years later, Twain's dispatches from a Mediterranean tour were published as a book titled *The Innocents Abroad.* This satirical travelogue poked fun at the traditional American pilgrimage to the monuments of European civilization. Over five thousand copies were sold in the first month, and more than thirty-one thousand within the year. Twain had launched a prosperous literary career.

An American Masterpiece

At thirty-five, with a raffish, barroom air about him, Twain was a dubious candidate for marriage, but he courted Olivia Langdon, the daughter of an affluent family from Elmira, New York. She was a delicate, proper woman, but Twain overcame all resistance, and, in 1870, Livy's father gave the couple his consent and a lavish wedding. Twain embarked on a marriage of unceasing devotion.

In 1871, Twain moved to Hartford, Connecticut, where he built an enormous home that is still visited today by thousands of tourists. The next year he published *Roughing It,* which drew on his experiences as a tenderfoot in the West. Then William Dean Howells invited Twain to do a series for *The Atlantic Monthly* about his days as a riverboat pilot. Those reminiscences eventually were expanded into the book *Life on the Mississippi* (1883).

By the mid-1870s, Twain was also at work on *The Adventures of Tom Sawyer* (1876). This celebration of boyhood absorbed him but presented difficulties of voice and point of view. Twain could not be sure if he was writing a book for children or for adults. Nevertheless, in writing the book, he made an imaginative return to the Hannibal of his childhood and succeeded in transforming it into a compelling myth.

In *Adventures of Huckleberry Finn* (1884), Twain found the voice he had been seeking. Through Huck's natural, slangy, first-person narration, Twain forged a new relation between expression and content, causing a revolution in American literature. As Ernest Hemingway (page 650), speaking through a fictional character, later put it, "All modern American literature comes from one book by Mark Twain called *Huckleberry Finn.*" T. S. Eliot (page 661), a fellow Missourian, added that Twain's was "a new way of writing . . . a literary language based on American colloquial speech."

> "**A**ll modern American literature comes from one book by Mark Twain. . . ."

Loss and Legacy

Twain was never able to duplicate the success of *Huckleberry Finn,* but he continued to produce popular books, including *A Connecticut Yankee in King Arthur's Court* (1889) and *Pudd'nhead Wilson* (1894). Twain's later years were marked by financial and professional disappointment as well as personal tragedy. His fascination with business and getting ahead financially, so typical of the new middle class, led him to invest disastrously in the Paige typesetting machine. The economic panic of 1893 bankrupted him.

Then illness overtook the close-knit Clemens family. Suzy, Twain's eldest daughter, died of meningitis in 1896. His wife, a permanent invalid during her last years, died in 1904. In a final blow, Jean, his youngest daughter, died in an epileptic seizure in 1909. "Possibly," said Twain after Jean's death, "I know now what the soldier feels when a bullet crashes through his heart." Four months later, he, too, was dead.

As loss followed loss, and as the whole country seemed to lose its vitality and become more complex, Twain had turned into an obsessive, embittered old man. In his final years, the subject matter of his work was his own disillusionment on a grand scale; the great comic writer appeared to be at war not only with the human race, but also with the God who had created it.

Make the Connection

Losing Its Luster

Sometimes, gaining something we've looked forward to isn't half as pleasurable as the anticipation of getting it. The person whose biggest wish is to be a movie actor might imagine all the glamorous trappings of that profession, but the reality of being an actor has more to do with hard work, discipline, and daily repetition than it does with adulation and fame. Experience brings its own rewards, but it can also make things seem too ordinary and familiar—lacking mystery and magic.

Quickwrite

Think about something you wished for—a skill or ability, or perhaps an honor or award—and then successfully gained. Were you in any way disappointed after achieving your goal? Write a few sentences describing how you felt before and after your wish came true.

Elements of Literature

Extended Metaphor

An **extended metaphor** is a **figure of speech** that makes a comparison between two unlike things and extends the comparison as far as the writer wants to take it. Much of Twain's humor comes from the surprise of two very unlike things joined to create an extended—and hilarious—comic metaphor.

> **A**n **extended metaphor** is a figure of speech that makes a comparison between two unlike things and extends the comparison as far as the writer wants to take it.
>
> *For more on Extended Metaphor, see page 188 and the Handbook of Literary Terms.*

Background

As a youth, Twain was so fascinated by riverboats that he persuaded Horace Bixby, the locally famous pilot of the *Paul Jones,* to teach him how to navigate the river between New Orleans and St. Louis (a distance of about seven hundred miles) for five hundred dollars. Twain was not alone in his dream; every boy along the Mississippi, black or white, yearned to work on a steamboat. It didn't matter whether the job was clerk, engineer, mate, or pilot; life on the river meant adventure. "Once a day a cheap, gaudy packet [boat] arrived upward from St. Louis," Twain wrote, "and another downward from Keokuk. Before these events, the day was glorious with expectancy; after them, the day was a dead and empty thing."

Twain did succeed in becoming a steamboat pilot. These two chapters from *Life on the Mississippi* describe a time when he was still an apprentice, or "cub," pilot being trained by Horace Bixby.

Champions of the Mississippi by Currier & Ives. Lithograph.

Museum of the City of New York. Scala/Art Resource, NY.

from Life on the Mississippi

Mark Twain

Perplexing Lessons

At the end of what seemed a tedious while, I had managed to pack my head full of islands, towns, bars, "points," and bends;[1] and a curiously <u>inanimate</u> mass of lumber it was, too. However, inasmuch as I could shut my eyes and reel off a good long string of these names without leaving out more than ten miles of river in every fifty, I began to feel that I could take a boat down to New Orleans if I could make her skip those little gaps. But of course my <u>complacency</u> could hardly get start enough to lift my nose a trifle into the air,

1. **islands . . . bends:** geographic features used in river navigation. Each numbered point was a landmark on a curve or bend in the river.

WORDS TO OWN
inanimate (in·an′ə·mit) *adj.*: lifeless.
complacency (kəm·plā′sən·sē) *n.*: self-satisfaction.

before Mr. Bixby would think of something to fetch it down again. One day he turned on me suddenly with this settler[2]—

"What is the shape of Walnut Bend?"

He might as well have asked me my grandmother's opinion of protoplasm.[3] I reflected respectfully, and then said I didn't know it had any particular shape. My gunpowdery chief went off with a bang, of course, and then went on loading and firing until he was out of adjectives.

I had learned long ago that he only carried just so many rounds of ammunition, and was sure to subside into a very placable and even remorseful old smooth-bore[4] as soon as they were all gone. That word "old" is merely affectionate; he was not more than thirty-four. I waited. By and by he said—

"My boy, you've got to know the *shape* of the river perfectly. It is all there is left to steer by on a very dark night. Everything else is blotted out and gone. But mind you, it hasn't the same shape in the night that it has in the daytime."

"How on earth am I ever going to learn it, then?"

"How do you follow a hall at home in the dark? Because you know the shape of it. You can't see it."

"Do you mean to say that I've got to know all the million trifling variations of shape in the banks of this interminable river as well as I know the shape of the front hall at home?"

"On my honor, you've got to know them *better* than any man ever did know the shapes of the halls in his own house."

"I wish I was dead!"

"Now I don't want to discourage you, but"—

"Well, pile it on me; I might as well have it now as another time."

"You see, this has got to be learned; there isn't any getting around it. A clear starlight night throws such heavy shadows that if you didn't know the

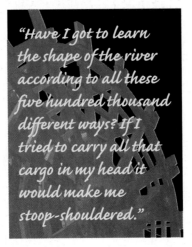

"Have I got to learn the shape of the river according to all these five hundred thousand different ways? If I tried to carry all that cargo in my head it would make me stoop-shouldered."

shape of a shore perfectly you would claw away from every bunch of timber, because you would take the black shadow of it for a solid cape;[5] and you see you would be getting scared to death every fifteen minutes by the watch.[6] You would be fifty yards from shore all the time when you ought to be within fifty feet of it. You can't see a snag[7] in one of those shadows, but you know exactly where it is, and the shape of the river tells you when you are coming to it. Then there's your pitch-dark night; the river is a very different shape on a pitch-dark night from what it is on a starlight night. All shores seem to be straight lines, then, and mighty dim ones, too; and you'd *run* them for straight lines only you know better. You boldly drive your boat right into what seems to be a solid, straight wall (you knowing very well that in reality there is a curve there), and that wall falls back and makes way for you. Then there's your gray mist. You take a night when there's one of these grisly, drizzly, gray mists, and then there isn't *any* particular shape to a shore. A gray mist would tangle the head of the oldest man that ever lived. Well, then, different kinds of *moonlight* change the shape of the river in different ways. You see"—

"Oh, don't say anymore, please! Have I got to learn the shape of the river according to all these five hundred thousand different ways? If I tried to carry all that cargo in my head it would make me stoop-shouldered."

"*No!* you only learn *the* shape of the river; and you learn it with such absolute certainty that you can always steer by the shape that's *in your head*, and never mind the one that's before your eyes."

5. **cape:** land projecting into water.
6. **by the watch:** The workday on a steamboat was divided into three four-hour periods, or watches, every twelve hours: two watches for work and one off-watch for rest.
7. **snag:** tree trunk dangerous to navigation because it is partly or completely underwater.

2. **settler:** colloquial for "something [such as Bixby's question] that does a person in."
3. **protoplasm:** living matter basic to all plant and animal cells.
4. **smoothbore:** gun with no grooves inside its barrel.

WORDS TO OWN

subside (səb·sīd′) v.: to settle down.
interminable (in·tur′mi·nə·bəl) adj.: endless.

"Very well, I'll try it; but after I have learned it can I depend on it? Will it keep the same form and not go fooling around?"

Before Mr. Bixby could answer, Mr. W—— came in to take the watch, and he said—

"Bixby, you'll have to look out for President's Island and all that country clear away up above the Old Hen and Chickens. The banks are caving and the shape of the shores changing like everything. Why, you wouldn't know the point above 40.[8] You can go up inside the old sycamore snag,[9] now."

So that question was answered. Here were leagues[10] of shore changing shape. My spirits were down in the mud again. Two things seemed pretty apparent to me. One was, that in order to be a pilot a man had got to learn more than any one man ought to be allowed to know; and the other was, that he must learn it all over again in a different way every twenty-four hours.

That night we had the watch until twelve. Now it was an ancient river custom for the two pilots to chat a bit when the watch changed. While the relieving pilot put on his gloves and lit his cigar, his partner, the retiring pilot, would say something like this—

"I judge the upper bar is making down a little at Hale's Point; had quarter twain with the lower lead and mark twain[11] with the other."

"Yes, I thought it was making down a little, last trip. Meet any boats?"

"Met one abreast the head of 21,[12] but she was away over hugging the bar, and I couldn't make her out entirely. I took her for the 'Sunny South'—hadn't any skylights forward of the chimneys."

And so on. And as the relieving pilot took the wheel his partner[13] would mention that we were in such and such a bend, and say we were abreast of such and such a man's woodyard or plantation. This was courtesy; I supposed it was *necessity.* But Mr. W—— came on watch full twelve minutes late on this particular night—a tremendous breach of etiquette; in fact, it is the unpardonable sin among pilots. So Mr. Bixby gave him no greeting whatever, but simply surrendered the wheel and marched out of the pilothouse without a word. I was appalled; it was a villainous night for blackness, we were in a particularly wide and blind part of the river, where there was no shape or substance to anything, and it seemed incredible that Mr. Bixby should have left that poor fellow to kill the boat trying to find out where he was. But I resolved that I would stand by him anyway. He should find that he was not wholly friendless. So I stood around, and waited to be asked where we were. But Mr. W—— plunged on serenely through the solid firmament of black cats that stood for an atmosphere, and never opened his mouth. Here is a proud devil, thought I; here is a limb of Satan that would rather send us all to destruction than put himself under obligations to me, because I am not yet one of the salt of the earth and privileged to snub captains and lord it over everything dead and alive in a steamboat. I presently climbed up on the bench; I did not think it was safe to go to sleep while this lunatic was on watch.

However, I must have gone to sleep in the course of time, because the next thing I was aware of was the fact that day was breaking, Mr. W—— gone, and Mr. Bixby at the wheel again. So it was four o'clock and all well—but me; I felt like a skinful of dry bones and all of them trying to ache at once.

Mr. Bixby asked me what I had stayed up there for. I confessed that it was to do Mr. W—— a benevolence—tell him where he was. It took five minutes for the entire preposterousness of the thing to filter into Mr. Bixby's system, and then I judge it filled him nearly up to the chin; because he paid me a compliment—and not much of a one either. He said—

---

8. **point above 40:** numbered navigational point on the river beyond the landmark numbered 40.

9. **inside . . . snag:** It may not be necessary but still can do no harm to explain that "inside" means between the snag and the shore. [Twain's note]

10. **leagues:** One league equals about 3 miles.

11. **quarter . . . mark twain:** Two fathoms. Quarter twain is 2¼ fathoms, [or] 13½ feet. Mark three is three fathoms. [Twain's note] These measures of water depth are calculated by using a lead weight attached to a rope. One fathom, or "mark one," equals 6 feet. Two fathoms, or "mark twain," equals 12 feet.

12. **abreast . . . 21:** beside landmark, or point, 21.

13. **partner:** "Partner" is technical for "the other pilot." [Twain's note]

WORDS TO OWN

serenely (sə·rēn′lē) *adv.*: calmly.
benevolence (bə·nev′ə·ləns) *n.*: kindness.

"Well, taking you by and large, you do seem to be more different kinds of an ass than any creature I ever saw before. What did you suppose he wanted to know for?"

I said I thought it might be a convenience to him.

"Convenience! D-nation! Didn't I tell you that a man's got to know the river in the night the same as he'd know his own front hall?"

"Well, I can follow the front hall in the dark if I know it *is* the front hall; but suppose you set me down in the middle of it in the dark and not tell me which hall it is; how am *I* to know?"

"Well, you've *got* to, on the river!"

"All right. Then I'm glad I never said anything to Mr. W——"

"I should say so. Why, he'd have slammed you through the window and utterly ruined a hundred dollars' worth of window sash[14] and stuff."

I was glad this damage had been saved, for it would have made me unpopular with the owners. They always hated anybody who had the name of being careless, and injuring things.

I went to work now to learn the shape of the river; and of all the eluding and ungraspable objects that ever I tried to get mind or hands on, that was the chief. I would fasten my eyes upon a sharp, wooded point that projected far into the river some miles ahead of me, and go to laboriously photographing its shape upon my brain; and just as I was beginning to succeed to my satisfaction, we would draw up toward it and the exasperating thing would begin to melt away and fold back into the bank! If there had been a conspicuous dead tree standing upon the very point of the cape, I would find that tree inconspicuously merged into the general forest, and occupying the middle of a straight shore, when I got abreast of it! No prominent hill would stick to its shape long enough for me to make up my mind what its form really was, but it was as dissolving and changeful as if it had been a mountain of butter in the hottest corner of the tropics. Nothing ever had the same shape when I was coming downstream that it had borne when I went up. I mentioned these little difficulties to Mr. Bixby. He said—

"That's the very main virtue of the thing. If the shapes didn't change every three seconds they

wouldn't be of any use. Take this place where we are now, for instance. As long as that hill over yonder is only one hill, I can boom right along the way I'm going; but the moment it splits at the top and forms a V, I know I've got to scratch to starboard[15] in a hurry, or I'll bang this boat's brains out against a rock; and then the moment one of the prongs of the V swings behind the other, I've got to waltz to larboard[16] again, or I'll have a misunderstanding with a snag that would snatch the keelson[17] out of this steamboat as neatly as if it were a sliver in your hand. If that hill didn't change its shape on bad nights there would be an awful steamboat graveyard around here inside of a year."

It was plain that I had got to learn the shape of the river in all the different ways that could be thought of—upside down, wrong end first, inside out, fore-and-aft, and "thort-ships"[18]—and then know what to do on gray nights when it hadn't any shape at all. So I set about it. In the course of time I began to get the best of this knotty lesson, and my self-complacency moved to the front once more. Mr. Bixby was all fixed, and ready to start it to the rear again. He opened on me after this fashion—

"How much water did we have in the middle crossing at Hole-in-the-Wall, trip before last?"

I considered this an outrage. I said—

"Every trip, down and up, the leadsmen[19] are singing through that tangled place for three quarters of an hour on a stretch. How do you reckon I can remember such a mess as that?"

"My boy, you've got to remember it. You've got to remember the exact spot and the exact marks the boat lay in when we had the shoalest[20] water, in every one of the five hundred shoal places between St. Louis and New Orleans; and you mustn't get the shoal soundings and marks[21] of

14. **window sash:** frame that holds window glass.

15. **scratch to starboard:** move quickly to the right side of the boat.
16. **larboard:** the left side of the boat.
17. **keelson:** wood or metal beams fastened along a boat's keel to strengthen it. The keel is the timber along the boat's bottom that supports the frame.
18. **fore-and-aft, and "thort-ships":** end to end and shore to shore.
19. **leadsmen:** workers who use a lead line to measure the water's depth.
20. **shoalest:** most shallow.
21. **soundings and marks:** measurements of water depth.

one trip mixed up with the shoal soundings and marks of another, either, for they're not often twice alike. You must keep them separate."

When I came to myself again, I said—

"When I get so that I can do that, I'll be able to raise the dead, and then I won't have to pilot a steamboat to make a living. I want to retire from this business. I want a slush-bucket and a brush; I'm only fit for a roustabout.[22] I haven't got brains enough to be a pilot; and if I had I wouldn't have strength enough to carry them around, unless I went on crutches."

"Now drop that! When I say I'll learn[23] a man the river, I mean it. And you can depend on it, I'll learn him or kill him."

Continued Perplexities

There was no use in arguing with a person like this. I promptly put such a strain on my memory

22. **roustabout:** deckhand; laborer on a boat.
23. **learn:** "Teach" is not in the river vocabulary. [Twain's note]

that by and by even the shoal water and the countless crossing marks[24] began to stay with me. But the result was just the same. I never could more than get one knotty thing learned before another presented itself. Now I had often seen pilots gazing at the water and pretending to read it as if it were a book; but it was a book that told me nothing. A time came at last, however, when Mr. Bixby seemed to think me far enough advanced to bear a lesson on water-reading. So he began—

"Do you see that long slanting line on the face of the water? Now, that's a reef. Moreover, it's a bluff reef.[25] There is a solid sandbar under it that is nearly as straight up and down as the side of a house. There is plenty of water close up to it, but mighty little on top of it. If you were to hit it you would knock the boat's brains out. Do you see where the line fringes out at the upper end and begins to fade away?"

24. **crossing marks:** points on the river where a boat could cross safely.
25. **bluff reef:** hidden sandbar with a high, steep front. Its position is indicated by lines or ripples on the water.

The pilothouse of *The Great Republic.*

The Bettmann Archive.

LITERATURE AND FOLKLORE

The Lure and Lore of the Mississippi

It was a monstrous big river down there—sometimes a mile and a half wide; we run nights, and laid up and hid daytimes. . . . we slid into the river and had a swim, so as to freshen up and cool off; then we set down on the sandy bottom where the water was about knee deep, and watched the daylight come.

—Mark Twain, *Adventures of Huckleberry Finn*

In the folklore of the Mississippi (Algonquian for "big river"), the river has many contradictory aspects: It is god, devil, giver of prosperity, destroyer of life and property, even trickster-hero. (The river is seen as a trickster because, when its course periodically changes, its changing configurations sometimes alter state lines, actually "moving" plantations and farms from one state to another.) The African American folklorist Ruth Bass once described the river's power and unpredictability: "Ole Miss' was lying mighty peaceful and tenderlike now, but she could be high-handed when she took a notion." That unpredictability has given rise to hundreds of superstitions and folk sayings. According to one African American folk belief, the river's evil spirit becomes angry and drowns anyone who dares swim across. Mississippi navigators claim the river never lets go of a person who falls in the water with clothes on. A Louisiana saying has it that it's bad luck to throw an animal into the river. On the other hand, according to some folk beliefs, if a person washes his or her face in the Mississippi, bad luck can change to good luck.

Sea monsters and other scares. Tales and legends associated with the "big river" run a vast course as long as the river itself. On the bluffs along the Mississippi, Native Americans made rock carvings, or petroglyphs, to depict supernatural beings they saw around them. Members of the Illinois people told Father Hennepin, a seventeenth-century explorer, that on the bluffs near present-day Minneapolis were "some Tritons and other Sea Monsters painted

---

"Yes, sir."

"Well, that is a low place; that is the head of the reef. You can climb over there, and not hurt anything. Cross over, now, and follow along close under the reef—easy water there—not much current."

I followed the reef along till I approached the fringed end. Then Mr. Bixby said—

"Now get ready. Wait till I give the word. She won't want to mount the reef: a boat hates shoal water. Stand by—wait—*wait*—keep her well in

hand. *Now* cramp her down![26] Snatch her![27] Snatch her!"

He seized the other side of the wheel and helped to spin it around until it was hard down, and then we held it so. The boat resisted, and refused to answer for a while, and next she came surging to starboard, mounted the reef, and sent a

26. **cramp her down:** turn the wheel sharply.
27. **Snatch her:** Act quickly.

which the boldest Men durst not look upon, there being some Enchantment in their face." Farther south, near Alton, Illinois, inmates of the state prison who were quarrying rock in the 1850s came upon the traces of two huge bird petroglyphs. Their origin, according to a tradition of the Illinois people, involves a gigantic bird that preyed on humans long before the white settlers came. After whole villages were destroyed, a chief offered himself to the bird as armed warriors lay in ambush. The Great Spirit, in admiration of the chief's cunning and bravery, allowed the chief to live, and the murderous bird died with a "wild, fearful scream." In memory of the event, the bird's image was engraved on the bluff.

The haunted river. The Mississippi also has its share of ghost stories. One Chippewa legend from Minnesota tells of a white panther that spoke the people's language and served as their prophet. A young warrior killed the panther and brought upon himself the curse of roaming forever, "a starving and undying skeleton." When the moon has a red cast or the sky is purple, legends say, the ghost of the warrior can be seen wandering the banks of the river. Another story, this one from Creole folklore, warns that zombies haunt a number of Louisiana bayous. On a shoal called Devil Flats, a zombie who carries his own dismembered head under his arm takes care on his evening walks to turn the head so that its eyes can take in the tranquil twilight scene.

On somewhat more scientific footing are the mysterious reports from Devil's Punch Bowl, near Natchez, Mississippi. The Bowl is a several-acre pit in a river bluff; it may have been caused by a prehistoric meteorite. Ship captains report that when their ship approaches the spot, their compass needles go wild and sometimes spin around completely. Some people theorize that this happens because of the iron sunk into the earth by the meteorite. But Devil's Punch Bowl is also said to have been a meeting place for pirates who preyed upon river traffic, and a hiding place for their stolen loot. Thus, the more romantic explanation for the erratic behavior of compasses is that it is caused by the huge pots of gold and silver coins buried by the pirates.

The Mississippi may or may not guard lost treasure, but it most certainly has riches in legend and lore.

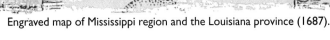

Engraved map of Mississippi region and the Louisiana province (1687).

long, angry ridge of water foaming away from her bows.[28]

"Now watch her; watch her like a cat, or she'll get away from you. When she fights strong and the tiller slips a little, in a jerky, greasy sort of way, let up on her a trifle; it is the way she tells you at night that the water is too shoal; but keep edging her up, little by little, toward the point. You are well up on the bar, now; there is a bar under every point, because the water that comes down around it forms an eddy and allows the sediment to sink. Do you see those fine lines on the face of the water that branch out like the ribs of a fan? Well, those are little reefs; you want to just miss the ends of them, but run them pretty close. Now look out—look out! Don't you crowd that slick, greasy-looking place; there ain't nine feet there; she won't stand it. She begins to smell it; look

28. **bows:** front part of a boat.

sharp, I tell you! Oh blazes, there you go! Stop the starboard wheel! Quick! Ship up to back! Set her back!"[29]

The engine bells jingled and the engines answered promptly, shooting white columns of steam far aloft out of the 'scape pipes, but it was too late. The boat had "smelt"[30] the bar in good earnest; the foamy ridges that radiated from her bows suddenly disappeared, a great dead swell[31] came rolling forward and swept ahead of her, she careened far over to larboard, and went tearing away toward the other shore as if she were about scared to death. We were a good mile from where we ought to have been, when we finally got the upper hand of her again.

During the afternoon watch the next day, Mr. Bixby asked me if I knew how to run the next few miles. I said—

"Go inside the first snag above the point, outside the next one, start out from the lower end of Higgins's woodyard, make a square crossing[32] and"—

"That's all right. I'll be back before you close up on the next point."

But he wasn't. He was still below when I rounded it and entered upon a piece of river which I had some misgivings about. I did not know that he was hiding behind a chimney to see how I would perform. I went gaily along, getting prouder and prouder, for he had never left the boat in my sole charge such a length of time before. I even got to "setting" her and letting the wheel go, entirely, while I vaingloriously turned my back and inspected the stern marks[33] and hummed a tune, a sort of easy indifference which I had prodigiously admired in Bixby and other great pilots. Once I inspected rather long, and

> The engine bells jingled and the engines answered promptly, shooting white columns of steam far aloft out of the 'scape pipes, but it was too late.

when I faced to the front again my heart flew into my mouth so suddenly that if I hadn't clapped my teeth together I should have lost it. One of those frightful bluff reefs was stretching its deadly length right across our bows! My head was gone in a moment; I did not know which end I stood on; I gasped and could not get my breath; I spun the wheel down with such rapidity that it wove itself together like a spider's web; the boat answered and turned square away from the reef, but the reef followed her! I fled, and still it followed still it kept—right across my bows! I never looked to see where I was going, I only fled. The awful crash was imminent—why didn't that villain come! If I committed the crime of ringing a bell, I might get thrown overboard. But better that than kill the boat. So in blind desperation I started such a rattling "shivaree"[34] down below as never had astounded an engineer in this world before, I fancy. Amidst the frenzy of the bells the engines began to back and fill in a furious way, and my reason forsook its throne—we were about to crash into the woods on the other side of the river. Just then Mr. Bixby stepped calmly into view on the hurricane deck.[35] My soul went out to him in gratitude. My distress vanished; I would have felt safe on the brink of Niagara, with Mr. Bixby on the hurricane deck. He blandly and sweetly took his toothpick out of his mouth between his fingers, as if it were a cigar— we were just in the act of climbing an overhanging big tree, and the passengers were scudding astern[36] like rats—and lifted up these commands to me ever so gently—

"Stop the starboard. Stop the larboard. Set her back on both."[37]

34. shivaree (shiv′ə·rē′): noisy celebration.
35. hurricane deck: topmost deck of a steamboat.
36. scudding astern: running to the back of the boat.
37. Stop . . . both: Halt the forward motion of the boat by stopping both the right and left paddle wheels, and put both wheels in reverse.

WORDS TO OWN

misgivings (mis′giv′iŋz) *n. pl.:* doubts; worries.
blandly (bland′lē) *adv.:* mildly.

---

29. Ship . . . back: Put it in reverse.
30. smelt: dialect for "smelled." That is, the boat recognized water too shallow for safety.
31. great dead swell: huge wave.
32. make a square crossing: go directly between crossing marks.
33. stern marks: landmarks already passed and thus astern of, or behind, the boat.

The boat hesitated, halted, pressed her nose among the boughs a critical instant, then reluctantly began to back away.

"Stop the larboard. Come ahead on it. Stop the starboard. Come ahead on it. Point her for the bar."

I sailed away as serenely as a summer's morning. Mr. Bixby came in and said, with mock simplicity—

"When you have a hail,[38] my boy, you ought to tap the big bell three times before you land, so that the engineers can get ready."

I blushed under the sarcasm, and said I hadn't had any hail.

"Ah! Then it was for wood, I suppose. The officer of the watch will tell you when he wants to wood up."

I went on consuming, and said I wasn't after wood.

"Indeed? Why, what could you want over here in the bend, then? Did you ever know of a boat following a bend upstream at this stage of the river?"

"No, sir—and I wasn't trying to follow it. I was getting away from a bluff reef."

"No, it wasn't a bluff reef; there isn't one within three miles of where you were."

"But I saw it. It was as bluff as that one yonder."

"Just about. Run over it!"

"Do you give it as an order?"

"Yes. Run over it."

"If I don't, I wish I may die."

"All right; I am taking the responsibility."

I was just as anxious to kill the boat, now, as I had been to save her before. I impressed my orders upon my memory, to be used at the inquest,[39] and made a straight break for the reef. As it disappeared under our bows I held my breath; but we slid over it like oil.

"Now don't you see the difference? It wasn't anything but a *wind* reef. The wind does that."

"So I see. But it is exactly like a bluff reef. How am I ever going to tell them apart?"

"I can't tell you. It is an instinct. By and by you will just naturally *know* one from the other, but you never will be able to explain why or how you know them apart."

It turned out to be true. The face of the water, in time, became a wonderful book—a book that was a dead language to the uneducated passenger, but which told its mind to me without reserve, delivering its most cherished secrets as clearly as if it uttered them with a voice. And it was not a book to be read once and thrown aside, for it had a new story to tell every day. Throughout the long twelve hundred miles there was never a page that was <u>void</u> of interest, never one that you could leave unread without loss, never one that you would want to skip, thinking you could find higher enjoyment in some other thing. There never was so wonderful a book written by man; never one whose interest was so absorbing, so unflagging, so sparklingly renewed with every reperusal. The passenger who could not read it was

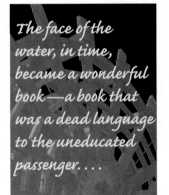

The face of the water, in time, became a wonderful book—a book that was a dead language to the uneducated passenger. . . .

charmed with a peculiar sort of faint dimple on its surface (on the rare occasions when he did not overlook it altogether); but to the pilot that was an *italicized* passage; indeed, it was more than that, it was a legend[40] of the largest capitals, with a string of shouting exclamation points at the end of it; for it meant that a wreck or a rock was buried there that could tear the life out of the strongest vessel that ever floated. It is the faintest and simplest expression the water ever makes, and the most hideous to a pilot's eye. In truth, the passenger who could not read this book saw nothing but all manner of pretty pictures in it, painted by the sun and shaded by the clouds, whereas to the trained eye these were not pictures at all, but the grimmest and most dead earnest of reading matter.

Now when I had mastered the language of this water and had come to know every trifling feature that bordered the great river as familiarly as I

40. **legend:** inscription.

---

38. **hail:** call to land.
39. **inquest:** inquiry by a jury or panel investigating a crime.

The Bettmann Archive.

knew the letters of the alphabet, I had made a valuable acquisition. But I had lost something, too. I had lost something which could never be restored to me while I lived. All the grace, the beauty, the poetry had gone out of the majestic river! I still keep in mind a certain wonderful sunset which I witnessed when steamboating was new to me. A broad expanse of the river was turned to blood; in the middle distance the red hue brightened into gold, through which a solitary log came floating, black and conspicuous; in one place a long, slanting mark lay sparkling upon the water; in another the surface was broken by boiling, tumbling rings, that were as many-tinted as an opal; where the ruddy flush was faintest, was a smooth spot that was covered with graceful circles and radiating lines, ever so delicately traced; the shore on our left was densely wooded, and the <u>somber</u> shadow that fell from this forest was broken in one place by a long, ruffled trail that shone like silver; and high above the forest wall a clean-stemmed dead tree waved a single leafy bough that glowed like a flame in the unobstructed splendor that was flowing from the sun. There were graceful curves, reflected images, woody heights, soft distances; and over the whole scene, far and near, the dissolving lights drifted steadily, enriching it, every passing moment, with new marvels of coloring.

I stood like one bewitched. I drank it in, in a speechless rapture. The world was new to me, and I had never seen anything like this at home. But as I have said, a day came when I began to cease from noting the glories and the charms which the moon and the sun and the twilight wrought upon the river's face; another day came when I ceased altogether to note them. Then, if that sunset scene had been repeated, I should have looked upon it without rapture, and should have commented upon it, inwardly, after this fashion: This sun means that we are going to have wind tomorrow; that floating log means that the river is rising, small thanks to it; that slanting mark on the water refers to a bluff reef which is going to kill somebody's steamboat one of these nights, if it keeps on stretching out like that; those tumbling "boils" show a dissolving bar and a changing channel there; the lines and circles in the slick water over yonder are a warning that that troublesome place is shoaling up dangerously; that silver streak in the shadow of the forest is the "break" from a new snag,[41] and he has located himself in the very best place he could have found to fish for steamboats; that tall dead tree, with a single living branch, is not going to last long, and then how is a body ever going to get through this blind place at night without the friendly old landmark?

No, the romance and the beauty were all gone from the river. All the value any feature of it had for me now was the amount of usefulness it could furnish toward compassing the safe piloting of a steamboat. Since those days, I have pitied doctors from my heart. What does the lovely flush in a beauty's cheek mean to a doctor but a "break" that ripples above some deadly disease? Are not all her visible charms sown thick with what are to him the signs and symbols of hidden decay? Does he ever see her beauty at all, or doesn't he simply view her professionally, and comment upon her unwholesome condition all to himself? And doesn't he sometimes wonder whether he has gained most or lost most by learning his trade?

41. **"break" . . . snag:** ripple or line in the water indicating a newly fallen tree.

WORDS TO OWN

somber (säm′bər) *adj.:* gloomy; dark.

MAKING MEANINGS

First Thoughts

1. Twain ruefully reports that "the romance and the beauty were all gone from the river." Do you think he is describing a common human reaction? Can you identify another example of this kind of experience?

Shaping Interpretations

2. In "Perplexing Lessons," what does Bixby mean when he says that Twain must learn the shape of the river?

3. In the chapter titled "Continued Perplexities," an **extended metaphor** compares the river with a book that "had a new story to tell every day" (page 461). Find three specific comparisons Twain makes between reading a book and "reading" the river.

4. Twain says that "All the grace, the beauty, the poetry had gone out of the majestic river!" (page 462). In what sense is he describing a loss of "innocence" that comes about as a result of increased experience?

Connecting with the Text

5. Think about the episode in which Bixby lets Twain get into trouble before giving him quiet guidance. On the basis of your own experience with a variety of teachers, do you rate Bixby as a good teacher or a poor one? Give the reasons for your answer.

Challenging the Text

6. Twain first wrote about his Mississippi experiences for *The Atlantic Monthly*, a magazine edited by William Dean Howells. Howells said of Twain's first installment, "It almost made the water in our ice pitcher muddy as I read it." Does Twain bring the river to life as vividly as Howells implies? Support your response with examples from the text.

Reading Check

a. What huge body of information is Twain told he must learn as well as he knows a hall in his own home?

b. What happens the night Twain believes he is left at the wheel alone?

c. Explain the factors that make "learning the river" a great challenge.

d. What does Twain say he has lost when he finally learns the language of the river?

READING SKILLS AND STRATEGIES

Identifying Comic Devices

Humor is hard to explain, but we do know that certain comic devices are used in humorous writings; and when they are used by a genius like Twain, they make us laugh.

- **Hyperbole:** outrageous exaggeration made for effect: ". . . when I faced to the front again my heart flew into my mouth so suddenly that if I hadn't clapped my teeth together I should have lost it" (page 460).

- **Comic metaphors:** comparisons between two unlike things that create colorful, hilarious images. Twain's metaphors often involve incongruity—two seemingly mismatched or even opposite images, events, or elements are unexpectedly joined: "My gunpowdery chief went off with a bang . . . and then went on loading and firing until he was out of adjectives" (page 454). Many of Twain's funniest comparisons are **extended metaphors.**

- **Understatement:** saying less than what is meant, usually for ironic purposes: "I was glad this damage had been saved, for it would have made me unpopular with the owners" (page 456).

1. Review the excerpt, and locate at least one more example of each of the three comic devices listed above. Read aloud the passages in which Twain uses each of these techniques.

2. Which of these comic devices is used most frequently in this excerpt from *Life on the Mississippi*? Overall, what adjectives would you use to describe Twain's humor?

3. Compare the comic devices in *Life on the Mississippi* with those in Twain's **tall tale** classic "The Celebrated Jumping Frog of Calaveras County." See if you can spot hyperbole, comic metaphors, and understatement in that tall tale about a jumping-frog contest held in a mining camp in California.

CHOICES: Building Your Portfolio

Writer's Notebook

1. Collecting Ideas for a Research Paper

Think of a place you would like to do research on—perhaps a historical place in your neighborhood or town, or a place that is threatened, such as a landmark slated for demolition. List some ideas of how you might approach your topic. You could focus your research on a question about the place, or how it has changed over time, or why it has meaning for you and others. You might also make some notes of ideas for drawings or maps you could use in your research paper. Save your notes for possible use in the Writer's Workshop on page 515.

(circular logo: WORK IN PROGRESS)

Analyzing Humor

2. Does Twain Hold Up?

Twain's use of humorous devices is one of the strongest characteristics of his work. With reference to both *Life on the Mississippi* and Spotlight On Mark Twain's Humor (page 465), explore in a brief essay how Twain's use of humor is like or unlike the use of humor by today's humorists and comedians. How do contemporary comics appeal to their particular audiences? Would Twain hold up today as a stand-up comic or a humorous writer? Explain.

Creative Writing

3. Double Take

The last three paragraphs of this excerpt from *Life on the Mississippi* examine two very different ways of looking at the river. Try writing your own essay in which you compare and contrast two different views of something:

- your feelings before and after taking a particular action
- how you see some aspect of your life now and how you saw it in the past
- how a favorite place of yours looks in the daytime and at night

Be sure to check your Quickwrite notes.

Speaking and Listening

4. In Character

Alone or with a partner, rehearse an oral reading of Twain's writing—either from the excerpts in this text or from another book. To prepare for your reading, you might want to watch the video *Mark Twain Gives an Interview,* with the actor Hal Holbrook portraying Mark Twain. You might also want to use simple props—a hat or an object representing a pilot's wheel—to help keep you in character. Perform your reading for the class.

Art/Research

5. Big Muddy

Locate paintings, drawings, or engravings of the Mississippi River. Select three to five works that in your opinion best capture the Mississippi that Twain portrays in this excerpt. For each work, write a brief paragraph explaining why you chose it, and cite appropriate descriptions from Twain. Set up a display for your class, mounting your explanatory paragraph next to a photocopy or reproduction of each visual you've selected.

Creative Writing/Research/Art

6. It Just Keeps Paddlin' Along

The editor of a travel magazine has asked you to write an article about the traditions and history of the Mississippi steamboat. Research the answers to such questions as these: When was the peak of the steamboat era? Did certain boats, captains, or pilots become famous? Where are the old steamboats now? How accurate are depictions like the musical *Show Boat* (available on video) in portraying the realities of the steamboat era? Write up your findings as a magazine story; include pictures for your article.

Mark Twain's Humor

During his lifetime, Mark Twain was better known as a lecturer than as a novelist, and he found considerable financial reward on the lecture circuit. Eyewitnesses reported that Twain had a genius for deadpan delivery, deliberately drawing out his remarks—and ending them with a perturbed expression. The **anecdotes** and maxims he delivered on stage would later be published in book form and sold by subscription in elaborate, illustrated volumes.

Twain's maxims have taken on the force of **proverbs,** a phenomenon securing his position as a pioneer of American humor. Here is a sampling of his many and varied one-liners.

Caricature of Mark Twain by Keppler. Lithograph.

The Bettmann Archive.

It's better to keep your mouth shut and appear stupid than to open it and remove all doubt.

By trying, we can easily learn to endure adversity. Another man's, I mean.

If the man doesn't believe as we do, we say he is a crank, and that settles it. I mean, it does nowadays, because now we can't burn him.

There are many humorous things in the world; among them, the white man's notion that he is less savage than the other savages.

There are several good protections against temptations, but the surest is cowardice.

If you pick up a starving dog and make him prosperous, he will not bite you. This is the principal difference between a dog and a man.

Few things are harder to put up with than the annoyance of a good example.

When I was a boy of fourteen, my father was so ignorant I could hardly stand to have the old man around. But when I got to be twenty-one, I was astonished at how much he had learned in seven years.

It takes your enemy and your friend, working together, to hurt you to the heart; the one to slander you and the other to get the news to you.

Nothing so needs reforming as other people's habits.

A sin takes on new and real terrors when there seems a chance that it is going to be found out.

Behold, the fool saith, "Put not all thine eggs in the one basket"—which is but a manner of saying, "Scatter your money and your attention"; but the wise man saith, "Put all your eggs in the one basket and—*watch that basket*."

Ambrose Bierce

(1842–1914?)

Ambrose Bierce infused his writing with an attitude of scorn for all the sentimental illusions human beings cling to. His dark vision of life centers on warfare and the cruel joke it plays on humanity. This bleak vision assures Bierce's place in our literary history.

Bierce was born in 1842, the tenth of thirteen children in the family of an eccentric and unsuccessful farmer named Marcus Aurelius Bierce. The Bierces lived in a log cabin in Meigs County, Ohio. Bierce was educated primarily through exploring his father's small library.

At nineteen, Bierce joined the Ninth Indiana Volunteers and saw action at the bloody Civil War battles of Shiloh and Chickamauga. He was also part of General Sherman's march to the sea in 1864. Bierce was once severely wounded and was cited for bravery no fewer than fifteen times.

At the war's end, Bierce reenlisted, but several years in the peacetime army left him discouraged about his prospects. He left the army and joined his brother Albert to work at the United States Mint in San Francisco. He began to contribute caustically witty, short pieces to the city's weeklies.

A growing reputation as a muckraking reporter brought Bierce the editorship of the San Francisco *News Letter* and the acquaintance of the literary community, including Mark Twain (page 450). When the financier Collis P. Huntington, head of the Southern Pacific Railroad, asked Bierce's price for silence on the railroad's tax fraud case, Bierce is said to have replied: "My price is about seventy-five million dollars, to be handed to the Treasurer of the United States." Bierce's disillusionment with the deceit and greed of his times continued to spur his pen and earned him the nickname "Bitter Bierce."

Bierce married in 1871 and moved to England, where he spent the next four years editing and contributing to humor magazines and making his first attempts at fiction. On his return to

Ambrose Bierce by J.H.E. Partington (1843–1899). Oil on canvas.

San Francisco in 1876, he wrote a regular column. This was the most active and fruitful time of Bierce's life. He became the witty scholar and literary dictator of the West Coast, but he never achieved wide recognition for his stories.

The Devil's Dictionary, first published in 1906 as *The Cynic's Word Book,* was more successful. In his dictionary, Bierce offered a collection of definitions filled with irony and sardonic humor. He defined war as a "by-product of the arts of peace," and peace as "a period of cheating between two periods of fighting." A cynic was a person who "sees things as they are, not as they ought to be. Hence the custom among the Scythians of plucking out a cynic's eyes to improve his vision."

In 1913, when Bierce was lonely and weary of his life, he asked his few friends to "forgive him in not perishing where he was." He set off for Mexico to report on, or join in, its revolution. "Goodbye," he wrote. "If you hear of my being stood up against a Mexican stone wall and shot to rags please know that I think it a pretty good way to depart this life. It beats old age, disease, or falling down the cellar stairs." No further word was ever heard from him.

Make the Connection

All in the Mind

Can we ever really understand the complexities of the human mind? What's real? What's imaginary? When someone we love is long overdue, we can conjure up the details of disaster in a few seconds and make ourselves sick with worry. On the other hand, we can lift ourselves out of a blue mood by focusing on an event we can look forward to. Imagine, then, the extremes to which the human imagination might go in a time of severe, even life-threatening, stress. If a person were threatened with imminent death, what kinds of thoughts might pass through his or her mind? Would the mind provide a calming refuge or intensify the fear and horror?

Reading Skills and Strategies

Clarifying Responses to a Text

As you journey with Bierce's hero, pause three or four times to write down your own feelings, thoughts, or observations. What developments make you afraid for the hero? When do you feel relieved or even happy for him? What doubts, questions, or other reactions arise in your mind at other times?

Elements of Literature

Point of View

In the different sections of Bierce's story, watch for these variations in **point of view:** (1) **omniscient,** in which the narrator seems to know everything about all characters or events; (2) **objective,** in which the narrator reports without comment, much as a camera would record a scene; and (3) **third-person limited,** in which the narrator zooms in on the thoughts and feelings of a single character.

Point of view is the vantage point from which a writer tells the story.

For more on Point of View, see the Handbook of Literary Terms.

Background

The belief that life will prove gratifying and will reward our virtues is so strong that it has become a main current in storytelling. But this romantic notion has its inevitable counterpart in realism and naturalism—fiction that conforms to the truth as it is experienced rather than as we would like it to be.

Bierce's no-punches-pull story is set in the deep South during the Civil War (1861–1865). He invites us sympathize with the hero, Southerner who has tried help the Confederate cause and he portrays the Union side as brutal and treacherous. Yet the horrors of war may serve only as an external setting for the landscape that *really* interests the writer. That landscape is the inside of the mind of a man condemned to death.

An Occurrence at Owl Creek Bridge

Ambrose Bierce

I

A man stood upon a railroad bridge in northern Alabama, looking down into the swift water twenty feet below. The man's hands were behind his back, the wrists bound with a cord. A rope closely encircled his neck. It was attached to a stout cross-timber above his head, and the slack fell to the level of his knees. Some loose boards laid upon the sleepers[1] supporting the metals of the railway supplied a footing for him and his executioners—two private soldiers of the Federal army, directed by a sergeant who in civil life may have been a deputy sheriff. At a short remove upon the same temporary platform was an officer in the uniform of his rank, armed. He was a captain. A sentinel at each end of the bridge stood with his rifle in the position known as "support," that is to say, vertical in front of the left shoulder, the hammer resting on the forearm thrown straight across the chest—a formal and unnatural position, enforcing an erect carriage of the body. It did not appear to be the duty of these two men to know what was occurring at the center of the bridge; they merely blockaded the two ends of the foot planking that traversed it.

Beyond one of the sentinels nobody was in sight; the railroad ran straight away into a forest for a hundred yards, then, curving, was lost to view. Doubtless there was an outpost farther along. The other bank of the stream was open ground —a gentle acclivity[2] topped with a stockade of vertical tree trunks, loopholed for rifles, with a single embrasure through which protruded the muzzle of a brass cannon commanding the bridge. Midway of the slope between bridge and fort were the spectators—a single company of infantry in line, at "parade rest," the butts of the rifles on the ground, the barrels inclining slightly backward against the right shoulder, the hands crossed upon the stock. A lieutenant stood at the right of the line, the point of his sword upon the ground, his left hand resting upon his right. Excepting the group of four at the center of the bridge, not a man moved. The company faced the bridge, staring stonily, motionless. The sentinels, facing the banks of the stream, might have been statues to adorn the bridge. The captain stood with folded arms, silent, observing the work of his subordinates, but making no sign. Death is a dignitary who when he comes announced is to be received with formal manifestations of respect,

---

WORDS TO OWN

sentinel (sen′ti·nəl) *n.*: guard; sentry.

---

1. **sleepers:** railroad ties.
2. **acclivity:** uphill slope.

even by those most familiar with him. In the code of military etiquette, silence and fixity are forms of <u>deference</u>.

The man who was engaged in being hanged was apparently about thirty-five years of age. He was a civilian, if one might judge from his habit, which was that of a planter. His features were good—a straight nose, firm mouth, broad forehead, from which his long, dark hair was combed straight back, falling behind his ears to the collar of his well-fitting frock coat. He wore a moustache and pointed beard, but no whiskers; his eyes were large and dark gray, and had a kindly expression which one would hardly have expected in one whose neck was in the hemp. Evidently this was no vulgar assassin. The liberal military code makes provision for hanging many kinds of persons, and gentlemen are not excluded.

The preparations being complete, the two private soldiers stepped aside and each drew away the plank upon which he had been standing. The sergeant turned to the captain, saluted, and placed himself immediately behind that officer, who in turn moved apart one pace. These movements left the condemned man and the sergeant standing on the two ends of the same plank, which spanned three of the crossties of the bridge. The end upon which the civilian stood almost, but not quite, reached a fourth. This plank had been held in place by the weight of the captain; it was now held by that of the sergeant. At a signal from the former, the latter would step aside, the plank would tilt and the condemned man go down between two ties. The arrangement commended itself to his judgment as simple and effective. His face had not been covered nor his eyes bandaged. He looked a moment at his "unsteadfast footing," then let his gaze wander to the swirling water of the stream racing madly beneath his feet. A piece of dancing driftwood caught his attention, and his eyes followed it down the current. How slowly it appeared to move! What a sluggish stream!

He closed his eyes in order to fix his last thoughts upon his wife and children. The water, touched to gold by the early sun, the brooding mists under the banks at some distance down the stream, the fort, the soldiers, the piece of drift—all had distracted him. And now he became conscious of a new disturbance. Striking through the thought of his dear ones was a sound which he could neither ignore nor understand, a sharp, distinct, metallic percussion like the stroke of a blacksmith's hammer upon the anvil; it had the same ringing quality. He wondered what it was, and whether immeasurably distant or nearby—it seemed both. Its recurrence was regular, but as slow as the tolling of a death knell. He awaited each stroke with impatience and—he knew not why—apprehension. The intervals of silence grew progressively longer; the delays became maddening. With their greater infrequency the sounds increased in strength and sharpness. They hurt his ear like the thrust of a knife; he feared he would shriek. What he heard was the ticking of his watch.

He unclosed his eyes and saw again the water below him. "If I could free my hands," he thought, "I might throw off the noose and spring into the stream. By diving I could evade the bullets and, swimming vigorously, reach the bank, take to the woods, and get away home. My home, thank God, is as yet outside their lines; my wife and little ones are still beyond the invader's farthest advance."

As these thoughts, which have here to be set down in words, were flashed into the doomed man's brain rather than evolved from it, the captain nodded to the sergeant. The sergeant stepped aside.

II

Peyton Farquhar was a well-to-do planter, of an old and highly respected Alabama family. Being a slave owner and, like other slave owners, a politician, he was naturally an original secessionist and ardently devoted to the Southern cause. Circumstances of an imperious nature, which it is unnecessary to relate here, had prevented him from taking service with the gallant army that had fought the disastrous campaigns ending with the fall of Corinth,[3] and he <u>chafed</u> under the inglorious

---

3. **Corinth:** Union forces under General William S. Rosecrans (1819-1898) took Corinth, Mississippi, on October 4, 1862.

WORDS TO OWN

deference (def′ər·əns) *n*.: respect.
chafed (chāft) *v*.: became impatient.

restraint, longing for the release of his energies, the larger life of the soldier, the opportunity for distinction. That opportunity, he felt, would come, as it comes to all in wartime. Meanwhile he did what he could. No service was too humble for him to perform in aid of the South, no adventure too <u>perilous</u> for him to undertake if consistent with the character of a civilian who was at heart a soldier, and who in good faith and without too much qualification assented to at least a part of the frankly villainous dictum that all is fair in love and war.

One evening while Farquhar and his wife were sitting on a rustic bench near the entrance to his grounds, a gray-clad soldier rode up to the gate and asked for a drink of water. Mrs. Farquhar was only too happy to serve him with her own white hands. While she was fetching the water, her husband approached the dusty horseman and inquired eagerly for news from the front.

"The Yanks are repairing the railroads," said the man, "and are getting ready for another advance. They have reached the Owl Creek bridge, put it in order, and built a stockade on the north bank. The commandant has issued an order, which is posted everywhere, declaring that any civilian caught interfering with the railroad, its bridges, tunnels, or trains will be summarily hanged. I saw the order."

"How far is it to the Owl Creek bridge?" Farquhar asked.

"About thirty miles."

"Is there no force on this side the creek?"

"Only a picket post half a mile out, on the railroad, and a single sentinel at this end of the bridge."

"Suppose a man—a civilian and student of hanging—should elude the picket post and perhaps get the better of the sentinel," said Farquhar, smiling, "what could he accomplish?"

The soldier reflected. "I was there a month ago," he replied. "I observed that the flood of last winter had lodged a great quantity of driftwood against the wooden pier at this end of the bridge. It is now dry and would burn like tow."

The lady had now brought the water, which the soldier drank. He thanked her ceremoniously, bowed to her husband, and rode away. An hour later, after nightfall, he repassed the plantation, going northward in the direction from which he had come. He was a Federal scout.

III

As Peyton Farquhar fell straight downward through the bridge, he lost consciousness and was as one already dead. From this state he was awakened—ages later, it seemed to him—by the pain of a sharp pressure upon his throat, followed by a sense of suffocation. Keen, poignant agonies seemed to shoot from his neck downward through every fiber of his body and limbs. These pains appeared to flash along well-defined lines of ramification and to beat with an inconceivably rapid periodicity. They seemed like streams of pulsating fire heating him to an intolerable temperature. As to his head, he was conscious of nothing but a feeling of fullness—of congestion. These sensations were unaccompanied by thought. The intellectual part of his nature was already effaced; he had power only to feel, and feeling was torment. He was conscious of motion. Encompassed in a luminous cloud, of which he was now merely the fiery heart, without material

WORDS TO OWN
perilous (per′ə·ləs) *adj.*: dangerous.

substance, he swung through unthinkable arcs of <u>oscillation</u>, like a vast pendulum. Then all at once, with terrible suddenness, the light about him shot upward with the noise of a loud plash; a frightful roaring was in his ears, and all was cold and dark. The power of thought was restored; he knew that the rope had broken and he had fallen into the stream. There was no additional strangulation; the noose about his neck was already suffocating him and kept the water from his lungs. To die of hanging at the bottom of a river!—the idea seemed to him ludicrous. He opened his eyes in the darkness and saw above him a gleam of light, but how distant, how inaccessible! He was still sinking, for the light became fainter and fainter until it was a mere glimmer. Then it began to grow and brighten, and he knew that he was rising toward the surface—knew it with reluctance, for he was now very comfortable. "To be hanged and drowned," he thought, "that is not so bad; but I do not wish to be shot. No; I will not be shot; that is not fair."

He was not conscious of an effort, but a sharp pain in his wrist apprised him that he was trying to free his hands. He gave the struggle his attention, as an idler might observe the feat of a juggler, without interest in the outcome. What splendid effort!—what magnificent, what superhuman strength! Ah, that was a fine endeavor! Bravo! The cord fell away; his arms parted and floated upward, the hands dimly seen on each side in the growing light. He watched them with a new interest as first one and then the other pounced upon the noose at his neck. They tore it away and thrust it fiercely aside, its undulations resembling those of a water snake. "Put it back, put it back!" He thought he shouted these words to his hands, for the undoing of the noose had been succeeded by the direst pang that he had yet experienced. His neck ached horribly; his brain was on fire; his heart, which had been fluttering faintly, gave a great leap, trying to force itself out at his mouth. His whole body was racked and wrenched with an insupportable anguish! But his disobedient hands gave no heed to the command. They beat the water vigorously with quick, downward strokes, forcing him to the surface. He felt his head emerge; his eyes were blinded by the sunlight; his chest expanded convulsively, and with a supreme and crowning agony his lungs engulfed a great draft of air, which instantly he expelled in a shriek!

He was now in full possession of his physical senses. They were, indeed, preternaturally keen and alert. Something in the awful disturbance of his organic system had so exalted and refined them that they made record of things never before perceived. He felt the ripples upon his face and heard their separate sounds as they struck. He looked at the forest on the bank of the stream, saw the individual trees, the leaves, and the veining of each leaf—saw the very insects upon them: the locusts, the brilliant-bodied flies, the gray spiders stretching their webs from twig to twig. He noted the prismatic colors in all the dewdrops upon a million blades of grass. The humming of the gnats that danced above the eddies of the stream, the beating of the dragonflies' wings, the strokes of the water spiders' legs, like oars which had lifted their boat—all these made audible music. A fish slid along beneath his eyes, and he heard the rush of its body parting the water.

He had come to the surface facing down the stream; in a moment the visible world seemed to wheel slowly round, himself the <u>pivotal</u> point, and he saw the bridge, the fort, the soldiers upon the bridge, the captain, the sergeant, the two privates, his executioners. They were in silhouette against the blue sky. They shouted and gesticulated, pointing at him. The captain had drawn his pistol, but did not fire; the others were unarmed. Their movements were grotesque and horrible, their forms gigantic.

Suddenly he heard a sharp report and something struck the water smartly within a few inches of his head, spattering his face with spray. He heard a second report, and saw one of the sentinels with his rifle at his shoulder, a light cloud of blue smoke rising from the muzzle. The man in the water saw the eye of the man on the bridge gazing into his own through the sights of the rifle. He observed that it was a gray eye and remembered having read that gray eyes were keenest,

WORDS TO OWN

oscillation (äs′ə·lā′shən) *n*.: regular back-and-forth movement.
pivotal (piv′ə·təl) *adj*.: central; acting as a point around which other things turn.

and that all famous marksmen had them. Nevertheless, this one had missed.

A counterswirl had caught Farquhar and turned him half round; he was again looking into the forest on the bank opposite the fort. The sound of a clear, high voice in monotonous singsong now rang out behind him and came across the water with a distinctness that pierced and subdued all other sounds, even the beating of the ripples in his ears. Although no soldier, he had frequented camps enough to know the dread significance of that deliberate, drawling, aspirated chant; the lieutenant on shore was taking a part in the morning's work. How coldly and pitilessly—with what an even, calm intonation, presaging, and enforcing tranquility in the men—with what accurately measured intervals fell those cruel words:

"Attention, company! . . . Shoulder arms! . . . Ready! . . . Aim! . . . Fire!"

Farquhar dived—dived as deeply as he could. The water roared in his ears like the voice of Niagara, yet he heard the dulled thunder of the volley and, rising again toward the surface, met shining bits of metal, singularly flattened, oscillating slowly downward. Some of them touched him on the face and hands, then fell away, continuing their descent. One lodged between his collar and neck; it was uncomfortably warm and he snatched it out.

As he rose to the surface, gasping for breath, he saw that he had been a long time underwater; he was perceptibly farther downstream—nearer to safety. The soldiers had almost finished reloading; the metal ramrods flashed all at once in the sunshine as they were drawn from the barrels, turned in the air, and thrust into their sockets. The two sentinels fired again, independently and ineffectually.

The hunted man saw all this over his shoulder; he was now swimming vigorously with the current. His brain was as energetic as his arms and legs; he thought with the rapidity of lightning.

"The officer," he reasoned, "will not make that martinet's[4] error a second time. It is as easy to dodge a volley as a single shot. He has probably already given the command to fire at will. God help me, I cannot dodge them all!"

4. **martinet's:** A martinet is a disciplinarian of military rigidity.

An appalling plash within two yards of him was followed by a loud, rushing sound, *diminuendo,*[5] which seemed to travel back through the air to the fort and died in an explosion which stirred the very river to its deeps! A rising sheet of water curved over him, fell down upon him, blinded him, strangled him! The cannon had taken a hand in the game. As he shook his head free from the commotion of the smitten water, he heard the deflected shot humming through the air ahead, and in an instant it was cracking and smashing the branches in the forest beyond.

"They will not do that again," he thought; "the next time they will use a charge of grape.[6] I must keep my eye upon the gun; the smoke will apprise me—the report arrives too late; it lags behind the missile. That is a good gun."

Suddenly he felt himself whirled round and round—spinning like a top. The water, the banks, the forests, the now distant bridge, fort and men—all were commingled and blurred. Objects were represented by their colors only; circular horizontal streaks of color—that was all he saw. He had been caught in a vortex and was being whirled on with a velocity of advance and gyration that made him giddy and sick. In a few moments he was flung upon the gravel at the foot of the left bank of the stream—the southern bank—and behind a projecting point which concealed him from his enemies. The sudden arrest of his motion, the abrasion of one of his hands on the gravel, restored him, and he wept with delight. He dug his fingers into the sand, threw it over himself in handfuls, and audibly blessed it. It looked like diamonds, rubies, emeralds; he could think of nothing beautiful which it did not resemble. The trees upon the bank were giant garden plants; he noted a definite order in their arrangement, inhaled the fragrance of their blooms. A strange, roseate light shone through the spaces

5. *diminuendo* (də·min′yo͞o·en′dō): decreasing in loudness.
6. **charge of grape:** cannon charge of small iron balls, called grapeshot.

- -

WORDS TO OWN

appalling (ə·pôl′iŋ) *adj.*: dismaying.
gyration (jī·rā′shən) *n.*: circular movement; whirling.
abrasion (ə·brā′zhən) *n.*: scrape.

- -

among their trunks, and the wind made in their branches the music of aeolian harps.[7] He had no wish to perfect his escape—was content to remain in that enchanting spot until retaken.

A whiz and rattle of grapeshot among the branches high above his head roused him from his dream. The baffled cannoneer had fired him a random farewell. He sprang to his feet, rushed up the sloping bank, and plunged into the forest.

All that day he traveled, laying his course by the rounding sun. The forest seemed interminable; nowhere did he discover a break in it, not even a woodsman's road. He had not known that he lived in so wild a region. There was something uncanny in the revelation.

By nightfall he was fatigued, footsore, famishing. The thought of his wife and children urged him on. At last he found a road which led him in what he knew to be the right direction. It was as wide and straight as a city street, yet it seemed untraveled. No fields bordered it, no dwelling anywhere. Not so much as the barking of a dog suggested human habitation. The black bodies of the trees formed a straight wall on both sides, terminating on the horizon in a point, like a diagram in a lesson in perspective. Overhead, as he looked up through this rift in the wood, shone great golden stars looking unfamiliar and grouped in strange constellations. He was sure they were arranged in some order which had a secret and <u>malign</u> significance. The wood on either side was full of singular noises, among which— once, twice, and again—he distinctly heard whispers in an unknown tongue.

His neck was in pain and lifting his hand to it he found it horribly swollen. He knew that it had a circle of black where the rope had bruised it. His eyes felt congested; he could no longer close them. His tongue was swollen with thirst; he relieved its fever by thrusting it forward from between his teeth into the cold air. How softly the turf had carpeted the untraveled avenue—he could no longer feel the roadway beneath his feet!

Doubtless, despite his suffering, he had fallen asleep while walking, for now he sees another scene—perhaps he has merely recovered from a delirium. He stands at the gate of his own home. All is as he left it, and all bright and beautiful in the morning sunshine. He must have traveled the entire night. As he pushes open the gate and passes up the wide white walk, he sees a flutter of female garments; his wife, looking fresh and cool and sweet, steps down from the veranda to meet him. At the bottom of the steps she stands waiting, with a smile of ineffable joy, an attitude of matchless grace and dignity. Ah, how beautiful she is! He springs forward with extended arms. As he is about to clasp her he feels a stunning blow upon the back of the neck; a blinding white light blazes all about him with a sound like the shock of a cannon—then all is darkness and silence!

Peyton Farquhar was dead; his body, with a broken neck, swung gently from side to side beneath the timbers of the Owl Creek bridge.

WORDS TO OWN

malign (mə·līn′) *adj.:* harmful; evil.

---

7. **aeolian harps:** stringed instruments that are played by the wind. Aeolus is the god of the winds in Greek mythology.

MAKING MEANINGS

First Thoughts

1. Did you feel that the outcome of this story was credible and powerful, or did you feel cheated by the surprise ending? What kind of ending had you been led to anticipate? Explain your response.

Reading Check

a. State the situation Peyton Farquhar faces in Part I.

b. Part II of the story is a flashback. List its events in **chronological order.**

c. **Summarize** in one sentence what Farquhar imagines in Part III.

Shaping Interpretations

2. What **point of view** does the writer use in the third part of the story, which occurs within the few seconds before Farquhar dies? Why is this point of view particularly appropriate?

3. Do you think Bierce tries to enlist your sympathies toward either the Union or the Confederate side? Or does the story seem to be focused on a more general **theme** about the nature of the war? Cite evidence from the story.

4. Review the notes you took on your responses to the story. How did Bierce manipulate your feelings? How did he prepare you for the ending?

Extending the Text

5. What does this story reveal about the psychology of a person in a life-or-death situation? Do you find this psychology believable or far-fetched? Explain.

Challenging the Text

6. The critics Cleanth Brooks and Robert Penn Warren have said that Bierce's story depends too much on a quirk of human psychology and is thus a mere "case study" that does not reveal anything important about human nature, as good fiction does. Do you agree? Why or why not?

CHOICES:
Building Your Portfolio

Writer's Notebook

1. Collecting Ideas for a Research Paper

Make some notes about interesting topics this story suggests (perhaps the use of spies during the Civil War or current psychological theories of stress). Then, write down a list of possible sources of information you could consult for your research: library resources, community sources (local museums or historical societies), and so on. Save your notes for possible use in the Writer's Workshop on page 515.

Adapting a Story to Another Medium

2. Film Version

Write a memorandum to a film producer outlining your plans for adapting "Occurrence" into a movie. Point out scenes where you would use each of the following techniques: (a) close-up shot; (b) panoramic shot; (c) moving-camera shot; (d) quick cut to new scene; (e) fast motion; (f) slow motion; (g) fuzzy image; (h) sound effects. Before you write your final draft of the memo, you might view the Academy Award®–winning short film (available on videocassette) of the story. It was made in 1962 in France and became a favorite episode of the old TV series *The Twilight Zone.* Compare your plans with the actual film, and then, if you choose, modify your memorandum.

Creative Writing

3. Variations on Bierce

Write a brief narrative in which you explore the inner workings of the mind of a character subjected to a moment of intense pressure or an extraordinary crisis. Try to imitate Bierce by shifting your narrative between external reality and internal thoughts.

Reading Skills and Strategies

VOCABULARY: AFFIXES—THE LONG AND SHORT OF IT

Prefixes and suffixes are examples of **affixes,** word parts attached to the beginning or end of a base word or root to make a new word. Knowing some frequently used affixes can help you quickly unlock the meanings of words that seem long and inaccessible.

In fact, *inaccessible* is a good word to start with. Ambrose Bierce uses it in "An Occurrence at Owl Creek Bridge": "He opened his eyes in the darkness and saw above him a gleam of light, but how distant, how inaccessible!" (page 471). Context tells you that *inaccessible* has a similar meaning to *distant.* To fully understand the word, try affix analysis.

There are many prefixes and suffixes in English, but some are more commonly used than others. **Prefixes** are added to the beginning of a **base word** or **root** and always change its meaning. Some prefixes adjust their spelling so that the resulting word will be easier to say.

Prefixes	Meanings	Examples
co–, col–, com–	with, together	coexist, collide, compare
con–, cor–	with, together	convene, correspond
de–	away, from, off	defect, desert
dis–	away, off, opposing	dismount, dissent
em–, en–	cause to be, put into	empower, enrobe
ex–, e–, ef–	away from, out, up	excise, emigrate efface
in–, im–, il–, ir–	not	incapable, impious, illegal, irregular
pro–	forward, in place of, favoring	proceed, pronoun, pro-American
re–	back, again	recede, recur
un–	not, reverse of	untrue, unfold

Suffixes are added to the end of a base word or root. **Inflectional suffixes,** like *-ed* and *-ing,* usually just change the tense, person, or number of a word (generally a verb). **Derivational suffixes,** like the ones listed below, change the entire meaning of a root or base word.

Suffixes	Meanings	Examples
–able, –ible	able, likely	capable, flexible
–al	doer, pertaining to	rival, autumnal
–ant, –ent	doer, showing	servant, super-intendent
–ate	having, characteristic of	collegiate
–ence	act, condition, fact	patience, evidence
–er, –or	doer	baker, director
–ic	dealing with, caused by, showing	classic, choleric, workaholic
–ion, –tion	action, result, state	union, fusion, selection
–ive	belonging or tending to	detective, native
–ous	marked by, given to	religious, furious
–y	quality, action	jealousy, inquiry

The chart below shows one way that you can use affixes to analyze the meaning of a word.

Word	Prefix	Base/Root	Suffix(es)	Meaning of Word
inacces-sible	in–meaning: not	access meaning: to obtain	–ible meaning: able	not able to be obtained

Try It Out
Make your own affix-analysis chart for these words from "Occurrence."

1. inglorious
2. roseate
3. infrequency
4. commandant
5. manifestations
6. recurrence
7. deflected
8. disobedient
9. encircled
10. exalted

SPOTLIGHT ON
Voices from the Civil War

There are few literary records of the Civil War, but there are many personal testimonies in the form of letters, diaries, and memoirs. Some of these were written by well-known figures, but most were the work of ordinary people caught up in the most extraordinary and painful events of America's history. The following excerpts provide a brief history of the war in the voices of those who experienced it, including an Indiana farm boy, President Lincoln, Frederick Douglass, a Southern gentlewoman, and a Union soldier who witnessed the surrender of General Robert E. Lee.

It is often said that any civil war is a war of brother against brother, but we must think a moment to realize what this meant in nineteenth-century America. The United States at the time was a mobile society, and many families, especially in the border states, had friends and relatives in both the North and the South. For such families, the Civil War was a profoundly personal conflict.

In April 1861, several months after seven Southern states had formally seceded from the Union, Confederate forces demanded the surrender of the Union garrison on Fort Sumter, located on an island in the harbor of Charleston, South Carolina. At dawn on the twelfth of April, fighting began. Here is the response of Theodore Upson, a teenage farm boy in Indiana, to the news of the attack on Fort Sumter.

The Granger Collection, New York (cannon).

Theodore Upson

APRIL 1861

Father and I were husking out some corn. We could not finish before it wintered up. When William Cory came across the field (he had been down after the mail) he was excited and said, "Jonathan, the Rebs have fired upon and taken Fort Sumter." Father got white and couldn't say a word.

William said, "The president will soon fix them. He has called for 75,000 men and is going to blockade their ports, and just as soon as those fellows find out that the North means business, they will get down off their high horse."

Father said little. We did not finish the corn and drove to the barn. Father left me to unload and put out the team and went to the house. After I had finished I went in to dinner. Mother said, "What is the matter with Father?" He had gone right upstairs. I told her what we had heard. She went to him. After a while they came down. Father looked ten years older. We sat down to the table. Grandma wanted to know what was the trouble. Father told her and she began to cry. "Oh, my poor children in the South! Now they will suffer! God knows how they will suffer! I knew it would come! Jonathan, I told you it would come!"

"They can come here and stay," said Father.

"No, they will not do that. There is their home. There they will stay. Oh, to think that I should have lived to see the day when brother should rise against brother. . . ."

Mother had a letter from the Hales. Charlie and his father are in their [that is, the Confederate] army and Dayton wanted to go but was too young. I wonder if I were in our army and they should meet me would they shoot me. I suppose they would.

—from *The Blue and the Gray: The Story of the Civil War as Told by Participants,* edited by Henry Steele Commager

Walt Whitman (page 348) was too old to fight in the Civil War, but he did volunteer his services as a nurse in army hospitals. The following is an excerpt from his description of the wounded after the Battle of Chancellorsville, one of the bloodiest in the war, and one that Stephen Crane depicts in *The Red Badge of Courage*.

Walt Whitman

Then the camps of the wounded—O heavens, what scene is this?—is this indeed *humanity*—these butchers' shambles? There are several of them. There they lie, in the largest, in an open space in the woods, from 200 to 300 poor fellows—the groans and screams—the odor of blood, mixed with the fresh scent of the night, the grass, the trees—that slaughterhouse! O well is it their mothers, their sisters cannot see them—cannot conceive, and never conceived, these things. One man is shot by a shell, both in the arm and leg—both are amputated—there lie the rejected members. Some have their legs blown off—some bullets through the breast—some indescribably horrid wounds in the face or head, all mutilated, sickening, torn, gouged out— some in the abdomen—some mere boys—many rebels, badly hurt—they take their regular turns with the rest, just the same as any—the surgeons use them just the same. Such is the camp of the wounded—such a fragment, a reflection afar off of the bloody scene—while over all the clear, large moon comes out at times softly, quietly shining.

—Walt Whitman, *from Specimen Days*

Wounded soldiers (1864). Library of Congress.

In July 1861, Major Ballou wrote to his wife, Sarah, in Rhode Island. One week after he wrote this letter, Major Ballou was killed in the First Battle of Bull Run, Virginia.

Major Sullivan Ballou

. . . I know I have but few claims upon Divine Providence, but something whispers to me—perhaps it is the wafted prayer of my little Edgar, that I shall return to my loved ones unharmed. If I do not, my dear Sarah, never forget how much I love you, nor that when my last breath escapes me on the battlefield, it will whisper your name.

Forgive my many faults, and the many pains I have caused you. How thoughtless, how foolish I have sometimes been! How gladly would I wash out with my tears every little spot upon your happiness. . . .

But, O Sarah! If the dead can come back to this earth and flit unseen around those they love, I shall be always with you in the brightest day and the darkest night . . . *always, always,* and when the soft breeze fans your cheek, it shall be my breath, or the cool air your throbbing temple, it shall be my spirit passing by. Sarah, do not mourn me dead: Think I am gone and wait for me, for we shall meet again. . . .

(Below) Unidentified women, photographed around 1850.

The Granger Collection, New York.

The Granger Collection, New York.

Alexander Hunter was a college boy who joined the Seventeenth Virginia Regiment at the outbreak of the war. His book, *Johnny Reb and Billy Yank*, provides a lively look at life in the Confederate Army. Here he describes a meeting between Union and Confederate soldiers.

Alexander Hunter

Johnny Reb and Billy Yank

It was in the latter part of August [1863]; orders were given to be prepared to go on [guard duty] early in the morning; and until a late hour the men were busy cooking rations and cleaning equipment.

Before the mists had been chased by the rising sun, the company in close column of fours marched down the road. Men and animals were in perfect condition, brimful of mettle and in buoyant spirits.

The route lay along the banks of the river; upon the winding course of which, after several hours riding, the regiment reached its destination and relieved the various [guards]. A sergeant and squad of men were left at each post . . . to watch the enemy on the other side of the Rappahannock. . . .

The Rappahannock, which was at this place about two hundred yards wide, flowing slowly oceanward, its bosom reflecting the roseate-hued morn, was as lovely a body of water as the sun ever shone upon. The sound of the gentle ripple of its waves upon the sand was broken by a faint "halloo" which came from the other side.

"Johnny Reb; I say, J-o-h-n-n-y R-e-b, don't shoot!"

Joe Reid shouted back, "All right!"

"What command are you?"

The spoken words floated clear and distinct across the water, "The Black Horse Cavalry. Who are you?"

"The Second Michigan Cavalry."

"Come to the bank," said our spokesman, "and show yourselves; we won't fire."

"On your honor, Johnny Reb?"

"On our honor, Billy Yank."

In a second a large squad of blue-coats across the way advanced to the water's brink. The Southerners did the same; then the former put the query.

"Have you any tobacco?"

"Plenty of it," went out our reply.

"Any sugar and coffee?" they questioned.

"Not a taste nor a smell."

"Let's trade," was shouted with eagerness.

"Very well," was the reply, ". . . meet us here this evening."

"All right," they answered; then added, "Say, Johnny, want some newspapers?"

"Y-e-s!"

"Then look out, we are going to send you some."

"How are you going to do it?"

"Wait and see. . . ."

Eagerly he watched. . . . Presently he shouted:

"Here they come!" and then in a tone of intense admiration, "I'll be doggoned if these Yanks are not the smartest people in the world."

On the other side were several miniature boats and ships—such as schoolboys delight in—with sails set; the gentle breeze impelled the little crafts across the river, each freighted with a couple of newspapers. . . .

Drawing lots, Joe Boteler, who found luck against him, started to town, with a muttered curse, to buy tobacco. . . .

Joe returned in the evening with a box of plug tobacco about a foot square; but how to get it across was the question. The miniature boats could not carry it, and we shouted over to the Yanks that we had about twenty pounds of cut plug, and asked them what we must do? They hallooed back to let one of us swim across, and declared that it was perfectly safe. . . . I volunteered. Having lived on the banks of the Potomac most of my life, I was necessarily a swimmer. . . .

As I approached the shore the news of my coming reached camp, and nearly all the Second Michigan were lined up along the bank.

I felt a little queer, but had perfect faith in their promise and kept on without missing a stroke. . . . The blue-coats crowded around me and gave me a hearty welcome, . . . and heaped the craft with offerings of sugar, coffee, lemons, and even candy.

Bidding my friends the enemy good-bye, I swam back with the precious cargo, and we had a feast that night.

—Alexander Hunter, *from* *Johnny Reb and Billy Yank*

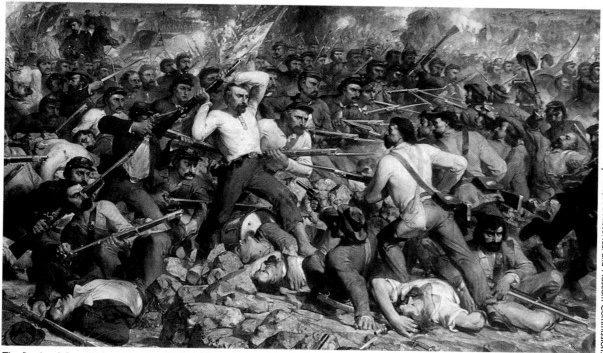

The Battle of Gettysburg: Pickett's Charge by Peter F. Rothermel.

The State Museum of Pennsylvania, PA. Historical and Museum Commission.

On July 7, 1863, a few days after the Battle of Gettysburg, Lincoln noted in an informal address how important this battle had been, but concluded that he was "not prepared to make [a speech] worthy of the occasion."

Several months later, in November of that year, Lincoln in fact delivered a speech on this theme, perhaps the most memorable of his career, at the dedication of the cemetery in Gettysburg.

Abraham Lincoln
The Gettysburg Address

Fourscore and seven years ago our fathers brought forth on this continent a new nation, conceived in Liberty, and dedicated to the proposition that all men are created equal.

Now we are engaged in a great civil war, testing whether that nation, or any nation so conceived and so dedicated, can long endure. We are met on a great battlefield of that war. We have come to dedicate a portion of that field as a final resting place for those who here gave their lives that that nation might live. It is altogether fitting and proper that we should do this.

But, in a larger sense, we cannot dedicate—we cannot consecrate—we cannot hallow—this ground. The brave men, living and dead, who struggled here, have consecrated it far above our poor power to add or detract. The world will little note nor long remember what we say here, but it can never forget what they did here. It is for us the living, rather, to be dedicated here to the unfinished work which they who fought here have thus far so nobly advanced. It is rather for us to be here dedicated to the great task remaining before us—that from these honored dead we take increased devotion to that cause for which they gave the last full measure of devotion—that we here highly resolve that these dead shall not have died in vain—that this nation, under God, shall have a new birth of freedom—and that government of the people, by the people, for the people, shall not perish from the earth.

—Abraham Lincoln
November 19, 1863

Susie King Taylor was born in slavery near Savannah, Georgia, in 1848. In April 1862, when she was fourteen, her uncle took her and his own seven children behind the Union lines. Taylor found work as a launderer for an African American troop, and soon found herself doing emergency work tending the wounded.

In 1902, Taylor wrote down her memory of her experiences with an African American regiment at Camp Saxton in Georgia.

Sgt. Balldwin of Company G, Fifty-sixth U.S. Colored Infantry (1863). Tintype.

The Granger Collection, New York.

Susie King Taylor

The first colored troops did not receive any pay for eighteen months, and the men had to depend wholly on what they received from the commissary established by General Saxton. A great many of these men had large families, and as they had no money to give them, their wives were obliged to support themselves and children by washing for the officers of the gunboats and the soldiers, and making cakes and pies which they sold to the boys in camp. Finally, in 1863, the government decided to give them half pay, but the men would not accept this. They wanted "full pay" or nothing. They preferred rather to give their services to the state, which they did until 1864, when the government granted them full pay, with all the back pay due. . . .

About four o'clock, July 2, the charge [into battle] was made. . . . [The first] one [of the wounded] brought in was Samuel Anderson of our company. . . . Then others of our boys, some with their legs off, arm gone, foot off, and wounds of all kinds imaginable. They had to wade through creeks and marshes, as they were discovered by the enemy and shelled very badly. A number of the men were lost. . . .

My work now began. I gave my assistance to try to alleviate their sufferings. I asked the doctor at the hospital what I could get for them to eat. They wanted soup, but that I could not get; but I had a few cans of condensed milk and some turtle eggs, so I thought I would try to make some custard. I had doubts as to my success, for cooking with turtle eggs was something new to me; but the adage has it, "Nothing ventured, nothing done," so I made a venture and the result was a very delicious custard. This I carried to the men, who enjoyed it very much.

—Susie King Taylor, *from Reminiscences of My Life in Camp*

Harriet Tubman Series No. 29 (1939–1940) by Jacob Lawrence. Casein tempera on gessoed hardboard (17 7/8" × 12").

Hampton University Museum, Hampton, Virginia.

Courtesy of the artist and the Francine Seders Gallery, Seattle, WA.

The most famous African American spokesperson during the Civil War was Frederick Douglass (page 424). Douglass used all of his eloquence and passionate oratory to persuade African Americans in the North to enlist in the Union Army. Eventually, a number of all-black volunteer regiments were formed and trained. (The 1989 film *Glory* reenacts the tragic exploits of one such regiment.) About 180,000 African Americans enlisted, including two of Douglass's sons. The following call to action first appeared in Douglass's own newspaper in March 1863.

Frederick Douglass

When first the rebel cannon shattered the walls of Sumter and drove away its starving garrison, I predicted that the war then and there inaugurated would not be fought out entirely by white men. Every month's experience during these dreary years has confirmed that opinion. A war undertaken and brazenly carried on for the perpetual enslavement of colored men, calls logically and loudly for colored men to help suppress it. Only a moderate share of sagacity was needed to see that the arm of the slave was the best defense against the arm of the slaveholder. Hence with every reverse to the national arms, with every exulting shout of victory raised by the slaveholding rebels, I have implored the imperiled nation to unchain against her foes, her powerful black hand. Slowly and reluctantly that appeal is beginning to be heeded. Stop not now to complain that it was not heeded sooner. It may or it may not have been best that it should not. This is not the time to discuss that question. Leave it to the future. When the war is over, the country is saved, peace is established, and the black man's rights are secured, as they will be, history with an impartial hand will dispose of that and sundry other questions. Action! Action! not criticism, is the plain duty of this hour. Words are now useful only as they stimulate to blows. The office of speech now is only to point out when, where, and how to strike to the best advantage. There is no time to delay. The tide is at its flood that leads on to fortune. From East to West, from North to South, the sky is written all over, "Now or never." Liberty won by white men would lose half its luster. "Who would be free themselves must strike the blow." "Better even die free, than to live slaves." This is the sentiment of every brave colored man amongst us.

—from *The Life and Times of Frederick Douglass*

Unidentified Union Army soldier with his wife, around 1865.

The following is just a small sample of memorable quotations from Frederick Douglass's speeches and writings.

We are *Americans,* speaking the same language, adopting the same customs, holding the same general opinions . . . and shall rise and fall with Americans.

Once let the black man get upon his person the brass letters "U.S."; let him get an eagle on his button, and a musket on his shoulder, and bullets in his pocket, and there is no power on the earth or under the earth which can deny that he has earned the right of citizenship in the United States.

The day dawns; the morning star is bright upon the horizon! The iron gate of our prison stands half open. One gallant rush from the North will fling it wide open, while four millions of our brothers and sisters shall march out into liberty. The chance is now given you to end in a day the bondage of centuries, and to rise in one bound from social degradation to the plane of common equality with all other varieties of men.

—from *The Life and Times of Frederick Douglass*

The Granger Collection, New York.

Mary Boykin Chesnut was the wife of James Chesnut, ex-senator from South Carolina and aide to Jefferson Davis, president of the Confederacy. During the course of the war, Mary Chesnut traveled from city to city in the South as the capital of the Confederacy changed. She kept up with the latest war news through her husband and their wide circle of knowledgeable and influential friends. Mary Chesnut was sophisticated, witty, and sensitive. Her diaries present an invaluable firsthand view of the war.

In April 1861, Mary Chesnut had been in Charleston, South Carolina, when the attack on Fort Sumter took place, beginning the Civil War. As she had been present at the beginning of the war, Mary Chesnut was also present at its end. In Columbia, South Carolina, she received the news, increasingly depressing, from the field.

Mary Boykin Chesnut (1856) by Samuel Osgood (1801–1885). Oil on canvas adhered to masonite (48″ × 30″).

National Portrait Gallery, Smithsonian Institution; on loan from Serena Williams Miles Van Rensselaer. Courtesy Art Resource, NY.

Mary Chesnut

SEPTEMBER 1, 1864

The battle is raging at Atlanta, our fate hanging in the balance.

SEPTEMBER 2, 1864

Atlanta is gone. Well that agony is over. Like David, when the child was dead, I will get up from my knees, will wash my face and comb my hair. There is no hope, but we will try to have no fear. . . .

SEPTEMBER 21, 1864

The president [of the Confederacy] has gone West. He has sent for Mr. Chesnut.

I went with Mrs. Rhett to hear Dr. Palmer [a minister]. I did not know before how utterly hopeless was our situation. This man is so eloquent; it was hard to listen and not give way. Despair was his word, and martyrdom. He offered us nothing more in this world than the martyr's crown. He is not for slavery, he says; he is for freedom, the freedom to govern our own country as we see fit. He is against foreign interference in our state matters. That is what Mr. Palmer went to war for, it appears. Every day shows that slavery is doomed the world over. For that he thanked God. He spoke of this time of our agony; and then came the cry: "Help us, Oh God! Vain is the help of man." So we came away shaken to the depths. . . .

The end has come, no doubt of the fact. . . . We are going to be wiped off the face of the earth. Now what is there to prevent Sherman taking General Lee in the rear. We have but two armies, and Sherman is between them now.

SEPTEMBER 29, 1864

These stories of our defeats in the Valley fall like blows upon a dead body. Since Atlanta, I have felt as if all were dead within me, forever. Captain Ogden of General Chesnut's staff dined here today. Had ever a Brigadier with little or no brigade so magnificent a staff? The reserves, as somebody said, are gathered by robbing the cradle and the grave of men too old and boys too young. . . .

OCTOBER 30, 1864

Every man is being hurried to the front. Today Mr. Chesnut met a poor creature coming from the surgeon's with a radiant face and a certificate. "General, see! I am exempt from service; one leg utterly useless, the other not warranted to last three months."

—Mary Chesnut, *from A Diary from Dixie*

Archive Photos.

Surrender of General Lee.

O n April 9, 1865, Lee surrendered to Grant at Appomattox Court House. Seth Flint, a Union soldier who witnessed the event, described the scene.

Seth M. Flint

I Saw Lee Surrender

Grant looked like an old and battered campaigner as he rode into the yard. His blue blouse was unbuttoned and underneath could be seen his undershirt. He was unlike Lee.

What a brave pair of thoroughbreds Lee and Traveler were. That horse would have attracted attention anywhere. General Lee's uniform was immaculate and he presented a superb martial figure. But it was the face beneath the gray felt hat that made the deepest impression on me. I have been trying to find a single word that describes it and I have concluded that "benign" is the adjective I'm after, because it means *kindly* and *gracious.* There was something else about him that aroused my deep pity that so great a warrior should be acknowledging defeat. . . .

Four o'clock—the door opened. Out came General Lee, his soldierly figure erect, even in defeat. We stiffened and gave him a salute, and the man in gray courteously returned it. At the moment his soul must have been heavy with sorrow—the years of desperate struggle fruitless—and yet he could return the salute of some Yankee troopers.

After the departure of General Lee, we quickly learned the happy news of the surrender and it spread like wildfire through the army. That night was one of the happiest I have ever known.

When I sounded taps, the sweetest of all bugle calls, the notes had scarcely died away when from the distance—it must have come from General Lee's headquarters—came, silvery clear, the same call. The boys on the other side welcomed peace.

Soldiers don't carry hatred.

—Seth M. Flint, *from* "I Saw Lee Surrender"

Stephen Crane
(1871–1900)

UPI/Bettmann.

Stephen Crane was the youngest of the fourteen children of a Methodist minister and his devout wife. Although frail as a child, Stephen grew up in upstate New York with a yearning to become a baseball star. He put in a year first at Lafayette College and then at Syracuse University (where he was captain of the baseball team) before he decided to try earning a living as a writer.

When Crane was about sixteen years old, he went to work for his brother Townley's news agency in Asbury Park, New Jersey. Later, struggling to make a living as a reporter in New York City, Crane was drawn to the city's underside. What he called his "artistic education" on the Bowery (Skid Row) kept him hungry and often ill.

Crane lived at the Art Students' League on East Twenty-third Street, writing his first significant fiction based on his explorations of the city's slums and saloons. This was *Maggie: A Girl of the Streets* (1893), a somber, somewhat shocking novel, whose plot involved brutality, alcoholism, prostitution, and suicide.

Maggie revealed Crane as a pioneer of **naturalism**—a literary movement that dissected human instincts and behavior and examined the social environment that "conditioned" people to turn out as they did. The novel was impossibly grim for popular magazines, and Crane borrowed $700 to have it printed. The copies of the little yellow paperback lay piled in his rented room for want of readers.

Crane's apparent failure with *Maggie* was followed by a triumph—a short novel titled *The Red Badge of Courage* (1895). Using an impressionistic technique, Crane filtered the events of the novel through the eyes of Henry Fleming, a young soldier at the Civil War battle of Chancellorsville. (In fiction, **impressionism** is a technique whereby the writer gives us not objective reality, but one character's impression of that reality.) As William Dean Howells observed, Crane's genius seemed to "spring to life fully armed" with this book. Crane had been

born after the Civil War, but he had read about it and had seen the famous battlefield photographs (page 408) attributed to Mathew Brady. "I have never been in a battle, of course," wrote Crane later, "and I believe that I got my sense of the rage of conflict on the football field. The psychology is the same. The opposing team is an enemy tribe."

The Red Badge of Courage made Crane into a celebrity, a national expert on war, and he spent the rest of his short life writing about it for the newspapers. In fact, he became the prototype of the adventurous correspondent who not only writes about sensational events but also lives a sensational life, delighting in shocking conservative readers.

One of the fascinating elements of Crane's life was the degree to which he interwove his fiction and his real-life experiences. It was as if he had invented a war in his novels and then

had to pursue the brush fires of his own times in order to confirm what he had written. Nor was experience wasted on him. When he sailed from Florida in late 1896 to cover a gunrunning operation to Cuba, he was shipwrecked off the Florida coast and endured a thirty-hour struggle against the sea. The result was his superb story "The Open Boat" (1898).

Before this ill-fated journey, Crane had stopped off at the Hotel de Dream in Jacksonville, Florida, and had taken up with the hostess, Cora Taylor. She soon decided that she would stay with him and become the first female war correspondent. This oddly matched couple later went off to Greece to cover a war. They settled eventually in England, renting a huge, dilapidated, medieval house in Sussex.

All of these adventures were taking their toll on Crane's always delicate health. Still, he continued to travel and write, desperate now to pay for Cora's extravagant domestic life. In 1899, he produced his second volume of poems, *War Is Kind* (page 494). But tuberculosis was sapping his strength. Crane died in June 1900, at a sanitarium in the Black Forest of Germany. He was only twenty-eight years old.

Detail from original manuscript page:
The Red Badge of Courage by Stephen Crane.
University of Virginia Library.

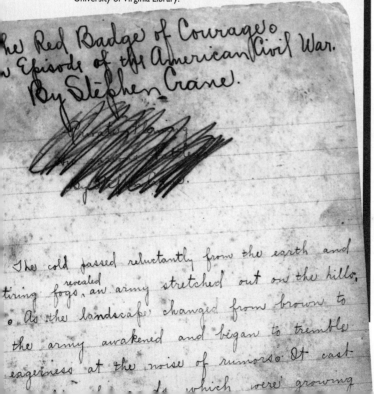

Before You Read
A MYSTERY OF HEROISM

Make the Connection
Fool or Hero?
What is heroism? Is it exceptional courage? fearlessness? If a person ignores normal human fear and risks his or her life for something others regard as trivial, is it an act of heroism or a deed of utmost foolishness?

Quickwrite
Imagine this scene, and then write down your thoughts about it: In the midst of all the frightful noise and bloody destruction of a Civil War battlefield, with death all around, a soldier suddenly has a mind to run straight into the battle on an impulse which, to his comrades, seems simply crazy. Right into the line of enemy fire—for *that*? Under what circumstances would such an action be regarded as heroic? When would such an action be considered foolhardy—even insane?

Elements of Literature
Situational Irony
Situational irony occurs when what actually happens differs from what one expects will happen. Such an irony is at the heart of this story.

> **S**ituational irony takes place when there is a discrepancy between what is expected to happen and what actually happens.
>
> *For more on Irony, see the Handbook of Literary Terms.*

Background
Firsthand accounts of Civil War battles speak of the stifling smoke and crashing noise of battle. Often, one soldier would escape death and another would die by the merest chance. Dazed by battle, soldiers could find it difficult later on to explain the reasons for their actions.

The Hornet's Nest (1895) by Thomas Corwin Lindsay. Oil on canvas.

A Mystery of Heroism

Stephen Crane

The dark uniforms of the men were so coated with dust from the incessant wrestling of the two armies that the regiment almost seemed a part of the clay bank which shielded them from the shells. On the top of the hill a battery[1] was arguing in tremendous roars with some other guns, and to the eye of the infantry, the artillerymen, the guns, the caissons,[2] the horses, were distinctly outlined upon the blue sky. When a piece was fired, a red streak as round as a log flashed low in the heavens, like a monstrous bolt of lightning. The men of the battery wore white duck trousers, which somehow emphasized their legs, and when they ran and crowded in little groups at the bidding of the shouting officers, it was more impressive than usual to the infantry.

1. **battery:** set of heavy guns.
2. **caissons** (kā′sənz): ammunition wagons.

Fred Collins of A Company was saying: "Thunder, I wisht I had a drink. Ain't there any water round here?" Then somebody yelled: "There goes th' bugler!"

As the eyes of half of the regiment swept in one machine-like movement, there was an instant's picture of a horse in a great convulsive leap of a death wound and a rider leaning back with a crooked arm and spread fingers before his face. On the ground was the crimson terror of an exploding shell, with fibers of flame that seemed like lances. A glittering bugle swung clear of the rider's back as fell headlong the horse and the man. In the air was an odor as from a conflagration.

WORDS TO OWN
conflagration (kän′flə·grā′shən) *n.:* huge fire.

Union soldier.

demeanors of <u>stolidity</u> and courage, were typical of something infinitely self-possessed in this clamor of death that swirled around the hill.

One of a "swing" team was suddenly smitten quivering to the ground and his maddened brethren dragged his torn body in their struggle to escape from this turmoil and danger. A young soldier astride one of the leaders swore and fumed in his saddle and furiously jerked at the bridle. An officer screamed out an order so violently that his voice broke and ended the sentence in a falsetto[3] shriek.

The leading company of the infantry regiment was somewhat exposed and the colonel ordered it moved more fully under the shelter of the hill. There was the clank of steel against steel.

A lieutenant of the battery rode down and passed them, holding his right arm carefully in his left hand. And it was as if this arm was not at all a part of him, but belonged to another man. His sober and reflective charger went slowly. The officer's face was grimy and perspiring and his uniform was tousled as if he had been in direct grapple with an enemy. He smiled grimly when the men stared at him. He turned his horse toward the meadow.

Collins of A Company said: "I wisht I had a drink. I bet there's water in that there ol' well yonder!"

"Yes; but how you goin' to git it?"

For the little meadow which intervened was now suffering a terrible onslaught of shells. Its green and beautiful calm had vanished utterly. Brown earth was being flung in monstrous handfuls. And there was a massacre of the young blades of grass. They were being torn, burned, <u>obliterated</u>. Some curious fortune of the battle had made this gentle little meadow the object of the red hate of the shells and each one as it exploded seemed like an imprecation[4] in the face of a maiden.

The wounded officer who was riding across this expanse said to himself: "Why, they couldn't

3. **falsetto:** artificially high voice.
4. **imprecation:** curse.

WORDS TO OWN
stolidity (stə·lid′ə·tē) *n.:* showing no emotion.
obliterated (ə·blit′ər·āt′əd) *v.:* destroyed.

Sometimes they of the infantry looked down at a fair little meadow which spread at their feet. Its long, green grass was rippling gently in a breeze. Beyond it was the gray form of a house half torn to pieces by shells and by the busy axes of soldiers who had pursued firewood. The line of an old fence was now dimly marked by long weeds and by an occasional post. A shell had blown the well house to fragments. Little lines of gray smoke ribboning upward from some embers indicated the place where had stood the barn.

From beyond a curtain of green woods there came the sound of some stupendous scuffle as if two animals of the size of islands were fighting. At a distance there were occasional appearances of swift-moving men, horses, batteries, flags, and, with the crashing of infantry, volleys were heard, often, wild and frenzied cheers. In the midst of it all, Smith and Ferguson, two privates of A Company, were engaged in a heated discussion, which involved the greatest questions of the national existence.

The battery on the hill presently engaged in a frightful duel. The white legs of the gunners scampered this way and that way and the officers redoubled their shouts. The guns, with their shoot any harder if the whole army was massed here!"

A shell struck the gray ruins of the house and as, after the roar, the shattered wall fell in fragments, there was a noise which resembled the flapping of shutters during a wild gale of winter. Indeed the infantry paused in the shelter of the bank, appeared as men standing upon a shore contemplating a madness of the sea. The angel of calamity had under its glance the battery upon the hill. Fewer white-legged men labored about the guns. A shell had smitten one of the pieces, and after the flare, the smoke, the dust, the wrath of this blow was gone, it was possible to see white legs stretched horizontally upon the ground. And at that interval to the rear, where it is the business of battery horses to stand with their noses to the fight awaiting the command to drag their guns out of the destruction or into it or wheresoever these incomprehensible humans demanded with whip and spur—in this line of passive and dumb spectators, whose fluttering hearts yet would not let them forget the iron laws of man's control of them—in this rank of brute soldiers there had been relentless and hideous carnage. From the ruck[5] of bleeding and prostrate horses, the men of the infantry could see one animal raising its stricken body with its forelegs and turning its nose with mystic and profound eloquence toward the sky.

Some comrades joked Collins about his thirst. "Well, if yeh want a drink so bad, why don't yeh go git it?"

"Well, I will in a minnet if yeh don't shut up."

A lieutenant of artillery floundered his horse straight down the hill with as great concern as if it were level ground. As he galloped past the colonel of the infantry, he threw up his hand in swift salute. "We've got to get out of that," he roared angrily. He was a black-bearded officer, and his eyes, which resembled beads, sparkled like those of an insane man. His jumping horse sped along the column of infantry.

The fat major standing carelessly with his sword held horizontally behind him and with his legs far apart, looked after the receding horseman and laughed. "He wants to get back with orders pretty quick or there'll be no batt'ry left," he observed.

The wise young captain of the second company hazarded[6] to the lieutenant colonel that the enemy's infantry would probably soon attack the hill, and the lieutenant colonel snubbed him.

A private in one of the rear companies looked out over the meadow and then turned to a companion and said: "Look there, Jim." It was the wounded officer from the battery, who some time before had started to ride across the meadow, supporting his right arm carefully with his left hand. This man had encountered a shell apparently at a time when no one perceived him and he could now be seen lying face downward with a stirruped foot stretched across the body of his dead horse. A leg of the charger extended slantingly upward precisely as stiff as a stake. Around this motionless pair the shells still howled.

There was a quarrel in A Company. Collins was shaking his fist in the faces of some laughing comrades. "Dern yeh! I ain't afraid t' go. If yeh say much, I will go!"

"Of course, yeh will! Yeh'll run through that there medder, won't yeh?"

Collins said, in a terrible voice: "You see, now!" At this ominous threat his comrades broke into renewed jeers.

Collins gave them a dark scowl and went to find his captain. The latter was conversing with the colonel of the regiment.

"Captain," said Collins, saluting and standing at attention. In those days all trousers bagged at the knees. "Captain, I want t' git permission to go git some water from that there well over yonder!"

The colonel and the captain swung about simultaneously and stared across the meadow.

> . . . there was a noise which resembled the flapping of shutters during a wild gale of winter.

6. **hazarded:** risked saying.

WORDS TO OWN

prostrate (präs′trāt′) *adj.*: lying flat on the ground.
ominous (äm′ə·nəs) *adj.*: sinister; foreboding.

---

5. **ruck:** mass; crowd.

The captain laughed. "You must be pretty thirsty, Collins?"

"Yes, sir; I am."

"Well—ah," said the captain. After a moment he asked: "Can't you wait?"

"No, sir."

The colonel was watching Collins's face. "Look here, my lad," he said, in a pious sort of a voice. "Look here, my lad." Collins was not a lad. "Don't you think that's taking pretty big risks for a little drink of water?"

"I dunno," said Collins, uncomfortably. Some of the resentment toward his companions, which perhaps had forced him into this affair, was beginning to fade. "I dunno wether 'tis."

The colonel and the captain contemplated him for a time.

"Well," said the captain finally.

"Well," said the colonel, "if you want to go, why go."

Collins saluted. "Much obliged t' yeh."

As he moved away the colonel called after him. "Take some of the other boys' canteens with you an' hurry back now."

"Yes, sir. I will."

The colonel and the captain looked at each other then, for it had suddenly occurred that they could not for the life of them tell whether Collins wanted to go or whether he did not.

They turned to regard Collins and as they perceived him surrounded by <u>gesticulating</u> comrades the colonel said: "Well, by thunder! I guess he's going."

Collins appeared as a man dreaming. In the midst of the questions, the advice, the warnings, all the excited talk of his company mates, he maintained a curious silence.

They were very busy in preparing him for his ordeal. When they inspected him carefully it was somewhat like the examination that grooms give a horse before a race; and they were amazed, staggered by the whole affair. Their astonishment found vent in strange repetitions.

"Are yeh sure a-goin'?" they demanded again and again.

"Certainly I am," cried Collins, at last furiously.

He strode sullenly away from them. He was swinging five or six canteens by their cords. It seemed that his cap would not remain firmly on his head, and often he reached and pulled it down over his brow.

There was a general movement in the compact column. The long animal-like thing moved slightly. Its four hundred eyes were turned upon the figure of Collins.

"Well, sir, if that ain't th' derndest thing. I never thought Fred Collins had the blood in him for that kind of business."

"What's he goin' to do, anyhow?"

"He's goin' to that well there after water."

"We ain't dyin' of thirst, are we? That's foolishness."

"Well, somebody put him up to it an' he's doin' it."

"Say, he must be a desperate cuss."

When Collins faced the meadow and walked away from the regiment, he was vaguely conscious that a chasm, the deep valley of all prides, was suddenly between him and his comrades. It was <u>provisional</u>, but the provision was that he return as a victor. He had blindly been led by quaint emotions and laid himself under an obligation to walk squarely up to the face of death.

But he was not sure that he wished to make a <u>retraction</u> even if he could do so without shame. As a matter of truth he was sure of very little. He was mainly surprised.

It seemed to him supernaturally strange that he had allowed his mind to maneuver his body into such a situation. He understood that it might be called dramatically great.

However, he had no full appreciation of anything excepting that he was actually conscious of being dazed. He could feel his dulled mind groping after the form and color of this incident.

Too, he wondered why he did not feel some keen agony of fear cutting his sense like a knife. He wondered at this because human expression had said loudly for centuries that men should feel

---

WORDS TO OWN

gesticulating (jes·tik′yo͞o·lāt′iŋ) v. used as adj.: gesturing, especially with the hands and arms, while speaking.

provisional (prō·vizh′ə·nəl) adj.: temporary; for the time being.

retraction (ri·trak′shən) n.: withdrawal.

---

afraid of certain things and that all men who did not feel this fear were phenomena, heroes.

He was then a hero. He suffered that disappointment which we would all have if we discovered that we were ourselves capable of those deeds which we most admire in history and legend. This, then, was a hero. After all, heroes were not much.

No, it could not be true. He was not a hero. Heroes had no shames in their lives and, as for him, he remembered borrowing fifteen dollars from a friend and promising to pay it back the next day, and then avoiding that friend for ten months.

Charge of VMI Cadets at New Market (1914) by Benjamin West Clinedinst. Oil on canvas (18″ × 23″).

rush for the house, which he viewed as a man submerged to the neck in a boiling surf might view the shore. In the air, little pieces of shell howled and the earthquake explosions drove him insane with the menace of their roar. As he ran the canteens knocked together with a rhythmical tinkling.

As he neared the house, each detail of the scene became vivid to him. He was aware of some bricks of the vanished chimney lying on the sod. There was a door which hung by one hinge.

Rifle bullets called forth by the insistent skirmishers came from the far-off bank of foliage. They mingled with the shells and the pieces of shells until the air was torn in all directions by hootings, yells, howls. The sky was full of fiends who directed all their wild rage at his head.

When at home his mother had aroused him for the early labor of his life on the farm, it had often been his fashion to be irritable, childish, diabolical, and his mother had died since he had come to the war.

He saw that in this matter of the well, the canteens, the shells, he was an intruder in the land of fine deeds.

He was now about thirty paces from his comrades. The regiment had just turned its many faces toward him.

From the forest of terrific noises there suddenly emerged a little uneven line of men. They fired fiercely and rapidly at distant foliage on which appeared little puffs of white smoke. The spatter of skirmish firing was added to the thunder of the guns on the hill. The little line of men ran forward. A color sergeant fell flat with his flag as if he had slipped on ice. There was hoarse cheering from this distant field.

Collins suddenly felt that two demon fingers were pressed into his ears. He could see nothing but flying arrows, flaming red. He lurched from the shock of this explosion, but he made a mad

When he came to the well he flung himself face downward and peered into its darkness. There were furtive silver glintings some feet from the surface. He grabbed one of the canteens and, unfastening its cap, swung it down by the cord. The water flowed slowly in with an <u>indolent</u> gurgle.

And now as he lay with his face turned away he was suddenly smitten with the terror. It came upon his heart like the grasp of claws. All the power faded from his muscles. For an instant he was no more than a dead man.

The canteen filled with a maddening slowness in the manner of all bottles. Presently he recovered his strength and addressed a screaming oath

- -

WORDS TO OWN

indolent (in′də·lənt) *adj.:* lazy.

- -

to it. He leaned over until it seemed as if he intended to try to push water into it with his hands. His eyes as he gazed down into the well shone like two pieces of metal and in their expression was a great appeal and a great curse. The stupid water derided him.

There was the blaring thunder of a shell. Crimson light shone through the swift-boiling smoke and made a pink reflection on part of the wall of the well. Collins jerked out his arm and canteen with the same motion that a man would use in withdrawing his head from a furnace.

He scrambled erect and glared and hesitated. On the ground near him lay the old well bucket, with a length of rusty chain. He lowered it swiftly into the well. The bucket struck the water and then turning lazily over, sank. When, with hand reaching tremblingly over hand, he hauled it out, it knocked often against the walls of the well and spilled some of its contents.

In running with a filled bucket, a man can adopt but one kind of gait. So through this terrible field over which screamed practical angels of death Collins ran in the manner of a farmer chased out of a dairy by a bull.

His face went staring white with anticipation—anticipation of a blow that would whirl him around and down. He would fall as he had seen other men fall, the life knocked out of them so suddenly that their knees were no more quick to touch the ground than their heads. He saw the long blue line of the regiment, but his comrades were standing looking at him from the edge of an impossible star. He was aware of some deep wheel ruts and hoof prints in the sod beneath his feet.

The artillery officer who had fallen in this meadow had been making groans in the teeth of the tempest of sound. These futile cries, wrenched from him by his agony, were heard only by shells, bullets. When wild-eyed Collins came running, this officer raised himself. His face contorted and <u>blanched</u> from pain, he was about to utter some great beseeching cry. But suddenly his face straightened and he called: "Say, young man, give me a drink of water, will you?"

Collins had no room amid his emotions for surprise. He was mad from the threats of destruction.

"I can't," he screamed, and in this reply was a full description of his quaking apprehension. His cap was gone and his hair was riotous. His clothes made it appear that he had been dragged over the ground by the heels. He ran on.

The officer's head sank down and one elbow crooked. His foot in its brass-bound stirrup still stretched over the body of his horse and the other leg was under the steed.

But Collins turned. He came dashing back. His face had now turned gray and in his eyes was all terror. "Here it is! Here it is!"

The officer was as a man gone in drink. His arm bended like a twig. His head drooped as if his neck was of willow. He was sinking to the ground, to lie face downward.

Collins grabbed him by the shoulder. "Here it is. Here's your drink. Turn over! Turn over, man, for God's sake!"

With Collins hauling at his shoulder, the officer twisted his body and fell with his face turned toward that region where lived the unspeakable noises of the swirling missiles. There was the faintest shadow of a smile on his lips as he looked at Collins. He gave a sigh, a little primitive breath like that from a child.

Collins tried to hold the bucket steadily, but his shaking hands caused the water to splash all over the face of the dying man. Then he jerked it away and ran on.

The regiment gave him a welcoming roar. The grimed faces were wrinkled in laughter.

His captain waved the bucket away. "Give it to the men!"

The two genial, skylarking young lieutenants were the first to gain possession of it. They played over it in their fashion.

When one tried to drink, the other teasingly knocked his elbow. "Don't, Billie! You'll make me spill it," said the one. The other laughed.

Suddenly there was an oath, the thud of wood on the ground, and a swift murmur of astonishment from the ranks. The two lieutenants glared at each other. The bucket lay on the ground empty.

WORDS TO OWN
blanched (blancht) *v.* used as *adj.*: drained of color.

What About Glory

Ask the child,
Who, without an answer,
Asks her brother,
"What is he like?"

Ask the brother,
Who, missing the memory,
Asks his mother,
"When will he be back?"

And ask the mother
Who, without a husband,
Asks herself, "Why'd
He have to be a hero?"

—Pindar VanArman
Gonzaga College High School
Washington, D.C.

MAKING MEANINGS

First Thoughts

1. What was your first reaction to the story? Did you consider Collins a hero or a fool? Why? Review your Quick-write notes before you answer.

Shaping Interpretations

2. There is a good deal of "rank" in this story—several lieutenants, a captain, a major, a colonel, and a lieutenant colonel. But Collins is a private. Discuss whether or not you think his lowly rank is significant in any way.

3. When Crane "paints" the battle scene in colorful language, he draws our attention to the legs of certain men who are wearing white duck (linen) trousers. Why do you think Crane emphasizes the **image** of the men's white legs? What does the white contrast with?

4. In modern war, it has been said, machines resemble humans, and humans resemble machines. Find two or three examples from this story showing that Crane believes war **personifies** machines and dehumanizes people. What do you think of this idea about the dehumanizing effects of war and the glorification of its machines?

5. What **situational irony** occurs at the end of the story as a result of Collins's action?

Connecting with the Text

6. What do you think is Collins's **motive** for his daring act? Simple thirst? The reactions of his comrades? Some other force within him? In what sense might the "mystery" in the title of the story refer to Collins's motivation?

Challenging the Text

7. The ending of the story is **ambiguous**—that is, it is open to more than one interpretation. Do you think the lieutenants spilled the water, or was the bucket empty by the time Collins got back? Does the empty bucket mean something? Explain how you interpreted the final lines of the story, and comment on whether or not you think this is a good ending.

Reading Check

a. What happens to the lieutenant who holds his wounded right arm carefully in his left hand?

b. Why is Collins disappointed when it occurs to him that he could be called a hero?

c. What does the maddened Collins do when the wounded lieutenant asks him for water?

d. How much of the water in the bucket does Collins get to drink?

Stephen Crane.

Drawing by David Levine.
Reprinted with permission from
The New York Review of Books.
Copyright © 1968 NYREV, Inc.

CHOICES: Building Your Portfolio

Writer's Notebook

1. Collecting Ideas for a Research Paper

One approach to researching a topic might involve surveying people about their attitudes. To gather information about current attitudes toward war, you could distribute copies of Crane's "A Mystery of Heroism" or "War Is Kind" to ten people, together with a questionnaire that explores their feelings about war. Write up a summary of the responses you get, and keep your notes for possible use in the Writer's Workshop on page 515.

Interpreting Texts

2. The Outrage of War

Write a brief essay in which you summarize Stephen Crane's attitudes toward war, based on your reading of "A Mystery of Heroism" and the Crane poem, "War Is Kind," on this page. In your essay, respond to these questions: (a) Is anyone in the story or the poem a hero in the sense of being willing to risk his life for a high moral principle? (b) Does any scene in the poem remind you of a scene in the story? (c) Do you find **irony** in Crane's attitudes toward war? (d) Does Crane really show you that war is kind?

Creative Writing

3. War Is . . .

Write a poem or a short prose piece about war based on one of the subjects or themes in Crane's works. Your work should be clearly focused on the topic, and the content should be gritty and true to life. For an example, see the Student to Student poem "What About Glory" on page 493.

War Is Kind

Do not weep, maiden, for war is kind.
Because your lover threw wild hands toward the sky
And the affrighted steed ran on alone,
Do not weep.
5 War is kind.

Hoarse, booming drums of the regiment,
Little souls who thirst for fight,
These men were born to drill and die.
The unexplained glory flies above them,
10 Great is the Battle-God, great, and his Kingdom—
A field where a thousand corpses lie.

Do not weep, babe, for war is kind.
Because your father tumbled in the yellow trenches,
Raged at his breast, gulped and died,
15 Do not weep.
War is kind.

Swift blazing flag of the regiment,
Eagle with crest of red and gold,
These men were born to drill and die.
20 Point for them the virtue of slaughter,
Make plain to them the excellence of killing
And a field where a thousand corpses lie.

Mother whose heart hung humble as a button
On the bright splendid shroud of your son,
25 Do not weep.
War is kind.

—Stephen Crane, 1896

Jack London

(1876–1916)

In his teens and twenties, Jack London adventured on sea and ice. Then, in the sixteen remaining years of his life, he turned out nearly fifty volumes of essays and fiction. Known during his lifetime as a passionate socialist, London is remembered today not for his political convictions, but for his exciting, fast-paced adventure stories. Even his harshest critic, Ambrose Bierce (page 466), called London's novel *The Sea Wolf* a "rattling good story."

London was born into a poor family in San Francisco. As a boy, he was largely uncared for by his parents. He delivered newspapers, worked on an ice wagon, set up pins in a bowling alley, and worked in a cannery. "Almost the first thing I realized were responsibilities," he says. "I worked hard from my eighth year." He graduated from grammar school in Oakland, across the bay from San Francisco.

Meanwhile, London read everything he could find in the public library, especially stories of real-life adventure. In his teens, he plunged into danger. "I joined the oyster pirates in the bay; shipped as sailor on a schooner; took a turn at salmon fishing; shipped before the mast and sailed for the Japanese coast on a seal-hunting expedition. After sealing for seven months I came back to California, and took odd jobs. . . ."

London was still in his teens when he settled in Oakland again. He began to write, selling a few pieces to local papers. After attending high school for one year, he managed to pass the entrance exams for the University of California at Berkeley by cramming on his own. The combination of work, school, and writing proved to be too much, however, and he quit halfway through his freshman year. He submerged himself in writing for the next three months. But he earned practically nothing, so in 1897 he took off to prospect for gold in the Klondike—part of the Yukon Territory in northwestern Canada.

London became sick and had to leave the Klondike in less than a year, but the experience convinced him that life is a struggle in which the strong survive and the weak do not. London's short stories and novels dramatize his belief that "civilized" beings are either destroyed or re-created in savage environments.

London's first major success was a story collection, *The Son of the Wolf* (1900). Readers were thrilled by the shocking brutality of his stories, then hooked by the action and adventure. His most famous short story, "To Build a Fire" (1908), focuses on survival. His most famous novel, *The Call of the Wild* (1903), celebrates the escape to freedom of a sled dog named Buck.

London became a millionaire from his writings, and success greatly altered his life. In 1900, he married and had two daughters, but his wife sued him for divorce in 1905. He remarried and established his home at Glen Ellen in Sonoma County, north of San Francisco. There he intended to create a magnificent ranch estate, but he lost interest when Wolf House, his nearly completed mansion, burned down in 1913. London, for years an alcoholic, suffered in his later years from kidney disease and depression. One evening in November 1916, when the physical pain finally became unendurable, London took a lethal dose of narcotics and lapsed into a coma. He died the next evening; he was forty years old.

Before You Read

TO BUILD A FIRE

Make the Connection

Cold, Cruel World

"To Build a Fire" must be the coldest story ever written. It is also one of the most effective examples of a conflict between a human being and the elements of nature. London draws on his own experience of prospecting for gold in the Yukon—a bleak, nearly sunless region of northwestern Canada—to give authenticity to the story.

But this is ultimately far more than a "person versus nature" story. It is a grimly realistic tale about a man who is "quick and alert in the things of life, but only in the things, and not in the significances"—an "innocent" who is not prepared for a cruel and unforgiving environment.

You may want to dress warmly before you read.

To Build

Day had broken cold and gray, exceedingly cold and g

Reading Skills and Strategies

Analyzing Text Structures: Cause and Effect

Science tells us that for every action there is a reaction. In literature, we call this the relationship of **cause** and **effect**. A plot is made up of a string of causes and effects. As you read London's story, keep notes on each action the protagonist takes and note its effect. You will find that an action as small as a misstep or the lighting of a match can take on critical importance.

Elements of Literature

Naturalism

The naturalists were a group of nineteenth-century writers who went beyond realism in an attempt to portray life exactly as it is. Naturalist writers, influenced by the scientist Charles Darwin's (1809–1882) theories of natural selection and survival of the fittest, believed human behavior is determined by heredity and environment. Relying on new theories in sociology and psychology, the naturalists dissected human behavior with detachment and objectivity, like scientists dissecting laboratory specimens. **Naturalism** presents human beings as subject to natural forces beyond their control. This idea is at the center of "To Build a Fire."

> **N**aturalism was a nineteenth-century literary movement that claimed to portray life exactly as it is, with detachment and objectivity.
>
> *For more on Naturalism, see page 421 and the Handbook of Literary Terms.*

a Fire

Jack London

n the man turned aside from the main Yukon trail and climbed the high earth bank . . .

Day had broken cold and gray, exceedingly cold and gray, when the man turned aside from the main Yukon trail and climbed the high earth bank, where a dim and little-traveled trail led eastward through the fat spruce timberland. It was a steep bank, and he paused for breath at the top, excusing the act to himself by looking at his watch. It was nine o'clock. There was no sun or hint of sun, though there was not a cloud in the sky. It was a clear day, and yet there seemed an intangible pall over the face of things, a subtle gloom that made the day dark, and that was due to the absence of sun. This fact did not worry the man. He was used to the lack of sun. It had been days since he had seen the sun, and he knew that a few more days must pass before that cheerful orb, due south, would just peep above the skyline and dip immediately from view.

The man flung a look back along the way he had come. The Yukon lay a mile wide and hidden under three feet of ice. On top of this ice were as many feet of snow. It was all pure white, rolling in gentle undulations where the ice jams of the freeze-up had formed. North and south, as far as his eye could see, it was unbroken white, save for a dark hairline that curved and twisted from around the spruce-covered island to the south, and that curved and twisted away into the north, where it disappeared behind another spruce-covered island.

WORDS TO OWN
intangible (in·tan′jə·bəl) *adj.*: difficult to define; vague.
undulations (un′dyo͞o·lā′shənz) *n. pl.*: wavelike motions.

This dark hairline was the trail—the main trail—that led south five hundred miles to the Chilkoot Pass, Dyea, and salt water; and that led north seventy miles to Dawson, and still on to the north a thousand miles to Nulato, and finally to St. Michael on the Bering Sea, a thousand miles and half a thousand more.

But all this—the mysterious, far-reaching hairline trail, the absence of sun from the sky, the tremendous cold, and the strangeness and weirdness of it all—made no impression on the man. It was not because he was long used to it. He was a newcomer in the land, a *cheechako*,[1] and this was his first winter. The trouble with him was that he was without imagination. He was quick and alert in the things of life, but only in the things, and not in the significances. Fifty degrees below zero meant eighty-odd degrees of frost. Such fact impressed him as being cold and uncomfortable, and that was all. It did not lead him to meditate upon his frailty as a creature of temperature, and upon man's frailty in general, able only to live within certain narrow limits of heat and cold, and from there on it did not lead him to the conjectural[2] field of immortality and man's place in the universe. Fifty degrees below zero stood for a bite of frost that hurt and that must be guarded against by the use of mittens, earflaps, warm moccasins, and thick socks. Fifty degrees below zero was to him just precisely fifty degrees below zero. That there should be anything more to it than that was a thought that never entered his head.

As he turned to go on, he spat speculatively. There was a sharp, explosive crackle that startled him. He spat again. And again, in the air, before it could fall to the snow, the spittle crackled. He knew that at fifty below, spittle crackled on the snow, but this spittle had crackled in the air. Undoubtedly it was colder than fifty below—how much colder he did not know. But the temperature did not matter. He was bound for the old claim on the left fork of Henderson Creek, where the boys were already. They had come over across the divide from the Indian Creek country, while he had come the roundabout way to take a look at the possibilities of getting out logs in the spring

from the islands in the Yukon. He would be into camp by six o'clock; a bit after dark, it was true, but the boys would be there, a fire would be going, and a hot supper would be ready. As for lunch, he pressed his hand against the <u>protruding</u> bundle under his jacket. It was also under his shirt, wrapped up in a handkerchief and lying against the naked skin. It was the only way to keep the biscuits from freezing. He smiled agreeably to himself as he thought of those biscuits, each cut open and sopped in bacon grease, and each enclosing a generous slice of fried bacon.

He plunged in among the big spruce trees. The trail was faint. A foot of snow had fallen since the last sled had passed over, and he was glad he was without a sled, traveling light. In fact, he carried nothing but the lunch wrapped in the handkerchief. He was surprised, however, at the cold. It certainly was cold, he concluded, as he rubbed his numb nose and cheekbones with his mittened hand. He was a warm-whiskered man, but the hair on his face did not protect the high cheekbones and the eager nose that thrust itself aggressively into the frosty air.

At the man's heels trotted a dog, a big native husky, the proper wolf dog, gray-coated and without any visible or temperamental difference from its brother, the wild wolf. The animal was depressed by the tremendous cold. It knew that it was no time for traveling. Its instinct told it a truer tale than was told to the man by the man's judgment. In reality, it was not merely colder than fifty below zero; it was colder than sixty below, than seventy below. It was seventy-five below zero. Since the freezing point is thirty-two above zero, it meant that one hundred and seven degrees of frost obtained. The dog did not know anything about thermometers. Possibly in its brain there was no sharp consciousness of a condition of very cold such as was in the man's brain. But the brute had its instinct. It experienced a vague but menacing apprehension that subdued it and made it slink along at the man's heels, and that made it question eagerly every unwonted[3] movement of

3. **unwonted:** unusual.

----

1. *cheechako* (chē·chä′kō): Chinook jargon for "newcomer" or "tenderfoot."
2. **conjectural:** based on guesswork or uncertain evidence.

WORDS TO OWN

protruding (prō·trōōd′iŋ) v. used as *adj.*: sticking out.

----

the man, as if expecting him to go into camp or to seek shelter somewhere and build a fire. The dog had learned fire, and it wanted fire, or else to burrow under the snow and cuddle its warmth away from the air.

The frozen moisture of its breathing had settled on its fur in a fine powder of frost, and especially were its jowls, muzzle, and eyelashes whitened by its crystaled breath. The man's red beard and moustache were likewise frosted, but more solidly, the deposit taking the form of ice and increasing with every warm, moist breath he exhaled. Also, the man was chewing tobacco, and the muzzle of ice held his lips so rigidly that he was unable to clear his chin when he expelled the juice. The result was that a crystal beard of the color and solidity of amber was increasing its length on his chin. If he fell down it would shatter itself, like glass, into brittle fragments. But he did not mind the appendage. It was the penalty all tobacco chewers paid in that country, and he had been out before in two cold snaps. They had not been so cold as this, he knew, but by the spirit thermometer[4] at Sixty Mile he knew they had been registered at fifty below and at fifty-five.

He held on through the level stretch of woods for several miles, crossed a wide flat, and dropped down a bank to the frozen bed of a small stream. This was Henderson Creek, and he knew he was ten miles from the forks. He looked at his watch. It was ten o'clock. He was making four miles an hour, and he calculated that he would arrive at the forks at half past twelve. He decided to celebrate that event by eating his lunch there.

The dog dropped in again at his heels, with a tail drooping discouragement, as the man swung along the creek bed. The furrow of the old sled trail was plainly visible, but a dozen inches of snow covered the marks of the last runners. In a month no man had come up or down that silent creek. The man held steadily on. He was not much given to thinking, and just then particularly, he had nothing to think about save that he would eat lunch at the forks and that at six o'clock he would be in camp with the boys. There was nobody to talk to; and, had there been, speech

would have been impossible because of the ice muzzle on his mouth. So he continued monotonously to chew tobacco and to increase the length of his amber beard.

Once in a while the thought reiterated itself that it was very cold and that he had never experienced such cold. As he walked along he rubbed his cheekbones and nose with the back of his mittened hand. He did this automatically, now and again changing hands. But rub as he would, the instant he stopped his cheekbones went numb, and the following instant the end of his nose went numb. He was sure to frost his cheeks; he knew that, and experienced a pang of regret that he had not devised a nose strap of the sort Bud wore in the cold snaps. Such a strap passed across the cheeks, as well, and saved them. But it didn't matter much, after all. What were frosted cheeks? A bit painful, that was all; they were never serious.

Empty as the man's mind was of thought, he was keenly observant, and he noticed the changes in the creek, the curves and bends and timber jams, and always he sharply noted where he placed his feet. Once, coming around a bend, he shied abruptly, like a startled horse, curved away from the place where he had been walking, and retreated several paces back along the trail. The creek, he knew, was frozen clear to the bottom—no creek could contain water in that arctic winter—but he knew also that there were springs that bubbled out from the hillsides and ran along under the snow and on top of the ice of the creek. He knew that the coldest snaps never froze these springs, and he knew likewise their danger. They were traps. They hid pools of water under the snow that might be three inches deep, or three feet. Sometimes a skin of ice half an inch thick covered them, and in turn was covered by the snow. Sometimes there were alternate layers of water and ice skin, so that when one broke through he kept on breaking through for a while, sometimes wetting himself to the waist.

That was why he had shied in such panic. He had felt the give under his feet and heard the crackle of a snow-hidden ice skin. And to get his feet wet in such a temperature meant trouble and

---

4. **spirit thermometer:** alcohol thermometer. In places where the temperature often drops below the freezing point of mercury, alcohol is used in thermometers.

WORDS TO OWN
solidity (sə·lid′ə·tē) *n.:* firmness; solidness.

He did not expose his fingers more

than a minute, and was astonished at

the swift numbness that smote them.

danger. At the very least it meant delay, for he would be forced to stop and build a fire, and under its protection to bare his feet while he dried his socks and moccasins. He stood and studied the creek bed and its banks, and decided that the flow of water came from the right. He reflected awhile, rubbing his nose and cheeks, then skirted to the left, stepping gingerly and testing the footing for each step. Once clear of the danger, he took a fresh chew of tobacco and swung along at his four-mile gait.

In the course of the next two hours he came upon several similar traps. Usually the snow above the hidden pools had a sunken, candied appearance that advertised the danger. Once again, however, he had a close call; and once, suspecting danger, he compelled the dog to go on in front. The dog did not want to go. It hung back until the man shoved it forward, and then it went quickly across the white, unbroken surface. Suddenly it broke through, floundered to one side, and got away to firmer footing. It had wet its forefeet and legs, and almost immediately the water that clung to it turned to ice. It made quick efforts to lick the ice off its legs, then dropped down in the snow and began to bite out the ice that had formed between the toes. This was a matter of instinct. To permit the ice to remain would mean sore feet. It did not know this. It merely obeyed the mysterious prompting that arose from the deep crypts[5] of

5. **crypts:** hidden recesses.

its being. But the man knew, having achieved a judgment on the subject, and he removed the mitten from his right hand and helped tear out the ice particles. He did not expose his fingers more than a minute, and was astonished at the swift numbness that smote[6] them. It certainly was cold. He pulled on the mitten hastily, and beat the hand savagely across his chest.

At twelve o'clock the day was at its brightest. Yet the sun was too far south on its winter journey to clear the horizon. The bulge of the earth intervened between it and Henderson Creek, where the man walked under a clear sky at noon and cast no shadow. At half past twelve, to the minute, he arrived at the forks of the creek. He was pleased at the speed he had made. If he kept it up, he would certainly be with the boys by six. He unbuttoned his jacket and shirt and drew forth his lunch. The action consumed no more than a quarter of a minute, yet in that brief moment the numbness laid hold of the exposed fingers. He did not put the mitten on, but instead struck the fingers a dozen sharp smashes against his leg. Then he sat down on a snow-covered log to eat. The sting that followed upon the striking of his fingers against his leg ceased so quickly that he was startled. He had had no chance to take a bite of biscuit. He struck the fingers repeatedly and returned them to the mitten, baring the other hand for the purpose of eating. He tried to take a mouthful, but the ice muzzle prevented. He had forgotten to build a fire and thaw out. He chuckled at his foolishness, and as he chuckled he noted the numbness creeping into the exposed fingers. Also, he noted that the stinging which had first come to his toes when he sat down was already passing away. He wondered whether the toes were warm or numb. He moved them inside the moccasins and decided that they were numb.

He pulled the mitten on hurriedly and stood up. He was a bit frightened. He stamped up and down until the stinging returned into the feet. It certainly was cold, was his thought. That man from Sulfur Creek had spoken the truth when telling how cold it sometimes got in the country. And he had laughed at him at the time! That showed one must not be too sure of things. There was no mistake about it, it *was* cold. He strode up

6. **smote:** powerfully struck; past tense of *smite.*

and down, stamping his feet and threshing his arms, until reassured by the returning warmth. Then he got out matches and proceeded to make a fire. From the undergrowth, where high water of the previous spring had lodged a supply of seasoned twigs, he got his firewood. Working carefully from a small beginning, he soon had a roaring fire, over which he thawed the ice from his face and in the protection of which he ate his biscuits. For the moment the cold of space was outwitted. The dog took satisfaction in the fire, stretching out close enough for warmth and far enough away to escape being singed.

When the man had finished, he filled his pipe and took his comfortable time over a smoke. Then he pulled on his mittens, settled the earflaps of his cap firmly about his ears, and took the creek trail up the left fork. The dog was disappointed and yearned back toward the fire. This man did not know cold. Possibly all the generations of his ancestry had been ignorant of cold, of real cold, of cold one hundred and seven degrees below freezing point. But the dog knew; all its ancestry knew, and it had inherited the knowledge. And it knew that it was not good to walk abroad in such fearful cold. It was the time to lie snug in a hole in the snow and wait for a curtain of cloud to be drawn across the face of outer space whence this cold came. On the other hand, there was no keen intimacy between the dog and the man. The one was the toil slave of the other, and the only caresses it had ever received were the caresses of the whiplash and of harsh and menacing throat sounds that threatened the whiplash. So the dog made no effort to communicate its apprehension to the man. It was not concerned in the welfare of the man; it was for its own sake that it yearned back toward the fire. But the man whistled, and spoke to it with the sound of whiplashes, and the dog swung in at the man's heels and followed after.

The man took a chew of tobacco and proceeded to start a new amber beard. Also, his moist breath quickly powdered with white his moustache, eyebrows, and lashes. There did not seem to be so many springs on the left fork of the Henderson, and for half an hour the man saw no signs of any. And then it happened. At a place where there were no signs, where the soft, unbroken snow seemed to advertise solidity beneath, the man broke through. It was not deep. He wet himself halfway to the knees before he floundered out to the firm crust.

He was angry, and cursed his luck aloud. He had hoped to get into camp with the boys at six o'clock, and this would delay him an hour, for he would have to build a fire and dry out his footgear. This was imperative at that low temperature—he knew that much; and he turned aside to the bank, which he climbed. On top, tangled in the underbrush about the trunks of several small spruce trees, was a high-water deposit of dry firewood—sticks and twigs, principally, but also larger portions of seasoned branches and fine, dry, last year's grasses. He threw down several large pieces on top of the snow. This served for a foundation and prevented the young flame from drowning itself in the snow it otherwise would melt. The flame he got by touching a match to a small shred of birch bark that he took from his pocket. This burned even more readily than paper. Placing it on the foundation, he fed the young flame with wisps of dry grass and with the tiniest dry twigs.

He worked slowly and carefully, keenly aware of his danger. Gradually, as the flame grew stronger, he increased the size of the twigs with which he fed it. He squatted in the snow, pulling the twigs out from their entanglement in the brush and feeding directly to the flame. He knew there must be no failure. When it is seventy-five below zero, a man must not fail in his first attempt to build a fire—that is, if his feet are wet. If his feet are dry, and he fails, he can run along the trail for a half a mile and restore his circulation. But the circulation of wet and freezing feet cannot be restored by running when it is seventy-five below. No matter how fast he runs, the wet feet will freeze the harder.

All this the man knew. The old-timer on Sulfur Creek had told him about it the previous fall, and now he was appreciating the advice. Already all sensation had gone out of his feet. To build the fire, he had been forced to remove his mittens, and the fingers had quickly gone numb. His pace of four miles an hour had kept his heart pumping blood to the surface of his body and to all the extremities. But the instant he stopped, the action of the pump eased down. The cold of space smote the unprotected tip of the planet, and he, being on that unprotected tip, received the full force of the blow. The blood of his body recoiled before it. The blood was alive, like the dog, and like the dog it wanted to hide away and cover itself up from the fearful cold. So long as he walked four miles an hour, he pumped that blood, willy-nilly, to the surface; but now it ebbed away and sank down into the recesses of his body. The extremities were the first to feel its absence. His wet feet froze the faster, and his exposed fingers numbed the faster, though they had not yet begun to freeze. Nose and cheeks were already freezing, while the skin of all his body chilled as it lost its blood.

But he was safe. Toes and nose and cheeks would be only touched by the frost, for the fire was beginning to burn with strength. He was feeding it twigs the size of his finger. In another minute he would be able to feed it with branches the size of his wrist, and then he could remove his wet footgear, and, while it dried, he could keep his naked feet warm by the fire, rubbing them at first, of course, with snow. The fire was a success. He was safe. He remembered the advice of the old-timer on Sulfur Creek, and smiled. The old-timer had been very serious in laying down the law that no man must travel alone in the Klondike after fifty below. Well, here he was; he had had the accident; he was alone; and he had saved himself. Those old-timers were rather womanish, some of them, he thought. All a man had to do was to keep his head and he was all right. Any man who was a man could travel alone. But it was surprising, the rapidity with which his cheeks and nose were freezing. And he had not thought his fingers could go lifeless in so short a time. Lifeless they were, for he could scarcely make them move together to grip a twig, and they seemed remote from his body and from him. When he touched a twig, he had to look and see whether or not he had hold of it. The wires were pretty well down between him and his finger ends.

All of which counted for little. There was the fire, snapping and crackling and promising life

---

WORDS TO OWN

imperative (im·per′ə·tiv) *adj.*: absolutely necessary; compulsory.

extremities (ek·strem′ə·tēz) *n. pl.*: limbs of the body, especially hands and feet.

recoiled (ri′koild′) *v.*: shrank away; drew back.

Even if he succeeded, he would most likely lose some toes. His feet must be badly frozen by now, and there would be some time before the second fire was ready.

with every dancing flame. He started to untie his moccasins. They were coated with ice; the thick German socks were like sheaths of iron halfway to the knees; and the moccasin strings were like rods of steel all twisted and knotted as by some conflagration. For a moment he tugged with his numb fingers, then, realizing the folly of it, he drew his sheath knife.

But before he could cut the strings it happened. It was his own fault, or, rather, his mistake. He should not have built the fire under the spruce tree. He should have built it in the open. But it had been easier to pull the twigs from the bush and drop them directly on the fire. Now the tree under which he had done this carried a weight of snow on its boughs. No wind had blown for weeks, and each bough was fully freighted. Each time he had pulled a twig he had communicated a slight agitation to the tree—an imperceptible agitation, so far as he was concerned, but an agitation sufficient to bring about the disaster. High up in the tree one bough capsized its load of snow. This fell on the boughs beneath, capsizing them. This process continued, spreading out and involving the whole tree. It grew like an avalanche, and it descended without warning upon the man and

the fire, and the fire was blotted out! Where it had burned was a mantle of fresh and disordered snow.

The man was shocked. It was as though he had just heard his own sentence of death. For a moment he sat and stared at the spot where the fire had been. Then he grew very calm. Perhaps the old-timer on Sulfur Creek was right. If he had only had a trail mate, he would have been in no danger now. The trail mate could have built the fire. Well, it was up to him to build the fire over again, and this second time there must be no failure. Even if he succeeded, he would most likely lose some toes. His feet must be badly frozen by now, and there would be some time before the second fire was ready.

Such were his thoughts, but he did not sit and think them. He was busy all the time they were passing through his mind. He made a new foundation for a fire, this time in the open, where no treacherous tree could blot it out. Next he

WORDS TO OWN

imperceptible (im′pər·sep′tə·bəl) *adj.*: not easily perceived.

gathered dry grasses and tiny twigs from the high-water flotsam.[7] He could not bring his fingers together to pull them out, but he was able to gather them by the handful. In this way he got many rotten twigs and bits of green moss that were undesirable, but it was the best he could do. He worked methodically, even collecting an armful of the larger branches to be used later when the fire gathered strength. And all the while the dog sat and watched him, a certain yearning wistfulness in its eyes, for it looked upon him as the fire provider, and the fire was slow in coming.

When all was ready, the man reached in his pocket for a second piece of birch bark. He knew the bark was there, and, though he could not feel it with his fingers, he could hear its crisp rustling as he fumbled for it. Try as he would, he could not clutch hold of it. And all the time, in his consciousness, was the knowledge that each instant his feet were freezing. This thought tended to put him in a panic, but he fought against it and kept calm. He pulled on his mittens with his teeth, and threshed his arms back and forth, beating his hands with all his might against his sides. He did this sitting down, and he stood up to do it; and all the while the dog sat in the snow, its wolf brush of a tail curled around warmly over its forefeet, its sharp wolf ears pricked forward intently as it watched the man. And the man, as he beat and threshed with his arms and hands, felt a great surge of envy as he regarded the creature that was warm and secure in its natural covering.

After a time he was aware of the first faraway signals of sensation in his beaten fingers. The faint tingling grew stronger till it evolved into a stinging ache that was excruciating, but which the man hailed with satisfaction. He stripped the mitten from his right hand and fetched forth the birch bark. The exposed fingers were quickly going numb again. Next he brought out his bunch of sulfur matches. But the tremendous cold had already driven the life out of his fingers. In his effort to separate one match from the others, the whole bunch fell in the snow. He tried to pick it out of the snow, but failed. The dead fingers could neither touch nor clutch. He was very careful. He drove the thought of his freezing feet, and nose,

and cheeks, out of his mind, devoting his whole soul to the matches. He watched, using the sense of vision in place of that of touch, and when he saw his fingers on each side of the bunch, he closed them—that is, he willed to close them, for the wires were down, and the fingers did not obey. He pulled the mitten on the right hand, and beat it fiercely against his knee. Then, with both mittened hands, he scooped the bunch of matches, along with much snow, into his lap. Yet he was no better off.

After some manipulation he managed to get the bunch between the heels of his mittened hands. In this fashion he carried it to his mouth. The ice crackled and snapped when by a violent effort he opened his mouth. He drew the lower jaw in, curled the upper lip out of the way, and scraped the bunch with his upper teeth in order to separate a match. He succeeded in getting one, which he dropped on his lap. He was no better off. He could not pick it up. Then he devised a way. He picked it up in his teeth and scratched it on his leg. Twenty times he scratched before he succeeded in lighting it. As it flamed he held it with his teeth to the birch bark. But the burning brimstone went up his nostrils and into his lungs, causing him to cough spasmodically. The match fell into the snow and went out.

The old-timer on Sulfur Creek was right, he thought in the moment of controlled despair that ensued: After fifty below, a man should travel with a partner. He beat his hands, but failed in exciting any sensation. Suddenly he bared both hands, removing the mittens with his teeth. He caught the whole bunch between the heels of his hands. His arm muscles, not being frozen, enabled him to press the hand heels tightly against the matches. Then he scratched the bunch along his leg. It flared into flame, seventy sulfur matches at once! There was no wind to blow them out. He kept his head to one side to escape the strangling fumes, and held the blazing bunch to the birch bark. As he so held it, he became aware of sensation in his hand. His flesh was burning. He could smell it.

7. **high-water flotsam:** branches and debris washed ashore by a stream or river during the warm months when the water is high.

WORDS TO OWN

excruciating (eks·krōō′shē·āt′iŋ) *adj.:* extreme; intense.

ensued (en·sōōd′) *v.:* resulted.

Deep down below the surface he could feel it. The sensation developed into pain that grew acute. And still he endured it, holding the flame of matches clumsily to the bark that would not light readily because his own burning hands were in the way, absorbing most of the flame.

At last, when he could endure no more, he jerked his hands apart. The blazing matches fell sizzling into the snow, but the birch bark was alight. He began laying dry grass and the tiniest twigs on the flame. He could not pick and choose, for he had to lift the fuel between the heels of his hands. Small pieces of rotten wood and green moss clung to the twigs, and he bit them off as well as he could with his teeth. He cherished the flame carefully and awkwardly. It meant life, and it must not perish. The withdrawal of blood from the surface of his body now made him begin to shiver, and he grew more awkward. A large piece of green moss fell squarely on the little fire. He tried to poke it out with his fingers, but his shivering frame made him poke too far, and he disrupted the nucleus of the little fire, the burning grasses and tiny twigs separating and scattering. He tried to poke them together again, but in spite of the tenseness of the effort, his shivering got away with him, and the twigs were hopelessly scattered. Each twig gushed a puff of smoke and went out. The fire provider had failed. As he looked apathetically about him, his eyes chanced on the dog, sitting across the ruins of the fire from him, in the snow, making restless, hunching movements, slightly lifting one forefoot and then the other, shifting its weight back and forth on them with wistful eagerness.

The sight of the dog put a wild idea into his head. He remembered the tale of the man, caught in a blizzard, who killed a steer and crawled inside the carcass, and so was saved. He would kill the dog and bury his hands in the warm body until the numbness went out of them. Then he could build another fire. He spoke to the dog, calling it to him; but in his voice was a strange note of fear that frightened the animal, who had never known the man to speak in such a way before. Something was the matter, and its suspicious nature sensed danger—it knew not what danger, but somewhere, somehow, in its brain arose an apprehension of the man. It flattened its ears down at the sound of the man's voice, and its restless, hunch-ing movements and the liftings and shiftings of its forefeet became more pronounced; but it would not come to the man. He got on his hands and knees and crawled toward the dog. This unusual posture again excited suspicion, and the animal sidled mincingly away.

The man sat up in the snow for a moment and struggled for calmness. Then he pulled on his mittens, by means of his teeth, and got up on his feet. He glanced down at first in order to assure himself that he was really standing up, for the absence of sensation in his feet left him unrelated to the earth. His erect position in itself started to drive the webs of suspicion from the dog's mind; and when he spoke peremptorily,[8] with the sound of whiplashes in his voice, the dog rendered its customary allegiance and came to him. As it came within reaching distance, the man lost his control. His arms flashed out to the dog, and he experienced genuine surprise when he discovered that his hands could not clutch, that there was neither bend nor feeling in the fingers. He had forgotten for the moment that they were frozen and that they were freezing more and more. All this happened quickly, and before the animal could get away, he encircled its body with his arms. He sat down in the snow, and in this fashion held the dog, while it snarled and whined and struggled.

But it was all he could do, hold its body encircled in his arms and sit there. He realized that he could not kill the dog. There was no way to do it. With his helpless hands he could neither draw nor hold his sheath knife nor throttle the animal. He released it, and it plunged wildly away, its tail between its legs and still snarling. It halted forty feet away and surveyed him curiously, with ears sharply pricked forward. The man looked down at his hands in order to locate them, and found them hanging on the ends of his arms. It struck him as curious that one should have to use his eyes in order to find out where his hands were. He began threshing his arms back and forth, beating the mit-tened hands against his sides. He did this for five minutes, violently, and his heart pumped enough blood up to the surface to put a stop to his shivering. But no sensation was aroused in his hands. He had an impression that they hung like weights on

8. **peremptorily** (pər·emp′tə·ri·lē): in a commanding way.

the ends of his arms, but when he tried to run the impression down, he could not find it.

A certain fear of death, dull and oppressive, came to him. This fear quickly became poignant as he realized that it was no longer a mere matter of freezing his fingers and toes, or of losing his hands and feet, but that it was a matter of life and death, with the chances against him. This threw him into a panic, and he turned and ran up the creek bed along the old, dim trail. The dog joined in behind and kept up with him. He ran blindly, without intention, in fear such as he had never known in his life. Slowly, as he plowed and floundered through the snow, he began to see things again—the banks of the creek, the old timber jams, the leafless aspens, and the sky. The running made him feel better. He did not shiver. Maybe, if he ran on, his feet would thaw out; and, anyway, if he ran far enough, he would reach the camp and the boys. Without doubt he would lose some fingers and toes and some of his face; but the boys would take care of him, and save the rest of him when he got there. And, at the same time, there was another thought in his mind that said he would never get to the camp and the boys; that it was too many miles away, that the freezing had too great a start on him, and that he would soon be stiff and dead. This thought he kept in the background and refused to consider. Sometimes it pushed itself forward and demanded to be heard, but he thrust it back and strove to think of other things.

It struck him as curious that he could run at all on feet so frozen that he could not feel them when they struck the earth and took the weight of his body. He seemed to himself to skim along above the surface, and to have no connection with the earth. Somewhere he had once seen a winged Mercury,[9] and he wondered if Mercury felt as he felt when skimming over the earth.

His theory of running until he reached camp and the boys had one flaw in it: He lacked the endurance. Several times he stumbled, and finally he tottered, crumpled up, and fell. When he tried to rise, he failed. He must sit and rest, he decided, and next time he would merely walk and keep on going. As he sat and regained his breath, he noted that he was feeling quite warm and comfortable. He was not shivering, and it even seemed that a warm glow had come to his chest and trunk. And yet, when he touched his nose or cheeks, there was no sensation. Running would not thaw them out. Nor would it thaw out his hands and feet. Then the thought came to him that the frozen portions of his body must be extending. He tried to keep this thought down, to forget it, to think of something else; he was aware of the panicky feeling that it caused, and he was afraid of the panic. But the thought asserted itself, and persisted, until it produced a vision of his body totally frozen. This was too much, and he made another wild run along the trail. Once he slowed down to a walk, but the thought of the freezing extending itself made him run again.

And all the time the dog ran with him, at his heels. When he fell down a second time, it curled its tail over its forefeet and sat in front of him, facing him, curiously eager and intent. The warmth and security of the animal angered him, and he cursed it till it flattened down its ears appeasingly. This time the shivering came more quickly upon the man. He was losing in this battle with the frost. It was creeping into his body from all sides. The thought of it drove him on, but he ran no more than a hundred feet when he staggered and pitched headlong. It was his last panic. When he had recovered his breath and control, he sat up and entertained in his mind the conception of meeting death with dignity. However, the conception did not come to him in such terms. His idea of it was that he had been making a fool of himself, running around like a chicken with its head cut off—such was the simile that occurred to him. Well, he was bound to freeze anyway, and he might as well take it decently. With this newfound peace of mind came the first glimmerings of drowsiness. A good idea, he thought, to sleep off to death. It was like taking an anesthetic. Freezing was not so bad as people thought. There were lots worse ways to die.

He pictured the boys finding his body next day. Suddenly he found himself with them, coming along the trail and looking for himself. And, still with them, he came around a turn in the trail and found himself lying in the snow. He did not belong with himself anymore, for even then he was out of himself, standing with the boys and looking

9. **Mercury:** messenger of the gods in Roman mythology. He wears winged sandals and a winged hat.

. . . he came around a turn in the trail and found

himself lying in the snow. He did not belong with

himself anymore, for even then he was out of him-

self, standing with the boys and looking at himself

in the snow.

at himself in the snow. It certainly was cold, was his thought. When he got back to the States, he could tell the folks what real cold was. He drifted on from this to a vision of the old-timer on Sulfur Creek. He could see him quite clearly, warm and comfortable, and smoking a pipe.

"You were right, old hoss; you were right," the man mumbled to the old-timer of Sulfur Creek.

Then the man drowsed off into what seemed to him the most comfortable and satisfying sleep he had ever known. The dog sat facing him and waiting. The brief day drew to a close in a long, slow twilight. There were no signs of a fire to be made, and, besides, never in the dog's experience had it known a man to sit like that in the snow and make

no fire. As the twilight drew on, its eager yearning for the fire mastered it, and with a great lifting and shifting of forefeet, it whined softly, then flattened its ears down in anticipation of being chidden[10] by the man. But the man remained silent. Later, the dog whined loudly. And still later it crept close to the man and caught the scent of death. This made the animal bristle and back away. A little longer it delayed, howling under the stars that leaped and danced and shone brightly in the cold sky. Then it turned and trotted up the trail in the direction of the camp it knew, where were the other food providers and fire providers.

10. chidden: scolded; past participle of *chide.*

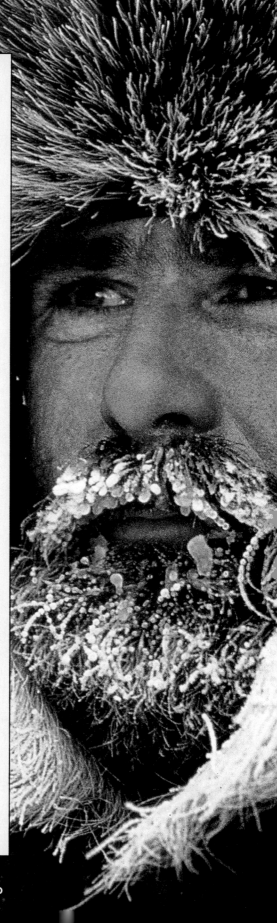

Cold Kills: Hypothermia

Here's what happens when you develop frostbite. After sitting out in the cold for a few hours, you develop hypothermia. The blood vessels in your skin and extremities clamp down in order to minimize further heat loss. Standing on ice or cold ground draws the warmth out of your feet, and the skin and subcutaneous tissues of your toes freeze. Chilled arterioles beneath the frozen tissue constrict, and blood flow through the capillaries slows as the blood becomes thick and syrupy. Clots form and block the capillary bed, thus depriving the tissues of oxygen and nutrients. Blood running into the limb is then diverted away from the capillary beds by shunts that cyclically open and close, allowing waves of warm blood to surge into the hands and feet at intervals. When your core temperature drops further, these shunts remain open, and the tissues begin to freeze. The feet, hands, ears, and nose are most vulnerable to frostbite because they are more likely to be exposed to the cold, they are distant from the warm core, and their large surface-to-volume ratio causes them to cool rapidly.

Frostnip is the mildest form of cold injury. It causes stinging pain, then numbness and a small white patch on the cheeks, nose, or ears. Immediate rewarming is the treatment.

Frostnip that is ignored progresses to superficial frostbite involving the skin and the subcutaneous tissues. The skin remains bloodless, pale and cold to the touch, but the tissue beneath the surface remains soft and pliable. A day or so after the injury, large blisters develop. After a few more days, the blisters heal and a hard, dry eschar forms. This is a thick, black scar that separates from the underlying tissue in a few weeks and is replaced by new skin.

Deep frostbite is freezing of the superficial as well as deep structures, including nerve, muscle, tendon, and even bone. The affected part is hard as wood, purple or red in color, cool to the touch, and has no feeling. In contrast to superficial frostbite, in which the injured part is sensitive, warm, and pink after rewarming, the part remains cold and blue after thawing. Small blood blisters may form after one to three weeks, and the part may remain swollen for months. Eventually, it mummifies and falls off.

—Paul G. Gill, Jr., M.D., *from* "Winning the Cold War," *Outdoor Life*, February 1993

MAKING MEANINGS

First Thoughts

1. How did you feel about the way the story ended? Did you predict this kind of ending? Explain.

Shaping Interpretations

2. Several times in the story, the man recalls the old-timer from Sulfur Creek. What key advice did the old-timer give him? Why do you think the man did not follow his advice?

3. Early in the story, London writes, "The animal was depressed by the tremendous cold. It knew that it was no time for traveling" (page 498). This passage alerts you to possible trouble ahead. Locate four other passages that **foreshadow** later events. Explain the link between each passage and the later event.

4. London does not merely tell you that it is extremely cold. He gives details that make you *feel* the cold. For example, he notes the "sharp, explosive crackle" when the man spits into the frigid air. List five other details from the story that make the cold real to you.

5. In the story, a man who thinks is contrasted with a dog who reacts by instinct. How do the man and the dog differ in the ways they approach the intense cold? What point do you think London is making?

6. Reread the definition of **naturalism** that precedes this selection (page 496). How does this story reflect key naturalist beliefs? How do you feel about this philosophy's view of human beings?

Reading Check

Summarize the **plot** of the story by listing its string of major **causes** and **effects**. Start by identifying the man's mission. Then, review your reading notes and explain *why* the man builds two different fires, what happens to each fire, and what results from each of these events. Be sure to include what happens to the man and to the dog by the end of the story.

Connecting with the Text

7. The central character is not particularly likable. He's described as "without imagination," he ignores the advice of his elders, and he has no love for dogs. Would you have enjoyed the story more—or less—if the man were portrayed in a more sympathetic light? (For instance, suppose that he were a more humble and insightful man who loved animals.) Give specific reasons to support your opinion.

Challenging the Text

8. London wrote another, more commercially acceptable ending for an earlier version of "To Build a Fire." In the first version, the man survives, returns to camp, and learns an important lesson: Never travel alone. Do you think this ending improves the story or weakens it? Explain your opinion.

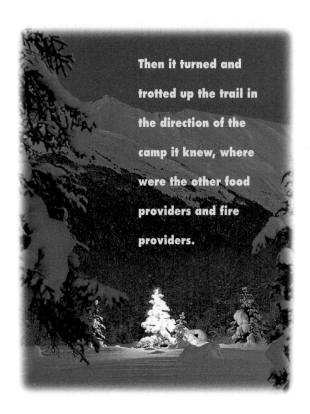

Then it turned and trotted up the trail in the direction of the camp it knew, where were the other food providers and fire providers.

CHOICES: Building Your Portfolio

Writer's Notebook

1. Collecting Ideas for a Research Paper

When you write a research paper, you will want to adjust your writing to suit your audience. For practice, think of a topic this story made you want to learn more about (for example, Jack London's life, the effects of cold on humans, the geography of the Yukon, or the naturalist literary movement). Imagine that you want to share the results of your research with three different audiences (for example, third-graders, a wilderness-exploration group, and a group of parents in your neighborhood). Make some notes about how you would tailor your coverage for each audience. Save your notes for possible use in the Writer's Workshop on page 515.

Analyzing Conflict

2. Opposing Forces

"To Build a Fire" contains both **internal** and **external conflict.** Identify what you consider the most important conflict of the story. In a brief essay, identify the opposing forces in this conflict. Use passages from the text to support your choice of this conflict as central to the story. Which force in the story wins?

Creative Writing / Role-Playing

3. Talk Before Leaving

Imagine that it's just before the story "To Build a Fire" begins. The man in the story is saying goodbye to his partners as he prepares to start out alone on the Yukon trail. Create a **dialogue** that occurs between the man and two of his partners. Then, with two classmates, role-play the dialogue for the class.

Crossing the Curriculum: Science

4. Survival Manual

You've been hired by a wilderness adventure company to create a "survival manual" for a group of people who will be traveling by foot in Yukon Territory during the winter, when the ground is covered by several feet of snow. Based on what you have learned from London's story, from reading about hypothermia in *Connections* (page 508), and from further research, work with a partner to make a list of the equipment and supplies these trekkers must assemble before they start out. After each item, write a sentence or two explaining its importance. To accompany the list of supplies, create a list of safety precautions. Illustrate your survival manual, if you wish.

Performance

5. Sound Matters

Consider how different sounds—or lack of all sound at some points—could enhance the drama if this story were recorded on audiocassette. With three or four other students, plan a recording of the story. First, break the story into small scenes. For each scene, list the **sound effects** you would use to heighten the tension. Be sure to include short, specific sounds, such as the matches that fall "sizzling into the snow." Also, select background music for various parts of the story. (Consider all kinds of music, from classical to rock to rap.) Finally, practice reading the story aloud, and record your reading together with sound effects and music. Play your recording for the class.

Creative Writing

6. Against All Odds

Write a survival story of your own, in which a character's life is threatened by a hostile environment: a weather condition, an isolated place, a terrain that poses difficulties. Like "To Build a Fire," your story should be built on realistic details that create suspense and a "you are there" feeling. For further inspiration, read *Into Thin Air* by Jon Krakauer, about the ill-fated Everest expeditions of 1996.

Follow the Drinking Gourd

Henry Brown nailed himself into a box and had it shipped to Philadelphia. Harriet Tubman risked her own life many times to lead fugitives north and out of slavery. They are just two of the many daring "passengers" and "conductors" whose firsthand accounts describe the flight from slavery to freedom in *The Underground Railroad* (Prentice Hall), edited by Charles L. Blockson.

Where the Buffalo Roamed

What was the westward expansion like from the American Indian point of view? Dee Brown's *Bury My Heart at Wounded Knee* (Holt, Rinehart and Winston) is a powerful, well-documented American Indian history of the West. For an exploration of Native American culture, consider *Dee Brown's Folktales of the Native American: Retold for Our Times* (Henry Holt). In this book, Brown narrates thirty-six stories, which include examples of the rich mythology and spirituality that make up much of the Native American oral tradition.

The Great American Novel

Ernest Hemingway wrote, "All modern American literature comes from one book by Mark Twain called *Huckleberry Finn*." Widely regarded as Twain's masterpiece, *Adventures of Huckleberry Finn* is a wise and funny novel about a young boy coming of age on the Mississippi River. Several film adaptations are also available on video. This title is available in the HRW Library.

The War Between the States

Though Stephen Crane never fought in the Civil War, he carefully researched it for *The Red Badge of Courage,* his famous novel about a young Union soldier. On video are both *The Red Badge of Courage* and Crane's *Three Miraculous Soldiers,* based on his ironic story of a young girl's encounters with both Union and Confederate soldiers. For a nonfiction account of the war, consider *The Civil War: An Illustrated History* (Alfred A. Knopf), by Geoffrey C. Ward, et al., the companion volume to the popular PBS TV series, which is also available on video.

The Frozen North

If "To Build a Fire" piqued your interest in cold and desolate places, try *Arctic Dreams* (Scribner's), Barry Lopez's exciting account of a real-life journey through northern climes. For more outdoor adventure from Jack London, try *The Call of the Wild*—another "dog story" of undisputed literary merit, which is also available in a film adaptation. This title is available in the HRW Library.

The American Language

American Dialects
by Gary Q. Arpin

James Fenimore Cooper, writing for a British audience in 1828, boasted about the absence of American dialects: "In America, while there are provincial or state peculiarities in tone, and even in the pronunciation and use of certain words, there is no patois [dialect]. An American may distinguish between the Georgian and the New England man, but you cannot." Americans, Cooper claimed, were too active and mobile for dialects to establish themselves—a point with which many other observers agreed.

Yet, a little over fifty years later, another American writer claimed to be using no less than seven dialects from a fairly small region in a single novel, *Adventures of Huckleberry Finn*. "In this book," Mark Twain wrote in an explanatory note, "a number of dialects are used, to wit: the Missouri Negro dialect; the extremest form of the backwoods South-Western dialect; the ordinary 'Pike-County' dialect; and four modified varieties of this last."

Unity or Variety?

Quite a bit had changed in America in that fifty years, but not enough to create a wholesale explosion of dialects where none had existed before. Even if Twain was exaggerating about his "four modified varieties" of the "'Pike-County' dialect," *Huckleberry Finn* depends for part of its effect on its use of dialect. Who was right about American dialects—Cooper or Twain?

Cooper was looking at an America that he was contrasting with England—a young, unified, mobile, democratic country, in which differences, if there were any, were kept within the family. Moreover, Cooper saw the country evolving toward even greater unity.

Twain, on the other hand, was looking very closely at a particular region of America and at distinctions of ethnicity, education, upbringing, and geography, all of which had small but significant effects on speech. He was also looking at a country whose recent Civil War had underscored the disunity of its people.

The views of Cooper and Twain toward American dialects represent two ways of looking at America and American speech. The Cooper view saw America as a unified nation marked principally by its distinctness from England. Twain saw the nation in terms of regional distinctions.

The Cooper view was shared by people like Noah Webster. Webster's dream was to stamp out local dialects and further unify the country (see page 195). He stated his attitude in this comparison between American and British language: "We are less infected with various dialects, the remains of the different conquerors of the English nation, than the inhabitants of England." A dialect in Webster's view was a weakness, an infection to be cured by education and spelling reform.

But Twain and other regional writers saw the local speech as one of the best ways of describing the inhabitants of a region. Dialect stories and poems, in fact, were very popular in the late nineteenth and early

"There wuz Maw and me, surrounded by screamin' Frenchmen, our Michelin-book lost and our faithful Cook's tour-guide nowhar in sight! . . ."

Fisher/Punch/Rothco.

twentieth centuries. They were usually comic, and much of their humor derived from funny pronunciations and peculiar local words. At the same time, these stories and poems in regional dialect illustrated the wisdom of the common person.

A New Englander called Hosea Biglow was a famous "common-sense" character created by James Russell Lowell in his First Series of *The Biglow Papers,* a collection of dialect poems. In the following excerpt, Hosea's New England speech patterns are shown, as he addresses recruiting officers for the Mexican War—a conflict which Hosea, in his common sense, strongly disapproves of.

> Ez fer war, I call it murder—
> There you hev it plain an' flat;
> I don't want to go no furder
> Than my Testyment fer that;
> God hez sed so plump an' fairly,
> It's ez long ez it is broad,
> An' you've gut to git up airly
> Ef you want to take in God.

What Is a Dialect?

In his novel about the Great Depression of the 1930s, *The Grapes of Wrath,* John Steinbeck records a conversation between migrant workers from different parts of the country. Here, the Joads, from Oklahoma, meet Ivy Wilson, from Kansas:

> "We're Joads," said Pa. "We come from right near Sallisaw."
> "Well, we're proud to meet you folks," said Ivy Wilson. "Sairy, these is Joads."
> "I knowed you wasn't

Oklahomy folks. You talk queer kinda—that ain't no blame, you understan'."

> "Ever'body says words different," said Ivy. "Arkansas folks says 'em different, and Oklahomy folks says 'em different. And we seen a lady from Massachusetts, an' she said 'em differentest of all. Couldn't hardly make out what she was sayin'."

What makes these Americans so different in speech is, of course, what linguists call dialect. A **dialect** can be defined as the characteristic language habits of a particular speech community. A speech community can be looked at in a very broad sense (as "American" versus "British"), or it can be subdivided almost endlessly. In fact, since no two people speak in exactly the same way, we might even say that each person speaks in his or her own dialect. (Linguists even have a term—*idiolect*—for the speech peculiar to one individual at one specific period of his or her life.) Though there are differences in the way the Joads, the Wilsons, and the puzzling lady from Massachusetts speak, they all are still clearly "American."

Dialects are distinguished from standard English and from each other in three principal ways:

1. In pronunciation: Pa Joad says "Oklahomy" and drops the final "d" in

understand. ("Kinda" for *kind of* is a form of rapid speech, not dialect.)

2. In vocabulary: Pa Joad uses an expression typical of his region when he says they come from "right near" Sallisaw.

3. In grammar: Pa says "knowed" instead of *knew*, "you wasn't" instead of *you weren't,* and "that ain't no blame."

The grammar of a language is its most profound element—like the skeleton of an animal. Grammar is likely to be changed only superficially in a dialect.

There can be an English dialect in which a person can say "Them was good peaches," but not one in which a person can say "Peaches good was them." When fundamental grammar rules are violated, the language becomes incoherent. Differences in vocabulary between dialects are more common, and most common are differences in pronunciation.

The main factors contributing to the formation of American dialects have been (1) settlement patterns—who settled in a region, where they came from, and how long they stayed there; (2) distance from a major cultural center; (3) influence of new immigrants; and (4) migration patterns.

English speakers settled first in the East, and the greatest profusion of dialects still exists

> Since no two people speak in exactly the same way, we might even say that each person speaks in his or her own dialect.

there. As settlers moved westward, they mixed dialects in the new communities in the West, and their original dialects became less and less evident.

Three Major Dialect Regions

Scholars have divided eastern American speech into three basic types of English: Northern, Midland, and Southern. Western states, in general, have blended these dialects, since their English-speaking settlers originally came from all three areas.

As a rule, regional differences in vocabulary and pronunciation are the easiest to pinpoint. If you take a *pail of swill* out to feed the hogs, you're probably a Northern farmer. If you take out a *bucket of slops,* you're probably from the South. If you pronounce *greasy* to rhyme with *we see,* you're probably from the North. If you pronounce it to rhyme with *easy,* you're probably from the Midland or South. Speakers in the Midland usually sound the *r* in words like *barn* and *horse,* while older speakers in the Northern and Southern regions tend to eliminate it. Bostonians, as we know, "pahk the cah." Southerners say something like "pawk the caw." Bostonians sometimes add an *r* to the end of a word, as President John F. Kennedy did when he spoke of "Cuber" rather than "Cuba." Midlanders usually make no distinction between the pronunciations of *horse* and *hoarse* and *mourning* and *morning.* Older Northerners and Southerners usually distinguish

"hawss" from "hohse," and "mawnin' " from "mohnin'." Southerners pronounce the *u* sound in words like *duty* and *news* as "you": "dyuty" and "nyews." Most Northern and Midland speakers say "dooty" and "nooz."

In literature, the accurate portrayal of regional speech is an excellent way of creating both an individual character and a member of a class. The South, with its rich oral culture, is the region where dialect has been most effectively used in literature, in the works of such writers as William Faulkner (page 713), Flannery O'Connor (page 672), and Bobbie Ann Mason. All of these writers—and more—have made it clear that speech patterns are an essential aspect of both our character and our environment.

Try It Out

1. **Examining regional dialects.** The objects or activities named by the words in each group below are all the same, but people in different regions of the country give them different names. Which word do you use? Do all of your classmates agree?

   a. *couch, sofa,* or *divan?*
   b. *faucet, spigot,* or *tap?*
   c. *spider, skillet,* or *frying pan?*
   d. *stand in line* or *stand on line?*
   e. *soda* or *pop?*

   Draw up a list of five words that you think are used only in your region. Then, swap lists with two other stu-

dents. Do you all agree that the words are regional dialect?

2. **Identifying dialect.** For each of the following passages, list examples of dialect in (a) vocabulary, (b) pronunciation, and (c) grammar.

African American, New York City, 1980s

"I'm axin you all a simple question. You keep talkin bout what's proper for a woman my age. How old am I anyhow?" And Joe Lee slams his eyes shut and squinches up his face to figure. And Task run a hand over his ear and stare into his glass like the ice cubes goin calculate for him. And Elo just starin at the top of my head like she goin rip the wig off any minute now.

—Toni Cade Bambara,
from "My Man Bovanne"

Kentucky, 1970s

"Law, I wouldn't want to be cremated the way some of them are doing now," says Edda. "To save space."

"Me neither," says Clausie with a whoop. "Did y'all see one of them Russians on television while back? At his funeral there was this horse and buggy pulling the body, and instead of a casket there was this little-bitty vase propped up there. It was real odd looking."

—Bobbie Ann Mason,
from "The Rookers"

Writer's Workshop

The history
of the written
word is rich ar
Page 1

EXPOSITORY WRITING

RESEARCH PAPER

Informative writing is the kind of writing you'll do most often during your school career and, in most cases, during your working life. A vast amount of the writing you encounter every day—the textbook you hold in your hands, the liner notes for a music recording, or the articles in your print or electronic newspaper—serves to inform you of something. Your goal as the writer of a research paper—also known as an informative report—is to collect, organize, synthesize, and present facts in order to expand your readers' knowledge of a topic.

Prewriting

1. **Find a topic.** Whether the choice of a topic is up to you or whether you're required to focus on a narrow topic within a general subject area, begin by brainstorming a list of topics you are interested in. Write a brief list of potential subjects. If you kept any of your Writer's Notebook jottings from Collections 9 and 10, you may already have some potential subjects and notes on those subjects. Highlight a couple of the strongest possibilities, and decide which one most appeals to you and might be most interesting to readers. Any of these historical topics could in turn suggest contemporary topics that interest you: an aspect of current African American music, groups who stage reenactments of Civil War battles, or contemporary war-story writers, such as Tim O'Brien.

2. **Narrow your topic, and freewrite about it.** In most cases, the first topic you come up with will be too broad to effectively handle in a research paper. Your next step, then, will be to narrow the focus of the broad topic you're considering—to go from "the Civil War," for example, to the more specific topic "women's roles during the Civil War."

   Once you have narrowed your topic, freewrite on what you already know about it, and generate questions that you will want to find answers to.

3. **Be sure you have a topic that can be researched.** The questions you decide to explore should be ones for which answers exist in reliable research sources that you can obtain. For any topic you choose, you should be able to find five or six good sources that are readily available to you through a library, the Internet, or other research facilities.

Technology HELP

See Writer's Workshop 2 CD-ROM. *Assignment: Informative Report.*

ASSIGNMENT
Write a research paper on a factual topic readers would be interested in learning more about.

AIM
To inform.

AUDIENCE
Your teacher; your classmates; other people interested in your topic.

Try It Out
With a partner or small group, review the introduction to "The Rise of Realism: The Civil War and Postwar Period" (pages 408–422). Then, brainstorm a list of possible subjects mentioned in the introduction that you think would make interesting topics to write about.

go.hrw.com
LE0 Research Paper

4. **Anticipate audience needs.** Before you start to write, it's important to think about the audience you'll be writing for. To anticipate your audi-ence's needs, ask yourself the following questions:

- What will my readers probably already know about the topic?
- What will they need to know in order to understand the topic?
- What will they be curious about? What will they be most interested in?

5. **Research your topic.** Though general reference books are often the first step in researching an informative paper, specialized reference books, such as biographical dictionaries and subject encyclopedias, are even more valuable once you begin digging into your topic. Check the card or on-line catalog of a library, the *Readers' Guide to Periodical Literature,* the indexes to major newspapers, and the library's vertical file. Also, look elsewhere for sources of information: Depending on your subject, you might contact gov-ernment offices, museums, historical societies, newspapers, and experts.

Throughout your research, you should be aware of striking a balance between primary and secondary sources. A **primary source** is original, firsthand information, such as a letter, a journal entry, a memorandum, an autobiography, or a historical document. A **secondary source** is informa-tion about, or derived from, primary sources: critical writings, reviews, en-cyclopedia entries, biographies, and so on. If primary sources are available, make use of them; secondary sources are usually plentiful, but try not to use them exclusively. Be sure to evaluate all sources carefully for accuracy and balance. Take notes from both primary and secondary sources on index cards, or use some other method that you find helpful.

6. **Examine your approach.** The nature of your subject, your sources, and your attitudes go into shaping your approach, or angle. Some research papers are concerned with presenting the newest findings about a subject. Others explore the development of the subject over time or its importance in a larger context. A research paper may show the causes and effects of a phenomenon or compare and contrast it to a related phenomenon.

7. **State a controlling idea.** Reread your notes, and summarize the **con-trolling idea,** or **thesis,** of your research paper in a brief statement. In informative writing, the controlling idea is an objective statement of the main concern of the paper; it defines the boundaries of the subject. Here are some examples of controlling ideas:

- Harriet Beecher Stowe, though initially not an abolitionist herself, fur-thered the abolitionist cause and helped pave the way to the Civil War with her book *Uncle Tom's Cabin.*
- The gambler with a heart of gold, the gentle farmer driven to a gunfight to defend his family, the tough-but-tender dance-hall girl—all of these familiar, stereotypical western characters owe their existence to one writer: Bret Harte.

8. **Organize.** Present your information in a logical sequence. You can cre-ate a framework for organizing a research paper using one of the following methods:

- chronological order (usually, from earliest to latest)

- order of importance (from most to least important, or least to most important)
- block comparison and contrast (Examine a series of aspects of one subject, then the same aspects, in the same order, for a second subject.)
- point-by-point comparison and contrast (Examine one aspect for the first subject, then the same aspect for the second subject, and so on.)

9. **Outline.** List as main headings the major aspects of your topic in an order that reflects your approach to the subject. Your preliminary outline may change during the course of drafting and revising. For now, you might make separate piles of index cards—or computer documents—to represent your major headings. Within each pile or document, cluster information into subheadings. Look for holes in your outline—headings that haven't been fully explored, relevant questions that haven't been answered. Do additional research to fill in the holes.

Drafting

1. **Begin forcefully.** The introductory paragraph of a research paper has two purposes: to define the subject and to get the reader interested. Try to accomplish both purposes in one stroke by defining your subject in a memorable, engaging way. You might begin with a surprising fact or statistic that has a bearing on your thesis; a quotation from an expert on your subject; or a question that balances different views of the subject. Describing a scene or narrating an anecdote can also be effective ways to open your research paper.

2. **Develop your points.** Follow your outline, checking off each item as you cover it to make sure you don't omit any essential information. As you develop your draft, though, you can rework your outline to match your increased understanding of what is important about the subject, what can be left out, and where each subtopic naturally falls into place.

3. **Define terms.** Define the terms your intended audience probably hasn't encountered before. If you were writing an article on Civil War weaponry for a general audience, you would probably need to define *Gatling gun* and *Arkansas toothpick*. In an article for Civil War buffs, though, you could give specialized information about those weapons without first having to explain what they are.

4. **Support your points.** Back up generalizations with specific examples and, if space permits, anecdotes. Flesh out the subject with details. Try to use concrete words rather than abstract ones to ease the reader's understanding of new concepts. Use facts and figures to demonstrate the validity of your statements, and provide necessary background information.

5. **Use quotations as seasoning.** The exact words of expert sources can add interest and authority to a research paper, but you should avoid overusing direct quotations. In general, use quotations when they are memorable or when the wording of the statement makes a difference. Otherwise, summarize or paraphrase—but be sure to use your own wording and sentence structure, and to credit your source.

Outline Form

Title: _____

Thesis Statement: _____

I. Main point
  A. Supporting point
    1. Detail 1
    2. Detail 2
    3. Detail 3
  B. Supporting point
    1. Detail 1
    2. Detail 2
    3. Detail 3
II. Main point
  A. Supporting point
    1. Detail 1
    2. Detail 2
    3. Detail 3
(etc.)

Language Handbook HELP

See Quotation Marks, page 1246.

Communications Handbook H E L P

Taking Notes and Documenting Sources; Proofreading.

Revision S T R A T E G I E S

Clear transitions smoothly guide your reader from subtopic to subtopic, from idea to idea. If you are dealing with the development of a subject over time, transitions such as first, then, next, last, *and* finally *will be important. For discussions of cause and effect, transitions such as* therefore, thus, so, *and* because *come into play. So do transitions that show exceptions or contrasts, such as* but, however, although, yet, rather, instead, *and* nevertheless.

▌ *Evaluation Criteria*

A good research paper
1. *sets forth its subject clearly*
2. *has an identifiable controlling idea, or thesis*
3. *supports its points adequately, using a variety of strategies*
4. *is organized in a way that supports the writer's purpose and is suitable to the subject*
5. *presents facts objectively*
6. *uses formal language*
7. *includes a Works Cited list at the end of the paper*

Documenting Sources: Parenthetical Citations and Works Cited

One crucial aspect of writing a research paper is deciding which information you must document. Use these guidelines to help determine whether you need to document a piece of information.

- In general, don't document basic information that appears in several reference works.
- Document unusual, little known facts, or facts and statistics your readers might question.
- Document the source of each direct quotation and paraphrase.
- Document theories or opinions that are not your own.
- Document any data from surveys, experiments, or research studies.

When you do document, you'll credit sources in two places—in parenthetical citations and in the Works Cited list at the end of your paper.

Parenthetical citations occur within the body of your essay. They are references that appear in parentheses after quoted or paraphrased material from a particular source. In many cases, all that you'll need in a parenthetical citation is the author's last name and a page number. For example, here's what a parenthetical citation might look like in a report on slave narratives:

> According to one critic, Equiano's story became "the prototype for the nineteenth-century slave narrative" (Gates xiv).

Your parenthetical citation tells the reader that you have picked up your quotation from a critical work by Gates that they will find documented in full in your Works Cited list at the end of your paper. (Note that the citation is placed before the final punctuation mark of the sentence, phrase, or clause you're documenting.)

Here's how your Works Cited entry for the same source will look:

> Gates, Henry Louis, Jr., ed. <u>The Classic Slave Narratives</u>. New York: New American Library, 1987.

The list of Works Cited contains all the works cited in your paper, with full bibliographic information that will enable readers to locate the sources you used. For more complete information on documenting sources in a research paper, be sure to consult the latest edition of the *MLA Handbook for Writers of Research Papers*.

6. **Establish an authoritative stance.** Your tone and point of view should consistently make your audience feel that you know what you are writing about. Depending on your intended audience, your paper may be either formal or somewhat informal in its level of language. Most research papers written as class assignments are relatively formal; they are serious and objective in tone and use the third-person point of view.

7. **Wrap it up neatly.** The ending of a research paper usually repeats the main point, or points, in a different way. It might also put the subject in a larger context or suggest topics for further exploration.

Language Workshop

CLAVDIVS
ONSOL-DEE

The history
of the written
word is rich and

Page 1

APPROPRIATE ADDITIONS: ADVERB AND ADJECTIVE CLAUSES

You can give your writing flavor, variety, and a smooth flow by using adjective and adverb clauses in your sentences. An **adjective clause** is a clause that modifies a noun or pronoun. Adjective clauses begin with the pronouns *who, whom, whose, which,* or *that.* An **adverb clause** is a clause that modifies a verb, an adjective, or another adverb. Adverb clauses begin with subordinating conjunctions such as *after, although, because, before, if, since, unless, until, when,* and *while.*

Use adverb and adjective clauses to combine two simple sentences into a single complex sentence.

EXAMPLE   Sojourner Truth wrote passionately for the abolition of slavery. Her first name means "visitor."

Joined by adjective clause:

Sojourner Truth, **whose first name means "visitor,"** wrote passionately for the abolition of slavery.

(**Note:** If an adjective clause is not essential to the meaning of a sentence, it is a **nonrestrictive clause** and needs to be set off from the rest of the sentence with a comma or commas, as in the example above. If the clause is essential to the meaning of the sentence, it is a **restrictive clause,** and no commas are necessary.)

EXAMPLE   Frederick Douglass fought with a slaveholder. Douglass was still enslaved then.

Joined by adverb clause:

While Frederick Douglass was still enslaved, he fought with a slaveholder.

(**Note:** When you place an adverb clause at the beginning of a sentence, separate it from the independent clause with a comma, as in the example above.)

Writer's Workshop Follow-Up: Revising

Look again at the research paper you wrote for the Writer's Workshop on page 515. Where can you improve your style by using adverb and adjective clauses to combine two simple sentences into a single complex sentence?

**Technology
H E L P**

See Language Workshop CD-ROM. *Key word entry: adverb clauses* or *adjective clauses.*

**Language
Handbook
H E L P**

The subordinate clause: pages 1231–1232.

Try It Out

Combine each pair of sentences by using either an adjective clause or an adverb clause. State which kind of clause you have used.

1. Mark Twain's humor became caustic. It happened in his old age.
2. The hero of "To Build a Fire" is lost and alone in the snow. He fears dying from hypothermia.
3. Kate Chopin's fiction has been rediscovered in recent years. Her fiction shows women struggling against obstacles to their freedom.
4. Code songs often contained directions for enslaved people escaping to freedom. These songs were often sung in the presence of slaveholders.
5. Ambrose Bierce was nicknamed "Bitter Bierce." He was disillusioned by the greed and deceit of humanity.

Reading for Life

Reading a College Guide

College in Southwest		College in Pacific Northwest	
Type of School	public	Type of School	public
Environment	suburban	Environment	city
Student Body		**Student Body**	
Total undergrad enrollment	14,000	Total undergrad enrollment	6,200
% male/female	48/52	% male/female	43/57
% from out of state	11	% from out of state	29
% transfers	32	% transfers	47
% live on campus	35	% live on campus	52
% international	3	% international	1
# of countries represented	100	% of countries represented	19
Academics		**Academics**	
Overall Rating	75	**Overall Rating**	88
Calendar	quarter	Calendar	quarter
Student/teacher ratio	21:1	Student/teacher ratio	20:1
Profs Interesting rating	66	Profs Interesting rating	89
% UG courses taught by profs	64	% UG courses taught by profs	100
Hours of study per day	2.90	Hours of study per day	3.32
Most Popular Majors		**Most Popular Majors**	
Biology		Education	
Psychology		Environmental studies	

Situation

As you make crucial choices about your own life, good reading skills will prove to be important. For instance, if you plan to attend college after high school, you will probably want to examine a college guide in order to compare the academic programs, financial-aid options, location, student body, and social life of various colleges and universities.

Strategies

Establish your purpose.
Before you open the guide, establish your purpose: For example, you may decide that you need to select four public colleges to apply to for admission next fall. You lean toward staying in the Southwest but will also consider schools in the Pacific Northwest. These decisions have narrowed your college search considerably.

Establish your criteria.
What are your priorities when choosing a college? Are you looking for a strong academic program or a specialized research center? Are there other features of a college—such as a competitive sports team, a diverse student body, or a generous financial-aid program—that are especially important to you?

Compare and contrast.
As you read the information about each college or university,

check to see how well it meets each of your priorities. Then, compare it to the other schools in your narrowed search field.

Adjust your purpose and priorities.
Don't be afraid to alter your purpose and your priorities as you analyze data on colleges.

Using the Strategies

Suppose you are committed to finding an academically strong public school in the Southwest or in the Pacific Northwest. You intend to major in biology, and you hope to work closely with your professors during your first years of college. You'd also like, if possible, to go to a school located in a city, with a diverse student body. Review the information on this page. Then, answer the following questions:

1. Is one school more likely to have a stronger biology department? How are the

schools rated for academics in general?

2. At which school are you likely to interact more with professors? At which school do students seem more enthusiastic about their professors?

3. Which school has a larger percentage of international students? Which school has more out-of-state students?

4. Which school is in a city?

5. Which school seems to best suit your needs?

Extending the Strategies

After looking through a college guide, make a list of additional pieces of information that you would like to find out about each college. Look for that information in other guide books, in college publications, in viewbooks, and on the Internet, where many colleges and universities offer details about themselves.

Learning for Life

Monitoring the Media

Problem

For centuries, painters and sketch artists had recorded wars visually, but the new eye of the camera lens made the Civil War and its aftermath more immediate and horribly real to people than earlier conflicts had been. How do the different news media today (television, newspapers, magazines, the Internet) affect the messages we receive and the assumptions we make about events of consequence taking place in our world?

Project

Compare and contrast television and print media coverage of an important current event in order to evaluate the power of different media to shape perceptions.

Preparation

1. As a group, choose a current event to monitor: a war or other political situation; a disaster; or an ongoing social problem, such as gang violence or drug abuse. The event should be one that has been in the news for a while and that will probably have a high profile for a time.

2. Divide the group into halves, one to monitor television coverage of the event and one to monitor print coverage (newspapers, magazines).

Procedure

1. Monitor your medium for coverage of the current event. Examine such aspects as
   - how frequently the event or situation is reported
   - how prominently the event is featured in the coverage
   - the types of coverage that are most common (reports, interviews, news analyses, newsmagazine segments, Internet features, lengthy articles, editorials, polls, and so on)

2. You may want to address these questions:
   - Does the coverage seem to take sides, or is it neutral?
   - How does the medium use visual images?
   - How does *seeing* something on the news differ from *reading* about it?

3. Make notes about how your perceptions of the current event are shaped by the medium's coverage. What are the particular strengths and weaknesses of the medium you have monitored? Are there differences in coverage among TV networks or newspapers and magazines?

Presentation

Present your findings about media coverage in one of the following formats (or another that your teacher approves):

1. **Panel Discussion**
   As a group, conduct a panel discussion on differences in media coverage. Address issues you have focused on during your monitoring. Also, evaluate each medium's strengths and shortcomings, and recommend how coverage could be improved.

2. **The Medium and the Message**
   Create a *Consumer Reports*–style bulletin rating the media you monitored. Summarize characteristics that set each particular news medium apart from others—strengths and weaknesses in reporting, tendencies toward bias, the influence of personalities on news coverage, and so on.

3. **Interview with a Newscaster or Journalist**
   Arrange an in-class interview with a local television news reporter, a writer or editor for a local newspaper or magazine, or a freelance journalist. Prepare beforehand a list of questions on media coverage. Ask the interviewee to share his or her perceptions of news coverage.

Processing

What did you learn about the power of media to shape perceptions? How can you watch for possible media bias? Write a reflection for your portfolio.

John Sloan

The Moderns
1900–1950

Men travel faster now, but I do not know if they go to better things.

—Willa Cather,
Death Comes for
the Archbishop

Sixth Avenue Elevated at Third Street (1928) by John Sloan. Oil on canvas (30″ × 40″).

The Moderns

by **John Leggett** *and*
John Malcolm Brinnin

I had a world, and it slipped away from me. The War blew up more than the bodies of men. . . . It blew ideas away—

—Sherwood Anderson, in a letter to his son, November 1929

The so-called Great War (1914–1918) was one of the events that changed the American voice in fiction. Before that clash of armies from the old and new worlds, American fiction had spoken in youthful tones—brash, but not fully original, and at times as uncertain as an adolescent's. Then, in 1917, the United States entered World War I, a conflict which was fought under the bright banners of humanity and democratic righteousness, but which, in fact, became a bloodbath. In 1916, more than a half-million soldiers were killed in a ten-month-long battle near the town of Verdun in northeastern France.

Although America emerged from the war as a victor, something was beginning to change. The country seemed to have lost its innocence. Idealism was turning into cynicism, and a few American writers began to question the authority and tradition that had seemed to be America's bedrock. The war introduced new moral codes, as well as short skirts, bobbed hair, and even new slang expressions. Americans' sense of a connection to their past seemed to be deteriorating.

This great nation will endure as it has endured, will revive and will prosper. So, first of all, let me assert my firm belief that the only thing we have to fear is fear itself.

—President Franklin D. Roosevelt, First Inaugural Address, March 1933

There were other reasons for this change in outlook. The Great Depression that followed the crash of the New York stock market in 1929 brought suffering to millions of Americans—to those same hard-working people who had put their faith in the boundless capacity of America to provide them with jobs and their children with brighter futures.

American writers, like their European counterparts, were also being profoundly affected by the **modernist** movement. This movement in literature, painting, music, and the other arts—swept along by disillusionment with traditions that seemed to have become spiritually empty—called for bold experimentation and a wholesale rejection of traditional themes and styles.

World War I was a turning point in American life, marking a loss of innocence and a strong disillusionment with tradition.

The American Dream: Pursuit of a Promise

If we try to identify our uniquely American beliefs, we find three central ideas that we have come to call the **American dream.**

First, there is admiration for America as a new Eden: a land of beauty, bounty, and unlimited promise. Both the promise and the disappointment of this idea are reflected in one of the greatest American novels, *The Great Gatsby* (1925), by F. Scott Fitzgerald (page 584). This work appeared at a time when great wealth and the pursuit of pleasure had become ends in themselves for many people. The title character, Gatsby, is a self-made man whose wealth has mysterious and clearly illegal origins. Moving into a pretentious mansion near New York City, Gatsby tries to woo both society and the woman he loves with a series of lavish parties. His extravagant gestures are in pursuit of a dream. Unfortunately, Gatsby's capacity for dreaming is far greater than any opportunity offered by the Roaring Twenties, and he meets a grotesquely violent end. But Gatsby's greatness is bound up with his tragedy: He believes in an America that has virtually disappeared under the degradations of modern life.

It is left to Nick Carraway, the narrator, to reflect at the end of the novel on the original promise of the American dream:

> . . . gradually I became aware of the old island here that flowered once for Dutch sailors' eyes—a fresh, green breast of the new world. Its vanished trees, the trees that had made way for Gatsby's house, had once pandered in whispers to the last and greatest of all human dreams; for a transitory enchanted moment man must have held his breath in the presence of this continent, compelled into an aesthetic contemplation he neither understood nor desired, face to face for the last time in history with something commensurate to his capacity for wonder.
>
> —F. Scott Fitzgerald, *from The Great Gatsby*

Eaton's Neck, Long Island (1872) by John Frederick Kensett. Oil on canvas (18″ × 36″).

The Metropolitan Museum of Art, gift of Thomas Kensett, 1874. (74.29) Photograph © 1979 The Metropolitan Museum of Art.

The Moderns 1900–1950

England's Joseph Conrad publishes the psychological novel *Heart of Darkness,* 1902

•

Frank Norris publishes *The Octopus,* a naturalistic novel about California wheat farmers fighting the railroad, 1901

William Carlos Williams's first collection of poems published, 1909

•

W.E.B. Du Bois publishes an influential collection of essays, *The Souls of Black Folk,* 1903

•

Jack London publishes *The Call of the Wild,* 1903

Carl Sandburg publishes *Chicago Poems,* 1916

•

Edgar Lee Masters publishes *Spoon River Anthology,* 1915

•

Willa Cather publishes *O Pioneers!,* 1913

•

Robert Frost publishes his first poetry collection, 1913

Edna St. Vincent Millay wins Pulitzer Prize in poetry, 1923

•

T. S. Eliot publishes *The Waste Land,* 1922

•

Irish writer James Joyce publishes *Ulysses,* 1922

•

Sinclair Lewis publishes *Main Street,* a novel about small-town Minnesota, 1920

1900–1909 | **1910–1919** | **1920–1929**

Queen Victoria of England dies, 1901

•

South African (or Boer) War ends in costly British victory, 1902

Einstein formulates his theory of relativity, 1905

•

Earthquake and fire ravage San Francisco, 1906

•

Freud lectures on psychoanalysis in U.S., 1909

British ocean liner *Titanic* sinks after striking an iceberg off Newfoundland, 1912

•

Armory Show in New York City introduces modern art to U.S., 1913

•

Panama Canal opens, 1914

•

World War I begins in Europe, 1914

•

U.S. enters World War I, 1917

•

Russian Revolution ends czarist regime, 1917

Harlem Renaissance begins, 1920

•

19th Amendment to Constitution grants U.S. women the right to vote, 1920

•

Charles A. Lindbergh completes first transatlantic solo flight by airplane, 1927

Albert Einstein. The Granger Collection, New York.

Charles Lindbergh and the *Spirit of St. Louis.*

Ernest Hemingway publishes noted World War I novel, *A Farewell to Arms,* 1929

•

Langston Hughes publishes his first poetry collection, *The Weary Blues,* 1926

•

The novels *An American Tragedy,* by Theodore Dreiser, and *The Great Gatsby,* by F. Scott Fitzgerald, are published, 1925

John Steinbeck publishes *The Grapes of Wrath,* 1939, and wins the Pulitzer Prize

•

Thornton Wilder's *Our Town* opens and wins Pulitzer Prize, 1938

•

Zora Neale Hurston publishes *Their Eyes Were Watching God,* 1937

•

Eugene O'Neill's dramatic trilogy *Mourning Becomes Electra* opens, 1931

Tennessee Williams's play *The Glass Menagerie* opens on Broadway, 1945

•

Richard Wright publishes *Native Son,* 1940

The play *Death of a Salesman,* by Arthur Miller, opens, 1949

•

William Faulkner publishes *Intruder in the Dust,* 1948

•

William Carlos Williams publishes first part of his long poem *Paterson,* 1946

1920–1929   1930–1939   1940–1950

The Jazz Singer, one of the first sound films with dialogue, opens, 1927

•

U.S. stock market crashes, leading to Great Depression, 1929

Mohandas Gandhi leads protest against British salt tax in India, 1930

•

Franklin D. Roosevelt becomes U.S. president; New Deal program to counter Great Depression begins, 1933

•

Nazi leader Adolf Hitler comes to power in Germany, 1933

•

Nationalist forces of Francisco Franco win Spanish civil war, 1939

•

Germany invades Poland; World War II begins in Europe, 1939

U.S. enters World War II after Japan attacks Pearl Harbor in Hawaii, 1941

•

Oklahoma!, a groundbreaking musical play by Richard Rodgers and Oscar Hammerstein, opens, 1943

•

Allies begin final drive against German forces on D-day, June 6, 1944

•

Germany surrenders, 1945

•

U.S. explodes atom bombs over Hiroshima and Nagasaki, Japan; Japan surrenders, 1945

United Nations established, 1945

•

India gains independence from British rule, 1947

•

State of Israel established, 1948

•

Communist forces under Mao Zedong win control of mainland China, 1949

•

Korean War begins, 1950

•

U.S. population is about 151 million, 1950

Franklin D. Roosevelt.

Attack on Pearl Harbor.

United Nations Building, New York City.

THE BEST OF TIMES, THE WORST OF TIMES

The era of the 1930s in the United States was marked by triumph and tragedy, growth and hardship. Between 1890 and 1940, the U.S. population more than doubled, rising from 63 million to 132 million. African Americans made up about 10 percent of the population, and other ethnic groups about 0.5 percent. Families were slightly larger than they are today, but people died younger—on average, around age sixty.

By 1933, the United States was in the depths of the Great Depression. Anywhere from one fourth to one third of American workers were unemployed. People waited in bread lines, foraged for food in garbage dumps, and slept in sewer pipes. Homeless families lived in tents and shacks in camps called Hoovervilles, named for President Herbert Hoover. In 1933, the new president, Franklin Delano Roosevelt (FDR), ignited a spark of hope with his promise to help

the "forgotten man." True to his word, FDR launched a blizzard of agencies, such as the Works Progress Administration and the Civilian Conservation Corps, that put millions of Americans back to work.

Despite hard times, human and technological marvels were a hallmark of the

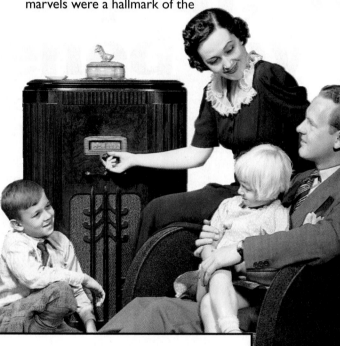

FPG International.

The second element in the American dream is optimism, justified by the ever-expanding opportunity and abundance that many people have come to expect. Most of the time, Americans have believed in progress—that life keeps getting better and that we are moving toward an era of prosperity, justice, and joy that always seems just around the corner.

Finally, the third important element in the American dream has been the importance and ultimate triumph of the individual—the independent, self-reliant person. This ideal of the self-reliant individual was championed by Ralph Waldo Emerson (page 216), who probably deserves most of the credit for defining the essence of the American dream, including its roots in the promise of the "new Eden" and its faith that "things are getting better all the time." Trust the universe and trust yourself, Emerson wrote. "If the single man plant himself indomitable on his instincts, and there abide, the huge world will come round to him."

Detroit Industry, West Wall (detail)
(1932–1933) by Diego M. Rivera. Fresco.
Gift of Edsel B. Ford. Photograph ©1998
The Detroit Institute of Art.

era. Amelia Earhart became the first woman to fly solo across the Atlantic (1932). Three famous structures were built during this decade: the Empire State Building in New York City (1931), Boulder (now Hoover) Dam on the Arizona-Nevada border (1936), and the Golden Gate Bridge in San Francisco (1937).

Happily, during a decade of severe shortages, there was no shortage of entertainment. Mystery fans devoured whodunits featuring Dashiell Hammett's hard-boiled investigator, Sam Spade, while both young and old listened to the Dorseys' jazz orchestra and danced to the swing music of Count Basie.

By the late 1930s, the Depression had eased, and people could again afford one of the most popular entertainments: movies. The golden age of motion pictures had begun. Each week, over a hundred million Americans flocked to watch cartoons, newsreels, and feature films at elaborate movie palaces with names such as the Bijou, the Roxy, and the Ritz. Audiences loved slapstick comics like Laurel and Hardy or the Marx brothers. Lines spoken by Mae West, such as "Come up and see me sometime," became household phrases. To top off the decade, audiences in 1939 thronged to behold the long-awaited blockbuster movie epic, *Gone with the Wind.*

But perhaps the most popular form of entertainment during the 1930s was the radio. By 1933, two thirds of American households owned at least one radio, and families gathered together to listen to comedies like *Fibber McGee and Molly* and adventures like *The Shadow.* People also relied on radios for news, as was demonstrated by a famous Halloween broadcast of 1938. Six million listeners tuned in to Orson Welles's radio play "Invasion from Mars"—a series of convincing but fictional news bulletins about a Martian invasion near New York City, based on H. G. Wells's science fiction novel *War of the Worlds.* At the time, some people feared that the German dictator Adolf Hitler might actually invade the United States. Believing that the broadcast was describing a real invasion, hundreds of people clogged eastern highways, fleeing for their lives.

> Fitzgerald's greatest work shows what happens to people who pursue illusory American dreams, and how society . . . fails to sustain them in their desperate hour.
>
> —Jeffrey Meyers, *Scott Fitzgerald: A Biography,* 1994

The three underpinnings of the American dream are a belief in the land as a bountiful new Eden, an unwavering faith in progress, and a confidence in the ultimate triumph of the individual.

A Crack in the World: Breakdown of Beliefs and Traditions

The cannonades of World War I and the economic crash a decade later severely damaged these inherited ideas of an Edenic land, an optimism in the future, and faith in individualism. Postwar writers became skeptical of the New England Puritan tradition and the gentility that had been central to the literary

The Tenets of the American Dream

- America is a new Eden, a "promised land" of beauty, unlimited resources, and endless opportunities.
- The American birthright is one of ever-expanding opportunity. Progress is a good thing, and we can optimistically expect life to keep getting better and better.
- The independent, self-reliant individual will triumph. Everything is possible for the person who places trust in his or her own powers and potential.

ideal. In fact, the center of American literary life now finally started to shift away from New England, which had been the native region of America's most brilliant writers during the nineteenth century. Many of the modernist writers you will read in the collections that follow were born in the South, the Midwest, or the West.

In the postwar period, two new intellectual trends or movements, **Marxism** and **psychoanalysis,** combined to increase the pressure on traditional beliefs and values. In Russia during World War I, a Marxist revolution had toppled and even murdered an anointed ruler, the czar. The socialistic beliefs of Karl Marx (1818–1883) that had powered the Russian Revolution in 1917 were in direct opposition to the American system of capitalism and free enterprise, and Marxists threatened to export their revolution everywhere. After visiting Russia, American writer Lincoln Steffens reported: "I have seen the future and it works."

In Vienna, there was another unsettling movement. Sigmund Freud (1856–1939), the founder of psychoanalysis, had opened the workings of the unconscious mind to scrutiny and called for a new understanding of human sexuality and the role it plays in our unconscious thoughts. Throughout America, there was a growing interest in this new field of psychology, and a resultant anxiety about the amount of freedom an individual really had. If our actions were influenced by our subconscious, and if we had no control over our subconscious, there seemed to be little room left for "free will."

One literary result of this interest in the psyche was the narrative technique called **stream of consciousness.** This writing style abandoned chronology and attempted to imitate the moment-by-moment flow of a character's perceptions and memories. The Irish writer James Joyce (1882–1941) radically changed the very concept of the novel by using stream of consciousness in *Ulysses* (1922), his monumental "odyssey" set in Dublin. Soon afterward, the American writers Katherine Anne Porter (page 702) and William Faulkner (page 713) used the stream-of-consciousness technique in their works.

> *Two important trends, Marxism and psychoanalysis, were noteworthy factors in the breakdown of traditional beliefs and values. Psychoanalysis led to the literary technique of stream-of-consciousness narration.*

At Home and Abroad: The Jazz Age

In 1919, the Constitution was amended to prohibit the manufacture and sale of alcohol, which was singled out as a central social evil. But far from shoring up traditional values, Prohibition ushered in an age characterized by the bootlegger, the speakeasy, the cocktail, the short-skirted flapper, the new rhythms of jazz, and the dangerous

William Faulkner.
The Granger Collection, New York.

> The liberty of the individual is no gift of civilization. It was greatest before there was any civilization.
>
> —Sigmund Freud, *Civilization and Its Discontents,* 1930

Manuscript page, "A Rose for Emily" by William Faulkner.

William Faulkner Collection, Special Collections Department, Manuscripts Division, University of Virginia Library.

but lucrative profession of the gangster. Recording the Roaring Twenties and making the era a vivid chapter in our history, F. Scott Fitzgerald gave it its name: the Jazz Age. Other writers also became emblems of the era. The poet Edna St. Vincent Millay (page 697)—"Vincent" to her friends—became a symbol of the liberated woman of the era. Her bold, carefree public identity as a romantic, extravagant female Casanova made her a national celebrity while she was still in her twenties. In 1920, women had finally won the right to vote, and Millay's poems, as well as her public persona, assigned women social, intellectual, and romantic roles that society had previously reserved for men.

As energetic as the Roaring Twenties were in America, the pursuit of pleasure abroad was even more attractive to some than its enjoyment at home. F. Scott Fitzgerald was among the many American writers and artists who abandoned their own shores after the war for the expatriate life in France. After World War I, living was not only cheap in Paris and on the sunny French Riviera, but also somehow better; it was more exotic, more filled with grace and luxury, and there was no need to go down a cellar stairway to get a drink. This wave of expatriates was another signal that something had gone wrong with the American dream—with the idea that America was Eden, with our notion of inherent virtue, and especially with the conviction that America was a land of heroes.

> **The Jazz Age at home was racy and unconventional. The same decade of the 1920s witnessed the flight of many American authors to an expatriate life abroad, especially in France.**

Grace Under Pressure: The New American Hero

Disillusionment was a major theme in the fiction of the time. In 1920, Sinclair Lewis (1885–1951) lashed out satirically at the

> The United States . . . is a country the right age to have been born in and the wrong age to live in.
>
> —Gertrude Stein, *transition* magazine, Fall 1928

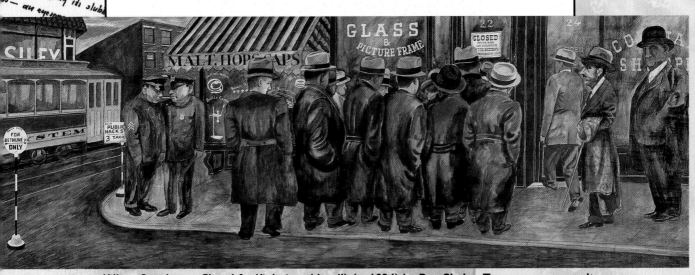

Village Speakeasy, Closed for Violations (detail) (c. 1934) by Ben Shahn. Tempera on masonite (16½" × 48"). Museum of the City of New York. Permanent Deposit of the Public Art Project through the Whitney Museum.
© Estate of Ben Shahn/Licensed by VAGA, New York, NY.

narrow-mindedness of small-town life in his immensely popular novel, *Main Street*. In 1925, Theodore Dreiser (1871–1945) produced a literary landmark with his prototype of the realistic novel, *An American Tragedy*, the story of an ambitious but luckless man who takes a path that leads him not to the success he seeks, but to the execution chamber.

The most influential of all the post–World War I writers, however, was Ernest Hemingway (page 650). Hemingway is perhaps most famous for his literary style, which affected the style of American prose fiction for several generations. Like the Puritans who strove for a "plain style" centuries earlier, Hemingway reduced the flamboyance of literary language to a minimum, to the bare bones of the truth it must express.

Hemingway also introduced a new kind of hero to American fiction, a character type that many readers embraced as a protagonist and a role model. This Hemingway hero is a man of action, a warrior, and a tough competitor; he has a code of honor, courage, and endurance. He shows, in Hemingway's own words, "grace under pressure." But the most important trait of this Hemingway hero is that he is thoroughly disillusioned, a quality that reflected the author's own outlook. For Hemingway feared, a little like Herman Melville (page 311), that at the inscrutable center of creation lay nothing at all.

Hemingway found his own "answer" to this crisis of faith in a belief in the self and in such qualities as decency, bravery, competence, and skill. He clung to this conviction in spite of what he saw as the absolutely unbeatable odds ranged against us all. A further part of the Hemingway code was the importance of recognizing and snatching up the rare, good, rich moments that life offers before those moments elude us.

Hemingway summed up the values of many post–World War I writers, both in his spare, plain style and in his creation of a new kind of hero, disillusioned but also honorable and courageous.

Modernist Voices in Poetry: A Dazzling Period

After the deaths of Emily Dickinson (page 372) and Walt Whitman (page 348), American poetry went into something of a decline. But time would show that the comparatively uneventful period between 1890 and 1910 was but the trough of a wave that was about to break. The force of this wave, when it arrived, would be strong enough to wash away the last traces of British influence on American poetry and to carry our poets into their most dazzling period of variety and experimentation.

During this period, many poets began to explore the artistic life of Europe, especially Paris. With other writers, artists, and composers from all over the world, they

Gary Cooper as Robert Jordan in the 1943 movie *For Whom the Bell Tolls,* **based on Hemingway's novel.**

Guernica (1937) by Pablo Picasso. Museo Nacional Centro de Arte Reina Sofia, Madrid. On permanent loan from the Museo del Prado, Madrid. © 2000 The Estate of Pablo Picasso/Artists Rights Society (ARS), New York.

> Literature is news that *stays* news.
>
> —Ezra Pound

absorbed the lessons of modernist painters like Henri Matisse and Pablo Picasso, who were exploring new ways to see and represent reality. In the same way, poets sought to create poems that invited new ways of seeing and thinking. Ezra Pound (page 773) and T. S. Eliot (page 661) used the suggestive techniques of **Symbolism** to fashion a new, modernist poetry (see page 770).

Pound also spearheaded a related poetic movement called **Imagism.** Exemplified by brilliant poets like William Carlos Williams (page 778), Marianne Moore (page 787), E. E. Cummings (page 796), and Wallace Stevens (page 783), the Imagist and Symbolist styles would prevail in poetry until midway into the twentieth century.

After an uneventful period between 1890 and 1910, an explosion of modernist poetry, heavily influenced by developments in Europe, began. Ezra Pound and T. S. Eliot, associated with the Symbolist and Imagist movements, were especially important in charting a modernist direction for American poetry.

The Elements of Modernism in American Literature

- Emphasis on bold experimentation in style and form, reflecting the fragmentation of society
- Rejection of traditional themes and subjects
- Sense of disillusionment and loss of faith in the American dream
- Rejection of the ideal of a hero as infallible in favor of a hero who is flawed and disillusioned but shows "grace under pressure"
- Interest in the inner workings of the human mind, sometimes expressed through new narrative techniques such as stream of consciousness

Voices of American Character: Poetry in New England and the Midwest

Meanwhile, other American poets rejected modernist trends. While their colleagues found inspiration in Paris, these poets stayed at home, ignoring or defying the revolution of modernism. These poets preferred to say what they had to say in plain American speech. Their individual accents reveal the regional diversity of American life and character.

Edwin Arlington Robinson (page 644) lightly disguised the people of his own "Down East" home—Gardiner, Maine—as characters representing American "types" whose fates were manifestations of their characters.

The greatest poetic voice in New England, however, was that of Robert Frost (page 558). Frost's independence was grounded in his ability to handle ordinary New England speech and in his surprising skill at taking the most conventional poetic forms and giving them a twist all his own. In an era when "good" was being equated by many artists with "new," the only new thing about Robert Frost was old: individual poetic genius. Using this gift to impose his own personality on the iambic line in verse, Frost created a poetic voice that was unique and impossible to imitate.

At the same time, poets of the Midwest brought the American heartland to life in slightly more adventuresome verse forms. They used rougher stanzas and looser lines. Best known of these poets is Edgar Lee Masters (page 692), who assembled a sort of town biography in his *Spoon River Anthology* (1915). Masters took the lid off sentimentalized small-town life— the *coffin* lid, to be exact—and allowed the dead of Spoon River to speak their own shocking litanies of greed, frustration, and spiritual poverty. His best-selling collection of poems received the same kind of interest Americans were beginning to give to Freudian case histories.

> *Poets like Edwin Arlington Robinson and Robert Frost from New England and Edgar Lee Masters from the Midwest continued to use traditional verse forms and offered penetrating insights into a variety of American character types.*

The Harlem Renaissance: Voices of the African American Experience

African American culture found expression in poetry in two different ways. The works of black poets who wrote in conventional forms, like Paul Laurence Dunbar (1872–1906), were most quickly accepted by white readers. These metrically regular and rhymed verse forms tended to make even the most urgent and desperate of African American concerns seem undisturbing. A second

> Tell me what America is and I'll tell you what its poetry is.
>
> —Robert Frost

125th Street Apollo Theatre. Harlem, 1934. Many great African American artists performed here.

group of black poets, however, focused directly on the unique contributions of African American culture to America. Their poetry based its rhythms on spirituals and jazz, its lyrics on songs known as the blues, and its diction on the street talk of the ghettos.

Foremost among African American lyric poets were James Weldon Johnson (page 736), Claude McKay (page 743), Langston Hughes (page 760), and Countee Cullen (page 746). These poets brought literary distinction to the broad movement of artists known as the **Harlem Renaissance** (page 734). The geographical center of the movement was Harlem, the section of New York City north of 110th Street in Manhattan. But its spiritual center was a place in the consciousness of African Americans—a people too long ignored, patronized, or otherwise shuffled to the margins of American art. When African American poetry, hand in hand with the music echoing from New Orleans, Memphis, and Chicago, became part of the Jazz Age, it was a catalyst for a new appreciation of the role of black talent in American culture.

The poets of the Harlem Renaissance revolutionized the African American contribution to American literature by introducing ghetto speech and the rhythms of jazz and blues into their verse.

Against the Grain: Poetic Voices of the West and South

The most distinctive poetic voice from the West in the early twentieth century was that of Robinson Jeffers (page 580), who carved out an isolated and almost hermitlike existence in a California town by the Pacific shore. Jeffers steered a wavering course between convention and experiment: Sometimes he worked in meter and rhyme, but more often he wrote in long lines of free verse. He became widely known less for his craftsmanship than for his unorthodox attitudes toward progress, religion, and the nature of humanity. While his contemporaries celebrated democracy and the rise of the common man, Jeffers took a very dim view of both. After his death, his poems became an inspiration to the Beats and other West Coast literary groups in the 1960s.

The South offered an equally distinctive literary voice in John Crowe Ransom (page 577). Ransom stood for wit, gentility, subtle intellect, and the manners of an earlier century. Ransom's formal grace and polish intimidated some readers, but others found in him a gentle nature and a passionate concern for the beauty and elegance of the English language.

Poetic voices of the West and the South included Robinson Jeffers, who was skeptical of social progress, and John Crowe Ransom, a Southerner who wrote with the courtly grace of an earlier age.

> . . . O, let America
> be America again—
> The land that never
> has been yet—
> And yet must be.
>
> —Langston Hughes

Paul Laurence Dunbar.

Culver Pictures.

(Background) Museum of African Art/Smithsonian Institution/Courtesy Aldo Tutino/Art Resource, NY.

The American Dream Revised

Even though the modernists rejected Emerson's optimism, a belief in self-reliance persisted, as did the old idea of America as Eden. Hemingway is really telling us about Eden in his *Up in Michigan* stories, where he describes the lakes and streams and woods he knew as a boy and where he extols the restorative power of nature in a way that Emerson might have recognized. This is the same Edenic America that has come down to us through Mark Twain's Mississippi, through Faulkner's Yoknapatawpha County, and through John Steinbeck's Salinas Valley.

As we explore this period of American writing—in some respects, the richest period since the flowering of New England in the first half of the nineteenth century—we stand at the threshold of our own time. Though this part of our own century has seen major changes in American attitudes, you'll recognize many concerns that are consistent with concerns of the past. These writers—some of the best that America has produced—experimented boldly with forms and subject matter. But they were also still trying to find the answers to the basic human questions: Who are we? Where are we going? And what values should guide us on that search for our human identity?

> I began to gather these impressions. There was a thing called happiness toward which men were striving. They never got to it. All of life was amazingly accidental. Love, moments of tenderness and despair, came to the poor and the miserable as to the rich and successful.
>
> It began to seem to me that what was most wanted by all people was love, understanding. Our writers, our storytellers, in wrapping life up into neat little packages, were only betraying life.
>
> —Sherwood Anderson, in a letter to George Freitag, August 27, 1938

American modernist writers both echoed and challenged the American dream. They constituted a broader, more resonant voice than ever before, resulting in a second American renaissance. With all the changes, however, writers continued to ask fundamental questions about the meaning and purpose of human existence.

Quickwrite
What Is Today's American Dream?

In 1929, Gertrude Stein, a leading modernist literary figure among the American expatriates in Paris, declared, "Everything is the same and everything is different." Apply her remark to the American dream today—and tomorrow. How do you define the American dream now? (Is there even an American dream anymore?) How has it remained the same? How has it changed? What forces might shape it in the future?

Collection 11

LOSS AND REDEMPTION

Cather
Wolfe
Frost
Ransom
Jeffers

On the rough wet grass of the back yard my father and mother have spread quilts. We all lie there, my mother, my father, my uncle, my aunt, and I too am lying there. First we were sitting up, then one of us lay down, and then we all lay down, on our stomachs, or on our sides, or on our backs, and they have kept on talking. They are not talking much, and the talk is quiet, of nothing in particular, or nothing at all in particular, of nothing at all. The stars are wide and alive, they seem each like a smile of great sweetness, and they seem very near. All my people are larger bodies than mine, quiet, with voices gentle and meaningless like the voices of sleeping birds. One is an artist, he is living at home. One is a musician, she is living at home. One is my mother who is good to me. One is my father who is good to me. By some chance, here they are, all on this earth; and who shall ever tell the sorrow of being on this earth, lying, on quilts, on the grass, in a summer evening, among the sounds of the night. May God bless my people, my uncle, my aunt, my mother, my good father, oh, remember them kindly in their time of trouble; and in the hour of their taking away.

—James Agee (1909–1955),
from "Knoxville: Summer 1915,"
from A Death in the Family

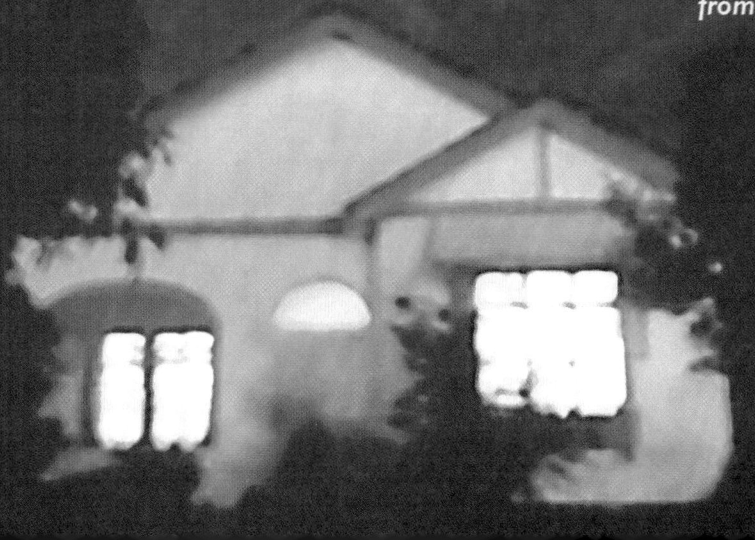

Willa Cather

(1873–1947)

Willa Cather, 1926 by Edward Steichen.
Courtesy George Eastman House. Reprinted with permission of Joanna T. Steichen.

Willa Cather was born in rural Virginia, the first of seven children. When she was nine, her father uprooted the family and headed for the untried lands of the West, settling in Webster County, Nebraska. She would later recall that this first encounter with the prairie was so striking that she felt "a kind of erasure of personality."

Nevertheless, Cather was stimulated by the hard life of the soil she saw around her, and she absorbed the stories of the immigrant families who were her neighbors. She read widely and became an outstanding student at the Red Cloud, Nebraska, school. In her boyish clothes and haircut, Willa was an unusual figure, and her teachers recognized in her an adolescent nonconformist.

While a freshman at the University of Nebraska, Cather published an essay in a Lincoln newspaper. She became a regular contributor to the newspaper and began to write poetry and stories. By the time Cather graduated in 1895, she had won a statewide reputation for brash, bright reviews. She moved to Pittsburgh and for a decade continued to work as a journalist. In 1903, she published her first book, a collection of verse entitled *April Twilights,* followed by *The Troll Garden,* a group of stories.

In 1906, the publisher S. S. McClure persuaded Cather to move to New York and join the staff of his dynamic, muckraking magazine, *McClure's.* For six years she served as a writer and editor, immersed in the social and political currents of the time; in 1912, she resigned from the magazine to give herself completely to writing fiction.

In 1908, Cather had met the Maine writer Sarah Orne Jewett (1849–1909), who had encouraged Cather to write about the themes and settings she knew best: the moral values of the hard-working immigrant families on the Midwestern prairie. Cather believed that these pioneers, who had sought to bring the wild, new land under cultivation, were heroic and that their era was the heart of the so-called American dream. She saw these immigrant settlers as contributing a cultural richness and an earthy love of life that were lacking in the pale, self-satisfied inhabitants of Eastern Seaboard cities. Cather developed these themes in *O Pioneers!* (1913), a novel whose title she borrowed from Walt Whitman, and in her novel *My Ántonia* (1918).

As Cather witnessed the decline of the agrarian ideal, her work became increasingly elegiac about the past and disillusioned with the present. *One of Ours* (1922), which was far from Cather's best novel but which won her the Pulitzer Prize, reflects Cather's dissatisfaction with the new people and machines who were betraying the pioneer ideal. "The world broke in two in 1922 or thereabout," Cather wrote, explaining that no one born in the twentieth century could grasp her own vision of America. She had seen her beloved Nebraska devastated by the machine, and she lamented the end of her epic vision of a noble society.

Cather reminds us of the novelist's duty to keep a wary eye on our relation to scientific progress. It was her profound intuition that a science that offers us new comfort, new speed, new security, and longer life will almost surely demand something of our spirit in return.

HRW go.hrw.com
LEO 11-11

Before You Read

A WAGNER MATINÉE

Make the Connection

Lost Pleasures

Most people can name at least one thing they enjoy that's a source of personal "bliss"— something they'd rather see, do, own, or listen to than anything else in the world. Sometimes circumstances in life force people to give up that beloved source of pleasure. Here is a story of a woman who has had to go without something important to her. As you will see, although Cather believed that Midwestern farm life fostered essential values, she was hardly a romantic who underestimated the hardships of that life, or the lost opportunities for some of the people who lived that life.

Quickwrite

Suppose you were deprived of your "bliss"— your favorite personal pleasure— for many years, and then you had the opportunity to experience it again, but only briefly. Write your ideas about how you would respond. Would you seize the opportunity or pass up the chance for fear that it would be too painful to realize what you had been missing?

Elements of Literature

Setting

As in most of Cather's works, **setting** plays a central role in this story. Here, however, there are really two settings: Rural Nebraska—in which the narrator, like Cather, spent his formative years—is contrasted with Boston and its thriving cultural life.

> **S**etting is the time and location in which a story takes place.
>
> *For more on Setting, see the Handbook of Literary Terms.*

Background

Willa Cather loved music and was herself an accomplished musician. The story's title refers to the German composer Richard Wagner (rish'ärt väg'nər) (1813–1883), an outstanding Romantic composer of the nineteenth century. A matinée is an afternoon performance of a play or concert.

Beneath the soiled linen duster which, on her arrival, was the most conspicuous feature of her costume, she wore a black stuff dress, whose ornamentation showed that she had surrendered herself unquestioningly into the hands of a country dressmaker.

A Wagner Matinée

Willa Cather

I received one morning a letter, written in pale ink on glassy, blue-lined note paper, and bearing the postmark of a little Nebraska village. This communication, worn and rubbed, looking as though it had been carried for some days in a coat pocket that was none too clean, was from my Uncle Howard and informed me that his wife had been left a small legacy by a bachelor relative who had recently died, and that it would be necessary for her to go to Boston to attend to the settling of the estate. He requested me to meet her at the station and render her whatever services might be necessary. On examining the date indicated as that of her arrival, I found it no later than tomorrow. He had characteristically delayed writing until, had I been away from home for a day, I must have missed the good woman altogether.

The name of Aunt Georgiana called up not alone her own figure, at once pathetic and grotesque, but opened before my feet a gulf of recollection so wide and deep, that, as the letter dropped from my hand, I felt suddenly a stranger to all the present conditions of my existence, wholly ill at ease and out of place amid the familiar surroundings of my study. I became, in short, the gangling farmer-boy my aunt had known, scourged with chilblains[1] and bashfulness, my hands cracked and sore from the cornhusking. I felt the knuckles of my thumb tentatively, as

1. **chilblains** (chil′blāns′): inflammation of the hands and feet, caused by exposure to cold.

though they were raw again. I sat again before her parlor organ, fumbling the scales with my stiff, red hands, while she, beside me, made canvas mittens for the huskers.

The next morning, after preparing my landlady somewhat, I set out for the station. When the train arrived I had some difficulty in finding my aunt. She was the last of the passengers to alight, and it was not until I got her into the carriage that she seemed really to recognize me. She had come all the way in a day coach; her linen duster had become black with soot and her black bonnet gray with dust during the journey. When we arrived at my boardinghouse the landlady put her to bed at once and I did not see her again until the next morning.

Whatever shock Mrs. Springer experienced at my aunt's appearance, she considerately concealed. As for myself, I saw my aunt's misshapen figure with that feeling of awe and respect with which we behold explorers who have left their ears and fingers north of Franz Josef Land,[2] or their health somewhere along the upper Congo. My Aunt Georgiana had been a music teacher at

2. **Franz Josef Land:** group of islands in the Arctic Ocean.

WORDS TO OWN

legacy (leg′ə·sē) *n.:* inheritance.
grotesque (grō·tesk′) *adj.:* strange; absurd.

Edith Mahon (1904) by Thomas Eakins. Oil on canvas (20″ x 16″).

Smith College Museum of Art, Northampton, Massachusetts. Purchased Drayton Hillyer Fund, 1931.

the Boston Conservatory, somewhere back in the latter sixties. One summer, while visiting in the little village among the Green Mountains where her ancestors had dwelt for generations, she had kindled the callow fancy of the most idle and shiftless of all the village lads, and had conceived for this Howard Carpenter one of those extravagant passions which a handsome country boy of twenty-one sometimes inspires in an angular, spectacled woman of thirty. When she returned to her duties in Boston, Howard followed her, and the upshot of this inexplicable infatuation was that she eloped with him, <u>eluding</u> the reproaches of her family and the criticisms of her friends by going with him to the Nebraska frontier. Carpenter, who, of course, had no money, had taken a homestead in Red Willow County, fifty miles from the railroad. There they had measured off their quarter section themselves by driving across the prairie in a wagon, to the wheel of which they had tied a red cotton handkerchief, and counting off its revolutions. They built a dugout in the red hillside, one of those cave dwellings whose inmates so often reverted to primitive conditions. Their water they got from the lagoons where the buffalo drank, and their slender stock of provisions was always at the mercy of bands of roving Indians. For thirty years my aunt had not been further than fifty miles from the homestead.

But Mrs. Springer knew nothing of all this, and must have been considerably shocked at what was left of my kinswoman. Beneath the soiled linen duster which, on her arrival, was the most conspicuous feature of her costume, she wore a black stuff[3] dress, whose ornamentation showed that she had surrendered herself unquestioningly into the hands of a country dressmaker. My poor aunt's figure, however, would have presented astonishing difficulties to any dressmaker. Originally stooped, her shoulders were now almost bent together over her sunken chest. She wore no stays,[4] and her gown, which trailed unevenly behind, rose in a sort of peak over her abdomen. She wore ill-fitting false teeth, and her skin was as yellow as a Mongolian's from constant exposure to a pitiless wind and to the alkaline water which hardens the most transparent cuticle into a sort of flexible leather.

I owed to this woman most of the good that ever came my way in my boyhood, and had a <u>reverential</u> affection for her. During the years when I was riding herd for my uncle, my aunt, after cooking the three meals—the first of which was ready at six o'clock in the morning—and putting the six children to bed, would often stand until midnight at her ironing board, with me at the kitchen table beside her, hearing me recite Latin declensions and conjugations, gently shaking me when my drowsy head sank down over a page of irregular verbs. It was to her, at her ironing or mending, that I read my first Shakespeare, and her old textbook on mythology was the first that ever came into my empty hands. She taught me my scales and exercises, too—on the little parlor organ, which her husband had bought her after fifteen years, during which she had not so much as seen any instrument, but an accordion that belonged to one of the Norwegian farmhands. She would sit beside me by the hour, darning and counting while I struggled with the "Joyous Farmer," but she seldom talked to me about music, and I understood why. She was a <u>pious</u> woman; she had the consolations of religion and, to her at least, her martyrdom was not wholly sordid. Once when I had been doggedly beating out some easy passages from an old score of *Euryanthe* I had found among her music books, she came up to me and, putting her hands over my eyes, gently drew my head back upon her shoulder, saying tremulously, "Don't love it so well, Clark, or it may be taken from you. Oh! dear boy, pray that whatever your sacrifice may be, it be not that."

When my aunt appeared on the morning after her arrival, she was still in a semisomnambulant[5] state. She seemed not to realize that she was in the city where she had spent her youth, the place longed for hungrily half a lifetime. She had been so wretchedly trainsick throughout the journey

---

5. semisomnambulant (sem′ē · säm · nam′byŏŏ · lənt): confused and unperceiving, as if sleepwalking.

WORDS TO OWN

eluding (ē · lōōd′iŋ) *v.* used as *adj.*: escaping.
reverential (rev′ə · ren′shəl) *adj.*: deeply respectful.
pious (pī′əs) *adj.*: devoted to one's religion.

---

3. stuff: cloth, usually woolen.
4. stays: a corset, or figure-enhancing women's undergarment, stiffened as with whalebone.

that she had no recollection of anything but her discomfort, and, to all intents and purposes, there were but a few hours of nightmare between the farm in Red Willow County and my study on Newbury Street. I had planned a little pleasure for her that afternoon, to repay her for some of the glorious moments she had given me when we used to milk together in the straw-thatched cowshed and she, because I was more than usually tired, or because her husband had spoken sharply to me, would tell me of the splendid performance of the *Huguenots*[6] she had seen in Paris, in her youth. At two o'clock the Symphony Orchestra was to give a Wagner program, and I intended to take my aunt; though, as I conversed with her, I grew doubtful about her enjoyment of it. Indeed, for her own sake, I could only wish her taste for such things quite dead, and the long struggle mercifully ended at last. I suggested our visiting the Conservatory and the Common before lunch, but she seemed altogether too timid to wish to venture out. She questioned me absently about various changes in the city, but she was chiefly concerned that she had forgotten to leave instructions about feeding half-skimmed milk to a certain weakling calf, "old Maggie's calf, you know, Clark," she explained, evidently having forgotten how long I had been away. She was further troubled because she had neglected to tell her daughter about the freshly opened kit of mackerel in the cellar, which would spoil if it were not used directly.

I asked her whether she had ever heard any of the Wagnerian operas, and found that she had not, though she was perfectly familiar with their respective situations, and had once possessed the piano score of *The Flying Dutchman*. I began to think it would have been best to get her back to Red Willow County without waking her, and regretted having suggested the concert.

From the time we entered the concert hall, however, she was a trifle less passive and <u>inert</u>, and for the first time seemed to perceive her surroundings. I had felt some <u>trepidation</u> lest she might become aware of the absurdities of her attire, or might experience some painful embarrassment at stepping suddenly into the world to

which she had been dead for a quarter of a century. But, again, I found how superficially I had judged her. She sat looking about her with eyes as impersonal, almost as stony, as those with which the granite Ramses[7] in a museum watches the froth and fret[8] that ebbs and flows about his pedestal—separated from it by the lonely stretch of centuries. I have seen this same aloofness in old miners who drift into the Brown Hotel at Denver, their pockets full of bullion, their linen soiled, their haggard faces unshaven; standing in the thronged corridors as solitary as though they were still in a frozen camp on the Yukon, conscious that certain experiences have isolated them from their fellows by a gulf no haberdasher[9] could bridge.

We sat at the extreme left of the first balcony, facing the arc of our own and the balcony above us, veritable hanging gardens, brilliant as tulip beds. The matinée audience was made up chiefly of women. One lost the contour of faces and figures, indeed any effect of line whatever, and there was only the color of bodices past counting, the shimmer of fabrics soft and firm, silky and sheer; red, mauve, pink, blue, lilac, purple, ecru, rose, yellow, cream, and white, all the colors that an impressionist finds in a sunlit landscape, with here and there the dead shadow of a frock coat. My Aunt Georgiana regarded them as though they had been so many daubs of tube paint on a palette.

When the musicians came out and took their places, she gave a little stir of anticipation and looked with quickening interest down over the rail at that invariable grouping, perhaps the first wholly familiar thing that had greeted her eye since she had left old Maggie and her weakling calf. I could feel how all those details sank into her soul, for I had not forgotten how they had

7. **Ramses** (ram′sēz′): one of the kings of ancient Egypt.
8. **froth and fret:** agitated waters moving around obstacles.
9. **haberdasher** (hab′ər·dash′ər): one who sells men's clothing. A men's clothing store is sometimes called a haberdashery.

WORDS TO OWN

inert (in·ʉrt′) *adj.*: inactive; dull.
trepidation (trep′ə·dā′shən) *n.*: anxious uncertainty.

---

6. *Huguenots* (hyo͞o′gə·näts): opera by Giacomo Meyerbeer about the violent struggle between Catholics and Protestants in sixteenth-century France.

sunk into mine when I came fresh from plowing forever and forever between green aisles of corn, where, as in a treadmill, one might walk from daybreak to dusk without perceiving a shadow of change. The clean profiles of the musicians, the gloss of their linen, the dull black of their coats, the beloved shapes of the instruments, the patches of yellow light thrown by the green shaded lamps on the smooth, varnished bellies of the cellos and the bass viols in the rear, the restless, wind-tossed forest of fiddle necks and bows—I recalled how, in the first orchestra I had ever heard, those long bow strokes seemed to draw the heart out of me, as a conjurer's stick reels out yards of paper ribbon from a hat.

The first number was the *Tannhäuser*[10] overture. When the horns drew out the first strain of the Pilgrim's chorus, my Aunt Georgiana clutched my coat sleeve. Then it was I first realized that for her this broke a silence of thirty years; the inconceivable silence of the plains. With the battle between the two motives, with the frenzy of the Venusberg theme and its ripping of strings, there came to me an overwhelming sense of the waste and wear we are so powerless to combat; and I saw again the tall, naked house on the prairie, black and grim as a wooden fortress; the black pond where I had learned to swim, its margin pitted with sun-dried cattle tracks; the rain-gullied clay banks about the naked house, the four dwarf ash seedlings where the dishcloths were always hung to dry before the kitchen door. The world there was the flat world of the ancients; to the east, a cornfield that stretched to daybreak; to the west, a corral that reached to sunset; between, the conquests of peace, dearer bought than those of war.

The overture closed, my aunt released my coat sleeve, but she said nothing. She sat staring at the orchestra through a dullness of thirty years, through the films made little by little by each of the three hundred and sixty-five days in every one of them. What, I wondered, did she get from it? She had been a good pianist in her day I knew, and her musical education had been broader than that of most music teachers of a quarter of a century ago. She had often told me of Mozart's operas

and Meyerbeer's, and I could remember hearing her sing, years ago, certain melodies of Verdi's. When I had fallen ill with a fever in her house she used to sit by my cot in the evening—when the cool, night wind blew in through the faded mosquito netting tacked over the window and I lay watching a certain bright star that burned red above the cornfield—and sing "Home to our mountains, O, let us return!" in a way fit to break the heart of a Vermont boy near dead of homesickness already.

I watched her closely through the prelude to *Tristan and Isolde,* trying vainly to conjecture what that seething turmoil of strings and winds might mean to her, but she sat mutely staring at the violin bows that drove obliquely downward, like the pelting streaks of rain in a summer shower. Had this music any message for her? Had she enough left to at all comprehend this power which had kindled the world since she had left it? I was in a fever of curiosity, but Aunt Georgiana sat silent upon her peak in Darien.[11] She preserved this utter immobility throughout the number from *The Flying Dutchman,* though her fingers worked mechanically upon her black dress, as though, of themselves, they were recalling the piano score they had once played. Poor old hands! They had been stretched and twisted into mere tentacles to hold and lift and knead with; the palms unduly swollen, the fingers bent and knotted—on one of them a thin, worn band that had once been a wedding ring. As I pressed and gently quieted one of those groping hands, I remembered with quivering eyelids their services for me in other days.

Soon after the tenor began the "Prize Song,"[12] I heard a quick drawn breath and turned to my aunt. Her eyes were closed, but the tears were glistening on her cheeks, and I think, in a moment more, they were in my eyes as well. It never really died, then—the soul that can suffer so excruciatingly

11. **silent . . . Darien:** allusion to John Keats's "On First Looking into Chapman's Homer," a poem about Keats's awe in the presence of a literary work of art.

12. **"Prize Song":** aria from the third act of Wagner's opera *Die Meistersinger von Nürnberg.*

10. *Tannhäuser* (tän′hoi′zər): Wagner's opera about German minstrels in the thirteenth century.

WORDS TO OWN

obliquely (ō·blēk′lē) *adv.:* at a slant.

watched
her
closely
through
the
prelude
to
*Tristan
and
Isolde,*
trying
vainly
to

At the Opera (1879) by Mary Cassatt.
Oil on canvas (31½″ × 25½″).

conjecture what that seething
turmoil of strings and winds might
mean to her, but she sat mutely
staring at the violin bows that drove
obliquely downward...

and so interminably; it withers to the outward eye only; like that strange moss which can lie on a dusty shelf half a century and yet, if placed in water, grows green again. She wept so throughout the development and elaboration of the melody.

During the intermission before the second half of the concert, I questioned my aunt and found that the "Prize Song" was not new to her. Some years before there had drifted to the farm in Red Willow County a young German, a tramp cowpuncher, who had sung the chorus at Bayreuth,[13] when he was a boy, along with the other peasant boys and girls. Of a Sunday morning he used to sit on his gingham-sheeted bed in the hands' bedroom which opened off the kitchen, cleaning the leather of his boots and saddle, singing the "Prize Song," while my aunt went about her work in the kitchen. She had hovered about him until she had prevailed upon him to join the country church, though his sole fitness for this step, in so far as I could gather, lay in his boyish face and his possession of this divine melody. Shortly afterward he had gone to town on the Fourth of July, been drunk for several days, lost his money at a faro[14] table, ridden a saddled Texan steer on a bet, and disappeared with a fractured collarbone. All this my aunt told me huskily, wanderingly, as though she were talking in the weak lapses of illness.

"Well, we have come to better things than the old *Trovatore*[15] at any rate, Aunt Georgie?" I queried, with a well-meant effort at jocularity.

Her lip quivered and she hastily put her handkerchief up to her mouth. From behind it she murmured, "And you have been hearing this ever since you left me, Clark?" Her question was the gentlest and saddest of reproaches.

The second half of the program consisted of four numbers from the *Ring,*[16] and closed with Siegfried's funeral march. My aunt wept quietly, but almost continuously, as a shallow vessel overflows in a rainstorm. From time to time her dim eyes looked up at the lights which studded the ceiling, burning softly under their dull glass globes; doubtless they were stars in truth to her. I was still perplexed as to what measure of musical comprehension was left to her, she who had heard nothing but the singing of gospel hymns at Methodist services in the square frame schoolhouse on Section Thirteen for so many years. I was wholly unable to gauge how much of it had been dissolved in soapsuds, or worked into bread, or milked into the bottom of a pail.

The deluge of sound poured on and on; I never knew what she found in the shining current of it; I never knew how far it bore her, or past what happy islands. From the trembling of her face I could well believe that before the last numbers she had been carried out where the myriad graves are, into the gray, nameless burying grounds of the sea; or into some world of death vaster yet, where, from the beginning of the world, hope has lain down with hope and dream with dream and, renouncing, slept.

The concert was over; the people filed out of the hall chattering and laughing, glad to relax and find the living level again, but my kinswoman made no effort to rise. The harpist slipped its green felt cover over his instrument; the flute players shook the water from their mouthpieces; the men of the orchestra went out one by one, leaving the stage to the chairs and music stands, empty as a winter cornfield.

I spoke to my aunt. She burst into tears and sobbed pleadingly. "I don't want to go, Clark, I don't want to go!"

I understood. For her, just outside the door of the concert hall, lay the black pond with the cattle-tracked bluffs; the tall, unpainted house, with weather-curled boards; naked as a tower, the crook-backed ash seedlings where the dishcloths hung to dry; the gaunt, molting turkeys picking up refuse about the kitchen door.

---

13. **Bayreuth** (bī·roit′): Bavarian city that hosts an annual festival of Wagnerian music.
14. **faro** (fer′ō): gambling game played with cards.
15. ***Trovatore*** (trô′vä·tô′rā): opera by the Italian composer Giuseppe Verdi.
16. ***Ring:*** Wagner's *Der Ring des Nibelungen,* a cycle of four operas based on traditional Germanic, Scandinavian, and Icelandic myths and legends.

WORDS TO OWN

deluge (del′yōōj′) *n.:* rush; flood.
myriad (mir′ē·əd) *adj.:* countless.

MAKING MEANINGS

First Thoughts

1. Georgiana says about music, "Don't love it so well, Clark, or it may be taken from you." How do you feel about her attitude?

Shaping Interpretations

2. Locate passages in which Clark, the first-person narrator, actually acts as an **omniscient narrator.** How would you characterize Clark? Why do you think Cather didn't use a woman's voice to tell this story?

3. In contrast to the music and the concert hall is the emotional effect of the Nebraska frontier—the **setting** we hear about over and over again in the story. How does Cather want you to feel about the Nebraska setting? What specific images create this "feeling"?

4. Summarize in your own words what you think Clark "understands" at the end of the story.

5. What seems to be Cather's **theme** in the story? How would you say the central episode of the concert contributes to this theme?

Connecting with the Text

6. Would you have attended the concert or avoided it? Why? (Refer to your Quick-write notes in your answer.)

Extending the Text

7. If this story were told by a Romantic, how would Aunt Georgiana's visit to Boston have turned out? How do you think a Romantic writer would have described the Nebraska farm setting?

Reading Check

a. Numerous **flash-backs** in the story provide information about Aunt Georgiana's life after her move to Nebraska. Describe some of her hardships and disappointments.

b. Explain why the narrator feels he owes a great debt to Aunt Georgiana. What special treat has he planned for Aunt Georgiana in Boston? How does she react to this opportunity?

CHOICES: Building Your Portfolio

Writer's Notebook

1. Collecting Ideas for an Analysis of Causes and Effects

The powerful attraction of music is a **theme** that often recurs in Cather's fiction. Find recordings of some of the works of Richard Wagner. As you listen, write down your feelings about the emotional effects of this music. Speculate on the effect Wagner's music might have had on Georgiana's imagination and feelings. Do you think Cather succeeded in conveying the emotional effects anyone might experience in listening to any kind of music? Save your notes for possible use in the Writer's Workshop on page 685.

Comparing Characters Across Texts

2. Linked Lives

In what ways is Aunt Georgiana's experience like the experience of Mrs. Sommers in Kate Chopin's story "A Pair of Silk Stockings" (page 437)? Write a brief essay comparing the two women and their afternoons of escape. For each character, consider her life at the beginning of the story, her past life, her wants and needs, and her reactions to her "escape."

Creative Writing

3. The Power of a Setting

Cather's imagery creates a striking contrast between two very different **settings**—a bustling city with its rich cultural life and an isolated, windswept farm. Write a description of two very different settings that you might use in a short story. Create clear images and details to convey the distinct emotional impact of each setting.

Thomas Wolfe

(1900–1938)

Thomas Wolfe is among the most autobiographical of all American writers. His fiction actually chronicles the events of his Southern upbringing and his later life in New York and Europe.

The youngest of eight children, Wolfe was born in the Smoky Mountains of Asheville, North Carolina. Much of his fiction centers on a character named Eugene Gant, who is the youngest child in a large Southern family and whose life parallels Wolfe's own. When Wolfe was six years old, his parents separated. His mother ran a boardinghouse, which she called The Old Kentucky Home; Wolfe's father, given to bouts of violent drinking, lived a few blocks away behind his stonecutting shop. The boy, very unhappy with the new situation, lived with his mother. Her boardinghouse appears repeatedly in Wolfe's fiction, usually depicted in an unpleasant light.

Culver Pictures.

Wolfe entered the University of North Carolina when he was sixteen. His extraordinary height, six feet six inches, was one reason he was so self-conscious all his life. After graduating in 1920, Wolfe studied playwriting at Harvard. In 1924, he moved to New York City, where he taught at New York University and tried, without success, to have his plays produced. That same year he made the first of seven trips to Europe that he would make during his lifetime.

In 1925, Wolfe became involved with Aline Bernstein, a woman much older than he was; he later wrote extensively about this affair in *The Web and the Rock*. Bernstein and Wolfe spent five years together, in England and in New York, where Wolfe continued to teach and to work on his first and best novel, *Look Homeward, Angel*.

Wolfe completed *Look Homeward, Angel* in 1928; the first draft is said to have filled up more than one suitcase. After several publishers rejected it, Scribner's showed interest. As a result, Wolfe began what would become a remarkable association with Maxwell Perkins, the famous editor who persuaded Wolfe to cut three hundred pages, or about one third, from his enormous story and saw the novel through to publication in 1929.

Wolfe eventually ended his association with Perkins and Scribner's. Before his sudden death in 1938 from an illness, Wolfe had signed up with another publisher, Harper's, and had delivered to them enormous chunks of a new manuscript. Another editor labored over the mass of material and, after Wolfe's death, published several posthumous books, including *You Can't Go Home Again* (1940).

Some readers believe that Wolfe's editors did Wolfe a disservice by reducing his manuscripts to the size of manageable novels. They think that Wolfe wanted to create one huge epic work of fiction based on his own life, just as Walt Whitman had crafted an American epic in "Song of Myself" (page 353). In many ways, Wolfe's greatness can be measured by the magnitude of what he tried, and failed, to accomplish. As William Faulkner (page 713) noted, Thomas Wolfe was "the best failure," a writer who dared "to throw away style, coherence, all the rules of preciseness, to try to put all the experience of the human heart on the head of a pin."

548 THE MODERNS

go.hrw.com
LEO 11-11

Make the Connection

When the Circus Comes to Town

In the past, when much of the United States was made up of small towns and rural areas, the most exciting annual event was the coming of the circus. It began with a parade—colorfully dressed band members, a calliope piping its shrill steam-whistle notes, wild animals roaring in rolling cages, elephants lumbering along in single file, bareback riders on prancing ponies, and a wild array of clowns, acrobats, and jugglers. No wonder many young observers harbored the secret dream of running away to join the circus—it was the embodiment of fantasy and adventure.

Reading Skills and Strategies

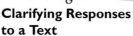

Clarifying Responses to a Text

The young dreamer in this story—perhaps Wolfe himself—imagines himself joining the circus to sell tickets, put up posters, and barter with farmers for fresh food. As you read, take notes on the effects his fantasy has on you. In what ways is it like a fairy tale? Do you feel pleasantly swept along in his fantasy, or does it create another response in you? As you read through to the end of the story, write your ideas about what "magic congruence" is shared by his "father's earth" and the circus as Wolfe describes it.

Elements of Literature

Description

Just as Napoleon realized the importance of food for his troops ("An army marches on its stomach"), so Wolfe in this story envisions a circus troupe eating its way through forty states. Wolfe's daydream, an exuberant **description** of the states' geographical features and abundant crops, coincides with the daydream of arriving at his father's house—a place that is not real but is pure fantasy. As you read, look for Wolfe's long descriptive lists of foods, people, and places.

> **D**escription is a form of writing that uses sensory language to create images and to convey moods or emotions.
>
> *For more on Description, see the Handbook of Literary Terms.*

American circus posters from the 1920s and 1930s.

The Granger Collection, New York.

Stone City, Iowa (1930) by Grant Wood. Oil on wood panel (30¼″ x 40″).
Joslyn Art Museum, Omaha, Nebraska (1930.35). © Estate of Grant Wood/Licensed by VAGA, New York, NY.

His Father's Earth

Thomas Wolfe

As the boy stood looking at the circus with his brother, there came to him two images, which had haunted his childhood and the life of every boy who ever lived, but were now for the first time seen together with an instant and magic congruence.[1] And these two images were the images of the circus and his father's earth.

He thought then he had joined a circus and started on the great tour of the nation with it. It was spring: The circus had started in New England and worked westward and then southward as the summer and autumn came on. His nominal

duties—for, in his vision, every incident, each face and voice and circumstance were blazing real as life itself—were those of ticket seller, but in this tiny show, everyone did several things: The performers helped put up and take down the tents, load and unload the wagons, and the roustabouts[2] and business people worked wherever they were needed.

The boy sold tickets, but he also posted bills and bartered with tradesmen and farmers in new places for fresh food. He became very shrewd and clever at this work, and loved to do it—some old,

2. **roustabouts** (roust′ə·bouts′): circus workers who handle various duties, including setting up and taking down tents.

- -

WORDS TO OWN
nominal (näm′ə·nəl) *adj.*: very small.

- -

1. **congruence** (kän′grōō·əns): harmony.

sharp, buried talent for shrewd trading, that had come to him from his mountain blood, now aided him. He could get the finest, freshest meats and vegetables at the lowest prices. The circus people were tough and hard, they always had a fierce and ravenous hunger, they would not accept bad food and cooking, they fed stupendously, and they always had the best of everything.

Usually the circus would arrive at a new town very early in the morning, before daybreak. He would go into town immediately: He would go to the markets, or with farmers who had come in for the circus. He felt and saw the purity of first light, he heard the sweet and sudden lutings of first birds, and suddenly he was filled with the earth and morning in new towns, among new men: He walked among the farmers' wagons, and he dealt with them on the spot for the <u>prodigal</u> plenty of their wares—the country melons bedded in sweet hay of wagons, the cool sweet prints of butter wrapped in clean wet cloths, with dew and starlight still on them, the enormous battered cans foaming with fresh milk, the new laid eggs which he bought by the gross and hundred dozens, the tender limy pullets by the score, the rude country wagons laden to the rim with heaped abundancies—with delicate bunches of green scallions, the heavy red ripeness of huge tomatoes, the sweet-leaved lettuces crisp as celery, the fresh podded peas and the succulent young beans, as well as the potatoes spotted with the loamy earth, the powerful winey odor of the apples, the peaches, and the cherries, the juicy corn stacked up in shocks of living green, and the heavy blackened rinds of home-cured hams and bacons.

As the market opened, he would begin to trade and dicker with the butchers for their finest cuts of meat: They would hold great roasts up in their gouted[3] fingers, they would roll up tubs of fresh ground sausage, they would smack with their long palms the flanks of beeves[4] and porks: He would drive back to the circus with a wagon full of meat and vegetables.

At the circus ground the people were already in full activity. He could hear the wonderful timed tattoo[5] of sledges on driven stakes, the shouts of men riding animals down to water, the slow clank and pull of mighty horses, the heavy rumble of the wagons as they rolled down off the circus flatcars. By now the eating table would be erected, and as he arrived, he could see the cooks already busy at their ranges, the long tables set up underneath the canvas with their rows of benches, their tin plates and cups, their strong readiness. There would be the amber indescribable pungency of strong coffee, and the smell of buckwheat batter.

And the circus people would come in for their breakfast: Hard and tough, for the most part decent and serious people, the performers, the men and women, the acrobats, the riders, the tumblers, the clowns, the jugglers, the contortionists, and the balancers would come in quietly and eat with a savage and inspired intentness.

The food they ate was as masculine and fragrant as the world they dwelt in: It belonged to the stained world of mellow sun-warmed canvas, the clean and healthful odor of the animals, and the mild sweet lyric nature of the land in which they lived as wanderers, and it was there for the asking with a fabulous and stupefying plenty, golden and embrowned: They ate stacks of buckwheat cakes, smoking hot, soaked in hunks of yellow butter which they carved at will with a wide free gesture from the piled prints on the table, and which they <u>garnished</u> (if they pleased) with ropes of heavy black molasses, or with the lighter, freer maple syrup.

They ate big steaks for breakfast, hot from the pan and lashed with onions, they ate whole melons, crammed with the ripeness of the deep pink meat, rashers of bacon, and great platters of fried eggs, or eggs scrambled with calves' brains, they helped themselves from pyramids of fruit piled up at intervals on the table—plums, peaches, apples, cherries, grapes, oranges, and bananas—they had great pitchers of thick cream to pour on everything, and they washed their hunger down with pint mugs of strong deep-savored coffee.

---

5. tattoo: pounding.

- -

WORDS TO OWN

prodigal (präd′i·gəl) *adj.*: extremely abundant.
garnished (gär′nisht) *v.*: topped.

- -

---

3. gouted (gout′id): swollen from gout, a kind of arthritis that usually affects the joints in the fingers or toes.
4. beeves: alternate plural of *beef*.

For their midday meal they would eat fiercely, hungrily, with wolfish gusts, mightily, with knit brows and convulsive movements of their corded throats. They would eat great roasts of beef with crackled hides, browned in their juices, rare and tender, hot chunks of delicate pork with hems of fragrant fat, delicate young boiled chickens, only a mouthful for these ravenous jaws, twelve-pound pot roasts cooked for hours in an iron pot with new carrots, onions, sprouts, and young potatoes, together with every vegetable that the season yielded: huge roasting ears of corn, smoking hot, stacked like cordwood on two-foot platters, tomatoes cut in slabs with wedges of okra and succotash, and raw onion, mashed potatoes whipped to a creamy smother, boats swimming with pure beef gravy, new carrots, turnips, fresh peas cooked in butter, and fat string beans seasoned with the flavor of big chunks of cooking-pork. In addition, they had every fruit that the place and time afforded: hot crusty apple, peach and cherry pies, encrusted with cinnamon, puddings and cakes of every sort, and blobbering cobblers inches deep.

Thus the circus moved across America, from town to town, from state to state, eating its way from Maine into the great plains of the West, eating its way along the Hudson and the Mississippi Rivers, eating its way across the prairies and from the North into the South, eating its way across the flat farmlands of the Pennsylvania Dutch colony, the eastern shore of Maryland and back again across the states of Virginia, North Carolina, Tennessee, and Florida—eating all good things that this enormous, this inevitably bountiful and abundant cornucopia[6] of a continent yielded.

They ate the cod, bass, mackerel, halibut, clams, and oysters of the New England coast, the terrapin[7] of Maryland, the fat beeves, porks, and cereals of the Middle West, and they had, as well, the heavy juicy peaches, watermelons, cantaloupes of Georgia, the fat sweet shad of the Carolina coasts, and the rounded and exotic citrus fruits of the tropics: the oranges, tangerines, bananas, kumquats, lemons, guavas down in Florida,

together with a hundred other fruits and meats—the Vermont turkeys, the mountain trout, the bunched heaviness of the Concord grapes, the red winey bulk of the Oregon apples, as well as the clawed, shelled, and crusted dainties, the crabs, the clams, the pink-meated lobsters that grope their way along the sea floors of America.

The boy awoke at morning in three hundred towns with the glimmer of starlight on his face; he was the moon's man; then he saw light quicken in the east, he saw the pale stars drown, he saw the birth of light, he heard the lark's wing, the bird tree, the first liquorous liquefied lutings, the ripe-aired trillings, the plumskinned bird-notes, and he heard the hoof and wheel come down the streets of the nation. He exulted in his work as food-producer for the circus people, and they loved him for it. They said there had never been anyone like him—they banqueted exult-antly, with hoarse gulpings and with joy, and they loved him.

Slowly, day by day, the circus worked its way across America, through forty states and through a dozen weathers. It was a little world that moved across the enormous loneliness of the earth, a little world that each day began a new life in new cities, and that left nothing to betray where it had been save a litter of beaten papers, the droppings of the camel and the elephant in Illinois, a patch of trampled grass, and a magical memory.

The circus men knew no other earth but this; the earth came to them with the smell of the canvas and the lion's roar. They saw the world behind the lights of the carnival, and everything beyond these lights was phantasmal and unreal to them; it lived for them within the circle of the tent as men and women who sat on benches, as the posts they came to, and sometimes as the enemy.

Their life was filled with the strong joy of food, with the love of traveling, and with danger and hard labor. Always there was the swift violence of change and movement, of putting up and tearing down, and sometimes there was the misery of rain and sleet, and mud above the ankles, of wind that shook their flimsy residence, that ripped the tent stakes from their moorings in the earth and

---

6. **cornucopia** (kôr′nyo͞o·kō′pē·ə): Also called a horn of plenty, a cornucopia is a symbol of fullness and abundance.

7. **terrapin** (ter′ə·pin): turtles.

WORDS TO OWN

exulted (eg·zult′id) v.: rejoiced greatly.

lifted out the great center pole as if it were a match. Now they must wrestle with the wind and hold their dwelling to the earth; now they must fight the weariness of mud and push their heavy wagons through the slime; now, cold and wet and wretched, they must sleep on piles of canvas, upon the flatcars in a driving rain, and sometimes they must fight the enemy—the drunk, the savage, the violent enemy, the bloody man, who dwelt in every place. Sometimes it was the city thug, sometimes the mill hands of the South, sometimes the miners in a Pennsylvania town— the circus people cried, "Hey, rube!"[8] and fought them with fist and foot, with pike and stake, and the boy saw and knew it all.

8. rube: unsophisticated person, usually from the country. The term is used as a taunt.

When the men in a little town barricaded the street against their parade, they charged the barricade with their animals, and once the sheriff tried to stop the elephant by saying: "Now, damn ye, if you stick your . . . damned trunk another inch, I'll shoot."

The circus moved across America foot by foot, mile by mile. He came to know the land. It was rooted in his blood and his brain forever—its food, its fruit, its fields and forests, its deserts, and its mountains, its savage lawlessness. He saw the crimes and the violence of the people with pity, with mercy, and with tenderness: He thought of them as if they were children. They smashed their neighbors' brains out with an ax, they disemboweled one another with knives, they were murderous and lost upon this earth they dwelt upon as strangers.

Fall Plowing (1931) by Grant Wood. Oil on canvas.
From the Deere & Company Art Collection, Moline, Illinois.

The tongueless blood of the murdered men ran down into the earth, and the earth received it. Upon this enormous and indifferent earth the little trains rattled on over ill-joined rails that loosely bound the sprawling little towns together. Lost and lonely, brief sawings of wood and plaster and cheap brick ugliness, the little towns were scattered like encampments through the wilderness. Only the earth remained, which all these people had barely touched, which all these people dwelt upon but could not possess.

Only the earth remained, the savage and lyrical earth with its rude potency, its thousand <u>vistas</u>, its heights and slopes and levels, with all its violence and delicacy, the terrible fecundity,[9] decay, and growth, its fierce colors, its vital bite and sparkle, its exultancy of space and wandering. And the memory of this earth, the memory of all this universe of sight and sense, was rooted in this boy's heart and brain forever. It fed the hungers of desire and wandering, it breached the walls of his secret and withdrawn spirit. And for every memory of place and continent, of enormous coffee-colored rivers and eight hundred miles of bending wheat, of Atlantic coast and midland prairie, of raw red Piedmont[10] and tropic flatness, there was always the small, fecund, perfect memory of his father's land, the dark side of his soul and his heart's desire, which he had never seen, but which he knew with every atom of his life, the strange phantasmal haunting of man's memory. It was a fertile, nobly swelling land, and it was large enough to live in, walled with fulfilled desire.

Abroad in this ocean of earth and vision he thought of his father's land, of its great red barns and nobly swelling earth, its clear familiarity and its haunting strangeness, and its dark and secret heart, its magnificent, its lovely and tragic beauty. He thought of its smell of harbors and its rumors of the seas, the city, and the ships, its wine-red apples and its brown-red soil, its snug weathered houses, and its lyric unutterable ecstasy.

A wonderful thing happened. One morning he awoke suddenly to find himself staring straight up at the pulsing splendor of the stars. At first he did not know where he was, but he knew instantly,

even before he looked about him, that he had visited this place before. The circus train had stopped in the heart of the country, for what reason he did not know. He could hear the <u>languid</u> and <u>intermittent</u> breathing of the engine, the strangeness of men's voices in the dark, the casual stamp of the horses in their cars, and all around him the attentive and vital silence of the earth.

Suddenly he raised himself from the pile of canvas on which he slept. It was the moment just before dawn: Against the east, the sky had already begun to whiten with the first faint luminosity of day, the invading tides of light crept up the sky, drowning the stars out as they went. The train had halted by a little river which ran swift and deep next to the tracks, and now he knew that what at first had been the sound of silence was the swift and ceaseless music of the river.

There had been rain the night before, and now the river was filled with the sweet clean rain-drenched smell of earthy deposits. He could see the delicate white glimmer of young birch trees leaning from the banks, and on the other side he saw the winding whiteness of the road. Beyond the road, and bordering it, there was an orchard with a wall of lichened stone: A row of apple trees, gnarled and sweet, spread their squat twisted branches out across the road, and in the faint light he saw that they were dense with blossoms: The cool intoxication of their fragrance overpowered him.

As the wan light grew, the earth and all its contours emerged sharply, and he saw again the spare, gaunt loneliness of the earth at dawn, with all its sweet and sudden cries of spring. He saw the worn and ancient design of lichened rocks, the fertile soil of the baked fields, he saw the kept order, the <u>frugal</u> cleanliness, with its springtime overgrowth, the mild tang of <u>opulent</u> greenery. There was an earth with fences, as big as a man's heart, but not so great as his desire, and after his

---

9. **fecundity** (fē·kun′də·tē): fertility.
10. **Piedmont** (pēd′mänt): hilly land east of the Appalachian Mountains.

WORDS TO OWN

vistas (vis′təz) *n. pl.*: views.
languid (laŋ′gwid) *adj.*: weak, as from exhaustion.
intermittent (in′tər·mit′′nt) *adj.*: pausing occasionally.
frugal (frōo′gəl) *adj.*: thrifty; economical.
opulent (äp′yōo·lənt) *adj.*: abundant; plentiful.

Spring Turning (1936) by Grant Wood. Oil on Masonite panel (18⅛″ x 40″).
Reynolda House, Museum of American Art, Winston-Salem, North Carolina. © Estate of Grant Wood/Licensed by VAGA, New York, NY.

giant wanderings over the prodigal fecundity of the continent, this earth was like a room he once had lived in. He returned to it as a sailor to a small closed harbor, as a man, spent with the hunger of his wandering, comes home.

Instantly he recognized the scene. He knew that he had come at last into his father's land. It was a magic that he knew but could not speak; he stood upon the lip of time, and all of his life now seemed the mirage of some wizard's spell—the spell of canvas and the circus ring, the spell of the tented world which had possessed him. Here was his home, brought back to him while he slept, like a forgotten dream. Here was the dark side of his soul, his heart's desire, his father's country, the earth his spirit dwelt on as a child. He knew every inch of the landscape, and he knew, past reason, doubt, or argument, that home was not three miles away.

He got up at once and leaped down to the earth; he knew where he would go. Along the track there was the slow swing and dance of the brakemen's lamps, that moving, mournful, and beautiful cloud of light along the rails of the earth, that he had seen so many times. Already the train was in motion; its bell tolled and its heavy trucks rumbled away from him. He began to walk back along the tracks, for

less than a mile away, he knew, where the stream boiled over the lip of a dam, there was a bridge. When he reached the bridge, a deeper light had come: The old red brick of the mill emerged sharply and with the tone and temper of deep joy fell sheer into bright shining waters.

He crossed the bridge and turned left along the road: Here it moved away from the river, among fields and through dark woods—dark woods bordered with stark poignancy of fir and pine, with the noble spread of maples, shot with the naked whiteness of birch. Here was the woodland maze: the sweet density of the brake[11] and growth. Sharp thrummings, woodland flitters broke the silence. His steps grew slow, he sat upon a wall, he waited.

Now rose the birdsong in first light, and suddenly he heard each sound the birdsong made. Like a flight of shot the sharp fast skaps of sound arose. With chittering bicker, fast-fluttering skirrs of sound, the palmy honeyed bird-cries came. Smooth drops and nuggets of bright gold they were. Now sang the birdtrees filled with lutings in bright air: The thrums, the lark's wing, and tongue-trilling chirrs arose now. The little name-

11. **brake:** thicket; marshy, overgrown area.

less cries arose and fell with liquorous liquefied lutings, with lirruping chirp, plumbellied smoothness, sweet lucidity.

And now there was the rapid kweet kweet kweet kweet kweet of homing birds and their pwee pwee pwee: others with sharp cricketing stitch, a mosquito buzz with thin metallic tongues, while some with rusty creakings, high shrew's caws, with eerie rasp, with harsh far calls—all birds that are awake in the sweet woodland tangles: And above, there passed the whirr of hidden wings, the strange lost cry of the unknown birds, in full flight now; in which the sweet confusion of their cries was mingled.

Then he got up and went along that road where, he knew, like the prophetic surmise of a dream, the house of his father's blood and kin lay hidden. At length, he came around a bending in the road, he left the wooded land, he passed by hedges and saw the old white house, set in the shoulder of the hill, worn like care and habit in the earth; clean and cool, it sat below the clean dark shelter of its trees: A twist of morning smoke coiled through its chimney.

Then he turned in to the rutted road that led up to the house, and at this moment the enormous figure of a powerful old man appeared around the corner prophetically bearing a smoked ham in one huge hand. And when the boy saw the old man, a cry of greeting burst from his throat, and the old man answered with a roar of welcome that shook the earth.

Then the old man dropped his ham, and waddled forward to meet the boy: They met half down the road, and the old man crushed him in his hug; they tried to speak but could not; they embraced again and in an instant all the years of wandering, the pain of loneliness and the fierce hungers of desire, were scoured away like a scum of frost from a bright glass.

He was a child again, he was a child that had stood upon the lip and leaf of time and heard the quiet tides that move us to our death, and he knew that the child could not be born again, the book of the days could never be turned back, old errors and confusions never righted. And he wept with sorrow for all that was lost and could never be regained, and with joy for all that had been recovered.

Suddenly he saw his youth as men on hilltops might look at the whole winding course of rivers to the sea, he saw the blind confusions of his wanderings across the earth, the horror of man's little stricken mote of earth against immensity, and he remembered the proud exultancy of his childhood when all the world lay like a coin between his palms, when he could have touched the horned rim of the moon, when heroes and great actions bent before him.

And he wept, not for himself, but out of love and pity for every youth that ever hoped and wandered and was alone. He had become a man, and he had in him unique glory that belongs to men alone, and that makes them great, and from which they shape their mightiest songs and legends. For out of their pain they utter first a cry for wounded self, then, as their vision deepens, widens, the universe of their marvelous sense leaps out and grips the universe; they feel contempt for gods, respect for men alone, and with the indifference of a selfless passion, enact earth out of a lyric cry.

At this moment, also, two young men burst from the house and came running down the road to greet him. They were powerful and heavy young men, already beginning to show signs of that epic and sensual grossness that distinguished their father. Like their father, they recognized the boy instantly, and in a moment he was engulfed in their mighty energies, borne up among them to the house. And they understood all he wanted to say, but could not speak, and they surrounded him with love and lavish heapings of his plate. And the boy knew the strange miracle of return to the dark land of his heart's desire, the father's land which haunts men like a dream they never knew.

Such were the twin images of the circus and his father's land which were to haunt his dreams and waking memory and which now, as he stood there with his brother looking at the circus, fused instantly to a living whole and came to him in a blaze of light.

And in this way, before he had ever set foot upon it, he came for the first time to his father's earth.

WORDS TO OWN
surmise (sər·mīz′) *n.*: guess.

MAKING MEANINGS

First Thoughts

1. Look back over the notes you made while reading. What words would you use to describe your response to this story?

Reading Check

a. Which words or passages tell you that Wolfe is describing a fantasy and not reality?

b. What examples of **onomatopoeia, alliteration,** and other poetic devices give Wolfe's story the "sound" of poetry?

Shaping Interpretations

2. Wolfe depicts the father as a nurturer—a male version of the "earth mother." What details help create that picture?

3. How does the world of the circus differ from "his father's earth"? What similarities are there in what the boy does and what the father represents?

4. How do **descriptions** of birdsong bring together descriptions of circus life and of home?

5. Wolfe is famous for evocative descriptions that are presented like the **catalogs** of Walt Whitman (page 348). Select one passage of description in Wolfe's story, and identify the sense or senses to which each image appeals: sight, taste, smell, hearing, or touch.

Extending the Text

6. Scenes in this story resemble other famous "reunion" scenes in literature. In Homer's *Odyssey*, Odysseus returns home after a twenty-year absence and is reunited with his aged father, who is tending vines. If you are familiar with the parable of the Prodigal Son in the New Testament (Luke 15:11–32), explain whether you think Wolfe's father-son reunion bears any resemblance to the reunion described there. Is the boy in this story a prodigal son? Why or why not?

CHOICES: Building Your Portfolio

Writer's Notebook

1. Collecting Ideas for an Analysis of Causes and Effects

Imagine that you are writing a biography of a writer. Brainstorm a list of questions you would ask your subject about what had influenced him or her. Influences might include family, friends, ideas, and the work of other writers. Save your notes for possible use in the Writer's Workshop on page 685.

Comparing Prose and Poetry

2. Two Grand Styles

Reread Walt Whitman's poetry (pages 352–362), especially the verses from "Song of Myself." In a brief essay, compare Whitman's style with Wolfe's. Gather details in a chart like the one below.

	Whitman	Wolfe
1. Use of catalogs		
2. Celebration of everyday people		
3. Celebration of America		
4. Emotional effect		

Creative Writing

3. Details, Details

Write a Wolfe-like description of a place you know well. Include a wide variety of people or items, and build up a **catalog** of details that capture the atmosphere of the place. Use rich, sensory details to imitate Wolfe's exuberant style.

Robert Frost

(1874–1963)

Although Robert Frost is the poet whom Americans most closely identify with New England, he was born in San Francisco, California. Frost was about ten years old before he first saw the New England landscapes and knew the changing seasons that he would later describe with the familiarity of a native son. The boy's move across the country was the result of his father's early death and his mother's decision to settle in the industrial town of Lawrence, Massachusetts. After high school in Lawrence, Frost entered Dartmouth College in New Hampshire. He decided after a few months that he was not yet ready for higher education, and he returned to Lawrence to work in the cotton mills and to write. His verse, however, found little favor with magazine editors.

Married and with a growing family, Frost in his early twenties finally began to feel the need for a more formal education than his random reading could provide. He took his family to Cambridge, Massachusetts, where he entered Harvard and stayed for less than two years. He later wrote of his decision to leave: "Harvard had taken me away from the question of whether I could write or not."

Frost earned a living as a schoolteacher and as an editor before deciding to try farming. For ten years, Frost tilled the stony New Hampshire soil on thirty acres that his grandfather had bought for him. But he decided that the concentration necessary for writing poetry did not mix with the round-the-clock physical effort of working the land. Discouraged, he returned to teaching full time for a few years; then, in 1912, he sought a complete change of scene by taking his family to England.

From Scribbler to Scribe

The move turned out to be a wise one. Stimulated by meeting English poets, Frost continued to write poetry, though he found his subjects in

The Bettmann Archive.

New England. In the three years he spent in England, he completed the two volumes that would make him famous—*A Boy's Will* (1913) and *North of Boston* (1914). These collections included several poems that would stand among Frost's best-known works: "The Tuft of Flowers," "In Hardwood Groves," "Mending Wall," "The Death of the Hired Man," and "After Apple-Picking." These poems were marked by a flinty realism and an impressive mastery of iambic rhythm, narrative dialogue, and the dramatic monologue.

When Frost returned to New Hampshire in 1915, he was no longer an obscure scribbler intent on turning New England folkways into poetry; he was an accomplished writer who had already extended the scope and character of

go.hrw.com

LE0 11-11

American literature into the twentieth century. In 1916, the publication of *Mountain Interval*—a collection that included such favorites as "The Road Not Taken," "'Out, Out—,'" and "Birches"—solidified his fame. Rewarded with many prizes (including four Pulitzer Prizes and a Congressional Medal), numerous honorary degrees, and the faithful attention of a wide readership, Frost spent the rest of his life as a lecturer at a number of colleges and as a public performer who, as he put it, liked to "say" rather than to recite his poetry.

Poet of the People

On stage, Frost in his later years became a character of his own creation—a lovable, fumbling old gent who could nevertheless pierce the minds and hearts of those able to see beyond his playacting. In private, he was apt to put aside this guileless character and become a sometimes wicked commentator on the pretensions of rival poets; and he could be just as cutting to gushing devotees, who were unaware that he held in contempt the very flattery he demanded.

On Inauguration Day, 1961, standing bareheaded in a bright, cold wind beside President John F. Kennedy on the Capitol steps in Washington, D.C., Frost recited "The Gift Outright." His art with words had brought him not only the friendship of a president (who was half his age) but also, by means of radio and television, the largest single audience in history for a poet up until that time.

In a period when poetry was being changed by verbal experiment and by exotic influences from abroad, Frost remained devoted to traditional forms and firmly rooted in American soil. If, at the time of his death, he seemed to belong more to the past than to the present, his reputation today is secure. Neither the cranky realism nor the homely philosophy of self-reliance and spiritual independence that mark his work have been forgotten. He was an artist who developed his talents with stubborn persistence, and he created a unique voice that remained unaffected by the clamor of modernism.

Frost on Frost's Diction

It has been a long time since I used any word not common in everyday speech. For example, I would never think of using the word "casement" for window in general. Whenever I have used that word, which I have occasionally, it was because I was writing about *that* kind of a window—never for window as such. In this, perhaps, I have unconsciously tried to do just what Chaucer did when the language was young and untried and virile. I have sought only those words I have met up with as a boy in New Hampshire, working on farms during the summer vacations. I listened to the men with whom I worked, and found that I could make out their conversation as they talked together out of ear-shot, even when I had not plainly heard the words they spoke. When I started to carry their conversation over into poetry, I could hear their voices, and the sound posture differentiated between one and the other. It was the sense of sound I have been talking about. In some sort of way like this I have been able to write poetry, where characters talk, and, though not without infinite pains, to make it plain to the reader which character is saying the lines, without having to place his name before it, as is done in the drama.

—Robert Frost, quoted in
*Robert Frost: Life and
Talks—Walking* (1965)
by Louis Mertins

Make the Connection

Design of Darkness

Anyone who has had a direct experience of nature knows that sudden violence and grisly death are facts of life: The strong eat the weak; the slow are overcome by the quick; the healthy ultimately die and decay. By human standards, nature can be cold and merciless. To paraphrase Frost in this poem, nature can be "appalling."

Quickwrite

Read the first line of the poem, and write down your prediction about what the tone of the poem will be. What words lead you to that conclusion?

Background

Frost was particularly proud of his **sonnets,** which are considered among the finest in the English language. He often expressed regret that more of them were not reprinted in the hundreds of anthologies in which his work appeared. "Design" reveals how densely packed with ideas his sonnets can be. (For more about sonnets, see page 180 and the Handbook of Literary Terms.)

Butterflies (1950) by M. C. Escher.
Wood engraving (28 cm × 26 cm).

Design

Robert Frost

I found a dimpled spider, fat and white,
On a white heal-all,° holding up a moth
Like a white piece of rigid satin cloth—
Assorted characters of death and blight
5 Mixed ready to begin the morning right,
Like the ingredients of a witches' broth—
A snowdrop spider, a flower like a froth,°
And dead wings carried like a paper kite.

What had that flower to do with being white,
10 The wayside blue and innocent heal-all?
What brought the kindred spider to that height,
Then steered the white moth thither° in the night?
What but design of darkness to appall?—
If design govern in a thing so small.

  2. heal-all: flowering plant of the mint family. The flowers, leaves, and stems are used in folk medicine to treat sore throats and other minor ailments.
  7. froth: foam.
  12. thither: archaic for "there."

MAKING MEANINGS

First Thoughts

1. Did your prediction in the Quickwrite about the **tone** of the poem prove correct, or did the poem surprise you? Explain.

Shaping Interpretations

2. What **similes** occur in the octave (first eight lines) of this sonnet? How do they affect the **tone** of the poem?

3. Identify the three "characters" of the poem, and tell what is happening to each one. What color is each character? What justifies the poet's description of these things as "characters of death and blight"?

4. Look up the word *character* in a dictionary. Explain which definitions of the word Frost might be applying in line 4. How does each definition affect the meaning of the line?

5. Describe the **rhyme scheme** of the poem. In your view, what key words or concepts do the limited rhyming sounds focus on?

6. In line 13, the poet answers his own questions with another question. Explain how his final question answers the previous ones. How would you define a "design of darkness"?

7. In line 14, Frost qualifies his answer with a reservation, beginning with a crucial "If." What is the reservation that remains in his mind?

8. How does the last line affect the whole **tone** and meaning of the poem?

Extending the Text

9. How do you think a Puritan (page 9) writer would have answered the questions Frost asks in this poem? How do you think a rationalist (page 13), or deist (page 16), would answer them?

Challenging the Text

10. The critic Laurence Perrine made this comment about "Design":

> Frost's brief poem, like the wayside blue or white heal-all, seems from the outside innocent enough. But within its fourteen innocent-seeming lines, Frost chillingly poses the problem of evil.
>
> —Laurence Perrine

Do you agree or disagree with this comment? Give reasons for your response. If you disagree, state what *you* think is the poem's central issue.

Calvin and Hobbes © 1993 Watterson. Distributed by Universal Press Syndicate. Reprinted with permission. All rights reserved.

Make the Connection

Good as Gold

"Gold," whether it refers to the metal or to the color, conjures up a myriad of images and meanings. Over the centuries, writers and artists have used gold as a symbol of perfection.

Quickwrite

Briefly write what you predict the poem is going to be about, based on its title.

Background

To understand this little lyric, you need to know about two other literary accounts: the Biblical account of Adam and Eve's loss of innocence and their expulsion from the Garden of Eden; and, in Greek mythology, the loss of the Golden Age, a time of innocent happiness that was an image of paradise for the ancient Greeks and Romans.

Nothing Gold Can Stay

Robert Frost

Nature's first green is gold,
Her hardest hue to hold.
Her early leaf's a flower;
But only so an hour.
Then leaf subsides to leaf.
So Eden sank to grief,
So dawn goes down to day.
Nothing gold can stay.

Expulsion from the Garden of Eden
(detail) (1828) by Thomas Cole.

Gift of Mrs. Maxim Karolik for the M. and M. Karolik Collection of American Paintings, 1815–1856. Courtesy, Museum of Fine Arts, Boston.

MAKING MEANINGS

First Thoughts

1. Review your Quickwrite, and explain whether the **title** of the poem helped you predict its message.

Shaping Interpretations

2. Identify four specific things that the poem says cannot, or did not, "stay."

3. Think what the first buds of leaves look like in spring, and explain what line 1 means.

4. Explain the natural process described in line 5.

5. What Biblical event is alluded to in line 6? What state of mind or situation might "Eden" **symbolize** here?

6. What different ideas might "gold" symbolize in the poem? Why can't gold stay—or do you disagree?

7. Show how **rhyme** and **rhythm** contribute to this poem's compactness and completeness. How do **alliteration, slant rhyme,** and echo-ing **sound effects** contribute to the poem's tightly woven unity?

Extending the Text

8. In *Connections* below, Naomi Shihab Nye tries to name things that don't change. How are her poem and Frost's poem alike and different in **tone** and **message**? Identify the central point you think each poet is trying to convey about change and loss.

Connections
A POEM

Trying to Name What Doesn't Change

Naomi Shihab Nye

Roselva says the only thing that doesn't change
is train tracks. She's sure of it.
The train changes, or the weeds that grow up spidery
by the side, but not the tracks.
5 I've watched one for three years, she says,
and it doesn't curve, doesn't break, doesn't grow.

Peter isn't sure. He saw an abandoned track
near Sabinas, Mexico, and says a track without a train
is a changed track. The metal wasn't shiny anymore.
10 The wood was split and some of the ties were gone.

Every Tuesday on Morales Street
butchers crack the necks of a hundred hens.
The widow in the tilted house
spices her soup with cinnamon.
15 Ask her what doesn't change.

Stars explode.
The rose curls up as if there is fire in the petals.
The cat who knew me is buried under the bush.

The train whistle still wails its ancient sound
20 but when it goes away, shrinking back
from the walls of the brain,
it takes something different with it every time.

ONCE BY THE PACIFIC

Make the Connection

The End of All Things
In the Bible, when God creates
the universe, he says, "Let there
be light." After each stage of
creation, the Bible says, "And
God saw that it was good." Keep
these ideas in mind as you read
Frost's vision of an event that is
the opposite of creation.

Quickwrite

You've seen waves
pounding against the
shore, in person or on film. In a
few sentences, describe your
thoughts as you watched the
watery assault.

Once by the Pacific

Robert Frost

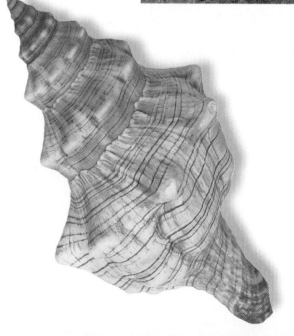

The shattered water made a misty din.
Great waves looked over others coming in,
And thought of doing something to the shore
That water never did to land before.
5 The clouds were low and hairy in the skies,
Like locks blown forward in the gleam of eyes.
You could not tell, and yet it looked as if
The shore was lucky in being backed by cliff,
The cliff in being backed by continent;
10 It looked as if a night of dark intent
Was coming, and not only a night, an age.
Someone had better be prepared for rage.
There would be more than ocean-water broken
Before God's last *Put out the Light* was spoken.

The Pennsylvania Academy of the Fine Arts, Philadelphia. Joseph E. Temple Fund.

Rocks and Breakers, California (1913) by William Ritschel. Oil on canvas.

Make the Connection

Ocean Reveries

For some, the sea is an object of reverie, inspiring a sense of peace and oneness with the world. For others, the sea represents a powerful, mysterious force of nature. What other things might the sea symbolize?

Quickwrite

Before you read the poem, write down your guess as to the meaning of Frost's puzzling title.

Neither Out Far Nor In Deep

Robert Frost

The people along the sand
All turn and look one way.
They turn their back on the land.
They look at the sea all day.

5 As long as it takes to pass
A ship keeps raising its hull;
The wetter ground like glass
Reflects a standing gull.

The land may vary more;
10 But wherever the truth may be—
The water comes ashore,
And the people look at the sea.

They cannot look out far.
They cannot look in deep.
15 But when was that ever a bar°
To any watch they keep?

15. bar: barrier; obstruction.

MAKING MEANINGS

Once by the Pacific

First Thoughts

1. Review the notes you made in your Quick-write. How do the speaker's thoughts in the poem compare to the thoughts you had while watching crashing waves?

Shaping Interpretations

2. Describe the scene presented in the poem. What does the scene remind the speaker of?

3. Explain what you think the speaker means by "a night of dark intent /. . . not only a night, an age" (lines 10–11). Whose "intent" is he referring to?

4. Who do you think is the "someone" who "had better be prepared for rage" (line 12)? Whose "rage"?

5. Besides ocean water, what else might be "bro-ken" during that rage?

6. "Put out the light" is something anyone might say on an ordinary evening at home. How does the use of this casual, domestic phrase make the poem's **message** even more chilling? What would you say that message is?

7. The poem's title suggests that Frost is describing a scene he once saw as he gazed at the Pacific Ocean. What larger event might this scene **symbolize**?

Connecting with the Text

8. Do you view this poem as a warning? Or, do you think Frost is just expressing a certain philoso-phy of life? Explain what the warning might be, or discuss the philosophy revealed in the poem.

Neither Out Far Nor In Deep

First Thoughts

1. Review your Quickwrite. Why do you think Frost included the words *out far* and *in deep* in the poem's title?

Shaping Interpretations

2. What is the one **simile** that Frost uses in the poem? How does it affect the scene described?

3. In what way are lines 11–12 tinged with **irony**?

4. What might the sea and the land **symbolize** in this poem? What larger meaning might the "watch" (line 16) take on?

5. Comment on the poet's **tone** in the last line. Does he admire the watchers for keeping their vigil, or does he feel scorn or pity for their fail-ure to recognize their limitations? Do you have another interpretation? Explain.

6. On a literal level, why is it that the people in the poem can look neither "out far" nor "in deep"? What more general human limitations might be symbolized by our inability to probe the dis-tance and depth of the sea?

Make the Connection

Life Lessons

A **parable** is a short story in which an ordinary event from everyday life is used to teach a much wider moral or religious lesson. In this poem, Frost draws a lesson from nature—from the sight of the bent branches of birch trees.

Reading Skills and Strategies

Reading Poetry

Frost's poems are written in a form that is very close to conversational English. (See Primary Sources, page 559, and **blank verse,** page 575.) Read the poem aloud to hear the rise and fall of the speaker's voice. When you come to a period, whether at the end of a line or in the middle of a line, make a full stop. When you come to a comma, semicolon, or dash, pause slightly. If there is no mark of punctuation at the end of a line, read right on to the next without pausing.

Background

As spindly and awkward as a giraffe's legs, the birch trees of Robert Frost's New England have white bark ringed with black. Their trunks are remarkably pliable—a fact that gives this poem its realistic base. Children do, in fact, climb and swing on birch trees.

Birches

Robert Frost

When I see birches bend to left and right
Across the lines of straighter darker trees,
I like to think some boy's been swinging them.
But swinging doesn't bend them down to stay
5 As ice storms do. Often you must have seen them
Loaded with ice a sunny winter morning
After a rain. They click upon themselves
As the breeze rises, and turn many-colored
As the stir cracks and crazes their enamel.
10 Soon the sun's warmth makes them shed crystal shells
Shattering and avalanching on the snow crust—
Such heaps of broken glass to sweep away
You'd think the inner dome of heaven had fallen.
They are dragged to the withered bracken° by the load,
15 And they seem not to break; though once they are bowed
So low for long, they never right themselves:
You may see their trunks arching in the woods
Years afterwards, trailing their leaves on the ground
Like girls on hands and knees that throw their hair
20 Before them over their heads to dry in the sun.
But I was going to say when Truth broke in
With all her matter of fact about the ice storm,
I should prefer to have some boy bend them
As he went out and in to fetch the cows—
25 Some boy too far from town to learn baseball,
Whose only play was what he found himself,
Summer or winter, and could play alone.
One by one he subdued his father's trees
By riding them down over and over again
30 Until he took the stiffness out of them,
And not one but hung limp, not one was left
For him to conquer. He learned all there was
To learn about not launching out too soon
And so not carrying the tree away

14. bracken: large, coarse fern.

35 Clear to the ground. He always kept his poise°
    To the top branches, climbing carefully
    With the same pains you use to fill a cup
    Up to the brim, and even above the brim.
    Then he flung outward, feet first, with a swish,
40 Kicking his way down through the air to the ground.
    So was I once myself a swinger of birches.
    And so I dream of going back to be.
    It's when I'm weary of considerations,
    And life is too much like a pathless wood
45 Where your face burns and tickles with the cobwebs
    Broken across it, and one eye is weeping
    From a twig's having lashed across it open.
    I'd like to get away from earth awhile
    And then come back to it and begin over.
50 May no fate willfully misunderstand me
    And half grant what I wish and snatch me away
    Not to return. Earth's the right place for love:
    I don't know where it's likely to go better.
    I'd like to go by climbing a birch tree,
55 And climb black branches up a snow-white trunk
    Toward heaven, till the tree could bear no more,
    But dipped its top and set me down again.
    That would be good both going and coming back.
    One could do worse than be a swinger of birches.

35. poise: balance.

MAKING MEANINGS

First Thoughts

1. Which passages of this poem do you think are especially interesting or true to life?

Shaping Interpretations

2. Describe the scenario that the speaker imagines when he sees birch trees. What realistic objection to his idea does he recognize in lines 4–5? What "matter of fact" does "Truth" break in with in lines 5–10?

3. Find at least three examples of **metaphor** and **onomatopoeia** in the poem.

4. Two strong **similes** give the poem a richness that is both imaginative and the result of close observation. What are these similes?

5. What does the playful activity of birch swinging seem to **symbolize** in the poem?

6. Summarize in your own words what you think is the **moral** or **message** of Frost's **parable** about birch swinging. What complex, conflicting attitudes toward life does it reveal?

7. How does the sound of Frost's poem differ from the sound of any of Whitman's poems (pages 352–362)?

Extending the Text

8. If a Puritan writer were to come upon the bent birches, what response do you think he or she would have to the natural scene? What response would a Transcendentalist like Ralph Waldo Emerson (page 216) have had?

Challenging the Text

9. In a famous remark about the nature of poetry, Frost said that a poem "begins in delight and ends in wisdom." Do you agree or disagree that this applies to "Birches"? Explain your view, including what you think *delight* and *wisdom* mean.

Make the Connection

Home Is Where the Heart Is
Embedded in this poem is one of Frost's most famous sayings, one often quoted by many people who probably have no idea where it comes from: "'Home is the place where, when you have to go there, / They have to take you in.'" Another definition of home is also offered in the poem: "'Something you somehow haven't to deserve.'" To some people, "home" is a definite place; to others, it is a state of mind, a sense of connectedness and belonging.

Reading Skills and Strategies

Drawing Inferences About Characters
Read this poem as if it were a short story. As you read, make notes about the feelings that you sense operate between Warren and Mary. What complex feelings do you think each of them has toward Silas, the hired man? Also, note your own feelings or impressions about each of these three characters. Do your feelings change as the poem goes on?

Elements of Literature

Dialogue in Verse
Most of this poem is a **dialogue** in **blank verse** (see page 575). The poem's main character never speaks for himself, yet his presence dominates the poem through the dialogue of the other characters. By the last line, we have heard enough about the hired man to understand his background, habits, and attitudes. In gradually coming to know him, we also come to know the personalities of the husband and wife whose dialogue carries the drama.

The Death of the Hired Man

Robert Frost

Mary sat musing on the lamp-flame at the table,
Waiting for Warren. When she heard his step,
She ran on tiptoe down the darkened passage
To meet him in the doorway with the news
5 And put him on his guard. "Silas is back."
She pushed him outward with her through the door
And shut it after her. "Be kind," she said.
She took the market things from Warren's arms
And set them on the porch, then drew him down
10 To sit beside her on the wooden steps.

"When was I ever anything but kind to him?
But I'll not have the fellow back," he said.
"I told him so last haying, didn't I?
If he left then, I said, that ended it.
15 What good is he? Who else will harbor° him
At his age for the little he can do?
What help he is there's no depending on.
Off he goes always when I need him most.
He thinks he ought to earn a little pay,
20 Enough at least to buy tobacco with,
So he won't have to beg and be beholden.°
'All right,' I say, 'I can't afford to pay

15. harbor: provide safe shelter for.

21. beholden: indebted.

The Veteran in a New Field (1865) by Winslow Homer. Oil on canvas.

The Metropolitan Museum of Art. Bequest of Miss Adelaide Milton de Groot, 1967 (67.187.131). Photograph © The Metropolitan Museum of Art.

Any fixed wages, though I wish I could.'
'Someone else can.' 'Then someone else will have to.'
25 I shouldn't mind his bettering himself
If that was what it was. You can be certain,
When he begins like that, there's someone at him
Trying to coax him off with pocket money—
In haying time, when any help is scarce.
30 In winter he comes back to us. I'm done."

"Sh! not so loud: He'll hear you," Mary said.

"I want him to: He'll have to soon or late."

"He's worn out. He's asleep beside the stove.
When I came up from Rowe's I found him here,
35 Huddled against the barn door fast asleep,
A miserable sight, and frightening, too—
You needn't smile—I didn't recognize him—
I wasn't looking for him—and he's changed.
Wait till you see."

          "Where did you say he'd been?"

40 "He didn't say. I dragged him to the house,
And gave him tea and tried to make him smoke.
I tried to make him talk about his travels.

Nothing would do: He just kept nodding off."

"What did he say? Did he say anything?"

"But little."

45   "Anything? Mary, confess
He said he'd come to ditch° the meadow for me."

"Warren!"

        "But did he? I just want to know."

"Of course he did. What would you have him say?
Surely you wouldn't grudge the poor old man
50 Some humble way to save his self-respect.
He added, if you really care to know,
He meant to clear the upper pasture, too.
That sounds like something you have heard before?
Warren, I wish you could have heard the way
55 He jumbled everything. I stopped to look
Two or three times—he made me feel so queer°—
To see if he was talking in his sleep.
He ran on° Harold Wilson—you remember—
The boy you had in haying four years since.
60 He's finished school, and teaching in his college.
Silas declares you'll have to get him back.
He says they two will make a team for work:
Between them they will lay this farm as smooth!
The way he mixed that in with other things.
65 He thinks young Wilson a likely lad, though daft
On education—you know how they fought
All through July under the blazing sun,
Silas up on the cart to build the load,
Harold along beside to pitch it on."

70 "Yes, I took care to keep well out of earshot."

"Well, those days trouble Silas like a dream.
You wouldn't think they would. How some things linger!
Harold's young college-boy's assurance piqued° him.
After so many years he still keeps finding
75 Good arguments he sees he might have used.
I sympathize. I know just how it feels
To think of the right thing to say too late.
Harold's associated in his mind with Latin.
He asked me what I thought of Harold's saying
80 He studied Latin, like the violin,
Because he liked it—that an argument!
He said he couldn't make the boy believe
He could find water with a hazel prong°—
Which showed how much good school had ever done him.
85 He wanted to go over that. But most of all
He thinks if he could have another chance

46. ditch: dig drainage channels in.

56. queer: uncomfortable; ill at ease.

58. ran on: kept talking in a rambling way about.

73. piqued: provoked.

83. hazel prong: forked branch used to find water underground.

To teach him how to build a load of hay——"

"I know, that's Silas' one accomplishment.
He bundles every forkful in its place,
90 And tags and numbers it for future reference,
So he can find and easily dislodge it
In the unloading. Silas does that well.
He takes it out in bunches like big birds' nests.
You never see him standing on the hay
95 He's trying to lift, straining to lift himself."

"He thinks if he could teach him that, he'd be
Some good perhaps to someone in the world.
He hates to see a boy the fool of books.
Poor Silas, so concerned for other folk,
100 And nothing to look backward to with pride,
And nothing to look forward to with hope,
So now and never any different."

Part of a moon was falling down the west,
Dragging the whole sky with it to the hills.
105 Its light poured softly in her lap. She saw it
And spread her apron to it. She put out her hand
Among the harplike morning-glory strings,
Taut with the dew from garden bed to eaves,
As if she played unheard some tenderness
110 That wrought° on him beside her in the night.
"Warren," she said, "he has come home to die:
You needn't be afraid he'll leave you this time."

"Home," he mocked gently.

                  "Yes, what else but home?
It all depends on what you mean by home.
115 Of course he's nothing to us, any more
Than was the hound that came a stranger to us
Out of the woods, worn out upon the trail."

"Home is the place where, when you have to go there,
They have to take you in."

                  "I should have called it
120 Something you somehow haven't to deserve."

Warren leaned out and took a step or two,
Picked up a little stick, and brought it back
And broke it in his hand and tossed it by.
"Silas has better claim on us you think
125 Than on his brother? Thirteen little miles
As the road winds would bring him to his door.
Silas has walked that far no doubt today.
Why doesn't he go there? His brother's rich,
A somebody—director in the bank."

110. wrought: worked.

"He never told us that."

130   "We know it, though."

"I think his brother ought to help, of course.
I'll see to that if there is need. He ought of right
To take him in, and might be willing to—
He may be better than appearances.
135 But have some pity on Silas. Do you think
If he had any pride in claiming kin
Or anything he looked for from his brother,
He'd keep so still about him all this time?"

"I wonder what's between them."

                         "I can tell you.
140 Silas is what he is—we wouldn't mind him—
But just the kind that kinsfolk can't abide.
He never did a thing so very bad.
He don't know why he isn't quite as good
As anybody. Worthless though he is,
145 He won't be made ashamed to please his brother."

"*I* can't think Si ever hurt anyone."

"No, but he hurt my heart the way he lay
And rolled his old head on that sharp-edged chair-back.
He wouldn't let me put him on the lounge.
150 You must go in and see what you can do.
I made the bed up for him there tonight.
You'll be surprised at him—how much he's broken.
His working days are done; I'm sure of it."

"I'd not be in a hurry to say that."

155 "I haven't been. Go, look, see for yourself.
But, Warren, please remember how it is:
He's come to help you ditch the meadow.
He has a plan. You mustn't laugh at him.
He may not speak of it, and then he may.
160 I'll sit and see if that small sailing cloud
Will hit or miss the moon."

                        It hit the moon.
Then there were three there, making a dim row,
The moon, the little silver cloud, and she.

Warren returned—too soon, it seemed to her—
165 Slipped to her side, caught up her hand and waited.

"Warren?" she questioned.
                    "Dead," was all he answered.

"I must have the pulse beat of rhythm . . ."

These comments are from an interview held on October 21, 1923, with *New York Times* reporter Rose C. Feld. Not long after the interview, Frost won his first Pulitzer Prize. Here, Frost has been talking about American poetry.

. . . We're still a bit afraid. America, for instance, was afraid to accept Walt Whitman when he first sang the songs of democracy. His influence on American poetry began to be felt only after the French had hailed him as a great writer, a literary revolutionist. Our own poet had to be imported from France before we were sure of his strength.

Today almost every man who writes poetry confesses his debt to Whitman. Many have gone very much further than Whitman would have traveled with them. They are the people who believe in wide straddling.

I, myself, as I said before, don't like it for myself. I do not write free verse; I write blank verse. I must have the pulse beat of rhythm, I like to hear it beating under the things I write.

That doesn't mean I do not like to read a bit of free verse occasionally. I do. It sometimes succeeds in painting a picture that is very clear and startling. It's good as something created momentarily for its sudden startling effect; it hasn't the qualities, however, of something lastingly beautiful.

And sometimes my objection to it is that it's a pose. It's not honest. When a man sets out consciously to tear up forms and rhythms and measures, then he is not interested in giving you poetry. He just wants to perform; he wants

Robert Frost at John F. Kennedy's inauguration, January 20, 1961.

Jim Brown/Black Star.

to show you his tricks. He will get an effect; nobody will deny that, but it is not a harmonious effect.

Sometimes it strikes me that the free-verse people got their idea from incorrect proof sheets. I have had stuff come from the printers with lines half left out or positions changed about. I read the poems as they stood, distorted and half finished, and I confess I get a rather pleasant sensation from them. They make a sort of nightmarish half-sense. . . .

—Robert Frost

MAKING MEANINGS

First Thoughts

1. Look back over your reading notes. How did you feel about each of the three characters in this poem?

Shaping Interpretations

2. Based on their **dialogue,** what inferences can you make about the relationship between Warren and Mary, and about how each relates to Silas?

3. Describe the basic problem facing Warren, Mary, and Silas. Some might say that Mary sees Silas as a hired man in an emotional sense, Warren in a work sense. Do you agree? Explain.

4. Identify the details in lines 103–110 that create a vivid image of the **setting.** What does this passage tell us about Mary's character?

5. Does the conclusion of this poem strike you as inevitable? Why or why not? What would your feelings have been if Warren, instead of answering "Dead" to Mary's question, had answered "Asleep," or "Sharpening his scythe"?

6. Find the two definitions of "home" offered in the poem. One critic has said that one definition is based on law and duty, the other definition on mercy. Identify each. Do you agree with the critic's observation? Which definition do you favor?

7. In Primary Sources on page 559, Frost says he aimed to give the speech of each character in his poetry a distinct sound, just as people's voices sound different in real life. Does he successfully differentiate Warren's and Mary's speech? Explain.

Extending the Text

8. State in your own words the poem's **message.** How would the message apply to the problem of homelessness in our society today?

READING SKILLS AND STRATEGIES

Understanding Blank Verse

"The poet goes in like a rope skipper to make the most of his opportunities," said Frost in an essay called "The Constant Symbol." "If he trips himself he stops the rope. He is of our stock and has been brought up by ear to choice of two meters, strict iambic and loose iambic (not to count varieties of the latter)." "The Death of the Hired Man" is written in **blank verse,** which is unrhymed iambic pentameter. It is called *blank* verse because the lines do not have end rhymes. Iambic pentameter means that there are five iambs to each line; an *iamb* is an unaccented syllable followed by an accented syllable: da DUM ($\smile \prime$).

1. Scan the first ten lines, and recite them aloud to hear the meter.

2. Look over the poem, and find examples of strict iambic and loose iambic meter.

3. Do you think Frost ever "trips" himself in this poem?

4. Take ten lines from this poem, and rewrite them in the free-verse style of Walt Whitman (page 348). Where will you break the lines? What rearrangement of words will have to be made to break the iambic meter?

5. Look at Frost's comments on free verse in Primary Sources (page 574). What is *your* opinion of Frost's ideas?

CHOICES: Building Your Portfolio

Writer's Notebook

1. Collecting Ideas for an Analysis of Causes and Effects

Jot down your own list of speculative questions suggested by the Frost poems you have read. Why is the speaker so appalled at the sight he sees in "Design"? Why are the people in "Neither Out Far Nor In Deep" looking out to sea? What motivated Silas in "The Death of the Hired Man" to come back to Warren and Mary? Keep your notes for possible use in the Writer's Workshop on page 685.

WORK IN PROGRESS

Interpreting a Poem

2. Frost Bites

The critic Louise Bogan pointed out the "tensions, dark conflicts, and passionate involvements" that appear in Frost's poetry and "pervade certain poems with almost nightmare intensity." In a brief essay, explore examples of the "dark conflicts" in Frost's poetry. What does Frost share with the Dark Romantics (page 213)? In what sense do Frost's poems have "bite"?

Comparing Poems

3. Accident or Design?

In a brief essay, compare and contrast "Design" and Emily Dickinson's poem "Apparently with no surprise" (page 385). Before you write, gather your data in a chart like the one below:

	Dickinson	Frost
Message in poem		
Use of symbols		
Tone		
Use of rhymes and rhythms		
Use of imagery		

Creative Writing

4. Updated "Hired Man"

In a poem, narrative, or screenplay, set "The Death of the Hired Man" in contemporary surroundings with up-to-date characters. You might set the story in a city, in a rural area, in a suburb, on a modern-day farm, or in a migrant worker camp. Be sure to include **dialogue, conflict,** and **resolution** in your story.

Speaking and Listening

5. Reading Nature

The Puritans and later the Romantics "read" lessons into nature. Lead a class discussion about whether or not Frost's poems "Design" and "Birches" are part of this same tradition. Discuss whether Frost is more like the Puritans or the Romantics in his attitude.

Art

6. Dark Design

Create a collage that captures some of the central themes and images that you feel sum up Frost's poetry. In choosing appropriate visuals, consider **similes, metaphors,** and **images** from the Frost poems you have read. Write a brief explanation of the thought that went behind each image you chose.

Music / Art

7. Frost Three Ways

With a partner or a team, choose several Frost poems from this collection or from a book of Frost's poetry, and select music and works of art that relate to the poems' **themes, images,** and **tones.** Prepare slides, video, or overhead transparencies to show your accompanying visuals, and play recorded music (or perform your own compositions) as you read aloud Frost's poems, creating your own multimedia presentation.

John Crowe Ransom
(1888–1974)

UPI/Bettmann.

He was the son of a minister and perhaps the most intellectually elegant conservative of twentieth-century American writers, but John Crowe Ransom—poet, teacher, editor, and critic—was nevertheless an innovator in his own way. He was the founder of a group of renegade Southern poets. He helped form a new and innovative school of critical thought called New Criticism. He was also mentor to some of the most important young poets and critics of the time. His students—among them Randall Jarrell (page 932), Robert Lowell (page 948), Robert Penn Warren, and James Wright (page 151)—found a larger audience than their teacher ever did, but Ransom did more than any of them to keep alive the delicacy, beauty, and endless resources of the English language.

Ransom was born in Pulaski, Tennessee. His illustrious teaching career at his alma mater, Vanderbilt University in Tennessee, lasted for more than twenty years, and it was during this stage of his life that he became a leader of the group of Southern writers called the "Fugitives." The Fugitives were determined to assert Southern cultural values, and they idealized a genteel, agrarian way of life that seemed to offer a more stable environment than Northern industrialism could. Their poetry was known for a combination of intellectual wit and the fatalism associated with Greek tragedy.

Changing times made Ransom's work—with its tone of wit, ironic detachment, and almost classical elegance of expression—seem like the echo of another age. Yet, today Ransom is appreciated not only for his considerable influence on some of the best poets of the modern era, but also for the shining perfection of his small but memorable body of work.

Before You Read

BELLS FOR JOHN WHITESIDE'S DAUGHTER

Make the Connection
Preserved in Memory
Everyone experiences losses in life; but poets, through their art, try to redeem what we have lost.

Quickwrite
The following poem is an **elegy,** written to mark a young girl's death. In a few sentences, list some aspects of the girl's life that you would expect the poet to mention.

Elements of Literature
Tone
Tone is the attitude a writer takes toward the subject of a work, the characters in it, or the audience. Ransom often combines two different tones—tenderness and detachment, for example—in one poem.

Eleanor (1901) by Frank Benson.
Oil on canvas (29½″ × 25″).

Bells for John Whiteside's Daughter

John Crowe Ransom

There was such speed in her little body,
And such lightness in her footfall,
It is no wonder that her brown study°
Astonishes us all.

5 Her wars were bruited° in our high window.
We looked among orchard trees and beyond.
Where she took arms against her shadow
Or harried° unto the pond

The lazy geese, like a snow cloud
10 Dripping their snow on the green grass,

Tricking and stopping, sleepy and proud,
Who cried in goose, Alas,

For the tireless heart within the little
Lady with rod that made them rise
15 From their noon apple-dreams, and scuttle
Goose-fashion under the skies!

But now go the bells, and we are ready;
In one house we are sternly stopped
To say we are vexed° at her brown study,
20 Lying so primly propped.

3. brown study: state of being lost in deep thought.
5. bruited (bro͞ot′id): reported.
8. harried (har′ēd): forced; pushed along.

19. vexed: disturbed; annoyed.

MAKING MEANINGS

First Thoughts

1. How does the speaker feel about the little girl who died? How did the poet make *you* feel about the Whitesides' daughter and about death itself?

Shaping Interpretations

2. What characteristics of the girl make the speaker astonished at her "brown study"?

3. What action of the little girl caused the geese to cry "Alas"? What additional overtones does this cry take on, given the poem's subject?

4. What details in the last stanza make it clear what the speaker is looking at?

5. What do you associate with the verb *vexed* in the next to last line of the poem? What verb would you expect the speaker to use to describe his reaction to the dead child?

Challenging the Text

6. The critic Babette Deutsch once said of Ransom:

> [W]hatever his subject . . . his tone is right. The glint of irony is there, deepened as well as softened by a sensitiveness without a grain of sentimentality.
>
> —Babette Deutsch

Do you think Ransom's **tone** is appropriate, given the highly emotional nature of the subject? Do you think he should also have covered other aspects of the girl's life? Explain.

CHOICES: Building Your Portfolio

Writer's Notebook

1. Collecting Ideas for an Analysis of Causes and Effects

If you are interested in literature and in the ways it is studied in school, you might find a topic for investigation in the work of John Crowe Ransom. Do some preliminary research on one of these topics: New Criticism (or New Critics) or the Fugitives. What effect did the New Criticism have on the way literature was (and still is) studied in schools and colleges? What effect did the Fugitives have on Southern writing? Save your notes for possible use in the Writer's Workshop on page 685.

Interpreting a Poem

2. The Human Condition

A critic wrote that Ransom's poems emphasize **themes** like the following:

> mortality and the fleetingness of youthful vigor and grace . . . [and] the disparity between the world as man would have it and as it actually is, between what [people] want and need emotionally and what is available for them. . . .
>
> —Thomas Daniel Young

In a brief essay, explain whether or not you believe this comment is supported by the poem. Use specific references to the poem.

Comparing Poems

3. Remembrances

Write a brief essay comparing "Bells for John Whiteside's Daughter" with Henry Wadsworth Longfellow's "The Cross of Snow" (page 178). Compare the poems' **tone, imagery,** and views of death. Support your comparison with lines from the poems.

Robinson Jeffers

(1887–1962)

The son of a theology teacher, Robinson Jeffers was born in Pittsburgh. His parents moved from place to place, and, by the time he was fifteen, he had already spent several years in Europe before the family settled in California. There Jeffers earned a degree from Occidental College and went on to do postgraduate work, including a term at medical school. But Jeffers did not pursue any of the careers he studied for. Fascinated with poetry, he found he could make no serious commitment to anything else.

In 1912 Jeffers inherited money from an uncle. This allowed him the freedom to live on his own terms and to provide for his wife and two sons without ever holding a job. Asserting his sudden independence, Jeffers bought property in the coastal village of Carmel, California. With his own hands he built a stone tower that would serve as a retreat and working studio for the rest of his life. As in the case of the Irish poet William Butler Yeats, the tower became symbolic for Jeffers of his worldview and his way of life; he lived a monklike existence apart from neighborly society and the literary world, marked by a lonely devotion to nature.

A man against the American grain, Jeffers had little confidence in the virtues of religion or democracy; he also kept a skeptical eye fixed on scientific progress and social advances. His philosophical outlook, combining fatalism with pessimism, was closer to that of the ancient Greeks than to that of the common American. For wayward humankind, aware of everything but its insignificance, he had little hope. He regarded awareness itself as a kind of disease to which natural forces are immune.

Much of Jeffers's poetic inspiration came from nature's power to endure and silently witness the absurdities of civilization. Rocks and the sea, hawks in the wind, sea creatures thrown upon the sea-washed ledges of the Pacific shore—these are Jeffers's recurring images and emblems. Although humorless, grandly isolated, and nourished by disgust, Jeffers was able to attract readers who were impressed by the integrity of his single-minded convictions and by his dark vision of the limited life of human beings.

Robinson Jeffers by Edward Weston.
© 1981 Arizona Board of Regents, Center for Creative Photography. Courtesy Richard A. Gleeson. University of San Francisco Library.

Before You Read

SHINE, PERISHING REPUBLIC

Make the Connection

Self-Sufficiency

This poem was written in the Big Sur region in California, where great mountains emerge like dripping shoulders out of the Pacific Ocean. The circumstance is that of a remote homestead built with the speaker's own hands. The speaker is a father determined to live apart from civilization and to have his children learn the lessons of nature rather than those of schoolbooks.

Quickwrite

Quickwrite your own feelings about America today. Do you consider it a "perishing republic" that has lost its positive qualities, or do you think the nation's values and strengths are still intact?

go.hrw.com
LE0 11-11

Old Mill, Big Sur (1933) by Millard Sheets. Watercolor on paper.
The E. Gene Crain Collection, Laguna Beach, California.

Shine, Perishing Republic

Robinson Jeffers

While this America settles in the mold of its vulgarity, heavily
    thickening to empire,
And protest, only a bubble in the molten mass, pops and sighs
    out, and the mass hardens,

I sadly smiling remember that the flower fades to make fruit,
    the fruit rots to make earth.
Out of the mother; and through the spring exultances,
    ripeness and decadence; and home to the mother.

You making haste, haste on decay: not blameworthy; life is
5   good, be it stubbornly long or suddenly
A mortal splendor: meteors are not needed less than
        mountains: shine, perishing republic.

But for my children, I would have them keep their distance
        from the thickening center; corruption
Never has been compulsory, when the cities lie at the
        monster's feet there are left the mountains.

And boys, be in nothing so moderate as in love of man, a
        clever servant, insufferable master.
There is the trap that catches noblest spirits, that caught—
10   they say—God, when he walked on earth.

MAKING MEANINGS

First Thoughts

1. What thoughts or feelings did you have about the speaker's advice in the last stanza? In what ways is this advice quite the opposite of "love thy neighbor"?

Shaping Interpretations

2. The first stanza contains an **implied metaphor.** What is America compared to? What does "vulgarity" mean here, and why does the republic thicken to *empire*?

3. What attitude toward America does the second stanza express?

4. What is the speaker's attitude in the last stanza? Do you think he really means what he says in line 9?

5. What does the speaker seem to think is the cause of the republic's condition?

Connecting with the Text

6. Review the Quickwrite you wrote before reading the poem. Did the poem make you rethink any of your responses? Explain.

7. If it were possible, would you like to take the speaker aside and instill a little optimism in him or her? What would you tell the speaker?

CHOICES:
Building Your Portfolio

Writer's Notebook

1. Collecting Ideas for an Analysis of Causes and Effects

Brainstorm a list of possible topics suggested by Jeffers's poem: why a civilization might decay, why someone would choose to live apart from society, why someone would feel as Jeffers does about America. Save your notes for possible use in the Writer's Workshop on page 685.

Critical Writing

2. Taking Stock

This poem was published in 1925. In a brief essay, explain why you think Jeffers's view of the condition of American society is or is not still valid. Summarize the view expressed in the poem. Then tell whether or not you think this view applies to contemporary America. Support your position with specific references to the poem and to contemporary life.

Fitzgerald
Steinbeck
Thurber
Welty

THE DREAM AND THE REALITY

"Did you ever see an amusement park?"

"No, Father."

"Well, go and see an amusement park." The priest waved his
hand vaguely. "It's a thing like a
fair, only much more glittering. Go
to one at night and stand a little
way off from it in a dark place—
under dark trees. You'll see a big
wheel made of lights turning in
the air, and a long slide shooting
boats down into the water. A band
playing somewhere, and a smell of
peanuts—and everything will twin-
kle. But it won't remind you of
anything, you see. It will all just
hang out there in the night like a
colored balloon—like a big yellow
lantern on a pole."

Father Schwartz frowned as he
suddenly thought of something.

"But don't get up close," he
warned Rudolph, "because if you
do you'll only feel the heat and the
sweat and the life."

—F. Scott Fitzgerald,
from "Absolution"

F. Scott Fitzgerald

(1896–1940)

If ever there was a writer whose life and fiction were one, it was F. Scott Fitzgerald. Fitzgerald—handsome, charming, and uncommonly gifted—was not only part of the crazy, wonderful, irresponsible era of the 1920s; he helped to name it the Jazz Age. He made a literary legend of it and, with his wife Zelda, lived it out in all of its excesses. He also almost certainly died of it.

Early Failures—and a Smash Hit

Fitzgerald was born in 1896 in St. Paul, Minnesota, the son of a father with claims to an aristocratic Maryland family. Scott was named for an ancestor, Francis Scott Key, the composer of "The Star-Spangled Banner." His mother was the daughter of a rich Irish immigrant. The young Scott was a spoiled boy, a failure at schoolwork and—to his own great disappointment—at sports. But he was a success at daydreaming and, while still in his teens, at writing stories and plays.

At Princeton University, which he entered in 1913, he wrote one of the Triangle Club musical shows, contributed to the *Nassau Literary Magazine,* and befriended the serious writers Edmund Wilson and John Peale Bishop. When the United States entered the First World War in 1917, Fitzgerald left college for officers' training school, yearning for heroic adventure on the battlefields of France. He was never sent overseas, but in camp he began to work on a novel, *The Romantic Egoist,* which was twice turned down by Scribner's.

While he was stationed at Camp Sheridan in Alabama, romance of a different sort overtook him. He fell deeply in love with Zelda Sayre, a high-spirited and gorgeous woman whose escapades had scandalized her hometown of Montgomery. Like Scott, Zelda hungered for new experiences. She was sure of her appeal and felt it was bound to bring her a full measure

of luxury and gaiety. Although Scott courted her persistently, he had not nearly enough money to offer her the kind of marriage she wanted, and at first she turned him down.

Now out of the army, Fitzgerald took a low-paying job he hated; he sent his novel, rewritten and retitled *This Side of Paradise,* off to Scribner's for the third time. In 1919, they agreed to publish it.

"I was an empty bucket," he said of the experience, "so mentally blunted by the summer's writing that I'd taken a job repairing car roofs at the Northern Pacific shops. Then the postman rang, and that day I quit work and ran along the streets, stopping automobiles to tell friends and acquaintances about it—my novel *This Side of Paradise* was accepted for publication. That week the postman rang and rang, and I paid off my terrible small debts, bought a suit, and woke up every morning with a world of ineffable toploftiness and promise."

When it was published in 1920, *This Side of Paradise* was a sensation. The old, prewar world with its Victorian code of behavior had been dumped in favor of a great, gaudy spree of new freedoms. Girls bobbed their hair and shortened their skirts, while boys filled their flasks with bootleg gin. To the wail of saxophones, couples danced the Charleston across the nation's dance floors. In young Fitzgerald's novel, the Jazz Age had found its definition.

> The Jazz Age had found its definition.

Taking Aim at the American Dream

Zelda married Scott in April of that year. The newlyweds moved to New York and became the center of a round of parties, while Scott turned out scores of stories. In the first years of the decade, he published two collections of stories and a second novel. After a stay in France, the Fitzgeralds returned to St. Paul, where their only child, a daughter named Frances, was born.

Scott announced to Maxwell Perkins, his editor at Scribner's, that he was going to write "something *new*—something extraordinary and beautiful and simple and intricately patterned." He fulfilled that ambition in *The Great Gatsby,* his nearly flawless masterpiece, which was published in 1925. It tells the story of James Gatz, a poor boy from the Middle West who dreams of success and elegance and finds their incarnation in a Louisville girl named Daisy Fay. When Gatz returns from the war, he learns that she has become Daisy Buchanan, married to a rich Chicagoan and leading a careless, sumptuous life on Long Island. The hero, now a successful bootlegger known as Jay Gatsby, hopes to win Daisy from what he believes is a loveless, unhappy marriage. The story ends in Gatsby's death, but we can see that his dreams and his feelings are admirable. The Buchanans, on the other hand, are insulated from life's possibilities by their wealth and self-indulgence.

The central triumph of *The Great Gatsby* was its revelation of the rich in all their seductive luxury and heedlessness, accompanied by an implicit condemnation of their way of life. In a remarkably concise work, Fitzgerald probed deeply the ambiguities of the American dream.

An Epitaph for the Jazz Age

The Great Gatsby won some critical praise, but it was a financial disappointment. Fitzgerald had to work even harder to keep up with the high cost of his and Zelda's international life. He turned out more potboiling short stories (mediocre in quality and written for money) and went to Hollywood to write movie scripts. In 1930, the tenth year of their marriage, Zelda suffered a mental breakdown and spent the rest of her life in and out of asylums. Hers was a search for both sanity and identity, an identity that seemed to have been devoured by Scott's productiveness. She aspired to be a dancer and a writer, and in 1932 produced her own novel, *Save Me the Waltz.* This was her thinly disguised account of her troubled marriage.

Scott's novel *Tender Is the Night,* published in 1934, was his rebuttal to Zelda's novel. Its hero, Dick Diver, is the protector and healer of the mad heroine, Nicole. However, the stock market crash of 1929 had put an end to Fitzgerald's era, and readers had lost interest in the problems of expatriates like Dick Diver. Still, the book displays Fitzgerald's hard-won experience of life, the commitment to early dreams, the self-destructiveness of charm, and a whole generation's craving for endless youth and irresponsibility. In its despair, *Tender Is the Night* is an epitaph for the Jazz Age.

It was Fitzgerald's epitaph as well. After its publication, he struggled with mounting debts, failing health, drinking, and depression. Zelda was hospitalized, and although Scott suffered under the drudgery of the Hollywood studios, he was bound to them. When he could, he continued to do serious work. Through his love affair with Sheilah Graham, a British journalist, he grew interested in the work of Hollywood producer Irving Thalberg and began to write a novel about him. He was at work on this novel, *The Last Tycoon,* in 1940 when he died of heart failure. *The Last Tycoon* was compiled and edited by his friend Edmund Wilson and was published to wide critical praise after Fitzgerald's death.

Before You Read

WINTER DREAMS

Make the Connection

You Can't Always Get What You Want

Have you ever met someone and thought, "That's the person I want to marry"? If you have had this thought—or if you ever do someday—you might find yourself facing the same kinds of problems that Dexter Green faces. In fiction, as well as in life, what individuals hope and long for is not always what they get.

Reading Skills and Strategies

Drawing Inferences About Characters

As you read this story, jot down your responses to these questions: How are Dexter's two ambitions—achieving material success and winning Judy's hand—tied together? What picture of Judy do you put together from what you learn about her? Why can't Dexter fully escape from Judy's magnetic charms?

Elements of Literature

Motivation

Motivation refers to the reasons for a character's behavior. Motivation can come from internal sources (ambition, insecurity, shyness) or from external factors (poverty, an ambitious parent, the crash of the stock market). In one-dimensional literature, motivation comes from a single cause. But in more sophisticated fiction, as in the complexity of life itself, motivation may come from many sources and is sometimes hard to pin down. In many stories, characters aren't even aware of their own motivation.

> **M**otivation refers to the reasons for a character's behavior.
>
> *For more on Motivation, see the Handbook of Literary Terms.*

Background

This story is one of several that Fitzgerald wrote about the dreams and illusions that marked the Jazz Age. "Winter Dreams" was written in 1922, when Fitzgerald's stories were commanding top prices from the *Saturday Evening Post* and other popular magazines. The story opens around 1911, when fourteen-year-old Dexter is caddying for wealthy golfers, and spans eighteen years of Dexter's life.

Winter Dreams

F. Scott Fitzgerald

Some of the caddies were poor as sin and lived in one-room houses with a neurasthenic[1] cow in the front yard, but Dexter Green's father owned the second best grocery-store in Black Bear—the best one was "The Hub," patronized by the wealthy people from Sherry Island—and Dexter caddied only for pocket-money.

1. neurasthenic (noo′ras·then′ik): thin and weak, as though suffering from a nervous disorder.

In the fall when the days became crisp and gray, and the long Minnesota winter shut down like the white lid of a box, Dexter's skis moved over the snow that hid the fairways[2] of the golf course. At these times the country gave him a feeling of profound melancholy—it offended him that the links should lie in enforced fallowness, haunted by ragged sparrows for the long season. It was dreary, too, that on the tees where the gay colors fluttered in summer there were now only the desolate sand-boxes knee-deep in crusted ice. When he crossed the hills the wind blew cold as misery, and if the sun was out he tramped with his eyes squinted up against the hard dimensionless glare.

In April the winter ceased abruptly. The snow ran down into Black Bear Lake scarcely tarrying[3] for the early golfers to brave the season with red and black balls. Without elation, without an interval of moist glory, the cold was gone.

Dexter knew that there was something dismal about this Northern spring, just as he knew there was something gorgeous about the fall. Fall made him clinch his hands and tremble and repeat idiotic sentences to himself, and make brisk abrupt gestures of command to imaginary audiences and armies. October filled him with hope which November raised to a sort of ecstatic triumph, and in this mood the fleeting brilliant impressions of the summer at Sherry Island were ready grist to his mill.[4] He became a golf champion and defeated Mr. T. A. Hedrick in a marvellous match played a hundred times over the fairways of his imagination, a match each detail of which he changed about untiringly—sometimes he won with almost laughable ease, sometimes he came up magnificently from behind. Again, stepping from a Pierce-Arrow automobile, like Mr. Mortimer Jones, he strolled frigidly into the lounge of the Sherry Island Golf Club—or perhaps, surrounded by an admiring crowd, he gave an exhibition of fancy diving from the spring-board of the club raft. . . . Among those who watched him in open-mouthed wonder was Mr. Mortimer Jones.

And one day it came to pass that Mr. Jones—himself and not his ghost—came up to Dexter with tears in his eyes and said that Dexter was the ——best caddy in the club, and wouldn't he decide not to quit if Mr. Jones made it worth his while, because every other——caddy in the club lost one ball a hole for him—regularly——

"No, sir," said Dexter decisively, "I don't want to caddy any more." Then, after a pause: "I'm too old."

"You're not more than fourteen. Why the devil did you decide just this morning that you wanted to quit? You promised that next week you'd go over to the State tournament with me."

"I decided I was too old."

Dexter handed in his "A Class" badge, collected what money was due him from the caddy master, and walked home to Black Bear Village.

"The best——caddy I ever saw," shouted Mr. Mortimer Jones over a drink that afternoon. "Never lost a ball! Willing! Intelligent! Quiet! Honest! Grateful!"

The little girl who had done this was eleven—beautifully ugly as little girls are apt to be who are destined after a few years to be inexpressibly lovely and bring no end of misery to a great number of men. The spark, however, was perceptible. There was a general ungodliness in the way her lips twisted down at the corners when she smiled, and in the—Heaven help us!—in the almost passionate quality of her eyes. Vitality is born early in such women. It was utterly in evidence now, shining through her thin frame in a sort of glow.

She had come eagerly out on to the course at nine o'clock with a white linen nurse and five small new golf-clubs in a white canvas bag which the nurse was carrying. When Dexter first saw her she was standing by the caddy house, rather ill at ease and trying to conceal the fact by engaging her nurse in an obviously unnatural conversation graced by startling and irrelevant grimaces from herself.

"Well, it's certainly a nice day, Hilda," Dexter heard her say. She drew down the corners of her

---

2. fairways: mowed parts of a golf course. The fairway of most holes starts at the tee and ends near the green.
3. tarrying: waiting.
4. grist to his mill: something that can be used to advantage.

mouth, smiled, and glanced furtively around, her eyes in transit falling for an instant on Dexter.

Then to the nurse:

"Well, I guess there aren't very many people out here this morning, are there?"

The smile again—radiant, blatantly artificial—convincing.

"I don't know what we're supposed to do now," said the nurse, looking nowhere in particular.

"Oh, that's all right. I'll fix it up."

Dexter stood perfectly still, his mouth slightly ajar. He knew that if he moved forward a step his stare would be in her line of vision—if he moved backward he would lose his full view of her face. For a moment he had not realized how young she was. Now he remembered having seen her several times the year before—in bloomers.

Suddenly, involuntarily, he laughed, a short abrupt laugh—then, startled by himself, he turned and began to walk quickly away.

"Boy!"

Dexter stopped.

"Boy——"

Beyond question he was addressed. Not only that, but he was treated to that absurd smile, that preposterous smile—the memory of which at least a dozen men were to carry into middle age.

"Boy, do you know where the golf teacher is?"

"He's giving a lesson."

"Well, do you know where the caddy-master is?"

"He isn't here yet this morning."

"Oh." For a moment this baffled her. She stood alternately on her right and left foot.

"We'd like to get a caddy," said the nurse. "Mrs. Mortimer Jones sent us out to play golf, and we don't know how without we get a caddy."

Here she was stopped by an ominous glance from Miss Jones, followed immediately by the smile.

"There aren't any caddies here except me," said Dexter to the nurse, "and I got to stay here in charge until the caddy-master gets here."

"Oh."

Miss Jones and her retinue[5] now withdrew, and at a proper distance from Dexter became involved in a heated conversation, which was concluded by Miss Jones taking one of the clubs and hitting it on the ground with violence. For further emphasis she raised it again and was about to bring it down smartly upon the nurse's bosom, when the nurse seized the club and twisted it from her hands.

"You damn little mean old *thing!*" cried Miss Jones wildly.

Another argument ensued. Realizing that the elements of the comedy were implied in the scene, Dexter several times began to laugh, but each time restrained the laugh before it reached audibility. He could not resist the monstrous conviction that the little girl was justified in beating the nurse.

The situation was resolved by the fortuitous[6] appearance of the caddy-master, who was appealed to immediately by the nurse.

"Miss Jones is to have a little caddy, and this one says he can't go."

"Mr. McKenna said I was to wait here till you came," said Dexter quickly.

"Well, he's here now." Miss Jones smiled cheerfully at the caddy-master. Then she dropped her bag and set off at a haughty mince[7] toward the first tee.

"Well?" the caddy-master turned to Dexter. "What you standing there like a dummy for? Go pick up the young lady's clubs."

"I don't think I'll go out to-day," said Dexter.

"You don't——"

"I think I'll quit."

The enormity of his decision frightened him. He was a favorite caddy, and the thirty dollars a month he earned through the summer were not to be made elsewhere around the lake. But he had received a strong emotional shock, and his perturbation required a violent and immediate outlet.

It is not so simple as that, either. As so frequently would be the case in the future, Dexter was unconsciously dictated to by his winter dreams.

6. **fortuitous** (fôr·tōō′ə·təs): fortunate.
7. **mince:** prim, affected walk.

WORDS TO OWN

perturbation (pʉr′tər·bā′shən) *n*.: feeling of alarm or agitation.

---

5. **retinue** (ret′'n·yōō′): group of followers or servants attending to a person of rank.

II

Now, of course, the quality and the seasonability of these winter dreams varied, but the stuff of them remained. They persuaded Dexter several years later to pass up a business course at the State university—his father, prospering now, would have paid his way—for the precarious[8] advantage of attending an older and more famous university in the East, where he was bothered by his scanty funds. But do not get the impression, because his winter dreams happened to be concerned at first with musings on the rich, that there was anything merely snobbish in the boy. He wanted not association with glittering things and glittering people—he wanted the glittering things themselves. Often he reached out for the best without knowing why he wanted it— and sometimes he ran up against the mysterious denials and prohibitions in which life indulges. It is with one of those denials and not with his career as a whole that this story deals.

He made money. It was rather amazing. After college he went to the city from which Black Bear Lake draws its wealthy patrons. When he was only twenty-three and had been there not quite two years, there were already people who liked to say: "Now *there's* a boy—" All about him rich men's sons were peddling bonds precariously, or investing patrimonies[9] precariously, or plodding through the two dozen volumes of the "George Washington Commercial Course," but Dexter borrowed a thousand dollars on his college degree and his confident mouth, and bought a partnership in a laundry.

It was a small laundry when he went into it but Dexter made a specialty of learning how the English washed fine woolen golf-stockings without shrinking them, and within a year he was catering to the trade that wore knickerbockers. Men were insisting that their Shetland hose and sweaters go to his laundry just as they had insisted on a caddy who could find golf-balls. A little later he was doing their wives' lingerie as well—and running five branches in different parts of the city. Before he was twenty-seven he owned the largest string of laundries in his section of the country. It was

then that he sold out and went to New York. But the part of his story that concerns us goes back to the days when he was making his first big success.

When he was twenty-three Mr. Hart—one of the gray-haired men who like to say "Now there's a boy"—gave him a guest card to the Sherry Island Golf Club for a week-end. So he signed his name one day on the register, and that afternoon played golf in a foursome with Mr. Hart and Mr. Sandwood and Mr. T. A. Hedrick. He did not consider it necessary to remark that he had once carried Mr. Hart's bag over this same links, and that he knew every trap and gully with his eyes shut— but he found himself glancing at the four caddies who trailed them, trying to catch a gleam or gesture that would remind him of himself, that would lessen the gap which lay between his present and his past.

It was a curious day, slashed abruptly with fleeting, familiar impressions. One minute he had the sense of being a trespasser—in the next he was impressed by the tremendous superiority he felt toward Mr. T. A. Hedrick, who was a bore and not even a good golfer any more.

Then, because of a ball Mr. Hart lost near the fifteenth green, an enormous thing happened. While they were searching the stiff grasses of the rough there was a clear call of "Fore!"[10] from behind a hill in their rear. And as they all turned abruptly from their search a bright new ball sliced abruptly over the hill and caught Mr. T. A. Hedrick in the abdomen.

"By Gad!" cried Mr. T. A. Hedrick, "they ought to put some of these crazy women off the course. It's getting to be outrageous."

A head and a voice came up together over the hill:

"Do you mind if we go through?"

"You hit me in the stomach!" declared Mr. Hedrick wildly.

"Did I?" The girl approached the group of men. "I'm sorry. I yelled 'Fore!'"

Her glance fell casually on each of the men— then scanned the fairway for her ball.

"Did I bounce into the rough?"

It was impossible to determine whether this

---

8. **precarious** (prē·ker′ē·əs): uncertain.
9. **patrimonies** (pa′trə·mō′nēz): inheritances.

10. **fore:** warning cry that a golfer gives before hitting a ball down the fairway.

question was ingenuous[11] or malicious. In a moment, however, she left no doubt, for as her partner came up over the hill she called cheerfully:

"Here I am! I'd have gone on the green except that I hit something."

As she took her stance for a short mashie[12] shot, Dexter looked at her closely. She wore a blue gingham dress, rimmed at throat and shoulders with a white edging that accentuated her tan. The quality of exaggeration, of thinness, which had made her passionate eyes and down-turning mouth absurd at eleven, was gone now. She was arrestingly beautiful. The color in her cheeks was centered like the color in a picture— it was not a "high" color, but a sort of fluctuating and feverish warmth, so shaded that it seemed at any moment it would recede and disappear. This color and the mobility of her mouth gave a continual impression of flux, of intense life, of passionate vitality—balanced only partially by the sad luxury of her eyes.

She swung her mashie impatiently and without interest, pitching the ball into a sand-pit on the other side of the green. With a quick, insincere smile and a careless "Thank you!" she went on after it.

"That Judy Jones!" remarked Mr. Hedrick on the next tee, as they waited—some moments—for her to play on ahead. "All she needs is to be turned up and spanked for six months and then to be married off to an old-fashioned cavalry captain."

"My God, she's good-looking!" said Mr. Sandwood, who was just over thirty.

"Good-looking!" cried Mr. Hedrick contemptuously, "she always looks as if she wanted to be kissed! Turning those big cow-eyes on every calf in town!"

It was doubtful if Mr. Hedrick intended a reference to the maternal instinct.

"She'd play pretty good golf if she'd try," said Mr. Sandwood.

"She has no form," said Mr. Hedrick solemnly.

"She has a nice figure," said Mr. Sandwood.

"Better thank the Lord she doesn't drive a swifter ball," said Mr. Hart, winking at Dexter.

Later in the afternoon the sun went down with a riotous swirl of gold and varying blues and scarlets, and left the dry, rustling night of Western summer. Dexter watched from the veranda of the Golf Club, watched the even overlap of the waters in the little wind, silver molasses under the harvest-moon. Then the moon held a finger to her lips and the lake became a clear pool, pale and quiet. Dexter put on his bathing-suit and swam out to the farthest raft, where he stretched dripping on the wet canvas of the springboard.

There was a fish jumping and a star shining and the lights around the lake were gleaming. Over on a dark peninsula a piano was playing the songs of last summer and of summers before that—songs from "Chin-Chin" and "The Count of Luxemburg" and "The Chocolate Soldier"—and because the sound of a piano over a stretch of water had always seemed beautiful to Dexter he lay perfectly quiet and listened.

The tune the piano was playing at that moment had been gay and new five years before when Dexter was a sophomore at college. They had played it at a prom once when he could not afford the luxury of proms, and he had stood outside the gymnasium and listened. The sound of the tune precipitated in him a sort of ecstasy and it was with that ecstasy he viewed what happened to him now. It was a mood of intense appreciation, a sense that, for once, he was magnificently attuned to life and that everything about him was radiating a brightness and a glamour he might never know again.

A low, pale oblong detached itself suddenly from the darkness of the Island, spitting forth the reverberate sound of a racing motor-boat. Two white streamers of cleft water rolled themselves out behind it and almost immediately the boat

> *She was arrestingly beautiful. The color in her cheeks was centered like the color in a picture —*

---

11. **ingenuous** (in·jen′yo͞o·əs): innocent; without guile.
12. **mashie**: a number 5 iron golf club.

WORDS TO OWN

malicious (mə·lish′əs) *adj.*: intentionally hurtful.

F. SCOTT FITZGERALD **591**

was beside him, drowning out the hot tinkle of the piano in the drone of its spray. Dexter raising himself on his arms was aware of a figure standing at the wheel, of two dark eyes regarding him over the lengthening space of water—then the boat had gone by and was sweeping in an immense and purposeless circle of spray round and round in the middle of the lake. With equal eccentricity one of the circles flattened out and headed back toward the raft.

"Who's that?" she called, shutting off her motor. She was so near now that Dexter could see her bathing-suit, which consisted apparently of pink rompers.

The nose of the boat bumped the raft, and as the latter tilted rakishly, he was precipitated[13] toward her. With different degrees of interest they recognized each other.

"Aren't you one of those men we played through this afternoon?" she demanded.

He was.

"Well, do you know how to drive a motor-boat? Because if you do I wish you'd drive this one so I can ride on the surf-board behind. My name is Judy Jones"—she favored him with an absurd smirk—rather, what tried to be a smirk, for, twist her mouth as she might, it was not grotesque, it was merely beautiful—"and I live in a house over there on the Island, and in that house there is a man waiting for me. When he drove up at the door I drove out of the dock because he says I'm his ideal."

There was a fish jumping and a star shining and the lights around the lake were gleaming. Dexter sat beside Judy Jones and she explained how her boat was driven. Then she was in the water, swimming to the floating surf-board with a sinuous[14] crawl. Watching her was without effort to the eye, watching a branch waving or a sea-gull flying. Her arms, burned to butternut, moved sinuously among the dull platinum ripples, elbow appearing first, casting the forearm back with a cadence of falling water, then reaching out and down, stabbing a path ahead.

They moved out into the lake; turning, Dexter saw that she was kneeling on the low rear of the now uptilted surf-board.

"Go faster," she called, "fast as it'll go."

13. **precipitated:** thrown headlong.
14. **sinuous:** curving back and forth; snakelike.

Obediently he jammed the lever forward and the white spray mounted at the bow. When he looked around again the girl was standing up on the rushing board, her arms spread wide, her eyes lifted toward the moon.

"It's awful cold," she shouted. "What's your name?"

He told her.

"Well, why don't you come to dinner to-morrow night?"

His heart turned over like the fly-wheel[15] of the boat, and, for the second time, her casual whim gave a new direction to his life.

III

Next evening while he waited for her to come down-stairs, Dexter peopled the soft deep summer room and the sun-porch that opened from it with the men who had already loved Judy Jones. He knew the sort of men they were—the men who when he first went to college had entered from the great prep schools with graceful clothes and the deep tan of healthy summers. He had seen that, in one sense, he was better than these men. He was newer and stronger. Yet in acknowledging to himself that he wished his children to be like them he was admitting that he was but the rough, strong stuff from which they eternally sprang.

When the time had come for him to wear good clothes, he had known who were the best tailors in America, and the best tailors in America had made him the suit he wore this evening. He had acquired that particular <u>reserve</u> peculiar to his university, that set it off from other universities. He recognized the value to him of such a mannerism and he had adopted it; he knew that to be careless in dress and manner required more confidence than to be careful. But carelessness was for his children. His mother's name had been Krimslich. She was a Bohemian of the peasant class and she had talked broken English to the end of her days. Her son must keep to the set patterns.

15. **fly-wheel:** wheel that regulates the speed of a machine.

WORDS TO OWN
reserve (ri·zʉrv′) *n.*: self-restraint.

At a little after seven Judy Jones came downstairs. She wore a blue silk afternoon dress, and he was disappointed at first that she had not put on something more elaborate. This feeling was accentuated when, after a brief greeting, she went to the door of a butler's pantry and pushing it open called: "You can serve dinner, Martha." He had rather expected that a butler would announce dinner, that there would be a cocktail. Then he put these thoughts behind him as they sat down side by side on a lounge and looked at each other.

"Father and mother won't be here," she said thoughtfully.

He remembered the last time he had seen her father, and he was glad the parents were not to be here to-night—they might wonder who he was. He had been born in Keeble, a Minnesota village fifty miles farther north, and he always gave Keeble as his home instead of Black Bear Village. Country towns were well enough to come from if they weren't inconveniently in sight and used as footstools by fashionable lakes.

They talked of his university, which she had visited frequently during the past two years, and of the near-by city which supplied Sherry Island with its patrons, and whither Dexter would return next day to his prospering laundries.

During dinner she slipped into a moody depression which gave Dexter a feeling of uneasiness. Whatever <u>petulance</u> she uttered in her throaty voice worried him. Whatever she smiled at—at him, at a chicken liver, at nothing—it disturbed him that her smile could have no root in <u>mirth</u>, or even in amusement. When the scarlet corners of her lips curved down, it was less a smile than an invitation to a kiss.

Then, after dinner, she led him out on the dark sun-porch and deliberately changed the atmosphere.

"Do you mind if I weep a little?" she said.

"I'm afraid I'm boring you," he responded quickly.

"You're not. I like you. But I've just had a terrible afternoon. There was a man I cared about, and

> *During dinner she slipped into a moody depression which gave Dexter a feeling of uneasiness.*

this afternoon he told me out of a clear sky that he was poor as a church-mouse. He'd never even hinted it before. Does this sound horribly mundane?"[16]

"Perhaps he was afraid to tell you."

"Suppose he was," she answered. "He didn't start right. You see, if I'd thought of him as poor—well, I've been mad about loads of poor men, and fully intended to marry them all. But in this case, I hadn't thought of him that way, and my interest in him wasn't strong enough to survive the shock. As if a girl calmly informed her fiancé that she was a widow. He might not object to widows, but——"

"Let's start right," she interrupted herself suddenly. "Who are you, anyhow?"

For a moment Dexter hesitated. Then:

"I'm nobody," he announced. "My career is largely a matter of futures."

"Are you poor?"

"No," he said frankly, "I'm probably making more money than any man my age in the Northwest. I know that's an obnoxious remark, but you advised me to start right."

There was a pause. Then she smiled and the corners of her mouth drooped and an almost imperceptible sway brought her closer to him, looking up into his eyes. A lump rose in Dexter's throat, and he waited breathless for the experiment, facing the unpredictable compound that would form mysteriously from the elements of their lips. Then he saw—she communicated her excitement to him, lavishly, deeply, with kisses that were not a promise but a fulfillment. They aroused in him not hunger demanding renewal but surfeit that would demand more surfeit . . . kisses that were like charity, creating want by holding back nothing at all.

It did not take him many hours to decide that he had wanted Judy Jones ever since he was a proud, desirous little boy.

16. **mundane:** ordinary; everyday.

WORDS TO OWN
petulance (pech′ə·ləns) *n.*: irritability; impatience.
mirth (murth) *n.*: joyfulness.

premeditation of effects—there was a very little mental side to any of her affairs. She simply made men conscious to the highest degree of her physical loveliness. Dexter had no desire to change her. Her deficiencies were knit up with a passionate energy that transcended and justified them.

When, as Judy's head lay against his shoulder that first night, she whispered, "I don't know what's the matter with me. Last night I thought I was in love with a man and to-night I think I'm in love with you——" —it seemed to him a beautiful and romantic thing to say. It was the exquisite excitability that for the moment he controlled and owned. But a week later he was compelled to view this same quality in a different light. She took him in her roadster to a picnic supper, and after supper she disappeared, likewise in her roadster, with another man. Dexter became enormously upset and was scarcely able to be decently civil to the other people present. When she assured him that she had not kissed the other man, he knew she was lying—yet he was glad that she had taken the trouble to lie to him.

He was, as he found before the summer ended, one of a varying dozen who circulated about her. Each of them had at one time been favored above all others—about half of them still basked in the solace of occasional sentimental revivals. Whenever one showed signs of dropping out through long neglect, she granted him a brief honeyed hour, which encouraged him to tag along for a year or so longer. Judy made these forays[18] upon the helpless and defeated without malice, indeed half unconscious that there was anything mischievous in what she did.

When a new man came to town every one dropped out—dates were automatically cancelled.

The helpless part of trying to do anything about it was that she did it all herself. She was not a girl who could be "won" in the kinetic[19] sense— she was proof against[20] cleverness, she was proof

18. **forays** (fôr′āz): raids.
19. **kinetic** (ki·net′ik): coming about through action or energy.
20. **proof against:** able to withstand.

Words to Own
divergence (dī·vʉr′jəns) n.: variance; difference.

IV

It began like that—and continued, with varying shades of intensity, on such a note right up to the dénouement.[17] Dexter surrendered a part of himself to the most direct and unprincipled personality with which he had ever come in contact. Whatever Judy wanted, she went after with the full pressure of her charm. There was no <u>divergence</u> of method, no jockeying for position or

17. **dénouement** (dā′nōō·män′): final outcome.

against charm; if any of these assailed her too strongly she would immediately resolve the affair to a physical basis, and under the magic of her physical splendor the strong as well as the brilliant played her game and not their own. She was entertained only by the gratification of her desires and by the direct exercise of her own charm. Perhaps from so much youthful love, so many youthful lovers, she had come, in self-defense, to nourish herself wholly from within.

Succeeding Dexter's first exhilaration came restlessness and dissatisfaction. The helpless ecstasy of losing himself in her was opiate rather than tonic.[21] It was fortunate for his work during the winter that those moments of ecstasy came in-

21. **opiate . . . tonic:** calming rather than stimulating.

frequently. Early in their acquaintance it had seemed for a while that there was a deep and spontaneous mutual attraction—that first August, for example—three days of long evenings on her dusky veranda, of strange wan kisses through the late afternoon, in shadowy alcoves or behind the protecting trellises of the garden arbors, of mornings when she was fresh as a dream and almost shy at meeting him in the clarity of the rising day. There was all the ecstasy of an engagement about it, sharpened by his realization that there was no engagement. It was during those three days that, for the first time, he had asked her to marry him. She said "maybe some day," she said "kiss me," she said "I'd like to marry you," she said "I love you"—she said—nothing.

The three days were interrupted by the arrival of a New York man who visited at her house for half September. To Dexter's agony, rumor engaged them. The man was the son of the president of a great trust company. But at the end of a month it was reported that Judy was yawning. At a dance one night she sat all evening in a motor-boat with a local beau, while the New Yorker searched the club for her frantically. She told the local beau that she was bored with her visitor, and two days later he left. She was seen with him at the station, and it was reported that he looked very mournful indeed.

On this note the summer ended. Dexter was twenty-four, and he found himself increasingly in a position to do as he wished. He joined two clubs in the city and lived at one of them. Though he was by no means an integral part of the stag-lines[22] at these clubs, he managed to be on hand at dances where Judy Jones was likely to appear. He could have gone out socially as much as he liked—he was an eligible young man, now, and popular with down-town fathers. His confessed devotion to Judy Jones had rather solidified his position. But he had no social aspirations and rather despised the dancing men who were always on tap for the Thursday or Saturday parties and who filled in at dinners with the younger married set. Already he was playing with the idea of going East to New York. He wanted to take Judy Jones with him. No disillusion as to the world in which she had grown up could cure his illusion as to her desirability.

Remember that—for only in the light of it can what he did for her be understood.

Eighteen months after he first met Judy Jones he became engaged to another girl. Her name was Irene Scheerer, and her father was one of the men who had always believed in Dexter. Irene was light-haired and sweet and honorable, and a little stout, and she had two suitors whom she pleasantly relinquished when Dexter formally asked her to marry him.

Summer, fall, winter, spring, another summer, another fall—so much he had given of his active life to the incorrigible[23] lips of Judy Jones. She had treated him with interest, with encouragement, with malice, with indifference, with contempt. She had inflicted on him the innumerable little slights and indignities possible in such a case—as if in revenge for having ever cared for him at all. She had beckoned him and yawned at him and beckoned him again and he had responded often with bitterness and narrowed eyes. She had brought him ecstatic happiness and intolerable agony of spirit. She had caused him untold inconvenience and not a little trouble. She had insulted him, and she had ridden over him, and she had played his interest in her against his interest in his work—for fun. She had done everything to him except to criticize him—this she had not done—it seemed to him only because it might have sullied the utter indifference she manifested and sincerely felt toward him.

When autumn had come and gone again it occurred to him that he could not have Judy Jones. He had to beat this into his mind but he convinced himself at last. He lay awake at night for a while and argued it over. He told himself the trouble and the pain she had caused him, he enumerated her glaring deficiences as a wife. Then he said to himself that he loved her, and after a while he fell asleep. For a week, lest he imagined her husky voice over the telephone or her eyes opposite him at lunch, he worked hard and late, and at night he went to his office and plotted out his years.

At the end of a week he went to a dance and cut in on her once. For almost the first time since they had met he did not ask her to sit out with him or tell her that she was lovely. It hurt him that she did not miss these things—that was all. He was not jealous when he saw that there was a new man to-night. He had been hardened against jealousy long before.

He stayed late at the dance. He sat for an hour with Irene Scheerer and talked about books and about music. He knew very little about either. But he was beginning to be master of his own time now, and he had a rather priggish[24] notion that he—the young and already fabulously successful Dexter Green—should know more about such things.

That was in October, when he was twenty-five. In January, Dexter and Irene became engaged. It

22. **stag-lines:** lines of unaccompanied men at a dance, waiting for available dance partners.
23. **incorrigible:** incapable of correction or reform.
24. **priggish:** annoyingly precise and proper.

was to be announced in June, and they were to be married three months later.

The Minnesota winter prolonged itself interminably, and it was almost May when the winds came soft and the snow ran down into Black Bear Lake at last. For the first time in over a year Dexter was enjoying a certain tranquility of spirit. Judy Jones had been in Florida, and afterward in Hot Springs, and somewhere she had been engaged, and somewhere she had broken it off. At first, when Dexter had definitely given her up, it had made him sad that people still linked them together and asked for news of her, but when he began to be placed at dinner next to Irene Scheerer people didn't ask him about her any more—they told him about her. He ceased to be an authority on her.

May at last. Dexter walked the streets at night when the darkness was damp as rain, wondering that so soon, with so little done, so much of ecstasy had gone from him. May one year back had been marked by Judy's poignant, unforgivable, yet forgiven turbulence—it had been one of those rare times when he fancied she had grown to care for him. That old penny's worth of happiness he had spent for this bushel of content. He knew that Irene would be no more than a curtain spread behind him, a hand moving among gleaming tea-cups, a voice calling to children . . . fire and loveliness were gone, the magic of nights and the wonder of the varying hours and seasons . . . slender lips, down-turning, dropping to his lips and bearing him up into a heaven of eyes. . . . The thing was deep in him. He was too strong and alive for it to die lightly.

In the middle of May when the weather balanced for a few days on the thin bridge that led to deep summer he turned in one night at Irene's house. Their engagement was to be announced in a week now—no one would be surprised at it. And to-night they would sit together on the lounge at the University Club and look on for an hour at the dancers. It gave him a sense of solidity to go with her—she was so sturdily popular, so intensely "great."

He mounted the steps of the brownstone house and stepped inside.

"Irene," he called.

Mrs. Scheerer came out of the living-room to meet him.

"Dexter," she said, "Irene's gone up-stairs with a splitting headache. She wanted to go with you but I made her go to bed."

"Nothing serious, I——"

"Oh, no. She's going to play golf with you in the morning. You can spare her for just one night, can't you, Dexter?"

Her smile was kind. She and Dexter liked each other. In the living-room he talked for a moment before he said good-night.

Returning to the University Club, where he had rooms, he stood in the doorway for a moment and watched the dancers. He leaned against the doorpost, nodded at a man or two—yawned.

"Hello, darling."

The familiar voice at his elbow startled him. Judy Jones had left a man and crossed the room to him—Judy Jones, a slender enamelled doll in cloth of gold: gold in a band at her head, gold in two slipper points at her dress's hem. The fragile glow of her face seemed to blossom as she smiled at him. A breeze of warmth and light blew through the room. His hands in the pockets of his dinner-jacket tightened spasmodically. He was filled with a sudden excitement.

"When did you get back?" he asked casually.

"Come here and I'll tell you about it."

She turned and he followed her. She had been away—he could have wept at the wonder of her return. She had passed through enchanted streets, doing things that were like provocative music. All mysterious happenings, all fresh and quickening hopes, had gone away with her, come back with her now.

She turned in the doorway.

"Have you a car here? If you haven't, I have."

"I have a coupé."

In then, with a rustle of golden cloth. He slammed the door. Into so many cars she had stepped—like this—like that—her back against the leather, so—her elbow resting on the door—waiting. She would have been soiled long since had there been anything to soil her—except herself—but this was her own self outpouring.

With an effort he forced himself to start the car and back into the street. This was nothing, he

must remember. She had done this before, and he had put her behind him, as he would have crossed a bad account from his books.

He drove slowly down-town and, affecting abstraction, traversed the deserted streets of the business section, peopled here and there where a movie was giving out its crowd or where consumptive[25] or pugilistic[26] youth lounged in front of pool halls. The clink of glasses and the slap of hands on the bars issued from saloons, cloisters of glazed glass and dirty yellow light.

She was watching him closely and the silence was embarrassing, yet in this crisis he could find no casual word with which to profane the hour. At a convenient turning he began to zigzag back toward the University Club.

"Have you missed me?" she asked suddenly.

"Everybody missed you."

25. **consumptive:** destructive; wasteful.
26. **pugilistic** (pyo͞o′jil·is′tik): eager to fight.

laugh. It was the sort of thing that was said to sophomores. Yet it stabbed at him.

"I'm awfully tired of everything, darling." She called every one darling, endowing the endearment with careless, individual comraderie. "I wish you'd marry me."

The directness of this confused him. He should have told her now that he was going to marry another girl, but he could not tell her. He could as easily have sworn that he had never loved her.

"I think we'd get along," she continued, on the same note, "unless probably you've forgotten me and fallen in love with another girl."

Her confidence was obviously enormous. She had said, in effect, that she found such a thing impossible to believe, that if it were true he had merely committed a childish indiscretion—and probably to show off. She would forgive him, because it was not a matter of any moment but rather something to be brushed aside lightly.

"Of course you could never love anybody but me," she continued. "I like the way you love me. Oh, Dexter, have you forgotten last year?"

"No, I haven't forgotten."

"Neither have I!"

Was she sincerely moved—or was she carried along by the wave of her own acting?

"I wish we could be like that again," she said, and he forced himself to answer:

"I don't think we can."

"I suppose not. . . . I hear you're giving Irene Scheerer a violent rush."

There was not the faintest emphasis on the name, yet Dexter was suddenly ashamed.

"Oh, take me home," cried Judy suddenly; "I don't want to go back to that idiotic dance—with those children."

Then, as he turned up the street that led to the residence district, Judy began to cry quietly to herself. He had never seen her cry before.

The dark street lightened, the dwellings of the rich loomed up around them, he stopped his coupé in front of the great white bulk of the Mortimer Joneses house, somnolent,[27] gorgeous, drenched with the splendor of the damp moonlight. Its solidity startled him. The strong walls, the steel of the girders, the breadth and beam and pomp of it were there only to bring out the

He wondered if she knew of Irene Scheerer. She had been back only a day—her absence had been almost contemporaneous with his engagement.

"What a remark!" Judy laughed sadly—without sadness. She looked at him searchingly. He became absorbed in the dashboard.

"You're handsomer than you used to be," she said thoughtfully. "Dexter, you have the most rememberable eyes."

He could have laughed at this, but he did not

27. somnolent: sleepy.

contrast with the young beauty beside him. It was sturdy to accentuate her slightness—as if to show what a breeze could be generated by a butterfly's wing.

He sat perfectly quiet, his nerves in wild clamor, afraid that if he moved he would find her irresistibly in his arms. Two tears had rolled down her wet face and trembled on her upper lip.

"I'm more beautiful than anybody else," she said brokenly, "why can't I be happy?" Her moist eyes tore at his stability—her mouth turned slowly downward with an exquisite sadness: "I'd like to marry you if you'll have me, Dexter. I suppose you think I'm not worth having, but I'll be so beautiful for you, Dexter."

A million phrases of anger, pride, passion, hatred, tenderness fought on his lips. Then a perfect wave of emotion washed over him, carrying off with it a sediment of wisdom, of convention,[28] of doubt, of honor. This was his girl who was speaking, his own, his beautiful, his pride.

"Won't you come in?" He heard her draw in her breath sharply.

Waiting.

"All right," his voice was trembling, "I'll come in."

"I'm more beautiful than anybody else . . . why can't I be happy?"

V

It was strange that neither when it was over nor a long time afterward did he regret that night. Looking at it from the perspective of ten years, the fact that Judy's flare for him endured just one month seemed of little importance. Nor did it matter that by his yielding he subjected himself to a deeper agony in the end and gave serious hurt to Irene Sheerer and to Irene's parents, who had befriended him. There was nothing sufficiently pictorial about Irene's grief to stamp itself on his mind.

28. **convention:** accepted practices of social behavior.

Dexter was at bottom hard-minded. The attitude of the city on his action was of no importance to him, not because he was going to leave the city, but because any outside attitude on the situation seemed superficial. He was completely indifferent to popular opinion. Nor, when he had seen that it was no use, that he did not possess in himself the power to move fundamentally or to hold Judy Jones, did he bear any malice toward her. He loved her, and he would love her until the day he was too old for loving—but he could not have her. So he tasted the deep pain that is reserved only for the strong, just as he had tasted for a little while the deep happiness.

Even the ultimate falsity of the grounds upon which Judy terminated the engagement, that she did not want to "take him away" from Irene—Judy, who had wanted nothing else—did not revolt him. He was beyond any revulsion or any amusement.

He went East in February with the intention of selling out his laundries and settling in New York—but the war came to America in March and changed his plans. He returned to the West, handed over the management of the business to his partner, and went into the first officers' training-camp in late April. He was one of those young thousands who greeted the war with a certain amount of relief, welcoming the liberation from webs of tangled emotion.

VI

This story is not his biography, remember, although things creep into it which have nothing to do with those dreams he had when he was young. We are almost done with them and with him now. There is only one more incident to be related here, and it happens seven years farther on.

It took place in New York, where he had done well—so well that there were no barriers too high for him. He was thirty-two years old, and, except for one flying trip immediately after the war, he had not been West in seven years. A man named Devlin from Detroit came into his office to see him in a business way, and then and there this incident occurred, and closed out, so to speak, this particular side of his life.

"So you're from the Middle West," said the man Devlin with careless curiosity. "That's funny—I thought men like you were probably born and raised on Wall Street. You know—wife of one of my best friends in Detroit came from your city. I was an usher at the wedding."

Dexter waited with no apprehension of what was coming.

"Judy Simms," said Devlin with no particular interest; "Judy Jones she was once."

"Yes, I knew her." A dull impatience spread over him. He had heard, of course, that she was married—perhaps deliberately he had heard no more.

"Awfully nice girl," brooded Devlin meaninglessly, "I'm sort of sorry for her."

"Why?" Something in Dexter was alert, receptive, at once.

"Oh, Lud Simms has gone to pieces in a way. I don't mean he ill-uses her, but he drinks and runs around——"

"Doesn't she run around?"

"No. Stays at home with her kids."

"Oh."

"She's a little too old for him," said Devlin.

"Too old!" cried Dexter. "Why, man, she's only twenty-seven."

He was possessed with a wild notion of rushing out into the streets and taking a train to Detroit. He rose to his feet spasmodically.

"I guess you're busy," Devlin apologized quickly. "I didn't realize——"

"No, I'm not busy," said Dexter, steadying his voice. "I'm not busy at all. Not busy at all. Did you say she was—twenty-seven? No, I said she was twenty-seven."

"Yes, you did," agreed Devlin dryly.

"Go on, then. Go on."

"What do you mean?"

"About Judy Jones."

Devlin looked at him helplessly.

"Well, that's—I told you all there is to it. He treats her like the devil. Oh, they're not going to get divorced or anything. When he's particularly outrageous she forgives him. In fact, I'm inclined to think she loves him. She was a pretty girl when she first came to Detroit."

A pretty girl! The phrase struck Dexter as ludicrous.

"Isn't she—a pretty girl, any more?"

"Oh, she's all right."

"Look here," said Dexter, sitting down suddenly, "I don't understand. You say she was a 'pretty girl' and now you say she's 'all right.' I don't understand what you mean—Judy Jones wasn't a pretty girl, at all. She was a great beauty. Why, I knew her, I knew her. She was——"

Devlin laughed pleasantly.

"I'm not trying to start a row," he said. "I think Judy's a nice girl and I like her. I can't understand how a man like Lud Simms could fall madly in love with her, but he did." Then he added: "Most of the women like her."

Dexter looked closely at Devlin, thinking wildly that there must be a reason for this, some insensitivity in the man or some private malice.

"Lots of women fade just like *that*," Devlin snapped his fingers. "You must have seen it happen. Perhaps I've forgotten how pretty she was at her wedding. I've seen her so much since then, you see. She has nice eyes."

A sort of dullness settled down upon Dexter. For the first time in his life he felt like getting very drunk. He knew that he was laughing loudly at something Devlin had said, but he did not know what it was or why it was funny. When, in a few minutes, Devlin went, he lay down on his lounge and looked out the window at the New York skyline into which the sun was sinking in dull lovely shades of pink and gold.

He had thought that having nothing else to lose he was invulnerable at last—but he knew that he had just lost something more, as surely as if he had married Judy Jones and seen her fade away before his eyes.

The dream was gone. Something had been taken from him. In a sort of panic he pushed the

---

WORDS TO OWN

ludicrous (lōō′di·krəs) *adj.*: laughable; absurd.

The dream was gone. Something had been taken from him.

palms of his hands into his eyes and tried to bring up a picture of the waters lapping on Sherry Island and the moonlit veranda, and gingham on the golf-links and the dry sun and the gold color of her neck's soft down. And her mouth damp to his kisses and her eyes <u>plaintive</u> with melancholy and her freshness like new fine linen in the morning. Why, these things were no longer in the world! They had existed and they existed no longer.

For the first time in years the tears were streaming down his face. But they were for himself now. He did not care about mouth and eyes and moving hands. He wanted to care, and he could not care. For he had gone away and he could never go back any more. The gates were closed, the sun was gone down, and there was no beauty but the gray beauty of steel that withstands all time. Even the grief he could have borne was left behind in the country of illusion, of youth, of the richness of life, where his winter dreams had flourished.

"Long ago," he said, "long ago, there was something in me, but now that thing is gone. Now that thing is gone, that thing is gone. I cannot cry. I cannot care. That thing will come back no more."

Words to Own

plaintive (plān′tiv) *adj.*: expressing sadness.

A Letter to His Daughter

La Paix, Rodgers' Forge,
Towson, Maryland,
August 8, 1933

F. Scott Fitzgerald with his daughter, Scottie.

Dear Pie:

I feel very strongly about you doing duty. Would you give me a little more documentation about your reading in French? I am glad you are happy—but I never believe much in happiness. I never believe in misery either. Those are things you see on the stage or the screen or the printed page, they never really happen to you in life.

All I believe in in life is the rewards for virtue (according to your talents) and the *punishments* for not fulfilling your duties, which are doubly costly. If there is such a volume in the camp library, will you ask Mrs. Tyson to let you look up a sonnet of Shakespeare's in which the line occurs *"Lilies that fester smell far worse than weeds."*

Have had no thoughts today, life seems composed of getting up a *Saturday Evening Post* story. I think of you, and always pleasantly; but if you call me "Pappy" again I am going to take the White Cat out and beat his bottom *hard, six times for every time you are impertinent.* Do you react to that?

I will arrange the camp bill.

Halfwit, I will conclude. Things to worry about:

    Worry about courage
    Worry about cleanliness
    Worry about efficiency
    Worry about horsemanship . . .

Things not to worry about:

    Don't worry about popular opinion
    Don't worry about dolls
    Don't worry about the past
    Don't worry about the future
    Don't worry about growing up
    Don't worry about anybody getting ahead of you
    Don't worry about triumph
    Don't worry about failure unless it comes through your own fault
    Don't worry about mosquitoes
    Don't worry about flies
    Don't worry about insects in general
    Don't worry about parents
    Don't worry about boys
    Don't worry about disappointments
    Don't worry about pleasures
    Don't worry about satisfactions

Things to think about:

What am I really aiming at?

How good am I really in comparison to my contemporaries in regard to:

    (a) Scholarship
    (b) Do I really understand about people and am I able to get along with them?
    (c) Am I trying to make my body a useful instrument or am I neglecting it?

                With dearest love,

MAKING MEANINGS

First Thoughts

1. Did you sympathize with Dexter Green in his tangled feelings for Judy Jones? Explain why or why not.

Shaping Interpretations

2. What details does Fitzgerald use to persuade us that Dexter is an ambitious young man? What does the story suggest are Dexter's **motivations**? Explain how Dexter's actions reveal his deepest motivations and conform to what the narrator and the other characters say about him.

3. In *Richard III,* Shakespeare refers to "the winter of our discontent." How do Dexter's "winter dreams" reflect his discontent? Does his sense of deprivation subside when he fulfills his ambition to become rich? Explain.

4. When they meet again as adults, Dexter decides that he has "wanted Judy Jones ever since he was a proud, desirous little boy" (page 593). What does Judy represent to Dexter? (Refer to the notes you made while reading.) Explain why you think he really does—or does not—love her.

5. What makes Dexter "newer and stronger" (page 592) than the wealthy people he meets? Why, then, does he want his children to be like those people?

6. A recurring **theme** of Fitzgerald's work is the pursuit of the American dream. Based on this story, explain what you think Fitzgerald saw as the American dream. (Be sure to include Dexter's quest for Judy as part of your answer.) What, if anything, do you think is left out of his vision?

> ### Reading Check
>
> **a.** How does his first meeting with Judy Jones lead Dexter to quit his job?
>
> **b.** How does Dexter encounter Judy again after nearly a decade?
>
> **c.** Why does Dexter break his engagement to Irene? Is he sorry later?
>
> **d.** At the end of the story, what has happened to Judy?

7. Why do you think Dexter feels a profound sense of loss when he hears about Judy at the end of the story?

Connecting with the Text

8. According to the story, Dexter and Judy did not know each other during their high school years. Imagine that they did and that they asked you for advice. What would you tell Judy about Dexter's crush on her? What would you advise Dexter to do about Judy's coolness?

9. Do you think Dexter would have been happier in the end if Judy had married him? Why or why not?

Challenging the Text

10. Do you think the **themes** of this story are universal and timeless, or is this a story that could only have happened in its specific time and place? Explain.

READING SKILLS AND STRATEGIES

Understanding Paradoxes

A **paradox** is a seemingly contradictory statement which may, upon closer inspection, prove to illuminate a deeper truth. F. Scott Fitzgerald uses paradox frequently in "Winter Dreams," particularly in his descriptions of Judy Jones. For example:

> "The smile again—radiant, blatantly artificial—convincing." (page 589)

> ". . . kisses that were like charity, creating want by holding back nothing at all." (page 593)

Find three more paradoxical descriptions of Judy's behavior. How does this method of phrasing help convey the enigmatic complexity Dexter perceives in her?

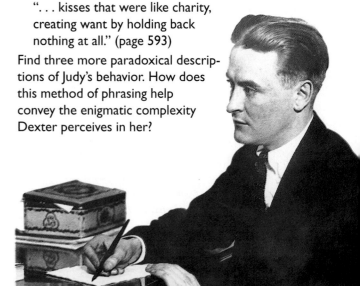

F. Scott Fitzgerald.
The Bettmann Archive.

CHOICES: Building Your Portfolio

Writer's Notebook

1. Collecting Ideas for an Analysis of Causes and Effects

In the Writer's Workshop on page 685, you'll write an essay that speculates about causes and effects. One of your choices will be to analyze the **motivations** of a fictional character that interests you. Record a series of questions you'd like to ask either Judy Jones or Dexter Green. (For example, you could ask Judy questions like these: "Were you in love with all, some, or none of your suitors? Was your main goal to be the center of attention, or was it something else? Did you enjoy making your boyfriends jealous? Did you intend to hurt anyone?") Then, record the answers you'd expect to receive from the character. Keep your notes for possible use in the Writer's Workshop.

Interpreting a Story

2. A Dreamy Fairy Tale?

In a book review of Fitzgerald's stories, the novelist Jay McInerney wrote the following:

> . . . the young (poor) boy's quest for the hand of the beautiful, rich princess is undoubtedly Fitzgerald's best plot, the fairy-tale skeleton of his jazz age tales. One supposes that magazine editors preferred the stories in which the quest is successful, but in the better ones, like "Winter Dreams" (1922) and "The Sensible Thing" (1924), the success is qualified or the quest ends in failure.
>
> —Jay McInerney

In a brief essay, analyze the ways in which "Winter Dreams" is like and unlike a fairy tale. Consider the story's **plot, atmosphere, tone,** and **characterization.**

Performance/Improvising

3. Dexter and Judy, Talking

Imagine that it is a year after the end of "Winter Dreams." Dexter and Judy meet by chance in a railroad station, where they are waiting for different trains. In their few minutes together, they discuss their past and present feelings and what they have learned about life. With a partner, briefly plan the content and direction of their conversation, based on your understanding of the characters. Then, improvise the conversation in front of the class.

Music

4. Jazz Age

"Winter Dreams" mentions three musical works: *Chin-Chin, The Count of Luxemburg,* and *The Chocolate Soldier.* Learn about the "soundtrack" of Dexter's and Judy's life by listening to music composed from about 1920 to 1930. Try the jazz, blues, operetta, symphonic, and popular vocals sections of a library or music store. Report your findings to the class. Your report might focus on a particular aspect— for example, how jazz influences abound in George Gershwin's wonderful *Rhapsody in Blue* (1924). Bring recordings to share.

Louis Armstrong.
Culver Pictures.

John Steinbeck

(1902–1968)

Most writers would probably agree that fiction that delivers a political message may be effective propaganda, but it is unlikely to be art. John Steinbeck would *not* have agreed with this precept, and he is a notable exception to it.

During the 1930s, the Great Depression cost millions of people their jobs and shook their faith in the American dream. But big business and the corporate farm seemed untouched by hard times; they were angrily perceived by many as impersonal and indifferent to human hardship.

Many novelists of the time were moved by this sense of injustice and turned their pens to a by-product of the Depression known as "the protest novel." Among these writers, John Steinbeck was the most widely praised and successful.

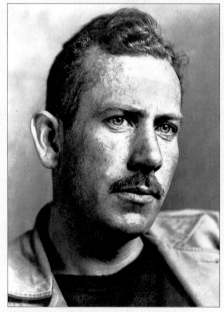

UPI/Bettmann.

Steinbeck was born in California's Salinas Valley in 1902, the son of a county treasurer and a schoolteacher. Although he graduated from high school and spent some time at Stanford University, he took more pride in the many jobs he held as a young man than in his formal education. He worked as a hod carrier, fruit picker, apprentice painter, laboratory assistant, caretaker, surveyor, and journalist. He also wrote seventeen novels, in addition to stories, plays, and screenplays.

Steinbeck's first major success came in 1937 with *Of Mice and Men,* a short, best-selling novel that Steinbeck himself adapted into a Broadway play. It is a tale of two itinerant farmhands: George and the powerful but simple-minded Lennie. Steinbeck took a pathetic situation and transformed it into an affirmative acceptance of life's brutal conflicts, along with life's possibilities for fellowship and courage.

He followed this success by living and working with some Oklahoma farmers—known as "Okies"—over the next two years. The result was his strongest and most enduring novel, *The Grapes of Wrath* (1939). It tells of the Joad family and their forced migration from the Dust Bowl of Oklahoma to California, the region that promised work at decent wages and a chance to buy land. Once in California, however, the Joads find only the exploitation and poverty of labor camps. Gradually they learn what "Okies" really means—people who never even had a chance.

The Grapes of Wrath was an angry book that spoke out on behalf of the migrant workers. Steinbeck sharply criticized a system that bankrupted thousands of farmers and turned them from their own land, making them into paid help for the big growers. When the novel appeared, it was greeted with outbursts of praise and condemnation, and it became the most widely read of all the protest novels of the 1930s.

The Grapes of Wrath won a Pulitzer Prize in 1940. After this major success, however, Steinbeck's eminence waned. Toward the end of his life, Steinbeck achieved a gratifying success with the award of the Nobel Prize in literature in 1962 and with the publication in that year of *Travels with Charley,* a nostalgic account of his odyssey across America with his aged poodle Charley. But Steinbeck's reputation is grounded on those earlier novels that portray California as the real and symbolic land of American promise.

Before You Read

THE LEADER OF THE PEOPLE

Make the Connection

The Golden Age

It seems that in every generation older people say to younger people, "It was different in my day." Most people feel nostalgic about the past, dreaming of it as a "golden age" that was somehow cleaner or more heroic or happier than the present. In fact, some people end up living mainly in memories of a past that might never have existed.

Quickwrite

There's a jaded point of view that holds that the time of heroes is long past. Who are our heroes today (or are there none)? Would you consider them role models? What opportunities do you see for heroism today? Quickwrite your thoughts.

Elements of Literature

Conflict

"The Leader of the People" shows three generations of a family in conflict because of differences in age, gender, personal histories, and the roles they play on the family ranch. Some conflicts in the story are **external conflicts:** They occur between two or more people. Others are **internal conflicts,** occurring inside one person's mind. One conflict involves a close look at that recurring dream of a more heroic American past.

Conflict is a struggle between opposing forces or characters in a story. Conflict can be internal (a character struggles with conscience, for example) or external (a character struggles against a blizzard).

For more about Conflict, see the Handbook of Literary Terms.

Background

In "The Leader of the People," John Steinbeck explores the conflict between dream and reality at the heart of so much American fiction. This story appears as the fourth and final part of Steinbeck's novel *The Red Pony* (1945). Each part of this novel was published as a complete short story. The stories, all connected by their characters and settings, are "The Gift," "The Great Mountains," "The Promise," and "The Leader of the People."

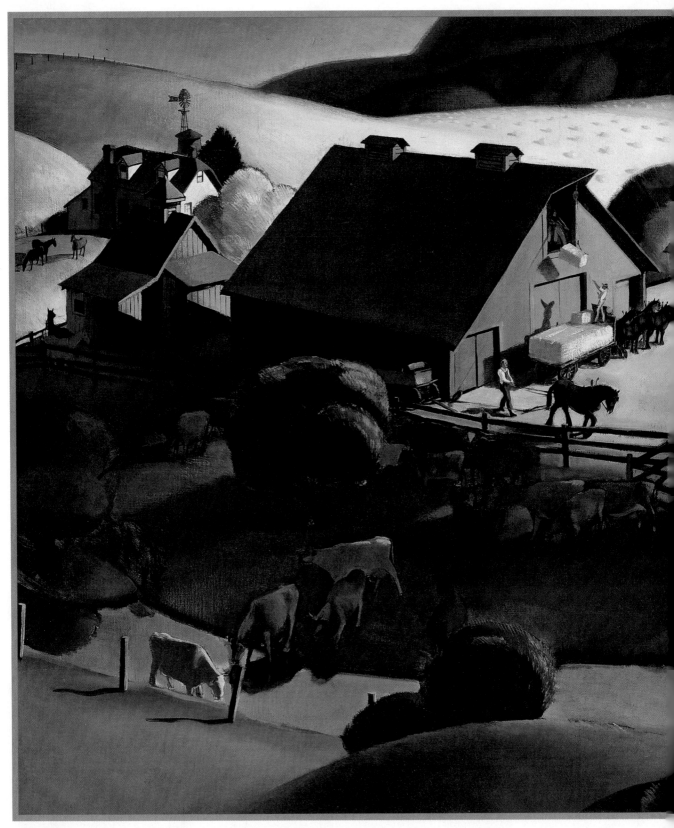

Ranch Near San Luis Obispo, Evening Light (c. 1935) by Phil Paradise. Oil on canvas (28″ × 34″).

The Leader of the People

John Steinbeck

O n Saturday afternoon Billy Buck, the ranch-hand, raked together the last of the old year's haystack and pitched small forkfuls over the wire fence to a few mildly interested cattle. High in the air small clouds like puffs of cannon smoke were driven eastward by the March wind. The wind could be heard whishing in the brush on the ridge crests, but no breath of it penetrated down into the ranch-cup.

The little boy, Jody, emerged from the house eating a thick piece of buttered bread. He saw Billy working on the last of the haystack. Jody tramped down scuffing his shoes in a way he had been told was destructive to good shoe-leather. A flock of white pigeons flew out of the black cypress tree as Jody passed, and circled the tree and landed again. A half-grown tortoise-shell[1] cat leaped from the bunkhouse porch, galloped on stiff legs across the road, whirled and galloped back again. Jody picked up a stone to help the game along, but he was too late, for the cat was under the porch before the stone could be discharged. He threw the stone into the cypress tree and started the white pigeons on another whirling flight.

Arriving at the used-up haystack, the boy leaned against the barbed wire fence. "Will that be all of it, do you think?" he asked.

The middle-aged ranch-hand stopped his careful raking and stuck his fork[2] into the ground. He took off his black hat and smoothed down his hair. "Nothing left of it that isn't soggy from ground moisture," he said. He replaced his hat and rubbed his dry leathery hands together.

"Ought to be plenty mice," Jody suggested.

"Lousy with them," said Billy. "Just crawling with mice."

"Well, maybe, when you get all through, I could call the dogs and hunt the mice."

"Sure, I guess you could," said Billy Buck. He lifted a forkful of the damp ground-hay and threw it into the air. Instantly three mice leaped out and burrowed frantically under the hay again.

Jody sighed with satisfaction. Those plump, sleek, <u>arrogant</u> mice were doomed. For eight months they had lived and multiplied in the haystack. They had been <u>immune</u> from cats, from traps, from poison and from Jody. They had grown smug in their security, overbearing and fat. Now the time of disaster had come; they would not survive another day.

1. **tortoise-shell:** having a pattern of brown and yellow markings, as commonly seen on the shell of a tortoise.
2. **fork:** pitchfork.

- -

WORDS TO OWN

arrogant (ar′ə·gənt) *adj.*: proud and overly confident.
immune (im·myo͞on′) *adj.*: protected.

- -

The Buck Collection, Laguna Hills, California.

Billy looked up at the top of the hills that surrounded the ranch. "Maybe you better ask your father before you do it," he suggested.

"Well, where is he? I'll ask him now."

"He rode up to the ridge ranch after dinner. He'll be back pretty soon."

Jody slumped against the fence post. "I don't think he'd care."

As Billy went back to his work he said ominously, "You'd better ask him anyway. You know how he is."

Jody did know. His father, Carl Tiflin, insisted upon giving permission for anything that was done on the ranch, whether it was important or not. Jody sagged farther against the post until he was sitting on the ground. He looked up at the little puffs of wind-driven cloud. "Is it like to rain, Billy?"

"It might. The wind's good for it, but not strong enough."

"Well, I hope it don't rain until after I kill those damn mice." He looked over his shoulder to see whether Billy had noticed the mature profanity. Billy worked on without comment.

Jody turned back and looked at the side-hill where the road from the outside world came down. The hill was washed with lean March sunshine. Silver thistles, blue lupins[3] and a few poppies bloomed among the sage bushes. Halfway up the hill Jody could see Doubletree Mutt, the black dog, digging in a squirrel hole. He paddled for a while and then paused to kick bursts of dirt out between his hind legs, and he dug with an earnestness which belied the knowledge he must have had that no dog had ever caught a squirrel by digging in a hole.

Suddenly, while Jody watched, the black dog stiffened, and backed out of the hole and looked up the hill toward the <u>cleft</u> in the ridge where the road came through. Jody looked up too. For a moment Carl Tiflin on horseback stood out against the pale sky and then he moved down the road toward the house. He carried something white in his hand.

The boy started to his feet. "He's got a letter," Jody cried. He trotted away toward the ranch house, for the letter would probably be read aloud and he wanted to be there. He reached the house before his father did, and ran in. He heard Carl dismount from his creaking saddle and slap the horse on the side to send it to the barn where Billy would unsaddle it and turn it out.

Jody ran into the kitchen. "We got a letter!" he cried.

His mother looked up from a pan of beans. "Who has?"

"Father has. I saw it in his hand."

Carl strode into the kitchen then, and Jody's mother asked, "Who's the letter from, Carl?"

He frowned quickly. "How did you know there was a letter?"

She nodded her head in the boy's direction. "Big-Britches Jody told me."

Jody was embarrassed.

His father looked down at him <u>contemptuously.</u> "He *is* getting to be a Big-Britches," Carl said. "He's minding everybody's business but his own. Got his big nose into everything."

Mrs. Tiflin relented a little. "Well, he hasn't enough to keep him busy. Who's the letter from?"

Carl still frowned on Jody. "I'll keep him busy if he isn't careful." He held out a sealed letter. "I guess it's from your father."

Mrs. Tiflin took a hairpin from her head and slit open the flap. Her lips pursed judiciously. Jody saw her eyes snap back and forth over the lines. "He says," she translated, "he says he's going to drive out Saturday to stay for a little while. Why, this is Saturday. The letter must have been delayed." She looked at the postmark. "This was mailed day before yesterday. It should have been here yesterday." She looked up questioningly at her husband, and then her face darkened angrily. "Now what have you got that look on you for? He doesn't come often."

Carl turned his eyes away from her anger. He could be stern with her most of the time, but when occasionally her temper arose, he could not combat it.

"What's the matter with you?" she demanded again.

WORDS TO OWN

cleft (kleft) *n*.: opening.
contemptuously (kən·temp′choo·əs·lē) *adv*.: scornfully.

---

3. **lupins** (loo′pinz): flowering plants of the bean family; more often spelled *lupines*.

In his explanation there was a tone of apology Jody himself might have used. "It's just that he talks," Carl said lamely. "Just talks."

"Well, what of it? You talk yourself."

"Sure I do. But your father only talks about one thing."

"Indians!" Jody broke in excitedly. "Indians and crossing the plains!"

Carl turned fiercely on him. "You get out, Mr. Big-Britches! Go on, now! Get out!"

Jody went miserably out the back door and closed the screen with elaborate quietness. Under the kitchen window his shamed, downcast eyes fell upon a curiously shaped stone, a stone of such fascination that he squatted down and picked it up and turned it over in his hands.

The voices came clearly to him through the open kitchen window. "Jody's damn well right," he heard his father say. "Just Indians and crossing the plains. I've heard that story about how the horses got driven off about a thousand times. He just goes on and on, and he never changes a word in the things he tells."

When Mrs. Tiflin answered her tone was so changed that Jody, outside the window, looked up from his study of the stone. Her voice had become soft and explanatory. Jody knew how her face would have changed to match the tone. She said quietly, "Look at it this way, Carl. That was the big thing in my father's life. He led a wagon train clear across the plains to the coast, and when it was finished, his life was done. It was a big thing to do, but it didn't last long enough. Look!" she continued, "it's as though he was born to do that, and after he finished it, there wasn't anything more for him to do but think about it and talk about it. If there'd been any farther west to go, he'd have gone. He's told me so himself. But at last there was the ocean. He lives right by the ocean where he had to stop."

She had caught Carl, caught him and entangled him in her soft tone.

"I've seen him," he agreed quietly. "He goes down and stares off west over the ocean." His voice sharpened a little. "And then he goes up to the Horseshoe Club in Pacific Grove, and he tells people how the Indians drove off the horses."

She tried to catch him again. "Well, it's everything to him. You might be patient with him and pretend to listen."

Carl turned impatiently away. "Well, if it gets too bad, I can always go down to the bunkhouse and sit with Billy," he said irritably. He walked through the house and slammed the front door after him.

Jody ran to his chores. He dumped the grain to the chickens without chasing any of them. He gathered the eggs from the nests. He trotted into the house with the wood and interlaced it so carefully in the wood-box that two armloads seemed to fill it to overflowing.

His mother had finished the beans by now. She stirred up the fire and brushed off the stove-top with a turkey wing. Jody peered cautiously at her to see whether any rancor toward him remained. "Is he coming today?" Jody asked.

"That's what his letter said."

"Maybe I better walk up the road to meet him."

Mrs. Tiflin clanged the stove-lid shut. "That would be nice," she said. "He'd probably like to be met."

"I guess I'll just do it then."

Outside, Jody whistled shrilly to the dogs. "Come on up the hill," he commanded. The two dogs waved their tails and ran ahead. Along the roadside the sage had tender new tips. Jody tore off some pieces and rubbed them on his hands until the air was filled with the sharp wild smell. With a rush the dogs leaped from the road and yapped into the brush after a rabbit. That was the last Jody saw of them, for when they failed to catch the rabbit, they went back home.

Jody plodded on up the hill toward the ridge top. When he reached the little cleft where the road came through, the afternoon wind struck him and blew up his hair and ruffled his shirt. He looked down on the little hills and ridges below and then out at the huge green Salinas Valley. He could see the white town of Salinas far out in the flat and the flash of its windows under the waning sun. Directly below him, in an oak tree, a crow congress had convened. The tree was black with crows all cawing at once.

Then Jody's eyes followed the wagon road down from the ridge where he stood, and lost it

---

WORDS TO OWN

rancor (raŋ′kər) *n.*: anger.
convened (kən·vēnd′) *v.*: assembled.

---

behind a hill, and picked it up again on the other side. On that distant stretch he saw a cart slowly pulled by a bay[4] horse. It disappeared behind the hill. Jody sat down on the ground and watched the place where the cart would reappear again. The wind sang on the hilltops and the puff-ball clouds hurried eastward.

Then the cart came into sight and stopped. A man dressed in black dismounted from the seat and walked to the horse's head. Although it was so far away, Jody knew he had unhooked the check-rein, for the horse's head dropped forward. The horse moved on, and the man walked slowly up the hill beside it. Jody gave a glad cry and ran down the road toward them. The squirrels bumped along off the road, and a road-runner flirted its tail and raced over the edge of the hill and sailed out like a glider.

Jody tried to leap into the middle of his shadow at every step. A stone rolled under his foot and he went down. Around a little bend he raced, and there, a short distance ahead, were his grandfather and the cart. The boy dropped from his <u>unseemly</u> running and approached at a dignified walk.

The horse plodded stumble-footedly up the hill and the old man walked beside it. In the lowering sun their giant shadows flickered darkly behind them. The grandfather was dressed in a black broadcloth suit and he wore kid congress gaiters[5] and a black tie on a short, hard collar. He carried his black slouch hat in his hand. His white beard was cropped close and his white eyebrows overhung his eyes like mustaches. The blue eyes were sternly merry. About the whole face and figure there was a granite dignity, so that every motion seemed an impossible thing. Once at rest, it seemed the old man would be stone, would never move again. His steps were slow and certain. Once made, no step could ever be retraced; once headed in a direction, the path would never bend nor the pace increase nor slow.

When Jody appeared around the bend, Grandfather waved his hat slowly in welcome, and he called, "Why, Jody! Come down to meet me, have you?"

Jody sidled[6] near and turned and matched his step to the old man's step and stiffened his body and dragged his heels a little. "Yes, sir," he said. "We got your letter only today."

"Should have been here yesterday," said Grandfather. "It certainly should. How are all the folks?"

"They're fine, sir." He hesitated and then suggested shyly, "Would you like to come on a mouse hunt tomorrow, sir?"

"Mouse hunt, Jody?" Grandfather chuckled. "Have the people of this generation come down to hunting mice? They aren't very strong, the new people, but I hardly thought mice would be game for them."

"No, sir. It's just play. The haystack's gone. I'm going to drive out the mice to the dogs. And you can watch, or even beat the hay a little."

The stern, merry eyes turned down on him. "I see. You don't eat them, then. You haven't come to that yet."

Jody explained, "The dogs eat them, sir. It wouldn't be much like hunting Indians, I guess."

"No, not much—but then later, when the troops were hunting Indians and shooting children and burning teepees, it wasn't much different from your mouse hunt."

They topped the rise and started down into the ranch cup, and they lost the sun from their shoulders. "You've grown," Grandfather said. "Nearly an inch, I should say."

"More," Jody boasted. "Where they mark me on the door, I'm up more than an inch since Thanksgiving even."

Grandfather's rich throaty voice said, "Maybe you're getting too much water and turning to pith and stalk. Wait until you head out, and then we'll see."[7]

Jody looked quickly into the old man's face to see whether his feelings should be hurt, but there was no will to injure, no punishing nor putting-in-your-place light in the keen blue eyes. "We might kill a pig," Jody suggested.

---

6. **sidled** (sīd′ld): approached sideways.
7. **Maybe . . . we'll see:** Like an overwatered plant, Jody may grow tall but not be very productive. Not until he "heads out" will anyone know what he is capable of.

---

4. **bay:** reddish brown.
5. **kid congress gaiters:** high leather boots with elastic inserts in each side.

WORDS TO OWN
unseemly (un·sēm′lē) *adj.*: improper.

"Oh, no! I couldn't let you do that. You're just humoring me. It isn't the time and you know it."

"You know Riley, the big boar, sir?"

"Yes. I remember Riley well."

"Well, Riley ate a hole into that same haystack, and it fell down on him and smothered him."

"Pigs do that when they can," said Grandfather.

"Riley was a nice pig, for a boar, sir. I rode him sometimes, and he didn't mind."

A door slammed at the house below them, and they saw Jody's mother standing on the porch waving her apron in welcome. And they saw Carl Tiflin walking up from the barn to be at the house for the arrival.

The sun had disappeared from the hills by now. The blue smoke from the house chimney hung in flat layers in the purpling ranch-cup. The puff-ball clouds, dropped by the falling wind, hung listlessly in the sky.

Billy Buck came out of the bunkhouse and flung a wash basin of soapy water on the ground. He had been shaving in mid-week, for Billy held Grandfather in reverence, and Grandfather said that Billy was one of the few men of the new generation who had not gone soft. Although Billy was in middle age, Grandfather considered him a boy. Now Billy was hurrying toward the house too.

When Jody and Grandfather arrived, the three were waiting for them in front of the yard gate.

Carl said, "Hello, sir. We've been looking for you."

Mrs. Tiflin kissed Grandfather on the side of his beard, and stood still while his big hand patted her shoulder. Billy shook hands solemnly, grinning under his straw mustache. "I'll put up your horse," said Billy, and he led the rig away.

Grandfather watched him go, and then, turning back to the group, he said as he had said a hundred times before, "There's a good boy. I knew his father, old Mule-tail Buck. I never knew why they called him Mule-tail except he packed mules."

Mrs. Tiflin turned and led the way into the house. "How long are you going to stay, Father? Your letter didn't say."

"Well, I don't know. I thought I'd stay about two weeks. But I never stay as long as I think I'm going to."

In a short while they were sitting at the white oilcloth table eating their supper. The lamp with the tin reflector hung over the table. Outside the dining-room windows the big moths battered softly against the glass.

Grandfather cut his steak into tiny pieces and chewed slowly. "I'm hungry," he said. "Driving out here got my appetite up. It's like when we were crossing. We all got so hungry every night we could hardly wait to let the meat get done. I could eat about five pounds of buffalo meat every night."

"It's moving around does it," said Billy. "My father was a government packer. I helped him when I was a kid. Just the two of us could about clean up a deer's ham."

"I knew your father, Billy," said Grandfather. "A fine man he was. They called him Mule-tail Buck. I don't know why except he packed mules."

"That was it," Billy agreed. "He packed mules."

Grandfather put down his knife and fork and looked around the table. "I remember one time we ran out of meat—" His voice dropped to a curious low sing-song, dropped into a tonal groove the story had worn for itself. "There was no buffalo, no antelope, not even rabbits. The hunters couldn't even shoot a coyote. That was the time for the leader to be on the watch. I was the leader, and I kept my eyes open. Know why? Well, just the minute the people began to get hungry they'd start slaughtering the team oxen. Do you believe that? I've heard of parties that just ate up their draft cattle. Started from the middle and worked toward the ends. Finally they'd eat the lead pair, and then the wheelers. The leader of a party had to keep them from doing that."

In some manner a big moth got into the room and circled the hanging kerosene lamp. Billy got up and tried to clap it between his hands. Carl struck with a cupped palm and caught the moth and broke it. He walked to the window and dropped it out.

"As I was saying," Grandfather began again, but Carl interrupted him. "You'd better eat some more meat. All the rest of us are ready for our pudding."

Jody saw a flash of anger in his mother's eyes. Grandfather picked up his knife and fork. "I'm pretty hungry, all right," he said. "I'll tell you about that later."

WORDS TO OWN

humoring (hyōō′mər·iŋ) v.: indulging.

When supper was over, when the family and Billy Buck sat in front of the fireplace in the other room, Jody anxiously watched Grandfather. He saw the signs he knew. The bearded head leaned forward; the eyes lost their sternness and looked wonderingly into the fire; the big lean fingers laced themselves on the black knees. "I wonder," he began, "I just wonder whether I ever told you how those thieving Piutes[8] drove off thirty-five of our horses."

"I think you did," Carl interrupted. "Wasn't it just before you went up into the Tahoe country?"

Grandfather turned quickly toward his son-in-law. "That's right. I guess I must have told you that story."

"Lots of times," Carl said cruelly, and he avoided his wife's eyes. But he felt the angry eyes on him, and he said, "'Course I'd like to hear it again."

Grandfather looked back at the fire. His fingers unlaced and laced again. Jody knew how he felt, how his insides were collapsed and empty. Hadn't Jody been called a Big-Britches that very afternoon? He arose to heroism and opened himself to the term Big-Britches again. "Tell about Indians," he said softly.

Grandfather's eyes grew stern again. "Boys always want to hear about Indians. It was a job for men, but boys want to hear about it. Well, let's see. Did I ever tell you how I wanted each wagon to carry a long iron plate?"

Everyone but Jody remained silent. Jody said, "No. You didn't."

"Well, when the Indians attacked, we always put the wagons in a circle and fought from between the wheels. I thought that if every wagon carried a long plate with rifle holes, the men could stand the plates on the outside of the wheels when the wagons were in the circle and they would be protected. It would save lives and that would make up for the extra weight of the iron. But of course the party wouldn't do it. No party had done it before and they couldn't see why they should go to the expense. They lived to regret it, too."

Jody looked at his mother, and knew from her expression that she was not listening at all. Carl picked at a callus on his thumb and Billy Buck watched a spider crawling up the wall.

Grandfather's tone dropped into its narrative groove again. Jody knew in advance exactly what words would fall. The story droned on, speeded up for the attack, grew sad over the wounds, struck a dirge[9] at the burials on the great plains. Jody sat quietly watching Grandfather. The stern blue eyes were detached. He looked as though he were not very interested in the story himself.

When it was finished, when the pause had been politely respected as the frontier of the story, Billy Buck stood up and stretched and hitched his trousers. "I guess I'll turn in," he said. Then he faced Grandfather. "I've got an old powder horn and a cap and ball pistol down to the bunkhouse. Did I ever show them to you?"

Grandfather nodded slowly. "Yes, I think you did, Billy. Reminds me of a pistol I had when I was leading the people across." Billy stood politely

8. **Piutes** (pī'yo͞ots'): usually spelled *Paiutes.* The Paiutes are an American Indian people who originally lived in Utah, Arizona, Nevada, and California.
9. **dirge** (durj): sad song that accompanies a funeral or expresses grief.

National Museum of American Art, Washington D.C./Courtesy Art Resource, NY.

Pioneers of the West (1934) by Helen Lundeberg. Oil on canvas (40″ × 50¼″).

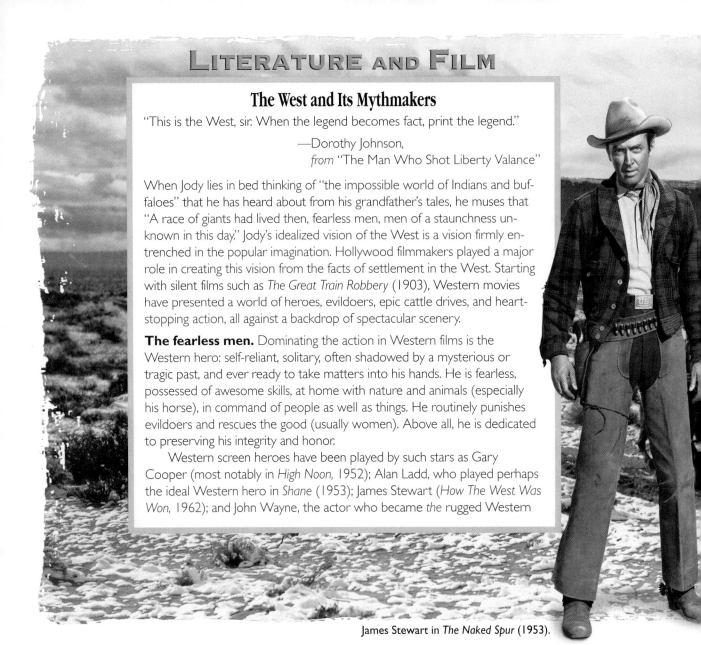

LITERATURE AND FILM

The West and Its Mythmakers

"This is the West, sir. When the legend becomes fact, print the legend."

—Dorothy Johnson,
from "The Man Who Shot Liberty Valance"

When Jody lies in bed thinking of "the impossible world of Indians and buffaloes" that he has heard about from his grandfather's tales, he muses that "A race of giants had lived then, fearless men, men of a staunchness unknown in this day." Jody's idealized vision of the West is a vision firmly entrenched in the popular imagination. Hollywood filmmakers played a major role in creating this vision from the facts of settlement in the West. Starting with silent films such as *The Great Train Robbery* (1903), Western movies have presented a world of heroes, evildoers, epic cattle drives, and heart-stopping action, all against a backdrop of spectacular scenery.

The fearless men. Dominating the action in Western films is the Western hero: self-reliant, solitary, often shadowed by a mysterious or tragic past, and ever ready to take matters into his hands. He is fearless, possessed of awesome skills, at home with nature and animals (especially his horse), in command of people as well as things. He routinely punishes evildoers and rescues the good (usually women). Above all, he is dedicated to preserving his integrity and honor.

Western screen heroes have been played by such stars as Gary Cooper (most notably in *High Noon,* 1952); Alan Ladd, who played perhaps the ideal Western hero in *Shane* (1953); James Stewart (*How The West Was Won,* 1962); and John Wayne, the actor who became *the* rugged Western

James Stewart in *The Naked Spur* (1953).

until the little story was done, and then he said, "Good night," and went out of the house.

Carl Tiflin tried to turn the conversation then. "How's the country between here and Monterey? I've heard it's pretty dry."

"It is dry," said Grandfather. "There's not a drop of water in the Laguna Seca. But it's a long pull from '87. The whole country was powder then, and in '61 I believe all the coyotes starved to death. We had fifteen inches of rain this year."

"Yes, but it all came too early. We could do with some now." Carl's eye fell on Jody. "Hadn't you better be getting to bed?"

Jody stood up obediently. "Can I kill the mice in the old haystack, sir?"

"Mice? Oh! Sure, kill them all off. Billy said there isn't any good hay left."

Jody exchanged a secret and satisfying look with Grandfather. "I'll kill every one tomorrow," he promised.

Jody lay in his bed and thought of the impossible world of Indians and buffaloes, a world that had ceased to be forever. He wished he could have been living in the heroic time, but he knew he was not of heroic timber.[10] No one living now,

10. **timber:** character.

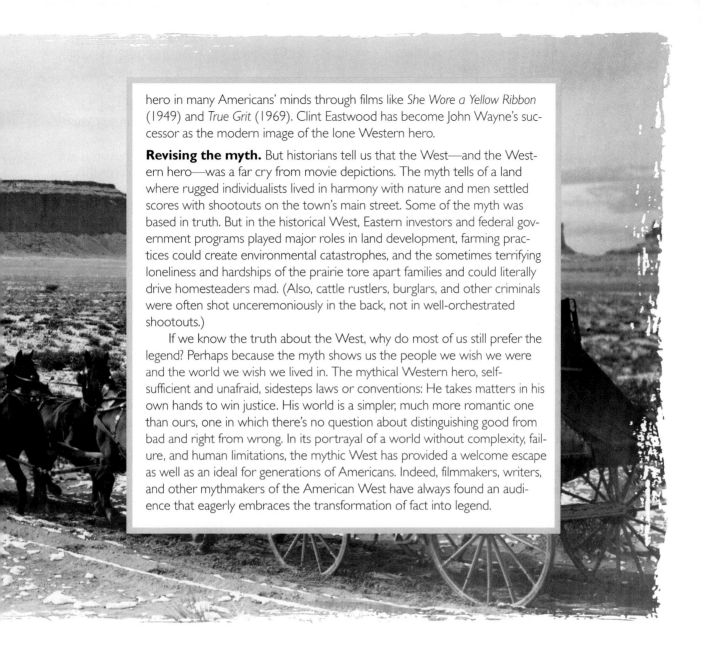

hero in many Americans' minds through films like *She Wore a Yellow Ribbon* (1949) and *True Grit* (1969). Clint Eastwood has become John Wayne's successor as the modern image of the lone Western hero.

Revising the myth. But historians tell us that the West—and the Western hero—was a far cry from movie depictions. The myth tells of a land where rugged individualists lived in harmony with nature and men settled scores with shootouts on the town's main street. Some of the myth was based in truth. But in the historical West, Eastern investors and federal government programs played major roles in land development, farming practices could create environmental catastrophes, and the sometimes terrifying loneliness and hardships of the prairie tore apart families and could literally drive homesteaders mad. (Also, cattle rustlers, burglars, and other criminals were often shot unceremoniously in the back, not in well-orchestrated shootouts.)

If we know the truth about the West, why do most of us still prefer the legend? Perhaps because the myth shows us the people we wish we were and the world we wish we lived in. The mythical Western hero, self-sufficient and unafraid, sidesteps laws or conventions: He takes matters in his own hands to win justice. His world is a simpler, much more romantic one than ours, one in which there's no question about distinguishing good from bad and right from wrong. In its portrayal of a world without complexity, failure, and human limitations, the mythic West has provided a welcome escape as well as an ideal for generations of Americans. Indeed, filmmakers, writers, and other mythmakers of the American West have always found an audience that eagerly embraces the transformation of fact into legend.

save possibly Billy Buck, was worthy to do the things that had been done. A race of giants had lived then, fearless men, men of a staunchness unknown in this day. Jody thought of the wide plains and of the wagons moving across like centipedes. He thought of Grandfather on a huge white horse, <u>marshaling</u> the people. Across his mind marched the great phantoms, and they marched off the earth and they were gone.

He came back to the ranch for a moment, then. He heard the dull rushing sound that space and silence make. He heard one of the dogs, out in the doghouse, scratching a flea and bumping his elbow against the floor with every stroke. Then the wind arose again and the black cypress groaned and Jody went to sleep.

He was up half an hour before the triangle sounded for breakfast. His mother was rattling the stove to make the flames roar when Jody went through the kitchen. "You're up early," she said. "Where are you going?"

"Out to get a good stick. We're going to kill the mice today."

WORDS TO OWN
marshaling (mär′shəl·iŋ) *v.* used as *adj.*: leading; guiding.

"Who is 'we'?"

"Why, Grandfather and I."

"So you've got him in it. You always like to have someone in with you in case there's blame to share."

"I'll be right back," said Jody. "I just want to have a good stick ready for after breakfast."

He closed the screen door after him and went out into the cool blue morning. The birds were noisy in the dawn and the ranch cats came down from the hill like blunt snakes. They had been hunting gophers in the dark, and although the four cats were full of gopher meat, they sat in a semi-circle at the back door and mewed piteously for milk. Doubletree Mutt and Smasher moved sniffing along the edge of the brush, performing the duty with rigid ceremony, but when Jody whistled, their heads jerked up and their tails waved. They plunged down to him, wriggling their skins and yawning. Jody patted their heads seriously, and moved on to the weathered scrap pile. He selected an old broom handle and a short piece of inch-square scrap wood. From his pocket he took a shoelace and tied the ends of the sticks loosely together to make a flail.[11] He whistled his new weapon through the air and struck the ground experimentally, while the dogs leaped aside and whined with apprehension.

Jody turned and started down past the house toward the old haystack ground to look over the field of slaughter, but Billy Buck, sitting patiently on the back steps, called to him, "You better come back. It's only a couple of minutes till breakfast."

Jody changed his course and moved toward the house. He leaned his flail against the steps. "That's to drive the mice out," he said. "I'll bet they're fat. I'll bet they don't know what's going to happen to them today."

"No, nor you either," Billy remarked philosophically, "nor me, nor anyone."

Jody was staggered by this thought. He knew it was true. His imagination twitched away from the mouse hunt. Then his mother came out on the back porch and struck the triangle, and all thoughts fell in a heap.

---

11. **flail:** farm tool for hand threshing grain. A flail is made of a short stick fastened with a leather strap to a longer handle. The user lets the short stick swing freely from the handle to knock the heads from the grain stalks.

Grandfather hadn't appeared at the table when they sat down. Billy nodded at his empty chair. "He's all right? He isn't sick?"

"He takes a long time to dress," said Mrs. Tiflin. "He combs his whiskers and rubs up his shoes and brushes his clothes."

Carl scattered sugar on his mush. "A man that's led a wagon train across the plains has got to be pretty careful how he dresses."

Mrs. Tiflin turned on him. "Don't do that, Carl! Please don't!" There was more of threat than of request in her tone. And the threat irritated Carl.

"Well, how many times do I have to listen to the story of the iron plates, and the thirty-five horses? That time's done. Why can't he forget it, now it's done?" He grew angrier while he talked, and his voice rose. "Why does he have to tell them over and over? He came across the plains. All right! Now it's finished. Nobody wants to hear about it over and over."

The door into the kitchen closed softly. The four at the table sat frozen. Carl laid his mush spoon on the table and touched his chin with his fingers.

Then the kitchen door opened and Grandfather walked in. His mouth smiled tightly and his eyes were squinted. "Good morning," he said, and he sat down and looked at his mush dish.

Carl could not leave it there. "Did—did you hear what I said?"

Grandfather jerked a little nod.

"I don't know what got into me, sir. I didn't mean it. I was just being funny."

Jody glanced in shame at his mother, and he saw that she was looking at Carl, and that she wasn't breathing. It was an awful thing that he was doing. He was tearing himself to pieces to talk like that. It was a terrible thing to him to retract a word, but to retract it in shame was infinitely worse.

Grandfather looked sidewise. "I'm trying to get right side up," he said gently. "I'm not being mad. I don't mind what you said, but it might be true, and I would mind that."

"It isn't true," said Carl. "I'm not feeling well this morning. I'm sorry I said it."

"Don't be sorry, Carl. An old man doesn't see things sometimes. Maybe you're right. The crossing is finished. Maybe it should be forgotten, now it's done."

Carl got up from the table. "I've had enough to eat. I'm going to work. Take your time, Billy!" He walked quickly out of the dining-room. Billy gulped the rest of his food and followed soon after. But Jody could not leave his chair.

"Won't you tell any more stories?" Jody asked.

"Why, sure I'll tell them, but only when—I'm sure people want to hear them."

"I like to hear them, sir."

"Oh! Of course you do, but you're a little boy. It was a job for men, but only little boys like to hear about it."

Jody got up from his place. "I'll wait outside for you, sir. I've got a good stick for those mice."

He waited by the gate until the old man came out on the porch. "Let's go down and kill the mice now," Jody called.

"I think I'll just sit in the sun, Jody. You go kill the mice."

"You can use my stick if you like."

"No, I'll just sit here a while."

Jody turned disconsolately away, and walked down toward the old haystack. He tried to whip up his enthusiasm with thoughts of the fat juicy mice. He beat the ground with his flail. The dogs coaxed and whined about him, but he could not go. Back at the house he could see Grandfather sitting on the porch, looking small and thin and black.

Jody gave up and went to sit on the steps at the old man's feet.

"Back already? Did you kill the mice?"

"No, sir. I'll kill them some other day."

The morning flies buzzed close to the ground and the ants dashed about in front of the steps. The heavy smell of sage slipped down the hill. The porch boards grew warm in the sunshine.

Jody hardly knew when Grandfather started to talk. "I shouldn't stay here, feeling the way I do." He examined his strong old hands. "I feel as though the crossing wasn't worth doing." His eyes moved up the side-hill and stopped on a motionless hawk perched on a dead limb. "I tell those old stories, but they're not what I want to tell. I only know how I want people to feel when I tell them.

"It wasn't Indians that were important, nor adventures, nor even getting out here. It was a whole bunch of people made into one big crawling beast. And I was the head. It was westering and westering. Every man wanted something for himself, but the big beast that was all of them wanted only westering. I was the leader, but if I hadn't been there, someone else would have been the head. The thing had to have a head.

"Under the little bushes the shadows were black at white noonday. When we saw the mountains at last, we cried—all of us. But it wasn't getting here that mattered, it was movement and westering.

"We carried life out here and set it down the way those ants carry eggs. And I was the leader. The westering was as big as God, and the slow steps that made the movement piled up and piled up until the continent was crossed.

"Then we came down to the sea, and it was done." He stopped and wiped his eyes until the rims were red. "That's what I should be telling instead of stories."

When Jody spoke, Grandfather started and looked down at him. "Maybe I could lead the people some day," Jody said.

The old man smiled. "There's no place to go. There's the ocean to stop you. There's a line of old men along the shore hating the ocean because it stopped them."

"In boats I might, sir."

"No place to go, Jody. Every place is taken. But that's not the worst—no, not the worst. Westering has died out of the people. Westering isn't a hunger any more. It's all done. Your father is right. It is finished." He laced his fingers on his knee and looked at them.

Jody felt very sad. "If you'd like a glass of lemonade I could make it for you."

Grandfather was about to refuse, and then he saw Jody's face. "That would be nice," he said. "Yes, it would be nice to drink a lemonade."

Jody ran into the kitchen where his mother was wiping the last of the breakfast dishes. "Can I have a lemon to make a lemonade for Grandfather?"

His mother mimicked—"And another lemon to make a lemonade for you."

"No, ma'am. I don't want one."

"Jody! You're sick!" Then she stopped suddenly. "Take a lemon out of the cooler," she said softly. "Here, I'll reach the squeezer down to you."

WORDS TO OWN

disconsolately (dis·kän′sə·lit·lē) *adv.*: unhappily.

Nobel Prize Acceptance Speech, 1962

I thank the Swedish Academy for finding my work worthy of this highest honor.

In my heart there may be doubt that I deserve the Nobel award over other men of letters whom I hold in respect and reverence—but there is no question of my pleasure and pride in having it for myself.

It is customary for the recipient of this award to offer personal or scholarly comment on the nature and the direction of literature. At this particular time, however, I think it would be well to consider the high duties and the responsibilities of the makers of literature.

Such is the prestige of the Nobel award and of this place where I stand that I am impelled, not to squeak like a grateful and apologetic mouse, but to roar like a lion out of pride in my profession and in the great and good men who have practiced it through the ages.

Literature was not promulgated by a pale and emasculated critical priesthood singing their litanies in empty churches—nor is it a game for the cloistered elect, the tinhorn mendicants of low-calorie despair.

Literature is as old as speech. It grew out of human need for it, and it has not changed except to become more needed.

The skalds, the bards, the writers are not separate and exclusive. From the beginning, their functions, their duties, their responsibilities have been decreed by our species.

Humanity has been passing through a gray and desolate time of confusion. My great predecessor, William Faulkner, speaking here, referred to it as a tragedy of universal fear so long sustained that there were no longer problems of the spirit, so that only the human heart in conflict with itself seemed worth writing about [see page 723].

Faulkner, more than most men, was aware of human strength as well as of human weakness. He knew that the understanding and the resolution of fear are a large part of the writer's reason for being.

This is not new. The ancient commission of the writer has not changed. He is charged with exposing our many grievous faults and failures, with dredging up to the light our dark and dangerous dreams for the purpose of improvement.

Furthermore, the writer is delegated to declare and to celebrate man's proven capacity for greatness of heart and spirit—for gallantry in defeat—for courage, compassion, and love. In the endless war against weakness and despair, these are the bright rally-flags of hope and of emulation.

I hold that a writer who does not passionately believe in the perfectibility of man has no dedication nor any membership in literature.

The present universal fear has been the result of a forward surge in our knowledge and manipulation of certain dangerous factors in the physical world.

It is true that other phases of understanding have not yet caught up with this great step, but there is no reason to presume that they cannot or will not draw abreast. Indeed, it is a part of the writer's responsibility to make sure that they do.

With humanity's long, proud history of standing firm against natural enemies, sometimes in the face of almost certain defeat and extinction, we would be cowardly and stupid to leave the field on the eve of our greatest potential victory.

Understandably, I have been reading the life of Alfred Nobel—a solitary man, the books say, a thoughtful man. He perfected the release of explosive forces, capable of creative good or of destructive evil, but lacking choice, ungoverned by conscience or judgment.

Nobel saw some of the cruel and bloody misuses of his inventions. He may even have foreseen the end result of his probing—access to ultimate violence—to final destruction. Some say that he became cynical, but I do not believe this. I think he strove to invent a control, a safety valve. I think he found it finally only in the human mind and the human spirit. To me, his thinking is clearly indicated in the categories of these awards.

They are offered for increased and continuing knowledge of man and of his world—for understanding and communication, which are the functions of literature. And they are offered for demonstrations of the capacity for peace—the culmination of all the others.

Less than fifty years after his death, the door of nature was unlocked and we were offered the dreadful burden of choice.

We have usurped many of the powers we once ascribed to God.

Fearful and unprepared, we have assumed lordship over the life or death of the whole world—of all living things.

The danger and the glory and the choice rest finally in man. The test of his perfectibility is at hand.

Having taken Godlike power, we must seek in ourselves for the responsibility and the wisdom we once prayed some deity might have.

Man himself has become our greatest hazard and our only hope.

So that today, Saint John the apostle may well be paraphrased: In the end is the Word, and the Word is Man—and the Word is with Men.

—John Steinbeck

MAKING MEANINGS

First Thoughts

1. How does Grandfather's statement "Westering has died out of the people" make Jody feel? How did it make *you* feel?

Shaping Interpretations

2. What seems to have been the significance of "the crossing" for Jody's grandfather?

3. There are several **conflicts** in the story—between Carl Tiflin and his wife, between Jody and his father, and between Jody's father and his grandfather. Describe the source of each

Reading Check

a. Why does Jody look forward to his grandfather's visit, while his father dreads it? How does Jody feel about his grandfather?

b. What are Grandfather's stories about? In what way was he "the leader of the people"?

conflict. Would you say this story is more about family relationships or more about the changing attitudes of each new generation?

4. The story holds many **ironies**. How does Steinbeck ironically characterize the modern age with his use of the mouse hunt?

5. What would you say is the **theme** of the story? What does it say about the relation between dreams and reality and the loss of the heroic ideal?

6. Is Jody right to want to listen to the same stories over and over, or is Carl right in wanting the past to be forgotten? Or are these two characters both right *and* wrong? Give reasons to support your views.

Extending the Text

7. Look back at your Quickwrite. Do you believe, as Jody's grandfather does, that there are no longer any frontiers for young Americans—no opportunities for heroism? Where do you think young people today might look for frontiers?

READING SKILLS AND STRATEGIES

Interpreting Figures of Speech

Scholars have defined over three hundred different figures of speech, but most people are familiar with five types: **(1) simile,** which compares two unlike things by using words of specific comparison (such as *like, as,* or *resembles*); **(2) metaphor,** which identifies two unlike things directly without using a specific word of comparison; **(3) personification,** a type of metaphor that speaks of something non-human as if it were human; **(4) oxymoron,** a combination of words that seem to contradict each other (*wise fool, death in life, sweet sorrow*); and **(5) hyperbole,** which uses exaggeration for effect.

Read the following figures of speech from the story, and see if you can identify the type being used from the list above. Then, paraphrase the literal meaning of each phrase in your own words.

1. "plump, sleek, arrogant mice" (page 609)
2. "a crow congress had convened" (page 611)
3. "a road-runner . . . sailed out like a glider" (page 612)
4. "blue eyes were sternly merry" (page 612)
5. "a granite dignity" (page 612)
6. "a race of giants had lived then" (page 617)
7. "wagons moving across like centipedes" (page 617)
8. "a whole bunch of people made into one big crawling beast" (page 619)

CHOICES: Building Your Portfolio

Writer's Notebook

1. Collecting Ideas for an Analysis of Causes and Effects

Reread the story's ending, this time thinking about what Jody and his mother are feeling and what their quiet words and actions signify. Then, write an extension of the ending, speculating on something Jody does afterward. You may continue the scene in the story, or skip to a new scene. In your scene, speculate on how Jody has been affected by his experiences with his grandfather and his father. Save your notes for possible use in the Writer's Workshop on page 685.

Comparing Texts

2. Variations on a Theme

Identify one of the basic **themes** of Steinbeck's story. It may have to do with the contrast between dream and reality, the loss of heroism, conflicts between generations, disillusionment, the limitations of the American dream, or some other subject. Choose another story from this textbook that deals with a similar theme. Write an essay comparing and contrasting the ways each story develops the theme. Focus on the stories' similarities and differences in **plot, character, setting,** and **tone.**

Speaking and Listening

3. Do Giants Walk the Earth?

With several students, organize a panel to discuss whether there are heroes today, and if so, who they are and what makes them heroic. As preparation for the panel, share your Quickwrite notes and exchange reactions to "The Leader of the People." In addition, try to obtain a video recording of Bill Moyers's interview of the anthropologist Joseph Campbell titled "The Hero's Adventure" (part of the PBS series *Joseph Campbell and the Power of Myth*). Play the interview as the opener of your presentation to the class or as a coda to it.

James Thurber
(1894–1961)

UPI/Bettmann.

James Thurber is generally acknowledged to be the foremost American humorist of the twentieth century. He was a supremely gifted cartoonist and a writer of essays, sketches, and stories. He once mocked the typical puffed-up biographies of literary figures by presenting this self-portrait:

> James Thurber was born in Columbus, Ohio, where so many awful things happened to him, on December 8, 1894. He was unable to keep anything on his stomach until he was seven years old, but grew to six feet one and a quarter inches tall and to weigh a hundred and fifty-four pounds fully dressed for winter. He began to write when he was ten years old . . . and to draw when he was fourteen. . . . Quick to arouse, he is very hard to quiet and people often just go away. . . . He never listens when anybody else is talking, preferring to keep his mind a blank until they get through, so he can talk. His favorite book is *The Great Gatsby.* His favorite author is Henry James. He wears excellent clothes very badly and can never find his hat. . . . He is Sagittarius with the moon in Aries and gets along fine with persons born between the 20th and 24th of August.

Thurber did grow up in Columbus, where he attended Ohio State University. He worked as a reporter in Columbus and Chicago for a number of years. He moved east, went to work for *The New Yorker* magazine in 1927, and remained on the staff for the rest of his life. Thurber's literary career peaked in the 1940s, even as his eyesight, damaged in a boyhood accident, worsened despite a series of operations. In addition to many collections of essays, stories, and children's books, he collaborated on a successful Broadway play.

His humor often turned on the chaos of contemporary American life. Thurber focused on the "little man," who cannot quite assert himself in a confusing world where women seem surer of their way. Walter Mitty, the antihero of Thurber's most famous story, seeks in fantasy a release from a wife who overwhelms him.

In many of his stories and cartoons, Thurber focused on relationships between men and women. While Thurber claimed to hope the feminist movement would seize power and prevent men from blowing the world to bits, he viewed women with a certain ambivalence—as intimidating to their mates, and as mother figures rather than partners. (His attitude toward women is comically revealed in the cartoons that illustrate his stories.)

Thurber defined humor as "a kind of emotional chaos told about calmly and quietly in retrospect." But humor is not subject to rational explanation. Perhaps this was in the mind of Thurber's friend, the writer Mark Van Doren, when he said of Thurber: "He was an extraordinary man . . . with so many quick changes: gentle and fierce, fascinating and boring, sophisticated and boorish, kind and cruel, broadminded and parochial. You can't explain Thurber."

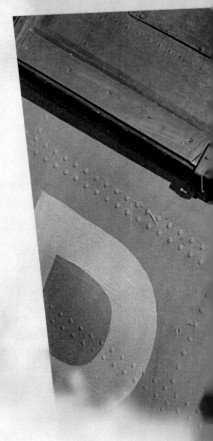

Before You Read

THE SECRET LIFE OF WALTER MITTY

Make the Connection

Daydream Believer

The name "Walter Mitty" has entered our language as the epitome of the "little guy" who is dominated by an assertive wife. You might recognize Mitty and the formidable Mrs. Mitty—they are character types that have formed the basis of many TV situation comedies. Mitty is based on a stereotype of the henpecked husband, but Mitty himself is an original. In fact, the term "Walter Mitty" is found in *Webster's Third New International Dictionary,* where it is defined as "a commonplace unadventurous person who seeks escape from reality through daydreaming and typically imagines himself leading a glamorous life and becoming famous."

Reading Skills and Strategies

Analyzing Text Structures: Cause/Effect

In this famous story, James Thurber adapts the basic plot structure of **cause** and **effect** in a highly original way. He describes a pattern of free association, in which trivial details from real life cause grand adventures in Walter Mitty's daydreams. Thus, Mitty's daydream is the effect. As you read the story, jot down the decidedly unheroic event that triggers each daydream, as well as the subjects of the daydreams. Note also what snaps Mitty out of each fantasy.

Elements of Literature

Parody

A **parody** makes fun of another work by imitating aspects of its style or contents. You've probably encountered parodies of shows, songs, and movies in humor magazines, TV sitcoms, commercials, and movies.

After you've read the first paragraph of this story, ask yourself what kind of movie it parodies.

> **A parody** is a work that makes fun of another work by imitating some aspect of its style or content.
>
> *For more about Parody, see the Handbook of Literary Terms.*

"Why don't you let me know what it is, if it's so pleasant?"

From *Men, Women and Dogs.* Copyright © 1943 by James Thurber. Copyright © renewed 1971 by Helen Thurber and Rosemary A. Thurber. Reprinted by arrangement with Rosemary A. Thurber and the Barbara Hogenson Agency.

All photos pages 625, 627, 628 from the movie
The Secret Life of Walter Mitty (1947) with Danny Kaye.
Photofest.

The Secret Life of Walter Mitty

James Thurber

We're going through!" The commander's voice was like thin ice breaking. He wore his full-dress uniform, with the heavily braided white cap pulled down <u>rakishly</u> over one cold gray eye. "We can't make it, sir. It's spoiling for[1] a hurricane, if you ask me." "I'm not asking you, Lieutenant Berg," said the commander. "Throw on the power lights! Rev her up to 8,500! We're going through!" The pounding of the cylinders increased: ta-pocketa-pocketa-pocketa-*pocketa-pocketa*. The commander stared at the ice forming on the pilot window. He walked over and twisted a row of complicated dials. "Switch on No. 8 auxiliary!" he shouted. "Switch on No. 8 auxiliary!" repeated Lieutenant Berg. "Full strength in No. 3 turret!" shouted the commander. "Full strength in No. 3 turret!" The

crew, bending to their various tasks in the huge, hurtling eight-engined navy hydroplane, looked at each other and grinned. "The Old Man'll get us through," they said to one another. "The Old Man ain't afraid of Hell!" . . .

"Not so fast! You're driving too fast!" said Mrs. Mitty. "What are you driving so fast for?"

"Hmm?" said Walter Mitty. He looked at his wife, in the seat beside him, with shocked astonishment. She seemed grossly unfamiliar, like a strange woman who had yelled at him in a crowd. "You were up to fifty-five," she said. "You know I don't like to go more than forty. You were up to fifty-five." Walter Mitty drove on toward Waterbury in silence, the roaring of the SN202 through

---

1. **it's spoiling for:** slang for "conditions are right for."

WORDS TO OWN

rakishly (rāk′·ish·lē) *adv.*: dashingly; jauntily.

---

the worst storm in twenty years of navy flying fading in the remote, intimate airways of his mind. "You're tensed up again," said Mrs. Mitty. "It's one of your days. I wish you'd let Dr. Renshaw look you over."

Walter Mitty stopped the car in front of the building where his wife went to have her hair done. "Remember to get those overshoes while I'm having my hair done," she said. "I don't need overshoes," said Mitty. She put her mirror back into her bag. "We've been all through that," she said, getting out of the car. "You're not a young man any longer." He raced the engine a little. "Why don't you wear your gloves? Have you lost your gloves?" Walter Mitty reached in a pocket and brought out the gloves. He put them on, but after she had turned and gone into the building and he had driven on to a red light, he took them off again. "Pick it up, brother!" snapped a cop as the light changed, and Mitty hastily pulled on his gloves and lurched ahead. He drove around the streets aimlessly for a time, and then he drove past the hospital on his way to the parking lot.

. . . "It's the millionaire banker, Wellington McMillan," said the pretty nurse. "Yes?" said Walter Mitty, removing his gloves slowly. "Who has the case?" "Dr. Renshaw and Dr. Benbow, but there are two specialists here, Dr. Remington from New York and Mr. Pritchard-Mitford from London. He flew over." A door opened down a long, cool corridor and Dr. Renshaw came out. He looked <u>distraught</u> and <u>haggard</u>. "Hello, Mitty," he said. "We're having the devil's own time with McMillan, the millionaire banker and close personal friend of Roosevelt. Obstreosis of the ductal tract. Tertiary. Wish you'd take a look at him." "Glad to," said Mitty.

In the operating room there were whispered introductions: "Dr. Remington, Dr. Mitty. Mr. Pritchard-Mitford, Dr. Mitty." "I've read your book on streptothricosis," said Pritchard-Mitford, shaking hands. "A brilliant performance, sir." "Thank you," said Walter Mitty. "Didn't know you were in the States, Mitty," grumbled Remington. "Coals to Newcastle,[2] bringing Mitford and me up here for a tertiary." "You are very kind," said Mitty. A huge, complicated machine, connected to the operating

table, with many tubes and wires, began at this moment to go pocketa-pocketa-pocketa. "The new anesthetizer is giving way!" shouted an intern. "There is no one in the East who knows how to fix it!" "Quiet, man!" said Mitty, in a low, cool voice. He sprang to the machine, which was now going pocketa-pocketa-queep-pocketa-queep. He began fingering delicately a row of glistening dials. "Give me a fountain pen!" he snapped. Someone handed him a fountain pen. He pulled a faulty piston out of the machine and inserted the pen in its place. "That will hold for ten minutes," he said. "Get on with the operation." A nurse hurried over and whispered to Renshaw, and Mitty saw the man turn pale. "Coreopsis has set in," said Renshaw nervously. "If you would take over, Mitty?" Mitty looked at him and at the <u>craven</u> figure of Benbow, who drank, and at the <u>grave</u>, uncertain faces of the two great specialists. "If you wish," he said. They slipped a white gown on him; he adjusted a mask and drew on thin gloves; nurses handed him shining . . .

"Back it up, Mac! Look out for that Buick!" Walter Mitty jammed on the brakes. "Wrong lane, Mac," said the parking-lot attendant, looking at Mitty closely. "Gee. Yeh," muttered Mitty. He began cautiously to back out of the lane marked "Exit Only." "Leave her sit there," said the attendant. "I'll put her away." Mitty got out of the car. "Hey, better leave the key." "Oh," said Mitty, handing the man the ignition key. The attendant vaulted into the car, backed it up with <u>insolent</u> skill, and put it where it belonged.

They're so damn cocky, thought Walter Mitty, walking along Main Street; they think they know everything. Once he had tried to take his chains[3] off, outside New Milford, and he had got them wound around the axles. A man had had to come out in a wrecking car and unwind them, a young, grinning garageman. Since then Mrs. Mitty always made him drive to a garage to have the chains

3. **chains:** chains attached to automobile tires to increase traction in snow and ice.

- -

WORDS TO OWN

distraught (di·strôt′) *adj.:* troubled.
haggard (hag′ərd) *adj.:* wasted or worn in appearance.
craven (krā′vən) *adj.:* very fearful; cowardly.
insolent (in′sə·lənt) *adj.:* arrogant.

- -

2. **coals to Newcastle:** an unnecessary effort. Newcastle, England, was a major coal-producing city.

taken off. The next time, he thought, I'll wear my right arm in a sling; they won't grin at me then. I'll have my right arm in a sling, and they'll see I couldn't possibly take the chains off myself. He kicked at the slush on the sidewalk. "Overshoes," he said to himself, and he began looking for a shoe store.

When he came out into the street again, with the overshoes in a box under his arm, Walter Mitty began to wonder what the other thing was his wife had told him to get. She had told him, twice, before they set out from their house for Waterbury. In a way he hated these weekly trips to town— he was always getting something wrong. Kleenex, he thought, Squibb's,[4] razor blades? No. Toothpaste, toothbrush, bicarbonate, carborundum, initiative and referendum? He gave it up. But she would remember it. "Where's the what's-its-name?" she would ask. "Don't tell me you forgot the what's-its-name." A newsboy went by shouting something about the Waterbury trial.

. . . "Perhaps this will refresh your memory." The district attorney suddenly thrust a heavy automatic at the quiet figure on the witness stand. "Have you ever seen this before?" Walter Mitty took the gun and examined it expertly. "This is my Webley-Vickers 50.80," he said calmly. An excited buzz ran around the courtroom. The judge rapped for order. "You are a crack shot with any sort of firearms, I believe?" said the district attorney, insinuatingly. "Objection!" shouted Mitty's attorney. "We have shown that the defendant could not have fired the shot. We have shown that he wore his right arm in a sling on the night of the fourteenth of July." Walter Mitty raised his hand briefly

"A brilliant performance, sir." "Thank you," said Walter Mitty.

Photofest.

and the bickering attorneys were stilled. "With any known make of gun," he said evenly, "I could have killed Gregory Fitzhurst at three hundred feet *with my left hand.*" Pandemonium broke loose in the courtroom. A woman's scream rose above the bedlam and suddenly a lovely, dark-haired girl was in Walter Mitty's arms. The district attorney struck at her savagely. Without rising from his chair, Mitty let the man have it on the point of the chin. "You miserable cur!"[5] . . .

"Puppy biscuit," said Walter Mitty. He stopped walking and the buildings of Waterbury rose up out of the misty courtroom and surrounded him again. A woman who was passing laughed. "He said 'Puppy biscuit,'" she said to her companion. "That man said 'Puppy biscuit' to himself." Walter Mitty hurried on. He went into an A & P, not the first one he came to but a smaller one farther up the street. "I want some biscuit for small, young dogs," he said to the clerk. "Any special brand, sir?" The greatest pistol shot in the world thought a moment. "It says 'Puppies Bark for It' on the box," said Walter Mitty.

His wife would be through at the hairdresser's in fifteen minutes, Mitty saw in looking at his watch, unless they had trouble drying it; sometimes they had trouble drying it. She didn't like to get to the hotel first; she would want him to be there waiting for her as usual. He found a big

---

4. **Squibb's:** Squibb (now part of Bristol-Myers Squibb) was a U.S. pharmaceutical company, established in 1858, that manufactured a variety of prescription drugs and health-care products, such as cough and cold medicines and vitamins. It is not clear which product Mitty is thinking about.

5. **cur:** a cowardly or contemptible person; also, a mongrel dog.

WORDS TO OWN

insinuatingly (in·sin′yoo·āt′iŋ·lē) *adv.:* suggestively.
pandemonium (pan′də·mō′nē·əm) *n.:* wild confusion.
bedlam (bed′ləm) *n.:* place or condition of noise and confusion.

"We only live once, Sergeant," said Mitty, with his faint, fleeting smile.

Photofest.

leather chair in the lobby, facing a window, and he put the overshoes and the puppy biscuit on the floor beside it. He picked up an old copy of *Liberty* and sank down into the chair. "Can Germany Conquer the World Through the Air?" Walter Mitty looked at the pictures of bombing planes and of ruined streets.

. . . "The <u>cannonading</u> has got the wind up in young Raleigh, sir," said the sergeant. Captain Mitty looked up at him through tousled hair. "Get him to bed," he said wearily. "With the others. I'll fly alone." "But you can't, sir," said the sergeant anxiously. "It takes two men to handle that bomber and the Archies[6] are pounding hell out of the air. Von Richtman's circus[7] is between here and Saulier." "Somebody's got to get to that ammunition dump," said Mitty. "I'm going over. Spot of brandy?" He poured a drink for the sergeant and one for himself. War thundered and whined around the dugout and battered at the door. There was a <u>rending</u> of wood and splinters flew through the room. "A bit of a near thing," said Captain Mitty carelessly. "The box barrage is closing in," said the sergeant. "We only live once, Sergeant," said Mitty, with his faint, fleeting smile. "Or do we?" He poured another brandy and

tossed it off. "I never see a man could hold his brandy like you, sir," said the sergeant. "Begging your pardon, sir." Captain Mitty stood up and strapped on his huge Webley-Vickers automatic. "It's forty kilometers through hell, sir," said the sergeant. Mitty finished one last brandy. "After all," he said softly, "what isn't?" The pounding of the cannon increased; there was the rat-tat-tatting of machine guns, and from somewhere came the menacing pocketa-pocketa-pocketa of the new flamethrowers. Walter Mitty walked to the door of the dugout humming "Auprès de Ma Blonde,"[8] He turned and waved to the sergeant. "Cheerio!" he said. . . .

Something struck his shoulder. "I've been looking all over this hotel for you," said Mrs. Mitty. "Why do you have to hide in this old chair? How did you expect me to find you?" "Things close in," said Walter Mitty vaguely. "What?" Mrs. Mitty said. "Did you get the what's-its-name? The puppy biscuit? What's in that box?" "Overshoes," said Mitty. "Couldn't you have put them on in the store?" "I was thinking," said Walter Mitty. "Does it ever occur to you that I am sometimes thinking?" She looked at him. "I'm going to take your temperature when I get you home," she said.

They went out through the revolving doors that made a faintly derisive whistling sound when you pushed them. It was two blocks to the parking lot. At the drugstore on the corner she said, "Wait here for me. I forgot something. I won't be a minute." She was more than a minute. Walter Mitty lighted a cigarette. It began to rain, rain with sleet in it. He stood up against the wall of the drugstore, smoking. . . . He put his shoulders back and his heels together. "To hell with the handkerchief," said Walter Mitty scornfully. He took one last drag on his cigarette and snapped it away. Then, with that faint, fleeting smile playing about his lips, he faced the firing squad; erect and motionless, proud and disdainful, Walter Mitty the Undefeated, inscrutable[9] to the last.

8. Auprès de Ma Blonde (ō·prä′ də mä blônd): French song. The title means "Near My Blonde."
9. inscrutable (in·skrōōt′ə·bəl): mysterious.

WORDS TO OWN

cannonading (kan′ən·ād′iŋ) *v.* used as *n.:* artillery fire.
rending (rend′iŋ) *v.* used as *n.:* violent ripping apart.

6. Archies: German antiaircraft guns or gunners in World War I.
7. circus: squadron of planes.

Thurber's longtime associate on *The New Yorker*, E. B. White, wrote this parting tribute to his friend on November 11, 1961.

The New Yorker's Farewell

I am one of the lucky ones; I knew him before blindness hit him, before fame hit him, and I tend always to think of him as a young artist in a small office in a big city, with all the world still ahead. It was a fine thing to be young and at work in New York for a new magazine when Thurber was young and at work, and I will always be glad that this happened to me.

It was fortunate that we got on well; the office we shared was the size of a hall bedroom. There was just room enough for two men, two typewriters, and a stack of copy paper. The copy paper disappeared at a scandalous rate—not because our production was high (although it was) but because Thurber used copy paper as the natural receptacle for discarded sorrows, immediate joys, stale dreams, golden prophecies, and messages of good cheer to the outside world and to fellow workers. His mind was never at rest, and his pencil was connected to his mind by the best conductive tissue I have ever seen in action. The whole world knows what a funny man he was, but you had to sit next to him day after day to understand the extravagance of his clowning, the wildness and subtlety of his thinking, and the intensity of his interest in others and his sympathy for their dilemmas—dilemmas that he instantly enlarged, put in focus, and made immortal, just as he enlarged and made immortal the strange goings-on in the Ohio home of his boyhood. His waking dreams and his sleeping dreams commingled shamelessly and uproariously. Ohio was never far from his thoughts, and when he received a medal from his home state in 1953, he wrote, "The clocks that strike in my dreams are often the clocks of Columbus." It is a beautiful sentence and a revealing one.

From *The Owl In The Attic.* Copyright © 1931 by James Thurber. Copyright © renewed 1959 by James Thurber. Reprinted by arrangement with Rosemary A. Thurber and the Barbara Hogenson Agency.

He was both a practitioner of humor and a defender of it. The day he died, I came on a letter from him, dictated to a secretary and signed in pencil with his sightless and enormous "Jim." "Every time is a time for humor," he wrote. "I write humor the way a surgeon operates, because it is a livelihood, because I have a great urge to do it, because many interesting challenges are set up, and because I have the hope it may do some good." Once, I remember, he heard someone say that humor is a shield, not a sword, and it made him mad. He wasn't going to have anyone beating his sword into a shield. That "surgeon," incidentally, is pure Mitty. During his happiest years, Thurber did not write the way a surgeon operates, he wrote the way a child skips rope, the way a mouse waltzes.

Although he is best known for "Walter Mitty" and *The Male Animal,* the book of his I like best is *The Last Flower.* In it you will find his faith in the renewal of life, his feeling for the beauty and fragility of life on earth. Like all good writers, he fashioned his own best obituary notice. Nobody else can add to the record, much as he might like to. And of all the flowers, real and figurative, that will find their way to Thurber's last resting place, the one that will remain fresh and wiltproof is the little flower he himself drew, on the last page of that lovely book.

—E. B. White

One of the most familiar Walter Mitty–like characters in popular culture is Snoopy, Charles M. Schulz's (1922–2000) beloved creation from the famous "Peanuts" comic strip.

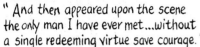

MAKING MEANINGS

First Thoughts

1. Do you think there's a little of Mitty in everyone? Explain.

Reading Check

a. List the errands Mitty is doing in real life.

b. In contrast, what deeds does Mitty perform in his fantasy life?

Shaping Interpretations

2. What is the central **irony** of Mitty's life? Is this irony humorous, serious, or partly both?

3. Thurber's story uses a technique called free association, in which words and sounds from real life become associated with elements of Mitty's daydreams. Review the notes you made while reading, and identify what causes Mitty to lapse into each daydream. What decidedly unheroic event snaps him out of each episode?

4. Where does Thurber use **parody** in the story? Who or what are the targets of his satire? (To help identify the targets, look especially at the jargon being bandied about in each daydream.)

5. Why do you think Mitty daydreams so much, and about these specific events? Do you think that his daydreaming enriches his life, or does it work as a handicap? Why?

Some nights she threw them all.

Extending the Text

6. Walter Mitty could be seen as one of a line of archetypal American characters, beginning with Benjamin Franklin's "self-made man." What does Mitty's life reveal about the opportunities for heroism and "self making" today? Do you agree with Thurber's assessment of modern life?

7. Walter Mitty and the formidable Mrs. Mitty have become **stock character** types in American popular culture. Brainstorm a list of popular movies and TV sitcoms in which similar husbands and wives can be found. Why do these character types endure? Do you think changing views of gender roles will eventually make these stock characters obsolete? Explain.

He always half suspected that something would get him.

From "The Night the Bed Fell" (top) and "The Night the Ghost Got In" (bottom) from *My Life and Hard Times*. Copyright © 1933 by James Thurber. Copyright © renewed 1961 by James Thurber. Reprinted by arrangement with Rosemary A. Thurber and the Barbara Hogenson Agency.

CHOICES: Building Your Portfolio

Comparing Characters

2. The Gender Gap

Thurber has been accused of being "tough" on women, a criticism that has also been leveled against Washington Irving for his portrait of Dame Van Winkle (page 154). In a brief essay, compare and contrast these two famous American couples—Rip and Dame Van Winkle, and Walter and Mrs. Mitty. At the end of your essay, describe your response to the character types used in each story to make us laugh.

Creative Writing

3. The Secret Life of Mrs. Mitty

Everybody has fantasies in which they escape from their everyday lives. What do you think *Mrs.* Mitty daydreams about? Brainstorm a list of elements you would include in a story about Mrs. Mitty's everyday experiences and her contrasting daydreams. Use your list to write an episode in "The Secret Life of Mrs. Mitty."

Art / Creative Writing

4. Thoroughly Modern Mitty

Charles M. Schulz's character Snoopy (see *Connections* on page 630) is truly cast in the Walter Mitty mold. Try creating your own cartoon version of a contempory Walter Mitty. What heroic fantasies might he or she escape to?

Drama / Performance

5. Dramatic Action

Because it contains five different fantasy settings and a recurring real-life setting, this story translates well into drama or film. (In fact, in 1947 the story was made into a movie starring Danny Kaye.) Work with a group of classmates to create a short play or video drama based on the story. Assign parts, and create costumes and props. Perform the scene for your class, or videotape it.

Creative Writing

6. Dear Mr. Thurber

In his lifetime, James Thurber sometimes complained that he received too many letters from students. Yet he answered such letters graciously and candidly. Write a letter in which you tell Thurber what you think of his story, giving reasons for your opinion.

From "The Dog That Bit People" from *My Life and Hard Times.* Copyright © 1933 by James Thurber. Copyright © renewed 1961 by James Thurber. Reprinted by arrangement with Rosemary A. Thurber and the Barbara Hogenson Agency.

Eudora Welty

(1909–2001)

Eudora Welty was born in the quintessentially Southern city of Jackson, Mississippi, and she has lived in Jackson almost her whole life. As the daughter of an insurance man and a schoolteacher, she enjoyed a conventional girlhood. She recalls pleading with her brothers to teach her golf, sharing their enthusiasm for baseball, and bicycling to the library in *two* petticoats to forestall the librarian's caustic remark, "I can practically see through you."

Welty attended Mississippi State College for Women, graduated from the University of Wisconsin, and did graduate work at Columbia University, anticipating a career in advertising. However, the Depression sent her home to Jackson with a belief, which did not fail her, that she would succeed as a writer of fiction.

Welty's widely recognized triumph is a painstaking accuracy in colloquial speech. The exactly right word always matters to her. She has always been fascinated by words, by the *way* people say things, by snatches of overheard dialogue. She was once delighted to hear a country woman confess to "a gnawing and a craving" for something. Telling a friend about it, Welty added, "Wasn't that a wonderful way of putting it? A gnawing and a craving!"

She greatly admires the work of Katherine Anne Porter (page 702), who befriended her when she was sending out stories and getting back rejection slips. It was the literary agent Diarmuid Russell who shared Welty's belief in an ultimate success. He not only took her on as a client, but also said of a certain Welty story that if the editor didn't accept it, the two ought to "horsewhip the offending editor for his insult to literature." (The editor in question bought the story.)

Welty's first collections of stories, *A Curtain of Green* and *The Wide Net,* appeared in the 1940s. These were followed by *The Golden Apples* (1949), one of her best-known volumes of short stories. Then came a novella, *The Ponder Heart* (1954), which was made into a Broadway play. *Losing Battles,* Welty's fine comic novel about a family reunion in the rural South, was published in 1970. Two years later, Welty produced *The Optimist's Daughter,* a poignant short novel about family conflicts; this book won her the Pulitzer Prize. An autobiographical memoir entitled *One Writer's Beginnings,* based on lectures Welty gave at Harvard University, was published in 1983 to wide critical acclaim.

Welty admits to being blessed with a visual mind, and she says that this gift makes for "the best shorthand a writer can have." She once wrote, "To watch everything about me I regarded grimly and possessively as a *need.*" Clearly, that need became an enviable artistic vision.

© Rollie McKenna.

Before You Read

A WORN PATH

Make the Connection

The Perilous Journey

From earliest times, storytellers have used the perilous journey as a metaphor for life. When we think of a perilous journey, we might conjure up images of a steely, larger-than-life hero or heroine who endures incredible hardships and faces monstrous adversaries. But a perilous journey can be a much more ordinary—even everyday—affair, on a road as modest and simple as a worn path.

Quickwrite

The major character in this story is named Phoenix Jackson. Before you read, look up the word *phoenix* in a dictionary. Then, write down your prediction of what a character named Phoenix might be like.

Elements of Literature

Theme

The plot of the story you are about to read is very simple, but its **themes**—its main insights into life—are subtle and complex. You may need a second reading to be sure you have grasped what Eudora Welty is implying in her low-key narrative about Phoenix Jackson's walk down a worn path.

To get a handle on the theme, first visualize the story and characters in a literal sense: who they are, where they are, and what they are doing. Then, visualize people and circumstances that are very different—perhaps your own life or the lives of other people you know. Ask yourself how knowing about Phoenix Jackson's path might help you understand your own path or that of someone you know.

> The **theme** of a story is its main idea or insight into life.
>
> *For more on Theme, see the Handbook of Literary Terms.*

Background

Phoenix makes her journey in rural Mississippi, late in the Depression era of the 1930s. This story offers several clues to how a person's race determined his or her social status in that time and place.

Pages 634 and 640: A woman of the thirties, Hinds County (1935) by Eudora Welty. Photograph.

Eudora Welty Collection, Mississippi Department of Archives and History.

A Worn Path

Eudora Welty

It was December—a bright frozen day in the early morning. Far out in the country there was an old Negro woman with her head tied in a red rag, coming along a path through the pinewoods. Her name was Phoenix Jackson. She was very old and small and she walked slowly in the dark pine shadows, moving a little from side to side in her steps, with the balanced heaviness and lightness of a <u>pendulum</u> in a grandfather clock. She carried a thin, small cane made from an umbrella, and with this she kept tapping the frozen earth in front of her. This made a grave and <u>persistent</u> noise in the still air, that seemed <u>meditative</u> like the chirping of a solitary little bird.

She wore a dark striped dress reaching down to her shoe tops, and an equally long apron of bleached sugar sacks, with a full pocket: all neat and tidy, but every time she took a step she might have fallen over her shoelaces, which dragged from her unlaced shoes. She looked straight ahead. Her eyes were blue with age. Her skin had a pattern all its own of numberless branching wrinkles and as though a whole little tree stood in the middle of her forehead, but a golden color ran underneath, and the two knobs of her cheeks were <u>illumined</u> by a yellow burning under the dark. Under the red rag her hair came down on her neck in the frailest of ringlets, still black, and with an odor like copper.

Now and then there was a quivering in the thicket. Old Phoenix said, "Out of my way, all you foxes, owls, beetles, jack rabbits, coons, and wild animals! . . . Keep out from under these feet, little bobwhites. . . . Keep the big wild hogs out of my path. Don't let none of those come running in my direction. I got a long way." Under her small black-freckled hand her cane, limber as a buggy whip, would switch at the brush as if to rouse up any hiding things.

> *Finally, trembling all over, she stood free, and after a moment dared to stoop for her cane.*

On she went. The woods were deep and still. The sun made the pine needles almost too bright to look at, up where the wind rocked. The cones dropped as light as feathers. Down in the hollow was the mourning dove—it was not too late for him.

The path ran up a hill. "Seem like there is chains about my feet, time I get this far," she said, in the voice of argument old people keep to use with themselves. "Something always take a hold of me on this hill—pleads I should stay."

After she got to the top she turned and gave a full, severe look behind her where she had come. "Up through pines," she said at length. "Now down through oaks."

Her eyes opened their widest, and she started down gently. But before she got to the bottom of the hill a bush caught her dress.

Her fingers were busy and in-tent, but her skirts were full and long, so that before she could pull them free in one place they were caught in another. It was not possible to allow the dress to tear. "I in the thorny bush," she said. "Thorns, you doing your <u>appointed</u> work. Never want to let folks pass, no sir. Old eyes thought you was a pretty little *green* bush."

Finally, trembling all over, she stood free, and after a moment dared to stoop for her cane.

"Sun so high!" she cried, leaning back and

WORDS TO OWN

pendulum (pen′dyo͞o·ləm) *n.*: freely swinging weight suspended from a fixed point to regulate a clock's movement.

persistent (pər·sist′ənt) *adj.*: continuing.

meditative (med′ə·tāt′iv) *adj.*: deeply thoughtful; reflective.

illumined (i·lo͞o′mənd) *v.*: lighted up.

intent (in·tent′) *adj.*: purposeful.

appointed (ə·point′id) *v.* used as *adj.*: assigned.

looking, while the thick tears went over her eyes. "The time getting all gone here."

At the foot of this hill was a place where a log was laid across the creek.

"Now comes the trial," said Phoenix.

Putting her right foot out, she mounted the log and shut her eyes. Lifting her skirt, leveling her cane fiercely before her, like a festival figure in some parade, she began to march across. Then she opened her eyes and she was safe on the other side.

"I wasn't as old as I thought," she said.

But she sat down to rest. She spread her skirts on the bank around her and folded her hands over her knees. Up above her was a tree in a pearly cloud of mistletoe. She did not dare to close her eyes, and when a little boy brought her a plate with a slice of marble cake on it she spoke to him. "That would be acceptable," she said. But when she went to take it there was just her own hand in the air.

So she left that tree, and had to go through a barbed-wire fence. There she had to creep and crawl, spreading her knees and stretching her fingers like a baby trying to climb the steps. But she talked loudly to herself: She could not let her dress be torn now, so late in the day, and she could not pay for having her arm or her leg sawed off if she got caught fast where she was.

At last she was safe through the fence and risen up out in the clearing. Big dead trees, like black men with one arm, were standing in the purple stalks of the withered cotton field. There sat a buzzard.

"Who you watching?"

In the furrow she made her way along.

"Glad this not the season for bulls," she said, looking sideways, "and the good Lord made his snakes to curl up and sleep in the winter. A pleasure I don't see no two-headed snake coming around that tree, where it come once. It took a while to get by him, back in the summer."

She passed through the old cotton and went into a field of dead corn. It whispered and shook and was taller than her head. "Through the maze now," she said, for there was no path.

Then there was something tall, black, and skinny there, moving before her.

At first she took it for a man. It could have been a man dancing in the field. But she stood still and listened, and it did not make a sound. It was as silent as a ghost.

"Ghost," she said sharply, "who be you the ghost of? For I have heard of nary death close by."

But there was no answer—only the ragged dancing in the wind.

She shut her eyes, reached out her hand, and touched a sleeve. She found a coat and inside that an emptiness, cold as ice.

"You scarecrow," she said. Her face lighted. "I ought to be shut up for good," she said with laughter. "My senses is gone. I too old. I the oldest people I ever know. Dance, old scarecrow," she said, "while I dancing with you."

She kicked her foot over the furrow, and with mouth drawn down, shook her head once or twice in a little strutting way. Some husks blew down and whirled in streamers about her skirts.

Then she went on, parting her way from side to side with the cane, through the whispering field. At last she came to the end, to a wagon track where the silver grass blew between the red ruts. The quail were walking around like pullets, seeming all dainty and unseen.

"Walk pretty," she said. "This the easy place. This the easy going."

She followed the track, swaying through the quiet bare fields, through the little strings of trees silver in their dead leaves, past cabins silver from weather, with the doors and windows boarded shut, all like old women under a spell sitting there. "I walking in their sleep," she said, nodding her head vigorously.

In a ravine she went where a spring was silently flowing through a hollow log. Old Phoenix bent and drank. "Sweet gum makes the water sweet," she said, and drank more. "Nobody know who made this well, for it was here when I was born."

The track crossed a swampy part where the moss hung as white as lace from every limb. "Sleep on, alligators, and blow your bubbles." Then the track went into the road.

Deep, deep the road went down between the high green-colored banks. Overhead the live oaks met, and it was as dark as a cave.

WORDS TO OWN

furrow (fur′ō) *n.*: groove in the land made by a plow.

A black dog with a lolling tongue came up out of the weeds by the ditch. She was meditating, and not ready, and when he came at her she only hit him a little with her cane. Over she went in the ditch, like a little puff of milkweed.

Down there, her senses drifted away. A dream visited her, and she reached her hand up, but nothing reached down and gave her a pull. So she lay there and presently went to talking. "Old woman," she said to herself, "that black dog come up out of the weeds to stall you off, and now there he sitting on his fine tail, smiling at you."

A white man finally came along and found her—a hunter, a young man, with his dog on a chain. "Well, Granny!" he laughed. "What are you doing there?"

"Lying on my back like a June bug waiting to be turned over, mister," she said, reaching up her hand.

He lifted her up, gave her a swing in the air, and set her down. "Anything broken, Granny?"

"No sir, them old dead weeds is springy enough," said Phoenix, when she had got her breath. "I thank you for your trouble."

"Where do you live, Granny?" he asked, while the two dogs were growling at each other.

"Away back yonder, sir, behind the ridge. You can't even see it from here."

"On your way home?"

"No sir, I going to town."

"Why, that's too far! That's as far as I walk when I come out myself, and I get something for my trouble." He patted the stuffed bag he carried, and there hung down a little closed claw. It was one of the bobwhites, with its beak hooked bitterly to show it was dead. "Now you go on home, Granny!"

"I bound to go to town, mister," said Phoenix. "The time come around."

He gave another laugh, filling the whole landscape. "I know you old colored people! Wouldn't miss going to town to see Santa Claus!"

But something held old Phoenix very still. The deep lines in her face went into a fierce and different <u>radiation</u>. Without warning, she had seen with her own eyes a flashing nickel fall out of the man's pocket onto the ground.

"How old are you, Granny?" he was saying.

"There is no telling, mister," she said, "no telling."

Then she gave a little cry and clapped her hands and said, "Git on away from here, dog! Look! Look at that dog!" She laughed as if in admiration. "He ain't scared of nobody. He a big black dog." She whispered, "Sic him!"

"Watch me get rid of that cur," said the man. "Sic him, Pete! Sic him!"

Phoenix heard the dogs fighting, and heard the man running and throwing sticks. She even heard a gunshot. But she was slowly bending forward by that time, further and further forward, the lids stretched down over her eyes, as if she were doing this in her sleep. Her chin was lowered almost to her knees. The yellow palm of her hand came out from the fold of her apron. Her fingers slid down and along the ground under the piece of money with the grace and care they would have in lifting an egg from under a setting hen. Then she slowly straightened up, she stood erect, and the nickel was in her apron pocket. A bird flew by. Her lips moved. "God watching me the whole time. I come to stealing."

The man came back, and his own dog panted about them. "Well, I scared him off that time," he said, and then he laughed and lifted his gun and pointed it at Phoenix.

She stood straight and faced him.

"Doesn't the gun scare you?" he said, still pointing it.

"No, sir, I seen plenty go off closer by, in my day, and for less than what I done," she said holding utterly still.

He smiled, and shouldered the gun. "Well, Granny," he said, "you must be a hundred years old, and scared of nothing. I'd give you a dime if I had any money with me. But you take my advice and stay home, and nothing will happen to you."

"I bound to go on my way, mister," said Phoenix. She inclined her head in the red rag. Then they went in different directions, but she could hear the gun shooting again and again over the hill.

She walked on. The shadows hung from the oak trees to the road like curtains. Then she smelled woodsmoke, and smelled the river, and she saw a steeple and the cabins on their steep

---

WORDS TO OWN

radiation (rā′dē·ā′shən) *n.*: pattern; arrangement.

---

steps. Dozens of little black children whirled around her. There ahead was Natchez shining. Bells were ringing. She walked on.

In the paved city it was Christmas time. There were red and green electric lights strung and crisscrossed everywhere, and all turned on in the daytime. Old Phoenix would have been lost if she had not distrusted her eyesight and depended on her feet to know where to take her.

She paused quietly on the sidewalk where people were passing by. A lady came along in the crowd, carrying an armful of red-, green-, and silver-wrapped presents; she gave off perfume like the red roses in hot summer, and Phoenix stopped her.

"Please, missy, will you lace up my shoe?" She held up her foot.

"What do you want, Grandma?"

"See my shoe," said Phoenix. "Do all right for out in the country, but wouldn't look right to go in a big building."

"Stand still then, Grandma," said the lady. She put her packages down on the sidewalk beside her and laced and tied both shoes tightly.

"Can't lace 'em with a cane," said Phoenix. "Thank you, missy. I doesn't mind asking a nice lady to tie up my shoe, when I gets out on the street."

Moving slowly and from side to side, she went into the big building, and into a tower of steps, where she walked up and around and around until her feet knew to stop.

She entered a door, and there she saw nailed up on the wall the document that had been stamped with the gold seal and framed in the gold frame, which matched the dream that was hung up in her head.

"Here I be," she said. There was a fixed and ceremonial stiffness over her body.

"A charity case, I suppose," said an attendant who sat at the desk before her.

But Phoenix only looked above her head. There was sweat on her face, the wrinkles in her skin shone like a bright net.

"Speak up, Grandma," the woman said. "What's your name? We must have your history, you know. Have you been here before? What seems to be the trouble with you?"

Old Phoenix only gave a twitch to her face as if a fly were bothering her.

"Are you deaf?" cried the attendant.

But then the nurse came in.

"Oh, that's just old Aunt Phoenix," she said. "She doesn't come for herself—she has a little grandson. She makes these trips just as regular as clockwork. She lives away back off the Old Natchez Trace." She bent down. "Well, Aunt Phoenix, why don't you just take a seat? We won't keep you standing after your long trip." She pointed.

The old woman sat down, bolt upright in the chair.

"Now, how is the boy?" asked the nurse.

Old Phoenix did not speak.

"I said, how is the boy?"

But Phoenix only waited and stared straight ahead, her face very <u>solemn</u> and withdrawn into rigidity.

"Is his throat any better?" asked the nurse. "Aunt Phoenix, don't you hear me? Is your grandson's throat any better since the last time you came for the medicine?"

With her hands on her knees, the old woman waited, silent, erect and motionless, just as if she were in armor.

"You mustn't take up our time this way, Aunt Phoenix," the nurse said. "Tell us quickly about your grandson, and get it over. He isn't dead, is he?"

At last there came a flicker and then a flame of comprehension across her face, and she spoke.

"My grandson. It was my memory had left me. There I sat and forgot why I made my long trip."

"Forgot?" The nurse frowned. "After you came so far?"

Then Phoenix was like an old woman begging a dignified forgiveness for waking up frightened in the night. "I never did go to school, I was too old at the Surrender," she said in a soft voice. "I'm an old woman without an education. It was my memory fail me. My little grandson, he is just the same, and I forgot it in the coming."

"Throat never heals, does it?" said the nurse, speaking in a loud, sure voice to old Phoenix. By

---

WORDS TO OWN

ceremonial (ser′ə·mō′nē·əl) *adj.*: formal.
solemn (säl′əm) *adj.*: serious.

Old Phoenix held the bottle close to her eyes, and then carefully put it into her pocket.

Courthouse town, Grenada (1935), by Eudora Welty. Photograph.

now she had a card with something written on it, a little list. "Yes. Swallowed lye. When was it?—January—two-three years ago—"

Phoenix spoke unasked now. "No, missy, he not dead, he just the same. Every little while his throat begin to close up again, and he not able to swallow. He not get his breath. He not able to help himself. So the time come around, and I go on another trip for the soothing medicine."

"All right. The doctor said as long as you came to get it, you could have it," said the nurse. "But it's an obstinate case."

"My little grandson, he sit up there in the house all wrapped up, waiting by himself," Phoenix went on. "We is the only two left in the world. He suffer and it don't seem to put him back at all. He got a sweet look. He going to last. He wear a little patch quilt and peep out holding his mouth open like a little bird. I remembers so plain now. I not going to forget him again, no, the whole enduring time. I could tell him from all the others in creation."

"All right." The nurse was trying to hush her now. She brought her a bottle of medicine. "Charity," she said, making a check mark in a book.

Old Phoenix held the bottle close to her eyes, and then carefully put it into her pocket.

"I thank you," she said.

"It's Christmas time, Grandma," said the attendant. "Could I give you a few pennies out of my purse?"

"Five pennies is a nickel," said Phoenix stiffly.

"Here's a nickel," said the attendant.

Phoenix rose carefully and held out her hand. She received the nickel and then fished the other nickel out of her pocket and laid it beside the new one. She stared at her palm closely, with her head on one side.

Then she gave a tap with her cane on the floor.

"This is what come to me to do," she said. "I going to the store and buy my child a little windmill they sells, made out of paper. He going to find it hard to believe there such a thing in the world. I'll march myself back where he waiting, holding it straight up in this hand."

She lifted her free hand, gave a little nod, turned around, and walked out of the doctor's office. Then her slow step began on the stairs, going down.

EUDORA WELTY 639

Fayette (1930s), by Eudora Welty. Photograph.
Eudora Welty Collection, Mississippi Department of Archives and History.

PRIMARY Sources — AN ESSAY

"Is Phoenix Jackson's Grandson Really Dead?"

A story writer is more than happy to be read by students; the fact that these serious readers think and feel something in response to his work he finds life-giving. At the same time he may not always be able to reply to their specific questions in kind. I wondered if it might clarify something, for both the questioners and myself, if I set down a general reply to the question that comes to me most often in the mail, from both students and their teachers, after some classroom discussion. The unrivaled favorite is this: "Is Phoenix Jackson's grandson really *dead*?"

. . . I had not meant to mystify readers by withholding any fact; it is not a writer's business to tease. The story is told through Phoenix's mind as she undertakes her errand. As the author at one with the character as I tell it, I must assume that the boy is alive. As the reader, you are free to think as you like, of course: The story invites you to believe that no matter what happens, Phoenix for as long as she is able to walk and can hold to her purpose

Courthouse steps, Fayette (1930s), by Eudora Welty. Photograph.

will make her journey. The *possibility* that she would keep on even if he were dead is there in her devotion and its single-minded, single-track errand. Certainly the *artistic* truth, which should be good enough for the fact, lies in Phoenix's own answer to that question. When the nurse asks, "He isn't dead, is he?" she speaks for herself: "He still the same. He going to last."

The grandchild is the incentive. But it is the journey, the going of the errand, that is the story, and the question is not whether the grandchild is in reality alive or dead. It doesn't affect the outcome of the story or its meaning from start to finish. But it is not the question itself that has struck me as much as the idea, almost without exception implied in the asking, that for Phoenix's grandson to be dead would somehow make the story "better."

. . . The grandson's plight was real and it made the truth of the story, which is the story of an errand of love carried out. If the child no longer lived, the truth would persist in the "wornness" of the path. But his being dead can't increase the truth of the story, can't affect it one way or the other. I think I signal this, because the end of the story has been reached before old Phoenix gets home again:

she simply starts back. To the question "Is the grandson really dead?" I could reply that it doesn't make any difference. I could also say that I did not make him up in order to let him play a trick on Phoenix. But my best answer would be: "*Phoenix* is alive."

The origin of a story is sometimes a trustworthy clue to the author—or can provide him with the clue—to its key image; maybe in this case it will do the same for the reader. One day I saw a solitary old woman like Phoenix. She was walking; I saw her, at middle distance, in a winter country landscape, and watched her slowly make her way across my line of vision. That sight of her made me write the story. I invented an errand for her, but that only seemed a living part of the figure she was herself: What errand other than for someone else could be making her go? And her going was the first thing, her persisting in her landscape was the real thing, and the first and the real were what I wanted and worked to keep. I brought her up close enough, by imagination, to describe her face, make her present to the eyes, but the full-length figure moving across the winter fields was the indelible one and the image to keep, and the perspective extending into the vanishing distance the true one to hold in mind.

I invented for my character, as I wrote, some passing adventures—some dreams and harassments and a small triumph or two, some jolts to her pride, some flights of fancy to console her, one or two encounters to scare her, a moment that gave her cause to feel ashamed, a moment to dance and preen—for it had to be a *journey,* and all these things belonged to that, parts of life's uncertainty.

. . . What I hoped would come clear was that in the whole surround of this story, the world it threads through, the only certain thing at all is the worn path. The habit of love cuts through confusion and stumbles or contrives its way out of difficulty, it remembers the way even when it forgets, for a dumbfounded moment, its reason for being. The path is the thing that matters.

—Eudora Welty

MAKING MEANINGS

First Thoughts

1. What was your first reaction to the story: "Good story!" or "I don't get it"—or another response? What questions do you have about the story?

Reading Check

a. Describe the purpose of Phoenix Jackson's journey, and list the obstacles she overcomes.

b. At the end of Phoenix's perilous journey, does she get what she wants? Explain.

Shaping Interpretations

2. Why is Phoenix an appropriate name for the main character? (Review your Quickwrite notes.)

3. How do Welty's **descriptions** of Phoenix's appearance, speech, and behavior identify her with the world of nature and with time itself?

4. Describe what Phoenix's encounters with the little boy, the buzzard, the scarecrow, the thorny bush, and the hunter tell us about her **character**. Is she a heroine in the traditional sense of the word? Why or why not?

5. What is **ironic** about the reason the hunter suggests for Phoenix's long journey? Many people treat Phoenix in a condescending manner. Why would they do this?

6. When the nurse gives Phoenix the medicine, she says, "Charity," and makes a check mark in her book. Given the character of Phoenix, what is **ironic** about the nurse's statement and action?

7. Welty says that the worn path is a **metaphor** for the habit of love. Explain what Welty means by "the habit of love," and tell why this habit might be compared with a worn path (and not with a new road, or the shining path of a rocket, or a crystal stairway).

8. What do you consider Welty's major **theme** in "A Worn Path"? Put another way, what "worn path" is open to us all?

CHOICES:
Building Your Portfolio

Writer's Notebook

1. Collecting Ideas for an Analysis of Causes and Effects

This story reveals in an indirect way the effects of racism and segregation. Take notes on what you can infer about the effects of segregation on people like Phoenix—and on the white hunter. Or, you might want to approach the situation from another perspective: Take notes on what you infer to be the causes of segregation in Phoenix's community—why would people want to separate themselves from other people? Save your notes for the Writer's Workshop on page 685.

Analyzing a Story

2. Stages of the Journey

In her comment on the story (page 640), Welty summarizes the purposes of the adventures she invented for Phoenix. In an essay, identify the specific parts of the journey that can be characterized as **(a)** dreams, **(b)** harassments, **(c)** small triumphs, **(d)** some jolts to the traveler's pride, **(e)** some flights of fancy to console the traveler, **(f)** encounters to scare the traveler, **(g)** cause to be ashamed, and **(h)** a moment to dance and preen. In your essay, explain how Phoenix's journey takes on mythic significance. How is it like the quests of heroes like Odysseus or fairy-tale heroes and heroines?

Creative Writing

3. Enduring a Worn Path

Write a story of your own about a person who travels a worn path over and over again without complaint. Open your story with a description of your setting: the time and place of the action. Let us see your main traveler as clearly as Welty shows us Phoenix. Your story may be fiction, or it may be based on fact.

Collection 13

NO TIME FOR HEROES

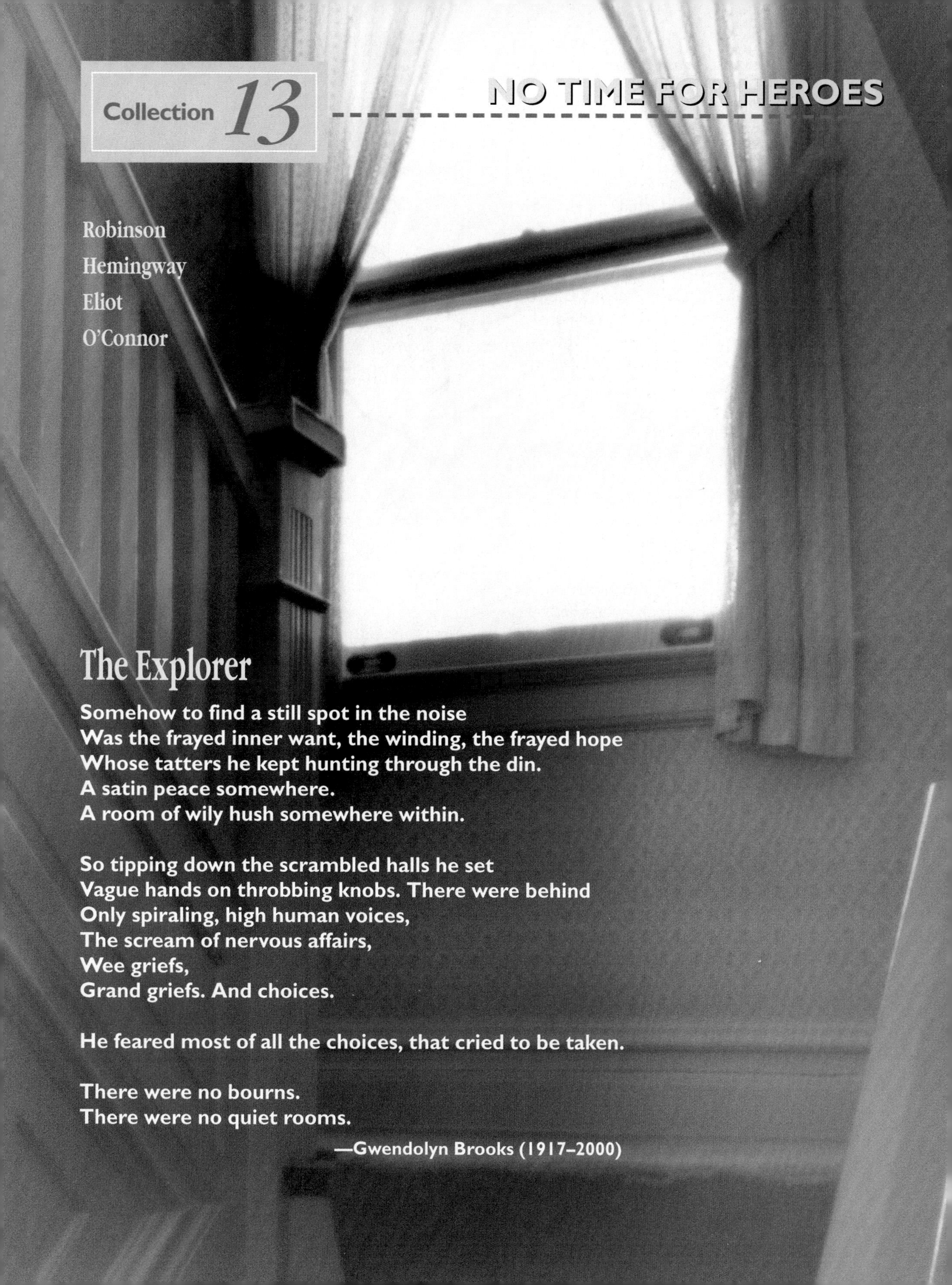

Robinson
Hemingway
Eliot
O'Connor

The Explorer

Somehow to find a still spot in the noise
Was the frayed inner want, the winding, the frayed hope
Whose tatters he kept hunting through the din.
A satin peace somewhere.
A room of wily hush somewhere within.

So tipping down the scrambled halls he set
Vague hands on throbbing knobs. There were behind
Only spiraling, high human voices,
The scream of nervous affairs,
Wee griefs,
Grand griefs. And choices.

He feared most of all the choices, that cried to be taken.

There were no bourns.
There were no quiet rooms.

—Gwendolyn Brooks (1917–2000)

Edwin Arlington Robinson

(1869–1935)

By the 1890s, the vitality of the nineteenth century seemed exhausted, and the gathering forces of modernism were still scattered and obscure. Between 1890 and 1910, many poets were churning out the same old rhymes and meters of Romanticism. But in those two decades, one voice spoke out in traditional forms enlivened with an authentic, contemporary American accent: the voice of Edwin Arlington Robinson.

The strengths that distinguish Robinson are his native voice and his wise and ironic view of human behavior. Robinson's bedrock realism informs even the most formal of his carefully wrought poems. In some of his poetic portraits of individuals, he anticipates by a decade the more loosely drawn portraits found in Edgar Lee Masters's *Spoon River Anthology* (page 692). In his skill with meter, Robinson foreshadows Robert Frost's gift for bending the strictly counted line to accommodate the ease and flow of vernacular speech.

Robinson was a Yankee from the rocky coast of Maine. Born at Head Tide in 1869, he lived for the next twenty-seven years in the town of Gardiner, except for the two years when he attended Harvard as a special student. Gardiner became the Tilbury Town of his poems, the home of some of his most famous characters. When he was in his late twenties, Robinson moved to New York City and published his first book. There he supported himself at various jobs, including one as a timekeeper at the construction site of the new subway system.

After a year of such work, Robinson's fortunes took a surprising turn for the better. Among the young poet's readers was none other than the president of the United States, Theodore Roosevelt. When Roosevelt learned that the poet he admired was barely scraping by on a laborer's salary, he arranged to have the

AP/Wide World Photos.

New York Custom House hire him as a clerk, a position Robinson held for almost five years. One year after Robinson resigned, he published *The Town Down the River* (1910) and dedicated the volume to Roosevelt.

Another form of assistance came in an invitation from the famous MacDowell Colony in Peterborough, New Hampshire. The colony is a center for composers, artists, and writers, established by the widow of the American composer Edward MacDowell. There Robinson spent long, working summers for the greater part of his life.

Robinson, a loner by temperament, became an increasingly popular poet. Even in a modernist age, Robinson's poetry, which was traditional in form, continued to be read and admired, and he was awarded a Pulitzer Prize three times. At the time of his death, Robinson's reputation had survived the tide of modernism that had once threatened to wash it away.

go.hrw.com
HRW
LE0 11-13

Make the Connection

Things Aren't Always What They Seem

One of the persistent themes of early-twentieth-century American poetry is that the conventions of small-town life are a façade that often obscures unpleasant realities. (Some say similar façades still exist today, in cities as well as in small towns.) In this famous poem, which contains a harsh, surprise ending, an unidentified speaker tells what happened to a prominent citizen.

Quickwrite

Can we accurately determine the inner feelings of a person by observing his or her outward behavior? Write a few sentences stating your opinion, supported by specific reasons.

Winter Twilight (1930) by Charles Burchfield.
Oil on composition board (27¾″ × 39½″).

Collection of Whitney Museum of American Art (31.128).
Photograph ©1998 Whitney Museum of American Art.

Richard Cory

Edwin Arlington Robinson

Whenever Richard Cory went downtown,
    We people on the pavement looked at him:
He was a gentleman from sole to crown,
    Clean favored, and imperially slim.

5 And he was always quietly arrayed,
    And he was always human when he talked;
But still he fluttered pulses when he said,
    "Good morning," and he glittered when he walked.

And he was rich—yes, richer than a king—
10   And admirably schooled in every grace:
In fine, we thought that he was everything
    To make us wish that we were in his place.

So on we worked, and waited for the light,
    And went without the meat, and cursed the bread;
15 And Richard Cory, one calm summer night,
    Went home and put a bullet through his head.

Make the Connection

Long Ago and Far Away
The glory and glamour of bygone days hold an irresistible charm for many of us. But sometimes a longing for the past leaves people sorely disappointed with the present.

Quickwrite

On a sheet of paper, write down some reasons why a person might be drawn to splendid times in the distant past.

Background

The title of this poem is not simply a man's name: It contains a clue to the poem's meaning. "Miniver" is the white fur trim, sometimes ermine, seen on the costumes of royalty in medieval and Renaissance portraits. The subjects of such portraits include rich and powerful members of the Medici family of Renaissance Italy. Other references in the poem also evoke heroic eras of the past.

Miniver Cheevy

Edwin Arlington Robinson

Miniver Cheevy, child of scorn,
    Grew lean while he assailed the seasons;
He wept that he was ever born,
    And he had reasons.

5 Miniver loved the days of old
    When swords were bright and steeds were prancing;
The vision of a warrior bold
    Would set him dancing.

  Miniver sighed for what was not,
10   And dreamed, and rested from his labors;
He dreamed of Thebes° and Camelot,°
    And Priam's° neighbors.

  Miniver mourned the ripe renown
    That made so many a name so fragrant;
15 He mourned Romance, now on the town,°
    And Art, a vagrant.

11. Thebes: city in ancient Greece associated with several myths.
Camelot: legendary site of King Arthur's court.
12. Priam's: In Homer's epic poem *The Iliad*, Priam (prī'əm) is the king of Troy during the Trojan War.
15. on the town: dependent on charity.

The Sentimental Yearner (1936) by Grant Wood. Pencil, black and white conté crayon, painted white around image.

Miniver loved the Medici,°
    Albeit° he had never seen one;
He would have sinned incessantly
20   Could he have been one.

Miniver cursed the commonplace
    And eyed a khaki suit with loathing;
He missed the medieval grace
    Of iron clothing.°

25 Miniver scorned the gold he sought,
    But sore annoyed was he without it;
Miniver thought, and thought, and thought,
    And thought about it.

Miniver Cheevy, born too late,
30   Scratched his head and kept on thinking;
Miniver coughed, and called it fate,
    And kept on drinking.

17. Medici (med′ə·chē′): members of a powerful Italian family of the fourteenth to sixteenth centuries. They were famous for their wealth, their sponsorship of the arts, and their control of the city of Florence.
18. albeit (ôl·bē′it): even though. The word combines and condenses "although it be."

24. iron clothing: armor worn by medieval knights.

PRIMARY
Sources
LETTERS

Robinson's Ruminations

I've written a nice little thing called "Richard Cory"—"Whenever Richard Cory went downtown, we people on the pavement looked at him . . . And Richard Cory, one calm summer night, went home and put a bullet through his head." There isn't any idealism in it, but there's lots of something else—humanity, maybe.

. . .

Why don't you like "Richard Cory"? You say it makes you feel cold, but that statement doesn't seem to agree with my impression of your character. It can't be you are squeamish after all. If you are, don't read "Reuben Bright" or he will knock you down. I used to read about clearness, force, and elegance in the rhetoric books, but I'm afraid I go in chiefly for force. So you will not be offended if I'm not always elegant. There are too many elegant men in the world just now, and they seem to be increasing.

. . .

I don't have trances, furors, or ecstasies. My poetic spells are of the most prosaic sort. I just sit down and grind it out and use a trifle more tobacco than is good for me.

. . .

You may call me anything you like—anything but Eddie. I had an aunt who called me Eddie and now she doesn't call me at all.

—Edwin Arlington Robinson,
from Letters to Edith Brower

MAKING MEANINGS

Richard Cory

First Thoughts

1. How did you respond to the ending of the poem?

Shaping Interpretations

2. What is **ironic** in the fact that Richard Cory takes his own life? What irony is there in the fact that the night was calm?

3. Find five words or phrases in "Richard Cory" that **connote** kingliness or royalty. How does the poet's choice of these words contribute to the **contrast** between the townspeople and Richard Cory?

4. Does the harsh surprise ending hint that the real story is the one that remains untold? What aspects of Richard Cory's life are *not* mentioned? How might these hidden or overlooked areas account for his fate?

5. Read Robinson's comments on "Richard Cory" (page 648). What do you think he means when he says there is a lot of "humanity" in the poem? Why do you think it made his correspondent feel "cold"? How did it make you feel?

Miniver Cheevy

First Thoughts

1. What were your thoughts or feelings about Cheevy and his attitude toward life?

Shaping Interpretations

2. What do you think "child of scorn" means?

3. Do Cheevy's problems really stem from his having been "born too late"? Explain. How does the disappointed Cheevy cope with his lot in life?

4. "Romance" and "Art" are **personified** in the fourth stanza. What does Cheevy think has happened to romance and art in his own time?

5. How would you describe the change of **tone** in the last stanza? How does this change affect the poem's meaning?

Extending the Texts

6. Explain whether or not you think the tales of Richard Cory and Miniver Cheevy have a moral or message for us today. Where can you find Corys and Cheevys in today's world?

7. Refer to your Quickwrite notes, and tell whether the poems indicate that appearances can be deceiving.

CHOICES:
Building Your Portfolio

Writer's Notebook

1. Collecting Ideas for an Analysis of Causes and Effects

Why does Richard Cory kill himself? Why does Miniver Cheevy suffer so much? Brainstorm a list of causes you could speculate on to answer these questions. With each cause, list details from the poem that might support your speculation. Save your notes for possible use in the Writer's Workshop on page 685.

Comparing and Contrasting Values

2. Rising Above or Mired Below?

In a brief essay, show how either Richard Cory or Miniver Cheevy demonstrates, or fails to demonstrate, the Transcendentalist ideals of self-reliance and individualism championed by Emerson (page 216) and Thoreau (page 230). As the focus of your essay, choose an appropriate quotation from either of these writers.

Creative Writing/Performance

3. From Page to Stage

In prose or verse, let Richard Cory tell his own story in the first person. Reveal the reasons for Cory's unhappiness and his true thoughts about the townspeople. Then, present his story to the class in a dramatic monologue. (For more on dramatic monologue, see page 663 and the Handbook of Literary Terms.)

Ernest Hemingway

(1899–1961)

Few American authors have offered as powerful a definition of the twentieth-century
hero as Ernest Hemingway has. Hemingway's
fiction presents a strict code of contemporary
heroism. His vision centers on disillusionment
with the conventions of an optimistic, patriotic
society and a belief that the essence of life is
violence, from which there is no refuge. As
Hemingway saw it, the only victory that can be
won from life lies in a graceful stoicism, a willingness to accept gratefully life's few moments
of pleasure.

Although this ideal of rugged machismo may
now seem superficial, it powerfully affected generations of American readers. Moreover, Hemingway launched a new style of writing so forceful in its simplicity that it became a measure of
excellence around the world.

Hemingway's life, like F. Scott Fitzgerald's,
bore a notable resemblance to the lives of his
fictional characters. He was born in the Chicago
suburb of Oak Park on July 21, 1899. His father,
a doctor, initiated him early into a love for the
Michigan woods and the hunting and fishing that
could be found there. Growing up, Hemingway
boxed and played football devotedly, but he also
wrote poetry, short stories, and a column for
the school newspaper. Graduating from high
school just as the United States entered World
War I in 1917, he yearned to enlist, but he
was rejected by the army because of a boxing
injury to his eye. He landed a job as a reporter
for the *Kansas City Star.* Hemingway reached the
war a year later as an ambulance driver for the
Red Cross in Italy, but after six weeks he was
wounded in the knee, seriously enough
to require a dozen operations. This wound
was a central episode in both Hemingway's real
and creative life. During his long convalescence
in an Italian hospital, he fell in love with a nurse
who became the model for the heroine of his
novel *A Farewell to Arms.*

After the armistice in 1918, Hemingway re-

Karsh/Woodfin Camp and Associates.

turned to Michigan. His experience of coming
to terms with the war is reflected in his story
"Big Two-Hearted River." In the story, Nick
Adams, a war veteran, camps and fishes alone in
the woods, escaping from the world in order to
heal himself from both a physical and psychological shattering.

An American in Paris

In 1921, newly married and with a commission
as a roving reporter for the *Toronto Star,*
Hemingway set off for Paris. It was the era of
the American expatriates, when writers and
painters crowded the cafes of the Left Bank of
the Seine. Here Hemingway worked at the craft
of fiction and met other important writers,
among them F. Scott Fitzgerald, James Joyce,
and Ezra Pound. But most important, he
met the American writer Gertrude Stein
(1874–1946). She read all his work and advised
him to prune his descriptions and to "concentrate." Hemingway took her advice and spoke
fervently of writing "the truest sentence that
you know," and of arriving through straight

presentation of unvarnished fact at a "true, simple declarative sentence."

Hemingway's first book, *Three Stories and Ten Poems* (1923), along with *The Torrents of Spring* (1926), a parody of his friend Sherwood Anderson's work, drew scant notice. Then, late in 1926, he published *The Sun Also Rises,* a novel based on his life in Paris but transplanted to Pamplona, the Spanish town famous for its annual running of the bulls through the streets. The novel brought Hemingway widespread critical attention. Gertrude Stein's remark, "You are all a lost generation," was the novel's epigraph, and the book did reveal the postwar epoch to itself. Many readers of Hemingway's age embraced it as a portrait of their shattered lives.

> "You are all a lost generation."

Hemingway, around thirty years old and married for the second time, went on to write an even more powerful and successful novel, *A Farewell to Arms* (1929). This is the beautifully told story of Frederic Henry, a wounded ambulance driver. Disillusioned with the war, he falls in love with Catherine Barkley, an English nurse, and flees with her to Switzerland, where she dies in childbirth. Frederic's farewell to the dying Catherine is one of the great love scenes in fiction.

Author and Adventurer

After the major success of *A Farewell to Arms,* Hemingway established himself as a worldwide adventurer, as though a heroic style was as important to his life as to his fiction. He fished and hunted wherever new seas and continents beckoned. And he periodically resumed his role as war correspondent, most notably during the Spanish civil war (1936–1939).

During the early 1930s, Hemingway brought out two nonfiction books that revealed his fascination with bullfighting and with big-game hunting—*Death in the Afternoon* (1932) and *Green Hills of Africa* (1935). Significantly, both books centered on the art of killing. In 1940,

just as the literary world was writing Hemingway off as a has-been novelist, he presented another triumph, *For Whom the Bell Tolls.*

The outbreak of World War II drew Hemingway back into uniform. Although officially a correspondent, he gathered around himself a small army of adventurers. During one battle, a First Army commander reported that Hemingway's band was sixty miles in front of the Americans' advancing line. When the Allies at last reached Paris in 1944, they found that Hemingway had already "liberated" the bar at the Ritz Hotel.

By 1952, Hemingway's celebrated literary accomplishments and his continuous pursuit of excitement and danger had made him as famous as any film star. In spite of his flamboyant exploits, he produced yet another widely acclaimed novel in that year, *The Old Man and the Sea,* which won the 1953 Pulitzer Prize. It tells of an old Cuban fisherman who hooks a giant marlin far out at sea and battles the fish for two days and nights. Although he finally succeeds in subduing the great fish and lashing it to the side of his boat, sharks tear at the carcass until the man is left with only the marlin's skeleton. The tale has been interpreted as Hemingway's metaphor for life: a vision of the hero, weighed down by the years, but still able to use his skill to taunt fate and so win a kind of victory from it.

In 1954, Hemingway won the Nobel Prize in literature. He now divided his time between his house in Ketchum, Idaho, and his restless travels all over the world: to Cuba, China, Venice, Spain, and Africa. His health deteriorated, and periods of elation alternated with episodes of severe depression. After a visit to the Mayo Clinic for treatment, he returned to Idaho. On the morning of July 2, 1961, he rose early, and with two charges of a double-barreled shotgun, he killed himself.

"He put life back on the page," wrote the critic Alfred Kazin, "made us see, feel, and taste the gift of life. . . . To read Hemingway was always to feel more alive."

Before You Read

SOLDIER'S HOME

Make the Connection

A Hero's Welcome

World War I was greeted as the "war to end all wars," and songs like "Over There" celebrated the heroism of hundreds of thousands of American soldiers who were shipped off to fight in the trenches of Europe. But advances in weaponry made the Great War devastating, both physically and psychologically. Returning soldiers sometimes couldn't readjust to life back home, which seemed to offer little they could relate to or believe in. As you can imagine, some became disillusioned, cynical, isolated, and overwhelmed by hopelessness. They became the most lost of Gertrude Stein's lost generation.

Reading Skills and Strategies

Reading for Details

As you read the story, try to piece together a **character profile** of the returned soldier Harold Krebs. Take notes on Krebs's feelings, attitudes, and views on the following: the war, his return home, his family, other people, his hometown, and his future.

Background

Soldiers who returned home from World War I were often described as shellshocked—suffering from a mental and emotional condition of confusion, exhaustion, anxiety, and depression. In the past, the condition—now termed *post-traumatic stress disorder*—was not well understood, and friends and relatives often found themselves at a loss. They expected returning soldiers to plunge directly back into civilian life and could not understand why some young men seemed unable to do so.

(Left and opposite page) Photos of Ernest Hemingway in Italy and France during World War I (1918).

Department of Rare Books and Special Collections/Princeton University Libraries.

Leib Image Archives.

Department of Rare Books and Special Collections/Princeton University Libraries.

John F. Kennedy Library, Boston, Massachusetts.

Soldier's Home

Ernest Hemingway

Krebs went to the war from a Methodist college in Kansas. There is a picture which shows him among his fraternity brothers, all of them wearing exactly the same height and style collar. He enlisted in the Marines in 1917 and did not return to the United States until the second division returned from the Rhine[1] in the summer of 1919.

There is a picture which shows him on the Rhine with two German girls and another corporal. Krebs and the corporal look too big for their uniforms. The German girls are not beautiful. The Rhine does not show in the picture.

By the time Krebs returned to his home town in Oklahoma the greeting of heroes was over. He came back much too late. The men from the town who had been drafted had all been welcomed

1. **Rhine:** river that flows through Germany toward the North Sea.

elaborately on their return. There had been a great deal of hysteria. Now the reaction had set in. People seemed to think it was rather ridiculous for Krebs to be getting back so late, years after the war was over.

At first Krebs, who had been at Belleau Wood, Soissons, the Champagne, St. Mihiel and in the Argonne[2] did not want to talk about the war at all. Later he felt the need to talk but no one wanted to hear about it. His town had heard too many atrocity stories to be thrilled by actualities. Krebs found that to be listened to at all he had to lie, and after he had done this twice he, too, had a reaction against the war and against talking about it. A distaste for everything that had happened to him in the war set in because of the lies he had told.

2. **Belleau** (be·lō′) **Wood . . . Argonne** (är′gän′): sites of World War I battles that demonstrated the Allies' superior strength against the Germans.

WORDS TO OWN

elaborately (ē·lab′ə·rit·lē) *adv.*: with great care.
hysteria (hi·ster′ē·ə) *n.*: uncontrolled excitement.
atrocity (ə·träs′ə·tē) *n.* used as *adj.*: horrible; brutal.

All of the times that had been able to make him feel cool and clear inside himself when he thought of them; the times so long back when he had done the one thing, the only thing for a man to do, easily and naturally, when he might have done something else, now lost their cool, valuable quality and then were lost themselves.

His lies were quite unimportant lies and consisted in attributing to himself things other men had seen, done or heard of, and stating as facts certain apocryphal incidents familiar to all soldiers. Even his lies were not sensational at the pool room. His acquaintances, who had heard detailed accounts of German women found chained to machine guns in the Argonne forest and who could not comprehend, or were barred by their patriotism from interest in, any German machine gunners who were not chained, were not thrilled by his stories.

Krebs acquired the nausea in regard to experience that is the result of untruth or exaggeration, and when he occasionally met another man who had really been a soldier and they talked a few minutes in the dressing room at a dance he fell into the easy pose of the old soldier among other soldiers: that he had been badly, sickeningly frightened all the time. In this way he lost everything.

During this time, it was late summer, he was sleeping late in bed, getting up to walk down town to the library to get a book, eating lunch at home, reading on the front porch until he became bored and then walking down through the town to spend the hottest hours of the day in the cool dark of the pool room. He loved to play pool.

In the evening he practised on his clarinet, strolled down town, read and went to bed. He was still a hero to his two young sisters. His mother would have given him breakfast in bed if he had wanted it. She often came in when he was in bed and asked him to tell her about the war, but her attention always wandered. His father was non-committal.

Before Krebs went away to the war he had never been allowed to drive the family motor car. His father was in the real estate business and always wanted the car to be at his command when he required it to take clients out into the country to show them a piece of farm property. The car always stood outside the First National Bank building where his father had an office on the second floor. Now, after the war, it was still the same car.

Nothing was changed in the town except that the young girls had grown up. But they lived in such a complicated world of already defined alliances and shifting feuds that Krebs did not feel the energy or the courage to break into it. He liked to look at them, though. There were so many good-looking young girls. Most of them had their hair cut short. When he went away only little girls wore their hair like that or girls that were fast. They all wore sweaters and shirt waists with round Dutch collars. It was a pattern. He liked to look at them from the front porch as they walked on the other side of the street. He liked to watch them walking under the shade of the trees. He liked the round Dutch collars above their sweaters. He liked their silk stockings and flat shoes. He liked their bobbed hair and the way they walked.

When he was in town their appeal to him was not very strong. He did not like them when he saw them in the Greek's ice cream parlor. He did not want them themselves really. They were too complicated. There was something else. Vaguely he wanted a girl but he did not want to have to work to get her. He would have liked to have a girl but he did not want to have to spend a long time getting her. He did not want to get into the intrigue and the politics. He did not want to have to do any courting. He did not want to tell any more lies. It wasn't worth it.

He did not want any consequences. He did not want any consequences ever again. He wanted to live along without consequences. Besides he did not really need a girl. The army had taught him that. It was all right to pose as though you had to have a girl. Nearly everybody did that. But it

---

WORDS TO OWN

apocryphal (ə·päk′rə·fəl) *adj.*: of questionable authority; false.

exaggeration (eg·zaj′ər·ā·shən) *n.*: overstatement.

alliances (ə·lī′əns·iz) *n. pl.*: close associations for common objectives.

intrigue (in′trēg′) *n.*: scheming.

consequences (kän′si·kwens·iz) *n. pl.*: results of an action.

---

wasn't true. You did not need a girl. That was the funny thing. First a fellow boasted how girls mean nothing to him, that he never thought of them, that they could not touch him. Then a fellow boasted that he could not get along without girls, that he had to have them all the time, that he could not go to sleep without them.

That was all a lie. It was all a lie both ways. You did not need a girl unless you thought about them. He learned that in the army. Then sooner or later you always got one. When you were really ripe for a girl you always got one. You did not have to think about it. Sooner or later it would come. He had learned that in the army.

Now he would have liked a girl if she had come to him and not wanted to talk. But here at home it was all too complicated. He knew he could never get through it all again. It was not worth the trouble. That was the thing about French girls and German girls. There was not all this talking. You couldn't talk much and you did not need to talk. It was simple and you were friends. He thought about France and then he began to think about Germany. On the whole he had liked Germany better. He did not want to leave Germany. He did not want to come home. Still, he had come home. He sat on the front porch.

He liked the girls that were walking along the other side of the street. He liked the look of them much better than the French girls or the German girls. But the world they were in was not the world he was in. He would like to have one of them. But it was not worth it. They were such a nice pattern. He liked the pattern. It was exciting. But he would not go through all the talking. He did not want one badly enough. He liked to look at them all, though. It was not worth it. Not now when things were getting good again.

He sat there on the porch reading a book on the war. It was a history and he was reading about all the engagements he had been in. It was the most interesting reading he had ever done. He wished there were more maps. He looked forward with a good feeling to reading all the really good histories when they would come out with good detail maps. Now he was really learning about the war. He had been a good soldier. That made a difference.

One morning after he had been home about a month his mother came into his bedroom and sat on the bed. She smoothed her apron.

"I had a talk with your father last night, Harold," she said, "and he is willing for you to take the car out in the evenings."

"Yeah?" said Krebs, who was not fully awake. "Take the car out? Yeah?"

"Yes. Your father has felt for some time that you should be able to take the car out in the evenings whenever you wished but we only talked it over last night."

"I'll bet you made him," Krebs said.

"No. It was your father's suggestion that we talk the matter over."

"Yeah. I'll bet you made him," Krebs sat up in bed.

"Will you come down to breakfast, Harold?" his mother said.

"As soon as I get my clothes on," Krebs said.

His mother went out of the room and he could hear her frying something downstairs while he washed, shaved and dressed to go down into the dining-room for breakfast. While he was eating breakfast his sister brought in the mail.

"Well, Hare," she said. "You old sleepy-head. What do you ever get up for?"

Krebs looked at her. He liked her. She was his best sister.

"Have you got the paper?" he asked.

She handed him *The Kansas City Star* and he shucked off its brown wrapper and opened it to the sporting page. He folded *The Star* open and propped it against the water pitcher with his cereal dish to steady it, so he could read while he ate.

"Harold," his mother stood in the kitchen doorway, "Harold, please don't muss up the paper. Your father can't read his *Star* if it's been mussed."

"I won't muss it," Krebs said.

His sister sat down at the table and watched him while he read.

"We're playing indoor over at school this afternoon," she said. "I'm going to pitch."

"Good," said Krebs. "How's the old wing?"[3]

"I can pitch better than lots of the boys. I tell them all you taught me. The other girls aren't much good."

3. **wing:** arm.

WORDS TO OWN

engagements (en·gāj′mənts) *n. pl.:* battles.

LITERATURE AND POPULAR CULTURE

Charleston endurance contest (1926).

UPI/Bettmann.

The Decade That Roared

Harold Krebs finds his hometown much the same as he left it before the war, except for new styles in women's hair and clothing. He especially notices girls' short, bobbed hair—a style that marked a girl as "fast" only a few years earlier when he shipped out to the trenches of France.

The flap over flappers. Krebs was right on target. As the slick, sophisticated ads of the era show, nothing symbolized the decade after World War I so well as the "flapper"—a liberated young woman who cropped her hair into a caplike shape, wore half the amount of clothing of her Victorian-era counterpart, and boldly wore rouge and lipstick. The flapper abandoned the confines of the corset and opted instead for loose, long-waisted dresses that ended at or above the knee. She showed off her legs in the new silk or rayon stockings that were affordable at every income level. And she kicked, shimmied, and swayed in a wild, new dance called the Charleston.

An era of excess. Tired of war and disillusioned with political and social causes, city dwellers and even small-town residents yearned for fun and excitement in the Roaring Twenties. Millions of Americans purchased automobiles and took to the road on touring

---

"Yeah?" said Krebs.

"I tell them all you're my beau.[4] Aren't you my beau, Hare?"

"You bet."

"Couldn't your brother really be your beau just because he's your brother?"

"I don't know."

"Sure you know. Couldn't you be my beau, Hare, if I was old enough and if you wanted to?"

"Sure. You're my girl now."

"Am I really your girl?"

"Sure."

"Do you love me?"

"Uh, huh."

"Will you love me always?"

"Sure."

"Will you come over and watch me play in-door?"

"Maybe."

"Aw, Hare, you don't love me. If you loved me, you'd want to come over and watch me play in-door."

Krebs's mother came into the dining-room from the kitchen. She carried a plate with two fried eggs and some crisp bacon on it and a plate of buckwheat cakes.

"You run along, Helen," she said. "I want to talk to Harold."

4. **beau** (bō): boyfriend.

vacations. Consumerism grew by leaps and bounds, fueled by abundant advertising and easy credit plans. Popular entertainment filled people's leisure time: Commercial radio and the movies changed American life by forming a national mass culture. People devoured the sensational stories of the day—vivid reports of scandals, crimes, freak disasters, and sports exploits. Young and old alike reveled in learning details of the private lives of movie stars like Rudolph Valentino, writers like Edna St. Vincent Millay (page 697), sports figures like Babe Ruth and the American Indian athlete Jim Thorpe, and celebrities like the pilot Charles Lindbergh. Crazes spread throughout the country—manias for the Chinese game of mahjong, six-day bicycle races, dance marathons, and even flagpole sitting. Jazz, one of the great African American contributions to popular culture, provided the exciting soundtrack to the era.

The young rebels. Women and men alike became more aware of modernist thought and the psychological theories of Sigmund Freud, calling for new social freedoms. Young people rebelled against the tight moral codes and even the good manners of the prewar years. They scoffed at the prohibition on alcohol by inventing the private cocktail party. With the new availability of motorcars, people roared off to dances in places where no one knew them, where they could feel free of their inhibitions. Couples danced closer together than ever before, tangoing and fox-trotting cheek to cheek to the sound of the saxophone.

The twenties' emphasis on youth and openness is recognizably "modern." At the time, many Americans were shocked and outraged by what they saw as the deterioration of culture and values. The 1920s were a rowdy, roisterous time—a decade that roared.

Archive Photos.

She put the eggs and bacon down in front of him and brought in a jug of maple syrup for the buckwheat cakes. Then she sat down across the table from Krebs.

"I wish you'd put down the paper a minute, Harold," she said.

Krebs took down the paper and folded it.

"Have you decided what you are going to do yet, Harold?" his mother said, taking off her glasses.

"No," said Krebs.

"Don't you think it's about time?" His mother did not say this in a mean way. She seemed worried.

"I hadn't thought about it," Krebs said.

"God has some work for every one to do," his mother said. "There can be no idle hands in His Kingdom."

"I'm not in His Kingdom," Krebs said.

"We are all of us in His Kingdom."

Krebs felt embarrassed and resentful as always.

"I've worried about you so much, Harold," his mother went on. "I know the temptations you must have been exposed to. I know how weak men are. I know what your own dear grandfather, my own father, told us about the Civil War and I have prayed for you. I pray for you all day long, Harold."

Krebs looked at the bacon fat hardening on his plate.

East Wind over Weehawken (1934) by Edward Hopper. Oil on canvas (34″ × 50 ¼″).

"Your father is worried, too," his mother went on. "He thinks you have lost your ambition, that you haven't got a definite aim in life. Charley Simmons, who is just your age, has a good job and is going to be married. The boys are all settling down; they're all determined to get somewhere; you can see that boys like Charley Simmons are on their way to being really a credit to the community."

Krebs said nothing.

"Don't look that way, Harold," his mother said. "You know we love you and I want to tell you for your own good how matters stand. Your father does not want to hamper your freedom. He thinks you should be allowed to drive the car. If you want to take some of the nice girls out riding with you, we are only too pleased. We want you to enjoy yourself. But you are going to have to settle down to work, Harold. Your father doesn't care what you start in at. All work is honorable as he says. But you've got to make a start at something. He asked me to speak to you this morning and then you can stop in and see him at his office."

"Is that all?" Krebs said.

"Yes. Don't you love your mother, dear boy?"

"No," Krebs said.

His mother looked at him across the table. Her eyes were shiny. She started crying.

"I don't love anybody," Krebs said.

It wasn't any good. He couldn't tell her, he couldn't make her see it. It was silly to have said it. He had only hurt her. He went over and took hold of her arm. She was crying with her head in her hands.

"I didn't mean it," he said. "I was just angry at something. I didn't mean I didn't love you."

His mother went on crying. Krebs put his arm on her shoulder.

"Can't you believe me, mother?"

His mother shook her head.

"Please, please, mother. Please believe me."

"All right," his mother said chokily. She looked up at him. "I believe you, Harold."

Krebs kissed her hair. She put her face up to him.

"I'm your mother," she said. "I held you next to my heart when you were a tiny baby."

Krebs felt sick and vaguely nauseated.

"I know, Mummy," he said. "I'll try and be a good boy for you."

"Would you kneel and pray with me, Harold?" his mother asked.

They knelt down beside the dining-room table and Krebs's mother prayed.

"Now, you pray, Harold," she said.

"I can't," Krebs said.

"Try, Harold."

"I can't."

"Do you want me to pray for you?"

"Yes."

So his mother prayed for him and then they stood up and Krebs kissed his mother and went out of the house. He had tried so to keep his life from being complicated. Still, none of it had touched him. He had felt sorry for his mother and she had made him lie. He would go to Kansas City and get a job and she would feel all right about it. There would be one more scene maybe before he got away. He would not go down to his father's office. He would miss that one. He wanted his life to go smoothly. It had just gotten going that way. Well, that was all over now, anyway. He would go over to the schoolyard and watch Helen play indoor baseball.

WORDS TO OWN

nauseated (nô'zhē·āt'id) *v.* used as *adj.*: feeling sickness or discomfort in the stomach.

PRIMARY Sources — A SPEECH

Nobel Prize Acceptance Speech, 1954

Having no facility for speech making and no command of oratory nor any domination of rhetoric, I wish to thank the administrators of the generosity of Alfred Nobel for this prize.

No writer who knows the great writers who did not receive the prize can accept it other than with humility. There is no need to list these writers. Everyone here may make his own list according to his knowledge and his conscience.

It would be impossible for me to ask the ambassador of my country to read a speech in which a writer said all of the things which are in his heart. Things may not be immediately discernible in what a man writes, and in this sometimes he is fortunate; but eventually they are quite clear and by these and the degree of alchemy[1] that he possesses he will endure or be forgotten.

Writing, at its best, is a lonely life. Organizations for writers palliate[2] the writer's loneliness, but I doubt if they improve his writing. He grows in public stature as he sheds his loneliness, and often his work deteriorates. For he does his work alone, and if he is a good enough writer he must face eternity, or the lack of it, each day.

For a true writer each book should be a new beginning where he tries again for something that is beyond attainment. He should always try for something that has never been done or that others have tried and failed. Then sometimes, with great luck, he will succeed.

How simple the writing of literature would be if it were only necessary to write in another way what has been well written. It is because we have had such great writers in the past that a writer is driven far out past where he can go, out to where no one can help him.

I have spoken too long for a writer. A writer should write what he has to say and not speak it. Again I thank you.

—Ernest Hemingway

1. alchemy: magical power to transform the ordinary into the extraordinary. Alchemy was a branch of medieval science in which one aim was to change common metals such as lead into gold.

2. palliate (pal'ē·āt'): ease; lessen.

MAKING MEANINGS

First Thoughts

1. Review your notes on Harold Krebs. What are your thoughts and feelings about Krebs's view of life? What advice would you give him?

Shaping Interpretations

2. By the time Krebs returns, his hometown has quit "the greeting of heroes" and "the reaction had set in." What is this reaction, and how does it affect Krebs?

3. What does Krebs's attitude toward the girls in town reveal about his state of mind?

4. What does Krebs mean by wanting "to live along without consequences"? Why do you suppose he feels that way?

5. Describe the **conflicts** expressed in the conversation between Mrs. Krebs and Harold at the end of the story. From this talk, what do we learn about the losses Harold has experienced?

6. How would you state the **theme** of "Soldier's Home"? What does the story reveal to you about the effects of war on the young?

Extending the Text

7. The "antihero" is a type of **protagonist** found in much modern literature. In contrast to the traditional hero, who responds to fate with strength and self-sacrifice, the antihero is generally disillusioned, passive, and defeated by life. Explain whether or not you consider Krebs to be an antihero. What does he have in common with antiheroes portrayed in contemporary books and movies? How is he different?

Reading Check

a. Describe the way Krebs spends his days.

b. What is Krebs's reaction to reading a history of all the battles he has been in?

c. How does Krebs's younger sister Helen feel about him?

d. What makes Krebs decide he should leave home?

CHOICES: Building Your Portfolio

Writer's Notebook

1. Collecting Ideas for an Analysis of Causes and Effects

Freewrite your speculation about the effects that Krebs's war experience and homecoming might have on his future. Will he leave home after all? If so, where will he go, and what will he do? Will he maintain contact with his family? Save your notes for possible use in the Writer's Workshop on page 685.

Interpreting a Character

2. The Lost Generation

Gertrude Stein's remark "You are all a lost generation" summarized her perception of the pain and disillusionment experienced by many young people after World War I. In a brief essay, explain how Stein's quotation applies to Krebs. Is Krebs like or unlike someone you could meet today? Why or why not?

Analyzing a Writer's Style

3. The Tip of the Iceberg

Ernest Hemingway once remarked of his writing style: "I always try to write on the principle of the iceberg. There is seven-eighths of it under water for every part that shows." In a brief essay, explain what you think he means, and tell whether you feel that "Soldier's Home" illustrates the "iceberg principle."

Creative Writing / Performance

4. What Can We Do About Harold?

With another student, write and perform a script of the discussion between Krebs's parents that leads to Mrs. Krebs's talk with Harold. Why are Mr. and Mrs. Krebs worried about Harold? After your performance, tell how you think his parents should have dealt with Krebs's problems.

T. S. Eliot

(1888–1965)

At the time when he was regarded as America's most eminent living poet, T. S. Eliot announced that he was a "classicist in literature, royalist in politics, and Anglo-Catholic in religion." In 1927, Eliot gave up his U.S. citizenship and became a subject of the king of England. The same year he was received into the Church of England. By a kind of poetic justice, this loss to America was later to be made up for: W. H. Auden (1907–1973), the leading British poet of his time, became a naturalized American citizen in 1946. But residence in an adopted country does not necessarily change the philosophy or the style of a poet. Eliot continued to speak in a voice first heard in the Puritan pulpits of Massachusetts. And Auden retained a British sense of language unaffected by the inroads of American speech.

Thomas Stearns Eliot's family was rooted in New England, though he was born in St. Louis, Missouri, where his grandfather had been a founder and chancellor of Washington University. Eliot's childhood awareness of his native city would show itself in his poetry, but only after he had moved far away from St. Louis. He graduated from Harvard and went on to postgraduate work at the Sorbonne in Paris.

Just before the outbreak of World War I, Eliot took up residence in London, the city that would become his home for the rest of his life. There he worked for a time in a bank, suffered a nervous breakdown, married an emotionally troubled Englishwoman, and finally took up the business of literature. He became active as a publisher in the outstanding firm of Faber and Faber and, on his own, edited *The Criterion,* a literary magazine. As a critic, he was responsible for reviving interest in many neglected poets, notably the seventeenth-century English poet John Donne.

Complex Poetry for a Complex World

Long before he decided to live abroad permanently, Eliot had developed a taste for classical

UPI/Bettmann.

literature. He was as familiar with European and Eastern writings as he was with the masterpieces of English. But the most crucial influence upon his early work came from the late-nineteenth-century French poets who, as a group, came to be known as the Symbolists. (For more on the Symbolists, see page 770.) When he was nineteen, Eliot came upon a book by the British critic Arthur Symons titled *The Symbolist Movement in Literature.* "I myself owe Mr. Symons a great debt," wrote Eliot. "But for having read his book, I should not . . . have heard of Laforgue and Rimbaud; I should probably not have begun to read Verlaine; and but for reading Verlaine, I should not have heard of Corbière. So the Symons book is one of those which have affected the course of my life."

The poets Eliot mentions were men of distinctly different talents. Yet they all believed in poetry as an art of suggestion rather than statement. They saw poetry as an art of re-creating states of mind and feeling, as opposed to reporting or confessing them. These beliefs became the basis of Eliot's own poetic methods. When people complained that this poetic method of sugges-tion was complex and diffi-cult to understand, Eliot retorted that poetry had to be complex to express the complexities of modern life. More or less ignor-ing the still undervalued contribution of Walt Whitman, Eliot and other American poets also believed that, divorced from British antecedents, they would once and for all bring the rhythms of their native speech into the mainstream of world literature. Eliot and these other poets are often referred to as modernists.

> **E**liot retorted that poetry had to be complex to express the complexities of modern life.

Words for a Wasteland

Eliot had an austere view of poetic creativity; he disagreed with those who regarded a poem as a means of self-expression, as a source of com-fort, or as a kind of spiritual pep talk. Practicing what he preached, Eliot startled his contempo-raries with "The Love Song of J. Alfred Prufrock" in 1915 and "Portrait of a Lady" in 1917. Then, in 1922, with the editorial advice and encouragement of Ezra Pound, Eliot pub-lished *The Waste Land,* a long work considered the most significant poem of the early twentieth century. The poem describes a civilization that is spiritually empty and paralyzed by indecision.

Assembled in the manner of a painter's collage or a moviemaker's montage, *The Waste Land* proved that it was possible to write an epic poem of classical scope in the space of 434 lines. Critics pored over the poem's complex structure and its dense network of allusions to world literature, Oriental religion, and anthropology. A few years after *The Waste Land* appeared, Eliot published a series of notes identifying many of his key references. (He was dismayed to find that some of his more ardent admirers were more interested in the notes than in the poem itself.)

In 1925, Eliot published a kind of lyrical post-script to *The Waste Land* called "The Hollow Men," which predicted in its somber conclusion that the world would end not with a bang but with a whimper. In "The Hollow Men," Eliot re-peats and expands some of the themes of his longer poem and arrives at that point of despair beyond which lie but two alternatives: renewal or annihilation.

A Submission to Peace

For critics surveying Eliot's career, it has be-come commonplace to say that, after the spirit-ual dead end of "The Hollow Men," Eliot chose hope over despair, and faith over the world-weary cynicism that marked his early years. But there is much evidence in his later poems to in-dicate that, for Eliot, hope and faith were not conscious choices. Instead, they were the con-sequences of a submission, even a surrender, to that "peace which passeth understanding" re-ferred to in the last line of *The Waste Land.*

Eliot spent the remainder of his poetic ca-reer in an extended meditation upon the limits of individual will and the limitless power of faith in the presence of grace.

Cited for his work as a pioneer of modern poetry, Eliot was awarded the Nobel Prize in literature in 1948. In the decades that followed, he came frequently to the United States to lecture and to read his poems, sometimes to audiences so large that he had to appear in football stadiums. Some of those who fought to buy tickets on the fifty-yard line were probably unaware of the irony in all of this: that a man once regarded as the most difficult and obscure poet of his era had achieved the drawing power of a rock star.

Ezra Pound (who called Eliot "Possum") wrote a few final words on the death of his old friend, ending with this passage:

"Am I to write 'about' the poet Thomas Stearns Eliot? Or my friend 'the Possum'? Let him rest in peace, I can only repeat, but with the urgency of fifty years ago: READ HIM."

Make the Connection

Where Have All the Heroes Gone?

In the PBS television series *The Power of Myth*, the noted student of myths Joseph Campbell says, "The hero is today running up against a hard world that is in no way responsive to his spiritual need." Modern society has become a "stagnation of inauthentic lives and living . . . that evokes nothing of our spiritual life, our potentialities, or even our physical courage." According to Campbell, the times we live in are hostile to heroism. Heroes are people of action, but the drudgery of modern life has made many people observers rather than participants in life's adventures. See whether you agree that the protagonist of this poem is a person of profound self-absorption and passivity, who fits the profile of antihero, the disillusioned and ineffectual protagonist we find in much modern and contemporary literature.

Reading Skills and Strategies

Identifying Main Ideas and Supporting Details

Read the poem through twice. The first time, aim for a general sense of Prufrock's thoughts. As you read the poem again, write down examples of how his thoughts reflect the following ideas about his own time (the poem was published in 1915, during World War I), and perhaps about our time as well: (1) the idea that people are spiritually empty, and (2) the idea that contemporary life is unromantic and unheroic.

Elements of Literature

Dramatic Monologue

This poem is written as a **dramatic monologue**—a poem in which a character speaks directly to one or more listeners. The words are being spoken by a man named Prufrock.

In a dramatic monologue, we must learn everything about the setting, situation, other characters, and the personality of the speaker through what the speaker tells us. Sometimes Prufrock's line of reasoning is interrupted by an unexpected thought. You will often have to supply the missing connections in the speaker's stream of thoughts and associations.

> A **dramatic monologue** is a poem in which a character speaks directly to one or more listeners.
>
> *For more on Dramatic Monologue, see the Handbook of Literary Terms.*

The Love Song of J. Alfred Prufrock

T. S. Eliot

> *S'io credessi che mia risposta fosse*
> *a persona che mai tornasse al mondo,*
> *questa fiamma staria senza più scosse.*
> *Ma per ciò che giammai di questo fondo*
> *non tornò vivo alcun, s'i'odo il vero,*
> *senza tema d'infamia ti rispondo.*

Let us go then, you and I,
When the evening is spread out against the sky
Like a patient etherized upon a table;
Let us go, through certain half-deserted streets,
5 The muttering retreats

Epigraph: This quotation is from Dante's epic poem *The Divine Comedy* (1321). The speaker is Guido da Montefeltro, a man consigned to Hell for dispensing evil advice. He speaks from a flame that quivers when he talks: "If I thought my answer were to one who ever could return to the world, this flame should shake no more; but since none ever did return alive from this depth, if what I hear be true, without fear of infamy I answer this." (*Inferno*, Canto 27, lines 61–66) Think of Prufrock as speaking from his own personal hell.

? **3.** *What is the evening compared with?*

Of restless nights in one-night cheap hotels
And sawdust restaurants with oyster-shells:
Streets that follow like a tedious argument
Of insidious intent
10 To lead you to an overwhelming question . . .
Oh, do not ask, "What is it?"
Let us go and make our visit.

In the room the women come and go
Talking of Michelangelo.°

15 The yellow fog that rubs its back upon the window-panes,
The yellow smoke that rubs its muzzle on the window-panes,
Licked its tongue into the corners of the evening,
Lingered upon the pools that stand in drains,
Let fall upon its back the soot that falls from chimneys,
20 Slipped by the terrace, made a sudden leap,
And seeing that it was a soft October night,
Curled once about the house, and fell asleep.

And indeed there will be time
For the yellow smoke that slides along the street
25 Rubbing its back upon the window-panes;
There will be time, there will be time
To prepare a face to meet the faces that you meet;
There will be time to murder and create,
And time for all the works and days of hands
30 That lift and drop a question on your plate;
Time for you and time for me,
And time yet for a hundred indecisions,
And for a hundred visions and revisions,
Before the taking of a toast and tea.

35 In the room the women come and go
Talking of Michelangelo.

And indeed there will be time
To wonder, "Do I dare?" and, "Do I dare?"
Time to turn back and descend the stair,
40 With a bald spot in the middle of my hair—
(They will say: "How his hair is growing thin!")
My morning coat, my collar mounting firmly to the chin,
My necktie rich and modest, but asserted by a simple pin—
(They will say: "But how his arms and legs are thin!")
45 Do I dare
Disturb the universe?
In a minute there is time
For decisions and revisions which a minute will reverse.

For I have known them all already, known them all—

7. *Where does the speaker want to take his companion? Whom could he be talking to?*

14. **Michelangelo:** Michelangelo Buonarroti (1475–1564), a great artist of the Italian Renaissance.

22. *What details are you given about this setting? What is the fog compared to?*

27. *How would you paraphrase this line?*

34. *What words are repeated in this stanza for poetic effect?*

38. *What could he want to dare to do?*

41. *Who are "they"?*

42. *A morning coat is formal daytime dress for men. What does Prufrock look like? Is he young, middle-aged, or elderly?*

50 Have known the evenings, mornings, afternoons,
    I have measured out my life with coffee spoons;
    I know the voices dying with a dying fall°
    Beneath the music from a farther room.
        So how should I presume?

55 And I have known the eyes already, known them all—
    The eyes that fix you in a formulated° phrase,
    And when I am formulated, sprawling on a pin,
    When I am pinned and wriggling on the wall,
    Then how should I begin
60 To spit out all the butt-ends of my days and ways?
        And how should I presume?

    And I have known the arms already, known them all—
    Arms that are braceleted and white and bare
    (But in the lamplight, downed with light brown hair!)
65 Is it perfume from a dress
    That makes me so digress?
    Arms that lie along a table, or wrap about a shawl.
        And should I then presume?
        And how should I begin?
            .   .   .   .   .   .

70 Shall I say, I have gone at dusk through narrow streets
    And watched the smoke that rises from the pipes
    Of lonely men in shirt-sleeves, leaning out of windows? . . .

    I should have been a pair of ragged claws
    Scuttling across the floors of silent seas.
            .   .   .   .   .   .

75 And the afternoon, the evening, sleeps so peacefully!
    Smoothed by long fingers,
    Asleep . . . tired . . . or it malingers,
    Stretched on the floor, here beside you and me.
    Should I, after tea and cakes and ices,
80 Have the strength to force the moment to its crisis?
    But though I have wept and fasted, wept and prayed,
    Though I have seen my head (grown slightly bald) brought in
        upon a platter,°
    I am no prophet—and here's no great matter;
    I have seen the moment of my greatness flicker,
    And I have seen the eternal Footman hold my coat, and
85   snicker,
    And in short, I was afraid.

    And would it have been worth it, after all,
    After the cups, the marmalade, the tea,
    Among the porcelain, among some talk of you and me,
90 Would it have been worth while,

51. *Has a life that is measured in coffee spoons been very exciting or heroic?*

52. dying fall: in music, notes that fade away.

56. formulated: reduced to a formula and made insignificant.

58. *What do you see here?*

60. *What are his days compared to? Is this a positive or a negative image?*

72. *What has Prufrock done in early evening?*

74. *What is the speaker comparing himself to here?*

77. Malingers *means "pretends to be sick." How is this image of the evening connected to the one that opens the poem?*

82. my head . . . a platter: allusion to the execution of John the Baptist (Mark 6:17–28 and Matthew 14:3–11). The dancing of Salome so pleased Herod Antipas, ruler of ancient Galilee, that he offered her any reward she desired. Goaded by her mother, who hated John, Salome asked for John's head. Herod ordered the prophet beheaded and his head delivered on a serving plate.

85. The "eternal Footman" is *death. What does this line tell you about Prufrock's confidence?*

To have bitten off the matter with a smile,
To have squeezed the universe into a ball
To roll it towards some overwhelming question,
To say: "I am Lazarus, come from the dead,
95 Come back to tell you all, I shall tell you all"—
If one, settling a pillow by her head,
    Should say: "That is not what I meant at all.
    That is not it, at all."

And would it have been worth it, after all,
100 Would it have been worth while,
After the sunsets and the dooryards and the sprinkled streets,
After the novels, after the teacups, after the skirts that trail
    along the floor—
And this, and so much more?—
It is impossible to say just what I mean!
But as if a magic lantern° threw the nerves in patterns on a
105   screen:
Would it have been worth while
If one, settling a pillow or throwing off a shawl,
And turning toward the window, should say:
    "That is not it at all,
110   That is not what I meant, at all."
    .   .   .   .   .

No! I am not Prince Hamlet, nor was meant to be;
Am an attendant lord, one that will do
To swell a progress,° start a scene or two,
Advise the prince; no doubt, an easy tool,
115 Deferential, glad to be of use,
Politic, cautious, and meticulous;
Full of high sentence,° but a bit obtuse;
At times, indeed, almost ridiculous—
Almost, at times, the Fool.

120 I grow old . . . I grow old . . .
I shall wear the bottoms of my trousers rolled.

Shall I part my hair behind? Do I dare to eat a peach?
I shall wear white flannel trousers, and walk upon the beach.
I have heard the mermaids singing, each to each.

125 I do not think that they will sing to me.

I have seen them riding seaward on the waves
Combing the white hair of the waves blown back
When the wind blows the water white and black.

We have lingered in the chambers of the sea
130 By sea-girls wreathed with seaweed red and brown
Till human voices wake us, and we drown.

94. *In the Bible, a man named Lazarus is raised from the dead by Jesus (John 11:38-44). How do these lines connect with the opening quote from Dante?*

98. *What is he afraid would happen if he "squeezed the universe into a ball"?*

105. magic lantern: early type of projector that could magnify and project opaque photographs or book pages as well as transparent slides.

110. *Who do you think might say this to Prufrock? Is it the same person as in lines 97–98?*

111. *Hamlet is the hero of Shakespeare's tragedy about a prince of Denmark. What is Prufrock saying "No!" to?*

113. swell a progress: fill out a scene in a play or pageant by serving as an extra.

117. high sentence: pompous talk.

119. *How does Prufrock feel about himself?*

121. *The style of the time called for fashionable young men to turn up the cuffs of their trousers. What is Prufrock hoping for here?*

125. *If the mermaids do not sing to him, what will he miss in life?*

128. *What does he see here?*

131. *What breaks the romantic spell cast by the sight of the mermaids? What could "drown" mean here?*

The Oddest Love Song

Of all the love songs ever written, this must be one of the oddest and most pathetic. The man who "sings" it has feelings but no one to share them with and ideas that are realized nowhere but in his own mind. Sensitive emotions and sophisticated thoughts do nothing to help him come to grips with the real world of the streets. He knows that life is "out there," but he also knows that he will never join it, and so he takes refuge in self-dramatization and heroic fantasy. Yet the man himself is not pitiful. He has sufficient knowledge of himself to control his longings and enough of a sense of humor to portray himself as a victim without being victimized.

"I am not Prince Hamlet," he says; and yet, he shares with Hamlet a breadth of vision to see two sides or more of every issue and the inability to act decisively upon any of his insights. If, in the jargon of today, we'd ask, "What's his problem?" the answer might be "self-consciousness—the egocentric trap that keeps an extraordinarily sophisticated man from enjoying the pleasures of this world that simpler men and women pursue and embrace without a thought."

One way to read the poem is to think of it as a movie—scenes follow one another immediately, without the connections or transitions that a conventional writer would provide. Consequently, the poem is demanding. What it demands is that, in the absence of logical connections, the reader must make the *psychological* connections that underlie the poem's structure and content.

"Let us go then," says the speaker, and so invites us (or someone) to join him on a "visit." But, instead of going wherever it is he has in mind, we soon find ourselves observers in the course of the man's search. Our companion seems to be looking for answers to the meaning of life and the nature of romantic love. He tries, without success, to find some place for himself even in the world he knows well. In line 10, we read that he has an "overwhelming question." But he impatiently brushes us aside before we can ask what it is.

Quick as a flash, we're confronted with something unexpected: women passing back and forth in a room and discussing Michelangelo, one of the greatest artists of all time. This little glimpse from the corner of the eye, so to speak, introduces an aspect of Prufrock's character that we'll find illustrated time and again. Focusing on one thing, he can't help thinking of something else. Everything actual has its counterpart in an image or a metaphor or a situation, by means of which Eliot can dramatize the dilemma of a man suffering a kind of emotional paralysis. As for the women who "come and go," they may be in an art gallery or in a museum or at a party or someplace else. The importance of their early and sudden appearance is to prepare us for the *method* of the poem. It is made up of a sequence of disjointed scenes that are psychologically related to the speaker's half-formed thoughts.

Time is a motif that recurs throughout the poem. Prufrock is conscious of time, and toward the end of his "love song," he makes his preoccupation clear: "I grow old . . . I grow old. . . ." Oppressed by time, he makes fun of his own obsession with it when he says, "There will be time . . . for a hundred visions." This statement might make us think of a religious revelation and the promise of salvation. But only for a moment. Prufrock soon drops us back into reality by the workaday word *revisions*—as if he is suggesting that the grandeur of imagination could be edited with a blue pencil, and that this would all take place before teatime.

For a number of years, John Malcolm Brinnin was the director of the noted Poetry Center of the 92nd Street YM-YWHA, in New York City. The center features public readings by leading poets.

from Mr. Eliot, I Presume

from Sextet *by* John Malcolm Brinnin

This late in his life (he was sixty-one) Eliot had given less than a handful of readings in the United States and, I believe, had read only once before in New York. The response to our announcement of the event suggested that many people thought his reading at the Poetry Center might well be his last. On the morning after we had named his date in *The New York Times*, fifteen or twenty requests were made for every seat available. Pursued and badgered to use my influence to produce tickets, I found that people who'd never read a sonnet since the seventh grade were suddenly lovers of poetry whose devotion I was implored not to dismiss. Whatever else he might have been in the eyes of the world, T. S. Eliot in 1950 was for New Yorkers a hot ticket....

On the appointed evening early in December, I got to the Poetry Center an hour before the reading and found myself barred from even entering the building. Crowds on the sidewalk were being kept in check by uniformed policemen, one of whom, as I attempted to identify myself, looked at me like a Thurber dog confronted by an insect. Rescued by an usher, I was finally able to muscle my way to the Green Room, where Eliot was chatting with a man of cherubic countenance who turned out to be his American editor, Robert Giroux.

Eliot's face seemed weighted with weariness, and when he stood up, I thought he was even more deeply bent than he'd been in London. But his sad, lingering hint of a smile suggested he was at ease with the circumstance. "Do you suppose I might read 'Prufrock'?" he asked. "Or would that be altogether too familiar to a sophisticated audience?"

As far as I was concerned, I told him, to hear him read "Prufrock" would be a very special pleasure.

"I want to make a good appearance," he said. The directness and humility of this left me with nothing to say.

When I presented him with his check, he gave it a glance. "Are you entirely sure you can afford as much as this?"

Since the figure was the one agreed upon, I took his question as a form of solicitude, or an indication of embarrassment. In any case, the check went into his pocket and in a few minutes he was onstage, not quite smiling into the waves of an ovation that kept him standing, bowing, unable to speak.

In the wings, entranced by the particular nuances he gave to words I'd long ago memorized, I felt again what had occurred to me in the course of our talk in London: He was a man trapped, condemned to live up to an image he could not live down. By all accounts I'd read or heard, he was masked and Parnassian[1]—an oracle who spoke in many voices, all his own. In actuality I had found him to be gentle and open, with a slow-fused kind of humor and a slightly wicked sense of conspiracy he seemed to want to share. Had he, in life as in poetry, carried his conviction about the self-effacement of the artist too far?

1. Parnassian: of the mountain Parnassus, seen by the ancient Greeks as the seat of poetry and music; here, forbidding and mysterious.

MAKING MEANINGS

First Thoughts

1. What words would you use to describe Prufrock's emotional difficulty in the poem?

Shaping Interpretations

2. What hints does the name "J. Alfred Prufrock" give us about the **character** of the "hero"?

3. How could the famous **simile** in lines 2–3 reveal that the speaker's mind or will is paralyzed?

4. What is the speaker inviting someone to do in lines 1–12? What is suggested by the **images** of the place they are going to travel through?

5. What does the name Michelangelo contribute in lines 13–14? What would be the effect if, for instance, the women were "talking of Joe DiMaggio" or "discussing detergents"?

6. In lines 15–25, we have one of the most famous **extended metaphors** in modern poetry. What is being indirectly compared to what? How many details extend the metaphor?

7. The self-consciousness of the speaker is nowhere more evident than in lines 37–44.

What do you think he is self-conscious and worried about in these lines?

8. What does line 51 imply about the way Prufrock has lived? What other measuring devices would suggest a different kind of life?

9. What references to women does Prufrock make in the poem? How do you think he feels about women and his attractiveness to them?

10. How are the **setting** and people described in lines 70–72 different from those familiar to Prufrock? What might this experience with another segment of city life tell us about Prufrock?

11. In lines 73–74, the speaker creates a **metaphor** to pointedly dramatize his alienation from the rest of the world. Can you explain why Prufrock thinks he should have been a clawed creature on the floor of the sea?

12. Lines 87–98 echo the widely heard complaint that a "lack of communication" between people is the cause of misunderstanding. What do you think Prufrock would like to tell people?

13. In lines 99–104, Prufrock considers summarizing his life to another person and reaches a point of exasperation that seems close to surrender: "It is impossible to say just what I mean!" Why does Prufrock find it so difficult to express himself to others?

Drawing by C. Barsotti. © 1987
The New Yorker Magazine, Inc.

14. In *Sextet* (see **Connections**, page 668), John Malcolm Brinnin says that at a poetry reading in 1950, Eliot asked him whether it would be all right to read "Prufrock." "'I want to make a good appearance,'" Eliot said. Do you think Eliot's concern was Prufrockian, or would appearances not have troubled Prufrock? Cite evidence from the poem to back up your interpretation.

15. Identify the brilliant visual **metaphor** in line 105. How does it relate to the rest of the poem? How does the speaker think people will respond to his "exposure"?

16. Read lines 120–125 closely. Explain how the speaker sees his role in life. Do you think he has overcome his doubts?

17. How would you characterize someone who worries about the part in his hair and about what he should dare to eat (line 122)?

18. In lines 125–128, the speaker thinks that the mermaids are indifferent to him, yet he is held by this romantic vision. Why do you think he is so fascinated by these mythological creatures, and what might they represent for him? Why does he believe they will not sing to him?

19. By means of **paraphrase,** can you restate the meaning of lines 129–131? When "human voices wake us," what do we "drown" in?

Connecting with the Text

20. Think about this poem as a journey, a quest that begins with an invitation to join the man who makes it. What do you think the journey has finally led us to? Or do you think that the point of the poem is not so much an answer arrived at as an experience lived? Explain.

Extending the Text

21. Review the notes you made in your second reading, about how Prufrock's thoughts reflect the times he lived in. Explain why this poem—one of the most famous poems of the twentieth century—has been described as a reflection of spiritual emptiness and emotional paralysis. Do you think its depiction of life in Eliot's day or our own is accurate? Why or why not?

Challenging the Text

22. Why do you think Eliot called this a "love song"? How is it different from the usual love song? If you were titling it, would you keep "love song" or use some other phrase?

READING SKILLS AND STRATEGIES

Understanding Rhythm, Rhymes, Metaphors, and Allusions

"No *vers* [verse] is *libre* [free] for the man who wants to do a good job," Eliot once remarked. Though Eliot's poem is written in free verse (page 355), it makes use of rhythm, rhyme, and, of course, figurative language.

1. Reread the first stanza, and identify the lines that conform to a particular **metrical pattern.**

2. How does repetition in the first thirty-six lines help create **rhythm** in the poem?

3. How many **end rhymes** can you find in the poem? How many **internal rhymes**?

4. Make a list of at least five **metaphors** in the poem that you think are particularly original and memorable.

5. Note the terms of comparison in the metaphors. Has Eliot based his comparison on "things" from modern life? Or has he used comparisons based mostly on elements from the world of nature?

It is characteristic of many poets who are highly educated and intimately aware of the history of their art to make use of **allusions.** Eliot expects that his readers will identify his references and see their relationship to the poem. Here is a list of a few of the allusions in "Prufrock." What do you think each one means in the **context** of the poem?

1. Dante's *Inferno,* a section of *The Divine Comedy* (opening quotation)

2. Michelangelo (line 14)

3. Salome and John the Baptist (line 82)

4. Jesus's raising of Lazarus from the dead (line 94)

5. Hamlet, Prince of Denmark, in Shakespeare's play (line 111)

Writer's Notebook

1. Collecting Ideas for an Analysis of Causes and Effects

What is the matter with J. Alfred Prufrock? Join the critics who have been debating this question for years. Write down thoughts of your own about the possible causes of Prufrock's isolation and his difficulty acting on or committing himself to anything. You could collect your ideas in a cluster diagram or other graphic organizer. Be sure to cite lines from the poem that support your interpretation. Save your notes for possible use in the Writer's Workshop on page 685.

Comparing Poems

2. Soul Searching

Write a short essay in which you compare "the explorer" in Gwendolyn Brooks's poem (page 643) with Prufrock. Consider how the explorer's search differs from Prufrock's, the fears each of them has, and the discoveries they each make. What does each poem have to say about the difficulty of making choices in today's world?

Responding to a Review of the Poem

3. Triumph or Tragedy?

Ezra Pound made the following comments about "Prufrock" in a personal letter to Harriet Monroe, the editor of *Poetry* magazine. Pound defends the ending of Eliot's poem against Monroe's objection that it goes "off at the end" (that it lacks a strong, triumphant **resolution**). In a brief essay, respond to Pound's comments.

> Now as to Eliot: "Mr. Prufrock" does not "go off at the end." It is a portrait of failure, or of a character which fails, and it would be false art to make it end on a note of triumph. I dislike the paragraph about Hamlet, but it is an early and cherished bit and T. E. won't give it up, and as it is the only portion of the poem that most readers will like at first reading, I don't see that it will do much harm. . . .
>
> —Ezra Pound

Art

4. Prufrock in Cartoons

Draw a cartoon based on a line or two from the poem. You will probably get best results if you focus on a figure of speech, as the artist of the cartoon on page 669 did.

Creative Writing

5. "Let Us Go Then . . ."

Write a **dramatic monologue** spoken by someone who wants to invite another person to do something. Let your monologue reflect the random process of the speaker's thoughts. Try to find **images** that suggest your speaker's feeling and state of mind. Open with Eliot's words: "Let us go then, you and I."

Comparing Characters

6. A Modern Trio

Is J. Alfred Prufrock like Walter Mitty in James Thurber's story (page 625)? Is he like Miniver Cheevy in Edwin Arlington Robinson's poem (page 646)? In a brief essay, compare these three characters. In what ways are they different? In what ways are they all types of the modern antihero?

Creative Writing/ Performance

7. Talking It Through

Write a dialogue between Prufrock and another person. Include references to topics in the poem that concern Prufrock. You might even imagine the conversation as being with Ralph Waldo Emerson (page 216), with references to Emerson's advice in the essay "Self-Reliance" (page 224). With another student, present your dialogue to the class.

Flannery O'Connor

(1925–1964)

The Bettmann Archive.

Flannery O'Connor with self-portrait.

Flannery O'Connor was born in Savannah, Georgia, and spent her short life almost entirely in nearby Milledgeville, where her family had lived since before the Civil War. Although she limited herself to a rural, Southern literary terrain and the body of her work was small, her place in American literature is secure.

O'Connor wrote steadily from 1948 until her death sixteen years later. For fourteen of those sixteen years, she was plagued by lupus, a painful, wasting disease that she had inherited from her father and that kept her ever more confined and immobile. "I have never been anywhere but sick," she wrote. "In a sense sickness is a place, more instructive than a long trip to Europe, and it's always a place where there's no company, where nobody can follow. Sickness before death is a very appropriate thing and I think those who don't have it miss one of God's mercies."

O'Connor graduated from the Women's College of Georgia in 1945. She then went to the Writers' Workshop at the University of Iowa. Her first novel, *Wise Blood,* was published in 1952. She followed that novel with a short-story collection, *A Good Man Is Hard to Find,* in 1955; a second novel, *The Violent Bear It Away,* in 1960; and a second set of stories, *Everything That Rises Must Converge,* in 1965 (posthumous).

Always disciplined as a writer, O'Connor forced herself to sit at her desk without conscious distraction of any sort at the same time every day for two hours, even if no inspiration came. "Sometimes I work for months and have to throw everything away," she commented, "but I don't think any of that was time wasted." While her central concern in her fiction was the abstract idea of good and evil, she felt compelled to confine herself to the concrete. She noted that the short-story writer has "only a short space" to "reveal as much of the mystery of existence as possible" and must therefore "do it by showing, not by saying, and by showing the concrete. . . ."

From the first, O'Connor was recognized as a satirist of astonishing originality and vigor, whose targets were smugness, optimism, and self-righteousness. However, the essential element of O'Connor's life and work is that she remained a Roman Catholic without the slightest wavering of faith throughout her thirty-nine years. A thunder-and-lightning Christian belief pervades every story and novel she wrote. Her attraction to the grotesque and the violent puts off many critics and readers. They fail to appreciate that the violent motifs in her fiction grow from her passionate, Christian vision of our secular times.

What O'Connor wants to tell us is that, in our rationality, we have lost the one essential—a spiritual center for our lives. "Redemption is meaningless," O'Connor wrote, "unless there is cause for it in the actual life we live, and for the last few centuries there has been operating in our culture the secular belief that there is no such cause."

In her works, O'Connor seems to be saying that we have become so accustomed to the lack of God in our lives that a writer must use violent means to make a point. Just as we are made to feel comfortable, enjoying O'Connor's carnival show, the comedy is miraculously transcended, and we realize that the situation has a philosophical meaning. All the freaks and clowns have taken on God's meaning. God is here, and the devil is, too.

Make the Connection

Truth in the Grotesque

The characters in this story act out a classic **theme**—that of innocence beset by evil. But, from the very beginning, we are confronted with dark hints that this is no comforting fairy tale or noble heroic epic. In this exquisite piece of storytelling, ideals of romance and heroism are turned upside down.

There are three vivid characters here, each one a masterful portrait from the rural South. With all their peculiarities, O'Connor's characters are disturbingly familiar. They are homespun figures, as real as any Georgia barnyard or roadside cafe, drawn with a kind of humor that balances on the edge of terror. They find themselves in a situation that is both tragic and comic, an odd mixture that O'Connor often used in order to communicate her points.

Reading Skills and Strategies

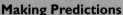

Making Predictions

You won't have to read very far to discover that this story is both disturbing and funny. Pay special attention to the way the characters speak, but don't let their casual, down-home voices fool you.

As you read, fill in a prediction chart like the one below. Record events or details from the story, along with your predictions about what these events or details suggest might happen later in the story. As you continue reading, write down what actually happens.

Detail or Event in Story	My Prediction	Actual Outcome

Elements of Literature

Foreshadowing

Writers often **foreshadow** what will happen later on in a story by giving hints or clues. These hints, which often create **suspense** and arouse curiosity, can carry potentially ominous or menacing undertones, so subtle sometimes as to escape notice on a first reading.

> **F**oreshadowing is the use of hints and clues to suggest what will happen later in a plot.
>
> *For more on Foreshadowing, see the Handbook of Literary Terms.*

Lilacs (1924–1927) by Charles Burchfield.
Oil on board.

The Delaware Art Museum, Bequest of John Saxon.

The Life You Save May Be Your Own

Flannery O'Connor

The old woman and her daughter were sitting on their porch when Mr. Shiftlet came up their road for the first time. The old woman slid to the edge of her chair and leaned forward, shading her eyes from the piercing sunset with her hand. The daughter could not see far in front of her and continued to play with her fingers. Although the old woman lived in this desolate spot with only her daughter and she had never seen Mr. Shiftlet before, she could tell, even from a distance, that he was a tramp and no one to be afraid of. His left coat sleeve was folded up to show there was only half an arm in it and his gaunt figure listed slightly to the side as if the breeze were pushing him. He had on a black town suit and a brown felt hat that was turned up in the front and down in the back and he carried a tin toolbox by a handle. He came on, at an amble, up her road, his face turned toward the sun which appeared to be balancing itself on the peak of a small mountain.

The old woman didn't change her position until he was almost into her yard; then she rose

WORDS TO OWN

gaunt (gônt) *adj.*: very thin.
listed (list'id) *v.*: tilted.
amble (am'bəl) *n.*: leisurely pace.

with one hand fisted on her hip. The daughter, a large girl in a short blue organdy dress, saw him all at once and jumped up and began to stamp and point and make excited speechless sounds.

Mr. Shiftlet stopped just inside the yard and set his box on the ground and tipped his hat at her as if she were not in the least afflicted; then he turned toward the old woman and swung the hat all the way off. He had long black slick hair that hung flat from a part in the middle to beyond the tips of his ears on either side. His face descended in forehead for more than half its length and ended suddenly with his features just balanced over a jutting steel-trap jaw. He seemed to be a young man but he had a look of composed dissatisfaction as if he understood life thoroughly.

"Good evening," the old woman said. She was about the size of a cedar fence post and she had a man's gray hat pulled down low over her head.

The tramp stood looking at her and didn't answer. He turned his back and faced the sunset. He swung both his whole and his short arm up slowly so that they indicated an expanse of sky and his figure formed a crooked cross. The old woman watched him with her arms folded across her chest as if she were the owner of the sun, and the daughter watched, her head thrust forward and her fat helpless hands hanging at the wrists. She had long pink-gold hair and eyes as blue as a peacock's neck.

He held the pose for almost fifty seconds and then he picked up his box and came on to the porch and dropped down on the bottom step. "Lady," he said in a firm nasal voice, "I'd give a fortune to live where I could see me a sun do that every evening."

"Does it every evening," the old woman said and sat back down. The daughter sat down too and watched him with a cautious sly look as if he were a bird that had come up very close. He leaned to one side, rooting in his pants pocket, and in a second he brought out a package of chewing gum and offered her a piece. She took it and unpeeled it and began to chew without taking her eyes off him. He offered the old woman a piece but she only raised her upper lip to indicate she had no teeth.

Mr. Shiftlet's pale sharp glance had already passed over everything in the yard—the pump near the corner of the house and the big fig tree that three or four chickens were preparing to roost in—and had moved to a shed where he saw the square rusted back of an automobile. "You ladies drive?" he asked.

"That car ain't run in fifteen year," the old woman said. "The day my husband died, it quit running."

"Nothing is like it used to be, lady," he said. "The world is almost rotten."

"That's right," the old woman said. "You from around here?"

"Name Tom T. Shiftlet," he murmured, looking at the tires.

"I'm pleased to meet you," the old woman said. "Name Lucynell Crater and daughter Lucynell Crater. What you doing around here, Mr. Shiftlet?"

He judged the car to be about a 1928 or '29 Ford. "Lady," he said, and turned and gave her his full attention, "lemme tell you something. There's one of these doctors in Atlanta that's taken a knife and cut the human heart—the human heart," he repeated, leaning forward, "out of a man's chest and held it in his hand," and he held his hand out, palm up, as if it were slightly weighted with the human heart, "and studied it like it was a day-old chicken, and lady," he said, allowing a long significant pause in which his head slid forward and his clay-colored eyes brightened, "he don't know no more about it than you or me."

"That's right," the old woman said.

"Why, if he was to take that knife and cut into every corner of it, he still wouldn't know no more than you or me. What you want to bet?"

"Nothing," the old woman said wisely. "Where you come from, Mr. Shiftlet?"

He didn't answer. He reached into his pocket and brought out a sack of tobacco and a package of cigarette papers and rolled himself a cigarette, expertly with one hand, and attached it in a hanging position to his upper lip. Then he took a box of wooden matches from his pocket and struck one on his shoe. He held the burning match as if he were studying the mystery of flame while it traveled dangerously toward his skin. The daughter began to make loud noises and to point to his hand and shake her finger at him, but when the flame was just before touching him, he leaned down with his hand cupped over it as if he were going to set fire to his nose and lit the cigarette.

He flipped away the dead match and blew a stream of gray into the evening. A sly look came over his face. "Lady," he said, "nowadays, people'll do anything anyways. I can tell you my name is Tom T. Shiftlet, and I come from Tarwater, Tennessee, but you never have seen me before: How you know I ain't lying? How you know my name ain't Aaron Sparks, lady, and I come from Singleberry, Georgia, or how you know it's not George Speeds and I come from Lucy, Alabama, or how you know I ain't Thompson Bright from Toolafalls, Mississippi?"

"I don't know nothing about you," the old woman muttered, <u>irked</u>.

"Lady," he said, "people don't care how they lie. Maybe the best I can tell you is, I'm a man; but listen lady," he said and paused and made his tone more ominous still, "what is a man?"

The old woman began to gum a seed. "What you carry in that tin box, Mr. Shiftlet?" she asked.

"Tools," he said, put back. "I'm a carpenter."

"Well, if you come out here to work, I'll be able to feed you and give you a place to sleep but I can't pay. I'll tell you that before you begin," she said.

There was no answer at once and no particular expression on his face. He leaned back against the two-by-four that helped support the porch roof. "Lady," he said slowly, "there's some men that some things mean more to them than money." The old woman rocked without comment and the daughter watched the trigger that moved up and down in his neck. He told the old woman then that all most people were interested in was money, but he asked what a man was made for. He asked her if a man was made for money, or what. He asked her what she thought she was made for but she didn't answer, she only sat rocking and wondered if a one-armed man could put a new roof on her garden house. He asked a lot of questions that she didn't answer. He told her that he was twenty-eight years old and had lived a varied life. He had been a gospel singer, a foreman on the railroad, an assistant in an undertaking parlor, and he come over the radio for three months with Uncle Roy and his Red Creek Wranglers. He said he had fought and bled in the Arm Service of his country and visited every foreign land and that everywhere he had seen people that didn't care if they did a thing one way or another. He said he hadn't been raised thataway.

A fat yellow moon appeared in the branches of the fig tree as if it were going to roost there with the chickens. He said that a man had to escape to the country to see the world whole and that he wished he lived in a desolate place like this where he could see the sun go down every evening like God made it to do.

"Are you married or are you single?" the old woman asked.

There was a long silence. "Lady," he asked finally, "where would you find you an innocent woman today? I wouldn't have any of this trash I could just pick up."

The daughter was leaning very far down, hanging her head almost between her knees watching him through a triangular door she had made in her overturned hair; and she suddenly fell in a heap on the floor and began to whimper. Mr. Shiftlet straightened her out and helped her get back in the chair.

"Is she your baby girl?" he asked.

"My only," the old woman said, "and she's the sweetest girl in the world. I would give her up for nothing on earth. She's smart too. She can sweep the floor, cook, wash, feed the chickens, and hoe. I wouldn't give her up for a casket of jewels."

"No," he said kindly, "don't ever let any man take her away from you."

"Any man come after her," the old woman said, "'ll have to stay around the place."

Mr. Shiftlet's eye in the darkness was focused on a part of the automobile bumper that glittered in the distance. "Lady," he said, jerking his short arm up as if he could point with it to her house and yard and pump, "there ain't a broken thing on this plantation that I couldn't fix for you, one-arm jackleg[1] or not. I'm a man," he said with a sullen dignity, "even if I ain't a whole one. I got," he said, tapping his knuckles on the floor to emphasize the immensity of what he was going to say, "a moral intelligence!" and his face pierced out of the darkness into a shaft of doorlight and he stared at her as if he were astonished himself at this impossible truth.

The old woman was not impressed with the

---

1. jackleg: not properly trained; amateur. O'Connor is possibly playing on the word's other meaning: "dishonest."

WORDS TO OWN

irked (ʉrkt) *v.* used as *adj.*: annoyed; irritated.

---

phrase. "I told you you could hang around and work for food," she said, "if you don't mind sleeping in that car yonder."

"Why listen, lady," he said with a grin of delight, "the monks of old slept in their coffins!"

"They wasn't as advanced as we are," the old woman said.

The next morning he began on the roof of the garden house while Lucynell, the daughter, sat on a rock and watched him work. He had not been around a week before the change he had made in the place was apparent. He had patched the front and back steps, built a new hog pen, restored a fence, and taught Lucynell, who was completely deaf and had never said a word in her life, to say the word "bird." The big rosy-faced girl followed him everywhere, saying "Burrttddt ddbirrrttdt," and clapping her hands. The old woman watched from a distance, secretly pleased. She was <u>ravenous</u> for a son-in-law.

In the evenings he sat on the steps and talked while the old woman and Lucynell rocked violently in their chairs on either side of him.

Mr. Shiftlet slept on the hard narrow back seat of the car with his feet out the side window. He had his razor and a can of water on a crate that served him as a bedside table and he put up a piece of mirror against the back glass and kept his coat neatly on a hanger that he hung over one of the windows.

In the evenings he sat on the steps and talked while the old woman and Lucynell rocked violently in their chairs on either side of him. The old woman's three mountains were black against the dark blue sky and were visited off and on by various planets and by the moon after it had left the chickens. Mr. Shiftlet pointed out that the reason he had improved this plantation was because he had taken a personal interest in it. He said he was even going to make the automobile run.

He had raised the hood and studied the mechanism and he said he could tell that the car had been built in the days when cars were really built. You take now, he said, one man puts in one bolt and another man puts in another bolt and another man puts in another bolt so that it's a man for a bolt. That's why you have to pay so much for a car: you're paying all those men. Now if you didn't have to pay but one man, you could get you a cheaper car and one that had had a personal interest taken in it, and it would be a better car. The old woman agreed with him that this was so.

Mr. Shiftlet said that the trouble with the world was that nobody cared, or stopped and took any trouble. He said he never would have been able to teach Lucynell to say a word if he hadn't cared and stopped long enough.

"Teach her to say something else," the old woman said.

"What you want her to say next?" Mr. Shiftlet asked.

The old woman's smile was broad and toothless and suggestive. "Teach her to say 'sugarpie,'" she said.

Mr. Shiftlet already knew what was on her mind.

The next day he began to tinker with the automobile and that evening he told her that if she would buy a fan belt, he would be able to make the car run.

The old woman said she would give him the money. "You see that girl yonder?" she asked, pointing to Lucynell who was sitting on the floor a foot away, watching him, her eyes blue even in the dark. "If it was ever a man wanted to take her away, I would say, 'No man on earth is going to take that sweet girl of mine away from me!' but if he was to say, 'Lady, I don't want to take her away, I want her right here,' I would say, 'Mister, I don't blame you none. I wouldn't pass up a chance to live in a permanent place and get the sweetest girl

WORDS TO OWN

ravenous (rav′ə·nəs) *adj.*: very eager; hungry.

in the world myself. You ain't no fool,' I would say."

"How old is she?" Mr. Shiftlet asked casually.

"Fifteen, sixteen," the old woman said. The girl was nearly thirty but because of her innocence it was impossible to guess.

"It would be a good idea to paint it too," Mr. Shiftlet remarked. "You don't want it to rust out."

"We'll see about that later," the old woman said.

The next day he walked into town and returned with the parts he needed and a can of gasoline. Late in the afternoon, terrible noises

In the darkness, Mr. Shiftlet's smile stretched like a weary snake waking up by a fire.

issued from the shed and the old woman rushed out of the house, thinking Lucynell was somewhere having a fit. Lucynell was sitting on a chicken crate, stamping her feet and screaming, "Burrddttt! bddurrddtttt!" but her fuss was drowned out by the car. With a volley of blasts it emerged from the shed, moving in a fierce and stately way. Mr. Shiftlet was in the driver's seat, sitting very erect. He had an expression of serious modesty on his face as if he had just raised the dead.

That night, rocking on the porch, the old woman began her business, at once. "You want you an innocent woman, don't you?" she asked sympathetically. "You don't want none of this trash."

"No'm, I don't," Mr. Shiftlet said.

"One that can't talk," she continued, "can't sass you back or use foul language. That's the kind for you to have. Right there," and she pointed to Lucynell sitting cross-legged in her chair, holding both feet in her hands.

"That's right," he admitted. "She wouldn't give me any trouble."

"Saturday," the old woman said, "you and her and me can drive into town and get married."

Mr. Shiftlet eased his position on the steps.

"I can't get married right now," he said. "Everything you want to do takes money and I ain't got any."

"What you need with money?" she asked.

"It takes money," he said. "Some people'll do anything anyhow these days, but the way I think, I wouldn't marry no woman that I couldn't take on a trip like she was somebody. I mean take her to a hotel and treat her. I wouldn't marry the Duchesser Windsor," he said firmly, "unless I could take her to a hotel and giver something good to eat.

"I was raised thataway and there ain't a thing I can do about it. My old mother taught me how to do."

"Lucynell don't even know what a hotel is," the old woman muttered. "Listen here, Mr. Shiftlet," she said, sliding forward in her chair, "you'd be getting a permanent house and a deep well and the most innocent girl in the world. You don't need no money. Lemme tell you something: there ain't any place in the world for a poor disabled friendless drifting man."

The ugly words settled in Mr. Shiftlet's head like a group of buzzards in the top of a tree. He didn't answer at once. He rolled himself a cigarette and lit it and then he said in an even voice, "Lady, a man is divided into two parts, body and spirit."

The old woman clamped her gums together.

"A body and a spirit," he repeated. "The body, lady, is like a house: it don't go anywhere; but the spirit, lady, is like a automobile: always on the move, always . . ."

"Listen, Mr. Shiftlet," she said, "my well never goes dry and my house is always warm in the winter and there's no mortgage on a thing about this place. You can go to the courthouse and see for yourself. And yonder under that shed is a fine automobile." She laid the bait carefully. "You can have it painted by Saturday. I'll pay for the paint."

In the darkness, Mr. Shiftlet's smile stretched like a weary snake waking up by a fire. After a second he recalled himself and said, "I'm only saying

---

WORDS TO OWN

volley (väl′ē) n.: firing of many shots at once.

---

a man's spirit means more to him than anything else. I would have to take my wife off for the weekend without no regards at all for cost. I got to follow where my spirit says to go."

"I'll give you fifteen dollars for a weekend trip," the old woman said in a crabbed voice. "That's the best I can do."

"That wouldn't hardly pay for more than the gas and the hotel," he said. "It wouldn't feed her."

"Seventeen-fifty," the old woman said. "That's all I got so it isn't any use you trying to milk me. You can take a lunch."

Mr. Shiftlet was deeply hurt by the word "milk." He didn't doubt that she had more money sewed up in her mattress but he had already told her he was not interested in her money. "I'll make that do," he said and rose and walked off without treating[2] with her further.

On Saturday the three of them drove into town in the car that the paint had barely dried on and Mr. Shiftlet and Lucynell were married in the Ordinary's[3] office while the old woman witnessed. As they came out of the courthouse, Mr. Shiftlet began twisting his neck in his collar. He looked <u>morose</u> and bitter as if he had been insulted while someone held him. "That didn't satisfy me none," he said. "That was just something a woman in an office did, nothing but paperwork and blood

old woman said, "Don't Lucynell look pretty? Looks like a baby doll." Lucynell was dressed up in a white dress that her mother had uprooted from a trunk and there was a Panama hat on her head with a bunch of red wooden cherries on the brim. Every now and then her placid expression was changed by a sly isolated little thought like a shoot of green in the desert. "You got a prize!" the old woman said.

Mr. Shiftlet didn't even look at her.

They drove back to the house to let the old woman off and pick up the lunch. When they were ready to leave, she stood staring in the window of the car, with her fingers clenched around the glass. Tears began to seep sideways out of her eyes and run along the dirty creases in her face. "I ain't ever been parted with her for two days before," she said.

Mr. Shiftlet started the motor.

"And I wouldn't let no man have her but you because I seen you would do right. Good-bye, Sugarbaby," she said, clutching at the sleeve of the white dress. Lucynell looked straight at her and didn't seem to see her there at all. Mr. Shiftlet eased the car forward so that she had to move her hands.

The early afternoon was clear and open and surrounded by pale blue sky. Although the car

Occasionally he stopped his thoughts long enough to look at Lucynell in the seat beside him.

tests. What do they know about my blood? If they was to take my heart and cut it out," he said, "they wouldn't know a thing about me. It didn't satisfy me at all."

"It satisfied the law," the old woman said sharply.

"The law," Mr. Shiftlet said and spit. "It's the law that don't satisfy me."

He had painted the car dark green with a yellow band around it just under the windows. The three of them climbed in the front seat and the

would go only thirty miles an hour, Mr. Shiftlet imagined a terrific climb and dip and swerve that went entirely to his head so that he forgot his morning bitterness. He had always wanted an automobile but he had never been able to afford one before. He drove very fast because he wanted to make Mobile by nightfall.

Occasionally he stopped his thoughts long enough to look at Lucynell in the seat beside him. She had eaten the lunch as soon as they were out

2. **treating:** dealing; negotiating.
3. **Ordinary's:** judge's.

of the yard and now she was pulling the cherries off the hat one by one and throwing them out the window. He became depressed in spite of the car. He had driven about a hundred miles when he decided that she must be hungry again and at the next small town they came to, he stopped in front of an aluminum-painted eating place called The Hot Spot and took her in and ordered her a plate of ham and grits. The ride had made her sleepy and as soon as she got up on the stool, she rested her head on the counter and shut her eyes. There

set directly in front of the automobile. It was a reddening ball that through his windshield was slightly flat on the bottom and top. He saw a boy in overalls and a gray hat standing on the edge of the road and he slowed the car down and stopped in front of him. The boy didn't have his hand raised to thumb the ride, he was only standing there, but he had a small cardboard suitcase and his hat was set on his head in a way to indicate that he had left somewhere for good. "Son," Mr. Shiftlet said, "I see you want a ride."

Occasionally he saw a sign that warned: "Drive carefully. The life you save may be your own."

was no one in The Hot Spot but Mr. Shiftlet and the boy behind the counter, a pale youth with a greasy rag hung over his shoulder. Before he could dish up the food, she was snoring gently.

"Give it to her when she wakes up," Mr. Shiftlet said. "I'll pay for it now."

The boy bent over her and stared at the long pink-gold hair and the half-shut sleeping eyes. Then he looked up and stared at Mr. Shiftlet. "She looks like an angel of Gawd," he murmured.

"Hitchhiker," Mr. Shiftlet explained. "I can't wait. I got to make Tuscaloosa."

The boy bent over again and very carefully touched his finger to a strand of the golden hair and Mr. Shiftlet left.

He was more depressed than ever as he drove on by himself. The late afternoon had grown hot and <u>sultry</u> and the country had flattened out. Deep in the sky a storm was preparing very slowly and without thunder as if it meant to drain every drop of air from the earth before it broke. There were times when Mr. Shiftlet preferred not to be alone. He felt too that a man with a car had a responsibility to others and he kept his eye out for a hitchhiker. Occasionally he saw a sign that warned: "Drive carefully. The life you save may be your own."

The narrow road dropped off on either side into dry fields and here and there a shack or a filling station stood in a clearing. The sun began to

The boy didn't say he did or he didn't but he opened the door of the car and got in, and Mr. Shiftlet started driving again. The child held the suitcase on his lap and folded his arms on top of it. He turned his head and looked out the window away from Mr. Shiftlet. Mr. Shiftlet felt oppressed. "Son," he said after a minute, "I got the best old mother in the world so I reckon you only got the second best."

The boy gave him a quick dark glance and then turned his face back out the window.

"It's nothing so sweet," Mr. Shiftlet continued, "as a boy's mother. She taught him his first prayers at her knee, she give him love when no other would, she told him what was right and what wasn't, and she seen that he done the right thing. Son," he said, "I never <u>rued</u> a day in my life like the one I rued when I left that old mother of mine."

The boy shifted in his seat but he didn't look at Mr. Shiftlet. He unfolded his arms and put one hand on the door handle.

"My mother was a angel of Gawd," Mr. Shiftlet said in a very strained voice. "He took her from heaven and giver to me and I left her." His eyes

- -

WORDS TO OWN

sultry (sul′trē) *adj.*: humid and still.
rued (ro͞od) *v.*: regretted.

- -

Death on Ridge Road (1935) by Grant Wood.
Oil on masonite (39″ × 46 1/16″).

were instantly clouded over with a mist of tears. The car was barely moving.

The boy turned angrily in the seat. "You go to the devil!" he cried. "My old woman is a fleabag and yours is a stinking polecat!" and with that he flung the door open and jumped out with his suitcase into the ditch.

Mr. Shiftlet was so shocked that for about a hundred feet he drove along slowly with the door still open. A cloud, the exact color of the boy's hat and shaped like a turnip, had descended over the sun, and another, worse looking, crouched behind the car. Mr. Shiftlet felt that the rottenness of the world was about to engulf him. He raised his arm and let it fall again to his breast. "Oh Lord!"

he prayed. "Break forth and wash the slime from this earth!"

The turnip continued slowly to descend. After a few minutes there was a guffawing peal of thunder from behind and fantastic raindrops, like tin-can tops, crashed over the rear of Mr. Shiftlet's car. Very quickly he stepped on the gas and with his stump sticking out the window he raced the galloping shower into Mobile.

WORDS TO OWN

guffawing (gu·fô′iŋ) *v.* used as *adj.*: like a loud burst of laughter. "Guffaw" is an echoic word—one that imitates the sound it stands for.

The Adventures of Mr. Shiftlet

› The following comments are from *The Habit of Being* (1979), a collection of O'Connor's letters.

I am going to New York on the 30th to be, if you please, interviewed by Mr. Harvey Breit (on the 31st) on a program he is starting over at NBC-TV [called *Galley-Proof*]. They are also going to dramatize the opening scene from "The Life You Save" etc. Do you reckon this is going to corrupt me? I already feel like a combination of Msgr. Sheen[1] and Gorgeous George [a wrestler]. Everybody who has read *Wise Blood* thinks I'm a hillbilly nihilist, whereas I would like to create the impression over the television that I'm a hillbilly Thomist,[2] but I will probably not be able to think of anything to say to Mr. Harvey Breit but "Huh?" and "Ah dunno." When I come back I'll probably have to spend three months day and night in the chicken pen to counteract these evil influences.

. . .

I have just sold the television rights to "The Life You Save May Be Your Own" to what I understand is called the General Electric Playhouse. All I know about television is hearsay but somebody told me that this was a production conducted by Ronald Regan (?). I don't know if this means RR will be Mr. Shiftlet or not. A staggering thought. Mr. Shiftlet and the idiot daughter will no doubt go off in a Chrysler and live happily ever after. Anyway, on account of this, I am buying my mother a new refrigerator. While they make hash out of my story, she and me will make ice in the new refrigerator.

. . .

I have just learned via one of those gossip columns that the story I sold for a TV play is going to be put on in the spring and that a

1. Msgr. Sheen: Monsignor Fulton J. Sheen, a Catholic priest who had a popular TV show in the 1950s.
2. Thomist (tō′mist): someone who follows the thinking of the thirteenth-century philosopher Thomas Aquinas.

tap-dancer by the name of Gene Kelly is going to make his tellyvision debut in it. The punishment always fits the crime. They must be going to make a musical out of it.

. . .

A letter from my agent today announces that "The Life You Save" will be presented February 1 on the Schlitz Playhouse at 9:30 New York time. My eager beaver friend in NY keeps sending me clippings of gossip columns, one announcing that Kelly will star in Flannery O'Connor's "backwoods love story." Another saying Kelly says "It's a kind of hillbilly thing in which I play a guy who *befriends* a deaf-mute girl in the hills of Kentucky. It gives me a great chance to do some straight acting, something I really have no opportunity to do in movies." See? He ain't had the opportunity before. There'll be no singing & dancing, Kelly says. I think it's channel 5 and people tell me you can't get it very good here, so I hope you will absolutely be in front of your set this time at the correct hour, as I must have some representative there to give Kelly a good leer every now and then for me. I don't know who his leading lady will be, but doubtless my NY friend will be providing that information before long. She thinks this is all hilariously funny and keeps writing me, "Has dignity no value for you?" etc. It will probably be appropriate to smoke a corncob pipe while watching this. All my kinfolks are going to think that it is a great improvement over the original story.

. . .

Someone has just called my attention to the fact that this . . . text which has "The Life You Save" in it has it with the last paragraph omitted. I would be much obliged if you would call Harcourt [O'Connor's publisher] and tell them. I think some kind of protest ought to be lodged. I suppose there is nothing that can be done about it now but I certainly don't like the idea of my story being in a textbook and the last paragraph omitted. . . ."

—Flannery O'Connor

MAKING MEANINGS

First Thoughts

1. Were you surprised at the way the story ended? Review your prediction chart, and describe how the story's outcome affected you.

Shaping Interpretations

2. In the opening pages of the story, what details of setting, of characterization, and of dialogue carry menacing undertones and seem to **foreshadow** later events? (Look back over your prediction chart.)

3. What is the significance of the remarks made by the hitchhiker just before he leaps from the moving car?

4. What are we to make of the fact that Mr. Shiftlet feels that "the rottenness of the world [is] about to engulf him"? What **irony** do you sense in Mr. Shiftlet's realization?

5. Find four **figures of speech** and several words with strong **connotations** that reveal the narrator's attitude toward Mr. Shiftlet. Consider, for example, why the narrator says that Shiftlet's "figure formed a crooked cross" (page 675) and describes his eyes as "clay-colored" (page 675). How does the narrator want us to regard Mr. Shiftlet? Is he a prophet or a demon or both?

6. What do you think is the significance of the peculiar clouds and storm that pursue Mr. Shiftlet toward Mobile at the end of the story?

7. Do you sense **irony** in the story's title? How would you state the story's **theme,** based on the warning implied in the title?

Reading Check

a. Describe the improvements Mr. Shiftlet makes in the Craters' place during his first week there.

b. Explain how Mr. Shiftlet seems to want to exploit the Craters.

c. How does the older Lucynell want to exploit Mr. Shiftlet?

d. What has become of young Lucynell and Mr. Shiftlet by story's end?

8. Are there any heroes in this story? Do you think it is a story about innocence versus evil, or is it a story about a world in which everyone is morally questionable? Explain.

ELEMENTS OF LITERATURE

The Four "Modes" of Fiction

According to some critics, all narrative literature can be more or less described in terms of four basic "modes," or story patterns. These modes are tragedy, comedy, romance, and irony. Tragedy and comedy are opposites, as are romance and irony.

In a typical **tragedy,** the hero is a noble, admirable character who falls from a position of some prominence to disaster or even death. This tragic hero is overcome by evil, but in the course of the struggle, he or she gains self-knowledge and wisdom. Watching a tragedy, we feel exhilarated, for we have seen the best that human beings are capable of in the face of overwhelming adversity. Greek tragedies such as *Antigone* and Shakespearean plays such as *Hamlet* best exemplify the tragic mode.

In a **comedy,** on the other hand, the central characters are often two lovers who want to marry despite parental and societal obstacles. By the end of a comedy, the young lovers have triumphed over the forces blocking them and are to be married. Many comedies end with a wedding, suggesting the renewal of life and love. Shakespeare's comedies, such as *Much Ado About Nothing* and *A Midsummer Night's Dream,* are perfect examples of comedy.

In the typical **romance** story, a hero undertakes a quest, during which his or her heroic qualities are put to the test. The hero is usually successful and returns having learned something of value. In such a story, beauty, innocence, and goodness prevail over evil, often with the help of magic or supernatural intervention. If you've ever read a fairy tale or a superhero comic, watched *Star Wars* or *Star Trek,* or gotten caught up in an adventure like *Raiders of the Lost Ark,* you've encountered the world of romance.

In the world of **irony,** as opposed to romance, there are no heroes and no triumphs. The world is a place where injustice, crime, and general foolishness prevail. The characters who triumph in such a world are often crafty rascals and even con artists—people who learn how to manipulate the world for their own gain. In other forms of irony, the characters are ordinary human beings like ourselves and are caught in a world that offers little opportunity for heroism. Walter Mitty (page 625) is an example of this type of character, one who longs for heroism but is limited to shopping for puppy biscuits in Waterbury, Connecticut. The characters in ironic fiction often find themselves in settings that are confining, that offer no opportunities for free choice: prisons, totalitarian societies, or even madhouses.

What modes are used in the stories you have read in the modern literature collections thus far?

CHOICES:
Building Your Portfolio

Writer's Notebook

1. Collecting Ideas for an Analysis of Causes and Effects

The dominant mode in today's stories, novels, and plays is irony. In Arthur Miller's famous  play *The Death of a Salesman,* for example, the characters and their problems are very ordinary. No longer do we find larger-than-life heroes struggling admirably against some malign fate, emerging with increased self-knowledge, even if the conflict ends in death. In Miller's play, the main character is an antihero named, appropriately, Loman. He is not a king or superman, but a failed salesman. His troubles are not caused by the gods or by fate, but by a boss who wants to make more money. Think of other ironic stories or novels you've read or ironic movies or plays you've seen. Then, write down some ideas about why the dominant mode in literature today is irony. In other words, why do we rarely write about great heroes anymore? Save your ideas for possible use in the Writer's Workshop on page 685.

Analyzing a Story
2. Romantic Reversal

In a brief essay, analyze O'Connor's story as an **ironic** commentary on a **romance.** (See Elements of Literature, page 683.) Account for the ironic reversals of these typical elements of a romance story: (a) the nurturing mother; (b) the beautiful, innocent young woman; (c) the hero who rescues the young woman; and (d) the romantic setting in a fairy-tale kingdom.

Critical Thinking / Speaking and Listening
3. Have Things Changed?

Lead a discussion in class analyzing O'Connor's comments about this story in Primary Sources (page 682). Consider (a) why TV producers would change the story, (b) whether the story would be popular if it were dramatized on TV today or made into a movie, and (c) why a textbook might omit the last paragraph (which is not omitted in this text).

Creative Writing
4. What Fate Awaits?

What becomes of Lucynell, asleep in The Hot Spot, and Mr. Shiftlet, driving on toward Mobile? In the form of a screenplay, story, magazine interview, or newspaper article, relate what their futures hold.

Creative Writing / Art
5. Mr. Shiftlet's Motto

Design a bumper sticker for Mr. Shiftlet that, in a very few words, expresses his philosophy of life. Include a logo or graphic device appropriate to his saying. Here's an example:

"The world is almost rotten."

Writer's Workshop

The history
of the written
word is rich a
Page 1

EXPOSITORY WRITING

ANALYZING CAUSES AND EFFECTS

In our everyday lives we frequently think about what caused an event to occur, or we predict the effects of an event or a situation that has already occurred. Whether we're discussing why the basketball team lost last week's game, deciding what electives will most benefit us in our school careers, or determining why there's been an increase in crime in our neighborhood, we are thinking about causes and effects. In fact, the world would make almost no sense to us unless we made connections between causes and effects. Thus, when you write a cause-and-effect essay, you're simply doing in a more formal and careful way what you informally or even unconsciously do most of the time.

A cause-and-effect essay is one in which the writer analyzes either the causes or the effects of an event, a situation, or a trend. (An *event* is a specific occurrence, such as an automobile accident; a *situation* is a continuing state of affairs, such as the lack of genuine heroes in movies today; and a *trend* is a pattern that changes over time, such as the increasing use of home computers.) To write an effective cause-and-effect essay, you must present reasons, evidence, and examples to convince your readers that your argument is correct. One way to think of the cause-and-effect essay is as an analysis that answers the questions *Why?* (by identifying causes) and *What's the result?* (by describing or predicting effects).

Prewriting

1. **Choosing a topic.** Changes often give rise to thinking about causes and effects: Perhaps there has been a change in the number of homeless people in a city park and we want to determine the cause or causes. Change is also involved when we predict the effects or results of an event, a situation, or a trend. For instance, we might want to predict the effects of a school's new policy on locker searches.

    Puzzling issues also lend themselves to weighing causes or effects. Literary works, for example, can suggest many possible topics for contemplation: Why does Richard Cory take his own life? Why is J. Alfred Prufrock so indecisive? What if Walter Mitty accomplished a heroic feat in real life?

    Your Writer's Notebook jottings from Collections 11–13 probably contain ideas for a cause or an effect essay about a literary topic. If you lack ideas for an essay topic, try listing events, situations, and trends you would

Technology HELP

See Writer's Workshop 2 CD-ROM. *Assignment: Cause and Effect.*

ASSIGNMENT
Write an essay analyzing the causes and/or the effects of an event, a situation, or a trend.

AIM
To explain or inform; to persuade; to explore.

AUDIENCE
Your teacher, classmates, and perhaps the readers of a particular magazine or newspaper.

When you brainstorm topics, it is useful to consider different categories. You can analyze causes and effects, for example, in the physical, social, economic, ecological, political, cultural, educational, and technological spheres.

Choose two topics from the above categories. For each topic, explore possible causes and effects by completing these sentence beginnings:

- This (event, situation, trend) occurred because

  _____.

- As a result of this (event, situation, trend), _____.

enjoy analyzing. If you are not really interested in your topic, you'll probably have trouble engaging your reader.

After you list five or more topics, participate in a classwide brainstorming session led by your teacher or a classmate. The group should write as many topics as possible on the chalkboard, where everyone can see them. Seeing the ideas of others may prompt you to come up with additional topics. For each topic, make sure you can ask either *Why?* (for causes) or *What's the result?* (for effects). Look at your list, and choose the topic that you find most interesting. Decide whether you are going to address causes, effects, or both.

2. **Charting causes and effects.** Depending on your topic, organize your information using a table, cluster diagram, or other graphic organizer (see models).

Model

Topic: What are the causes of decreasing voter turnout in local elections?

Causes	Possible Explanations
People are not interested in local issues.	The issues have become so complicated that people are confused. People don't have time to watch local news programs or read newspaper articles on local issues.
Polling places are not conveniently located.	Working people often must vote during a lunch hour or short break; if it takes too long to reach a polling place, many people may not want to expend the time or energy. The downtown polling places often have long lines, while the polling places near people's homes are hardly used.
People don't trust local politicians.	The media have portrayed politicians as dishonest. The city is so large that few people have a chance to meet politicians.
People are apathetic.	People hear the results of opinion polls and figure their vote won't matter. People feel powerless to bring about desired changes; this becomes a self-fulfilling prophecy.
People are not interested in candidates' ideas.	People feel there is no real choice among candidates because all the candidates' ideas are virtually the same.

Study your graphic organizer, and select the elements you want to include in your essay. Make an outline of the major structure of your essay. If possible, meet with one or two classmates and exchange outlines. Briefly discuss each other's outlines, pointing out major causes or effects that may have been overlooked.

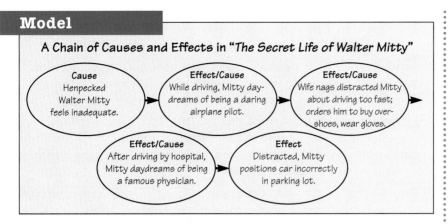

A Chain of Causes and Effects in "The Secret Life of Walter Mitty"

Cause
Henpecked Walter Mitty feels inadequate.

Effect/Cause
While driving, Mitty daydreams of being a daring airplane pilot.

Effect/Cause
Wife nags distracted Mitty about driving too fast; orders him to buy overshoes, wear gloves.

Effect/Cause
After driving by hospital, Mitty daydreams of being a famous physician.

Effect
Distracted, Mitty positions car incorrectly in parking lot.

3. **Swaying the crowd.** If you are examining a social issue, will your audience be citizens of your town? members of the student body? readers of a particular magazine or newspaper in which the essay might appear? If you are analyzing the causes of a character's actions in a literary work, will your audience be other students who have read the work? Once you have identified your audience, think about background information you may need to provide. You will also need to use sound reasoning.

Inductive Thinking: Drawing Conclusions

Analyzing causes and effects requires that you use a critical-thinking process called **induction.** When you use induction to figure out something, you begin with a specific set of facts or observations, study them carefully, and then draw a general conclusion from them. In other words, induction is a kind of thinking in which you reason from the specific to the general. Here's a model:

Evidence:	A local defense plant with 10,000 employees has closed down in our city.
Evidence:	The local jobless rate has risen by 2 percent.
Evidence:	Local retail sales are off significantly from the same time last year. Retailers are worried.
Generalization:	The closing of a defense plant has had a noticeably negative effect on our local economy.

You need to be sure of the validity of the generalization you've made. Here are some questions to ask yourself in order to test the validity of your conclusion:

1. Do I have enough evidence to support my generalization? Is the sample I have selected truly representative of a larger population?
2. Is the source of my evidence trustworthy? Have I used a mixture of sound research sources—published statistics, opinions of authorities, eyewitness testimonies—and not just personal observations?
3. Does all my evidence lead to the generalization, or does some evidence refute it? What can I make of such discrepancies?

With a partner, study the inductive statements below, and brainstorm possible sources of evidence to support or refute each generalization.

1. Traffic fatalities will increase if the speed limit is raised to 70 miles per hour.
2. A law allowing people to carry concealed weapons will reduce crime.
3. Students who have above-average aptitude in mathematics will have higher earning potential in their future careers.

Questions for Gathering Data

Causes
- What are the obvious causes?
- Are there any hidden causes?
- Is there a most important cause?
- What is the most recent cause?
- Did any causes occur much earlier?

Effects
- What are the obvious effects?
- Are there any hidden effects?
- What was (or will be) the first effect?
- What effect(s) might occur much later?

Evidence
- What constitutes sufficient evidence?
- Do experts support my analysis?

Strategies for Elaboration

- Supply historical evidence, statistics, analogous cases, or other facts to underpin your analysis.
- Cite experts in order to support your conclusions.
- Apply observations or anecdotes from your own experience.
- In writing about a literary work, quote relevant passages.
- Include less obvious causes and effects.

Drafting

With your audience firmly in mind, begin drafting your essay.

1. **Lead.** Begin by grabbing your reader's attention. You might open with a startling observation, an anecdote, an interesting situation, a telling quotation, or a vivid what-if scenario.

2. **Introduction.** State the event, situation, or trend that you will analyze. Include sufficient—but not too much—background information. Then, briefly state your topic as a **thesis statement.** In your statement, be sure you say whether you will discuss causes, effects, or both.

3. **Body.** In the body of your paper, present your analysis of causes or effects or both. For each cause or effect, you should elaborate by explaining the cause or effect and providing logical and convincing evidence of connections. You may organize your arguments in order of importance or in chronological order. Use separate paragraphs to make your method of organization clear to the reader. It is also helpful to use **subordinating conjunctions** when discussing causes and effects. (For more on subordinating conjunctions, see the Language Workshop on page 689.)

4. **Conclusion.** Conclude your essay by summarizing your main points. Perhaps end with a thought-provoking comment or a prediction of future effects.

Evaluating and Revising

1. **Peer review.** Share your draft with a classmate, and have him or her act as a critical reader by answering these questions:

   • Is the event, situation, or trend well-defined? Has the writer provided enough elaboration to convince the reader?

   • Are the essay's statements clear and unambiguous? Are they presented in a logical order?

   • Has the writer provided several causes or effects or both? Are there too many elements? too few?

   • Has the writer overlooked important matters?

   • Are the introduction and conclusion original and engaging?

2. **Self-evaluation.** Review your critical-reader's comments, and make needed revisions. Consult the list above to evaluate your own work.

SHOWING RELATIONSHIPS: USING SUBORDINATING CONJUNCTIONS

When you write, part of your job is to sort out and define for your readers the relationships between the ideas you present. In the following sentence, two clauses are joined with the conjunction *and*. As you will see, this conjunction fails to indicate the relationship between the two clauses.

EXAMPLE   Flannery O'Connor was sick for fourteen years, and she wrote critically acclaimed novels and short stories.

By using a subordinating conjunction instead, you can join the same clauses above in a way that more clearly conveys the relationship between the ideas expressed:

EXAMPLE   *Although* Flannery O'Connor was sick for fourteen years, she wrote critically acclaimed novels and short stories.

   A **subordinating conjunction** begins a subordinate clause and indicates the relationship of this clause to an independent clause in the same sentence. A subordinating conjunction may come between two clauses, or it may appear at the beginning of a sentence.

EXAMPLES   Lucynell was sitting on the porch *when* Mr. Shiftlet arrived.

   When Mr. Shiftlet arrived, Lucynell was sitting on the porch.

The chart below shows some subordinating conjunctions.

Subordinating Conjunctions		
although	in order that	until
as	since	when
because	so that	whereas
before	that	while

Writer's Workshop Follow-Up: Revising

In writing about causes and/or effects for the Writer's Workshop on page 685, you analyzed the relationships among events, situations, or trends. Now, review your essay to see whether you can better pinpoint the connections by using subordinating conjunctions in your sentences.

Technology HELP

See Language Workshop CD-ROM. *Key word entry: subordinating conjunctions.*

Language Handbook HELP

Subordinating ideas: pages 1235 and 1238.

Try It Out

Rewrite these sentences, replacing *and* with a subordinating conjunction that more precisely explains the relationship between the two clauses.

1. Mr. Shiftlet claimed to be honest, and he betrayed the old woman and her daughter.

2. The old woman gave Mr. Shiftlet her car, and he married her daughter.

3. Mr. Shiftlet worked hard at fixing up the old woman's place, and he planned to con her.

Reading for Life

Interpreting and Constructing a Graphic Organizer

Situation

You and a classmate want to settle an argument about the range of ethnic diversity in the United States. You've compiled information about America's major ethnic groups (see box) and want to display that information in graphic form. You need to learn how to interpret and construct a graphic organizer.

Strategies

Recognize the different kinds of graphic organizers.

- A **line graph** charts a pattern over time, such as the yearly increase in immigration of a certain group over a ten-year period.

- A **pie graph** (it looks like a pie cut into wedge-shaped pieces) shows percentages of elements that make up a whole, such as the percentages of earnings from a farm's various crops.

- A **bar graph** uses parallel bars to compare two or more kinds of information in relation to time and quantity. A bar graph might compare student enrollment by ethnic group for a given year.

Examine your information and decide which kind of graph would best illustrate your data.

- In creating your own graphic organizer, use appropriate measurements and labels. For example, to make a bar graph, you

```
          1998 Population Estimate
Total United States population: 270,733,000.
• White Americans constituted 233,401,000, or 82.5
percent.
• African Americans constituted 34,489,000, or 12.7
percent.
• Persons of Hispanic origin constituted 30,680,000
or 11.3 percent.
• Members of the American Indian, Eskimo, and Aleut
groups constituted 2,366,000, or 0.9 percent.
• Members of Asian and Pacific Island groups
constituted 10,476,000, or 3.9 percent.

Note: The groups listed above total 311,412,000, or
111.3 percent, because persons may belong in more than
one category.
Source: U.S. Bureau of the Census.
```

will need to show a scale divided into numerical units (such as "thousands," or "millions") that encompasses the range of data you are comparing. To make a pie graph, you'll need to create wedge-shaped segments that are scaled to the percentages that they represent.

Using the Strategies

1. Based on the data on this page, which two groups made up the smallest percentage of the U.S. population?

2. Which two groups had about the same percentage of the total population?

3. Which of the three kinds of graphs described above would you use to illustrate this data? On a separate

sheet of paper, sketch the graph using appropriate labels.

Extending the Strategies

- Using the Internet or printed materials, research information about a selected aspect of your community, city, or school (population makeup, income, growth, voting patterns, reading scores, etc.). Display the information on a graph.

- Be aware of the different kinds of graphic organizers used in print and electronic media. Bring in examples of graphic organizers for a permanent classroom exhibit. Note that newsmagazines often use elaborate pictorial graphics. Be sure to find some of these for your exhibit.

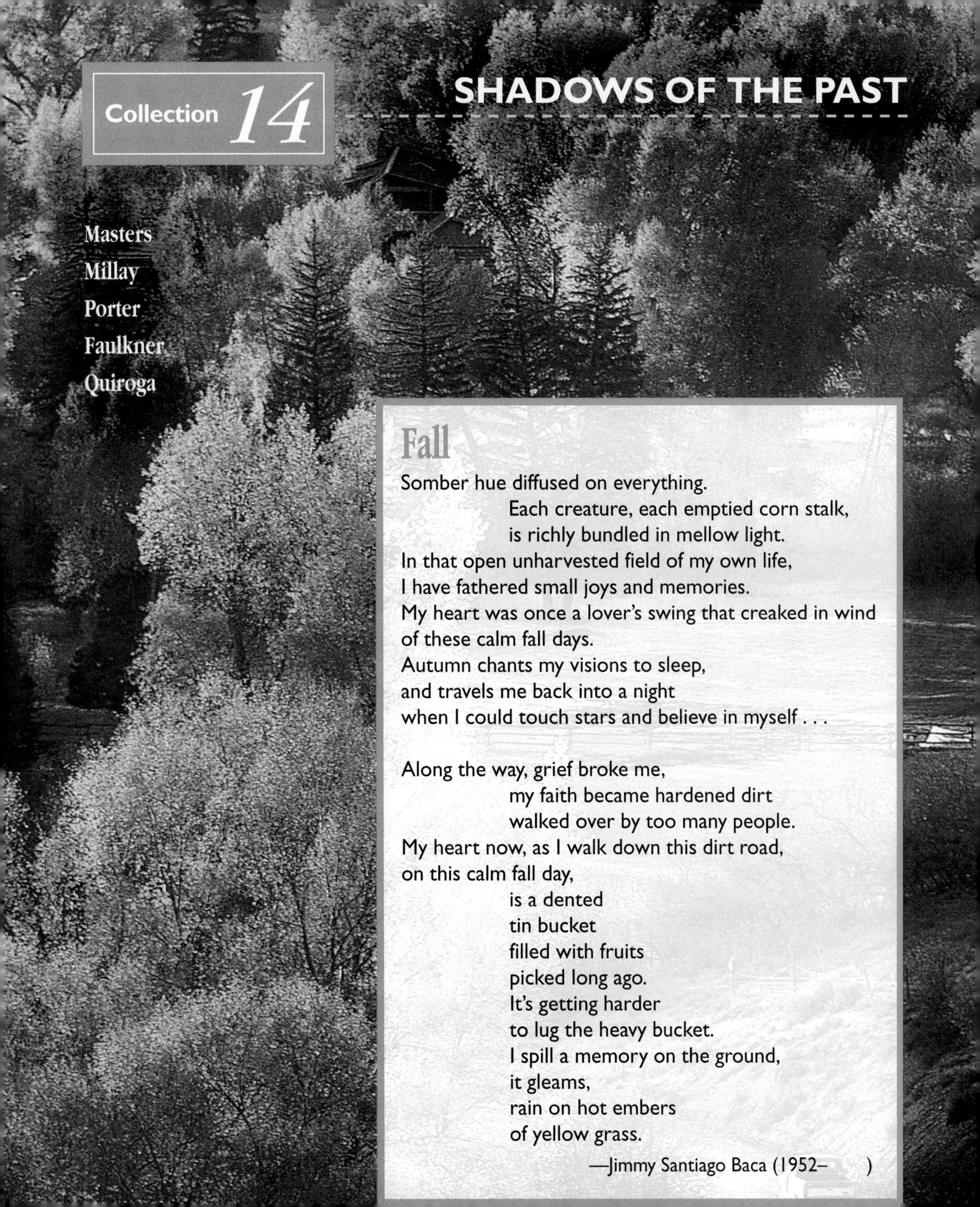

SHADOWS OF THE PAST

Masters

Millay

Porter

Faulkner

Quiroga

Fall

Somber hue diffused on everything.
        Each creature, each emptied corn stalk,
        is richly bundled in mellow light.
In that open unharvested field of my own life,
I have fathered small joys and memories.
My heart was once a lover's swing that creaked in wind
of these calm fall days.
Autumn chants my visions to sleep,
and travels me back into a night
when I could touch stars and believe in myself . . .

Along the way, grief broke me,
        my faith became hardened dirt
        walked over by too many people.
My heart now, as I walk down this dirt road,
on this calm fall day,
        is a dented
        tin bucket
        filled with fruits
        picked long ago.
        It's getting harder
        to lug the heavy bucket.
        I spill a memory on the ground,
        it gleams,
        rain on hot embers
        of yellow grass.

                    —Jimmy Santiago Baca (1952–   )

Edgar Lee Masters

(1869–1950)

AP/Wide World Photos.

Edgar Lee Masters was born in Garnett, Kansas. Like Carl Sandburg (page 792), he was a product of that part of the Middle West known as the Corn Belt or Bible Belt. Also like Sandburg, he found his voice in the free verse that characterized the second decade of the twentieth century. But unlike Sandburg, Masters produced just one book in a spare style that served his homely subject matter. After that he reverted to a more conventional poetic style: pretty, romantic, and wordy.

Yet this one book, *Spoon River Anthology* (1915), was a landmark in American literature, and it made Masters famous. It is a collection of some 250 epitaphs—memorial inscriptions on gravestones—spoken by the inhabitants of a cemetery in the fictional town of Spoon River: drunkards, bankers, judges, poets, atheists, preachers, gamblers, druggists, and housewives.

The dramatic device of having dead people speak their own epitaphs served Masters brilliantly. Drawing upon his memories of Petersburg and Lewistown—the Illinois towns he knew during his first twenty years—he used these epitaphs to show the hidden underside of American life. Victims of that life, freed by death to speak without fear of consequences, tell their stories. Bit by bit, they fill in a picture of small-town life that is vastly different from the folksy, sentimental magazine cover images of the time. Masters's speakers from beyond the grave bring buried truth into the daylight.

Spoon River Anthology became one of the most widely read books of an age that was fascinated by psychology. Better than any scientific study, it revealed how the conventions of society warred with people's real needs and beliefs. By turning psychological "case histories" into lyric poems, Masters gave speech to the inarticulate and, at the same time, brought a new kind of realism to poetry.

Before You Read

FROM SPOON RIVER ANTHOLOGY

Make the Connection

Having Their Say

Have you ever stood in a graveyard and thought of all the hundreds of stories that lie buried there—all the secrets, the loves, the angers, the disappointments, all the unfinished business of lives that have ended? Have you ever thought of how the people in that graveyard were connected in life—by family, by occupation, by feuds, even by scandal?

Reading Skills and Strategies

Oral Interpretations

In *Spoon River Anthology*, Masters captures the sounds and rhythms of American English spoken by ordinary people from a small Midwestern town. Read each poem aloud in order to appreciate how Masters imitates real speech and conveys a sense of the person who is speaking. Can you interpret the poems in different ways by using different tones of voice?

Masters often gives his speakers names that are clues to their character. As a stonecutter, Bone engraved words that identified skeletons. As a spokesman for his own conscience, he speaks words that cut to the bone.

Richard Bone

Edgar Lee Masters

When I first came to Spoon River
I did not know whether what they told me
Was true or false.
They would bring me the epitaph
5 And stand around the shop while I worked
And say "He was so kind," "He was wonderful,"
"She was the sweetest woman," "He was a consistent Christian."
And I chiseled for them whatever they wished,
All in ignorance of its truth.
10 But later, as I lived among the people here,
I knew how near to the life
Were the epitaphs that were ordered for them as they died.
But still I chiseled whatever they paid me to chisel
And made myself party to the false chronicles°
15 Of the stones,
Even as the historian does who writes
Without knowing the truth,
Or because he is influenced to hide it.

14. **chronicles:** historical accounts.

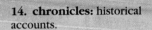

PRIMARY Sources — AN AUTOBIOGRAPHY

The Genesis of Spoon River [1914]

About the 20th of May my mother came to visit us, and we had many long talks. . . . In our talks now we went over the whole past of Lewistown and Petersburg, bringing up characters and events that had passed from my mind. We traced these persons to their final fates, to the positions in life that they were then in. We had many sessions at this recalling of old days. . . .

The psychological experience of this was truly wonderful. Finally on the morning she was leaving for Springfield we had a last and a rather sobering talk. It was Sunday, too, and after putting her on the train at 53rd Street I walked back home full of strange pensiveness. The little church bell was ringing, but spring was in the air. I went to my room and immediately wrote "The Hill," and two or three of the portraits of *Spoon River Anthology.* Almost at once the idea came to me: Why not make this book the book I had thought about in 1906, in which I should draw the macrocosm by portraying the microcosm? Why not put side by side the stories of two characters interlocked in fate, thus giving both misunderstood souls a chance to be justly weighed? . . .

—Edgar Lee Masters, *from Across Spoon River: An Autobiography*

Many of the stories from *Spoon River* are interlocking. The villain of the whole book is Deacon Thomas Rhodes, who "ran the church as well as the store and the bank." We hear about Rhodes from a number of his victims, including "Butch" Weldy. "Butch" refers to Jack the Fiddler, a blind man also buried in the cemetery. Jack was killed when "Butch," who had been drinking, drove a carriage into a ditch.

"Butch" Weldy

Edgar Lee Masters

After I got religion and steadied down
They gave me a job in the canning works,
And every morning I had to fill
The tank in the yard with gasoline,
5　That fed the blow-fires in the sheds
To heat the soldering irons.
And I mounted a rickety ladder to do it,
Carrying buckets full of the stuff.
One morning, as I stood there pouring,
10　The air grew still and seemed to heave,
And I shot up as the tank exploded,
And down I came with both legs broken
And my eyes burned crisp as a couple of
　　eggs,
For someone left a blow-fire going,
15　And something sucked the flame in the
　　tank.
The Circuit Judge said whoever did it
Was a fellow-servant of mine, and so
Old Rhodes' son didn't have to pay me.
And I sat on the witness stand as blind
20　As Jack the Fiddler, saying over and over,
"I didn't know him at all."

Like many characters in *Spoon River Anthology,* Fiddler Jones is based on a real person, a Petersburg-area fiddler named John Jones. Cooney Potter was a hard-working farmer, and Red-Head Sammy Watkins was a local musician.

Fiddler Jones

Edgar Lee Masters

The earth keeps some vibration going
There in your heart, and that is you.
And if the people find you can fiddle,
Why, fiddle you must, for all your life.
5　What do you see, a harvest of clover?
Or a meadow to walk through to the river?
The wind's in the corn; you rub your hands
For beeves° hereafter ready for market;
Or else you hear the rustle of skirts
10　Like the girls when dancing at Little Grove.
To Cooney Potter a pillar of dust
Or whirling leaves meant ruinous drouth;°
They looked to me like Red-Head Sammy
Stepping it off, to "Toor-a-Loor."
15　How could I till my forty acres
Not to speak of getting more,
With a medley of horns, bassoons and
　　piccolos
Stirred in my brain by crows and robins
And the creak of a wind-mill—only these?
20　And I never started to plow in my life
That someone did not stop in the road
And take me away to a dance or picnic.
I ended up with forty acres;
I ended up with a broken fiddle—
25　And a broken laugh, and a thousand
　　memories,
And not a single regret.

8. beeves: alternative plural of *beef;* here, the meaning is "cattle."
12. drouth: archaic spelling of *drought.*

• Petit is largely based on Ernest McGaffey, a friend of Masters' in Chicago during the 1890s who wrote several books of undistinguished poetry. Petit also resembles Masters himself, a writer whose best poetry deals simply and directly with everyday life around him.

• This epitaph refers to a real-life bank failure in Lewistown in 1894, which Masters blamed on Henry Phelps (here renamed Thomas Rhodes) and Phelps's son. The bank collapse caused enormous hardship for the town's citizens, and Masters's father helped prosecute the bank officials. Contrary to this poem, none were sent to prison.

Petit, the Poet

Edgar Lee Masters

Seeds in a dry pod, tick, tick, tick,
Tick, tick, tick, like mites in a quarrel—
Faint iambics that the full breeze wakens—
But the pine tree makes a symphony thereof.
5   Triolets, villanelles, rondels, rondeaus,
Ballades° by the score with the same old
      thought:
The snows and the roses of yesterday are
      vanished;
And what is love but a rose that fades?
Life all around me here in the village:
10 Tragedy, comedy, valor and truth,
Courage, constancy, heroism, failure—
All in the loom, and oh what patterns!
Woodlands, meadows, streams and rivers—
Blind to all of it all my life long.
15 Triolets, villanelles, rondels, rondeaus,
Seeds in a dry pod, tick, tick, tick,
Tick, tick, tick, what little iambics,
While Homer and Whitman roared in the
      pines.

6. Triolets . . . Ballades: various complicated forms of poetry.

Mrs. George Reece

Edgar Lee Masters

To this generation I would say:
Memorize some bit of verse of truth or
      beauty.
It may serve a turn in your life.
My husband had nothing to do
5   With the fall of the bank—he was only
      cashier.
The wreck was due to the president, Thomas
      Rhodes,
And his vain, unscrupulous son.
Yet my husband was sent to prison,
And I was left with the children,
10 To feed and clothe and school them.
And I did it, and sent them forth
Into the world all clean and strong,
And all through the wisdom of Pope, the
      poet:°
"Act well your part, there all the honor lies."

13. Pope, the poet: The English poet Alexander Pope (1688-1744), whose wise sayings are often quoted.

MAKING MEANINGS

First Thoughts

1. Think of the people you know in your own town or neighborhood. Compared with them, do these Spoon River characters sound real to you? Cite reasons to support your responses.

Shaping Interpretations

2. What does Richard Bone, the stone carver, come to realize about the people of Spoon River? What does he come to realize about himself?

3. How does Butch Weldy feel about the accident that ruined his life? What is the **tone** of his epitaph?

4. How does Fiddler Jones feel about his life? Cite passages from the poem to support your interpretation.

5. Appropriately, Petit, the poet, uses **metaphors** to talk about his experiences. In lines 1–3, what is he comparing his own poetry to? How does this small-town poet feel about his work—and why does he mention Homer and Whitman at the end of his epitaph?

6. Summarize Mrs. George Reece's advice. Do you think her husband would have agreed with her? Explain.

7. What significance can you find in some of the names that Masters gave his characters?

8. Compare the ways any two of these Spoon River speakers feel about life. Consider their feelings about their own work, their attitudes toward other people, and their responses to chance or fate.

Connecting with the Texts

9. If you had the chance, how would you reply to these speakers of *Spoon River Anthology*?

Extending the Texts

10. In what ways do the speakers' feelings—such as Bone's remorse or Petit's regrets—suggest universal **themes**? What experiences in today's world might produce a contemporary Butch Weldy, Fiddler Jones, or Mrs. George Reece?

CHOICES: Building Your Portfolio

Writer's Notebook

1. Collecting Ideas for an Interpretive Essay

A good focus for an interpretive essay is the writer's tone.

Tone refers to the writer's attitude toward his or her subject. Tone can be ironic, sentimental, critical, admiring, condescending, and so on. Read each *Spoon River* poem several times. Pay particular attention to word choice. How do you think Masters himself feels about each speaker? Cite specific details from the poems to support your interpretation. Keep your notes for possible use in the Writer's Workshop on page 804.

Analyzing the Poems

2. The American Way

In a brief essay, tell what the five *Spoon River* poems in this text say about life in a Midwestern American town in the early twentieth century. Consider the values of the people, their hopes and dreams, their problems, and their sense of community. What beliefs and experiences, in your opinion, make Masters's characters especially American? (You might want to read more *Spoon River* poems before writing.)

Speaking and Listening

3. *Spoon River* in Performance

The entire *Spoon River Anthology* has been performed onstage, with several actors taking the parts of the speakers. Prepare these five poems for a performance of your own. The performers' first task is to analyze each character: What is this person's attitude toward life? What tone of voice would he or she speak in? You might wish to include music in your performance and to dress your speakers in some kind of costume (perhaps they could all dress in black). You might also add other Spoon Riverites to your performance. Ask your listeners to evaluate your performance.

Edna St. Vincent Millay

(1892–1950)

Like Edwin Arlington Robinson (page 644), Edna St. Vincent Millay was born on the granite coast of Maine and established her poetic reputation in New York. Also like Robinson, she lived to see the day when, despite

AP/Wide World Photos.

many honors and the devotion of a wide audience, she had to realize that her reputation had barely withstood the onslaught of modernism.

Millay achieved fame even before she graduated from Vassar College, with the publication of her first collection of verse, *Renascence and Other Poems* (1917). After World War I, she moved to Greenwich Village. This was an era when that section of New York City was not only a haven for artists, but also a place where women were as free as men to speak their minds, to live by their own rules, and to pursue careers—activities that most Americans still considered improper for women. Taking advantage of this liberated atmosphere, Millay became one of its leading voices—a free spirit who wrote saucy and slightly scandalous lyrics in a style that occasionally evoked Elizabethan verse. Millay's philosophy might best be described in her own words:

First Fig

My candle burns at both ends;
It will not last the night;
But ah, my foes, and oh, my friends—
It gives a lovely light!

Millay also became caught up in the radical dissent of the time, and she worked passionately, if vainly, to save the anarchists Sacco and Vanzetti, who were executed in Massachusetts in 1927 after a celebrated trial.

"Vincent," as she was familiarly known, was a skilled actress and speaker with the flair of a seasoned performer. She gave recitals during long, nationwide tours in which she won a degree of celebrity seldom associated with poets.

Both shocking and fascinating to her audiences, Millay grew in popularity even as her poetic achievements began to decline. Her most productive period was between the two world wars, when she published seven collections of poetry, as well as a series of dramas written for the Provincetown Players in New York. In 1923, she became the first woman to win the Pulitzer Prize in poetry.

During World War II, Millay determined to write "public" poetry to contribute to the Allied cause. She produced scores of poems which, although widely read, proved that outrage and passion could not substitute for the verbal artistry that poetry demands. The lyricist had been overtaken by the propagandist.

One of the brightest literary stars of a generation was all but faded from sight when, in her fifty-eighth year, Edna St. Vincent Millay died alone at her home, Steepletop.

Make the Connection

Happy Memories

Remembering a happy event can cast a sudden glow over our lives. The title of this poem is a Spanish word meaning "remembrance" or "souvenir." Here the poet evokes a happy memory of time past—a carefree night spent riding one of the ferry boats that connect the island of Manhattan with other parts of New York City.

Quickwrite

Without pausing for critical thought, free-write a list of three or four memories of happy times that pop into your mind.

The Normandie (1938) by Reginald Marsh. Watercolor (30″ × 50″).

The Butler Institute of American Art, Youngstown, Ohio. Purchased 1962.

Recuerdo

Edna St. Vincent Millay

We were very tired, we were very merry—
We had gone back and forth all night on the ferry.
It was bare and bright, and smelled like a stable—
But we looked into a fire, we leaned across a table,
5 We lay on a hill-top underneath the moon;
And the whistles kept blowing, and the dawn came soon.

We were very tired, we were very merry—
We had gone back and forth all night on the ferry;
And you ate an apple, and I ate a pear,
10 From a dozen of each we had bought somewhere;
And the sky went wan, and the wind came cold,
And the sun rose dripping, a bucketful of gold.

We were very tired, we were very merry,
We had gone back and forth all night on the ferry.
15 We hailed, "Good morrow, mother!" to a shawl-covered head,
And bought a morning paper, which neither of us read;
And she wept, "God bless you!" for the apples and pears,
And we gave her all our money but our subway fares.

In 1912, two talented young poets wrote a letter to the editor of a poetry anthology saying that "Renascence," the poem submitted by E. St. Vincent Millay, Esq., must surely be the work of a forty-five-year-old brawny male. When she heard of the letter, Millay replied as follows.

"The brawny male sends his picture"

[December 5, 1912]

To Mr. Ficke and Mr. Bynner:

Mr. Earle has acquainted me with your wild surmises. Gentlemen: I must convince you of your error; my reputation is at stake. I simply will not be a "brawny male." Not that I have an aversion to brawny males; *au contraire, au contraire.* But I cling to my femininity!

Is it that you consider brain and brawn so inseparable?—I have thought otherwise. Still, that is all a matter of personal opinion. But, gentlemen: When a woman insists that she is twenty, you must not, must not call her forty-five. That is more than wicked; it is indiscreet.

Mr. Ficke, you are a lawyer. I am very much afraid of lawyers. Spare me, kind sir! Take into consideration my youth—for I am indeed but twenty—and my fragility—for "I do protest I am a maid"—and—sleuth me no sleuths!

Seriously: I thank you also for the compliment you have unwittingly given me. For tho I do not yet aspire to be forty-five and brawny, if my verse so represents me, I am more gratified than I can say. When I was a little girl, this is what I thought and wrote:

Let me not shout into the world's great ear
Ere I have something for the world to hear.
Then let my message like an arrow dart
And pierce a way into the world's great
    heart.

You cannot know how much I appreciate what you have said about my *Renascence.*

If you should care to look up the April, 1907, number of *Current Literature,* you

Portrait of Edna St. Vincent Millay (1934) by Charles Ellis.
National Portrait Gallery, Washington, D.C./Courtesy Art Resource.

would find a review of my *Land of Romance* (near a review of Mr. Bynner's *Fair of My Fancy*). And you might be interested in Mr. Edward Wheeler's comment: "The poem which follows (by E. St. Vincent Millay) seems to me to be phenomenal. The author, whether boy or girl we do not know, is just fourteen years of age."

E. St. V. M.

P. S. The brawny male sends his picture. I *have* to laugh.

MAKING MEANINGS

First Thoughts

1. Do you recognize the feelings described in this poem? When have you ever had similar feelings?

Shaping Interpretations

2. Whom do you think the "we" in the poem refers to? What do lines 4–5 suggest about their feelings for each other?

3. Why do you think the people in the poem gave their money to the "shawl-covered head"? What does this action say about the power of love?

4. Identify the **metaphor** in line 12. What does this image reveal about the speaker's feelings?

5. Describe the poem's **meter** and **rhyme scheme**.

6. How would you describe the **tone** of "Recuerdo"? (You may find it easier to answer this question if you first read the poem aloud.)

READING SKILLS AND STRATEGIES

Appreciating Imagery

Imagery in poetry is more than decoration. It helps express the poet's feelings, and it evokes feelings in the reader. Imagery depends a great deal on the **connotations** of words—their suggestive power. For example, "smelled like a stable" in line 3 of Millay's "Recuerdo" might create a feeling of distaste in someone who despises the odor of stables. But for other readers, the image might evoke something pleasant—earthiness, the warmth of animals, the coziness of a place protected from the out-of-doors. The image would have been quite different if the poet had said "smelled of manure."

Try your hand at changing the effect Millay created with her words and images in the poem "Recuerdo."

a. In line 6, replace "blowing" with a word that creates a negative or unpleasant feeling.

b. In line 12, think of an image to replace "a bucketful of gold" that would make the rising sun seem unpleasant.

c. Think of the image suggested by the phrase "shawl-covered head." Replace that image with one suggesting that the woman is threatening or dangerous.

CHOICES: Building Your Portfolio

Writer's Notebook

1. Collecting Ideas for an Interpretive Essay

Nowadays, Millay's name is better known than her work. Some critics see her as lacking depth and complexity, in spite of her knack for simple, evocative descriptions of nature and human emotions. Jot down your own assessment of Millay's abilities, based on "Recuerdo." Save your notes for possible use in the Writer's Workshop on page 804.

Comparing Poems

2. Art and Life

The contrasts between America's most famous early-twentieth-century female poet (Millay) and America's most famous nineteenth-century female poet (Emily Dickinson) are interesting. Dickinson—quiet, reserved, and a social hermit—was an experimenter in poetry, a true original. Millay—socially unconventional and adventuresome—was more imitative and conservative as a poet. In a brief essay, contrast "Recuerdo" with at least one of Dickinson's poems (perhaps "Heart! We will forget him!" on page 374). Consider differences in **message, imagery, rhyme, meter,** and **tone.** Which poem do you prefer?

Creative Writing

3. Merry Memory

Review the Quickwrite you wrote before reading "Recuerdo," and use it as a springboard for a poem about a happy memory in your life. Your poem can be written as you like, rhymed or unrhymed, but it should have a **tone** and **rhythm** that convey joy and lightheartedness.

© Rollie McKenna.

Katherine Anne Porter

(1890–1980)

Katherine Anne Porter was born in a Texas log cabin. She was raised, mostly by her grandmother, as a member of a sprawling family on close terms with hardship and deprivation. Her schooling was fragmentary. In later life, Porter tended to embroider these plain origins with a certain romantic opulence, as though her past could be revised like a novel in progress.

The first of Porter's four marriages took place when she was sixteen. She was consistently impatient with lasting marital relationships, and yet she disliked being alone. Her early years were a struggle to define herself as an individual, as a Southern woman, and as the writer that, so very slowly, she was becoming.

After her Texas youth, Porter traveled widely, living at various times in the West, New York City's Greenwich Village, New England, Washington, Mexico, Paris, and Berlin. She supported herself as a newspaper reporter and editor and as a translator of French and Spanish literature.

As a creative writer, Porter was largely self-taught. She became well read and had a natural talent for clear, flowing language. She could tell a seemingly effortless story, combining a searching intelligence, honesty, sound psychology, a flawless memory, and a vivid sense of scene. The grace of her objective style concealed the labor that went into it. Porter worked slowly and painstakingly, and she did not begin publishing until she was over thirty. Her first book of stories, *Flowering Judas* (1930), grew out of her recollections of her experiences in Mexico immediately after World War I. This collection won her a critical reputation as a stylist.

Much of Porter's work presents Southern women caught up in a web of custom and obligation. Her main themes include the burden of past evil and the strain with which that evil holds us captive in the present. Miranda, the clearly autobiographical central figure of so many of her stories, is forever trying to separate the fictions of family legend from objective truth. She knows that people do not always tell the truth, and she is skeptical of the romantic sheen with which they disguise the realities of poverty and sexuality.

With the publication of her finest story collection, *Pale Horse, Pale Rider* (1939), Porter's growing audience eagerly awaited a promised novel. In 1941, Porter began her novel, titled *Ship of Fools*. The novel takes place during the early days of Hitler's rise to power and chronicles the passage of a steamer ship whose passengers, in escaping their loneliness, search for fantasy rather than friendship or love. *Ship of Fools* is really about the seeds of World War II—a bitter portrait of the Nazi state and the human race's capacity for cruelty. When it finally appeared in 1962, the novel enjoyed a wide popular success. It was followed by the many awards and tributes (including the National Book Award and the Pulitzer Prize) that embellished the final years of Porter's long life.

HRW go.hrw.com
LE0 11-14

Before You Read

THE JILTING OF GRANNY WEATHERALL

Make the Connection

Alive in Memory

Most of the people we know and come across in the course of a day are looking ahead. Even for those in middle or old age, much of life seems to lie before them. What's the weather going to be next Sunday? Where shall we go on vacation?

Often, older persons can vividly recall events of long ago but have more difficulty remembering the recent past. That is surely true of Ellen Weatherall. Ellen is nearly eighty years old, and she has little interest in the future, which she knows is over for her. But the past! Now *there's* something to think about.

The point of this story is what Granny Weatherall recalls most vividly of all. It happened sixty years ago, Granny tells us, and the memory still hurts.

Reading Skills and Strategies

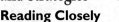

Reading Closely

You will need to be a good detective as you sift clues to learn who all the people in Granny's mind are. As you meet them, take notes on their relationship to Granny and note whether they are living or dead.

Here are some suggestions: Pay careful attention to **tenses of verbs,** since they help distinguish past from present. Also, pay attention to the use of **quotation marks**. They enclose words actually spoken as opposed to unspoken thoughts. Finally, be patient. If a character is mentioned but not immediately identified, wait until more clues are given.

Elements of Literature

Stream of Consciousness

Although this story uses some dialogue, it mostly employs a modernist narrative technique called **stream of consciousness.** This technique allows the reader to overhear Granny's thoughts and memories. These occur to her in no special order, her mind switching back and forth from what is going on around her to what happened long ago, including the central episode of the story.

> **S**tream of consciousness is a style of writing that conveys the inner—and sometimes chaotic—workings of a character's mind.
>
> *For more on Stream of Consciousness, see the Handbook of Literary Terms.*

The Jilting of Granny Weatherall

Katherine Anne Porter

She flicked her wrist neatly out of Doctor Harry's pudgy careful fingers and pulled the sheet up to her chin. The brat ought to be in knee breeches. Doctoring around the country with spectacles on his nose! "Get along now, take your schoolbooks and go. There's nothing wrong with me."

Doctor Harry spread a warm paw like a cushion on her forehead where the forked green vein danced and made her eyelids twitch. "Now, now, be a good girl, and we'll have you up in no time."

"That's no way to speak to a woman nearly eighty years old just because she's down. I'd have you respect your elders, young man."

"Well, Missy, excuse me." Doctor Harry patted her cheek. "But I've got to warn you, haven't I? You're a marvel, but you must be careful or you're going to be good and sorry."

"Don't tell me what I'm going to be. I'm on my feet now, morally speaking. It's Cornelia. I had to go to bed to get rid of her."

Her bones felt loose, and floated around in her skin, and Doctor Harry floated like a balloon around the foot of the bed. He floated and pulled down his waistcoat and swung his glasses on a cord. "Well, stay where you are, it certainly can't hurt you."

New England Woman (1895) by Cecilia Beaux. Oil on canvas (43″ × 24¼″).

The Pennsylvania Academy of the Fine Arts, Philadelphia. Joseph E. Temple Fund.

"Get along and doctor your sick," said Granny Weatherall. "Leave a well woman alone. I'll call for you when I want you. . . . Where were you forty years ago when I pulled through milk leg[1] and double pneumonia? You weren't even born. Don't let Cornelia lead you on," she shouted, because Doctor Harry appeared to float up to the ceiling and out. "I pay my own bills, and I don't throw my money away on nonsense!"

She meant to wave goodbye, but it was too much trouble. Her eyes closed of themselves, it was like a dark curtain drawn around the bed. The pillow rose and floated under her, pleasant as a hammock in a light wind. She listened to the leaves rustling outside the window. No, somebody was swishing newspapers: No, Cornelia and Doctor Harry were whispering together. She leaped broad awake, thinking they whispered in her ear.

"She was never like this, *never* like this!" "Well, what can we expect?" "Yes, eighty years old. . . ."

Well, and what if she was? She still had ears. It was like Cornelia to whisper around doors. She always kept things secret in such a public way. She was always being tactful and kind. Cornelia was dutiful; that was the trouble with her. Dutiful and good: "So good and dutiful," said Granny, "that I'd like to spank her." She saw herself spanking Cornelia and making a fine job of it.

"What'd you say, Mother?"

Granny felt her face tying up in hard knots.

"Can't a body think, I'd like to know?"

"I thought you might want something."

"I do. I want a lot of things. First off, go away and don't whisper."

She lay and drowsed, hoping in her sleep that the children would keep out and let her rest a minute. It had been a long day. Not that she was tired. It was always pleasant to snatch a minute now and then. There was always so much to be done, let me see: tomorrow.

Tomorrow was far away and there was nothing to trouble about. Things were finished somehow when the time came; thank God there was always a little margin over for peace: Then a person could spread out the plan of life and tuck in the edges orderly. It was good to have everything clean and folded away, with the hairbrushes and tonic bottles sitting straight on the white embroidered linen: the day started without fuss and the pantry shelves laid out with rows of jelly glasses and brown jugs and white stone-china jars with blue whirligigs and words painted on them: coffee, tea, sugar, ginger, cinnamon, allspice: and the bronze clock with the lion on top nicely dusted off. The dust that lion could collect in twenty-four hours! The box in the attic with all those letters tied up, well, she'd have to go through that tomorrow. All those letters—George's letters and John's letters and her letters to them both—lying around for the children to find afterward made her uneasy. Yes, that would be tomorrow's business. No use to let them know how silly she had been once.

While she was rummaging around she found death in her mind and it felt clammy and unfamiliar. She had spent so much time preparing for death there was no need for bringing it up again. Let it take care of itself now. When she was sixty she had felt very old, finished, and went around making farewell trips to see her children and grandchildren, with a secret in her mind: This is the very last of your mother, children! Then she made her will and came down with a long fever. That was all just a notion like a lot of other things, but it was lucky too, for she had once for all got over the idea of dying for a long time. Now she couldn't be worried. She hoped she had better sense now. Her father had lived to be one hundred and two years old and had drunk a noggin[2] of strong hot toddy[3] on his last birthday. He told the reporters it was his daily habit, and he owed his long life to that. He had made quite a scandal and was very pleased about it. She believed she'd just plague Cornelia a little.

"Cornelia! Cornelia!" No footsteps, but a sudden hand on her cheek. "Bless you, where have you been?"

---

1. **milk leg:** painful swelling of the leg, usually as a result of an infection during childbirth.

2. **noggin:** mug.
3. **hot toddy:** drink made of liquor mixed with hot water, sugar, and spices.

- - - - - - - - - - - - - - - - - -

WORDS TO OWN

tactful (takt'fəl) *adj.*: skilled in saying the right thing.
margin (mär'jən) *n.*: extra amount.
clammy (klam'ē) *adj.*: cold and damp.
plague (plāg) *v.*: annoy.

- - - - - - - - - - - - - - - - - -

"Here, Mother."

"Well, Cornelia, I want a noggin of hot toddy."

"Are you cold, darling?"

"I'm chilly, Cornelia. Lying in bed stops the circulation. I must have told you that a thousand times."

Well, she could just hear Cornelia telling her husband that Mother was getting a little childish and they'd have to humor her. The thing that most annoyed her was that Cornelia thought she was deaf, dumb, and blind. Little hasty glances and tiny gestures tossed around her and over her head saying, "Don't cross her, let her have her way, she's eighty years old," and she sitting there as if she lived in a thin glass cage. Sometimes Granny almost made up her mind to pack up and move back to her own house where nobody could remind her every minute that she was old. Wait, wait, Cornelia, till your own children whisper behind your back!

In her day she had kept a better house and had got more work done. She wasn't too old yet for Lydia to be driving eighty miles for advice when one of the children jumped the track, and Jimmy still dropped in and talked things over: "Now, Mammy, you've a good business head, I want to know what you think of this? . . ." Old. Cornelia couldn't change the furniture around without asking. Little things, little things! They had been so sweet when they were little. Granny wished the old days were back again with the children young and everything to be done over. It had been a hard pull, but not too much for her. When she thought of all the food she had cooked, and all the clothes she had cut and sewed, and all the gardens she had made—well, the children showed it. There they were, made out of her, and they couldn't get away from that. Sometimes she wanted to see John again and point to them and say, Well, I didn't do so badly, did I? But that would have to wait. That was for tomorrow. She used to think of him as a man, but now all the children were older than their father, and he would be a child beside her if she saw him now. It seemed strange and there was something wrong in the idea. Why, he couldn't possibly recognize her. She had fenced in a hundred acres once, digging the postholes herself and clamping the wires with just a Negro boy to help. That changed a woman. John would be looking for a young woman with the peaked Spanish comb in her hair and the painted fan. Digging postholes changed a woman. Riding country roads in the winter when women had their babies was another thing: sitting up nights with sick horses and sick Negroes and sick children and hardly ever losing one. John, I hardly ever lost one of them! John would see that in a minute, that would be something he could understand, she wouldn't have to explain anything!

It made her feel like rolling up her sleeves and putting the whole place to rights again. No matter if Cornelia was determined to be everywhere at once, there were a great many things left undone on this place. She would start tomorrow and do them. It was good to be strong enough for everything, even if all you made melted and changed and slipped under your hands, so that by the time you finished you almost forgot what you were working for. What was it I set out to do? she asked herself intently, but she could not remember. A fog rose over the valley, she saw it marching across the creek swallowing the trees and moving up the hill like an army of ghosts. Soon it would be at the near edge of the orchard, and then it was time to go in and light the lamps. Come in, children, don't stay out in the night air.

Lighting the lamps had been beautiful. The children huddled up to her and breathed like little calves waiting at the bars in the twilight. Their eyes followed the match and watched the flame rise and settle in a blue curve, then they moved away from her. The lamp was lit, they didn't have to be scared and hang on to mother any more. Never, never, never more. God, for all my life I thank Thee. Without Thee, my God, I could never have done it. Hail, Mary, full of grace.

I want you to pick all the fruit this year and see that nothing is wasted. There's always someone who can use it. Don't let good things rot for want of using. You waste life when you waste good food. Don't let things get lost. It's bitter to lose things. Now, don't let me get to thinking, not when I am tired and taking a little nap before supper. . . .

The pillow rose about her shoulders and pressed against her heart and the memory was being squeezed out of it: Oh, push down the pillow, somebody: It would smother her if she tried to hold it. Such a fresh breeze blowing and such a green day with no threats in it. But he had not come, just the same. What does a woman do when she has put on the white veil and set out the white cake for a man and he doesn't come? She tried to remember. No, I swear he never harmed me but in that. He never harmed me but in that . . . and what if he did? There was the day, the day, but a whirl of dark smoke rose and covered it, crept up and over into the bright field where everything was planted so carefully in orderly rows. That was hell, she knew hell when she saw it. For sixty years she had prayed against remembering him and against losing her soul in the deep pit of hell, and now the two things were mingled in one and the thought of him was a smoky cloud from hell that moved and crept in her head when she had just got rid of Doctor Harry and was trying to rest a minute. Wounded vanity, Ellen, said a sharp voice in the top of her mind. Don't let your wounded vanity get the upper hand of you. Plenty of girls get jilted. You were jilted, weren't you? Then stand up to it. Her eyelids wavered and let in streamers of blue-gray light like tissue paper over her eyes. She must get up and pull the shades down or she'd never sleep. She was in bed again and the shades were not down. How could that happen? Better turn over, hide from the light, sleeping in the light gave you nightmares. "Mother, how do you feel now?" and a stinging wetness on her forehead. But I don't like having my face washed in cold water!

Hapsy? George? Lydia? Jimmy? No, Cornelia, and her features were swollen and full of little puddles. "They're coming, darling, they'll all be here soon." Go wash your face, child, you look funny.

Instead of obeying, Cornelia knelt down and put her head on the pillow. She seemed to be talking but there was no sound. "Well, are you tongue-tied? Whose birthday is it? Are you going to give a party?"

Cornelia's mouth moved urgently in strange shapes. "Don't do that, you bother me, daughter."

"Oh, no, Mother. Oh, no . . ."

Nonsense. It was strange about children. They disputed your every word. "No what, Cornelia?"

"Here's Doctor Harry."

"I won't see that boy again. He just left five minutes ago."

"That was this morning, Mother. It's night now. Here's the nurse."

"This is Doctor Harry, Mrs. Weatherall. I never saw you look so young and happy!"

"Ah, I'll never be young again—but I'd be happy if they'd let me lie in peace and get rested."

She thought she spoke up loudly, but no one answered. A warm weight on her forehead, a warm bracelet on her wrist, and a breeze went on whispering, trying to tell her something. A shuffle of leaves in the everlasting hand of God, He blew on them and they danced and rattled. "Mother, don't mind, we're going to give you a little hypodermic."[4] "Look here, daughter, how do ants get in this bed? I saw sugar ants yesterday." Did you send for Hapsy too?

It was Hapsy she really wanted. She had to go a long way back through a great many rooms to find Hapsy standing with a baby on her arm. She seemed to herself to be Hapsy also, and the baby on Hapsy's arm was Hapsy and himself and herself, all at once, and there was no surprise in the meeting. Then Hapsy melted from within and turned flimsy as gray gauze and the baby was a gauzy shadow, and Hapsy came up close and said, "I thought you'd never come," and looked at her very searchingly and said, "You haven't changed a bit!" They leaned forward to kiss, when Cornelia began whispering from a long way off, "Oh, is there anything you want to tell me? Is there anything I can do for you?"

Yes, she had changed her mind after sixty years and she would like to see George. I want you to find George. Find him and be sure to tell him I forgot him. I want him to know I had my husband just the same and my children and my house like any other woman. A good house too and a good husband that I loved and fine children out of him. Better than I hoped for even. Tell him I was given back everything he took away and more. Oh, no, oh, God, no, there was something else besides the house and the man and the children. Oh, surely they were not all? What was it? Something not given back. . . . Her breath crowded down under

---

4. **hypodermic:** injection of medicine.

WORDS TO OWN

vanity (van′ə·tē) *n*.: excessive pride.
jilted (jilt′id) *v*.: rejected (as a lover).
disputed (di·spyōōt′id) *v*.: contested.

Evening Light (1908) by Frank Benson. Oil on canvas (25 ¼″ × 30 ½″).

her ribs and grew into a monstrous frightening shape with cutting edges; it bored up into her head, and the agony was unbelievable: Yes, John, get the Doctor now, no more talk, my time has come.

When this one was born it should be the last. The last. It should have been born first, for it was the one she had truly wanted. Everything came in good time. Nothing left out, left over. She was strong, in three days she would be as well as ever. Better. A woman needed milk in her to have her full health.

"Mother, do you hear me?"

"I've been telling you—"

"Mother, Father Connolly's here."

"I went to Holy Communion only last week. Tell him I'm not so sinful as all that."

"Father just wants to speak to you."

He could speak as much as he pleased. It was like him to drop in and inquire about her soul as if it were a teething baby, and then stay on for a cup of tea and a round of cards and gossip. He always had a funny story of some sort, usually about an Irishman who made his little mistakes and confessed them, and the point lay in some absurd thing he would blurt out in the confessional showing his struggles between native piety and original sin.[5] Granny felt easy about her soul. Cornelia, where are your manners? Give Father Connolly a chair. She had her secret comfortable understanding with a few favorite saints who cleared a straight road to God for her. All as surely signed and sealed as the papers for the new Forty Acres. Forever . . . heirs and assigns forever. Since the day the wedding cake was not cut, but thrown

5. original sin: in Christian theology, the sin of disobedience committed by Adam and Eve, the first man and woman, which is passed on to all persons.

out and wasted. The whole bottom dropped out of the world, and there she was blind and sweating with nothing under her feet and the walls falling away. His hand had caught her under the breast, she had not fallen, there was the freshly polished floor with the green rug on it, just as before. He had cursed like a sailor's parrot and said, "I'll kill him for you." Don't lay a hand on him, for my sake leave something to God. "Now, Ellen, you must believe what I tell you. . . ."

So there was nothing, nothing to worry about any more, except sometimes in the night one of the children screamed in a nightmare, and they both hustled out shaking and hunting for the matches and calling, "There, wait a minute, here we are!" John, get the doctor now, Hapsy's time has come. But there was Hapsy standing by the bed in a white cap. "Cornelia, tell Hapsy to take off her cap. I can't see her plain."

Her eyes opened very wide and the room stood out like a picture she had seen somewhere. Dark colors with the shadows rising toward the ceiling in long angles. The tall black dresser gleamed with nothing on it but John's picture, enlarged from a little one, with John's eyes very black when they should have been blue. You never saw him, so how do you know how he looked? But the man insisted the copy was perfect, it was very rich and handsome. For a picture, yes, but it's not my husband. The table by the bed had a linen cover and a candle and a crucifix. The light was blue from Cornelia's silk lampshades. No sort of light at all, just <u>frippery</u>. You had to live forty years with kerosene lamps to appreciate honest electricity. She felt very strong and she saw Doctor Harry with a rosy <u>nimbus</u> around him.

"You look like a saint, Doctor Harry, and I vow that's as near as you'll ever come to it."

"She's saying something."

"I heard you, Cornelia. What's all this carrying-on?"

"Father Connolly's saying—"

Cornelia's voice staggered and bumped like a cart in a bad road. It rounded corners and turned back again and arrived nowhere. Granny stepped up in the cart very lightly and reached for the reins, but a man sat beside her and she knew him by his hands, driving the cart. She did not look in his face, for she knew without seeing, but looked instead down the road where the trees leaned over and

bowed to each other and a thousand birds were singing a Mass. She felt like singing too, but she put her hand in the bosom of her dress and pulled out a rosary, and Father Connolly murmured Latin in a very solemn voice and tickled her feet.[6] My God, will you stop that nonsense? I'm a married woman. What if he did run away and leave me to face the priest by myself? I found another a whole world better. I wouldn't have exchanged my husband for anybody except St. Michael[7] himself, and you may tell him that for me with a thank you in the bargain.

Light flashed on her closed eyelids, and a deep roaring shook her. Cornelia, is that lightning? I hear thunder. There's going to be a storm. Close all the windows. Call the children in. . . . "Mother, here we are, all of us." "Is that you, Hapsy?" "Oh, no, I'm Lydia. We drove as fast as we could." Their faces drifted above her, drifted away. The rosary fell out of her hands and Lydia put it back. Jimmy tried to help, their hands fumbled together, and Granny closed two fingers around Jimmy's thumb. Beads wouldn't do, it must be something alive. She was so amazed her thoughts ran round and round. So, my dear Lord, this is my death and I wasn't even thinking about it. My children have come to see me die. But I can't, it's not time. Oh, I always hated surprises. I wanted to give Cornelia the amethyst[8] set—Cornelia, you're to have the amethyst set, but Hapsy's to wear it when she wants, and, Doctor Harry, do shut up. Nobody sent for you. Oh, my dear Lord, do wait a minute. I meant to do something about the Forty Acres, Jimmy doesn't need it and Lydia will later on, with that worthless husband of hers. I meant to finish the altar cloth and send six bottles of wine to Sister Borgia for her dyspepsia.[9] I want to send six

6. **murmured . . . feet:** The priest is performing the sacramental last rites of the Roman Catholic Church, which include anointing the dying person's feet with oil.
7. **Michael:** most powerful of the four archangels in Jewish and Christian doctrine. In Christian art, he is usually depicted as a handsome knight in white armor.
8. **amethyst** (am′i·thist): purple or violet quartz gemstone, used in jewelry.
9. **dyspepsia** (dis·pep′sē·ə): indigestion.

- -

WORDS TO OWN

frippery (frip′ər·ē) *n.:* something showy, frivolous, or unnecessary.

nimbus (nim′bəs) *n.:* aura; halo.

- -

bottles of wine to Sister Borgia, Father Connolly, now don't let me forget.

Cornelia's voice made short turns and tilted over and crashed. "Oh, Mother, oh, Mother, oh, Mother . . ."

"I'm not going, Cornelia. I'm taken by surprise. I can't go."

You'll see Hapsy again. What about her? "I thought you'd never come." Granny made a long journey outward, looking for Hapsy. What if I don't find her? What then? Her heart sank down and down, there was no bottom to death, she couldn't come to the end of it. The blue light from Cornelia's lampshade drew into a tiny point in the center of her brain, it flickered and winked like an eye, quietly it fluttered and <u>dwindled</u>. Granny lay curled down within herself, amazed and watchful, staring at the point of light that was herself; her body was now only a deeper mass of shadow in an endless darkness and this darkness would curl around the light and swallow it up. God, give a sign!

For the second time there was no sign. Again no bridegroom and the priest in the house. She could not remember any other sorrow because this grief wiped them all away. Oh, no, there's nothing more cruel than this—I'll never forgive it. She stretched herself with a deep breath and blew out the light.

WORDS TO OWN
dwindled (dwin′dəld) v.: diminished.

Connections
A POEM

Conrad Aiken (1889–1973), an influential American writer, was concerned with how we construct a personal identity. He was a friend of T.S. Eliot's, and in the 1920s he helped establish Emily Dickinson's reputation as a major poet. Aiken often wrote poetry that mimicked a musical form or referred to music. The following lines are taken from a longer poem in which the speaker tries to come to terms with the loss of a person he loved dearly.

from Discordants

Conrad Aiken

Music I heard with you was more than music,
And bread I broke with you was more than bread;
Now that I am without you, all is desolate;
All that was once so beautiful is dead.

5 Your hands once touched this table and this silver,
And I have seen your fingers hold this glass.
These things do not remember you, beloved,—
And yet your touch upon them will not pass.

For it was in my heart you moved among them,
10 And blessed them with your hands and with your eyes;
And in my heart they will remember always,—
They knew you once, O beautiful and wise.

The Green Blouse (1919) by Pierre Bonnard (1867–1947), French. Oil on canvas (40⅛″ × 26⅞″).

The Metropolitan Museum of Art, Mr. and Mrs. Henry Ittleson, Jr., Fund, 1963 (63.64). Photograph © 1993 The Metropolitan Museum of Art.

MAKING MEANINGS

First Thoughts

1. Granny's last thoughts revolve around a rejection that occurred six decades before. Do you find this believable? Why or why not?

Shaping Interpretations

2. When Granny recalls George, she thinks, "Find him and be sure to tell him I forgot him" (page 708). What is **ironic** in Granny's thought? How did George really affect her life?

3. **Ambiguity** is a technique by which a writer deliberately suggests two or more different, and possibly conflicting, meanings in a work. Granny feels that she was "given back everything" that was taken away by the jilting. Yet, she then says that something was "not given back." Identify what that something might be. What other ambiguities do you find in the story? How does Porter's use of **stream of consciousness** contribute to these ambiguities?

4. From what **point of view** is this story told? How would the effect of the story have been different if another point of view had been used?

5. What does Granny mean when she thinks, "That was hell, she knew hell when she saw it" (page 708)? How does she feel about heaven?

6. The end of the story suggests that Granny is jilted again. Who jilts her this time? How does Granny feel at this moment of revelation?

7. Read Conrad Aiken's lines from "Discordants" (see **Connections,** page 711). How would you compare the speaker's feelings toward the lost loved one with Granny's feelings about George?

Reading Check

a. Review the notes you made as you read the story. When the story opens, who is with Granny?

b. What are the names of Granny's children?

c. Which child was Granny's favorite? Is she still alive—or did she even exist at all?

d. What incident does the **title** of the story refer to?

CHOICES: Building Your Portfolio

Writer's Notebook

1. Collecting Ideas for an Interpretive Essay

Porter's story contains enough **ambiguities** to give a reader plenty of food for thought. Jot down some questions you have about the meanings of this story. Keep your notes for possible use in the Writer's Workshop on page 804.

Describing a Character

2. Portrait of Granny

Write an essay that tells Granny Weatherall's life story, based on the information in Porter's story. Include a description of her personality. Before you write, organize the information about Granny in a chart like the following one.

1. Key events in Granny's life	
2. Kind of life she led	
3. Attitude toward other people	
4. Feelings about death	

Creative Writing

3. Too Late the Bridegroom

George, now eighty years old, has returned just in time to visit Ellen at her bedside. Write a brief **monologue** in which you reproduce George's thoughts as he looks at the woman he jilted sixty years earlier. Use **stream of consciousness** to show George's flow of thoughts.

William Faulkner

(1897–1962)

Brown Brothers.

Yoknapatawpha County, Mississippi, is surely the hardest of American literary place names to pronounce. Still, it is wise to learn how (yäk′nə·pə·tô′fə), for it is famous as the imagined world of William Faulkner, the scene of his most celebrated novels and stories. Imaginary Yoknapatawpha is similar in many ways to the actual impoverished farmland, with its red clay hills, that rings Oxford, Mississippi, home of the state's main university. It was there that William's father, Murry Falkner (William added the *u* to the family name), ran a livery stable and later became the university's business manager. William Faulkner lived and wrote there throughout most of his life.

The South Provides a Theme

Faulkner was a mediocre student and quit high school in the tenth grade, but he read widely and he wrote poetry. At the outbreak of World War I, the United States Army rejected him because he failed to meet their height and weight requirements. However, he enlisted in the Royal Air Force of Canada and trained for flight duty, only to see the war end before he was commissioned. Returning to Oxford after the war, he took some courses at the university and did poorly in English. With neither profession nor skill, and a marked distaste for regular employment, he seemed a moody and puzzling young man to his neighbors.

Faulkner took several short-lived jobs, among them that of postmaster for the university. Resigning from this job, he wrote, "I will be damned if I propose to be at the beck and call of every itinerant scoundrel who has two cents to invest in a postage stamp."

In 1924, Faulkner left Oxford for New Orleans, where he met Sherwood Anderson, who had attracted much attention with the publication of *Winesburg, Ohio* (1919), his study of small-town life. Impressed and encouraged by Anderson, Faulkner tried his hand at fiction. In five months, he completed a first novel, *Soldier's Pay,* a self-conscious story about the lost generation. Thereafter, Faulkner wrote with a tireless energy.

Within the next three years, Faulkner found his great theme: the American South as a microcosm for the universal themes of time, the passions of the human heart, and the destruction of the wilderness. Faulkner saw the South as a nation unto itself, with a strong sense of its noble past and an array of myths by which it clung to its pride, despite the humiliating defeat of the Civil War and the acceptance of the distasteful values of an industrial North. Faulkner started to explore these themes in *Sartoris* (the first story set in mythical Yoknapatawpha) and *The Sound and the Fury,* two novels published within months of each other in 1929. *The Sound and the Fury* was a milestone in American literature, owing to Faulkner's bold manipulation of point of view and its stream-of-consciousness narrative technique.

In the decade that followed, Faulkner produced a succession of dazzling books: *As I Lay Dying* (1930), *Sanctuary* (1931), *Light in August* (1932), *Absalom, Absalom!* (1936)—considered by many readers to be his finest work—*The Unvanquished* (1938), and *The Hamlet* (1940). These works reveal Faulkner as equally skillful in the tragic or comic mode. He portrayed the South accurately, perceptively, and with a poignant ambivalence—on the one hand affectionate, on the other critical. He once said of the South, "Well, I love it and I hate it."

Faulkner's Fictional Families

Faulkner described his South through fictional families who often reappear from novel to novel. They resemble trees, attaining grandeur, casting much shade, and then growing old and dry, crumbling as the seedlings of social change grow up around their fallen limbs and stumps.

There are the aristocratic Sartorises, who resemble Faulkner's own ancestors. Colonel John Sartoris, for example, was patterned after Faulkner's great-grandfather, who rose from rural poverty to command the Second Mississippi Regiment, built a railroad, wrote a best-selling novel, and was murdered on the street by his business partner.

There are also the Compsons, who incorporate some characteristics of the author's immediate family. They form the centerpiece of *The Sound and the Fury,* which records the decline of a once great clan, and with it the passing of a traditionally Southern world.

As I Lay Dying tells of the poor-white Bundren family and its efforts to bring the body of its matriarch, Addie, back to the town of Jefferson for burial. The novel reveals these humble people as more enduring than their social betters. *Light in August* concerns other Southern families and explores the problem of racism through the character of the protagonist, Joe Christmas. Although he appears white, Joe's racial heritage is mixed. His failure to find a place in either white or black society leads to his murder.

And, finally, there is Faulkner's unforgettable portrayal of the Snopeses—a sprawling clan of irresponsible, depraved, socially ambitious varmints who rise from the dust and cheat their way to respectability and wealth, destroying the old values of aristocracy and peasantry alike.

Faulkner often forces the reader to piece together events from a seemingly random and fragmentary series of impressions experienced by a variety of narrators. Faulkner's style often strains conventional syntax; he might pile up clause upon clause in an effort to capture the complexity of thought. In *The Sound and the Fury,* for example, he entrusts part of the narra-

> **M**oral dilemmas are the perennial mysteries of human existence.

tive to the chaotic intelligence of one of the sons, Benjy Compson. But the efforts of patient readers are richly repaid, as they discover in book after book a mythical universe in which the moral dilemmas are the perennial mysteries of human existence.

"The Dream of Perfection"

By the time he received the Nobel Prize in literature in 1950, Faulkner's best work was behind him. After his richly productive period (1929–1942), he wrote many more stories and novels, including *Intruder in the Dust* (1948), *Requiem for a Nun* (1951), *A Fable* (1954), *The Town* (1957), *The Mansion* (1959), and *The Reivers* (1962). These works displayed his virtuosity and willingness to experiment, but his powers were clearly diminished.

Faulkner's writing surely diverged from that of his realist contemporaries—notably Ernest Hemingway, whom he put at the bottom of his own list of the best American contemporary writers. "I said we were all failures. All of us had failed to match the dream of perfection. . . . I rated Hemingway last because he stayed within what he knew. He did it fine, but he didn't try for the impossible."

Faulkner had this to say about the qualities of a novel: "The only mistake with any novel is if it fails to create pleasure. That it is not true is irrelevant; a novel is to be enjoyed. A book that fails to create enjoyment is not a good one."

Debate will always rage about the position of figures in our literary pantheon, but critics are now unanimous in their opinion that Faulkner is one of the greatest of all American novelists. There is certainly no argument over William Faulkner's preeminence among Southern writers. As Flannery O'Connor once put it: "The presence alone of Faulkner in our midst makes a great difference in what the writer can and cannot permit himself to do. Nobody wants his mule and wagon stalled on the same track the Dixie Limited is roaring down."

Before You Read

A ROSE FOR EMILY

Make the Connection

Skeletons in the Closet

Faulkner, the master of the Southern Gothic tale, knew first-hand the old American South and its powerful social traditions. It's all here in "A Rose for Emily"—the small-town social castes, the changing social values, the politeness with which people go about the routine of life, and the struggles they undergo to find joy in it.

The facts of this story tell a lurid tale, as sensational as any you will see headlined in those scandal sheets displayed at the supermarket checkouts. But what primarily turns this account of outrageous human behavior into literature is the relationship between the event and its setting. As the story of one eccentric woman unfolds, we learn some important truths about the rest of her community: its loyalty to family and the past, its pride, its faithfulness to old values, its fierce independence, and its scorn for all that is new and widely accepted.

Reading Skills and Strategies

Taking Notes on a Character

Miss Emily has a quality we all share to some degree: a tendency to retreat from a reality we don't like into a fantasy world where we can have things our own way. But is her bizarre behavior merely madness, or an extension of qualities admired in her community? As you read the story, take notes on Miss Emily's characteristics. Include your ideas about the motives for her strange actions.

Elements of Literature

Setting

Setting is the time and location in which a story takes place. Setting also includes the customs and social conditions of a time—including, in this case, such things as racial stereotyping. If parts of this story give off an offensive odor, it comes only in part from Miss Emily's house and her horrible deed: It comes also from the racial slurs used by some of the characters. Although we find this language offensive, we must remember that Faulkner used it to portray as realistically as

possible a racially segregated town of the rural South in the early part of the twentieth century.

> **S**etting is the time and location in which a story takes place.
>
> *For more on Setting, see the Handbook of Literary Terms.*

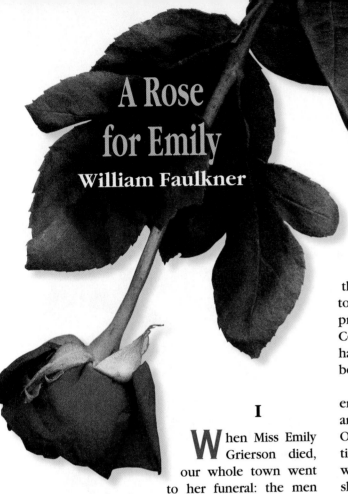

A Rose for Emily

William Faulkner

I

When Miss Emily Grierson died, our whole town went to her funeral: the men through a sort of respectful affection for a fallen monument, the women mostly out of curiosity to see the inside of her house, which no one save an old manservant—a combined gardener and cook—had seen in at least ten years.

It was a big, squarish frame house that had once been white, decorated with cupolas[1] and spires and scrolled balconies in the heavily lightsome style of the seventies,[2] set on what had once been our most select street. But garages and cotton gins had encroached and obliterated even the august names of that neighborhood; only Miss Emily's house was left, lifting its stubborn and coquettish decay above the cotton wagons and the gasoline pumps—an eyesore among eyesores. And now Miss Emily had gone to join the representatives of those august names where they lay in the cedar-bemused cemetery among the ranked and anonymous graves of Union and Confederate soldiers who fell at the battle of Jefferson.

Alive, Miss Emily had been a tradition, a duty, and a care; a sort of hereditary obligation upon the town, dating from that day in 1894 when Colonel Sartoris, the mayor—he who fathered the edict that no Negro woman should appear on the streets without an apron—remitted[3] her taxes, the dispensation dating from the death of her father on into perpetuity. Not that Miss Emily would have accepted charity. Colonel Sartoris invented an involved tale to the effect that Miss Emily's father had loaned money to the town, which the town, as a matter of business, preferred this way of repaying. Only a man of Colonel Sartoris' generation and thought could have invented it, and only a woman could have believed it.

When the next generation, with its more modern ideas, became mayors and aldermen, this arrangement created some little dissatisfaction. On the first of the year they mailed her a tax notice. February came, and there was no reply. They wrote her a formal letter, asking her to call at the sheriff's office at her convenience. A week later the mayor wrote her himself, offering to call or to send his car for her, and received in reply a note on paper of an archaic shape in a thin, flowing calligraphy in faded ink, to the effect that she no longer went out at all. The tax notice was also enclosed, without comment.

They called a special meeting of the Board of Aldermen. A deputation waited upon her, knocked at the door through which no visitor had passed since she ceased giving china-painting lessons eight or ten years earlier. They were admitted by the old Negro into a dim hall from which a stairway mounted into still more shadow. It smelled of dust and disuse—a close, dank smell. The Negro led them into the parlor. It was furnished in heavy, leather-covered furniture. When

---

3. **remitted:** refrained from enforcing payment of.

---

1. **cupolas** (kyo͞o′pə·ləz): small, dome-shaped structures built on a roof.
2. **the seventies:** the 1870s.

My Mother (1921)
by George Wesley Bellows.
American (1882–1925).
Oil on canvas
(210.9 cm × 124.5 cm).

the Negro opened the blinds of one window they could see that the leather was cracked; and when they sat down, a faint dust rose sluggishly about their thighs spinning with slow motes in the single sun-ray. On a tarnished gilt easel before the fireplace stood a crayon portrait of Miss Emily's father.

They rose when she entered—a small, fat woman in black, with a thin gold chain descending to her waist and vanishing into her belt, leaning on an ebony cane with a tarnished gold head. Her skeleton was small and spare; perhaps that was why what would have been merely plumpness in another was obesity in her. She looked bloated, like a body long submerged in motionless water, and of that pallid hue. Her eyes, lost in the fatty ridges of her face, looked like two small pieces of coal pressed into a lump of dough as they moved from one face to another while the visitors stated their errand.

She did not ask them to sit. She just stood in the door and listened quietly until the spokesman came to a stumbling halt. Then they could hear the invisible watch ticking at the end of the gold chain.

Her voice was dry and cold. "I have no taxes in Jefferson. Colonel Sartoris explained it to me. Perhaps one of you can gain access to the city records and satisfy yourselves."

"But we have. We are the city authorities, Miss Emily. Didn't you get a notice from the sheriff, signed by him?"

"I received a paper, yes," Miss Emily said. "Perhaps he considers himself the sheriff . . . I have no taxes in Jefferson."

"But there is nothing on the books to show that, you see. We must go by the—"

"See Colonel Sartoris. I have no taxes in Jefferson."

"But, Miss Emily—"

"See Colonel Sartoris." (Colonel Sartoris had been dead almost ten years.) "I have no taxes in Jefferson. Tobe!" The Negro appeared. "Show these gentlemen out."

II

So she vanquished them, horse and foot, just as she had vanquished their fathers thirty years before about the smell. That was two years after her father's death and a short time after her sweetheart—the one we believed would marry her—had deserted her. After her father's death she went out very little; after her sweetheart went away, people hardly saw her at all. A few of the ladies had the temerity[4] to call, but were not received, and the only sign of life about the place was the Negro man—a young man then—going in and out with a market basket.

"Just as if a man—any man—could keep a kitchen properly," the ladies said; so they were not surprised when the smell developed. It was another link between the gross, teeming world and the high and mighty Griersons.

A neighbor, a woman, complained to the mayor, Judge Stevens, eighty years old.

"But what will you have me do about it, madam?" he said.

"Why, send her word to stop it," the woman said. "Isn't there a law?"

"I'm sure that won't be necessary," Judge Stevens said. "It's probably just a snake or a rat that nigger of hers killed in the yard. I'll speak to him about it."

The next day he received two more complaints, one from a man who came in diffident deprecation.[5] "We really must do something about it, Judge. I'd be the last one in the world to bother Miss Emily, but we've got to do something." That night the Board of Aldermen met— three graybeards and one younger man, a member of the rising generation.

"It's simple enough," he said. "Send her word to have her place cleaned up. Give her a certain time to do it in, and if she don't . . ."

"Dammit, sir," Judge Stevens said, "will you accuse a lady to her face of smelling bad?"

So the next night, after midnight, four men crossed Miss Emily's lawn and slunk about the house like burglars, sniffing along the base of the brickwork and at the cellar openings while one of them performed a regular sowing motion with his hand out of a sack slung from his shoulder. They broke open the cellar door and sprinkled lime there, and in all the outbuildings. As they recrossed the lawn, a window that had been dark was lighted and Miss Emily sat in it, the light

4. **temerity:** foolish boldness; rashness.
5. **diffident deprecation:** timid disapproval.

behind her, and her upright torso motionless as that of an idol. They crept quietly across the lawn and into the shadow of the locusts that lined the street. After a week or two the smell went away.

That was when people had begun to feel really sorry for her. People in our town, remembering how old lady Wyatt, her great-aunt, had gone completely crazy at last, believed that the Griersons held themselves a little too high for what they really were. None of the young men were quite good enough for Miss Emily and such. We had long thought of them as a tableau,[6] Miss Emily a slender figure in white in the background, her father a spraddled silhouette in the foreground, his back to her and clutching a horsewhip, the two of them framed by the back-flung front door. So when she got to be thirty and was still single, we were not pleased exactly, but <u>vindicated</u>; even with insanity in the family she wouldn't have turned down all of her chances if they had really materialized.

When her father died, it got about that the house was all that was left to her; and in a way, people were glad. At last they could pity Miss Emily. Being left alone, and a <u>pauper</u>, she had become humanized. Now she too would know the old thrill and the old despair of a penny more or less.

The day after his death all the ladies prepared to call at the house and offer condolence and aid, as is our custom. Miss Emily met them at the door, dressed as usual and with no trace of grief on her face. She told them that her father was not dead. She did that for three days, with the ministers calling on her, and the doctors, trying to persuade her to let them dispose of the body. Just as they were about to resort to law and force, she broke down, and they buried her father quickly.

We did not say she was crazy then. We believed she had to do that. We remembered all the young men her father had driven away, and we knew that with nothing left, she would have to cling to that which had robbed her, as people will.

III

She was sick for a long time. When we saw her again, her hair was cut short, making her look like a girl, with a vague resemblance to those angels in colored church windows—sort of tragic and serene.

The town had just let the contracts for paving the sidewalks, and in the summer after her father's death they began the work. The construction company came with niggers and mules and machinery, and a foreman named Homer Barron, a Yankee—a big, dark, ready man, with a big voice and eyes lighter than his face. The little boys would follow in groups to hear him cuss the niggers, and the niggers singing in time to the rise and fall of picks. Pretty soon he knew everybody in town. Whenever you heard a lot of laughing anywhere about the square, Homer Barron would be in the center of the group. Presently we began to see him and Miss Emily on Sunday afternoons driving in the yellow-wheeled buggy and the matched team of bays from the livery stable.

At first we were glad that Miss Emily would have an interest, because the ladies all said, "Of course a Grierson would not think seriously of a Northerner, a day laborer." But there were still others, older people, who said that even grief could not cause a real lady to forget *noblesse oblige*[7]—without calling it *noblesse oblige*. They just said, "Poor Emily. Her kinsfolk should come to her." She had some kin in Alabama; but years ago her father had fallen out with them over the estate of old lady Wyatt, the crazy woman, and there was no communication between the two families. They had not even been represented at the funeral.

And as soon as the old people said, "Poor Emily," the whispering began. "Do you suppose it's really so?" they said to one another. "Of course it is. What else could . . ." This behind their hands; rustling of craned[8] silk and satin behind jalousies[9]

7. *noblesse oblige* (nō·bles′ ô·blēzh′): French for "nobility obliges"; that is, the supposed obligation of the upper classes to act nobly or kindly toward the lower classes.
8. **craned:** stretched.
9. **jalousies** (jal′ə·sēz′): windows, shades, or doors made of overlapping, adjustable slats.

- -

WORDS TO OWN

vindicated (vin′də·kāt′id) v. used as *adj.*: proved correct.
pauper (pô′pər) n.: extremely poor person.

- -

6. **tableau:** set scene, as in the theater.

That Which I Should Have Done I Did Not Do (1931–1941)
by Ivan Le Lorraine Albright (1897–1983). American.
Oil on canvas (246.5 cm × 91.5 cm).

closed upon the sun of Sunday afternoon as the thin, swift, clop-clop-clop of the matched team passed: "Poor Emily."

She carried her head high enough—even when we believed that she was fallen. It was as if she demanded more than ever the recognition of her dignity as the last Grierson; as if it had wanted that touch of earthiness to reaffirm her imperviousness. Like when she bought the rat poison, the arsenic. That was over a year after they had begun to say "Poor Emily," and while the two female cousins were visiting her.

"I want some poison," she said to the druggist. She was over thirty then, still a slight woman, though thinner than usual, with cold, haughty black eyes in a face the flesh of which was strained across the temples and about the eye-sockets as you imagine a lighthouse-keeper's face ought to look. "I want some poison," she said.

"Yes, Miss Emily. What kind? For rats and such? I'd recom—"

"I want the best you have. I don't care what kind."

The druggist named several. "They'll kill anything up to an elephant. But what you want is—"

"Arsenic," Miss Emily said. "Is that a good one?"

"Is . . . arsenic? Yes, ma'am. But what you want—"

"I want arsenic."

The druggist looked down at her. She looked back at him, erect, her face like a strained flag. "Why, of course," the druggist said. "If that's what you want. But the law requires you to tell what you are going to use it for."

Miss Emily just stared at him, her head tilted back in order to look him eye for eye, until he looked away and went and got the arsenic and wrapped it up. The Negro delivery boy brought her the package; the druggist didn't come back. When she opened the package at home there was written on the box, under the skull and bones: "For rats."

IV

So the next day we all said, "She will kill herself"; and we said it would be the best thing. When she had first begun to be seen with Homer Barron, we had said, "She will marry him." Then we said, "She will persuade him yet," because Homer himself had remarked—he liked men, and it was known that he drank with the younger men in the Elks' Club—that he was not a marrying man. Later we said, "Poor Emily," behind the jalousies as they passed on Sunday afternoon in the glittering buggy, Miss Emily with her head high and Homer Barron with his hat cocked and a cigar in his teeth, reins and whip in a yellow glove.

Then some of the ladies began to say that it was a disgrace to the town and a bad example to the young people. The men did not want to interfere, but at last the ladies forced the Baptist minister—Miss Emily's people were Episcopal—to call upon her. He would never divulge what happened during that interview, but he refused to go back again. The next Sunday they again drove about the streets, and the following day the minister's wife wrote to Miss Emily's relations in Alabama.

So she had blood-kin under her roof again and we sat back to watch developments. At first nothing happened. Then we were sure that they were to be married. We learned that Miss Emily had been to the jeweler's and ordered a man's toilet set[10] in silver, with the letters H. B. on each piece. Two days later we learned that she had bought a complete outfit of men's clothing, including a nightshirt, and we said, "They are married." We were really glad. We were glad because the two female cousins were even more Grierson than Miss Emily had ever been.

So we were not surprised when Homer Barron—the streets had been finished some time since—was gone. We were a little disappointed that there was not a public blowing-off, but we believed that he had gone on to prepare for Miss Emily's coming, or to give her a chance to get rid of the cousins. (By that time it was a cabal,[11] and we were all Miss Emily's allies to help circumvent the cousins.) Sure enough, after another week they departed. And, as we had expected all along, within three days Homer Barron was back in town. A neighbor saw the Negro man admit him at the kitchen door at dusk one evening.

And that was the last we saw of Homer Barron. And of Miss Emily for some time. The Negro man went in and out with the market basket, but the front door remained closed. Now and then we would see her at a window for a moment, as the men did that night when they sprinkled the lime, but for almost six months she did not appear on the streets. Then we knew that this was to be expected too; as if that quality of her father which had thwarted her woman's life so many times had been too virulent and too furious to die.

When we next saw Miss Emily, she had grown fat and her hair was turning gray. During the next few years it grew grayer and grayer until it attained an even pepper-and-salt iron-gray, when it ceased turning. Up to the day of her death at seventy-four it was still that vigorous iron-gray, like the hair of an active man.

From that time on her front door remained closed, save for a period of six or seven years, when she was about forty, during which she gave lessons in china-painting. She fitted up a studio in one of the downstairs rooms, where the daughters and granddaughters of Colonel Sartoris' contemporaries were sent to her with the same regularity and in the same spirit that they were sent to church on Sundays with a twenty-five-cent piece for the collection plate. Meanwhile her taxes had been remitted.

Then the newer generation became the backbone and the spirit of the town, and the painting pupils grew up and fell away and did not send their children to her with boxes of color and tedious brushes and pictures cut from the ladies' magazines. The front door closed upon the last one and remained closed for good. When the town got free postal delivery, Miss Emily alone refused to let them fasten the metal numbers above her door and attach a mailbox to it. She would not listen to them.

Daily, monthly, yearly we watched the Negro grow grayer and more stooped, going in and out with the market basket. Each December we sent her a tax notice, which would be returned by the post office a week later, unclaimed. Now and then we would see her in one of the downstairs windows—she had evidently shut up the top floor of

10. **toilet set:** set of grooming aids, such as a hand mirror, hairbrush, and comb.
11. **cabal** (kə·bäl′): small group involved in a secret intrigue.

WORDS TO OWN

circumvent (sʉr′kəm·vent′) v.: to get the better of by craft or ingenuity.
virulent (vir′yoo·lənt) adj.: full of hate; venomous.

the house—like the carven torso of an idol in a niche, looking or not looking at us, we could never tell which. Thus she passed from generation to generation—dear, inescapable, impervious, <u>tranquil</u>, and perverse.

And so she died. Fell ill in the house filled with dust and shadows, with only a <u>doddering</u> Negro man to wait on her. We did not even know she was sick; we had long since given up trying to get any information from the Negro. He talked to no one, probably not even to her, for his voice had grown harsh and rusty, as if from disuse.

She died in one of the downstairs rooms, in a heavy walnut bed with a curtain, her gray head propped on a pillow yellow and moldy with age and lack of sunlight.

V

The Negro met the first of the ladies at the front door and let them in, with their hushed, sibilant[12] voices and their quick, curious glances, and then he disappeared. He walked right through the house and out the back and was not seen again.

The two female cousins came at once. They held the funeral on the second day, with the town coming to look at Miss Emily beneath a mass of bought flowers, with the crayon face of her father musing profoundly above the bier[13] and the ladies sibilant and macabre;[14] and the very old men— some in their brushed Confederate uniforms—on the porch and the lawn, talking of Miss Emily as if she had been a contemporary of theirs, believing that they had danced with her and courted her perhaps, confusing time with its mathematical progression, as the old do, to whom all the past is not a diminishing road but, instead, a huge meadow which no winter ever quite touches, divided from them now by the narrow bottle-neck of the most recent decade of years.

Already we knew that there was one room in that region above stairs which no one had seen in forty years, and which would have to be forced. They waited until Miss Emily was decently in the ground before they opened it.

The violence of breaking down the door

12. **sibilant** (sib′əl·ənt): hissing.
13. **bier** (bir): coffin and its supporting platform.
14. **macabre** (mə·käb′rə): focused on the gruesome; horrible.

seemed to fill this room with pervading dust. A thin, <u>acrid</u> pall as of the tomb seemed to lie everywhere upon this room decked and furnished as for a bridal: upon the <u>valance</u> curtains of faded rose color, upon the rose-shaded lights, upon the dressing table, upon the delicate array of crystal and the man's toilet things backed with tarnished silver, silver so tarnished that the monogram was obscured. Among them lay a collar and tie, as if they had just been removed, which, lifted, left upon the surface a pale crescent in the dust. Upon a chair hung the suit, carefully folded; beneath it the two mute shoes and the discarded socks.

The man himself lay in the bed.

For a long while we just stood there, looking down at the profound and fleshless grin. The body had apparently once lain in the attitude of an embrace, but now the long sleep that outlasts love, that conquers even the grimace of love, had cuckolded[15] him. What was left of him, rotted beneath what was left of the nightshirt, had become inextricable from the bed in which he lay; and upon him and upon the pillow beside him lay that even coating of the patient and biding dust.

Then we noticed that in the second pillow was the indentation of a head. One of us lifted something from it, and leaning forward, that faint and invisible dust dry and acrid in the nostrils, we saw a long strand of iron-gray hair.

15. **cuckolded** (kuk′əld·id): betrayed, as in the sense of a husband whose wife has been unfaithful.

WORDS TO OWN

tranquil (tran′kwil) *adj.:* calm; quiet.
doddering (däd′ər·iŋ) *adj.:* shaky; trembling from old age.
acrid (ak′rid) *adj.:* bitter; irritating.
valance (val′əns) *n.* used as *adj.:* short decorative drapery.

Nobel Prize Acceptance Speech, 1950

I feel that this award was not made to me as a man, but to my work—a life's work in the agony and sweat of the human spirit, not for glory and least of all for profit, but to create out of the materials of the human spirit something which did not exist before. So this award is only mine in trust. It will not be difficult to find a dedication for the money part of it commensurate with the purpose and significance of its origin. But I would like to do the same with the acclaim too, by using this moment as a pinnacle from which I might be listened to by the young men and women already dedicated to the same anguish and travail, among whom is already that one who will someday stand here where I am standing.

Our tragedy today is a general and universal physical fear so long sustained by now that we can even bear it. There are no longer problems of the spirit. There is only the question: When will I be blown up? Because of this, the young man or woman writing today has forgotten the problems of the human heart in conflict with itself which alone can make good writing because only that is worth writing about, worth the agony and the sweat.

He must learn them again. He must teach himself that the basest of all things is to be afraid; and, teaching himself that, forget it forever, leaving no room in his workshop for anything but the old verities and truths of the heart, the old universal truths lacking which any story is ephemeral and doomed—love and honor and pity and pride and compassion and sacrifice. Until he does so, he labors under a curse. He writes not of love but of lust, of defeats in which nobody loses anything of value, of victories without hope and, worst of all, without pity or compassion. His griefs grieve on no universal bones, leaving no scars. He writes not of the heart but of the glands.

William Faulkner (right) receiving the Nobel Prize in literature (1950). AP/Wide World Photos.

Until he relearns these things, he will write as though he stood among and watched the end of man. I decline to accept the end of man. It is easy enough to say that man is immortal simply because he will endure: that when the last dingdong of doom has clanged and faded from the last worthless rock hanging tideless in the last red and dying evening, that even then there will still be one more sound: that of his puny inexhaustible voice, still talking. I refuse to accept this. I believe that man will not merely endure: he will prevail. He is immortal, not because he alone among creatures has an inexhaustible voice, but because he has a soul, a spirit capable of compassion and sacrifice and endurance. The poet's, the writer's, duty is to write about these things. It is his privilege to help man endure by lifting his heart, by reminding him of the courage and honor and hope and pride and compassion and pity and sacrifice which have been the glory of his past. The poet's voice need not merely be the record of man, it can be one of the props, the pillars to help him endure and prevail.

—William Faulkner

MAKING MEANINGS

First Thoughts

1. Did the ending of this story surprise you, or were you prepared for it? Explain.

Shaping Interpretations

2. The community thought of Emily and her father "as a tableau"— a kind of dramatic picture. This tableau suggests conflict. What **conflicts** do you think existed between Emily and her father? (For whom or what was that horsewhip intended?)

3. How is Colonel Sartoris's white lie to Miss Emily about her taxes an attempt to spare her any embarrassment? Explain how Judge Stevens has also taken steps to avoid embarrassing her. How do the later changes in attitude toward Miss Emily's taxes reflect wider social and economic changes in the South?

4. Why do you think Faulkner emphasizes the way Miss Emily's hair turned gray—and what do you think is significant about the time it started to happen?

5. What significance do you see in the long strand of iron-gray hair found on the second pillow?

6. What part do you think Tobe, the manservant, plays in Miss Emily's history?

7. What sort of person do you think the **narrator** of this story is? Is it a man or a woman? Does the narrator pity Miss Emily? admire her? hold her in contempt?

8. The critics Cleanth Brooks, R.W.B. Lewis, and Robert Penn Warren noted of this story: "The community is nearly everywhere in Faulkner's

> ### Reading Check
>
> a. What do people think is causing Miss Emily's house to smell? What really causes the odor?
>
> b. How does Miss Emily's odd behavior when her father dies **foreshadow** the end of the story?
>
> c. Why does the minister's wife send for Miss Emily's relations?
>
> d. Who is Homer Barron? What makes him disappear?

work as an important force and, diffused and anonymous though it be, it becomes one of the most important elements in the story. . . . Miss Emily Grierson is one of the numerous characters in Faulkner's work who are warped by their inheritance from the past and who are cut off from the community—sometimes by their own will—to their detriment." Do you agree with these critics? Why or why not?

9. Another observation made by the same critics is that Faulkner's story has significance far beyond its horror-story ending: "To read 'A Rose for Emily' as merely a piece of cheap Southern Gothicism, an attempt to shock and horrify, would be to miss the point." Do you agree or disagree with these critics? What is the point of the story, in your opinion?

Extending the Text

10. Historical details in this story reveal a great deal about its **setting.** What do you learn about the times from the townspeople's attitude toward the African Americans who live in Jefferson? In our time, have such attitudes changed or stayed much the same? Discuss how Faulkner might have changed his story if he'd written it today.

Challenging the Text

11. Faulkner once explained the title "A Rose for Emily" this way:

> "Oh, it's simply the poor woman had had no life at all. Her father had kept her more or less locked up and then she had a lover who was about to quit her, she had to murder him. It was just 'A Rose for Emily'—that's all."

Faulkner's answer is not very helpful. Consider what roses usually **symbolize.** Then defend the title of the story, or propose a more appropriate title.

CHOICES: Building Your Portfolio

Writer's Notebook

1. Collecting Ideas for an Interpretive Essay

See if you can better understand Miss Emily by 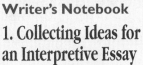 analyzing her **character.** Review the places in this story where the narrator directly describes what the townspeople thought of Miss Emily. For example, in part IV, the narrator says they thought of her as "dear, inescapable, impervious, tranquil, and perverse" (page 722). Use these descriptions, together with the notes you made while reading, to make a chart (see below). When you have finished your chart, write a few sentences summarizing your insights into Miss Emily. Save your work for possible use in the Writer's Workshop on page 804.

Analyzing a Story Line

2. Sequencing the Plot

The order in which the narrator *mentions* events in this story differs from the order in which they occurred. Go through the story, listing the key events as they are mentioned: Homer's arriving in town, Emily's buying the poison, the death of Emily's father, and so on. Then, rearrange your list in **chronological order.** Compare the lists, and write a brief essay in which you analyze Faulkner's **plot sequence.** Try to explain Faulkner's purpose in fragmenting time (presenting events out of order).

Creative Writing

3. Nightmare on *Your* Street

Write a short-short story (no more than 1,200 words) about a fictional solitary person who lives in your neighborhood. A shocking secret should lie hidden in this person's past. Before you begin writing, decide what the secret is and what events occur in the plot of your story. Include vivid, descriptive details that create a mysterious **atmosphere** and a believable **setting.** Save the startling truth for the last sentences, as Faulkner does in "A Rose for Emily."

Speaking and Listening

4. Literary Likenesses

With a small group, choose one of the statements below. Divide your group in half, and decide which side will argue in support of and which in opposition to each statement. Do whatever research is needed (using this book, a library, or the Internet) before deciding which side you can argue most convincingly.

a. Miss Emily's house is like Roderick Usher's house in "The Fall of the House of Usher" by Edgar Allan Poe (page 263). (You could also compare it with Julio Cortázar's "House Taken Over" on page 291.)

b. Miss Emily and Richard Cory in the poem by Edwin Arlington Robinson (page 645) are both victims of their extreme isolation from their communities.

c. Miss Emily is haunted by a lost love in much the same way that Granny Weatherall in Katherine Anne Porter's story (page 704) turns out to be haunted by the memory of the man who jilted her.

d. Miss Emily and Miss Havisham, in the novel *Great Expectations* by Charles Dickens, react to losing a lover in similar ways.

Reading Skills and Strategies

VOCABULARY: SEMANTIC FEATURES ANALYSIS

Semantic features analysis is a way of analyzing related words, or **synonyms**—words having nearly the same meaning—to highlight their similarities and differences. A good way to see distinctions between terms that have overlapping meanings or subtle differences in **connotation** is to analyze their semantic features.

Here's an example of an occasion when you might want to use this technique. Near the beginning of "A Rose for Emily," William Faulkner writes, "Alive, Miss Emily had been a tradition, a duty, and a care; a sort of hereditary obligation upon the town. . . ." You can be sure that Faulkner precisely chose the words *tradition, duty, care,* and *obligation* and made a considered decision to use all four to describe Miss Emily. Why? A semantic features analysis might help you understand why.

To make a semantic features chart, list the words being analyzed down the left-hand side. From a thesaurus and a dictionary, gather various meanings and connotations of the words to list along the top. (A **thesaurus** is a compilation of synonyms and antonyms.)

If a word has or suggests a particular meaning or connotation, mark +. If the word does *not* have that meaning or connotation, mark −. If a word potentially, but not necessarily, has a specific connotation, you may want to mark it *.

For the four words from "A Rose for Emily," you might need to begin with a dictionary definition to be sure you know the exact meaning—or **denotation**—of each word. Then you would choose connotations, and you might create a chart like the one below.

The analysis done in the chart shows that each word listed emphasizes a different aspect of responsibility. *Tradition* is the only word that suggests something that is necessarily passed along over generations. *Duty* emphasizes requirement. *Care* implies a burden. *Obligation* emphasizes the contractual nature of the responsibility. Thus, it could be argued, Faulkner has used these four words together to build a composite, or combined, meaning that is richer than the meaning of any one or two of the words alone.

	felt as burdensome	something long-established	something that is required	suggests a social obligation	has aspects of a law or contract
tradition	*	+	*	+	*
duty	+	*	+	*	+
care	+	*	−	*	−
obligation	+	*	+	*	+

. . . .

Try It Out

Choose words with similar meanings from a selection in this collection to form an appropriate group for a semantic features analysis. Make a chart, and use a thesaurus and a dictionary to help you identify definitions and connotations. Then, fill in the chart.

Finally, try to describe in your own words the similarities and differences in meaning of the words you chose. Think about the connotations as well as the denotations.

Horacio Quiroga
(1878–1937)

Horacio Quiroga (kē·rō′gä) was one of Latin America's finest and most celebrated short-story writers, a master of the taut, suspenseful, well-crafted tale. Born in Salto, Uruguay, Quiroga was an avid admirer of Edgar Allan Poe's fiction. Like Poe, Quiroga wrote stories that blend horror with psychological suspense. Also like Poe, Quiroga developed a philosophy of short-story writing. In his essay "Manual of the Perfect Short Story Writer," Quiroga presents an approach to writing not unlike Poe's theory of the "single effect": the idea that every word and detail in a story should build to a single, unified emotional effect. Quiroga warns writers to avoid unnecessary words and details and never to begin a story without knowing exactly where it is heading. He felt that in the perfect short story the first few sentences are as important as the last few, and inevitably lead to them. In his best stories— among which is "The Feather Pillow" (first published in 1907)—Quiroga achieves a compressed, sustained effect with every word and sentence. By the time of his death, he had written about two hundred works of fiction, including the classic story collections *Jungle Tales* (1918) and *The Decapitated Chicken and Other Stories* (1925).

A master of dramatic technique, Quiroga was also superb at creating setting. In his stories, as in the stories of William Faulkner and other American writers who explore in depth certain real or fictionalized regions, Quiroga makes setting almost a character in itself. He spent a good portion of his life in San Ignacio, a jungle province in Misiones (in northern Argentina) that provided inspiration for his settings. In many of his stories, he deals with fundamental conflicts between human beings and the world of nature—conflicts in which nature is invariably the victor. Many of his jungle stories illustrate his uncompromising vision of life as an eternal, often brutal, struggle for survival, not unlike some of the tales of Jack London, to whom Quiroga has also been compared.

Quiroga's Poe-like obsession with death and the grotesque is not surprising, given that his life was a patchwork of nightmares as disturbing as the tales he crafted. Quiroga came face to face with gruesome death early in his life. First, his father accidentally killed himself with a shotgun. When he was twenty-three, Quiroga accidentally shot to death one of his closest friends. There were more personal tragedies: Quiroga's attempts to start a business in the rugged and dangerous Argentine jungle failed; his first wife, in despair over their living conditions in the jungle, took her own life; and his second marriage ended unhappily in separation. Quiroga ended his own tragic life in 1937, after discovering that he was dying of cancer.

Before You Read

THE FEATHER PILLOW

Background

The Gothic tale has been well represented in literature of the United States, starting with Edgar Allan Poe, moving to Southern Gothic writers like William Faulkner and Flannery O'Connor, and continuing into the present with best-selling writers like Stephen King and Anne Rice.

Like their counterparts in the United States, many Latin American writers have used Gothic conventions to craft unsettling tales of the fantastic. One of the most successful of these writers is Horacio Quiroga, who used his fascination with the dark side of the human mind to craft a number of powerful stories with Gothic-horror overtones. A typical Quiroga story quickly reaches its terrible conclusion with not a word or detail wasted.

Be warned: The story you are about to read is one you won't soon forget. After you come to the stunning conclusion of this tale, you may never look at feather pillows the same way again.

Reading Skills and Strategies

Dialogue with the Text

As you read this story, pause to jot down

- questions that occur to you
- emotional reactions to the story
- predictions of where the story is heading
- thoughts about characters, details of the plot, or issues the story raises

The Lovers (1928) by René Magritte. Oil on canvas (21³⁄₈″ × 28⁷⁄₈″).

The Feather Pillow

Horacio Quiroga

translated from the Spanish by Margaret Sayers Peden

Her entire honeymoon gave her hot and cold shivers. A blond, angelic, and timid young girl, the childish fancies she had dreamed about being a bride had been chilled by her husband's rough character. She loved him very much, nonetheless, although sometimes she gave a light shudder when, as they returned home through the streets together at night, she cast a furtive glance at the impressive stature of her Jordan, who had been silent for an hour. He, for his part, loved her profoundly but never let it be seen.

For three months—they had been married in April—they lived in a special kind of bliss. Doubtless she would have wished less severity in the rigorous sky of love, more expansive and less cautious tenderness, but her husband's impassive manner always restrained her.

The house in which they lived influenced her chills and shuddering to no small degree. The whiteness of the silent patio—friezes,[1] columns, and marble statues—produced the wintry impression of an enchanted palace. Inside, the glacial brilliance of stucco, the completely bare walls, affirmed the sensation of unpleasant coldness. As one crossed from one room to another, the echo of his steps reverberated throughout the house, as if long abandonment had sensitized its resonance.

Alicia passed the autumn in this strange love nest. She had determined, however, to cast a veil over her former dreams and live like a sleeping beauty in the hostile house, trying not to think about anything until her husband arrived each evening.

It is not strange that she grew thin. She had a light attack of influenza that dragged on insidiously for days and days: After that Alicia's health never returned. Finally one afternoon she was able to go into the garden, supported on her husband's arm. She looked around listlessly. Suddenly Jordan, with deep tenderness, ran his hand very slowly over her head, and Alicia instantly burst into sobs, throwing her arms around his neck. For a long time she cried out all the fears she had kept silent, redoubling her weeping at Jordan's

---

1. **friezes** (frēz′iz): decorative, ornamental bands around a room or along a wall.

slightest caress. Then her sobs subsided, and she stood a long while, her face hidden in the hollow of his neck, not moving or speaking a word.

This was the last day Alicia was well enough to be up. On the following day she awakened feeling faint. Jordan's doctor examined her with minute attention, prescribing calm and absolute rest.

"I don't know," he said to Jordan at the street door. "She has a great weakness that I am unable to explain. And with no vomiting, nothing . . . if she wakes tomorrow as she did today, call me at once."

When she awakened the following day, Alicia was worse. There was consultation. It was agreed there was an anemia of incredible progression, completely inexplicable. Alicia had no more fainting spells, but she was visibly moving toward death. The lights were lighted all day long in her bedroom, and there was complete silence. Hours went by without the slightest sound. Alicia dozed. Jordan virtually lived in the drawing room, which was also always lighted. With tireless persistence he paced ceaselessly from one end of the room to the other. The carpet swallowed his steps. At times he entered the bedroom and continued his silent pacing back and forth alongside the bed, stopping for an instant at each end to regard his wife.

Suddenly Alicia began to have hallucinations, vague images, at first seeming to float in the air, then descending to floor level. Her eyes excessively wide, she stared continuously at the carpet on either side of the head of her bed. One night she suddenly focused on one spot. Then she opened her mouth to scream, and pearls of sweat suddenly beaded her nose and lips.

"Jordan! Jordan!" she clamored, rigid with fright, still staring at the carpet.

Jordan ran to the bedroom, and, when she saw him appear, Alicia screamed with terror.

"It's I, Alicia, it's I!"

Alicia looked at him confusedly; she looked at the carpet; she looked at him once again; and after a long moment of stupefied confrontation, she regained her senses. She smiled and took her husband's hand in hers, caressing it, trembling, for half an hour.

Among her most persistent hallucinations was that of an anthropoid[2] poised on his fingertips on the carpet, staring at her.

The doctors returned, but to no avail. They saw before them a diminishing life, a life bleeding away day by day, hour by hour, absolutely without their knowing why. During their last consultation Alicia lay in a stupor while they took her pulse, passing her inert wrist from one to another. They observed her a long time in silence and then moved into the dining room.

"Phew . . ." The discouraged chief physician shrugged his shoulders. "It is an inexplicable case. There is little we can do . . ."

"That's my last hope!" Jordan groaned. And he staggered blindly against the table.

Alicia's life was fading away in the subdelirium[3] of anemia, a delirium which grew worse throughout the evening hours but which let up somewhat after dawn. The illness never worsened during the daytime, but

2. **anthropoid** (an′thrə·poid′): humanlike creature, such as an ape.
3. **subdelirium** (sub·di·lir′ē·əm): restless, feverish state in which a person hallucinates.

each morning she awakened pale as death, almost in a swoon. It seemed only at night that her life drained out of her in new waves of blood. Always when she awakened she had the sensation of lying collapsed in the bed with a million-pound weight on top of her. Following the third day of this relapse she never left her bed again. She could scarcely move her head. She did not want her bed to be touched, not even to have her bedcovers arranged. Her crepuscular[4] terrors advanced now in the form of monsters that dragged themselves toward the bed and laboriously climbed upon the bedspread.

Then she lost consciousness. The final two days she raved ceaselessly in a weak voice. The lights funereally illuminated the bedroom and drawing room. In the deathly silence of the house the only sound was the monotonous delirium from the bedroom and the dull echoes of Jordan's eternal pacing.

Finally, Alicia died. The servant, when she came in afterward to strip the now empty bed, stared wonderingly for a moment at the pillow.

"Sir!" she called Jordan in a low voice. "There are stains on the pillow that look like blood."

Jordan approached rapidly and bent over the pillow. Truly, on the case, on both sides of the hollow left by Alicia's head, were two small, dark spots.

"They look like punctures," the servant murmured after a moment of motionless observation.

"Hold it up to the light," Jordan told her.

The servant raised the pillow but immediately dropped it and stood staring at it, livid and trembling. Without knowing why, Jordan felt the hair rise on the back of his neck.

"What is it?" he murmured in a hoarse voice.

"It's very heavy," the servant whispered, still trembling.

Jordan picked it up; it was extraordinarily heavy. He carried it out of the room, and on the dining room table he ripped open the case and the ticking with a slash. The top feathers floated away, and the servant, her mouth opened wide, gave a scream of horror and covered her face with her clenched fists: In the bottom of the pillowcase, among the feathers, slowly moving its hairy legs, was a monstrous animal, a living, viscous ball. It was so swollen one could scarcely make out its mouth.

Night after night, since Alicia had taken to her bed, this abomination had stealthily applied its mouth—its proboscis[5] one might better say—to the girl's temples, sucking her blood. The puncture was scarcely perceptible. The daily plumping of the pillow had doubtlessly at first impeded its progress, but as soon as the girl could no longer move, the suction became vertiginous.[6] In five days, in five nights, the monster had drained Alicia's life away.

These parasites of feathered creatures, diminutive in their habitual environment, reach enormous proportions under certain conditions. Human blood seems particularly favorable to them, and it is not rare to encounter them in feather pillows.

4. **crepuscular** (kri·pus′kyōō·lər): happening at or related to twilight.
5. **proboscis** (prō·bäs′is): tubular mouthpart used by parasites to attach to a host and withdraw blood.
6. **vertiginous** (vər·tij′ə·nəs): causing vertigo; dizzying.

FINDING COMMON GROUND

Now that you've finished the story, meet in small groups, and share the questions and comments you noted while reading.

- Read aloud your notes, or pass the notes around so that everyone can read the comments.
- Identify and discuss three or four issues, comments, or reactions that seem most interesting or widely shared within your group.
- Compare the effect of this story to that of "A Rose for Emily." For example, both stories end on a shocking note. But Faulkner does not spell out what happens to Miss Emily and Homer Barron; Quiroga, on the other hand, reveals Alicia's fate in graphic detail. In what other ways are Faulkner's and Quiroga's stories alike and different?

- Quiroga also has much in common with Edgar Allan Poe. Like Poe, he was fascinated by madness and obsession, and he mastered the short-story format, creating a single sustained effect in each story. What does "The Feather Pillow" have in common with "The Fall of the House of Usher" and other Poe stories you have read?
- Reconvene as a class, and share the results of your discussion.

LITERATURE AND POPULAR CULTURE

Reader Beware! Urban Legends We Hope Aren't True

What makes *your* skin crawl? Part of what makes Quiroga's story "The Feather Pillow" so effectively creepy is the sneaking but still embarrassing suspicion (or fear) we all have that *something like this could really happen*.

Our tendency to half believe in the grotesque possibilities of stories about creepy creatures lurking inside feather pillows (or wigs, or the linings of down jackets, or even the bedroom closet) is the fuel for what anthropologists call **urban folklore,** or urban belief tales. Like all folk tales, these anecdotes travel at lightning speed simply through word of mouth, probably the way fairy tales were transmitted hundreds of years ago. And they seem all too believable.

Not all urban folk tales are scary, but many of the most memorable ones are. You may have heard tales about giant alligators living in city sewers, spider eggs in bubble gum that later hatch inside a person's stomach, or earwigs that crawl into people's ears and drill right through their brains (sometimes leaving a supply of eggs behind). We don't know for certain whether Quiroga based his story on scary tales he had heard passed off as the truth, but one thing is certain: "The Feather Pillow" plays on the same emotions of fascination, fear, and disgust that we all feel when we hear a scary story that we *know* is not true, but that makes us sneak a few extra peeks in the closet or under the bed anyway.

Collection 15

I, TOO, SING AMERICA
THE HARLEM RENAISSANCE

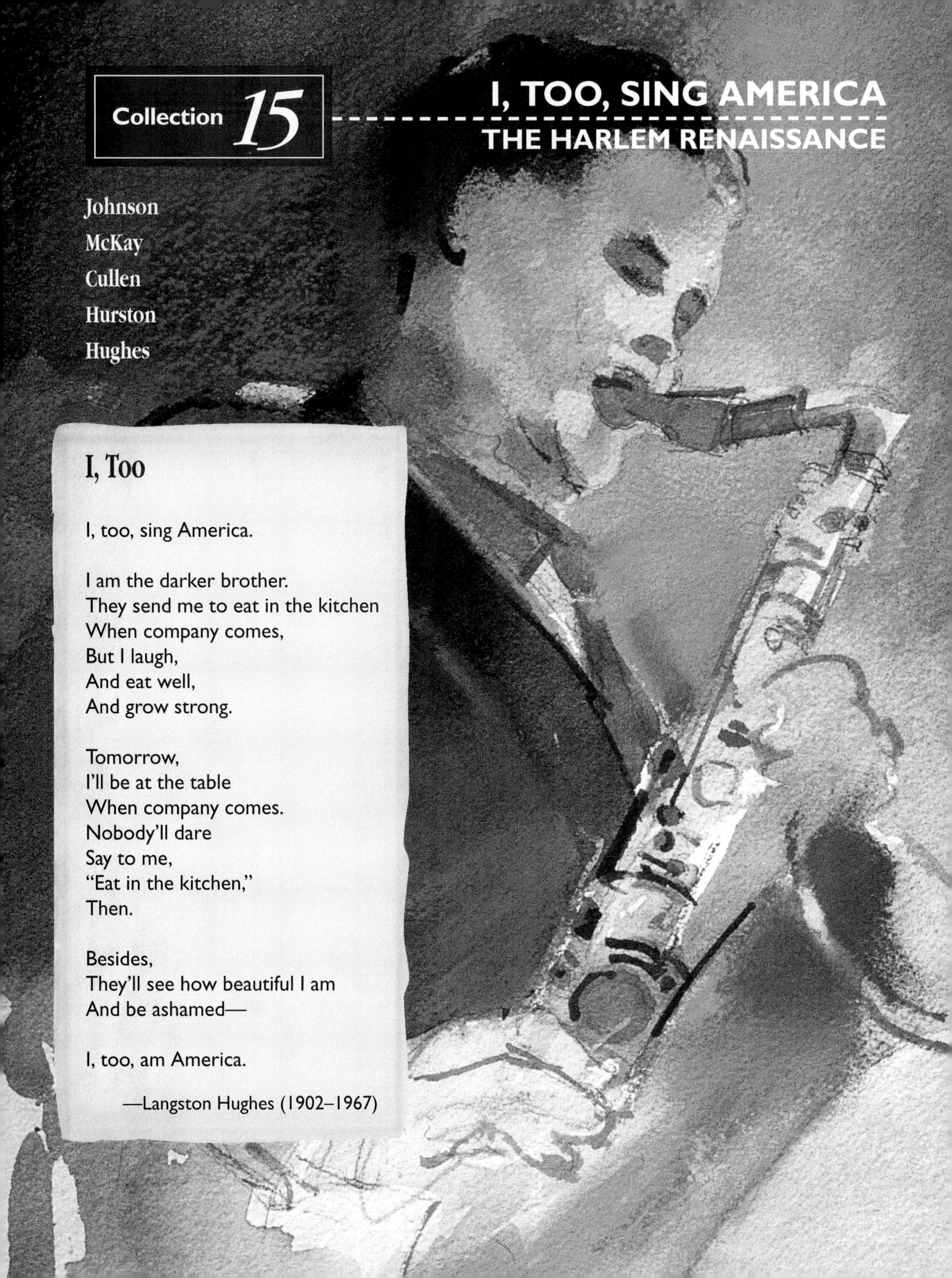

Johnson
McKay
Cullen
Hurston
Hughes

I, Too

I, too, sing America.

I am the darker brother.
They send me to eat in the kitchen
When company comes,
But I laugh,
And eat well,
And grow strong.

Tomorrow,
I'll be at the table
When company comes.
Nobody'll dare
Say to me,
"Eat in the kitchen,"
Then.

Besides,
They'll see how beautiful I am
And be ashamed—

I, too, am America.

—Langston Hughes (1902–1967)

The Harlem Renaissance

In the early 1920s, African American artists, writers, musicians, and performers were part of a great cultural movement known as the Harlem Renaissance. The huge migration to the north after World War I brought African Americans of all ages and walks of life to the thriving New York City neighborhood called Harlem. Doctors, singers, students, musicians, shopkeepers, painters, and writers congregated, forming a vibrant mecca of cultural affirmation and inspiration.

As Langston Hughes wrote, "It was the period when the Negro was in vogue." Marcus Garvey's "Back to Africa" movement was in full swing. The blues were vibrantly alive; jazz was just beginning. An all-black show, *Shuffle Along,* opened on Broadway with the performers Josephine Baker and Florence Mills, music composed by Eubie Blake, and lyrics by Noble Sissle. And mainstream America was developing a new respect for African art and culture, thanks in part to its reflection in the work of the modernist artists Pablo Picasso and Georges Braque.

Against this backdrop, Harlem Renaissance artists insisted that the African American be accepted as "a collaborator and participant in American civilization," in the words of the educator and critic Alain Locke. Writers such as Jean Toomer and Zora Neale Hurston (page 750) wrote about the African American experience. Artists such as Aaron Douglas and William H. Johnson painted it. The photographer James Van Der Zee recorded it with his camera. The trumpeter Louis Armstrong and the pianist Fletcher Henderson set it to music, and vocalists Bessie Smith and Ma Rainey sang it.

Harlem newspapers and journals, such as *Crisis* and *Opportunity,* published the work of both new and established African American writers. To promote and support intellectually gifted young people, the journals sponsored literary contests that encouraged creative writing and rewarded it with cash prizes and social introductions to the top writers of the time.

In autobiographies, poetry, short stories, novels, and folklore, African American writers affirmed the role of black talent in American culture and focused on different aspects of black life in Harlem, the South, Europe, the

Bessie Smith.
Brown Brothers.

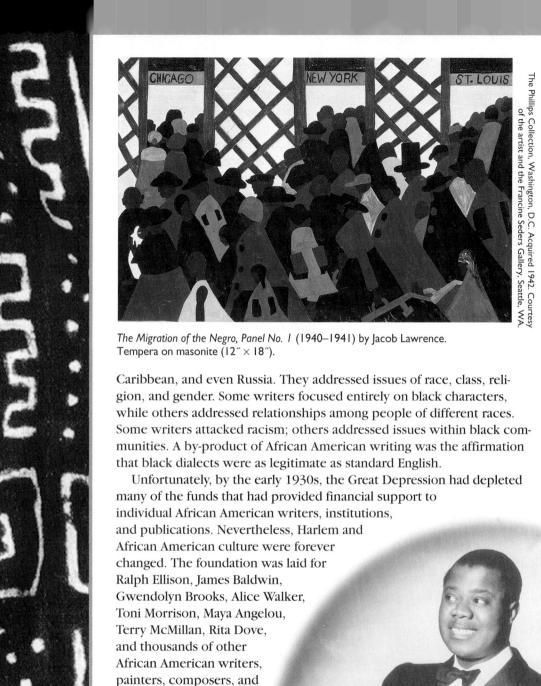

The Migration of the Negro, Panel No. 1 (1940–1941) by Jacob Lawrence. Tempera on masonite (12″ × 18″).

Caribbean, and even Russia. They addressed issues of race, class, religion, and gender. Some writers focused entirely on black characters, while others addressed relationships among people of different races. Some writers attacked racism; others addressed issues within black communities. A by-product of African American writing was the affirmation that black dialects were as legitimate as standard English.

Unfortunately, by the early 1930s, the Great Depression had depleted many of the funds that had provided financial support to individual African American writers, institutions, and publications. Nevertheless, Harlem and African American culture were forever changed. The foundation was laid for Ralph Ellison, James Baldwin, Gwendolyn Brooks, Alice Walker, Toni Morrison, Maya Angelou, Terry McMillan, Rita Dove, and thousands of other African American writers, painters, composers, and singers to make their feelings and experiences part of American artistic expression: "I, too, sing America."

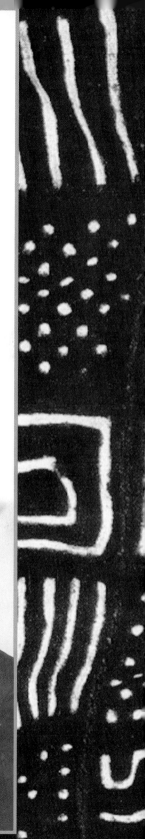

Louis Armstrong.

Brown Brothers.

James Weldon Johnson (c. 1925) by Winold Reiss. Pastel on artist board (30 1/16″ × 21 9/16″).

National Portrait Gallery, Washington, D.C. Courtesy Art Resource, NY.

James Weldon Johnson

(1871–1938)

James Weldon Johnson—poet, teacher, and lawyer—was born in Jacksonville, Florida. Educated at Atlanta University in Georgia and Columbia University in New York City, he was the first African American to be admitted to the Florida bar after Reconstruction. Throughout his career, Johnson was an energetic exponent of civil rights, and in his writing he constantly sought recognition for the contributions that African Americans had made to American culture.

After serving as U.S. consul in Venezuela and then in Nicaragua (1907–1913), Johnson worked as field secretary of the National Association for the Advancement of Colored People (NAACP) for four years and then served as the association's general secretary for the following ten years. In 1931, he was appointed professor of creative literature at Fisk University. Seven years later, he died in an automobile accident.

Although some of Johnson's early poems are in dialect, he soon abandoned that style for standard English, which he felt was capable of greater variety and power. His principal theme was black pride, which he celebrated in such poems as "Fifty Years," written on the fiftieth anniversary of the Emancipation Proclamation, and "O Black and Unknown Bards," a tribute to the anonymous authors of African American spirituals. With his brother, the composer John Rosamond Johnson, he wrote a number of very successful light operas and songs for Tin Pan Alley, and the brothers collaborated in editing two collections of spirituals.

Johnson was an important leader of the first phase of the Harlem Renaissance. His anthology, *The Book of American Negro Poetry* (1922), was one of the significant early collections of poems by African Americans. In addition to poetry, Johnson wrote fiction (most notably *The Autobiography of an Ex-Colored Man,* published in 1912), nonfiction studies of black life, and an autobiography, *Along This Way* (1933).

It was Johnson's extensive research for one collection, *The Book of American Negro Spirituals* (1925), that inspired his poem "Go Down, Death." Describing this experience, he said: "The research which I did in collecting the spirituals and gathering the data for my introductory essay had an effect on me similar to what I received from hearing the Negro evangelist preach. . . . I was in touch with the deepest revelation of the Negro's soul that has yet been made, and I felt myself attuned to it. I made an outline of the second poem that I wrote of this series. It was to be a 'funeral sermon.' I decided to call it 'Go Down, Death.'

"On Thanksgiving Day, 1926, I was at home. After breakfast I went to my desk and began work in earnest on the poem. As I worked, my own spirit rose till it reached a degree almost of ecstasy. The poem shaped itself easily and before the hour for dinner I had written it as it stands published."

HRW go.hrw.com
LEO 11-15

Make the Connection

Death at the Doorstep

Every religion has its own view of what happens when we die, and countless storytellers, philosophers, and writers have added their views to the sum of our understanding of the great mystery we call death. Is death a source of pain and sorrow, or is it a comfort—perhaps even a joyous affirmation of life?

Reading Skills and Strategies

Tracking Your Responses

This poem is one of seven "sermons" written by Johnson in the style of the old-time African American preachers. He collected the sermons in a book called *God's Trombones*—the trombone being "of just the tone and timbre to represent the old-time Negro preacher's voice."

Johnson tells us that the person reading "Go Down, Death" would intone, moan, plead, blare, crash, and thunder. As you read, jot down the words, lines, or stanzas that have the strongest emotional effect on you.

Elements of Literature

Personification

Personification is a figure of speech in which an animal, object, or abstract concept is portrayed with human qualities. In this poem, Johnson invites readers to see and understand Death as a character rather than as an abstract concept.

Go Down, Death

A Funeral Sermon

James Weldon Johnson

Weep not, weep not,
She is not dead;
She's resting in the bosom of Jesus.
Heart-broken husband—weep no more;
5 Grief-stricken son—weep no more;
Left-lonesome daughter—weep no more;
She's only just gone home.

Day before yesterday morning,
God was looking down from his great, high heaven,
10 Looking down on all his children,
And his eye fell on Sister Caroline,
Tossing on her bed of pain.
And God's big heart was touched with pity,
With the everlasting pity.

15 And God sat back on his throne,
And he commanded that tall, bright angel standing at his right
    hand:
Call me Death!
And that tall, bright angel cried in a voice
That broke like a clap of thunder:
20 Call Death!—Call Death!
And the echo sounded down the streets of heaven
Till it reached away back to that shadowy place,
Where Death waits with his pale, white horses.°

And Death heard the summons,
25 And he leaped on his fastest horse,
Pale as a sheet in the moonlight.
Up the golden street Death galloped,
And the hoofs of his horse struck fire from the gold,
But they didn't make no sound.
30 Up Death rode to the Great White Throne,
And waited for God's command.

And God said: Go down, Death, go down,
Go down to Savannah, Georgia,
Down in Yamacraw,

23. Death waits . . . horses: allusion to Revelation 6:8, "And I looked, and behold a pale horse: and his name that sat on him was Death."

Go Down Death (1927) by Aaron Douglas. Oil on masonite.

35   And find Sister Caroline.
     She's borne the burden and heat of the day,
     She's labored long in my vineyard,
     And she's tired—
     She's weary—
40   Go down, Death, and bring her to me.

     And Death didn't say a word,
     But he loosed the reins on his pale, white horse,
     And he clamped the spurs to his bloodless sides,
     And out and down he rode,
45   Through heaven's pearly gates,
     Past suns and moons and stars;
     On Death rode,
     And the foam from his horse was like a comet in the sky;
     On Death rode,
50   Leaving the lightning's flash behind;
     Straight on down he came.

     While we were watching round her bed,
     She turned her eyes and looked away,
     She saw what we couldn't see;
55   She saw Old Death. She saw Old Death
     Coming like a falling star.
     But Death didn't frighten Sister Caroline;
     He looked to her like a welcome friend.
     And she whispered to us: I'm going home,
60   And she smiled and closed her eyes.

     And Death took her up like a baby,
     And she lay in his icy arms,
     But she didn't feel no chill.
     And Death began to ride again—
65   Up beyond the evening star,
     Out beyond the morning star,°
     Into the glittering light of glory,
     On to the Great White Throne.
     And there he laid Sister Caroline
70   On the loving breast of Jesus.

     And Jesus took his own hand and wiped away her tears,
     And he smoothed the furrows from her face,
     And the angels sang a little song,
     And Jesus rocked her in his arms,
75   And kept a-saying: Take your rest,
     Take your rest, take your rest.

     Weep not—weep not,
     She is not dead;
     She's resting in the bosom of Jesus.

66. evening star . . . morning star: the planet Venus, which is traditionally referred to as both the morning star and the evening star. Its orbital path makes it visible for no more than about three hours after sunset and three hours before sunrise.

God's Trombones

❦ In his preface to *God's Trombones,* from which "Go Down, Death" is taken, Johnson describes the origin of his idea for his collection of poems.

The old-time preacher was generally a man far above the average in intelligence; he was, not infrequently, a man of positive genius. The earliest of these preachers must have virtually committed many parts of the Bible to memory through hearing the scriptures read or preached from in the white churches which the slaves attended. They were the first of the slaves to learn to read, and their reading was confined to the Bible, and specifically to the more dramatic passages of the Old Testament. A text served mainly as a starting point and often had no relation to the development of the sermon. Nor would the old-time preacher balk at any text within the lids of the Bible. There is the story of one who after reading a rather cryptic passage took off his spectacles, closed the Bible with a bang and by way of preface said, "Brothers and sisters, this morning—I intend to explain the unexplainable—find out the undefinable—ponder over the imponderable—and unscrew the inscrutable."

The old-time Negro preacher of parts was above all an orator, and in good measure an actor. He knew the secret of oratory, that at bottom it is a progression of rhythmic words more than it is anything else. Indeed, I have witnessed congregations moved to ecstasy by the rhythmic intoning of sheer incoherencies. He was a master of all the modes of eloquence. He often possessed a voice that was a marvelous instrument, a voice he could modulate from a sepulchral whisper to a crashing thunder clap. His discourse was generally kept at a high pitch of fervency, but occasionally he dropped into colloquialisms and, less often, into humor. He preached a personal and anthropomorphic God, a sure-enough heaven and a red-hot hell. His imagination was bold and unfettered. He had the power to sweep his hearers before him; and so himself was often swept away. At such times his language was not prose but poetry. It was from memories of such preachers there grew the idea of this book of poems.

—James Weldon Johnson

Prayer Meeting (1951) by Samella Sanders Lewis. Watercolor (17" × 14¾").

Hampton University Museum, Hampton, Virginia.

Borrowing from the spiritual "Swing Low, Sweet Chariot," the African American poet Gwendolyn Brooks (1917–2000) created a poem that also has the rhythm of a song. (For more on spirituals, see page 432.) Lincoln Cemetery is in Chicago.

# of De Witt Williams on his way to Lincoln Cemetery

Gwendolyn Brooks

He was born in Alabama.
He was bred in Illinois.
He was nothing but a
Plain black boy.

5   Swing low swing low sweet sweet chariot.
Nothing but a plain black boy.

Drive him past the Pool Hall.
Drive him past the Show.
Blind within his casket,
10   But maybe he will know.

Down through Forty-seventh Street:
Underneath the L,
And—Northwest Corner, Prairie,
That he loved so well.

15   Don't forget the Dance Halls—
Warwick and Savoy,
Where he picked his women, where
He drank his liquid joy.

Born in Alabama.
20   Bred in Illinois.
He was nothing but a
Plain black boy.

Swing low swing low sweet sweet chariot.
Nothing but a plain black boy.

Haitian Funeral Procession (c. 1950s) by Ellis Wilson. Oil on canvas (30 ½″ × 29 ¼″).

Aaron Douglas Collection, Amistad Research Center, Tulane University, New Orleans, Louisiana.

MAKING MEANINGS

First Thoughts

1. Review the notes you made as you read "Go Down, Death." Which words, lines, or stanzas had the strongest effect on you? Why?

Shaping Interpretations

2. Identify where God is in stanza 2, and where Death is in stanza 3. According to stanza 5, where is Sister Caroline? How does Sister Caroline respond to Death's arrival in stanza 7?

3. Find three **similes** that help to suggest the magnificence of the workings of heaven.

4. Does the speaker portray God and Jesus as distant, forbidding figures, or as familiar, gentle ones? Point out at least four **details** that support your interpretation.

5. Why do you think Death rides a "pale, white horse"? Where else have you seen the color white used in a similar **symbolic** way?

Extending the Text

6. While many of the traditional representations of death are fearful, the one in this poem is not. Discuss the ways Johnson **personifies** death in this poem. Then compare Johnson's image with images you have encountered in literature (see especially Emily Dickinson's "Because I could not stop for Death" on page 391) or on film.

ELEMENTS OF LITERATURE

Free Verse and the Orator's Style

When Johnson was working on the poems that would eventually become *God's Trombones,* he talked with the African American poet Paul Laurence Dunbar (1872–1906).

> I showed Paul the things I had done under the sudden influence of Whitman. He read them through and, looking at me with a queer smile, said, "I don't like them, and I don't see what you are driving at." He may be

> justified, but I was taken aback. I got out my copy of *Leaves of Grass* and read him some of the things I admired most. There was, at least, some personal consolation in the fact that his verdict was the same on Whitman himself.
>
> —James Weldon Johnson

Examine "Go Down, Death," and see if you can identify the influence of Whitman (page 348). Look for these elements of Whitman's style: (1) **repetition** and **parallel structure** to create rhythm; (2) the simple language of everyday conversation, including slang; (3) variation of line length, from very long to very short, to create a rolling **cadence;** (4) other **sound effects.**

CHOICES: Building Your Portfolio

Writer's Notebook

1. Collecting Ideas for an Interpretive Essay

Explore the similarities and differences in the attitudes toward death in Johnson's "Go Down, Death" and Gwendolyn Brooks's "of De Witt Williams on his way to Lincoln Cemetery" (see *Connections* on page 741). Take notes in a double-column comparison-contrast chart. Save your notes for possible use in the Writer's Workshop on page 804.

Comparing Sermons

2. Sermons Side by Side

Extracts from another famous sermon in American literature are on page 79—Jonathan Edwards's "Sinners in the Hands of an Angry God." In a brief essay, compare and contrast Johnson's sermon with Edwards's. Consider these elements of each sermon: (a) imagery, (b) figures of speech, (c) message, (d) tone, (e) audience, and (f) purpose.

Claude McKay (1941) by Carl Van Vechten.
The Beinecke Rare Book and Manuscript Library, Yale University, New Haven, Connecticut. Estate of Carl Van Vechten, Joseph Solomon, Executor.

Claude McKay

(1890–1948)

Claude McKay was born and raised on the Caribbean island of Jamaica, the eighth child of farmers. When he was nine, he went to live with his eldest brother, who was a school-master, and his early education came chiefly from his brother's classroom and library. McKay apprenticed as a wheelwright and cabinetmaker, then worked as a constable. All the while, he was writing poems in a Jamaican dialect of English. In 1912, with the help of an English friend, he published his first two collections of verse, *Songs of Jamaica* and *Constab Ballads,* then traveled to the United States to study agriculture. After briefly enrolling at Tuskegee Institute in Alabama, McKay transferred to Kansas State College, where he studied for two years.

In 1914, McKay moved to Harlem and opened a restaurant with a friend. When this venture failed, he supported himself with a variety of jobs, from janitor to butler, while he continued to refine his craft and publish poems in periodicals. In 1920, his third book, *Spring in New Hampshire,* was published. His most important book of poetry, *Harlem Shadows,* appeared in 1922.

By this time, McKay was a major figure in the Harlem Renaissance. He had served as an editor of the radical newspapers the *Liberator* and *The Masses.* Like many writers of the period, he was drawn to the "noble experiment" of communism. In 1922, he signed on as a stoker for a merchant ship and toured Russia for a year.

McKay lived abroad, principally in France, until 1934. During this time he concentrated on writing fiction and essays rather than poetry, and he published four novels, including the best-selling *Home to Harlem* (1928). Disillusioned with communism, in 1942 he converted to Roman Catholicism. McKay spent the rest of his life teaching in Catholic schools in Chicago.

Despite the use of Jamaican dialect early in his career, much of McKay's poetry shows the influence of the English Romantic poets, especially Wordsworth, Keats, and Shelley. In subject matter, however, the Romantics and McKay diverge widely: McKay's sonnets voice his ambivalent and often defiant feelings about African American life in the United States.

Make the Connection

America the Beautiful?

By expressing defiance as well as love, McKay reveals the complexity of the African American experience in the United States—an experience that requires a large measure of strength and courage.

Quickwrite

Write down four or five adjectives that you feel describe the heart of today's American society. Then, in two or three sentences, tell how you see yourself in relation to that society.

National Museum of American Art, Washington, D.C. Courtesy Art Resource, NY.

Lower East Side from *Scenes of New York* (Mural study, Madison Square Postal Station, New York City) by Kindred McLeary. Tempera on fiberboard (23¾″ × 20″).

America

Claude McKay

Although she feeds me bread of bitterness,°
And sinks into my throat her tiger's tooth,
Stealing my breath of life, I will confess
I love this cultured hell that tests my youth!
5 Her vigor flows like tides into my blood,
Giving me strength erect against her hate.
Her bigness sweeps my being like a flood.
Yet as a rebel fronts° a king in state,
I stand within her walls with not a shred
10 Of terror, malice, not a word of jeer.
Darkly I gaze into the days ahead,
And see her might and granite wonders there,
Beneath the touch of Time's unerring hand,
Like priceless treasures sinking in the sand.

1. bread of bitterness: allusion to Psalm 80:5, "Thou feedest them with the bread of tears; and givest them tears to drink in great measure."
8. fronts: confronts.

MAKING MEANINGS

First Thoughts

1. Review your Quickwrite. Then, compare your views of America, and your place in it, with McKay's.

Shaping Interpretations

2. In lines 1–3, what treatment does the poem's speaker say he receives from America? What qualities of America cause the speaker to love the country anyway?

3. America is **personified** in this poem as an entity both cruel and powerful. What **images** suggest America's cruelty and injustice? What images convey its power?

4. A rebel with "not a shred / Of terror, malice, not a word of jeer" might seem to be a rebel who does not really rebel. How does the poem resolve this **paradox,** or apparent contradiction?

Extending the Text

5. What does this speaker see happening to America as he gazes into "the days ahead"? What messages about America's future do you hear today in various sources—films, TV shows, news programs, magazines, and other media?

Street vendors in Harlem in the 1920s.

UPI/Bettmann.

CHOICES: Building Your Portfolio

Writer's Notebook

1. Collecting Ideas for an Interpretive Essay

Using a chart like the one below, compare McKay's "America" to Robinson Jeffers's "Shine, Perishing Republic" (page 581). Consider the **form, subject, point of view,** and **tone** of each poem. List similarities in the overlapping space. Use the remaining spaces to list the differences. Save your notes for possible use with the Writer's Workshop on page 804.

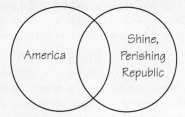

Creative Writing / Art

2. Get the Message

Design a poster or write a bumper sticker that the speaker in "America" might display. Try to capture in a phrase or two the main idea expressed in the poem.

Countee Cullen

(1903–1946)

Countee Cullen grew up in New York City as the adopted son of Rev. and Mrs. Frederick Cullen. He was a brilliant student, and during high school he was already writing accomplished poems in traditional forms. He graduated Phi Beta Kappa from New York University in 1925. While in college, Cullen won the Witter Bynner Poetry Prize; that same year, *Color*, his first volume of poetry, was published. This collection won a gold medal from the Harmon Foundation and established the young poet's reputation.

After earning his master's degree from Harvard in 1926, Cullen worked as an assistant editor of the important African American magazine *Opportunity*. His poems were published in such influential periodicals as *Harper's, Poetry*, and *Crisis*. In 1927, he published *Copper Sun*, a collection of poems, and *Caroling Dusk*, an anthology of poetry by African Americans. *Caroling Dusk* was a significant contribution to the Harlem Renaissance, but the introduction Cullen wrote for the book was controversial. He called for black poets to write traditional verse and to avoid the restrictions of solely racial themes.

At the peak of his career, Cullen married the daughter of the famous black writer W.E.B. Du Bois and published a third collection of poems, *The Ballad of the Brown Girl*. In 1929, he published a fourth volume, *The Black Christ*. Although he continued to write prose until the end of his life, this was his last collection of poetry. During the Great Depression of the 1930s, unable to make a living solely from writing, he began teaching in Harlem public schools, a job that he held until his early death.

Countee Porter Cullen (c. 1925) by Winold Reiss. Pastel on artist board (30 1/16″ × 21 1/2″).

Cullen's verse was heavily influenced by the poetry of the English Romantics, especially John Keats. He thought of himself primarily as a lyric poet in the Romantic tradition, not as a black poet writing about social and racial themes. Nevertheless, Cullen found himself repeatedly drawn to such themes: "Somehow or other I find my poetry of itself treating of the Negro, of his joys and his sorrows—mostly of the latter—and of the heights and depths of emotion which I feel as a Negro."

Before You Read

TABLEAU

Make the Connection

Still Life

Usually, *tableau* means a scene or an action stopped cold, like a still picture in a reel of film. Here we have a *tableau vivant;* that is, a little scene in which figures silently pose, a significant moment caught and preserved. This preserved moment is a disarmingly simple glimpse of a friendship—a friendship that speaks silently but forcefully of a much larger issue.

Quickwrite

If you were sure you were behaving correctly, how would you deal with critics of your actions? Write down your thoughts in a few sentences.

Tableau

(For Donald Duff)

Countee Cullen

Locked arm in arm they cross the way,
   The black boy and the white,
The golden splendor of the day,
   The sable pride of night.

5 From lowered blinds the dark folk stare,
   And here the fair folk talk,
Indignant that these two should dare
   In unison to walk.

Oblivious to look and word
10   They pass, and see no wonder
That lightning brilliant as a sword
   Should blaze the path of thunder.

Tony Galindo/The Image Bank

Make the Connection

A Word Remembered

The power of a word to taunt, to criticize, to dehumanize can't be underestimated. You might be shaken by the offensive word in this poem—imagine how it would affect a child.

Quickwrite

Before you read "Incident," quickwrite your response to the poem's title. Does it suggest something serious, or something relatively minor? How would you react if the title were "Catastrophe"?

Passengers (1953) by Raphael Soyer. Oil on canvas.

© Estate of Raphael Soyer, Forum Gallery, New York.

Incident

Countee Cullen

Once, riding in old Baltimore,
    Heart-filled, head-filled with glee,
I saw a Baltimorean
    Keep looking straight at me.

5 Now I was eight and very small,
    And he was no whit bigger,
And so I smiled, but he poked out
    His tongue, and called me "Nigger."

I saw the whole of Baltimore
10   From May until December;
Of all the things that happened there
    That's all that I remember.

MAKING MEANINGS

Tableau

First Thoughts

1. Review your Quickwrite. Do the boys in "Tableau" act toward their critics as you would act toward yours?

Shaping Interpretations

2. What **metaphors** describe the two boys in the first stanza?

3. In the third stanza, who or what is "lightning brilliant as a sword"? Who or what is the "path of thunder"?

4. Why should such a commonplace thing as the friendship between two boys evoke such a dramatic response? What larger **topic** do you think the poem is really about?

Incident

First Thoughts

1. Look at your Quickwrite notes. Does the poem describe a mere incident or something much larger? Explain.

Shaping Interpretations

2. What might lead a child to insult an eight-year-old boy in the way described here? In what ways is a child's prejudice even more disturbing than an adult's?

3. Review your response to First Thoughts. What **ironic** overtones does the title have?

4. The speaker never directly states his emotional response to the experience. How does the last stanza indirectly make clear the impact the event had on him?

Extending the Text

5. Do you think that the content and **message** of "Tableau" and "Incident" are outdated, or are the scenes described in these poems still occurring today? Explain.

CHOICES:
Building Your Portfolio

Writer's Notebook

1. Collecting Ideas for an Interpretive Essay

Compare and contrast the **diction** and **sentence structure** in "Tableau" and "Incident." Take notes that show how Cullen uses language to create two different effects in poems that are about very similar subjects. Save your notes for possible use in the Writer's Workshop on page 804.

Creative Writing

2. Kindred Spirits

Write a conversation in which the two boys who appear in "Tableau" discuss what happens in "Incident" with the eight-year-old boy who was the victim of the incident.

Creative Writing / Music

3. A Film Version

Suppose you were going to make a short film based on the poem "Incident." To convince a producer that you have a good idea, write a list of planned camera shots, in the order in which they would appear on screen. Then write a treatment, or summary, of your vision of the film. If you wish, find or compose music that you would use as an appropriate soundtrack for your film, and include a recording of that music with your film treatment.

Zora Neale Hurston

(c. 1903–1960)

Zora Neale Hurston was born in the all-black town of Eatonville, Florida. Her father was a preacher, and her mother, a schoolteacher, urged her talented daughter to "jump at the sun."

In her autobiography, Hurston recalls that as a young girl, "I used to climb to the top of one of the huge chinaberry trees which guarded our front gate and look out over the world. The most interesting thing that I saw was the horizon. . . . It grew upon me that I ought to walk out to the horizon and see what the end of the world was like."

When Hurston was about nine, her mother died, and Zora was passed among relatives and family friends, supporting herself from her early teens on. Eventually, she enrolled at Howard University in Washington, D.C., where she published her first story in 1921.

Four years later, she set out for New York City to attend Barnard College, arriving with

Zora Neale Hurston (1935) by Carl Van Vechten.

a dollar and a half in her pocket. Hurston was soon in the midst of the Harlem Renaissance, writing stories and plays that celebrated her African American heritage. She wore big hats and turbans, danced, gave parties, and sometimes shocked other African American artists, especially male writers like James Weldon Johnson and Langston Hughes.

Enrolling at prestigious Barnard College, Hurston met the famous anthropologist Franz Boas. Boas believed that Hurston's interest was really in his field, the study of human social and cultural behavior. Indeed, Hurston, who became his protégé, did eventually make her reputation not just as a fiction writer, but also as a folk-lorist. She traveled through Alabama, Florida, and Louisiana to gather folklore material, using a scholar's eye to evaluate oral tales, many of which were familiar to her from earliest child-hood. Eventually, she gathered enough folklore to fill two groundbreaking collections, *Mules and Men* (1935) and *Tell My Horse* (1938). Alice Walker (page 1101) says that the stories in *Mules and Men* gave back to her own relatives in the South all the stories they'd forgotten or grown ashamed of.

Hurston also wrote musical revues portraying black folk-culture, and these brought her initial success. But it was *Story* magazine's publication of her short story "The Gilded Six Bits" that launched her literary career. When the Philadelphia publisher J. B. Lippincott asked if she had a novel, Hurston promptly sat down and wrote *Jonah's Gourd Vine,* published in 1934. Three years later, Hurston published her best novel, *Their Eyes Were Watching God,* the story of a young African American woman who strikes out for a life beyond a conventional marriage, much as Hurston herself had done.

Throughout the last twenty years of her life, Hurston continued to produce fiction and nonfiction, including her autobiography, *Dust Tracks on a Road.* But she began to have difficulty finding a market for her work, some of which was criticized in the African American community for celebrating the life of black people in the United States rather than confronting the white community for its discrimination.

In the late 1940s, Hurston left New York and returned to Florida. In 1960, she died, broke, in a Florida welfare home. A collection had to be taken up to pay for her funeral. Ironically, in the years since her death, much of her work has been brought back into print, and Hurston is now recognized as the forerunner of such celebrated contemporary writers as Toni Morrison and Alice Walker.

 go.hrw.com

LEO 11-15

Before You Read

FROM DUST TRACKS ON A ROAD

Make the Connection

Looking for the Threads

It's no surprise that the auto-biographies of writers often include lovingly detailed memories of childhood interests and discoveries that paved the way for the adult writer. In her auto-biography, *One Writer's Beginnings,* Eudora Welty (page 633) notes, "Writing fiction has developed in me an abiding respect for the unknown in a human lifetime and a sense of where to look for the threads, how to follow, how to connect, find in the thick of the tangle what clear line persists. The strands are all there: To the memory nothing is ever really lost." Here, Zora Neale Hurston connects some of her own threads by recounting what is surely every writer's first experience of falling in love: the passion for hearing and reading stories.

Reading Skills and Strategies

Analyzing an Autobiography

As you read, write down what you learn about Hurston's character from her thoughts and actions, as well as any details that suggest Hurston's early interest in people, her fascination with storytelling, and her later devotion to anthropology and folklore research.

Background

Zora Neale Hurston's *Dust Tracks on a Road* is rich with cultural and historical meaning, as well as personal insight and data. Woven through these recollections of Hurston's childhood are her impressions of racial segregation, economic conditions, education, social customs, and family, as well as general attitudes of Southerners around 1900.

Her World (1948) by Philip Evergood. Oil on canvas (48″ × 35⅝″).

> *I used to take a seat on top of the gatepost and watch the world go by.*

from *Dust Tracks on a Road*

Zora Neale Hurston

Dunbar High School, Quincy, Florida (pages 752–753, 755, 756).
Florida State Archives.

I used to take a seat on top of the gatepost and watch the world go by. One way to Orlando ran past my house, so the carriages and cars would pass before me. The movement made me glad to see it. Often the white travelers would <u>hail</u> me, but more often I hailed them, and asked, "Don't you want me to go a piece of the way with you?"

They always did. I know now that I must have caused a great deal of amusement among them, but my self-assurance must have carried the point, for I was always invited to come along. I'd ride up the road for perhaps a half-mile, then walk back. I did not do this with the permission of my parents, nor with their foreknowledge. When they found out about it later, I usually got a whipping. My grandmother worried about my forward ways a great deal. She had known slavery and to her my <u>brazenness</u> was unthinkable.

She had known slavery and to her my brazenness was unthinkable.

"Git down offa dat gatepost! You li'l sow, you! Git down! Setting up dere looking dem white folks right in de face! They's gowine[1] to lynch you, yet. And don't stand in dat doorway gazing out at 'em neither. Youse too brazen to live long."

---

1. **gowine:** dialect for "going."

WORDS TO OWN
hail (hāl) *v.*: greet.
brazenness (brā′zən·nis) *n.*: boldness.

Nevertheless, I kept right on gazing at them, and "going a piece of the way" whenever I could make it. The village seemed dull to me most of the time. If the village was singing a chorus, I must have missed the tune.

Perhaps a year before the old man[2] died, I came to know two other white people for myself. They were women.

It came about this way. The whites who came down from the North were often brought by their friends to visit the village school. A Negro school was something strange to them, and while they were always sympathetic and kind, curiosity must have been present, also. They came and went, came and went. Always, the room was hurriedly put in order, and we were threatened with a prompt and bloody death if we cut one <u>caper</u> while the visitors were present. We always sang a spiritual, led by Mr. Calhoun himself. Mrs. Calhoun always stood in the back, with a palmetto switch[3] in her hand as a squelcher. We were all little angels for the duration, because we'd better be. She would cut her eyes[4] and give us a glare that meant trouble, then turn her face toward the visitors and beam as much as to say it was a great privilege and pleasure to teach lovely children like us. They couldn't see that palmetto hickory in her hand behind all those benches, but we knew where our angelic behavior was coming from.

Usually, the visitors gave warning a day ahead and we would be cautioned to put on shoes, comb our heads, and see to ears and fingernails. There was a close inspection of every one of us before we marched in that morning. Knotty heads, dirty ears, and fingernails got hauled out of line, strapped, and sent home to lick the calf[5] over again.

This particular afternoon, the two young ladies just popped in. Mr. Calhoun was flustered, but he put on the best show he could. He dismissed the class that he was teaching up at the front of the room, then called the fifth grade in reading. That was my class.

So we took our readers and went up front. We stood up in the usual line, and opened to the lesson. It was the story of Pluto and Persephone.[6] It was new and hard to the class in general, and Mr. Calhoun was very uncomfortable as the readers stumbled along, spelling out words with their lips, and in mumbling undertones before they exposed them experimentally to the teacher's ears.

Then it came to me. I was fifth or sixth down the line. The story was not new to me, because I had read my reader through from lid to lid, the first week that Papa had bought it for me.

That is how it was that my eyes were not in the book, working out the paragraph which I knew would be mine by counting the children ahead of me. I was observing our visitors, who held a book between them, following the lesson. They had shiny hair, mostly brownish. One had a looping gold chain around her neck. The other one was dressed all over in black and white with a pretty finger ring on her left hand. But the thing that held my eyes were their fingers. They were long and thin, and very white, except up near the tips. There they were baby pink. I had never seen such hands. It was a fascinating discovery for me. I wondered how they felt. I would have given those hands more attention, but the child before me was almost through. My turn next, so I got on my mark, bringing my eyes back to the book and made sure of my place. Some of the stories I had reread several times, and this Greco-Roman myth was one of my favorites. I was <u>exalted</u> by it, and that is the way I read my paragraph.

"Yes, Jupiter[7] had seen her (Persephone). He had seen the maiden picking flowers in the field. He had seen the chariot of the dark monarch pause by the maiden's side. He had seen him when he seized Persephone. He had seen the

---

2. **old man:** a white farmer who knew Hurston's family, took her fishing, and gave her advice.
3. **palmetto switch:** whip made from the stem of a large, fanlike leaf of a kind of palm tree. Teachers sometimes used these switches to discipline students.
4. **cut her eyes:** slang for "look scornfully."
5. **lick the calf:** slang for "wash up."

6. **Pluto and Persephone** (pər·sef′ə·nē): In classical mythology, Pluto, or Hades, is the god who rules the underworld; Persephone, also known as Proserpina, is his wife, queen of the underworld. In this version of the origin of the seasons, Hurston uses the names of Roman and Greek gods interchangeably.
7. **Jupiter:** in Roman mythology, king of the gods.

- -

WORDS TO OWN
caper (kā′pər) *n*.: foolish prank.
exalted (eg·zôlt′id) *v*.: lifted up.

- -

black horses leap down Mount Aetna's[8] fiery throat. Persephone was now in Pluto's dark <u>realm</u> and he had made her his wife."

The two women looked at each other and then back to me. Mr. Calhoun broke out with a proud smile beneath his bristly moustache, and instead of the next child taking up where I had ended, he nodded to me to go on. So I read the story to the end, where flying Mercury, the messenger of the Gods, brought Persephone back to the sunlit earth and restored her to the arms of Dame Ceres, her mother, that the world might have springtime and summer flowers, autumn and harvest. But because she had bitten the pomegranate while in Pluto's kingdom, she must return to him for three months of each year, and be his queen. Then the world had winter, until she returned to earth.

The class was dismissed and the visitors smiled us away and went into a low-voiced conversation with Mr. Calhoun for a few minutes. They glanced my way once or twice and I began to worry. Not only was I barefooted, but my feet and legs were dusty. My hair was more uncombed than usual, and my nails were not shiny clean. Oh, I'm going to catch it now. Those ladies saw me, too. Mr. Calhoun is promising to 'tend to me. So I thought.

Then Mr. Calhoun called me. I went up thinking how awful it was to get a whipping before company. Furthermore, I heard a snicker run over the room. Hennie Clark and Stell Brazzle did it out loud, so I would be sure to hear them. The smart aleck was going to get it. I slipped one hand behind me and switched my dress tail at them, indicating scorn.

"Come here, Zora Neale," Mr. Calhoun cooed as I reached the desk. He put his hand on my shoulder and gave me little pats. The ladies smiled and held out those flower-looking fingers toward me. I seized the opportunity for a good look.

"Shake hands with the ladies, Zora Neale," Mr. Calhoun prompted and they took my hand one after the other and smiled. They asked me if I loved school, and I lied that I did. There was *some* truth in it, because I liked geography and reading, and I liked to play at recess time. Whoever it was invented writing and arithmetic got no thanks from me. Neither did I like the arrangement where the teacher could sit up there with a palmetto stem and lick me whenever he saw fit. I hated things I couldn't do anything about. But I knew better than to bring that up right there, so I said yes, I *loved* school.

"I can tell you do," Brown Taffeta gleamed. She patted my head, and was lucky enough not to get sandspurs in her hand. Children who roll and tumble in the grass in Florida are apt to get sandspurs in their hair. They shook hands with me again and I went back to my seat.

When school let out at three o'clock, Mr. Calhoun told me to wait. When everybody had gone, he told me I was to go to the Park House, that was the hotel in Maitland, the next afternoon to call upon Mrs. Johnstone and Miss Hurd. I must tell Mama to see that I was clean and brushed from head to feet, and I must wear shoes and stockings. The ladies liked me, he said, and I must be on my best behavior.

The next day I was let out of school an hour early, and went home to be stood up in a tub of suds and be scrubbed and have my ears dug into. My sandy hair sported a red ribbon to match my red and white checked gingham dress, starched until it could stand alone. Mama saw to it that my shoes were on the right feet, since I was

> The ladies smiled and held out those flower-looking fingers toward me.

---

8. **Mount Aetna's:** Mount Aetna (also spelled Etna) is a volcanic mountain in eastern Sicily.

WORDS TO OWN

realm (relm) *n.*: kingdom.

careless about left and right. Last thing, I was given a handkerchief to carry, warned again about my behavior, and sent off, with my big brother John to go as far as the hotel gate with me.

First thing, the ladies gave me strange things, like stuffed dates and preserved ginger, and encouraged me to eat all that I wanted. Then they showed me their Japanese dolls and just talked. I was then handed a copy of *Scribner's Magazine,* and asked to read a place that was pointed out to me. After a paragraph or two, I was told with smiles, that that would do.

I was led out on the grounds and they took my picture under a palm tree. They handed me what was to me then a heavy cylinder done up in fancy paper, tied with a ribbon, and they told me goodbye, asking me not to open it until I got home.

My brother was waiting for me down by the lake, and we hurried home, eager to see what was in the thing. It was too heavy to be candy or anything like that. John insisted on toting it for me.

My mother made John give it back to me and let me open it. Perhaps, I shall never experience such joy again. The nearest thing to that moment was the telegram accepting my first book. One hundred goldy-new pennies rolled out of the cylinder. Their gleam lit up the world. It was not avarice that moved me. It was the beauty of the thing. I stood on the mountain. Mama let me play with my pennies for a while, then put them away for me to keep.

That was only the beginning. The next day I received an Episcopal hymnbook bound in white leather with a golden cross stamped into the front cover, a copy of *The Swiss Family Robinson,* and a book of fairy tales.

I set about to commit the song words to memory. There was no music written there, just the words. But there was to my consciousness music in between them just the same. "When I survey the Wondrous Cross" seemed the most beautiful to me, so I committed that to memory first of all. Some of them seemed dull and without life, and I pretended they were not there. If white people liked trashy singing like that, there must be something funny about them that I had not noticed before. I stuck to the pretty ones where the words marched to a throb I could feel.

Of the Greeks, Hercules moved me most.

WORDS TO OWN
avarice (av′ə·ris) *n.*: greed.

A month or so after the two young ladies returned to Minnesota, they sent me a huge box packed with clothes and books. The red coat with a wide circular collar and the red tam pleased me more than any of the other things. My chums pretended not to like anything that I had, but even then I knew that they were jealous. Old Smarty had gotten by them again. The clothes were not new, but they were very good. I shone like the morning sun.

But the books gave me more pleasure than the clothes. I had never been too keen on dressing up. It called for hard scrubbings with Octagon soap suds getting in my eyes, and none too gentle fingers scrubbing my neck and gouging in my ears.

In that box were *Gulliver's Travels, Grimm's Fairy Tales, Dick Whittington, Greek and Roman Myths,* and best of all, *Norse Tales.* Why did the Norse tales strike so deeply into my soul? I do not know, but they did. I seemed to remember seeing Thor swing his mighty short-handled hammer as he sped across the sky in rumbling thunder, lightning flashing from the tread of his steeds and the wheels of his chariot. The great and good Odin, who went down to the well of knowledge to drink, and was told that the price of a drink from that fountain was an eye. Odin drank deeply, then plucked out one eye without a murmur and handed it to the grizzly keeper, and walked away. That held majesty for me.

Of the Greeks, Hercules moved me most. I followed him eagerly on his tasks. The story of the choice of Hercules as a boy when he met Pleasure and Duty, and put his hand in that of Duty and followed her steep way to the blue hills of fame and glory, which she pointed out at the end, moved me profoundly. I resolved to be like him. The tricks and turns of the other gods and goddesses left me cold. There were other thin books about this and that sweet and gentle little girl who gave up her heart to Christ and good works. Almost always they died from it, preaching as they passed. I was utterly indifferent to their deaths. In the first place I could not conceive of death, and in the next place they never had any funerals that amounted to a hill of beans, so I didn't care how soon they rolled up their big, soulful, blue eyes and kicked the bucket. They had no meat on their bones.

But I also met Hans Andersen[9] and Robert Louis Stevenson.[10] They seemed to know what I wanted to hear and said it in a way that tingled me. Just a little below these friends was Rudyard Kipling in his Jungle Books.[11] I loved his talking snakes as much as I did the hero.

I came to start reading the Bible through my mother. She gave me a licking one afternoon for repeating something I had overheard a neighbor telling her. She locked me in her room after the whipping, and the Bible was the only thing in there for me to read. I happened to open to the place where David was doing some mighty smiting, and I got interested. David went here and he went there, and no matter where he went, he smote 'em hip and thigh. Then he sung songs to his harp awhile, and went out and smote some more. Not one time did David stop and preach about sins and things. All David wanted to know from God was who to kill and when. He took care of the other details himself. Never a quiet moment. I liked him a lot. So I read a great deal more in the Bible, hunting for some more active people like David. Except for the beautiful language of Luke and Paul, the New Testament still plays a poor second to the Old Testament for me. The Jews had a God who laid about Him[12] when they needed Him. I could see no use waiting till Judgment Day to see a man who was just crying for a good killing, to be told to go and roast.[13] My idea was to give him a good killing first, and then if he got roasted later on, so much the better.

---

9. Hans Andersen: Hans Christian Andersen (1805–1875), Danish writer known primarily for his fairy tales.
10. Robert Louis Stevenson (1850–1894): Scottish writer of adventure stories such as *Kidnapped* and *Treasure Island.*
11. Rudyard Kipling . . . Books: Kipling (1865–1936) was an English writer born in India. His *Jungle Book* and *Second Jungle Book* contain stories of the adventures of Mowgli, a boy raised by animals in the jungles of India.
12. laid about Him: slang for "struck blows in every direction."
13. roast: slang for "burn in hell."

WORDS TO OWN
tread (tred) *n.:* stepping.
profoundly (prō·found′lē) *adv.:* deeply.
resolved (rē·zälvd′) *v.:* made a decision; determined.
conceive (kən·sēv′) *v.:* think; imagine.

In Search of a Story

• In another section of *Dust Tracks on a Road,* Zora Neale Hurston tells of her passion, as a child, for hearing stories from the African American tradition.

For me, the store porch was the most interesting place that I could think of. I was not allowed to sit around there, naturally. But, I could and did drag my feet going in and out, whenever I was sent there for something, to allow whatever was being said to hang in my ear. I would hear an occasional scrap of gossip in what to me was adult double talk, but which I understood at times. . . .

But what I really loved to hear was the menfolks holding a "lying" session. That is, straining against each other in telling folks tales. God, Devil, Brer Rabbit, Brer Fox, Sis Cat, Brer Bear, Lion, Tiger, Buzzard, and all the wood folk walked and talked like natural men. The wives of the storytellers might yell from back yards for them to come and tote some water, or chop wood for the cookstove and never get a move out of the men. The usual rejoinder was, "Oh, she's got enough to go on. No matter how much wood you chop, a woman will burn it all up to get a meal. If she got a couple of pieces, she will make it do. If you chop up a whole boxful, she will burn every stick of it. Pay her no mind." So the storytelling would go right on.

• • •

• This passion for listening to stories from the oral tradition led Hurston to collect folklore as a field researcher. In this section of her autobiography, Hurston tells of studying anthropology at Barnard College in New York City and of how she went out among African Americans to gather their folk tales. In her first attempts as a folklore collector, she did not succeed. She had to learn the hard way that a folklorist must use just the right approach with his or her sources.

Mecklenburg Evening (1984) by Romare Bearden. Collage and watercolor on board.
© Romare Bearden Foundation/Licensed by VAGA, New York, NY.

Research is formalized curiosity. It is poking and prying with a purpose. It is a seeking that he who wishes may know the cosmic secrets of the world and they that dwell therein. . . .

My first six months were disappointing. I found out later that it was not because I had no talents for research, but because I did not have the right approach. The glamour of Barnard College was still upon me. I dwelt in marble halls. I knew where the material was all right. But, I went about asking, in carefully accented Barnardese, "Pardon me, but do you know any folk tales or folk songs?" The men and women who had whole treasuries of material just seeping through their pores looked at me and shook their heads. No, they had never heard of anything like that around there. Maybe it was over in the next county. Why didn't I try over there? I did, and got the selfsame answer. Oh, I got a few little items. But compared with what I did later, not enough to make a flea a waltzing jacket.

—Zora Neale Hurston

MAKING MEANINGS

First Thoughts

1. Did you identify with Hurston's love of books? What were your feelings about books when you were younger? Have your feelings changed?

Shaping Interpretations

2. Consulting the notes you took while reading, **characterize** the narrator. Find examples from the text to support your view of Hurston.

3. What qualities does the young Hurston exhibit when she reads aloud in class?

4. What does Hurston think about the two women who visit? How do you know?

5. Why do you think the visitors invite Hurston to their hotel?

6. Why does the young Hurston treasure the books the ladies from Minnesota send her?

Challenging the Text

7. Hurston was criticized by some of her contemporaries because they felt she did not place enough emphasis on the racial oppression of African Americans by the white community. Using references from this autobiographical excerpt, explain whether you agree or disagree with this criticism.

CHOICES: Building Your Portfolio

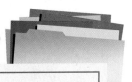

Writer's Notebook

1. Collecting Ideas for an Interpretive Essay

The **title** of an autobiography can tell you a great deal about how a writer views his or her life. Write down your reactions to the title *Dust Tracks on a Road*. Based on what you learned about Hurston in the biography on page 750 and in this excerpt, why do you think she chose this title? What does it reveal about her life experiences? Keep your notes for possible use in the Writer's Workshop on page 804.

Comparing Autobiographies

2. Real-Life Stories

In a brief essay, compare this passage from Hurston's autobiography with the selection from Benjamin Franklin's *Autobiography* (page 86). You might compare (a) the narrators' actions and motives; (b) the narrators' relationships with other people; (c) the incidents described and why the narrators might have chosen to write about them.

Creative Writing / Performance

3. *Dust Tracks* Onstage

Autobiographies are often successfully adapted and dramatized for the stage. Working with a group, prepare this excerpt from *Dust Tracks on a Road* for performance. You will have to assign scriptwriters, a director, actors, costume designers, and set designers. You might also need a narrator to tell the parts of the story that are not told directly in dialogue. Consider using music (such as orchestral, rock, folk, blues, jazz, or rap) to emphasize important moments.

Portrait of Langston Hughes by Winold Reiss.
National Portrait Gallery, Washington, D.C., U.S.A.

Langston Hughes

(1902–1967)

One evening toward the end of 1925, the poet Vachel Lindsay was eating dinner in the Wardman Park Hotel in Washington, D.C. The busboy, a twenty-three-year-old African American, left three poems near Lindsay's plate. Lindsay was so impressed by the poems that he presented them in his reading that night, telling the audience that he had discovered a true poet—a young black man who was working as a busboy in the hotel restaurant. Over the next few days, articles about the "busboy poet" appeared in newspapers up and down the East Coast.

The busboy, Langston Hughes, was no beginning writer. In fact, when he shyly approached Lindsay, Hughes's first book of poetry, *The Weary Blues,* was about to be published by a prestigious New York company, and individual poems had appeared in numerous places. Lindsay warned the young poet about literary "lionizers" who might exploit him for their own purpose: "Hide and write and study and think. I know what factions do. Beware of them. I know what lionizers do. Beware of them." In response to Lindsay, Hughes wrote back: "If anything is important, it is my poetry, not me. I do not want folks to know me, but if they know and like some of my poems I am glad. Perhaps the mission of an artist is to interpret beauty to the people—the beauty within themselves. That is what I want to do, if I consciously want to do anything with poetry."

Before this encounter, Hughes had attended Columbia University and worked his way to Africa and back as a crew member on an ocean freighter. Ambitious and energetic, Hughes had learned early to rely on himself. He spoke German and Spanish; he had lived in Mexico, France, and Italy. In the years that followed his "overnight" celebrity, he earned his degree at Lincoln University, wrote fifteen volumes of poetry, six novels, three books of short stories, eleven plays, and a variety of nonfiction works.

Born in Joplin, Missouri, Hughes spent most of his childhood in Lawrence, Kansas, with his grandmother. When he was thirteen, she died, and he moved to Lincoln, Illinois, and then to Cleveland, Ohio, to live with his mother and stepfather.

Hughes began writing poems in the eighth grade, and he began publishing his work as a high school student in his school literary magazine. He read voraciously and greatly admired the work of Edgar Lee Masters, Vachel Lindsay, Amy Lowell, Carl Sandburg, and Walt Whitman.

The most important influences on Hughes's poetry were Walt Whitman and Carl Sandburg. Both poets broke from traditional poetic forms and used free verse to express the humanity of all people regardless of their age, gender, race, and class. Encouraged by the examples of Whitman and Sandburg, Hughes celebrated the experiences of African Americans, often using jazz rhythms and the repetitive structure of the blues in his poems. Toward the end of his life, he wrote poems specifically for jazz accompaniment. He was also responsible for the founding of several black theater companies, and he wrote and translated a number of dramatic works. His work, he said, was an attempt to "explain and illuminate the Negro condition in America." It succeeded in doing that with both vigor and compassion.

Before You Read

THE WEARY BLUES

Make the Connection

Sweet Blues

Among the great contributions of American culture to the world is the music produced by African Americans: orchestral, blues, ragtime, jazz, rap, and new musical expressions that you can hear every day.

The kind of music known as the blues started to attract attention at the turn of the century, eventually becoming widely popular in the United States and abroad and making stars out of such blues singers as Bessie Smith and Ethel Waters. In this poem, Hughes tries both to report the experience of a "sad raggy tune" and to capture some of its rhythms in words.

Quickwrite

Blues music has influenced all kinds of popular music, from rock and soul to country, folk, and jazz. Jot down any associations you have with the word *blues*. What do you already know about blues music? Is there any blues influence in the kinds of music you like?

Elements of Literature

Rhythm

Rhythm in poetry is the rise and fall of the voice, produced by the alternation of stressed and unstressed syllables. Langston Hughes uses several different kinds of rhythms in "The Weary Blues." As he says in the first line, he uses the "syncopated tune" of a piano. He also uses the rhythm of everyday speech, the soulful rhythm of the blues, and even the formal meter of traditional poetry. His poems are true originals.

Background

On a March night in 1922, Langston Hughes sat in a small Harlem cabaret and wrote "The Weary Blues." In this poem, Hughes incorporated the many elements of his life—the music of Southern black speech, the lyrics of the first blues he ever heard, and conventional poetic forms he learned in school. While the body of the poem took shape quickly, it took the poet two years to get the ending right: "I could not achieve an ending I liked, although I worked and worked on it." When he at last completed the poem, "The Weary Blues" marked the beginning of his literary career.

The Weary Blues

Langston Hughes

Droning a drowsy syncopated tune,°
Rocking back and forth to a mellow croon,
   I heard a Negro play.
Down on Lenox Avenue° the other night
5 By the pale dull pallor of an old gas light
    He did a lazy sway . . .
    He did a lazy sway . . .
To the tune o' those Weary Blues.
With his ebony hands on each ivory key
10 He made that poor piano moan with melody.
    O Blues!
Swaying to and fro on his rickety stool
He played that sad raggy tune like a musical fool.
    Sweet Blues!

1. syncopated tune: melody in which accents are placed on normally unaccented beats.
4. Lenox Avenue: street in Harlem.

Out Chorus by Romare Bearden. Silkscreen (12⅜″ × 16½″).

15 Coming from a black man's soul.
     O Blues!
  In a deep song voice with a melancholy tone
  I heard that Negro sing, that old piano moan—
     "Ain't got nobody in all this world,
20   Ain't got nobody but ma salf.
     I's gwine to quit ma frownin'
     And put ma troubles on the shelf."
  Thump, thump, thump, went his foot on the floor.
  He played a few chords then he sang some more—
25   "I got the Weary Blues
     And I can't be satisfied.
     Got the Weary Blues
     And can't be satisfied—
     I ain't happy no mo'
30   And I wish that I had died."
  And far into the night he crooned that tune.
  The stars went out and so did the moon.
  The singer stopped playing and went to bed
  While the Weary Blues echoed through his head.
35 He slept like a rock or a man that's dead.

Birth of the Blues

When asked about the origins of the blues, a veteran New Orleans fiddler once said: "The blues? Ain't no first blues! The blues always been." The first form of blues, country blues, developed in several parts of the United States, most notably the Mississippi Delta, around 1900. Country blues tunes were typically sung by men—usually sharecroppers. The subject was often the relationship between men and women. As the contemporary blues singer B. B. King once said, the blues is about a man losing his woman.

From the start, blues music was improvisational—it changed with every singer and performance. Parts of lyrics were freely borrowed from other songs or based on folk songs or figures of speech. Lines might be repeated two or three times, with different accents and emphases, then answered or completed by a rhyming line:

> Black cat on my doorstep, black cat on my window sill. (repeat)
> If some black cat don't cross me, some other black cat will.
>
> —Ma Rainey

The blues catch on. The earliest blues singers, among them Charley Patton, Robert Johnson, and Blind Lemon Jefferson, played at country stores, at Friday- and Saturday-night dances, at cafes, and at picnics. The first popular blues recordings, made in the 1920s, featured female singers such as Ma Rainey and Bessie Smith backed by a piano or a jazz band.

When rural Southern African Americans migrated after World War I to cities like Chicago, New York, Detroit, St. Louis, and Memphis, the blues sound evolved further. Musicians sang about their experiences in the city, adding the electric guitar, amplified harmonica, bass, and drums to blues ensembles. Musicians such as Sunnyland Slim, T-Bone Walker, and Memphis Minnie pioneered the urban blues sound in the 1930s and 1940s; the next generation included the blues greats Muddy Waters, Howlin' Wolf, and B. B. King. Since then, blues music has influenced virtually every genre of music, including folk, country and western, and—most profoundly—rock. Elvis Presley, Bob Dylan, the Rolling Stones, Eric Clapton, and Bonnie Raitt have all borrowed freely from the blues tradition. Today, blues music is still being played and created by such artists as Buddy Guy, Etta James, Otis Rush, Koko Taylor, Keb' Mo', and Robert Cray. They are carrying on a musical tradition that was invented at a particular time and place—the American South in the early 1900s—to express the African American experience. The genius of the blues is that it has honored its origins even as it expresses universal hopes, fears, and sorrows.

Make the Connection

Feeling Trapped

The Harlem Renaissance writers created many poems that were responses to the feeling of oppression that pervaded the lives of Harlem residents. Hughes himself wrote several poems called "Harlem." This poem is set during the Great Depression, a time when even a one-cent increase in the price of bread could be disastrous, when being black and poor meant that there were limited opportunities.

Quickwrite

How would it feel to be the victim of discrimination? List some adjectives describing a victim's emotions.

Elements of Literature

Tone

Tone is the attitude a writer takes toward the subject of a literary work, the characters or events in it, or the audience that it is directed to. Some early African American writers conveyed their real emotions under masks of carefully shaped observations, images, and thoughts. In "Harlem," Langston Hughes manipulates the poem's tone to both hide and reveal his feelings.

Harlem

Langston Hughes

Here on the edge of hell
Stands Harlem—
Remembering the old lies,
The old kicks in the back,
5 The old "Be patient"
They told us before.

Sure, we remember.
Now when the man at the corner store
Says sugar's gone up another two cents,
10 And bread one,
And there's a new tax on cigarettes—
We remember the job we never had,
Never could get,
And can't have now
15 Because we're colored.

So we stand here
On the edge of hell
In Harlem
And look out on the world
20 And wonder
What we're gonna do
In the face of what
We remember.

Harlem Street Scene (1975) by Jacob Lawrence. Serigraph (27″ × 24″).

Heyday in Harlem

Langston Hughes describes the vigor and excitement of Harlem in the 1920s and 1930s.

White people began to come to Harlem in droves. For several years they packed the expensive Cotton Club on Lenox Avenue. But I was never there, because the Cotton Club was a Jim Crow club[1] for gangsters and monied whites. They were not cordial to Negro patronage, unless you were a celebrity like Bojangles.[2] So Harlem Negroes did not like the Cotton Club and never appreciated its Jim Crow policy in the very heart of their dark community. . . .

It was a period when, at almost every Harlem upper-crust dance or party, one would be introduced to various distinguished white

1. **Jim Crow club:** segregated nightclub.

2. **Bojangles:** Bill "Bojangles" Robinson (1879–1949), star of black musical comedies and vaudeville.

Jockey Club (1929) by Archibald John Motley, Jr. Oil on canvas.

Schomburg Center for Research in Black Culture. Art and Artifacts Division. The New York Public Library, Astor, Lenox and Tilden Foundations.

celebrities there as guests. It was a period when almost any Harlem Negro of any social importance at all would be likely to say casually: "As I was remarking the other day to Heywood—," meaning Heywood Broun.[3] Or: "As I said to George—," referring to George Gershwin.[4] It was a period when local and visiting royalty were not at all uncommon in Harlem. And when the parties of A'Lelia Walker, the Negro heiress, were filled with guests whose names would turn any Nordic[5] social climber green with envy. . . . It was a period when every season there was at least one hit play on Broadway acted by a Negro cast. And when books by Negro authors were being published with much greater frequency and much more publicity than ever before or since in history. It was a period when white writers wrote about Negroes more successfully (commercially speaking) than Negroes did about themselves. It was the period (God help us!) when Ethel Barrymore[6] appeared in blackface in *Scarlet Sister Mary*! It was the period when the Negro was in vogue. . . .

Then it was that house-rent parties began to flourish—and not always to raise the rent either. But, as often as not, to have a get-together of one's own, where you could do the blackbottom[7] with no stranger behind you trying to do it, too. Nontheatrical, nonintellectual Harlem was an unwilling victim of its own vogue. It didn't like to be stared at by white folks. But perhaps the downtowners never knew this—for the cabaret owners, the entertainers, and the speakeasy[8] proprietors treated them fine—as long as they paid.

The Saturday night rent parties that I attended were often more amusing than any night club, in small apartments where God knows who lived—because the guests seldom did—but where the piano would often be augmented by a guitar, or an odd cornet, or somebody with a pair of drums walking in off the street. And where awful bootleg whiskey and good fried fish or steaming chitterling[9] were sold at very low prices. And the dancing and singing and impromptu entertaining went on until dawn came in at the windows.

These parties, often termed whist[10] parties or dances, were usually announced by brightly colored cards stuck in the grille of apartment house elevators. Some of the cards were highly entertaining in themselves:

Some wear pajamas, some wear pants, what does it matter just so you can dance, at

A Social Whist Party

GIVEN BY

MR. & MRS. BROWN
AT 258 W. 115TH STREET, APT. 9
SATURDAY EVE., SEPT. 14, 1929

The music is sweet and everything good to eat!

Almost every Saturday night when I was in Harlem I went to a house-rent party. I wrote lots of poems about house-rent parties, and ate thereat many a fried fish and pig's foot—with liquid refreshments on the side. I met ladies' maids and truck drivers, laundry workers and shoeshine boys, seamstresses and porters. I can still hear their laughter in my ears, hear the soft slow music, and feel the floor shaking as the dancers danced.

—Langston Hughes,
*from "When the Negro Was in Vogue,"
from The Big Sea*

3. Heywood Broun (1888–1939): American journalist during the 1920s and 1930s.
4. George Gershwin (1898–1937): great American composer of both popular and serious music.
5. Nordic: white.
6. Ethel Barrymore (1879–1959): American stage and movie actress.
7. black-bottom: popular dance of the late 1920s.
8. speakeasy: club where alcoholic drinks were sold illegally during Prohibition.

9. chitterling (chit'lin): food made from small intestines of pigs, deep-fried in hot oil.
10. whist: card game.

MAKING MEANINGS

The Weary Blues

First Thoughts

1. What would you say is the most powerful **image** in "The Weary Blues"? Why?

Shaping Interpretations

2. How does the **message** of the blues singer's first verse contrast with that of his second?

3. What are some of the words in the poem that help to create a slow, weary, melancholy **mood**?

4. Review your Quickwrite to see how well this poem fits your concept of blues music. Describe how the poem's structure suggests the **rhythms** of blues music. Point out examples of **alliteration** and **onomatopoeia** that also add to the poem's wailing, musical effect.

5. How would you describe the emotional effect of the **image** in line 32?

6. What **similes** in the poem's last line describe how the singer sleeps? What do you think the last five words suggest?

Harlem

First Thoughts

1. Did any of the adjectives in your Quickwrite describe the feelings of the speaker in this poem? If not, what adjective would best describe the speaker's **tone**?

Shaping Interpretations

2. Name the specific hardships and injustices that the people of Harlem remember, according to the speaker in the poem.

3. In "Harlem," what does the speaker suggest when he says "Here on the edge of hell / Stands Harlem—"?

4. What is the effect of the repetition of "remember"?

5. Do you interpret the poem's final stanza as an expression of powerlessness, or as a threat? Defend your opinion.

6. How would you read this poem and "The Weary Blues" aloud to express the **tones** you hear in them?

CHOICES:
Building Your Portfolio

Writer's Notebook

1. Collecting Ideas for an Interpretive Essay

Create a chart analyzing the attitudes of the speakers in "Harlem" and "I, Too" (page 733). Note the ways the speakers are similar and the ways they are different. Save your notes for possible use in the Writer's Workshop on page 804.

Comparing Poems

2. Echoes of Whitman

In a brief essay, compare and contrast Walt Whitman's "I celebrate myself, and sing myself" (page 347) with Hughes's "I, Too" (page 733).

Creative Writing

3. The Harlem Beat

Write the opening paragraph for a newspaper article about the Harlem described in "Harlem." Include a portion of an interview with an imagined resident of Hughes's Harlem.

Describing Blues Music / Research

4. Liner Notes

Write brief liner notes (400 to 800 words) for a recording of classic blues songs. Your notes should briefly explain what the blues are and how they developed, as well as tell a bit about each of the blues artists (your choice) represented in the anthology.

Music / Performance

5. Blues Riff

Choose any passage in "The Weary Blues," and set it to a rhythmic or other musical accompaniment. Or adapt an existing blues melody to the poem. When you've brought music to Hughes's verse, perform your work for the class.

MAKE IT NEW!

Pound
Williams
Stevens
Moore
Sandburg
Cummings

Make it new! Art is a joyous thing.

—*Ezra Pound*

The Radiator Building— Night, New York, 1927 (1927) by Georgia O'Keeffe. Oil on canvas (48″ × 30″).

Collection of Fisk University, Nashville, Tennessee. ©1998 The Georgia O'Keeffe Foundation/Artists Rights Society (ARS), New York.

Symbolism, Imagism, and Beyond
by John Malcolm Brinnin

Sometime in the early twentieth century, Americans awoke to a sense that their own national culture had come of age. This was true in poetry and in painting, in music and in dance, even in the new architecture of the skyscraper. Ironically, American poets found their new inspiration in Paris rather than their homeland. Learning from the French Symbolist poets, who dominated French literature from about 1875 to 1895, Americans were able to produce a new type of poetry through which the true American genius could speak.

Symbolism: The Search for a New Reality

Symbolism is a form of expression in which the world of appearances is violently rearranged by artists who seek a different and more truthful version of reality. The Symbolist poets did not merely describe objects; they tried to portray the emotional effects that objects can suggest. But don't be misled by the term *symbolism.* It has nothing to do with the religious, national, or psychological symbols we are all familiar with. In fact, the Symbolists were concerned with getting rid of such symbols, which they saw as having become dull and meaningless through overuse. The Symbolists stressed instead the need for a trust in the nonrational. Imagination is more reliable than reason, the Symbolists argued, and just as precise. With their emphasis on the mysterious and the intuitive, Symbolists hoped to bring revelation—self-discovery—to the reader through poems that lead the imagination to discover truths.

Symbolism was a new manifestation of the **Romanticism** that had swept over Europe and the United States in the nineteenth century. The Romantics had stressed the importance of feeling and the independence of the individual, and they had made a great stand against the mechanization of human life. In the natural world, the Romantics found messages that spoke to the soul and gave it strength.

The Symbolists, however, could find neither solace nor spiritual renewal in nature. By the start of the twentieth century, nature had been subjected to so much scientific classification and interpretation that it had been stripped of much of its mystery. Artists now faced the onslaught of the modern world, which in spite of advances in science and technology suffered increased poverty, violence, and conflict. The Symbolist poets saw this new world as spiritually debased, and they faced it with a distaste amounting to outrage. They knew they could not transform or erase the modern world, though, so their revolt was spiritual. They tried to redefine what it meant to be human in a time when individualism was succumbing to the power of mass culture.

Night Fires (c. 1919) by Joseph Stella. Pastel on paper (22 ½″ × 29″).
Milwaukee Art Museum, Gift of Friends of Art.

Imagism: "The *Exact* Word"

The two Americans who first came into close contact with Symbolism and introduced the techniques of the movement to the United States were Ezra Pound (page 773) and T. S. Eliot (page 661). With the help of several British poets, a group of Americans led by Pound founded a school perhaps better known and understood in the United States than Symbolism itself. This was **Imagism,** which flourished in the years 1912–1917.

Like the Symbolists, Imagists believed that poetry can be made purer by concentration on the precise, clear, unqualified image. Imagery alone, the Imagists believed, could carry a poem's emotion and message. It could do this almost instantly, without all the elaborate metrics and stanza patterns that were part of poetry's traditional mode. The Imagists—including Pound, H. D. (Hilda Doolittle), and Amy Lowell—took on the role of reformers. They would rid poetry of its prettiness, sentimentality, and artificiality, concentrating instead on the raw power of the image to communicate feeling and thought.

The Imagists issued a "manifesto," or public declaration, proposing "to use the language of common speech," as well as "the *exact* word, not merely the decorative word." In the same spirit, they called for a poetry "hard and clear, never blurred or indefinite." Some of the Imagists' inspiration was drawn from Eastern art forms, particularly Japanese **haiku,** a verse form that often juxtaposes two distinct images and invites the reader to experience the emotion created by the juxtaposition.

Pound defined an *image* as "that which presents an intellectual and emotional complex in an instant of time." Here is a famous Imagist poem that illustrates this concept:

In a Station of the Metro
The apparition of these faces in the crowd;
Petals on a wet, black bough.

—Ezra Pound

A New Poetic Order

Today, poems with imagistic technique are commonplace. But at the time the Imagists published their manifesto on poetry's nature and function, their theory created a great stir. It insisted that the range of poetic subject matter might include the kitchen sink as well as the rising of the moon, the trash can as well as the Chinese porcelain vase. The strongest opposition to the Imagists was caused by their proposal "to create new rhythms—as the expression of new moods. . . . We do believe that the individuality of a poet may often be better expressed in free verse than in conventional forms." To tradition-minded poets, this **free verse**—poetry without regular rhyming and metrical patterns—was deplorable. It meant a loosening of poetic standards and an assault on the very craft of poetry. These poets did not yet realize that successful free verse was at least as difficult to create as verse written in traditional forms.

Although Imagism was a short-lived movement, it gave rise to some of our greatest poets. Many in the forefront of Imagism went beyond the movement's limitations and expanded its insights. Besides Pound, H. D., and Lowell, these included William Carlos Williams (page 778), Marianne Moore (page 787), E. E. Cummings (page 796), and Wallace Stevens (page 783). Eventually, Imagism came to stand for a whole new order of poetry in the United States. Most Americans became familiar with the movement mainly as the school of "free verse." But the Imagist program was not only a call for a new method of organizing lines and stanzas; it was also an invitation to a new way of seeing and experiencing the world.

Ezra Pound

(1885–1972)

Boris De Rachewiltz/New Directions Publishing.

Ezra Pound is remembered by many people as the man who was charged with treason during World War II and who spent many years in a psychiatric hospital. This notoriety has tended to obscure Pound's impact on American poetry. But his influence is still apparent everywhere; the generations of poets who have come after Pound have kept alive a complex memory of a man whose career wavered between brilliance and episodic madness.

Pound was born in Hailey, Idaho, and grew up in Pennsylvania. He taught at a conservative religious college for a while but his bohemian lifestyle was out of tune with his surroundings.

In search of greater personal freedom and contacts with European poets, Pound settled in London in 1908. There he became a self-appointed spokesperson for the new poetic movement known as Imagism. He also became a self-exiled critic of American life and torch-bearer for any art that challenged the complacent middle class.

Pound—whose slogan was "Make it new!"—was a born teacher whose advice was sought by the most brilliant writers of the period. T. S. Eliot acknowledged Pound's valuable advice when he dedicated his great poem *The Waste Land* (1922) to Pound.

After World War I, Pound felt the need for even broader horizons than London offered him. He moved to Paris in 1921, and to Italy three years later, where he continued to write poetry and criticism. And now came a tragic turning point in Pound's life. His interest in economics and social theory led him to support Benito Mussolini, the Fascist dictator of Italy.

When World War II broke out, Pound stayed in Italy and turned propagandist for Mussolini's policies. In his radio broadcasts from Italy, Pound denounced the struggle of the United States and its allies against Germany, Italy, and Japan. Many of these broadcasts were viciously antisemitic.

When the American army advanced northward up the Italian peninsula in 1945, Pound was taken prisoner. He was confined to a cage on an airstrip near Pisa and eventually returned to the United States to be tried for treason. But psychiatrists judged him to be mentally incompetent, and in 1946 the poet was committed to St. Elizabeth's, at the time designated as a hospital for the criminally insane, in Washington, D.C.

Twelve years later, he was released through the intercession of writers, including Archibald MacLeish and Robert Frost, who argued that his literary contributions outweighed his disastrous lack of judgment and his notorious bigotry. Pound returned to Italy, where he lived the rest of his life. During these last years of exile, a reporter once asked Pound where he was living. "In hell," Pound answered. "Which hell?" the reporter asked. "Here," said Pound, pressing his heart. "Here."

When he died in Venice, Pound left behind a body of work extending from the delicate lyrics he wrote at the turn of the century to *The Cantos*, an enormous epic he did not complete until well over fifty years later. He also left a public record that still uncomfortably involves scholars and historians in "The Case of Ezra Pound."

HRW go.hrw.com
LEO 11-16

EZRA POUND 773

THE RIVER-MERCHANT'S WIFE: A LETTER

Make the Connection

Missing You

Have you ever been moved to write a letter to someone you loved and missed? In this letter-poem, Pound assumes the voice of a river merchant's wife as she contemplates her life, love, and longing. This poem is a tribute to Li Po (701–762), one of the greatest Chinese poets. Though Pound crosses generations, cultures, continents, and gender, the intimate tone of the poem creates a bridge for the reader, inviting understanding and even identification with the eighth-century Chinese speaker.

Reading Skills and Strategies

Identifying Images

This poem is not a word-for-word translation of Li's poem but an adaptation based on the feelings and images that Pound experienced when reading translations of the original poem. As you read, note **images** that seem to suggest specific emotions.

Handscroll: *Wang Hsi-chih Watching Geese* (detail) (c. 1235–before 1307) by Ch'ien Hsüan. Ink and color on paper (9 1/8″ × 36 1/2″).

The River-Merchant's Wife: A Letter

Li T'ai Po

Ezra Pound

While my hair was still cut straight across my forehead
Played I about the front gate, pulling flowers.
You came by on bamboo stilts, playing horse,
You walked about my seat, playing with blue plums.
5 And we went on living in the village of Chokan:
Two small people, without dislike or suspicion.

At fourteen I married My Lord you.
I never laughed, being bashful.
Lowering my head, I looked at the wall.
10 Called to, a thousand times, I never looked back.

At fifteen I stopped scowling,
I desired my dust to be mingled with yours

Forever and forever and forever.
Why should I climb the lookout?

15 At sixteen you departed,
You went into far Ku-to-yen, by the river of swirling eddies,
And you have been gone five months.
The monkeys make sorrowful noise overhead.

You dragged your feet when you went out.
20 By the gate now, the moss is grown, the different mosses,
Too deep to clear them away!
The leaves fall early this autumn, in wind.
The paired butterflies are already yellow with August
Over the grass in the West garden;
25 They hurt me. I grow older.
If you are coming down through the narrows of the river Kiang,
Please let me know beforehand.
And I will come out to meet you
              As far as Cho-fu-Sa.

Ezra Pound wrote the following "rules" for poets in an article in the March 1913 issue of *Poetry* magazine. Many of them are useful to all writers.

A Few Don'ts by an Imagiste

It is better to present one Image in a lifetime than to produce voluminous works. . . .

Pay no attention to the criticism of men who have never themselves written a notable work. Consider the discrepancies between the actual writing of the Greek poets and dramatists, and the theories of the Greco-Roman grammarians, concocted to explain their meters.

Language

Use no superfluous word, no adjective, which does not reveal something.

Don't use such an expression as "dim lands of peace." It dulls the image. It mixes an abstraction with the concrete. It comes from the writer's not realizing that the natural object is always the *adequate* symbol.

Go in fear of abstractions. Don't retell in mediocre verse what has already been done in good prose. Don't think any intelligent person is going to be deceived when you try to shirk all the difficulties of the unspeakably difficult art of good prose by chopping your composition into line lengths. . . .

Don't imagine that the art of poetry is any simpler than the art of music, or that you can please the expert before you have spent at least as much effort on the art of verse as the average piano teacher spends on the art of music.

Be influenced by as many great artists as you can, but have the decency either to acknowledge the debt outright, or to try to conceal it. . . .

Rhythm and Rhyme

. . . Let the neophyte know assonance and alliteration, rhyme immediate and delayed, simple and polyphonic, as a musician would expect to know harmony and counterpoint and all the minutiae of his craft. No time is too great to give to these matters or to any one of them, even if the artist seldom have need of them. . . .

Consider the way of the scientists rather than the way of an advertising agent for a new soap.

The scientist does not expect to be acclaimed as a great scientist until he has *discovered* something. He begins by learning what has been discovered already. He goes from that point onward. He does not bank on being a charming fellow personally. He does not expect his friends to applaud the results of his freshman classwork. Freshmen in poetry are unfortunately not confined to a definite and recognizable classroom. They are "all over the shop." Is it any wonder "the public is indifferent to poetry"?

Don't chop your stuff into separate *iambs*. Don't make each line stop dead at the end, and then begin every next line with a heave. Let the beginning of the next line catch the rise of the rhythm wave, unless you want a definite longish pause. . . .

If you are using a symmetrical form, don't put in what you want to say and then fill up the remaining vacuums with slush.

—Ezra Pound

MAKING MEANINGS

First Thoughts

1. Which line or image in this poem do you think is most important or most vivid? Compare your choices in class.

Shaping Interpretations

2. What events are referred to in the first four stanzas?

3. How is the third stanza a **turning point** in the poem? What do you think the wife expresses in line 14?

4. What **image** suggests that the husband was reluctant to leave home?

5. How is the season appropriate to the **mood** of the poem?

6. What hurts the young wife in line 25, and why? In the same line, why does she say, after only five months, that she grows "older"?

7. What does the wife promise to do?

8. Think of possible reasons why the husband left. Do you think he will ever return? What may have delayed him?

ELEMENTS OF LITERATURE

The Objective Correlative

Throughout Pound's poem, the letter writer's feelings are expressed more often by references to objects and activities than by direct statements. This is a method often practiced by Pound and identified by T. S. Eliot as the **objective correlative.** Eliot defined this term as "a set of objects, a situation, a chain of events which shall be the formula of [a] *particular* emotion." According to Eliot, the only valid way to express an emotion in art is to find such an objective correlative.

The term *objective correlative* soon became a permanent part of the vocabulary of poetic analysis. Several years earlier, however, Pound had anticipated the essence of the term, when he referred to poetry as "a sort of inspired mathematics" that gives us "equations for the human emotions."

Both Eliot and Pound believed that poetry is a means of expressing emotions *indirectly* but

precisely. Poetry does this by finding the images and actions that best embody a feeling. (An example in Pound's poem might be the "river of swirling eddies.") This kind of poetic shorthand leaves the reader without the connections that usually join the parts of an argument, a story, or even most poems. Readers are forced to supply these connections and find the logic of a poem by themselves.

Not every poem deals in objective correlatives. Most poems have a logical or narrative sequence that is easy to recognize. But other poems are organized, not by a logical sequence, but by a *psychological* one. Such poems will make no logical sense until you supply the connecting links. These are the poems that can be analyzed according to Eliot's definition of the objective correlative.

CHOICES: Building Your Portfolio

Writer's Notebook

1. Collecting Ideas for an Interpretive Essay

Reread Emily Dickinson's poem "If you were coming in the Fall" (page 376), and compare it to "The River-Merchant's Wife: A Letter." Jot down the ways that Dickinson's poem is like and unlike Pound's poem in reference to its **speaker's expectations,** its **tone,** and its **imagery.** Save your notes for possible use in the Writer's Workshop on page 804.

Analyzing Imagery

2. Indirect Expression

Choose at least three **images** from the poem, and, in a paragraph, explain how each image is used as an **objective correlative** to convey emotion indirectly.

Creative Writing

3. Tell It Slant

Choose a topic you feel strongly about. Then, think of a single concrete **image** that suggests your feelings. In a paragraph, include your image in a way that communicates your feelings but doesn't express them directly.

William Carlos Williams

(1883–1963)

William Carlos Williams was born in Rutherford, New Jersey, where he lived and practiced medicine as a pediatrician and obstetrician for most of his adult life. While studying medicine at the University of Pennsylvania, he came in contact with Ezra Pound (page 773). Pound's theories of Imagism had a considerable influence on Williams's early verse, which was published in *Poems* (1909) and *The Tempers* (1913). During the next two decades, however, Williams went on to evolve his own distinctive poetic style, which he called *objectivism*.

Williams defined the source of his poetry as "the local," by which he meant a strict focus on the reality of individual life and its surroundings. Williams looked for a return to the barest essentials in poetry. In this respect, he opposed such contemporaries as T. S. Eliot (page 661) and, to a certain extent, Pound himself, in their frequent use of allusions to art, history, religion, and foreign cultures. (Williams and Eliot, in fact, made no secret of their dislike of each other's work.)

In addition to poetry, Williams produced novels, plays, essays, and several autobiographical memoirs. His influence on twentieth-century American poetry, especially since World War II, has been considerable, and he was awarded a Pulitzer Prize in 1963. His masterpiece is the long epic *Paterson,* a poem that appeared in five volumes over a twelve-year span (1946–1958). In this partly autobiographical epic, a poet wanders the neighborhoods of Paterson, New Jersey, an industrial town near Williams's home, and meditates on the variegated experiences of urban life.

In his insistence on local topics and colloquial speech, Williams was allying himself with the kind of poetic revolution championed by the

Pach/Bettmann.

English Romantics a century earlier. William Wordsworth, in his preface to the third edition of *Lyrical Ballads* (1802), had written that poetry should treat "incidents and situations from common life . . . in a selection of language really used by men."

Williams deliberately wrote in a spare, detached style about commonplace subjects, the very opposite of what many nineteenth-century American writers had thought of as poetic material. Using as his slogan "No ideas but in things," Williams wrote of such sights and events as animals at the zoo, schoolgirls walking down a street, a piece of paper blowing down a street, or a raid on the refrigerator. As Marianne Moore, an admirer, pointed out, Williams's topics are "American"—crowds at the movies, turkey nests, mushrooms among fir trees, mist rising from a duck pond, a ballgame.

go.hrw.com
LEO 11-16

THE RED WHEELBARROW
THE GREAT FIGURE

Make the Connection

A Recovery from Stodginess
The Imagists wanted to describe commonplace subjects, just as they are. These new poets were very different from many popular poets of the nineteenth century, who believed that poetry should be "about" certain poetic subjects. Do you think there is any limitation on subject matter?

Quickwrite

Make a list of at least six subjects from your ordinary world that might be subjects for a poem.

The Red Wheelbarrow

William Carlos Williams

so much depends
upon

a red wheel
barrow

glazed with rain
water

beside the white
chickens.

Critical Comment

So Much Depends

Williams's "The Red Wheelbarrow" at first glance seems to be very slight. But it has proved to have the leverage power that the ancient Greek inventor and mathematician Archimedes spoke of when he said, "Give me a place to stand, and I will move the world." Where William Carlos Williams stood was a place where ordinary things were *not* used as symbols or metaphors; they were simply ordinary things. The world he moved was the world of poetry. Before Williams, poets saw things not as things in themselves, but as objects to be used (to be compared, to be endowed with alien meaning, or to be played with); in themselves, things meant nothing.

How do we talk about this poem? When we consider analyzing it, where do we begin? Trying to answer these questions leads only to frustration. This poem is a composition of words so complete and simple that it denies all attempts to treat it as a poem.

And yet, there is the temptation to ask what happens in the brief course of the poem that has made it so durable. It was, after all, not a typographical accident; it was composed, and as such it can be analyzed. But our analysis must be concerned with the modest premises of the poem; we must not attempt to give it meanings that it does not claim.

The first line contains a vague but enormously suggestive phrase that leads the reader to expect an answer. (*What* depends on *what*?) But, except for the metaphorical lift of the word *glazed* in line 5, what the reader gets is only bare, flat reality—a moment captured as permanently as if it had been photographed. If the poem can be said to have some movement, some progress, from its first word to its last, it would be in what we call "reverse action." Our yearning toward what might be implicit in "so much depends" is quietly checked by the homely beauty of what *is*.

Do you like or dislike this poem? Why?

The Great Figure

William Carlos Williams

Among the rain
and lights
I saw the figure 5
in gold
5   on a red
fire truck
moving
tense
unheeded
10   to gong clangs
siren howls
and wheels rumbling
through the dark city.

The Figure 5
in Gold (1928)
by Charles
Henry Demuth.
Oil on com-
position board
(36″ × 29¾″).

PRIMARY Sources

AN AUTOBIOGRAPHY

Williams Talks About Poetry

I'll never forget the dream I had a few days after he [Williams's father] died, after a wasting illness, on Christmas Day, 1918. I saw him coming down a peculiar flight of exposed steps, steps I have since identified as those before the dais of Pontius Pilate in some well-known painting. But this was in a New York office building, Pop's office. He was bare-headed and had some business letters in his hand on which he was concentrating as he descended. I noticed him and with joy cried out, "Pop! So, you're *not* dead!" But he only looked up at me over his right shoulder and commented severely, "You know all that poetry you're writing. Well, it's no good." I was left speechless and woke trembling.

• • •

What were we seeking? No one knew consistently enough to formulate a "movement." We were restless and constrained, closely allied with the painters. Impressionism, dadaism, surrealism applied to both painting and the poem.

What a battle we made of it merely getting rid of capitals at the beginning of every line! The immediate image, which was impressionistic, sure enough, fascinated us all. We had followed Pound's instructions, his famous "Don'ts," eschewing inversions of the phrase. . . . Literary allusions, save in very attenuated form, were unknown to us. Few had the necessary reading.

We were looked at askance by scholars and those who turned to scholarship for their norm. To my mind the thing that gave us most a semblance of a cause was not Imagism, as some thought, but the line: the poetic line and our hopes for its recovery from stodginess. I say recovery in the sense that one recovers a salt from solution by chemical action. We were destroyers, vulgarians, obscurantists to most who read; though occasionally a witty line, an unusual reference, or a wrench of the simile to force it into approximation with experience rather than reading—bringing a whole proximate "material" into view—found some response from the alert.

—William Carlos Williams,
from The Autobiography

Make the Connection

Becoming Spring

Like many other poems by Williams, this one is about a process—a development, a transformation, or a condition at the point of change. Here the subject is the coming of spring, examined as seen under a magnifying glass. The poet also examines the feeling of spring, in which changes in nature are reflected in someone who observes them.

Quickwrite

Try to picture the look of nature as spring begins. Then, write down several visual images you associate with this turning point in the earth's yearly cycle. Be sure to mention the main colors of the images. Note also the feelings the images arouse in you.

Spring and All

William Carlos Williams

By the road to the contagious hospital°
under the surge of the blue
mottled clouds driven from the
northeast—a cold wind. Beyond, the
5 waste of broad, muddy fields
brown with dried weeds, standing and fallen

patches of standing water
the scattering of tall trees

All along the road the reddish
10 purplish, forked, upstanding, twiggy
stuff of bushes and small trees
with dead, brown leaves under them
leafless vines—

Lifeless in appearance, sluggish
15 dazed spring approaches—

They enter the new world naked,
cold, uncertain of all
save that they enter. All about them
the cold, familiar wind—

20 Now the grass, tomorrow
the stiff curl of wildcarrot leaf
One by one objects are defined—
It quickens:° clarity, outline of leaf

But now the stark dignity of
25 entrance—Still, the profound change
has come upon them: rooted, they
grip down and begin to awaken

1. contagious hospital: hospital for people with contagious diseases.

23. quickens: enlivens; revives. The speaker may also be referring to a less common meaning: "enters the stage of pregnancy when the fetus's movement can be felt."

MAKING MEANINGS

The Great Figure

Spring and All

First Thoughts

1. In "The Red Wheelbarrow" Williams says "so much depends" on an ordinary, workaday wheelbarrow. Do "The Great Figure" and "Spring and All" also focus on the very ordinary things in life? Explain.

Shaping Interpretations

2. The painter Charles Henry Demuth (1883–1935) was so moved by the dynamic imagery in "The Great Figure" that he painted *The Figure Five in Gold* (see page 780). What movement do you *see* in the painting? What do you *hear* in the poem itself?

3. How would the feeling of "The Great Figure" change if the colors were different? Try it.

4. What significance can you find in the **title** "Spring and All"?

5. The first three stanzas of "Spring and All" are about plants. The pronoun in line 16, however, may refer to more than plants. What broader meaning might the word *they* have?

6. Reread the last stanza of "Spring and All." Which two meanings of the word *still* make line 25 a **paradox**? (A paradox is a statement that appears self-contradictory but that reveals a kind of truth.)

7. As a physician, Williams delivered thousands of babies. Can you see any connections between that fact and the last three stanzas of "Spring and All"? What references would apply equally to the coming of spring and the birth of an infant?

8. The famous opening of *The Waste Land*, by T. S. Eliot, declares that "April is the cruelest month." Would the speaker of "Spring and All" agree with this view of the start of spring? Explain.

Extending the Texts

9. If you were an artist and wanted to paint what you see and feel in any of these poems by Williams, what images and feelings would you focus on? What colors would you use?

CHOICES:
Building Your Portfolio

Writer's Notebook
1. Collecting Ideas for an Interpretive Essay

Jot down some notes about Williams's use of concrete objects to make you think in new ways about people, art, or life in general. Save your notes for possible use in the Writer's Workshop on page 804.

Creative Writing
2. An Imagist Poem

Write a brief imagist poem describing some subject from your everyday life. Before you write, reread what Williams says in his comments on poetry on page 780. Strive to capture a thing and a moment as precisely as you can. Your Quickwrite notes might help you find a subject.

Creative Writing
3. Picture Poem

Find a painting or photograph that interests you (perhaps one from this book). Write a six-line poem describing the **images** you see in the picture. Try to record details exactly as they are, without using them as symbols or ascribing any significance to them beyond the fact that they simply are what they are.

Reviewing a Performance
4. Springs to Life?

Along with a group of three or four classmates, listen to the performance of "Spring and All" on the HRW Audio CD or have a group member read the poem aloud. Then, each student (except the student reader, if any) should write a short review of the performance. Did the performer catch the poem's meaning and rhythm? Was the pronunciation clear, with the correct words emphasized? Exchange reviews, and discuss the similarities and differences of your critiques.

Wallace Stevens

(1879–1955)

The Bettmann Archive.

Americans are often surprised to learn that one of their greatest poets was a business executive who walked to his downtown office, sat on boards of directors, served as a vice president of a major insurance company, and became one of the pillars of a local society dedicated to the collection, investment, and distribution of money. Wallace Stevens was all of these and, almost incidentally, a genius of such magnitude that his place in American literature is still being reassessed and the depth of his vision ever more closely examined. Yet Stevens's life was a remarkably quiet, undramatic, and private one.

Stevens was born in Reading, Pennsylvania. He was educated at Harvard College and the New York Law School. Married in 1909 (to a woman who modeled for the image on the liberty-head dime), he and his wife had one child, Holly, who after his death assumed the editorship of his letters and other posthumously published works.

When he was thirty-six, Stevens moved to Hartford, Connecticut, where he entered the insurance business. He kept his creative life completely apart from his preoccupations as a business executive and maintained his literary friendships almost exclusively by correspondence. Happy with routine, a connoisseur of wines and French painting, and a lover of music, Stevens traveled to Cuba and often to Key West. Unlike most of his equally eminent contemporaries, he refused all invitations (until the last years of his life) to give interviews or to recite his poetry in public.

Almost forty-four when he published his first book of verse, *Harmonium* (1923)—a volume that sold a meager few hundred copies—Stevens came late and very quietly onto a scene already occupied by two quite different kinds of poetic expression: the colloquial rhythms and down-to-earth concerns of Carl Sandburg and Edgar Lee Masters, and the intellectual style exemplified by Ezra Pound and T. S. Eliot. Stevens shared the aspirations of both movements; yet he made his way along a path that avoided the extreme practices of either. His sense of place and American character kept him firmly rooted on native ground, but his grasp of metaphysical precision allowed him to soar into realms of "pure" poetry. Stevens went beyond where any other American poet had gone before.

Stevens admired the work of many contemporary American poets with whom he would seem to have little in common. Long before critics or the reading public were aware of William Carlos Williams's common speech and of his flat, almost casual rendering of everyday experience, Stevens knew exactly what his friend was up to. His respect and affection for Marianne Moore, his beloved "Marianna," was lifelong, as was his admiration for the precisely intricate structures that were the hallmark of her poetry. Toward Robert Frost, his attitude was one of friendly rivalry. "The trouble with you, Robert," Stevens once remarked in the course of one of their meetings, "is that [all of your poems] have *subjects*." That statement contains a clue to the originality of Stevens's work: For him, objects are important only as touchstones for the play of the imagination.

In 1955, Stevens's *Collected Poems* won the Pulitzer Prize in poetry. In a poem called "Of Modern Poetry" (printed in full on page 790), Stevens said this of his craft:

> It has to be living, to learn the speech of the
> place.
> It has to face the men of the time and to
> meet
> The women of the time. It has to think about
> war
> And it has to find what will suffice. It has
> To construct a new stage.

Make the Connection

The World in Our Hands

People often say, "Life is what we make of it." Wallace Stevens developed that idea into a full-fledged philosophy of life and art. He built his poetry on the belief that our imaginations are always interacting with the world around us, with both engaged in a vital creative partnership. The result of this dynamic interplay of imagination and reality is our ever-changing experience of life.

Quickwrite

Do you think that most people you know have active and creative imaginations? Write down your thoughts in a few sentences.

Reading Skills and Strategies

Analyzing Metaphor

A **metaphor** is a figure of speech that makes a comparison between two unlike things. When you sense that a writer is using an **implied metaphor**—one that does not state explicitly the two things being compared—how do you determine the comparison being made?

For example, suppose a poem described a jar. You sense that the jar is more than a jar—but what? Start by listing the jar's qualities: It's made by skilled craftspeople; it comes in various sizes and shapes; it is useful; it often contains things; you can usually see through it. Now, use your imagination: Why didn't the poet describe a building or a statue or a stone? Why the *jar*?

Anecdote of the Jar

Wallace Stevens

I placed a jar in Tennessee,
And round it was, upon a hill.
It made the slovenly wilderness
Surround that hill.

5   The wilderness rose up to it,
And sprawled around, no longer wild.
The jar was round upon the ground
And tall and of a port in air.

It took dominion everywhere.
10 The jar was gray and bare.
It did not give of bird or bush,
Like nothing else in Tennessee.

Disillusionment of Ten O'Clock

Wallace Stevens

The houses are haunted
By white night-gowns.
None are green,
Or purple with green rings,
5 Or green with yellow rings,
Or yellow with blue rings.
None of them are strange,
With socks of lace
And beaded ceintures.°
10 People are not going
To dream of baboons and periwinkles.°
Only, here and there, an old sailor,
Drunk and asleep in his boots,
Catches tigers
15 In red weather.

9. ceintures (san′tyoŏrz): belts.
11. periwinkles (per′i·wiŋ′kəlz): saltwater snails.

Taking Dominion, Catching Tigers

Wallace Stevens's great subject—reality and the imagination—appears in virtually every poem he wrote. He knew of course that we live in the physical world that he called "things as they are." However, he knew too that we shape that world into something else, an imagined world that is the place where our deepest and truest experiences occur. The key to happiness is balancing those worlds. Too much reality leaves us dull, passive, overwhelmed by the ordinary. Too much imagina-tion makes us creatures of fantasy, light-weight, out of touch with the actual.

In "Anecdote of the Jar," the jar creates an ordered world out of the chaos of nature. It is a work of art standing at the center of a uni-verse that it has organized. It can't actually create a living bird or a bush, but without it all the birds and bushes have no meaning. In "Disillusionment of Ten O'Clock," the sailor's spectacular dream invigorates the environ-ment around him. For Stevens, the jar and the dream accomplish the same purpose—creat-ing a new, ordered, heroic world out of the real and the imagined.

MAKING MEANINGS

First Thoughts

1. Read "Anecdote of the Jar" and "Disillusionment of Ten O'Clock" at least twice. After each read-ing, write down what you think each poem is about. Exchange your ideas with a partner. How similar are your statements about the poems?

Anecdote of the Jar

Shaping Interpretations

2. Describe what the speaker does in the first stanza. What adjective does the speaker use to describe the jar? How does he describe the wilderness in which he places the jar?

3. In the second stanza, what effect does the jar have on the wilderness?

4. What does the jar "not give" in the last stanza?

5. Some critics say that the jar is a **meta-phor** for the poet's act of imagination in creating this poem, or for the poem itself. Do you agree with either interpretation? Why or why not? What else could the jar stand for?

6. If the jar stands for the poet's art (or for any kind of art), what is the "wilderness" that the jar has "dominion" or control over?

7. Some other critics think the jar is a **metaphor** for human interference with nature. Reread the poem and see if you could justify this interpretation.

Disillusionment of Ten O'Clock

Shaping Interpretations

1. Describe the nightgowns that do *not* haunt the houses.

2. What *won't* the people in these houses dream about?

3. Why do you suppose the poet says that the houses are "haunted" by white nightgowns?

4. What is the speaker implying about the old sailor, based on the sailor's dream? How does the sailor contrast with the other people?

5. What could the "disillusionment" of the **title** refer to? (What does the speaker expect? What does he discover?)

6. List other fantastic things that these people will never dream about.

CHOICES: Building Your Portfolio

Writer's Notebook

1. Collecting Ideas for an Interpretive Essay

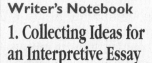

Use the following questions to analyze any poem in this collection. Then, freewrite a paragraph explaining how literary elements work together to help create the poem's meaning. Save your notes for possible use in the Writer's Workshop on page 804.

1. What is the **subject** of the poem?
2. What is the **tone** of the poem?
3. What **images** does the poet use?
4. What **figures of speech** does the poem contain?
5. What **symbols** does the poem contain?
6. How does the poet use **rhyme, meter,** and other **sound effects**?
7. Which elements are most important in the poem? Which are least important?
8. What does the poem's **title** mean?
9. What is the poem's **theme**?
10. What is your emotional response to the text?

Analyzing Poetry

2. A Poem's World

Choose one of Stevens's aphorisms in Primary Sources (see below), and in a short essay, apply it to either "Anecdote of the Jar" or "Disillusionment of Ten O'Clock." Explain the ways in which the poem reflects—or doesn't reflect—the aphorism.

Writing an Analytical Essay

3. Imagination: Necessary?

Refer to your Quick-write notes, and write an essay about people's imaginative lives today. Where is imagination needed? How can imagination be nourished? How do children lose their imagination? If you wish, refer to Stevens's poems to make your point.

PRIMARY Sources NOTEBOOKS

Wallace Stevens tried many times to define poetry. He often jotted down his ideas in the form of **aphorisms,** short, cleverly worded statements, which he kept in two notebooks called *Adagia*. Here are some of his most memorable attempts to put into words his unending engagement of imagination and reality.

- Poetry is a response to the daily necessity of getting the world right.
- Poetry is a renovation of experience.
- Poetry is the expression of the experience of poetry.
- Poetry must resist the intelligence almost successfully.
- Poetry is the statement of a relation between a man and the world.

- Every poem is a poem within a poem: the poem of the idea within the poem of the words.
- The theory of poetry is the theory of life.
- The poem is a nature created by the poet.
- The purpose of poetry is to contribute to man's happiness.
- The purpose of poetry is to make life complete in itself.

—Wallace Stevens

Marianne Moore

(1887–1972)

Esther Bubley/Life Magazine
© Time, Inc.

Marianne Moore is remembered by many people as the woman who wrote a poem in 1955 celebrating the only World Series the Brooklyn Dodgers ever won. Moore spent almost half her life in Brooklyn, where she became one of the most famous supporters of the local baseball team.

She was born in Kirkwood, a suburb of St. Louis, Missouri. After graduating from Bryn Mawr College outside Philadelphia, Moore worked as a teacher and a librarian, and later served as the editor of *The Dial,* a magazine that encouraged young writers. She spent a good part of her life caring for her brother and mother. When her mother died, Moore lost her best friend—and her toughest critic.

All the while, Moore was writing and publishing her poems in the prestigious journals of the time. By 1921, she was living in New York City and had just published her first collection of poetry, *Poems.* Among the literary celebrities in New York, she was easily identifiable by her antique capes and other nineteenth-century touches in costume.

Behind the costume, however, Moore was a serious poet of meticulous detail, clarity, and humor. Mixing with the *literati* did not mean that she endorsed their tolerance in matters of personal behavior or their embrace of anything in the arts that seemed new, or bold, or simply amusing.

In fact, the only thing "modern" about Moore was her poetry. Like a bird building an intricate nest, she carefully pieced together her poems by combining her own writing with quotations and excerpts from social science and natural history journals. It has been said of her that no one was ever more indebted to other writers for material and, at the same time, more original. Her poetry reflects some of the influence of the Imagists, and it also makes constant use of the concrete in the tradition of William Carlos Williams. Williams himself assessed his colleague's achievement when he said, "The magic name, Marianne Moore . . . I don't think there is a better poet writing in America today or one who touches so deftly a great range of our thought."

Like the visual artists of the twentieth century, Moore was able to join apparently unrelated elements of what she observed and bring them into a "picture" with a single focus. In some of her poems, Moore works like a painter whose nervous strokes and jagged edges capture a hundred details in one moment stopped in time. What she says in one famous poem, "The Steeple-Jack," might apply to readers approaching her work for the first time: "[i]t is a privilege to see so much confusion."

Poetry

Marianne Moore

I, too, dislike it: there are things that are important beyond all this fiddle.°
  Reading it, however, with a perfect contempt for it, one discovers in
  it after all, a place for the genuine.
    Hands that can grasp, eyes
5   that can dilate, hair that can rise
       if it must, these things are important not because a

high-sounding interpretation can be put upon them but because they are
  useful. When they become so derivative° as to become unintelligible,
  the same thing may be said for all of us, that we
10   do not admire what
     we cannot understand: the bat
       holding on upside down or in quest of something to

eat, elephants pushing, a wild horse taking a roll, a tireless wolf under
  a tree, the immovable critic twitching his skin like a horse that feels a flea, the base-
15   ball fan, the statistician—
     nor is it valid
       to discriminate against "business documents and

school-books"; all these phenomena are important. One must make a distinction
  however: when dragged into prominence by half poets, the result is not poetry,
20   nor till the poets among us can be
     'literalists of
     the imagination'—above
       insolence and triviality and can present

for inspection, "imaginary gardens with real toads in them," shall we have
25   it. In the meantime, if you demand on the one hand,
    the raw material of poetry in
     all its rawness and
     that which is on the other hand
       genuine, then you are interested in poetry.

1. fiddle: slang for "nonsense."
8. derivative: based on the work of others; unoriginal.

Netsuke carved in the shape of a
frog. Japanese (18th century).

Victoria & Albert Museum, London.

Archibald MacLeish (1892–1982), an American poet and Moore's contemporary, reflects on the means and ends of poetry in the following poem. *Ars poetica* translates from Latin as "the art of poetry." It is also the title of a work by the Roman poet Horace (65 B.C.–8 B.C.).

Ars Poetica

Archibald MacLeish

A poem should be palpable and mute
As a globed fruit,

Dumb
As old medallions to the thumb,

5 Silent as the sleeve-worn stone
Of casement ledges where the moss has grown—

A poem should be wordless
As the flight of birds.

•

A poem should be motionless in time
10 As the moon climbs,

Leaving, as the moon releases
Twig by twig the night-entangled trees,

Leaving, as the moon behind the winter leaves,
Memory by memory the mind—

15 A poem should be motionless in time
As the moon climbs.

•

A poem should be equal to:
Not true.

For all the history of grief
20 An empty doorway and a maple leaf.

For love
The leaning grasses and two lights above the sea—

A poem should not mean
But be.

Wallace Stevens (see page 783) was, like MacLeish, a contemporary of Marianne Moore. In the following *ars poetica*, Stevens is particularly concerned with the raw material a poem draws on and how a poem works in the mind of the reader or listener. Above all, a poem must be fresh—it must avoid outdated concerns and forms.

Of Modern Poetry

Wallace Stevens

The poem of the mind in the act of finding
What will suffice. It has not always had
To find: the scene was set; it repeated what
Was in the script.
　　　　　　　Then the theatre was changed
5　To something else. Its past was a souvenir.

It has to be living, to learn the speech of the place.
It has to face the men of the time and to meet
The women of the time. It has to think about war
And it has to find what will suffice. It has
10　To construct a new stage. It has to be on that stage
And, like an insatiable° actor, slowly and
With meditation, speak words that in the ear,
In the delicatest ear of the mind, repeat,
Exactly, that which it wants to hear, at the sound
15　Of which, an invisible audience listens,
Not to the play, but to itself, expressed
In an emotion as of two people, as of two
Emotions becoming one. The actor is
A metaphysician° in the dark, twanging
20　An instrument, twanging a wiry string that gives
Sounds passing through sudden rightnesses, wholly
Containing the mind, below which it cannot descend
Beyond which it has no will to rise.
　　　　　　　　　　　It must
25　Be the finding of a satisfaction, and may
Be of a man skating, a woman dancing, a woman
Combing. The poem of the act of the mind.

12. insatiable (in·sā′shə·bəl): incapable of being satisfied.
20. metaphysician (met′ə·fə·zish′ən): philosopher who studies the nature of being or reality.

MAKING MEANINGS

First Thoughts

1. How do *you* feel about poetry? Do you agree with Moore about what "real" poetry is? Review the notes you made in your Quickwrite.

Shaping Interpretations

2. Whom do you think Moore is addressing in this poem?

3. What kind of poetry does Moore dislike?

4. What elements does Moore think useful poetry should contain?

5. Moore says "literalists of the imagination" are necessary for true poetry. What do you think she means? How is this idea related to those "imaginary gardens with real toads in them"?

6. Identify the **end rhymes** of the fourth and fifth lines of stanzas 1, 2, 4, and 5. Which are **exact rhymes,** and which are **slant rhymes**?

Connecting with the Text

7. List five experiences from your life that Moore would consider the "raw material of poetry."

CHOICES: Building Your Portfolio

Writer's Notebook

1. Collecting Ideas for an Interpretive Essay

In your own words, **paraphrase** Moore's criteria for good poetry as stated in her poem. Which of these criteria would you apply to your own interpretation of a poem? Which of the criteria would you change or expand? Keep your notes for possible use in the Writer's Workshop on page 804.

Comparing Literary Theories

2. Poems About Poetry

In a brief essay, compare Marianne Moore's ideas about poetry with Archibald MacLeish's ideas in "Ars Poetica" (see *Connections,* page 789) or with Wallace Stevens's in "Of Modern Poetry" (*Connections,* page 790). What does each poet require in a poem? What do their descriptions of poetry have in common? For another poem on poetry, try Dickinson's "Tell all the Truth. . ." on page 386.

Evaluating a Poem

3. Letter to a Poet

Write a letter to Marianne Moore, describing your response to "Poetry." Cite specific passages from her poem.

Creative Writing

4. Poetry Is . . .

The most famous line in this poem is the one that says that poetry should show us " 'imaginary gardens with real toads in them.' " Write your own list of what poetry is. Start with the words "Poetry is."

Creative Writing

5. Moore's Method

Marianne Moore often used information that she took from science and nature publications. Look through nature magazines or journals, and find an article that includes illustrations of animals, insects, birds, or fish that interest you. Write a poem about your chosen subject. Incorporate quotations from the article into your poem.

Performance

6. "Poetry" Reading

With a partner, take turns reading "Poetry" aloud. Pay attention to line and stanza breaks and to the alternation of long and short lines. Note also the punctuation: Where would you read quickly, and where would you slow down for emphasis? Record or perform two or three renditions for your class, and discuss how responses and interpretations differ for each reading.

Carl Sandburg

(1878–1967)

Brown Brothers.

When he died in his nine-tieth year, Carl Sandburg was already an American myth. Sandburg's deeply lined, leathery face and his boyish shock of hair had been familiar to the American public for more than five decades. As the author of two of the most popular poems of the first half of the century—"Chicago" (1914) and "Fog" (1916)—and a six-volume biography of Abraham Lincoln, Sandburg had carved a place for himself in modern literature. As a poetic spokesperson for the American laborer, he had become part of the folklore from which he drew his inspiration. While he seemed on the page to be the roughest of American poets, Sandburg was actually a gentle and contemplative man. He found his most characteristic voice in the vernacular—in slang, street talk, and the common speech of clichés and plain expressions.

A descendant of Swedes who had settled in Galesburg, Illinois, where he was born, Sandburg was not so much schooled in a classroom as in the proverbial "school of hard knocks." Before he was twenty, he had ranged the Middle West from Illinois to Nebraska. He thus came in contact with workers in the fields and factories that would one day provide his own poetic landscape. Sandburg volunteered, more from restlessness than from patriotism, to fight in the Spanish-American War that broke out in 1898, and he served in the first Puerto Rican campaign. When the war ended, he was finally ready to go back to school. He attended Lombard College in his hometown, where he was captain of the basketball team and editor of the college newspaper. It was at Lombard that Sandburg first began to think of himself as a writer. But his first professional writing was in advertising, politics, and journalism.

After a succession of jobs, Sandburg became nationally known as a poet at the age of thirty-six when *Poetry* magazine published some of his shorter poems, including "Chicago." Sandburg's daring use of colloquialism and free verse (suggesting the influence of Walt Whitman) involved him in critical controversy and established his reputation as a major literary figure.

Sandburg's affirmation of American democracy and of the inherent nobility of labor and the working person culminated in one of his best-known collections of poems, *The People, Yes* (1936), a Whitmanesque panorama of American life that expressed a profound faith in his country. One of Sandburg's many enterprises was compiling a sort of folk-song history of America, consisting of songs collected coast to coast.

Before You Read

CHICAGO

Make the Connection

Echoes of Whitman

Free verse with a ring of oratory in its cadences is characteristic of Sandburg's poetry. Be sure to read the following poem aloud to hear the echoes of Whitman.

Quickwrite

Sandburg uses vivid words and **images** to portray a city of enormous energy. Jot down words or phrases that might capture a city's energy. What key image would best describe a city you are familiar with? (Be sure to name the city.)

Elements of Literature

Apostrophe

Apostrophe is a technique in which a writer addresses an inanimate object, an idea, or a person who is either dead or absent. In this poem, Sandburg addresses an entire city as though it were a kind of intelligent being, capable of understanding what he says.

go.hrw.com

LE0 11-16

Chicago (1923) by Louis Lozowick. Oil on canvas.

Chicago

Carl Sandburg

Hog Butcher for the World,
Tool Maker, Stacker of Wheat,
Player with Railroads and the Nation's Freight Handler;
Stormy, husky, brawling,
5   City of the Big Shoulders:

They tell me you are wicked and I believe them, for I have
seen your painted women under the gas lamps luring the
farm boys.

And they tell me you are crooked and I answer: Yes, it is true I
have seen the gunman kill and go free to kill again.

And they tell me you are brutal and my reply is: On the faces
of women and children I have seen the marks of wanton
hunger.

And having answered so I turn once more to those who sneer
at this my city, and I give them back the sneer and say to
them:

Come and show me another city with lifted head singing so
10   proud to be alive and coarse and strong and cunning.

Flinging magnetic curses amid the toil of piling job on job,
here is a tall bold slugger set vivid against the little soft
cities;

Fierce as a dog with tongue lapping for action, cunning as a
savage pitted against the wilderness,
      Bareheaded,
      Shoveling,
15   Wrecking,
      Planning,
      Building, breaking, rebuilding.

Under the smoke, dust all over his mouth, laughing with white
teeth,

Under the terrible burden of destiny laughing as a young man
laughs,

Laughing even as an ignorant fighter laughs who has never lost
20   a battle,

Bragging and laughing that under his wrist is the pulse, and
under his ribs the heart of the people,
          Laughing!

Laughing the stormy, husky, brawling laughter of Youth, half-
naked, sweating, proud to be Hog Butcher, Tool Maker,
Stacker of Wheat, Player with Railroads and Freight Handler
to the Nation.

MAKING MEANINGS

First Thoughts

1. How does Sandburg make you feel about the city he describes?

Shaping Interpretations

2. Sandburg opens with a series of **epithets,** or descriptive phrases, about Chicago. What does each of these epithets reveal about the city and the various activities that make up its economy?

3. What do "they" tell the speaker about Chicago? What is the speaker's answer to each of these comments about the city?

4. Many different **images** contribute to this portrait of Chicago, but its central image is never named. To what is Chicago really being compared? How is this image introduced and extended?

5. What are the city's main strengths and main weaknesses, according to Sandburg? What seems to be the poet's attitude toward the city?

Extending the Text

6. Which features of Chicago do you think have changed since this poem was written in 1914?

Challenging the Text

7. What would you say to those critics who have claimed that Sandburg's poetry is full of bluster and proclamation at the expense of thought?

CHOICES:
Building Your Portfolio

Writer's Notebook

1. Collecting Ideas for an Interpretive Essay

Reread Walt Whitman's "I Hear America Singing" (page 352). Then, write some notes comparing and contrasting Whitman's poem with Sandburg's "Chicago." Gather your data in a chart like the following one.

Save your notes for possible use in the Writer's Workshop on page 804.

	Whitman	Sandburg
Subject		
Imagery		
Figures of speech		
Rhythm		
Catalogs of details		
Slang and colloquial language		
Tone		

Creative Writing

2. Apt Epithets

Review the **epithets** Sandburg uses in addressing Chicago in the opening stanza. Then, choose a city, town, or other area you know well. Write an **apostrophe**— a direct address to an inanimate object—using at least five epithets about the place you have chosen. Be sure to refer to your Quickwrite notes.

Performance

3. Sing It Out

Prepare this famous poem for a group performance. Your first task will be to decide how many speakers you will need and whether you will use a group of voices to recite some passages. You will also want to decide whether you will use sound effects, even music. Perform the poem for your class.

Art

4. Chicago Illustrated

Using pictures from magazines and newspapers, create a collage to illustrate Sandburg's "Chicago." Look for references to specific images in the poem as you select drawings and photographs for the collage.

Self-Portrait by E. E. Cummings.

Berg Collection of English and American Literature, The New York Public Library. © Astor, Lenox, and Tilden Foundations. Photograph by John Lei.

E. E. Cummings

(1894–1962)

Edward Estlin (E. E.) Cummings was born in Cambridge, Massachusetts, the son of a Unitarian minister. After a childhood spent within walking distance of Harvard, he attended the university at a time when French Symbolism and free verse were major new influences on American poetry. Like other poets, Cummings found in the Imagist manifesto guidelines that allowed him to experiment and to break old rules.

If there is such a thing as "rugged individualism" in poetry, Cummings may be its prime example. All by himself, he altered conventional English syntax and made typography and the division of words part of the shape and meaning of a poem. And—in the age of celebration of the common person—he went against the grain by championing the virtues of elitism. "So far as I am concerned," he wrote, "poetry and every other art was and is and forever will be strictly and distinctly a question of individuality. . . . Poetry is being, not doing. If you wish to follow, even at a distance, the poet's calling . . . you've got to come out of the measurable doing universe into the immeasurable house of being. . . . Nobody else can be alive for you; nor can you be alive for anybody else."

Graduating from college in the midst of World War I, Cummings became part of the conflict well before American soldiers appeared on European battlefields in 1917. He volunteered for an ambulance corps privately financed by Americans and staffed by young men like himself. Crossing to Bordeaux on a French troop ship threatened by German U-boats, Cummings had hardly begun his duties when a French censor, intercepting one of his typographically odd letters, imprisoned him on suspicion of espionage. Released within three months, Cummings drew on the experience to produce his first important book of prose, *The Enormous Room* (1922).

After World War I, Cummings returned to France. He was one of the American literary expatriates who found in Paris the freedom and inspiration they felt were denied them by the restrictive Puritan climate of their own country. During this period, Cummings refined the eccentric shifts of syntax and typography that would become his trademark. In 1923, he published his first collection of verse, *Tulips and Chimneys,* which was followed by & (1925), *XLI Poems* (1925), and *is 5* (1926). His poetry is often marked by jubilant lyricism, as he celebrates love, nature's beauty, and an almost Transcendentalist affirmation of the individual. He reserved his mischievous wit for the satire of the "unman," by which he meant the unthinking, unfeeling temperament of urban "humans."

Back in the United States, Cummings split his time between an apartment in Greenwich Village in New York City and a house in Silver Lake, New Hampshire. He died still believing that "when skies are hanged and oceans drowned, / the single secret will still be man."

go.hrw.com

LEO 11-16

Make the Connection
The Prevailing Spirit

Modern literature is full of bleak images of destruction and the wane of civilization. At the same time, an extraordinary number of writers explore the determination of the human spirit to prevail in spite of hardship and even devastation. What tone about the future of this planet do you hear in Cummings's poem?

Quickwrite

Before you read this poem, jot down some of your predictions about the future of the planet. You could focus your thoughts on "What if . . . ?"

what if a much of a which of a wind

E. E. Cummings

what if a much of a which of a wind
gives the truth to summer's lie;
bloodies with dizzying leaves the sun
and yanks immortal stars awry?°
5   Blow king to beggar and queen to seem
(blow friend to fiend:blow space to time)
—when skies are hanged and oceans drowned,
the single secret will still be man

what if a keen of a lean wind flays°
10   screaming hills with sleet and snow:
strangles valleys by ropes of thing
and stifles forests in white ago?
Blow hope to terror;blow seeing to blind
(blow pity to envy and soul to mind)
15   —whose hearts are mountains,roots are trees,
it's they shall cry hello to the spring

what if a dawn of a doom of a dream
bites this universe in two,
peels forever out of his grave
20   and sprinkles nowhere with me and you?
Blow soon to never and never to twice
(blow life to isn't:blow death to was)
—all nothing's only our hugest home;
the most who die,the more we live

4. awry (ə·rī′): out of place.

9. flays: here, whips; lashes.

SPRIMARY Sources   AN INTRODUCTION

"Miracles are to come"

The poems to come are for you and for me and are not for mostpeople—it's no use trying to pretend that mostpeople and ourselves are alike. Mostpeople have less in common with ourselves than the squarerootofminusone. You and I are human beings;mostpeople are snobs. . . .

you and I are not snobs. We can never be born enough. We are human beings;for whom birth is a supremely welcome mystery,the mystery of growing:the mystery which happens only and whenever we are faithful to ourselves. You and I wear the dangerous looseness of doom and find it becoming. Life,for eternal us,is now;and now is much too busy being a little more than everything to seem anything, catastrophic included. . . .

Miracles are to come. With you I leave a remembrance of miracles:they are by somebody who can love and who shall be continually re-born,a human being;somebody who said to those near him,when his fingers would not hold a brush "tie it into my hand"—

—E. E. Cummings,
from New Poems

Before You Read

SOMEWHERE I . . .

Make the Connection

Searching for Words

Have you ever been at a loss for words, unable to find the right way to express a deep feeling or a complex thought? Poets, too, search for ways of using language that will at least approximate their complicated feelings and thoughts. In a sense, therefore, a poem is an attempt to put on paper what cannot quite be expressed in words.

Quickwrite

Maybe love is the hardest feeling of all to put into words. Poets often use figures of speech to try to express how they feel when they love someone very much. What comparisons would you use to describe that feeling of being in love—or of longing for a loved person?

somewhere i have never travelled,gladly beyond

E. E. Cummings

somewhere i have never travelled,gladly beyond
any experience,your eyes have their silence:
in your most frail gesture are things which enclose me,
or which i cannot touch because they are too near

5 your slightest look easily will unclose me
though i have closed myself as fingers,
you open always petal by petal myself as Spring opens
(touching skilfully,mysteriously)her first rose

or if your wish be to close me,i and
10 my life will shut very beautifully,suddenly,
as when the heart of this flower imagines
the snow carefully everywhere descending;

nothing which we are to perceive in this world equals
the power of your intense fragility:whose texture
15 compels me with the colour of its countries,
rendering death and forever with each breathing

(i do not know what it is about you that closes
and opens;only something in me understands
the voice of your eyes is deeper than all roses)
20 nobody,not even the rain,has such small hands

The Kiss (Der Kuss) (1907–1908) by Gustav Klimt.

Oesterreichische Galerie, Vienna, Austria.

MAKING MEANINGS

what if a much of a which of a wind

First Thoughts

1. How did you react to the poem's message? Did the message differ from the predictions you made in your Quickwrite?

Shaping Interpretations

2. If the world is destroyed, what will still survive?

3. What **images** describe the seasons of the year in the first two stanzas?

4. Describe the **rhyme scheme** of the poem. How is **slant rhyme** used?

5. What common human fears does Cummings refer to in the first six lines of each stanza? How does he comment on those fears in the last two lines of each stanza?

6. What do you think Cummings means by the last two lines? Is he celebrating life or death?

somewhere i have never travelled,gladly beyond

First Thoughts

1. Which line or **image** in the poem made the strongest impression on you? Explain.

Shaping Interpretations

2. What **figures of speech** does Cummings use to talk about his love? (How do they compare with your Quickwrite notes?)

3. The poem rises in intensity in stanza 4. **Paraphrase** this stanza, making clear what you think the speaker means by "death and forever."

4. In line 2 the phrase "your eyes have their silence" is an example of **synesthesia**—the juxtaposition of one sensory image with another image that appeals to a different sense. Where else does Cummings use synesthesia?

5. A **paradox** is a statement that appears contradictory but that reveals a kind of truth. Find at least two paradoxes in the poem and explain what you think they mean.

CHOICES: Building Your Portfolio

Writer's Notebook

1. Collecting Ideas for an Interpretive Essay

Cummings's style can be challenging because he uses a difficult **syntax** consisting of thought groupings that often don't have any punctuation or that use unusual punctuation. He also often uses verbs, adjectives, and adverbs as nouns. Go back over one of the two poems by Cummings, and determine where thought groupings begin and end. Paraphrase these thought groupings in a brief paragraph. Save your notes for possible use in the Writer's Workshop on page 804.

Evaluating Ideas

2. Snobs, Look Elsewhere

In Primary Sources (page 797), taken from the introduction to his collection *New Poems* (1938), Cummings makes several statements about poetry and his audience, and at the same time reveals an attitude toward life itself. In a brief essay, tell whether you find that any of these statements relate to the messages in "what if a much of a which of a wind" or "somewhere i have never travelled,gladly beyond." Use specific lines to support your opinions.

Comparing Poems

3. That Which Survives

In a brief essay, compare "what if a much of a which of a wind" with Robert Frost's "Once by the Pacific" (page 564). Consider in your essay the **theme** or **message, imagery, tone,** and **structure** of the poems.

Music / Performance

4. A Poem Is a Song

Create a melody to accompany either poem by Cummings. Then, with two or three classmates, perform the song for your class.

READ ON

Lifestyles of the Rich and Famous

He's rich, he's handsome, he throws great parties—so why does Jay Gatsby stand outside his opulent Long Island mansion, gazing longingly at a light across the water? The narrator Nick Carraway tries to unlock the puzzle in *The Great Gatsby*, F. Scott Fitzgerald's novel of American dreams and disappointments during the Jazz Age. This title is available in the HRW Library. A movie adaptation (1974) is also available on video.

Small-Town Americana

Like Edwin Arlington Robinson's Tilbury Town and Edgar Lee Masters' Spoon River, Sherwood Anderson's Winesburg is a typical American small town. In *Winesburg, Ohio* (Viking), Anderson explores the splendid hopes and stifled dreams of Winesburg's inhabitants in a series of interconnected stories set in the early decades of the twentieth century. For another view of a small town, read Thornton Wilder's classic play *Our Town*.

Wounds of War

Ernest Hemingway is famous for his realistic, almost journalistic accounts of the triumphs and tragedies of warfare. In *A Farewell to Arms* (Scribner's), he sets a tragic romance against the backdrop of World War I Italy. In *For Whom the Bell Tolls* (Scribner's), the backdrop changes to the Spanish civil war. Both novels have been adapted as films.

Take the "A" Train

From about 1919 to 1932, New York City experienced a blossoming of African American culture known as the Harlem Renaissance (see page 734). Langston Hughes, Zora Neale Hurston, and James Weldon Johnson are just three of the many creative talents featured in *When Harlem Was in Vogue* (Random House), a highly readable social history by David Levering Lewis.

Two Sisters Have Their Say

The Delany sisters, Sarah Louise and Annie Elizabeth, were 104 and 102 in 1993 when they wrote *Having Our Say* (Dell). Their father was born into slavery; the sisters lived through the northern migration of African Americans, the Harlem Renaissance, and the civil rights movement of the 1960s. Their story gives a unique perspective of life in the United States over the last hundred years. This nonfiction best-seller has been adapted as a stage play. In 1997, after the death of her younger sister, Sarah Louise Delaney published *On My Own at 107: Reflections on Life Without Bessie* (HarperCollins).

The American Language

American Slang

by Gary Q. Arpin

Many people think of slang as a kind of corrupt English, the product of ignorance and laziness. They see slang as a sort of linguistic disease that flourishes in the poorest and worst-maintained neighborhoods of the language. Slang, they feel, should be stamped out for the health and well-being of the general public.

But slang is as old as language itself. In fact, many words that at one time were considered slang later entered the language and are now used by all speakers. Perhaps Carl Sandburg (page 792) sized up the appeal of slang best: "Slang is language that rolls up its sleeves, spits on its hands, and goes to work."

Before the middle of the eighteenth century, slang as we know it today was called *cant* and *argot*. *Cant* referred to the secret language of thieves and beggars. *Argot* referred to the specialized vocabulary of occupations (sailors and farmers, for example). Gradually, the word *slang* came to refer to any informal, nonstandard, specialized language. Today, slang specifically refers to a kind of colorful, irreverent, lively language that quickly becomes popular and often just as quickly drops out of use. It has always been popular among the young.

Why Do We Use Slang?

Why do people use slang? Not usually out of ignorance, despite widespread misconceptions. Most slang terms are substitutes for fairly common words or phrases. A waitress who calls out the food order "Adam and Eve on a raft—wreck 'em," knows how to say "two scrambled eggs on toast." She is just using the **jargon,** or specialized vocabulary, of her occupation.

We ordinarily think of language only as a means of communication. But anthropologists point out that it has a more subtle function as well—marking relatedness. Members of a family or other group reinforce their connections by their language. If you think about it for a moment, you will probably realize that your family or group of friends does the same thing by using key words or unusual pronunciations. This is the most important function of slang: It marks members of a group and asserts the group's relatedness, thereby helping to keep it together.

The group can be of any size and come from any social class. It can be a single family or a large and widespread profession. Teenagers, athletes, actors, truck drivers, doctors, criminals, filmmakers, and soldiers all have their own slang. People outside the group who try to use its slang often appear ridiculous.

Walt Whitman (page 348) claimed that slang produced poets and poetry. This is an exaggeration, but it might point to another explanation for the persistence of slang. Slang may be used for the sheer pleasure of making sounds. It may also be a way to create new metaphors, sometimes just for the fun of it, sometimes to capture attention. Perhaps slang is used because as humans, we have an impulse to be wordsmiths. Certainly, people have persisted in making up new slang terms for concepts that already have more than enough terms to name them. Even some forty-five years ago, there were 180 slang terms for "having no money," 400 slang terms for "failing," and 200 slang terms for "getting angry." By now, who can tell how many new slang terms have been added to those lists?

People who do not speak a particular slang often are highly critical of it. This can be because some slang is vulgar or is a pointless corruption of standard

> Walt Whitman claimed that slang produced poets and poetry.

speech with no apparent justification other than novelty. Some slang can also be criticized for being imprecise. Often, however, naysayers are simply annoyed at not being part of the in-group associated with the slang they are criticizing.

Origins of American Slang

America has always been a fertile ground for the development of slang, especially since the 1830s, when informality began to be considered an almost essential aspect of democracy. The country's cowboys, railroad workers, politicians, and members of hundreds of new occupations introduced many slang terms, often to name things for which there were no existing words. The media then helped to popularize the new terms.

Slang words and phrases develop in the same ways as other additions to standard English.

1. Existing words may be given a new meaning. *Sack,* during World War II, became the almost universal slang word for "bed." It helped to create countless new phrases for "sleep": *hit the sack, sack out,* *sack time, sack duty,* and *sack drill.*

2. Two or more words may be combined to form a new expression. Americans' love affair with cars, for example, gave us the marvelously inventive *rattletrap* and the more recent *gas guzzler.* One witty compound verb, *to rubberneck,* meaning to stretch one's neck to see an accident or traffic tie-up, was once said to be the best slang term ever coined.

3. A word may be "clipped" to form a shortened word. *Fan,* as in *baseball fan,* was clipped from the word *fanatic.*

4. Words may also be borrowed from other languages. (These are often called *loanwords.*) During the westward expansion, for example, *bronco* was borrowed from the Spanish for "rough" and *mustang* from the Spanish for "stray."

5. Some slang words are simply invented. Among American backwoodsmen of the nineteenth century, the wilder the invention, the better. If you were *puckerstoppled,* you were embarrassed; confusion was *conbobberation;* and a heavy blow, in a fight or from the weather, was a *sockdologer.* Those words have disappeared, but other invented words have remained. *Blizzard,* for example, was first defined as a violent blow, perhaps from the German word *blitz,* for "lightning." In 1870, *blizzard* was applied by newspapers to violent snowstorms and was found to be so useful that it became standard English.

From Slang to Standard English

Most slang terms die quickly. There is a constant turnover, especially among "in" words. *Lounge lizard, hootchie-kootchie,* and *goo-goo eyes* came and went as fast as *cool cat, squaresville,* and *hep.* (*Hep's* offspring, *hip,* is still with us, however.) Terms that fill a need in standard English sometimes make the transition from slang to standard. *Plunder, fix, all right,* and *rough-*

"Luann" reprinted by permission of United Feature Syndicate, Inc.

neck all started as slang and were once condemned by one *highbrow* or another.

Who decides what is slang and what is standard usage? The answer to this is that we all do. Native speakers of a language have a finely tuned sense of the distinction between formal and informal language. As some slang words achieve wide popular usage, though, that distinction may blur. For example, which of these words would you say are slang, and which are standard: *corny, scrumptious, pinhead*? You might say, "Look it up in the dictionary." But the answer depends on which dictionary you use. Dictionaries whose primary purpose is to *describe* the language are apt to provide fewer usage distinctions than dictionaries prepared by lexicographers who feel that it is important to *prescribe* usage. The chart below shows the verdicts of three popular American dictionaries on whether or not our three test words are slang.

Obviously, lexicographers disagree on when a word becomes widely enough used to qualify as "standard." Some words, in fact, never make the jump at all. Terms that fill a real informal need often remain as slang for generations. Terms like *rubberneck, to squeal, baloney,* and *nifty* have endured, although regarded as slang for years. These words seem so informal that they resist incorporation into standard English, but they survive to remind us of our capacity for making poetry out of the commonplace.

Harbaugh/Rothco.

"Failure to do your homework on proper grammatical usage will result in a final grade of zero, zip, zilch . . ."

Try It Out

1. **Listing slang terms.** There are hundreds of slang terms for some common experiences or things. With two or three other students, list as many slang terms as you can for the following.

   a. an automobile
   b. failing a test
   c. getting angry
   d. stealing

   Once you've completed the lists, talk about the **metaphors** on which some of the slang terms may be based.

2. **Identifying full-word forms.** Here are some clipped forms of words in current use. Identify their full forms, referring to a dictionary if necessary.

ad lib	flu	pep
bus	gas	prom
cello	gym	prop

3. **Compiling local slang.** Join with the rest of the class in compiling a list of slang words that you believe are used only in your particular school or community. Try to explain the origin of each word.

Are They Slang? Three Verdicts			
Dictionary	**Word**		
	Corny	Scrumptious	Pinhead
Webster's Second International	No	Yes	No
Webster's Third International	No	No	No
American Heritage Dictionary	No	No	Yes

Writer's Workshop

ASSIGNMENT
Write an essay inter-
preting a work of lit-
erature, a movie, or
a work of visual art.

AIM
To inform; to ex-
plain; to persuade.

AUDIENCE
Your teacher; your
classmates; mem-
bers of a literature,
film, or art apprecia-
tion group.

Try It Out
With a partner or a
small group, choose a
poem, story, film, or
work of visual art.
Identify two or three
of the most impor-
tant elements in the
work, and discuss
how they relate to
the work's meaning.
Then, develop three
or four interpretive
claims you can make
about the work.

EXPOSITORY WRITING

INTERPRETIVE ESSAY

Every day you interpret information you receive from your environment and arrive at conclusions based on evidence presented to you. You might see dark clouds and infer that it's going to rain, or notice how shy a classmate is and infer that he may have difficulty making friends. Interpreting a literary work, a movie, or a painting isn't as straightforward as inferring the meaning of an ordinary event. However, it can be fascinating and satisfying to make sense of a work of verbal or visual art and to share your interpretation with others.

Prewriting

1. **What hooks your interest?** When you write an interpretation, it's important to feel strongly about the work
you're interpreting. Perhaps one poem or story in this book
or in your outside reading moved you in a way no other literary
work has. Perhaps you have had a similar response to a favorite painting or
film. Be sure to review your Writer's Notebook entries for Collections
14–16; you may have already made a head start on prewriting for an interpretive essay.

2. **Ask yourself about the work.** "What does this mean to me?" is
perhaps the most productive question to ask yourself about a literary
work or a work of visual art. Spend time developing a thorough answer.
Remember—this question can take you anywhere: into your own life experience; into the society around you; into historical events; into other subject areas; into other literary works, films, and other works of art; or into
an examination of the life and personality of a writer, a director, or an artist.

3. **Use a double-entry journal.** A double-entry journal is one of the simplest and best response tools you can use. Divide a sheet of paper into two
columns. In the left column, include quotations from the work you're analyzing (literature), descriptions of significant dialogue or images (film or video),
or notes on visual elements such as color and composition (fine art). In the
right column, write your response to each quotation or description. Then,
select those entries in the left column that you sense are crucial to the
work's meaning. Think of the double-entry journal as a written dialogue with
yourself, full of questions and unexpected discoveries.

The history
of the written
word is rich and
once upon a time
Page 1

Model: A Double-Entry Journal

"A Rose for Emily" by William Faulkner

title: "A Rose for Emily"	The title seems kind of romantic, maybe sentimental and nostalgic.
her house: "stubborn and coquettish decay"; "an eyesore among eyesores" (p. 716)	I had to look up the word "coquettish." It comes from the word coquette, a vain girl or woman who tries to get the attention of admirers. A clue to Miss Emily's personality? The house reminds me of the house in Poe's "Fall of the House of Usher." It's creepy.
"Miss Emily had been a tradition, a duty, and a care; a sort of hereditary obligation upon the town." (p. 716)	She sounds like a burden. I wonder if anyone really liked her? Sounds like they probably didn't.

4. **Make interpretive claims.** An **interpretive claim** is a general statement about what the work means. You might make several interpretive claims in one essay, especially if you focus on several key elements in the work. To make your interpretive claims, begin thinking in general terms about what the work means. For stories and novels, think about character, plot, setting, point of view, and theme. For poems, think about diction, imagery, symbolism, figurative language, and sound. For the visual arts, think about subject matter, colors, shapes, tone, and overall effect. Try to make at least one generalization for each element that is important to the work. For Faulkner's "A Rose for Emily," for example, you might write, "Events in the story are presented out of sequence so that Faulkner can explore the effects of the past on the present" (plot). (Unsupportable opinions such as "I like this poem" or "I have mixed feelings about this painting" are not interpretive claims.)

5. **Focus on a thesis.** Choose the interpretive claim that you feel is the strongest or most interesting, and make it your thesis: the central idea that will unify your essay. A thesis statement might be, "At first glance 'A Rose for Emily' seems to be merely a shocking horror story, but it has a serious theme: it explores the risks of clinging obstinately to the past and tradition."

6. **Support your claims.** Types of supporting evidence include quotations and paraphrases from the text, details from related works, and your own knowledge and experience. You might also wish to support your interpretive claim with quotations from critics. Be sure all quoted material is carefully documented.

Strategies for Elaboration

To ensure that your essay reads well:
- Use transitional words and phrases.
- Use definite, specific, concrete language instead of vague generalities.
- Use the literary present tense when appropriate (see page 807).
- Use a relatively formal tone, avoiding slang and colloquialisms.

Drafting

1. **Getting Started.**   At the beginning of your essay, identify the work you are writing about (by title and author, artist, or director), and provide necessary background information (perhaps a *very* brief summary of the work). You also need to give your readers a sense of where the essay as a whole is going. You might do that by stating your thesis directly in your opening paragraph.

2. **Organizing your thoughts.**   Choose a sensible order for presenting your ideas. An interpretive essay may be organized in one of several ways.

   • **Chronological order.**   Show the order in which certain details occur in the work (such as changes in a character).

   • **Order of importance.**   Move from your least important point to your most important point, or vice versa.

   • **Logical order.**   Group related ideas together. If, for example, you're focusing on plot and setting, present all your points about plot in one section and all your points about setting in another section. If you've chosen to compare and contrast two works, you can either treat the elements of one work before turning to elements of the other work (block method) or alternate between the works as you discuss each element in turn (point-by-point organization).

3. **Presenting and developing your interpretive claims.**   The heart of your essay is an organized presentation of your claim about the work. Stating your generalizations may only require a sentence or two. Many more sentences will be needed to support these claims, including evidence from the text and related works. You'll need to document your sources in two places—in parenthetical citations and in the list of Works Cited.

4. **Staying on topic.**   Keep your thesis in mind at all times; never lose the thread of your analysis; include only relevant points; be specific and concrete. Conclude your essay with an insight that sums up your thesis or leads to intriguing new questions.

Evaluating and Revising

1. **Peer review.**   Exchange papers with one or more classmates, and answer the following questions about the paper you read:

   • Can you clearly identify the writer's thesis? Does the writer provide sufficient background information about the work?

   • Does the writer present enough evidence to support his or her interpretive claims? Were you convinced of the writer's position?

   • Does the essay come to a conclusion that ties all the writer's ideas together and reinforces the thesis?

2. **Self-evaluation.**   Read your peers' comments; then, reread your own essay as if you were not the author. Decide if your essay needs more of something (more supporting evidence, more focus) or less of something (less padding, less personal opinion). Then, make appropriate revisions.

Language Workshop

The history
of the written
word is rich and
Page 1

THE RIGHT TENSE FOR SENSE: USING THE LITERARY PRESENT

When you write, you can help your readers to understand the order in which things occur by using verb tenses correctly—and consistently. Each of the six basic verb tenses—present, past, future, present perfect, past perfect, and future perfect—has its own applications. The present tense, for example, is used to express an action or state of being that is current, that is happening right now.

When you write about literature, you'll want to use a form of present tense called the **literary present.** You may write, for example, "'A Rose for Emily' *is* a story about a solitary individual with a shocking secret." You use the literary present because a work of literature is continually alive, re-created each time someone reads it. "A Rose for Emily" will *always* be a story about an individual with a shocking secret.

Strategies for Using the Literary Present

1. Use the present tense when analyzing a story or paraphrasing the author's ideas. Use the past tense when the characters themselves use the past tense. In other words, when you're quoting directly from a work, use the same tense the author uses. Otherwise, keep your essay in the literary present.

2. Sometimes, using the literary present and the past tense can create awkward situations. When your tenses sound awkward, try rewriting. For example, this sentence is awkward even though it correctly uses past and present tenses: "In 'A Rose for Emily,' William Faulkner, who *was* a Southerner, *shows* his understanding of the traditions of the American South." This could be rewritten in the following way: "In 'A Rose for Emily,' William Faulkner, a Southerner, *shows* his understanding of the traditions of the American South."

3. When you **summarize** the plot of a story or a poem, you can use the present or past tense, but you must be consistent. If you use the literary present and refer to an action that took place in the past, you must use the past tense. Thus you would say "After Miss Emily dies, the ladies go to her house and are met by the Negro servant who had worked for Miss Emily for years."

Writer's Workshop Follow-Up: Revising

Reread the interpretive essay you wrote for the Writer's Workshop on page 804, and make sure you use the literary present correctly. If you have summarized a plot, be sure your verb tenses are consistent.

**Technology
H E L P**

See Language Workshop CD-ROM. *Key word entry: consistency of tense.*

**Language
Handbook
H E L P**

See Tenses and Their Uses, pages 1224-1225.

Try It Out

Revise the paragraph below so that it consistently uses the literary present.

"A Rose for Emily" was a complex story that could be interpreted on several levels. On one level the story was about the conflict between the individual and the community. It was also about the conflicts between tradition and modern life. Faulkner, a modernist, contrasted the "New South" with the "Old South," which was symbolized by Miss Emily's old-style, crumbling house.

Reading for Life

Obtaining Information from an Internet Database

Situation

Like Marianne Moore, you're a sports fan and you want to research data on a baseball team in the American League. You have access to a commercial on-line service or to the Internet.

Strategies

When using an electronic database, apply the following strategies:

Focus on the data you need.

- Formulate a clear idea of the data you want to find and how you intend to use it. This will help you focus your search.

Search the Internet.

- Use the search feature of your on-line service provider or an Internet portal. You may need to enter the category of information you're looking for, such as "baseball statistics." You can also enter a specific Uniform Resource Locator (URL) for a Web site. See also the Communications Handbook.

Evaluate the database.

- Once you've found some data, scan through it to make sure it's what you want.

- Evaluate the source of the data. Is it a reputable source? Is the data current and updated regularly? Does the data agree with data from at least one other source?

- Cite the source of any data you use. For example, give the Web site or the name of the on-line service.

TEXAS RANGERS

1998 TEXAS RANGERS REGULAR SEASON BATTING STATISTICS

PLAYER	G	AB	R	H	2B	3B	HR	RBI	BB	SO	OBP	SLG	AVG
Roberto Kelly	75	257	48	83	7	3	16	46	8	46	.349	.560	.323
Ivan Rodriguez	145	579	88	186	40	4	21	91	32	88	.358	.513	.321
Juan Gonzalez	154	606	110	193	50	2	45	157	46	126	.366	.630	.318
Rusty Greer	155	598	107	183	31	5	16	108	80	93	.386	.455	.306
Will Clark	149	554	98	169	41	1	23	102	72	97	.384	.507	.305
Mike Simms	86	186	36	55	11	0	16	46	24	47	.381	.613	.296
Tom Goodwin	154	520	102	151	13	3	2	33	73	90	.378	.338	.290
Luis Alecea	101	259	51	71	15	3	6	33	37	40	.372	.425	.274
Todd Zeile	158	572	85	155	32	3	19	94	69	90	.350	.437	.271
...Tex	52	180	26	47	14	1	6	28	28	32	.358	.450	.261
...La	40	158	22	40	6	1	7	27	10	24	.300	.437	.253
...Fla	66	234	37	68	12	1	6	39	31	34	.374	.427	.291
Lee Stevens	120	344	52	91	17	4	20	59	31	93	.324	.512	.265
Domingo Cedeno	61	141	19	37	9	1	2	21	10	32	.309	.383	.262
Royce Clayton	142	541	89	136	31	2	9	53	53	83	.319	.366	.251
...Tex	52	186	30	53	12	1	5	24	13	32	.330	.441	.285
...StL	90	355	59	83	19	1	4	29	40	51	.313	.327	.234
Mark McLemore	126	461	79	114	15	1	5	53	89	64	.369	.317	.247
Kevin Elster	84	297	33	69	10	1	8	37	33	66	.311	.354	.232
Totals (including players not listed)	162	5672	940	1637	314	32	201	894	595	1045	.375	.462	.289

Using the Strategies

Examine the database on this page. Then, answer the following questions.

1. Which Texas Rangers player had the highest batting average?

2. Which player had the most official at-bats?

3. Which three players scored the most runs?

4. Who played for more than one team in 1998?

5. What does OBP mean?

6. What are two possible uses you might have for this data?

7. What resources might you use to corroborate the data?

8. Where did this data come from?

Extending the Strategies

Using the strategies you've learned, research data on another sports team or on a different subject that interests you. Focus on a specific topic, and in a paragraph or two report the information you found and the problems you encountered. If you like, suggest ways in which the database could be improved.

Learning for Life

Planning for the Future

Problem

Many of the stories and poems in the collections you have just read are told from the perspective of people looking back on their lives from the vantage point of old age. How do people in our society make fulfilling lives for themselves as they grow older? How can you plan for your later years so that life is meaningful and enjoyable?

Project

Research contemporary issues pertaining to aging: geriatric health care, the future of Social Security and retirement benefits, increases in life expectancy, older employees returning to the work force, changing perspectives of older adults, and so on.

Preparation

1. With a group, brainstorm a list of questions you have about the topic of aging.

2. Make a list of current books, periodicals, and other sources for information on aging.

Procedure

1. You might want to interview an older relative or friend about individual perspectives on aging and retirement. You might also choose to

   - interview a geriatric doctor or nurse about the medical aspects of aging

   - investigate retirement options by contacting the American Association of Retired Persons (AARP)

   - examine retirement financing with a planning expert

   - discuss social and emotional aspects of aging with a social worker or psychologist

   Set a time for your interview, and prepare questions.

2. Study current social views of aging and the elderly by paying attention to media representations. You might take notes on news programs devoted to the topic of the elderly, keep track of the number of elderly characters on TV shows and note how they are portrayed, and watch popular films such as *The Trip to Bountiful* and *Driving Miss Daisy*. What positive and negative messages about aging is society giving us?

Presentation

Present your information on aging in one of the following formats (or another that your teacher approves):

1. **Retirement Brochure**
   Write and design a brochure describing the ideal retirement plan for you. Be sure to include the following:

   - whether you plan to continue working part time, perform community service, and so on

   - a description of the living situation you would prefer

   - recreational activities you hope to participate in

2. **In Praise of Old Age**
   Put together a video documentary or a photo-essay of interviews with older adults. Show as many sides of the realities of aging as you can. If you wish, include interviews with people who work with the aged or who live with or know the particular persons you have interviewed.

3. **Graphic Communication**
   Share your findings about aging (what happens to the body as it ages, life expectancy in the twenty-first century, media depictions of the elderly, economic trends among retired people, and so on) in a visual display that combines two or more types of graphic communication: charts, graphs, diagrams, illustrations, and so on. Set up your graphic display in your school.

Processing

What did you learn about aging by completing this project? What can people do to develop more realistic ideas of what growing older entails? What can you do now to make sure that your own later years are meaningful and enjoyable? Write a reflection for your portfolio.

American Drama

Scene from Rodgers and Hammerstein's *Carousel*. Lincoln Center, New York City, 1994.

American Drama

by **Robert Anderson**

Theater is one of the most emotionally satisfying experiences imaginable. It touches our inner core, and gives insight into who we are.

—Theodore Mann

Drama is probably the most difficult form of writing; it certainly seems to take the longest to learn. According to a saying, young poets are eighteen, young novelists are twenty-four, and young playwrights are thirty.

George S. Kaufman, a noted American writer of comedies during the 1920s and 1930s, said that writing plays was not an art but a trick. Art or trick, it is difficult, possibly because when a play is written, it is not finished in the same way that a poem or novel is. There remains the painful and pleasurable process of bringing the play to life on stage, with the help of a director, actors, set designer, costume designer, lighting technician, stagehands, musicians—and a responsive audience. Producing a play is a team effort, and much can go wrong. A beautifully written and acted scene, for example, can be ruined if the lighting technician dims the lights too rapidly.

Another difference between drama and other literary forms is that movement and gesture are essential elements in drama. Some of the high points in a play may even be nonverbal. In *The Diary of Anne Frank*, for example, Mr. Frank realizes that the Nazis are downstairs and that the family's hiding place is about to be discovered. He turns to his family and friends and spreads his hands in resignation. This heartbreaking moment is conceived by the playwright, but its achievement on the stage—the exact gesture—requires the close and creative cooperation of actor and director.

Young writers are often drawn to the stage by the theatrical trappings: the gestures, the colorful sets, and the magical effects that drama can achieve. But playwrights soon learn that theatrical effects are rarely enough in themselves. The effects and gestures are there only to serve a story, and it must be a story that engages the passions of the collaborators—the director, the actors, and dozens of others who work to produce a play. Stage technicians may dazzle our senses with intricate and fascinating effects, but if a play doesn't have a significant story, we find nothing moving in the end, because our emotions have not been touched.

> . . . [W]hile I am working I toss papers right and left; at the end of each day I gather them helter-skelter and pile them together. So that the ultimate arrangement is a colossal job, which I do with actual groans and muttered curses, sitting on the floor with papers all about me, gradually going into little separate stacks, some order finally emerging, but not till I have died a thousand deaths. . . . Writing is not a happy profession.
>
> —Tennessee Williams

PLAYBILL®

THE MUSIC BOX

THE DIARY OF ANNE FRANK

Structure: Organizing Our Emotions

When a play goes wrong, it is almost always because the writer has failed to conceive the story in dramatic terms. There are, of course, some plays (such as Thornton Wilder's *Our Town*) that work in the theater even though they ignore the usual principles of drama. But over the centuries certain principles have developed, and they are usually observed by playwrights who want to catch, hold, and reward the attention of an audience.

The analogy is slightly oversimplified, but we respond to a play in very much the way we respond to a sports event. Let's assume that one summer evening you go to a professional baseball game. For some reason, you take a liking to one of the pitchers. Then someone sitting next to you says that the pitcher has been out for several weeks with an injured elbow and is trying to make a comeback. If he fails in this game, he is finished. You start rooting for him. He gets some bad calls from the plate umpire, and you boo or whistle. Then your neighbor tells you that the pitcher is not pitching his best. Unless he stops protecting his injured elbow and starts putting more speed in his pitches, he will not win.

Most plays have more psychological complexity than this situation does. With a little imagination, however, we can add to the pitcher's problems. Suppose, for instance, that the pitcher's wife is afraid that if he throws too hard, he will ruin his elbow and be unable to play. She tells him that if he damages his elbow further, she will leave him; but, to him, the glory of winning transcends practical matters. To his wife, he is a ball-playing "boy," careless and immature. And so forth. . . . What has happened in this scenario is what happens in almost every play. Early on, the playwright organizes our emotions behind some character or group of characters: We are "for" them. The playwright has placed these characters in a situation involving **conflict** and then has made us understand that it is not just any conflict: The character or characters have something vital at stake. They want to win, and they need to win in order to survive. In the baseball game, the situation is made difficult for the pitcher, who is the **protagonist** (the major character who wants something and who drives the action forward). The pitcher struggles against

> You have to hit the public when it is not looking . . . you have to make it real to them the way the subway is real. You can't depend on their embracing your work because it is art, but only because it somehow reaches into the part of them that is still alive and questing.
>
> —Arthur Miller

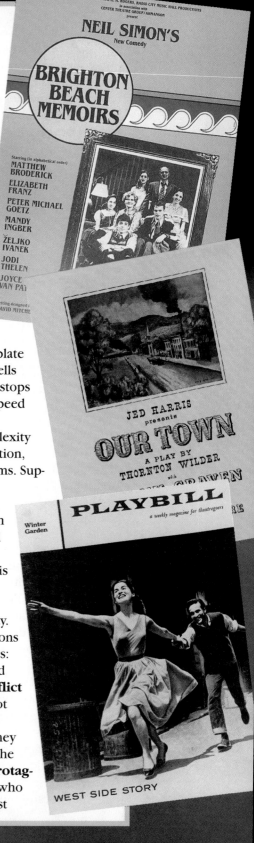

both **external conflict** (the opposing side) and **internal conflict** (his fears of damaging his arm, his feelings about the pressure from his wife). The fan sitting next to you has given us the background information, or **exposition** (who the pitcher is, what he wants to do, and what he has at stake). The story of a character who, against the odds, wants something meaningful has been set in motion. The tension mounts as the innings pass; we are witnessing, or participating in and enjoying, a drama.

The word *participation* is important. We have all heard ballplayers say how encouraged they are by the response of the spectators. Actors, too, may say as they come offstage after a scene, "That's a wonderful audience out there tonight!" And because of the audience, performances often rise to a higher level. It has often been said that a play exists halfway between the stage and the audience. What an audience gets from a performance is directly related to what it brings to the performance, not only in the way of understanding and feeling but also in enthusiasm. In successful dramatic performances, a note is sounded onstage, and a chord of recognition or responsiveness echoes back from the audience. A play performed in an empty theater is not a play.

> . . . I would say that the whole notion of going into a theater and sitting with a lot of other people and watching a spectacle, especially now when you can watch television or the movies with greater convenience, tells me that, apart from the fact that it's a little more exciting to see a live actor on the stage, it's also exciting to sit next to human beings.
>
> —Arthur Miller

The basic elements of drama include exposition, which gives us information, and a protagonist, the major character who struggles against internal conflict and external conflict.

How a Play Is Produced (It's a Miracle!)

The English plays of the late Middle Ages were called miracle plays because they often dealt with stories of miracles from the Bible or the lives of the saints. Any modern-day American play might also be called a miracle play, because it is a miracle that it was written and even more of a miracle that it was produced. In the United States today, drama is dependent on money. Only a few institutional theaters are able to present plays with little or no regard for profit. Most of the plays that are produced (and that therefore stand a chance of becoming part of our dramatic literature) are put on with the idea that they will make money.

To produce any writer's new play on Broadway costs a minimum of half a million dollars (at this writing). The **producers** (people who advance the money) willing to take such a risk are rare, although such risks *are* taken every season. Even though it operates in a very costly manner, the professional Broadway theater, to its credit, has been the launching pad for most of the distinguished plays in American dramatic literature.

Recently, regional theaters throughout the country have been presenting new plays by both new and established playwrights. The Broadway producers often visit, look, and take whatever they want for production. For the most part, only a successful Broadway production gives a playwright enough income to plunge in and take the years necessary to write the next play. For that reason, Broadway remains the goal of most playwrights.

There are many stops on the way to New York, some of which become full stops. Over ten thousand plays are copyrighted every year; this probably represents only half of the plays that are actually written. Perhaps several hundred new plays are produced onstage *somewhere* around the country; maybe ten appear on Broadway.

Producers could not hope to cope with reading thousands and thousands of plays, so playwrights must generally find an **agent** who will handle their work. The agent is the producer's first line of defense. Knowing their various tastes, the agent submits a play to likely producers, who may take three months to a year to read it. They may admire the play but still be unwilling to produce it. One playwright used to say, "If they take you to lunch, they're not going to invest in your play." A good lunch is a consolation prize, and many playwrights have eaten very well off plays that were never produced.

> To a certain extent I imagine a play is completely finished in my mind—in my case, at any rate—without my knowing it, before I sit down to write. So in that sense, I suppose, writing a play is *finding out* what the play is.
>
> —Edward Albee

But if the producer should decide to finance the play, he or she then sits down with the playwright to go over changes suggested for the script or ideas for directors and actors. Authors maintain control over their scripts, and the playwright is very much involved in the selection of the director and the actors. Of course, since theater is a collaborative medium, the playwright tries to get along with the producer. But if the playwright and producer discover during these preliminary talks that they have incompatible ideas, they can shake hands and part.

The director becomes the playwright's surrogate at rehearsals. In a sense, the director takes the play away from the playwright, and, finally, the actors take it away from both of them.

Rehearsals involve both pleasure and tension. Many temperaments must mesh as the actors move forward to the climactic moment of opening night. (Note that all the elements of drama itself are also present at play rehearsals: striving for a goal, having something at stake, dealing with internal and external conflicts, etc.)

Scenes from 1989 production
of *A Raisin in the Sun* by Lorraine Hansberry.

© Mitzi Trumbo for PBS
American Playhouse,
KCET Los Angeles.

The play opens in a smaller city for a tryout run or in New York for previews. Sometimes all goes well, and the production needs only some refining and sharpening. More often, the play needs work—rewriting, new sets, new costumes, sometimes a new director or a new star. Chaos reigns until opening night, when all the cast will suddenly come down with laryngitis, intestinal upsets, sinus trouble, or splitting headaches. Somehow, the curtain rises, and the show goes on.

The day after the opening, there may or may not be a line of eager theatergoers at the box office. If there is, the playwright has created what may later be called an American classic, which will be performed around the world and will find its way into the anthologies you study in school. If there isn't a line, the playwright will quickly look around for a way to make a living while writing the next play—if he or she has the courage. The second instance is the more usual. The theater has been called the "fabulous invalid," always teetering on the edge of extinction. If so, playwrights themselves might be called the walking wounded—working, barely surviving, but finally enduring to try once again.

The production of a play depends on a successful working relationship between the playwright, the producer, the director, and the actors.

. . . [T]he final evaluation of a play has nothing to do with immediate audience or critical response. The playwright, along with any writer, composer, painter in this society, has got to have a terribly private view of his own value, of his own work. He's got to listen to his own voice primarily.
—Edward Albee

The History of American Drama: The Caboose of Literature

Eugene O'Neill (1888–1953) is generally considered the first important figure in American drama. It is significant that decades after the 1920 production of his first full-length play, *Beyond the Horizon,* he is still regarded as the most important playwright the United States has produced.

American drama before O'Neill consisted mostly of shows and entertainments. These wildly theatrical spectacles often featured such delights as chariot races and burning cities, staged by means of special effects that dazzled audiences. Melodramas and farces were also written for famous actors, much as television shows today are created to display the personalities and talents of popular performers. In fact, O'Neill's own father, James O'Neill, spent the better part of his life touring in a spectacular melodrama based on Alexandre Dumas's *The Count of Monte Cristo.*

There was great theatrical activity in the United States in the nineteenth century, a time when there were no movies, radio, or television. Every town of any size had its theater or "opera house" in which touring companies performed. Given the hunger for entertainment, one may wonder why no significant American drama was staged in the century that produced, among others, Melville, Emerson, Whitman, Dickinson, and Twain.

nts are either
keen
psycholo-
they aren't
wrights.
gene O'Neill

PLAYBIL
WALTER KERR THEATRE

THE PIAN
LESSON

One explanation is that theater has usually followed the other arts, rather than pointing the way toward new directions. Robert Sherwood, one of a group of notable American playwrights between 1920 and 1940, once said, "Drama travels in the caboose of literature." Theater seems to take up new attitudes, subject matter, and forms only after they have been explored in the other arts. For the most part, theater tends to dramatize accepted attitudes and values.

The reason for this is that theater is a social art, one we attend as part of a large group; we seem to respond to something new much more slowly as a group than we do as individuals. When you laugh or cry in the theater, your response is noticed. You are, in a sense, giving your approval, and this approval may be subject to criticism or condemnation by those sitting around you who are not laughing or crying. Furthermore, you may not be shocked to *read* about your secret thoughts, dreams, and desires; but if you *see* them shown on stage as you sit among a thousand people, you may refuse to respond, refuse to acknowledge them. You may even rise up and stalk out of the theater.

Thus, the novel and, to some extent, the poetry of the nineteenth and early twentieth centuries were more daring than the theater in giving us a record of experience, in showing us life as it *is* lived rather than as it *should be* lived.

During the period before Eugene O'Neill, American drama tended to be mild and sentimental, rarely questioning the life and attitudes it depicted, almost never challenging the accepted traditions of its times.

The Influence of Europe: Psychology and Taboo Subjects

European drama, which was to influence modern American drama profoundly, matured in the last third of the nineteenth century with the achievements of three playwrights: the Norwegian Henrik Ibsen, the Swede August Strindberg, and the Russian Anton Chekhov. Ibsen deliberately tackled subjects such as guilt, sexuality, and mental illness—subjects that had never before been so realistically and disturbingly portrayed on stage. Strindberg brought to his characterizations an unprecedented level of psychological complexity. And Chekhov, along with Ibsen and Strindberg, shifted the subject matter of drama from wildly theatrical displays of external action to inner action and emotions and the concerns of everyday life. Chekhov once remarked, "People don't go to the North Pole and fall off icebergs. They go to the office and quarrel with their wives and eat cabbage soup."

Ibsen, Strindberg, and Chekhov bequeathed to their American heirs plays about life as it is actually lived. They presented characters and situations more or less realistically, in what has been called the "slice-of-life" dramatic technique.

Realism and Eugene O'Neill: Putting American Drama on the Map

Realistic drama is based on the illusion that when we watch a play, we are looking at life through a "fourth wall" that has been removed so that we can see the action. Soon after the beginning of the twentieth century, realism became the dominant mode of American drama.

As with all theatrical revolutions, the movement toward realism began apart from the commercial theater. But very soon after the new drama succeeded in the little theaters off Broadway (about 1916), the commercial theater adopted realism, too.

In 1916 and 1917, two small theater groups in New York—the Provincetown Players and the Washington Square Players—began to produce new American plays. They provided a congenial home for new American playwrights, notably Eugene O'Neill, whose first one-act plays about the sea were produced by the Provincetown Players in Greenwich Village in 1916. (New movements in the theater have often begun with one-act plays. In addition to O'Neill, Tennessee Williams, Clifford Odets, and Edward Albee all started with short plays.)

These theater groups seemed to have no program. They were not sure what they were for, but they were sure what they were against: the established commercial theater. They would produce any play, in any style, that commercial theater would not touch.

O'Neill gravitated there naturally. Well aware of Sigmund Freud and his new theories about the complex self, O'Neill tried especially hard to reveal more than realism—or Naturalism—could normally reveal. "The old naturalism," he wrote, "no longer applies. We have taken too many snapshots of each other in every graceless position; we have endured too much from the banality of surfaces."

In *The Great God Brown* (1926), O'Neill experimented with using masks to differentiate between two sides of a personality. In *Days Without End* (1934), he had two actors play one character to achieve the same end. And in *Strange Interlude* (1928), characters spoke in asides to the audience, revealing thoughts and feelings that could not be expressed in dialogue to other characters.

Goodspeed Opera House, East Haddam, Connecticut.

Inge Morath/Magnum.

Sure, I'll write about happiness if I ever happen to meet up with that luxury and find it sufficiently dramatic and in harmony with any deep rhythm of life. But happiness is a word. What does it mean? Exaltation, an intensified feeling of the significant worth of man's being and becoming? Well, if it means that—and not a mere smirking contentment with one's lot—I know that there is more of it in one real tragedy than in all the happy ending plays ever written.

—Eugene O'Neill

Scene from *Death of a Salesman* by Arthur Miller.

With his experimental flair, his enormous output, and his high aspirations for the theater, Eugene O'Neill dominated American drama in his generation; he can be said to have put it on the map. His plays were widely produced abroad, and he was awarded the Nobel Prize in literature in 1936.

Americans fancy themselves . . . to be openhanded, on the side of justice, a little bit careless about what they buy, wasteful, but essentially good guys, optimistic. But under that level of awareness there is another one, which gets expressed in very few movies and very few plays, but in more plays in proportion than in the movies: the level which confronts our bewilderment, our lonely naïveté, our hunger for purpose.

—Arthur Miller

Arthur Miller: Playwright of Our Social Conscience

The post–World War II years brought two important figures to prominence in American drama: Arthur Miller (1915-   ) and Tennessee Williams (1911-1983). Although other playwrights, such as William Inge (1913-1973), have contributed striking and effective plays, Miller and Williams remain the dominant figures of the second half of the century. Miller and Williams represent the two principal movements in modern American drama: realism, and realism combined with an attempt at something more imaginative. From the beginning, American playwrights have tried to break away from realism or to blend it with more poetic expression, as in Miller's *Death of a Salesman* (1949), Williams's *The Glass Menagerie* (1944), and Thornton Wilder's *Our Town* (1938) and *The Skin of Our Teeth* (1942).

Arthur Miller's best work, *Death of a Salesman,* is one of the most successful in fusing the realistic and the imaginative; in all of his other plays, however, Miller is the master of realism. He is a true disciple of Henrik Ibsen, not only in his realistic technique but also in his concern about society's impact on his characters' lives.

In Miller's plays, the course of the action and the development of characters depend not only on the characters' psychological makeup but also on the social, philosophical, and economic atmosphere of their times. Miller's most notable character, Willy Loman in *Death of a Salesman,* is a self-deluded man; but he is also a product of the American dream of success and a victim of the American business machine, which disposes of him when he has outlived his usefulness.

Miller is a writer of high moral seriousness, whether he is dealing with personal versus social responsibility, as in *All My Sons* (1947), or with witch hunts past and present, as in *The Crucible* (1953), which you are about to read. Miller writes a plain and muscular prose that under the force of emotion often becomes eloquent, as in Linda Loman's famous speech in *Death of a Salesman,* in which she talks to her two sons about their father:

> I don't say he's a great man. Willy Loman never made a lot of money. His name was never in the paper. He's not the finest character that ever lived. But he's a human being, and a terrible thing is happening to him. So attention must be paid. He's not to be allowed to fall into his grave like an old dog. Attention, attention must finally be paid to such a person.

—Arthur Miller,
from Death of a Salesman

Tennessee Williams: Playwright of Our Souls

Although Tennessee Williams was Miller's contemporary, his concern was not with social matters, but with personal ones. If Miller was often the playwright of our social conscience, then Williams was the playwright of our souls. In play after play, he probed the psychological complexities of his characters, especially of his female characters: Amanda and Laura in *The Glass Menagerie* (1944), Blanche in *A Streetcar Named Desire* (1947), and Alma in *Summer and Smoke* (1948).

In contrast to Miller's spare, plain language, Williams's writing is delicate and sensuous; it is often colored with lush imagery and evocative rhythms. Miller's characters are, by and large, ordinary people with whom we identify because they are caught up in the social tensions of our times. Williams's characters are often women who are lost ladies, drowning in their own neuroses, but somehow mirroring a part of our own complex psychological selves.

The actual scenes in Williams's plays are usually purely realistic, even though these scenes may deal with colorful and extreme characters. But Williams usually theatricalized the realism with "music in the wings" or symbolic props, such as Laura's unicorn in *The Glass Menagerie* or the looming statue of Eternity in *Summer and Smoke.* He always conceived his plays in visually arresting, colorful, theatrical environments—an effort in which he was aided by the imaginative designer Jo Mielziner, who designed the sets for many of his plays.

In the works of Arthur Miller and Tennessee Williams, we see the two strongest strands in American drama: pure realism, and realism blended with an imaginative, poetic sensibility.

The Revolt Against Realism: Theater of Fragmentation

In the mid–nineteenth century, realism in drama was conceived as a revolt against crude theatricalism. Currently, there is a revolt against realism itself in American drama. Naturally, the movement is toward theatricalism again, with its emphasis on stage effects and imaginative settings. This revolt does not confine itself to a particular manner of staging; instead, it extends to the texture of language and plot in the scripts themselves.

The moral and religious certainties that once bound people together exert little or no force on many modern audiences. Some people believe that survival itself depends on a willingness to accept life as formless or meaningless.

Some American playwrights found this new outlook on life impossible to express in the orderly "beginning, middle, end" format of realism. They borrowed, again from Europe, a theater of fragmentation, impressions, and stream of consciousness that was called "expressionist." **Expressionist drama** aimed at the revelation of characters' interior consciousness without reference to a logical sequence of surface actions. Many writers who used expressionist techniques in drama came to be called playwrights of the Theater of the Absurd. Samuel Beckett (1906–1989) and Eugene Ionesco (1912–1994) were among the founders of the Theater of the Absurd. The drama critic Martin Esslin has written this about the Absurdists:

The action of a play of the Theater of the Absurd is not intended to tell a story but to communicate a pattern of poetic images. To give but one example: Things happen in [Samuel Beckett's] *Waiting*

Scene from *The Glass Menagerie* by Tennessee Williams. Long Wharf Theater, New Haven, Connecticut, 1986.

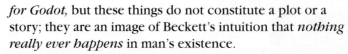

for Godot, but these things do not constitute a plot or a story; they are an image of Beckett's intuition that *nothing really ever happens* in man's existence.

—Martin Esslin

The trouble with a static play that mirrors a static life is that it is static. It is an image, a picture; and a picture can absorb our interest for only so long because it lacks the progression and development of a dramatic story. We can observe a situation without development for about the length of a one-act play. Perhaps this is why so many of the Absurdist plays *are* only one act, such as Beckett's *Krapp's Last Tape* and Ionesco's *The Bald Soprano.*

The most significant Absurdist in the United States has been Edward Albee (1928–   ). Albee is not a pure Absurdist, since, like all innovative playwrights, he experiments with many forms. From 1959 to 1970, Albee produced a play a year. These works ranged from his startling one-act debut, *The Zoo Story* (1959), through the Absurdist play *The American Dream* (1961), to the savage and electrifying domestic drama *Who's Afraid of Virginia Woolf?* (1962), which made Albee world famous.

Experimental drama has increased the options that are open to playwrights. There are practically no conventions in the theater anymore; there is simply a stage and an audience. Playwrights are free to load the stage with scenery, lights, and special effects; but they are equally free—as the playwright was in the age of Shakespeare—to have an actor gesture toward one side of an utterly bare stage and say, "This is the Forest of Arden."

Dramatists now have the freedom to express their deepest feelings in almost any form they choose—provided that their approach can be made comprehensible to an audience and touch their emotions.

Scene from *Happy Days* by Samuel Beckett. The entire play takes place while the actors are half buried in a pile of sand.

Quickwrite What do you predict will happen to American drama in the next ten years? Consider subject matter, sets and costume design, popularity, and competition with movies, television, and the Internet. Jot down your thoughts, and then compare notes with your classmates.

Miller

In a sense I went naked to Salem, still unable to accept the most common experience of humanity, the shifts of interests that turned loving husbands and wives into stony enemies, loving parents into indifferent supervisors or even exploiters of their children, and so forth. As I already knew from my reading, that was the real story of ancient Salem Village, what they called then the breaking of charity with one another. The gray rain on my windshield was falling into my soul.

—Arthur Miller,
from *Timebends: A Life*

Arthur Miller
(1915–   )

by Robert Anderson

Arthur Miller, considered by many to be the pre-eminent American playwright of the second half of the twentieth century, was born in New York City. His father manufactured women's coats, and his mother was a schoolteacher. In high school, Arthur was more involved with sports than with literature. "Until the age of seventeen," Miller said, "I can safely say that I never read a book weightier than *Tom Swift* and *The Rover Boys,* and only verged on literature with some Dickens."

On graduation from high school, Miller applied to the University of Michigan, but his grades were not good enough for a scholarship, and the Depression left his father unable to finance his tuition. To earn money for college, Miller worked for two years in an automobile parts plant, where, incidentally, he read Tolstoy's *War and Peace.* The experience in the parts plant later supplied him with the material for his 1955 play *A Memory of Two Mondays.*

Miller eventually enrolled in the University of Michigan. To help finance his education, he took on various jobs. First, he was a mouse tender in the university science laboratory. Later, he moved on (and up) to become the night editor of the *Michigan Daily.* More important, he started to write plays.

After graduation, Miller returned to New York and, like many of us "playwrights-in-waiting," earned a living by writing radio scripts for such programs as *Cavalcade of America,* the *Columbia Workshop,* and *The Theatre Guild of the Air.*

Miller's first Broadway success, *All My Sons,* was produced in 1947 and won The New York Drama Critic's award for Best Play. That play struck a note that was to become familiar in Miller's work: the need for moral responsibility in families and society.

In 1949, with the production of his masterpiece, *Death of a Salesman* (written in a small studio he built with his own hands on his prop-

erty in northwestern Connecticut), all promises were fulfilled. Miller instantly joined the pantheon of the great American playwrights.

It was totally in character that Miller's next play, produced in 1953, should be *The Crucible*—about a witch hunt that took place in 1692 in Salem, Massachusetts. In that witch-hunt, Miller found parallels to the "Red hunt" being conducted in the 1950s in Washington, D.C., by Senator Joseph McCarthy. Writers, actors, politicians—and all kinds of other people—were summoned to appear before McCarthy to answer the question: "Are you now or were you ever a Communist?" Those summoned were required to inform on neighbors and friends or be sent to jail.

Three years after the production of *The Crucible* in New York, Miller was summoned before a congressional committee. He spoke freely about himself and his occasional attendance, years before, as a guest at Communist meetings; but he refused to name names of other people in attendance. Miller was found in contempt of Congress, but his conviction was later overturned by the Supreme Court.

The Crucible was not successful in its first production. Some critics questioned the comparison between the old witch-hunts and the contemporary hunt for Communists in government. In a later production, supervised by Miller himself, the play ran for over six hundred performances. It is now Miller's most produced play.

go.hrw.com

LEO 11-17

Why I Wrote *The Crucible*
An artist's answer to politics

by Arthur Miller

As I watched *The Crucible* taking shape as a movie over much of the past year, the sheer depth of time that it represents for me kept returning to mind. As those powerful actors blossomed on the screen, and the children and the horses, and the crowds and the wagons, I thought again about how I came to cook all this up nearly fifty years ago, in an America almost nobody I know seems to remember clearly. . . .

I remember those years—they formed *The Crucible's* skeleton—but I have lost the dead weight of the fear I had then. Fear doesn't travel well; just as it can warp judgment, its absence can diminish memory's truth. What terrifies one generation is likely to bring only a puzzled smile to the next. . . .

[Senator] McCarthy's power to stir fears of creeping Communism was not entirely based on illusion, of course. . . . From being our wartime ally, the Soviet Union rapidly became an expanding empire. In 1949, Mao Zedong took power in China. Western Europe also seemed ready to become Red, especially Italy, where the Communist Party was the largest outside Russia, and was growing. . . . McCarthy—brash and ill-mannered but to many authentic and true—boiled it all down to what anyone could understand: We had "lost China" and would soon lose Europe as well, because the State Department—staffed, of course, under Democratic presidents—was full of treasonous pro-Soviet intellectuals. It was as simple as that. . . .

The Crucible was an act of desperation. . . . By 1950 when I began to think of writing about the hunt for Reds in America, I was motivated in some great part by the paralysis that had set in among many liberals who, despite their discomfort with the inquisitors' violations of civil rights, were fearful, and with good reason, of being identified as covert Communists if they should protest too strongly. . . .

I visited Salem for the first time on a dismal spring day in 1952. . . . In the gloomy courthouse there I read the transcripts of the witchcraft trials of 1692, as taken down in a primitive shorthand by ministers who were spelling each other. But there was one entry in Upham° in which the thousands of pieces I had come across were jogged into place. It was from a report written by the Reverend Samuel Parris, who was one of the chief instigators of the witch-hunt. "During the examination of Elizabeth Proctor, Abigail Williams, and Ann Putnam"—the two were "afflicted" teen-age accusers, and Abigail was Parris's niece—"both made offer to strike at said Proctor; but when Abigail's hand came near, it opened, whereas it was made up, into a fist before, and came down exceeding lightly as it drew near to said Proctor, and at length, with open and extended fingers, touched Proctor's hood very lightly. Immediately Abigail cried out her fingers, her fingers, her fingers burned. . . ."

In this remarkably observed gesture of a troubled young girl, I believed, a play became possible. Elizabeth Proctor had been the orphaned Abigail's mistress, and they had lived together in the same small house until Elizabeth fired the girl. By this time, I was sure, John Proctor had bedded Abigail, who had to be dismissed most likely to appease Elizabeth. There was bad blood between the two women now. That Abigail started, in effect, to condemn Elizabeth to death with her touch, then stopped her hand, then went through with it, was quite suddenly the human center of all this turmoil.

All this I understood. I had not approached the witchcraft out of nowhere or from purely social and political considerations. My own marriage of twelve years was teetering and I knew more than I wished to know about where the blame lay. That John Proctor the sinner might overturn his paralyzing personal guilt and become the most forthright voice against the madness around him was a reassurance to me, and, I suppose, an inspiration: It demonstrated that a clear moral outcry could still spring even from an ambiguously unblemished soul. Moving crabwise across the profusion of evidence, I sensed that I had at last found something of myself in it, and a play began to accumulate around this man.

—from *The New Yorker*,
October 21 and 28, 1996

°Charles W. Upham, a mayor of Salem, published a two-volume study of the trials in 1867.

Before You Read

THE CRUCIBLE

cru·ci·ble (krōō'sə bəl) *n.*
[ML *crucibulum,* lamp, crucible, prob. < Gmc, as in OE *cruce,* pot, jug, MHG *kruse,* earthen pot (see CRUSE) a+ L suffix *-ibulum* (as in *thuribulum,* censer), but assoc. by folk etym. with L *crux,* CROSS, as if lamp burning before cross] **1** a container made of a substance that can resist great heat, for melting, fusing, or calcining ores, metals, etc. **2** the hollow at the bottom of an ore furnace, where the molten metal collects **3** a severe test or trial

Make the Connection

Public Voices, Private Lives

Most of us recognize and live with the difference between our public self and our private self. Sometimes, however, those selves—with all their convictions, passions, and values—come into conflict. Then, we must make a choice. Which self will triumph and which self must be sacrificed? Can we find a compromise? These choices are sometimes simply matters of avoiding embarrassment or preventing hurt feelings or confessing dishonesty. Sometimes they are matters of life and death.

Quickwrite

How do you think most people try to resolve conflicts between their public and their private lives?

How can people be true to their values? What situations might challenge their honesty and integrity? How can people sometimes slip into hypocrisy or conflicts of interest? Jot down your thoughts on these issues.

Reading Skills and Strategies

Interpreting a Text

To read a complex dramatic work like *The Crucible,* you need to **interpret** it—you need to offer your own explanations of who the characters really are, why they behave the way they do, and what the larger meaning of their tragedy is.

As you read *The Crucible,* take notes. (You might also want to start a **time line** to organize the events that lead up to the tragedy.) You can organize your notes by **character.** Jot down your interpretation of what the dialogue and the action reveal about the characters' values, emotions, motivations, and personal histories. Feel free to

include your own views of what the characters look like, how they speak, and how they perform the actions called for in the stage directions. If you become confused about any aspect of a particular character, don't be afraid to adjust your reading. Go back and reread sections of the play simply to find out information that will clarify what makes the character tick.

Elements of Literature

Motivation

Motivation is the reason for a character's behavior. Just as in life, character motivations are often complex, and a particular action is often produced by several motivating factors. Motivation provides the driving force of *The Crucible.*

Miller demonstrates that the residents of Salem were not simply a hysterical mob; every person had at least one reason for acting the way he or she did—psychological, sexual, financial, theological, or political.

In an essay about Nathaniel Hawthorne, a critic describes Salem and the past that still hung over the town when Hawthorne lived there in the early 1800s. Hawthorne's ancestor is Judge Hathorne, and he is in the play.

Salem bristled with old wives' tales and old men's legends. One heard of locked closets in haunted houses where skeletons had been found. One heard of walls that resounded with knocks where there had once been doorways, now bricked up. One heard of poisonous houses and blood-stained houses. . . .

—from "Hawthorne in Salem," Van Wyck Brooks

The Crucible

Arthur Miller

They believed that they held in their steady hands the candle that would light the world.

The photographs that illustrate this play are from the 1996 film adaptation starring Daniel Day-Lewis, Joan Allen, and Winona Ryder.

The Crucible *was first presented by Kermit Bloomgarden at the Martin Beck Theatre, New York City, January 22, 1953, with the following cast.*

(in order of appearance)

Reverend Parris . . . . .Fred Stewart
Betty Parris . . . . .Janet Alexander
Tituba .Jacqueline Andre
Abigail Williams . . . . .Madeleine Sherwood
Susanna Walcott . . . . .Barbara Stanton
Mrs. Ann Putnam . . . . .Jane Hoffman
Thomas Putnam . . . . .Raymond Bramley
Mercy Lewis . . . . .Dorothy Joliffe
Mary Warren . . . . .Jennie Egan
John Proctor . . . . .Arthur Kennedy
Rebecca Nurse . . . . .Jean Adair
Giles Corey . . . . .Joseph Sweeney
Reverend John Hale . . . . .E. G. Marshall
Elizabeth Proctor . . . . .Beatrice Straight
Francis Nurse . . . . .Graham Velsey
Ezekiel Cheever . . . . .Don McHenry
Marshal Herrick . . . . .George Mitchell
Judge Hathorne . . . . .Philip Coolidge
Deputy Governor Danforth . . .Walter Hampden
Sarah Good . . . . .Adele Fortin
Hopkins . . . . .Donald Marye

Staged by Jed Harris

Settings by Boris Aronson

Costumes made and designed by Edith Lutyens

The play is set in Salem, Massachusetts, in 1692.

Act One (An Overture)
 Home of Rev. Samuel Parris.

Act Two
 John Proctor's house, eight days later.

Act Three
 Salem meeting house, serving as the General Court.

Act Four
 A cell in Salem jail, fall 1692.

Act One

(An Overture)

A small upper bedroom in the home of REVEREND SAMUEL PARRIS, *Salem, Massachusetts, in the spring of the year 1692.*

There is a narrow window at the left. Through its leaded panes the morning sunlight streams. A candle still burns near the bed, which is at the right. A chest, a chair, and a small table are the other furnishings. At the back a door opens on the landing of the stairway to the ground floor. The room gives off an air of clean spareness. The roof rafters are exposed, and the wood colors are raw and unmellowed.

As the curtain rises, REVEREND PARRIS *is discovered kneeling beside the bed, evidently in prayer. His daughter,* BETTY PARRIS, *aged ten, is lying on the bed, inert.*

At the time of these events Parris was in his middle forties. In history he cut a villainous path, and there is very little good to be said for him. He believed he was being persecuted wherever he went, despite his best efforts to win people and God to his side. In meeting, he felt insulted if someone rose to shut the door without first asking his permission. He was a widower with no interest in children, or talent with them. He regarded them as young adults, and until this strange crisis he, like the rest of Salem, never conceived that the children were anything but thankful for being permitted to walk straight, eyes slightly lowered, arms at the sides, and mouths shut until bidden to speak.

His house stood in the "town"—but we today would hardly call it a village. The meeting house was nearby, and from this point outward—toward the bay or inland—there were a few small-windowed, dark houses snuggling against the raw Massachusetts winter. Salem had been established hardly forty years before. To the European world the whole province was a barbaric frontier inhabited by a sect of fanatics who, nevertheless, were shipping out products of slowly increasing quantity and value.

No one can really know what their lives were like. They had no novelists—and would not have permitted anyone to read a novel if one were handy. Their creed forbade anything resembling a theater or "vain enjoyment." They did not celebrate Christmas, and a holiday from work meant only that they must concentrate even more upon prayer.

Which is not to say that nothing broke into this strict and somber way of life. When a new farmhouse was built, friends assembled to "raise the roof," and there would be special foods cooked and probably some potent cider passed around. There was a good supply of ne'er-do-wells in Salem, who dallied at the shovelboard in Bridget Bishop's tavern. Probably more than the creed, hard work kept the morals of the place from spoiling, for the people were forced to fight the land like heroes for every grain of corn, and no man had very much time for fooling around.

That there were some jokers, however, is indicated by the practice of appointing a two-man patrol whose duty was to "walk forth in the time of God's worship to take notice of such as either lye about the meeting house, without attending to the word and ordinances, or that lye at home or in the fields without giving good account thereof, and to take the names of such persons, and to present them to the magistrates, whereby they may be accordingly proceeded against." This predilection for minding other people's business was time-honored among the people of Salem, and it undoubtedly created many of the suspicions which were to feed the coming madness. It was also, in my opinion, one of the things that a John Proctor would rebel against, for the time of the armed camp had almost passed, and since the country was reasonably—although not wholly—safe, the old disciplines were beginning to rankle. But, as in all such matters, the issue was not clear-cut, for danger was still a possibility, and in unity still lay the best promise of safety.

The edge of the wilderness was close by. The American continent stretched endlessly west, and it was full of mystery for them. It stood, dark and threatening, over their shoulders night and day, for out of it Indian tribes marauded from time to time, and Reverend Parris had parishioners who had lost relatives to these heathen.

The parochial snobbery of these people was partly responsible for their failure to convert the Indians. Probably they also preferred to take land from heathens rather than from fellow Christians. At any rate, very few Indians were converted, and the Salem folk believed that the virgin forest was the Devil's last preserve, his home base and the citadel of his final stand. To the best of their knowledge the American forest was the last place on earth that was not paying homage to God.

For these reasons, among others, they carried about an air of innate resistance, even of persecution. Their fathers had, of course, been persecuted in England. So now they and their church found it necessary to deny any other sect its freedom, lest their New Jerusalem[2] be defiled and corrupted by wrong ways and deceitful ideas.

They believed, in short, that they held in their steady hands the candle that would light the world. We have inherited this belief, and it has helped and hurt us. It helped them with the discipline it gave them. They were a dedicated folk, by and large, and they had to be to survive the life they had chosen or been born into in this country.

The proof of their belief's value to them may be taken from the opposite character of the first Jamestown settlement, farther south, in Virginia. The Englishmen who landed there were motivated mainly by a hunt for profit. They had thought to pick off the wealth of the new country and then return rich to England. They were a band of individualists, and a much more ingratiating group than the Massachusetts men. But Virginia destroyed them. Massachusetts tried to kill off the Puritans, but they combined; they set up a communal society which, in the beginning, was little more than an armed camp with an autocratic and very devoted leadership. It was, however, an autocracy by consent, for they were united from top to bottom by a commonly held ideology whose perpetuation was the reason and justification for all their sufferings. So their self-denial, their purposefulness, their suspicion of all vain pursuits, their hard-handed justice were altogether perfect instruments for the conquest of this space so antagonistic to man.

But the people of Salem in 1692 were not quite the dedicated folk that arrived on the *Mayflower.*

2. **New Jerusalem:** in the Bible (Revelations 21), the holy city of heaven.

A vast differentiation had taken place, and in their own time a revolution had unseated the royal government and substituted a junta which was at this moment in power. The times, to their eyes, must have been out of joint, and to the common folk must have seemed as insoluble and complicated as do ours today. It is not hard to see how easily many could have been led to believe that the time of confusion had been brought upon them by deep and darkling forces. No hint of such speculation appears on the court record, but social disorder in any age breeds such mystical suspicions, and when, as in Salem, wonders are brought forth from below the social surface, it is too much to expect people to hold back very long from laying on the victims with all the force of their frustrations.

The Salem tragedy, which is about to begin in these pages, developed from a paradox. It is a paradox in whose grip we still live, and there is no prospect yet that we will discover its resolution. Simply, it was this: for good purposes, even high purposes, the people of Salem developed a theocracy, a combine of state and religious power whose function was to keep the community together, and to prevent any kind of disunity that might open it to destruction by material or ideological enemies. It was forged for a necessary purpose and accomplished that purpose. But all organization is and must be grounded on the idea of exclusion and prohibition, just as two objects cannot occupy the same space. Evidently the time came in New England when the repressions of order were heavier than seemed warranted by the dangers against which the order was organized. The witch-hunt was a perverse manifestation of the panic which set in among all classes when the balance began to turn toward greater individual freedom.

When one rises above the individual villainy displayed, one can only pity them all, just as we shall be pitied someday. It is still impossible for man to organize his social life without repressions, and the balance has yet to be struck between order and freedom.

The witch-hunt was not, however, a mere repression. It was also, and as importantly, a long overdue opportunity for everyone so inclined to express publicly his guilt and sins, under the cover of accusations against the victims. It suddenly became possible—and patriotic and holy—for a man to say that Martha Corey had come into his bedroom at night, and that, while his wife was sleeping at his side, Martha laid herself down on his chest and "nearly suffocated him." Of course it was her spirit only, but his satisfaction at confessing himself was no lighter than if it had been Martha herself. One could not ordinarily speak such things in public.

Long-held hatreds of neighbors could now be openly expressed, and vengeance taken, despite the Bible's charitable injunctions. Land-lust, which had been expressed by constant bickering over boundaries and deeds, could now be elevated to the arena of morality; one could cry witch against one's neighbor and feel perfectly justified in the bargain. Old scores could be settled on a plane of heavenly combat between Lucifer and the Lord; suspicions and the envy of the miserable toward the happy could and did burst out in the general revenge.

REVEREND PARRIS *is praying now, and, though we cannot hear his words, a sense of his confusion hangs about him. He mumbles, then seems about to weep; then he weeps, then prays again; but his daughter does not stir on the bed.*

The door opens, and his Negro slave enters. TITUBA *is in her forties.* PARRIS *brought her with him from Barbados, where he spent some years as a merchant before entering the ministry. She enters as one does who can no longer bear to be barred from the sight of her beloved, but she is also very frightened because her slave sense has warned her that, as always, trouble in this house eventually lands on her back.*

Tituba, *already taking a step backward:* My Betty be hearty soon?
Parris: Out of here!
Tituba, *backing to the door:* My Betty not goin' die . . .
Parris, *scrambling to his feet in a fury:* Out of my sight! *She is gone.* Out of my— *He is overcome with sobs. He clamps his teeth against them and closes the door and leans against it, exhausted.* Oh, my God! God help me! *Quaking with fear, mumbling to himself through his sobs, he goes to the bed and gently takes* BETTY*'s hand.*

Betty. Child. Dear child. Will you wake, will you open up your eyes! Betty, little one . . .

He is bending to kneel again when his niece, ABIGAIL WILLIAMS, *seventeen, enters—a strikingly beautiful girl, an orphan, with an endless capacity for dissembling. Now she is all worry and apprehension and propriety.*

Abigail: Uncle? *He looks to her.* Susanna Walcott's here from Doctor Griggs.
Parris: Oh? Let her come, let her come.
Abigail, *leaning out the door to call to* SUSANNA, *who is down the hall a few steps:* Come in, Susanna.

SUSANNA WALCOTT, *a little younger than* ABIGAIL, *a nervous, hurried girl, enters.*

Parris, *eagerly:* What does the doctor say, child?
Susanna, *craning around* PARRIS *to get a look at* BETTY: He bid me come and tell you, reverend sir, that he cannot discover no medicine for it in his books.
Parris: Then he must search on.
Susanna: Aye, sir, he have been searchin' his books since he left you, sir. But he bid me tell you, that you might look to unnatural things for the cause of it.
Parris, *his eyes going wide:* No—no. There be no unnatural cause here. Tell him I have sent for Reverend Hale of Beverly, and Mr. Hale will surely confirm that. Let him look to medicine and put out all thought of unnatural causes here. There be none.
Susanna: Aye, sir. He bid me tell you. *She turns to go.*
Abigail: Speak nothin' of it in the village, Susanna.
Parris: Go directly home and speak nothing of unnatural causes.
Susanna: Aye, sir. I pray for her. *She goes out.*
Abigail: Uncle, the rumor of witchcraft is all about; I think you'd best go down and deny it yourself. The parlor's packed with people, sir. I'll sit with her.
Parris, *pressed, turns on her:* And what shall I say to them? That my daughter and my niece I discovered dancing like heathen in the forest?
Abigail: Uncle, we did dance; let you tell them I confessed it—and I'll be whipped if I must be. But they're speakin' of witchcraft. Betty's not witched.

Parris: Abigail, I cannot go before the congregation when I know you have not opened with me. What did you do with her in the forest?
Abigail: We did dance, uncle, and when you leaped out of the bush so suddenly, Betty was frightened and then she fainted. And there's the whole of it.
Parris: Child. Sit you down.
Abigail, *quavering, as she sits:* I would never hurt Betty. I love her dearly.
Parris: Now look you, child, your punishment will come in its time. But if you trafficked with spirits in the forest I must know it now, for surely my enemies will, and they will ruin me with it.
Abigail: But we never conjured spirits.
Parris: Then why can she not move herself since midnight? This child is desperate! ABIGAIL *lowers her eyes.* It must come out—my enemies will bring it out. Let me know what you done there. Abigail, do you understand that I have many enemies?
Abigail: I have heard of it, uncle.
Parris: There is a faction that is sworn to drive me from my pulpit. Do you understand that?
Abigail: I think so, sir.
Parris: Now then, in the midst of such disruption, my own household is discovered to be the very center of some obscene practice. Abominations are done in the forest—
Abigail: It were sport, uncle!
Parris, *pointing at* BETTY: You call this sport? *She lowers her eyes. He pleads:* Abigail, if you know something that may help the doctor, for God's sake tell it to me. *She is silent.* I saw Tituba waving her arms over the fire when I came on you. Why was she doing that? And I heard a screeching and gibberish coming from her mouth. She were swaying like a dumb beast over that fire!
Abigail: She always sings her Barbados songs, and we dance.
Parris: I cannot blink what I saw, Abigail, for my enemies will not blink it. I saw a dress lying on the grass.
Abigail, *innocently:* A dress?
Parris—*it is very hard to say:* Aye, a dress. And I thought I saw—someone naked running through the trees!
Abigail, *in terror:* No one was naked! You mistake yourself, uncle!

Parris, *with anger:* I saw it! *He moves from her. Then, resolved:* Now tell me true, Abigail. And I pray you feel the weight of truth upon you, for now my ministry's at stake, my ministry and perhaps your cousin's life. Whatever abomination you have done, give me all of it now, for I dare not be taken unaware when I go before them down there.

Abigail: There is nothin' more. I swear it, uncle.

Parris, *studies her, then nods, half convinced:* Abigail, I have fought here three long years to bend these stiff-necked people to me, and now, just now when some good respect is rising for me in the parish, you compromise my very character. I have given you a home, child, I have put clothes upon your back—now give me upright answer. Your name in the town—it is entirely white, is it not?

Abigail, *with an edge of resentment:* Why, I am sure it is, sir. There be no blush about my name.

Parris, *to the point:* Abigail, is there any other cause than you have told me, for your being discharged from Goody[3] Proctor's service? I have

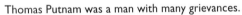

3. **Goody:** formerly a title (short for *goodwife*) for a woman, especially a housewife or older woman.

heard it said, and I tell you as I heard it, that she comes so rarely to the church this year for she will not sit so close to something soiled. What signified that remark?

Abigail: She hates me, uncle, she must, for I would not be her slave. It's a bitter woman, a lying, cold, sniveling woman, and I will not work for such a woman!

Parris: She may be. And yet it has troubled me that you are now seven month out of their house, and in all this time no other family has ever called for your service.

Abigail: They want slaves, not such as I. Let them send to Barbados for that. I will not black my face for any of them! *With ill-concealed resentment at him:* Do you begrudge my bed, uncle?

Parris: No—no.

Abigail, *in a temper:* My name is good in the village! I will not have it said my name is soiled! Goody Proctor is a gossiping liar!

Enter MRS. ANN PUTNAM. *She is a twisted soul of forty-five, a death-ridden woman, haunted by dreams.*

Parris, *as soon as the door begins to open:* No—no, I cannot have anyone. *He sees her, and a certain deference springs into him, although his*

Thomas Putnam was a man with many grievances.

worry remains. Why, Goody Putnam, come in.

Mrs. Putnam, *full of breath, shiny-eyed:* It is a marvel. It is surely a stroke of hell upon you.

Parris: No, Goody Putnam, it is—

Mrs. Putnam, *glancing at* BETTY: How high did she fly, how high?

Parris: No, no, she never flew—

Mrs. Putnam, *very pleased with it:* Why, it's sure she did. Mr. Collins saw her goin' over Ingersoll's barn, and come down light as bird, he says!

Parris: Now, look you, Goody Putnam, she never— *Enter* THOMAS PUTNAM, *a well-to-do, hard-handed landowner, near fifty.* Oh, good morning, Mr. Putnam.

Putnam: It is a providence the thing is out now! It is a providence. *He goes directly to the bed.*

Parris: What's out, sir, what's—?

MRS. PUTNAM *goes to the bed.*

Putnam, *looking down at* BETTY: Why, *her* eyes is closed! Look you, Ann.

Mrs. Putnam: Why, that's strange. *To* PARRIS: Ours is open.

Parris, *shocked:* Your Ruth is sick?

Mrs. Putnam, *with vicious certainty:* I'd not call it sick; the Devil's touch is heavier than sick. It's death, y'know, it's death drivin' into them, forked and hoofed.

Parris: Oh, pray not! Why, how does Ruth ail?

Mrs. Putnam: She ails as she must—she never waked this morning, but her eyes open and she walks, and hears naught, sees naught, and cannot eat. Her soul is taken, surely.

PARRIS *is struck.*

Putnam, *as though for further details:* They say you've sent for Reverend Hale of Beverly?

Parris, *with dwindling conviction now:* A precaution only. He has much experience in all demonic arts, and I—

Mrs. Putnam: He has indeed; and found a witch in Beverly last year, and let you remember that.

Parris: Now, Goody Ann, they only thought that were a witch, and I am certain there be no element of witchcraft here.

Putnam: No witchcraft! Now look you, Mr. Parris—

Parris: Thomas, Thomas, I pray you, leap not to witchcraft. I know that you—you least of all, Thomas, would ever wish so disastrous a charge laid upon me. We cannot leap to witchcraft. They will howl me out of Salem for such corruption in my house.

A word about Thomas Putnam. He was a man with many grievances, at least one of which appears justified. Some time before, his wife's brother-in-law, James Bayley, had been turned down as minister of Salem. Bayley had all the qualifications, and a two-thirds vote into the bargain, but a faction stopped his acceptance, for reasons that are not clear.

Thomas Putnam was the eldest son of the richest man in the village. He had fought the Indians at Narragansett, and was deeply interested in parish affairs. He undoubtedly felt it poor payment that the village should so blatantly disregard his candidate for one of its more important offices, especially since he regarded himself as the intellectual superior of most of the people around him.

His vindictive nature was demonstrated long before the witchcraft began. A former Salem minister, George Burroughs, had had to borrow money to pay for his wife's funeral, and, since the parish was remiss in his salary, he was soon bankrupt. Thomas and his brother John had Burroughs jailed for debts the man did not owe. The incident is important only in that Burroughs succeeded in becoming minister where Bayley, Thomas Putnam's brother-in-law, had been rejected; the motif of resentment is clear here. Thomas Putnam felt that his own name and the honor of his family had been smirched by the village, and he meant to right matters however he could.

Another reason to believe him a deeply embittered man was his attempt to break his father's will, which left a disproportionate amount to a stepbrother. As with every other public cause in which he tried to force his way, he failed in this.

So it is not surprising to find that so many accusations against people are in the handwriting of Thomas Putnam, or that his name is so often found as a witness corroborating the supernatural testimony, or that his daughter led the crying-out at the most opportune junctures of the trials, especially when—But we'll speak of that when we come to it.

Putnam—*at the moment he is intent upon getting* PARRIS, *for whom he has only contempt, to move toward the abyss:* Mr. Parris, I have taken your part in all contention here, and I would continue; but I cannot if you hold back in this. There are hurtful, vengeful spirits layin' hands on these children.

Parris: But, Thomas, you cannot—

Putnam: Ann! Tell Mr. Parris what you have done.

Mrs. Putnam: Reverend Parris, I have laid seven babies unbaptized in the earth. Believe me, sir, you never saw more hearty babies born. And yet, each would wither in my arms the very night of their birth. I have spoke nothin', but my heart has clamored intimations. And now, this year, my Ruth, my only— I see her turning strange. A secret child she has become this year, and shrivels like a sucking mouth were pullin' on her life too. And so I thought to send her to your Tituba—

Parris: To Tituba! What may Tituba—?

Mrs. Putnam: Tituba knows how to speak to the dead, Mr. Parris.

Parris: Goody Ann, it is a formidable sin to conjure up the dead!

Mrs. Putnam: I take it on my soul, but who else may surely tell us what person murdered my babies?

Parris, *horrified:* Woman!

Mrs. Putnam: They were murdered, Mr. Parris! And mark this proof! Mark it! Last night my Ruth were ever so close to their little spirits; I know it, sir. For how else is she struck dumb now except some power of darkness would stop her mouth? It is a marvelous sign, Mr. Parris!

Putnam: Don't you understand it, sir? There is a murdering witch among us, bound to keep herself in the dark. PARRIS *turns to* BETTY, *a frantic terror rising in him.* Let your enemies make of it what they will, you cannot blink it more.

Parris, *to* ABIGAIL: Then you were conjuring spirits last night.

Abigail, *whispering:* Not I, sir—Tituba and Ruth.

Parris, *turns now, with new fear, and goes to* BETTY, *looks down at her, and then, gazing off:* Oh, Abigail, what proper payment for my charity! Now I am undone.

Putnam: You are not undone! Let you take hold here. Wait for no one to charge you—declare it yourself. You have discovered witchcraft—

Parris: In my house? In my house, Thomas? They will topple me with this! They will make of it a—

Enter MERCY LEWIS, *the* PUTNAMS' *servant, a fat, sly, merciless girl of eighteen.*

Mercy: Your pardons. I only thought to see how Betty is.

Putnam: Why aren't you home? Who's with Ruth?

Mercy: Her grandma come. She's improved a little, I think—she give a powerful sneeze before.

Mrs. Putnam: Ah, there's a sign of life!

Mercy: I'd fear no more, Goody Putnam. It were a grand sneeze; another like it will shake her wits together, I'm sure. *She goes to the bed to look.*

Parris: Will you leave me now, Thomas? I would pray a while alone.

Abigail: Uncle, you've prayed since midnight. Why do you not go down and—

Parris: No—no. *To* PUTNAM: I have no answer for that crowd. I'll wait till Mr. Hale arrives. *To get* MRS. PUTNAM *to leave:* If you will, Goody Ann . . .

Putnam: Now look you, sir. Let you strike out against the Devil, and the village will bless you for it! Come down, speak to them—pray with them. They're thirsting for your word, Mister! Surely you'll pray with them.

Parris, *swayed:* I'll lead them in a psalm, but let you say nothing of witchcraft yet. I will not discuss it. The cause is yet unknown. I have had enough contention since I came; I want no more.

Mrs. Putnam: Mercy, you go home to Ruth, d'y'hear?

Mercy: Aye, mum.

MRS. PUTNAM *goes out.*

Parris, *to* ABIGAIL: If she starts for the window, cry for me at once.

Abigail: I will, uncle.

Parris, *to* PUTNAM: There is a terrible power in her arms today. *He goes out with* PUTNAM.

Abigail, *with hushed trepidation:* How is Ruth sick?

Mercy: It's weirdish, I know not—she seems to walk like a dead one since last night.

Abigail, *turns at once and goes to* BETTY, *and now, with fear in her voice:* Betty? BETTY *doesn't move. She shakes her.* Now stop this! Betty! Sit up now!

BETTY *doesn't stir.* MERCY *comes over.*

Mercy: Have you tried beatin' her? I gave Ruth a good one and it waked her for a minute. Here, let me have her.

Abigail, *holding* MERCY *back:* No, he'll be comin' up. Listen, now; if they be questioning us, tell them we danced—I told him as much already.

Mercy: Aye. And what more?

Abigail: He knows Tituba conjured Ruth's sisters to come out of the grave.

Mercy: And what more?

Abigail: He saw you naked.

Mercy, *clapping her hands together with a frightened laugh:* Oh, Jesus!

Enter MARY WARREN, *breathless. She is seventeen, a subservient, naïve, lonely girl.*

Mary Warren: What'll we do? The village is out! I just come from the farm; the whole country's talkin' witchcraft! They'll be callin' us witches, Abby!

Mercy, *pointing and looking at* MARY WARREN: She means to tell, I know it.

Mary Warren: Abby, we've got to tell. Witchery's a hangin' error, a hangin' like they done in Boston two year ago! We must tell the truth, Abby! You'll only be whipped for dancin', and the other things!

Abigail: Oh, *we'll* be whipped!

Mary Warren: I never done none of it, Abby. I only looked!

Mercy, *moving menacingly toward* MARY: Oh, you're a great one for lookin', aren't you, Mary Warren? What a grand peeping courage you have!

BETTY, *on the bed, whimpers.* ABIGAIL *turns to her at once.*

Abigail: Betty? *She goes to* BETTY. Now, Betty, dear, wake up now. It's Abigail. *She sits* BETTY *up and furiously shakes her.* I'll beat you, Betty! BETTY *whimpers.* My, you seem improving. I talked to your papa and I told him everything. So there's nothing to—

Betty, *darts off the bed, frightened of* ABIGAIL, *and flattens herself against the wall:* I want my mama!

Abigail, *with alarm, as she cautiously approaches* BETTY: What ails you, Betty? Your mama's dead and buried.

Betty: I'll fly to Mama. Let me fly! *She raises her arms as though to fly, and streaks for the window, gets one leg out.*

Abigail, *pulling her away from the window:* I told him everything; he knows now, he knows everything we—

Betty: You drank blood, Abby! You didn't tell him that!

Abigail: Betty, you never say that again! You will never—

Betty: You did, you did! You drank a charm to kill John Proctor's wife! You drank a charm to kill Goody Proctor!

Abigail, *smashes her across the face:* Shut it! Now shut it!

Betty, *collapsing on the bed:* Mama, Mama! *She dissolves into sobs.*

Abigail: Now look you. All of you. We danced. And Tituba conjured Ruth Putnam's dead sisters. And that is all. And mark this. Let either of you breathe a word, or the edge of a word, about the other things, and I will come to you in the black of some terrible night and I will bring a pointy reckoning that will shudder you. And you know I can do it; I saw Indians smash my dear parents' heads on the pillow next to mine, and I have seen some reddish work done at night, and I can make you wish you had never seen the sun go down! *She goes to* BETTY *and roughly sits her up.* Now, you—sit up and stop this!

But BETTY *collapses in her hands and lies inert on the bed.*

Mary Warren, *with hysterical fright:* What's got her? ABIGAIL *stares in fright at* BETTY. Abby, she's going to die! It's a sin to conjure, and we—

Abigail, *starting for* MARY: I say shut it, Mary Warren!

Enter JOHN PROCTOR. *On seeing him,* MARY WARREN *leaps in fright.*

Proctor was a farmer in his middle thirties. He need not have been a partisan of any faction in the town, but there is evidence to suggest that he had a sharp and biting way with hypocrites. He was the kind of man—powerful of body, even-tempered, and not easily led—who cannot refuse support to partisans without drawing their deepest resentment. In Proctor's presence a fool felt his foolishness instantly—and a Proctor is always marked for calumny therefore.

But as we shall see, the steady manner he displays does not spring from an untroubled soul. He is a sinner, a sinner not only against the moral fashion of the time, but against his own vision of decent conduct. These people had no ritual for the washing away of sins. It is another trait we inherited from them, and it has helped to discipline us as well as to breed hypocrisy among us. Proctor, respected and even feared in Salem, has come to regard himself as a kind of fraud. But no hint of this has yet appeared on the surface, and as he enters from the crowded parlor below it is a man in his prime we see, with a quiet confidence and an unexpressed, hidden force. Mary Warren, his servant, can barely speak for embarrassment and fear.

Mary Warren: Oh! I'm just going home, Mr. Proctor.

Proctor: Be you foolish, Mary Warren? Be you deaf? I forbid you leave the house, did I not? Why shall I pay you? I am looking for you more often than my cows!

Mary Warren: I only come to see the great doings in the world.

Proctor: I'll show you a great doin' on your arse one of these days. Now get you home; my wife is waitin' with your work! *Trying to retain a shred of dignity, she goes slowly out.*

Mercy Lewis, *both afraid of him and strangely titillated:* I'd best be off. I have my Ruth to watch. Good morning, Mr. Proctor.

MERCY *sidles out. Since* PROCTOR'*s entrance,* ABIGAIL *has stood as though on tiptoe, absorbing his presence, wide-eyed. He glances at her, then goes to* BETTY *on the bed.*

Abigail: Gah! I'd almost forgot how strong you are, John Proctor!

Proctor, *looking at* ABIGAIL *now, the faintest suggestion of a knowing smile on his face:* What's this mischief here?

Abigail, *with a nervous laugh:* Oh, she's only gone silly somehow.

Proctor: The road past my house is a pilgrimage to Salem all morning. The town's mumbling witchcraft.

Abigail: Oh, posh! *Winningly she comes a little closer, with a confidential, wicked air.* We were dancin' in the woods last night, and my uncle leaped in on us. She took fright, is all.

Proctor, *his smile widening:* Ah, you're wicked yet, aren't y'! *A trill of expectant laughter escapes her, and she dares come closer, feverishly looking into his eyes.* You'll be clapped in the stocks before you're twenty.

He takes a step to go, and she springs into his path.

Abigail: Give me a word, John. A soft word. *Her concentrated desire destroys his smile.*

Proctor: No, no, Abby. That's done with.

Abigail, *tauntingly:* You come five mile to see a silly girl fly? I know you better.

Proctor, *setting her firmly out of his path:* I come to see what mischief your uncle's brewin' now. *With final emphasis:* Put it out of mind, Abby.

Abigail, *grasping his hand before he can release her:* John—I am waitin' for you every night.

Proctor: Abby, I never give you hope to wait for me.

Abigail, *now beginning to anger—she can't believe it:* I have something better than hope, I think!

Proctor: Abby, you'll put it out of mind. I'll not be comin' for you more.

Abigail: You're surely sportin' with me.

Proctor: You know me better.

Abigail: I know how you clutched my back behind your house and sweated like a stallion when

ever I come near! Or did I dream that? It's she put me out, you cannot pretend it were you. I saw your face when she put me out, and you loved me then and you do now!

Proctor: Abby, that's a wild thing to say—

Abigail: A wild thing may say wild things. But not so wild, I think. I have seen you since she put me out; I have seen you nights.

Proctor: I have hardly stepped off my farm this sevenmonth.

Abigail: I have a sense for heat, John, and yours has drawn me to my window, and I have seen you looking up, burning in your loneliness. Do you tell me you've never looked up at my window?

Proctor: I may have looked up.

Abigail, *now softening:* And you must. You are no wintry man. I know you, John. I *know* you. *She is weeping.* I cannot sleep for dreamin'; I cannot dream but I wake and walk about the house as though I'd find you comin' through some door. *She clutches him desperately.*

Proctor, *gently pressing her from him, with great sympathy but firmly:* Child—

Abigail, *with a flash of anger:* How do you call me child!

Proctor: Abby, I may think of you softly from time to time. But I will cut off my hand before I'll ever reach for you again. Wipe it out of mind. We never touched, Abby.

Abigail: Aye, but we did.

Proctor: Aye, but we did not.

Abigail, *with a bitter anger:* Oh, I marvel how such a strong man may let such a sickly wife be—

Proctor, *angered—at himself as well:* You'll speak nothin' of Elizabeth!

Abigail: She is blackening my name in the village! She is telling lies about me! She is a cold, sniveling woman, and you bend to her! Let her turn you like a—

Proctor, *shaking her:* Do you look for whippin'?

A psalm is heard being sung below.

Abigail, *in tears:* I look for John Proctor that took me from my sleep and put knowledge in my heart! I never knew what pretense Salem was, I never knew the lying lessons I was taught by all these Christian women and their covenanted men! And now you bid me tear the light out of my eyes? I will not, I cannot! You loved me, John Proctor,

"We never touched, Abby."

and whatever sin it is, you love me yet! *He turns abruptly to go out. She rushes to him.* John, pity me, pity me!

The words "going up to Jesus" are heard in the psalm, and BETTY *claps her ears suddenly and whines loudly.*

Abigail: Betty? *She hurries to* BETTY, *who is now sitting up and screaming.* PROCTOR *goes to* BETTY *as* ABIGAIL *is trying to pull her hands down, calling "Betty!"*

Proctor, *growing unnerved:* What's she doing? Girl, what ails you? Stop that wailing!

The singing has stopped in the midst of this, and now PARRIS *rushes in.*

Parris: What happened? What are you doing to her? Betty! *He rushes to the bed, crying, "Betty, Betty!"* MRS. PUTNAM *enters, feverish with curiosity, and with her* THOMAS PUTNAM *and* MERCY LEWIS. PARRIS, *at the bed, keeps lightly slapping* BETTY's *face, while she moans and tries to get up.*

Abigail: She heard you singin' and suddenly she's up and screamin'.

Mrs. Putnam: The psalm! The psalm! She cannot bear to hear the Lord's name!

Parris: No, God forbid. Mercy, run to the doctor! Tell him what's happened here! MERCY LEWIS *rushes out.*

Mrs. Putnam: Mark it for a sign, mark it!

REBECCA NURSE, *seventy-two, enters. She is white-haired, leaning upon her walking-stick.*

Putnam, *pointing at the whimpering* BETTY: That is a notorious sign of witchcraft afoot, Goody Nurse, a prodigious sign!

Mrs. Putnam: My mother told me that! When they cannot bear to hear the name of—

Parris, *trembling:* Rebecca, Rebecca, go to her, we're lost. She suddenly cannot bear to hear the Lord's—

GILES COREY, *eighty-three, enters. He is knotted with muscle, canny, inquisitive, and still powerful.*

Rebecca: There is hard sickness here, Giles Corey, so please to keep the quiet.

Giles: I've not said a word. No one here can testify I've said a word. Is she going to fly again? I hear she flies.

Putnam: Man, be quiet now!

Everything is quiet. REBECCA *walks across the room to the bed. Gentleness exudes from her.* BETTY *is quietly whimpering, eyes shut.* REBECCA *simply stands over the child, who gradually quiets.*

And while they are so absorbed, we may put a word in for Rebecca. Rebecca was the wife of Francis Nurse, who, from all accounts, was one of those men for whom both sides of the argument had to have respect. He was called upon to arbitrate disputes as though he were an unofficial judge, and Rebecca also enjoyed the high opinion most people had for him. By the time of the delusion, they had three hundred acres, and their children were settled in separate homesteads within the same estate. However, Francis had originally rented the land, and one theory has it that, as he gradually paid for it and raised his social status, there were those who resented his rise.

Another suggestion to explain the systematic campaign against Rebecca, and inferentially against Francis, is the land war he fought with his neighbors, one of whom was a Putnam. This squabble grew to the proportions of a battle in the woods between partisans of both sides, and it is said to have lasted for two days. As for Rebecca herself, the general opinion of her character was so high that to explain how anyone dared cry her out for a witch—and more, how adults could bring themselves to lay hands on her—we must look to the fields and boundaries of that time.

As we have seen, Thomas Putnam's man for the Salem ministry was Bayley. The Nurse clan had been in the faction that prevented Bayley's taking office. In addition, certain families allied to the Nurses by blood or friendship, and whose farms were contiguous with the Nurse farm or close to it, combined to break away from the Salem town authority and set up Topsfield, a new and independent entity whose existence was resented by old Salemites.

That the guiding hand behind the outcry was Putnam's is indicated by the fact that, as soon as it began, this Topsfield-Nurse faction absented themselves from church in protest and disbelief. It was Edward and Jonathan Putnam who signed the first complaint against Rebecca; and Thomas Putnam's little daughter was the one who fell into a fit at the hearing and pointed to Rebecca as her attacker. To top it all, Mrs. Putnam—who is now staring at the bewitched child on the bed—soon accused Rebecca's spirit of "tempting her to iniquity," a charge that had more truth in it than Mrs. Putnam could know.

Mrs. Putnam, *astonished:* What have you done?

REBECCA, *in thought, now leaves the bedside and sits.*

Parris, *wondrous and relieved:* What do you make of it, Rebecca?

Putnam, *eagerly:* Goody Nurse, will you go to my Ruth and see if you can wake her?

Rebecca, *sitting:* I think she'll wake in time. Pray calm yourselves. I have eleven children, and I am twenty-six times a grandma, and I have seen them all through their silly seasons, and when it come on them they will run the Devil bowlegged keeping up with their mischief. I think she'll wake when she tires of it. A child's spirit is like a child, you can never catch it by running after it; you must stand still, and, for love, it will soon itself come back.

Proctor: Aye, that's the truth of it, Rebecca.

Mrs. Putnam: This is no silly season, Rebecca. My Ruth is bewildered, Rebecca; she cannot eat.

Rebecca: Perhaps she is not hungered yet. *To* PARRIS: I hope you are not decided to go in search of loose spirits, Mr. Parris. I've heard promise of that outside.

Parris: A wide opinion's running in the parish that the Devil may be among us, and I would satisfy them that they are wrong.

Proctor: Then let you come out and call them wrong. Did you consult the wardens before you called this minister to look for devils?

Parris: He is not coming to look for devils!

Proctor: Then what's he coming for?

Putnam: There be children dyin' in the village, Mister!

Proctor: I seen none dyin'. This society will not be a bag to swing around your head, Mr. Putnam. *To* PARRIS: Did you call a meeting before you—?

Putnam: I am sick of meetings; cannot the man turn his head without he have a meeting?

Proctor: He may turn his head, but not to Hell!

Rebecca: Pray, John, be calm. *Pause. He defers to her.* Mr. Parris, I think you'd best send Reverend Hale back as soon as he come. This will set us all to arguin' again in the society, and we thought to have peace this year. I think we ought rely on the doctor now, and good prayer.

Mrs. Putnam: Rebecca, the doctor's baffled!

Rebecca: If so he is, then let us go to God for the cause of it. There is prodigious danger in the seeking of loose spirits. I fear it, I fear it. Let us rather blame ourselves and—

Putnam: How may we blame ourselves? I am one of nine sons; the Putnam seed have peopled this province. And yet I have but one child left of eight—and now she shrivels!

Rebecca: I cannot fathom that.

Mrs. Putnam, *with a growing edge of sarcasm:* But I must! You think it God's work you should never lose a child, nor grandchild either, and I bury all but one? There are wheels within wheels in this village, and fires within fires!

Putnam, *to* PARRIS: When Reverend Hale comes, you will proceed to look for signs of witchcraft here.

Proctor, *to* PUTNAM: You cannot command Mr. Parris. We vote by name in this society, not by acreage.

Putnam: I never heard you worried so on this society, Mr. Proctor. I do not think I saw you at Sabbath meeting since snow flew.

Proctor: I have trouble enough without I come five mile to hear him preach only hellfire and bloody damnation. Take it to heart, Mr. Parris. There are many others who stay away from church these days because you hardly ever mention God any more.

Parris, *now aroused:* Why, that's a drastic charge!

Rebecca: It's somewhat true; there are many that quail to bring their children—

Parris: I do not preach for children, Rebecca. It is not the children who are unmindful of their obligations toward this ministry.

Rebecca: Are there really those unmindful?

Parris: I should say the better half of Salem village—

Putnam: And more than that!

Parris: Where is my wood? My contract provides I be supplied with all my firewood. I am waiting since November for a stick, and even in November I had to show my frostbitten hands like some London beggar!

Giles: You are allowed six pound a year to buy your wood, Mr. Parris.

Parris: I regard that six pound as part of my salary. I am paid little enough without I spend six pound on firewood.

Proctor: Sixty, plus six for firewood—

Parris: The salary is sixty-six pound, Mr. Proctor! I am not some preaching farmer with a book under my arm; I am a graduate of Harvard College.

Giles: Aye, and well instructed in arithmetic!

Parris: Mr. Corey, you will look far for a man of my kind at sixty pound a year! I am not used to this poverty; I left a thrifty business in the Barbados to serve the Lord. I do not fathom it, why am I persecuted here? I cannot offer one proposition but there be a howling riot of argument. I have often wondered if the Devil be in it somewhere; I cannot understand you people otherwise.

Proctor: Mr. Parris, you are the first minister ever did demand the deed to this house—

Parris: Man! Don't a minister deserve a house to live in?

Proctor: To live in, yes. But to ask ownership is like you shall own the meeting house itself; the last meeting I were at you spoke so long on deeds and mortgages I thought it were an auction.

Parris: I want a mark of confidence, is all! I am your third preacher in seven years. I do not wish to be put out like the cat whenever some majority feels the whim. You people seem not to comprehend that a minister is the Lord's man in the

parish; a minister is not to be so lightly crossed and contradicted—

Putnam: Aye!

Parris: There is either obedience or the church will burn like Hell is burning!

Proctor: Can you speak one minute without we land in Hell again? I am sick of Hell!

Parris: It is not for you to say what is good for you to hear!

Proctor: I may speak my heart, I think!

Parris, *in a fury:* What, are we Quakers?[4] We are not Quakers here yet, Mr. Proctor. And you may tell that to your followers!

Proctor: My followers!

Parris—*now he's out with it:* There is a party in this church. I am not blind; there is a faction and a party.

Proctor: Against you?

Putnam: Against him and all authority!

Proctor: Why, then I must find it and join it.

There is shock among the others.

Rebecca: He does not mean that.

Putnam: He confessed it now!

Proctor: I mean it solemnly, Rebecca; I like not the smell of this "authority."

Rebecca: No, you cannot break charity with your minister. You are another kind, John. Clasp his hand, make your peace.

Proctor: I have a crop to sow and lumber to drag home. *He goes angrily to the door and turns to* COREY *with a smile.* What say you, Giles, let's find the party. He says there's a party.

Giles: I've changed my opinion of this man, John. Mr. Parris, I beg your pardon. I never thought you had so much iron in you.

Parris, *surprised:* Why, thank you, Giles!

Giles: It suggests to the mind what the trouble be among us all these years. *To all:* Think on it. Wherefore is everybody suing everybody else? Think on it now, it's a deep thing, and dark as a pit. I have been six time in court this year—

Proctor, *familiarly, with warmth, although he knows he is approaching the edge of* GILES' *tolerance with this:* Is it the Devil's fault that a man cannot say you good morning without you clap him for defamation? You're old, Giles, and you're not hearin' so well as you did.

Giles—*he cannot be crossed:* John Proctor, I have only last month collected four pound damages for you publicly sayin' I burned the roof off your house, and I—

Proctor, *laughing:* I never said no such thing, but I've paid you for it, so I hope I can call you deaf without charge. Now come along, Giles, and help me drag my lumber home.

Putnam: A moment, Mr. Proctor. What lumber is that you're draggin', if I may ask you?

Proctor: My lumber. From out my forest by the riverside.

Putnam: Why, we are surely gone wild this year. What anarchy is this? That tract is in my bounds, it's in my bounds, Mr. Proctor.

Proctor: In your bounds! *Indicating* REBECCA: I bought that tract from Goody Nurse's husband five months ago.

Putnam: He had no right to sell it. It stands clear in my grandfather's will that all the land between the river and—

Proctor: Your grandfather had a habit of willing land that never belonged to him, if I may say it plain.

Giles: That's God's truth; he nearly willed away my north pasture but he knew I'd break his fingers before he'd set his name to it. Let's get your lumber home, John. I feel a sudden will to work coming on.

Putnam: You load one oak of mine and you'll fight to drag it home!

Giles: Aye, and we'll win too, Putnam—this fool and I. Come on! *He turns to* PROCTOR *and starts out.*

Putnam: I'll have my men on you, Corey! I'll clap a writ on you!

Enter REVEREND JOHN HALE *of Beverly.*

Mr. Hale is nearing forty, a tight-skinned, eager-eyed intellectual. This is a beloved errand for him; on being called here to ascertain witchcraft he felt the pride of the specialist whose unique knowledge has at last been publicly called for. Like almost all men of learning, he spent a good deal of his time pondering the invisible world, especially

---

4. **Quakers:** Most Quakers believe that no rite or formally trained priest is needed to commune with God; instead, divine truth can be found in one's "inner light."

since he had himself encountered a witch in his parish not long before. That woman, however, turned into a mere pest under his searching scrutiny, and the child she had allegedly been afflicting recovered her normal behavior after Hale had given her his kindness and a few days of rest in his own house. However, that experience never raised a doubt in his mind as to the reality of the underworld or the existence of Lucifer's many-faced lieutenants. And his belief is not to his discredit. Better minds than Hale's were—and still are—convinced that there is a society of spirits beyond our ken. One cannot help noting that one of his lines has never yet raised a laugh in any audience that has seen this play; it is his assurance that "We cannot look to superstition in this. The Devil is precise." Evidently we are not quite certain even now whether diabolism is holy and not to be scoffed at. And it is no accident that we should be so bemused.

Like Reverend Hale and the others on this stage, we conceive the Devil as a necessary part of a respectable view of cosmology. Ours is a divided empire in which certain ideas and emotions and actions are of God, and their opposites are of Lucifer. It is as impossible for most men to conceive of a morality without sin as of an earth without "sky." Since 1692 a great but superficial change has wiped out God's beard and the Devil's horns, but the world is still gripped between two diametrically opposed absolutes. The concept of unity, in which positive and negative are attributes of the same force, in which good and evil are relative, ever-changing, and always joined to the same phenomenon—such a concept is still reserved to the physical sciences and to the few who have grasped the history of ideas. When it is recalled that until the Christian era the underworld was never regarded as a hostile area, that all gods were useful and essentially friendly to man despite occasional lapses; when we see the steady and methodical inculcation into humanity of the idea of man's worthlessness—until redeemed—the necessity of the Devil may become evident as a weapon, a weapon designed and used time and time again in every age to whip men into a surrender to a particular church or church-state.

Our difficulty in believing the—for want of a better word—political inspiration of the Devil is due in great part to the fact that he is called up and damned not only by our social antagonists but by our own side, whatever it may be. The Catholic Church, through its Inquisition,[5] is famous for cultivating Lucifer as the arch-fiend, but the Church's enemies relied no less upon the Old Boy to keep the human mind enthralled. Luther[6] was himself accused of alliance with Hell, and he in turn accused his enemies. To complicate matters further, he believed that he had had contact with the Devil, and had argued theology with him. I am not surprised at this, for at my own university a professor of history—a Lutheran, by the way—used to assemble his graduate students, draw the shades, and commune in the classroom with Erasmus.[7] He was never, to my knowledge, officially scoffed at for this, the reason being that the university officials, like most of us, are the children of a history which still sucks at the Devil's teats. At this writing, only England has held back before the temptations of contemporary diabolism. In the countries of the Communist ideology, all resistance of any import is linked to the totally malign capitalist succubi,[8] and in America any man who is not reactionary in his views is open to the charge of alliance with the Red hell. Political opposition, thereby, is given an inhumane overlay which then justifies the abrogation of all normally applied customs of civilized intercourse. A political policy is equated with moral right, and opposition to it with diabolical malevolence. Once such an equation is effectively made, society becomes a congerie of plots and counterplots, and the main role of government changes from that of the arbiter to that of the scourge of God.

The results of this process are no different now from what they ever were, except sometimes in the degree of cruelty inflicted, and not always

5. Inquisition: suppression and punishment, begun in the thirteenth century, by the Roman Catholic Church of people thought to hold heretical beliefs.
6. Luther: Martin Luther (1483–1546), a German theologian and leader of the Protestant Reformation.
7. Erasmus (i·raz′məs) (c. 1466–1536): Dutch scholar and humanist, who came into conflict with Luther over predestination. (Erasmus believed in free will.)
8. succubi (suk′yoo·bī): plural of *succubus,* a female evil spirit or demon thought in medieval times to have sexual intercourse with sleeping men.

even in that department. Normally the actions and deeds of a man were all that society felt comfortable in judging. The secret intent of an action was left to the ministers, priests, and rabbis to deal with. When diabolism rises, however, actions are the least important manifests of the true nature of a man. The Devil, as Reverend Hale said, is a wily one, and, until an hour before he fell, even God thought him beautiful in Heaven.

The analogy, however, seems to falter when one considers that, while there were no witches then, there are Communists and capitalists now, and in each camp there is certain proof that spies of each side are at work undermining the other. But this is a snobbish objection and not at all warranted by the facts. I have no doubt that people *were* communing with, and even worshiping, the Devil in Salem, and if the whole truth could be known in this case, as it is in others, we should discover a regular and conventionalized propitiation of the dark spirit. One certain evidence of this is the confession of Tituba, the slave of Reverend Parris, and another is the behavior of the children who were known to have indulged in sorceries with her.

There are accounts of similar *klatches* in Europe, where the daughters of the towns would assemble at night and, sometimes with fetishes, sometimes with a selected young man, give themselves to love, with some bastardly results. The Church, sharp-eyed as it must be when gods long dead are brought to life, condemned these orgies as witchcraft and interpreted them rightly, as a resurgence of the Dionysiac[9] forces it had crushed long before. Sex, sin, and the Devil were early linked, and so they continued to be in Salem, and are today. From all accounts there are no more puritanical mores in the world than those enforced by the Communists in Russia, where women's fashions, for instance, are as prudent and all-covering as any American Baptist would desire. The divorce laws lay a tremendous responsibility on the father for the care of his children. Even the laxity of divorce regulations in the early years of the revolution was undoubtedly a revulsion from the nineteenth-century Victorian immobility of marriage and the consequent hypocrisy that developed from it. If for no other reasons, a state so powerful, so jealous of the uniformity of its citizens, cannot long tolerate the atomization of the family. And yet, in American eyes at least, there remains the conviction that the Russian attitude toward women is lascivious. It is the Devil working again, just as he is working within the Slav who is shocked at the very idea of a woman's disrobing herself in a burlesque show. Our opposites are always robed in sexual sin, and it is from this unconscious conviction that demonology gains both its attractive sensuality and its capacity to infuriate and frighten.

Coming into Salem now, Reverend Hale conceives of himself much as a young doctor on his first call. His painfully acquired armory of symptoms, catchwords, and diagnostic procedures is now to be put to use at last. The road from Beverly is unusually busy this morning, and he has passed a hundred rumors that make him smile at the ignorance of the yeomanry in this most precise science. He feels himself allied with the best minds of Europe—kings, philosophers, scientists, and ecclesiasts of all churches. His goal is light, goodness and its preservation, and he knows the exaltation of the blessed whose intelligence, sharpened by minute examinations of enormous tracts, is finally called upon to face what may be a bloody fight with the Fiend himself.

He appears loaded down with half a dozen heavy books.

Hale: Pray you, someone take these!
Parris, *delighted:* Mr. Hale! Oh! it's good to see you again! *Taking some books:* My, they're heavy!
Hale, *setting down his books:* They must be; they are weighted with authority.
Parris, *a little scared:* Well, you do come prepared!
Hale: We shall need hard study if it comes to tracking down the Old Boy. *Noticing* REBECCA: You cannot be Rebecca Nurse?
Rebecca: I am, sir. Do you know me?
Hale: It's strange how I knew you, but I suppose you look as such a good soul should. We have all heard of your great charities in Beverly.
Parris: Do you know this gentleman? Mr. Thomas Putnam. And his good wife Ann.

---

9. Dionysiac (dī′ə·nis′ē·ak): like Dionysius (dī′ə·nish′əs), the ancient Greek god of wine and revelry.

Hale: Putnam! I had not expected such distinguished company, sir.

Putnam, *pleased:* It does not seem to help us today, Mr. Hale. We look to you to come to our house and save our child.

Hale: Your child ails too?

Mrs. Putnam: Her soul, her soul seems flown away. She sleeps and yet she walks . . .

Putnam: She cannot eat.

Hale: Cannot eat! *Thinks on it. Then, to* PROCTOR *and* GILES COREY: Do you men have afflicted children?

Parris: No, no, these are farmers. John Proctor—

Giles Corey: He don't believe in witches.

Proctor, *to* HALE: I never spoke on witches one way or the other. Will you come, Giles?

Giles: No—no, John, I think not. I have some few queer questions of my own to ask this fellow.

Proctor: I've heard you to be a sensible man, Mr. Hale. I hope you'll leave some of it in Salem.

PROCTOR *goes.* HALE *stands embarrassed for an instant.*

Parris, *quickly:* Will you look at my daughter, sir? *Leads* HALE *to the bed.* She has tried to leap out the window; we discovered her this morning on the highroad, waving her arms as though she'd fly.

Hale, *narrowing his eyes:* Tries to fly.

Putnam: She cannot bear to hear the Lord's name, Mr. Hale; that's a sure sign of witchcraft afloat.

Hale, *holding up his hands:* No, no. Now let me instruct you. We cannot look to superstition in this. The Devil is precise; the marks of his presence are definite as stone, and I must tell you all that I shall not proceed unless you are prepared to believe me if I should find no bruise of Hell upon her.

Parris: It is agreed, sir—it is agreed—we will abide by your judgment.

Hale: Good then. *He goes to the bed, looks down at* BETTY. *To* PARRIS: Now, sir, what were your first warning of this strangeness?

Parris: Why, sir—I discovered her—*indicating* ABIGAIL—and my niece and ten or twelve of the other girls, dancing in the forest last night.

Hale, *surprised:* You permit dancing?

Parris: No, no, it were secret—

Mrs. Putnam, *unable to wait:* Mr. Parris's slave has knowledge of conjurin', sir.

Parris, *to* MRS. PUTNAM: We cannot be sure of that, Goody Ann—

Mrs. Putnam, *frightened, very softly:* I know it, sir. I sent my child—she should learn from Tituba who murdered her sisters.

Rebecca, *horrified:* Goody Ann! You sent a child to conjure up the dead?

Mrs. Putnam: Let God blame me, not you, not you, Rebecca! I'll not have you judging me any more! *To* HALE: Is it a natural work to lose seven children before they live a day?

Parris: Sssh!

REBECCA, *with great pain, turns her face away. There is a pause.*

Hale: Seven dead in childbirth.

Mrs. Putnam, *softly:* Aye. *Her voice breaks; she looks up at him. Silence.* HALE *is impressed.* PARRIS *looks to him. He goes to his books, opens one, turns pages, then reads. All wait, avidly.*

Parris, *hushed:* What book is that?

Mrs. Putnam: What's there, sir?

Hale, *with a tasty love of intellectual pursuit:* Here is all the invisible world, caught, defined, and calculated. In these books the Devil stands stripped of all his brute disguises. Here are all your familiar spirits—your incubi and succubi; your witches that go by land, by air, and by sea; your wizards of the night and of the day. Have no fear now—we shall find him out if he has come among us, and I mean to crush him utterly if he has shown his face! *He starts for the bed.*

Rebecca: Will it hurt the child, sir?

Hale: I cannot tell. If she is truly in the Devil's grip we may have to rip and tear to get her free.

Rebecca: I think I'll go, then. I am too old for this. *She rises.*

Parris, *striving for conviction:* Why, Rebecca, we may open up the boil of all our troubles today!

Rebecca: Let us hope for that. I go to God for you, sir.

"I mean to crush him utterly . . ."

Parris, *with trepidation—and resentment:* I hope you do not mean we go to Satan here! *Slight pause.*

Rebecca: I wish I knew. *She goes out; they feel resentful of her note of moral superiority.*

Putnam, *abruptly:* Come, Mr. Hale, let's get on. Sit you here.

Giles: Mr. Hale, I have always wanted to ask a learned man—what signifies the readin' of strange books?

Hale: What books?

Giles: I cannot tell; she hides them.

Hale: Who does this?

Giles: Martha, my wife. I have waked at night many a time and found her in a corner, readin' of a book. Now what do you make of that?

Hale: Why, that's not necessarily—

Giles: It discomfits me! Last night—mark this—I tried and tried and could not say my prayers. And then she close her book and walks out of the house, and suddenly—mark this—I could pray again!

Old Giles must be spoken for, if only because his fate was to be so remarkable and so different from that of all the others. He was in his early eighties at this time, and was the most comical hero in the history. No man has ever been blamed for so much. If a cow was missed, the first thought was to look for her around Corey's house; a fire blazing up at night brought suspicion of arson to his door. He didn't give a hoot for public opinion, and only in his last years—after he had married Martha—did he bother much with the church. That she stopped his prayer is very probable, but he forgot to say that he'd only recently learned any prayers and it didn't take much to make him stumble over them. He was a crank and a nuisance, but withal a deeply innocent and brave man. In court, once, he was asked if it were true that he had been frightened by the strange behavior of a hog and had then said he knew it to be the Devil in an animal's shape. "What frighted you?" he was asked. He forgot everything but the word "frighted," and instantly replied, "I do not know that I ever spoke that word in my life."

Hale: Ah! The stoppage of prayer—that is strange. I'll speak further on that with you.

Giles: I'm not sayin' she's touched the Devil, now, but I'd admire to know what books she reads and why she hides them. She'll not answer me, y' see.

Hale: Aye, we'll discuss it. *To all:* Now mark me, if the Devil is in her you will witness some frightful wonders in this room, so please to keep your wits about you. Mr. Putnam, stand close in case she flies. Now, Betty, dear, will you sit up? PUTNAM *comes in closer, ready-handed.* HALE *sits* BETTY *up, but she hangs limp in his hands.* Hmmm. *He observes her carefully. The others watch breathlessly.* Can you hear me? I am John Hale, minister of Beverly. I have come to help you, dear. Do you remember my two little girls in Beverly? *She does not stir in his hands.*

Parris, *in fright:* How can it be the Devil? Why would he choose my house to strike? We have all manner of licentious people in the village!

Hale: What victory would the Devil have to win a soul already bad? It is the best the Devil wants, and who is better than the minister?

Giles: That's deep, Mr. Parris, deep, deep!

Parris, *with resolution now:* Betty! Answer Mr. Hale! Betty!

Hale: Does someone afflict you, child? It need not be a woman, mind you, or a man. Perhaps some bird invisible to others comes to you—perhaps a pig, a mouse, or any beast at all. Is there some figure bids you fly? *The child remains limp in his hands. In silence he lays her back on the pillow. Now, holding out his hands toward her, he intones:* In nomine Domini Sabaoth sui filiique ite ad infernos.[10] *She does not stir. He turns to* ABIGAIL, *his eyes narrowing.* Abigail, what sort of dancing were you doing with her in the forest?

Abigail: Why—common dancing is all.

Parris: I think I ought to say that I—I saw a kettle in the grass where they were dancing.

Abigail: That were only soup.

Hale: What sort of soup were in this kettle, Abigail?

Abigail: Why, it were beans—and lentils, I think, and—

Hale: Mr. Parris, you did not notice, did you, any living thing in the kettle? A mouse, perhaps, a spider, a frog—?

10. In nomine Domini Sabaoth sui filiique ite ad infernos: Latin for "In the name of the Lord of Hosts and his son, get thee to hell."

Parris, *fearfully:* I—do believe there were some movement—in the soup.

Abigail: That jumped in, we never put it in!

Hale, *quickly:* What jumped in?

Abigail: Why, a very little frog jumped—

Parris: A frog, Abby!

Hale, *grasping* ABIGAIL: Abigail, it may be your cousin is dying. Did you call the Devil last night?

Abigail: I never called him? Tituba, Tituba . . .

Parris, *blanched:* She called the Devil?

Hale: I should like to speak with Tituba.

Parris: Goody Ann, will you bring her up? MRS. PUTNAM *exits.*

Hale: How did she call him?

Abigail: I know not—she spoke Barbados.

Hale: Did you feel any strangeness when she called him? A sudden cold wind, perhaps? A trembling below the ground?

Abigail: I didn't see no Devil! *Shaking* BETTY: Betty, wake up. Betty! Betty!

Hale: You cannot evade me, Abigail. Did your cousin drink any of the brew in that kettle?

Abigail: She never drank it!

Hale: Did you drink it?

Abigail: No, sir!

Hale: Did Tituba ask you to drink it?

Abigail: She tried, but I refused.

Hale: Why are you concealing? Have you sold yourself to Lucifer?

Abigail: I never sold myself! I'm a good girl! I'm a proper girl!

MRS. PUTNAM *enters with* TITUBA, *and instantly* ABIGAIL *points at* TITUBA.

Abigail: She made me do it! She made Betty do it!

Tituba, *shocked and angry:* Abby!

Abigail: She makes me drink blood!

Parris: Blood!!

Mrs. Putnam: My baby's blood?

Tituba: No, no, chicken blood. I give she chicken blood!

Hale: Woman, have you enlisted these children for the Devil?

Tituba: No, no, sir, I don't truck with no Devil!

Hale: Why can she not wake? Are you silencing this child?

Tituba: I love me Betty!

Hale: You have sent your spirit out upon this child, have you not? Are you gathering souls for the Devil?

Abigail: She sends her spirit on me in church; she makes me laugh at prayer!

Parris: She have often laughed at prayer!

Abigail: She comes to me every night to go and drink blood!

Tituba: You beg *me* to conjure! She beg *me* make charm—

Abigail: Don't lie! *To* HALE: She comes to me while I sleep; she's always making me dream corruptions!

Tituba: Why you say that, Abby?

Abigail: Sometimes I wake and find myself standing in the open doorway and not a stitch on my body! I always hear her laughing in my sleep. I hear her singing her Barbados songs and tempting me with—

Tituba: Mister Reverend, I never—

Hale, *resolved now:* Tituba, I want you to wake this child.

Tituba: I have no power on this child, sir.

Hale: You most certainly do, and you will free her from it now! When did you compact with the Devil?

Tituba: I don't compact with no Devil!

Parris: You will confess yourself or I will take you out and whip you to your death, Tituba!

Putnam: This woman must be hanged! She must be taken and hanged!

Tituba, *terrified, falls to her knees:* No, no, don't hang Tituba! I tell him I don't desire to work for him, sir.

Parris: The Devil?

Hale: Then you saw him! TITUBA *weeps.* Now Tituba, I know that when we bind ourselves to Hell it is very hard to break with it. We are going to help you tear yourself free—

Tituba, *frightened by the coming process:* Mister Reverend, I do believe somebody else be witchin' these children.

Hale: Who?

Tituba: I don't know, sir, but the Devil got him numerous witches.

Hale: Does he! *It is a clue.* Tituba, look into my eyes. Come, look into me. *She raises her eyes to his fearfully.* You would be a good Christian woman, would you not, Tituba?

Tituba: Aye, sir, a good Christian woman.

Hale: And you love these little children?

Tituba: Oh, yes, sir, I don't desire to hurt little children.

Hale: And you love God, Tituba?

Tituba: I love God with all my bein'.

Hale: Now, in God's holy name—

Tituba: Bless Him. Bless Him. *She is rocking on her knees, sobbing in terror.*

Hale: And to His glory—

Tituba: Eternal glory. Bless Him—bless God . . .

Hale: Open yourself, Tituba—open yourself and let God's holy light shine on you.

Tituba: Oh, bless the Lord.

Hale: When the Devil comes to you does he ever come—with another person? *She stares up into his face.* Perhaps another person in the village? Someone you know.

Parris: Who came with him?

Putnam: Sarah Good? Did you ever see Sarah Good with him? Or Osburn?

Parris: Was it man or woman came with him?

Tituba: Man or woman. Was—was woman.

Parris: What woman? A woman, you said. What woman?

Tituba: It was black dark, and I—

Parris: You could see him, why could you not see her?

Tituba: Well, they was always talking; they was always runnin' round and carryin' on—

Parris: You mean out of Salem? Salem witches?

Tituba: I believe so, yes, sir.

Now HALE *takes her hand. She is surprised.*

Hale: Tituba. You must have no fear to tell us who they are, do you understand? We will protect you. The Devil can never overcome a minister. You know that, do you not?

Tituba—she kisses HALE's hand: Aye, sir, oh, I do.

Hale: You have confessed yourself to witchcraft, and that speaks a wish to come to Heaven's side. And we will bless you, Tituba.

Tituba, *deeply relieved:* Oh, God bless you, Mr. Hale!

Hale, *with rising exaltation:* You are God's instrument put in our hands to discover the Devil's agents among us. You are selected, Tituba, you are chosen to help us cleanse our village. So speak utterly, Tituba, turn your back on him and face God—face God, Tituba, and God will protect you.

Tituba, *joining with him:* Oh, God, protect Tituba!

Hale, *kindly:* Who came to you with the Devil? Two? Three? Four? How many?

TITUBA *pants and begins rocking back and forth again, staring ahead.*

Tituba: There was four. There was four.

Parris, *pressing in on her:* Who? Who? Their names, their names!

Tituba, *suddenly bursting out:* Oh, how many times he bid me kill you, Mr. Parris!

Parris: Kill me!

Tituba, *in a fury:* He say Mr. Parris must be kill! Mr. Parris no goodly man, Mr. Parris mean man and no gentle man, and he bid me rise out of my bed and cut your throat! *They gasp.* But I tell him "No! I don't hate that man. I don't want kill that man." But he say, "You work for me, Tituba, and I make you free! I give you pretty dress to wear, and put you way high up in the air, and you gone fly back to Barbados!" And I say, "You lie, Devil, you lie!" And then he come one stormy night to me, and he say, "Look! I have *white* people belong to me." And I look—and there was Goody Good.

Parris: Sarah Good!

Tituba, *rocking and weeping:* Aye, sir, and Goody Osburn.

Mrs. Putnam: I knew it! Goody Osburn were midwife to me three times. I begged you, Thomas, did I not? I begged him not to call Osburn because I feared her. My babies always shriveled in her hands!

Hale: Take courage, you must give us all their names. How can you bear to see this child suffering? Look at her, Tituba. *He is indicating* BETTY *on the bed.* Look at her God-given innocence; her soul is so tender; we must protect her, Tituba; the Devil is out and preying on her like a beast upon the flesh of the pure lamb. God will bless you for your help.

ABIGAIL *rises, staring as though inspired, and cries out.*

Abigail: I want to open myself! *They turn to her, startled. She is enraptured, as though in a pearly light.* I want the light of God, I want the sweet love of Jesus! I danced for the Devil; I saw him; I wrote in his book; I go back to Jesus; I kiss His hand. I saw Sarah Good with the Devil! I saw Goody Osburn with the Devil! I saw Bridget Bishop with the Devil!

As she is speaking, BETTY *is rising from the bed, a fever in her eyes, and picks up the chant.*

Betty, *staring too:* I saw George Jacobs with the Devil! I saw Goody Howe with the Devil!
Parris: She speaks! *He rushes to embrace* BETTY. She speaks!
Hale: Glory to God! It is broken, they are free!
Betty, *calling out hysterically and with great relief:* I saw Martha Bellows with the Devil!
Abigail: I saw Goody Sibber with the Devil! *It is rising to a great glee.*

Putnam: The marshal, I'll call the marshal!

PARRIS *is shouting a prayer of thanksgiving.*

Betty: I saw Alice Barrow with the Devil!

The curtain begins to fall.

Hale, *as* PUTNAM *goes out:* Let the marshal bring irons!
Abigail: I saw Goody Hawkins with the Devil!
Betty: I saw Goody Bibber with the Devil!
Abigail: I saw Goody Booth with the Devil!

On their ecstatic cries

The curtain falls

Making Meanings

Act One

First Thoughts

1. What do you think of Abigail, and what would you have said to her if you had been present at the end of Act One?

Reading Check

a. When Abigail is alone with Proctor, what claim does she make?
b. Whom has Parris invited to Salem?
c. Why are both Mrs. Putnam and Abigail interested in Tituba's "conjuring"?

Shaping Interpretations

2. Why is Reverend Parris so terrified by the events in Salem? What possible result does he fear?

3. How would you explain the "illnesses" of Betty and Ruth?

4. Using your reading notes as a guide, reread the background information that Miller provides about the history of Salem, in order to find out when important events occurred. Then make a **time line** that places in rough **chronological order** events such as the murder of Abigail's parents, the dispute over the election of the minister, the battle over Francis Nurse's land, and the death of Mrs. Putnam's babies.

5. How would you interpret Abigail's relationship to the other girls and her relationship to Proctor? Be sure to check your reading notes.

6. Summarize Hale's view of his mission in Salem. What does he mean when he says the Devil is "precise"?

7. At the beginning of the act, Tituba enters Betty's bedroom in fright because she knows "trouble in this house eventually lands on her back." Are her fears justified? To what extent is Tituba a scapegoat for Abigail and the other girls, and to what extent does she share responsibility for the witch hunt?

8. At the end of the act, what do you think is Abigail's **motivation** to "open" herself and begin naming names?

9. A **static character** changes little or not at all during a story. A **dynamic character** changes in an important way as a result of the story's action. Among the characters introduced in Act One, which do you think have potential for change as the play progresses?

Connecting with the Text

10. When someone is accused of a crime today, do people still have a tendency to "jump on the bandwagon" with the accusers? Explain your answer.

Act Two

The common room of PROCTOR'S *house, eight days later.*

At the right is a door opening on the fields outside. A fireplace is at the left, and behind it a stairway leading upstairs. It is the low, dark, and rather long living room of the time. As the curtain rises, the room is empty. From above, ELIZABETH *is heard softly singing to the children. Presently the door opens and* JOHN PROCTOR *enters, carrying his gun. He glances about the room as he comes toward the fireplace, then halts for an instant as he hears her singing. He continues on to the fireplace, leans the gun against the wall as he swings a pot out of the fire and smells it. Then he lifts out the ladle and tastes. He is not quite pleased. He reaches to a cupboard, takes a pinch of salt, and drops it into the pot. As he is tasting again, her footsteps are heard on the stair. He swings the pot into the fireplace and goes to a basin and washes his hands and face.* ELIZABETH *enters.*

Elizabeth: What keeps you so late? It's almost dark.

Proctor: I were planting far out to the forest edge.

Elizabeth: Oh, you're done then.

Proctor: Aye, the farm is seeded. The boys asleep?

Elizabeth: They will be soon. *And she goes to the fireplace, proceeds to ladle up stew in a dish.*

Proctor: Pray now for a fair summer.

Elizabeth: Aye.

Proctor: Are you well today?

Elizabeth: I am. *She brings the plate to the table, and, indicating the food:* It is a rabbit.

Proctor, *going to the table:* Oh, is it! In Jonathan's trap?

Elizabeth: No, she walked into the house this afternoon; I found her sittin' in the corner like she come to visit.

Proctor: Oh, that's a good sign walkin' in.

Elizabeth: Pray God. It hurt my heart to strip her, poor rabbit. *She sits and watches him taste it.*

Proctor: It's well seasoned.

Elizabeth, *blushing with pleasure:* I took great care. She's tender?

Proctor: Aye. *He eats. She watches him.* I think we'll see green fields soon. It's warm as blood beneath the clods.

Elizabeth: That's well.

PROCTOR *eats, then looks up.*

Proctor: If the crop is good I'll buy George Jacobs' heifer. How would that please you?

Elizabeth: Aye, it would.

Proctor, *with a grin:* I mean to please you, Elizabeth.

Elizabeth—*it is hard to say:* I know it, John.

He gets up, goes to her, kisses her. She receives it. With a certain disappointment, he returns to the table.

Proctor, *as gently as he can:* Cider?

Elizabeth, *with a sense of reprimanding herself for having forgot:* Aye! *She gets up and goes and pours a glass for him. He now arches his back.*

Proctor: This farm's a continent when you go foot by foot droppin' seeds in it.

Elizabeth, *coming with the cider:* It must be.

Proctor, *he drinks a long draught, then, putting the glass down:* You ought to bring some flowers in the house.

Elizabeth: Oh! I forgot! I will tomorrow.

Proctor: It's winter in here yet. On Sunday let you come with me, and we'll walk the farm together; I never see such a load of flowers on the earth. *With good feeling he goes and looks up at the sky through the open doorway.* Lilacs have a purple smell. Lilac is the smell of nightfall, I think. Massachusetts is a beauty in the spring!

Elizabeth: Aye, it is.

There is a pause. She is watching him from the table as he stands there absorbing the night. It is as though she would speak but cannot. Instead, now, she takes up his plate and glass and fork and goes with them to the basin. Her back is turned to him. He turns to her and watches her. A sense of their separation rises.

Proctor: I think you're sad again. Are you?

Elizabeth—*she doesn't want friction, and yet she must:* You come so late I thought you'd gone to Salem this afternoon.

Proctor: Why? I have no business in Salem.

Elizabeth: You did speak of going, earlier this week.

Proctor—*he knows what she means:* I thought better of it since.

Elizabeth: Mary Warren's there today.

Proctor: Why'd you let her? You heard me forbid her to go to Salem any more!

Elizabeth: I couldn't stop her.

Proctor, *holding back a full condemnation of her:* It is a fault, it is a fault, Elizabeth—you're the mistress here, not Mary Warren.

Elizabeth: She frightened all my strength away.

Proctor: How may that mouse frighten you, Elizabeth? You—

Elizabeth: It is a mouse no more. I forbid her go, and she raises up her chin like the daughter of a prince and says to me, "I must go to Salem, Goody Proctor; I am an official of the court!"

Proctor: Court! What court?

Elizabeth: Aye, it is a proper court they have now. They've sent four judges out of Boston, she says, weighty magistrates of the General Court, and at the head sits the Deputy Governor of the Province.

Proctor, *astonished:* Why, she's mad.

Elizabeth: I would to God she were. There be fourteen people in the jail now, she says. PROCTOR *simply looks at her, unable to grasp it.* And they'll be tried, and the court have power to hang them too, she says.

Proctor, *scoffing, but without conviction:* Ah, they'd never hang—

Elizabeth: The Deputy Governor promise hangin' if they'll not confess, John. The town's gone wild, I think. She speak of Abigail, and I thought she were a saint, to hear her. Abigail brings the other girls into the court, and where she walks the crowd will part like the sea for Israel. And folks are brought before them, and if they scream and howl and fall to the floor—the person's clapped in the jail for bewitchin' them.

Proctor, *wide-eyed:* Oh, it is a black mischief.

Elizabeth: I think you must go to Salem, John. *He turns to her.* I think so. You must tell them it is a fraud.

Proctor, *thinking beyond this:* Aye, it is, it is surely.

Elizabeth: Let you go to Ezekiel Cheever—he knows you well. And tell him what she said to you last week in her uncle's house. She said it had naught to do with witchcraft, did she not?

Proctor, *in thought:* Aye, she did, she did. *Now a pause.*

Elizabeth, *quietly, fearing to anger him by prodding:* God forbid you keep that from the court, John. I think they must be told.

Proctor, *quietly, struggling with his thought:* Aye, they must, they must. It is a wonder they do believe her.

Elizabeth: I would go to Salem now, John—let you go tonight.

Proctor: I'll think on it.

Elizabeth, *with her courage now:* You cannot keep it, John.

Proctor, *angering:* I know I cannot keep it. I say I will think on it!

Elizabeth, *hurt, and very coldly:* Good, then, let you think on it. *She stands and starts to walk out of the room.*

Proctor: I am only wondering how I may prove what she told me, Elizabeth. If the girl's a saint now, I think it is not easy to prove she's fraud, and the town gone so silly. She told it to me in a room alone—I have no proof for it.

Elizabeth: You were alone with her?

Proctor, *stubbornly:* For a moment alone, aye.

Elizabeth: Why, then, it is not as you told me.

Proctor, *his anger rising:* For a moment, I say. The others come in soon after.

Elizabeth, *quietly—she has suddenly lost all faith in him:* Do as you wish, then. *She starts to turn.*

Proctor: Woman. *She turns to him.* I'll not have your suspicion any more.

Elizabeth, *a little loftily:* I have no—

Proctor: I'll not have it!

Elizabeth: Then let you not earn it.

Proctor, *with a violent undertone:* You doubt me yet?

Elizabeth, *with a smile, to keep her dignity:* John, if it were not Abigail that you must go to hurt, would you falter now? I think not.

Proctor: Now look you—

Elizabeth: I see what I see, John.

Proctor, *with solemn warning:* You will not judge me more, Elizabeth. I have good reason to think before I charge fraud on Abigail, and I will think on it. Let you look to your own improvement before you go to judge your husband any more. I have forgot Abigail, and—

Elizabeth: And I.

Proctor: Spare me! You forget nothin' and forgive nothin.' Learn charity, woman. I have gone tiptoe in this house all seven month since she is gone. I have not moved from there to there without I think to please you, and still an everlasting funeral marches round your heart. I cannot speak but I am doubted, every moment judged for lies, as though I come into a court when I come into this house!

Elizabeth: John, you are not open with me. You saw her with a crowd, you said. Now you—

Proctor: I'll plead my honesty no more, Elizabeth.

Elizabeth—*now she would justify herself:* John, I am only—

Proctor: No more! I should have roared you down when first you told me your suspicion. But I wilted, and, like a Christian, I confessed. Confessed! Some dream I had must have mistaken you for God that day. But you're not, you're not, and let you remember it! Let you look sometimes for the goodness in me, and judge me not.

Elizabeth: I do not judge you. The magistrate sits in your heart that judges you. I never thought you but a good man, John—*with a smile*—only somewhat bewildered.

Proctor, *laughing bitterly:* Oh, Elizabeth, your justice would freeze beer! *He turns suddenly toward a sound outside. He starts for the door as* MARY WARREN *enters. As soon as he sees her, he goes directly to her and grabs her by her cloak, furious.* How do you go to Salem when I forbid it? Do you mock me? *Shaking her:* I'll whip you if you dare leave this house again!

Strangely, she doesn't resist him but hangs limply by his grip.

Mary Warren: I am sick, I am sick, Mr. Proctor. Pray, pray, hurt me not. *Her strangeness throws him off, and her evident pallor and weakness. He frees her.* My insides are all shuddery; I am in the proceedings all day, sir.

Proctor, *with draining anger—his curiosity is draining it:* And what of these proceedings here?

When will you proceed to keep this house, as you are paid nine pound a year to do—and my wife not wholly well?

As though to compensate, MARY WARREN *goes to* ELIZABETH *with a small rag doll.*

Mary Warren: I made a gift for you today, Goody Proctor. I had to sit long hours in a chair, and passed the time with sewing.

Elizabeth, *perplexed, looking at the doll:* Why, thank you, it's a fair poppet.[1]

Mary Warren, *with a trembling, decayed voice:* We must all love each other now, Goody Proctor.

Elizabeth, *amazed at her strangeness:* Aye, indeed, we must.

Mary Warren, *glancing at the room:* I'll get up early in the morning and clean the house. I must sleep now. She turns and starts off.

Proctor: Mary. *She halts.* Is it true? There be fourteen women arrested?

Mary Warren: No, sir. There be thirty-nine now— *She suddenly breaks off and sobs and sits down, exhausted.*

Elizabeth: Why, she's weepin'! What ails you, child?

Mary Warren: Goody Osburn—will hang! *There is a shocked pause, while she sobs.*

Proctor: Hang! *He calls into her face.* Hang, y'say?

Mary Warren, *through her weeping:* Aye.

Proctor: The Deputy Governor will permit it?

Mary Warren: He sentenced her. He must. *To ameliorate it:* But not Sarah Good. For Sarah Good confessed, y'see.

Proctor: Confessed! To what?

Mary Warren: That she—*in horror at the memory*—she sometimes made a compact with Lucifer, and wrote her name in his black book—with her blood—and bound herself to torment Christians till God's thrown down—and we all must worship Hell forevermore.

Pause.

Proctor: But—surely you know what a jabberer she is. Did you tell them that?

Mary Warren: Mr. Proctor, in open court she near to choked us all to death.

Proctor: How, choked you?

Mary Warren: She sent her spirit out.

1. **poppet:** doll; puppet.

The girls of Salem "scream and howl and fall to the floor . . ."

Elizabeth: Oh, Mary, Mary, surely you—

Mary Warren, *with an indignant edge:* She tried to kill me many times, Goody Proctor!

Elizabeth: Why, I never heard you mention that before.

Mary Warren: I never knew it before. I never knew anything before. When she come into the court I say to myself, I must not accuse this woman, for she sleep in ditches, and so very old and poor. But then—then she sit there, denying and denying, and I feel a misty coldness climbin' up my back, and the skin on my skull begin to creep, and I feel a clamp around my neck and I cannot breathe air; and then—*entranced*—I hear a voice, a screamin' voice, and it were my voice—and all at once I remember everything she done to me!

Proctor: Why? What did she do to you?

Mary Warren, *like one awakened to a marvelous secret insight:* So many time, Mr. Proctor, she come to this very door, beggin' bread and a cup of cider—and mark this: whenever I turned her away empty, she *mumbled.*

Elizabeth: Mumbled! She may mumble if she's hungry.

Mary Warren: But *what* does she mumble? You must remember, Goody Proctor. Last month—a Monday, I think—she walked away, and I thought my guts would burst for two days after. Do you remember it?

Elizabeth: Why—I do, I think, but—

Mary Warren: And so I told that to Judge Hathorne, and he asks her so. "Goody Osburn," says he, "what curse do you mumble that this girl must fall sick after turning you away?" And then she replies—*mimicking an old crone*—"Why, your excellence, no curse at all. I only say my commandments; I hope I may say my commandments," says she!

Elizabeth: And that's an upright answer.

Mary Warren: Aye, but then Judge Hathorne say, "Recite for us your commandments!"—*leaning avidly toward them*—and of all the ten she could not say a single one. She never knew no commandments, and they had her in a flat lie!

Proctor: And so condemned her?

Mary Warren, *now a little strained, seeing his stubborn doubt:* Why, they must when she condemned herself.

Proctor: But the proof, the proof!

Mary Warren, *with greater impatience with him:* I told you the proof. It's hard proof, hard as rock, the judges said.

Proctor—*he pauses an instant, then:* You will not go to court again, Mary Warren.

Mary Warren: I must tell you, sir, I will be gone every day now. I am amazed you do not see what weighty work we do.

Proctor: What work you do! It's strange work for a Christian girl to hang old women!

Mary Warren: But, Mr. Proctor, they will not hang them if they confess. Sarah Good will only sit in jail some time—*recalling*—and here's a wonder for you; think on this. Goody Good is pregnant!

Elizabeth: Pregnant! Are they mad? The woman's near to sixty!

Mary Warren: They had Doctor Griggs examine her, and she's full to the brim. And smokin' a pipe all these years, and no husband either! But she's safe, thank God, for they'll not hurt the innocent child. But be that not a marvel? You must see it, sir, it's God's work we do. So I'll be gone every day for some time. I'm—I am an official of the court, they say, and I— *She has been edging toward offstage.*

Proctor: I'll official you! *He strides to the mantel, takes down the whip hanging there.*

Mary Warren, *terrified, but coming erect, striving for her authority:* I'll not stand whipping any more!

Elizabeth, *hurriedly, as* PROCTOR *approaches:* Mary, promise now you'll stay at home—

Mary Warren, *backing from him, but keeping her erect posture, striving, striving for her way:* The Devil's loose in Salem, Mr. Proctor; we must discover where he's hiding!

Proctor: I'll whip the Devil out of you! *With whip raised he reaches out for her, and she streaks away and yells.*

Mary Warren, *pointing at* ELIZABETH: I saved her life today!

Silence. His whip comes down.

Elizabeth, *softly:* I am accused?

Mary Warren, *quaking:* Somewhat mentioned. But I said I never see no sign you ever sent your spirit out to hurt no one, and seeing I do live so closely with you, they dismissed it.

Elizabeth: Who accused me?

Mary Warren: I am bound by law, I cannot tell it. *To* PROCTOR: I only hope you'll not be so sarcastical no more. Four judges and the King's deputy sat to dinner with us but an hour ago. I—I would have you speak civilly to me, from this out.

Proctor, *in horror, muttering in disgust at her:* Go to bed.

Mary Warren, *with a stamp of her foot:* I'll not be ordered to bed no more, Mr. Proctor! I am eighteen and a woman, however single!

Proctor: Do you wish to sit up? Then sit up.

Mary Warren: I wish to go to bed!

Proctor, *in anger:* Good night, then!

Mary Warren: Good night. *Dissatisfied, uncertain of herself, she goes out. Wide-eyed, both* PROCTOR *and* ELIZABETH *stand staring.*

Elizabeth, *quietly:* Oh, the noose, the noose is up!

Proctor: There'll be no noose.

Elizabeth: She wants me dead. I knew all week it would come to this!

Proctor, *without conviction:* They dismissed it. You heard her say—

Elizabeth: And what of tomorrow? She will cry me out until they take me!

Proctor: Sit you down.

Elizabeth: She wants me dead, John, you know it!

Proctor: I say sit down! *She sits, trembling. He speaks quietly, trying to keep his wits.* Now we must be wise, Elizabeth.

Elizabeth, *with sarcasm, and a sense of being lost:* Oh, indeed, indeed!

Proctor: Fear nothing. I'll find Ezekiel Cheever. I'll tell him she said it were all sport.

Elizabeth: John, with so many in the jail, more than Cheever's help is needed now, I think. Would you favor me with this? Go to Abigail.

Proctor, *his soul hardening as he senses . . . :* What have I to say to Abigail?

Elizabeth, *delicately:* John—grant me this. You have a faulty understanding of young girls. There is a promise made in any bed—

Proctor, *striving against his anger:* What promise!

Elizabeth: Spoke or silent, a promise is surely made. And she may dote on it now—I am sure she does—and thinks to kill me, then to take my place.

PROCTOR's *anger is rising; he cannot speak.*

Elizabeth: It is her dearest hope, John, I know it. There be a thousand names; why does she call mine? There be a certain danger in calling such a name—I am no Goody Good that sleeps in ditches, nor Osburn, drunk and half-witted. She'd dare not call out such a farmer's wife but there be monstrous profit in it. She thinks to take my place, John.

Proctor: She cannot think it! *He knows it is true.*

Elizabeth, *"reasonably":* John, have you ever shown her somewhat of contempt? She cannot pass you in the church but you will blush—

Proctor: I may blush for my sin.

Elizabeth: I think she sees another meaning in that blush.

Proctor: And what see you? What see you, Elizabeth?

Elizabeth, *"conceding":* I think you be somewhat ashamed, for I am there, and she so close.

Proctor: When will you know me, woman? Were I stone I would have cracked for shame this seven month!

Elizabeth: Then go and tell her she's a whore. Whatever promise she may sense—break it, John, break it.

Proctor, *between his teeth:* Good, then. I'll go. *He starts for his rifle.*

Elizabeth, *trembling, fearfully:* Oh, how unwillingly!

Proctor, *turning on her, rifle in hand:* I will curse her hotter than the oldest cinder in hell. But pray, begrudge me not my anger!

Elizabeth: Your anger! I only ask you—

Proctor: Woman, am I so base? Do you truly think me base?

Elizabeth: I never called you base.

Proctor: Then how do you charge me with such a promise? The promise that a stallion gives a mare I gave that girl!

Elizabeth: Then why do you anger with me when I bid you break it?

Proctor: Because it speaks deceit, and I am honest! But I'll plead no more! I see now your spirit twists around the single error of my life, and I will never tear it free!

Elizabeth, *crying out:* You'll tear it free—when you come to know that I will be your only wife, or no wife at all! She has an arrow in you yet, John Proctor, and you know it well!

Quite suddenly, as though from the air, a figure appears in the doorway. They start slightly. It is MR. HALE. *He is different now—drawn a little, and there is a quality of deference, even of guilt, about his manner now.*

Hale: Good evening.

Proctor, *still in his shock:* Why, Mr. Hale! Good evening to you, sir. Come in, come in.

Hale, *to* ELIZABETH: I hope I do not startle you.

Elizabeth: No, no, it's only that I heard no horse—

Hale: You are Goodwife Proctor.

Proctor: Aye; Elizabeth.

Hale, *nods, then:* I hope you're not off to bed yet.

Proctor, *setting down his gun:* No, no. HALE *comes further into the room. And* PROCTOR, *to explain his nervousness:* We are not used to visitors after dark, but you're welcome here. Will you sit you down, sir?

Hale: I will. *He sits.* Let you sit, Goodwife Proctor.

She does, never letting him out of her sight. There is a pause as HALE *looks about the room.*

Proctor, *to break the silence:* Will you drink cider, Mr. Hale?

Hale: No, it rebels my stomach; I have some further traveling yet tonight. Sit you down, sir. PROCTOR *sits.* I will not keep you long, but I have some business with you.

Proctor: Business of the court?

Hale: No—no, I come of my own, without the court's authority. Hear me. *He wets his lips.* I know not if you are aware, but your wife's name is—mentioned in the court.

Proctor: We know it, sir. Our Mary Warren told us. We are entirely amazed.

Hale: I am a stranger here, as you know. And in my ignorance I find it hard to draw a clear opinion of them that come accused before the court. And so this afternoon, and now tonight, I go from house to house—I come now from Rebecca Nurse's house and—

Elizabeth, *shocked:* Rebecca's charged!

Hale: God forbid such a one be charged. She is, however—mentioned somewhat.

Elizabeth, *with an attempt at a laugh:* You will never believe, I hope, that Rebecca trafficked with the Devil.

Hale: Woman, it is possible.

Proctor, *taken aback:* Surely you cannot think so.

Hale: This is a strange time, Mister. No man may longer doubt the powers of the dark are gathered in monstrous attack upon this village. There is too much evidence now to deny it. You will agree, sir?

Proctor, *evading:* I—I have no knowledge in that line. But it's hard to think so pious a woman be secretly a Devil's bitch after seventy year of such good prayer.

Hale: Aye. But the Devil is a wily one, you cannot deny it. However, she is far from accused, and I know she will not be. *Pause.* I thought, sir, to put some questions as to the Christian character of this house, if you'll permit me.

Proctor, *coldly, resentful:* Why, we—have no fear of questions, sir.

Hale: Good, then. *He makes himself more comfortable.* In the book of record that Mr. Parris keeps, I note that you are rarely in the church on Sabbath Day.

Proctor: No, sir, you are mistaken.

Hale: Twenty-six time in seventeen month, sir. I must call that rare. Will you tell me why you are so absent?

Proctor: Mr. Hale, I never knew I must account to that man for I come to church or stay at home. My wife were sick this winter.

Hale: So I am told. But you, Mister, why could you not come alone?

Proctor: I surely did come when I could, and when I could not I prayed in this house.

Hale: Mr. Proctor, your house is not a church; your theology must tell you that.

Proctor: It does, sir, it does; and it tells me that a minister may pray to God without he have golden candlesticks upon the altar.

Hale: What golden candlesticks?

Proctor: Since we built the church there were pewter candlesticks upon the altar; Francis Nurse made them, y'know, and a sweeter hand never touched the metal. But Parris came, and for twenty week he preach nothin' but golden candlesticks until he had them. I labor the earth from dawn of day to blink of night, and I tell you true, when I look to heaven and see my money glaring at his elbows—it hurt my prayer, sir, it hurt my prayer. I think, sometimes, the man dreams cathedrals, not clapboard meetin' houses.

Hale, *thinks, then:* And yet, Mister, a Christian on Sabbath Day must be in church. *Pause.* Tell me— you have three children?

Proctor: Aye. Boys.

Hale: How comes it that only two are baptized?

Proctor, *starts to speak, then stops, then, as though unable to restrain this:* I like it not that Mr. Parris should lay his hand upon my baby. I see no light of God in that man. I'll not conceal it.

Hale: I must say it, Mr. Proctor; that is not for you to decide. The man's ordained, therefore the light of God is in him.

Proctor, *flushed with resentment but trying to smile:* What's your suspicion, Mr. Hale?

Hale: No, no, I have no—

Proctor: I nailed the roof upon the church, I hung the door—

Hale: Oh, did you! That's a good sign, then.

Proctor: It may be I have been too quick to bring the man to book, but you cannot think we ever desired the destruction of religion. I think that's in your mind, is it not?

Hale, *not altogether giving way:* I—have—there is a softness in your record, sir, a softness.

Elizabeth: I think, maybe, we have been too hard with Mr. Parris. I think so. But sure we never loved the Devil here.

Hale, *nods, deliberating this. Then, with the voice of one administering a secret test:* Do you know your Commandments, Elizabeth?

Elizabeth, *without hesitation, even eagerly:* I surely do. There be no mark of blame upon my life, Mr. Hale. I am a covenanted Christian woman.

Hale: And you, Mister?

Proctor, *a trifle unsteadily:* I—am sure I do, sir.

Hale, *glances at her open face, then at* JOHN, *then:* Let you repeat them, if you will.

Proctor: The Commandments.

Hale: Aye.

Proctor, *looking off, beginning to sweat:* Thou shalt not kill.

Hale: Aye.

Proctor, *counting on his fingers:* Thou shalt not steal. Thou shalt not covet thy neighbor's goods, nor make unto thee any graven image. Thou shalt not take the name of the Lord in vain; thou shalt have no other gods before me. *With some hesitation:* Thou shalt remember the Sabbath Day and keep it holy. *Pause. Then:* Thou shalt honor thy father and mother. Thou shalt not bear false witness. *He is stuck. He counts back on his fingers, knowing one is missing.* Thou shalt not make unto thee any graven image.

Hale: You have said that twice, sir.

Proctor, *lost:* Aye. *He is flailing for it.*

Elizabeth, *delicately:* Adultery, John.

Proctor, *as though a secret arrow had pained his heart:* Aye. *Trying to grin it away—to* HALE: You see, sir, between the two of us we do know them all. HALE *only looks at* PROCTOR, *deep in his attempt to define this man.* PROCTOR *grows more uneasy.* I think it be a small fault.

Hale: Theology, sir, is a fortress; no crack in a fortress may be accounted small. *He rises; he seems worried now. He paces a little, in deep thought.*

Proctor: There be no love for Satan in this house, Mister.

Hale: I pray it, I pray it dearly. *He looks to both of them, an attempt at a smile on his face, but his misgivings are clear.* Well, then—I'll bid you good night.

Elizabeth, *unable to restrain herself:* Mr. Hale. *He turns.* I do think you are suspecting me somewhat? Are you not?

Hale, *obviously disturbed—and evasive:* Goody Proctor, I do not judge you. My duty is to add what I may to the godly wisdom of the court. I pray you both good health and good fortune. *To* JOHN: Good night, sir. *He starts out.*

Elizabeth, *with a note of desperation:* I think you must tell him, John.

Hale: What's that?

Elizabeth, *restraining a call:* Will you tell him?

Slight pause. HALE *looks questioningly at* JOHN.

Proctor, *with difficulty:* I—I have no witness and cannot prove it, except my word be taken. But I know the children's sickness had naught to do with witchcraft.

Hale, *stopped, struck:* Naught to do—?

Proctor: Mr. Parris discovered them sportin' in the woods. They were startled and took sick.

Pause.

Hale: Who told you this?

Proctor, *hesitates, then:* Abigail Williams.

Hale: Abigail!

Proctor: Aye.

Hale, *his eyes wide:* Abigail Williams told you it had naught to do with witchcraft!

Proctor: She told me the day you came, sir.

Hale, *suspiciously:* Why—why did you keep this?

Proctor: I never knew until tonight that the world is gone daft with this nonsense.

Hale: Nonsense! Mister, I have myself examined Tituba, Sarah Good, and numerous others that have confessed to dealing with the Devil. They have *confessed* it.

Proctor: And why not, if they must hang for denyin' it? There are them that will swear to anything before they'll hang; have you never thought of that?

Hale: I have. I—I have indeed. *It is his own suspicion, but he resists it. He glances at* ELIZABETH, *then at* JOHN. And you—would you testify to this in court?

Proctor: I—had not reckoned with goin' into court. But if I must I will.

Hale: Do you falter here?

Proctor: I falter nothing, but I may wonder if my story will be credited in such a court. I do wonder on it, when such a steady-minded minister as you will suspicion such a woman that never lied, and cannot, and the world knows she cannot! I may falter somewhat, Mister; I am no fool.

Hale, *quietly—it has impressed him:* Proctor, let you open with me now, for I have a rumor that troubles me. It's said you hold no belief that there may even be witches in the world. Is that true, sir?

Proctor—*he knows this is critical, and is*

striving against his disgust with HALE *and with himself for even answering:* I know not what I have said, I may have said it. I have wondered if there be witches in the world—although I cannot believe they come among us now.

Hale: Then you do not believe—

Proctor: I have no knowledge of it; the Bible speaks of witches, and I will not deny them.

Hale: And you, woman?

Elizabeth: I—I cannot believe it.

Hale, *shocked:* You cannot!

Proctor: Elizabeth, you bewilder him!

Elizabeth, *to* HALE: I cannot think the Devil may own a woman's soul, Mr. Hale, when she keeps an upright way, as I have. I am a good woman, I know it; and if you believe I may do only good work in the world, and yet be secretly bound to Satan, then I must tell you, sir, I do not believe it.

Hale: But, woman, you do believe there are witches in—

Elizabeth: If you think that I am one, then I say there are none.

Hale: You surely do not fly against the Gospel, the Gospel—

Proctor: She believe in the Gospel, every word!

Elizabeth: Question Abigail Williams about the Gospel, not myself!

HALE *stares at her.*

Proctor: She do not mean to doubt the Gospel, sir, you cannot think it. This be a Christian house, sir, a Christian house.

Hale: God keep you both; let the third child be quickly baptized, and go you without fail each Sunday in to Sabbath prayer; and keep a solemn, quiet way among you. I think—

GILES COREY *appears in doorway.*

Giles: John!

Proctor: Giles! What's the matter?

Giles: They take my wife.

FRANCIS NURSE *enters.*

Giles: And his Rebecca!

Proctor, *to* FRANCIS: Rebecca's in the *jail!*

Francis: Aye, Cheever come and take her in his wagon. We've only now come from the jail, and they'll not even let us in to see them.

Elizabeth: They've surely gone wild now, Mr. Hale!

Francis, *going to* HALE: Reverend Hale! Can you not speak to the Deputy Governor? I'm sure he mistakes these people—

Hale: Pray calm yourself, Mr. Nurse.

Francis: My wife is the very brick and mortar of the church, Mr. Hale—*indicating* GILES—and Martha Corey, there cannot be a woman closer yet to God than Martha.

Hale: How is Rebecca charged, Mr. Nurse?

Francis, *with a mocking, half-hearted laugh:* For murder, she's charged! *Mockingly quoting the warrant:* "For the marvelous and supernatural murder of Goody Putnam's babies." What am I to do, Mr. Hale?

Hale, *turns from* FRANCIS, *deeply troubled, then:* Believe me, Mr. Nurse, if Rebecca Nurse be tainted, then nothing's left to stop the whole green world from burning. Let you rest upon the justice of the court; the court will send her home, I know it.

Francis: You cannot mean she will be tried in court!

Hale, *pleading:* Nurse, though our hearts break, we cannot flinch; these are new times, sir. There is a misty plot afoot so subtle we should be criminal to cling to old respects and ancient friendships. I have seen too many frightful proofs in court—the Devil is alive in Salem, and we dare not quail to follow wherever the accusing finger points!

Proctor, *angered:* How may such a woman murder children?

Hale, *in great pain:* Man, remember, until an hour before the Devil fell, God thought him beautiful in Heaven.

Giles: I never said my wife were a witch, Mr. Hale; I only said she were reading books!

Hale: Mr. Corey, exactly what complaint were made on your wife?

Giles: That bloody mongrel Walcott charge her. Y'see, he buy a pig of my wife four or five year ago, and the pig died soon after. So he come dancin' in for his money back. So my Martha, she says to him, "Walcott, if you haven't the wit to feed a pig properly, you'll not live to own many," she says. Now he goes to court and claims that from that day to this he cannot keep a pig alive for more than four weeks because my Martha bewitch them with her books!

Enter EZEKIEL CHEEVER. *A shocked silence.*

Cheever: Good evening to you, Proctor.
Proctor: Why, Mr. Cheever. Good evening.
Cheever: Good evening, all. Good evening, Mr. Hale.
Proctor: I hope you come not on business of the court.
Cheever: I do, Proctor, aye. I am clerk of the court now, y'know.

Enter MARSHAL HERRICK, *a man in his early thirties, who is somewhat shamefaced at the moment.*

Giles: It's a pity, Ezekiel, that an honest tailor might have gone to Heaven must burn in Hell. You'll burn for this, do you know it?
Cheever: You know yourself I must do as I'm told. You surely know that, Giles. And I'd as lief² you'd not be sending me to Hell. I like not the sound of it, I tell you; I like not the sound of it. *He fears* PROCTOR, *but starts to reach inside his coat.* Now believe me, Proctor, how heavy be the law, all its tonnage I do carry on my back tonight. *He takes out a warrant.* I have a warrant for your wife.
Proctor, *to* HALE: You said she were not charged!
Hale: I know nothin' of it. *To* CHEEVER: When were she charged?
Cheever: I am given sixteen warrant tonight, sir, and she is one.
Proctor: Who charged her?
Cheever: Why, Abigail Williams charge her.
Proctor: On what proof, what proof?
Cheever, *looking about the room:* Mr. Proctor, I have little time. The court bid me search your house, but I like not to search a house. So will you hand me any poppets that your wife may keep here?
Proctor: Poppets?
Elizabeth: I never kept no poppets, not since I were a girl.
Cheever, *embarrassed, glancing toward the mantel where sits* MARY WARREN'*s poppet:* I spy a poppet, Goody Proctor.
Elizabeth: Oh! *Going for it:* Why, this is Mary's.

2. **lief:** gladly.

"The Devil is alive in Salem, and we dare not quail to follow wherever the accusing finger points!"

Cheever, *shyly:* Would you please to give it to me?
Elizabeth, *handing it to him, asks* HALE: Has the court discovered a text in poppets now?
Cheever, *carefully holding the poppet:* Do you keep any others in this house?
Proctor: No, not this one either till tonight. What signifies a poppet?
Cheever: Why, a poppet—*he gingerly turns the poppet over*—a poppet may signify— Now, woman, will you please to come with me?
Proctor: She will not! *To* ELIZABETH: Fetch Mary here.
Cheever, *ineptly reaching toward* ELIZABETH: No, no, I am forbid to leave her from my sight.
Proctor, *pushing his arm away:* You'll leave her out of sight and out of mind, Mister. Fetch Mary, Elizabeth. ELIZABETH *goes upstairs.*
Hale: What signifies a poppet, Mr. Cheever?
Cheever, *turning the poppet over in his hands:* Why, they say it may signify that she— *He has lifted the poppet's skirt, and his eyes widen in astonished fear.* Why, this, this—
Proctor, *reaching for the poppet:* What's there?
Cheever: Why—*he draws out a long needle from the poppet*—it is a needle! Herrick, Herrick, it is a needle!

HERRICK *comes toward him.*

Proctor, *angrily, bewildered:* And what signifies a needle!
Cheever, *his hands shaking:* Why, this go hard with her, Proctor, this—I had my doubts, Proctor, I had my doubts, but here's calamity. *To* HALE, *showing the needle:* You see it, sir, it is a needle!
Hale: Why? What meanin' has it?
Cheever, *wide-eyed, trembling:* The girl, the Williams girl, Abigail Williams, sir. She sat to dinner in Reverend Parris's house tonight, and

without word nor warnin' she falls to the floor. Like a struck beast, he says, and screamed a scream that a bull would weep to hear. And he goes to save her, and, stuck two inches in the flesh of her belly, he draw a needle out. And demandin' of her how she come to be so stabbed, she—*to* PROCTOR *now*—testify it were your wife's familiar spirit pushed it in.

Proctor: Why, she done it herself! *To* HALE: I hope you're not takin' this for proof, Mister!

HALE, *struck by the proof, is silent.*

Cheever: 'Tis hard proof! *To* HALE: I find her a poppet Goody Proctor keeps. I have found it, sir. And in the belly of the poppet a needle's stuck. I tell you true, Proctor, I never warranted to see such proof of Hell, and I bid you obstruct me not, for I—

Enter ELIZABETH *with* MARY WARREN. PROCTOR, *seeing* MARY WARREN, *draws her by the arm to* HALE.

Proctor: Here now! Mary, how did this poppet come into my house?

Mary Warren, *frightened for herself, her voice very small:* What poppet's that, sir?

Proctor, *impatiently, pointing at the doll in* CHEEVER's *hand:* This poppet, this poppet.

Mary Warren, *evasively, looking at it:* Why, I—I think it is mine.

Proctor: It is your poppet, is it not?

Mary Warren, *not understanding the direction of this:* It—is, sir.

Proctor: And how did it come into this house?

Mary Warren, *glancing about at the avid faces:* Why—I made it in the court, sir, and—give it to Goody Proctor tonight.

Proctor, *to* HALE: Now, sir—do you have it?

Hale: Mary Warren, a needle have been found inside this poppet.

Mary Warren, *bewildered:* Why, I meant no harm by it, sir.

Proctor, *quickly:* You stuck that needle in yourself?

Mary Warren: I—I believe I did, sir, I—

Proctor, *to* HALE: What say you now?

Hale, *watching* MARY WARREN *closely:* Child, you are certain this be your natural memory? May it be, perhaps, that someone conjures you even now to say this?

Mary Warren: Conjures me? Why, no, sir, I am entirely myself, I think. Let you ask Susanna Walcott—she saw me sewin' it in court. *Or better still:* Ask Abby, Abby sat beside me when I made it.

Proctor, *to* HALE, *of* CHEEVER: Bid him begone. Your mind is surely settled now. Bid him out, Mr. Hale.

Elizabeth: What signifies a needle?

Hale: Mary—you charge a cold and cruel murder on Abigail.

Mary Warren: Murder! I charge no—

Hale: Abigail were stabbed tonight; a needle were found stuck into her belly—

Elizabeth: And she charges me?

Hale: Aye.

Elizabeth, *her breath knocked out:* Why—! The girl is murder! She must be ripped out of the world!

Cheever, *pointing at* ELIZABETH: You've heard that, sir! Ripped out of the world! Herrick, you heard it!

Proctor, *suddenly snatching the warrant out of* CHEEVER's *hands:* Out with you.

Cheever: Proctor, you dare not touch the warrant.

Proctor, *ripping the warrant:* Out with you!

Cheever: You've ripped the Deputy Governor's warrant, man!

Proctor: Damn the Deputy Governor! Out of my house!

Hale: Now, Proctor, Proctor!

Proctor: Get y'gone with them! You are a broken minister.

Hale: Proctor, if she is innocent, the court—

Proctor: If *she* is innocent! Why do you never wonder if Parris be innocent, or Abigail? Is the accuser always holy now? Were they born this morning as clean as God's fingers? I'll tell you what's walking Salem—vengeance is walking Salem. We are what we always were in Salem, but now the little crazy children are jangling the keys of the kingdom, and common vengeance writes the law! This warrant's vengeance! I'll not give my wife to vengeance!

Elizabeth: I'll go, John—

Proctor: You will not go!

Herrick: I have nine men outside. You cannot keep her. The law binds me, John, I cannot budge.

Proctor, *to* HALE, *ready to break him:* Will you see her taken?

Hale: Proctor, the court is just—

Proctor: Pontius Pilate![3] God will not let you wash your hands of this!

Elizabeth: John—I think I must go with them. *He cannot bear to look at her.* Mary, there is bread enough for the morning; you will bake, in the afternoon. Help Mr. Proctor as you were his daughter—you owe me that, and much more. *She is fighting her weeping. To* PROCTOR: When the children wake, speak nothing of witchcraft—it will frighten them. *She cannot go on.*

Proctor: I will bring you home. I will bring you soon.

Elizabeth: Oh, John, bring me soon!

Proctor: I will fall like an ocean on that court! Fear nothing, Elizabeth.

Elizabeth, *with great fear:* I will fear nothing. *She looks about the room, as though to fix it in her mind.* Tell the children I have gone to visit someone sick.

She walks out the door, HERRICK *and* CHEEVER *behind her. For a moment,* PROCTOR *watches from the doorway. The clank of chain is heard.*

Proctor: Herrick! Herrick, don't chain her! *He rushes out the door. From outside:* Damn you, man, you will not chain her! Off with them! I'll not have it! I will not have her chained!

There are other men's voices against his. HALE, *in a fever of guilt and uncertainty, turns from the door to avoid the sight;* MARY WARREN *bursts into tears and sits weeping.* GILES COREY *calls to* HALE.

Giles: And yet silent, minister? It is fraud, you know it is fraud! What keeps you, man?

PROCTOR *is half braced, half pushed into the room by two deputies and* HERRICK.

Proctor: I'll pay you, Herrick, I will surely pay you!

Herrick, *panting:* In God's name, John, I cannot help myself. I must chain them all. Now let you keep inside this house till I am gone! *He goes out with his deputies.*

PROCTOR *stands there, gulping air. Horses and a wagon creaking are heard.*

3. **Pontius Pilate** (pun′chəs pī′lət) (1st century A.D.): Roman official who unwillingly condemned Christ to death. Pilate is said to have declared, "I am innocent of the blood of this just man" (Matthew 27:24).

Hale, *in great uncertainty:* Mr. Proctor—

Proctor: Out of my sight!

Hale: Charity, Proctor, charity. What I have heard in her favor, I will not fear to testify in court. God help me, I cannot judge her guilty or innocent—I know not. Only this consider: the world goes mad, and it profit nothing you should lay the cause to the vengeance of a little girl.

Proctor: You are a coward! Though you be ordained in God's own tears, you are a coward now!

Hale: Proctor, I cannot think God be provoked so grandly by such a petty cause. The jails are packed—our greatest judges sit in Salem now—and hangin's promised. Man, we must look to cause proportionate. Were there murder done, perhaps, and never brought to light? Abomination? Some secret blasphemy that stinks to Heaven? Think on cause, man, and let you help me to discover it. For there's your way, believe it, there is your only way, when such confusion strikes upon the world. *He goes to* GILES *and* FRANCIS. Let you counsel among yourselves; think on your village and what may have drawn from heaven such thundering wrath upon you all. I shall pray God open up our eyes.

HALE *goes out.*

Francis, *struck by* HALE's *mood:* I never heard no murder done in Salem.

Proctor—*he has been reached by* HALE's *words:* Leave me, Francis, leave me.

Giles, *shaken:* John—tell me, are we lost?

Proctor: Go home now, Giles. We'll speak on it tomorrow.

Giles: Let you think on it. We'll come early, eh?

Proctor: Aye. Go now, Giles.

Giles: Good night, then.

GILES COREY *and* FRANCIS NURSE *go out. After a moment:*

Mary Warren, *in a fearful squeak of a voice:* Mr. Proctor, very likely they'll let her come home once they're given proper evidence.

Proctor: You're coming to the court with me, Mary. You will tell it in the court.

Mary Warren: I cannot charge murder on Abigail.

Proctor, *moving menacingly toward her:* You will tell the court how that poppet come here and who stuck the needle in.

Mary Warren: She'll kill me for sayin' that! PROC-TOR *continues toward her.* Abby'll charge lechery on you, Mr. Proctor!

Proctor, *halting:* She's told you!

Mary Warren: I have known it, sir. She'll ruin you with it, I know she will.

Proctor, *hesitating, and with deep hatred of himself:* Good. Then her saintliness is done with. MARY *backs from him.* We will slide together into our pit; you will tell the court what you know.

Mary Warren, *in terror:* I cannot, they'll turn on me—

PROCTOR *strides and catches her, and she is re-peating, "I cannot, I cannot!"*

Proctor: My wife will never die for me! I will bring your guts into your mouth but that good-ness will not die for me!

Mary Warren, *struggling to escape him:* I cannot do it, I cannot!

Proctor, *grasping her by the throat as though he would strangle her:* Make your peace with it! Now Hell and Heaven grapple on our backs, and all our old pretense is ripped away—make your peace! *He throws her to the floor, where she sobs, "I cannot, I cannot . . ." And now, half to himself, staring, and turning to the open door:* Peace. It is a providence, and no great change; we are only what we always were, but naked now. *He walks as though toward a great horror, facing the open sky.* Aye, naked! And the wind, God's icy wind, will blow!

And she is over and over again sobbing, "I can-not, I cannot, I cannot," as

The curtain falls

MAKING MEANINGS

Act Two

First Thoughts

1. At this point in the play, what would you do if you were John Proctor?

Shaping Interpretations

2. Describe the relationship between John and Elizabeth. In your own words, explain the **meta-phor** of the "everlasting funeral" that John sees in Elizabeth's heart.

3. Based on Mary's statements, what do you infer is the real reason Mary gives Elizabeth the gift?

4. Using your reading notes as a starting point, how do you interpret Mary's visions and accusations? What clues does Miller give us about her **motivation**?

Reading Check

a. At the beginning of the act, why does Elizabeth want John to go to Salem?

b. What gift does Mary Warren give to Eliza-beth?

c. According to Eliza-beth, what is Abigail's true objective in court?

d. Why has Rebecca Nurse been jailed?

e. What does John Proctor want Mary to testify?

---

5. Why does Hale become suspicious of the Proc-tors? What is the **irony** in Hale's urging Proctor to show "charity"?

6. The **protagonist** of a story is the central character who drives the action, and is usually considered the hero or heroine. The **antago-nist** is the character who struggles against the protagonist, often with cruel or destructive intent. By the end of Act Two, which character seems to have emerged as the protagonist? Which character is most clearly the antagonist? Support your answer with specific evidence from the text.

7. Identify at least three **external conflicts** in the play. Then describe the **internal conflict** that Proctor faces. How could Proctor's conflict relate to a broader conflict in the play—between public appearance and private reality?

Extending the Text

8. What insights about the Puritans do you gain from reading *The Crucible*—insights that you don't usually find in a history textbook? What dangers would there be in relying only on later literature for historical truth?

Act Three

The vestry room of the Salem meeting house, now serving as the anteroom of the General Court.

As the curtain rises, the room is empty, but for sunlight pouring through two high windows in the back wall. The room is solemn, even forbidding. Heavy beams jut out, boards of random widths make up the walls. At the right are two doors leading into the meeting house proper, where the court is being held. At the left another door leads outside.

There is a plain bench at the left, and another at the right. In the center a rather long meeting table, with stools and a considerable armchair snugged up to it.

Through the partitioning wall at the right we hear a prosecutor's voice, JUDGE HATHORNE*'s, asking a question; then a woman's voice,* MARTHA COREY*'s, replying.*

Hathorne's Voice: Now, Martha Corey, there is abundant evidence in our hands to show that you have given yourself to the reading of fortunes. Do you deny it?

Martha Corey's Voice: I am innocent to a witch. I know not what a witch is.

Hathorne's Voice: How do you know, then, that you are not a witch?

Martha Corey's Voice: If I were, I would know it.

Hathorne's Voice: Why do you hurt these children?

Martha Corey's Voice: I do not hurt them. I scorn it!

Giles' Voice, *roaring:* I have evidence for the court!

Voices of townspeople rise in excitement.

Danforth's Voice: You will keep your seat!

Giles' Voice: Thomas Putnam is reaching out for land!

Danforth's Voice: Remove that man, Marshal!

Giles' Voice: You're hearing lies, lies!

A roaring goes up from the people.

Hathorne's Voice: Arrest him, Excellency!

Giles' Voice: I have evidence. Why will you not hear my evidence?

The door opens and GILES *is half carried into the vestry room by* HERRICK. FRANCIS NURSE *enters, trailing anxiously behind* GILES.

Giles: Hands off, damn you, let me go!

Herrick: Giles, Giles!

Giles: Out of my way, Herrick! I bring evidence—

Herrick: You cannot go in there, Giles; it's a court!

Enter HALE *from the court.*

Hale: Pray be calm a moment.

Giles: You, Mr. Hale, go in there and demand I speak.

Hale: A moment, sir, a moment.

Giles: They'll be hangin' my wife!

JUDGE HATHORNE *enters. He is in his sixties, a bitter, remorseless Salem judge.*

Hathorne: How do you dare come roarin' into this court! Are you gone daft, Corey?

Giles: You're not a Boston judge yet, Hathorne. You'll not call me daft!

Enter DEPUTY GOVERNOR DANFORTH *and, behind him,* EZEKIEL CHEEVER *and* PARRIS. *On his appearance, silence falls.* DANFORTH *is a grave man in his sixties, of some humor and sophistication that do not, however, interfere with an exact loyalty to his position and his cause. He comes down to* GILES, *who awaits his wrath.*

Danforth, *looking directly at* GILES: Who is this man?

Parris: Giles Corey, sir, and a more contentious—

Giles, *to* PARRIS: I am asked the question, and I am old enough to answer it! *To* DANFORTH, *who impresses him and to whom he smiles through his strain:* My name is Corey, sir, Giles Corey. I have six hundred acres, and timber in addition. It is my wife you be condemning now. *He indicates the courtroom.*

Danforth: And how do you imagine to help her cause with such contemptuous riot? Now be gone. Your old age alone keeps you out of jail for this.

Giles, *beginning to plead:* They be tellin' lies about my wife, sir, I—

Danforth: Do you take it upon yourself to determine what this court shall believe and what it shall set aside?

Giles: Your Excellency, we mean no disrespect for—

Danforth: Disrespect indeed! It is disruption, Mister. This is the highest court of the supreme government of this province, do you know it?

Giles, *beginning to weep:* Your Excellency, I only said she were readin' books, sir, and they come and take her out of my house for—

Danforth, *mystified:* Books! What books?

Giles, *through helpless sobs:* It is my third wife, sir; I never had no wife that be so taken with books, and I thought to find the cause of it, d'y'see, but it were no witch I blamed her for. *He is openly weeping.* I have broke charity with the woman, I have broke charity with her. *He covers his face, ashamed.* DANFORTH *is respectfully silent.*

Hale: Excellency, he claims hard evidence for his wife's defense. I think that in all justice you must—

Danforth: Then let him submit his evidence in proper affidavit.[1] You are certainly aware of our procedure here, Mr. Hale. *To* HERRICK: Clear this room.

Herrick: Come now, Giles. *He gently pushes* COREY *out.*

Francis: We are desperate, sir; we come here three days now and cannot be heard.

Danforth: Who is this man?

Francis: Francis Nurse, Your Excellency.

Hale: His wife's Rebecca that were condemned this morning.

Danforth: Indeed! I am amazed to find you in such uproar. I have only good report of your character, Mr. Nurse.

Hathorne: I think they must both be arrested in contempt, sir.

Danforth, *to* FRANCIS: Let you write your plea, and in due time I will—

Francis: Excellency, we have proof for your eyes; God forbid you shut them to it. The girls, sir, the girls are frauds.

Danforth: What's that?

Francis: We have proof of it, sir. They are all deceiving you.

DANFORTH *is shocked, but studying* FRANCIS.

---

1. **affidavit** (af′ə·dā′vit): written statement made under oath before a legal authority.

Hathorne: This is contempt, sir, contempt!

Danforth: Peace, Judge Hathorne. Do you know who I am, Mr. Nurse?

Francis: I surely do, sir, and I think you must be a wise judge to be what you are.

Danforth: And do you know that near to four hundred are in the jails from Marblehead to Lynn, and upon my signature?

Francis: I—

Danforth: And seventy-two condemned to hang by that signature?

Francis: Excellency, I never thought to say it to such a weighty judge, but you are deceived.

Enter GILES COREY *from left. All turn to see as he beckons in* MARY WARREN *with* PROCTOR. MARY *is keeping her eyes to the ground;* PROCTOR *has her elbow as though she were near collapse.*

Parris, *on seeing her, in shock:* Mary Warren! *He goes directly to bend close to her face.* What are you about here?

Proctor, *pressing* PARRIS *away from her with a gentle but firm motion of protectiveness:* She would speak with the Deputy Governor.

Danforth, *shocked by this, turns to* HERRICK: Did you not tell me Mary Warren were sick in bed?

Herrick: She were, Your Honor. When I go to fetch her to the court last week, she said she were sick.

Giles: She has been strivin' with her soul all week, Your Honor; she comes now to tell the truth of this to you.

Danforth: Who is this?

Proctor: John Proctor, sir. Elizabeth Proctor is my wife.

Parris: Beware this man, Your Excellency, this man is mischief.

Hale, *excitedly:* I think you must hear the girl, sir, she—

Danforth, *who has become very interested in* MARY WARREN *and only raises a hand toward* HALE: Peace. What would you tell us, Mary Warren?

PROCTOR *looks at her, but she cannot speak.*

Proctor: She never saw no spirits, sir.

Danforth, *with great alarm and surprise, to* MARY: Never saw no spirits!

Giles, *eagerly:* Never.

Proctor, *reaching into his jacket:* She has signed a deposition, sir—

Danforth, *instantly:* No, no, I accept no depositions. *He is rapidly calculating this; he turns from her to* PROCTOR. Tell me, Mr. Proctor, have you given out this story in the village?

Proctor: We have not.

Parris: They've come to overthrow the court, sir! This man is—

Danforth: I pray you, Mr. Parris. Do you know, Mr. Proctor, that the entire contention of the state in these trials is that the voice of Heaven is speaking through the children?

Proctor: I know that, sir.

Danforth, *thinks, staring at* PROCTOR, *then turns to* MARY WARREN: And you, Mary Warren, how came you to cry out people for sending their spirits against you?

Mary Warren: It were pretense, sir.

Danforth: I cannot hear you.

Proctor: It were pretense, she says.

Danforth: Ah? And the other girls? Susanna Walcott, and—the others? They are also pretending?

Mary Warren: Aye, sir.

Danforth, *wide-eyed:* Indeed. *Pause. He is baffled by this. He turns to study* PROCTOR's *face.*

Parris, *in a sweat:* Excellency, you surely cannot think to let so vile a lie be spread in open court!

Danforth: Indeed not, but it strike hard upon me that she will dare come here with such a tale. Now, Mr. Proctor, before I decide whether I shall hear you or not, it is my duty to tell you this. We burn a hot fire here; it melts down all concealment.

Proctor: I know that, sir.

Danforth: Let me continue. I understand well, a husband's tenderness may drive him to extravagance in defense of a wife. Are you certain in your conscience, Mister, that your evidence is the truth?

Proctor: It is. And you will surely know it.

Danforth: And you thought to declare this revelation in the open court before the public?

Proctor: I thought I would, aye—with your permission.

Danforth, *his eyes narrowing:* Now, sir, what is your purpose in so doing?

Proctor: Why, I—I would free my wife, sir.

Danforth: There lurks nowhere in your heart, nor hidden in your spirit, any desire to undermine this court?

Proctor, *with the faintest faltering:* Why, no, sir.

Cheever, *clears his throat, awakening:* I— Your Excellency.

Danforth: Mr. Cheever.

Cheever: I think it be my duty, sir—*Kindly, to* PROCTOR: You'll not deny it, John. *To* DANFORTH: When we come to take his wife, he damned the court and ripped your warrant.

Parris: Now you have it!

Danforth: He did that, Mr. Hale?

Hale, *takes a breath:* Aye, he did.

Proctor: It were a temper, sir. I knew not what I did.

Danforth, *studying him:* Mr. Proctor.

Proctor: Aye, sir.

Danforth, *straight into his eyes:* Have you ever seen the Devil?

Proctor: No, sir.

Danforth: You are in all respects a Gospel Christian?

Proctor: I am, sir.

Parris: Such a Christian that will not come to church but once in a month!

Danforth, *restrained—he is curious:* Not come to church?

Proctor: I—I have no love for Mr. Parris. It is no secret. But God I surely love.

Cheever: He plow on Sunday, sir.

Danforth: Plow on Sunday!

Cheever, *apologetically:* I think it be evidence, John. I am an official of the court, I cannot keep it.

Proctor: I—I have once or twice plowed on Sunday. I have three children, sir, and until last year my land give little.

Giles: You'll find other Christians that do plow on Sunday if the truth be known.

Hale: Your Honor, I cannot think you may judge the man on such evidence.

Danforth: I judge nothing. *Pause. He keeps watching* PROCTOR, *who tries to meet his gaze.* I tell you straight, Mister—I have seen marvels in this court. I have seen people choked before my eyes by spirits; I have seen them stuck by pins and slashed by daggers. I have until this moment not the slightest reason to suspect that the children may be deceiving me. Do you understand my meaning?

Proctor: Excellency, does it not strike upon you that so many of these women have lived so long with such upright reputation, and—

Parris: Do you read the Gospel, Mr. Proctor?

Proctor: I read the Gospel.

Parris: I think not, or you should surely know that Cain were an upright man, and yet he did kill Abel.[2]

Proctor: Aye, God tells us that. *To* DANFORTH: But who tells us Rebecca Nurse murdered seven babies by sending out her spirit on them? It is the children only, and this one will swear she lied to you.

DANFORTH *considers, then beckons* HATHORNE *to him.* HATHORNE *leans in, and he speaks in his ear.* HATHORNE *nods.*

Hathorne: Aye, she's the one.

Danforth: Mr. Proctor, this morning, your wife send me a claim in which she states that she is pregnant now.

Proctor: My wife pregnant!

Danforth: There be no sign of it—we have examined her body.

Proctor: But if she say she is pregnant, then she must be! That woman will never lie, Mr. Danforth.

Danforth: She will not?

Proctor: Never, sir, never.

Danforth: We have thought it too convenient to be credited. However, if I should tell you now that I will let her be kept another month; and if she begin to show her natural signs, you shall have her living yet another year until she is delivered—what say you to that? JOHN PROCTOR *is struck silent.* Come now. You say your only purpose is to save your wife. Good, then, she is saved at least this year, and a year is long. What say you, sir? It is done now. *In conflict,* PROCTOR *glances at* FRANCIS *and* GILES. Will you drop this charge?

Proctor: I—I think I cannot.

Danforth, *now an almost imperceptible hardness in his voice:* Then your purpose is somewhat larger.

Parris: He's come to overthrow this court, Your Honor!

Proctor: These are my friends. Their wives are also accused—

Danforth, *with a sudden briskness of manner:* I judge you not, sir. I am ready to hear your evidence.

Proctor: I come not to hurt the court; I only—

Danforth, *cutting him off:* Marshal, go into the court and bid Judge Stoughton and Judge Sewall declare recess for one hour. And let them go to the tavern, if they will. All witnesses and prisoners are to be kept in the building.

Herrick: Aye, sir. *Very deferentially:* If I may say it, sir, I know this man all my life. It is a good man, sir.

Danforth—*it is the reflection on himself he resents:* I am sure of it, Marshal. HERRICK *nods, then goes out.* Now, what deposition do you have for us, Mr. Proctor? And I beg you be clear, open as the sky, and honest.

Proctor, *as he takes out several papers:* I am no lawyer, so I'll—

Danforth: The pure in heart need no lawyers. Proceed as you will.

Proctor, *handing* DANFORTH *a paper:* Will you read this first, sir? It's a sort of testament. The people signing it declare their good opinion of Rebecca, and my wife, and Martha Corey. DANFORTH *looks down at the paper.*

Parris, *to enlist* DANFORTH'*s sarcasm:* Their good opinion! *But* DANFORTH *goes on reading, and* PROCTOR *is heartened.*

Proctor: These are all landholding farmers, members of the church. *Delicately, trying to point out a paragraph:* If you'll notice, sir—they've known the women many years and never saw no sign they had dealings with the Devil.

PARRIS *nervously moves over and reads over* DANFORTH'*s shoulder.*

Danforth, *glancing down a long list:* How many names are here?

Francis: Ninety-one, Your Excellency.

Parris, *sweating:* These people should be summoned. DANFORTH *looks up at him questioningly.* For questioning.

Francis, *trembling with anger:* Mr. Danforth, I gave them all my word no harm would come to them for signing this.

Parris: This is a clear attack upon the court!

---

2. **Cain...Abel:** according to the Book of Genesis, Cain, the oldest son of Adam and Eve, killed his brother Abel.

Hale, *to* PARRIS, *trying to contain himself:* Is every defense an attack upon the court? Can no one—?

Parris: All innocent and Christian people are happy for the courts in Salem! These people are gloomy for it. *To* DANFORTH *directly:* And I think you will want to know, from each and every one of them, what discontents them with you!

Hathorne: I think they ought to be examined, sir.

Danforth: It is not necessarily an attack, I think. Yet—

Francis: These are all covenanted Christians, sir.

Danforth: Then I am sure they may have nothing to fear. *Hands* CHEEVER *the paper.* Mr. Cheever, have warrants drawn for all of these—arrest for examination. *To* PROCTOR: Now, Mister, what other information do you have for us? FRANCIS *is still standing, horrified.* You may sit, Mr. Nurse.

Francis: I have brought trouble on these people; I have—

Danforth: No, old man, you have not hurt these people if they are of good conscience. But you must understand, sir, that a person is either with this court or he must be counted against it, there be no road between. This is a sharp time, now, a precise time—we live no longer in the dusky afternoon when evil mixed itself with good and befuddled the world. Now, by God's grace, the shining sun is up, and them that fear not light will surely praise it. I hope you will be one of those. MARY WARREN *suddenly sobs.* She's not hearty, I see.

Proctor: No, she's not, sir. *To* MARY, *bending to her, holding her hand, quietly:* Now remember what the angel Raphael said to the boy Tobias.[3] Remember it.

Mary Warren, *hardly audible:* Aye.

Proctor: "Do that which is good, and no harm shall come to thee."

Mary Warren: Aye.

Danforth: Come, man, we wait you.

MARSHAL HERRICK *returns, and takes his post at the door.*

Giles: John, my deposition, give him mine.

Proctor: Aye. *He hands* DANFORTH *another paper.* This is Mr. Corey's deposition.

Danforth: Oh? *He looks down at it. Now*

HATHORNE *comes behind him and reads with him.*

Hathorne, *suspiciously:* What lawyer drew this, Corey?

Giles: You know I never hired a lawyer in my life, Hathorne.

Danforth, *finishing the reading:* It is very well phrased. My compliments. Mr. Parris, if Mr. Putnam is in the court, will you bring him in? HATHORNE *takes the deposition, and walks to the window with it.* PARRIS *goes into the court.* You have no legal training, Mr. Corey?

Giles, *very pleased:* I have the best, sir—I am thirty-three time in court in my life. And always plaintiff, too.

Danforth: Oh, then you're much put-upon.

Giles: I am never put-upon; I know my rights, sir, and I will have them. You know, your father tried a case of mine—might be thirty-five year ago, I think.

Danforth: Indeed.

Giles: He never spoke to you of it?

Danforth: No, I cannot recall it.

Giles: That's strange, he give me nine pound damages. He were a fair judge, your father. Y'see, I had a white mare that time, and this fellow come to borrow the mare— *Enter* PARRIS *with* THOMAS PUTNAM. *When he sees* PUTNAM, GILES' *ease goes; he is hard.* Aye, there he is.

Danforth: Mr. Putnam, I have here an accusation by Mr. Corey against you. He states that you coldly prompted your daughter to cry witchery upon George Jacobs that is now in jail.

Putnam: It is a lie.

Danforth, *turning to* GILES: Mr. Putnam states your charge is a lie. What say you to that?

Giles, *furious, his fists clenched:* A fart on Thomas Putnam, that is what I say to that!

Danforth: What proof do you submit for your charge, sir?

Giles: My proof is there! *Pointing to the paper.* If Jacobs hangs for a witch he forfeit up his property—that's law! And there is none but Putnam with the coin to buy so great a piece. This man is killing his neighbors for their land!

Danforth: But proof, sir, proof.

Giles, *pointing at his deposition:* The proof is there! I have it from an honest man who heard Putnam say it! The day his daughter cried out on Jacobs, he said she'd given him a fair gift of land.

---

3. **Raphael...Tobias:** in the Old Testament Apocrypha, the archangel Raphael guides Tobias, an exiled Jew.

Hathorne: And the name of this man?

Giles, *taken aback:* What name?

Hathorne: The man that give you this information.

Giles, *hesitates, then:* Why, I—I cannot give you his name.

Hathorne: And why not?

Giles, *hesitates, then bursts out:* You know well why not! He'll lay in jail if I give his name!

Hathorne: This is contempt of the court, Mr. Danforth!

Danforth, *to avoid that:* You will surely tell us the name.

Giles: I will not give you no name. I mentioned my wife's name once and I'll burn in hell long enough for that. I stand mute.

Danforth: In that case, I have no choice but to arrest you for contempt of this court, do you know that?

Giles: This is a hearing; you cannot clap me for contempt of a hearing.

Danforth: Oh, it is a proper lawyer! Do you wish me to declare the court in full session here? Or will you give me good reply?

Giles, *faltering:* I cannot give you no name, sir, I cannot.

Danforth: You are a foolish old man. Mr. Cheever, begin the record. The court is now in session. I ask you, Mr. Corey—

Proctor, *breaking in:* Your Honor—he has the story in confidence, sir, and he—

Parris: The Devil lives on such confidences! *To* DANFORTH: Without confidences there could be no conspiracy, Your Honor!

Hathorne: I think it must be broken, sir.

Danforth, *to* GILES: Old man, if your informant tells the truth let him come here openly like a decent man. But if he hide in anonymity I must know why. Now sir, the government and central church demand of you the name of him who reported Mr. Thomas Putnam a common murderer.

Hale: Excellency—

Danforth: Mr. Hale.

Hale: We cannot blink it more. There is a prodigious fear of this court in the country—

Danforth: Then there is a prodigious guilt in the country. Are *you* afraid to be questioned here?

Hale: I may only fear the Lord, sir, but there is fear in the country nevertheless.

Danforth, *angered now:* Reproach me not with the fear in the country; there is fear in the country because there is a moving plot to topple Christ in the country!

Hale: But it does not follow that everyone accused is part of it.

Danforth: No uncorrupted man may fear this court, Mr. Hale! None! *To* GILES. You are under arrest in contempt of this court. Now sit you down and take counsel with yourself, or you will be set in the jail until you decide to answer all questions.

GILES COREY *makes a rush for* PUTNAM. PROCTOR *lunges and holds him.*

Proctor: No, Giles!

Giles, *over* PROCTOR's *shoulder at* PUTNAM: I'll cut your throat, Putnam, I'll kill you yet!

Proctor, *forcing him into a chair:* Peace, Giles, peace. *Releasing him.* We'll prove ourselves. Now we will. *He starts to turn to* DANFORTH.

Giles: Say nothin' more, John. *Pointing at* DANFORTH: He's only playin' you! He means to hang us all!

MARY WARREN *bursts into sobs.*

Danforth: This is a court of law, Mister. I'll have no effrontery here!

Proctor: Forgive him, sir, for his old age. Peace, Giles, we'll prove it all now. *He lifts up* MARY's *chin.* You cannot weep, Mary. Remember the angel, what he say to the boy. Hold to it, now; there is your rock. MARY *quiets. He takes out a paper, and turns to* DANFORTH. This is Mary Warren's deposition. I—I would ask you remember, sir, while you read it, that until two week ago she were no different than the other children are today. *He is speaking reasonably, restraining all his fears, his anger, his anxiety.* You saw her scream, she howled, she swore familiar spirits choked her; she even testified that Satan, in the form of women now in jail, tried to win her soul away, and then when she refused—

Danforth: We know all this.

Proctor: Aye, sir. She swears now that she never saw Satan; not any spirit, vague or clear, that Satan may have sent to hurt her. And she declares her friends are lying now.

PROCTOR *starts to hand* DANFORTH *the deposition,*

and HALE *comes up to* DANFORTH *in a trembling state.*

Hale: Excellency, a moment. I think this goes to the heart of the matter.

Danforth, *with deep misgivings:* It surely does.

Hale: I cannot say he is an honest man; I know him little. But in all justice, sir, a claim so weighty cannot be argued by a farmer. In God's name, sir, stop here; send him home and let him come again with a lawyer—

Danforth, *patiently:* Now look you, Mr. Hale—

Hale: Excellency, I have signed seventy-two death warrants; I am a minister of the Lord, and I dare not take a life without there be a proof so immaculate no slightest qualm of conscience may doubt it.

Danforth: Mr. Hale, you surely do not doubt my justice.

Hale: I have this morning signed away the soul of Rebecca Nurse, Your Honor. I'll not conceal it, my hand shakes yet as with a wound! I pray you, sir, *this* argument let lawyers present to you.

Danforth: Mr. Hale, believe me; for a man of such terrible learning you are most bewildered—I hope you will forgive me. I have been thirty-two year at the bar, sir, and I should be confounded were I called upon to defend these people. Let you consider, now— *To* PROCTOR *and the others:* And I bid you all do likewise. In an ordinary crime, how does one defend the accused? One calls up witnesses to prove his innocence. But witchcraft is *ipso facto,*[4] on its face and by its nature, an invisible crime, is it not? Therefore, who may possibly be witness to it? The witch and the victim. None other. Now we cannot hope the witch will accuse herself; granted? Therefore, we must rely upon her victims—and they do testify, the children certainly do testify. As for the witches, none will deny that we are most eager for all their confessions. Therefore, what is left for a lawyer to bring out? I think I have made my point. Have I not?

Hale: But this child claims the girls are not truthful, and if they are not—

Danforth: That is precisely what I am about to consider, sir. What more may you ask of me? Unless you doubt my probity?[5]

4. *ipso facto:* by that very fact.
5. *probity:* integrity.

Hale, *defeated:* I surely do not, sir. Let you consider it, then.

Danforth: And let you put your heart to rest. Her deposition, Mr. Proctor.

PROCTOR *hands it to him.* HATHORNE *rises, goes beside* DANFORTH, *and starts reading.* PARRIS *comes to his other side.* DANFORTH *looks at* JOHN PROCTOR, *then proceeds to read.* HALE *gets up, finds position near the judge, reads too.* PROCTOR *glances at* GILES. FRANCIS *prays silently, hands pressed together.* CHEEVER *waits placidly, the sublime official, dutiful.* MARY WARREN *sobs once.* JOHN PROCTOR *touches her head reassuringly. Presently* DANFORTH *lifts his eyes, stands up, takes out a kerchief and blows his nose. The others stand aside as he moves in thought toward the window.*

Parris, *hardly able to contain his anger and fear:* I should like to question—

Danforth—*his first real outburst, in which his contempt for* PARRIS *is clear:* Mr. Parris, I bid you be silent! *He stands in silence, looking out the window. Now, having established that he will set the gait:* Mr. Cheever, will you go into the court and bring the children here? CHEEVER *gets up and goes out upstage.* DANFORTH *now turns to* MARY. Mary Warren, how came you to this turnabout? Has Mr. Proctor threatened you for this deposition?

Mary Warren: No, sir.

Danforth: Has he ever threatened you?

Mary Warren, *weaker:* No, sir.

Danforth, *sensing a weakening:* Has he threatened you?

Mary Warren: No, sir.

Danforth: Then you tell me that you sat in my court, callously lying, when you knew that people would hang by your evidence? *She does not answer.* Answer me!

Mary Warren, *almost inaudibly:* I did, sir.

Danforth: How were you instructed in your life? Do you not know that God damns all liars? *She cannot speak.* Or is it now that you lie?

Mary Warren: No, sir—I am with God now.

Danforth: You are with God now.

Mary Warren: Aye, sir.

Danforth, *containing himself:* I will tell you this—you are either lying now, or you were lying in the court, and in either case you have commit-

ted perjury and you will go to jail for it. You cannot lightly say you lied, Mary. Do you know that?

Mary Warren: I cannot lie no more. I am with God, I am with God.

But she breaks into sobs at the thought of it, and the right door opens, and enter SUSANNA WALCOTT, MERCY LEWIS, BETTY PARRIS, *and finally* ABIGAIL. CHEEVER *comes to* DANFORTH.

Cheever: Ruth Putnam's not in the court, sir, nor the other children.

Danforth: These will be sufficient. Sit you down, children. *Silently they sit.* Your friend, Mary Warren, has given us a deposition. In which she swears that she never saw familiar spirits, apparitions, nor any manifest of the Devil. She claims as well that none of you have seen these things either. *Slight pause.* Now, children, this is a court of law. The law, based upon the Bible, and the Bible, writ by Almighty God, forbid the practice of witchcraft, and describe death as the penalty thereof. But likewise, children, the law and Bible damn all bearers of false witness. *Slight pause.* Now then. It does not escape me that this deposition may be devised to blind us; it may well be that Mary Warren has been conquered by Satan, who sends her here to distract our sacred purpose. If so, her neck will break for it. But if she speak true, I bid you now drop your guile and confess your pretense, for a quick confession will go easier with you. *Pause.* Abigail Williams, rise. ABIGAIL *slowly rises.* Is there any truth in this?

Abigail: No, sir.

Danforth, *thinks, glances at* MARY, *then back to* ABIGAIL: Children, a very augur bit[6] will now be turned into your souls until your honesty is proved. Will either of you change your positions now, or do you force me to hard questioning?

Abigail: I have naught to change, sir. She lies.

Danforth, *to* MARY: You would still go on with this?

Mary Warren, *faintly:* Aye, sir.

Danforth, *turning to* ABIGAIL: A poppet were discovered in Mr. Proctor's house, stabbed by a needle. Mary Warren claims that you sat beside her in the court when she made it, and that you saw her make it and witnessed how she herself stuck her

needle into it for safe-keeping. What say you to that?

Abigail, *with a slight note of indignation:* It is a lie, sir.

Danforth, *after a slight pause:* While you worked for Mr. Proctor, did you see poppets in that house?

Abigail: Goody Proctor always kept poppets.

Proctor: Your Honor, my wife never kept no poppets. Mary Warren confesses it was her poppet.

Cheever: Your Excellency.

Danforth: Mr. Cheever.

Cheever: When I spoke with Goody Proctor in that house, she said she never kept no poppets. But she said she did keep poppets when she were a girl.

Proctor: She has not been a girl these fifteen years, Your Honor.

Hathorne: But a poppet will keep fifteen years, will it not?

Proctor: It will keep if it is kept, but Mary Warren swears she never saw no poppets in my house, nor anyone else.

Parris: Why could there not have been poppets hid where no one ever saw them?

Proctor, *furious:* There might also be a dragon with five legs in my house, but no one has ever seen it.

Parris: We are here, Your Honor, precisely to discover what no one has ever seen.

Proctor: Mr. Danforth, what profit this girl to turn herself about? What may Mary Warren gain but hard questioning and worse?

Danforth: You are charging Abigail Williams with a marvelous cool plot to murder, do you understand that?

Proctor: I do, sir. I believe she means to murder.

Danforth, *pointing at* ABIGAIL, *incredulously:* This child would murder your wife?

Proctor: It is not a child. Now hear me, sir. In the sight of the congregation she were twice this year put out of this meetin' house for laughter during prayer.

Danforth, *shocked, turning to* ABIGAIL: What's this? Laughter during—!

Parris: Excellency, she were under Tituba's power at that time, but she is solemn now.

Giles: Aye, now she is solemn and goes to hang people!

---

6. **augur bit:** drilling tool with pointed end and spiral grooves. (The conventional spelling is *auger.*)

Danforth: Quiet, man.

Hathorne: Surely it have no bearing on the question, sir. He charges contemplation of murder.

Danforth: Aye. *He studies* ABIGAIL *for a moment, then:* Continue, Mr. Proctor.

Proctor: Mary. Now tell the Governor how you danced in the woods.

Parris, *instantly:* Excellency, since I come to Salem this man is blackening my name. He—

Danforth: In a moment, sir. *To* MARY WARREN, *sternly, and surprised:* What is this dancing?

Mary Warren: I— *She glances at* ABIGAIL, *who is staring down at her remorselessly. Then, appealing to* PROCTOR: Mr. Proctor—

Proctor, *taking it right up:* Abigail leads the girls to the woods, Your Honor, and they have danced there naked—

Parris: Your Honor, this—

Proctor, *at once:* Mr. Parris discovered them himself in the dead of night! There's the "child" she is!

Danforth—*it is growing into a nightmare, and he turns, astonished, to* PARRIS: Mr. Parris—

Parris: I can only say, sir, that I never found any of them naked, and this man is—

Danforth: But you discovered them dancing in the woods? *Eyes on* PARRIS, *he points at* ABIGAIL. Abigail?

Hale: Excellency, when I first arrived from Beverly, Mr. Parris told me that.

Danforth: Do you deny it, Mr. Parris?

Parris: I do not, sir, but I never saw any of them naked.

Danforth: But she have *danced?*

Parris, *unwillingly:* Aye, sir.

DANFORTH, *as though with new eyes, looks at* ABIGAIL.

Hathorne: Excellency, will you permit me? *He points at* MARY WARREN.

Danforth, *with great worry:* Pray, proceed.

Hathorne: You say you never saw no spirits, Mary, were never threatened or afflicted by any manifest of the Devil or the Devil's agents.

Mary Warren, *very faintly:* No, sir.

Hathorne, *with a gleam of victory:* And yet, when people accused of witchery confronted you in court, you would faint, saying their spirits came out of their bodies and choked you—

Mary Warren: That were pretense, sir.

Danforth: I cannot hear you.

Mary Warren: Pretense, sir.

Parris: But you did turn cold, did you not? I myself picked you up many times, and your skin were icy. Mr. Danforth, you—

Danforth: I saw that many times.

Proctor: She only pretended to faint, Your Excellency. They're all marvelous pretenders.

Hathorne: Then can she pretend to faint now?

Proctor: Now?

Parris: Why not? Now there are no spirits attacking her, for none in this room is accused of witchcraft. So let her turn herself cold now, let her pretend she is attacked now, let her faint. *He turns to* MARY WARREN. Faint!

Mary Warren: Faint?

Parris: Aye, faint. Prove to us how you pretended in the court so many times.

Mary Warren, *looking to* PROCTOR: I—cannot faint now, sir.

Proctor, *alarmed, quietly:* Can you not pretend it?

Mary Warren: I— *She looks about as though searching for the passion to faint.* I—have no *sense* of it now, I—

Danforth: Why? What is lacking now?

Mary Warren: I—cannot tell, sir, I—

Danforth: Might it be that here we have no afflicting spirit loose, but in the court there were some?

Mary Warren: I never saw no spirits.

Parris: Then see no spirits now, and prove to us that you can faint by your own will, as you claim.

Mary Warren, *stares, searching for the emotion of it, and then shakes her head:* I—cannot do it.

Parris: Then you will confess, will you not? It were attacking spirits made you faint!

Mary Warren: No, sir, I—

Parris: Your Excellency, this is a trick to blind the court!

Mary Warren: It's not a trick! *She stands.* I—I used to faint because I—I thought I saw spirits.

Danforth: *Thought* you saw them!

Mary Warren: But I did not, Your Honor.

Hathorne: How could you think you saw them unless you saw them?

Mary Warren: I—I cannot tell how, but I did. I—I heard the other girls screaming, and you, Your Honor, you seemed to believe them, and I— It were only sport in the beginning, sir, but then the whole world cried spirits, spirits, and I—I promise you, Mr. Danforth, I only thought I saw them but I did not.

DANFORTH *peers at her.*

Parris, *smiling, but nervous because* DANFORTH *seems to be struck by* MARY WARREN'*s story:* Surely Your Excellency is not taken by this simple lie.

Danforth, *turning worriedly to* ABIGAIL: Abigail. I bid you now search your heart and tell me this—and beware of it, child, to God every soul is precious and His vengeance is terrible on them that take life without cause. Is it possible, child, that the spirits you have seen are illusion only, some deception that may cross your mind when—

Abigail: Why, this—this—is a base question, sir.

Danforth: Child, I would have you consider it—

Abigail: I have been hurt, Mr. Danforth; I have seen my blood runnin' out! I have been near to murdered every day because I done my duty pointing out the Devil's people—and this is my reward? To be mistrusted, denied, questioned like a—

Danforth, *weakening:* Child, I do not mistrust you—

Abigail, *in an open threat:* Let *you* beware, Mr. Danforth. Think you to be so mighty that the power of Hell may not turn *your* wits? Beware of it! There is— *Suddenly, from an accusatory attitude, her face turns, looking into the air above—it is truly frightened.*

Danforth, *apprehensively:* What is it, child?

Abigail, *looking about in the air, clasping her arms about her as though cold:* I—I know not. A wind, a cold wind, has come. *Her eyes fall on* MARY WARREN.

Mary Warren, *terrified, pleading:* Abby!

Mercy Lewis, *shivering:* Your Honor, I freeze!

Proctor: They're pretending!

Hathorne, *touching* ABIGAIL*'s hand:* She is cold, Your Honor, touch her!

Mercy Lewis, *through chattering teeth:* Mary, do you send this shadow on me?

Mary Warren: Lord, save me!

Susanna Walcott: I freeze, I freeze!

Abigail, *shivering visibly:* It is a wind, a wind!

Mary Warren: Abby, don't do that!

"Do you witch her?"

Danforth, *himself engaged and entered by* ABIGAIL: Mary Warren, do you witch her? I say to you, do you send your spirit out?

With a hysterical cry MARY WARREN *starts to run.* PROCTOR *catches her.*

Mary Warren, *almost collapsing:* Let me go, Mr. Proctor, I cannot, I cannot—
Abigail, *crying to Heaven:* Oh, Heavenly Father, take away this shadow!

Without warning or hesitation, PROCTOR *leaps at* ABIGAIL *and, grabbing her by the hair, pulls her to her feet. She screams in pain.* DANFORTH, *astonished, cries,* "What are you about?" *and* HATHORNE *and* PARRIS *call,* "Take your hands off her!" *and out of it all comes* PROCTOR's *roaring voice.*

Proctor: How do you call Heaven! Whore! Whore!

HERRICK *breaks* PROCTOR *from her.*

Herrick: John!
Danforth: Man! Man, what do you—
Proctor, *breathless and in agony:* It is a whore!
Danforth, *dumfounded:* You charge—?
Abigail: Mr. Danforth, he is lying!
Proctor: Mark her! Now she'll suck a scream to stab me with, but—
Danforth: You will prove this! This will not pass!
Proctor, *trembling, his life collapsing about him:* I have known her, sir. I have known her.
Danforth: You—you are a lecher?
Francis, *horrified:* John, you cannot say such a—
Proctor: Oh, Francis, I wish you had some evil in you that you might know me! *To* DANFORTH: A man will not cast away his good name. You surely know that.
Danforth, *dumfounded:* In—in what time? In what place?
Proctor, *his voice about to break, and his shame great:* In the proper place—where my beasts are bedded. On the last night of my joy, some eight months past. She used to serve me in my house, sir. *He has to clamp his jaw to keep from weeping.* A man may think God sleeps, but God sees everything, I know it now. I beg you, sir, I beg you—see her what she is. My wife, my dear good wife, took this girl soon after, sir, and put her out on the highroad. And being what she is, a lump of vanity, sir— *He is being overcome.* Excellency, forgive me, forgive me. *Angrily against himself, he turns away from the Governor for a moment. Then, as though to cry out is his only means of speech left:* She thinks to dance with me on my wife's grave! And well she might, for I thought of her softly. God help me, I lusted, and there *is* a promise in such sweat. But it is a whore's vengeance, and you must see it; I set myself entirely in your hands. I know you must see it now.
Danforth, *blanched, in horror, turning to* ABIGAIL: You deny every scrap and tittle of this?
Abigail: If I must answer that, I will leave and I will not come back again!

DANFORTH *seems unsteady.*

Proctor: I have made a bell of my honor! I have rung the doom of my good name—you will believe me, Mr. Danforth! My wife is innocent, except she knew a whore when she saw one!
Abigail, *stepping up to* DANFORTH: What look do you give me? DANFORTH *cannot speak.* I'll not have such looks! *She turns and starts for the door.*
Danforth: You will remain where you are! HERRICK *steps into her path. She comes up short, fire in her eyes.* Mr. Parris, go into the court and bring Goodwife Proctor out.
Parris, *objecting:* Your Honor, this is all a—
Danforth, *sharply to* PARRIS: Bring her out! And tell her not one word of what's been spoken here. And let you knock before you enter. PARRIS *goes out.* Now we shall touch the bottom of this swamp. *To* PROCTOR: Your wife, you say, is an honest woman.
Proctor: In her life, sir, she have never lied. There are them that cannot sing, and them that cannot weep—my wife cannot lie. I have paid much to learn it, sir.
Danforth: And when she put this girl out of your house, she put her out for a harlot?
Proctor: Aye, sir.
Danforth: And knew her for a harlot?
Proctor: Aye, sir, she knew her for a harlot.
Danforth: Good then. *To* ABIGAIL: And if she tell me, child, it were for harlotry, may God spread His mercy on you! *There is a knock. He calls to the door:* Hold! *To* ABIGAIL: Turn your back. Turn your

back. *To* PROCTOR: Do likewise. *Both turn their backs*— ABIGAIL *with indignant slowness.* Now let neither of you turn to face Goody Proctor. No one in this room is to speak one word, or raise a gesture aye or nay. *He turns toward the door, calls:* Enter! *The door opens.* ELIZABETH *enters with* PARRIS. PARRIS *leaves her. She stands alone, her eyes looking for* PROCTOR. Mr. Cheever, report this testimony in all exactness. Are you ready?

Cheever: Ready, sir.

Danforth: Come here, woman. ELIZABETH *comes to him, glancing at* PROCTOR'*s back.* Look at me only, not at your husband. In my eyes only.

Elizabeth, *faintly:* Good, sir.

Danforth: We are given to understand that at one time you dismissed your servant, Abigail Williams.

Elizabeth: That is true, sir.

Danforth: For what cause did you dismiss her? *Slight pause. Then* ELIZABETH *tries to glance at* PROCTOR. You will look in my eyes only and not at your husband. The answer is in your memory and you need no help to give it to me. Why did you dismiss Abigail Williams?

Elizabeth, *not knowing what to say, sensing a situation, wetting her lips to stall for time:* She— dissatisfied me. *Pause.* And my husband.

Danforth: In what way dissatisfied you?

Elizabeth: She were— *She glances at* PROCTOR *for a cue.*

Danforth: Woman, look at me! ELIZABETH *does.* Were she slovenly? Lazy? What disturbance did she cause?

Elizabeth: Your Honor, I—in that time I were sick. And I—My husband is a good and righteous man. He is never drunk as some are, nor wastin' his time at the shovelboard, but always at his work. But in my sickness—you see, sir. I were a long time sick after my last baby, and I thought I saw my husband somewhat turning from me. And this girl— *She turns to* ABIGAIL.

Danforth: Look at me.

Elizabeth: Aye, sir. Abigail Williams— *She breaks off.*

Danforth: What of Abigail Williams?

Elizabeth: I came to think he fancied her. And so one night I lost my wits, I think, and put her out on the highroad.

Danforth: Your husband—did he indeed turn from you?

Elizabeth, *in agony:* My husband—is a goodly man, sir.

Danforth: Then he did not turn from you.

Elizabeth, *starting to glance at* PROCTOR: He—

Danforth, *reaches out and holds her face, then:* Look at me! To your own knowledge, has John Proctor ever committed the crime of lechery? *In a crisis of indecision she cannot speak.* Answer my question! Is your husband a lecher!

Elizabeth, *faintly:* No, sir.

Danforth: Remove her, Marshal.

Proctor: Elizabeth, tell the truth!

Danforth: She has spoken. Remove her!

Proctor, *crying out:* Elizabeth, I have confessed it!

Elizabeth: Oh, God! *The door closes behind her.*

Proctor: She only thought to save my name!

Hale: Excellency, it is a natural lie to tell; I beg you, stop now before another is condemned! I may shut my conscience to it no more—private vengeance is working through this testimony! From the beginning this man has struck me true. By my oath to Heaven, I believe him now, and I pray you call back his wife before we—

Danforth: She spoke nothing of lechery, and this man has lied!

Hale: I believe him! *Pointing at* ABIGAIL: This girl has always struck me false! She has—

ABIGAIL, *with a weird, wild, chilling cry, screams up to the ceiling.*

Abigail: You will not! Begone! Begone, I say!

Danforth: What is it, child? *But* ABIGAIL, *pointing with fear, is now raising up her frightened eyes, her awed face, toward the ceiling—the girls are doing the same—and now* HATHORNE, HALE, PUTNAM, CHEEVER, HERRICK, *and* DANFORTH *do the same.* What's there? *He lowers his eyes from the ceiling, and now he is frightened; there is real tension in his voice.* Child! *She is transfixed—with all the girls, she is whimpering open-mouthed, agape at the ceiling.* Girls! Why do you—?

Mercy Lewis, *pointing:* It's on the beam! Behind the rafter!

Danforth, *looking up:* Where!

Abigail: Why—? *She gulps.* Why do you come, yellow bird?

Proctor: Where's a bird? I see no bird!

Abigail, *to the ceiling:* My face? My face?

Proctor: Mr. Hale—

Danforth: Be quiet!

Proctor, *to* HALE: Do you see a bird?

Danforth: Be quiet!!

Abigail, *to the ceiling, in a genuine conversation with the "bird," as though trying to talk it out of attacking her:* But God made my face; you cannot want to tear my face. Envy is a deadly sin, Mary.

Mary Warren, *on her feet with a spring, and horrified, pleading:* Abby!

Abigail, *unperturbed, continuing to the "bird":* Oh, Mary, this is a black art to change your shape. No, I cannot, I cannot stop my mouth; it's God's work I do.

Mary Warren: Abby, I'm *here!*

Proctor, *frantically:* They're pretending, Mr. Danforth!

Abigail—*now she takes a backward step, as though in fear the bird will swoop down momentarily:* Oh, please, Mary! Don't come down.

Susanna Walcott: Her claws, she's stretching her claws!

Proctor: Lies, lies.

Abigail, *backing further, eyes still fixed above:* Mary, please don't hurt me!

Mary Warren, *to* DANFORTH: I'm not hurting her!

Danforth, *to* MARY WARREN: Why does she see this vision?

Mary Warren: She sees nothin'!

Abigail, *now staring full front as though hypnotized, and mimicking the exact tone of* MARY WARREN*'s cry:* She sees nothin'!

Mary Warren, *pleading:* Abby, you mustn't!

Abigail and All the Girls, *all transfixed:* Abby, you mustn't!

Mary Warren, *to all the girls:* I'm here, I'm here!

Girls: I'm here, I'm here!

Danforth, *horrified:* Mary Warren! Draw back your spirit out of them!

Mary Warren: Mr. Danforth!

Girls, *cutting her off:* Mr. Danforth!

Danforth: Have you compacted with the Devil? Have you?

Mary Warren: Never, never!

Girls: Never, never!

Danforth, *growing hysterical:* Why can they only repeat you?

Proctor: Give me a whip—I'll stop it!

Mary Warren: They're sporting. They—!

Girls: They're sporting!

Mary Warren, *turning on them all hysterically and stamping her feet:* Abby, stop it!

Girls, *stamping their feet:* Abby, stop it!

Mary Warren: Stop it!

Girls: Stop it!

Mary Warren, *screaming it out at the top of her lungs, and raising her fists:* Stop it!!

Girls, *raising their fists:* Stop it!!

MARY WARREN, *utterly confounded, and becoming overwhelmed by* ABIGAIL*'s—and the girls'—utter conviction, starts to whimper, hands half raised, powerless, and all the girls begin whimpering exactly as she does.*

Danforth: A little while ago you were afflicted. Now it seems you afflict others; where did you find this power?

Mary Warren, *staring at* ABIGAIL: I—have no power.

Girls: I have no power.

Proctor: They're gulling you, Mister!

Danforth: Why did you turn about this past two weeks? You have seen the Devil, have you not?

Hale, *indicating* ABIGAIL *and the girls:* You cannot believe them!

Mary Warren: I—

Proctor, *sensing her weakening:* Mary, God damns all liars!

Danforth, *pounding it into her:* You have seen the Devil, you have made compact with Lucifer, have you not?

Proctor: God damns liars, Mary!

MARY *utters something unintelligible, staring at* ABIGAIL, *who keeps watching the "bird" above.*

Danforth: I cannot hear you. What do you say? MARY *utters again unintelligibly.* You will confess yourself or you will hang! *He turns her roughly to face him.* Do you know who I am? I say you will hang if you do not open with me!

Proctor: Mary, remember the angel Raphael—do that which is good and—

Abigail, *pointing upward:* The wings! Her wings are spreading! Mary, please, don't, don't—!

Hale: I see nothing, Your Honor!

Danforth: Do you confess this power! *He is an inch from her face.* Speak!

Abigail: She's going to come down! She's walking the beam!

Danforth: Will you speak!

Mary Warren, *staring in horror:* I cannot!

Girls: I cannot!

Parris: Cast the Devil out! Look him in the face! Trample him! We'll save you, Mary, only stand fast against him and—

Abigail, *looking up:* Look out! She's coming down!

She and all the girls run to one wall, shielding their eyes. And now, as though cornered, they let out a gigantic scream, and MARY, *as though infected, opens her mouth and screams with them. Gradually* ABIGAIL *and the girls leave off, until only* MARY *is left there, staring up at the "bird," screaming madly. All watch her, horrified by this evident fit.* PROCTOR *strides to her.*

Proctor: Mary, tell the Governor what they— *He has hardly got a word out, when, seeing him coming for her, she rushes out of his reach, screaming in horror.*

Mary Warren: Don't touch me—don't touch me! *At which the girls halt at the door.*

Proctor, *astonished:* Mary!

Mary Warren, *pointing at* PROCTOR: You're the Devil's man!

He is stopped in his tracks.

Parris: Praise God!

Girls: Praise God!

Proctor, *numbed:* Mary, how—?

Mary Warren: I'll not hang with you! I love God, I love God.

Danforth, *to* MARY: He bid you do the Devil's work?

Mary Warren, *hysterically, indicating* PROCTOR: He come at me by night and every day to sign, to sign, to—

Danforth: Sign what?

Parris: The Devil's book? He come with a book?

Mary Warren, *hysterically, pointing at* PROCTOR, *fearful of him:* My name, he want my name. "I'll murder you," he says, "if my wife hangs! We must go and overthrow the court," he says!

DANFORTH's *head jerks toward* PROCTOR, *shock and horror in his face.*

Proctor, *turning, appealing to* HALE: Mr. Hale!

Mary Warren, *her sobs beginning:* He wake me every night, his eyes were like coals and his fingers claw my neck, and I sign, I sign . . .

Hale: Excellency, this child's gone wild!

Proctor, *as* DANFORTH's *wide eyes pour on him:* Mary, Mary!

Mary Warren, *screaming at him:* No, I love God; I go your way no more. I love God, I bless God. *Sobbing, she rushes to* ABIGAIL. Abby, Abby, I'll never hurt you more! *They all watch, as* ABIGAIL, *out of her infinite charity, reaches out and draws the sobbing* MARY *to her, and then looks up to* DANFORTH.

Danforth, *to* PROCTOR: What are you? PROCTOR *is beyond speech in his anger.* You are combined with anti-Christ,[7] are you not? I have seen your power; you will not deny it! What say you, Mister?

Hale: Excellency—

Danforth: I will have nothing from you, Mr. Hale! *To* PROCTOR: Will you confess yourself befouled with Hell, or do you keep that black allegiance yet? What say you?

Proctor, *his mind wild, breathless:* I say—I say—God is dead!

Parris: Hear it, hear it!

Proctor, *laughs insanely, then:* A fire, a fire is burning! I hear the boot of Lucifer, I see his filthy face! And it is my face, and yours, Danforth! For them that quail to bring men out of ignorance, as I have quailed, and as you quail now when you know in all your black hearts that this be fraud— God damns our kind especially, and we will burn, we will burn together!

Danforth: Marshal! Take him and Corey with him to the jail!

Hale, *starting across to the door:* I denounce these proceedings!

Proctor: You are pulling Heaven down and raising up a whore!

Hale: I denounce these proceedings, I quit this court! *He slams the door to the outside behind him.*

Danforth, *calling to him in a fury:* Mr. Hale! Mr. Hale!

The curtain falls

7. **anti-Christ:** in the Bible, Christ's great enemy, expected to spread evil before Christ conquers him and the world ends (1 John 2:18).

MAKING MEANINGS

Act Three

First Thoughts

1. Identify one phrase or expression in Act Three that made a strong impression on you. Tell why the phrase affected you.

Shaping Interpretations

2. Danforth believes that he is living in a "sharp time" in which good and evil are not "mixed" in people, but are easily distinguishable. Do you agree with his viewpoint? Why or why not?

Reading Check

a. How does Mary respond when Danforth asks her to explain the "crying out"?

b. What does Danforth do with the list of people supporting Rebecca and Martha?

c. What test does Danforth devise to determine why Abigail was put out of the Proctor house?

d. What is Abigail's "vision"?

3. Serious dramatic works often include **comic relief**—the inclusion of a comic episode or element to relieve emotional tension. In Shakespeare's tragedies, comic relief is often provided by the absurd wisdom of a clown or fool (such as the gravedigger in *Hamlet*). Do you think Giles Corey's eccentric and earthy dialogue provides **comic relief** in *The Crucible?* Support your answer with specific examples from the play.

4. What does Hale mean when he asks if every defense is an attack upon the court? How has Hale changed by the end of this act? Use your reading notes to help explain the transformation of this **dynamic** character.

5. When John reveals his true relationship to Abigail, what do you think he also reveals about his character and his **motivation**?

Extending the Text

6. In sports, in politics, and in war, people often *demonize* their opponents—that is, they portray their enemies as incarnations of evil. Can you think of examples? Why do you think people do this? What effect do you think such behavior has on society as a whole?

Act Four

A cell in Salem jail, that fall.

At the back is a high barred window; near it, a great, heavy door. Along the walls are two benches.

The place is in darkness but for the moonlight seeping through the bars. It appears empty. Presently footsteps are heard coming down a corridor beyond the wall, keys rattle, and the door swings open. MARSHAL HERRICK *enters with a lantern.*

He is nearly drunk, and heavy-footed. He goes to a bench and nudges a bundle of rags lying on it.

Herrick: Sarah, wake up! Sarah Good! *He then crosses to the other bench.*

Sarah Good, *rising in her rags:* Oh, Majesty! Comin', comin'! Tituba, he's here, His Majesty's come!

Herrick: Go to the north cell; this place is wanted now. *He hangs his lantern on the wall.* TITUBA *sits up.*

Tituba: That don't look to me like His Majesty; look to me like the marshal.

Herrick, *taking out a flask:* Get along with you now, clear this place. *He drinks, and* SARAH GOOD *comes and peers up into his face.*

Sarah Good: Oh, is it you, Marshal! I thought sure you be the Devil comin' for us. Could I have a sip of cider for me goin'-away?

Herrick, *handing her the flask:* And where are you off to, Sarah?

Tituba, *as* SARAH *drinks:* We goin' to Barbados, soon the Devil gits here with the feathers and the wings.

Herrick: Oh? A happy voyage to you.

Sarah Good: A pair of bluebirds wingin' southerly, the two of us! Oh, it be a grand transformation, Marshal! *She raises the flask to drink again.*

Herrick, *taking the flask from her lips:* You'd best give me that or you'll never rise off the ground. Come along now.

Tituba: I'll speak to him for you, if you desires to come along, Marshal.

Herrick: I'd not refuse it, Tituba; it's the proper morning to fly into Hell.

Tituba: Oh, it be no Hell in Barbados. Devil, him be pleasureman in Barbados, him be singin' and dancin' in Barbados. It's you folks—you riles him up 'round here; it be too cold 'round here for that Old Boy. He freeze his soul in Massachusetts, but in Barbados he just as sweet and— *A bellowing cow is heard, and* TITUBA *leaps up and calls to the window:* Aye, sir! That's him, Sarah!

Sarah Good: I'm here, Majesty! *They hurriedly pick up their rags as* HOPKINS, *a guard, enters.*

Hopkins: The Deputy Governor's arrived.

Herrick, *grabbing* TITUBA: Come along, come along.

Tituba, *resisting him:* No, he comin' for me. I goin' home!

Herrick, *pulling her to the door:* That's not Satan, just a poor old cow with a hatful of milk. Come along now, out with you!

Tituba, *calling to the window:* Take me home, Devil! Take me home!

Sarah Good, *following the shouting* TITUBA *out:* Tell him I'm goin', Tituba! Now you tell him Sarah Good is goin' too!

In the corridor outside TITUBA *calls on—"Take me home, Devil; Devil take me home!" and* HOPKINS' *voice orders her to move on.* HERRICK *returns and begins to push old rags and straw into a corner. Hearing footsteps, he turns, and enter* DANFORTH *and* JUDGE HATHORNE. *They are in greatcoats and wear hats against the bitter cold. They are followed in by* CHEEVER, *who carries a dispatch case and a flat wooden box containing his writing materials.*

Herrick: Good morning, Excellency.

Danforth: Where is Mr. Parris?

Herrick: I'll fetch him. *He starts for the door.*

Danforth: Marshal. HERRICK *stops.* When did Reverend Hale arrive?

Herrick: It were toward midnight, I think.

Danforth, *suspiciously:* What is he about here?

Herrick: He goes among them that will hang, sir. And he prays with them. He sits with Goody Nurse now. And Mr. Parris with him.

Danforth: Indeed. That man have no authority to enter here, Marshal. Why have you let him in?

Herrick: Why, Mr. Parris command me, sir. I cannot deny him.

Danforth: Are you drunk, Marshal?

Herrick: No, sir; it is a bitter night, and I have no fire here.

Danforth, *containing his anger:* Fetch Mr. Parris.

Herrick: Aye, sir.

Danforth: There is a prodigious stench in this place.

Herrick: I have only now cleared the people out for you.

Danforth: Beware hard drink, Marshal.

Herrick: Aye, sir. *He waits an instant for further orders. But* DANFORTH, *in dissatisfaction, turns his back on him, and* HERRICK *goes out. There is a pause.* DANFORTH *stands in thought.*

Hathorne: Let you question Hale, Excellency; I should not be surprised he have been preaching in Andover lately.

Danforth: We'll come to that; speak nothing of Andover. Parris prays with him. That's strange. *He blows on his hands, moves toward the window, and looks out.*

Hathorne: Excellency, I wonder if it be wise to let Mr. Parris so continuously with the prisoners. DANFORTH *turns to him, interested.* I think, sometimes, the man has a mad look these days.

Danforth: Mad?

Hathorne: I met him yesterday coming out of his house, and I bid him good morning—and he wept and went his way. I think it is not well the village sees him so unsteady.

Danforth: Perhaps he have some sorrow.

Cheever, *stamping his feet against the cold:* I think it be the cows, sir.

Danforth: Cows?

Cheever: There be so many cows wanderin' the highroads, now their masters are in the jails, and much disagreement who they will belong to now. I know Mr. Parris be arguin' with farmers all yesterday—there is great contention, sir, about the cows. Contention make him weep, sir; it were always a man that weep for contention. *He turns, as do* HATHORNE *and* DANFORTH, *hearing someone coming up the corridor.* DANFORTH *raises his head as* PARRIS *enters. He is gaunt, frightened, and sweating in his greatcoat.*

Parris, *to* DANFORTH, *instantly:* Oh, good morning, sir, thank you for coming, I beg your pardon wakin' you so early. Good morning, Judge Hathorne.

Danforth: Reverend Hale have no right to enter this—

Parris: Excellency, a moment. *He hurries back and shuts the door.*

Hathorne: Do you leave him alone with the prisoners?

Danforth: What's his business here?

Parris, *prayerfully holding up his hands:* Excellency, hear me. It is a providence. Reverend Hale has returned to bring Rebecca Nurse to God.

Danforth, *surprised:* He bids her confess?

Parris, *sitting:* Hear me. Rebecca have not given me a word this three month since she came. Now she sits with him, and her sister and Martha Corey and two or three others, and he pleads with them, confess their crimes and save their lives.

Danforth: Why—this is indeed a providence. And they soften, they soften?

Parris: Not yet, not yet. But I thought to summon you, sir, that we might think on whether it be not wise, to— *He dares not say it.* I had thought to put a question, sir, and I hope you will not—

Danforth: Mr. Parris, be plain, what troubles you?

Parris: There is news, sir, that the court—the court must reckon with. My niece, sir, my niece—I believe she has vanished.

Danforth: Vanished!

Parris: I had thought to advise you of it earlier in the week, but—

Danforth: Why? How long is she gone?

Parris: This be the third night. You see, sir, she told me she would stay a night with Mercy Lewis. And next day, when she does not return, I send to Mr. Lewis to inquire. Mercy told him she would sleep in *my* house for a night.

Danforth: They are both gone?!

Parris, *in fear of him:* They are, sir.

Danforth, *alarmed:* I will send a party for them. Where may they be?

Parris: Excellency, I think they be aboard a ship. DANFORTH *stands agape.* My daughter tells me how she heard them speaking of ships last week, and tonight I discover my—my strongbox is broke into. *He presses his fingers against his eyes to keep back tears.*

Hathorne, *astonished:* She have robbed you?

Parris: Thirty-one pound is gone. I am penniless. *He covers his face and sobs.*

Danforth: Mr. Parris, you are a brainless man! *He walks in thought, deeply worried.*

Parris: Excellency, it profit nothing you should

blame me. I cannot think they would run off except they fear to keep in Salem any more. *He is pleading.* Mark it, sir, Abigail had close knowledge of the town, and since the news of Andover has broken here—

Danforth: Andover is remedied. The court returns there on Friday, and will resume examinations.

Parris: I am sure of it, sir. But the rumor here speaks rebellion in Andover, and it—

Danforth: There is no rebellion in Andover!

Parris: I tell you what is said here, sir. Andover has thrown out the court, they say, and will have no part of witchcraft. There be a faction here, feeding on that news, and I tell you true, sir, I fear there will be riot here.

Hathorne: Riot! Why at every execution I have seen naught but high satisfaction in the town.

Parris: Judge Hathorne—it were another sort that hanged till now. Rebecca Nurse is no Bridget that lived three year with Bishop before she married him. John Proctor is not Isaac Ward that drank his family to ruin. *To* DANFORTH: I would to God it were not so, Excellency, but these people have great weight yet in the town. Let Rebecca stand upon the gibbet[1] and send up some righteous prayer, and I fear she'll wake a vengeance on you.

Hathorne: Excellency, she is condemned a witch. The court have—

Danforth, *in deep concern, raising a hand to* HATHORNE: Pray you. *To* PARRIS: How do you propose, then?

Parris: Excellency, I would postpone these hangin's for a time.

Danforth: There will be no postponement.

Parris: Now Mr. Hale's returned, there is hope, I think—for if he bring even one of these to God, that confession surely damns the others in the public eye, and none may doubt more that they are all linked to Hell. This way, unconfessed and claiming innocence, doubts are multiplied, many honest people will weep for them, and our good purpose is lost in their tears.

Danforth, *after thinking a moment, then going to* CHEEVER: Give me the list.

---

1. **gibbet** (jib′it): gallows, or structure from which a person is executed by hanging.

CHEEVER *opens the dispatch case, searches.*

Parris: It cannot be forgot, sir, that when I summoned the congregation for John Proctor's excommunication there were hardly thirty people come to hear it. That speak a discontent, I think, and—

Danforth, *studying the list:* There will be no postponement.

Parris: Excellency—

Danforth: Now, sir—which of these in your opinion may be brought to God? I will myself strive with him till dawn. *He hands the list to* PARRIS, *who merely glances at it.*

Parris: There is not sufficient time till dawn.

Danforth: I shall do my utmost. Which of them do you have hope for?

Parris, *not even glancing at the list now, and in a quavering voice, quietly:* Excellency—a dagger— *He chokes up.*

Danforth: What do you say?

Parris: Tonight, when I open my door to leave my house—a dagger clattered to the ground. *Silence.* DANFORTH *absorbs this. Now* PARRIS *cries out:* You cannot hang this sort. There is danger for me. I dare not step outside at night!

REVEREND HALE *enters. They look at him for an instant in silence. He is steeped in sorrow, exhausted, and more direct than he ever was.*

Danforth: Accept my congratulations, Reverend Hale; we are gladdened to see you returned to your good work.

Hale, *coming to* DANFORTH *now:* You must pardon them. They will not budge.

HERRICK *enters, waits.*

Danforth, *conciliatory:* You misunderstand, sir; I cannot pardon these when twelve are already hanged for the same crime. It is not just.

Parris, *with failing heart:* Rebecca will not confess?

Hale: The sun will rise in a few minutes. Excellency, I must have more time.

Danforth: Now hear me, and beguile yourselves no more. I will not receive a single plea for pardon or postponement. Them that will not confess will hang. Twelve are already executed; the names of

these seven are given out, and the village expects to see them die this morning. Postponement now speaks a floundering on my part; reprieve or pardon must cast doubt upon the guilt of them that died till now. While I speak God's law, I will not crack its voice with whimpering. If retaliation is your fear, know this—I should hang ten thousand that dared to rise against the law, and an ocean of salt tears could not melt the resolution of the statutes. Now draw yourselves up like men and help me, as you are bound by Heaven to do. Have you spoken with them all, Mr. Hale?

Hale: All but Proctor. He is in the dungeon.

Danforth, *to* HERRICK: What's Proctor's way now?

Herrick: He sits like some great bird; you'd not know he lived except he will take food from time to time.

Danforth, *after thinking a moment:* His wife—his wife must be well on with child now.

Herrick: She is, sir.

Danforth: What think you, Mr. Parris? You have closer knowledge of this man; might her presence soften him?

Parris: It is possible, sir. He have not laid eyes on her these three months. I should summon her.

Danforth, *to* HERRICK: Is he yet adamant? Has he struck at you again?

Herrick: He cannot, sir, he is chained to the wall now.

Danforth, *after thinking on it:* Fetch Goody Proctor to me. Then let you bring him up.

Herrick: Aye, sir. HERRICK *goes. There is silence.*

Hale: Excellency, if you postpone a week and publish to the town that you are striving for their confessions, that speak mercy on your part, not faltering.

Danforth: Mr. Hale, as God have not empowered me like Joshua to stop this sun from rising,[2] so I cannot withhold from them the perfection of their punishment.

Hale, *harder now:* If you think God wills you to raise rebellion, Mr. Danforth, you are mistaken!

Danforth, *instantly:* You have heard rebellion spoken in the town?

---

2. Joshua . . . rising: in the Bible, Joshua, the successor of Moses, commands the sun and moon to stand still while his people take vengeance on their enemies.

Hale: Excellency, there are orphans wandering from house to house; abandoned cattle bellow on the highroads, the stink of rotting crops hangs everywhere, and no man knows when the harlots' cry will end his life—and you wonder yet if rebellion's spoke? Better you should marvel how they do not burn your province!

Danforth: Mr. Hale, have you preached in Andover this month?

Hale: Thank God they have no need of me in Andover.

Danforth: You baffle me, sir. Why have you returned here?

Hale: Why, it is all simple. I come to do the Devil's work. I come to counsel Christians they should belie themselves. *His sarcasm collapses.* There is blood on my head! Can you not see the blood on my head!!

Parris: Hush! *For he has heard footsteps. They all face the door.* HERRICK *enters with* ELIZABETH. *Her wrists are linked by heavy chain, which* HERRICK *now removes. Her clothes are dirty; her face is pale and gaunt.* HERRICK *goes out.*

Danforth, *very politely:* Goody Proctor. *She is silent.* I hope you are hearty?

Elizabeth, *as a warning reminder:* I am yet six month before my time.

Danforth: Pray be at your ease, we come not for your life. We—*uncertain how to plead, for he is not accustomed to it.* Mr. Hale, will you speak with the woman?

Hale: Goody Proctor, your husband is marked to hang this morning.

Pause.

Elizabeth, *quietly:* I have heard it.

Hale: You know, do you not, that I have no connection with the court? *She seems to doubt it.* I come of my own, Goody Proctor. I would save your husband's life, for if he is taken I count myself his murderer. Do you understand me?

Elizabeth: What do you want of me?

Hale: Goody Proctor, I have gone this three month like our Lord into the wilderness. I have sought a Christian way, for damnation's doubled on a minister who counsels men to lie.

Hathorne: It is no lie, you cannot speak of lies.

Hale: It is a lie! They are innocent!

Danforth: I'll hear no more of that!

Hale, *continuing to* ELIZABETH: Let you not mistake your duty as I mistook my own. I came into this village like a bridegroom to his beloved, bearing gifts of high religion; the very crowns of holy law I brought, and what I touched with my bright confidence, it died; and where I turned the eye of my great faith, blood flowed up. Beware, Goody Proctor—cleave to no faith when faith brings blood. It is mistaken law that leads you to sacrifice. Life, woman, life is God's most precious gift; no principle, however glorious, may justify the taking of it. I beg you, woman, prevail upon your husband to confess. Let him give his lie. Quail not before God's judgment in this, for it may well be God damns a liar less than he that throws his life away for pride. Will you plead with him? I cannot think he will listen to another.

Elizabeth, *quietly:* I think that be the Devil's argument.

Hale, *with a climactic desperation:* Woman, before the laws of God we are as swine! We cannot read His will!

Elizabeth: I cannot dispute with you, sir; I lack learning for it.

Danforth, *going to her:* Goody Proctor, you are not summoned here for disputation. Be there no wifely tenderness within you? He will die with the sunrise. Your husband. Do you understand it? *She only looks at him.* What say you? Will you contend with him? *She is silent.* Are you stone? I tell you true, woman, had I no other proof of your unnatural life, your dry eyes now would be sufficient evidence that you delivered up your soul to Hell! A very ape would weep at such calamity! Have the Devil dried up any tear of pity in you? *She is silent.* Take her out. It profit nothing she should speak to him!

Elizabeth, *quietly:* Let me speak with him, Excellency.

Parris, *with hope:* You'll strive with him? *She hesitates.*

Danforth: Will you plead for his confession or will you not?

Elizabeth: I promise nothing. Let me speak with him.

A sound—the sibilance of dragging feet on stone. They turn. A pause. HERRICK *enters with* JOHN PROCTOR. *His wrists are chained. He is an-other man, bearded, filthy, his eyes misty as though webs had overgrown them. He halts inside the doorway, his eye caught by the sight of* ELIZABETH. *The emotion flowing between them prevents anyone from speaking for an instant. Now* HALE, *visibly affected, goes to* DANFORTH *and speaks quietly.*

Hale: Pray, leave them, Excellency.

Danforth, *pressing* HALE *impatiently aside:* Mr. Proctor, you have been notified, have you not? PROCTOR *is silent, staring at* ELIZABETH. I see light in the sky, Mister; let you counsel with your wife, and may God help you turn your back on Hell. PROCTOR *is silent, staring at* ELIZABETH.

Hale, *quietly:* Excellency, let—

DANFORTH *brushes past* HALE *and walks out.* HALE *follows.* CHEEVER *stands and follows,* HATHORNE *behind.* HERRICK *goes.* PARRIS, *from a safe distance, offers:*

Parris: If you desire a cup of cider, Mr. Proctor, I am sure I— PROCTOR *turns an icy stare at him, and he breaks off.* PARRIS *raises his palms toward* PROCTOR. God lead you now. PARRIS *goes out.*

Alone. PROCTOR *walks to her, halts. It is as though they stood in a spinning world. It is beyond sorrow, above it. He reaches out his hand as though toward an embodiment not quite real, and as he touches her, a strange soft sound, half laughter, half amazement, comes from his throat. He pats her hand. She covers his hand with hers. And then, weak, he sits. Then she sits, facing him.*

Proctor: The child?

Elizabeth: It grows.

Proctor: There is no word of the boys?

Elizabeth: They're well. Rebecca's Samuel keeps them.

Proctor: You have not seen them?

Elizabeth: I have not. *She catches a weakening in herself and downs it.*

Proctor: You are a—marvel, Elizabeth.

Elizabeth: You—have been tortured?

Proctor: Aye. *Pause. She will not let herself be drowned in the sea that threatens her.* They come for my life now.

Elizabeth: I know it.

Pause.

Proctor: None—have yet confessed?

Elizabeth: There be many confessed.

Proctor: Who are they?

Elizabeth: There be a hundred or more, they say. Goody Ballard is one; Isaiah Goodkind is one. There be many.

Proctor: Rebecca?

Elizabeth: Not Rebecca. She is one foot in Heaven now; naught may hurt her more.

Proctor: And Giles?

Elizabeth: You have not heard of it?

Proctor: I hear nothin', where I am kept.

Elizabeth: Giles is dead.

He looks at her incredulously.

Proctor: When were he hanged?

Elizabeth, *quietly, factually:* He were not hanged. He would not answer aye or nay to his indictment; for if he denied the charge they'd hang him surely, and auction out his property. So he stand mute, and died Christian under the law. And so his sons will have his farm. It is the law, for he could not be condemned a wizard without he answer the indictment, aye or nay.

Proctor: Then how does he die?

Elizabeth, *gently:* They press him, John.

Proctor: Press?

Elizabeth: Great stones they lay upon his chest until he plead aye or nay. *With a tender smile for the old man:* They say he give them but two words. "More weight," he says. And died.

Proctor, *numbed—a thread to weave into his agony:* "More weight."

Elizabeth: Aye. It were a fearsome man, Giles Corey.

Pause.

Proctor, *with great force of will, but not quite looking at her:* I have been thinking I would confess to them, Elizabeth. *She shows nothing.* What say you? If I give them that?

Elizabeth: I cannot judge you, John.

Pause.

Proctor, *simply—a pure question:* What would you have me do?

Elizabeth: As you will, I would have it. *Slight pause.* I want you living, John. That's sure.

Proctor—*he pauses, then with a flailing of hope:* Giles' wife? Have she confessed?

Elizabeth: She will not.

Pause.

Proctor: It is a pretense, Elizabeth.

Elizabeth: What is?

Proctor: I cannot mount the gibbet like a saint. It is a fraud. I am not that man. *She is silent.* My honesty is broke, Elizabeth; I am no good man. Nothing's spoiled by giving them this lie that were not rotten long before.

Elizabeth: And yet you've not confessed till now. That speak goodness in you.

Proctor: Spite only keeps me silent. It is hard to give a lie to dogs. *Pause, for the first time he turns directly to her.* I would have your forgiveness, Elizabeth.

Elizabeth: It is not for me to give, John, I am—

Proctor: I'd have you see some honesty in it. Let them that never lied die now to keep their souls. It is pretense for me, a vanity that will not blind God nor keep my children out of the wind. *Pause.* What say you?

Elizabeth, *upon a heaving sob that always threatens:* John, it come to naught that I should forgive you, if you'll not forgive yourself. *Now he turns away a little, in great agony.* It is not my soul, John, it is yours. *He stands, as though in physical pain, slowly rising to his feet with a great immortal longing to find his answer. It is difficult to say, and she is on the verge of tears.* Only be sure of this, for I know it now: Whatever you will do, it is a good man does it. *He turns his doubting, searching gaze upon her.* I have read my heart this three month, John. *Pause.* I have sins of my own to count. It needs a cold wife to prompt lechery.

> **"Only be sure of this: Whatever you will do, it is a good man does it."**

Proctor, *in great pain:* Enough, enough—

Elizabeth, *now pouring out her heart:* Better you should know me!

Proctor: I will not hear it! I know you!

Elizabeth: You take my sins upon you, John—

Proctor, *in agony:* No, I take my own, my own!

Elizabeth: John, I counted myself so plain, so poorly made, no honest love could come to me! Suspicion kissed you when I did; I never knew how I should say my love. It were a cold house I kept! *In fright, she swerves, as* HATHORNE *enters.*

Hathorne: What say you, Proctor? The sun is soon up.

PROCTOR, *his chest heaving, stares, turns to* ELIZABETH. *She comes to him as though to plead, her voice quaking.*

Elizabeth: Do what you will. But let none be your judge. There be no higher judge under Heaven than Proctor is! Forgive me, forgive me, John—I never knew such goodness in the world! *She covers her face, weeping.*

PROCTOR *turns from her to* HATHORNE; *he is off the earth, his voice hollow.*

Proctor: I want my life.

Hathorne, *electrified, surprised:* You'll confess yourself?

Proctor: I will have my life.

Hathorne, *with a mystical tone:* God be praised! It is a providence! *He rushes out the door, and his voice is heard calling down the corridor:* He will confess! Proctor will confess!

Proctor, *with a cry, as he strides to the door:* Why do you cry it? *In great pain he turns back to her.* It is evil, is it not? It is evil.

Elizabeth, *in terror, weeping:* I cannot judge you, John, I cannot!

Proctor: Then who will judge me? *Suddenly clasping his hands:* God in Heaven, what is John Proctor, what is John Proctor? *He moves as an animal, and a fury is riding in him, a tantalized search.* I think it is honest, I think so; I am no saint. *As though she had denied this he calls angrily at her:* Let Rebecca go like a saint; for me it is fraud!

Voices are heard in the hall, speaking together in suppressed excitement.

Elizabeth: I am not your judge, I cannot be. *As though giving him release:* Do as you will, do as you will!

Proctor: Would you give them such a lie? Say it. Would you ever give them this? *She cannot answer.* You would not; if tongs of fire were singeing you you would not! It is evil. Good, then—it is evil, and I do it!

HATHORNE *enters with* DANFORTH, *and, with them,* CHEEVER, PARRIS, *and* HALE. *It is a businesslike, rapid entrance, as though the ice had been broken.*

Danforth, *with great relief and gratitude:* Praise to God, man, praise to God; you shall be blessed in Heaven for this. CHEEVER *has hurried to the bench with pen, ink, and paper.* PROCTOR *watches him.* Now then, let us have it. Are you ready, Mr. Cheever?

Proctor, *with a cold, cold horror at their efficiency:* Why must it be written?

Danforth: Why, for the good instruction of the village, Mister; this we shall post upon the church door! *To* PARRIS, *urgently:* Where is the marshal?

Parris, *runs to the door and calls down the corridor:* Marshal! Hurry!

Danforth: Now, then, Mister, will you speak slowly, and directly to the point, for Mr. Cheever's sake. *He is on record now, and is really dictating to* CHEEVER, *who writes.* Mr. Proctor, have you seen the Devil in your life? PROCTOR's *jaws lock.* Come, man, there is light in the sky; the town waits at the scaffold; I would give out this news. Did you see the Devil?

Proctor: I did.

Parris: Praise God!

Danforth: And when he come to you, what were his demand? PROCTOR *is silent.* DANFORTH *helps.* Did he bid you to do his work upon the earth?

Proctor: He did.

Danforth: And you bound yourself to his service? DANFORTH *turns, as* REBECCA NURSE *enters, with* HERRICK *helping to support her. She is barely able to walk.* Come in, come in, woman!

Rebecca, *brightening as she sees* PROCTOR: Ah, John! You are well, then, eh?

PROCTOR *turns his face to the wall.*

Danforth: Courage, man, courage—let her witness your good example that she may come to God herself. Now hear it, Goody Nurse! Say on, Mr. Proctor. Did you bind yourself to the Devil's service?

Rebecca, *astonished:* Why, John!

Proctor, *through his teeth, his face turned from* REBECCA: I did.

Danforth: Now, woman, you surely see it profit nothin' to keep this conspiracy any further. Will you confess yourself with him?

Rebecca: Oh, John—God send his mercy on you!

Danforth: I say, will you confess yourself, Goody Nurse?

Rebecca: Why, it is a lie, it is a lie; how may I damn myself? I cannot, I cannot.

Danforth: Mr. Proctor. When the Devil came to you did you see Rebecca Nurse in his company? PROCTOR *is silent.* Come, man, take courage—did you ever see her with the Devil?

Proctor, *almost inaudibly:* No.

DANFORTH, *now sensing trouble, glances at* JOHN *and goes to the table, and picks up a sheet—the list of condemned.*

Danforth: Did you ever see her sister, Mary Easty, with the Devil?

Proctor: No, I did not.

Danforth, *his eyes narrow on* PROCTOR: Did you ever see Martha Corey with the Devil?

Proctor: I did not.

Danforth, *realizing, slowly putting the sheet down:* Did you ever see anyone with the Devil?

Proctor: I did not.

Danforth: Proctor, you mistake me. I am not empowered to trade your life for a lie. You have most certainly seen some person with the Devil. PROCTOR *is silent.* Mr. Proctor, a score of people have already testified they saw this woman with the Devil.

Proctor: Then it is proved. Why must I say it?

Danforth: Why "must" you say it! Why, you should rejoice to say it if your soul is truly purged of any love for Hell!

Proctor: They think to go like saints. I like not to spoil their names.

Danforth, *inquiring, incredulous:* Mr. Proctor, do you think they go like saints?

Proctor, *evading:* This woman never thought she done the Devil's work.

Danforth: Look you, sir. I think you mistake your duty here. It matters nothing what she thought—she is convicted of the unnatural murder of children, and you for sending your spirit out upon Mary Warren. Your soul alone is the issue here, Mister, and you will prove its whiteness or you cannot live in a Christian country. Will you tell me now what persons conspired with you in the Devil's company? PROCTOR *is silent.* To your knowledge was Rebecca Nurse ever—

Proctor: I speak my own sins; I cannot judge another. *Crying out, with hatred:* I have no tongue for it.

Hale, *quickly to* DANFORTH: Excellency, it is enough he confess himself. Let him sign it, let him sign it.

Parris, *feverishly:* It is a great service, sir. It is a weighty name; it will strike the village that Proctor confess. I beg you, let him sign it. The sun is up, Excellency!

Danforth, *considers; then with dissatisfaction:* Come, then, sign your testimony. *To* CHEEVER: Give it to him. CHEEVER *goes to* PROCTOR, *the confession and a pen in hand.* PROCTOR *does not look at it.* Come, man, sign it.

Proctor, *after glancing at the confession:* You have all witnessed it—it is enough.

Danforth: You will not sign it?

Proctor: You have all witnessed it; what more is needed?

Danforth: Do you sport with me? You will sign your name or it is no confession, Mister! *His breast heaving with agonized breathing,* PROCTOR *now lays the paper down and signs his name.*

Parris: Praise be to the Lord!

PROCTOR *has just finished signing when* DANFORTH *reaches for the paper. But* PROCTOR *snatches it up, and now a wild terror is rising in him, and a boundless anger.*

Danforth, *perplexed, but politely extending his hand:* If you please, sir.

Proctor: No.

Danforth, *as though* PROCTOR *did not understand:* Mr. Proctor, I must have—

Proctor: No, no. I have signed it. You have seen me. It is done! You have no need for this.

Parris: Proctor, the village must have proof that—

Proctor: Damn the village! I confess to God, and God has seen my name on this! It is enough!

Danforth: No, sir, it is—

Proctor: You came to save my soul, did you not? Here! I have confessed myself; it is enough!

Danforth: You have not con—

Proctor: I have confessed myself! Is there no good penitence but it be public? God does not need my name nailed upon the church! God sees my name; God knows how black my sins are! It is enough!

Danforth: Mr. Proctor—

Proctor: You will not use me! I am no Sarah Good or Tituba, I am John Proctor! You will not use me! It is no part of salvation that you should use me!

Danforth: I do not wish to—

Proctor: I have three children—how may I teach them to walk like men in the world, and I sold my friends?

Danforth: You have not sold your friends—

Proctor: Beguile me not! I blacken all of them when this is nailed to the church the very day they hang for silence!

Danforth: Mr. Proctor, I must have good and legal proof that you—

Proctor: You are the high court, your word is good enough! Tell them I confessed myself; say Proctor broke his knees and wept like a woman; say what you will, but my name cannot—

Danforth, *with suspicion:* It is the same, is it not? If I report it or you sign to it?

Proctor—*he knows it is insane:* No, it is not the same! What others say and what I sign to is not the same!

Danforth: Why? Do you mean to deny this confession when you are free?

Proctor: I mean to deny nothing!

Danforth: Then explain to me, Mr. Proctor, why you will not let—

Proctor, *with a cry of his whole soul:* Because it is my name! Because I cannot have another in my life! Because I lie and sign myself to lies! Because I am not worth the dust on the feet of them that hang! How may I live without my name? I have given you my soul; leave me my name!

Danforth, *pointing at the confession in* PROC-TOR'*s hand:* Is that document a lie? If it is a lie I will not accept it! What say you? I will not deal in lies, Mister! PROCTOR *is motionless.* You will give me your honest confession in my hand, or I cannot keep you from the rope. PROCTOR *does not reply.* Which way do you go, Mister?

His breast heaving, his eyes staring, PROCTOR *tears the paper and crumples it, and he is weeping in fury, but erect.*

Danforth: Marshal!

Parris, *hysterically, as though the tearing paper were his life:* Proctor, Proctor!

Hale: Man, you will hang! You cannot!

Proctor, *his eyes full of tears:* I can. And there's your first marvel, that I can. You have made your magic now, for now I do think I see some shred of goodness in John Proctor. Not enough to weave a banner with, but white enough to keep it from such dogs. ELIZABETH, *in a burst of terror, rushes to him and weeps against his hand.* Give them no tear! Tears pleasure them! Show honor now, show a stony heart and sink them with it! *He has lifted her, and kisses her now with great passion.*

Rebecca: Let you fear nothing! Another judgment waits us all!

Danforth: Hang them high over the town! Who weeps for these, weeps for corruption! *He sweeps out past them.* HERRICK *starts to lead* REBECCA, *who*

almost collapses, but PROCTOR *catches her, and she glances up at him apologetically.*

Rebecca: I've had no breakfast.

Herrick: Come, man.

HERRICK *escorts them out,* HATHORNE *and* CHEEVER *behind them.* ELIZABETH *stands staring at the empty doorway.*

Parris, *in deadly fear, to* ELIZABETH: Go to him, Goody Proctor! There is yet time!

From outside a drumroll strikes the air. PARRIS *is startled.* ELIZABETH *jerks about toward the window.*

Parris: Go to him! *He rushes out the door, as though to hold back his fate.* Proctor! Proctor!

Again, a short burst of drums.

"He have his goodness now."

Hale: Woman, plead with him! *He starts to rush out the door, and then goes back to her.* Woman! It is pride, it is vanity. *She avoids his eyes, and moves to the window. He drops to his knees.* Be his helper! What profit him to bleed? Shall the dust praise him? Shall the worms declare his truth? Go to him, take his shame away!

Elizabeth, *supporting herself against collapse, grips the bars of the window, and with a cry:* He have his goodness now. God forbid I take it from him!

The final drumroll crashes, then heightens violently. HALE *weeps in frantic prayer, and the new sun is pouring in upon her face, and the drums rattle like bones in the morning air.*

The curtain falls

MAKING MEANINGS

Act Four

First Thoughts

1. Which character do you most identify with? Why? Whom did Miller identify with? (Check his comments on page 827.)

Shaping Interpretations

2. Why does Hale say he has come "to do the Devil's work"? What **motivates** his actions?

3. What events precede the sudden disappearance of Abigail and Mercy?

4. What does Parris fear about the response of the people in Andover?

5. Why does Hale counsel Elizabeth to persuade John Proctor to lie? Do you think he is right to do so?

6. How do you interpret Arthur Miller's statement that John and Elizabeth inhabit a world "beyond sorrow, above it"?

7. What **motivations** does Proctor have for confessing? At the same time, why does he see his confession as deeply **ironic**?

8. In the play's **climax,** Proctor destroys his own confession. Review your reading notes interpreting Proctor's character: Why does he ultimately choose his "goodness"?

The Play as a Whole

Shaping Interpretations

1. Refer back to the dictionary definition of *crucible* on page 828, and explain the **title** of the play.

2. Miller has said he wrote *The Crucible* with the

Reading Check

a. Why has Reverend Hale returned to Salem?

b. What news about Abigail does Parris give Danforth?

c. What two things does Elizabeth say she is unable to do for John?

d. Why does Danforth want a written confession from Proctor?

conviction that "there were moments when an individual conscience was all that could keep the world from falling apart." Do you agree with his conviction? Do you think the play actually demonstrates a triumph of individual conscience? Explain your answers.

3. What, in your opinion, is the difference between the ways Proctor and Hale resolve the **conflicts** between their public and their private lives? Whose solution is better? Could their conflicts be found in people today? Support your answers with examples from the text and from life.

Extending the Text

4. In Act One, after the introduction of Proctor, Miller writes that modern Americans have "inherited" the Puritan idea that sin cannot be washed away—an idea that has disciplined us, but has also bred hypocrisy. Explain why you agree or disagree with Miller's assessment of American culture.

Challenging the Text

5. The writer of a literary work may have responsibilities not only to readers and publishers but also to the people he or she chooses to write about. Do you think Arthur Miller had a responsibility to portray the Salem witchcraft trials accurately? Is his use of "artistic license" with respect to some of the historical facts justifiable? To what extent do you think a writer, artist, or filmmaker should be accurate when basing a work of fiction on historical events? Explain your opinion.

6. Miller has called *The Crucible* a tragedy. Do you think it is a tragedy? Why or why not?

7. Some critics have claimed that Miller's play is really only a vehicle for his own political viewpoints. How do you feel about these criticisms of the play? Miller's lengthy comments on his characters, on their problems, and on history in general are certainly unusual in a play. How do you respond to Miller's commentary throughout the play? Be specific in your answers.

CHOICES: Building Your Portfolio

Writer's Notebook

1. Collecting Ideas for a Problem-Solution Essay

Think of a social or political problem suggested by *The Crucible*. To analyze the problem, answer as many of the following questions as you can.

Description:
What is the problem? How widespread is it?

Narration:
What is the problem's history? What are its causes? What are its effects?

Classification:
What are the major parts of the problem? How is the problem similar to other problems? How is it unique?

Evaluation:
Why is the problem important? What solutions have been tried? Which solution is most practical? Which does the most good for the most people? Which has moral and ethical justification?

Keep your notes for possible use in the Writer's Workshop on page 895.

Interpreting Theme

2. The Breaking of Charity

In his autobiography, *Timebends,* Arthur Miller writes that "the real story" of the Salem witch trials is to be found in "the breaking of charity" within a human community. Write a brief essay explaining what you think Miller means by this interesting statement, and support your opinion with evidence from the text. Conclude your essay with your reflection on whether "the breaking of charity" could destroy a community today.

Analyzing Character

3. Private Lives

In an essay, analyze one of the characters in *The Crucible*. (You can use the notes you took on an interesting character as you read the play.) Some possible characters are John Proctor, Elizabeth Proctor, Judge Danforth, and Abigail Williams. In your essay, focus on these aspects of the character:

- conflicts
- motivation
- significant actions or decisions
- changes or discoveries

Include at the end of the essay your response to the character: Did you find the character believable? Did he or she do the right thing? Did you admire this person? Were your feelings negative? Or was your response mixed or complex?

Comparing Text and History

4. Is It True?

Compare details of the actual Salem witchcraft trials with details presented in *The Crucible*. You'll find information on the trials on pages 10–11 of this book. Use this feature and other resources, including the Internet, to gather data on the trials. Before looking further, formulate questions that will guide your research. Present your findings in an essay.

Researching Historical Context

5. Naming Names

Research the 1950s Congressional hearings into "un-American activities," and analyze the relationship of Miller's play to this painful American event. Examine Miller's own comments about his intentions (see the playwright's essay "Why I Wrote *The Crucible*," on page 827), as well as the reactions of contemporary literary and social critics. Include your own assessment of how effectively a work of fiction can comment on a real-life political or social situation.

Reading Skills and Strategies

VOCABULARY: DOING ANALOGIES

A kind of comparison called an **analogy** often appears as a logic problem in standardized tests. An analogy begins with a related pair of words or phrases. The goal is to create or identify a second pair that has a similar relationship.

Analogies appearing on tests are always written in a set form. Often the last word is omitted, and you must supply it.

TREE : FLORA :: mammal : _____

The colon (:) stands for the phrase "is related to." The double colon (::) between the capitalized word pair and the first word of the incomplete pair can be read as "in the same way that." Thus, you'd read the above analogy like this: "Tree is related to flora in the same way that mammal is related to . . ."

Now you have to do two things: Identify the relationship between the first two elements as precisely as possible, and choose a word that will make the final pair have a parallel relationship. In this case, you could say TREE **is a type of** FLORA. **Is a type of** is the relationship. Now read the first word of the second pair, supplying the same relationship: "mammal **is a type of** _____." The only word that fits this blank adequately is "fauna," a term often paired with "flora."

TREE : FLORA :: mammal : fauna

The chart in the next column shows the relationships that are most frequently used in formal analogies. In reading an analogy, you can substitute the phrasing of the relationship—"is a type of," for example, or "is similar in meaning to"—for the colon.

Sometimes only the first pair of an analogy will be presented, and you have to come up with a parallel second pair. If you are doing this type of analogy exercise, keep the following guidelines in mind:

1. Look for a second pair with a clear, precise relationship.

2. Compare the relationship, not the words.

3. Knowing the precise denotation (dictionary definition) of words will help. Consult a dictionary frequently.

4. Don't be tricked by choices in which the order is reversed. For example, if the first pair has first the part and then the whole, the second pair must appear in the same order.

TYPES OF ANALOGY RELATIONSHIPS		
TYPE	RELATIONSHIP	EXAMPLE
Classification	. . . is a type of . . .	TREE : FLORA
Performer and related object	. . . is the tool of . . .	BATON : CONDUCTOR
Characteristic quality	. . . is characteristic of . . .	SURLINESS : CURMUDGEON
Cause and effect	. . . is a cause (or effect) of . . .	FIRE : SMOKE
Part and whole	. . . is a part of . . .	STOMACH : DIGESTIVE TRACT
Synonym	. . . is similar in meaning to . . .	DRY : ARID
Antonym	. . . is opposite in meaning to . . .	KIND : CRUEL
Function	. . . is used to . . .	PEN : WRITE
Degree	. . . is a small (or large) . . .	CHUCKLE : LAUGH
Performer and related action	. . . does/performs . . .	CHEF : COOKS

Try It Out

Write an analogy exercise for each of the ten relationships defined above. Leave out the last word in each analogy, and trade papers with a partner. See if you can complete his or her exercises. Then, discuss the answers and any differences between the responses expected and those given.

More from Miller

Arthur Miller has produced a great body of work. Some of his notable plays, besides *The Crucible* and *Death of a Salesman,* include *A View from the Bridge* (1955), about longshoremen without immigration papers; *Incident At Vichy* (1965), about French citizens arrested by the Nazis in 1942; and *The Price* (1968), about two adult brothers comparing their lives. He also wrote the screenplay for *The Misfits* (1961), a drama starring Clark Gable and Miller's then-wife Marilyn Monroe.

The Beginning of Black Theater

When *A Raisin in the Sun,* by Lorraine Hansberry, opened in 1959, it was an instant success. This play about an African American family in Chicago marked the beginning of a vigorous black theater movement, which became one of the most vital forces in the modern American theater. Lloyd Richards directed a superb cast, which included Sidney Poitier, Claudia McNeil, Diana Sands, Ruby Dee, and Louis Gossett. The play was translated into thirty languages and won the New York Drama Critics' Circle Award. At twenty-nine, Hansberry became the youngest person—and the first African American playwright—ever to win this award. The play is available in the HRW Library. A 1961 film adaptation starring Sidney Poitier and Ruby Dee is available on videotape, as is a 1989 American Playhouse television production.

Lessons and Legacies

Would you part with a cherished family heirloom if you thought that by selling it you could make a better life for your family? This is the question the Charles family must answer in August Wilson's 1990 Pulitzer Prize-winning play *The Piano Lesson.* An antique piano thus becomes the catalyst for the discovery of the family's African American heritage.

A Long Drive Together

For twenty-five years in midcentury Atlanta, Hoke Coleburn, an African American, works as the chauffeur for Daisy Werthan, an elderly white woman. Their evolving relationship is traced in *Driving Miss Daisy* (Theatre Communications), a gentle depiction of prejudice and aging that won the play-wright Alfred Uhry a Pulitzer Prize in 1988. The Academy Award-winning film adaptation (1989) is available on videotape.

Dreams vs. Reality

Shy Laura Wingfield finds it easier to talk to her collection of glass animals than to people, but her mother insists that Laura prepare for "gentleman callers." Their poignant story is recounted in Tennessee Williams's *The Glass Menagerie* (1944), one of the best-loved dramas of the American Stage. Another Williams classic, *A Streetcar Named Desire* (1947), depicts a monumental clash of dream and reality in New Orleans. Both plays were made into notable films, available on videotape.

Euphemisms

by **Gary Q. Arpin**

One day in 1837, Captain Frederick Marryat, a British naval officer visiting the United States, was escorting a young lady in Niagara Falls, New York. She slipped and grazed her shin, and Marryat asked, "Did you hurt your leg much?" What he said seemed to offend her.

"She turned from me," Marryat wrote, "evidently much shocked." Puzzled, he asked her what he had done wrong. The word *leg,* she told him, was never used in the presence of ladies. What word was used for "such articles," the captain asked her. "Her reply," he wrote, "was that the word *limb* was used."

Victorian Prudery

The young lady did not invent the delicacy that had caused a leg to become a limb. The year 1837 marked the beginning of the long reign of Queen Victoria in England. One of the meanings of the adjective formed from her name—*Victorian*—is "having excessively severe standards of respectability." The Victorian Age became known for its prudery, an attitude that was as common in some American social circles as it was in England.

During this period in America, the only polite word for women's stockings was *hose,* and undergarments were referred to as *unmentionables.* Even the word *woman* was considered vulgar; *female* and *lady* became its acceptable substitutes.

Victorians were so offended by the names of body parts that they developed a new vocabulary for meals. A chicken or turkey leg became a *drumstick* or a *first joint;* the *thigh* became the *second joint;* chicken or turkey breast came to be called simply *white meat.*

Euphemisms for Taboo Words

A **euphemism** is a word or phrase that is substituted for another word or phrase considered offensive or upsetting. The word *euphemism* comes from a Greek term meaning "to use words of good omen." People use euphemisms in an attempt to hide a reality they find unpleasant, or to politely communicate something that another person might find offensive.

Why do certain words become taboo or forbidden, while other words with the same meaning are acceptable? There is no simple answer, because the role that language plays in our lives is so complex. One thing is certain, though. There is nothing inherent in any word that makes it good or bad. Words become acceptable or offensive only because people give them those qualities.

Some words become taboo because they refer to experiences we find psychologically overwhelming. The more terrifying the experience, the more euphemisms we are likely to devise for it. For example, we have dozens of ways of talking about death without using that word. Some of our euphemisms for death are respectful, such as *departed, breathed her last, went to her final reward,* and *met his Maker.* Some are neutral, like *passed on, passed away,* and *deceased.* Others are humorous: *kicked the bucket, went West, bought the farm,* and *cashed in his chips* are flippant ways of reducing the horror of death.

Euphemisms and "Civilized Behavior"

For a number of reasons, Americans have been especially prone to using euphemisms. The early Puritans were concerned with

> People use euphemisms in an attempt to hide a reality they find unpleasant, or to politely communicate something that another person might find offensive.

purifying language as well as religious practice. While they did not completely eradicate profanity, they certainly created an atmosphere hostile to vulgar speech. Though Americans who later moved westward were not averse to using profanity, it was in the pioneer communities that linguistic delicacy often was most prevalent. "The essentially English word *bull*," William Bartlett wrote, "is refined beyond the mountains . . . into *cow-creature, male-cow, and even gentleman-cow*!"

"The Language of Anticipation"

Another aspect of the need to provide a kind of instant civilization through gentility in language is what the historian Daniel Boorstin has called "the language of anticipation." This form of "good speaking" described things as they were to be in the future, rather than as they actually were at the time. Wealthy City, Kansas, which never fulfilled the promise of its name and dwindled into extinction, is an example of this kind of positive thinking. This linguistic optimism was a common phenomenon in a country where someone confronting a muddy, stump-filled plain might imagine a prosperous farm in its place. As Boorstin points out, even the country's name, "United States of America," which appears in the Constitution, was anticipatory. "It expressed hope that the new nation be *united,* that the components really be *states,* and that somehow they could be identified with the whole of

America." (*State*, until that time, referred only to sovereign nations.)

Examples of this kind of anticipatory euphemism abound in American history. Americans needed to talk "big." For instance, *city* was preferred over the more modest (if more accurate) *town* or *village*. Many cities boasted an *opera house*, even if it usually was only a tiny auditorium that presented troupes of traveling jugglers. "The elegant *hotel*," Boorstin writes, "was widely applied to ramshackle, flea-bitten inns and taverns. Americans thought they were not exaggerating but only anticipating—describing things which had not quite yet 'gone through the formality of taking place.'"

Euphemisms and Democracy

A love of inflated descriptive terms has a long history in America. Relentlessly democratic, Americans declared every man a "gentleman," while the British restricted the term to men of a particular social standing. Proud of being a nation with no inherited titles, Americans almost immediately began to generate countless acquired titles.

A British traveler in New York in 1744 remarked on the great many colonels he encountered. "It is a common saying here," he wrote, "that a man has no right to that dignity unless he has killed a rattlesnake." Governors of states were later empowered to bestow the title (along with *captain* and *major*) on virtually anyone they wished,

and many did so with great zeal, notably in Kentucky.

Americans applied a similar principle to occupations. Any occupation that was in danger of falling below a certain level of acceptability was usually yanked up by its linguistic bootstraps. This relentless linguistic upgrading of occupational titles is especially popular today. At times, this upgrading is very subtle; at other times, very obvious.

What is the difference, for example, between a *teacher* and an *educator*? Most people would agree that *educator* has a slightly more prestigious ring to it. This can be accounted for by taking a look at where English words come from.

English is composed primarily of Anglo-Saxon and Latin-based words. Historically, the Anglo-Saxon words have been the property of the common people, while the Latinate words have filtered down from the upper classes. This was especially the case following the Norman conquest of England in 1066. After that invasion, French (which is derived ultimately from Latin) was the official language of England for generations. Most people in England, however, continued to speak their own Anglo-Saxon language. During this bilingual period, the language was further enriched with synonyms. In most cases, the French word became the genteel word, while the Anglo-Saxon word became the common word. This explains the difference between the Latin *educare* (to educate) and the Anglo-Saxon word *taecan* (to teach).

Latinate words usually have more syllables than Anglo-Saxon words. Hence, a greater number of syllables often indicates a slide up the scale of acceptability. A *profession* (Latinate) somehow seems more important than a *job* (Anglo-Saxon). American job titles (or "career designations") have undergone frequent upgradings as a result of this tendency toward linguistic respectability. Thus, *mortician* (Latinate) was coined in the 1890s as a more dignified term than *undertaker* (Anglo-Saxon) for a person who manages a funeral home.

Euphemism and Distortion

Euphemisms can demonstrate sensitivity to the feelings of others. But euphemisms can also obscure meaning. Language can provide a veil to hide behind.

A boss would rather "excess" an employee than "fire" her, not because it makes the employee feel any better but because it makes the boss feel better. A government does not like to think of itself as "invading" another country, for example. It will make an *incursion,* or *liberate* the country instead. It is wrong to be the aggressor in a war, and *invasion* is a very aggressive word.

Many people have attacked the bureaucratic tendency to use long Latinate words where a short Anglo-Saxon word would serve just as well. The state and federal governments are particularly creative in generating euphemisms: prison guards have become "correctional officers," budget deficits are "negative growth," and taxes are sometimes called "revenue enhancement." This tendency has also spilled over to the general public in the language of advertising. Secondhand clothes are now sold as "vintage clothing," and used cars are called "previously owned" or "pre-driven." Even in this so-called modern age, softening blunt or distasteful names for things sometimes seems as prevalent now as in those prudish Victorian times.

Try It Out

1. **Interpreting connotations.** With another student, look through the local Yellow Pages or another business directory. Find at least three examples of euphemistic titles for occupations or businesses. Write the titles on a sheet of paper, and next to each write the ordinary word it is replacing. (For example, "resale boutique" is a euphemism that sometimes replaces "thrift shop.")

2. **Researching word origins.** Make two columns on a sheet of paper. Write the column titles *Plain* and *Fancy* at the top of the page. Decide which word in each of the following pairs belongs in each column. Then find each word in a dictionary. Write *L* next to the word if it is derived from Latin. Write *OE* if it is derived from Old English—that is, if it has Anglo-Saxon roots. What patterns do you notice?

   eat / dine
   spit / expectorate
   love / cherish
   cheap / inexpensive
   achieve / win
   beef / cow
   pig / pork
   work / career
   veal / calf
   father / parent

3. **Replacing euphemisms.** The following words are commonly used euphemisms. See if you can come up with a word or phrase that is a more direct way of saying the same thing.

   a. restroom
   b. passed on
   c. underprivileged
   d. senior citizens
   e. custodian
   f. sanitation engineers
   g. work stoppage
   h. expecting
   i. resting places

Writer's Workshop

The history
of the written
word is rich a
Page 1

PERSUASIVE WRITING

PROBLEM-SOLUTION ESSAY

If you've ever tried to work out a problem or dilemma by writing about it in a diary, journal, or letter, you know how the simple act of writing can help you think through problems and possible solutions. When you write a **problem-solution essay,** you thoroughly explore a problem and its possible solutions in a formal, methodical way. In a problem-solution essay, you identify and describe a problem and then propose one or more solutions to that problem.

Prewriting

1. Looking for problems.   The problems you think about in a given day may range from how to save enough money for a new bicycle to how to implement world peace. The problem of saving money is probably going to be too personal and specific to be of interest to a general audience. The problem of world peace is, on the other hand, far too broad for an essay. In selecting a topic for a problem-solution essay, think of a problem that is interesting to other people and manageable in a short paper.

You might already have an idea for a problem to explore if you completed the Writer's Notebook assignment on page 889. If you are starting from scratch, you might begin by thinking of problems that affect the everyday life of yourself, your family, and your friends. Think about problems you have observed firsthand in your school or community. Are students having a problem getting access to computers? Does your community need to do more to respond to the needs of people with disabilities by improving wheelchair access and increasing handicapped parking? Are families failing to participate fully in your local recycling program? Quickwrite a list of problems you would like to write about.

You might focus on the theme of this collection, "the breaking of charity." How is "charity" broken in the world today? How does the breaking of charity cause problems in families, in communities, and in the wider society?

In selecting a problem to write about, consider these questions:

* Which problem do I care most about solving?

* Which problem do I most want to learn about?

* Which problem could I, or others, act on?

Technology HELP

See Writer's Workshop 2 CD-ROM. *Assignment: Controversial Issue.*

ASSIGNMENT

Describe a problem, and then propose and defend the solution or solutions you believe are best.

AIM

To explore; to explain; to persuade.

AUDIENCE

People who are affected by the problem; people who can carry out your suggested solution; your teacher and classmates.

2. **Defining the problem.** Once you've chosen a problem to write about, you need to define it: You can't solve a problem that you don't understand. To define the problem you want to write about, ask yourself these questions:

- Why is it a problem?

- What causes this problem?

- What or whom does the problem affect?

- How does it affect them?

If you don't have the answers to all these questions, you'll want to do some research, which will probably involve reading, interviewing, viewing, or listening. For example, if you are interested in the effectiveness of neighborhood crime-prevention efforts in your community, you might want to interview local police officers.

3. **Brainstorming solutions.** Once you have thoroughly investigated your problem, you can move on to finding some answers. Remember, don't censor yourself. Often, good solutions come from seemingly improbable ideas.

One way to thoroughly explore multiple solutions is to make a chart in which you list the advantages and disadvantages of each solution. Don't forget to include solutions that have already been tried, perhaps in other schools or communities, and to note how effective these solutions have been. The chart below explores the topic of community recycling.

Model

Problem: *Families in the community do not recycle cans, glass, and newspapers.*

Possible Solutions	Advantages	Disadvantages
Give an award to one family each week, on the basis of that family's recycling	*Encourages family participation; enhances public awareness of problem*	*Cost of awards; people who don't promptly win awards may lose interest*
Provide recycling containers and pickup service	*Makes participation easier; can use existing volunteer groups*	*Expense of containers and pickup service; requires long-term management*
Fine people who do not recycle	*Provides incentive to recycle*	*Requires regulatory staff; may foster negative feelings*

Review your chart, and ask these questions to help you evaluate all possible solutions and select the best one:

- What are possible objections to these solutions?

- What are the counterarguments to these objections?

- Which solutions seem better than others?

- Is one solution more practical than the others?

- Does one solution do the most good for the most people?

4. **Outlining.** Once you have decided on a solution, pull all the information you've gathered together, and plan your essay. Outline the following items:

- the problem

- your proposed solution

- the steps necessary to implement your solution

Try It Out
Together with one or more classmates, choose a problem from the Quickwrite list you made while prewriting, and use a cluster diagram, map, double-entry journal, or other graphic organizer to list possible solutions.

- evidence to support your solution, including reasons, facts, examples, and statistics (If you need more support, now is the time to gather it.)

- possible objections to your solution

- other possible solutions and the reasons you rejected them

5. **Targeting your audience.**   When you write a problem-solution essay, it's crucial to know who your audience is: Remember, you are trying to convince people that (a) your problem is serious and (b) your proposed solution is the best one. To convince your readers, you have to know what point of view and what concerns they bring to your essay.

After you decide who your audience is, ask these questions: Are your target readers aware that there is a problem? If so, what do they already know about it? In other words, what background information do you need to provide?

Drafting

A problem-solution essay can take many different forms. One effective pattern is as follows:

1. **Introducing the problem.**   Think about how you can best engage your readers' interest. If you're confident that your readers share your interest in the problem, you might simply introduce it directly, together with a statement of its importance. Or, you might start with an anecdote or attention-getting fact. For example, in an essay about recycling, you may open with this detail: "Every day, thousands of pounds of newspapers, glass jars, and aluminum cans are needlessly thrown into our town dump."

2. **Stating the problem.**   State the problem clearly. In an essay about recycling, you might write, "Most of the families in our community are simply not recycling their newspapers, glass jars, and cans." In describing the problem, you might want to use anecdotes or testimonies from interviews to engage the readers' interest. You might also want to use **connotative language**—words and phrases that create a specific emotional response.

3. **Discussing the solutions.**   Use your chart as a guide to touch briefly on two or three solutions that have been suggested or tried. You might choose the solutions you think your audience is inclined to favor. Discuss the disadvantages of these solutions in a balanced, fair way, being as thorough and persuasive as you can.

Devote about a paragraph to describing your solution and how it would be implemented. Be sure to outline the steps involved in implementing your solution. Remember that one purpose of your essay is to persuade your reader that, having considered all factors, you have chosen the best solution. Think of arguments you might make for your solution based on, for example, its practicality, feasibility, low cost, easy implementation, or other benefits.

4. **Producing the evidence.**   Use the most persuasive reasoning and information you've collected to show your readers that your solution is the best. Bolster your argument, if possible, with evidence from some other community or school that has tried this solution. You may even be able to locate statistics that back up your claim that this is an effective solution.

Strategies for Elaboration

The evidence you plan to use in your essay should be evaluated against these standards, or **criteria:**

1. Is the evidence **trustworthy**? Is it from a reliable source or from an expert?

2. Is the evidence **accurate**? If it seems suspect, check it against other sources.

3. Is the evidence **useful**? Is it logically connected to your problem or your solution?

Communications Handbook
H E L P

See Taking Notes and Documenting Sources; List of Sources Cited; Proofreading.

Proofreading Tips
H E L P

Double-check all statistics against your sources. Be sure you have used quotation marks when quoting from your sources and experts.

*Reread your essay from the
viewpoint of your readers.
Ask yourself: Have I presented
the problem in a compelling
way? How strong a case have
I made for my solution? Have
I responded to all likely objections? Have I addressed alternative solutions?*

**Language
Handbook
H E L P**

*See Revising to Reduce
Wordiness, page 1237.*

■ *Evaluation Criteria*

*A good problem-solution
essay*

1. *has a strong opening that
   elicits interest in the topic*
2. *clearly states the problem
   and its importance*
3. *addresses solutions other
   than your own and ex-
   plains their disadvantages*
4. *clearly explains your solution and supports it
   with evidence*
5. *addresses possible objections to your proposed
   solution*
6. *takes into account the
   reader's point of view*
7. *has an objective, authoritative tone that reflects
   your commitment to your
   solution*
8. *leaves the reader feeling
   convinced of the sound-
   ness of the solution*

Remember that you will want to credit your sources with full documentation. In your essay, you'll credit sources in two places—in parenthetical
citations and in the list of Works Cited at the end of your essay. (For more
information on documenting sources, see page 518.)

5. **Answering possible objections.**   In presenting your solution, you will
   have to respond to the logical arguments your readers may raise against it.
   What concerns and objections to your solution might your audience raise?
   Your paper will be most persuasive if you directly address all possible disadvantages to your solution that you can think of. Explain why you consider
   these disadvantages negligible compared to the advantages.

6. **Concluding.**   Conclude by again stating your solution and briefly restating
   its advantages. You might conclude your essay with your personal conviction that this solution should be implemented, or end with a clear call to
   action—advice about what readers themselves can do.

Evaluating and Revising

1. **Peer review.**   After you have a rough draft, ask one or more classmates
   who are interested in the problem to read your essay. Then, ask them the
   following questions.

   - Did I help you to understand the problem, and did I convince you that
     it is a significant one? If not, how can I persuade you to care about this
     problem as I do?
   - Do you think I clearly and fully described my proposed solution? Did I
     provide sound reasons for adopting my solution? If not, what reasons
     should I add?
   - Which solution is the most convincing? the least convincing? Should any
     proposed solutions be omitted?
   - Do you feel I have overlooked a potential solution? If so, how can I ad-
     dress this other solution while still showing why I think my solution is
     preferable?
   - Are my tone and approach appropriate for the subject?
   - What is the strongest aspect of my essay? What parts of the essay need
     more work?

2. **Self-evaluation.**   Revise your essay according to the feedback that you
   find most helpful. Then, do your own critique using the same list of questions. Eliminate any unnecessary words in your essay so that your arguments are forceful and easy to grasp.

Language Workshop

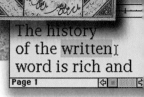

The history
of the written
word is rich and

Page 1

FITTING IT ALL TOGETHER: USING TRANSITIONAL EXPRESSIONS

Transitional expressions are words or phrases that provide a transition between ideas, making writing more coherent. Often these expressions show chronological or spatial relationships. They may also show relationships of cause and effect, definition, or contrast.

EXAMPLE   Arthur Miller was worried about a climate of fear in the United States in the early 1950s. **Therefore,** he wrote *The Crucible,* about a similar period of public anxiety in Colonial America. (**Therefore** indicates a cause-and-effect relationship.)

TRANSITIONAL WORDS AND PHRASES		
Comparing Ideas / Classification and Definition		
also	another	similarly
and	moreover	too
Contrasting Ideas / Classification and Definition		
although	in spite of	on the other hand
but	instead	still
however	nevertheless	yet
Showing Cause and Effect / Narration		
as a result	consequently	so that
because	since	therefore
Showing Time / Narration		
after	eventually	next
at last	finally	then
at once	first	thereafter
before	meanwhile	when
Showing Place / Description		
above	down	next
across	here	over
around	in	there
before	inside	to
beyond	into	under
Showing Importance / Evaluation		
first	mainly	then
last	more important	to begin with

Writer's Workshop Follow-Up: Revising

Reread the problem-solution essay you wrote for the Writer's Workshop (page 895). If some of your ideas seem disconnected, or if cause-and-effect and other relationships are unclear, revise your essay by adding transitions for coherence.

**Technology
H E L P**

See Language Workshop CD-ROM. *Key word entry: transitional expressions.*

**Language
Handbook
H E L P**

See Commas, pages 1243-1244.

Try It Out

Use transitional words or phrases to combine sentences as you rewrite the following paragraph about *The Crucible.*

   Reverend Parris's daughter Betty engages in some type of ritual with Tituba, Parris's slave. Betty becomes very ill. Tituba is forced to admit she practices witchcraft, with the power to harm other people. Leading citizens of Salem, including John Proctor, are accused of doing the devil's work. Proctor is sentenced to hang.

Reading for Life

Reading a Film Review

Situation

Suppose you've seen the film adaptation (available on videotape) of Arthur Miller's play *The Crucible*, and you want to compare your opinions with those of a film critic. An excerpt from a critic's review appears in the box to the right. Here are strategies you can follow in comparing your response to that of the critic.

Strategies

Recognize the critic's criteria.

• Note which elements of the film the critic focuses on. What elements, if any, does the critic ignore?

• What seem to be the critic's criteria for a good film?

Compare the criteria with those elements you look for in a good film.

• Your criteria might include an original **plot;** believable **dialogue** and **characters;** skillful **directing;** an interesting **setting;** realistic **acting;** good camera **work, costume design,** and **pacing.** Which of these are most important to you?

Be aware of bias.

• Does the reviewer seem biased against anyone involved in the film?

• Does the reviewer seem biased against the film's topic? Are any loaded words used?

The Crucible

JANET MASLIN

We've grown so accustomed to seeing classic works transposed to jazzier settings that it's startling to see what Nicholas Hytner has done to *The Crucible*: played it straight. Yet it is precisely by leaving Arthur Miller's 1953 play so emphatically in the Salem, Mass., of 1692 that Hytner's vibrant screen version succeeds so well in transcending time and place. . . .

As adapted gamely by the playwright into a screenplay that takes advantage of scenic backgrounds and photogenic stars, *The Crucible* now speaks to subtler forms of dishonesty and opportunism than it did before.

This agile film is so simply, abstractly rooted in Salem's soil that it becomes free to suggest anything from the impact of religious fundamentalism on politics to the hysterical excess of tabloid television. Along the way, this *Crucible* heats up its dramatic tale of marital betrayal and redemption without losing track of its central concern, the murderous power of lies.

Hytner . . . is particularly adept at balancing the film's look of museum realism with its frankly theatrical ways of heightening its drama. . . . The actors speak quaintly ("Are the accusers always holy now, were they born this morning pure as God's fingers?") without ever making their meaning less than resoundingly clear. Especially impressive here is Ms. Allen, whose look of luminous simplicity suits the film's visual style and whose immensely dignified performance captures the essence of Miller's concerns.

—*The New York Times*, November 27, 1996

• What evidence does the critic provide to support his or her opinions? Is the evidence credible, even if you disagree with the critic's opinions?

• Note the **tone** of the review and how it affects your reading.

Using the Strategies

1. In this excerpt from her review of *The Crucible,* what elements does critic Janet Maslin focus on?

2. What are her criteria for a good film (insofar as you can tell from this excerpt)?

3. What are the critic's opinions of this film? Does she support her opinions effectively? Cite specific examples.

4. Decide if you agree or disagree with the critic's main opinions, and why.

Extending the Strategies

• Make a list of what *you* look for in a good film.

• Look for two different reviews of the same film. Do you find one review more convincing than the other? (Note: The Internet is a good source.)

• Read the reviews in several different newspapers and magazines. Which publication publishes the best reviews, in your opinion?

Problem

Evaluating a drama means more than just saying "I liked that play" or "It stinks." Sometimes we may need to evaluate a play's suitability for a specific purpose or its appropriateness for a certain audience, setting, or physical location. A play that addresses adult themes would be suitable for a professional theater but inappropriate in a middle school. One that calls for elaborate costumes, special effects, and a huge stage belongs on Broadway—not in a small community playhouse. How can we evaluate a play's suitability for a particular situation, purpose, and audience?

Project

Collect and evaluate information on a number of plays in order to recommend one to be performed next year by your school.

Preparation

1. Form a team of evaluators.
2. In your school or community library, research eight to ten plays to evaluate. You can consult with a librarian, your English teacher, or the school drama teacher. Start with plays commonly taught and/or performed in high schools.
3. Decide the role each team member will play in evaluating the eight to ten plays.
4. Come to a consensus on the criteria you will use to evaluate the plays. Some criteria you might use are
   - general quality and value
   - number and types of roles
   - staging requirements
   - subject matter and language suitability for high school

   Include any other criteria you think are important in making your recommendation.
5. Prepare an evaluation form that each team member will fill out for each play that is being considered. Your form should list the various criteria your team agreed upon.

Procedure

1. Read the plays and any critical literature you can find about them. Fill out your evaluation forms.
2. As a group, convene to discuss the plays and your evaluations.
3. Reach consensus on one play you will recommend as being suitable for your school to perform next year.

Presentation

Present your drama evaluations and recommendations in one of the following formats (or another your teacher approves):

1. **Letter to the Drama Teacher**
   Working as a group, compose a detailed, persuasive letter to a drama or English teacher in your school, describing your project and the evaluation process, listing the plays you examined, and justifying your recommendation.

2. **Informational Display**
   As a group, create an informational display about the plays. Include excerpts from your evaluations, dialogue from the plays, photographs of the playwrights or performances of the plays, and any other elements that will make your display attractive and informative. Exhibit your display in your school or your community library.

3. **Critics' Corner**
   Prepare a "Sneak Previews"–style presentation of your reviews. Each member of your group should orally present his or her evaluation of a play. If individuals from different groups evaluated the same play, you could pair reviewers from the different groups and have them present a spirited discussion of the play.

Processing

What did this project teach you about evaluating drama? How could you apply techniques you used to make decisions and choose from various alternatives in your everyday life? Write a reflection for your portfolio.

Swing Landscape
(1938) by Stuart Davis.
Oil on canvas
(86¾″ x 172⅛″)
(220.3 cm x 437.2 cm).

Contemporary Literature

1950 to Present

Contemporary Literature

by John Leggett, Susan Allen Toth,
John Malcolm Brinnin, *and* Thomas Hernacki

"You mean there's a catch?"

"Sure there's a catch," Doc Daneeka replied. "Catch-22. Anyone who wants to get out of combat duty isn't really crazy."

There was only one catch and that was Catch-22, which specified that a concern for one's own safety in the face of dangers that were real and immediate was the process of a rational mind. Orr was crazy and could be grounded. All he had to do was ask; and as soon as he did, he would no longer be crazy and would have to fly more missions. Orr would be crazy to fly more missions and sane if he didn't, but if he was sane he had to fly them. If he flew them he was crazy and didn't have to; but if he didn't want to he was sane and had to. Yossarian was moved very deeply by the absolute simplicity of this clause of Catch-22 and let out a respectful whistle.

"That's some catch, that Catch-22," he observed.

"It's the best there is," Doc Daneeka agreed.

—Joseph Heller, from Catch-22

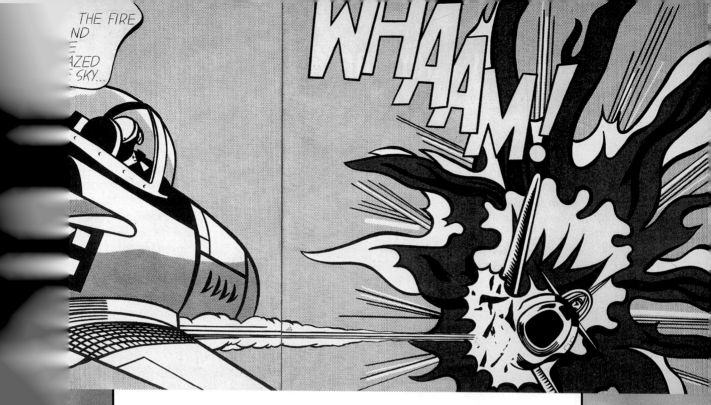

THE FIRE
ND
=AZED
SKY...

On August 6, 1945, at 8:15 A.M., an atomic bomb was dropped on the Japanese city of Hiroshima from the U.S. airplane *Enola Gay.* Within seconds, the center of Hiroshima had disappeared. The bomb, in effect, ended World War II, and its mushroom cloud has cast a shadow over each generation since.

Although many Americans disapproved of the use of the atomic bomb to end World War II, most Americans agreed with the purpose of the war itself. They were fighting against tyranny, against regimes that would destroy the American way of life. Only twenty years later, however, the United States became deeply involved in another overseas war—this time in Vietnam—that would sharply divide the nation. In the 1960s, demonstrations, both peaceful and violent, became commonplace. To some writers, such as Kurt Vonnegut, Jr., the madness of the war-torn world was an inescapable condition of modern life, and the only appropriate response was hard-edged laughter at life's tragic ironies. The term *gallows humor*—ironic humor arising from an acknowledgment of the absurd or grotesque—was often used to describe Vonnegut's work, as well as that of Joseph Heller, Terry Southern, and others. Heller's novel *Catch-22* (1961) is set in World War II, but the absurdities it describes belong to postwar life. In *Catch-22,* madness and war are inextricably mixed, not because madness is a result of war but because war is the result of our madness.

Whaam! (1963) by Roy Lichtenstein. Acrylic on canvas (172.7cm × 406.4cm).

© Copyright Contemporary Art Services, New York. Tate Gallery, London. Courtesy Art Resource, NY.

At all times, an old world is collapsing and a new world arising; we have better eyes for the collapse than the rise, for the old one is the world we know. The artist, in focusing on his own creation, finds, and offers, relief from the tension and sadness of being burdened not just with consciousness but with historical consciousness. . . .

—John Updike, *from Hugging the Shore*

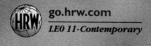

Contemporary Literature 1950–Present

LITERARY EVENTS

A Raisin in the Sun, a play by Lorraine Hansberry, opens, 1959

•

Ralph Ellison publishes his novel *Invisible Man,* 1952

•

J. D. Salinger publishes his novel *The Catcher in the Rye,* 1951

The Autobiography of Malcolm X published, 1965

•

Edward Albee's play *Who's Afraid of Virginia Woolf?* opens, 1962

•

John Steinbeck wins the Nobel Prize for Literature, 1962

•

Harper Lee publishes her novel *To Kill a Mockingbird,* 1960

Colombian **Gabriel García Márquez** publishes *One Hundred Years of Solitude,* 1967

•

Bernard Malamud publishes *The Fixer,* a novel about Jewish life in czarist Russia, 1966

•

Truman Capote publishes his "nonfiction novel" *In Cold Blood,* 1966

Aleksandr Solzhenitsyn publishes the first volume of *The Gulag Archipelago,* documenting oppression in the Soviet Union, 1973

•

James Dickey publishes *Deliverance,* a novel about a violent canoe trip in Georgia, 1970

| 1950–1959 | 1960–1964 | 1965–1969 | 1970–1974 |

CULTURAL/HISTORICAL EVENTS

Senator Joseph McCarthy charges that 205 Communists infiltrated the State Department, February 1950

•

Korean War ends, 1953

•

U.S. Supreme Court rules that segregation in public schools is unconstitutional, 1954

•

Soviet Union launches first artificial satellite, *Sputnik I,* thereby beginning the "space race" with the U.S., 1957

•

Federal troops enforce the integration of Central High School in Little Rock, Arkansas, 1957

Arkansas student heckled during enforced integration, September 4, 1957.

U.S. population is about 179 million, 1960

•

Many African countries, including Nigeria and Senegal, achieve independence, 1960

•

Bay of Pigs invasion of Cuba fails, 1961

•

Rev. Martin Luther King, Jr., delivers "I Have a Dream" speech during the March on Washington, 1963

•

President John F. Kennedy is assassinated, 1963

U.S. escalates involvement in Vietnam War, 1965

•

Israel occupies nearby territory as a result of Six-Day War with Arab countries, 1967

•

Rev. Martin Luther King, Jr., and Senator Robert F. Kennedy are assassinated, 1968

•

Two U.S. astronauts become first humans to walk on the moon, 1969

•

Woodstock music festival takes place in Bethel, NY, August 1969

Peace treaty provides for cease-fire in Vietnam and withdrawal of U.S. forces, 1973

•

World economy is jolted by a sharp rise in petroleum prices, 1973

•

Watergate scandal forces Richard M. Nixon to resign as U.S. president, 1974

President John F. Kennedy's funeral procession, November 25, 1963.

Toni Morrison.

Alex Haley publishes *Roots*, a history of his family from its origins in Africa, 1976

•

Saul Bellow publishes his novel *Humboldt's Gift*, 1975

•

E. L. Doctorow publishes *Ragtime*, a novel mixing fictional and real characters, 1975

Raymond Carver publishes *Cathedral*, a collection of his stories, 1983

•

Alice Walker publishes her novel *The Color Purple*, 1982

•

John Updike publishes his novel *Rabbit Is Rich*, 1981

Amy Tan publishes her novel *The Joy Luck Club*, 1989

•

Richard Wilbur publishes *New and Collected Poems*, 1988

•

Anne Tyler publishes her novel *Breathing Lessons*, 1988

•

Larry McMurtry publishes his novel *Lonesome Dove*, 1985

Garrett Hongo publishes *Volcano: A Memoir of Hawaii*, 1995

•

Steven Spielberg directs the film *Schindler's List*, based on the novel (1982) by Australia's Thomas Keneally, 1993

•

Toni Morrison wins the Nobel Prize for Literature, 1993

•

Tim O'Brien publishes *The Things They Carried*, 1990

1975–1979	1980–1984	1985–1989	1990–

Israel and Egypt agree to a landmark peace treaty, 1978–1979

•

Iranian militants seize the U.S. embassy in Tehran and take 52 Americans hostage, thus beginning 444-day "hostage crisis," 1979

•

Soviet Union invades Afghanistan, 1979

Eight-year war between Iran and Iraq begins, 1980

•

Sandra Day O'Connor becomes the first female justice on U.S. Supreme Court, 1981

•

United States invades Grenada after a military coup there, 1983

Era of great change in Soviet Union begins as Mikhail Gorbachev rises to power, 1985

•

U.S. space shuttle *Challenger* explodes soon after liftoff, 1986

•

U.S. stock market crashes, 1987

•

United States and Soviet Union sign treaty reducing medium-range nuclear weapons, 1987

•

Berlin Wall comes down, 1989

•

Pro-democracy demonstrations crushed in Tiananmen Square, Beijing, 1989

U.S. population is about 249 million, 1990

•

Iraq invades Kuwait but is forced to retreat by Operation Desert Storm, led by the United States, 1990–1991

•

West Germany and East Germany unite, 1990

•

Soviet Union is dissolved, 1991

•

British transfer sovereignty over Hong Kong to China, 1997

•

Internet becomes major form of communication, late 1990s

View of the shuttle *Atlantis* docked to the *Kristall* module of the Russian space agency's MIR space station.

ATOMIC ANXIETY

Things are probably going to look different when you get outside.

—from *How to Survive an Atomic Bomb* (1950)

At the end of World War II, Americans confronted two unsettling new facts of life: the atomic bomb and the cold war with the Soviet Union. U.S. scientists published chilling calculations of what would happen if atomic (and later, hydrogen) bombs were dropped on American cities. Meanwhile, a vivid image of a malignant Soviet leadership with its collective finger poised over the red button that would launch a nuclear attack was created in the American psyche—an image memorably evoked in the 1963 film *Dr. Strangelove: or, How I Learned to Stop Worrying and Love the Bomb.* Politicians warned that war would come, in the words of New York Governor Thomas E. Dewey, "whenever the fourteen evil men in Moscow decide to have it break out." It was high time, experts of various stripes agreed, to devise a new national civil defense plan.

The possible responses to nuclear attack were succinctly described by one U.S. government official as "dig, die, or get out." The second option aside, "getting out" meant leaving big cities, which presumably would be targets of Soviet bombs. Some policymakers urged that major cities be relocated under mountain ranges or in 30-foot strips alongside highways. Government officials ultimately rejected these and other relocation schemes. Even the less ambitious idea of evacuating cities drove planners to despair as they pondered maps of New York City and Los Angeles.

What was left but to dig? The notion of burrowing underground took root, partly because it allowed every citizen a personal response to nuclear war: Build a bomb shelter. Companies selling shelters proliferated in the 1950s, and marketing creativity soared. Using fictitious "protection factor" ratings, shelter ads boasted blastproof rooms; one ad featured a decontamination room for latecomers to the shelter. Aesthetic considerations came into play in one prefab shelter that featured a window with a woodland view painted on one wall. Ingenious designs and vigorous advertising

By permission of the artist. National Museum of American Art, Washington, D.C.

The 1970s saw the winding down of the Vietnam War, but another focus of disillusion filled the news: the Watergate scandal that in 1974 forced the only resignation of an American president. On the other hand, the celebration in 1976 of the bicentennial of the Declaration of Independence witnessed a prideful restatement of fundamental American values.

Then came the 1980s, which many Americans now regard as the time of the Me Generation, when individual enjoyment and material success seemed to overshadow other concerns.

Miss Liberty (1987) by Malcah Zeldis. Oil on corrugated cardboard.

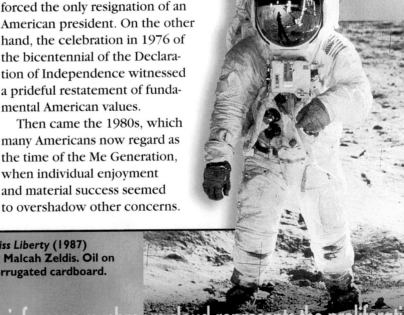

Its infamous mushroom cloud represents the proliferatio

were essential, because bomb shelters were a considerable investment: Models typically cost several hundred dollars (a large sum in those days), and that didn't include the requisite first-aid kit, flashlights, sandbags, periscope, supply of water and canned food, and pliers (in case of toothache). Economy-minded citizens were encouraged to improvise a shelter in their homes by stacking brick-filled dresser drawers on a table, and to crawl underneath in the event of a nuclear strike. (Helpful instructions warned the builder to "be careful not to overload the table to the point where it will collapse.") Bomb shelters generated so much enthusiasm that, by the end of 1960, industrious Americans had constructed about one million of them.

Although shelters and other civil defense schemes of the fifties sound far-fetched today, the fears that inspired them were entirely justified. In

Bomb shelter in New York, 1952.

fact, interest in civil defense waned in the early 1960s partly because people began to understand just how disastrous nuclear war could be. Antiradiation suits and community loudspeaker systems began to seem ridiculous in light of dangerously high and long-lived radiation levels. Moreover, weapons delivery systems had been improved so that bombs could reach the United States in minutes—hardly time to alert entire communities. The final blow to civil defense programs, however, was a positive development: The signing of the Limited Test Ban Treaty in 1963 officially ended above-ground nuclear testing—and thus the fallout that had aroused so much alarm. The bomb shelters of the fifties have long since been converted into toolsheds and wine cellars—or storage spaces for the home Geiger counters and antiradiation pills of another era.

As the 1980s ended, so did the cold war, the struggle between the United States and the Soviet Union that had dominated international politics since shortly after the end of World War II. The Soviet Union collapsed as its republics and satellite nations declared independence. The end of the cold war reduced but did not end the threat of nuclear warfare.

In many ways, the nuclear bomb is the dramatic symbol of the last half of the twentieth century. Its infamous mushroom cloud represents the proliferation of science and technology, the purpose of which was, ironically enough, to benefit humankind, to make life richer and easier for all.

In some ways, science and technology have fulfilled their promise. They have increased the life spans of many and have fed and housed many people better. They have moved us faster from place to place—even allowing a few of us to stroll on the surface of the moon.

But at the same time, poverty and crime have increased, not diminished. Science and technology have standardized and "assembly-lined" our lives and displaced countless workers. The era of the computer chip has

Peace Today by Rube Goldberg.

The Granger Collection, New York.

Neil Armstrong on the moon, 1969.

ence and technology, the purpose of which was, ironically enough, to benefit humankind, to

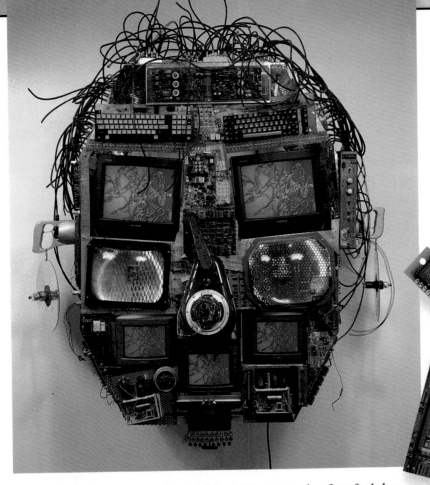

often seems

lost

fast-paced,

computerized

world.

diminished Emerson's rugged individual. Many people often feel they are only a number on a computer disk or credit card. Even our thoughts seem to be shaped or controlled by mass advertising, mass journalism, and mass entertainment. Some people even predict that our new technologies will deliver the planet itself back to lower organisms—to the cockroaches and ants, perhaps—who may survive the nuclear holocaust that might one day engulf us.

> *The aftermath of World War II ushered in an age of rapid developments in science and technology. The postwar years have offered many Americans increased opportunities for economic and cultural growth, but the individual person often seems lost in the fast-paced, computerized world.*

Contemporary Fiction: Diversity and Vitality

Probably the most common word used to describe American culture at the end of the twentieth century is **postmodern,** a term that, like our age, is still in the process of being defined. Postmodernism sees contemporary culture as a change—a development or a departure—from modernism, the dominant movement in the arts from about 1890 to 1945. In literature, the great American modernists, notably Ezra Pound, T. S. Eliot, Willa Cather, William Carlos Williams, Marianne Moore, Wallace Stevens, Katherine Anne Porter, William Faulkner, and Ernest Hemingway, forged new styles and new forms to express the sensibility of the twentieth century. Postmodern writers build with many of the tools provided by the modernists, and they are now constructing a body of literature that is strikingly different from that of the first half of the century.

New perspectives in postmodern fiction.

Postmodern fiction writers allow for multiple meanings and multiple worlds in their works. Realistic and literal worlds, future worlds, and dreamlike metaphorical worlds may merge, as they do in Thomas Pynchon's dazzling novel *Gravity's Rainbow* (1973). Narrators and characters may tell different versions of a story, or a story may deliberately accommodate several valid interpretations, as in *Pale Fire* (1962), by the Russian American novelist Vladimir Nabokov. The postmodernist asks, Why choose only one version? Why limit ourselves?

Writers of our time often structure their works in a variety of nontraditional forms and do not abide by conventional rules of shaping fiction. Sometimes these forms are quite arbitrary. Donald Barthelme's story "Sentence," for example, is a nine-page tale that consists entirely of one sentence. In Walter Abish's novel *Alphabetical Africa* (1974), every word in the first chapter begins with the letter *a;* every word in the second chapter begins with *a* or *b,* and so on through the alphabet to *z* and then, in reverse, all the way back to *a.*

Some postmodern works are also intensely self-conscious: They comment upon themselves, criticize themselves, take themselves apart, and encourage us to put

> The past is not a terrible burden to be sustained but a box of images to be resorted to for pleasure.
>
> —Denis Donoghue

Why choose only one version? Why limit ourselves?

Untitled (Ralph Ellison) (1994) by Glenn Ligon. Oil stick on paper (32″ x 15⅝″).

them together again. In his novel *Operation Shylock* (1993), the author Philip Roth meets a character named Philip Roth and wonders which one of them is "real." In other words, postmodern literature is aware of itself as literature and encourages the reader's self-awareness as well.

The vitality of contemporary fiction lies in its cultural diversity, in its enthusiasm for blending fiction with nonfiction, and in its extraordinary sense of play. It also demonstrates a typically American ability to invigorate the old with the new.

> *Contemporary fiction allows for multiple meanings and multiple worlds, uses nontraditional forms, and comments upon itself. But it embraces traditional storytellers as well as postmodern risk-takers. It features cultural diversity, crisscrosses the boundaries between fiction and nonfiction, and uses subjects, images, and themes from the past fearlessly.*

Contemporary Nonfiction: Breaking the Barriers

Until fairly recently, "nonfiction" meant whatever was *not* fiction—suggesting that nonfiction was a nonliterary form and a nonart. Nonfiction writers were lumped together with journalists, who were in turn defined as nonliterary folk whose work was quickly written, read, and discarded. Critics tended to concentrate on the search for the elusive Great American Novel, which was thought to be more important than anything a nonfiction writer could produce.

> . . . [N]onfiction is the place where much of the best writing of the day is being done. Yet many writers and teachers of writing continue to feel vaguely guilty if they prefer it to fiction—nonfiction is the slightly disreputable younger brother in the royal house of literature. No such guilt is necessary. While the keepers of the temple weren't looking, nonfiction crept in and occupied the throne.
>
> —William Zinsser

Since the 1970s, however, nonfiction has come into its own. Featured reviews now discuss the art (not just the factual content) of books on computers, architecture, travel, history, film, and other subjects. Bestseller lists, which have always included self-help books, cookbooks, and exercise manuals, now also regularly feature memoirs, biographies, and histories.

"*On the Internet, nobody knows you're a dog.*"

Peter Steiner, ©1997. From The New Yorker Collection. All Rights Reserved.

Questions of terminology and accuracy.

Critics, however, are still uncertain about the terminology we should apply to nonfiction. For instance, when discussing fiction, we can talk about point of view, character, plot, theme, and setting; with more complex fiction, we can analyze irony, metaphors, symbols, and levels of meaning. But these traditional literary terms don't always apply to nonfiction.

More troubling is the problem of accuracy. No one expects a novel to be true, although it may be based on verifiable facts. But truth or accuracy is often a test applied to nonfiction, with frequently unsatisfactory results. A class recently read Peter Matthiessen's *The Snow Leopard* (1978), a travel memoir about wildlife in the Himalayas and the writer's search for the meaning of life. The class praised the book for its penetrating observations, philosophical depth, and narrative technique. Students were then asked if they would like it just as much if they learned that it was fiction, that Matthiessen had done extensive library research but had never gone to the Himalayas at all. (This is, of course, *not* the case.) No, many students said, they would not like the book as well. It would no longer be true. Wasn't truth what distinguished nonfiction from fiction?

The New Journalism.

This question was often raised in the 1960s when the New Journalism (also called Literary Journalism) began to appear. Truman Capote, Tom Wolfe, Joan Didion, Norman Mailer, and others attracted attention by describing contemporary culture and actual events in strongly individual voices. They employed many of the devices of fiction, including complex characterization, plot, suspense, setting, symbolism, and irony.

A New Journalist did not feel obliged to keep personal opinion and his or her presence out of the writing; in fact, presence and participation were often crucial. Joan Didion bought a dress for a defendant in a trial she was covering as a journalist. Truman Capote befriended the murderers he was writing about in his book *In Cold Blood,* which he called a nonfiction novel—a perfect example of the overlapping of genres. Readers wanted to know just what the writer was thinking or feeling about the subject, and so the tone of a book became nearly as important as its facts.

If facts alone do not distinguish nonfiction from fiction, what does? No one is sure. What readers *are* sure about is their interest in nonfiction that uses the traditional attractions of accomplished fiction:

> ### Characteristics of Postmodern Literature
>
> - Allows for multiple meanings and multiple worlds
> - Structures works in nontraditional forms
> - Comments upon itself
> - Features cultural diversity
> - Blends and overlaps fiction and nonfiction
> - Uses the past fearlessly

Don't Buy (1988) by Phoebe Beasley. Collage (36″ × 28″).
Courtesy of the artist.

characters to care about, suspense, and compelling use of language. Many readers, eager for literature that will illuminate their lives, enrich their knowledge, and entertain them, have become as willing to pursue those goals in nonfiction as they are in fiction. They find what they are looking for in the works of the writers mentioned above and many others, including Annie Dillard, Lewis Thomas, Paul Theroux, Alice Walker, and Barry Lopez.

> *Contemporary nonfiction has become a field equal to fiction, though questions about terminology and accuracy still give rise to controversy. New Journalism (or Literary Journalism) has added personal and fictional elements to nonfiction, enhancing its popularity with today's readers.*

Contemporary Poetry: Varied and Intensely Personal

It is difficult to describe the course of American poetry since 1945, because recent trends are still too close to be viewed objectively. Moreover, in recent years, unprecedented numbers of Americans have been writing poetry, so it is a special challenge to determine which poets and which movements will last.

The decline of modernism. There are a number of clear, significant differences between American poetry written before 1945 and the poetry written in the decades since. The twenty years between World War I and World War II marked the flowering and near monopoly of modernist poetry. This was the kind of poetry defined, by and large, by the theory and practice of T. S. Eliot, Ezra Pound, and, somewhat later, W. H. Auden.

In 1917, Eliot had called for an impersonal, objective poetry that would transcend the subjective emotions of the poet. The poem, said Eliot, should be impersonal, allusive (it should make references, or allusions, to other works), and intellectually challenging. Modernist writers followed Ezra Pound's insistence that the image was all-important and that all unnecessary words should be omitted; but in doing this, they often eliminated material that could have made their poetry more accessible to readers.

By the early 1950s, though, there was a growing sense that modernism was somehow becoming played out, that it was no longer appropriate for the times. The era itself may have had something to do with the shift away from modernism. A generation had returned from war to a country where conformity and material success were predominant values. The Soviet Union and the atomic bomb worried Americans in the late

Maya Angelou reciting her poem "On the Pulse of Morning" at the presidential inauguration in 1993.

1940s and early 1950s, but acquiring a house and a car and making money were generally of more immediate importance. "These are the tranquilized *Fifties*," Robert Lowell wrote in a poem toward the end of that decade, as he ironically described the complacent scene around him:

> I hog a whole house on Boston's
> "hardly passionate Marlborough Street,"
> where even the man
> scavenging filth in the back alley trash cans,
> has two children, a beach wagon, a helpmate,
> and is a "young Republican."
>
> —Robert Lowell, *from*
> "Memories of West Street and Lepke"

By the early 1950s, many writers and readers felt that modernist poetry—impersonal, allusive, difficult—was no longer appropriate. The times called for a more personal and accessible approach that challenged complacency and convention.

The Beat poets. In 1956, a long poem called *Howl* was published by Allen Ginsberg, who could by no stretch of the imagination be described as dull. A cry of outrage against the conformity of the 1950s, *Howl* was as far removed from the safe confines of modernism as could be imagined. It begins, "I saw the best minds of my generation destroyed by madness, starving hysterical naked," and it continues at the same intense pitch for hundreds of lines.

Student reading at the 1995 Dodge Poetry Festival.

American Flag: A Mosaic of Faces is part of an exhibit at the Ellis Island Immigration Museum. From 1891 to 1954 this New York Harbor island processed over 16 million immigrants.

Together with *On the Road* (1957), Jack Kerouac's novel celebrating the bohemian life, *Howl* quickly became a kind of bible for young nonconformists known as the Beat Generation. Beat poetry and the Beat lifestyle of poetry readings, jazz, and late-night coffeehouses in San Francisco and New York's Greenwich Village had an immediate impact on American popular culture. *Life* magazine even ran illustrated stories about the new bohemians.

> One judges an age, just as one judges a poet, by its best poems.
>
> —Randall Jarrell

Howl provided the first clear alternative to academic poetry—intellectual poetry that seemed to be written for analysis in the classroom rather than poetry that addressed the real concerns of contemporary life. Many of Ginsberg's concerns—the injustices of modern life, the importance of the imagination—would become the principal themes of poetry a decade later.

Poetry and personal experience. In 1959, Robert Lowell published *Life Studies,* one of the most important and influential volumes of verse to appear since World War II. These poems are about personal experiences that modernist poets had avoided dealing with directly: emotional problems, alcoholism, illness, and depression. In *Life Studies,* Lowell clearly and decisively broke with Eliot's theory that poetry should be impersonal; in doing so, he helped to reunite, both for himself and for other writers, "the man who suffers and the mind which creates."

Shortly after *Life Studies* appeared, a critic described Lowell's poems as "confessional." The label stuck, and the **Confessional School** of poets, mostly friends or students of Lowell, was officially born. These poets—including Sylvia Plath, Anne Sexton, and John Berryman—wrote frank, sometimes brutal poems about their private lives. Nothing could have been further from Eliot's model.

By the mid-1970s, many of the first generation of major postwar poets were dead, as were some of the second generation. William Carlos Williams, Theodore Roethke, and Plath all died in 1963. The 1970s saw the deaths of Berryman, Sexton, and Lowell. With Lowell's death, the American literary world was again without a major poet to provide it with definition and a common sense of direction.

Landmarks in the revolt against modernist poetry include Allen Ginsberg's Howl (1956) and Robert Lowell's Life Studies (1959), both of which deal vividly with the poets' personal experience. The Confessional School of poets, which included Lowell, Sylvia Plath, and Anne Sexton, wrote frank and revealing poems about their private lives.

A time of diversity. Since the 1970s, American poetry has been characterized by diversity. Extraordinary variety in style and attitude has attracted large new audiences to poetry. Oral performance of poetry has increased, with live poetry "slams" at such places as the Nuyorican Poets Cafe in New York City. Technology has made available thousands of readings on audio-tape and videotape, and even some television broadcasts devoted to poetry.

Much contemporary poetry reflects a democratic quality, often influenced by the works of Walt Whitman and William Carlos Williams. Poetry lives in the people, contemporary poets seem to say, and any walk of life, any everyday experience, any style of expression can result in authentic poetry. These poets often write in the vernacular, the language of common speech, and do not hesitate to surprise or even shock with their language, attitudes, and details of their private lives.

Poetry today is anything but impersonal.

There are good reasons for suggesting that the modern age has ended. Many things indicate that we are going through a transitional period, when it seems that something is on the way out and something else is painfully being born. It is as if something were crumbling, decaying, and exhausting itself, while something else, still indistinct, were arising from the rubble.

The distinguishing features of transitional periods are a mixing and blending of cultures and a plurality or parallelism of intellectual and spiritual worlds. These are periods when all consistent value systems collapse, when cultures distant in time and space are discovered or rediscovered. New meaning is gradually born from the encounter, or the intersection, of many different elements.

Today, this state of mind, or of the human world, is called postmodernism. For me, a symbol of that state is a Bedouin mounted on a camel and clad in traditional robes under which he is wearing jeans, with a transistor radio in his hands and an ad for Coca-Cola on the camel's back.

—Vaclav Havel, political leader of the Czech Republic, on receiving the Philadelphia Liberty Medal, July 4, 1994

Where the Present Meets the Past on the Way to the Future

The literature that captures a wide audience often does so by offering a fresh voice and a new attitude, for these are the powerful needs of each new generation. Yet much of contemporary American literature still deals with the same themes that concerned our greatest writers of the nineteenth century: Poe, Hawthorne, Whitman, Dickinson, Melville, Emerson, and Thoreau. The characters of the novelist John Updike, for example, seek spiritual revelations in ordinary life. "The invariable mark of wisdom," Emerson wrote, "is to find the miraculous in the common." But it is more difficult to find transcendent spiritual values in the cheap clutter of modern life than it was in the woods around Emerson's Concord. Still, Updike's characters continue the search. "I find myself . . . circling back to man's religious nature," Updike has written of his own work, "and the real loss to man and art alike when that nature has nowhere to plug itself in. . . ." These words could serve to describe the work of a great number of contemporary writers whose intellectual roots can be traced to the Transcendentalists of the nineteenth century, and even further back to those hardy, practical Puritans who braved that two-month voyage in a small wooden boat.

> Everything is connected in the end.
> —Don DeLillo
> from *Underworld*

Today, this

state of mind,

or of the

human

world, is

called

postmodernism.

Untitled, 1980 by Keith Haring. Black ink on Bristol board (20″ x 25¾″).

© The Estate of Keith Haring

Quickwrite

Read the quote about postmodernism by Vaclav Havel at the bottom of page 917. How do you think contemporary literature bears out his assertion that new meanings arise from the meeting of a variety of old and new elements? What striking image—like Havel's camel-riding, jeans-clad Bedouin listening to a radio—can you think of that would symbolize the qualities of contemporary American culture?

Wiesel

Jarrell

Hersey

Lowell

Barthelme

O'Brien

Komunyakaa

At the Bomb Testing Site

At noon in the desert a panting lizard
waited for history, its elbows tense,
watching the curve of a particular road
as if something might happen.

It was looking at something farther off
than people could see, an important scene
acted in stone for little selves
at the flute end of consequences.

There was just a continent without much on it
under a sky that never cared less.
Ready for a change, the elbows waited.
The hands gripped hard on the desert.

—William Stafford
(1914–1993)

Elie Wiesel

(1928–   )

In March of 1944, when Elie Wiesel (el´ē wi·zel´) was fifteen, his life changed forever. At the time, Wiesel was living in the little town where he was born—Sighet, a remote village in the Carpathian Mountains of Hungary (now Romania). Raised in the Jewish mystical tradition of Hasidism, Wiesel had spent his childhood years immersed in the heritage of his extended family and in intense religious study. But in March 1944, the German army invaded Hungary. Soon Wiesel, his family, and some fifteen thousand other Jews from his region were rounded up and deported to extermination camps in Nazi-occupied Poland.

What Wiesel experienced in the camps was an unremitting horror. He saw his mother and youngest sister sent to die in a gas chamber, he saw his father succumb to dysentery and senseless violence, and he saw great numbers of fellow prisoners, many of them children, tortured and murdered by the Nazis.

After Wiesel was liberated from Buchenwald concentration camp in April 1945, he could not bring himself to write of the Holocaust for a decade, for fear "that words might betray it." Yet he also remembered the promise he had made to himself: "If, by some miracle, I survive, I will devote my life to testifying on behalf of all those whose shadows will be bound to mine forever." The result of this promise was *Night,* Wiesel's devastating memoir of his experiences under the Nazi terror, originally published in Yiddish as *Un di Velt Hot geshvigen (And the World Kept Silent)* in 1956. In the same year, he came to the United States to cover the United Nations as a reporter. He became a U.S. citizen in 1963 and is now a professor at Boston University.

For over four decades, Wiesel has continued to be a powerful advocate for human dignity—as a novelist, dramatist, journalist, religious scholar, and international activist. Seeking to maintain global awareness of the Nazi atrocities, and to prevent similar crimes against humanity, he has spoken out against human rights abuses in Cambodia, the former Soviet Union, Bosnia and Herzegovina, and South Africa under the Apartheid regime. Such work earned Wiesel a Nobel Peace Prize in 1986. In his acceptance speech, he reflected on his past and his purpose in life.

"This is what I say to the young Jewish boy wondering what I have done with his years. It is in his name that I speak to you and that I express to you my deepest gratitude. No one is as capable of gratitude as one who has emerged from the Kingdom of Night. We know that every moment is a moment of grace, every hour an offering; not to share them would mean to betray them. Our lives no longer belong to us alone; they belong to all those who need us desperately."

Before You Read

FROM **NIGHT**

Make the Connection

Part of the power of Wiesel's memoir lies in its ability to make us feel both enormous empathy and deep fear. How can these feelings change a person? When a writer fulfills his responsibility as a witness, what is your responsibility as a reader?

Quickwrite

Think about a difficult time in your life, one in which you felt afraid, hopeless, or helpless. Jot down your thoughts on how you responded and how you feel you ought to have responded (or how you would respond now).

Elements of Literature

Atmosphere: Witnessing the Scene

As you read these sections of *Night*, notice how Wiesel evokes

the terrifying and brutal **atmosphere** of the Nazi extermination camps without using elaborate figures of speech or ornamentation. How does Wiesel's unadorned style make this atmosphere all the more powerful and disturbing?

Background

World War II forced people to face not only battlefield atrocities, but also the grim reality that an industrialized, civilized society was capable of profound evil. In the Holocaust, or Shoah, the German Nazis and their collaborators made a systematic attempt to destroy all of Europe's Jewish people, who were deemed "racially inferior" by Nazi ideology. By the war's end in 1945, the Nazis had killed over 6 million Jews in what their leaders termed "The

Final Solution." In all, the Nazis murdered more than 11 million civilians—among whom were gypsies, homosexuals, "non-Aryans," political opponents, and captured resistance fighters.

This was an appalling evil: the deliberate torture, starvation, and murder of millions of men, women, and children—without even the pretense that they posed a military threat. But it happened.

On the following pages, you will find three excerpts from Wiesel's memoir. The first excerpt occurs on a train headed for Auschwitz (oush'vits'), the most infamous of the "concentration camps." The account opens after Wiesel and his family have been forced into a railroad car with eighty other Hungarian Jews. They are only beginning to comprehend the horror that awaits them.

Arriving at Auschwitz from Hungary in Spring, 1944.

from Night

Elie Wiesel

translated from the French by **Stella Rodway**

The train stopped at Kaschau,[1] a little town on the Czechoslovak frontier. We realized then that we were not going to stay in Hungary. Our eyes were opened, but too late.

The door of the car slid open. A German officer, accompanied by a Hungarian lieutenant-interpreter, came up and introduced himself.

"From this moment, you come under the authority of the German army. Those of you who

---

1. Kaschau (käsh'ou'): Polish; Košice (kô'shē·tse).

still have gold, silver, or watches in your possession must give them up now. Anyone who is later found to have kept anything will be shot on the spot. Secondly, anyone who feels ill may go to the hospital car. That's all."

The Hungarian lieutenant went among us with a basket and collected the last possessions from those who no longer wished to taste the bitterness of terror.

"There are eighty of you in this wagon," added the German officer. "If anyone is missing, you'll all be shot, like dogs. . . ."

They disappeared. The doors were closed. We were caught in a trap, right up to our necks. The doors were nailed up; the way back was finally cut off. The world was a cattle wagon hermetically sealed.[2]

We had a woman with us named Madame Schächter.[3] She was about fifty; her ten-year-old son was with her, crouched in a corner. Her husband and two eldest sons had been deported with the first transport by mistake. The separation had completely broken her.

I knew her well. A quiet woman with tense, burning eyes, she had often been to our house. Her husband, who was a pious man, spent his days and nights in study, and it was she who worked to support the family.

Madame Schächter had gone out of her mind. On the first day of the journey she had already begun to moan and to keep asking why she had been separated from her family. As time went on, her cries grew hysterical.

On the third night, while we slept, some of us sitting one against the other and some standing, a piercing cry split the silence:

"Fire! I can see a fire! I can see a fire!"

There was a moment's panic. Who was it who had cried out? It was Madame Schächter. Standing in the middle of the wagon, in the pale light from the windows, she looked like a withered tree in a cornfield. She pointed her arm toward the window, screaming:

"Look! Look at it! Fire! A terrible fire! Mercy! *Oh, that fire!*"

Some of the men pressed up against the bars. There was nothing there; only the darkness.

2. **hermetically** (hər·met′ik·lē) **sealed:** airtight.
3. **Schächter** (shekh′tər).

The shock of this terrible awakening stayed with us for a long time. We still trembled from it. With every groan of the wheels on the rail, we felt that an abyss was about to open beneath our bodies. Powerless to still our own anguish, we tried to console ourselves:

"She's mad, poor soul. . . ."

Someone had put a damp cloth on her brow, to calm her, but still her screams went on:

"Fire! Fire!"

Her little boy was crying, hanging onto her skirt, trying to take hold of her hands. "It's all right, Mummy! There's nothing there. . . . Sit down. . . ." This shook me even more than his mother's screams had done.

Some women tried to calm her. "You'll find your husband and your sons again. . . . in a few days. . . ."

She continued to scream, breathless, her voice broken by sobs. "Jews, listen to me! I can see a fire! There are huge flames! It is a furnace!"

It was as though she were possessed by an evil spirit which spoke from the depths of her being.

We tried to explain it away, more to calm ourselves and to recover our own breath than to comfort her. "She must be very thirsty, poor thing! That's why she keeps talking about a fire devouring her."

But it was in vain. Our terror was about to burst the sides of the train. Our nerves were at breaking point. Our flesh was creeping. It was as though madness were taking possession of us all. We could stand it no longer. Some of the young men forced her to sit down, tied her up, and put a gag in her mouth.

Silence again. The little boy sat down by his mother, crying. I had begun to breathe normally again. We could hear the wheels churning out that monotonous rhythm of a train traveling through the night. We could begin to doze, to rest, to dream. . . .

An hour or two went by like this. Then another scream took our breath away. The woman had broken loose from her bonds and was crying out more loudly than ever:

WORDS TO OWN

abyss (ə·bis′) *n.:* gulf or void too deep for measurement.

"Look at the fire! Flames, flames everywhere. . . ."

Once more the young men tied her up and gagged her. They even struck her. People encouraged them:

"Make her be quiet! She's mad! Shut her up! She's not the only one. She can keep her mouth shut. . . ."

They struck her several times on the head—blows that might have killed her. Her little boy clung to her; he did not cry out; he did not say a word. He was not even weeping now.

An endless night. Toward dawn, Madame Schächter calmed down. Crouched in her corner, her bewildered gaze <u>scouring</u> the emptiness, she could no longer see us.

She stayed like that all through the day, dumb, absent, isolated among us. As soon as night fell, she began to scream: "There's a fire over there!" She would point at a spot in space, always the same one. They were tired of hitting her. The heat, the thirst, the pestilential[4] stench, the suffocating lack of air—these were as nothing compared with these screams which tore us to shreds. A few days more and we should all have started to scream too.

But we had reached a station. Those who were next to the windows told us its name:

"Auschwitz."

No one had ever heard that name.

The train did not start up again. The afternoon passed slowly. Then the wagon doors slid open. Two men were allowed to get down to fetch water.

When they came back, they told us that, in exchange for a gold watch, they had discovered that this was the last stop. We would be getting out here. There was a labor camp. Conditions were good. Families would not be split up. Only the young people would go to work in the factories. The old men and invalids would be kept occupied in the fields.

The barometer of confidence soared. Here was a sudden release from the terrors of the previous nights. We gave thanks to God.

Madame Schächter stayed in her corner, wilted, dumb, indifferent to the general confidence. Her little boy stroked her hand.

4. **pestilential** (pes′tə·len′shəl): like a pestilence or deadly infection; dangerous and harmful.

As dusk fell, darkness gathered inside the wagon. We started to eat our last provisions. At ten in the evening, everyone was looking for a convenient position in which to sleep for a while, and soon we were all asleep. Suddenly:

"The fire! The furnace! Look, over there! . . ."

Waking with a start, we rushed to the window. Yet again we had believed her, even if only for a moment. But there was nothing outside save the darkness of night. With shame in our souls, we went back to our places, gnawed by fear, in spite of ourselves. As she continued to scream, they began to hit her again, and it was with the greatest difficulty that they silenced her.

The man in charge of our wagon called a German officer who was walking about on the platform, and asked him if Madame Schächter could be taken to the hospital car.

"You must be patient," the German replied. "She'll be taken there soon."

Toward eleven o'clock, the train began to move. We pressed against the windows. The convoy was moving slowly. A quarter of an hour later, it slowed down again. Through the windows we could see barbed wire; we realized that this must be the camp.

We had forgotten the existence of Madame Schächter. Suddenly, we heard terrible screams:

"Jews, look! Look through the window! Flames! Look!"

And as the train stopped, we saw this time that flames were gushing out of a tall chimney into the black sky.

Madame Schächter was silent herself. Once more she had become dumb, indifferent, absent, and had gone back to her corner.

We looked at the flames in the darkness. There was an abominable odor floating in the air. Suddenly, our doors opened. Some odd-looking characters, dressed in striped shirts and black trousers, leapt into the wagon. They held electric torches[5] and truncheons.[6] They began to strike out to right and left, shouting:

5. **electric torches:** flashlights.
6. **truncheons** (trun′chənz): short, thick clubs.

WORDS TO OWN

scouring (skour′iŋ) v.: roaming about, searching.

"Everybody get out! Everyone out of the wagon! Quickly!"

We jumped out. I threw a last glance toward Madame Schächter. Her little boy was holding her hand.

In front of us flames. In the air that smell of burning flesh. It must have been about midnight. We had arrived—at Birkenau,[7] reception center for Auschwitz. . . .

7. Birkenau (bir′kə·nou).

The following section of Night *takes place in Buna* (bōō′nə), *another camp in Poland, where Wiesel and his father were sent from Auschwitz. It documents the horrifying process of selection, by which the Nazis separated those prisoners judged fit to perform slave labor from those who were to be killed immediately. It was after just such a selection that Wiesel's mother and sister were murdered in the Auschwitz gas chamber.*

The head of our block had never been outside concentration camps since 1933. He had already been through all the slaughterhouses, all the factories of death. At about nine o'clock, he took up his position in our midst:

"Achtung!"[8]

There was instant silence.

"Listen carefully to what I am going to say." (For the first time, I heard his voice quiver.) "In a few moments the selection will begin. You must get completely undressed. Then one by one you go before the SS[9] doctors. I hope you will all succeed in getting through. But you must help your own chances. Before you go into the next room, move about in some way so that you give yourselves a little color. Don't walk slowly, run! Run as if the devil were after you! Don't look at the SS. Run, straight in front of you!"

He broke off for a moment, then added:

"And, the essential thing, don't be afraid!"

Here was a piece of advice we should have liked very much to be able to follow.

I got undressed, leaving my clothes on the bed. There was no danger of anyone stealing them this evening.

Tibi and Yossi, who had changed their unit at the same time as I had, came up to me and said:

"Let's keep together. We shall be stronger."

Yossi was murmuring something between his teeth. He must have been praying. I had never realized that Yossi was a believer. I had even always

thought the reverse. Tibi was silent, very pale. All the prisoners in the block stood naked between the beds. This must be how one stands at the last judgment.

"They're coming!"

There were three SS officers standing round the notorious Dr. Mengele,[10] who had received us at Birkenau. The head of the block, with an attempt at a smile, asked us:

"Ready?"

Yes, we were ready. So were the SS doctors. Dr. Mengele was holding a list in his hand: our numbers.[11] He made a sign to the head of the block: "We can begin!" As if this were a game!

The first to go by were the "officials" of the block: *Stubenaelteste,*[12] Kapos,[13] foremen, all in perfect physical condition of course! Then came the ordinary prisoners' turn. Dr. Mengele took stock of them from head to foot. Every now and then, he wrote a number down. One single thought filled my mind: not to let my number be taken; not to show my left arm.

There were only Tibi and Yossi in front of me. They passed. I had time to notice that Mengele had not written their numbers down. Someone pushed me. It was my turn. I ran without looking

8. Achtung (əkh′tooŋ): German for "attention."
9. SS: Abbreviation for the German *Schutzstaffel* (shoots′shtä′fəl), meaning "protection squad," the elite Nazi guards who oversaw the operation of the concentration camps.

10. Dr. Mengele: Josef Mengele (yō′zef′ meŋ′ə·lə) (1911-1979) was a Nazi doctor and SS officer infamous for torturing camp prisoners, often children, sometimes in pseudoscientific experiments.
11. our numbers: Concentration camp prisoners were identified by a number, which was usually tattooed on the left arm shortly after arrival.
12. *Stubenaelteste* (shtoob′ən·el′təst·ə): German for "barracks leaders" or "room leaders."
13. Kapos (kä′pōz): prisoners appointed by the Nazis to head work gangs, often in exchange for better treatment.

back. My head was spinning: you're too thin, you're weak, you're too thin, you're good for the furnace. . . . The race seemed interminable. I thought I had been running for years. . . . You're too thin, you're too weak. . . . At last I had arrived exhausted. When I regained my breath, I questioned Yossi and Tibi:

"Was I written down?"

"No," said Yossi. He added, smiling: "In any case, he couldn't have written you down, you were running too fast. . . ."

I began to laugh. I was glad. I would have liked to kiss him. At that moment, what did the others matter! I hadn't been written down.

Those whose numbers had been noted stood apart, abandoned by the whole world. Some were weeping in silence. . . .

Several days had elapsed. We no longer thought about the selection. We went to work as usual, loading heavy stones into railway wagons. Rations had become more meager: this was the only change.

We had risen before dawn, as on every day. We had received the black coffee, the ration of bread. We were about to set out for the yard as usual. The head of the block arrived, running.

"Silence for a moment. I have a list of numbers here. I'm going to read them to you. Those whose numbers I call won't be going to work this morning; they'll stay behind in the camp."

And, in a soft voice, he read out about ten numbers. We had understood. These were numbers chosen at the selection. Dr. Mengele had not forgotten.

The head of the block went toward his room. Ten prisoners surrounded him, hanging onto his clothes:

"Save us! You promised . . . ! We want to go to the yard. We're strong enough to work. We're good workers. We can . . . we will. . . ."

He tried to calm them, to reassure them about their fate, to explain to them that the fact that they were staying behind in the camp did not mean much, had no tragic significance.

"After all, I stay here myself every day," he added.

It was a somewhat feeble argument. He realized it, and without another word went and shut himself up in his room.

The bell had just rung.

"Form up!"

It scarcely mattered now that the work was hard. The essential thing was to be as far away as possible from the block, from the crucible of death, from the center of hell.

I saw my father running toward me. I became frightened all of a sudden.

"What's the matter?"

Out of breath, he could hardly open his mouth.

"Me, too . . . me, too . . . ! They told me to stay behind in the camp."

They had written down his number without his being aware of it.

"What will happen?" I asked in anguish.

But it was he who tried to reassure me.

"It isn't certain yet. There's still a chance of escape. They're going to do another selection today . . . a decisive selection."

I was silent.

He felt that his time was short. He spoke quickly. He would have liked to say so many

Identity card and yellow star for a Jew living in Amsterdam in 1943.

things. His speech grew confused; his voice choked. He knew that I would have to go in a few moments. He would have to stay behind alone, so very alone.

"Look, take this knife," he said to me. "I don't need it any longer. It might be useful to you. And take this spoon as well. Don't sell them. Quickly! Go on. Take what I'm giving you!"

The inheritance.

"Don't talk like that, Father." (I felt that I would break into sobs.) "I don't want you to say that. Keep the spoon and knife. You need them as much as I do. We shall see each other again this evening, after work."

He looked at me with his tired eyes, veiled with despair. He went on:

"I'm asking this of you. . . . Take them. Do as I ask, my son. We have no time. . . . Do as your father asks."

Our Kapo yelled that we should start.

The unit set out toward the camp gate. Left, right! I bit my lips. My father had stayed by the block, leaning against the wall. Then he began to run, to catch up with us. Perhaps he had forgotten something he wanted to say to me. . . . But we were marching too quickly . . . Left, right!

We were already at the gate. They counted us, to the din of military music. We were outside.

The whole day, I wandered about as if sleepwalking. Now and then Tibi and Yossi would throw me a brotherly word. The Kapo, too, tried to reassure me. He had given me easier work today. I felt sick at heart. How well they were treating me! Like an orphan! I thought: even now, my father is still helping me.

I did not know myself what I wanted—for the day to pass quickly or not. I was afraid of finding myself alone that night. How good it would be to die here!

At last we began the return journey. How I longed for orders to run!

The military march. The gate. The camp.

I ran to Block 36.

Were there still miracles on this earth? He was alive. He had escaped the second selection. He had been able to prove that he was still useful. . . . I gave him back his knife and spoon.

Akiba Drumer left us, a victim of the selection. Lately, he had wandered among us, his eyes glazed, telling everyone of his weakness: "I can't go on . . . It's all over. . . ." It was impossible to raise his morale. He didn't listen to what we told him. He could only repeat that all was over for him, that he could no longer keep up the struggle, that he had no strength left, nor faith. Suddenly his eyes would become blank, nothing but two open wounds, two pits of terror.

He was not the only one to lose his faith during those selection days. I knew a rabbi from a little town in Poland, a bent old man, whose lips were always trembling. He used to pray all the time, in the block, in the yard, in the ranks. He would recite whole pages of the Talmud from memory, argue with himself, ask himself questions and answer himself. And one day he said to me: "It's the end. God is no longer with us."

And, as though he had repented of having spoken such words, so clipped, so cold, he added in his faint voice:

"I know. One has no right to say things like that. I know. Man is too small, too humble and inconsiderable to seek to understand the mysterious ways of God. But what can I do? I'm not a sage, one of the elect, nor a saint. I'm just an ordinary creature of flesh and blood. I've got eyes, too, and I can see what they're doing here. Where is the divine Mercy? Where is God? How can I believe, how could anyone believe, in this merciful God?"

Poor Akiba Drumer, if he could have gone on believing in God, if he could have seen a proof of God in this Calvary,[14] he would not have been taken by the selection. But as soon as he felt the first cracks forming in his faith, he had lost his reason for struggling and had begun to die.

When the selection came, he was condemned in advance, offering his own neck to the executioner. All he asked of us was:

"In three days I shall no longer be here. . . . Say the Kaddish[15] for me."

---

14. Calvary: Wiesel compares Drumer's tragedy to the crucifixion of Jesus, which took place at the site near Jerusalem called Golgotha, or Calvary.

15. Kaddish (käd'ish): Jewish prayer in praise of God, one form of which is recited to mourn a death.

We promised him. In three days' time, when we saw the smoke rising from the chimney, we would think of him. Ten of us would gather together and hold a special service. All his friends would say the Kaddish.

Then he went off toward the hospital, his step steadier, not looking back. An ambulance was waiting to take him to Birkenau.

These were terrible days. We received more blows than food; we were crushed with work. And three days after he had gone we forgot to say the Kaddish. . . .

Concentration Camp (1944) by Ben Shahn. Tempera (24″ x 24″).
©Estate of Ben Shahn/Licensed by VAGA, New York, NY. Courtesy Sotheby's N.Y.

The next section of Night *occurs toward the end of Wiesel's eleven months in the concentration camps. It opens during a brutal march toward a new camp, Gleiwitz (glī'vits). The Nazi guards have forced the prisoners to run for miles in the snow without adequate rest or clothing. As a result, hundreds will die before they reach the dangerously overcrowded barracks.*

The door of the shed opened. An old man appeared, his moustache covered with frost, his lips blue with cold. It was Rabbi Eliahou,[16] the rabbi of a small Polish community. He was a very good man, well loved by everyone in the camp, even by the Kapos and the heads of the blocks. Despite the trials and privations, his face still shone with his inner purity. He was the only rabbi who was always addressed as "Rabbi" at Buna. He was like one of the old prophets, always in the midst of his people to comfort them. And, strangely, his words of comfort never provoked rebellion; they really brought peace.

He came into the shed and his eyes, brighter than ever, seemed to be looking for someone:

"Perhaps someone has seen my son somewhere?"

He had lost his son in the crowd. He had looked in vain among the dying. Then he had scratched up the snow to find his corpse. Without result.

For three years they had stuck together. Always near each other, for suffering, for blows, for the ration of bread, for prayer. Three years, from camp to camp, from selection to selection. And now—when the end seemed near—fate had separated them. Finding himself near me, Rabbi Eliahou whispered:

"It happened on the road. We lost sight of one another during the journey. I had stayed a little to the rear of the column. I hadn't any strength left for running. And my son didn't notice. That's all I know. Where has he disappeared? Where can I find him? Perhaps you've seen him somewhere?"

"No, Rabbi Eliahou, I haven't seen him."

He left then as he had come: like a wind-swept shadow.

He had already passed through the door when I suddenly remembered seeing his son running by my side. I had forgotten that, and I didn't tell Rabbi Eliahou!

Then I remembered something else: his son had seen him losing ground, limping, staggering back to the rear of the column. He had seen him. And he had continued to run on in front, letting the distance between them grow greater.

A terrible thought loomed up in my mind: he had wanted to get rid of his father! He had felt that his father was growing weak, he had believed that the end was near and had sought this separation in order to get rid of the burden, to free himself from an <u>encumbrance</u> which could lessen his own chances of survival.

I had done well to forget that. And I was glad that Rabbi Eliahou should continue to look for his beloved son.

And, in spite of myself, a prayer rose in my heart, to that God in whom I no longer believed.

My God, Lord of the Universe, give me strength never to do what Rabbi Eliahou's son has done.

Shouts rose outside in the yard, where darkness had fallen. The SS ordered the ranks to form up.

The march began again. The dead stayed in the yard under the snow, like faithful guards assassinated, without burial. No one had said the prayer for the dead over them. Sons abandoned their fathers' remains without a tear.

On the way it snowed, snowed, snowed endlessly. We were marching more slowly. The guards themselves seemed tired. My wounded foot no longer hurt me. It must have been completely frozen. The foot was lost to me. It had detached itself from my body like the wheel of a car. Too bad. I should have to resign myself; I could live with only one leg. The main thing was not to think about it. Above all, not at this moment. Leave thoughts for later.

Our march had lost all <u>semblance</u> of discipline.

WORDS TO OWN
encumbrance (en·kum'brəns) *n.*: hindrance; burden.
semblance (sem'bləns) *n.*: appearance, resemblance.

---

16. **Eliahou** (el·ē·ä'hōō').

We went as we wanted, as we could. We heard no more shots. Our guards must have been tired.

But death scarcely needed any help from them. The cold was <u>conscientiously</u> doing its work. At every step someone fell and suffered no more.

From time to time, SS officers on motorcycles would go down the length of the column to try and shake us out of our growing apathy:

"Keep going! We are getting there!"

"Courage! Only a few more hours!"

"We're reaching Gleiwitz."

These words of encouragement, even though they came from the mouths of our assassins, did us a great deal of good. No one wanted to give up now, just before the end, so near to the goal. Our eyes searched the horizon for the barbed wire of Gleiwitz. Our only desire was to reach it as quickly as possible.

The night had now set in. The snow had ceased to fall. We walked for several more hours before arriving.

We did not notice the camp until we were just in front of the gate.

Some Kapos rapidly installed us in the barracks. We pushed and jostled one another as if this were the supreme refuge, the gateway to life. We walked over pain-racked bodies. We trod on wounded faces. No cries. A few groans. My father and I were ourselves thrown to the ground by this rolling tide. Beneath our feet someone let out a rattling cry:

"You're crushing me . . . mercy!"

A voice that was not unknown to me.

"You're crushing me . . . mercy! mercy!"

The same faint voice, the same rattle, heard somewhere before. That voice had spoken to me one day. Where? When? Years ago? No, it could only have been at the camp.

"Mercy!"

I felt that I was crushing him. I was stopping his breath. I wanted to get up. I struggled to disengage myself, so that he could breathe. But I was crushed myself beneath the weight of other bodies. I could hardly breathe. I dug my nails into unknown faces. I was biting all round me, in order to get air. No one cried out.

Suddenly I remembered. Juliek![17] The boy from Warsaw who played the violin in the band at Buna. . . .

"Juliek, is it you?"

"Eliezer[18]. . . the twenty-five strokes of the whip. Yes . . . I remember."

He was silent. A long moment elapsed.

"Juliek! Can you hear me, Juliek?"

"Yes . . . ," he said, in a feeble voice. "What do you want?"

He was not dead.

"How do you feel, Juliek?" I asked, less to know the answer than to hear that he could speak, that he was alive.

"All right, Eliezer. . . . I'm getting on all right . . . hardly any air . . . worn out. My feet are swollen. It's good to rest, but my violin . . ."

I thought he had gone out of his mind. What use was the violin here?

"What, your violin?"

He gasped.

"I'm afraid . . . I'm afraid . . . that they'll break my violin. . . . I've brought it with me."

I could not answer him. Someone was lying full length on top of me, covering my face. I was unable to breathe, through either mouth or nose. Sweat beaded my brow, ran down my spine. This was the end—the end of the road. A silent death, suffocation. No way of crying out, of calling for help.

I tried to get rid of my invisible assassin. My whole will to live was centered in my nails. I scratched. I battled for a mouthful of air. I tore at decaying flesh which did not respond. I could not free myself from this mass weighing down my chest. Was it a dead man I was struggling against? Who knows?

I shall never know. All I can say is that I won. I succeeded in digging a hole through this wall of dying people, a little hole through which I could drink in a small quantity of air.

"Father, how are you?" I asked, as soon as I could utter a word.

I knew he could not be far from me.

18. **Eliezer** (ā·lē·ā′zər).

17. **Juliek** (yoo′lē·ek).

WORDS TO OWN

conscientiously (kän′shē·en′shəs·lē) adv.: diligently; thoroughly.

"Well!" answered a distant voice, which seemed to come from another world. I tried to sleep.

He tried to sleep. Was he right or wrong? Could one sleep here? Was it not dangerous to allow your vigilance to fail, even for a moment, when at any minute death could pounce upon you?

I was thinking of this when I heard the sound of a violin. The sound of a violin, in this dark shed, where the dead were heaped on the living. What madman could be playing the violin here, at the brink of his own grave? Or was it really an hallucination?

It must have been Juliek.

He played a fragment from Beethoven's concerto. I had never heard sounds so pure. In such a silence.

How had he managed to free himself? To draw his body from under mine without my being aware of it?

It was pitch-dark. I could hear only the violin, and it was as though Juliek's soul were the bow. He was playing his life. The whole of his life was gliding on the strings—his lost hopes, his charred past, his extinguished future. He played as he would never play again.

I shall never forget Juliek. How could I forget that concert, given to an audience of dying and dead men! To this day, whenever I hear Beethoven played my eyes close and out of the dark rises the sad, pale face of my Polish friend, as he said farewell on his violin to an audience of dying men.

I do not know for how long he played. I was overcome by sleep. When I awoke, in the daylight, I could see Juliek, opposite me, slumped over, dead. Near him lay his violin, smashed, trampled, a strange overwhelming little corpse.

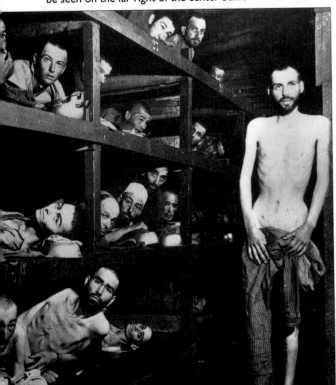

Slave laborers in the barracks of Buchenwald concentration camp, April 16, 1945. Elie Wiesel is the man whose face can be seen on the far right of the center bunk.

MAKING MEANINGS

First Thoughts

1. Wiesel was just fifteen years old when he arrived at Auschwitz. Imagine what it would have been like to experience what he experienced at that age. How might it have changed you? Look over your Quickwrite notes as you formulate your answer.

Shaping Interpretations

2. In the first excerpt, what do you think is the cause of Madame Schächter's terrible vision?

3. In the second excerpt, how has Akiba Drumer "begun to die" when he starts to lose his faith in God? What do you think kept Wiesel from giving up?

4. In the third excerpt, why is it **ironic** that Rabbi Eliahou will "continue to look for his beloved son"? Why is Wiesel glad that he will keep looking?

Reading Check

a. What does Madame Schächter see on the journey? What effects do her cries have on her fellow prisoners?

b. When they arrive at Auschwitz, what do the prisoners find that shows Madame Schächter's vision was tragically accurate?

c. In the second excerpt, what does the head of Wiesel's block advise the prisoners to do before the selection process? Why?

d. What is Akiba Drumer's last request?

e. In the third excerpt, what does Juliek play at Gleiwitz? Who is his audience?

5. At the end of the third excerpt, why do you think Wiesel uses the **metaphor** of "a strange overwhelming little corpse" to describe Juliek's violin? What might the violin **symbolize** for Wiesel?

6. Select at least two passages from this text that create, for you, the dreadful **atmosphere** of the camps where Wiesel was held prisoner. Which specific words help create that atmosphere? Be sure to share your passages in class.

Connecting with the Text

7. When Wiesel accepted the Nobel Peace Prize, he said that "[i]ndifference is the greatest source of evil and danger in the world." He also sug-gested that if humanity ever forgets the Holo-caust, "we are guilty, we are accomplices." What do you think Wiesel meant? Do you agree? What actions could people take to help combat such indifference to human suffering?

Extending the Text

8. In his humanitarian work, Wiesel struggles against what he calls "selective sensitivity," in which "people are sensitive only to one category of victims and not to the others." He demands instead that "[i]f one is sensitive to one injustice, one must be sensitive to all injustice." Discuss situations in the world today where you find this "selective sensitivity" at work.

CHOICES: Building Your Portfolio

Writer's Notebook

1. Collecting Ideas for an Evaluation

Wiesel and other sur-vivors of the Holocaust are living exam-ples of how the human spirit and its best impulses can endure in the worst, most immoral circumstances. Yet Wiesel also chooses not to ignore how cruelly some of his fellow prisoners treated one another in their terror and desperation. Do you approve of his decision? Is such **objective reporting** always necessary? Jot down some points in support of your position, using specific examples from the text. Save your notes for possible use in the Writer's Work-shop on page 1181.

Comparing Texts

2. Journeys into Night

Write a brief essay in which you compare Wiesel's nar-ration of his journey to Auschwitz with Olaudah Equiano's narration of his middle-passage journey in a slave ship (page 57). What **tone** does each narrator take when describing the conditions under which the captives are forced to live? How does each narrator feel about his captors? How does each narrator use **foreshadowing** to prepare readers for what lies ahead?

Comparing Texts

3. No One Left

The following tale was told by a German pastor named Martin Niemöller, who found the courage to resist the Nazis during World War II. Read Niemöller's cautionary tale carefully. In a brief essay, explain the **main point** of the tale and tell how it connects with Wiesel's experience. Is there any connection with world events today?

In Germany, the Nazis first came for the Communists and I didn't speak up because I wasn't a Communist. Then they came for the Jews and I did not speak up because I was not a Jew. Then they came for the trade unionists and I didn't speak up because I was not a trade unionist. Then they came for the Catholics and I was a Protestant so I didn't speak up. Then they came for me: by that time there was no one left to speak up.

—*Martin Niemöller*

Randall Jarrell

(1914–1965)

Elliott Erwitt/Magnum.

One of the most careful and erudite readers of contemporary poetry, Randall Jarrell was, at the same time, both an abrasive critic and a generous promoter of the art of poetry.

Born in Nashville, Tennessee, Jarrell was brought up in California. His childhood experiences included close observation of the gaudy remnants of the old Hollywood, a personal acquaintance with the MGM lion, and an appreciation of the difference between fantasy and fact—between life and myths about life—that would provide him with themes for poetry for years to come.

After graduating from Vanderbilt University in his native city, Jarrell began a career that led to positions in the English departments of many colleges and universities from Texas to New York. In 1942, he joined the Army Air Corps and served for a time as a pilot and then, for a longer time, as Celestial Navigation Trainer of pilots assigned to fly the famous B-29 bombers of World War II. Out of this experience came two notable books of poetry, *Little Friend, Little Friend* (1945) and *Losses* (1948). Many critics say these books rank among the best American contributions to the literature of World War II.

A man of extraordinary wit, Jarrell gave full play to his gifts in his often caustic and devastating critical articles and essays, particularly in the collection *A Sad Heart at the Supermarket* (1962). In poetry, however, his faculty for contemptuous criticism is kept under wraps: His wit shows itself only in mellow good humor ("I feel like the first men who read Wordsworth. / It's so simple I can't understand it.") and in a resigned toleration of the more absurd aspects of American life.

Jarrell died when struck by a car while walking on a North Carolina highway in 1965. His tragic death raised a question: Was it actually a suicide? But of his loss to American letters and to the poets who had counted upon him to explain, judge, and celebrate their art, there was no question at all.

Before You Read

THE DEATH OF THE BALL TURRET GUNNER

Make the Connection

Five Famous Lines

These five lines, written in 1945, make up the most famous poem to come out of World War II.

Quickwrite

Write your thoughts on these questions: What attitude toward war do you expect to find in most literature and films produced today? Is war literature today more cynical than it used to be?

The Death of the Ball Turret Gunner

Randall Jarrell

From my mother's sleep I fell into the State,
And I hunched in its belly till my wet fur froze.
Six miles from earth, loosed from its dream of life,
I woke to black flak and the nightmare fighters.
When I died they washed me out of the turret with a hose.

PRIMARY Sources — A COMMENT

The Ball Turret

A ball turret was a plexiglass sphere set into the belly of a B-17 or B-24, and inhabited by two .50 caliber machine guns and one man, a short, small man. When this gunner tracked with his machine guns a fighter attacking his bomber from below, he revolved with the turret; hunched upside down in his little sphere, he looked like the fetus in the womb. The fighters which attacked him were armed with cannon firing explosive shells. The hose was a steam hose.

—Randall Jarrell

MAKING MEANINGS

First Thoughts

1. Do you find this poem shocking? Why or why not?

Shaping Interpretations

2. "Belly" here can be read on two levels. What two bellies is the speaker talking about?

3. How do you know that the speaker didn't enter the army on the basis of a rational decision?

4. What is the speaker's "wet fur"? Why do you think he compares himself to an animal?

5. Do you think the speaker is a hero? Explain.

6. What, in the long run, do you think this poem is about? Is it about political dissent? Is it a statement about the way things in the world are regimented and mechanized? Is it about the destruction of the innocent? Explain your views.

Extending the Text

7. Hollywood has produced hundreds of movies about war. These movies reflect a wide spectrum of attitudes. Some show soldiers as heroes, some as victims; some evoke pride in one's country, some hatred of another country; some summon nostalgia for a past era. Think of some war movies you have seen, and analyze their attitudes toward war. (Be sure to check your Quickwrite notes.)

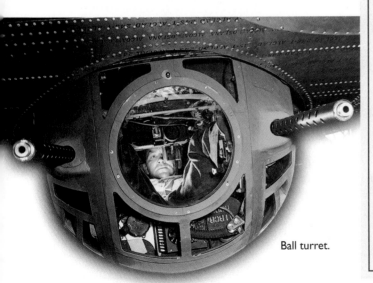
Ball turret.

CHOICES:
Building Your Portfolio

Writer's Notebook

1. Collecting Ideas for an Evaluation

If you were writing an evaluation of "The Death of the Ball Turret Gunner," what facts would a general audience need to know? Write down aspects of the real-world context of the poem—relevant information about World War II, the ball turret, and Jarrell's experiences. Keep your notes for possible use in the Writer's Workshop on page 1181.

Interpreting an Extended Metaphor

2. Hunched in the Belly

In a brief essay, explain the **extended metaphor** that runs through the poem. Is there something **ironic** about the metaphor? Explain your interpretation.

Creative Writing

3. Speaking Out

Find a newspaper article about someone who has died. Write a paragraph or a short poem from the point of view of that person as you imagine him or her. Imitate the style of "The Death of the Ball Turret Gunner." Speak as "I."

Speaking and Listening

4. Whose Emphasis?

Poems are musical. They are meant to be read aloud or recited from memory. When performing a poem aloud, each of us tends to emphasize different words as we give our particular spin to the poem. Together with another student, perform "The Death of the Ball Turret Gunner" before the class. The class should try to spot differences, even small differences, between the performances, and discuss how different interpretations affect the meaning of the poem.

John Hersey

(1914–1993)

Brown Brothers.

What book was considered so extraordinary that the great scientist Albert Einstein ordered one thousand copies? What book was thought so compelling that the Book-of-the-Month Club distributed free copies because no book "could be of more importance at this moment to the human race"? The book is *Hiroshima,* by John Hersey.

Hersey was born in China, where he lived until he was ten. He later graduated from Yale and studied at Cambridge University in England, served as private secretary to the American novelist Sinclair Lewis, and reported from the South Pacific and the Mediterranean during World War II for *Time* and *Life* magazines.

But journalism (if that means objective, factual reporting) could not contain Hersey's passionate concern about contemporary events. In 1945, he won a Pulitzer Prize for his novel *A Bell for Adano,* based on what he had seen of American military government in Italy. Some critics saw this novel as a troubling examination of democracy and its ideals, and the difficulties of putting it into practice.

In 1946, Hersey published *Hiroshima.* Combining techniques of a novel and the factual air of journalism to describe a real event, *Hiroshima* began what some critics call the genre of the "nonfiction novel." (Other examples include Truman Capote's *In Cold Blood* [1966] and Norman Mailer's *The Executioner's Song* [1979].) Hersey took an almost incomprehensible act, the dropping of an atomic bomb on a civilian population, and showed how it affected the lives of six survivors. Through their eyes, Americans could experience this catastrophe as if it were happening to them and to their friends and neighbors. Through Hersey's vivid narrative and his gift for characterization, the unimaginable became horrifyingly real.

Hiroshima became a national event, a precursor of the kind of celebrity status that best-sellers often enjoy today, with attention paid to the authors on talk shows and in interviews in magazines and newspapers. *Hiroshima* first appeared in *The New Yorker,* which devoted an entire issue to the book—a startling commitment for a magazine. The American Broadcasting Company had the book read aloud on its radio stations. *Hiroshima* has since been called the most significant piece of reportage in modern times.

After *Hiroshima,* Hersey became famous as a writer who could make history understandable. While serving as a teacher and mentor at Yale, he continued to dramatize issues and events, dealing with the Holocaust, racism, fascism, and other evils of modern life. He called his type of fiction "the novel of contemporary history" and wrote that "this kind of novel should make anyone who reads it better able to meet life in his generation—whenever that generation may be." He produced books in a steady stream from the 1940s to the 1990s, sending his publisher a manuscript of new short stories, *Key West Tales,* six weeks before his death. His books include the highly acclaimed novel *The Wall* (1950), about the annihilation of Polish Jews in the Warsaw ghetto, and *Blues* (1987), a brilliant meditation on Hersey's favorite sport, fishing. (The book, of course, turns out to be about much more than fly-casting and trolling.)

None of Hersey's other works achieved the impact of *Hiroshima.* The book continues to force readers to face the horrifying realities of nuclear war. In half a century, no book on nuclear warfare has come close to *Hiroshima*'s impact on our moral and ethical sensibilities.

Before You Read
A NOISELESS FLASH

Make the Connection
The Human Element

Modern war, waged with highly sophisticated weaponry, is often described in *numerical* terms: how many missiles fired, how many targets annihilated, how many people killed. In the face of such abstraction, writers and artists force us to confront the personal element in war. By telling us about the details of other people's lives, writers remind us that, even in war, we are all—friend and foe—human beings first and foremost.

Reading Skills and Strategies

Reading Closely for Details

As you read this account of the effects of the atomic bomb explosion on six people in Hiroshima, note the many precise details Hersey uses to lend his account authenticity. Skim the account before you start reading. Note the six sections, each set off by extra space. Locate the name of the person Hersey is focusing on in each section. Then, pick one of the six people, and, as you read, take notes on the key details Hersey gives you about that person.

Elements of Literature
Subjectivity and Objectivity

In **subjective reporting,** the writer openly expresses personal emotions and attitudes toward the events and characters he or she is writing about. In **objective reporting,** such as John Hersey's, the writer presents mainly observable, verifiable facts and keeps his or her own feelings at a distance. At times, the only way we can discover how such a writer feels about an event is by analyzing the details specifically chosen for inclusion or omission.

> In **subjective reporting,** the writer openly expresses emotions and attitudes toward events and characters. In **objective reporting,** the writer keeps his or her feelings at a distance.

Background

War between the United States and Japan began on December 7, 1941, when the Japanese suddenly attacked the U.S. naval base at Pearl Harbor, in Hawaii. By mid-1945, after many costly battles, the United States and its allies were nearing the final victory in World War II as they pressed toward an invasion of the main Japanese islands. As part of the endgame against Japan, the United States used its newest and most powerful weapon, the atomic bomb, twice—first to destroy Hiroshima, and then, three days later, to devastate another Japanese city, Nagasaki.

First photo taken of Hiroshima after the atomic explosion, August 6, 1945.

Matsushige/Sygma.

A Noiseless Flash

from Hiroshima

John Hersey

At exactly fifteen minutes past eight in the morning, on August 6, 1945, Japanese time, at the moment when the atomic bomb flashed above Hiroshima, Miss Toshiko Sasaki, a clerk in the personnel department of the East Asia Tin Works, had just sat down at her place in the plant office and was turning her head to speak to the girl at the next desk. At that same moment, Dr. Masakazu Fujii was settling down cross-legged to read the Osaka *Asahi*[1] on the porch of his private hospital, overhanging one of the seven deltaic rivers which divide Hiroshima; Mrs. Hatsuyo Nakamura, a tailor's widow, stood by the window of her kitchen, watching a neighbor tearing down

his house because it lay in the path of an air-raid-defense fire lane; Father Wilhelm Kleinsorge, a German priest of the Society of Jesus,[2] reclined in his underwear on a cot on the top floor of his order's three-story mission house, reading a Jesuit magazine, *Stimmen der Zeit*;[3] Dr. Terufumi Sasaki, a young member of the surgical staff of the city's large, modern Red Cross Hospital, walked along one of the hospital corridors with a blood specimen for a Wassermann test[4] in his hand; and the

1. *Asahi:* Japanese for "morning sun." The Osaka *Asahi* is the city newspaper.

2. **Society of Jesus:** Roman Catholic religious order of priests and brothers, also known as the Jesuit (jezh′o͞o·it) order.

3. *Stimmen der Zeit* (shtim′ən der tsīt): German for "Voices of the Times."

4. **Wassermann test:** blood test used to diagnose syphilis.

Reverend Mr. Kiyoshi Tanimoto, pastor of the Hiroshima Methodist Church, paused at the door of a rich man's house in Koi, the city's western suburb, and prepared to unload a handcart full of things he had evacuated from town in fear of the massive B-29 raid which everyone expected Hiroshima to suffer. A hundred thousand people were killed by the atomic bomb, and these six were among the survivors. They still wonder why they lived when so many others died. Each of them counts many small items of chance or volition—a step taken in time, a decision to go indoors, catching one streetcar instead of the next—that spared him. And now each knows that in the act of survival he lived a dozen lives and saw more death than he ever thought he would see. At the time, none of them knew anything.

The Reverend Mr. Tanimoto got up at five o'clock that morning. He was alone in the parsonage, because for some time his wife had been commuting with their year-old baby to spend nights with a friend in Ushida, a suburb to the north. Of all the important cities of Japan, only two, Kyoto[5] and Hiroshima, had not been visited in strength by *B-san*, or Mr. B, as the Japanese, with a mixture of respect and unhappy familiarity, called the B-29; and Mr. Tanimoto, like all his neighbors and friends, was almost sick with anxiety. He had heard uncomfortably detailed accounts of mass raids on Kure, Iwakuni, Tokuyama, and other nearby towns; he was sure Hiroshima's turn would come soon. He had slept badly the night before, because there had been several air-raid warnings. Hiroshima had been getting such warnings almost every night for weeks, for at that time the B-29s were using Lake Biwa, northeast of Hiroshima, as a <u>rendezvous</u> point, and no matter what city the Americans planned to hit, the Superfortresses streamed in over the coast near Hiroshima. The frequency of the warnings and the continued <u>abstinence</u> of Mr. B with respect to Hiroshima had made its citizens jittery; a rumor was going around that the Americans were saving something special for the city.

Mr. Tanimoto is a small man, quick to talk, laugh, and cry. He wears his black hair parted in the middle and rather long; the prominence of the frontal bones just above his eyebrows and the smallness of his moustache, mouth, and chin give him a strange, old-young look, boyish and yet wise, weak and yet fiery. He moves nervously and fast, but with a restraint which suggests that he is a cautious, thoughtful man. He showed, indeed, just those qualities in the uneasy days before the bomb fell. Besides having his wife spend the nights in Ushida, Mr. Tanimoto had been carrying all the portable things from his church, in the close-packed residential district called Nagaragawa, to a house that belonged to a rayon manufacturer in Koi, two miles from the center of town. The rayon man, a Mr. Matsui, had opened his then unoccupied estate to a large number of his friends and acquaintances, so that they might evacuate whatever they wished to a safe distance from the probable target area. Mr. Tanimoto had had no difficulty in moving chairs, hymnals, Bibles, altar gear, and church records by pushcart himself, but the organ console and an upright piano required some aid. A friend of his named Matsuo had, the day before, helped him get the piano out to Koi; in return, he had promised this day to assist Mr. Matsuo in hauling out a daughter's belongings. That is why he had risen so early.

Mr. Tanimoto cooked his own breakfast. He felt awfully tired. The effort of moving the piano the day before, a sleepless night, weeks of worry and unbalanced diet, the cares of his parish—all combined to make him feel hardly adequate to the new day's work. There was another thing, too: Mr. Tanimoto had studied theology at Emory College, in Atlanta, Georgia; he had graduated in 1940; he spoke excellent English; he dressed in American clothes; he had corresponded with many American friends right up to the time the war began; and among a people <u>obsessed</u> with a fear of being spied upon—perhaps almost obsessed himself—he found himself growing increasingly uneasy. The police had questioned him several times, and just a few days before, he had heard that an influential acquaintance, a Mr. Tanaka, a retired

---

5. **Kyoto:** city some 200 miles east of Hiroshima.

WORDS TO OWN

rendezvous (rän′dā·v̅o̅o̅′) *adj.*: meeting.
abstinence (ab′stə·nəns′) *n.*: staying away.
obsessed (əb·sest′) *v.* used as *adj.*: preoccupied; haunted.

---

officer of the Toyo Kisen Kaisha steamship line, an anti-Christian, a man famous in Hiroshima for his showy philanthropies and notorious for his personal tyrannies, had been telling people that Tanimoto should not be trusted. In compensation, to show himself publicly a good Japanese, Mr. Tanimoto had taken on the chairmanship of his local *tonarigumi,* or Neighborhood Association, and to his other duties and concerns this position had added the business of organizing air-raid defense for about twenty families.

Before six o'clock that morning, Mr. Tanimoto started for Mr. Matsuo's house. There he found that their burden was to be a *tansu,* a large Japanese cabinet, full of clothing and household goods. The two men set out. The morning was perfectly clear and so warm that the day promised to be uncomfortable. A few minutes after they started, the air-raid siren went off—a minute-long blast that warned of approaching planes but indicated to the people of Hiroshima only a slight degree of danger, since it sounded every morning at this time, when an American weather plane came over. The two men pulled and pushed the handcart through the city streets. Hiroshima was a fan-shaped city, lying mostly on the six islands formed by the seven estuarial[6] rivers that branch out from the Ota River; its main commercial and residential districts, covering about four square miles in the center of the city, contained three-quarters of its population, which had been reduced by several evacuation programs from a wartime peak of 380,000 to about 245,000. Factories and other residential districts, or suburbs, lay compactly around the edges of the city. To the south were the docks, an airport, and the island-studded Inland Sea. A rim of mountains runs around the other three sides of the delta. Mr. Tanimoto and Mr. Matsuo took their way through the shopping center, already full of people, and across two of the rivers to the sloping streets of Koi, and up them to the outskirts and foothills. As they started up a valley away from the tight-ranked houses, the all-clear sounded. (The Japanese radar operators, detecting only three planes, supposed that they comprised a reconnaissance.)[7] Pushing the hand-cart up to the rayon man's house was tiring, and the men, after they had maneuvered their load into the driveway and to the front steps, paused to rest awhile. They stood with a wing of the house between them and the city. Like most homes in this part of Japan, the house consisted of a wooden frame and wooden walls supporting a heavy tile roof. Its front hall, packed with rolls of bedding and clothing, looked like a cool cave full of fat cushions. Opposite the house, to the right of the front door, there was a large, finicky rock garden. There was no sound of planes. The morning was still; the place was cool and pleasant.

Then a tremendous flash of light cut across the sky. Mr. Tanimoto has a distinct recollection that it traveled from east to west, from the city toward the hills. It seemed a sheet of sun. Both he and Mr. Matsuo reacted in terror—and both had time to react (for they were 3,500 yards, or two miles, from the center of the explosion). Mr. Matsuo dashed up the front steps into the house and dived among the bedrolls and buried himself there. Mr. Tanimoto took four or five steps and threw himself between two big rocks in the garden. He bellied up very hard against one of them. As his face was against the stone, he did not see what happened. He felt a sudden pressure, and then splinters and pieces of board and fragments of tile fell on him. He heard no roar. (Almost no one in Hiroshima recalls hearing any noise of the bomb. But a fisherman in his sampan[8] on the Inland Sea near Tsuzu, the man with whom Mr. Tanimoto's mother-in-law and sister-in-law were living, saw the flash and heard a tremendous explosion; he was nearly twenty miles from Hiroshima, but the thunder was greater than when the B-29s hit Iwakuni, only five miles away.)

When he dared, Mr. Tanimoto raised his head and saw that the rayon man's house had collapsed. He thought a bomb had fallen directly on it. Such clouds of dust had risen that there was a sort of twilight around. In panic, not thinking for the moment of Mr. Matsuo under the ruins, he dashed out into the street. He noticed as he ran that the

8. sampan: small, flat-bottomed boat.

Words to Own

philanthropies (fə·lan′thrə·pēz) *n. pl.:* charitable gifts.

6. **estuarial** (es′tyo͞o·er′ē·əl): on the estuary, or mouth of a river, where freshwater meets saltwater.
7. **reconnaissance** (ri·kän′ə·səns): exploratory mission.

Yasuko Yamagata, age 49.

❢ Some thirty years later, the horror of the bombing of Hiroshima remained
etched in the mind of Yasuko Yamagata, a survivor. She explains her painting:

"About 8:00 A.M., August 7, on the street in front of the former Hiroshima Broadcasting Station.

"Since I was at school in Ujina I had been exposed to radiation separately from my parents. The next morning at 7:30 I started from school toward the ruins of my house in Nobori-cho. I passed by Hijiyama. There were few people to be seen in the scorched field. I saw for the first time a pile of burned bodies in a water tank by the entrance to the broadcasting station. Then I was suddenly frightened by a terrible sight on the street 40 to 50 meters from Shukkeien Garden. There was a charred body of a woman standing frozen in a running position with one leg lifted and her baby tightly clutched in her arms. Who on earth could she be? This cruel sight still vividly remains in my mind."

concrete wall of the estate had fallen over—toward the house rather than away from it. In the street, the first thing he saw was a squad of soldiers who had been burrowing into the hillside opposite, making one of the thousands of dugouts in which the Japanese apparently intended to resist invasion, hill by hill, life for life; the soldiers were coming out of the hole, where they should have been safe, and blood was running from their heads, chests, and backs. They were silent and dazed.

Under what seemed to be a local dust cloud, the day grew darker and darker.

At nearly midnight, the night before the bomb was dropped, an announcer on the city's radio station said that about two hundred B-29s were approaching southern Honshu[9] and advised the population of Hiroshima to evacuate to their designated "safe areas." Mrs. Hatsuyo Nakamura, the tailor's widow, who lived in the section called Noboricho and who had long had a habit of doing as she was told, got her three children—a ten-year-old boy, Toshio, an eight-year-old girl, Yaeko, and a five-year-old girl, Myeko—out of bed and dressed them and walked with them to the military area known as the East Parade Ground, on the northeast edge of the city. There she unrolled some mats and the children lay down on them. They slept until about two, when they were awakened by the roar of the planes going over Hiroshima.

As soon as the planes had passed, Mrs. Nakamura started back with her children. They reached home a little after two-thirty and she immediately turned on the radio, which, to her distress, was just then broadcasting a fresh warning. When she looked at the children and saw how tired they were, and when she thought of the number of trips they had made in past weeks, all to no purpose, to the East Parade Ground, she decided that in spite of the instructions on the radio, she simply could not face starting out all over again. She put the children in their bedrolls on the floor, lay down herself at three o'clock, and fell asleep at once, so soundly that when the planes passed over later, she did not waken to their sound.

The siren jarred her awake at about seven. She arose, dressed quickly, and hurried to the house of Mr. Nakamoto, the head of her Neighborhood Association, and asked him what she should do. He said that she should remain at home unless an urgent warning—a series of intermittent blasts of the siren—was sounded. She returned home, lit the stove in the kitchen, set some rice to cook, and sat down to read that morning's Hiroshima *Chugoku*.[10] To her relief, the all-clear sounded at eight o'clock. She heard the children stirring, so she went and gave each of them a handful of peanuts and told them to stay on their bedrolls, because they were tired from the night's walk. She had hoped that they would go back to sleep, but the man in the house directly to the south began to make a terrible hullabaloo of hammering, wedging, ripping, and splitting. The prefectural government,[11] convinced, as everyone in Hiroshima was, that the city would be attacked soon, had begun to press with threats and warnings for the completion of wide fire lanes, which, it was hoped, might act in conjunction with the rivers to localize any fires started by an incendiary raid; and the neighbor was reluctantly sacrificing his home to the city's safety. Just the day before, the prefecture had ordered all able-bodied girls from the secondary schools to spend a few days helping to clear these lanes, and they started work soon after the all-clear sounded.

Mrs. Nakamura went back to the kitchen, looked at the rice, and began watching the man next door. At first, she was annoyed with him for making so much noise, but then she was moved almost to tears by pity. Her emotion was specifically directed toward her neighbor, tearing down his home, board by board, at a time when there was so much unavoidable destruction, but undoubtedly she also felt a generalized, community pity, to say nothing of self-pity. She had not had an easy time. Her husband, Isawa, had gone into the

9. **Honshu:** largest island of Japan. Hiroshima is in southern Honshu.

10. *Chugoku:* newspaper named for the region where Hiroshima is located.
11. **prefectural government:** the regional administration of each Japanese district, called a prefecture.

WORDS TO OWN

incendiary (in·sen′dē·er′ē) *adj.:* designed to cause fires.

Army just after Myeko was born, and she had heard nothing from or of him for a long time, until, on March 5, 1942, she received a seven-word telegram: "Isawa died an honorable death at Singapore." She learned later that he had died on February 15th, the day Singapore fell, and that he had been a corporal. Isawa had been a not particularly prosperous tailor, and his only capital was a Sankoku sewing machine. After his death, when his allotments stopped coming, Mrs. Nakamura got out the machine and began to take in piece-work[12] herself, and since then had supported the children, but poorly, by sewing.

As Mrs. Nakamura stood watching her neighbor, everything flashed whiter than any white she had ever seen. She did not notice what happened to the man next door; the reflex of a mother set her in motion toward her children. She had taken a single step (the house was 1,350 yards, or three-quarters of a mile, from the center of the explosion) when something picked her up and she seemed to fly into the next room over the raised sleeping platform, pursued by parts of her house.

Timbers fell around her as she landed, and a shower of tiles pummeled her; everything became dark, for she was buried. The debris did not cover her deeply. She rose up and freed herself. She heard a child cry, "Mother, help me!," and saw her youngest—Myeko, the five-year-old—buried up to her breast and unable to move. As Mrs. Nakamura started frantically to claw her way toward the baby, she could see or hear nothing of her other children.

In the days right before the bombing, Dr. Masakazu Fujii, being prosperous, hedonistic, and at the time not too busy, had been allowing himself the luxury of sleeping until nine or nine-thirty, but fortunately he had to get up early the morning the bomb was dropped to see a house guest off on a train. He rose at six, and half an hour later walked with his friend to the station, not far away, across two of the rivers. He was back home by seven, just as the siren sounded its sustained warning. He ate breakfast and then, because the morning was already hot, undressed down to his underwear and went out on the porch to read the paper. This porch—in fact, the whole building—was curiously constructed. Dr. Fujii was the proprietor of a peculiarly Japanese institution: a private, single-doctor hospital. This building, perched beside and over the water of the Kyo River, and next to the bridge of the same name, contained thirty rooms for thirty patients and their kinfolk—for, according to Japanese custom, when a person falls sick and goes to a hospital, one or more members of his family go and live there with him, to cook for him, bathe, massage, and read to him, and to offer incessant familial sympathy, without which a Japanese patient would be miserable indeed. Dr. Fujii had no beds—only straw mats—for his patients. He did, however, have all sorts of modern equipment: an X-ray machine, diathermy[13] apparatus, and a fine tiled laboratory. The structure rested two-thirds on the land, one-third on piles over the tidal waters of the Kyo. This overhang, the part of the building where Dr. Fujii lived, was queer-looking, but it was cool in summer and from the porch, which faced away from the center of the city, the prospect of the river, with pleasure boats drifting up and down it, was always refreshing. Dr. Fujii had occasionally had anxious moments when the Ota and its mouth branches rose to flood, but the piling was apparently firm enough and the house had always held.

Dr. Fujii had been relatively idle for about a month because in July, as the number of untouched cities in Japan dwindled and as Hiroshima seemed more and more inevitably a target, he began turning patients away, on the ground that in case of a fire raid he would not be able to evacuate them. Now he had only two patients left—a woman from Yano, injured in the shoulder, and a young man of twenty-five recovering from burns he had suffered when the steel factory near Hiroshima in which he worked had been hit. Dr. Fujii had six nurses to tend his patients. His wife and children were safe; his wife

13. **diathermy:** heat treatment.

WORDS TO OWN

debris (də·brē′) *n*.: rubble; broken pieces.
hedonistic (hē′də·nis′tik) *adj*.: pleasure-loving; self-indulgent.
sustained (sə·stānd′) *v*. used as *adj*.: prolonged.

---

12. **piecework:** work paid at a fixed rate for each piece completed.

and one son were living outside Osaka, and another son and two daughters were in the country on Kyushu.[14] A niece was living with him, and a maid and a manservant. He had little to do and did not mind, for he had saved some money. At fifty, he was healthy, convivial, and calm, and he was pleased to pass the evenings drinking whiskey with friends, always sensibly and for the sake of conversation. Before the war, he had affected brands imported from Scotland and America; now he was perfectly satisfied with the best Japanese brand, Suntory.

Dr. Fujii sat down cross-legged in his underwear on the spotless matting of the porch, put on his glasses, and started reading the Osaka *Asahi.* He liked to read the Osaka news because his wife was there. He saw the flash. To him—faced away from the center and looking at his paper—it seemed a brilliant yellow. Startled, he began to rise to his feet. In that moment (he was 1,550 yards from the center), the hospital leaned behind his rising and, with a terrible ripping noise, toppled into the river. The doctor, still in the act of getting to his feet, was thrown forward and around and over; he was buffeted and gripped; he lost track of everything, because things were so speeded up; he felt the water.

Dr. Fujii hardly had time to think that he was dying before he realized that he was alive, squeezed tightly by two long timbers in a V across his chest, like a morsel suspended between two huge chopsticks—held upright, so that he could not move, with his head miraculously above water and his torso and legs in it. The remains of his hospital were all around him in a mad assortment of splintered lumber and materials for the relief of pain. His left shoulder hurt terribly. His glasses were gone.

Father Wilhelm Kleinsorge, of the Society of Jesus, was, on the morning of the explosion, in rather frail condition. The Japanese wartime diet had not sustained him, and he felt the strain of being a foreigner in an increasingly xenophobic[15] Japan; even a German, since the defeat of the Fatherland,[16] was unpopular. Father Kleinsorge had, at thirty-eight, the look of a boy growing too fast—thin in the face, with a prominent Adam's apple, a hollow chest, dangling hands, big feet. He walked clumsily, leaning forward a little. He was tired all the time. To make matters worse, he had suffered for two days, along with Father Cieslik, a fellow-priest, from a rather painful and urgent diarrhea, which they blamed on the beans and black ration bread they were obliged to eat. Two other priests then living in the mission compound, which was in the Noboricho section—Father Superior LaSalle and Father Schiffer—had happily escaped this affliction.

Father Kleinsorge woke up about six the morning the bomb was dropped, and half an hour later—he was a bit tardy because of his sickness—he began to read Mass in the mission chapel, a small Japanese-style wooden building which was without pews, since its worshipers knelt on the usual Japanese matted floor, facing an altar graced with splendid silks, brass, silver, and heavy embroideries. This morning, a Monday, the only worshipers were Mr. Takemoto, a theological student living in the mission house; Mr. Fukai, the secretary of the diocese;[17] Mrs. Murata, the mission's devoutly Christian housekeeper; and his fellow-priests. After Mass, while Father Kleinsorge was reading the Prayers of Thanksgiving, the siren sounded. He stopped the service and the missionaries retired across the compound to the bigger building. There, in his room on the ground floor, to the right of the front door, Father Kleinsorge changed into a military uniform which he had acquired when he was teaching at the Rokko Middle School in Kobe and which he wore during air-raid alerts.

After an alarm, Father Kleinsorge always went out and scanned the sky, and in this instance, when he stepped outside, he was glad to see only the single weather plane that flew over Hiroshima each day about this time. Satisfied that nothing

16. **defeat of the Fatherland:** Germany surrendered to the Allies on May 7, 1945, approximately three months before the bombing of Hiroshima.
17. **diocese** (dī′ə·sis): church district administered by a bishop.

WORDS TO OWN

convivial (kən·viv′ē·əl) *adj.*: jovial; sociable.

---

14. **Kyushu** (kyo͞o′sho͞o′): southernmost of the principal islands of Japan.
15. **xenophobic** (zen′ō·fō′bik): fearing or disliking foreigners.

would happen, he went in and breakfasted with the other Fathers on substitute coffee and ration bread, which, under the circumstances, was especially repugnant to him. The Fathers sat and talked awhile, until, at eight, they heard the all-clear. They went then to various parts of the building. Father Schiffer retired to his room to do some writing. Father Cieslik sat in his room in a straight chair with a pillow over his stomach to ease his pain, and read. Father Superior LaSalle stood at the window of his room, thinking. Father Kleinsorge went up to a room on the third floor, took off all his clothes except his underwear, and stretched out on his right side on a cot and began reading his *Stimmen der Zeit.*

After the terrible flash—which, Father Kleinsorge later realized, reminded him of something he had read as a boy about a large meteor colliding with the earth—he had time (since he was 1,400 yards from the center) for one thought: A bomb has fallen directly on us. Then, for a few seconds or minutes, he went out of his mind.

Father Kleinsorge never knew how he got out of the house. The next things he was conscious of were that he was wandering around in the mission's vegetable garden in his underwear, bleeding slightly from small cuts along his left flank; that all the buildings round about had fallen down except the Jesuits' mission house, which had long before been braced and double-braced by a priest named Gropper, who was terrified of earthquakes; that the day had turned dark; and that Murata-*san*, the housekeeper, was nearby, crying over and over, "*Shu Jesusu, awaremi tamai!* Our Lord Jesus, have pity on us!"

On the train on the way into Hiroshima from the country, where he lived with his mother, Dr. Teru-fumi Sasaki, the Red Cross Hospital surgeon, thought over an unpleasant nightmare he had had the night before. His mother's home was in Mukai-hara, thirty miles from the city, and it took him two hours by train and tram to reach the hospital. He had slept uneasily all night and had wakened an hour earlier than usual, and, feeling sluggish and slightly feverish, had debated whether to go to the hospital at all; his sense of duty finally forced him to go, and he had started out on an earlier train than he took most mornings. The dream had particularly frightened him

because it was so closely associated, on the surface at least, with a disturbing actuality. He was only twenty-five years old and had just completed his training at the Eastern Medical University, in Tsingtao, China. He was something of an idealist and was much distressed by the inadequacy of medical facilities in the country town where his mother lived. Quite on his own, and without a permit, he had begun visiting a few sick people out there in the evenings, after his eight hours at the hospital and four hours' commuting. He had recently learned that the penalty for practicing without a permit was severe; a fellow-doctor whom he had asked about it had given him a serious scolding. Nevertheless, he had continued to practice. In his dream, he had been at the bedside of a country patient when the police and the doctor he had consulted burst into the room, seized him, dragged him outside, and beat him up cruelly. On the train, he just about decided to give up the work in Mukai-hara, since he felt it would be impossible to get a permit, because the authorities would hold that it would conflict with his duties at the Red Cross Hospital.

At the terminus, he caught a streetcar at once. (He later calculated that if he had taken his customary train that morning, and if he had had to wait a few minutes for the streetcar, as often happened, he would have been close to the center at the time of the explosion and would surely have perished.) He arrived at the hospital at seven-forty and reported to the chief surgeon. A few minutes later, he went to a room on the first floor and drew blood from the arm of a man in order to perform a Wassermann test. The laboratory containing the incubators[18] for the test was on the third floor. With the blood specimen in his left hand, walking in a kind of distraction he had felt all morning, probably because of the dream and his restless night, he started along the main corridor on his way toward the stairs. He was one step beyond an open window when the light of the bomb was reflected, like a gigantic photographic

18. **incubators:** equipment providing a favorable environment for the growth of cell cultures.

Words to Own

idealist (ī·dē′əl·ist) *n.:* one who believes in noble, though often impractical, goals; dreamer.

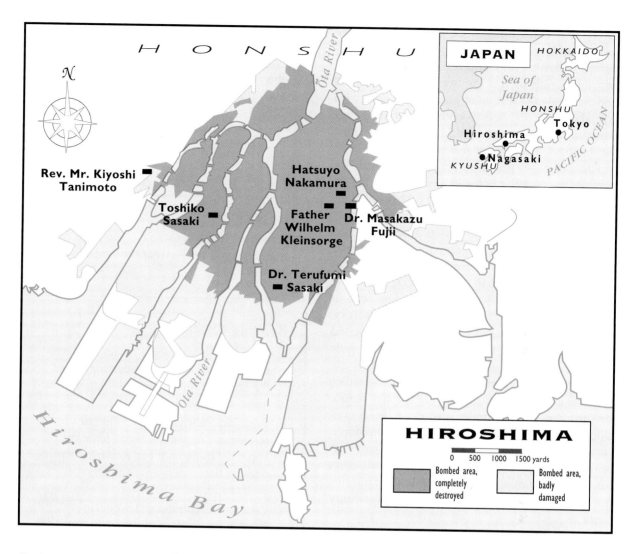

flash, in the corridor. He ducked down on one knee and said to himself, as only a Japanese would, "Sasaki, *gambare!* Be brave!" Just then (the building was 1,650 yards from the center), the blast ripped through the hospital. The glasses he was wearing flew off his face; the bottle of blood crashed against one wall; his Japanese slippers zipped out from under his feet—but otherwise, thanks to where he stood, he was untouched.

Dr. Sasaki shouted the name of the chief surgeon and rushed around to the man's office and found him terribly cut by glass. The hospital was in horrible confusion: Heavy partitions and ceilings had fallen on patients, beds had overturned, windows had blown in and cut people, blood was spattered on the walls and floors, instruments were everywhere, many of the patients were running about screaming, many more lay dead. (A colleague working in the laboratory to which Dr. Sasaki had been walking was dead; Dr. Sasaki's patient, whom he had just left and who a few moments before had been dreadfully afraid of syphilis, was also dead.) Dr. Sasaki found himself the only doctor in the hospital who was unhurt.

Dr. Sasaki, who believed that the enemy had hit only the building he was in, got bandages and began to bind the wounds of those inside the hospital; while outside, all over Hiroshima, maimed and dying citizens turned their unsteady steps toward the Red Cross Hospital to begin an invasion that was to make Dr. Sasaki forget his private nightmare for a long, long time.

Miss Toshiko Sasaki, the East Asia Tin Works clerk, who is not related to Dr. Sasaki, got up at three o'clock in the morning on the day the bomb fell.

There was extra housework to do. Her eleven-month-old brother, Akio, had come down the day before with a serious stomach upset; her mother had taken him to the Tamura Pediatric Hospital and was staying there with him. Miss Sasaki, who was about twenty, had to cook breakfast for her father, a brother, a sister, and herself, and—since the hospital, because of the war, was unable to provide food—to prepare a whole day's meals for her mother and the baby, in time for her father, who worked in a factory making rubber earplugs for artillery crews, to take the food by on his way to the plant. When she had finished and had cleaned and put away the cooking things, it was nearly seven. The family lived in Koi, and she had a forty-five-minute trip to the tin works, in the section of town called Kannon-machi. She was in charge of the personnel records in the factory. She left Koi at seven, and as soon as she reached the plant, she went with some of the other girls from the personnel department to the factory auditorium. A prominent local Navy man, a former employee, had committed suicide the day before by throwing himself under a train—a death considered honorable enough to warrant a memorial service, which was to be held at the tin works at ten o'clock that morning. In the large hall, Miss Sasaki and the others made suitable preparations for the meeting. This work took about twenty minutes.

Miss Sasaki went back to her office and sat down at her desk. She was quite far from the windows, which were off to her left, and behind her were a couple of tall bookcases containing all the books of the factory library, which the personnel department had organized. She settled herself at her desk, put some things in a drawer, and shifted papers. She thought that before she began to make entries in her lists of new employees, discharges, and departures for the Army, she would chat for a moment with the girl at her right. Just as she turned her head away from the windows, the room was filled with a blinding light. She was paralyzed by fear, fixed still in her chair for a long moment (the plant was 1,600 yards from the center).

Everything fell, and Miss Sasaki lost consciousness. The ceiling dropped suddenly and the wooden floor above collapsed in splinters and the people up there came down and the roof above

them gave way; but principally and first of all, the bookcases right behind her swooped forward and the contents threw her down, with her left leg horribly twisted and breaking underneath her. There, in the tin factory, in the first moment of the atomic age, a human being was crushed by books.

MAKING MEANINGS

First Thoughts

1. What aspect of *Hiroshima* did you focus on most intently as you read—what character, image, or idea?

Reading Check

a. Who are the six people presented in this section of *Hiroshima*? Besides surviving the atomic bomb explosion, what do they have in common?

b. What simple **images** does Hersey use to help us imagine the actual physical impact of the bomb? For example, how does he describe the flash as seen by each character?

c. What small, commonplace human-interest details does Hersey give about his characters so that they come alive and seem like people we might know?

d. How does Hersey explain the **ironic** fact that an all-clear signal sounded just before the bomb was dropped?

Shaping Interpretations

2. What **ironies** can you find in each character's story—including the irony of the last image?

3. While mostly recounting facts **objectively,** Hersey communicates a **subjective** attitude toward war. How does he accomplish that? How would you describe his attitude toward the Japanese? toward the Americans?

4. During World War II, most Americans felt that the Japanese, like the Germans, were enemies to be destroyed no matter what the cost. How do

you respond to Hersey's treatment of the Japanese in this account? How do you think readers in 1946—one year after the war had ended—would have responded?

Extending the Text

5. From what you know of history and from what you have read here, tell why, in human and political terms, the explosion at Hiroshima was a central event in the twentieth century. How has

this distant event affected our lives even today? How did it affect the poet William Stafford, whose "At the Bomb Testing Site" appears on the Collection 18 opener (page 919)?

Challenging the Text

6. What other methods might a historian or journalist have used to tell this story? What do you think of Hersey's method? Cite passages from the text to support your evaluation.

CHOICES: Building Your Portfolio

Writer's Notebook

1. Collecting Ideas for an Evaluation

Write down some of the facts and events in this excerpt from *Hiroshima* that are striking examples of **objective reporting**. Then, choose examples of vivid **subjective reporting** and personal involvement by the author. Which type of reporting dominates, and how effective is it? Keep your notes for possible use in the Writer's Workshop on page 1181.

Analyzing Suspense

2. Page Turner

Readers of Hersey's *Hiroshima* know the outcome of the narrative before they open the book. In a brief essay, show how in this excerpt Hersey manages, nevertheless, to create **suspense**. What questions does he plant in your mind? When does he answer them?

Crossing the Curriculum: History

3. Enormous Decision

Research the decision by U.S. President Harry S Truman to use the atomic bomb against Japan. You will find facts and opinions in biographies and memoirs of Truman and other U.S. and British government officials, in government reports, and in a wide variety of additional works by historians and journalists. In an essay, describe how the decision was made and what factors were considered. End the essay with your own reflections about whether Truman made the correct decision.

Critical Writing

4. Telling Words

Hersey notes that the Japanese had a nickname for the B-29 bomber planes that regularly damaged their cities: "*B-san,* or Mr. B" (page 938). The appositive (which is a context clue that directly defines the word) also gives us an idea of what *–san* means when attached to a noun. Hersey almost always helps his readers by including strong **context clues** with Japanese terms. In a brief essay, describe how Hersey's use of Japanese terms helps to establish the authenticity of his report, and explain the insight these terms provide into the people, the culture, or the events described. (For example, the information about the Japanese nickname "B-san" for the B-29 bomber might tell you something about how some Japanese were coping psychologically with the frequent bombings.)

UPI/Bettmann.

Robert Lowell

(1917–1977)

From virtually the beginning of his career, Robert Lowell was a major presence in American poetry. He was born into an aristocratic Boston family whose ancestors went back to the *Mayflower*. The nineteenth-century poet James Russell Lowell (1819–1891) was his great-uncle; the early-twentieth-century poet Amy Lowell (1874–1925), a promoter of Imagism, was his cousin. Lowell felt he had to rebel against his family's conservative, traditional background in order to carve out his own identity as an individual and as a poet.

Lowell left Harvard after two years to attend Kenyon College in Ohio, where the poet John Crowe Ransom was teaching. The summer before enrolling at Kenyon, Lowell lived in a tent on the poet Allen Tate's lawn in Nashville, Tennessee, soaking up all he could learn from Tate about writing poetry. Ransom and Tate were both supporters of what is called the New Criticism. They admired densely packed, "formal, difficult poems," as Lowell later put it, and Lowell began writing poems in this style.

Lowell graduated from Kenyon in 1940, married the novelist Jean Stafford, and started what would be a distinguished career of teaching and writing. Shortly thereafter, in what was at least partly another rebellious act against his family's Protestant roots, he converted to Roman Catholicism.

In the early days of World War II, Lowell tried several times to enlist in the Navy, but was rejected for his poor eyesight. By 1943, appalled at the destruction caused by American bombing in Europe, he refused induction into the Army and served a five-month prison sentence. His poems of this period—in the collections *Land of Unlikeness* (1944), *Lord Weary's Castle* (1946) (which won a Pulitzer Prize), and *The Mills of the Kavanaughs* (1951)—were tight, formal, and intellectually challenging. Most poems presented a grim vision of a world about to end.

In the 1950s, Lowell's style and subject matter gradually changed. At poetry readings with Allen Ginsberg, whose loose and freewheeling style immediately touched audiences, Lowell, an endless reviser, would sometimes simplify some of his own poems as he read them. He began writing a looser, freer verse, with more natural rhythms and more personal subject matter.

All his life, Lowell suffered great bouts of mental instability. In 1959, he published *Life Studies,* in which he wrote frankly about his condition. His tone was neither self-pitying nor self-indulgent. Instead, he described his suffering with a light irony.

Life Studies became one of the most influential works of poetry written after World War II. It helped to make acceptable the highly personal poetry being written by Sylvia Plath (page 1148), Anne Sexton (page 1088), and John Berryman (1914–1972)—the group now referred to as the Confessional School of poets.

In the 1960s, Lowell became more and more of a public figure. Like many writers of the time, he expressed opposition to the war in Vietnam. His poetry remained deeply personal, however, and he wrote a great many unrhymed sonnets, first published as *Notebooks* in 1969 and then revised as *History* in 1973. He also wrote several well-received plays, notably *The Old Glory* (1965), based on stories by Herman Melville and Nathaniel Hawthorne.

In 1977, returning to New York from London, Robert Lowell died of a heart attack in a taxi taking him home from the airport.

HRW go.hrw.com
LE0 11-18

Before You Read

FOR THE UNION DEAD

Make the Connection

What Have We Gained?

After all the wars that Americans have fought, after all the suffering and loss and sacrifice, what kind of a world have we created? Poets and politicians, sages and students ask this question in different ways every day: Are we satisfied with our world?

Reading Skills and Strategies

Gaining Understanding Through Questioning

As you read "For the Union

Dead," keep a record of your questions and uncertainties about the poem. If a passage seems confusing or obscure, try to write down exactly what you need to learn in order to understand the passage. Remember, no great work of art gives up all its secrets upon first acquaintance.

Elements of Literature

Imagery

"For the Union Dead" resonates with powerful **imagery**— language that evokes a picture or a concrete sensation of a person, a thing, a place, or an experience. Lowell wants us to do more than simply think about his ideas; he gives us the opportunity to *feel* what he means—in our noses, in our throats, and on our fingertips.

> **I**magery is language that evokes a picture or a concrete sensation of a person, a thing, a place, or an experience.
>
> *For more on Imagery, see the Handbook of Literary Terms.*

Background

"They give up everything to serve the Republic," says the Latin inscription preceding this poem. "They" are all the Union soldiers who served during the Civil War. But, more specifically, "they" are the members of the first regiment of African American soldiers from a free state, in this case Massachusetts. Under a white commander, Robert Gould Shaw, this regiment stormed Fort Wagner, South Carolina, in an assault resulting in many deaths, including that of the commander himself. The event is dramatized in the award-winning film *Glory*.

The subject of the poem is not that event, however, but its memorial—the bronze monument by the great sculptor Augustus Saint-Gaudens, which stands in Boston Common, the park directly across from the State House.

Today, Boston has a new aquarium that is a major tourist attraction. In 1960, when "For the Union Dead" was written, an older aquarium in South Boston—empty, deserted, and dilapidated—provided just the right image to set up the relationship between past and present.

Because this is a complex poem, you should read it at least twice. A comment follows the poem.

Henry Steward, Sergeant, Fifty-fourth Massachusetts Infantry Regiment, Company E.

Massachusetts Historical Society, Boston.

Civil War monument by Augustus Saint-Gaudens
honoring the Fifty-fourth Regiment of Black Soldiers,
led by Col. Robert Gould Shaw, Boston Common.

For the Union Dead

"Relinquunt Omnia Servare Rem Publicam."°

subtitle: They give up everything to serve the Republic.

Robert Lowell

The old South Boston Aquarium stands
in a Sahara of snow now. Its broken windows are boarded.
The bronze weathervane cod has lost half its scales.
The airy tanks are dry.

5 Once my nose crawled like a snail on the glass;
my hand tingled
to burst the bubbles
drifting from the noses of the cowed, compliant fish.

My hand draws back. I often sigh still
10 for the dark downward and vegetating kingdom
of the fish and reptile. One morning last March,
I pressed against the new barbed and galvanized

fence on the Boston Common. Behind their cage,
yellow dinosaur steamshovels were grunting

15 as they cropped up tons of mush and grass
to gouge their underworld garage.

Parking spaces luxuriate like civic
sandpiles in the heart of Boston.
A girdle of orange, Puritan-pumpkin colored girders
20 braces the tingling Statehouse,

shaking over the excavations, as it faces Colonel Shaw
and his bell-cheeked Negro infantry
on St. Gaudens' shaking Civil War relief,
propped by a plank splint against the garage's earthquake.

25 Two months after marching through Boston,
half the regiment was dead;
at the dedication,
William James° could almost hear the bronze Negroes breathe.

28. **William James** (1842–1910): American philosopher and psychologist who taught at Harvard University, which is adjacent to Boston.

Their monument sticks like a fishbone
30 in the city's throat.
Its Colonel is as lean
as a compass-needle.

He has an angry wrenlike vigilance,
a greyhound's gentle tautness;
35 he seems to wince at pleasure,
and suffocate for privacy.

He is out of bounds now. He rejoices in man's lovely,
peculiar power to choose life and die—
when he leads his black soldiers to death,
40 he cannot bend his back.

On a thousand small town New England greens,
the old white churches hold their air
of sparse, sincere rebellion; frayed flags
quilt the graveyards of the Grand Army of the Republic.

45 The stone statues of the abstract Union Soldier
grow slimmer and younger each year—
wasp-wasted, they doze over muskets
and muse through their sideburns . . .

Shaw's father wanted no monument
50 except the ditch,
where his son's body was thrown
and lost with his "niggers."

The ditch is nearer.
There are no statues for the last war° here;

54. **the last war:** World War II.

55   on Boylston Street, a commercial photograph
     shows Hiroshima boiling

     over a Mosler Safe, the "Rock of Ages"
     that survived the blast. Space is nearer.
     When I crouch to my television set,
60   the drained faces of Negro school-children rise like balloons.

     Colonel Shaw
     is riding on his bubble,
     he waits
     for the blesséd break.

65   The Aquarium *is* gone. Everywhere,
     giant finned cars nose forward like fish;
     a savage servility
     slides by on grease.

Aerial view of excavation site for Boston Common garage. Lowell's poem was inspired by the scene of this razing—a deep scar on a landscape that once boasted the old South Boston Aquarium.

A Vision of Blacks and Whites United

A good poem can withstand anything said about it. Understanding "For the Union Dead" depends on the knowledge and experiences you bring to it as much as it depends upon what the poem itself offers. After you read the poem, try to paraphrase it in order to clarify some of its references and to open possibilities of interpretation.

Looking at the ruined aquarium in its desert of snow, the poet remembers how, as a child, he used to press his nose right up against the glass of the great fish tanks; he recalls how his hand itched to get inside the tanks and play with the rising bubbles and all the marvelous sea creatures. But he is no longer a child. He draws back his hand, even though something in his nature still hungers to explore another order of life—that subconscious region where all beings in the "vegetating kingdom" had their beginnings.

The grown man presses himself against the fence that makes a "cage" in which steamshovels are gouging out space for an underground parking garage. The tremors of excavation work are so thunderous that both the State House and the bronze monument facing it have to be braced for protection. The jeopardy in which "progress" has placed both State House and monument brings the poet's central subject—the black regiment—into focus.

Having paraded through Boston as heroes on their way to the battlefield, half of these soldiers were dead within two months. When the monument to them was dedicated in 1897, the memory of these men was so much alive, and their faces and figures so faithfully rendered in bronze, that the great American psychologist William James felt that they almost breathed.

But now the poet observes that the monument "sticks like a fishbone / in the city's throat," meaning that it is an irritant. Ironically, Boston is not only one of the cities where the abolitionist movement was strongest; it is also, like many places in the United States, a place where racism has persisted. The poet compares Colonel Shaw, the regiment's leader, to the needle on a compass; this characterization suggests that Shaw pointed the way—a way in which whites and blacks united might become part of a nation's most honorable history. But Shaw is now "out of bounds" in a time and place where his special kind of vision and integrity are conspicuously lacking.

Then, instantaneously, like a change of scene in a movie, the poet's eye suddenly "pans" over the New England landscape (lines 41–48). Churches on village greens remind him of the Revolutionary War; cemeteries with their "quilt" of ragged flags recall the Civil War; the young soldiers of the Union, "stone statues" all alike, remain young and slim as their nation grows older and fatter.

Colonel Shaw's father, we learn, felt that the monument to his son was unnecessary; people had only to remember the ditch where the young commander's body was thrown with those of his soldiers. "The ditch," that common boneyard of blacks and whites, "is nearer." Why? Because nuclear holocaust threatens a world more preoccupied with sales and profits than with its own survival.

The bubbles that rose in the fish tanks of the old aquarium return at the end of the poem. They are now "balloons" that are compared to the "drained faces" of young African Americans. They also appear as the buried dream of Colonel Shaw that, like a bubble, may burst forth when idealism explodes into reality.

The old aquarium and everything it stood for in the speaker's childhood imagination no longer exist. "Finned" luxury cars now "slide by," just as the marvelous fish once glided through the bubbly depths of their tanks. To the speaker, the chrome-laden automobiles represent a "savage servility." They move "on grease," the by-product of the oil that supplies the modern world's energy, and the end product and sludgy residue of the world's great power.

MAKING MEANINGS

First Thoughts

1. What basic **message** does this poem suggest to you? Explain it briefly.

Shaping Interpretations

2. What do you think the poet means by saying Colonel Shaw "rejoices in man's lovely, / peculiar power to choose life and die" (lines 37–38)?

3. What historical events in Boston and other American cities might the poet be referring to with the mention of the "drained faces" of African American children on television (line 60)?

4. What do you think is the "savage servility" (line 67) mentioned in the last stanza?

5. Explain how the **title** of the poem could have at least two meanings. Does Lowell use the Latin subtitle **ironically,** or seriously? Explain.

6. How would you describe the poem's **tone?**

Reading Check

a. What **images** describe the old South Boston Aquarium?

b. What **images** describe what the speaker saw on Boston Common?

c. What **images** describe the Saint-Gaudens monument? How many things is the colonel compared with?

d. What details tell you what happened to Colonel Shaw and his men?

CHOICES: Building Your Portfolio

Writer's Notebook

1. Collecting Ideas for an Evaluation

When you write an evaluation, you need to be aware of your readers—the knowledge and experience they bring to a reading of the text. Review the notes you

made as you read Lowell's poem. Then, make a list of the historical information, allusions, vocabulary, and other data you would need to include in an evaluation of this poem written for students your own age who are not in your class. Save your notes for possible use in the Writer's Workshop on page 1181.

Comparing Poems

2. Monuments and Messages

In an essay, explain how the following poem by Henry Timrod (1828–1867) is like or unlike Lowell's poem in terms of (a) theme, (b) tone, (c) diction, and (d) form.

Ode on the Confederate Dead

Sung on the Occasion of Decorating the Graves of the Confederate Dead, at Magnolia Cemetery, Charleston, S.C., 1867

> Sleep sweetly in your humble graves,
>   Sleep, martyrs of a fallen cause;
> Though yet no marble column craves
>   The pilgrim here to pause.
>
> 5 In seeds of laurel in the earth
>   The blossom of your fame is blown,
> And somewhere, waiting for its birth,
>   The shaft is in the stone!°
>
> Meanwhile, behalf the tardy years
> 10   Which keep in trust your storied tombs,
> Behold! your sisters bring their tears,
>   And these memorial blooms.
>
> Small tributes! but your shades will smile
>   More proudly on these wreaths today,
> 15 Than when some cannon-molded pile
>   Shall overlook this bay.
>
> Stoop, angels, hither from the skies!
>   There is no holier spot of ground
> Than where defeated valor lies,
> 20   By mourning beauty crowned!

8. shaft . . . stone: allusion to Arthurian legend. Arthur proved he was the rightful king by pulling a sword out of a stone.

Donald Barthelme
(1931–1989)

Donald Barthelme (bär′thəl·mē) was an experimenter in fiction and a true member of the avant-garde. Sometimes known as a postmodernist, he is widely regarded as one of the ablest and most versatile American stylists—witty, adventurous, and profound.

In broad terms, Barthelme believed that while literature of the past functioned to revitalize the imagination, storytelling had largely lost the

© Nancy Crampton.

power to inspire, persuade, or even entertain us. He felt that our language had gone bankrupt. Since words no longer effectively communicated feelings, he said, they had lost the power to move us. Contemporary language, Barthelme asserted, is thick with sludge and stuffing. Its use of clichés and its verbosity obscure truth rather than reveal it. As Snow White, the title character of Barthelme's 1967 novel, says, "Oh I wish there were some words in the world that were not the words I always hear!"

Barthelme saw the problems with language as a reflection of a society so dehumanized, so lacking in quality, that it could no longer sustain the kinds of myths that once gave us our identity. Thus, he felt, the whole point of storytelling was lost.

In his fiction, Barthelme set out to create a banal world that fails to make distinctions of quality in people, things, and ideas. Then, since he felt it was no longer possible to write about real life or the real world, he took writing itself for his subject—the art of making art out of language. His interest lay in the form and sound of language, and he tended to play with words,

to make art out of fragments, much as some contemporary sculptors fashion works out of everyday objects and some pop artists transform cartoons into art.

Barthelme's plots are also unconventional. They are episodic, a clutter of styles, absurdities, and slapstick. "Fragments are the only forms I trust," says one of his narrators. His characters are types rather than fully developed individuals.

In Barthelme's hands, myth may turn into realism and realism into absurdity; readers can lose their way as they try to identify with the proceedings and wonder about the writer's point. Barthelme explained to the puzzled: "Art is not difficult because it wishes to be difficult, rather because it wishes to be art. However much the writer might long to be, in his work, simple, honest, straightforward, these virtues are no longer available to him. He discovers that in being simple, honest, straightforward, nothing much happens. . . . We are looking for the as yet unspeakable, the as yet unspoken."

Barthelme was born in Philadelphia, the son of an avant-garde architect, and was raised and educated in Texas. After serving with the U.S. Army, he worked as a reporter for the *Houston Post,* as a museum director, as the editor of an art and literature review, as a professor of English at the City University of New York, and as a teacher of creative writing at the University of Houston. He was a regular contributor to *The New Yorker* magazine. Collections of his stories include *Come Back, Dr. Caligari* (1964), *Unspeakable Practices, Unnatural Acts* (1968), in which "Game" appears, *Sixty Stories* (1981), and *Overnight to Many Distant Cities* (1983).

Before You Read

GAME

Make the Connection

Games People Play

We are all part of the physical and social world around us. How we view that world determines in large measure how we live our lives. The following story offers a rather quirky view of our times. "Game" won't give you a clear picture of your world, but it may start you thinking.

Reading Skills and Strategies

Interpreting Word Meanings and Connotations

How many distinct meanings can you think of for the word *game*? What does it mean to a child? to a professional athlete? to a hunter? Does the word connote, or suggest, something serious or something frivolous? Jot down the meanings of the word that occur to you as you read the story.

And don't forget: Barthelme said that art is difficult, and "Game" is no exception. Read the story slowly, and don't expect everything to be immediately understandable.

If I behave strangely Shotwell is supposed to shoot me.

Game

Donald Barthelme

Shotwell keeps the jacks and the rubber ball in his attaché case and will not allow me to play with them. He plays with them, alone, sitting on the floor near the <u>console</u> hour after hour, chanting "onesies, twosies, threesies, foursies" in a precise, well-modulated voice, not so loud as to be annoying, not so soft as to allow me to forget. I point out to Shotwell that two can derive more enjoyment from playing jacks than one, but he is not interested. I have asked repeatedly to be allowed to play by myself, but he simply shakes his head. "Why?" I ask. "They're mine," he says. And when he has finished, when he has <u>sated</u> himself, back they go into the attaché case.

It is unfair but there is nothing I can do about it. I am aching to get my hands on them.

Shotwell and I watch the console. Shotwell and I live under the ground and watch the console. If certain events take place upon the console, we are to insert our keys in the appropriate locks and turn our keys. Shotwell has a key and I have a key. If we turn our keys simultaneously the bird flies, certain switches are activated and the bird flies. But the bird never flies. In one hundred thirty-three days the bird has not flown. Meanwhile Shotwell and I watch each other. We each wear a .45 and if Shotwell behaves strangely I am supposed to shoot him. If I behave strangely Shotwell is supposed to shoot me. We watch the console and think about shooting each other and think about the bird. Shotwell's behavior with the jacks is strange. Is it strange? I do not know. Perhaps he is merely selfish . . . perhaps his character is flawed, perhaps his childhood was twisted. I do not know.

Each of us wears a .45 and each of us is supposed to shoot the other if the other is behaving strangely. How strangely is strangely? I do not know. In addition to the .45 I have a .38 which Shotwell does not know about concealed in my attaché case, and Shotwell has a .25 caliber Beretta which I do not know about strapped to his right calf. Sometimes instead of watching the console I pointedly watch Shotwell's .45, but this is simply a ruse, simply a maneuver, in reality I am watching his hand when it dangles in the vicinity of his right calf. If he decides I am behaving strangely he will shoot me not with the .45 but with the Beretta. Similarly, Shotwell pretends to watch my .45 but he is really watching my hand resting idly atop my attaché case, my hand resting idly atop my attaché case, my hand. My hand resting idly atop my attaché case.

In the beginning I took care to behave normally. So did Shotwell. Our behavior was painfully normal. Norms of politeness, consideration, speech, and personal habits were scrupulously observed. But then it became apparent that an error had been made, that our relief was not going to arrive. Owing to an oversight. Owing to an oversight we have been here for one hundred

thirty-three days. When it became clear that an error had been made, that we were not to be relieved, the norms were relaxed. Definitions of normality were redrawn in the agreement of January 1, called by us, The Agreement. Uniform regulations were relaxed, and mealtimes are no longer rigorously scheduled. We eat when we are hungry and sleep when we are tired. Considerations of rank and precedence were temporarily put aside, a handsome concession on the part of Shotwell, who is a captain, whereas I am only a first lieutenant. One of us watches the console at all times rather than two of us watching the console at all times, except when we are both on our feet. One of us watches the console at all times and if the bird flies then that one wakes the other and we turn our keys in the locks simultaneously and the bird flies. Our system involves a delay of perhaps twelve seconds but I do not care because I am not well, and Shotwell does not care because he is not himself. After the agreement was signed Shotwell produced the jacks and the rubber ball from his attaché case, and I began to write a series of descriptions of forms occurring in nature, such as a shell, a leaf, a stone, an animal. On the walls.

Shotwell plays jacks and I write descriptions of natural forms on the walls.

Shotwell is enrolled in a USAFI[1] course which leads to a master's degree in business administration from the University of Wisconsin (although we are not in Wisconsin, we are in Utah, Montana or Idaho). When we went down it was in either Utah, Montana or Idaho, I don't remember. We have been here for one hundred thirty-three days owing to an oversight. The pale green reinforced concrete walls sweat and the air conditioning zips on and off erratically and Shotwell reads *Introduction to Marketing* by Lassiter and Munk, making notes with a blue ballpoint pen. Shotwell is not himself but I do not know it, he presents a calm

1. **USAFI:** United States Armed Forces Information, an organization that supervises courses taken by service members.

WORDS TO OWN

ruse (ro͞oz) *n.*: trick; deception.
precedence (pres′ə·dəns) *n.*: order.
simultaneously (sī′məl·tā′nē·əs·lē) *adv.*: at the same time.

aspect and reads *Introduction to Marketing* and makes his <u>exemplary</u> notes with a blue ballpoint pen, meanwhile controlling the .38 in my attaché case with one-third of his attention. I am not well.

We have been here one hundred thirty-three days owing to an oversight. Although now we are not sure what is oversight, what is plan. Perhaps the plan is for us to stay here permanently, or if not permanently at least for a year, for three hundred sixty-five days. Or if not for a year for some number of days known to them and not known to us, such as two hundred days. Or perhaps they are observing our behavior in some way, <u>sensors</u> of some kind, perhaps our behavior determines the number of days. It may be that they are pleased with us, with our behavior, not in every detail but in sum. Perhaps the whole thing is very successful, perhaps the whole thing is an experiment and the experiment is very successful. I do not know. But I suspect that the only way they can persuade sun-loving creatures into their pale green sweating reinforced concrete rooms under the ground is to say that the system is twelve hours on, twelve hours off. And then lock us below for some number of days known to them and not known to us. We eat well although the frozen enchiladas are damp when defrosted and the frozen devil's food cake is sour and untasty. We sleep uneasily and <u>acrimoniously</u>. I hear Shotwell shouting in his sleep, objecting, denouncing, cursing sometimes, weeping sometimes, in his sleep. When Shotwell sleeps I try to pick the lock on his attaché case, so as to get at the jacks. Thus far I have been unsuccessful. Nor has Shotwell been successful in picking the locks on my attaché case so as to get at the .38. I have seen the marks on the shiny surface. I laughed, in the latrine, pale green walls sweating and the air conditioning whispering, in the latrine.

I write descriptions of natural forms on the walls, scratching them on the tile surface with a diamond. The diamond is a two and one-half carat solitaire I had in my attaché case when we went down. It was for Lucy. The south wall of the room containing the console is already covered. I have described a shell, a leaf, a stone, animals, a baseball bat. I am aware that the baseball bat is not a natural form. Yet I described it. "The baseball bat," I said, "is typically made of wood. It is typically one meter in length or a little longer, fat at one end, tapering to afford a comfortable grip at the other. The end with the handhold typically offers a slight rim, or lip, at the <u>nether</u> extremity, to prevent slippage." My description of the baseball bat ran to 4500 words, all scratched with a diamond on the south wall. Does Shotwell read what I have written? I do not know. I am aware that Shotwell regards my writing-behavior as a little strange. Yet it is no stranger than his jacks-behavior, or the day he appeared in black bathing trunks with the .25 caliber Beretta strapped to his right calf and stood over the console, trying to span with his two arms outstretched the distance between the locks. He could not do it, I had already tried, standing over

---

WORDS TO OWN

exemplary (eg·zem′plə·rē) *adj.*: serving as a model.
sensors (sen′sərz) *n. pl.*: detecting devices.
acrimoniously (ak′ri·mō′nē·əs·lē) *adv.*: bitterly; harshly.
nether (neth′ər) *adj.*: lower.

the console with my two arms outstretched, the distance is too great. I was moved to comment but did not comment, comment would have provoked counter-comment, comment would have led God knows where. They had in their infinite patience, in their infinite foresight, in their infinite wisdom already imagined a man standing over the console with his two arms outstretched, trying to span with his two arms outstretched the distance between the locks.

Shotwell is not himself. He has made certain overtures. The burden of his message is not clear. It has something to do with the keys, with the locks. Shotwell is a strange person. He appears to be less affected by our situation than I. He goes about his business stolidly, watching the console, studying *Introduction to Marketing*, bouncing his rubber ball on the floor in a steady, rhythmical, conscientious manner. He appears to be less affected by our situation than I am. He is stolid. He says nothing. But he has made certain overtures, certain overtures have been made. I am not sure that I understand them. They have something to do with the keys, with the locks. Shotwell has something in mind. Stolidly he shucks the shiny silver paper from the frozen enchiladas, stolidly he stuffs them into the electric oven. But he has something in mind. But there must be a quid pro quo.[2] I insist on a quid pro quo. I have something in mind.

I am not well. I do not know our target. They do not tell us for which city the bird is targeted. I do not know. That is planning. That is not my responsibility. My responsibility is to watch the console and when certain events take place upon the console, turn my key in the lock. Shotwell

2. quid pro quo: Latin for "something for something." The phrase is used here to mean an even exchange.

bounces the rubber ball on the floor in a steady, stolid, rhythmical manner. I am aching to get my hands on the ball, on the jacks. We have been here one hundred thirty-three days owing to an oversight. I write on the walls. Shotwell chants "onesies, twosies, threesies, foursies" in a precise, well-modulated voice. Now he cups the jacks and the rubber ball in his hands and rattles them suggestively. I do not know for which city the bird is targeted. Shotwell is not himself.

Sometimes I cannot sleep. Sometimes Shotwell cannot sleep. Sometimes when Shotwell cradles me in his arms and rocks me to sleep, singing Brahms' "Guten Abend, gute Nacht,"[3] or I cradle Shotwell in my arms and rock him to sleep, singing, I understand what it is Shotwell wishes me to do. At such moments we are very close. But only if he will give me the jacks. That is fair. There is something he wants me to do with my key, while he does something with his key. But only if he will give me my turn. That is fair. I am not well.

3. Guten Abend, gute Nacht (gōōt′'n ä′bənt gōōt′ə näkht): German for "good evening, good night." This line is from the musical composition popularly known as "Brahms' Lullaby" by Johannes Brahms (1833–1897).

WORDS TO OWN

overtures (ō′vər·chərz) *n. pl.*: approaches; offers.

Absurd World

Almost every element of Barthelme's story contributes to its satirical, absurdist tone. As in the plays of the Theater of the Absurd, such as those composed by Samuel Beckett and Eugene Ionesco, statements either do not follow each other logically, or they are connected by pseudologic. The narrator's constant repetition suggests the mind of someone on the brink of a precipice, desperately trying to hold on to words as symbols of reality and sanity.

The two characters, Shotwell and the unnamed narrator, are confined underground for an indefinite period. We never learn the exact details of the mission they may be called to carry out, but it seems to involve nuclear warfare and so could result in world destruction.

The first-person narration underscores the horror, as we know only what the speaker can tell us about his situation. Both he and Shotwell have been reduced to infantilism as they wait for the terrible contingency on the console: Childlike pastimes alternate with petty jealousies and disturbing nightmares. The two men's gradual dehumanization is relieved only when they rock each other to sleep. The men's eccentric behavior is portrayed as a desperate attempt to blot out the horror of their circumstances, but the story makes it clear that they are on the edge of madness: Note that Shotwell seems determined to destroy them by activating the two locks that apparently will launch a destructive event.

As you read Barthelme's vignette of life in the nuclear age, it may be easy to dismiss the particulars of his vision as exaggerated or surrealistic. But consider that a serious theme may underlie this apparently absurdist story. Our modern methods of warfare, Barthelme seems to be suggesting, are horrible not only because of their potential for physical destruction, but also because of the way their very existence corrodes and perverts humanity.

MAKING MEANINGS

First Thoughts

1. What was your emotional reaction to "Game"?

Shaping Interpretations

2. Which details in the first three paragraphs suggest the state of Shotwell's and the narrator's minds?

3. How would you explain the strange behavior of the men? What do you think happened before the story begins?

Reading Check

a. Despite his experimentation, Barthelme still uses essential elements of fiction. Who is the **narrator** of this story? What is the **setting**?

b. What is the narrator's problem, or **conflict**? Is there a **resolution** to it? If so, describe it.

4. How would you explain what the "bird" is?

5. What might be the "oversight" that has led to the men's confinement?

6. The narrator is apprehensive that Shotwell "has something in mind." What might that something be? How can you tell?

7. Barthelme uses a great deal of **repetition** in this story. What phrases are most often repeated? How does the repetition contribute to the **characterization**?

8. What meanings and connotations does the word *game* have in the story? How does the word *game* point to the story's **theme**?

Challenging the Text

9. Is the world as absurd as Barthelme describes it? Describe your response to the world Barthelme has created.

ELEMENTS OF LITERATURE

Satire

Satire—ridiculing human foolishness or wrong-doing—ultimately holds a moral. The sting of satire is meant to cure us of our pretensions and blindness. While a realistic, ironic writer wants us to come to terms with the world as it is, the satirist wants to reform that world. The satirist's premise is that when an unacceptable situation is exposed to ridicule and laughter, it cannot last very long.

The tools of satire.   Satire requires two ingredients to be successful: (1) either wit, humor based on fantasy, or humor based on a sense of the absurd and (2) a target.

The humor of the satirist almost always involves some use of **irony**—that is, it involves a discrepancy between what is said and what is actually meant, or between what we expect to happen and what actually happens. Satirists also use **hyperbole,** or exaggeration, for effect, and **incongruity,** a kind of irony that brings together two ideas (or events or people) that do not belong together (*incongruous* means "not fitting together"). Donald Barthelme uses all three devices in "Game."

A famous satirist: Jonathan Swift.   One of the greatest satirists of all time was the Irish-born writer Jonathan Swift. In *Gulliver's Travels* (1726), Swift took as his target the narrow-minded, hypocritical, and cruel English society of his time. Swift mocked his fellow citizens' pretensions to superiority by describing, among other wonders, a race of noble horses who are unquestionably superior to the English in intellect and in morals. In 1729, Swift published a satiric essay called *A Modest Proposal,* in which his fictional narrator suggests that the English could solve their vexing "Irish problem" (and also their food shortages) by serving poor Irish children up as food for the rich landlords, "who, as they have already devoured most of the parents, seem to have the best title to the children."

Fantasy and the collapse of common sense.
One of the greatest weapons of a certain type of satire is **fantasy,** the creation of a world where common sense has collapsed. Two of the most famous fantasies in the English language are Lewis Carroll's *Alice's Adventures in Wonderland* (1865) and

Through the Looking-Glass (1871). In these books, the whole world is turned on its head. Even language itself no longer means what we think it means. "When *I* use a word," proclaims Humpty Dumpty, "it means just what I choose it to mean—neither more nor less." This world of satiric fantasy is also found in *Gulliver's Travels.* There, for example, the horses not only speak, but also govern themselves in a way far superior to human governments.

Satire and the absurd.   At times, a satirist's fantasy will turn to the absurd or grotesque, and we can get what is known as *gallows humor,* an Americanism that means "morbid or cynical humor" (literally, humor when facing the executioner). Swift's *A Modest Proposal* becomes grotesque when the narrator dares to suggest cannibalism as a solution to an economic problem.

Satire in American literature.   Satire has a long history in American literature. The shrewd counsels of prudence we hear from Benjamin Franklin's Poor Richard (page 95) are a kind of satire, in which the writer suggests practical ways to succeed in a world that is less than ideal. Mark Twain (page 450) was more of a satirist than he generally receives credit for; his Mr. Bixby in *Life on the Mississippi* is part of a long line of boasters and rogues in literature who use wit and verbal exuberance to survive in an imperfect world. James Thurber created in Walter Mitty (page 625) an American version of the man bullied by a woman, an archetypal character popular in satire at least from the days of ancient Rome. And, of course, the daily newspapers are filled with biting editorial cartoons built on satire.

What elements of satire do you find in Barthelme's story?

The Mad Hatter at the tea party, after Sir John Tenniel's design for the first edition of Lewis Carroll's *Alice's Adventures in Wonderland* (1865).

The Granger Collection, New York.

CHOICES: Building Your Portfolio

Writer's Notebook

1. Collecting Ideas for an Evaluation

Suppose you want to evaluate the **theme** of "Game." Take notes now that you might use later in an essay of evaluation. First, try to state the theme as accurately as you can. Then, describe your responses to the theme. Here are some questions you can cover: Is the theme clearly presented, or is it ambiguous? Do I agree with the theme? Is the theme popular in contemporary literature and film? How does its presentation in "Game" compare with its presentation in other texts? What does the theme reveal about the writer's view of the world? Jot down evidence to support your responses. Save your work for possible use in the Writer's Workshop on page 1181.

Comparing Texts

2. The World According to Barthelme, Auden, and You

In the following famous poem, W. H. Auden (1907–1973) describes a citizen of the modern world. In a brief essay, tell whether you think Barthelme's characters and Auden's citizen live in the same world. Has society taken away their freedom and ignored their humanity? Do you agree with these views of the world?

The Unknown Citizen

To JS/07/M/378
This Marble Monument Is Erected by the State

He was found by the Bureau of Statistics to be
One against whom there was no official complaint,
And all the reports on his conduct agree
That, in the modern sense of an old-fashioned word,
    he was a saint,
5 For in everything he did he served the Greater Community.
Except for the War till the day he retired
He worked in a factory and never got fired,
But satisfied his employers, Fudge Motors Inc.
Yet he wasn't a scab or odd in his views,
10 For his Union reports that he paid his dues,
(Our report on his Union shows it was sound)
And our Social Psychology workers found
That he was popular with his mates and liked a drink.
The Press are convinced that he bought a paper every day
And that his reactions to advertisements were normal in
15   every way.
Policies taken out in his name prove that he was fully insured,
And his Health-card shows he was once in hospital but
    left it cured.
Both Producers Research and High-Grade Living declare
He was fully sensible to the advantages of the Installment Plan
20 And had everything necessary to the Modern Man,
A gramophone, a radio, a car, and a frigidaire.
Our researchers into Public Opinion are content
That he held the proper opinions for the time of year;
When there was peace, he was for peace; when there
    was war, he went.
25 He was married and added five children to the population,
Which our Eugenist says was the right number for a parent of
    his generation,
And our teachers report that he never interfered with
    their education.
Was he free? Was he happy? The question is absurd:
Had anything been wrong, we should certainly have heard.

—W. H. Auden

Tim O'Brien

(1946–   )

"All my work has been somewhat political in that it's been directed at big issues," Tim O'Brien once said. "My concerns have to do with the abstractions: What's courage and how do you get it? What's justice and how do you achieve it? How does one do right in an evil situation?" O'Brien turned those questions into powerful artistic tools in his gripping war novel *Going After Cacciato* (1978).

O'Brien was born in Austin, Minnesota, and graduated from Macalester College. In 1968, he was drafted and served with the U.S. Army in Vietnam, where he attained the rank of sergeant. Returning from the war, he went to Harvard for graduate work in English. A summer internship on the *Washington Post* led to a job as national affairs reporter for that newspaper.

O'Brien had been writing stories since childhood, and even in the midst of his academic work, he knew he wanted to write full time. It was his military experience in Vietnam that provided much of the material for his fiction and personal narratives. *If I Die in a Combat Zone, Box Me Up and Ship Me Home* (1973) is a collection of anecdotes and observations of his duty in Vietnam. The book drew widespread praise, particularly from veterans, as an authentic recreation of the foot soldier's experience in an unpopular war.

O'Brien's first novel, *Northern Lights,* appeared in 1974 and dealt with a veteran returned to civilian life. *Going After Cacciato,* his second novel, followed four years later. This novel returned to the jungle war and depicted a

© Jerry Bauer.

soldier's fantasy of quitting the battle and walking off across the mountains to find Paris. *Cacciato* was acclaimed as one of the few novels to have captured the essence of the Vietnam experience, and it won a prestigious National Book Award in 1979.

O'Brien has said of his novel, "It's not really Vietnam that I was concerned about when I wrote *Cacciato;* rather it was to have readers care about what's right and wrong and about the difficulty of doing right, the difficulty of saying no to a war."

In 1990, O'Brien published *The Things They Carried,* another remarkable book dealing with the Vietnam War and its human effects. At publication, he told an interviewer:

> My life is storytelling. I believe in stories, in their incredible power to keep people alive, to keep the living alive, and the dead. And if I have started now to play with the stories, inside the stories themselves, well, that's what people do all the time.
>
> Storytelling is the essential human activity. The harder the situation, the more essential it is. In Vietnam men were constantly telling one another stories about the war. Our unit lost a lot of guys around My Lai, but the stories they told stay around after them. I would be mad not to tell the stories I know.

O'Brien keeps the Vietnam experience at the core of his psychological thriller *In the Lake of the Woods* (1994). This is a novel about a politician who attempts to conceal his past involvement in the massacre of Vietnamese civilians by American soldiers at My Lai in 1968.

HRW

go.hrw.com

LE0 11-18

Three Flags (1958) by Jasper Johns. Encaustic on canvas (30⅞″ × 45½″ × 5″).

Collection of Whitney Museum of American Art. Fiftieth Anniversary Gift of the Gilman Foundation, Inc., The Lauder Foundation, A. Alfred Taubman, an anonymous donor, and purchase. 80.32. Photograph ©1998: Whitney Museum of American Art, ©Jasper Johns/Licensed by VAGA, New York, NY.

Before You Read

SPEAKING OF COURAGE

Make the Connection

Courage and Common Sense

What is courage? At what point does it become foolhardiness? In retrospect, Paul Berlin wishes he had been *really* courageous in war, especially during a particular incident. Maybe he was following good common sense, however, in acting as he did.

Quickwrite

Why might it be difficult for a young soldier to speak with a parent about a difficult experience in war? Write down some reasons why such a communication might be strained.

Elements of Literature

Conflict

A **conflict** is a struggle between opposing forces or characters. An **external conflict** can involve two people, a person and nature, a person and a machine, and many other situations. An **internal conflict** involves opposing forces within a person's mind. "Speaking of Courage" is largely about an internal conflict in Paul Berlin's mind.

> **A conflict** is a struggle between opposing forces or characters.
>
> *For more on Conflict, see page 607 and the Handbook of Literary Terms.*

Background

Before he published the full novel *Going After Cacciato,* O'Brien published portions of it as short stories in magazines. This story, which appeared in a different form in the novel, was named one of the O. Henry Prize Stories of 1978.

The novel about Cacciato is told through the eyes and sensibilities of a young soldier from Iowa named Paul Berlin. In this story, Paul has recently returned from battle duty in Vietnam. Like many veterans of that war, he is confused over the meaning of his experience. He is also vaguely dissatisfied with his performance in the war.

Speaking of Courage

Tim O'Brien

The war was over, and there was no place in particular to go. Paul Berlin followed the tar road in its seven-mile loop around the lake, then he started all over again, driving slowly, feeling safe inside his father's big Chevy, now and again looking out onto the lake to watch the boats and waterskiers and scenery. It was Sunday and it was summer, and things seemed pretty much the same. The lake was the same. The houses were the same, all low-slung and split level and modern, porches and picture windows facing the water. The lots were spacious. On the lake-side of the road, the houses were handsome and set deep in, well-kept and painted, with docks jutting out into the lake, and boats moored and covered with canvas, and gardens, and sometimes even gardeners, and stone patios with barbecue spits and grills, and wooden shingles saying who lived where. On the other side of the road, to his left, the houses were also handsome, though less expensive and on a smaller scale and with no docks or boats or wooden shingles. The road was a sort of boundary between the affluent and the almost affluent, and to live on the lake-side of the road was one of the few natural privileges in a town of the prairie—the difference between watching the sun set over cornfields or over the lake.

It was a good-sized lake. In high school he'd driven round and round and round with his friends and pretty girls, talking about urgent matters, worrying eagerly about the existence of God and theories of causation,[1] or wondering whether Sally Hankins, who lived on the lake-side of the road, would want to pull into the shelter of Sunset Park. Then, there had not been a war. But there had always been the lake. It had been dug out by the southernmost advance of the Wisconsin glacier. Fed by neither springs nor streams, it was a tepid, algaed lake that depended on fickle prairie rains for replenishment. Still, it was the town's only lake, the only one in twenty-six miles, and at night the moon made a white swath across its waters, and on sunny days it was nice to look at, and that evening it would dazzle with the reflections of fireworks, and it was the center of things from the very start, always there to be driven around, still mesmerizing and quieting and a good audience for silence, a seven-mile flat circumference that could

1. **theories of causation:** philosophical theories holding that events are connected through cause-and-effect relationships.

WORDS TO OWN

affluent (af′lōō·ənt) *adj.* used as *n.*: well-to-do people.
tepid (tep′id) *adj.*: lukewarm.
mesmerizing (mez′mər·īz′iŋ) *v.* used as *adj.*: hypnotic.

---

be traveled by slow car in twenty-five minutes. It was not such a good lake for swimming. After college, he'd caught an ear infection that had almost kept him out of the war. And the lake had drowned Max Arnold, keeping him out of the war entirely. Max had been one who liked to talk about the existence of God. "No, I'm not saying *that*," he would say carefully against the <u>drone</u> of the engine. "I'm saying it is possible as an idea, even necessary as an idea, a final cause in the whole structure of causation." Now he knew, perhaps. Before the war, they'd driven around the lake as friends, but now Max was dead and most of the others were living in Des Moines or Sioux City, or going to school somewhere, or holding down jobs. None of the girls was left. Sally Hankins was married. His father would not talk. His father had been in another war, so he knew the truth already, and he would not talk about it, and there was no one left to talk with.

He turned on the radio. The car's big engine fired machinery that blew cold air all over him. Clockwise, like an electron spinning forever around its nucleus, the big Chevy circled the lake, and he had little to do but sit in the air-conditioning, both hands on the wheel, letting the car carry him in orbit. It was a lazy Sunday. The town was small. Out on the lake, a man's motorboat had stalled, and the fellow was bent over the silver motor with a wrench and a frown, and beyond him there were waterskiers and smooth July waters and two mud hens.

The road curved west. The sun was low in front of him, and he figured it was close to five o'clock. Twenty after, he guessed. The war had taught him to figure time. Even without the sun, waking from sleep, he could usually place it within fifteen minutes either way. He wished his father were there beside him, so he could say, "Well, looks about five-twenty," and his father would look at his watch and say, "Hey! How'd you do that?" "One of those things you learn in the war," he would say. "I know exactly what you mean," his father would then say, and the ice would be broken, and then they would be able to talk about it as they circled the lake.

He drove past Slater Park and across the causeway and past Sunset Park. The radio announcer sounded tired. He said it was five-thirty. The temperature in Des Moines was eighty-one degrees,

and "All you on the road, drive carefully now, you hear, on this fine Fourth of July." Along the road, kicking stones in front of them, two young boys were hiking with knapsacks and toy rifles and canteens. He honked going by, but neither boy looked up. Already he'd passed them six times, forty-two miles, nearly three hours. He watched the boys <u>recede</u> in his rearview mirror. They turned purply colored, like clotted blood, before finally disappearing.

"How many medals did you win?" his father might have asked.

"Seven," he would have said, "though none of them were for <u>valor</u>."

"That's all right," his father would have answered, knowing full well that many brave men did not win medals for their bravery, and that others won medals for doing nothing. "What are the medals you won?"

And he would have listed them, as a kind of starting place for talking about the war: the Combat Infantryman's Badge, the Air Medal, the Bronze Star (without a V-device for valor), the Army Commendation Medal, the Vietnam Campaign Medal, the Good Conduct Medal, and the Purple Heart, though it wasn't much of a wound, and there was no scar, and it didn't hurt and never had. While none of them was for valor, the decorations still looked good on the uniform in his closet, and if anyone were to ask, he would have explained what each signified, and eventually he would have talked about the medals he did not win, and why he did not win them, and how afraid he had been.

"Well," his father might have said, "that's an impressive list of medals, all right."

"But none were for valor."

"I understand."

And that would have been the time for telling his father that he'd almost won the Silver Star, or maybe even the Medal of Honor.

"I almost won the Silver Star," he would have said.

"How's that?"

WORDS TO OWN

drone *n.*: monotonous hum.
recede (ri·sēd′) *v.*: become more distant and indistinct.
valor (val′ər) *n.*: great courage.

"Oh, it's just a war story."

"What's wrong with war stories?" his father would have said.

"Nothing, except I guess nobody wants to hear them."

"Tell me," his father would have said.

And then, circling the lake, he would have started the story by saying what a crazy hot day it had been when Frenchie Tucker crawled like a snake into the clay tunnel and got shot in the neck, going on with the story in great detail, telling how it smelled and what the sounds had been, everything, then going on to say how he'd almost won the Silver Star for valor.

"Well," his father would have said, "that's not a very pretty story."

"I wasn't very brave."

"You have seven medals."

"True, true," he would have said, "but I might have had eight," but even so, seven medals was pretty good, hinting at courage with their bright colors and heavy metals. "But I wasn't brave," he would have admitted.

"You weren't a coward, either," his father would have said.

"I might have been a hero."

"But you weren't a coward," his father would have insisted.

"No," Paul Berlin would have said, holding the wheel slightly right of center to produce the constant clockwise motion, "no, I wasn't a coward, and I wasn't brave, but I had the chance." He would have explained, if anyone were there to listen, that his most precious medal, except for the one he did not win, was the Combat Infantryman's Badge. While not strictly speaking a genuine medal—more an insignia of soldierdom—the CIB meant that he had seen the war as a real soldier, on the ground. It meant he'd had the opportunity to be brave, it meant that. It meant, too, that he'd . . . seen Frenchie Tucker crawl into the tunnel so that just his feet were left showing, and heard the sound when he got shot in the neck. With its crossed rifles and silver and blue colors, the CIB was really not such a bad decoration, not as good as the Silver Star or Medal of Honor, but still evidence that he'd once been there with the chance to be very brave. "I wasn't brave," he would have said, "but I might have been."

The road descended into the outskirts of town, turning northwest past the junior college and tennis courts, then past the city park where tables were spread with sheets of colored plastic as picnickers listened to the high school band, then past the <u>municipal</u> docks where a fat woman stood in pedal-pushers and white socks, fishing for bullheads.[2] There were no other fish in the lake, excepting some perch and a few worthless carp. It was a bad lake for swimming and fishing both.

He was in no great hurry. There was no place in particular to go. The day was very hot, but inside the Chevy the air was cold and oily and secure, and he liked the sound of the big engine and the radio and the air-conditioning. Through the windows, as though seen through one-way glass, the town shined like a stop-motion photograph, or a memory. The town could not talk, and it would not listen, and it was really a very small town anyway. "How'd you like to hear about the time I almost won the Silver Star for valor?" he might have said. The Chevy seemed to know its way around the lake.

It was late afternoon. Along an unused railway spur, four men were erecting steel launchers for the evening fireworks. They were dressed alike in khaki trousers, work shirts, visored caps and black boots. They were sweating. Two of them were unloading crates of explosives from a city truck, stacking the crates near the steel launchers. They were talking. One of them was laughing. "How'd you like to hear about it?" he might have murmured, but the men did not look up. Later they would blow color into the sky. The lake would be like a mirror, and the picnickers would sigh. The colors would open wide. "Well, it was this crazy hot day," he would have said to anyone who asked, "and Frenchie Tucker took off his helmet and pack and crawled into the tunnel with a forty-five and a knife, and the whole platoon stood in a circle around the mouth of the tunnel to watch him go down. 'Don't get blowed away,' said Stink Harris, but Frenchie was already inside and he didn't hear. You could see his feet wiggling,

2. **bullheads:** A bullhead is a type of freshwater catfish with hornlike growths near its mouth.

WORDS TO OWN

municipal (myoo·nis′ə·pəl) *adj.*: belonging to a city or town.

and you could smell the dirt and clay, and then, when he got shot through the neck, you could smell the gunpowder and you could see Frenchie's feet jerk, and that was the day I could have won the Silver Star for valor."

The Chevy rolled smoothly across the old railroad spur. To his right, there was only the open lake. To his left, the lawns were scorched dry like October corn. Hopelessly, round and round, a rotating sprinkler scattered water into Doctor Mason's vegetable garden. In August it would get worse. The lake would turn green, thick with bacteria and decay, and the golf course would dry up, and dragonflies would crack open for lack of good water. The summer seemed permanent.

The big Chevy curled past the A&W[3] and Centennial Beach, and he started his seventh revolution around the lake.

He followed the road past the handsome low-slung houses. Back to Slater Park, across the causeway, around to Sunset Park, as though riding on tracks.

Out on the lake, the man with the stalled motorboat was still fiddling with the engine.

The two boys were still trudging on their hike. They did not look up when he honked.

The pair of mud hens floated like wooden decoys. The waterskiers looked tan and happy, and the spray behind them looked clean.

It was all distant and pretty.

Facing the sun again, he figured it was nearly six o'clock. Not much later the tired announcer in Des Moines confirmed it, his voice seeming to rock itself into a Sunday afternoon snooze.

Too bad, he thought. If Max were there, he would say something meaningful about the announcer's fatigue, and relate it to the sun low and red now over the lake, and the war, and courage. Too bad that all the girls had gone away. And his father, who already knew the difficulties of being brave, and who preferred silence.

Circling the lake, with time to talk, he would have told the truth. He would not have faked it. Starting with the admission that he had not been truly brave, he would have next said he hadn't been a coward, either. "I almost won the Silver Star for valor," he would have said, and, even so, he'd learned many important things in the war.

3. **A&W:** chain of drive-in, fast-food restaurants.

Like telling time without a watch. He had learned to step lightly. He knew, just by the sound, the difference between friendly and enemy mortars, and with time to talk and with an audience, he could explain the difference in great detail. He could tell people that the enemy fired 82-millimeter mortar rounds, while we fired 81's, and that this was a real advantage to the enemy since they could steal our rounds and shoot them from their own weapons. He knew many lies. Simple, unprofound things. He knew it is a lie that only stupid men are brave. He knew that a man can die of fright, literally, because it had happened just that way to Billy Boy Watkins after his foot had been blown off. Billy Boy had been scared to death. Dead of a heart attack caused by fright, according to Doc Peret, who would know. He knew, too, that it is a lie, the old saying that you never hear the shot that gets you, because Frenchie Tucker was shot in the neck, and after they dragged him out of the tunnel he lay there and told everyone his great discovery; he'd heard it coming the whole way, he said excitedly; and then he raised his thumb and bled through his mouth, grinning at the great discovery. So the old saying was surely a lie, or else Frenchie Tucker was lying himself, which under the circumstances was hard to believe. He knew a lot of things. They were not new or profound, but they were true. He knew that he might have won a Silver Star, like Frenchie, if he'd been able to finish what Frenchie started in the foul tunnel. He knew many war stories, a thousand details, smells and the confusion of the senses, but nobody was there to listen, and nobody knew a damn about the war because nobody believed it was really a war at all. It was not a war for war stories, or talk of valor, and nobody asked questions about the details, such as how afraid you can be, or what the particular sounds were, or whether it hurts to be shot, or what you think about and hear and see on ambush, or whether you can really tell in a firefight which way to shoot, which you can't, or how you become brave enough to win the Silver Star, or how it smells of sulfur against your cheek after firing

WORDS TO OWN

mortars (môrt′ərz) *n. pl.:* cannons used to fire explosive shells.

eighteen fast rounds, or how you crawl on hands and knees without knowing direction, and how, after crawling into the red-mouthed tunnel, you close your eyes like a mole and follow the tunnel walls and smell Frenchie's fresh blood and know a bullet cannot miss in there, and how there is nowhere to go but forward or backward, eyes closed, and how you can't go forward, and lose all sense, and are dragged out by the heels, losing the Silver Star. All the details, without <u>profundity</u>, simple and age old, but nobody wants to hear war stories because they are age old and not new and not profound, and because everyone knows already that it hadn't been a war like other wars. If Max or his father were ever to ask, or anybody, he would say, "Well, first off, it was a war the same as any war," which would not sound profound at all, but which would be the truth. Then he would explain what he meant in great detail, explaining that, right or wrong or win or lose, at root it had been a real war, regardless of corruption in high places or politics or sociology or the existence of God. His father knew it already, though. Which was why he didn't ask. And Max could not ask. It was a small town, but it wasn't the town's fault, either.

He passed the sprawling ranch-style homes. He lit a cigarette. He had learned to smoke in the war. He opened the window a crack but kept the air-conditioner going full, and again he circled the lake. His thoughts were the same. Out on the lake, the man was frantically yanking the cord to his stalled outboard motor. Along the causeway, the two boys marched on. The pair of mud hens sought sludge at the bottom of the lake, heads under water and tails bobbing.

Six-thirty, he thought. The lake had divided into two halves. One half still glistened. The other was caught in shadow. Soon it would be dark. The

Vietnam Veterans Memorial (detail), Washington, D.C.

Bill Hickey/The Image Bank.

crew of workers would shoot the sky full of color, for the war was over, and the town would celebrate independence. He passed Sunset Park once again, and more houses, and the junior college and tennis courts, and the picnickers and the high school band, and the municipal docks where the fat woman patiently waited for fish.

Already, though it wasn't quite dusk, the A&W was awash in neon lights.

He maneuvered his father's Chevy into one of the parking slots, let the engine idle, and waited. The place was doing a good holiday business. Mostly kids in their fathers' cars, a few farmers in for the day, a few faces he thought he remembered, but no names. He sat still. With the sound of the engine and air-conditioning and radio, he could not hear the kids laughing, or the cars coming and going and burning rubber. But it didn't matter, it seemed proper, and he sat patiently and watched while mosquitoes and June bugs swarmed off the lake to attack the orange-colored lighting. A slim, hipless, deft young blonde delivered trays of food, passing him by as if the big Chevy were invisible, but he waited. The tired announcer in Des Moines gave the time, seven

WORDS TO OWN

profundity (prō·fun′də·tē) *n.*: intellectual depth.

o'clock. He could trace the fall of dusk in the orange lights which grew brighter and sharper. It was a bad war for medals. But the Silver Star would have been nice. Nice to have been brave. The <u>tactile</u>, certain substance of the Silver Star, and how he could have rubbed his fingers over it, remembering the tunnel and the smell of clay in his nose, going forward and not backward in simple bravery. He waited patiently. The mosquitoes were electrocuting themselves against a Pest-Rid machine. The slim young carhop ignored him, chatting with four boys in a Firebird, her legs in nylons even in mid-summer.

He honked once, a little embarrassed, but she did not turn. The four boys were laughing. He could not hear them, or the joke, but he could see their bright eyes and the way their heads moved. She patted the cheek of the driver.

He honked again, twice. He could not hear the sound. The girl did not hear, either.

He honked again, this time leaning on the horn. His ears buzzed. The air-conditioning shot cold air into his lap. The girl turned slowly, as though hearing something very distant, not at all sure. She said something to the boys, and they laughed, then she moved reluctantly toward him. EAT MAMA BURGERS said the orange and brown button on her chest. "How'd you like to hear about the war," he whispered, feeling vengeful. "The time I almost won the Silver Star."

She stood at the window, straight up so he could not see her face, only the button that said, EAT MAMA BURGERS. "Papa Burger, root beer, and french fries," he said, but the girl did not move or answer. She rapped on the window.

"Papa Burger, root beer, and french fries," he said, rolling it down.

She leaned down. She shook her head dumbly. Her eyes were as lovely and fuzzy as cotton candy.

"Papa Burger, root beer, and french fries," he said slowly, pronouncing the words separately and distinctly for her.

She stared at him with her strange eyes. "You blind?" she chirped suddenly. She gestured toward an intercom attached to a steel post. "You blind or something?"

"Papa Burger, root beer, and french fries."

"Push the button," she said, "and place your order." Then, first punching the button for him, she returned to her friends in the Firebird.

"Order," commanded a tinny voice.

"Papa Burger, root beer, and french fries."

"Roger-dodger," the voice said. "Repeat: one Papa, one beer, one fries. Stand by. That's it?"

"Roger," said Paul Berlin.

"Out," said the voice, and the intercom squeaked and went dead.

"Out," said Paul Berlin.

When the slim carhop brought him his tray, he ate quickly, without looking up, then punched the intercom button.

"Order," said the tinny voice.

"I'm done."

"That's it?"

"Yes, all done."

"Roger-dodger, over n' out," said the voice.

"Out."

On his ninth revolution around the lake he passed the hiking boys for the last time. The man with the stalled motorboat was paddling toward shore. The mud hens were gone. The fat woman was reeling in her line. The sun had left a smudge of watercolor on the horizon, and the bandshell[4] was empty, and Doctor Mason's sprinkler went round and round.

On his tenth revolution, he switched off the air-conditioning, cranked open a window, and rested his elbow comfortably on the sill, driving with one hand. He could trace the contours of the tunnel. He could talk about the scrambling sense of being lost, though he could not describe it even in his thoughts. He could talk about the terror, but he could not describe it or even feel it anymore. He could talk about emerging to see sunlight, but he could not feel the warmth, or see the faces of the men who looked away, or talk about his shame. There was no one to talk to, and nothing to say.

On his eleventh revolution, the sky went crazy with color.

He pulled into Sunset Park and stopped in the shadow of a picnic shelter. After a time, he got out and walked down to the beach and stood with his arms folded and watched the fireworks. For a small town, it was a pretty good show.

4. bandshell: open-air stage with a rear sounding board shaped like the shell of a scallop.

- -

WORDS TO OWN

tactile (tak′təl) *adj.*: able to be perceived by touch.

- -

MAKING MEANINGS

First Thoughts

1. How would you have felt if you had been in Paul Berlin's shoes?

Shaping Interpretations

2. Explain why it is so difficult for Paul and his father to talk. What do you think Paul means when he says that his father "knew the truth already"? What truth does his father know, and how does he know it?

3. Discuss the **symbolic** meaning of the repeated circular action in the story and of the repeated references to time.

4. What is the **symbolic** meaning of the date in the story's context?

5. Given his experiences, what is **ironic** about the military language in Paul's conversation with the disembodied voice on the drive-in restaurant's intercom system?

6. Find the passages in which Paul mentions conversations about God. What purpose do you think these passages serve?

7. Do you think Paul's **internal conflict** has been resolved by the end of the story? Explain.

8. Do you think Paul is or is not a courageous person? Explain your answer.

Extending the Text

9. What will happen to Paul next? Share your predictions about Paul's future, and explain your reasons.

Reading Check

a. Describe the story's **setting**. In contrast, what sights, sounds, and smells does Paul remember from his time in Vietnam?

b. What does Paul wish his father would do?

c. List the things Paul has learned as a result of the war. According to Paul, why don't people want to hear about the war?

d. What does Paul wish he had done in Vietnam? What does he want to tell his father?

CHOICES:
Building Your Portfolio

Writer's Notebook
1. Collecting Ideas for an Evaluation

What are your criteria for judging whether a writer has been successful in creating a character? List some qualities you expect to find in a well-conceived character. Then, note whether Paul Berlin meets those criteria. Save your notes for possible use in the Writer's Workshop on page 1181.

Analyzing Contrast
2. War and Peace, Peace and War

"Speaking of Courage" deals indirectly with the horror of warfare. In a brief essay, explain how the story uses **contrast** to deal with this subject. In planning your essay, consider how contrast is evident in the story's **setting**, **characterization**, and **tone**.

Comparing Stories
3. Soldiers' Homes

In a brief essay, compare and contrast the situation and character of Paul Berlin with that of Harold Krebs in Ernest Hemingway's "Soldier's Home" (page 653). What can you infer about the similarities and differences in the experiences of soldiers returning from World War I and soldiers returning from Vietnam?

Creative Writing / Performance
4. "What Did You Do in the War?"

Write the dialogue for a television interview about Vietnam with Paul Berlin to be broadcast on a July 4 newscast. Then, ask two students to perform the dialogue, with you as director. Instruct them in how to speak and how to incorporate gestures and facial expressions. Allow them to ad-lib a little as well.

© Nancy Crampton.

Yusef Komunyakaa

(1947–)

" Vietnam helped me to look at the horror and terror in the hearts of people and realize how we can't aim guns and set booby traps for people we have never spoken a word to. That kind of impersonal violence mystifies me." These are the heartfelt reflections of one of the finest poets to emerge from the Vietnam conflict, Yusef Komunyakaa (kō·mun·yä′kə), the soldier-writer-teacher who was awarded a Pulitzer Prize in 1994 for his poetry collection *Neon Vernacular*.

A poet of both unflinching honesty and emotional restraint, Komunyakaa was born and raised in Bogalusa, Louisiana. His impulse to write, he recalls, first came when he was sixteen and read a copy of James Baldwin's *Nobody Knows My Name,* which he had found in a tiny church library. After high school, he served as a soldier in Vietnam and was awarded the Bronze Star. He then worked as a military "information specialist," corresponding from the front for a service newspaper. After the war, Komunyakaa earned advanced degrees: a master's from Colorado State University in 1979 and a master's in creative writing from the University of California, Irvine, in 1980.

Like so many American poets, Komunyakaa has made his living as a teacher. He has taught at the University of New Orleans and Indiana University, and he has given special poetry classes to elementary school students. Essentially a private and even shy man, Komunyakaa once said, "I'm happier talking about the process of writing, yes. . . . I'm even happier to have people read my work. I'm uncomfortable with the focus on the poet and not on the poem." Nevertheless, he gives poetry readings across America and in other countries. One critic, Kirkland C. Jones, points out the close connection for Komunyakaa between the written and the spoken word:

> In his Vietnam verse he keeps before the world what it meant and still means to be American, black, and a soldier, and what the painful inequities of this combination add up to. His poetry is as rhythmic and fluid as his speaking voice, and just as mellow and introspective.

Komunyakaa's collections include *Lost in the Bonewheel Factory* (1979); *Copacetic* (1984), in which critics have noted jazzlike poems that recall the verse of Langston Hughes and Jean Toomer; *I Apologize for the Eyes in My Head* (1986); *Magic City* (1992), and *Thieves of Paradise* (1998). His poems cluster around themes of violent conflict and loss, of family and racial identity, of survival and memory, and of facing up to the harsh facts of life and death. In 1988, Komunyakaa published a powerful volume devoted entirely to his Vietnam experience, *Dien Cai Dau.* Kirkland Jones ranks this among the most highly accomplished books generated by the war because Komunyakaa

> focuses on the mental horrors of war—the anguish shared by the soldiers, those left at home to keep watch, and other observers, participants, objectors, who are all part of the "psychological terrain," as he has termed it, "that makes us all victims" and rages behind the eyes long after the actual fighting has ceased.

Before You Read

MONSOON SEASON

Make the Connection

Living with Dying

Memories of violence last far longer than the physical pain. Sometimes the most common things—a leaf, a breeze, a drop of rain—can trigger those memories and bring seemingly forgotten experiences back to life.

Elements of Literature

Imagery

Images in literature use language to evoke a picture or a sensation of a person or thing. Poetry is closely related to music, so it is not surprising that many poems contain **images** of sound. "Monsoon Season" includes several. Try to spot them as you read. It will probably help to read the poem aloud.

Quickwrite

Write down some **images** that you might find in a poem set during the Vietnam War in a heavy rainstorm. For ideas, you might look at the photographs on these pages.

Background

U.S. soldiers fighting the ground war during the Vietnam conflict had to contend with conditions completely alien to them. The moist, hot, tropical climate of Vietnam, its extensive jungles and mountains, and the ever-present threat of an often invisible enemy made fighting conditions unusually hazardous and frightening. And then there were the monsoons—year-round winds bringing torrents of seemingly unending rain in the hot summer and lighter but still frequent showers in the somewhat cooler winter.

Monsoon Season

Yusef Komunyakaa

A river shines in the jungle's
wet leaves. The rain's finally
let up but whenever wind shakes
the foliage it starts to fall.
5   The monsoon uncovers troubled
seasons we tried to forget.
Dead men slip through bad weather,
stamping their muddy boots to wake us,
their curses coming easier.
10   There's a bend in everything,
in elephant grass & flame trees,
raindrops pelting the sand-bagged
bunker like a muted gong.

White phosphorus° washed from the air,
15 wind sways with violet myrtle,°
beating it naked. Soaked to the bone,
jungle rot brings us down to earth.
We sit in our hooches°
with too much time,
20 where grounded choppers
can't fly out the wounded.
Somewhere nearby a frog
begs a snake.
I try counting droplets,
25 stars that aren't in the sky.
My poncho feels like a body bag.
I lose count. Red leaves
whirl by, the monsoon
unburying the dead.

14. white phosphorus: poisonous, highly flammable chemical element used in weapons during the Vietnam War.
15. myrtle: type of evergreen shrub.
18. hooches: U.S. military slang for huts and other simple buildings in which soldiers lived while at base camps.

U.S. soldier of the Second Battalion in Mekong Delta, Vietnam, 1967.

Larry Burrows © 1967 Time, Inc.

Poetry Emotion

ANNA QUINDLEN

Yusef Komunyakaa won the Pulitzer Prize this week, but he does not expect to become a household name, and not because his name itself, phonetically simple once parsed out bit by bit, looks at first glance so unpronounceable. Mr. Komunyakaa won the prize for poetry, and there is little premium in poetry in a world that thinks of Pound and Whitman as a weight and sampler, not an Ezra, a Walt, a thing of beauty, a joy forever.

It's hard to figure out why this should be true, why poetry has been shunted onto a siding at a time, a place, so in need of brevity and truth. We still use the word as a synonym for a kind of lovely perfection, for an inspired figure skater, an accomplished ballet dancer. Many of the finest books children read when young are poetry: "The Cat in the Hat," "Goodnight Moon," the free verse of "Where the Wild Things Are."

And then suddenly, just as their faces lose the soft curves of babyhood, the children harden into prose, and leave verse behind, or reject it entirely. Their summer reading lists rarely include poetry, only stories; *The Red Badge of Courage,* not Mr. Komunyakaa's spare and evocative poems about his hitch in Vietnam:

> *He danced with tall grass*
> *for a moment, like he was*
> *swaying*
> *with a woman. Our gun barrels*
> *glowed white-hot.*
> *When I got to him,*
> *a blue halo*
> *of flies had already claimed*
> *him.*

For some of those children who once were lulled to sleep by the rhythms of Seuss and Sendak, poetry comes now set to music: Nirvana and Arrested Development, Tori Amos and the Indigo Girls. Many readers are scared off young, put off by the belief that poetry is difficult and demanding. We complain that it doesn't sound like the way we talk, but if it sounds like the way we talk, we complain that it doesn't rhyme.

A poet who teaches in the schools tells of how one boy told him he couldn't, wouldn't write poetry. Then one day in class he heard Hayden Carruth's "Cows at Night" and cried, "I didn't know we were allowed to write poems about cows."

Or to write a poem about two women talking in the kitchen:

> *Crazy as a bessy bug.*
> *Jack wasn't cold*
> *In his grave before*
> *She done up & gave all*
> *The insurance money*
> *To some young pigeon*
> *Who never hit a lick*
> *At work in his life.*
> *He cleaned her out & left*
> *With Donna Faye's girl.*
> *Honey, hush. You don't*
> *Say . . .*

That's Mr. Komunyakaa, from the collection, *Neon Vernacular,* that won the Pulitzer. His publisher originally printed 2,500 copies, which is fairly large for poetry but a joke to the folks who stock those racks at the airport. Few are the parents who leap up with soundless joy when a son or daughter announces, "Mom, Dad, I've decided to become a poet."

People who are knowledgeable about poetry sometimes discuss it in that knowing, rather hateful way in which enophiles talk about wine: robust, delicate, muscular. This has nothing to do with how most of us experience it, the heart coming around the corner and unexpectedly running into the mind. Of all the words that have stuck to the ribs of my soul, poetry has been the most filling. Robert Frost, Robert Lowell, Elizabeth Bishop, Emily Dickinson, the divine W. B. Yeats. April is the cruelest month. O World, I cannot hold thee close enough! After the first death, there is no other. A terrible beauty is born.

Poems are now appearing on posters in subway trains; one commuter said of a Langston Hughes poem, "I can't express it, but I get it." Now rolling through the soot-black dark of the tunnels and the surprising sunshine where the subways suddenly shoot aboveground: Marianne Moore, William Carlos Williams, Audre Lorde, May Swenson, Rita Dove, and Gwendolyn Brooks, who wrote that exquisite evocation of *carpe diem,* and perhaps of poetry too:

> *Exhaust the little moment.*
> *Soon it dies.*
> *And be it gash or gold it will*
> *not come*
> *Again in this identical*
> *disguise.*

Says Mr. Komunyakaa, who teaches, "I never really approached it from the perspective of making a living. It was simply a need." Maybe it's a need for us all and we just forget it, as we move past bedtime-story rhythms and into a world without rhyme or reason.

—*The New York Times,*
April 16, 1994

MAKING MEANINGS

First Thoughts

1. How would you characterize the speaker's mood? Cite passages to support your opinion.

Shaping Interpretations

2. Where is the poem's speaker? What are the "troubled / seasons we tried to forget" (lines 5–6)?

3. How might the rainy weather have influenced the speaker's thoughts and feelings?

4. What specifically triggers the speaker's memory of past experiences?

5. In an **image** of sound, the speaker of "Monsoon Season" says the raindrops pelted the bunker "like a muted gong" (line 13). In your own words, tell what the sound of the raindrops was like to the speaker. Why is the image surprising?

6. When the speaker says "I lose count" (line 27), what does he *explicitly* say he is counting? What does he *imply* he has been counting?

7. Review your Quickwrite. In what ways were the **images** in the poem similar to or different from the ones you wrote down?

Extending the Text

8. In *Connections* on page 977, Anna Quindlen describes most people's experience of poetry as "the heart coming around the corner and unexpectedly running into the mind." Choose this or another observation of Quindlen's, and tell what you think it means and whether it seems to fit your experience of "Monsoon Season."

CHOICES:
Building Your Portfolio

Writer's Notebook

1. Collecting Ideas for an Evaluation

One criterion for evaluating a poem is the success with which it uses **imagery.** Review Komunyakaa's poem. Then, list some of the visual images in "Monsoon Season," and jot down notes evaluating whether the poet uses them effectively. Save your notes for possible use in the Writer's Workshop on page 1181.

Analyzing Symbolism

2. Frogs and Snakes

Poets frequently use **symbols**—persons, places, things, or events that have meaning in themselves but also stand for something more. In the passage "Somewhere nearby a frog / begs a snake," what might the frog and the snake symbolize? Do you think the poet has chosen his symbols wisely? Present your answers in a short essay.

Analyzing Our Culture / Speaking and Listening

3. "I have a real problem with that."

Komunyakaa struggles to understand the contemporary legacy of violence. He once said in an interview, "In our culture we celebrate violence. All of our heroes have blood on their hands. I have a real problem with that." Imagine that you are present at the interview in which Komunyakaa delivers this opinion. In a brief statement of your own, with no wasted words, tell him—and your class—why you agree or disagree with his statement.

U.S. Army helmet, Vietnam.

Henri Bureau / Sygma.

Collection 19

DISCOVERIES AND AWAKENINGS

Malamud
García Márquez
Roethke
Wilbur
Shapiro
Wright
Carver
Bishop
Harjo
Kingston
Heat-Moon

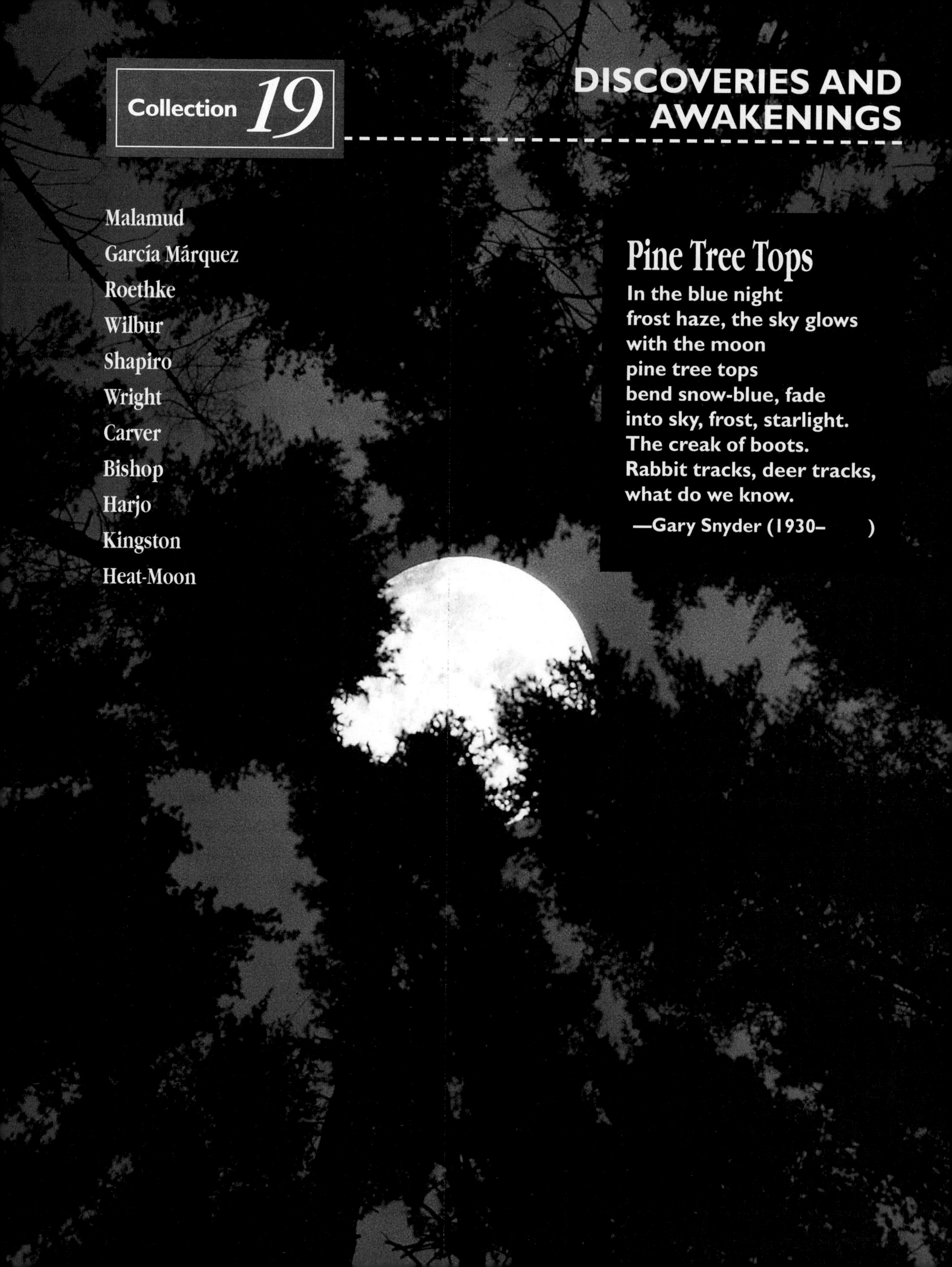

Pine Tree Tops

In the blue night
frost haze, the sky glows
with the moon
pine tree tops
bend snow-blue, fade
into sky, frost, starlight.
The creak of boots.
Rabbit tracks, deer tracks,
what do we know.

—Gary Snyder (1930–   )

Bernard Malamud

(1914–1986)

© Nancy Crampton.

Bernard Malamud is a principal figure in the group of Jewish writers whose work has enriched contemporary American literature. Yet Malamud preferred not to be easily pigeonholed. He did write *about* Jews, but he wrote *for* all people.

Malamud's characters usually live at a level of bare physical subsistence. Though we may feel compassion for them, they do not display the least self-pity. If their plight is sad, it is also triumphant, because they survive in heroic fashion against the odds all humans face.

"As you are grooved, so you are grieved," Malamud once wrote as preamble to an account of his own bleak upbringing. He was the older of two sons of a Russian immigrant storekeeper. His mother died when he was fourteen. He grew up in Brooklyn in a household without books, music, or pictures on the walls. During the Great Depression, he worked at a census office and a yarn factory to help support his family, but he felt these experiences were important to him as a writer. Getting down to essential needs and "turning inward," Malamud believed, are the best preparation for writing.

It was the suffering of European Jews during World War II that convinced Malamud he had something to say as a writer. "I for one believe that not enough has been made of the tragedy of the destruction of six million Jews," he said. "Somebody has to cry—even if it's just a writer, twenty years later."

Malamud's unique drama is spun out of the commonplace, the tragicomedy of survival in a brutal world. But his stories are always informed by love, and, indeed, his characters are largely redeemed by love. Philip Roth, whose own notable writing covers some of the same ground as Malamud's, wrote the following analysis:

"Malamud wrote of a meager world of pain in a language all his own. [It was] an English that often appeared, even outside the idiosyncratic dialogue, to have in large part been clipped together from out of what one might have thought to be the least promising stockpile, most unmagical barrel, around: the locutions, inversions, and diction of Jewish immigrant speech, a heap of broken verbal bones that looked, until he came along in those early stories to make them dance to his sad tune, to be of no use to anyone any longer other than the Borscht Belt comic and the professional nostalgia-monger."

Malamud taught English in New York City high schools and fiction at Oregon State University and Bennington College in Vermont. His first novel, *The Natural* (1952), whose central character is a baseball player, was made into a popular film in 1984. His other books include *The Assistant* (1957), a novel set in Brooklyn, considered by some critics to be his best work; the short-story collections *The Magic Barrel* (1958; National Book Award) and *Idiots First* (1963); and the novels *The Fixer* (1966; National Book Award and Pulitzer Prize), set in czarist Russia, and *The Tenants* (1971).

Malamud was a firm believer in the power of story. "The story will be with us as long as man is," he once said. "You know that, in part because of its effect on children. It's through story they realize that mystery won't kill them. Through story they learn they have a future."

go.hrw.com
LE0 11-19

Before You Read
THE MAGIC BARREL

Make the Connection

"When I fall in love . . ."

"Unbelievable!" "You're kidding!" Many of us react with exclamations like these when we hear of two seemingly mismatched people falling in love. After all, what do they have in common? A great deal, apparently. It may happen to friends or people in our families, to a famous actress who marries a quiet intellectual, to a king who gives up his throne for a commoner—to ourselves, even. Suddenly, deep emotional connections are made between people who, on the surface, inhabit different worlds.

Quickwrite

Why do people fall in love? Poets, philosophers, playwrights, and just about everybody else have been offering answers to that question for thousands of years. Yet we are still not sure about the answer. Is love purely emotional? Does it involve the mind as well as the heart? Write down some of your ideas on the subject.

Elements of Literature

Static and Dynamic Characters

A **static character** does not change much over the course of a story. A **dynamic character,** on the other hand, changes in an important way as the story unfolds. As you read, ask yourself: Which type of character is Leo Finkle? Which type is Pinye Salzman?

A **static character** does not change much over the course of a story. A **dynamic character** changes in an important way as a result of the story's action.

For more on Character, see the Handbook of Literary Terms.

Phyllis Seated (1952) by Moses Soyer. Oil on canvas (42″ × 36″).

Courtesy ACA Galleries, NY/Munich.

Birthday (L'Anniversaire) (1915) by Marc Chagall. Oil on cardboard.

The Magic Barrel

Bernard Malamud

"Love comes with the right person, not before."

Not long ago there lived in uptown New York, in a small, almost <u>meager</u> room, though crowded with books, Leo Finkle, a rabbinical student in the Yeshivah University.[1] Finkle, after six years of study, was to be ordained in June and had been advised by an acquaintance that he might find it easier to win himself a congregation if he were married. Since he had no present prospects of marriage, after two tormented days of turning it over in his mind, he called in Pinye Salzman, a marriage broker whose two-line advertisement he had read in the *Forward.*[2]

The matchmaker appeared one night out of the dark fourth-floor hallway of the graystone rooming house where Finkle lived, grasping a black, strapped portfolio that had been worn thin with use. Salzman, who had been long in the business, was of slight but dignified build, wearing an old hat, and an overcoat too short and tight for him. He smelled frankly of fish, which he loved to eat, and although he was missing a few teeth, his presence was not displeasing, because of an amiable manner curiously contrasted with mournful eyes. His voice, his lips, his wisp of beard, his bony fingers were animated, but give him a moment of repose and his mild blue eyes revealed a depth of sadness, a characteristic that put Leo a little at ease although the situation, for him, was inherently tense.

He at once informed Salzman why he had asked him to come, explaining that his home was in Cleveland, and that but for his parents, who had married comparatively late in life, he was alone in the world. He had for six years devoted himself almost entirely to his studies, as a result of which, understandably, he had found himself without time for a social life and the company of young women. Therefore he thought it the better part of trial and error—of embarrassing fumbling—to call in an experienced person to advise him on these matters. He remarked in passing that the function of the marriage broker was ancient and honorable, highly approved in the Jewish community, because it made practical the necessary without hindering joy. Moreover, his own parents had been brought together by a matchmaker. They had made, if not a financially profitable marriage—since neither had possessed any worldly goods to speak of—at least a successful one in the sense of their everlasting devotion to each other. Salzman listened in embarrassed surprise, sensing a sort of apology. Later, however, he experienced a glow of pride in his work, an emotion that had left him years ago, and he heartily approved of Finkle.

The two went to their business. Leo had led Salzman to the only clear place in the room, a table near a window that overlooked the lamp-lit city. He seated himself at the matchmaker's side but facing him, attempting by an act of will to <u>suppress</u> the unpleasant tickle in his throat. Salzman eagerly unstrapped his portfolio and removed a loose rubber band from a thin packet of much-handled cards. As he flipped through them, a gesture and sound that physically hurt Leo, the student pretended not to see and gazed steadfastly out the window. Although it was still February, winter was on its last legs, signs of which he had for the first time in years begun to notice. He now observed the round white moon, moving high in the sky through a cloud menagerie, and watched with half-open mouth as it penetrated a huge hen, and dropped out of her like an egg laying itself. Salzman, though pretending through eyeglasses he had just slipped on, to be engaged in scanning the writing on the cards, stole occasional glances at the young man's distinguished face, noting with pleasure the long, severe scholar's nose, brown eyes heavy with learning, sensitive yet <u>ascetic</u> lips, and a certain, almost hollow quality of the dark cheeks. He gazed around at shelves upon shelves of books and let out a soft, contented sigh.

When Leo's eyes fell upon the cards, he counted six spread out in Salzman's hand.

---

1. **Yeshivah** (ye·shē′və) **University:** prominent New York City school serving both as a general college and as a seminary for Orthodox Jewish rabbis.
2. *Forward:* formerly the *Jewish Daily Forward,* a newspaper published in New York City.

WORDS TO OWN

meager (mē′gər) *adj.:* poor; inadequate.
suppress (sə·pres′) *v.:* to restrain; to hold back.
ascetic (ə·set′ik) *adj.:* severe; stern.

"So few?" he asked in disappointment.

"You wouldn't believe me how much cards I got in my office," Salzman replied. "The drawers are already filled to the top, so I keep them now in a barrel, but is every girl good for a new rabbi?"

Leo blushed at this, regretting all he had revealed of himself in a curriculum vitae[3] he had sent to Salzman. He had thought it best to acquaint him with his strict standards and specifications, but in having done so, felt he had told the marriage broker more than was absolutely necessary.

He hesitantly inquired, "Do you keep photographs of your clients on file?"

"First comes family, amount of dowry, also what kind promises," Salzman replied, unbuttoning his tight coat and settling himself in the chair. "After comes pictures, rabbi."

"Call me Mr. Finkle. I'm not yet a rabbi."

Salzman said he would, but instead called him doctor, which he changed to rabbi when Leo was not listening too attentively.

Salzman adjusted his horn-rimmed spectacles, gently cleared his throat and read in an eager voice the contents of the top card:

"Sophie P. Twenty four year. Widow one year. No children. Educated high school and two years college. Father promises eight thousand dollars. Has wonderful wholesale business. Also real estate. On the mother's side comes teachers, also one actor. Well known on Second Avenue."

Leo gazed up in surprise. "Did you say a widow?"

"A widow don't mean spoiled, rabbi. She lived with her husband maybe four months. He was a sick boy she made a mistake to marry him."

"Marrying a widow has never entered my mind."

"This is because you have no experience. A widow, especially if she is young and healthy like this girl, is a wonderful person to marry. She will be thankful to you the rest of her life. Believe me, if I was looking now for a bride, I would marry a widow."

Leo reflected, then shook his head.

Salzman hunched his shoulders in an almost imperceptible gesture of disappointment. He placed the card down on the wooden table and began to read another:

"Lily H. High school teacher. Regular. Not a substitute. Has savings and new Dodge car. Lived in Paris one year. Father is successful dentist thirty-five years. Interested in professional man. Well Americanized family. Wonderful opportunity.

"I knew her personally," said Salzman. "I wish you could see this girl. She is a doll. Also very intelligent. All day you could talk to her about books and theyater and what not. She also knows current events."

"I don't believe you mentioned her age?"

"Her age?" Salzman said, raising his brows. "Her age is thirty-two years."

Leo said after a while, "I'm afraid that seems a little too old."

Salzman let out a laugh. "So how old are you, rabbi?"

"Twenty-seven."

"So what is the difference, tell me, between twenty-seven and thirty-two? My own wife is seven years older than me. So what did I suffer?—Nothing. If a Rothschild's[4] daughter wants to marry you, would you say on account her age, no?"

"Yes," Leo said dryly.

Salzman shook off the no in the yes. "Five years don't mean a thing. I give you my word that when you will live with her for one week you will forget her age. What does it mean five years—that she lived more and knows more than somebody who is younger? On this girl, God bless her, years are not wasted. Each one that it comes makes better the bargain."

"What subject does she teach in high school?"

"Languages. If you heard the way she speaks French, you will think it is music. I am in the business twenty-five years, and I recommend her

4. Rothschild's: The Rothschilds are a wealthy banking family.

WORDS TO OWN

dowry (dou′rē) *n.*: money or goods a bride brings with her in a marriage.

---

3. *curriculum vitae* (kə·rik′yoo·ləm vīt′ē): Latin for "course of life"; that is, a résumé or summary of one's career and qualifications.

with my whole heart. Believe me, I know what I'm talking, rabbi."

"What's on the next card?" Leo said abruptly.

Salzman reluctantly turned up the third card:

"Ruth K. Nineteen years. Honor student. Father offers thirteen thousand cash to the right bridegroom. He is a medical doctor. Stomach specialist with marvelous practice. Brother-in-law owns own garment business. Particular people."

Salzman looked as if he had read his trump card.

"Did you say nineteen?" Leo asked with interest.

"On the dot."

"Is she attractive?" He blushed. "Pretty?"

Salzman kissed his finger tips. "A little doll. On this I give you my word. Let me call the father tonight and you will see what means pretty."

But Leo was troubled. "You're sure she's that young?"

"This I am positive. The father will show you the birth certificate."

"Are you positive there isn't something wrong with her?" Leo insisted.

"Who says there is wrong?"

"I don't understand why an American girl her age should go to a marriage broker."

A smile spread over Salzman's face.

"So for the same reason you went, she comes."

Leo flushed. "I am pressed for time."

Salzman, realizing he had been tactless, quickly explained. "The father came, not her. He wants she should have the best, so he looks around himself. When we will locate the right boy he will introduce him and encourage. This makes a better marriage than if a young girl without experience takes for herself. I don't have to tell you this."

"But don't you think this young girl believes in love?" Leo spoke uneasily.

Salzman was about to guffaw but caught himself and said soberly, "Love comes with the right person, not before."

Leo parted dry lips but did not speak. Noticing that Salzman had snatched a glance at the next card, he cleverly asked, "How is her health?"

"Perfect," Salzman said, breathing with difficulty. "Of course, she is a little lame on her right foot from an auto accident that it happened to her when she was twelve years, but nobody notices on account she is so brilliant and also beautiful."

Leo got up heavily and went to the window. He felt curiously bitter and upbraided himself for having called in the marriage broker. Finally, he shook his head.

"Why not?" Salzman persisted, the pitch of his voice rising.

"Because I detest stomach specialists."

"So what do you care what is his business? After you marry her do you need him? Who says he must come every Friday night in your house?"

Ashamed of the way the talk was going, Leo dismissed Salzman, who went home with heavy, melancholy eyes.

Though he had felt only relief at the marriage broker's departure, Leo was in low spirits the next day. He explained it as arising from Salzman's failure to produce a suitable bride for him. He did not care for his type of clientele. But when Leo found himself hesitating whether to seek out another matchmaker, one more polished than Pinye, he wondered if it could be— his protestations to the contrary, and although he honored his father and mother—that he did not, in essence, care for the matchmaking institution? This thought he quickly put out of mind yet found himself still upset. All day he ran around in the woods—missed an important appointment, forgot to give out his laundry, walked out of a Broadway cafeteria without paying and had to run back with the ticket in his hand; had even not recognized his landlady in the street when she passed with a friend and courteously called out, "A good evening to you, Doctor Finkle." By nightfall, however, he had regained sufficient calm to sink his nose into a book and there found peace from his thoughts.

Almost at once there came a knock on the door. Before Leo could say enter, Salzman, commercial cupid, was standing in the room. His face was gray and meager, his expression hungry, and

---

WORDS TO OWN

upbraided (up·brād′id) v.: severely criticized.
clientele (klī′ən·tel′) n.: customers.

---

he looked as if he would expire on his feet. Yet the marriage broker managed, by some trick of the muscles, to display a broad smile.

"So good evening. I am invited?"

Leo nodded, disturbed to see him again, yet unwilling to ask the man to leave.

Beaming still, Salzman laid his portfolio on the table. "Rabbi, I got for you tonight good news."

"I've asked you not to call me rabbi. I'm still a student."

"Your worries are finished. I have for you a first-class bride."

"Leave me in peace concerning this subject." Leo pretended lack of interest.

"The world will dance at your wedding."

"Please, Mr. Salzman, no more."

"But first must come back my strength," Salzman said weakly. He fumbled with the portfolio straps and took out of the leather case an oily paper bag, from which he extracted a hard, seeded roll and a small, smoked whitefish. With a quick motion of his hand he stripped the fish out of its skin and began ravenously to chew. "All day in a rush," he muttered.

Leo watched him eat.

"A sliced tomato you have maybe?" Salzman hesitantly inquired.

"No."

The marriage broker shut his eyes and ate. When he had finished he carefully cleaned up the crumbs and rolled up the remains of the fish, in the paper bag. His spectacled eyes roamed the room until he discovered, amid some piles of books, a one-burner gas stove. Lifting his hat he humbly asked, "A glass tea you got, rabbi?"

Conscience-striken, Leo rose and brewed the tea. He served it with a chunk of lemon and two cubes of lump sugar, delighting Salzman.

After he had drunk his tea, Salzman's strength and good spirits were restored.

"So tell me, rabbi," he said amiably, "you considered some more the three clients I mentioned yesterday?"

"There was no need to consider."

"Why not?"

"None of them suits me."

"What then suits you?"

Leo let it pass because he could give only a confused answer.

Without waiting for a reply, Salzman asked, "You remember this girl I talked to you—the high school teacher?"

"Age thirty-two?"

But, surprisingly, Salzman's face lit in a smile. "Age twenty-nine."

Leo shot him a look. "Reduced from thirty-two?"

"A mistake," Salzman avowed. "I talked today with the dentist. He took me to his safety deposit box and showed me the birth certificate. She was twenty-nine years last August. They made her a party in the mountains where she went for her vacation. When her father spoke to me the first time I forgot to write the age and I told you thirty-two, but now I remember this was a different client, a widow."

"The same one you told me about? I thought she was twenty-four?"

"A different. Am I responsible that the world is filled with widows?"

"No, but I'm not interested in them, nor for that matter, in school teachers."

Salzman pulled his clasped hands to his breast. Looking at the ceiling he devoutly exclaimed, "Yiddishe kinder,[5] what can I say to somebody that he is not interested in high school teachers? So what then you are interested?"

Leo flushed but controlled himself.

"In what else will you be interested," Salzman went on, "if you not interested in this fine girl that she speaks four languages and has personally in the bank ten thousand dollars? Also her father guarantees further twelve thousand. Also she has a new car, wonderful clothes, talks on all subjects, and she will give you a first-class home and children. How near do we come in our life to paradise?"

"If she's so wonderful, why wasn't she married ten years ago?"

"Why?" said Salzman with a heavy laugh. "—Why? Because she is *partikiler*. This is why. She wants the *best*."

Leo was silent, amused at how he had entangled himself. But Salzman had aroused his interest in Lily H., and he began seriously to consider

5. *Yiddishe kinder:* Yiddish for "Jewish children."

calling on her. When the marriage broker observed how intently Leo's mind was at work on the facts he had supplied, he felt certain they would soon come to an agreement.

Late Saturday afternoon, conscious of Salzman, Leo Finkle walked with Lily Hirschorn along Riverside Drive. He walked briskly and erectly, wearing with distinction the black fedora he had that morning taken with trepidation out of the dusty hat box on his closet shelf, and the heavy black Saturday coat he had thoroughly whisked clean. Leo also owned a walking stick, a present from a distant relative, but quickly put temptation aside and did not use it. Lily, petite and not unpretty, had on something signifying the approach of spring. She was au courant,[6] animatedly, with all sorts of subjects, and he weighed her words and found her surprisingly sound—score another for Salzman, whom he uneasily sensed to be somewhere around, hiding perhaps high in a tree along the street, flashing the lady signals with a pocket mirror; or perhaps a cloven-hoofed Pan,[7] piping <u>nuptial</u> ditties as he danced his invisible way before them, strewing wild buds on the walk and purple grapes in their path, symbolizing fruit of a union, though there was of course still none.

Lily startled Leo by remarking, "I was thinking of Mr. Salzman, a curious figure, wouldn't you say?"

Not certain what to answer, he nodded.

She bravely went on, blushing, "I for one am grateful for his introducing us. Aren't you?"

He courteously replied, "I am."

"I mean," she said with a little laugh—and it was all in good taste, or at least gave the effect of being not in bad—"do you mind that we came together so?"

He was not displeased with her honesty, recognizing that she meant to set the relationship aright, and understanding that it took a certain amount of experience in life, and courage, to want to do it quite that way. One had to have some sort of past to make that kind of beginning.

He said that he did not mind. Salzman's function was <u>traditional</u> and honorable—valuable for what it might achieve, which, he pointed out, was frequently nothing.

Lily agreed with a sigh. They walked on for a while and she said after a long silence, again with a nervous laugh, "Would you mind if I asked you something a little bit personal? Frankly, I find the subject fascinating." Although Leo shrugged, she went on half embarrassedly, "How was it that you came to your calling? I mean was it a sudden passionate inspiration?"

Leo, after a time, slowly replied, "I was always interested in the Law."[8]

"You saw revealed in it the presence of the Highest?"

He nodded and changed the subject. "I understand that you spent a little time in Paris, Miss Hirschorn?"

"Oh, did Mr. Salzman tell you, Rabbi Finkle?" Leo winced but she went on, "It was ages ago and almost forgotten. I remember I had to return for my sister's wedding."

And Lily would not be put off. "When," she asked in a trembly voice, "did you become enamored of God?"

He stared at her. Then it came to him that she was talking not about Leo Finkle, but of a total stranger, some mystical figure, perhaps even passionate prophet that Salzman had dreamed up for her—no relation to the living or dead. Leo trembled with rage and weakness. The trickster had obviously sold her a bill of goods, just as he had him, who'd expected to become acquainted with a young lady of twenty-nine, only to behold, the moment he laid eyes upon her strained

---

8. Law: first five books of the Bible, the most sacred texts of Judaism. These books are also called the Torah or the Five Books of Moses.

---

6. *au courant* (ō kōō·rän): French for "in the current," that is, up-to-date on news or events.

7. Pan: in Greek mythology, a god associated with forests, pastures, flocks, and shepherds. Pan is usually pictured as having the legs, horns, and ears of a goat, and the head and upper body of a man. He plays music on reed pipes.

WORDS TO OWN

nuptial (nup′shəl) *adj.*: related to weddings or marriage.

traditional (trə·dish′ə·nel) *adj.*: established; customary.

and anxious face, a woman past thirty-five and aging rapidly. Only his self-control had kept him this long in her presence.

"I am not," he said gravely, "a talented religious person," and in seeking words to go on, found himself possessed by shame and fear. "I think," he said in a strained manner, "that I came to God not because I loved Him, but because I did not."

This confession he spoke harshly because its unexpectedness shook him.

Lily wilted. Leo saw a profusion of loaves of bread go flying like ducks high over his head, not unlike the winged loaves by which he had counted himself to sleep last night. Mercifully, then, it snowed, which he would not put past Salzman's machinations.

He was infuriated with the marriage broker and swore he would throw him out of the room the minute he reappeared. But Salzman did not come that night, and when Leo's anger had subsided, an unaccountable despair grew in its place. At first he thought this was caused by his disappointment in Lily, but before long it became evident that he had involved himself with Salzman without a true knowledge of his own intent. He gradually realized—with an emptiness that seized him with six hands—that he had called in the broker to find him a bride because he was incapable of doing it himself. This terrifying insight he had derived as a result of his meeting and conversation with Lily Hirschorn. Her probing questions had somehow irritated him into revealing—to himself more than her—the true nature of his relationship to God, and from that it had come upon him, with shocking force, that apart from his parents, he had never loved anyone. Or perhaps it went the other way, that he did not love God so well as he might, because he had not loved man. It seemed to Leo that his whole life stood starkly revealed and he saw himself for the first time as he truly was—unloved and loveless. This bitter but somehow not fully unexpected revelation brought him to a point of panic, controlled only by extraordinary effort. He covered his face with his hands and cried.

The week that followed was the worst of his life. He did not eat and lost weight. His beard darkened and grew ragged. He stopped attending seminars and almost never opened a book. He seriously considered leaving the Yeshivah, although he was deeply troubled at the thought of the loss of all his years of study—saw them like pages torn from a book, strewn over the city— and at the devastating effect of this decision upon his parents. But he had lived without knowledge of himself, and never in the Five Books and all the Commentaries—mea culpa[9]— had the truth been revealed to him. He did not know where to turn, and in all this desolating loneliness there was no *to whom,* although he often thought of Lily but not once could bring himself to go downstairs and make the call. He became touchy and irritable, especially with his landlady, who asked him all manner of personal questions; on the other hand, sensing his own disagreeableness, he waylaid her on the stairs and apologized abjectly, until mortified, she ran from him. Out of this, however, he drew the consolation that he was a Jew and that a Jew suffered. But gradually, as the long and terrible week drew to a close, he regained his composure and some idea of purpose in life: to go on as planned. Although he was imperfect, the ideal was not. As for his quest of a bride, the thought of continuing afflicted him with anxiety and heartburn, yet perhaps with this new knowledge of himself he would be more successful than in the past. Perhaps love would now come to him and a bride to that love. And for this sanctified seeking who needed a Salzman?

The marriage broker, a skeleton with haunted eyes, returned that very night. He looked, withal, the picture of frustrated expectancy—as if he had steadfastly waited the week at Miss Lily Hirschorn's side for a telephone call that never came.

Casually coughing, Salzman came immediately to the point: "So how did you like her?"

9. *mea culpa* (mā′ä kōōl′pä): Latin for "by my fault."

WORDS TO OWN

machinations (mak′ə·nā′shənz) *n. pl.:* plots; schemes.

evident (ev′ə·dənt) *adj.:* clear; obvious.

The Rabbi by Marc Chagall.

Leo's anger rose and he could not refrain from chiding the matchmaker: "Why did you lie to me, Salzman?"

Salzman's pale face went dead white, the world had snowed on him.

"Did you not state that she was twenty-nine?" Leo insisted.

"I give you my word—"

"She was thirty-five, if a day. *At least* thirty-five."

"Of this don't be too sure. Her father told me—"

"Never mind. The worst of it was that you lied to her."

"How did I lie to her, tell me?"

"You told her things about me that weren't true. You made me out to be more, consequently less than I am. She had in mind a totally different person, a sort of semi-mystical Wonder Rabbi."

"All I said, you was a religious man."

"I can imagine."

Salzman sighed. "This is my weakness that I have," he confessed. "My wife says to me I shouldn't be a salesman, but when I have two fine people that they would be wonderful to be married, I am so happy that I talk too much." He smiled wanly. "This is why Salzman is a poor man."

Leo's anger left him. "Well, Salzman, I'm afraid that's all."

The marriage broker fastened hungry eyes on him.

"You don't want any more a bride?"

"I do," said Leo, "but I have decided to seek her in a different way. I am no longer interested in an arranged marriage. To be frank, I now admit the necessity of premarital love. That is, I want to be in love with the one I marry."

"Love?" said Salzman, astounded. After a moment he remarked, "For us, our love is our life, not for the ladies. In the ghetto they—"

"I know, I know," said Leo. "I've thought of it often. Love, I have said to myself, should be a by-product of living and worship rather than its own end. Yet for myself I find it necessary to establish the level of my need and fulfill it."

Salzman shrugged but answered, "Listen, rabbi, if you want love, this I can find for you also. I have such beautiful clients that you will love them the minute your eyes will see them."

Leo smiled unhappily. "I'm afraid you don't understand."

But Salzman hastily unstrapped his portfolio and withdrew a manila packet from it.

"Pictures," he said, quickly laying the envelope on the table.

Leo called after him to take the pictures away, but as if on the wings of the wind, Salzman had disappeared.

March came. Leo had returned to his regular routine. Although he felt not quite himself yet—lacked energy—he was making plans for a more active social life. Of course it would cost something, but he was an expert in cutting corners; and when there were no corners left he would make circles rounder. All the while Salzman's pictures had lain on the table, gathering dust. Occasionally as Leo sat studying, or enjoying a cup of tea, his eyes fell on the manila envelope, but he never opened it.

The days went by and no social life to speak of developed with a member of the opposite sex—it was difficult, given the circumstances of his situation. One morning Leo toiled up the stairs to his room and stared out the window at the city. Although the day was bright his view of it was dark. For some time he watched the people in the street below hurrying along and then turned with a heavy heart to his little room. On the table was the packet. With a sudden relentless gesture he tore it open. For a half-hour he stood by the table in a state of excitement, examining the photographs of the ladies Salzman had included. Finally, with a deep sigh he put them down. There were six, of varying degrees of attractiveness, but look at them long enough and they all became Lily Hirschorn: all past their prime, all starved behind bright smiles, not a true personality in the lot. Life, despite their frantic yoohooings, had passed them by; they were pictures in a briefcase that stank of fish. After a while, however, as Leo attempted to return the photographs into the envelope, he found in it another, a snapshot of the type taken by a machine for a quarter. He gazed at it a moment and let out a cry.

Her face deeply moved him. Why, he could at first not say. It gave him the impression of youth—spring flowers, yet age—a sense of having been used to the bone, wasted; this came from the eyes, which were hauntingly familiar, yet absolutely strange. He had a vivid impression that he had met her before, but try as he might he could not place her although he could almost recall her name, as if he had read it in her own handwriting. No, this couldn't be; he would have remembered her. It was not, he affirmed, that she had an extraordinary beauty—no, though her face was attractive enough; it was that *something* about her moved him. Feature for feature, even some of the ladies of the photographs could do better; but she leaped forth to his heart—had *lived,* or wanted to—more than just wanted, perhaps regretted how she had lived—had somehow deeply suffered: It could be seen in the depths of those reluctant eyes, and from the way the light enclosed and shone from her, and within her, opening realms of possibility: This was her own. Her he desired. His head ached and eyes narrowed with the intensity of his gazing, then as if an obscure fog had blown up in the mind, he experienced fear of her and was aware that he had received an impression, somehow, of evil. He shuddered, saying softly, it is thus with us all. Leo brewed some tea in a small pot and sat sipping it without sugar, to calm himself. But before he had finished drinking, again with excitement he examined the face and found it good: good for Leo Finkle. Only such a one could understand him and help him seek whatever he was seeking. She might, perhaps, love him. How she had happened to be among the discards in Salzman's barrel he could never guess, but he knew he must urgently go find her.

Leo rushed downstairs, grabbed up the Bronx[10] telephone book, and searched for Salzman's home address. He was not listed, nor was his office. Neither was he in the Manhattan[11] book. But Leo remembered having written down the address on a slip of paper after he had read Salzman's advertisement in the "personals" column of the *Forward.* He ran up to his room and tore through his papers, without luck. It was

10. **Bronx:** borough of New York City.
11. **Manhattan:** borough of New York City, south of the Bronx.

exasperating. Just when he needed the matchmaker he was nowhere to be found. Fortunately Leo remembered to look in his wallet. There on a card he found his name written and a Bronx address. No phone number was listed, the reason—Leo now recalled—he had originally communicated with Salzman by letter. He got on his coat, put a hat on over his skullcap and hurried to the subway station. All the way to the far end of the Bronx he sat on the edge of his seat. He was more than once tempted to take out the picture and see if the girl's face was as he remembered it, but he refrained, allowing the snapshot to remain in his inside coat pocket, content to have her so close. When the train pulled into the station he was waiting at the door and bolted out. He quickly located the street Salzman had advertised.

The building he sought was less than a block from the subway, but it was not an office building, nor even a loft, nor a store in which one could rent office space. It was a very old tenement house. Leo found Salzman's name in pencil on a soiled tag under the bell and climbed three dark flights to his apartment. When he knocked, the door was opened by a thin, asthmatic, gray-haired woman, in felt slippers.

"Yes?" she said, expecting nothing. She listened without listening. He could have sworn he had seen her, too, before but knew it was an illusion.

"Salzman—does he live here? Pinye Salzman," he said, "the matchmaker?"

She stared at him a long minute. "Of course."

He felt embarrassed. "Is he in?"

"No." Her mouth, though left open, offered nothing more.

"The matter is urgent. Can you tell me where his office is?"

"In the air." She pointed upward.

"You mean he has no office?" Leo asked.

"In his socks."

He peered into the apartment. It was sunless and dingy, one large room divided by a half-open curtain, beyond which he could see a sagging metal bed. The near side of the room was crowded with rickety chairs, old bureaus, a three-legged table, racks of cooking utensils, and all the apparatus of a kitchen. But there was no sign of Salzman or his magic barrel, probably also a figment of the imagination. An odor of frying fish made Leo weak to the knees.

"Where is he?" he insisted. "I've got to see your husband."

At length she answered, "So who knows where he is? Every time he thinks a new thought he runs to a different place. Go home, he will find you."

"Tell him Leo Finkle."

She gave no sign she had heard.

He walked downstairs, depressed.

But Salzman, breathless, stood waiting at his door.

Leo was astounded and overjoyed. "How did you get here before me?"

"I rushed."

"Come inside."

They entered. Leo fixed tea, and a sardine sandwich for Salzman. As they were drinking he reached behind him for the packet of pictures and handed them to the marriage broker.

Salzman put down his glass and said expectantly, "You found somebody you like?"

"Not among these."

The marriage broker turned away.

"Here is the one I want." Leo held forth the snapshot.

Salzman slipped on his glasses and took the picture into his trembling hand. He turned ghastly and let out a groan.

"What's the matter?" cried Leo.

"Excuse me. Was an accident this picture. She isn't for you."

Salzman frantically shoved the manila packet into his portfolio. He thrust the snapshot into his pocket and fled down the stairs.

Leo, after momentary paralysis, gave chase and cornered the marriage broker in the vestibule. The landlady made hysterical outcries but neither of them listened.

"Give me back the picture, Salzman."

"No." The pain in his eyes was terrible.

"Tell me who she is then."

"This I can't tell you. Excuse me."

He made to depart, but Leo, forgetting himself, seized the matchmaker by his tight coat and shook him frenziedly.

"Please," sighed Salzman. "*Please.*"

Leo ashamedly let him go. "Tell me who she is," he begged. "It's very important for me to know."

"She is not for you. She is a wild one—wild, without shame. This is not a bride for a rabbi."

"What do you mean wild?"

"Like an animal. Like a dog. For her to be poor was a sin. This is why to me she is dead now."

"In God's name, what do you mean?"

"Her I can't introduce to you," Salzman cried.

"Why are you so excited?"

"Why, he asks," Salzman said, bursting into tears. "This is my baby, my Stella, she should burn in hell."

Leo hurried up to bed and hid under the covers. Under the covers he thought his life through. Although he soon fell asleep he could not sleep her out of his mind. He woke, beating his breast. Though he prayed to be rid of her, his prayers went unanswered. Through days of torment he endlessly struggled not to love her; fearing success, he escaped it. He then concluded to convert her to goodness, himself to God. The idea alternately nauseated and exalted him.

He perhaps did not know that he had come to a final decision until he encountered Salzman in a Broadway cafeteria. He was sitting alone at a rear table, sucking the bony remains of a fish. The marriage broker appeared haggard, and transparent to the point of vanishing.

Salzman looked up at first without recognizing him. Leo had grown a pointed beard and his eyes were weighted with wisdom.

"Salzman," he said, "love has at last come to my heart."

"Who can love from a picture?" mocked the marriage broker.

"It is not impossible."

"If you can love her, then you can love anybody. Let me show you some new clients that they just sent me their photographs. One is a little doll."

"Just her I want," Leo murmured.

"Don't be a fool, doctor. Don't bother with her."

"Put me in touch with her, Salzman," Leo said humbly. "Perhaps I can be of service."

Salzman had stopped eating and Leo understood with emotion that it was now arranged.

Leaving the cafeteria, he was, however, afflicted by a tormenting suspicion that Salzman had planned it all to happen this way.

Leo was informed by letter that she would meet him on a certain corner, and she was there one spring night, waiting under a street lamp. He appeared, carrying a small bouquet of violets and rosebuds. Stella stood by the lamppost, smoking. She wore white with red shoes, which fitted his expectations, although in a troubled moment he had imagined the dress red, and only the shoes white. She waited uneasily and shyly. From afar he saw that her eyes—clearly her father's—were filled with desperate innocence. He pictured, in her, his own redemption. Violins and lit candles revolved in the sky. Leo ran forward with flowers outthrust.

Around the corner, Salzman, leaning against a wall, chanted prayers for the dead.

*C*ritical *C*omment

A Tale of Self-Discovery

At the opening of this story, a lonely young rabbinical student decides to contact a marriage broker through a newspaper ad. Leo Finkle has been immersed in his studies for six years, he is painfully shy, and he can think of no other way to meet suitable young women. (If the custom seems strange, think of the thousands of people today who use dating services.)

Finkle's attitudes have been shaped by years of study and theological debate. It is not surprising that he has had very little time to think about his social life. The tradition of the marriage broker, seemingly exotic in America, was familiar to European Jews in the early part of this century. Brokers fulfilled a genuine social function by negotiating between families and easing embarrassment. It was inevitable that, in some of these arranged marriages, the chief feature was not the partners' mutual devotion but the financial or social advantages to the families involved.

Finkle is portrayed as wavering between two worlds. In the old world of his parents (who owed their marriage to a broker), social criteria for marriage were more important than love. Leo himself is originally impelled to look for a wife by an acquaintance's suggestion that "he might find it easier to win himself a congregation if he were married." In his first conversations with Salzman, Finkle is preoccupied by external, superficial criteria. But a profound change is at work in Leo, and he reaches a turning point when he suddenly finds himself admitting to the pleasant but superficial Lily that "I came to God not because I loved Him, but because I did not." The story then shows him dramatically, even transcendentally, caught up in love at first sight. As you think about the story, consider the possibility that Malamud's real interest is not in the probability—or even the future consequences—of Leo's change of heart. Perhaps the writer wants us to witness Leo Finkle's process of self-discovery: his initiation into a new world, where he can exist as an authentic person, capable of love.

Ketubbah (marriage contract) (detail) (1732), Padua, Italy.

Collection Israel Museum, Jerusalem. Photo Israel Museum.

MAKING MEANINGS

First Thoughts

1. What do you think caused Stella's father to regard her as dead?

Shaping Interpretations

2. Finkle confesses to Lily "...I came to God not because I loved Him, but because I did not." How would you explain this **paradox,** or seeming contradiction?

3. Why do you think Finkle pictures in Stella his own redemption? What does he want to be redeemed *from*?

4. **Summarize** what you think Finkle has learned about love and about himself by the end of the story. Has he changed in an important way?

5. What do you think of the scene with Finkle and Stella near the end of the story? Do you think Salzman arranged a marriage for Finkle after all?

6. Does Malamud end the story on a positive or a negative note? How would you explain the last sentence of the story: "Around the corner, Salzman, leaning against a wall, chanted prayers for the dead"?

7. Explain the story's **title.**

Extending the Text

8. What do you think will happen to Leo and Stella once they learn more about each other? Will they marry? Will they drift apart? Consult your Quickwrite notes for ideas.

Reading Check

a. According to the first paragraph, who is the story's **protagonist,** and what does he want?

b. Another character—Pinye Salzman—is introduced in the second paragraph. Find the descriptive details that hint of something tragic in his past.

c. Explain what Finkle discovers about himself after the experience with Lily.

d. Why does Finkle fall in love with the woman in the photograph?

CHOICES: Building Your Portfolio

Writer's Notebook

1. Collecting Ideas for an Evaluation

What makes for skillful characterization? Create a chart to organize the criteria you'd use to evaluate the characters Leo Finkle and Pinye Salzman in "The Magic Barrel." In column one, enter five or six qualities that make for skillful characterization. (Two criteria might be that a character be **believable** and **dynamic.**) In columns two and three (headed "Leo" and "Pinye"), list specific examples from the text that show how each character meets (or does not meet) each criterion. Save your notes for possible use in the Writer's Workshop on page 1181.

Interpreting a Story

2. What's at the Heart of Malamud?

Select one of the following comments about Bernard Malamud's fiction, and write a brief essay responding to it. Tell whether or not the comment has to do with the **plot, characters,** or **theme** of "The Magic Barrel."

a. "Malamud has always had a fondness for telling tales arranged for the purpose of a specific moral lesson." (Alan Lelchuk)

b. "What it is to be human, and to be humane, is his [Malamud's] deepest concern." (Philip Roth)

Telling a Story

3. Stella by Starlight

One spring night, Leo runs toward Stella "with flowers outthrust." That's about where "The Magic Barrel" ends. Tell a story to the class that extends Malamud's story. Include the dialogue that might take place as Leo and Stella meet. Bring your story to an ambiguous conclusion, in Malamud's style.

Gabriel García Márquez
(1928 –   )

Gabriel García Márquez (gä'brē·el' gär·sē'ä mär'kes) was born in Aracataca, Colombia, the town that became the model for the fictional village of Macondo in his popular novel *One Hundred Years of Solitude* (1967). He spent his early years with his maternal grandparents, whom he regards as "wonderful beings." According to García Márquez, "They had an enormous house, full of ghosts. They were people of great imagination and superstitions. In every corner there were dead people and memories, and after six o'clock in the [evening] the house was untraversable. It was a world prodigious with terror. There were conversations in code."

After attending universities in Bogotá and Cartagena, García Márquez worked as a journalist in Colombia and in Rome, Paris, Barcelona, Caracas, and New York. Newspaper work helped García Márquez (like Ernest Hemingway) develop a style of writing fiction. Even after ending his newspaper career in 1965, García Márquez considered himself to be at heart a journalist, which is one reason for the factual or realistic basis for his fiction. It also accounts for his occasional nonfiction books, such as *News of a Kidnapping* (1997). Because of serious political differences with the Colombian government, he lives in Mexico City.

García Márquez has achieved international renown mainly for his fiction, which includes, besides *One Hundred Years of Solitude, The Autumn of the Patriarch* (1976), *Love in the Time of Cholera* (1988), *Strange Pilgrims* (1993), and *Of Love and Other Demons* (1995). He was awarded the Nobel Prize in literature in 1982.

Gabriel García Márquez signing autographs in the streets of Cartagena.

Carlos Angel/Gamma Liaison.

Before You Read

THE HANDSOMEST DROWNED MAN IN THE WORLD

Background

Gabriel García Márquez blends **realism** with playful imagination to create a type of literature known as **magic realism**. Developed in Latin America around the middle of the twentieth century, the genre has proved popular and influential in much of the world. You can see echoes of magic (also called marvelous) realism in works by such noted U.S. authors as Donald Barthelme (page 955), Thomas Pynchon, and Kurt Vonnegut, Jr., and in the writing of Günter Grass of Germany and John Fowles of England. A key novel of magic realism is García Márquez's best-selling *Cien años de soledad* (1967), translated into English as *One Hundred Years of Solitude* (1970).

Art on pages 996, 997, 999 by Sergio Bustamente/Photo by Clint Clemens.

According to a perceptive analysis by the literary critic David Young, "One way to understand magic realism is as a kind of pleasant joke on realism, suggesting as it does a new kind of fiction, produced in reaction to the confining assumptions of realism. [Magic realism is] a hybrid that somehow manages to combine the truthful and verifiable aspects of realism with the magical effects we associate with myth, folk tale, tall story, and that being in all of us—our childhood self, perhaps—who loves the spell that narrative casts even when it is perfectly implausible." The critic James Park Sloan observes that an essential element of García Márquez's magic realism is "a steadily toneless background in which everyday events become marvelous and marvelous events are assimilated without comment into everyday life."

García Márquez identifies an additional important aspect of his writing: "There's no doubt nostalgia is one of the important ingredients of my books and life. I make decisions, basic decisions, out of sheer nostalgia. Nostalgia gives my books the distance they bear from reality."

Reading Skills and Strategies

Dialogue with the Text

As you read this story by García Márquez, write down your responses to the following questions. Where appropriate, back up your responses by quoting passages from the story.

- The author subtitles the story "A Tale for Children." In what ways do you need to become childlike again in order to really enjoy this work?

- Which passages remind you in general of a **myth, legend, or folk tale**? Are you reminded at any point of a specific myth or tale?

- How does the villagers' attitude toward the drowned man change over the course of the story?

- What ultimate effect does the arrival of the drowned man have on the villagers' lives?

- What did you find puzzling or difficult to understand about this story?

The Handsomest Drowned Man in the World

Gabriel García Márquez

translated by **Gregory Rabassa**

A Tale for Children

The first children who saw the dark and slinky bulge approaching through the sea let themselves think it was an enemy ship. Then they saw it had no flags or masts and they thought it was a whale. But when it was washed up on the beach, they removed the clumps of seaweed, the jellyfish tentacles, and the remains of fish and flotsam, and only then did they see that it was a drowned man.

They had been playing with him all afternoon, burying him in the sand and digging him up again, when someone chanced to see them and spread the alarm in the village. The men who carried him to the nearest house noticed that he weighed more than any dead man they had ever known, almost as much as a horse, and they said to each other that maybe he'd been floating too long and the water had got into his bones. When they laid him on the floor they said he'd been taller than all other men because there was barely enough room for him in the house, but they thought that maybe the ability to keep on growing after death was part of the nature of certain drowned men. He had the smell of the sea about him and only his shape gave one to suppose that it was the corpse of a human being, because the skin was covered with a crust of mud and scales.

They did not even have to clean off his face to know that the dead man was a stranger. The village was made up of only twenty-odd wooden houses that had stone courtyards with no flowers and which were spread about on the end of a desertlike cape. There was so little land that mothers always went about with the fear that the wind would carry off their children and the few dead that the years had caused among them had to be thrown off the cliffs. But the sea was calm and bountiful and all the men fit into seven boats. So when they found the drowned man they simply had to look at one another to see that they were all there.

That night they did not go out to work at sea. While the men went to find out if anyone was missing in neighboring villages, the women stayed behind to care for the drowned man. They took the mud off with grass swabs, they removed the underwater stones entangled in his hair, and they scraped the crust off with tools used for scaling fish. As they were doing that they noticed that the vegetation on him came from faraway oceans and deep water and that his clothes were in tatters, as if he had sailed through labyrinths of coral. They noticed too that he bore his death with pride, for he did not have the lonely look of other drowned men who came out of the sea or that haggard, needy look of men who drowned in rivers. But only when they finished cleaning him off did they become aware of the kind of man he was and it left them breathless. Not only was he the tallest, strongest, most virile, and best-built man they had ever seen, but even though they were looking at him there was no room for him in their imagination.

They could not find a bed in the village large enough to lay him on nor was there a table solid enough to use for his wake. The tallest men's holiday pants would not fit him, not the fattest ones' Sunday shirts, nor the shoes of the one with the biggest feet. Fascinated by his huge size and his beauty, the women then decided to make him some pants from a large piece of sail and a shirt from some bridal brabant linen[1] so that he could continue through his death with dignity. As they sewed, sitting in a circle and gazing at the corpse between stitches, it seemed to them that the wind had never been so steady nor the sea so restless as on that night and they supposed that the change had something to do with the dead man. They thought that if that magnificent man had lived in the village, his house would have had the widest doors, the highest ceiling, and the strongest floor, his bedstead would have been made from a midship frame held together by iron bolts, and his wife would have been the happiest woman. They thought that he would have had so much authority that he could have drawn fish out of the sea simply by calling their names and that he would have put so much work into his land that springs would have burst forth from among the rocks so that he would have been able to plant flowers on the cliffs. They secretly compared him to their own men, thinking that for all their lives theirs were incapable of doing what he could do in one night, and they ended up dismissing them deep in their hearts as the weakest, meanest, and most useless creatures on earth. They were wandering through that maze of fantasy when the oldest woman, who as the oldest had looked upon the drowned man with more compassion than passion, sighed:

"He has the face of someone called Esteban."[2]

It was true. Most of them had only to take another look at him to see that he could not have any other name. The more stubborn among them, who were the youngest, still lived for a few hours with the illusion that when they put his clothes on and he lay among the flowers in patent leather shoes his name might be Lautaro.[3] But it was a vain illusion. There had not been enough canvas, the poorly cut and worse sewn pants were too tight, and the hidden strength of his heart popped the buttons on his shirt. After midnight the whistling of the wind died down and the sea fell into its Wednesday drowsiness.[4] The silence put an end to any last doubts: he was Esteban. The women who had dressed him, who had combed his hair, had cut his nails and shaved him were unable to hold back a shudder of pity when they had to resign themselves to his being dragged along the ground. It was then that they understood how unhappy he must have been with that huge body since it bothered him even after death. They could see him in life, condemned to going through doors sideways, cracking his head on crossbeams, remaining on his feet during visits, not knowing what to do with his soft, pink, sea lion hands while the lady of the house looked for her most resistant chair and begged him, frightened to death, sit here, Esteban, please, and he, leaning against the wall, smiling, don't bother, ma'am, I'm fine where I am, his heels raw and his back roasted from having done the same thing so many times whenever he paid a visit, don't bother, ma'am, I'm fine where I am, just to avoid the embarrassment of breaking up the chair, and never knowing perhaps that the ones who said don't go, Esteban, at least wait till the coffee's ready, were the ones who later on would whisper the big boob finally left, how nice, the handsome fool has gone. That was what the women were thinking beside the body a little before dawn. Later, when they covered his face with a handkerchief so that the light would not bother him, he looked so forever dead, so defenseless, so much

---

1. **brabant** (brə·bant′) **linen:** linen from Brabant, a province of Belgium known for its fine lace and cloth.

2. **Esteban** (es·te′bän): Spanish equivalent for "Stephen." In Christian tradition, Stephen was the first martyr. He was stoned to death because of his beliefs.

3. **Lautaro** (lou·tä′rô): leader of Araucanian Indian people who resisted the Spanish conquistadors entering their land, in what is now Chile, during the sixteenth century. Lautaro is now seen as a Chilean national hero.

4. **Wednesday drowsiness** (and later **Wednesday meat** and **Wednesday dead body**): *Wednesday* is a colloquial expression for "tiresome." In many fishing villages, fishers returned from the sea on Thursday, so by Wednesday, people began running out of food and were generally weary and bored.

blind and divers die of nostalgia, and bad currents would not bring him back to shore, as had happened with other bodies. But the more they hurried, the more the women thought of ways to waste time. They walked about like startled hens, pecking with the sea charms[6] on their breasts, some interfering on one side to put a scapular[7] of the good wind on the drowned man, some on the other side to put a wrist compass on him, and after a great deal of *get away from there, woman, stay out of the way, look, you almost made me fall on top of the dead man,* the men began to feel mistrust in their livers and started grumbling about why so many main-altar decorations for a stranger, because no matter how many nails and holy-water jars he had on him, the sharks would chew him all the same, but the women kept piling on their junk relics, running back and forth, stumbling, while they released in sighs what they did not in tears, so that the men finally exploded with *since when has there ever been such a fuss over a drifting corpse, a drowned nobody, a piece of cold Wednesday meat.* One of the women, mortified by so much lack of care, then removed the handkerchief from the dead man's face and the men were left breathless too.

He was Esteban. It was not necessary to repeat it for them to recognize him. If they had been told Sir Walter Raleigh, even they might have been impressed with his gringo accent, the macaw[8] on his shoulder, his cannibal-killing blunderbuss,[9] but there could be only one Esteban in the world and there he was, stretched out like a sperm whale, shoeless, wearing the pants of an undersized child, and with those stony nails that had to be cut with a knife. They only had to take the handkerchief off his face to see that he was ashamed, that it was not his fault that he was so big or so heavy or so handsome, and if he had known that this

like their men that the first furrows of tears opened in their hearts. It was one of the younger ones who began the weeping. The others, coming to, went from sighs to wails, and the more they sobbed the more they felt like weeping, because the drowned man was becoming all the more Esteban for them, and so they wept so much, for he was the most destitute, most peaceful, and most obliging man on earth, poor Esteban. So when the men returned with the news that the drowned man was not from the neighboring villages either, the women felt an opening of jubilation in the midst of their tears.

"Praise the Lord," they sighed, "he's ours!"

The men thought the fuss was only womanish frivolity. Fatigued because of the difficult nighttime inquiries, all they wanted was to get rid of the bother of the newcomer once and for all before the sun grew strong on that arid, windless day. They improvised a litter with the remains of foremasts and gaffs,[5] tying it together with rigging so that it would bear the weight of the body until they reached the cliffs. They wanted to tie the anchor from a cargo ship to him so that he would sink easily into the deepest waves, where fish are

5. **gaffs:** poles used on a boat to support a sail.

6. **sea charms:** magic charms worn to protect the wearer from dangers at sea.
7. **scapular** (skap′yə·lər): pair of small cloth squares with images of saints, joined by string and worn under clothing by some Roman Catholics as a symbol of religious devotion.
8. **macaw:** large, brightly colored parrot.
9. **blunderbuss:** now-obsolete gun with a short, flaring muzzle.

was going to happen, he would have looked for a more discreet place to drown in, seriously, I even would have tied the anchor off a galleon around my neck and staggered off a cliff like someone who doesn't like things in order not to be upsetting people now with this Wednesday dead body, as you people say, in order not to be bothering anyone with this filthy piece of cold meat that doesn't have anything to do with me. There was so much truth in his manner that even the most mistrustful men, the ones who felt the bitterness of endless nights at sea fearing that their women would tire of dreaming about them and begin to dream of drowned men, even they and others who were harder still shuddered in the marrow of their bones at Esteban's sincerity.

That was how they came to hold the most splendid funeral they could conceive of for an abandoned drowned man. Some women who had gone to get flowers in the neighboring villages returned with other women who could not believe what they had been told, and those women went back for more flowers when they saw the dead man, and they brought more and more until there were so many flowers and so many people that it was hard to walk about. At the final moment it pained them to return him to the waters as an orphan and they chose a father and mother from among the best people, and aunts and uncles and cousins, so that through him all the inhabitants of the village became kinsmen. Some sailors who heard the weeping from a distance went off course and people heard of one who had himself tied to the mainmast, remembering ancient fables about sirens.[10] While they fought for the privilege of carrying him on their shoulders along the steep escarpment by the cliffs, men and women became aware for the first time of the desolation of their streets, the dryness of their courtyards, the narrowness of their dreams as they faced the splendor and beauty of their drowned man. They let him go without an anchor so that he could come back if he wished and whenever he wished, and they all held their breath for the fraction of centuries the body took to fall into the abyss. They did not need to look at one another to realize that they were no longer all present, that they would never be. But they also knew that everything would be different from then on, that their houses would have wider doors, higher ceilings, and stronger floors so that Esteban's memory could go everywhere without bumping into beams and so that no one in the future would dare whisper the big boob finally died, too bad, the handsome fool has finally died, because they were going to paint their house fronts gay colors to make Esteban's memory eternal and they were going to break their backs digging for springs among the stones and planting flowers on the cliffs so that in future years at dawn the passengers on great liners would awaken, suffocated by the smell of gardens on the high seas, and the captain would have to come down from the bridge in his dress uniform, with his astrolabe,[11] his polestar, and his row of war medals and, pointing to the promontory of roses on the horizon, he would say in fourteen languages, look there, where the wind is so peaceful now that it's gone to sleep beneath the beds, over there, where the sun's so bright that the sunflowers don't know which way to turn, yes, over there, that's Esteban's village.

10. **sirens:** In Greek mythology, the sirens are sea maidens whose seductive singing lures men to wreck their boats on coastal rocks. Odysseus, hero of Homer's *Odyssey,* fills his crew's ears with wax so that they can pass the sirens safely. Odysseus, however, has his crew tie him to the ship's mast so that he can listen to the sirens' songs without plunging into the sea.

11. **astrolabe** (as′trō·lāb′): instrument used to find a star's altitude and to help navigators determine their position at sea.

FINDING COMMON GROUND

Meet in small groups to discuss "The Handsomest Drowned Man in the World." As you talk about the story, refer to the notes you made while reading.

• First, decide how to run your discussion group. If you want a moderator, choose a group member to fill that role.

• Second, draw up an agenda of topics for consideration. (Refer to your reading notes for some ideas.) It will be helpful for a group member to act as a recorder, writing down the agenda as well as the main points brought up in the discussion.

UPI/Bettmann.

Theodore Roethke

(1908–1963)

"Everything that lives is holy: I call upon these holy forms of life." These words of Theodore Roethke (ret′kē), which sound like the words of a religious ceremony, are at the core of his intense vision. For Roethke, the function of poetry is to represent in words the sanctified forms and experiences of life.

A native of Saginaw, Michigan, Roethke grew up in a family situation that had an enormous influence on his poetry. His father owned the largest greenhouse complex in the state, and Roethke's childhood was spent close to nature, nurturing cuttings and small plants and walking in the vast acres of woodlands owned by his family. This childhood world provided the foundation for much of his poetry, which often looks at the smallest aspects of nature—worms, snails, tiny seedlings—through the eyes of a child. "I have a genuine love of nature," he

wrote when he was a sophomore in college. "When I get alone under an open sky where man isn't too evident—then I'm tremendously exalted and a thousand vivid ideas and sweet visions flood my consciousness."

Roethke studied law and worked in public relations for some time after graduating from college, but his desire to become a writer finally led him to graduate school. He began a teaching career at Lafayette College in Easton, Pennsylvania (where he also coached the tennis team); taught at Pennsylvania State University; and, from 1947 until his death, taught at the University of Washington.

A passionate and dedicated teacher, Roethke brought the same energy to the classroom that he brought to poetry. In teaching, he sought the same rewards he searched for in his writing: transcendence and illumination. "Most teaching is visceral," he wrote, "and the genial uproar that constitutes a verse class, especially so. It is as ephemeral as the dance. . . . [Teaching] is what is left after all the reading and thinking and reciting: the residue, the illumination."

The search for illumination and ecstasy was a fundamental concern for Roethke in life as well as in poetry. This search brought with it a psychological imbalance that he tried to face openly and employ honestly in his verse. "My heart keeps open house," he wrote in an early poem.

My truths are all foreknown,
This anguish self-revealed.
I'm naked to the bone,
With nakedness my shield.

—*from "Open House"*

Between 1947 and 1958, Roethke published four volumes of poetry and received a number of honors, including a Pulitzer Prize, a National Book Award, and a Bollingen Prize. A poet of both pain and joy, the dark and the light, Roethke tried to find in both extremes the same transcendent moment, "a consciousness beyond the mundane," as he once put it, "a purity, a final innocence."

ELEGY FOR JANE

Make the Connection

In Moments of Intensity

At the most intense and concentrated moments of our lives, we often focus on the tiniest things. Like one of Shakespeare's great tragic kings musing on a straw or a worm, people in crisis seem to search for a comforting balance between the infinite and the infinitesimal. On the one hand, we face love and death and grief and fate; on the other hand, we take note of a bird, a smile, a leaf, a strand of hair.

Quickwrite

Think of a person you hold dear. Then, write down five of his or her special characteristics.

Elements of Literature

Figures of Speech

A **figure of speech** is a word or phrase that describes one thing in terms of another and that is not meant to be taken literally. It always involves a comparison of two things that are very dissimilar. Many such figures of speech have been identified by scholars. Among the most common are the **simile,** which makes an explicit comparison, using *like, as, than, resembles,* or another connective; **metaphor,** which (in contrast to a simile) makes a comparison without using a connective; and **personification,** which ascribes to an object or animal human feelings, thoughts, or attitudes. Watch for all three figures of speech in "Elegy for Jane."

Elegy for Jane

My Student, Thrown by a Horse

Theodore Roethke

I remember the neckcurls, limp and damp as tendrils,°
And her quick look, a sidelong pickerel° smile;
And how, once startled into talk, the light syllables leaped
    for her,
And she balanced in the delight of her thought,
5 A wren, happy, tail into the wind,
Her song trembling the twigs and small branches.
The shade sang with her;
The leaves, their whispers turned to kissing;
And the mold sang in the bleached valleys under the rose.

Oh, when she was sad, she cast herself down into such a
10   pure depth,
Even a father could not find her:
Scraping her cheek against straw;
Stirring the clearest water.

My sparrow, you are not here,
15 Waiting like a fern, making a spiny shadow.
The sides of wet stones cannot console me,
Nor the moss, wound with the last light.

If only I could nudge you from this sleep,
My maimed darling, my skittery pigeon.
20 Over this damp grave I speak the words of my love:
I, with no rights in this matter,
Neither father nor lover.

1. **tendrils:** coiled strands, as of a climbing plant.
2. **pickerel:** small, North American pike fish.

Make the Connection

The Land I Love

The crack trains that once were the fastest way to cross America found their way into the works of poets and painters. Today, most of those trains have been replaced by airplanes. What do we miss when we cannot see the prairies, the lighted windows in small towns, the mountains, and the cities that those trains used to roar past? A cross-country train ride was once a real journey; on a plane, that journey becomes a mere trip.

Quickwrite

Recall a trip that you have made in a plane, train, bus, or car—whether it was a short one (like the trip to school) or a long one (like a journey to another state or country). Write down your memories and impressions of what you saw and felt along the way.

Night Journey

Theodore Roethke

Now as the train bears west,
Its rhythm rocks the earth,
And from my pullman berth
I stare into the night
5   While others take their rest.
Bridges of iron lace,
A suddenness of trees,
A lap of mountain mist
All cross my line of sight,
10 Then a bleak wasted place,
And a lake below my knees.
Full on my neck I feel
The straining at the curve;
My muscles move with steel,
15 I wake in every nerve.
I watch a beacon swing
From dark to blazing bright;
We thunder through ravines
And gullies washed with light.
20 Beyond the mountain pass
Mist deepens on the pane;
We rush into the rain
That rattles double glass.
Wheels shake the roadbed stone,
25 The pistons jerk and shove.
I stay up half the night
To see the land I love.

Railroad Sunset (1929) by Edward Hopper. Oil on canvas (28¼″ × 47¾″); (71.8 cm × 121.3 cm).

Collection of Whitney Museum of American Art, Josephine N. Hopper Bequest (Acq. 70.1170). Photograph ©1998 by Whitney Museum of American Art.

MAKING MEANINGS

Elegy for Jane

First Thoughts

1. Describe Jane's personality. Has Roethke focused on characteristics that you might focus on in a person you love? Explain. (Review your Quickwrite notes.)

Shaping Interpretations

2. In the poem, Jane is compared to three birds. Name them, and tell how the comparisons help build an overall impression of the young woman.

3. An **elegy** is a poem of mourning. Some elegies concentrate fully on the person who has died; others extend their subject to reflect on general matters, such as life, death, beauty, even politics. Which type of elegy is Roethke's poem? Explain.

4. The poem's speaker says he has "no rights in this matter" (line 21). In your own words, explain what he means. Do you think he is correct? Why or why not?

Night Journey

First Thoughts

1. What **image** in the poem strikes you as especially powerful or memorable? Explain.

Shaping Interpretations

2. Roethke uses **figurative language** to convey the physical intensity of the journey. Which lines suggest a kind of fusion between the speaker, the speeding train, and the countryside?

3. Read "Night Journey" aloud, emphasizing its **rhythm.** How does the rhythm give you the feeling of being on a train?

4. What are the speaker's attitudes toward the train and toward the land? Are his feelings similar to those you noted in your Quickwrite?

CHOICES: Building Your Portfolio

Writer's Notebook

1. Collecting Ideas for an Evaluation

A well-written evaluation of a work of literature includes an *orientation* for the audience, a clearly stated *judgment,* identification of the *criteria* used in judging, and *evidence* to back up the judgment. Make an informal outline for an evaluation of "Elegy for Jane" or "Night Journey." What would your readers need to know? What specific aspects of the poem would you evaluate— **figures of speech, theme, form, emotional effect, sounds,** some other element? What criteria would you apply? What evidence (examples, experiences, authorities) would you cite? Save your notes for possible use in the Writer's Workshop on page 1181.

Comparing Poems

2. Two Young Women

Write a brief essay comparing and contrasting "Elegy for Jane" with John Crowe Ransom's "Bells for John Whiteside's Daughter" (page 578). Consider especially the **figures of speech** and **tone** used in each elegy.

Responding to Art

3. Does It Fit?

In a brief essay tell whether or not you feel that the Edward Hopper painting used with "Night Journey" fits the **mood** of the poem. To support your response, refer to at least one specific detail in the painting.

Art

4. Painting a Poem

Draw or paint the landscape of Roethke's "Night Journey." Before you start, list all the specific **images** you'll want to consider including, starting with the "bridges of iron lace." Select a phrase from the poem as your title.

Richard Wilbur

(1921–   )

"No poetry can have any strength unless it continually bashes itself against the reality of things." This poetic credo of Richard Wilbur has given us some of the strongest poems of our time—rock hard at the center, subtle and delicate on the edges.

From the time of his first book, *The Beautiful Changes and Other Poems* (1947), Wilbur was recognized as one of the most graceful and technically adept poets in the generation then coming of age. His poetry reminds us of the meters and natural speech of Robert Frost and of the metaphysical elegance and emotional reticence of Wallace Stevens.

But the influences of Frost and Stevens are merely overtones. Wilbur's poetic character is forged of his own unassertive religious devotion, his political liberalism, and his irrepressible delight in "the things of this world." Wilbur writes at a time when poetry has often been marked by self-promotion and seeming form-lessness, as well as by uneasy borrowings from the paintings of minimalists and surrealists. But Wilbur has continued to write lyrics demanding scrupulous care and skill. His inward vision of delight finds expression in measured speech and indelible metaphor.

Wilbur was born in New York City but grew up in suburban New Jersey. He attended Amherst College in Massachusetts, served with

© Nancy Crampton.

combat troops in Europe during World War II, and went to graduate school at Harvard. There he prepared for the illustrious teaching career that has taken him to long-term appointments at Wellesley, Wesleyan (Connecticut), and Smith. During 1987–1988, Wilbur served as poet laureate of the United States.

When Wilbur is not embarked on reading tours that take him across the breadth of the continent, he divides his time between Cummington, Massachusetts, the Berkshire village where he lives within a stone's throw of the homestead where William Cullen Bryant (page 169) lived, and Key West, Florida.

In addition to poetry, Wilbur has produced sparkling translations of the plays of Molière, including *The Misanthrope* (1955) and *Tartuffe* (1963). These rhymed-verse versions of the seventeenth-century French playwright's work are both elegant and earthy, as well as practical enough to be successfully produced on stage.

Two of Wilbur's poetry collections, *Things of This World: Poems* (1956) and *New and Collected Poems* (1988), won Pulitzer Prizes. He has also published several noted books for children, including *A Bestiary* (1955), illustrated by Alexander Calder. Wilbur's fondness for wordplay is evident in his book *Pedestrian Flight: Twenty-one Clerihews for the Telephone* (1981). A *clerihew* is a humorous poem made up of two rhymed couplets that give some real and some imagined biographical information about a famous person.

Make the Connection

The Eye of the Beholder

Beauty often seems to have something magical about it. "Now you see it, now you don't" is a magician's cliché that could just as easily be a poet's catch phrase. The poet, like the magician, knows that beauty can be ever-shifting, forged in a fleeting moment by combining everyday people and things with the artist's creative eye.

Quickwrite

Think about a person or a thing you consider beautiful. Then, write down some of the special characteristics of this person or thing. For instance, a beautiful person might radiate an aura of kindness.

Elements of Literature

Ambiguity

The title of Wilbur's poem presents us with an **ambiguity**—an expression that deliberately suggests two or more different, and sometimes conflicting, meanings. Does "the beautiful changes" mean that our idea of the beautiful changes? Or is the poem about beautiful transformations? Do both meanings apply?

Background

Queen Anne's lace (or wild carrot) is a common weed. Its flower looks like a crocheted doily with a tiny ruby at its center. "Lucernes" (lo͞o·sᵘrnz') is a reference to the glacier-fed Lake of Lucerne in Switzerland.

Bonnie Sue/Photo Researchers.

The Beautiful Changes

Richard Wilbur

One wading a Fall meadow finds on all sides
The Queen Anne's Lace lying like lilies
On water; it glides
So from the walker, it turns
5 Dry grass to a lake, as the slightest shade of you
Valleys my mind in fabulous blue Lucernes.

The beautiful changes as a forest is changed
By a chameleon's tuning his skin to it;
As a mantis, arranged
10 On a green leaf, grows
Into it, makes the leaf leafier, and proves
Any greenness is deeper than anyone knows.

Your hands hold roses always in a way that says
They are not only yours; the beautiful changes
15 In such kind ways,
Wishing ever to sunder
Things and things' selves for a second finding, to lose
For a moment all that it touches back to wonder.

Spring by
Donald C. Martin.
Private Collection.

Before You Read

BOY AT THE WINDOW

Make the Connection

Inside and Outside

Indoors is warm, bright, and protected
from harsh weather. Outdoors is cold,
dark, and lashed by snow and rain.
Indoors and outdoors are very different—but there can be connections.
There may be, for instance, danger in
both places. Have you ever felt that outdoors was just an extension of indoors?

Quickwrite

At times, some
people feel that
inanimate objects—trees, clouds, snowmen—are almost human. Write down
some notes explaining why people might
personify such things in the natural
world.

Boy at the Window

Richard Wilbur

Seeing the snowman standing all alone
In dusk and cold is more than he can bear.
The small boy weeps to hear the wind prepare
A night of gnashings° and enormous moan.
5   His tearful sight can hardly reach to where
The pale-faced figure with bitumen° eyes
Returns him such a god-forsaken stare
As outcast Adam gave to Paradise.

The man of snow is, nonetheless, content,
10   Having no wish to go inside and die.
Still, he is moved to see the youngster cry.
Though frozen water is his element,
He melts enough to drop from one soft eye
A trickle of the purest rain, a tear
15   For the child at the bright pane surrounded by
Such warmth, such light, such love, and so much fear.

4. gnashings (nash′iŋz): grinding of teeth, as in anger.
6. bitumen (bi·too′mən): thick, coal-like substance.

MAKING MEANINGS

The Beautiful Changes

First Thoughts

1. Is anything in the poem similar to your own experience? Can you make a connection between the poem and anything you noted in your Quickwrite?

Shaping Interpretations

2. According to the poem's speaker, in what way does Queen Anne's lace change a meadow?

3. Who is "you"? In what way is the effect of "you" similar to the effect of Queen Anne's lace?

4. The third stanza makes a strong statement. Paraphrase that statement and tell what you think the "second finding" might be.

5. In your own words, explain the **ambiguity** of the **title**. Does the poem as a whole support one meaning or the other, or both?

6. Is this a love poem? If so, who or what does the speaker love? Pick out the lines that support your answer.

Boy at the Window

First Thoughts

1. What do you think the poem is suggesting about the boy and his fears? (How is the boy's indoor "weather" like the outdoors?)

Shaping Interpretations

2. Explain the **allusion** at the end of the first stanza. Could it apply to both the snowman and the boy? Why or why not?

3. Why do you think the boy feels a connection with the snowman?

4. Why does the snowman feel sympathy for the boy?

5. Who is more comfortable in his situation—the boy or the snowman? Do you think this indicates something about the difference between the human world and the world of nature?

CHOICES:
Building Your Portfolio

Writer's Notebook

1. Collecting Ideas for an Evaluation

"The Beautiful Changes" and "Boy at the Window" are **lyric poems,** or poems that express the personal feelings and thoughts of a speaker. In your opinion, what makes such a poem effective? Consider elements like **message, language, form,** and **tone.** Then, note how either of Wilbur's poems meets or does not meet each of your criteria. Save your notes for possible use in the Writer's Workshop on page 1181.

Interpreting a Poem

2. "Glorious Energy"

In an interview, Wilbur made this statement: "To put it simply, I feel that the universe is full of glorious energy, that the energy tends to take pattern and shape, and that the ultimate character of things is comely and good." In a brief essay, discuss how "The Beautiful Changes" demonstrates what Wilbur means in this statement. Do you agree or disagree with the poet?

A Reflection

3. The Motive for Metaphor

Why do you think we humans imagine that snowmen can feel the cold or that a storm can gnash its teeth? Get together with a partner and exchange some ideas about this question. Don't worry about a definite answer; philosophers still don't know the answer to that question, but that doesn't mean they stop asking. When you have some ideas about "the motive for metaphor," write them up in a brief essay. In your essay, refer to the little boy in the poem. Try to explain *why* the boy **personifies** the snowman—when he knows very well that the snowman cannot feel the cold. Be sure to refer to your Quickwrite notes.

Karl Shapiro

(1913–2000)

©Rollie McKenna.

Karl Shapiro made a career out of defying literary classification. As a poet, novelist, and literary critic, he had a self-acknowledged determination to "take the other side of almost any argument" and to pursue "the anti-poem" that cuts through "traditional poetic faking."

Shapiro's resistance to doctrine led him to reject contemporary wisdom about how a poem should be written and to take up forms and styles that were either radically new or unfashionably old. As the critic Michael True observed, "[i]f he were asked to speak at the White House, he would probably arrive dressed in a Hawaiian shirt, orange trousers, and sneakers; at a rock concert he would be the one in white tie and tails." In spite of—perhaps because of—this fierce independence, Shapiro's poetry reflects the conflicts and contradictions of a crucial transition period in American history and American literature.

Born in Baltimore, Maryland, in 1913, Shapiro was raised in a Jewish household in an urban environment, a world that was both inside and outside the centers of traditional American culture. While he was determined to become a poet from an early age, Shapiro had to be "coaxed and cajoled through grade after grade," and he dropped out of the University of Virginia after one unhappy semester. It was only after he was inducted into the Army Medical Corps and served for five years in the South Pacific that Shapiro began to achieve academic and literary success. During World War II, he wrote the hard-edged, tightly metered poems that would establish his literary reputation, culminating in the collection *V-Letter and Other Poems,* which won the Pulitzer Prize in 1945.

As one of the first young literary figures to emerge from the devastation of World War II, Shapiro was often seen as the voice of a new generation. Members of this literary group rejected the formalism, abstract subject matter, and occasional obscurity of modernist poets like T. S. Eliot and Ezra Pound. At the same time, they anticipated the rougher forms and nontraditional subject matter that characterized the Beat poetry of the 1950s and '60s. Indeed, Shapiro seemed to speak for the Beats and their literary forefathers, William Carlos Williams and Walt Whitman, with the credo "Between the poetry of language or symbol and that of situation, I choose situation." Yet Shapiro's frequent use of traditional metric forms distinguishes him from Beat poets like Allen Ginsberg and Lawrence Ferlinghetti.

Shapiro's later disillusionment with the artistic standards of the 1960s "counterculture" and with what he termed "the intellectual infantilism of the American radical" further established his stubborn independence as an artist and cultural critic. This mistrust of popular movements in poetry and politics remained a constant in Shapiro's long and varied career. It is also reflected in his searching, moving poems about his Jewish identity, his flirtations with both communism and Catholicism, and his service in World War II.

Shapiro said of "Elegy for a Dear Soldier," his celebrated war poem, "It was not a flag-waving poem, and it was not an anti-flag-waving poem, a hard balance which [I] always tried for." It is this kind of balance that has established Shapiro as one of America's most innovative poets, one whose work consistently challenges conventional assumptions about what constitutes good politics, good culture, and good art.

Make the Connection

Lack of Control

Most of us live under the assumption that we can control or at least understand events that happen to us and around us. Yet we often encounter accidents, mysterious events, and random tragedies that mock this sense of order. How have you dealt with unexpected and unexplained events in your own life?

Quickwrite

Shapiro's poem has the simple and powerful title "Auto Wreck." Before you read, think of a time that you witnessed or learned about an accident or a natural disaster. Jot down some of your responses at the time—sorrow, fear, curiosity, even guilt or shame.

Elements of Literature

Synesthesia

The first line of "Auto Wreck" contains a striking example of **synesthesia,** the juxtaposition of images that appeal to different kinds of sensory experience. As a literary technique, synesthesia is often an attempt to capture the complex blend of sensory data that helps make up human experience.

Auto Wreck

Karl Shapiro

Its quick soft silver bell beating, beating,
And down the dark one ruby flare
Pulsing out red light like an artery,
The ambulance at top speed floating down
5   Past beacons and illuminated clocks
Wings in a heavy curve, dips down,
And brakes speed, entering the crowd.
The doors leap open, emptying light;
Stretchers are laid out, the mangled lifted
10 And stowed into the little hospital.
Then the bell, breaking the hush, tolls once,
And the ambulance with its terrible cargo
Rocking, slightly rocking, moves away,
As the doors, an afterthought, are closed.

15 We are deranged, walking among the cops
Who sweep glass and are large and
    composed.
One is still making notes under the light.
One with a bucket douches° ponds of blood
Into the street and gutter.
20 One hangs lanterns on the wrecks that cling,
Empty husks of locusts, to iron poles.

Our throats were tight as tourniquets,
Our feet were bound with splints, but now,

---

18. douches (do͞osh′iz): splashes or flushes with water to clean; washes.

Like convalescents intimate and gauche,°
25 We speak through sickly smiles and warn
With the stubborn saw of common sense,
The grim joke and the banal resolution.
The traffic moves around with care,
But we remain, touching a wound
30 That opens to our richest horror.
Already old, the question Who shall die?
Becomes unspoken Who is innocent?

24. gauche (gōsh): lacking social grace; awkward.

For death in war is done by hands;
Suicide has cause and stillbirth, logic;
35 And cancer, simple as a flower, blooms.
But this invites the occult mind,
Cancels our physics with a sneer,
And spatters all we knew of
        denouement°
Across the expedient and wicked stones.

38. denouement (dā′nōō·mänʹ): outcome of a drama or story.

Making Meanings

First Thoughts

1. How do you think the speaker in "Auto Wreck" is changed by this experience of human tragedy?

Shaping Interpretations

2. In your own words, **summarize** very briefly what happens in each stanza.

3. Describe what you *see* and *hear* in the first two stanzas. Which details in the poem evoke those sensations?

4. What details in lines 22–27 tell you how the spectators are feeling and what they are saying to one another?

5. Which **images** in the poem are based on medical terminology? Why do you think the poet decided to choose these images?

6. According to the speaker, how are deaths by war, suicide, and stillbirth different from the kind of accidental death described in the poem? What do you think the speaker is really so disturbed about in the last lines?

7. What might the speaker mean by saying that his questions can be answered only by an "occult" mind? What verb in line 38 reminds you again of the auto wreck?

Extending the Text

8. Do you think someone the speaker knew was in the auto wreck, or is he just a bystander? Do you think it is important to know the answer to this question? Explain your response.

Choices:
Building Your Portfolio

Writer's Notebook

1. Collecting Ideas for an Evaluation

Shapiro's poetry is admired for its technical and intellectual brilliance, but some critics say his tone is too harsh and short on compassion. Based on your reading of "Auto Wreck," do you agree with this assessment? Does the speaker's focus on the witnesses make him seem indifferent to the victims? Write down some thoughts and cite details from the poem to support your ideas. Save your notes for possible use in the Writer's Workshop on page 1181.

Creative Writing

2. A Witness

Refer to your Quickwrite notes, and use them to write a brief essay about your own experience with an accident or disaster. The event need not be tragic, or even significant to anyone else. It should be something that affected you in some way, perhaps by raising some of the questions Shapiro raises in the poem. A broken arm, for example, might have made you think for the first time about how fragile our bodies really are and how we should take care of them. Be sure to write about something you don't mind sharing.

Richard Wright

(1908–1960)

"It had been only through books—at best, no more than vicarious cultural transfusions—that I had managed to keep myself alive. . . ." Richard Wright *did* keep himself alive, and he became a writer with a gift for conveying the intensity of his struggle. He is typically described as the first African American writer to expose American racism to a large white audience. But this cool academic assessment fails to capture the angry, relentless drive of his most famous novel, *Native Son* (1940), or of his autobiography, *Black Boy* (1945).

Critics have labored to justify Wright's twelve-year membership in the Communist Party and explain his self-exile in Paris for the last fourteen years of his life. Full of contradictions, Wright is hard to label, yet it is clear that African American writers who have followed him have had to emerge from his shadow.

When the University of Mississippi organized a symposium on Wright in 1985, it was front-page news. Part of the poignancy of such posthumous recognition comes from the fact that Wright had remembered his home state of Mississippi with "ambivalence." We can only speculate on how Wright might have reacted to an authority on Southern culture who told *The New York Times:* "Faulkner is considered the top Mississippi writer, but I would put Wright with Eudora Welty and Tennessee Williams in their international reputation."

Wright's life began in poverty. His father, a Mississippi sharecropper, abandoned his family when Wright was five; when the boy was twelve, his mother could no longer support the family. Raised by various relatives, Wright early learned the bitter lessons of survival on ghetto streets. He remembered living with "the sustained expectation of violence." By borrowing a white man's library card, he was finally able to gain access to books.

Richard Wright by Carl Van Vechten.

Before he was twenty, Wright fled the South forever, moving to Chicago and then to New York. He joined the WPA Federal Writers Project, a Depression-era government organization that provided a livelihood for unemployed writers. He began to explore Marxism and eventually joined the Communist Party at a time when many people thought it offered hope for a more equitable reorganization of society (and before the horrors of the Stalinist purges of the 1930s became public). Eventually disillusioned, Wright left the party in 1944.

Wright achieved his first real recognition with *Native Son,* a tale of a victimized black man, Bigger Thomas, who accidentally kills once, then murders again to avoid betrayal. *Black Boy* secured Wright's fame and became a best-seller. But in the fifteen years between its publication and his death, Wright wrote no other book that equaled its success. He struggled to understand the historical and cultural place of African Americans in modern life, visiting Africa and recording his observations in *Black Power* (1954) and *White Man, Listen!* (1957). But he felt as much an alien in Africa as anywhere else. He died in Paris, where he had found as much of a home as he could.

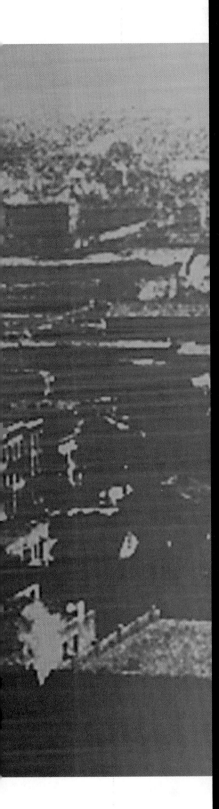

Before You Read

Make the Connection

**The Child Is Father
to the Man**
What does it mean to grow
up, to put away our toys, and
to participate in the world as
mature and responsible
adults? What elements of
childhood do we carry with
us forever? The discoveries
we make as children, awakening to what the world is
really like, can be harsh or
sweet, shocking or gradual,
depending on the specific
circumstances of our lives.
Yet in one way or another,
we are all deeply affected by
our childhood awakenings.

Reading Skills
and Strategies

Interpreting Details
In this excerpt, images of
"home" are associated
mainly with physical and
emotional hunger. As you
read, make note of details
that express the two kinds of
hunger the young Wright
feels—physical, gnawing
hunger and another, emo-
tional kind of hunger. Which
hunger do you think Wright
feels most acutely?

Elements of Literature

Dialogue
We often think of **dialogue,**
or the directly quoted words
of conversation between two
or more people, as the property of drama and fiction.
But dialogue can also play a
significant role in nonfiction.
   In nonfiction, though, dialogue can be controversial.
Reporters and biographers
are often challenged in court
to prove that the conversations they put in quotation
marks really occurred. In
this excerpt from Wright's
autobiography, most scenes
are dramatized through dialogue. By presenting conversations, Wright *shows,*
rather than describes, his
own thoughts and feelings.
With dialogue, he creates
vivid pictures of the people
in his life.

> **D**ialogue is the directly
> quoted words of conversa-
> tion between two or more
> people.

Boy with Tire (1952) by Hughie Lee-Smith. Oil on prestwood panel (60.3 cm × 82.6 cm).

Hunger stole upon me so slowly that at first I was not aware of what hunger really meant.

from

Black Boy

Richard Wright

One day my mother told me that we were going to Memphis on a boat, the *Kate Adams*, and my eagerness thereafter made the days seem endless. Each night I went to bed hoping that the next morning would be the day of departure.

"How big is the boat?" I asked my mother.

"As big as a mountain," she said.

"Has it got a whistle?"

"Yes."

"Does the whistle blow?"

"Yes."

"When?"

"When the captain wants it to blow."

"Why do they call it the *Kate Adams*?"

"Because that's the boat's name."

"What color is the boat?"

"White."

"How long will we be on the boat?"

"All day and all night."

"Will we sleep on the boat?"

"Yes, when we get sleepy, we'll sleep. Now, hush."

For days I had dreamed about a huge white boat floating on a vast body of water, but when my mother took me down to the levee on the day of leaving, I saw a tiny, dirty boat that was not at all like the boat I had imagined. I was disappointed and when time came to go on board I cried and my mother thought that I did not want to go with her to Memphis, and I could not tell her what the trouble was. Solace came when I wandered about the boat and gazed at Negroes throwing dice, drinking whiskey, playing cards, lolling on boxes, eating, talking, and singing. My father took me down into the engine room and the throbbing machines enthralled me for hours.

In Memphis we lived in a one-story brick tenement. The stone buildings and the concrete pavements looked bleak and hostile to me. The absence of green, growing things made the city seem dead. Living space for the four of us—my mother, my brother, my father, and me—was a kitchen and a bedroom. In the front and rear were paved areas in which my brother and I could play, but for days I was afraid to go into the strange city streets alone.

It was in this tenement that the personality of my father first came fully into the orbit of my concern. He worked as a night porter in a Beale Street drugstore and he became important and forbidding to me only when I learned that I could not make noise when he was asleep in the daytime. He was the lawgiver in our family and I never laughed in his presence. I used to lurk timidly in the kitchen doorway and watch his huge body sitting slumped at the table. I stared at him with awe as he gulped his beer from a tin bucket, as he ate long and heavily, sighed, belched, closed his eyes to nod on a stuffed belly. He was quite fat and his bloated stomach always lapped over his belt. He was always a stranger to me, always somehow alien and remote. . . .

Hunger stole upon me so slowly that at first I was not aware of what hunger really meant. Hunger had always been more or less at my elbow when I played, but now I began to wake up at night to find hunger standing at my bedside, staring at me gauntly. The hunger I had known before this had been no grim, hostile stranger; it had been a normal hunger that had made me beg constantly for bread, and when I ate a crust or two I was satisfied. But this new hunger baffled me, scared me, made me angry and insistent. Whenever I begged for food now my mother would pour me a cup of tea which would still the clamor in my stomach for a moment or two; but a little later I would feel hunger nudging my ribs, twisting my empty guts until they ached. I would grow dizzy and my vision would dim. I became less active in my play, and for the first time in my life I had to pause and think of what was happening to me.

"Mama, I'm hungry," I complained one afternoon.

"Jump up and catch a kungry," she said, trying to make me laugh and forget.

"What's a *kungry*?"

"It's what little boys eat when they get hungry," she said.

"What does it taste like?"

"I don't know."

"Then why do you tell me to catch one?"

"Because you said that you were hungry," she said, smiling.

I sensed that she was teasing me and it made me angry.

"But I'm hungry. I want to eat."

"You'll have to wait."

"But I want to eat now."

"But there's nothing to eat," she told me.

"Why?"

"Just because there's none," she explained.

"But I want to eat," I said, beginning to cry.

"You'll just have to wait," she said again.

"But why?"

"For God to send some food."

"When is He going to send it?"

"I don't know."

"But I'm hungry!"

Words to Own

enthralled (en·thrôld′) *v.*: fascinated.

lurk (lʉrk) *v.*: to hide unnoticed.

clamor (klam′ər) *n.*: loud noise; uproar.

She was ironing and she paused and looked at me with tears in her eyes.

"Where's your father?" she asked me.

I stared in bewilderment. Yes, it was true that my father had not come home to sleep for many days now and I could make as much noise as I wanted. Though I had not known why he was absent, I had been glad that he was not there to shout his restrictions at me. But it had never occurred to me that his absence would mean that there would be no food.

"I don't know," I said.

"Who brings food into the house?" my mother asked me.

"Papa," I said. "He always brought food."

"Well, your father isn't here now," she said.

"Where is he?"

"I don't know," she said.

"But I'm hungry," I whimpered, stomping my feet.

"You'll have to wait until I get a job and buy food," she said.

As the days slid past, the image of my father became associated with my pangs of hunger, and whenever I felt hunger I thought of him with a deep biological bitterness.

My mother finally went to work as a cook and left me and my brother alone in the flat each day with a loaf of bread and a pot of tea. When she returned at evening she would be tired and dispir-ited and would cry a lot. Sometimes, when she was in despair, she would call us to her and talk to us for hours, telling us that we now had no father, that our lives would be different from those of other children, that we must learn as soon as possible to take care of ourselves, to dress ourselves, to prepare our own food; that we must take upon ourselves the responsibility of the flat while she worked. Half frightened, we would promise solemnly. We did not understand what had happened between our father and our mother and the most that these long talks did to us was to make us feel a vague dread. Whenever we asked why father had left, she would tell us that we were too young to know.

One evening my mother told me that thereafter I would have to do the shopping for food. She took me to the corner store to show me the way. I was proud; I felt like a grownup. The next afternoon I looped the basket over my arm and went down the pavement toward the store. When I reached the corner, a gang of boys grabbed me, knocked me down, snatched the basket, took the money, and sent me running home in panic. That evening I told my mother what had happened, but she made no comment; she sat down at once, wrote another note, gave me more money, and sent me out to the grocery again. I crept down the steps and saw the same gang of boys playing down the street. I ran back into the house.

"What's the matter?" my mother asked.

"It's those same boys," I said. "They'll beat me."

"You've got to get over that," she said. "Now, go on."

"I'm scared," I said.

"Go on and don't pay any attention to them," she said.

I went out of the door and walked briskly down the sidewalk, praying that the gang would not molest me. But when I came abreast of them someone shouted.

"There he is!"

They came toward me and I broke into a wild run toward home. They overtook me and flung me to the pavement. I yelled, pleaded, kicked, but they wrenched the money out of my hand. They yanked me to my feet, gave me a few slaps, and sent me home sobbing. My mother met me at the door.

"They b-beat m-me," I gasped. "They t-t-took the m-money."

I started up the steps, seeking the shelter of the house.

"Don't you come in here," my mother warned me.

I froze in my tracks and stared at her.

"But they're coming after me," I said.

"You just stay right where you are," she said in a deadly tone. "I'm going to teach you this night to stand up and fight for yourself."

She went into the house and I waited, terrified, wondering what she was about. Presently she returned with more money and another note; she also had a long heavy stick.

"Take this money, this note, and this stick," she said. "Go to the store and buy those groceries. If those boys bother you, then fight."

WORDS TO OWN

dispirited (di·spir′it·id) *adj.*: discouraged.

I was baffled. My mother was telling me to fight, a thing that she had never done before.

"But I'm scared," I said.

"Don't you come into this house until you've gotten those groceries," she said.

"They'll beat me; they'll beat me," I said.

"Then stay in the streets; don't come back here!"

I ran up the steps and tried to force my way past her into the house. A stinging slap came on my jaw. I stood on the sidewalk, crying.

"Please, let me wait until tomorrow," I begged.

"No," she said. "Go now! If you come back into this house without those groceries, I'll whip you!"

She slammed the door and I heard the key turn in the lock. I shook with fright. I was alone upon the dark, hostile streets and gangs were after me. I had the choice of being beaten at home or away from home. I clutched the stick, crying, trying to reason. If I were beaten at home, there was absolutely nothing that I could do about it; but if I were beaten in the streets, I had a chance to fight and defend myself. I walked slowly down the sidewalk, coming closer to the gang of boys, holding the stick tightly. I was so full of fear that I could scarcely breathe. I was almost upon them now.

"There he is again!" the cry went up.

They surrounded me quickly and began to grab for my hand.

"I'll kill you!" I threatened.

They closed in. In blind fear I let the stick fly, feeling it crack against a boy's skull. I swung again, lamming another skull, then another. Realizing that they would retaliate if I let up for but a second, I fought to lay them low, to knock them cold, to kill them so that they could not strike back at me. I flayed with tears in my eyes, teeth clenched, stark fear making me throw every ounce of my strength behind each blow. I hit again and again, dropping the money and the grocery list. The boys scattered, yelling, nursing their heads, staring at me in utter disbelief. They had never seen such <u>frenzy</u>. I stood panting, egging them on, taunting them to come on and fight. When they refused, I ran after them and they tore out for their homes, screaming. The parents of the boys rushed into the streets and threatened me, and for the first time in my life I shouted at grownups, telling them that I would give them the same if they bothered me. I finally found my

grocery list and the money and went to the store. On my way back I kept my stick poised for instant use, but there was not a single boy in sight. That night I won the right to the streets of Memphis....

After my father's desertion, my mother's <u>ardently</u> religious disposition dominated the household and I was often taken to Sunday school where I met God's representative in the guise of a tall, black preacher. One Sunday my mother invited the tall, black preacher to a dinner of fried chicken. I was happy, not because the preacher was coming but because of the chicken. One or two neighbors also were invited. But no sooner had the preacher arrived than I began to resent him, for I learned at once that he, like my father, was used to having his own way. The hour for dinner came and I was wedged at the table between talking and laughing adults. In the center of the table was a huge platter of golden-brown fried chicken. I compared the bowl of soup that sat before me with the crispy chicken and decided in favor of the chicken. The others began to eat their soup, but I could not touch mine.

"Eat your soup," my mother said.

"I don't want any," I said.

"You won't get anything else until you've eaten your soup," she said.

The preacher had finished his soup and had asked that the platter of chicken be passed to him. It <u>galled</u> me. He smiled, cocked his head this way and that, picking out choice pieces. I forced a spoonful of soup down my throat and looked to see if my speed matched that of the preacher. It did not. There were already bare chicken bones on his plate, and he was reaching for more. I tried eating my soup faster, but it was no use; the other people were now serving themselves chicken and the platter was more than half empty. I gave up and sat staring in despair at the vanishing pieces of fried chicken.

"Eat your soup or you won't get anything," my mother warned.

I looked at her appealingly and could not answer. As piece after piece of chicken was eaten, I

WORDS TO OWN

frenzy (fren′zē) *n.*: frantic behavior; wildness.
ardently (ärd″nt·lē) *adv.*: intensely; eagerly.
galled (gôld) *v.*: irritated; angered.

My Brother (1942) by John Wilson. Oil on panel (12" × 10⅝").

Smith College Museum of Art, Northampton, Massachusetts.

was unable to eat my soup at all. I grew hot with anger. The preacher was laughing and joking and the grownups were hanging on his words. My growing hate of the preacher finally became more important than God or religion and I could no longer contain myself. I leaped up from the table, knowing that I should be ashamed of what I was doing, but unable to stop, and screamed, running blindly from the room.

"That preacher's going to eat *all* the chicken!" I bawled.

The preacher tossed back his head and roared with laughter, but my mother was angry and told me that I was to have no dinner because of my bad manners.

When I awakened one morning my mother told me that we were going to see a judge who would make my father support me and my brother. An hour later all three of us were sitting in a huge crowded room. I was overwhelmed by the many faces and the voices which I could not understand. High above me was a white face which my mother told me was the face of the judge. Across the huge room sat my father, smiling confidently, looking at us. My mother warned me not to be fooled by my father's friendly manner; she told me that the judge might ask me questions, and if he did I must tell him the truth. I agreed, yet I hoped that the judge would not ask me anything.

For some reason the entire thing struck me as being useless; I felt that if my father were going to feed me, then he would have done so regardless of what a judge said to him. And I did not want my father to feed me; I was hungry, but my thoughts of food did not now center about him. I waited, growing restless, hungry. My mother gave me a dry sandwich and I munched and stared, longing to go home. Finally I heard my mother's name called; she rose and began weeping so copiously that she could not talk for a few moments; at last she managed to say that her husband had deserted her and two children, that her children were hungry, that they stayed hungry, that she worked, that she was trying to raise them alone. Then my father was called; he came forward jauntily, smiling. He tried to kiss my mother, but she turned away from him. I only heard one sentence of what he said.

"I'm doing all I can, Your Honor," he mumbled, grinning.

It had been painful to sit and watch my mother crying and my father laughing and I was glad when we were outside in the sunny streets. Back at home my mother wept again and talked complainingly about the unfairness of the judge who had accepted my father's word. After the court scene, I tried to forget my father; I did not hate him; I simply did not want to think of him. Often when we were hungry my mother would beg me to go to my father's job and ask him for a dollar, a dime, a nickel . . . But I would never consent to go. I did not want to see him.

My mother fell ill and the problem of food became an acute, daily agony. Hunger was with us always. Sometimes the neighbors would feed us or a dollar bill would come in the mail from my grandmother. It was winter and I would buy a dime's worth of coal each morning from the corner coalyard and lug it home in paper bags. For a time I remained out of school to wait upon my mother, then Granny came to visit us and I returned to school.

At night there were long, halting discussions about our going to live with Granny, but nothing came of it. Perhaps there was not enough money for railroad fare. Angered by having been hauled into court, my father now spurned us completely. I heard long, angrily whispered conversations between my mother and grandmother to the effect that "that woman ought to be killed for breaking up a home." What irked me was the ceaseless talk and no action. If someone had suggested that my father be killed, I would perhaps have become interested; if someone had suggested that his name never be mentioned, I would no doubt have agreed; if someone had suggested that we move to another city, I would have been glad. But there was only endless talk that led nowhere and I began to keep away from home as much as possible, preferring the simplicity of the streets to the worried, <u>futile</u> talk at home.

Finally we could no longer pay the rent for our dingy flat; the few dollars that Granny had left us before she went home were gone. Half sick and in despair, my mother made the rounds of the charitable institutions, seeking help. She found an orphan home that agreed to assume the guidance of me and my brother provided my mother worked and made small payments. My mother hated to be separated from us, but she had no choice.

The orphan home was a two-story frame building set amid trees in a wide, green field. My mother ushered me and my brother one morning into the building and into the presence of a tall, gaunt, mulatto woman who called herself Miss Simon. At once she took a fancy to me and I was frightened speechless; I was afraid of her the moment I saw her and my fear lasted during my entire stay in the home.

The house was crowded with children and there was always a storm of noise. The daily routine was blurred to me and I never quite grasped it. The most abiding feeling I had each day was

---

WORDS TO OWN

futile (fyoot'l) *adj.*: useless; pointless.

---

hunger and fear. The meals were skimpy and there were only two of them. Just before we went to bed each night we were given a slice of bread smeared with molasses. The children were silent, hostile, vindictive, continuously complaining of hunger. There was an overall atmosphere of nervousness and intrigue, of children telling tales upon others, of children being deprived of food to punish them.

The home did not have the money to check the growth of the wide stretches of grass by having it mown, so it had to be pulled by hand. Each morning after we had eaten a breakfast that seemed like no breakfast at all, an older child would lead a herd of us to the vast lawn and we would get to our knees and wrench the grass loose from the dirt with our fingers. At intervals Miss Simon would make a tour of inspection, examining the pile of pulled grass beside each child, scolding or praising according to the size of the pile. Many mornings I was too weak from hunger to pull the grass; I would grow dizzy and my mind would become blank and I would find myself, after an interval of unconsciousness, upon my hands and knees, my head whirling, my eyes staring in bleak astonishment at the green grass, wondering where I was, feeling that I was emerging from a dream . . .

During the first days my mother came each night to visit me and my brother, then her visits stopped. I began to wonder if she, too, like my father, had disappeared into the unknown. I was rapidly learning to distrust everything and everybody. When my mother did come, I asked her why had she remained away so long and she told me that Miss Simon had forbidden her to visit us, that Miss Simon had said that she was spoiling us with too much attention. I begged my mother to take me away; she wept and told me to wait, that soon she would take us to Arkansas. She left and my heart sank.

Miss Simon tried to win my confidence; she asked me if I would like to be adopted by her if my mother consented and I said no. She would take me into her apartment and talk to me, but her words had no effect. Dread and mistrust had already become a daily part of my being and my memory grew sharp, my senses more impressionable; I began to be aware of myself as a distinct personality striving against others. I held myself in, afraid to act or speak until I was sure of my surroundings, feeling most of the time that I was suspended over a void. My imagination soared; I dreamed of running away. Each morning I vowed that I would leave the next morning, but the next morning always found me afraid.

One day Miss Simon told me that thereafter I was to help her in the office. I ate lunch with her and, strangely, when I sat facing her at the table, my hunger vanished. The woman killed something in me. Next she called me to her desk where she sat addressing envelopes.

"Step up close to the desk," she said. "Don't be afraid."

I went and stood at her elbow. There was a wart on her chin and I stared at it.

"Now, take a blotter from over there and blot each envelope after I'm through writing on it," she instructed me, pointing to a blotter that stood about a foot from my hand.

I stared and did not move or answer.

"Take the blotter," she said.

I wanted to reach for the blotter and succeeded only in twitching my arm.

"Here," she said sharply, reaching for the blotter and shoving it into my fingers.

She wrote in ink on an envelope and pushed it toward me. Holding the blotter in my hand, I stared at the envelope and could not move.

"Blot it," she said.

I could not lift my hand. I knew what she had said; I knew what she wanted me to do; and I had heard her correctly. I wanted to look at her and say something, tell her why I could not move; but my eyes were fixed upon the floor. I could not summon enough courage while she sat there looking at me to reach over the yawning space of twelve inches and blot the wet ink on the envelope.

"Blot it!" she spoke sharply.

Still I could not move or answer.

"Look at me!"

I could not lift my eyes. She reached her hand to my face and I twisted away.

"What's wrong with you?" she demanded.

I began to cry and she drove me from the room. I decided that as soon as night came I would run away. The dinner bell rang and I did not go to the table, but hid in a corner of the hallway. When I heard the dishes rattling at the table, I opened the door and ran down the walk to the street. Dusk was falling. Doubt made me stop. Ought I go back? No; hunger was back there, and fear. I went on, coming to concrete sidewalks. People passed me. Where was I going? I did not know. The farther I walked the more frantic I became. In a confused and vague way I knew that I was doing more running *away* from than running *toward* something. I stopped. The streets seemed dangerous. The buildings were massive and dark. The moon shone and the trees loomed frighteningly. No, I could not go on. I would go back. But I had walked so far and had turned too many corners and had not kept track of the direction. Which way led back to the orphan home? I did not know. I was lost.

I stood in the middle of the sidewalk and cried. A "white" policeman came to me and I wondered if he was going to beat me. He asked me what was the matter and I told him that I was trying to find my mother. His "white" face created a new fear in me. I was remembering the tale of the "white" man who had beaten the "black" boy. A crowd gathered and I was urged to tell where I lived. Curiously, I was too full of fear to cry now. I wanted to tell the "white" face that I had run off from an orphan home and that Miss Simon ran it, but I was afraid. Finally I was taken to the police station where I was fed. I felt better. I sat in a big chair where I was surrounded by "white" policemen, but they seemed to ignore me. Through the window I could see that night had completely fallen and that lights now gleamed in the streets. I grew sleepy and dozed. My shoulder was shaken gently and I opened my eyes and looked into a "white" face of another policeman who was sitting beside me. He asked me questions in a quiet, confidential tone, and quite before I knew it he was not "white" any more. I told him that I had run away from an orphan home and that Miss Simon ran it.

It was but a matter of minutes before I was walking alongside a policeman, heading toward the home. The policeman led me to the front gate and I saw Miss Simon waiting for me on the steps. She identified me and I was left in her charge. I begged her not to beat me, but she yanked me upstairs into an empty room and lashed me thoroughly. Sobbing, I slunk off to bed, resolved to run away again. But I was watched closely after that.

My mother was informed upon her next visit that I had tried to run away and she was terribly upset.

"Why did you do it?" she asked.

"I don't want to stay here," I told her.

"But you must," she said. "How can I work if I'm to worry about you? You must remember that you have no father. I'm doing all I can."

"I don't want to stay here," I repeated.

"Then, if I take you to your father . . ."

"I don't want to stay with him either," I said.

"But I want you to ask him for enough money for us to go to my sister's in Arkansas," she said.

Again I was faced with choices I did not like, but I finally agreed. After all, my hate for my father was not so great and urgent as my hate for the orphan home. My mother held to her idea and one night a week or so later I found myself standing in a room in a frame house. My father and a strange woman were sitting before a bright fire that blazed in a grate. My mother and I were standing about six feet away, as though we were afraid to approach them any closer.

"It's not for me," my mother was saying. "It's for your children that I'm asking you for money."

"I ain't got nothing," my father said, laughing.

"Come here, boy," the strange woman called to me.

I looked at her and did not move.

"Give him a nickel," the woman said. "He's cute."

"Come here, Richard," my father said, stretching out his hand.

I backed away, shaking my head, keeping my eyes on the fire.

"He is a cute child," the strange woman said.

"You ought to be ashamed," my mother said to the strange woman. "You're starving my children."

"Now, don't you-all fight," my father said, laughing.

"I'll take that poker and hit you!" I blurted at my father.

He looked at my mother and laughed louder.

"You told him to say that," he said.

"Don't say such things, Richard," my mother said.

"You ought to be dead," I said to the strange woman.

The woman laughed and threw her arms about my father's neck. I grew ashamed and wanted to leave.

"How can you starve your children?" my mother asked.

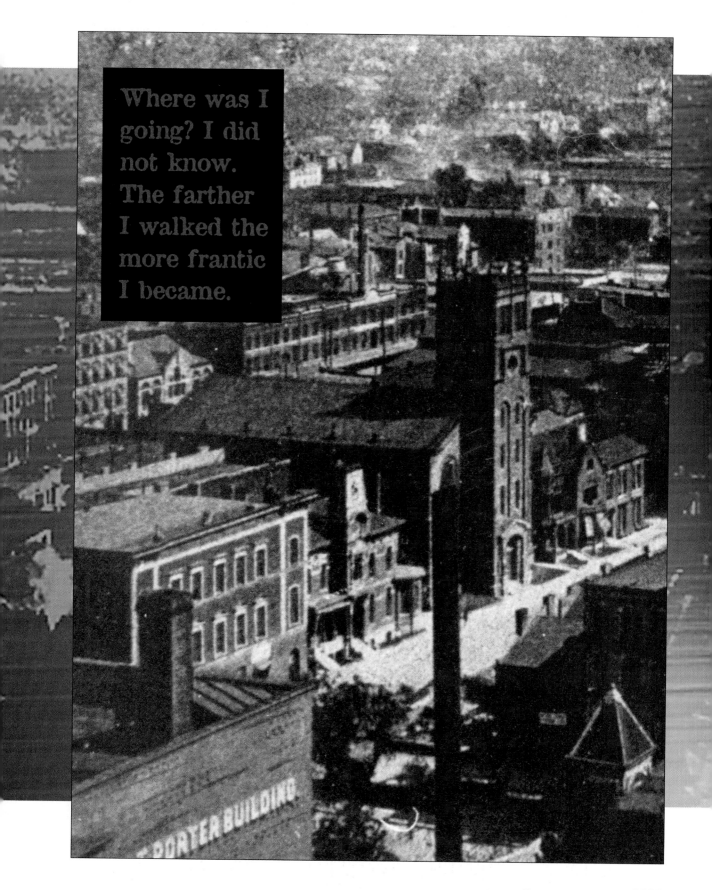

Where was I going? I did not know. The farther I walked the more frantic I became.

"Let Richard stay with me," my father said.

"Do you want to stay with your father, Richard?" my mother asked.

"No," I said.

"You'll get plenty to eat," he said.

"I'm hungry now," I told him. "But I won't stay with you."

"Aw, give the boy a nickel," the woman said.

My father ran his hand into his pocket and pulled out a nickel.

"Here, Richard," he said.

"Don't take it," my mother said.

"Don't teach him to be a fool," my father said. "Here, Richard, take it."

I looked at my mother, at the strange woman, at my father, then into the fire. I wanted to take the nickel, but I did not want to take it from my father.

"You ought to be ashamed," my mother said, weeping. "Giving your son a nickel when he's hungry. If there's a God, He'll pay you back."

"That's all I got," my father said, laughing again and returning the nickel to his pocket.

We left. I had the feeling that I had had to do with something unclean. Many times in the years after that the image of my father and the strange woman, their faces lit by the dancing flames, would surge up in my imagination so vivid and strong that I felt I could reach out and touch it; I would stare at it, feeling that it possessed some vital meaning which always eluded me.

A quarter of a century was to elapse between the time when I saw my father sitting with the strange woman and the time when I was to see him again, standing alone upon the red clay of a Mississippi plantation, a sharecropper,[1] clad in ragged overalls, holding a muddy hoe in his gnarled, veined hands—a quarter of a century during which my mind and consciousness had become so greatly and violently altered that when I tried to talk to him I realized that, though ties of blood made us kin, though I could see a shadow of my face in his face, though there was

an echo of my voice in his voice, we were forever strangers, speaking a different language, living on vastly distant planes of reality. That day a quarter of a century later when I visited him on the plantation—he was standing against the sky, smiling toothlessly, his hair whitened, his body bent, his eyes glazed with dim recollection, his fearsome aspect of twenty-five years ago gone forever from him—I was overwhelmed to realize that he could never understand me or the scalding experiences that had swept me beyond his life and into an area of living that he could never know. I stood before him, poised, my mind aching as it embraced the simple nakedness of his life, feeling how completely his soul was imprisoned by the slow flow of the seasons, by wind and rain and sun, how fastened were his memories to a crude and raw past, how chained were his actions and emotions to the direct, animalistic impulses of his withering body . . .

From the white landowners above him there had not been handed to him a chance to learn the meaning of loyalty, of sentiment, of tradition. Joy was as unknown to him as was despair. As a creature of the earth, he endured, hearty, whole, seemingly indestructible, with no regrets and no hope. He asked easy, drawling questions about me, his other son, his wife, and he laughed, amused, when I informed him of their destinies. I forgave him and pitied him as my eyes looked past him to the unpainted wooden shack. From far beyond the horizons that bound this bleak plantation there had come to me through my living the knowledge that my father was a black peasant who had gone to the city seeking life, but who had failed in the city; a black peasant whose life had been hopelessly snarled in the city, and who had at last fled the city—that same city which had lifted me in its burning arms and borne me toward alien and undreamed-of shores of knowing.

WORDS TO OWN

elapse (ē·laps′) v.: to pass by; to slip away.

withering (with′ər·iŋ) v. used as adj.: drying up; weakening.

---

1. **sharecropper:** farmer who works a piece of land for its owner and gets a small portion of the crop in return.

MAKING MEANINGS

First Thoughts

1. Wright works in swift strokes to draw sharp **images** of his life. Which images stand out most clearly in your mind?

Shaping Interpretations

2. When his mother gives Richard a stick and sends him back to confront the bullies, what lesson is she trying to teach? Was there anything else she could have done?

3. Why can't Richard eat his soup when the preacher is devouring the chicken? What does this incident reveal about the boy's **character**?

4. Remembering his father and the strange woman, "their faces lit by the dancing flames," Wright says this **image** "possessed some vital meaning which always eluded me" (page 1024). What do you think he means?

Connecting with the Text

5. The **image** of the boy pulling grass at the orphanage is a powerful one, although Wright makes no comment on it. Do you wish he had commented, or do you think it wasn't necessary? How does this scene make you feel?

Reading Check

a. What details does Wright use to make the reader feel the physical and emotional hunger he experienced as a boy? (Check your reading notes.)

b. How did Richard win the right to the streets of Memphis?

c. How does Wright's father behave in the courtroom scene and in the meeting with Richard, his mother, and the strange woman?

d. How is the city's effect on his father different from its effect on Wright?

CHOICES:
Building Your Portfolio

Writer's Notebook

1. Collecting Ideas for an Evaluation

In order to build an argument— an explanation of why you like or dislike a text—you need to select and present evidence to support your view. Evidence can include examples from the text, personal experiences that support your opinion, and critical testimonials (quotations and comments) from other people familiar with the text. Write down two examples, experiences, or critical testimonials that you think would support how you feel about Wright's autobiography. Save your notes for possible use in the Writer's Workshop on page 1181.

Analyzing a Character

2. "The simple nakedness of his life . . ."

The father changes tremendously in this excerpt from *Black Boy*. In a short essay, analyze the **character** of the father as Wright presents him. Consider the father when he lives in Memphis and, twenty-five years later, when he lives as a sharecropper. Why does he change? Does he see his son in a different light? What assessment does Wright make of his father at the end?

Speaking and Listening / Oral Interpretation

3. Interpreting Wright Aloud

Select a section of *Black Boy*, and present your interpretation of the text in an oral reading. (Be sure to choose a passage with dialogue.) In preparing for your performance, consider the following: Who is your audience? How many speakers will you use? Will you include sound or visual effects, such as music or dramatic lighting? What different tones of voice will you use to present your interpretation of different parts of the text?

Raymond Carver
(1938–1988)

AP/Wide World Photos.

" **W**e didn't have any youth," Raymond Carver remembered in a 1983 interview. He was thinking of the tough days he spent growing up in a working-class family in the Pacific Northwest. Carver was born in Oregon and raised in Yakima, Washington, where his father worked in a lumber mill and his mother worked periodically as a waitress and a clerk. Carver married soon after graduating from high school, and by the time he turned twenty he and his wife were raising two children. To support his family, he worked at a variety of blue-collar jobs: pumping gas, sweeping hospital corridors, picking tulips.

Given Carver's experiences, it is no surprise that in his stories—as the critic Thomas R. Edwards has commented—"people worry about whether their old cars will start, [and] unemployment or personal bankruptcy are present dangers." Carver's characters typically work as mechanics, factory workers, waitresses, or door-to-door salespeople in an America where making a living can be difficult and uncertain. Characters often survive their difficulties, however, and there is a sense of hope in many Carver stories. "I have a great deal of sympathy with [characters in my stories]," Carver once said. "They're my people. I know them. I could never write down to them."

In the late 1950s, the Carvers moved to California, where Raymond enrolled in college, taking a course in fiction writing with the novelist John Gardner. In 1963, he earned a college degree and then attended the University of Iowa's highly regarded Writers' Workshop.

In the 1960s and early 1970s, Carver published stories and poems, some dealing with favorite topics like hunting and fishing. A breakthrough came in 1976 with the publication of a collection of his stories, *Will You Please Be Quiet, Please?* The lavish praise bestowed upon this book earned Carver wide recognition as a hugely talented writer. The critic Margo Johnson noted that the stories "are filled with glass-sharp details, images and conversations, meticulously arranged." In 1977, Carver won a prestigious Guggenheim fellowship. Yet as he succeeded professionally, his personal life deteriorated, and his marriage ended.

In 1981, Carver published another collection of stories, *What We Talk About When We Talk About Love,* and in 1983, his story collection *Cathedral* enjoyed enormous critical and popular success. By now critics were talking of Carver's permanent place in American literature. The critic Irving Howe compared his work to that of Stephen Crane and Ernest Hemingway. The *Washington Post* book reviewer Jonathan Yardley called Carver "a writer of astonishing compassion and honesty, utterly free of pretense and affectation, his eye set only on describing and revealing the world as he sees it. His eye is so clear, it almost breaks your heart."

Carver's personal life brightened in the years before his early death from lung cancer. He formed a close relationship with the poet and short-story writer Tess Gallagher, who eventually became his wife. Since his death, and despite recent revelations about the significant role one editor played in shaping his stories, Carver's reputation as an important poet and short-story writer has remained firm. His work has been translated into more than twenty languages.

L. (1986) by Mike & Doug Starn. Toned silver print on polyester, tape, wood (48″ × 48″).

Before You Read

EVERYTHING STUCK TO HIM

Make the Connection

Life's Give-and-Take

If we think in simple terms about human feelings, reducing them to clear-cut patterns and easy definitions, we may be tricked into believing that feelings themselves are simple. Great fiction, no matter how simple on the surface, enables us to discover the depths of feelings. We respond to such fiction because we recognize in it the give-and-take of real experience, the gains and the losses, the complex interactions of people who defy stereotyping.

Reading Skills and Strategies

Learning Through Questioning

As you read "Everything Stuck to Him," make a list of questions that occur to you about the characters. You might ask, for instance, about their feelings and what they are *not* saying to each other.

Elements of Literature

Style

One of the most striking elements of Raymond Carver's writing is its **style,** the unique way in which he uses language. Carver's prose has a chiseled quality, as if he has chipped away every unnecessary word. There are some oddities, however. No quotation marks surround dialogue. Most characters aren't given names. You need to read carefully to catch every turn of Carver's meticulously crafted prose.

> **S**tyle is the unique way in which a writer uses language.
>
> *For more on Style, see the Handbook of Literary Terms.*

Everything Stuck to Him

Raymond Carver

They were kids themselves, but they were crazy in love.

She's in Milan[1] for Christmas and wants to know what it was like when she was a kid.

Tell me, she says. Tell me what it was like when I was a kid. She sips Strega, waits, eyes him closely.

She is a cool, slim, attractive girl, a survivor from top to bottom.

That was a long time ago. That was twenty years ago, he says.

You can remember, she says. Go on.

What do you want to hear? he says. What else can I tell you? I could tell you about something that happened when you were a baby. It involves you, he says. But only in a minor way.

Tell me, she says. But first fix us another so you won't have to stop in the middle.

He comes back from the kitchen with drinks, settles into his chair, begins.

They were kids themselves, but they were crazy in love, this eighteen-year-old boy and this seventeen-year-old girl when they married. Not all that long afterwards they had a daughter.

1. **Milan** (mi·lan′): city in northwestern Italy.

The baby came along in late November during a cold spell that just happened to coincide with the peak of the waterfowl season. The boy loved to hunt, you see. That's part of it.

The boy and girl, husband and wife, father and mother, they lived in a little apartment under a dentist's office. Each night they cleaned the dentist's place upstairs in exchange for rent and utilities. In summer they were expected to maintain the lawn and the flowers. In winter the boy shoveled snow and spread rock salt on the walks. Are you still with me? Are you getting the picture?

I am, she says.

That's good, he says. So one day the dentist finds out they were using his letterhead for their personal correspondence. But that's another story.

He gets up from his chair and looks out the window. He sees the tile rooftops and the snow that is falling steadily on them.

Tell the story, she says.

WORDS TO OWN

coincide (kō′in·sīd′) *v.*: to occur at the same time.
correspondence (kôr′ə·spän′dəns) *n.*: communication by letters.

Couple in Open Doorway (1977) by George Segal. Painted plaster, wood, and metal (96″ × 69″ × 52″).

The two kids were very much in love. On top of this they had great ambitions. They were always talking about the things they were going to do and the places they were going to go.

Now the boy and girl slept in the bedroom, and the baby slept in the living room. Let's say the baby was about three months old and had only just begun to sleep through the night.

On this one Saturday night after finishing his work upstairs, the boy stayed in the dentist's office and called an old hunting friend of his father's.

Carl, he said when the man picked up the receiver, believe it or not, I'm a father.

Congratulations, Carl said. How is the wife?

She's fine, Carl. Everybody's fine.

That's good, Carl said, I'm glad to hear it. But if you called about going hunting, I'll tell you something. The geese are flying to beat the band. I don't think I've ever seen so many. Got five today. Going back in the morning, so come along if you want to.

I want to, the boy said.

The boy hung up the telephone and went downstairs to tell the girl. She watched while he laid out his things. Hunting coat, shell bag, boots, socks, hunting cap, long underwear, pump gun.

What time will you be back? the girl said.

Probably around noon, the boy said. But maybe as late as six o'clock. Would that be too late?

It's fine, she said. The baby and I will get along fine. You go and have some fun. When you get back, we'll dress the baby up and go visit Sally.

The boy said, Sounds like a good idea.

Sally was the girl's sister. She was <u>striking</u>. I don't know if you've seen pictures of her. The boy was a little in love with Sally, just as he was a little in love with Betsy, who was another sister the girl had. The boy used to say to the girl, If we weren't married, I could go for Sally.

What about Betsy? the girl used to say. I hate to admit it, but I truly feel she's better looking than Sally and me. What about Betsy?

Betsy too, the boy used to say.

After dinner he turned up the furnace and helped her bathe the baby. He marveled again at the infant who had half his features and half the girl's. He powdered the tiny body. He powdered between fingers and toes.

He emptied the bath into the sink and went upstairs to check the air. It was <u>overcast</u> and cold. The grass, what there was of it, looked like canvas, stiff and gray under the street light.

Snow lay in piles beside the walk. A car went by. He heard sand under the tires. He let himself imagine what it might be like tomorrow, geese beating the air over his head, shotgun plunging against his shoulder.

Then he locked the door and went downstairs.

In bed they tried to read. But both of them fell asleep, she first, letting the magazine sink to the quilt.

It was the baby's cries that woke him up.

The light was on out there, and the girl was standing next to the crib rocking the baby in her arms. She put the baby down, turned out the light, and came back to the bed.

He heard the baby cry. This time the girl stayed where she was. The baby cried <u>fitfully</u> and stopped. The boy listened, then dozed. But the baby's cries woke him again. The living-room light was burning. He sat up and turned on the lamp.

I don't know what's wrong, the girl said, walking back and forth with the baby. I've changed her and fed her, but she keeps on crying. I'm so tired I'm afraid I might drop her.

You come back to bed, the boy said. I'll hold her for a while.

He got up and took the baby, and the girl went to lie down again.

Just rock her for a few minutes, the girl said from the bedroom. Maybe she'll go back to sleep.

The boy sat on the sofa and held the baby. He jiggled it in his lap until he got its eyes to close, his own eyes closing right along. He rose carefully and put the baby back in the crib.

It was a quarter to four, which gave him forty-five minutes. He crawled into bed and dropped off. But a few minutes later the baby was crying again, and this time they both got up.

The boy did a terrible thing. He swore.

For God's sake, what's the matter with you? the girl said to the boy. Maybe she's sick or something. Maybe we shouldn't have given her the bath.

The boy picked up the baby. The baby kicked its feet and smiled.

Look, the boy said, I really don't think there's anything wrong with her.

How do you know that? the girl said. Here, let me have her. I know I ought to give her something, but I don't know what it's supposed to be.

The girl put the baby down again. The boy and the girl looked at the baby, and the baby began to cry.

The girl took the baby. Baby, baby, the girl said with tears in her eyes.

Probably it's something on her stomach, the boy said.

The girl didn't answer. She went on rocking the baby, paying no attention to the boy.

The boy waited. He went to the kitchen and put on water for coffee. He drew his woolen underwear on over his shorts and T-shirt, buttoned up, then got into his clothes.

What are you doing? the girl said.

Going hunting, the boy said.

I don't think you should, she said. I don't want to be left alone with her like this.

Carl's planning on me going, the boy said. We've planned it.

I don't care about what you and Carl planned, she said. And I don't care about Carl, either. I don't even know Carl.

You've met Carl before. You know him, the boy said. What do you mean you don't know him?

That's not the point and you know it, the girl said.

What is the point? the boy said. The point is we planned it.

The girl said, I'm your wife. This is your baby. She's sick or something. Look at her. Why else is she crying?

I know you're my wife, the boy said.

The girl began to cry. She put the baby back in the crib. But the baby started up again. The girl dried her eyes on the sleeve of her nightgown and picked the baby up.

The boy laced up his boots. He put on his shirt, his sweater, his coat. The kettle whistled on the stove in the kitchen.

You're going to have to choose, the girl said. Carl or us. I mean it.

What do you mean? the boy said.

You heard what I said, the girl said. If you want a family, you're going to have to choose.

They stared at each other. Then the boy took up his hunting gear and went outside. He started the car. He went around to the car windows and, making a job of it, scraped away the ice.

He turned off the motor and sat awhile. And then he got out and went back inside.

The living-room light was on. The girl was asleep on the bed. The baby was asleep beside her.

The boy took off his boots. Then he took off everything else. In his socks and his long underwear, he sat on the sofa and read the Sunday paper.

The girl and the baby slept on. After a while, the boy went to the kitchen and started frying bacon.

The girl came out in her robe and put her arms around the boy.

Hey, the boy said.

I'm sorry, the girl said.

It's all right, the boy said.

I didn't mean to snap like that.

It was my fault, he said.

You sit down, the girl said. How does a waffle sound with bacon?

Sounds great, the boy said.

She took the bacon out of the pan and made waffle batter. He sat at the table and watched her move around the kitchen.

She put a plate in front of him with bacon, a waffle. He spread butter and poured syrup. But when he started to cut, he turned the plate into his lap.

I don't believe it, he said, jumping up from the table.

If you could see yourself, the girl said.

The boy looked down at himself, at everything stuck to his underwear.

I was starved, he said, shaking his head.

You were starved, she said, laughing.

He peeled off the woolen underwear and threw it at the bathroom door. Then he opened his arms and the girl moved into them.

We won't fight anymore, she said.

The boy said, We won't.

He gets up from his chair and refills their glasses.

That's it, he says. End of story. I admit it's not much of a story.

I was interested, she says.

He shrugs and carries his drink over to the window. It's dark now but still snowing.

Things change, he says. I don't know how they do. But they do without your realizing it or wanting them to.

Yes, that's true, only——But she does not finish what she started.

She drops the subject. In the window's reflection he sees her study her nails. Then she raises her head. Speaking brightly, she asks if he is going to show her the city, after all.

He says, Put your boots on and let's go.

But he stays by the window, remembering. They had laughed. They had leaned on each other and laughed until the tears had come, while everything else—the cold, and where he'd go in it—was outside, for a while anyway.

PRIMARY
Sources
AN
INTERVIEW

When Raymond Carver was interviewed by *The Paris Review* in 1983, he was asked, "What are your writing habits like? Are you always working on a story?" This was his reply.

"Paddlewheel of Days"

When I'm writing, I write every day. It's lovely when that's happening. One day dovetailing into the next. Sometimes I don't even know what day of the week it is. The "paddlewheel of days," John Ashbery has called it. When I'm not writing, like now, when I'm tied up with teaching duties as I have been the last while, it's as if I've never written a word or had any desire to write. I fall into bad habits. I stay up too late and sleep in too long. But it's okay. I've learned to be patient and to bide my time. I had to learn that a long time ago. Patience. If I believed in signs, I suppose my sign would be the sign of the turtle. I write in fits and starts. But when I'm writing, I put in a lot of hours at the desk, ten or twelve or fifteen hours at a stretch, day after day. I love that, when that's happening. Much of this work time, understand, is given over to revising and rewriting. There's not much that I like better than to take a story that I've had around the house for a while and work it over again. It's the same with the poems I write. I'm in no hurry to send something off just after I write it, and I sometimes keep it around the house for months doing this or that to it, taking this out and putting that in. It doesn't take that long to do the first draft of the story, that usually happens in one sitting, but it does take a while to do the various versions of the story. I've done as many as twenty or thirty drafts of a story. Never less than ten or twelve drafts. It's instructive, and heartening both, to look at the early drafts of great writers. I'm thinking of the photographs of galleys belonging to Tolstoy, to name one writer who loved to revise. I mean, I don't know if he loved it or not, but he did a great deal of it. He was always revising, right down to the time of page proofs. He went through and rewrote *War and Peace* eight times and was still making corrections in the galleys. Things like this should hearten every writer whose first drafts are dreadful, like mine are.

—Raymond Carver

MAKING MEANINGS

First Thoughts

1. What was your emotional reaction to "Everything Stuck to Him"?

Shaping Interpretations

2. What is the effect of not giving names to the main characters? Why do you think Carver uses the terms *boy* and *girl* rather than *man* and *woman* or *father* and *mother*?

3. How would you describe the main **conflict** between the husband and wife in the inner story?

4. What thoughts and emotions do you think the boy experienced as he "sat awhile" in the car?

5. The man, having told the tale of the boy and the girl, says that "things change." What has changed since the time of the inner story? What has the man discovered?

6. Near the end of the story, after the man offers statements about change, the woman replies "Yes, that's true, only——" She does not finish. What do you think she intended to say, and why did she stop?

7. The story's **title** refers to an incident in the inner story. Explain how the title also refers to something much more important to the man.

Challenging the Text

8. As Carver says in Primary Sources on page 1032, his **style** is the result of much revising. What scenes, speeches, or comments do you think might have been deleted from earlier drafts of this story? Do you think Carver should have provided more details? For ideas, refer to the notes you made while reading.

Reading Check

a. What is the **setting** and who are the **characters** in the **frame story**—the introductory narrative within which a character proceeds to tell a story (the **inner story**)?

b. What is the **setting** and who are the main **characters** in the inner story? Which characters appear in both stories?

c. What happened during the night when the baby kept crying?

d. What promise did the couple make on Sunday morning?

CHOICES:
Building Your Portfolio

Writer's Notebook
1. Collecting Ideas for an Evaluation

One strategy you might use in evaluating a text is to consider the reading experience of others. Interview three or four class members who have read "Everything Stuck to Him," and record their opinions of Carver's **characters, themes,** and **style.** Did you learn from their opinions? Save your notes for possible use in the Writer's Workshop on page 1181.

Interpreting a Story
2. Major or Minor?

Early on, the man says the inner story involves the woman, "but only in a minor way." Do you take this comment at face value, or is it an **understatement,** a statement that downplays the importance or magnitude of something? Explain your opinion in a short essay, defending it with evidence from the text.

Creative Writing
3. Words Unspoken

Write a **monologue** revealing the unspoken thoughts and feelings of one of the characters in "Everything Stuck to Him." Use the personal pronoun *I.* Choose one of the following scenes in the story to step into the character's mind: (a) the girl sitting up alone with the crying baby, (b) the boy sitting alone in the car, or (c) the woman looking at her fingernails after hearing the story.

UPI/Bettmann.

Elizabeth Bishop

(1911–1979)

A "poet's poet," Elizabeth Bishop has been, for many important poets of our time, an acknowledged master of the highest art and most meticulous craft. She has also been an unacknowledged inspiration for many others still trying to solve the mystery of her impenetrable simplicity. Her poetry has won wide formal recognition, including a Pulitzer Prize for *Poems: North and South—A Cold Spring* (1955) and a National Book Award for *Complete Poems* (1969).

Born in Worcester, Massachusetts, Bishop spent her early years in a Nova Scotia village—a childhood marked by the early death of her father and darkened by the long illness of her mother. These circumstances, in effect, made her an orphan whose upbringing was entrusted to relatives.

At the time of her mother's death in a psychiatric hospital, Bishop was a student at Vassar College. After graduation, she embarked on a career quietly devoted to poetry and, by means of a private income, to travels. During these travels, she discovered two places congenial enough to detain her for years—Key West, Florida, and Rio de Janeiro. *Questions of Travel* (1965), the title she gave to one of her books, might serve as an index to the story of a life told in poems that are always "letters from abroad." In these poems, places—near or far—provide temporary settings for an endless inquiry into the nature of perception and reality.

In the final years of her life, Bishop lived in a condominium on a Boston Harbor wharf and spent her summers on an island off the coast of Maine. These changes of scene came about when her close friend Robert Lowell (page 948) became ill, and Harvard University invited her to take over the classes he had been scheduled to teach. She continued to teach at Harvard until her death.

A shy woman with a taste for the exotic as well as a love of the ordinary, Bishop surrounded herself with artifacts acquired in the course of her travels. She conducted herself with a scrupulous conventionality much at odds with the audacity and profundity of her imagination. Her poems most truly reveal her character: a combination of the conservatism and moral rectitude many associate with "the North" and the casual sensuousness and cheerfully untidy sprawl many associate with nature and the everyday outdoor life of "the South." For Elizabeth Bishop, geography was less a matter of maps and place names than of states of mind and areas of feeling.

go.hrw.com
LE0 11-19

Before You Read

THE FISH

Make the Connection

Creature Teachers

Since ancient times, writers and storytellers have used creatures from the natural world to illustrate all aspects of human behavior, from the wisest to the most absurd. Ancient Greek myths, Aesop's fables, and Grimms' fairy tales contain famous examples. American literature also includes many notable examples, such as "The Chambered Nautilus" by Oliver Wendell Holmes (page 189) and *Moby-Dick; or The Whale* by Herman Melville (page 313).

Quickwrite

Read the first nine lines of the poem, and then stop: Write what you predict the poem's speaker will do with the fish.

Elements of Literature

Personification

A metaphor is a comparison between two unlike things. **Personification** is a kind of metaphor in which a nonhuman thing or quality is talked about as if it were human. It may be given human feelings, thoughts, or attitudes. In the poem that follows, the speaker uses many metaphors and similes to describe the fish. Watch for instances of personification.

The Fish

Elizabeth Bishop

I caught a tremendous fish
and held him beside the boat
half out of water, with my hook
fast in a corner of his mouth.
5 He didn't fight.
He hadn't fought at all.
He hung a grunting weight,
battered and venerable
and homely. Here and there
10 his brown skin hung in strips
like ancient wall-paper,
and its pattern of darker brown
was like wall-paper:
shapes like full-blown roses
15 stained and lost through age.
He was speckled with barnacles,
fine rosettes of lime,
and infested
with tiny white sea-lice,
20 and underneath two or three
rags of green weed hung down.
While his gills were breathing in
the terrible oxygen
—the frightening gills
25 fresh and crisp with blood,
that can cut so badly—
I thought of the coarse white flesh
packed in like feathers,
the big bones and the little bones,
30 the dramatic reds and blacks
of his shiny entrails,
and the pink swim-bladder
like a big peony.
I looked into his eyes
35 which were far larger than mine
but shallower, and yellowed,
the irises backed and packed
with tarnished tinfoil
seen through the lenses
40 of old scratched isinglass.°
They shifted a little, but not
to return my stare.

40. isinglass (ī′zin·glas′): mica, glasslike mineral that crystallizes in thin layers.

—It was more like the tipping
of an object toward the light.
45 I admired his sullen face,
the mechanism of his jaw,
and then I saw
that from his lower lip
—if you could call it a lip—
50 grim, wet, and weapon-like,
hung five old pieces of fish-line,
or four and a wire leader
with the swivel still attached,
with all their five big hooks
55 grown firmly in his mouth.
A green line, frayed at the end
where he broke it, two heavier lines,
and a fine black thread
still crimped from the strain and snap
60 when it broke and he got away.
Like medals with their ribbons
frayed and wavering,
a five-haired beard of wisdom
trailing from his aching jaw.
65 I stared and stared
and victory filled up
the little rented boat,
from the pool of bilge
where oil had spread a rainbow
70 around the rusted engine
to the bailer rusted orange,
the sun-cracked thwarts,
the oarlocks on their strings,
the gunnels—until everything
75 was rainbow, rainbow, rainbow!
And I let the fish go.

Leaping Trout (1889) by Winslow Homer.
Watercolor on paper (14″ × 19¾″).

Portland Museum of Art, Portland, Maine. Bequest of Charles Shipman
Payson (1988.55.7). Photo by Melville McLean.

MAKING MEANINGS

First Thoughts

1. Did the ending of "The Fish" surprise you? (Review the prediction you made in your Quickwrite notes.) Explain.

Shaping Interpretations

2. As the speaker examines the fish, a series of **similes** and **metaphors** are used to describe it. Find at least six figures of speech in lines 1–40 that help you see the fish.

3. Identify the two figures of speech in lines 61–64 that **personify** the fish. How would you characterize the type of person these comparisons suggest?

4. As the speaker stares at the fish, "victory filled up" the boat. What does this mean? Whose "victory" is it, and who or what was the enemy?

5. What clues suggest that the fish might have **symbolic** meaning? What might it symbolize?

6. As the speaker thinks "rainbow, rainbow, rainbow," she sees the pool of oil, the "rusted engine," and the "sun-cracked thwarts" in a totally new way. Why do you think she lets the fish go?

Connecting with the Text

7. Have you ever experienced a moment when the ordinary suddenly seemed full of beauty and wonder? Describe your experience.

8. What do you think of the speaker's decision to let the old fish go? What would you have done?

CHOICES:
Building Your Portfolio

Writer's Notebook

1. Collecting Ideas for an Evaluation

Comparing "The Fish" to another literary work could be an effective strategy for arriving at an evaluation of this

poem. List several American works that center around the conflict between a main character and an animal, such as Ernest Hemingway's *The Old Man and the Sea* or William Faulkner's "The Bear." Jot down your thoughts on **themes, plots, characters,** or **images** that each work might have in common with Bishop's "The Fish," or tell how each work might be different. Keep your notes for possible use in the Writer's Workshop on page 1181.

Analyzing a Poem
2. What Happened?

The first line of "The Fish" is a simple statement: "I caught a tremendous fish." So is the last line: "And I let the fish go." Between the moment the speaker announces the catch and the moment the fish is let go, something important happens, and that is what the poem is all about. Make a list of the speaker's actions in the poem. Then, in a brief essay, recount these actions in chronological order. At the conclusion of your essay, identify the moment when something happens that makes the speaker give up what most other fishers would be only too happy to keep. Explain this moment of discovery in a few sentences.

Creative Writing
3. A Fish's Story

Write a short poem telling the poem's story from the fish's point of view. You might begin with the line "I was caught," and end with the line "I was let go." How does the fish feel about being caught? about being set free? What does the fish think of the speaker? Try to imitate the style of "The Fish."

Joy Harjo
(1951–   )

And I write it to you
at this moment
never being able to get
the essence
    the true breath
in words, because we exist
not in words, but in the motion
set off by them. . . .

—from "Motion"

© Paul Abdoo.

Joy Harjo is a poet who puts words in their place, who doesn't let them take over life itself. Stymied, she says, by the limitations of language, she has written that "all poets / understand the final uselessness of words." Nevertheless, she produces vibrant poetry and screenplays, teaches Native American literature and creative writing, edits poetry journals, and holds a master's degree from the University of Iowa Writers' Workshop.

Harjo is mostly of mixed Muscogee Creek and Cherokee descent. She grew up in Oklahoma in difficult circumstances, as her divorced mother struggled to feed and clothe four children. Partly in response to the poverty and frustration of her mother's life, Harjo has said, she "wanted something different" for herself and for her son and her daughter. "I obtained two degrees as a single mother. I wrote poetry, screenplays, became a professor, and tried to live a life that would be a positive influence for both of my children." In addition to being a poet, the multitalented Harjo is an editor, filmmaker, painter, and jazz saxophonist.

Harjo's first collection of poems, *The Last Song,* appeared in 1975, when she was still a student at the University of New Mexico. Her 1983 volume, *She Had Some Horses,* met with particular acclaim, and she issued another poetry collection, *In Mad Love and War,* in 1990. Her ability to invest the contemporary scene with American Indian myths is evident in *The Woman Who Fell from the Sky* (1994), a book accompanied by an audiocassette of Harjo reading her words.

Harjo's work is rooted in the past and the present of her fellow Native Americans. She has written that "my work in this life has to do with reclaiming the memory stolen from our peoples when we were dispossessed from our lands east of the Mississippi; it has to do with restoring us. I am proud of our history." As she asks in her poem "Anchorage,"

who would believe
the fantastic and terrible story of all of our
    survival
those who were never meant to survive?

As an American Indian and as a contemporary woman, Harjo uses poetry as a vehicle for moving beyond survival to success. She writes, she tells us, because "if Indian people, Indian women, keep silent, then we will disappear."

Make the Connection

Connected

In this age of isolated computer modems, the impersonal information superhighway, and lonely flickering TV screens, it is easy to overlook the many ways we can connect with fellow humans and with the world around us. One of the main functions of poets through the ages has been to remind us of connections we have forgotten or take for granted and to show us new connections.

Quickwrite

Freewrite all the associations you make with the word *connection*. How many possible connections can human beings make with one another and with the world around them?

Remember

Joy Harjo

Remember the sky that you were born under,
know each of the stars' stories.
Remember the moon, know who she is.
Remember the suns' birth at dawn, that is the
5   strongest point of time. Remember sundown
and the giving away to night.
Remember your birth, how your mother struggled
to give you form and breath. You are evidence of
her life, and her mother's, and hers.
10   Remember your father. He is your life, also.
Remember the earth whose skin you are:
red earth, black earth, yellow earth, white earth
brown earth, we are earth.
Remember the plants, trees, animal life who all have their
15   tribes, their families, their histories, too. Talk to them,
listen to them. They are alive poems.
Remember the wind. Remember her voice. She knows the
origin of this universe.
Remember that you are all people and that all people
20   are you.
Remember that you are this universe and that this
universe is you.
Remember that all is in motion, is growing, is you.
Remember that language comes from this.
25   Remember the dance that language is, that life is.
Remember.

Sun (1943) by Arthur G. Dove. Wax emulsion on canvas (24″ × 32″).

National Museum of American Art, Washington, D.C. Bequest of Suzanne M. Smith.
By permission of D. Mullett Smith Trust. © 1976 by Suzanne Mullett Smith. Courtesy Art Resource, NY.

MAKING MEANINGS

First Thoughts

1. Which passage in the poem had the strongest effect on you? Why?

Shaping Interpretations

2. Who do you think is the **speaker** of "Remember"? Whom is the speaker addressing?

3. How would you state the main **theme** of the poem in your own words?

4. "Remember" includes several instances of **personification** (a figure of speech in which an object or animal is given human attributes). Identify two such instances, and explain what they add to the poem.

5. Identify the **refrain** of the poem. What does it contribute to the poem's message?

Connecting with the Text

6. The speaker asks the reader to talk to and listen to plants, trees, and animal life. Does this request make sense to you? Explain, referring to your Quickwrite notes.

David L. Brown/The Stock Market

CHOICES: Building Your Portfolio

Writer's Notebook

1. Collecting Ideas for an Evaluation

When writing an evaluation, you can cite your own experience to support your judgment of a text. Jot down experiences you can recall that relate to Harjo's "Remember." Do any match the speaker's? Based on your own experience, which of the speaker's requests could you follow easily? Which would be more difficult or even impossible to follow? Save your notes for possible use in the Writer's Workshop on page 1181.

Comparing Texts

2. The American Tradition

Ralph Waldo Emerson, born in a very different era, almost 150 years before Joy Harjo, shares with her a keen appreciation of the natural world. In a short essay, compare the messages of Harjo's "Remember" and the excerpt from Emerson's *Nature* (page 219). How are they similar and different?

Creative Writing / Speaking and Listening

3. All Your Yesterdays

Write a "Remember" poem in which you relate some of your own memories and experiences. Start each line or stanza with "Remember" or "I remember."

Oral Interpretation

4. Joy's Dance

Prepare the poem for an oral reading. You will have to decide if you will read the poem alone, or use solo voices and a chorus. Decide how you will pace your reading and how you will vary the tone of your voice. Be sure to ask your audience for evaluations.

Maxine Hong Kingston

(1940–   )

© Nancy Crampton.

Maxine Hong Kingston burst onto the literary scene in 1976 with an extraordinary and innovative book—*The Woman Warrior: Memoirs of a Girlhood Among Ghosts.* Kingston, who was born in California of Chinese immigrant parents, uses a mixture of autobiography, myth, poetic meditation, and fiction to convey her memories and feelings about growing up in a strange world (the United States) populated by what she and her family thought of as white-skinned "ghosts."

The book received immediate acclaim. William McPherson of the *Washington Post* wrote: "*The Woman Warrior* is a strange, sometimes savagely terrifying and, in the literal sense, wonderful story about growing up caught between two highly sophisticated and utterly alien cultures, both vivid, often menacing, and equally mysterious." Paul Gray said in *Time:* "Exiles and refugees tell sad stories of the life they left behind. Even sadder, sometimes, is the muteness of their children. They are likely to find the old ways and old language excess baggage, especially if their adopted homeland is the United States, where the race is to the swift and the adaptable. Thus a heritage of centuries can die in a generation of embarrassed silence. *The Woman Warrior* gives that silence a voice."

When *The Woman Warrior* won the National Book Critics Circle Award for general nonfiction in 1976, Kingston gained national attention. The suddenness of her appearance as an important literary figure was startling.

Where had Kingston been until the age of thirty-six? Named for an American woman in the gambling house where her father worked for a time, Maxine Hong grew up in the Chinatown of Stockton, California. She earned a B.A. from the University of California at Berkeley in 1962 and married the actor Earll Kingston. After their son was born, the Kingstons lived in Hawaii for a time, where Maxine taught English at the high school and college levels, before returning to California.

In 1980, Kingston published a companion piece to *The Woman Warrior,* a kind of ancestral history called *China Men.* The critic Susan Currier has described this book as "a sort of vindication of all the Chinese who helped build America but who were rewarded with abuse and neglect." In 1988, Kingston published an extravagant novel called *Tripmaster Monkey: His Fake Book,* blending Chinese history and myth and vivid storytelling in the adventures of a young Chinese American named Wittman Ah Sing. The noted novelist Anne Tyler called *Tripmaster Monkey* "a novel of satisfying complexity and bite and verve." In the 1990s, Kingston taught creative writing at the University of California at Berkeley and worked on a book of nonfiction.

Despite the attention given to her books, Kingston has remained relatively private. She seldom gives interviews or appears at public readings. In her two memoirs, she does not answer all of the personal questions raised by her writing. In the selection that follows, even a careful reader will not be able to decide what is truth, what is fiction, and what is simply left unsaid. This ambiguity gives Kingston's work much of its haunting quality.

Before You Read
THE GIRL WHO WOULDN'T TALK

Make the Connection
Things Left Unspoken
It happens just about every day to all of us: For one reason or another, we don't tell others about something important we know or feel. Out of self-doubt, politeness, love, fear, or many other reasons, we don't express in conversation certain thoughts or feelings that are near to us. Instead, we sometimes express them in writing, painting, dance, song, or some other art form.

Reading Skills and Strategies

Drawing Inferences About Characters
As you read "The Girl Who Wouldn't Talk," take notes on the author's **characterization** of the silent girl and the narrator. Then, stop near the end of page 1049, and write down what you think the silent girl is not saying—that is, what her unexpressed thoughts and feelings are. You might also jot down what you think the *narrator* is not saying.

Elements of Literature
Conflict
Conflict—the struggle between opposing forces or characters in a story—can be either external or internal. **External conflict** can take many forms. For example, it can involve two people, a person and a force of nature, a person and a machine, or a person and a society or community. **Internal conflict** involves opposing forces within a person's mind. Kingston's story presents both external and internal conflicts centering around childhood cruelty, a problem that knows no cultural or linguistic barriers.

> **C**onflict is the struggle between opposing forces or characters in a story.
>
> *For more on Conflict, see page 607 and the Handbook of Literary Terms.*

Background
The Chinese American family in this extract from *The Woman Warrior* lives in Stockton, California. Just before the episode starts, the narrator talks about speech and Chinese voices, which she says are louder than American voices. Describing her own voice, the narrator says: "You could hear splinters in my voice, bones rubbing jagged against one another. I was loud, though. I was glad I didn't whisper."

The "ghosts" mentioned by the narrator are white Americans, who seemed so strange to this Chinese family.

The Girl Who Wouldn't Talk

from The Woman Warrior

Maxine Hong Kingston

Normal Chinese women's voices are strong and bossy. We American-Chinese girls had to whisper to make ourselves American-feminine. Apparently we whispered even more softly than the Americans. Once a year the teachers referred my sister and me to speech therapy, but our voices would straighten out, unpredictably normal, for the therapists. Some of us gave up, shook our heads, and said nothing, not one word. Some of us could not even shake our heads. At times shaking my head no is more self-assertion than I can manage. Most of us eventually found some voice, however faltering. We invented an American-feminine speaking personality, except for that one girl who could not speak up even in Chinese school.

She was a year older than I and was in my class for twelve years. During all those years she read aloud but would not talk. Her older sister was usually beside her; their parents kept the older daughter back to protect the younger one. They were six and seven years old when they began school. Although I had flunked kindergarten, I was the same age as most other students in our class; my parents had probably lied about my age, so I had had a head start and came out even. My younger sister was in the class below me; we were normal ages and normally separated. The parents of the quiet girl, on the other hand, protected both daughters. When it sprinkled, they kept them home from school. The girls did not work for a living the way we did. But in other ways we were the same.

We were similar in sports. We held the bat on our shoulders until we walked to first base. (You got a strike only when you actually struck at the ball.) Sometimes the pitcher wouldn't bother to throw to us. "Automatic walk," the other children would call, sending us on our way. By fourth or fifth grade, though, some of us would try to hit the ball. "Easy out," the other kids would say. I hit the ball a couple of times. Baseball was nice in that there was a definite spot to run to after hitting the ball. Basketball confused me because when I caught the ball I didn't know whom to throw it to. "Me. Me," the kids would be yelling. "Over here." Suddenly it would occur to me I hadn't memorized which ghosts were on my team and which were on the other. When the kids said, "Automatic walk," the girl who was quieter than I kneeled with one end of the bat in each hand and placed it carefully on the plate. Then she dusted her hands as she walked to first base, where she rubbed her hands softly, fingers spread. She always got tagged out before second base. She would whisper-read but not talk. Her whisper was as soft as if she had no muscles. She seemed to be breathing from a distance. I heard no anger or tension.

I joined in at lunchtime when the other students, the Chinese too, talked about whether or not she was mute, although obviously she was not if she could read aloud. People told how *they* had tried *their* best to be friendly. *They* said hello, but if she refused to answer, well, they didn't see why they had to say hello anymore. She had no friends of her own but followed her sister everywhere, although people and she herself probably thought I was her friend. I also followed her sister about, who was fairly normal. She was almost two years older and read more than anyone else.

I hated the younger sister, the quiet one. I hated her when she was the last chosen for her team and I, the last chosen for my team. I hated her for her China doll hair cut. I hated her at music time for the wheezes that came out of her plastic flute.

One afternoon in the sixth grade (that year I was arrogant with talk, not knowing there were going to be high school dances and college seminars to set me back), I and my little sister and the quiet girl and her big sister stayed late after school for some reason. The cement was cooling, and the tetherball poles made shadows across the gravel. The hooks at the rope ends were clinking against the poles. We shouldn't have been so late; there was laundry work to do and Chinese school to get to by 5:00. The last time we had stayed late, my mother had phoned the police and told them we had been kidnapped by bandits. The radio stations broadcast our descriptions. I had to get home before she did that again. But sometimes if you loitered long enough in the schoolyard, the other children would have gone home and you could play with the equipment before the office took it away. We were chasing one another through the playground and in and out of the basement, where the playroom and lavatory were. During air raid drills (it was during the Korean War, which you knew about because every day the front page of the newspaper printed a map of Korea with the top part red and going up and down like a window shade), we curled up in this basement. Now everyone was gone. The playroom was army green and had nothing in it but a long trough with drinking spigots in rows. Pipes across the ceiling led to the drinking fountains and to the toilets in the next room. When someone flushed you could hear the water and other matter, which the children named, running inside the big pipe above the drinking spigots. There was one playroom for girls next to the girls' lavatory and one playroom for boys next to the boys' lavatory. The stalls were open and the toilets had no lids, by which we knew that ghosts have no sense of shame or privacy.

Inside the playroom the lightbulbs in cages had already been turned off. Daylight came in x-patterns through the caging at the windows. I looked out and, seeing no one in the schoolyard, ran outside to climb the fire escape upside down, hanging on to the metal stairs with fingers and toes.

I did a flip off the fire escape and ran across the schoolyard. The day was a great eye, and it was not paying much attention to me now. I could disappear with the sun; I could turn quickly sideways and slip into a different world. It seemed I could run faster at this time, and by evening I would be able to fly. As the afternoon wore on we could run into the forbidden places—the boys' big yard, the boys' playroom. We could go into the boys' lavatory and look at the urinals. The only time during school hours I had

crossed the boys' yard was when a flatbed truck with a giant thing covered with canvas and tied down with ropes had parked across the street. The children had told one another that it was a gorilla in captivity; we couldn't decide whether the sign said "Trail of the Gorilla" or "Trial of the Gorilla." The thing was as big as a house. The teachers couldn't stop us from hysterically rushing to the fence and clinging to the wire mesh. Now I ran across the boys' yard clear to the Cyclone fence and thought about the hair that I had seen sticking out of the canvas. It was going to be summer soon, so you could feel that freedom coming on too.

I ran back into the girls' yard, and there was the quiet sister all by herself. I ran past her, and she followed me into the girls' lavatory. My footsteps rang hard against cement and tile because of the taps I had nailed into my shoes. Her footsteps were soft, padding after me. There was no one in the lavatory but the two of us. I ran all around the rows of twenty-five open stalls to make sure of that. No sisters. I think we must have been playing hide-and-go-seek. She was not good at hiding by herself and usually followed her sister; they'd hide in the same place. They must have gotten separated. In this growing twilight, a child could hide and never be found.

I stopped abruptly in front of the sinks, and she came running toward me before she could stop herself, so that she almost collided with me. I walked closer. She backed away, puzzlement, then alarm in her eyes.

"You're going to talk," I said, my voice steady and normal, as it is when talking to the familiar, the weak, and the small. "I am going to make you talk, you sissy-girl." She stopped backing away and stood fixed.

I looked into her face so I could hate it close up. She wore black bangs, and her cheeks were pink and white. She was baby-soft. I thought that I could put my thumb on

WORDS TO OWN
loitered (loit′ərd) v.: spent time; hung around.

her nose and push it bonelessly in, indent her face. I could poke dimples into her cheeks. I could work her face around like dough. She stood still, and I did not want to look at her face anymore; I hated fragility. I walked around her, looked her up and down the way the Mexican and Negro girls did when they fought, so tough. I hated her weak neck, the way it did not support her head but let it droop; her head would fall backward. I stared at the curve of her nape. I wished I was able to see what my own neck looked like from the back and sides. I hoped it did not look like hers; I wanted a stout neck. I grew my hair long to hide it in case it was a flower-stem neck. I walked around to the front of her to hate her face some more.

I reached up and took the fatty part of her cheek, not dough, but meat, between my thumb and finger. This close, and I saw no pores. "Talk," I said. "Are you going to talk?" Her skin was fleshy, like squid out of which the glassy blades of bones had been pulled. I wanted tough skin, hard brown skin. I had callused my hands; I had scratched dirt to blacken the nails, which I cut straight across to make stubby fingers. I gave her face a squeeze. "Talk." When I let go, the pink rushed back into my white thumbprint on her skin. I walked around to her side. "Talk!" I shouted into the side of her head. Her straight hair hung, the same all these years, no ringlets or braids or permanents. I squeezed her other cheek. "Are you? Huh? Are you going to talk?" She tried to shake her head, but I had hold of her face. She had no muscles to jerk away. Her skin seemed to stretch. I let go in horror. What if it came away in my hand? "No, huh?" I said, rubbing the touch of her off my fingers. "Say 'No,' then," I said. I gave her another pinch and a twist. "Say 'No.'" She shook her head, her straight hair turning with her head, not swinging side to side like the pretty girls'. She was so neat. Her neatness bothered me. I hated the way she folded the wax paper from her lunch; she did not wad her brown paper bag and her school papers. I hated her clothes—the blue pastel cardigan, the white blouse with the collar that lay flat over the cardigan, the homemade flat, cotton skirt she wore when everybody else was wearing flared skirts. I hated pastels; I would wear black always. I squeezed again, harder, even though her cheek had a weak rubbery feeling I did not like. I squeezed one cheek, then the other, back and forth until the tears ran out of her eyes as if I had pulled them out. "Stop crying," I said, but although she habitually followed me around, she did not obey. Her eyes dripped; her nose dripped. She wiped her eyes with her papery fingers. The skin on her hands and arms seemed powdery-dry, like tracing paper, onion paper. I hated her fingers. I could snap them like breadsticks. I pushed her hands down. "Say 'Hi,'" I said. "'Hi.' Like that. Say your name. Go ahead. Say it. Or are you stupid? You're so stupid, you don't know your own name, is that it? When I say, 'What's your name?' you just blurt it out, O.K.? What's your name?" Last year the whole class had laughed at a boy who couldn't fill out a form because he didn't know his father's name. The teacher sighed, exasperated and was very sarcastic, "Don't you notice things? What does your mother call him?" she said. The class laughed at how dumb he was not to notice things. "She calls him father of me," he said. Even we laughed although we knew that his mother did not call his father by name, and a son does not know his father's name. We laughed and were relieved that our parents had had the foresight to tell us some names we could give the teachers. "If you're not stupid," I said to the quiet girl, "what's your name?" She shook her head, and some hair caught in the tears; wet black hair stuck to the side of the pink and white face. I reached up (she was taller than I) and took a strand of hair. I pulled it. "Well, then,

---

WORDS TO OWN

nape (nāp) *n.*: back of the neck.

habitually (hə·bich′ōō·əl·lē) *adv.*: usually; by habit.

sarcastic (sär·kas′tik) *adj.*: scornful; mocking.

---

let's honk your hair," I said. "Honk. Honk." Then I pulled the other side—"ho-o-n-nk"—a long pull; "ho-o-n-n-nk"—a longer pull. I could see her little white ears, like white cutworms curled underneath the hair. "Talk!" I yelled into each cutworm.

I looked right at her. "I know you talk," I said. "I've heard you." Her eyebrows flew up. Something in those black eyes was startled, and I pursued it. "I was walking past your house when you didn't know I was there. I heard you yell in English and in Chinese. You weren't just talking. You were shouting. I heard you shout. You were saying, 'Where are you?' Say that again. Go ahead, just the way you did at home." I yanked harder on the hair, but steadily, not jerking. I did not want to pull it out. "Go ahead. Say, 'Where are you?' Say it loud enough for your sister to come. Call her. Make her come help you. Call her name. I'll stop if she comes. So call. Go ahead."

She shook her head, her mouth curved down, crying. I could see her tiny white teeth, baby teeth. I wanted to grow big strong yellow teeth. "You do have a tongue," I said. "So use it." I pulled the hair at her tem-ples, pulled the tears out of her eyes. "Say, 'Ow'" I said. "Just 'Ow.' Say, 'Let go.' Go ahead. Say it. I'll honk you again if you don't say, 'Let me alone.' Say, 'Leave me alone,' and I'll let you go. I will. I'll let go if you say it. You can stop this anytime you want to, you know. All you have to do is tell me to stop. Just say, 'Stop.' You're just asking for it, aren't you? You're just asking for another honk. Well then, I'll have to give you another honk. Say, 'Stop.'" But she didn't. I had to pull again and again.

Sounds did come out of her mouth, sobs, chokes, noises that were almost words. Snot ran out of her nose. She tried to wipe it on her hands, but there was too much of it. She used her sleeve. "You're disgusting," I told her. "Look at you, snot streaming down your nose, and you won't say a word to stop it. You're such a nothing." I moved behind her and pulled the hair growing out of her weak neck. I let go. I stood silent for a long time.

Then I screamed, "Talk!" I would scare the words out of her. If she had had little bound feet, the toes twisted under the balls, I would have jumped up and landed on them—crunch!—stomped on them with my iron shoes. She cried hard, sobbing aloud. "Cry, 'Mama,'" I said. "Come on. Cry, 'Mama.' Say, 'Stop it.'"

I put my finger on her pointed chin. "I don't like you. I don't like the weak little toots you make on your flute. Wheeze. Wheeze. I don't like the way you don't swing at the ball. I don't like the way you're the last one chosen. I don't like the way you can't make a fist for tetherball. Why don't you make a fist? Come on. Get tough. Come on. Throw fists." I pushed at her long hands; they swung limply at her sides. Her fingers were so long, I thought maybe they had an extra joint. They couldn't possibly make fists like other people's. "Make a fist," I said. "Come on. Just fold those fingers up; fingers on the inside, thumbs on the outside. Say something. Honk me back. You're so tall, and you let me pick on you."

"Would you like a hanky? I can't get you one with embroidery on it or crocheting along the edges, but I'll get you some toilet paper if you tell me to. Go ahead. Ask me. I'll get it for you if you ask." She did not stop crying. "Why don't you scream, 'Help'?" I suggested. "Say, 'Help.' Go ahead." She cried on. "O.K. O.K. Don't talk. Just scream, and I'll let you go. Won't that feel good? Go ahead. Like this." I screamed not too loudly. My voice hit the tile and rang it as if I had thrown a rock at it. The stalls opened wider and the toilets wider and darker. Shadows leaned at angles I had not seen before. It was very late. Maybe a janitor had locked me in with this girl for the night. Her black eyes blinked and stared, blinked and stared. I felt dizzy from hunger. We had been in this lava-tory together forever. My mother would call

- -
WORDS TO OWN
temples (tem′pəlz) n. pl.: sides of the forehead, just above and in front of the ears.
- -

The Chinese American Family

In her story, Maxine Hong Kingston mentions that the girl who wouldn't talk was supported and protected by her family. This isn't surprising, given the importance of family relationships in Chinese culture. As the Chinese American writer Leslie Li notes, solitude is not a coveted state among most Chinese people. "They love their family and friends and want them around, along with the *renao* they bring, the heat and noise of human relationships."

Family ties. In Chinese culture, "name" does not so much signify individual identity as relationship to others, such as daughter, son, aunt, uncle, and so on. In Chinese tradition, the family name is given first—for example, "Chung Connie," not the Americanized "Connie Chung"—and family members are often introduced not by their names but by their family relationships. Children may address family members not by name but as Aunt, Second Older Brother, Grandfather, and so on. In Kingston's story, a boy is laughed at in class because he doesn't know his father's name; at home, he says, his father is called only "father of me." In the story "Rules of the Game" by the Chinese American writer Amy Tan (page 1110), the character Waverly is called "Waverly" for the benefit of outsiders, but at home she is "Meimei" (Little Sister).

Bridging two worlds. Ultimately, many Chinese Americans choose to integrate the cultures of both China and the United States in their family life. They embrace some traditional beliefs of their immigrant parents or grandparents, but they also take part in mainstream American traditions. They may celebrate both Chinese and American holidays, for example, or enjoy traditional Chinese foods one day, grilled steak the next. They may use American names with outsiders but their Chinese middle names at home. In addition to attending regular public or private school all day, some Chinese American children spend three or four hours at Chinese school (often held on Saturdays), where their

---

the police again if I didn't bring my sister home soon. "I'll let you go if you say just one word," I said. "You can even say 'a' or 'the,' and I'll let you go. Come on. Please." She didn't shake her head anymore, only cried steadily, so much water coming out of her. I could see the two duct holes where the tears welled out. Quarts of tears but no words. I grabbed her by the shoulder. I could feel bones. The light was coming in queerly through the frosted glass with the chicken wire embedded in it. Her crying was like an animal's—a seal's—and it echoed around the basement. "Do you want to stay here all night?" I asked. "Your mother is wondering what happened to her baby. You wouldn't want to have her mad at you. You'd better say something." I shook her shoulder. I pulled her hair again. I squeezed her face. "Come on! Talk! Talk! Talk!" She didn't seem to feel it anymore when I pulled her hair. "There's nobody here but you and me. This isn't a classroom or a playground or a crowd. I'm just one person. You can talk in front of one person. Don't make me pull harder and harder until you talk." But her hair seemed to stretch; she did not say a word. "I'm going to pull harder. Don't make me pull anymore, or your hair will come out and you're going to be bald. Do you want to be bald? You don't want to be bald, do you?"

Far away, coming from the edge of town, I

parents expect them to learn Chinese language, literature, history, and philosophy.

Reverence toward ancestors, a cornerstone of Chinese tradition, has been an important feature of traditional Chinese American family life. A memorial plaque inscribed with ancestors' names is sometimes displayed in the home, and one tradition requires family members to read the names aloud while bowing to the plaque. Some families make ritual visits to ancestors' graves each spring, honoring the spirits of the dead by bringing gifts of food and cleaning the graves. And, when the Chinese New Year arrives, families may rearrange their living quarters *feng-shui* style—that is, move the furniture around to achieve maximum harmony with nature. The belief behind *feng-shui* is that proper balancing of elements will pump *ch'i* (vital energy) throughout the home and enhance the family's experience of harmony and success during the coming year.

heard whistles blow. The cannery was changing shifts, letting out the afternoon people, and still we were here at school. It was a sad sound—work done. The air was lonelier after the sound died.

"Why won't you talk?" I started to cry. What if I couldn't stop, and everyone would want to know what happened? "Now look what you've done," I scolded. "You're going to pay for this. I want to know why. And you're going to tell me why. You don't see I'm trying to help you out, do you? Do you want to be like this, dumb (do you know what dumb means?), your whole life? Don't you ever want to be a cheerleader? Or a pompom girl? What are you going to do for a living? Yeah, you're going to have to work because you can't be a housewife. Somebody has to marry you before you can be a housewife. And you, you are a plant. Do you know that? That's all you are if you don't talk. If you don't talk, you can't have a personality. You'll have no personality and no hair. You've got to let people know you have a personality and a brain. You think somebody is going to take care of you all your stupid life? You think you'll always have your big sister? You think somebody's going to marry you, is that it? Well, you're not the type that gets dates, let alone gets married. Nobody's going to notice you. And you have to talk for interviews, speak right up in front of the boss. Don't you know that? You're so dumb. Why do I waste my time on you?" Sniffling and snorting, I couldn't stop crying and talking at the same time. I kept wiping my nose on my arm, my sweater lost somewhere (probably not worn because my mother said to wear a sweater). It seemed as if I had spent my life in that basement, doing the worst thing I had yet done to another person. "I'm doing this for your own good," I said. "Don't you dare tell anyone I've been bad to you. Talk. Please talk."

I was getting dizzy from the air I was gulping. Her sobs and my sobs were bouncing wildly off the tile, sometimes together, sometimes alternating. "I don't understand why you won't say just one word," I cried, clenching my teeth. My knees were shaking, and I hung on to her hair to stand up. Another time I'd stayed too late, I had had to walk around two Negro kids who were bonking each other's head on the concrete. I went back later to see if the concrete had cracks in it. "Look. I'll give you something if you talk. I'll give you my pencil box. I'll buy you some candy. O.K.? What do you want? Tell me. Just say it, and I'll give it to you. Just say, 'yes,' or, 'O.K.,' or, 'Baby Ruth.'" But she didn't want anything.

I had stopped pinching her cheek because I did not like the feel of her skin. I would go crazy if it came away in my hands. "I skinned her," I would have to confess.

Suddenly I heard footsteps hurrying through the basement, and her sister ran into the lavatory calling her name. "Oh, there you are," I said. "We've been waiting for you. I was only trying to teach her to talk. She wouldn't cooperate, though." Her sister went into one of the stalls and got handfuls of toilet paper and wiped her off. Then we found my sister, and we walked home together. "Your family really ought to force her to speak," I advised all the way home. "You mustn't pamper her."

The world is sometimes just, and I spent the next eighteen months sick in bed with a mysterious illness. There was no pain and no symptoms, though the middle line in my left palm broke in two. Instead of starting junior high school, I lived like the Victorian recluses[1] I read about. I had a rented hospital bed in the living room, where I watched soap operas on TV, and my family cranked me up and down. I saw no one but my family, who took good care of me. I could have no visitors, no other relatives, no villagers. My bed was against the west window, and I watched the seasons change the peach tree. I had a bell to ring for help. I used a bedpan. It was the best year and a half of my life. Nothing happened.

But one day my mother, the doctor, said, "You're ready to get up today. It's time to get up and go to school." I walked about outside to get my legs working, leaning on a staff I cut from the peach tree. The sky and trees, the sun were immense—no longer framed by a window, no longer grayed with a fly screen. I sat down on the sidewalk in amazement—the night, the stars. But at school I had to figure out again how to talk. I met again the poor girl I had tormented. She had not changed. She wore the same clothes, hair cut, and manner as when we were in elementary school, no make-up on the pink and white face, while the other Asian girls were starting to tape their eyelids. She continued to be able to read aloud. But there was hardly any reading aloud anymore, less and less as we got into high school.

I was wrong about nobody taking care of her. Her sister became a clerk-typist and stayed unmarried. They lived with their mother and father. She did not have to leave the house except to go to the movies. She was supported. She was protected by her family, as they would normally have done in China if they could have afforded it, not sent off to school with strangers, ghosts, boys.

1. **Victorian recluses:** like characters in Victorian novels who, because of some illness or incapacity, lived shut away from the world.

MAKING MEANINGS

First Thoughts

1. What is your reaction to the silent girl? How do you feel about the narrator?

Shaping Interpretations

2. The narrator's deep undercurrent of anger seems directed solely at the silent girl. What else do you think the narrator could be angry about? Is she affected by an **internal conflict**? Explain.

3. The silent girl is obviously able to speak. Review the notes you made while reading. Why do you think the girl does *not* speak? What **external** or **internal conflicts** might cause her to remain silent?

4. What inference do you draw from the fact that the narrator says that her time in bed "was the best year and a half of my life"? What discoveries about herself or about the silent girl might she have made during this time?

5. This episode comes from a chapter called "A Song for a Barbarian Reed Pipe." What could be the significance of that **title**? How is this story of the silent girl related to that title?

6. At times, Kingston's **images** can evoke powerful responses from us and can reveal the narrator's strong feelings as well. Find the images describing the silent girl's skin, her fingers, the skin of her hands and arms, her ears, and her crying. What feelings about the girl do these images reveal? How do they make you respond to the girl and to her tormentor, the narrator?

Reading Check

a. What reasons does the narrator give for hating the silent girl?

b. What do the other students think of the silent girl?

c. How does the narrator try to make the silent girl talk? (Note the physical and the psychological torments she applies.) What is the girl's response?

d. What happens to the narrator to make her say that "the world is sometimes just"?

Connecting with the Text

7. Why do you think the narrator cares so intensely about making the silent girl talk? Do her feelings strike you as believable—have you experienced or observed feelings like these?

CHOICES: Building Your Portfolio

Writer's Notebook

1. Collecting Ideas for an Evaluation

A well-written evaluation maintains a consistent and confident **tone**. Whether stating your judgment or offering evidence, express your thoughts clearly and with confidence. As practice, write several sentences evaluating the use of **imagery** in Kingston's work. Make sure your tone is crystal clear and consistent. Save your sentences for possible use in the Writer's Workshop on page 1181.

Interpreting Character

2. Tortured Tormentor

In a short essay, discuss the **character** of the narrator. As a first step, review your reading notes. Then, write about these basic elements of characterization: (a) appearance, (b) speech, (c) actions, (d) private thoughts and feelings, and (e) responses of other people to the character. Conclude by discussing your own response to the narrator.

Creative Writing

3. Time Out

The narrator says that "nothing happened" during her time sick in bed. Yet something must have happened, because one day her mother said that she was "ready" to return to school. In a brief story, reveal what you think happened to prepare the narrator to rejoin the world.

© Robert M. Lindholm.

Traveling Americans turned their journals into such classics as Henry David Thoreau's *The Maine Woods* (1864), Mark Twain's *Roughing It* (1872) and *Life on the Mississippi* (1883), and Henry James's *The American Scene* (1907). Modern writers have explored America—Jack Kerouac, in *On the Road* (1957); John Steinbeck, in *Travels with Charley* (1962); and Robert Pirsig, in *Zen and the Art of Motorcycle Maintenance* (1974). William Least Heat-Moon's *Blue Highways: A Journey into America* (1982) thus takes its place in a vital American literary tradition. In fact, the writer says that Steinbeck's *Charley* inspired him to embark on the journey described in *Blue Highways*.

William Least Heat-Moon is the pen name of William Trogdon, who is descended mainly from the Osage people in Missouri. His given name, he explains, comes from an immigrant English ancestor eight generations back, and the name Heat-Moon comes from his Osage father (William added the hyphen). "My father calls himself Heat Moon"—the name for the seventh month in the Osage calendar—"[and] my elder brother Little Heat Moon. I, coming last, am therefore Least. It has been a long lesson of a name to learn."

When Heat-Moon was thirty-eight, his first marriage was ending, and he was laid off from a teaching job. So he left Missouri in a converted van that became both transport and home. He called his van *Ghost Dancing*, after the name the Plains Indians gave to ceremonies of the 1890s

William Least Heat-Moon

(1939–   )

Some of the finest insights into American ways of life have appeared in the nonfiction accounts of travelers. As early as 1835, Alexis de Tocqueville, a visiting Frenchman, wrote *Democracy in America,* still treasured as a profound commentary on the American character.

go.hrw.com
HRW
LE0 11-19

in which they prayed for the return of their old life. And in a sense, Heat-Moon's trip was such a ceremony. "I took to the open road in search of places where change did not mean ruin and where time and men and deeds connected." At the start of the trip, he decided to use his Osage last name rather than Trogdon.

Blue Highways, the edited journal of his travels, shows that Heat-Moon found what he sought. He stayed on the back roads, the ones printed in blue on old highway maps, not the main routes printed in red. His quest took him east from Missouri to North Carolina, south to Louisiana, then west across Texas to New Mexico, north through Utah and California to Washington State, back across the northernmost boundary of the United States all the way to Maine, south again to New Jersey, and finally west back to Missouri. The roughly circular trip, he thought, "would give a purpose—to come around again."

Some contemporary travelers have found a sad, petty-minded, and materialistic America. But Heat-Moon usually liked the people he met in such places as Lookingglass and Simplicity, New Hope and New Freedom, Cutthroat Gulch and Calamity River, Why and Whynot. He found the inhabitants as vigorous, imaginative, and astonishing as the names of their towns. His journal celebrates these people— their struggles, their poverty, their spiritual wealth, and their dignity. They treated him well, and he admired them.

In 1991, Heat-Moon continued that celebration with *PrairyErth (a deep map).* Instead of offering a wide-ranging view of America, *PrairyErth* delves into the landscape and the people of one Kansas county.

Heat-Moon returned to a broader view of the United States in 1995, when he undertook an approximately 5,200-mile coast-to-coast journey of North America's inland waterways, almost all on a 22-foot cruiser named *Nikawa.* The four-month voyage began in New York and ended in Oregon. Perhaps we can look forward to a Heat-Moon celebration of America's "blue waterways" and the people who live along them.

Before You Read
FROM BLUE HIGHWAYS

Make the Connection
Discovering Harmony
"Where are you going?" We hear that question often, and the answer is usually something like "the gym" or "shopping" or "Omaha." Heat-Moon goes out to discover *harmony.* In music, harmony is the sounding of separate tones in a satisfying combination. In human experience, its definition is much more elusive. We search for harmony in our individual lives, families, communities, and nations. Perhaps the real discovery is that harmony has to be created, not found.

Quickwrite
Think about the community where you live. What's unusual or quirky about it? List some of the unconventional people, places, or things that make your community special.

Elements of Literature
Dialect
As he travels across America, Heat-Moon *listens* to the people he meets. By accurately transferring their dialects to the printed page, he lets us hear them too. **Dialect** is a way of speaking that is characteristic of a certain social group or of the inhabitants of a certain geographical area. It is an authentic link between people and the places they have made their own.

> **D**ialect is a way of speaking that is characteristic of a certain social group or of the inhabitants of a certain geographical area.
>
> *For more on Dialect, see page 512 and the Handbook of Literary Terms.*

Pee Wee's Diner, Warnerville, N.Y. (1977) by Ralph Goings. Oil on canvas (48″ × 48″).

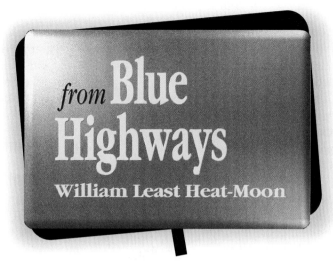

from Blue Highways

William Least Heat-Moon

Had it not been raining hard that morning on the Livingston square, I never would have learned of Nameless, Tennessee. Waiting for the rain to ease, I lay on my bunk and read the atlas to pass time rather than to see where I might go. In Kentucky were towns with fine names like Boreing, Bear Wallow, Decoy, Subtle, Mud Lick, Mummie, Neon; Belcher was just down the road from Mouthcard, and Minnie only ten miles from Mousie.

I looked at Tennessee. Turtletown eight miles from Ducktown. And also: Peavine, Wheel, Milky Way, Love Joy, Dull, Weakly, Fly, Spot, Miser Station, Only, McBurg, Peeled Chestnut, Clouds, Topsy, Isoline. And the best of all, Nameless. The logic! I was heading east, and Nameless lay forty-five miles west. I decided to go anyway.

The rain stopped, but things looked saturated, even bricks. In Gainesboro, a hill town with a square of businesses around the Jackson County Courthouse, I stopped for directions and breakfast. There is one almost infallible way to find honest food at just prices in blue-highway America: Count the wall calendars in a cafe.

No calendar: Same as an interstate pit stop.
One calendar: Preprocessed food assembled in
New Jersey.
Two calendars: Only if fish trophies present.
Three calendars: Can't miss on the farm-boy
breakfasts.
Four calendars: Try the ho-made pie too.
Five calendars: Keep it under your hat, or
they'll franchise.

One time I found a six-calendar cafe in the Ozarks, which served fried chicken, peach pie, and chocolate malts, that left me searching for another ever since. I've never seen a seven-calendar place. But old-time travelers—road men in a day when cars had running

WORDS TO OWN
saturated (sach′ə·rāt′id) *adj.*: completely soaked.
infallible (in·fal′ə·bəl) *adj.*: sure; never wrong.

boards and lunchroom windows said AIR COOLED in blue letters with icicles dripping from the tops—those travelers have told me the golden legends of seven-calendar cafes.

To the rider of back roads, nothing shows the tone, the voice of a small town more quickly than the breakfast grill or the five-thirty tavern. Much of what the people do and believe and share is evident then. The City Cafe in Gainesboro had three calendars that I could see from the walk. Inside were no interstate refugees with full bladders and empty tanks, no wild-eyed children just released from the glassy cell of a station-wagon backseat, no long-haul truckers talking in CB numbers.[1] There were only townspeople wearing overalls, or catalog-order suits with five-and-dime ties, or uniforms. That is, here were farmers and mill hands, bank clerks, the dry goods merchant, a policeman, and chiropractor's receptionist. Because it was Saturday, there were also mothers and children.

I ordered my standard on-the-road breakfast: two eggs up, hash browns, tomato juice. The waitress, whose pale, almost translucent skin shifted hue in the gray light like a thin slice of mother of pearl, brought the food. Next to the eggs was a biscuit with a little yellow Smiley button stuck in it. She said, "You from the North?"

"I guess I am." A Missourian gets used to Southerners thinking him a Yankee, a Northerner considering him a cracker, a Westerner sneering at his effete Easternness, and the Easterner taking him for a cowhand.

"So whata you doin' in the mountains?"

"Talking to people. Taking some pictures. Looking mostly."

"Lookin' for what?"

"A three-calendar cafe that serves Smiley buttons on the biscuits."

"You needed a smile. Tell me really."

"I don't know. Actually, I'm looking for some jam to put on this biscuit now that you've brought one."

She came back with grape jelly. In a land of quince jelly, apple butter, apricot jam, blueberry preserves, pear conserves, and lemon marmalade, you always get grape jelly.

"Whata you lookin' for?"

Like anyone else, I'm embarrassed to eat in front of a watcher, particularly if I'm getting interviewed. "Why don't you have a cup of coffee?"

"Cain't right now. You gonna tell me?"

"I don't know how to describe it to you. Call it harmony."

She waited for something more. "Is that it?" Someone called her to the kitchen. I had managed almost to finish by the time she came back. She sat on the edge of the booth. "I started out in life not likin' anything, but then it grew on me. Maybe that'll happen to you." She watched me spread the jelly. "Saw your van." She watched me eat the biscuit. "You sleep in there?" I told her I did. "I'd love to do that, but I'd be scared spitless."

"I don't mind being scared spitless. Sometimes."

"I'd love to take off cross country. I like to look at different license plates. But I'd take a dog. You carry a dog?"

"No dogs, no cats, no budgie birds. It's a one-man campaign to show Americans a person can travel alone without a pet."

"Cain't travel without a dog!"

"I like to do things the hard way."

"Shoot! I'd take me a dog to talk to. And for protection."

"It isn't traveling to cross the country and talk to your pug instead of people along the way. Besides, being alone on the road makes you ready to meet someone when you stop. You get sociable traveling alone."

She looked out toward the van again. "Time I get the nerve to take a trip, gas'll cost five dollars a gallon."

"Could be. My rig might go the way of the

---

1. **CB numbers:** Users of CB (citizens' band) shortwave radios substitute numbers for simple messages (such as "10–4" for "message received").

steamboat." I remembered why I'd come to Gainesboro. "You know the way to Nameless?"

"Nameless? I've heard of Nameless. Better ask the amlance driver in the corner booth." She pinned the Smiley on my jacket. "Maybe I'll see you on the road somewhere. His name's Bob, by the way."

"The ambulance driver?"

"The Smiley. I always name my Smileys—otherwise they all look alike. I'd talk to him before you go."

"The Smiley?"

"The amlance driver."

And so I went looking for Nameless, Tennessee, with a Smiley button named Bob.

"I don't know if I got directions for where you're goin'," the ambulance driver said. "I *think* there's a Nameless down the Shepardsville Road."

"When I get to Shepardsville, will I have gone too far?"

"Ain't no Shepardsville."

"How will I know when I'm there?"

"Cain't say for certain."

"What's Nameless look like?"

"Don't <u>recollect</u>."

"Is the road paved?"

"It's possible."

Those were the directions. I was looking for an unnumbered road named after a nonexistent town that would take me to a place called Nameless that nobody was sure existed.

Clumps of wild garlic lined the county highway that I hoped was the Shepardsville Road. It scrimmaged with the mountain as it tried to stay on top of the ridges; the hillsides were so steep and thick with oak, I felt as if I were following a trail through the misty treetops. Chickens, doing more work with their necks than legs, ran across the road, and, with a battering of wings, half leapt and half flew into the lower branches of oaks. A vicious

pair of mixed-breed German shepherds raced along trying to eat the tires. After miles, I decided I'd missed the town—assuming there truly *was* a Nameless, Tennessee. It wouldn't be the first time I'd qualified for the Ponce de Leon[2] Believe Anything Award.

I stopped beside a big man loading tools in a pickup. "I may be lost."

"Where'd you lose the right road?"

"I don't know. Somewhere around nineteen sixty-five."

"Highway fifty-six, you mean?"

"I came down fifty-six. I think I should've turned at the last junction."

"Only thing down that road's stumps and huckleberries, and the berries ain't there in March. Where you tryin' to get to?"

"Nameless. If there is such a place."

"You might not know Thurmond Watts, but he's got him a store down the road. That's Nameless at his store. Still there all right, but I might not <u>vouch</u> you that tomorrow." He came up to the van. "In my army days, I wrote Nameless, Tennessee, for my place of birth on all the papers, even though I lived on this end of the ridge. All these ridges and hollers got names of their own. That's Steam Mill Holler over yonder. Named after the steam engine in the gristmill. Miller had him just one arm but done a good business."

"What business you in?"

"I've always farmed, but I work in Cookeville now in a heatin' element factory. Bad back made me go to town to work." He pointed to a wooden building not much bigger than his truck. By the slanting porch, a faded Double Cola sign said J M WHEELER STORE. "That used to be my business. That's me—Madison Wheeler. Feller came by one day. From Detroit. He wanted to buy the sign because he carried my name too. But I didn't sell. Want to keep my name up." He gave a cigarette a good slow smoking. "Had a decent business for

2. **Ponce de Leon:** Juan Ponce de Leon, Spanish explorer and discoverer of Florida. According to legend, he searched for a fountain said to have the power to restore youth.

WORDS TO OWN
recollect (rek′ə·lekt′) *v.:* remember.
vouch (vouch) *v.:* guarantee.

Highway US 1, Panel 3 (1963) by Allan D'Arcangelo. Acrylic on canvas (69½″ × 81″).

five years, but too much of it was in credit. Then them supermarkets down in Cookeville opened, and I was buyin' higher than they was sellin'. With these hard roads now, everybody gets out of the hollers to shop or work. Don't stay up in here anymore. This tar road under my shoes done my business in, and it's likely to do Nameless in."

"Do you wish it was still the old way?"

"I got no debts now. I got two boys raised, and they never been in trouble. I got a brick house and some corn and tobacco and a few Hampshire hogs and Herefords. A good bull. Bull's pumpin' better blood than I do. Real generous man in town let me put my cow in with his stud. I couldna paid the fee on that specimen otherwise." He took an-

other long, meditative pull on his filter tip. "If you're satisfied, that's all they are to it. I'll tell you, people from all over the nation—Florida, Mississippi—are comin' in here to retire because it's good country. But our young ones don't stay on. Not much way to make a livin' in here anymore. Take me. I been beatin' on these stumps all my life, tryin' to farm these hills. They don't give much up to you. Fightin' rocks and briars all the time. One of the first things I recollect is swingin' a briar blade—filed out of an old saw it was. Now they come in with them crawlers and push out a pasture in a day. Still, it's a grudgin' land—like the gourd. Got to hard cuss gourd seed, they say, to get it up out of the ground."

The whole time, my rig sat in the middle of the right lane while we stood talking next to it and wiped at the mist. No one else came or went. Wheeler said, "Factory work's easier on the back, and I don't mind it, understand, but a man becomes what he does. Got to watch that. That's why I keep at farmin', although the crops haven't ever throve. It's the doin' that's important." He looked up suddenly. "My apologies. I didn't ask what you do that gets you into these hollers."

I told him. I'd been gone only six days, but my account of the trip already had taken on some polish.

He nodded. "Satisfaction is doin' what's important to yourself. A man ought to honor other people, but he's got to honor what he believes in too."

As I started the engine, Wheeler said, "If you get back this way, stop in and see me. Always got beans and taters and a little piece of meat."

Down along the ridge, I wondered why it's always those who live on little who are the ones to ask you to dinner.

Nameless, Tennessee, was a town of maybe ninety people if you pushed it, a dozen houses along the road, a couple of barns, same number of churches, a general merchandise store selling Fire Chief gasoline, and a community center with a lighted volleyball court. Behind the center was an open-roof, rusting metal privy with PAINT ME on the door; in the hollow of a nearby oak lay a full pint of Jack Daniel's Black Label. From the houses, the odor of coal smoke.

Next to a red tobacco barn stood the general merchandise with a poster of Senator Albert Gore, Jr.,[3] smiling from the window. I knocked. The door opened partway. A tall, thin man said, "Closed up. For good," and started to shut the door.

"Don't want to buy anything. Just a question for Mr. Thurmond Watts."

The man peered through the slight opening.

He looked me over. "What question would that be?"

"If this is Nameless, Tennessee, could he tell me how it got that name?"

The man turned back into the store and called out, "Miss Ginny! Somebody here wants to know how Nameless come to be Nameless."

Miss Ginny edged to the door and looked me and my truck over. Clearly, she didn't approve. She said, "You know as well as I do, Thurmond. Don't keep him on the stoop in the damp to tell him." Miss Ginny, I found out, was Mrs. Virginia Watts, Thurmond's wife.

I stepped in and they both began telling the story, adding a detail here, the other correcting a fact there, both smiling at the foolishness of it all. It seems the hilltop settlement went for years without a name. Then one day the Post Office Department told the people if they wanted mail up on the mountain they would have to give the place a name you could properly address a letter to. The community met; there were only a handful, but they commenced debating. Some wanted patriotic names, some names from nature, one man recommended in all seriousness his own name. They couldn't agree, and they ran out of names to argue about. Finally, a fellow tired of the talk; he didn't like the mail he received anyway.

"Forget the durn Post Office," he said. "This here's a nameless place if I ever seen one, so leave it be." And that's just what they did.

Watts pointed out the window. "We used to have signs on the road, but the Halloween boys keep tearin' them down."

"You think Nameless is a funny name," Miss Ginny said. "I see it plain in your eyes. Well, you take yourself up north a piece to Difficult or Defeated or Shake Rag. Now them are silly names."

The old store, lighted only by three fifty-watt bulbs, smelled of coal oil and baking bread. In the middle of the rectangular room, where the oak floor sagged a little, stood an iron stove. To the right was a wooden table with an unfinished

---

3. Senator Albert Gore, Jr. (1948–): United States senator from Tennessee, 1985–1992; elected vice president of the United States in 1992 and 1996.

WORDS TO OWN
commenced (kə·mensd′) v.: started.

game of checkers and a stool made from an apple-tree stump. On shelves around the walls sat earthen jugs with corncob stoppers, a few canned goods, and some of the two thousand old clocks and clockworks Thurmond Watts owned. Only one was ticking; the others he just looked at. I asked how long he'd been in the store.

"Thirty-five years, but we closed the first day of the year. We're hopin' to sell it to a churchly couple. Upright people. No athians."[4]

"Did you build this store?"

"I built this one, but it's the third general store on the ground. I fear it'll be the last. I take no pleasure in that. Once you could come in here for a gallon of paint, a pickle, a pair of shoes, and a can of corn."

"Or horehound candy," Miss Ginny said. "Or corsets and salves. We had cough syrups and all that for the body. In season, we'd buy and sell blackberries and walnuts and chestnuts, before the blight got them. And outside, Thurmond milled corn and sharpened plows. Even shoed a horse sometimes."

"We could fix up a horse or a man or a baby," Watts said.

"Thurmond, tell him we had a doctor on the ridge in them days."

"We had a doctor on the ridge in them days. As good as any doctor alivin'. He'd cut a crooked toenail or deliver a woman. Dead these last years."

"I got some bad ham meat one day," Miss Ginny said, "and took to vomitin'. All day, all night. Hangin' on the drop edge of yonder. I said to Thurmond, 'Thurmond, unless you want shut of me, call the doctor.'"

"I studied on it," Watts said.

"You never did. You got him right now. He come over and put three drops of iodeen in half a glass of well water. I drank it down and the vomitin' stopped with the last swallow. Would you think iodeen could do that?"

"He put Miss Ginny on one teaspoon of spirits of ammonia in well water for her nerves. Ain't nothin' works better for her to this day."

"Calms me like the hand of the Lord."

Hilda, the Wattses' daughter, came out of the backroom. "I remember him," she said. "I was just a baby. Y'all were talkin' to him, and he lifted me up on the counter and gave me a stick of Juicy Fruit and a piece of cheese."

"Knew the old medicines," Watts said. "Only drugstore he needed was a good kitchen cabinet. None of them antee-beeotics that hit you worsen your ailment. Forgotten lore now, the old medicines, because they ain't profit in iodeen."

Miss Ginny started back to the side room where she and her sister Marilyn were taking apart a duck-down mattress to make bolsters. She stopped at the window for another look at *Ghost Dancing*.[5] "How do you sleep in that thing? Ain't you all cramped and cold?"

"How does the clam sleep in the shell?" Watts said in my defense.

"Thurmond, get the boy a piece of buttermilk pie afore he goes on."

"Hilda, get him some buttermilk pie." He looked at me. "You like good music?" I said I did. He cranked up an old Edison phonograph, the kind with the big morning-glory blossom for a speaker, and put on a wax cylinder. "This will be 'My Mother's Prayer,'" he said.

While I ate buttermilk pie, Watts served as disc jockey of Nameless, Tennessee. "Here's 'Mountain Rose.'" It was one of those moments that you know at the time will stay with you to the grave: the sweet pie, the

5. ***Ghost Dancing:*** Least Heat-Moon's van, named for the Plains Indian ceremony performed for the restoration of the buffalo and old ways of life.

- -

WORDS TO OWN
lore (lôr) *n*.: traditional knowledge or teachings.

- -

4. **athians:** Mr. Watts means "atheists," people who deny the existence of God.

gaunt man playing the old music, the coals in the stove glowing orange, the scent of kerosene and hot bread. "Here's 'Evening Rhapsody.'" The music was so heavily romantic we both laughed. I thought: It is for this I have come.

Feathered over and giggling, Miss Ginny stepped from the side room. She knew she was a sight. "Thurmond, give him some lunch. Still looks hungry."

Hilda pulled food off the woodstove in the backroom: home-butchered and canned whole-hog sausage, home-canned June apples, turnip greens, coleslaw, potatoes, stuffing, hot cornbread. All delicious.

Watts and Hilda sat and talked while I ate. "Wish you would join me."

"We've ate," Watts said. "Cain't beat a woodstove for flavorful cookin'."

He told me he was raised in a one-hundred-fifty-year-old cabin still standing in one of the hollows. "How many's left," he said, "that grew up in a log cabin? I ain't the last surely, but I must be climbin' on the list."

Hilda cleared the table. "You Watts ladies know how to cook."

"She's in nursin' school at Tennessee Tech. I went over for one of them football games last year there at Coevul." To say *Cookeville*, you let the word collapse in upon itself so that it comes out "Coevul."

"Do you like football?" I asked.

"Don't know. I was so high up in that stadium, I never opened my eyes."

Watts went to the back and returned with a fat spiral notebook that he set on the table. His expression had changed. "Miss Ginny's *Deathbook*."

The thing startled me. Was it something I was supposed to sign? He opened it but said nothing. There were scads of names written in a tidy hand over pages incised to crinkliness by a ballpoint. Chronologically, the names had piled up: wives, grandparents, a stillborn infant, relatives, friends close and distant. Names, names. After each, the date of *the* unknown finally known and transcribed. The last entry bore yesterday's date.

"She's wrote out twenty years' worth. Ever day she listens to the hospital report on the radio and puts the names in. Folks come by to check a date. Or they just turn through the books. Read them like a scrapbook."

Hilda said, "Like Saint Peter at the gates inscribin' the names."

Watts took my arm. "Come along." He led me to the fruit cellar under the store. As we went down, he said, "Always take a newborn baby upstairs afore you take him downstairs, otherwise you'll incline him downwards."

The cellar was dry and full of cobwebs and jar after jar of home-canned food, the bottles organized as a shopkeeper would: sausage, pumpkin, sweet pickles, tomatoes, corn relish, blackberries, peppers, squash, jellies. He held a hand out toward the dusty bottles. "Our tomorrows."

Upstairs again, he said, "Hope to sell the store to the right folk. I see now, though, it'll be somebody offen the ridge. I've studied on it, and maybe it's the end of our place." He stirred the coals. "This store could give a comfortable livin', but not likely get you rich. But just gettin' by is dice rollin' to people nowadays. I never did see my day guaranteed."

When it was time to go, Watts said, "If you find anyone along your way wants a good store—on the road to Cordell Hull Lake—tell them about us."

I said I would. Miss Ginny and Hilda and Marilyn came out to say goodbye. It was cold and drizzling again. "Weather to give a man the weary dismals," Watts grumbled. "Where you headed from here?"

"I don't know."

"Cain't get lost then."

Miss Ginny looked again at my rig. It had worried her from the first as it had my mother. "I hope you don't get yourself kilt in that durn thing gallivantin' around the country."

"Come back when the hills dry off," Watts said. "We'll go lookin' for some of them round rocks all sparkly inside."

I thought a moment. "Geodes?"[6]

"Them's the ones. The county's properly full of them."

6. **geodes** (jē′ōdz′): stones having cavities lined with crystals or minerals.

WORDS TO OWN

incised (in·sīzd′): v. used as adj.: deeply marked.
chronologically (krän′ō·läj′i·kə·lē) adv.: arranged in order of occurrence.
transcribed (tran·skrībd′) v. used as adj.: written down.

James Agee (1909–1955) was a Tennessee-born author who is now remembered primarily for his Pulitzer Prize–winning autobiographical novel, *A Death in the Family* (1957). He also wrote poetry, much-admired movie criticism for *The Nation* and *Time* magazines, and several screenplays, including adaptations of two of Stephen Crane's short stories.

In 1936, during the Great Depression, *Fortune* magazine assigned Agee to write about sharecroppers in the South. The result was too passionate for the magazine, but was eventually published as a book, *Let Us Now Praise Famous Men* (1941), one of the lesser-known master-pieces of American literature. Like Heat-Moon, Agee wrote about the people he discovered along back roads in rural America. Issued with photographs by Walker Evans, *Let Us Now Praise Famous Men* is Agee's dignified and heart-rending portrait of three Alabama families.

In the following passage, the young journalist shares a meal with a family he calls the Gudgers. As you read, notice how Agee's meditative style adds a layer of personal interpretation over the spare reality he is observing. He avoids quota-tion marks, and his long sentences and stream of thoughts are reminiscent of the modernist style of William Faulkner (page 713).

from Let Us Now Praise Famous Men

James Agee

So it was there was neither any fake warmth and heartiness nor any coldness in his saying, Sure, come on in, to my asking could he put me up for the night after all, and he added, Better eat some supper. I was in fact very hungry, but I did all I was able to stop this, finally trying to compromise it to a piece of bread and some milk, that needn't be prepared; I'm making you enough bother already; but no; Can't go to bed without no supper; you just hold on a second or two; and he leans his head through the bed-room door and speaks to his wife, explaining, and lights the lamp for her. After a few mo-ments, during which I hear her breathing and a weary shuffling of her heels, she comes out barefooted carrying the lamp, frankly and pro-foundly sleepy as a child; feeling disgusted to wake her further with so many words I say, Hello, Mrs. Gudger: say I want to tell you I'm *aw*ful sorry to give you all this bother: you just, honest I don't need much of anything, if you'd just tell me where a piece of bread is, it'll be *plenty,* I'd hate for you to bother to cook any-thing up for me: but she answers me while passing, looking at me, trying to get me into focus from between her sticky eyelashes, that 'tain't no bother at all, and for me not to worry over that, and goes on into the kitchen; and how quickly I don't understand, for I am too much occupied to see, with Gudger, and with holding myself from the cardinal error of hov-ering around her, or of offering to help her, she has built a pine fire and set in front of me, on the table in the hall, warmed-over biscuit and butter and blackberry jam and a jelly-glass full of buttermilk, and warmed field peas, fried pork, and four fried eggs, and she sits a little away from the table out of courtesy, trying to hold her head up and her eyes open, until I shall have finished eating, saying at one time how it's an awful poor sort of supper and at an-other how it's awful plain, mean food; I tell her different, and eat as rapidly as possible and a good deal more than I can hold, in fact, all the eggs, a second large plateful of peas, most of the biscuit, feeling it is better to keep them awake and to eat too much than in the least to let them continue to believe I am what they assume I must be: 'superior' to them or to their food, eating only so much as I need to be 'polite'; and I see that they are, in fact, quietly surprised and gratified in my appetite.

But somehow I have lost hold of the reality of all this, I scarcely can understand how; a loss of the reality of simple actions upon the specific surface of the earth. This country, these roads, these odors and noises, the action of walking the dark in mud, the approach, just what a slow succession of certain trees past your walking can implant in you, can mean to you, the house as it stands there dark in darkness, the indecisiveness and the bellowing dog, the conversations of questioning, defense, assurance, acceptance, the subtle yet strong distinctions of attitude, the walking between the walls of wood and the sitting and eating, the tastes of the several foods, the weights of our bodies in our chairs, the look of us in the lamplight in the presence of the walls of the house and of the country night, the beauty and the stress of our tiredness, how we held quietness, gentleness,

Depression-era photo of living room by Walker Evans.
Library of Congress.

and care toward one another like three mild lanterns held each at the met heads of strangers in darkness: such things, and these are just a few, I have not managed to give their truth in words, which are a soft, plain-featured, and noble music, each part in the experience of it and in the memory so cleanly and so simply defined in its own terms, striking so many chords and relationships at once, which I can but have blurred in the telling at all.

MAKING MEANINGS

First Thoughts

1. What would you most like to ask Heat-Moon about his travels?

Shaping Interpretations

2. Heat-Moon knows that food tells a lot about the people who serve and eat it. Where in this excerpt does food tell us about **character**?

3. What concrete details help paint a vivid picture of the Wattses' home? What details keep the Wattses' story from being a depressing one?

4. Heat-Moon captures the flavor of the country in re-creating the **dialect** of Madison Wheeler and the Watts family. Find examples of **images, expressions, proverbs,** and uncommon **grammar** that tell us who and what these people are.

5. Heat-Moon eats buttermilk pie while an old man plays music on a hand-cranked phonograph. Heat-Moon thinks, "It is for this I have come." What does he mean?

6. In *Let Us Now Praise Famous Men* (see *Connections* on page 1064), James Agee spends the night with the Gudger family in Alabama. Why does Agee eat so heartily there? Does Heat-Moon eat a huge meal at the Wattses' for the same reasons? Explain.

Reading Check

a. What can you learn about a small town by observing people eating breakfast at a restaurant?

b. According to what he tells the waitress, what is Heat-Moon searching for?

c. Explain how Nameless, Tennessee, got its name.

d. What does the Watts family share with the narrator?

READING SKILLS AND STRATEGIES

Analyzing Metaphors

When a man asks Heat-Moon, "Where'd you lose the right road?" his reply is "Somewhere around nineteen sixty-five" (page 1059). This befuddles the man, because he doesn't grasp that Heat-Moon is using a **metaphor,** a figure of speech in which one thing is compared to another thing, as in "the voyage of life."

1. In the metaphor of "the right road," what two things is Heat-Moon comparing?

2. Explain what is meant by these metaphors:
   a. "Hangin' on the drop edge of yonder" (page 1062)
   b. "How does the clam sleep in the shell?" (page 1062)

CHOICES: Building Your Portfolio

Writer's Notebook

1. Collecting Ideas for an Evaluation

Comparing and contrasting are effective methods of evaluation. Try comparing or contrasting Heat-Moon's narrative with the excerpt from Thoreau's *Walden* (page 233). Make a chart in which you compare the two works in terms of **topics, tone, style,** and each narrator's **quest.** Save your notes for possible use in the Writer's Workshop on page 1181.

Creative Writing

2. My Neighborhood

In a brief essay, describe your own neighborhood or community. Imitate Heat-Moon and pick up all the small, seemingly insignificant details about where you live. Think of things like where people eat, what they eat, what they hang on their wall, what they talk about, how they talk, how they feel about strangers. Be sure to check your Quickwrite notes.

Crossing the Curriculum: Geography

3. What's in a Name?

Heat-Moon delights in American place names. Find a detailed map of your state, and write an essay about the place names that amuse or please you, telling why they do so. What do the names suggest about your state's geography or history?

Updike

Alvarez

Sexton

Momaday

Walker

Tan

Hongo

Speaking

I take him outside
under the trees,
have him stand on the ground.
We listen to the crickets,
cicadas, million years old sound.
Ants come by us.
I tell them,
"This is he, my son.
This boy is looking at you.
I am speaking for him."

The crickets, cicadas,
the ants, the millions of years
are watching us,
hearing us.
My son murmurs infant words,
speaking, small laughter
bubbles from him.
Tree leaves tremble.
They listen to this boy
speaking for me.

—Simon J. Ortiz (1941–   )

John Updike

(1932–   )

© Nancy Crampton.

Accepting the National Book Award in 1982, John Updike offered this advice to young writers: "Have faith. May you surround yourselves with parents, editors, mates, and children as supportive as mine have been. But the essential support and encouragement of course come from within, arising out of the mad notion that your society needs to know what only you can tell it." That "mad notion" has generated some of our finest contemporary short stories.

John Updike spent his youth in the small town of Shillington in rural Pennsylvania. Gifted with what seems like total recall of growing up in the American middle class, Updike also displays a skill with language that can evoke responses to the most ordinary and familiar events, endowing them with importance.

In his memoir, "The Dogwood Tree: A Boyhood" (published in *Assorted Prose* in 1965), Updike crafts an image of his youthful artistic ambition: ". . . riding a thin pencil line out of Shillington, out of time altogether, into an infinity of unseen and even unborn hearts." As a mature and successful writer, he confronts that image and senses disappointment: "Like some phantom conjured by this child from a glue bottle, I have executed his commands; acquired pencils, paper, and an office. Now I wait apprehensively for his next command, or at least a nod of appreciation, and he smiles through me as if I am already transparent with failure."

After graduating *summa cum laude* from Harvard University in 1954, Updike studied drawing in England for a year, and on his return to the United States went to work for *The New Yorker* magazine. After two years, he made the courageous decision to support his young family entirely by writing. He left New York for Massachusetts and has since produced a long shelf of impressive novels, stories, poems, memoirs, and critical essays.

Although critics are a cantankerous lot, nearly all agree with Rachael C. Burchard that Updike's "style is superb. His work is worth reading if for no reason other than to enjoy the piquant phrase, the lyric vision, the fluent rhetoric."

Among his successful novels have been the tales in the Rabbit series—*Rabbit, Run* (1960), *Rabbit Redux* (1971), *Rabbit Is Rich* (1981; Pulitzer Prize), and *Rabbit at Rest* (1990).

The Rabbit novels mark the ends of four consecutive decades and embody the concerns of their time. They chronicle the life of Harry "Rabbit" Angstrom, who lives, as his creator might have, an outwardly conventional life in a small Pennsylvania town. In revealing Rabbit's yearnings and disappointments and the fluctuations of his relationships, Updike gives us a portrait of forty years of American social behavior. As always with an Updike novel, readers enjoy the feel of life—the sights, smells, and sounds that bring life into focus.

Among Updike's other novels are *The Centaur* (1963; National Book Award) and a trilogy, *A Month of Sundays* (1975), *Roger's Version* (1986), and *S.* (1988), which make up a modern version of Nathaniel Hawthorne's *The Scarlet Letter*. In 1996 he published *In the Beauty of the Lilies*, a novel that spans the twentieth century and focuses, in Updike's characteristic way, on generations of a family and on the mysteries of faith—and, as something new, on the American love affair with the movies.

Eli (1963) by Alex Katz. Oil on canvas (72" × 86").

Before You Read

SON

Make the Connection

Fathers and Sons

"Fathers and sons"—simple words that hide complex, mystifying, and aching relationships. Why do a father's good intentions and thoughts go astray? Why does a son feel antagonized and trapped by a well-meaning father? These are age-old questions that always intrigue us and never seem to receive satisfactory answers.

Reading Skills and Strategies

Analyzing Text Structures: Non-chronological Order

Updike has used an unusual narrative structure for this story about generations. As you read, or after you read, you will want to organize these events into chronological order. One way to do this is to create a time line.

On the time line, plot the story's important time periods and information concerning the son whose life is described in that period. Here is an example:

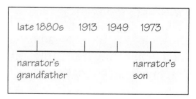

late 1880s   1913   1949   1973

narrator's grandfather   narrator's son

Son

John Updike

He is often upstairs, when he has to be home. He prefers to be elsewhere. He is almost sixteen, though beardless still, a man's mind indignantly captive in the frame of a child. I love touching him, but don't often dare. The other day, he had the flu, and a fever, and I gave him a back rub, marvelling at the symmetrical knit of muscle, the organic tension. He is high-strung. Yet his sleep is so solid he sweats like a stone in the wall of a well. He wishes for perfection. He would like to destroy us, for we are, variously, too fat, too jocular, too sloppy, too affectionate, too grotesque and heedless in our ways. His mother smokes too much. His younger brother chews with his mouth open. His older sister leaves unbuttoned the top button of her blouses. His younger sister tussles with the dogs, getting them overexcited, avoiding doing her homework. Everyone in the house talks nonsense. He would be a better father than his father. But time has tricked him, has made him a son. After a quarrel, if he cannot go outside and kick a ball, he retreats to a corner of the house and reclines on the beanbag chair in an attitude of strange—infantile or leonine—torpor.[1] We exhaust him, without meaning to. He takes an interest in the newspaper now, the front page as well as the sports, in this tiring year of 1973.

He is upstairs, writing a musical comedy. It is a Sunday in 1949. He has volunteered to prepare a high-school assembly program; people will sing. Songs of the time go through his head, as he scribbles new words. *Up in de mornin', down at de school, work like a debil for my grades.* Below him, irksome voices grind on, like machines working their way through tunnels. His parents each want something from the other. "Marion, you don't understand that man like I do; he has a heart of gold." His father's charade is very complex: the

world, which he fears, is used as a flail[2] on his wife. But from his cringing attitude he would seem to an outsider the one being flailed. With burning red face, the woman accepts the role of aggressor as penance for the fact, the incessant shameful fact, that *he* has to wrestle with the world while she hides here, in solitude, at home. This is normal, but does not seem to them to be so. Only by convolution[3] have they arrived at the dominant/submissive relationship society has assigned them. For the man is maternally kind and with a smile hugs to himself his jewel, his certainty of being victimized; it is the mother whose tongue is sharp, who sometimes strikes. "Well, he gets you out of the house, and I guess that's gold to you." His answer is "Duty calls," pronounced mincingly. "The social contract is a balance of compromises." This will infuriate her, the son knows; as his heart thickens, the downstairs overflows with her hot voice. "*Don't* wear that smile at me! And *take* your hands off your hips; you look like a sissy!" Their son tries not to listen. When he does, visual details of the downstairs flood his mind: the two antagonists, circling with their coffee cups; the shabby mismatched furniture; the hopeful books; the docile framed photographs of the dead, docile and still like cowed students. This matrix of pain that bore him—he

2. **flail:** a kind of whip.
3. **convolution:** twisting together until distinctions are obscured.

- -

WORDS TO OWN

symmetrical (si·me′tri·kəl) *adj.:* equally balanced.
jocular (jäk′yo͞o·lər) *adj.:* joking; comical.
irksome (ʉrk′səm) *adj.:* irritating.
mincingly (mins′iŋ·lē) *adv.:* in an affectedly dainty manner.
antagonists (an·tag′ə·nists) *n. pl.:* adversaries; opponents.
docile (däs′əl) *adj.:* passive.

- -

1. **torpor** (tôr′pər): sluggishness; dormancy.

Laurence Typing (1952) by Fairfield Porter. Oil on canvas (40″ × 30⅛″).

feels he is floating above it, sprawled on the bed as on a cloud, stealing songs as they come into his head (*Across the hallway from the guidance room / Lives a French instructor called Mrs. Blum*), contemplating the view from the upstairs window (last summer's burdock[4] stalks like the beginnings of an alphabet, an apple tree holding three rotten apples as if pondering why they failed to fall), yearning for Monday, for the ride to school with his father, for the bell that calls him to homeroom, for the excitements of class, for Broadway, for fame, for the cloud that will carry him away, out of this, out.

He returns from his paper-delivery route and finds a few Christmas presents for him on the kitchen table. I must guess at the year. 1913? Without opening them, he knocks them to the floor, puts his head on the table, and falls asleep. He must have been consciously dramatizing his plight: His father was sick, money was scarce, he had to work, to win food for the family when he was still a child. In his dismissal of Christmas, he touched a nerve: his love of anarchy, his distrust of the social contract. He treasured this moment of revolt; else why remember it, hoard a memory so bitter, and confide it to his son many Christmases later? He had a teaching instinct, though he claimed that life miscast him as a schoolteacher. I suffered in his classes, feeling the confusion as a persecution of him, but now wonder if his rebellious heart did not court confusion, not as Communists do, to intrude their own order, but, more radical still, as an end pleasurable in itself, as truth's very body. Yet his handwriting (an old pink permission slip recently fluttered from a book where it had been marking a page for twenty years) was always considerately legible, and he was sitting up doing arithmetic the morning of the day he died.

And letters survive from that yet prior son, written in brown ink, in a tidy tame hand, home to his mother from the Missouri seminary where he was preparing for his vocation. The dates are 1887, 1888, 1889. Nothing much happened: He missed New Jersey, and was teased at a church social for escorting a widow. He wanted to do the right

thing, but the little sheets of faded penscript exhale a dispirited calm, as if his heart already knew he would not make a successful minister, or live to be old. His son, my father, when old, drove hundreds of miles out of his way to visit the Missouri town from which those letters had been sent. Strangely, the town had not changed; it looked just as he had imagined, from his father's descriptions: tall wooden houses, rain-soaked, stacked on a bluff. The town was a sepia[5] postcard mailed homesick home and preserved in an attic. My father cursed: His father's old sorrow bore him down into depression, into hatred of life. My mother claims his decline in health began at that moment.

He is wonderful to watch, playing soccer. Smaller than the others, my son leaps, heads, dribbles, feints, passes. When a big boy knocks him down, he tumbles on the mud, in his green-and-black school uniform, in an ecstasy of falling. I am envious. Never for me the jaunty pride of the school uniform, the solemn ritual of the coach's pep talk, the camaraderie of shook hands and slapped backsides, the shadow-striped hush of late afternoon and last quarter, the solemn vaulted universe of official combat, with its cheering mothers and referees exotic as zebras and the bespectacled timekeeper alert with his claxon.[6] When the boy scores a goal, he runs into the arms of his teammates with upraised arms and his face alight as if blinded by triumph. They lift him from the earth in a union of muddy hugs. What spirit! What valor! What skill! His father, watching from the sidelines, inwardly registers only one complaint: He feels the boy, with his talent, should be more aggressive.

5. sepia (sē′pē·ə): brownish ink used in artwork and photography.
6. claxon (klaks′ən): more correctly, Klaxon, the trademark for a type of electric horn with a distinctively loud, shrill sound. Such a horn is often used to mark the end of a time period in sporting events.

---

4. burdock: coarse, hairy weed with thick stalks, heart-shaped leaves, and prickly purple flowers.

WORDS TO OWN

anarchy (an′ər·kē) *n.*: complete disorder.
seminary (sem′ə·ner′ē) *n.*: school for training ministers, priests, or rabbis.
jaunty (jônt′ē) *adj.*: confident; carefree.

They drove across the Commonwealth of Pennsylvania to hear their son read in Pittsburgh. But when their presence was announced to the audience, they did not stand; the applause groped for them and died. My mother said afterwards she was afraid she might fall into the next row if she tried to stand in the dark. Next morning was sunny, and the three of us searched for the house where once they had lived. They had been happy there; I imagined, indeed, that I had been conceived there, just before the slope of the Depression steepened and fear gripped my family. We found the library where she used to read Turgenev,[7] and the little park where the bums slept close as paving stones in the summer night; but their street kept eluding us, though we circled in the car. On foot, my mother found the tree. She claimed she recognized it, the sooty linden tree she would gaze into from their apartment windows. The branches, though thicker, had held their pattern. But the house itself, and the entire block, was gone. Stray bricks and rods of iron in the grass suggested that the demolition had been recent. We stood on the empty spot and laughed. They knew it was right, because the railroad tracks were the right distance away. In confirmation, a long freight train pulled itself east around the curve, its great weight gliding as if on a river current; then a silver passenger train came gliding as effortlessly in the other direction. The curve of the tracks tipped the cars slightly toward us. The Golden Triangle,[8] gray and hazed, was off to our left, beyond a forest of bridges. We stood on the grassy rubble that morning, where something once had been, beside the tree still there, and were intensely happy. Why? We knew.

"'No,' Dad said to me, 'the Christian ministry isn't a job you choose, it's a vocation for which you got to receive a call.' I could tell he wanted me to ask him. We never talked much, but we understood each other, we were both scared devils, not like you and the kid. I asked him, Had he ever received the call? He said No. He said No, he never

had. Received the call. That was a terrible thing, for him to admit. And I was the one he told. As far as I knew he never admitted it to anybody, but he admitted it to me. He felt like hell about it, I could tell. That was all we ever said about it. That was enough."

He has made his younger brother cry, and justice must be done. A father enforces justice. I corner the rat in our bedroom; he is holding a cardboard mailing tube like a sword. The challenge flares white-hot; I roll my weight toward him like a rock down a mountain, and knock the weapon from his hand. He smiles. Smiles! Because my facial expression is silly? Because he is glad that he can still be overpowered, and hence is still protected? Why? I do not hit him. We stand a second, father and son, and then as nimbly as on the soccer field he steps around me and out the door. He slams the door. He shouts obscenities in the hall, slams all the doors he can find on the way to his room. Our moment of smilingly shared silence was the moment of compression; now the explosion. The whole house rocks with it. Downstairs, his <u>siblings</u> and mother come to me and offer advice and psychological analysis. I was too aggressive. He is spoiled. What they can never know, my grief alone to treasure, was that lucid many-sided second of his smiling and my relenting, before the world's wrathful pantomime of power resumed.

As we huddle whispering about him, my son takes his revenge. In his room, he plays his guitar. He has greatly improved this winter; his hands getting bigger is the least of it. He has found in the guitar an escape. He plays the Romanza[9] wherein repeated notes, with a sliding like the heart's valves, let themselves fall along the scale:

The notes fall, so gently he bombs us, drops feathery notes down upon us, our visitor, our prisoner.

---

7. **Turgenev** (toor·gān′əf): Ivan Turgenev (1818–1883), Russian writer.
8. **The Golden Triangle:** wedge-shaped piece of land formed by the junction of the Allegheny and Monongahela Rivers in Pittsburgh, Pennsylvania. The two rivers join to form the Ohio River at this point.

9. **Romanza** (rō·män′zə): musical term. Italian for "romance."

WORDS TO OWN

siblings (sib′liŋz) *n. pl.:* brothers or sisters.

One of contemporary America's best fiction writers, Anne Tyler (1941–   ) has written several widely read novels, including *Dinner at the Homesick Restaurant* (1982), *The Accidental Tourist* (1985), which was made into a popular film, and *A Patchwork Planet* (1998). In the following passage, Tyler talks about writing as a craft and about how she discovered that one can write interestingly about ordinary people. "Even the most ordinary person, in real life," she says, "will turn out to have something unusual at his center."

from "Still Just Writing"

Anne Tyler

I was standing in the schoolyard waiting for a child when another mother came up to me. "Have you found work yet?" she asked. "Or are you still just writing?"

Now, how am I supposed to answer that?

I could take offense, come to think of it. Maybe the reason I didn't is that I halfway share her attitude. They're *paying* me for this? For just writing down untruthful stories? I'd better look around for more permanent employment. For I do consider writing to be a finite job. I expect that any day now, I will have said all I have to say; I'll have used up all my characters, and then I'll be free to get on with my real life. When I make a note of new ideas on index cards, I imagine I'm clearing out my head, and that soon it will be empty and spacious. I file the cards in a little blue box, and I can picture myself using the final card one day—ah! through at last!—and throwing the blue box away. I'm like a dentist who continually fights tooth decay, working toward the time when he's conquered it altogether and done himself out of a job. But my head keeps loading up again; the little blue box stays crowded and messy. Even when I feel I have no ideas at all, and can't possibly start the next chapter, I have a sense of something still bottled in me, trying to get out. . . .

Walker/Gamma Liaison.

I spent my adolescence planning to be an artist, not a writer. After all, books had to be about major events, and none had ever happened to me. All I knew were tobacco workers, stringing the leaves I handed them and talking up a storm. Then I found a book of Eudora Welty's short stories in the high school library. She was writing about Edna Earle, who was so slow-witted she could sit all day just pondering how the tail of the *C* got through the loop of the *L* on the Coca-Cola sign. Why, I knew Edna Earle. You mean you could *write* about such people? I have always meant to send Eudora Welty a thank-you note, but I imagine she would find it a little strange.

MAKING MEANINGS

First Thoughts

1. What thoughts about parents and children did you have as you read "Son"?

Shaping Interpretations

2. This story includes a variety of incidents that range over several different time periods. What **thematic** thread unifies the story? How does the time frame relate to the story's meaning?

3. In the long line of the generations, hope keeps reappearing. In what ways are the characters' hopes for each other disappointed? How are they fulfilled?

4. In the context of the story, what do you think Updike means by the phrase "the social contract"? Would he say that this contract is or is not honored between fathers and sons? Explain.

5. At the end of the story, why does the narrator refer to his son as "our visitor, our prisoner"?

6. Why do you think Updike gave the story the title "Son" instead of "Father"? Would you read the story differently if it had been called "Father"?

7. How would you describe the narrator's **tone** in telling this story? How does he feel about the people in this family?

8. Updike is known as a great wordsmith. Describe some aspects of "Son" that show him to be a skilled practitioner of the writer's craft.

Extending the Text

9. What discovery about writing, described by Anne Tyler in "Still Just Writing" (see *Connections* on page 1074), is also apparent in "Son"? Explain.

Reading Check

a. For each of the story's eight sections, identify the time period and the characters. Refer to your time line as necessary.

b. Find passages in each section in which the narrator reveals private thoughts of the characters.

c. What test does the father-narrator face in the last section?

d. How does the son respond to the father's discipline?

CHOICES:
Building Your Portfolio

Writer's Notebook

1. Collecting Ideas for an Evaluation

When you evaluate a short story, you need to show how separate elements work (or do not work) together. Use a graphic organizer, such as a cluster diagram, to demonstrate how the eight sections of Updike's "Son" contribute to the story's main theme. Write the theme in the center of the cluster, and, in each of the eight bubbles, identify the words, images, characters, or ideas that help convey the theme. Save your notes for possible use in the Writer's Workshop on page 1181.

Interpreting Theme

2. "A contact barely reached"

Analyzing Updike's book *Problems and Other Stories* (1979), in which "Son" appears, the critic Donald J. Greiner wrote:

> The stories were written from 1971 to 1978, a period of unsettling family conditions for Updike himself. Although the tales are not autobiography, the specter of domestic loss, of love moving forward from all sides toward a contact barely reached, hovers around most of them. It is not that love is denied but that it is difficult to sustain.

Write a brief essay applying Greiner's statement to "Son." What does this story say about loss, love, and "a contact barely reached"?

Creative Writing

3. "Daughter"

Imitating the structure of "Son," write some episodes of a story called "Daughter." Let your narrator reveal the thoughts and feelings of at least three generations of one family.

Julia Alvarez

(1950–   )

"All my childhood I had dressed like an American, eaten American foods, and befriended American children. I had gone to an American school and spent most of the day speaking and reading English. At night, my prayers were full of blond hair and blue eyes and snow. . . . All my childhood I had longed for this moment of arrival. And here I was, an American girl, coming home at last."

With these words, Julia (pronounced hoo'lē·ä) Alvarez describes stepping back into America. Although born in New York City, Alvarez spent her early childhood in the Dominican Republic. In 1960, just before her father was to be arrested for his involvement in a secret plot to overthrow the dictator Rafael Trujillo Molina, Alvarez and her family were tipped off by an American agent and escaped to the United States.

Paradoxically, her homecoming was filled with all the difficulties of adjusting to a brand-new life. Learning contemporary American English was only part of the adjustment. Alvarez also had to learn to compromise in order to resolve conflicts between American customs and her parents' more traditional views. This theme is at the heart of her fiction—particularly her short stories and her best-known work, the novel *How the Garcia Girls Lost Their Accents* (1991).

Before concentrating on writing fiction, Alvarez taught courses in poetry for twelve years in schools in Kentucky, California, Vermont, Illinois, and Washington, D.C. Her first collection of poems, appropriately titled *Homecoming,* was published in 1984. Alvarez has also won the American Academy of Poetry Prize, but it is as a novelist that she has received the most notice.

How the Garcia Girls Lost Their Accents is a novel of fifteen interlocking stories with engaging and memorable characters. The Garcia family, with its four daughters, struggles to overcome a variety of cultural and generational conflicts, and comparisons with Alvarez's own

family make it clear that the novel is highly autobiographical. Her 1994 novel, *In the Time of the Butterflies,* is a fictionalized account of the lives and deaths of three sisters, Patria, Minerva, and María Teresa Mirabal, the wives of political prisoners in the Dominican Republic. The women, who had been visiting their husbands, were murdered in 1960 by thugs connected to the Trujillo regime. Alvarez's 1997 novel *Yo!* is populated by some of the *Garcia Girls* characters.

It is clear that Alvarez has forged, out of memory and imagination, a novelist's sensibility. As one critic said about *Garcia Girls,* Alvarez has "beautifully captured the threshold experience of the new immigrant, where the past is not yet a memory and the future remains an anxious dream."

Theo Westenberger/Gamma Liaison.

Make the Connection

Generations

From the Biblical parable of the prodigal son to a short story written this morning, literature will probably never end its chronicle of children and parents struggling to understand and make peace with each other. "Experience is the greatest teacher, so trust us," says the older generation. "We want to live our own lives, not yours," say the children. Both have valid points, of course, and the search for equilibrium goes on.

Reading Skills and Strategies

Drawing Inferences About Characters

It is fascinating to see how the three characters in the following story have adapted so differently to the liberty the family enjoys in its new country. As you read, jot down notes on how Cukita, Mami, and Papi adjust to the United States.

"Daughters of Invention" is one of the fifteen interlocking stories in *How the Garcia Girls Lost Their Accents.*

Elements of Literature

Conflict

Do you doubt that a story runs on **conflict**? Here is a splendid example that takes its strength and much of its fun from the clash between the anxious values of Latin American parents and the liberated ones of their New York–raised daughter. Each major character in this story experiences both **external conflict** (with other people, a government, or society in general) and **internal conflict** (within his or her own mind).

> **E**xternal conflict exists between two people, between a person and a thing, or between a person and society. **Internal conflict** involves opposing forces within a person's mind.
>
> *For more on Conflict, see the Handbook of Literary Terms.*

Daughter of Invention

Julia Alvarez

She wanted to invent something, my mother. There was a period after we arrived in this country, until five or so years later, when my mother was inventing. They were never pressing, global needs she was addressing with her pencil and pad. She would have said that was for men to do, rockets and engines that ran on gasoline and turned the wheels of the world. She was just fussing with little house things, don't mind her.

She always invented at night, after settling her house down. On his side of the bed my father would be conked out for an hour already, his Spanish newspaper draped over his chest, his glasses, propped up on his bedside table, looking out eerily at the darkened room like a <u>disembodied</u> guard. But in her lighted corner, like some devoted scholar burning the midnight oil, my mother was inventing, sheets pulled to her lap, pillows propped up behind her, her reading glasses riding the bridge of her nose like a schoolmarm's. On her lap lay one of those innumerable pads of paper my father always brought home from his office, compliments of some pharmaceutical company, advertising tranquilizers or antibiotics or skin cream; in her other hand, my mother held a pencil that looked like a pen with a little cylinder of lead inside. She would work on a sketch of something familiar, but drawn at such close range so she could attach a special nozzle or handier handle, the thing looked peculiar. Once, I mistook the spiral of a corkscrew for a nautilus shell, but it could just as well have been a galaxy forming.

It was the only time all day we'd catch her sitting down, for she herself was living proof of the *perpetuum mobile*[1] machine so many inventors had sought over the ages. My sisters and I would seek her out now when she seemed to have a moment to talk to us: We were having trouble at school or we wanted her to persuade my father to give us permission to go into the city or to a shopping mall or a movie—in broad daylight! My mother would wave us out of her room. "The problem with you girls . . ." I can tell you right now what the problem always boiled down to: We wanted to become Americans and my father—and my mother, at first—would have none of it.

"You girls are going to drive me crazy!" She always threatened if we kept nagging. "When I end up in Bellevue,[2] you'll be safely sorry!"

She spoke in English when she argued with us, even though, in a matter of months, her daughters were the fluent ones. Her English was much better than my father's, but it was still a mishmash of mixed-up idioms and sayings that showed she was "green behind the ears," as she called it.

If my sisters and I tried to get her to talk in Spanish, she'd snap, "When in Rome, do unto the Romans . . ."

I had become the spokesman for my sisters, and I would stand my ground in that bedroom. "We're not going to that school anymore, Mami!"

"You have to." Her eyes would widen with worry. "In this country, it is against the law not to go to school. You want us to get thrown out?"

"You want us to get killed? Those kids were throwing stones today!"

"Sticks and stones don't break bones . . ." she chanted. I could tell, though, by the look on her face, it was as if one of those stones the kids had aimed at us had hit her. But she always pretended we were at fault. "What did you do to provoke them? It takes two to tangle, you know."

"Thanks, thanks a lot, Mom!" I'd storm out of that room and into mine. I never called her *Mom* except when I wanted her to feel how much she had failed us in this country. She was a good enough Mami, fussing and scolding and giving advice, but a terrible girlfriend parent, a real failure of a Mom.

Back she'd go to her pencil and pad, scribbling and tsking and tearing off paper, finally giving up,

2. **Bellevue:** large New York City hospital known for its psychiatric department.

1. *perpetuum mobile* (per·pe′tōō·əm′ mō′bi·le): Latin for "perpetual motion."

Madre e hija (1995) by Oscar Pardo. Pastel on paper (19″ × 12½″). Courtesy of the artist.

and taking up her *New York Times*. Some nights, though, she'd get a good idea, and she'd rush into my room, a flushed look on her face, her tablet of paper in her hand, a cursory knock on the door she'd just thrown open: "Do I have something to show you, Cukita!"

This was my time to myself, after I'd finished my homework, while my sisters were still downstairs watching TV in the basement. Hunched over my small desk, the overhead light turned off, my lamp shining poignantly on my paper, the rest of the room in warm, soft, uncreated darkness, I wrote my secret poems in my new language.

"You're going to ruin your eyes!" My mother would storm into my room, turning on the overly bright overhead light, scaring off whatever shy passion I had just begun coaxing out of a <u>labyrinth</u> of feelings with the blue thread of my writing.

"Oh Mami!" I'd cry out, my eyes blinking up at her. "I'm writing."

"Ay, Cukita." That was her <u>communal</u> pet name for whoever was in her favor. "Cukita, when I make a million, I'll buy you your very own typewriter." (I'd been nagging my mother for one just like the one father had bought her to do his order forms at home.) "Gravy on the turkey" was what she called it when someone was buttering her up. She'd butter and pour. "I'll hire you your very own typist."

Down she'd plop on my bed and hold out her pad to me. "Take a guess, Cukita?" I'd study her rough sketch a moment: soap sprayed from the nozzle head of a shower when you turned the knob a certain way? Coffee with creamer already mixed in? Time-released water capsules for your plants when you were away? A key chain with a timer that would go off when your parking meter was about to expire? (The ticking would help you find your keys easily if you mislaid them.) The famous one, famous only in hindsight, was the stick person dragging a square by a rope—a suitcase with wheels? "Oh, of course," we'd humor her. "What every household needs: a shower like a car wash, keys ticking like a bomb, luggage on a leash!" By now, as you can see, it'd become something of a family joke, our Thomas Edison Mami, our Benjamin Franklin Mom.

Her face would fall. "Come on now! Use your head." One more wrong guess, and she'd tell me,

pressing with her pencil point the different highlights of this incredible new wonder. "Remember that time we took the car to Bear Mountain, and we re-ah-lized that we had forgotten to pack an opener with our pick-a-nick?" (We kept correcting her, but she insisted this is how it should be said.) "When we were ready to eat we didn't have any way to open the refreshments cans?" (This before fliptop lids, which she claimed had crossed her mind.) "You know what this is now?" A shake of my head. "Is a car bumper, but see this part is a removable can opener. So simple and yet so necessary, no?"

"Yeah, Mami. You should patent it." I'd shrug. She'd tear off the scratch paper and fold it, carefully, corner to corner, as if she were going to save it. But then, she'd toss it in the wastebasket on her way out of the room and give a little laugh like a <u>disclaimer</u>. "It's half of one or two dozen of another . . ."

I suppose none of her daughters was very encouraging. We resented her spending time on those dumb inventions. Here, we were trying to fit in America among Americans; we needed help figuring out who we were, why these Irish kids whose grandparents were micks two generations ago, why they were calling us spics. Why had we come to the country in the first place? Important, crucial, final things, you see, and here was our own mother, who didn't have a second to help us puzzle any of this out, inventing gadgets to make life easier for American moms. Why, it seemed as if she were arming our own enemy against us!

One time, she did have a moment of triumph. Every night, she liked to read *The New York Times* in bed before turning off her light, to see what the Americans were up to. One night, she let out a yelp to wake up my father beside her, bolt upright, reaching for his glasses which, in his haste, he knocked across the room. *"Que pasa? Que pasa?"*[3] What is wrong? There was terror in

3. ***Que pasa?*** (kä pä′sä): Spanish for "What's going on?"

WORDS TO OWN

labyrinth (lab′ə·rinth′) *n.*: place full of intricate passageways; maze.
communal (kə·myo͞on′əl) *adj.*: belonging to an entire group (in this case, Mami's daughters).
disclaimer (dis·klām′ər) *n.*: a giving up of a claim or connection.

---

his voice, fear she'd seen in his eyes in the Dominican Republic before we left. We were being watched there; he was being followed; he and mother had often exchanged those looks. They could not talk, of course, though they must have whispered to each other in fear at night in the dark bed. Now in America, he was safe, a success even; his Centro Medico in Brooklyn was thronged with the sick and the homesick. But in dreams, he went back to those awful days and long nights, and my mother's screams confirmed his secret fear: We had not gotten away after all; they had come for us at last.

"Ay, Papi, I'm sorry. Go back to sleep, Cukito. It's nothing, nothing really." My mother held up the *Times* for him to squint at the small print, back page headline, one hand tapping all over the top of the bedside table for his glasses, the other rubbing his eyes to wakefulness.

"Remember, remember how I showed you that suitcase with little wheels so we would not have to carry those heavy bags when we traveled? Someone stole my idea and made a million!" She shook the paper in his face. She shook the paper in all our faces that night. "See! See! This man was no *bobo*![4] He didn't put all his pokers on a back burner. I kept telling you, one of these days my ship would pass me by in the night!" She wagged her finger at my sisters and my father and me, laughing all the while, one of those eerie laughs crazy people in movies laugh. We had congregated in her room to hear the good news she'd been yelling down the stairs, and now we eyed her and each other. I suppose we were all thinking the same thing: Wouldn't it be weird and sad if Mami did end up in Bellevue as she'd always threatened she might?

"*Ya, ya!* Enough!" She waved us out of her room at last. "There is no use trying to drink spilt milk, that's for sure."

It was the suitcase rollers that stopped my mother's hand; she had weather vaned a minor brainstorm. She would have to start taking herself seriously. That blocked the free play of her ingenuity. Besides, she had also begun working at my father's office, and at night, she was too tired and busy filling in columns with how much money they had made that day to be fooling with gadgets!

4. *bobo:* Spanish for "fool."

She did take up her pencil and pad one last time to help me out. In ninth grade, I was chosen by my English teacher, Sister Mary Joseph, to deliver the teacher's day address at the school assembly. Back in the Dominican Republic, I was a terrible student. No one could ever get me to sit down to a book. But in New York, I needed to settle somewhere, and the natives were unfriendly, the country inhospitable, so I took root in the language. By high school, the nuns were reading my stories and compositions out loud to my classmates as examples of imagination at work.

This time my imagination jammed. At first I didn't want and then I couldn't seem to write that speech. I suppose I should have thought of it as a "great honor," as my father called it. But I was mortified. I still had a pronounced lilt to my accent, and I did not like to speak in public, subjecting myself to my classmates' ridicule. Recently, they had begun to warm toward my sisters and me, and it took no great figuring to see that to deliver a eulogy for a convent full of crazy, old overweight nuns was no way to endear myself to the members of my class.

But I didn't know how to get out of it. Week after week, I'd sit down, hoping to polish off some quick, noncommittal little speech. I couldn't get anything down.

The weekend before our Monday morning assembly I went into a panic. My mother would just have to call in and say I was in the hospital, in a coma. I was in the Dominican Republic. Yeah, that was it! Recently, my father had been talking about going back home to live.

My mother tried to calm me down. "Just remember how Mister Lincoln couldn't think of anything to say at the Gettysburg, but then, Bang! 'Four score and once upon a time ago,'" she began reciting. Her version of history was half invention and half truths and whatever else she needed to prove a point. "Something is going to come if you just relax. You'll see, like the Americans say, 'Necessity is the daughter of invention.' I'll help you."

All weekend, she kept coming into my room with help. "Please, Mami, just leave me alone, please," I pleaded with her. But I'd get rid of the goose only to have to contend with the gander. My father kept poking his head in the door just to see if I had "fulfilled my obligations," a phrase he'd used when we were a little younger, and he'd check to see whether we had gone to the bathroom before a car trip. Several times that weekend around the supper table, he'd recite his valedictorian speech from when he graduated from high school. He'd give me pointers on delivery, on the great orators and their tricks. (Humbleness and praise and falling silent with great emotion were his favorites.)

My mother sat across the table, the only one who seemed to be listening to him. My sisters and I were forgetting a lot of our Spanish, and my father's formal, <u>florid</u> diction was even harder to understand. But my mother smiled softly to herself, and turned the Lazy Susan at the center of the table around and around as if it were the prime mover,[5] the first gear of attention.

That Sunday evening, I was reading some poetry to get myself inspired: Whitman in an old book with an engraved cover my father had picked up in a thrift shop next to his office a few weeks back. "I celebrate myself and sing myself . . ." "He most honors my style who learns under it to destroy the teacher." The poet's words shocked and thrilled me. I had gotten used to the nuns, a literature of appropriate sentiments, poems with a message, expurgated texts. But here was a flesh and blood man, belching and laughing and sweating in poems. "Who touches this book touches a man."

That night, at last, I started to write, recklessly, three, five pages, looking up once only to see my father passing by the hall on tiptoe. When I was done, I read over my words, and my eyes filled. I finally sounded like myself in English!

As soon as I had finished that first draft, I called my mother to my room. She listened attentively, as she had to my father's speech, and in the end, her eyes were glistening too. Her face was soft and warm and proud. "That is a beautiful, beautiful speech, Cukita. I want for your father to hear it before he goes to sleep. Then I will type it for you, all right?"

Down the hall we went, the two of us, faces flushed with accomplishment. Into the master bedroom where my father was propped up on his pillows, still awake, reading the Dominican papers, already days old. He had become interested in his country's fate again. The dictatorship had been toppled. The interim government was going to hold the first free elections in thirty years. There was still some question in his mind whether or not we might want to move back. History was in the making, freedom and hope were in the air again! But my mother had gotten used to the life here. She did not want to go back to the old country where she was only a wife and a mother (and a failed one at that, since she had never had the required son). She did not come straight out and disagree with my father's plans. Instead, she fussed with him about reading the papers in bed, soiling those sheets with those poorly printed, foreign tabloids. "*The Times* is not that bad!" she'd claim if my father tried to humor her by saying they shared the same dirty habit.

The minute my father saw my mother and me, filing in, he put his paper down, and his face brightened as if at long last his wife had delivered a son, and that was the news we were bringing him. His teeth were already grinning from the glass of water next to his bedside lamp, so he lisped when he said, "Eh-speech, eh-speech!"

"It is so beautiful, Papi," my mother previewed him, turning the sound off on his TV. She sat down at the foot of the bed. I stood before both of them, blocking their view of the soldiers in helicopters landing amid silenced gun reports and explosions. A few weeks ago it had been the shores of the Dominican Republic. Now it was the jungles of Southeast Asia they were saving. My mother gave me the nod to begin reading.

I didn't need much encouragement. I put my nose to the fire, as my mother would have said, and read from start to finish without looking up. When I was done, I was a little embarrassed at my pride in my own words. I pretended to quibble with a phrase or two I was sure I'd be talked out of changing. I looked questioningly to my mother. Her face was radiant. She turned to share her pride with my father.

---

5. prime mover: in philosophy, the self-moved being that is the source of all motion; in machinery, the source of power, such as a windmill or an engine.

WORDS TO OWN
florid (flôr′id) *adj.*: showy.

Uno (1920) by Alejandro Xul Solar. Watercolor and pencil on paper on card (5⁹/₃₂″ × 7½″).

But the expression on his face shocked us both. His toothless mouth had collapsed into a dark zero. His eyes glared at me, then shifted to my mother, accusingly. In barely audible Spanish, as if secret microphones or informers were all about, he whispered, "You will permit her to read *that*?"

My mother's eyebrows shot up, her mouth fell open. In the old country, any whisper of a challenge to authority could bring the secret police in their black V.W.'s. But this was America. People could say what they thought. "What is wrong with her speech?" my mother questioned him.

"What ees wrrrong with her eh-speech?" My father wagged his head at her. His anger was always more frightening in his broken English. As if he had mutilated the language in his fury—and now there was nothing to stand between us and his raw, dumb anger. "What is wrong? I will tell you what is wrong. It shows no gratitude. It is boastful. 'I celebrate myself'? 'The best student learns to destroy the teacher'?" He mocked my plagiarized words. "That is insubordinate. It is improper. It is

disrespecting of her teachers—" In his anger he had forgotten his fear of lurking spies: Each wrong he voiced was a decibel higher than the last outrage. Finally, he was yelling at me, "As your father, I forbid you to say that eh-speech!"

My mother leapt to her feet, a sign always that she was about to make a speech or deliver an <u>ultimatum</u>. She was a small woman, and she spoke all her pronouncements standing up, either for more protection or as a carry-over from her girlhood in convent schools where one asked for, and literally took, the floor in order to speak. She stood by my side, shoulder to shoulder; we looked down at my father. "That is no tone of voice, Eduardo—" she began.

By now, my father was truly furious. I suppose it was bad enough I was rebelling, but here was

---

WORDS TO OWN

ultimatum (ul'tə·māt'əm) *n.:* last offer; final proposition.

Courtesy Rachel Adler Gallery, New York.

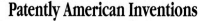

Patently American Inventions

Have an invention of your own you'd like to protect? Consider patenting it. A U.S. patent gives you the right to exclude all others from making, using, or selling your invention within the United States for a limited number of years. To start, put your idea in writing, illustrate your device or process, and sign and date the document (use indelible ink). But before you reach for pad and pen, you might want to learn a little more about patents and inventions.

Patents are granted by the U.S. Patent and Trademark Office, in Arlington, Virginia. The Patent Office is flooded with over 150,000 applications a year, each of which takes about two years to process. If you can convince the patent officer that your invention is (1) new, (2) useful, and (3) original, a patent is yours. But be warned: You'll need deep pockets, since patent fees typically exceed $1,000.

Patented inventions we haven't seen in stores. Anyone wanting an afternoon's—or a lifetime's—entertainment could do worse than browse through the five million patents on record at the Patent Office. Ideas on record include these:

- eye protectors for chickens
- suspenders that convert into ropes in case the wearer needs to escape a burning building
- a device combining a plow and a gun
- a locket for storing used chewing gum
- a wake-up device consisting of suspended wood blocks that fall on the sleeper's face
- a device to create or maintain dimples
- balloons powered by large birds
- farms that rest on giant saucers floating in the sea

---

my mother joining forces with me. Soon he would be surrounded by a house full of independent American women. He too leapt from his bed, throwing off his covers. The Spanish newspapers flew across the room. He snatched my speech out of my hands, held it before my panicked eyes, a vengeful, mad look in his own, and then once, twice, three, four, countless times, he tore my prize into shreds.

"Are you crazy?" My mother lunged at him. "Have you gone mad? That is her speech for tomorrow you have torn up!"

"Have *you* gone mad?" He shook her away. "You were going to let her read that . . . that insult to her teachers?"

"Insult to her teachers!" My mother's face had

crumpled up like a piece of paper. On it was written a love note to my father. Ever since they had come to this country, their life together was a constant war. "This is America, Papi, America!" she reminded him now. "You are not in a savage country any more!"

I was on my knees, weeping wildly, collecting all the little pieces of my speech, hoping that I could put it back together before the assembly tomorrow morning. But not even a sibyl[6] could

---

6. **sibyl** (sib′əl): in ancient Greece and Rome, a woman who foretold the future.

WORDS TO OWN
vengeful (venj′fəl) *adj.*: intent on revenge.

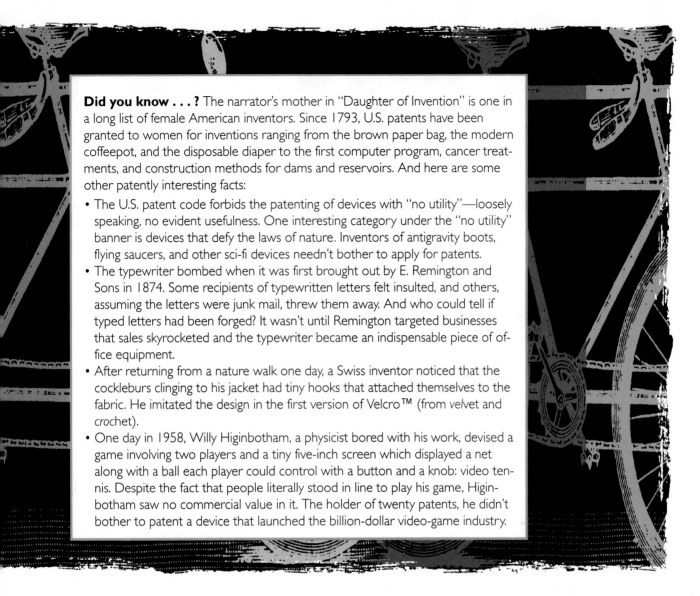

Did you know . . . ? The narrator's mother in "Daughter of Invention" is one in a long list of female American inventors. Since 1793, U.S. patents have been granted to women for inventions ranging from the brown paper bag, the modern coffeepot, and the disposable diaper to the first computer program, cancer treatments, and construction methods for dams and reservoirs. And here are some other patently interesting facts:

- The U.S. patent code forbids the patenting of devices with "no utility"—loosely speaking, no evident usefulness. One interesting category under the "no utility" banner is devices that defy the laws of nature. Inventors of antigravity boots, flying saucers, and other sci-fi devices needn't bother to apply for patents.

- The typewriter bombed when it was first brought out by E. Remington and Sons in 1874. Some recipients of typewritten letters felt insulted, and others, assuming the letters were junk mail, threw them away. And who could tell if typed letters had been forged? It wasn't until Remington targeted businesses that sales skyrocketed and the typewriter became an indispensable piece of office equipment.

- After returning from a nature walk one day, a Swiss inventor noticed that the cockleburs clinging to his jacket had tiny hooks that attached themselves to the fabric. He imitated the design in the first version of Velcro™ (from *velvet* and *crochet*).

- One day in 1958, Willy Higinbotham, a physicist bored with his work, devised a game involving two players and a tiny five-inch screen which displayed a net along with a ball each player could control with a button and a knob: video tennis. Despite the fact that people literally stood in line to play his game, Higinbotham saw no commercial value in it. The holder of twenty patents, he didn't bother to patent a device that launched the billion-dollar video-game industry.

have made sense of all those scattered pieces of paper. All hope was lost. "He broke it, he broke it," I moaned as I picked up a handful of pieces.

Probably, if I had thought a moment about it, I would not have done what I did next. I would have realized my father had lost brothers and comrades to the dictator Trujillo.[7] For the rest of his life, he would be haunted by blood in the streets and late night disappearances. Even after he had been in the states for years, he jumped if a black Volkswagen passed him on the street. He feared anyone in uniform: the meter maid giving out parking tickets, a museum guard approaching to tell him not to touch his favorite Goya at the Metropolitan.[8]

I took a handful of the scraps I had gathered, stood up, and hurled them in his face. "Chapita!" I said in a low, ugly whisper. "You're just another Chapita!"

It took my father only a moment to register the hated nickname of our dictator, and he was after me. Down the halls we raced, but I was quicker than he and made it to my room just in time to lock the door as my father threw his weight

7. Trujillo (trōō·hē′yō): Rafael Leonidas Trujillo Molina, general who took over as president of the Dominican Republic and ruled oppressively from 1930 to 1938 and from 1942 until he was assassinated in 1961.

8. Goya . . . Metropolitan: a painting by the Spanish artist Francisco José de Goya y Lucientes at the Metropolitan Museum of Art in New York City.

against it. He called down curses on my head, ordered me on his authority as my father to open that door this very instant! He throttled that doorknob, but all to no avail. My mother's love of gadgets saved my hide that night. She had hired a locksmith to install good locks on all the bedroom doors after our house had been broken into while we were away the previous summer. In case burglars broke in again, and we were in the house, they'd have a second round of locks to contend with before they got to us.

"Eduardo," she tried to calm him down. "Don't you ruin my new locks."

He finally did calm down, his anger spent. I heard their footsteps retreating down the hall. I heard their door close, the clicking of their lock. Then, muffled voices, my mother's peaking in anger, in persuasion, my father's deep murmurs of explanation and of self-defense. At last, the house fell silent, before I heard, far off, the gun blasts and explosions, the serious, self-important voices of newscasters reporting their TV war.

A little while later, there was a quiet knock at my door, followed by a tentative attempt at the doorknob. "Cukita?" my mother whispered. "Open up, Cukita."

"Go away," I wailed, but we both knew I was glad she was there, and I needed only a moment's protest to save face before opening that door.

What we ended up doing that night was putting together a speech at the last moment. Two brief pages of stale compliments and the polite commonplaces on teachers, wrought by necessity without much invention by mother for daughter late into the night in the basement on the pad of paper and with the same pencil she had once used for her own inventions, for I was too upset to compose the speech myself. After it was drafted, she typed it up while I stood by, correcting her misnomers and mis-sayings.

She was so very proud of herself when I came home the next day with the success story of the assembly. The nuns had been flattered, the audience had stood up and given "our devoted teachers a standing ovation," what my mother had suggested they do at the end of my speech.

She clapped her hands together as I recreated the moment for her. "I stole that from your father's speech, remember? Remember how he put that in at the end?" She quoted him in Spanish, then translated for me into English.

That night, I watched him from the upstairs hall window where I'd retreated the minute I heard his car pull up in front of our house. Slowly, my father came up the driveway, a grim expression on his face as he grappled with a large, heavy cardboard box. At the front door, he set the package down carefully and patted all his pockets for his house keys—precisely why my mother had invented her ticking key chain. I heard the snapping open of the locks downstairs. Heard as he struggled to maneuver the box through the narrow doorway. Then, he called my name several times. But I would not answer him.

"My daughter, your father, he love you very much," he explained from the bottom of the stairs. "He just want to protect you." Finally, my mother came up and pleaded with me to go down and reconcile with him. "Your father did not mean to harm. You must pardon him. Always it is better to let bygones be forgotten, no?"

I guess she was right. Downstairs, I found him setting up a brand new electric typewriter on the kitchen table. It was even better than the one I'd been begging to get like my mother's. My father had outdone himself with all the extra features: a plastic carrying case with my initials, in decals, below the handle, a brace to lift the paper upright while I typed, an erase cartridge, an automatic margin tab, a plastic hood like a toaster cover to keep the dust away. Not even my mother, I think, could have invented such a machine!

But her inventing days were over just as mine were starting up with my schoolwide success. That's why I've always thought of that speech my mother wrote for me as her last invention rather than the suitcase rollers everyone else in the family remembers. It was as if she had passed on to me her pencil and pad and said, "Okay, Cukita, here's the buck. You give it a shot."

WORDS TO OWN

misnomers (mis·nō′merz) n. pl.: wrong terms or names.
reconcile (rek′ən·sīl′) v.: to make peace.

MAKING MEANINGS

First Thoughts

1. Did your feelings about any of the characters change as you read the story? Explain.

Shaping Interpretations

2. The narrator wants to use Whitman's words: "He most honors my style who learns under it to destroy the teacher" (page 1082). How does the girl's father interpret the words? What do you think Whitman was really saying?

3. The narrator says, "She was a good enough Mami, fussing and scolding and giving advice, but a terrible girlfriend parent, a real failure of a Mom" (page 1079). What does the narrator mean?

4. What **conflicts** does the father face in this story? How does the narrator address the conflicts?

5. Review the notes you made while reading, and **compare** and **contrast** how Cukita, Mami, and Papi have adjusted to life in the United States. What adjustments occur over the course of the story?

Extending the Text

6. In this story, the father's experience of politics in his country of origin clearly influences his behavior in the United States. Can you identify other contemporary or past immigrants who have vivid memories of politics in their native lands?

Reading Check

a. Which of the mother's ideas for an invention is a huge success for somebody else?

b. Why did the daughters resent the time the mother spent on inventions?

c. The narrator's mother is fond of English-language **aphorisms** (brief, wise sayings), but she gets them slightly wrong. Provide corrected versions of some of her sayings.

d. How does the daughter insult her father after he destroys her speech?

CHOICES: Building Your Portfolio

Writer's Notebook

1. Collecting Ideas for an Evaluation

Readers often evaluate a story according to the power of its conflicts. "Daughter of Invention" offers a variety of **external** and **internal conflicts.** Make a four-column chart to help organize your thoughts about them. In the first column, list all the conflicts you can identify, such as interpersonal, social, cultural, and political conflicts. In the second column, tell who is involved in each conflict: for example, mother/ daughter, father/daughter, husband/wife. In the third column, describe the resolution—if any—of each conflict in the story. In the fourth column, evaluate each conflict's power to hold your interest and to evoke emotions and thoughts. Save your chart for possible use in the Writer's Workshop on page 1181.

Interpreting a Title

2. Resonance

A good **title** often has what might be called resonance—it echoes with meaning. In an essay, explain how Alvarez's title touches on (a) a humorous detail of the story, (b) a **theme** of the story, and (c) the **climax** of the story.

Creative Writing / Speaking and Listening

3. "All these I feel or am"

The narrator's Walt Whitman–inspired speech ends up as little pieces of paper on the floor. Reread the Whitman selections in this book (beginning on page 352), and then write the first page of the speech the narrator might have written. You can use the lines she uses or any other appropriate Whitman lines. If you like, read the opening of your speech to the class.

Anne Sexton

(1928–1974)

© Rollie McKenna.

From the very beginning of her literary career, Anne Sexton was recognized as a spirit in turmoil. The writer James Dickey (page 1155) put it this way: "Anne Sexton's poems so obviously come out of deep, painful sections of the author's life that one's literary opinions scarcely seem to matter; one feels tempted to drop them furtively into the nearest ashcan, rather than be caught with them in the presence of so much naked suffering."

Sexton's poetry was an eruption into art of her stormy emotional life. The titles of her most gripping volumes indicate a preoccupation with bouts of mental illness and anxiety and with the need to confront ultimate questions: *To Bedlam and Part Way Back* (1960), *Live or Die* (1966), *The Death Notebooks* (1974), and *The Awful Rowing Toward God* (1975).

Anne Gray Harvey was born in Newton, Massachusetts, and attended the public schools in nearby Wellesley. In 1947, she enrolled in the Garland School, a finishing school for women, and in 1948 married Alfred Sexton. Anne Sexton worked for a time as a fashion model, gave birth to two daughters, and then, at age 28, began writing poetry.

Sexton studied with Robert Lowell (page 948) in his graduate writing seminar at Boston University, and developed friendships with other important poets, including Sylvia Plath (page 1148), Maxine Kumin, and George Starbuck. One of the strongest influences on her was the work of her friend W. D. Snodgrass, whose volume of poetry, *Heart's Needle* (1959),

traced the emotional consequences of a difficult midlife divorce.

Sexton traveled to Europe and Africa, taught at Boston University, gave readings, and earned several honorary doctorates and numerous poetry prizes, including a Pulitzer Prize for *Live or Die*. In 1968, she formed a rock music group called Anne Sexton and Her Kind. In performance, Sexton read her poems while musicians accompanied her on guitar, flute, saxophone, drums, bass, and keyboards. She believed, she said, that the music "opens up my poems in a new way, by involving them in the sound of rock music."

Sexton's poetry was intended to be, as she said, "a shock to the senses." In her second book, *All My Pretty Ones* (1962), she quoted Franz Kafka: ". . . the books we need are the kind that act upon us like a misfortune, that make us suffer like the death of someone we love more than ourselves . . . [A] book should serve as the ax for the frozen sea within us." Her books were personal axes, but they also opened up a wider vision of contemporary women. Many of her poems are dramatic monologues that portray women in moments of crisis.

The general public as well as other poets responded enthusiastically to Sexton's poems. But artistic success did not strengthen her fragile personality. As her close friend Robert Lowell remembered: "At a time when poetry readings were expected to be boring, no one ever fell asleep at Anne's. I see her as having the large, transparent, breakable, and increasingly ragged wings of a dragonfly—her poor, shy, driven life, the blind terror behind her bravado, her deadly increasing pace . . . her bravery while she lasted."

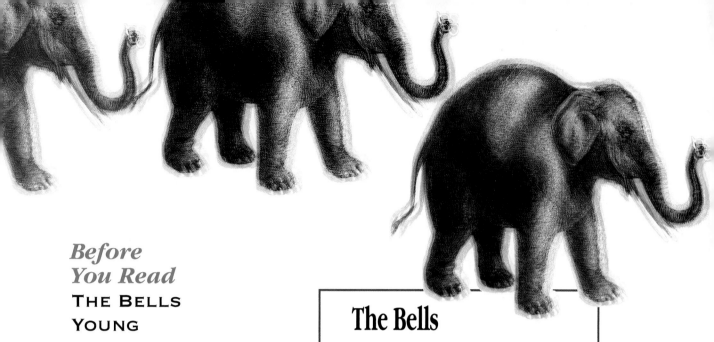

Make the Connection

**Remembrance of
Things Past**

Some events, major or minor at the time, stick in our minds many years later. A parade, a kiss, a summer night—it could be anything that brings back the past for us, reminding us of our younger selves.

Quickwrite

Jot down an experience from the past that makes you feel joy. What image or sound prompts your memory of the experience?

Elements of Literature

Imagery

Imagery is the use of language to evoke a picture or a concrete sensation of a person, place, thing, or experience. Most images in literature appeal to our sense of sight. An image can, however, also appeal to our senses of taste, smell, hearing, and touch. In the following poems, look for images of sight, hearing, and touch.

The Bells

Anne Sexton

Today the circus poster
is scabbing off the concrete wall
and the children have forgotten
if they knew at all.
5 Father, do you remember?
Only the sound remains,
the distant thump of the good elephants,
the voice of the ancient lions
and how the bells
10 trembled for the flying man.
I, laughing,
lifted to your high shoulder
or small at the rough legs of strangers,
was not afraid.
15 You held my hand
and were instant to explain
the three rings of danger.
Oh see the naughty clown
and the wild parade
20 while love love
love grew rings around me.
This was the sound where it began;
our breath pounding up to see
the flying man breast out
25 across the boarded sky
and climb the air.
I remember the color of music
and how forever
all the trembling bells of you
30 were mine.

Young

Anne Sexton

A thousand doors ago
when I was a lonely kid
in a big house with four
garages and it was summer
5 as long as I could remember,
I lay on the lawn at night,
clover wrinkling under me,
the wise stars bedding over me,
my mother's window a funnel
10 of yellow heat running out,
my father's window, half shut,
an eye where sleepers pass,
and the boards of the house
were smooth and white as wax
15 and probably a million leaves
sailed on their strange stalks
as the crickets ticked together
and I, in my brand new body,
which was not a woman's yet,
20 told the stars my questions
and thought God could really see
the heat and the painted light,
elbows, knees, dreams, goodnight.

Me and the Moon (1937) by Arthur G. Dove. Graphite on paper (7″ x 10″; 17.9 cm x 25.5 cm).

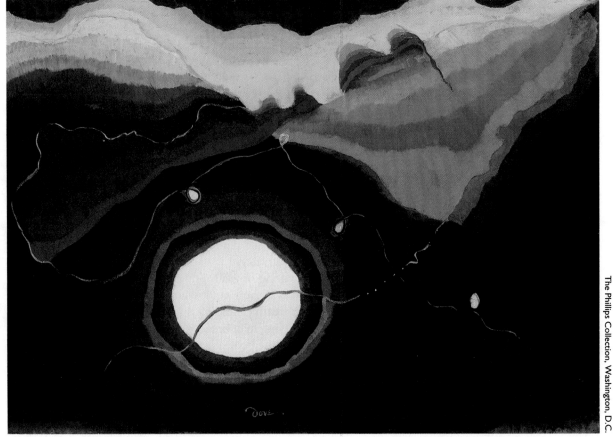

MAKING MEANINGS

The Bells

First Thoughts

1. What emotions did you feel as you read "The Bells"?

Shaping Interpretations

2. What prompts the speaker to remember the scene from her past? (How do her memories compare with your own, as recorded in your Quickwrite notes?)

3. According to line 6, what "remains"? Where does it remain, and why do you think it does so?

4. What feelings does the poem's speaker remember? How would you describe the poem's **tone**?

5. "Rings" are mentioned twice in the poem. At first they are "rings of danger." What do they become, and what is it that transforms them?

6. Describing a perception of one sense in terms of another sense is called **synesthesia.** What senses does Sexton mix in line 27?

7. One **theme** of the poem is conveyed with childlike simplicity in the last two lines. How would you paraphrase this message?

Young

First Thoughts

1. Is this a happy memory for the speaker? Compare it with the memory you described in the Quickwrite.

Shaping Interpretations

2. Why do you think the speaker says her youth took place "a thousand doors ago"?

3. Identify the **metaphors** used to describe the windows. Do you think the metaphors reflect the speaker's feelings about her mother and father? Explain your responses.

4. Describe the **tone** of the poem, as you "hear" it. Which words in the poem convey this tone?

5. Read the poem aloud, which Sexton recommended. Where would you pause slightly for breath and emphasis? Do you think the poem sounds like a young girl speaking?

CHOICES:
Building Your Portfolio

Writer's Notebook

1. Collecting Ideas for an Evaluation

What are your criteria for evaluating **images** in a poem? Do they need to be powerful? If so, what gives them power? Must they be universal, or can they be solely personal? List the qualities that you think an image ought to have, and then apply your criteria to Sexton's images in either poem. Save your notes for possible use in the Writer's Workshop on page 1181.

Analyzing Sounds

2. The Poet's Craft

Sexton uses **rhymes** very subtly and very skillfully. Many are **approximate rhymes** (words that have some correspondence in sound but not an exact one), and therefore they may not be apparent at first. (Reading the poems aloud should help reveal these "hidden" rhymes.) In a short essay, identify some of the rhymes and other sound effects, such as **alliteration,** in "The Bells" and "Young." In your essay, answer these questions about the use of sound in the poems:

- What are the effects of the sounds in the poem? Are the sounds harsh, discordant, pleasing, harmonious?
- How do the sounds affect the tone of the poem? How do they reinforce its sense?
- Do the rhymes and other sound effects call attention to certain key words or ideas?

Viewing and Representing

3. A Poem's Pictures

"Young" overflows with visual **imagery.** Draw or paint the speaker, her family's house and its surroundings, or whatever else interests you. You might want to focus on a detail, such as one of those windows. (As a starting point, you may wish to respond visually to the painting on page 1090.)

N. Scott Momaday

(1934–   )

Among American voices, one of the most poignant and powerful to make itself heard at long last has been that of the Native American. In the past, the American Indian appeared in literature and the other arts mostly in the baldest of stereotypes, either as a noble, primitive warrior or as a fearsome, ignorant savage. One has only to look at Western movies from the 1940s and 1950s to see how blatant the stereotypes were. Even American history textbooks seldom questioned the popular view that the white settlers' gradual "winning" of the West was a virtuous struggle against the unwarranted resistance of American Indians. Few Americans gave much thought either to the moral basis on which the United States expanded or to the history of the American Indians.

Courtesy N. Scott Momaday.

When the civil rights movement of the 1950s and 1960s brought discrimination against African Americans to the forefront of public discussion, other minority groups began to demand a fairer social and political standing for themselves. Native Americans spoke loudly and clearly of loss, injustice, and prejudice. Among the notable books on the Native American experience are Vine Deloria, Jr.'s novel *Custer Died for Your Sins* (1969), the historian Dee Brown's *Bury My Heart at Wounded Knee* (1970), Louise Erdrich's novel *Love Medicine* (1984), and the works of N. Scott Momaday.

Navarre Scott Momaday was born in Lawton, Oklahoma, of Kiowa ancestry on his father's side, and some Cherokee on his mother's. After receiving an undergraduate degree from the University of New Mexico in 1958, Momaday studied creative writing at Stanford University, where he earned a Ph.D. in 1963.

But Momaday broke loose from the standard academic mold with three works grounded in his knowledge of American Indian life: a Pulitzer Prize–winning novel, *House Made of Dawn* (1968), and two memoirs, *The Way to Rainy Mountain* (1969) and *The Names* (1976).

The Way to Rainy Mountain is part legend, part history, and part poetry, with an artistic addition of striking illustrations by Momaday's father, Alfred Momaday. Following the introduction, Momaday describes Kiowa history in a form that is associative and imagistic; it works on the reader's imagination in subtle ways that do not depend on a straightforward narrative. On one page, he sets down a Kiowa myth or legend; on the facing page, he places a short excerpt from a traditional history and then a personal memory of his own. In the mind of the reader, the inner truth blends with the outer; emotion mixes with fact.

The Kiowas' journey to Rainy Mountain begins in the hidden mists of time, when a tribe of unknown origin descends from the headwaters of the Yellowstone River eastward to the Black Hills (in present-day South Dakota) and south to the Wichita Mountains. It ends in a cemetery where many of Momaday's Kiowa relatives are buried. Momaday says that "the journey is an evocation of three things in particular: a landscape that is incomparable, a time that is gone forever, and the human spirit, which endures."

The incomparable landscape is the Great Plains, wind-swept and lonely, in turn brilliant with summer sun and buried in winter snows. Momaday's love of the land where he grew up suffuses everything he writes. He reminds us of both the spiritual richness and the rigors of living close to the land, under a wide, open sky, in harmony with the changing seasons. In his work, Momaday has looked at his own particular landscape from so many angles that his pictures often shimmer like prisms.

go.hrw.com
LE0 11-20

Before You Read

FROM THE WAY TO RAINY MOUNTAIN

Make the Connection

Knowledge of Ancient Days
What is it that we honor about the generations that preceded us? Perhaps it's the realization that not only did they build civilizations and give us life—but also that they *knew* something. We search in thousands of ways for the secret of what they must have known. We search in history, archaeology, anthropology, art, linguistics, architecture, music, mythology, literature. In many ways, we search for knowledge of ourselves as we search the past.

Reading Skills and Strategies

Identifying Main Ideas and Supporting Details
As you read (or as you reread), take notes on Momaday's **main ideas** and their **supporting details.** Use the following format for your notes.

> **Main idea**
> • supporting detail
> • supporting detail
> **Main idea**
> • supporting detail
> • supporting detail

Elements of Literature

Setting
Momaday is a master at describing **setting,** the time and location in which events occur or in which characters are placed. The following excerpt contains descriptions of numerous settings, which help to create mood and atmosphere. In some cases, the description is made up of just one or two well-chosen images.

> **S**etting is the time and location in which events occur or in which characters are placed.
>
> *For more on Setting, see the Handbook of Literary Terms.*

Background

This excerpt from *The Way to Rainy Mountain* is not a simple narrative. Momaday uses frequent **flashbacks** to earlier times and often omits transitional passages. The text is like a poem in which the narrator traces, in his imagination, the heroic and ultimately tragic history of his people, the Kiowas. Keep in mind Momaday's telling comment at the end of the book: "Once in his life a man ought to concentrate his mind upon the remembered earth. . . ."

from **The Way to Rainy Mountain**

N. Scott Momaday

Blind Kiowa woman at Carnegie, Oklahoma, powwow (1946). Photo by P. Tartoue.

Devils Tower, Wyoming.

A single knoll rises out of the plain in Oklahoma north and west of the Wichita Range. For my people, the Kiowas, it is an old landmark, and they gave it the name Rainy Mountain. The hardest weather in the world is there. Winter brings blizzards, hot tornadic winds arise in the spring, and in summer the prairie is an anvil's edge. The grass turns brittle and brown, and it cracks beneath your feet. There are green belts along the rivers and creeks, linear groves of hickory and pecan, willow and witch hazel. At a distance in July or August the steaming foliage seems almost to writhe in fire. Great green and yellow grasshoppers are everywhere in the tall grass, popping up like corn to sting the flesh, and tortoises crawl about on the red earth, going nowhere in the plenty of time. Loneliness is an aspect of the land. All things in the plain are isolate; there is no confusion of objects in the eye, but *one* hill or *one* tree or *one* man. To look upon that landscape in the early morning, with the sun at your back, is to lose the sense of proportion. Your imagination comes to life, and this, you think, is where Creation was begun.

I returned to Rainy Mountain in July. My grandmother had died in the spring, and I wanted to be at her grave. She had lived to be very old and at last infirm. Her only living daughter was with her when she died, and I was told that in death her face was that of a child.

I like to think of her as a child. When she was born, the Kiowas were living that last great moment of their history. For more than a hundred years they had controlled the open range from the Smoky Hill River to the Red, from the headwaters of the Canadian to the fork of the Arkansas and Cimarron. In alliance with the Comanches, they had ruled the whole of the southern Plains. War was their sacred business, and they were among the finest horsemen the world has ever known. But warfare for the Kiowas was preeminently a matter of disposition rather than of survival, and they never understood the grim, unrelenting advance of the U.S. Cavalry. When at last, divided and ill-provisioned, they were driven onto the Staked Plains in the cold rains of autumn, they fell into panic. In Palo Duro Canyon they abandoned their crucial stores to pillage and had nothing then but their lives. In order to save themselves, they surrendered to the soldiers at Fort Sill and were imprisoned in the old stone corral that now stands as a military museum. My grandmother was spared the humiliation of those high gray walls by eight or ten years, but she must have known from birth the affliction of defeat, the dark brooding of old warriors.

Her name was Aho, and she belonged to the last culture to evolve in North America. Her forebears came down from the high country in western Montana nearly three centuries ago. They were a mountain people, a mysterious tribe of hunters whose language has never been positively classified in any major group. In the late seventeenth century they began a long migration to the south and east. It was a journey toward the dawn, and it led to a golden age. Along the way the Kiowas were befriended by the Crows, who gave them the culture and religion of the Plains. They acquired horses, and their ancient nomadic spirit was suddenly free of the ground. They acquired Tai-me, the sacred Sun Dance doll, from that moment the object and symbol of their worship, and so shared in the divinity of the sun. Not least, they acquired the sense of destiny, therefore courage and pride. When they entered upon the southern Plains they had been transformed. No longer were they slaves to the simple necessity of survival; they were a lordly and dangerous society of fighters and thieves, hunters and priests of the sun. According to their origin myth, they entered the world through a hollow log. From one point of view, their migration was the fruit of an old prophecy, for indeed they emerged from a sunless world.

Although my grandmother lived out her long life in the shadow of Rainy Mountain, the immense landscape of the continental interior lay like memory in her blood. She could tell of the Crows, whom she had never seen, and of the

WORDS TO OWN

infirm (in·fʉrm′) *adj*.: physically weak.
preeminently (prē·em′ə·nənt·lē) *adv*.: above all else.

Black Hills, where she had never been. I wanted to see in reality what she had seen more perfectly in the mind's eye, and traveled fifteen hundred miles to begin my pilgrimage.

Yellowstone, it seemed to me, was the top of the world, a region of deep lakes and dark timber, canyons and waterfalls. But, beautiful as it is, one might have the sense of confinement there. The skyline in all directions is close at hand, the high wall of the woods and deep cleavages of shade. There is a perfect freedom in the mountains, but it belongs to the eagle and the elk, the badger and the bear. The Kiowas reckoned their stature by the distance they could see, and they were bent and blind in the wilderness.

Descending eastward, the highland meadows are a stairway to the plain. In July the inland slope of the Rockies is <u>luxuriant</u> with flax and buckwheat, stonecrop and larkspur. The earth unfolds and the limit of the land recedes. Clusters of trees, and animals grazing far in the distance, cause the vision to reach away and wonder to build upon the mind. The sun follows a longer course in the day, and the sky is immense beyond all comparison. The great billowing clouds that sail upon it are shadows that

move upon the grain like water, dividing light. Farther down, in the land of the Crows and Blackfeet, the plain is yellow. Sweet clover takes hold of the hills and bends upon itself to cover and seal the soil. There the Kiowas paused on their way; they had come to the place where they must change their lives. The sun is at home on the plains. Precisely there does it have the certain character of a god. When the Kiowas came to the land of the Crows, they could see the dark lees of the hills at dawn across the Bighorn River, the profusion of light on the grain shelves, the oldest deity ranging after the solstices.[1] Not yet would they veer southward to the caldron of the land that lay below; they must

wean their blood from the northern winter and hold the mountains a while longer in their view. They bore Tai-me in procession to the east.

A dark mist lay over the Black Hills, and the land was like iron. At the top of a ridge I caught sight of Devils Tower upthrust against the gray sky as if in the birth of time the core of the earth had broken through its crust and the motion of the world was begun. There are things in nature that engender an awful quiet in the heart of man; Devils Tower is one of them. Two centuries ago, because they could not do otherwise, the Kiowas made a legend at the base of the rock. My grandmother said:

Eight children were there at play, seven sisters and their brother. Suddenly the boy was struck dumb; he trembled and began to run upon his hands and feet. His fingers became claws, and his body was covered with fur. Directly there was a bear where the boy had been. The sisters were terrified; they ran, and the bear after them. They came to the stump of a great tree, and the tree spoke to them. It bade them climb upon it, and as they did so it began to rise into the air. The bear came to kill them, but they were just beyond its reach. It reared against the tree and scored the bark all around with its claws. The seven sisters were borne into the sky, and they became the stars of the Big Dipper.

From that moment, and so long as the legend lives, the Kiowas have kinsmen in the night sky. Whatever they were in the mountains, they could be no more. However <u>tenuous</u> their well-being, however much they had suffered and would suffer again, they had found a way out of the wilderness.

My grandmother had a reverence for the sun, a holy regard that now is all but gone out of mankind. There was a <u>wariness</u> in her, and an an-

1. **solstices:** The solstices are the points where the sun is farthest north and farthest south of the celestial equator, creating the longest day (June 21) and the shortest day (December 21) of sunlight in the Northern Hemisphere.

WORDS TO OWN
luxuriant (lug·zhoor'ē·ənt) *adj.*: rich; abundant.
tenuous (ten'yo͞o·əs) *adj.*: slight; insubstantial; not firm.
wariness (wer'ē·nis) *n.*: caution; carefulness.

John Stevens/The Stock Solution.

cient awe. She was a Christian in her later years, but she had come a long way about, and she never forgot her birthright. As a child she had been to the Sun Dances; she had taken part in those annual rites, and by them she had learned the restoration of her people in the presence of Tai-me. She was about seven when the last Kiowa Sun Dance was held in 1887 on the Washita River above Rainy Mountain Creek. The buffalo were gone. In order to consummate the ancient sacrifice—to impale the head of a buffalo bull upon the medicine tree—a delegation of old men journeyed into Texas, there to beg and barter for an animal from the Goodnight herd. She was ten when the Kiowas came together for the last time as a living Sun Dance culture. They could find no buffalo;

they had to hang an old hide from the sacred tree. Before the dance could begin, a company of soldiers rode out from Fort Sill under orders to disperse the tribe. Forbidden without cause the essential act of their faith, having seen the wild herds slaughtered and left to rot upon the ground, the Kiowas backed away forever from the medicine tree. That was July 20, 1890, at the great bend of the Washita. My grandmother was there. Without bitterness, and for as long as she lived, she bore a vision of deicide.[2]

2. **deicide** (dē′ə·sīd′): murder of a god.

WORDS TO OWN

disperse (di·spʉrs′) v.: to scatter.

Now that I can have her only in memory, I see my grandmother in the several postures that were peculiar to her: standing at the wood stove on a winter morning and turning meat in a great iron skillet; sitting at the south window, bent above her beadwork, and afterwards, when her vision failed, looking down for a long time into the fold of her hands; going out upon a cane, very slowly as she did when the weight of age came upon her; praying. I remember her most often at prayer. She made long, rambling prayers out of suffering and hope, having seen many things. I was never sure that I had the right to hear, so exclusive were they of all mere custom and company. The last time I saw her she prayed standing by the side of her bed at night, naked to the waist, the light of a kerosene lamp moving upon her dark skin. Her long, black hair, always drawn and braided in the day, lay upon her shoulders and against her breasts like a shawl. I do not speak Kiowa, and I never understood her prayers, but there was something inherently sad in the sound, some merest hesitation upon the syllables of sorrow. She began in a high and descending pitch, exhausting her breath to silence; then again and again—and always the same intensity of effort, of something that is, and is not, like urgency in the human voice. Transported so in the dancing light among the shadows of her room, she seemed beyond the reach of time. But that was illusion; I think I knew then that I should not see her again.

Houses are like sentinels in the plain, old keepers of the weather watch. There, in a very little while, wood takes on the appearance of great age. All colors wear soon away in the wind and rain, and then the wood is burned gray and the grain appears

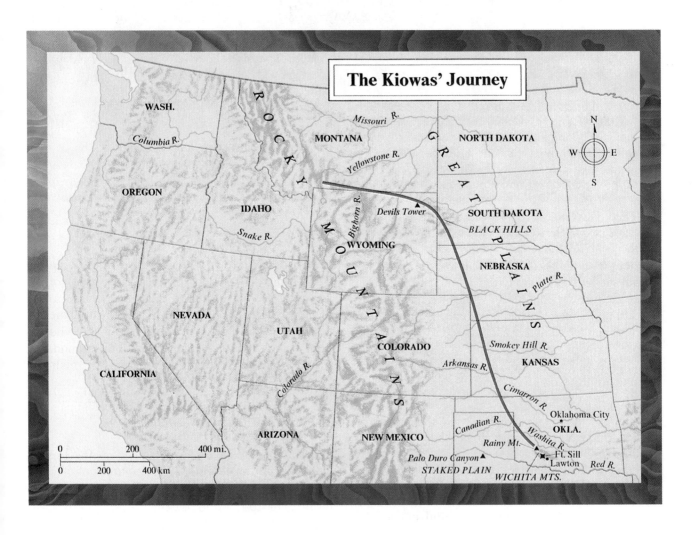

and the nails turn red with rust. The window-panes are black and opaque; you imagine there is nothing within, and indeed there are many ghosts, bones given up to the land. They stand here and there against the sky, and you approach them for a longer time than you expect. They belong in the distance; it is their domain.

Once there was a lot of sound in my grandmother's house, a lot of coming and going, feasting and talk. The summers there were full of excitement and reunion. The Kiowas are a summer people; they abide the cold and keep to themselves, but when the season turns and the land becomes warm and vital they cannot hold still; an old love of going returns upon them. The aged visitors who came to my grandmother's house when I was a child were made of lean and leather, and they bore themselves upright. They wore great black hats and bright ample shirts that shook in the wind. They rubbed fat upon their hair and wound their braids with strips of colored cloth. Some of them painted their faces and carried the scars of old and cherished enmities. They were an old council of warlords, come to remind and be reminded of who they were. Their wives and daughters served them well. The women might indulge themselves; gossip was at once the mark and compensation of their servitude. They made loud and elaborate talk among themselves, full of jest and gesture, fright and false alarm. They went abroad in fringed and flowered shawls, bright beadwork and German silver. They were at home in the kitchen, and they prepared meals that were banquets.

There were frequent prayer meetings, and great nocturnal feasts. When I was a child I played with my cousins outside, where the lamplight fell upon the ground and the singing of the old people rose up around us and carried away into the darkness. There were a lot of good things to eat, a lot of laughter and surprise. And afterwards, when the quiet returned, I lay down with my grandmother and could hear the frogs away by the river and feel the motion of the air.

Now there is a funeral silence in the rooms, the endless wake of some final word. The walls have closed in upon my grandmother's house. When I returned to it in mourning, I saw for the first time in my life how small it was. It was late at night, and there was a white moon, nearly full. I sat for a long time on the stone steps by the kitchen door. From there I could see out across the land; I could see the long row of trees by the creek, the low light upon the rolling plains, and the stars of the Big Dipper. Once I looked at the moon and caught sight of a strange thing. A cricket had perched upon the handrail, only a few inches away from me. My line of vision was such that the creature filled the moon like a fossil.[3] It had gone there, I thought, to live and die, for there, of all places, was its small definition made whole and eternal. A warm wind rose up and purled[4] like the longing within me.

The next morning I awoke at dawn and went out on the dirt road to Rainy Mountain. It was already hot, and the grasshoppers began to fill the air. Still, it was early in the morning, and the birds sang out of the shadows. The long yellow grass on the mountain shone in the bright light, and a scissortail[5] hied above the land. There, where it ought to be, at the end of a long and legendary way, was my grandmother's grave. Here and there on the dark stones were ancestral names. Looking back once, I saw the mountain and came away.

3. fossil: hardened remains of plant or animal life from a previous geological time period.
4. purled (pʉrld): moved in ripples.
5. scissortail: a species of flycatcher bird. The bird's distinctive tail is an average of thirteen inches long and is divided like scissors near its end.

WORDS TO OWN

opaque (ō·pāk′) *adj.*: not transparent; not letting light pass through.
vital (vīt″l) *adj.*: filled with life.
enmities (en′mə·tēz) *n. pl.*: hatreds.
indulge (in·dulj′) *v.*: to satisfy; to please; to humor.

MAKING MEANINGS

First Thoughts

1. What single visual **image** in Momaday's text strikes you as the most memorable? Why?

Shaping Interpretations

2. What do you think Momaday means when he calls the Kiowa migration "a journey toward the dawn"?

3. Describe Momaday's grandmother Aho, noting her physical appearance and her thoughts. What is Momaday's attitude toward her?

4. When Momaday tells of a cricket near the end of the excerpt, he says: "It had gone there, I thought, to live and die, for there, of all places, was its small definition made whole and eternal." How do you interpret this comment? What do you think the cricket might **symbolize**?

5. List **images** that Momaday uses to convey strongly contrasting feelings of light and life versus darkness and death. Is the overall **mood** of this essay light or dark? Explain your answer.

6. Momaday writes in gracefully evocative poetic prose. On page 1096, reread the paragraph that begins "Descending eastward . . .". Then, identify at least three figures of speech (**metaphor, simile, personification**) in the paragraph that refer to the **setting**. How do they contribute to the overall effect of the writing?

7. *The Way to Rainy Mountain* is in part an **elegy**, a song or poem contemplating a dead person—or, by extension, a way of life that has been destroyed. What does Momaday praise about the Kiowas? What loss does he mourn?

Reading Check

a. Why does the narrator return to Rainy Mountain?

b. What does this memoir tell about the Kiowa religion and the role of the sun in their rituals?

c. According to Kiowa legend, what is the origin of the Big Dipper? How does this myth explain the peculiar formation called Devils Tower?

d. What eventually happens to the Kiowa?

8. Do you think Momaday and the Kiowas, like earlier Puritans and Romantics, read lessons in nature? Explain.

9. Referring to your reading notes, **summarize** the **main ideas** in Momaday's piece. Include at least two **details** that support each main idea.

CHOICES: Building Your Portfolio

Writer's Notebook

1. Collecting Ideas for an Evaluation

Just about every work of literature has at least one **setting**. One criterion for evaluating a work is the skill with which setting is evoked. In a few sentences, evaluate Momaday's success in describing setting, giving specific reasons for your judgment. Consider these uses of setting:

• creates an impression or mood
• tells about society's manners, beliefs, values, customs, etc.
• helps reveal character

Save your notes for possible use in the Writer's Workshop on page 1181.

Interpreting a Statement

2. "An awful quiet"

Momaday writes "There are things in nature that engender an awful quiet in the heart of man" (page 1096). In a two-paragraph essay, explain in your own words what the writer means by this statement. Then, tell whether you agree with him, and why.

Creative Writing

3. The Remembered Earth

For Momaday, the land around Rainy Mountain is associated with childhood and ancestral traditions. Think of a place you associate with your own childhood—a store, a park, a play area. Write a description of this place, using vivid imagery to describe what it looked like and to suggest what it meant to you.

Alice Walker

(1944–   )

In her poetry, essays, and novels, Alice Walker has celebrated the endurance, the strength, and the creativity of African American women like her mother—unsung women who carried immense familial and social burdens even as they struggled against low status and a complete lack of recognition.

Walker was born in Eatonton, Georgia, and grew up on a succession of farms in the area. Her father was a sharecropper, and her mother labored side-by-side with him in the fields, cared for their eight children, and still never failed, wherever they were living, to cultivate a large and beautiful flower garden. Her mother's hard work and determination to enrich her own life have served as an inspiration to Walker throughout her career.

A childhood accident that blinded Walker in one eye made her feel for a time disfigured and outcast. Seeking solace, she turned to writing poetry and reading, and also to closely observing people around her. Walker later attended Spelman College in Atlanta for two and a half years, before transferring to Sarah Lawrence College, near New York City. There she studied with the noted poet Muriel Rukeyser (1913–1980) before graduating in 1965.

During her college years, Walker was active in the civil rights movement in Georgia and Mississippi, and she traveled in Africa. Many of the poems in her first published collection, *Once: Poems* (1968), were inspired by these activities. The poems were written in a burst of creativity while Walker was at Sarah Lawrence. As quickly as she completed a poem, she would rush over to Muriel Rukeyser's classroom (a converted gardener's cottage in the center of the campus) and shove it under the door, then go back to her own room and write some more. This immense outpouring of creative energy continued night and day for the short period it lasted, but

© Jeff Reinking.

Walker didn't even care what Rukeyser did with the poems—the point was the creative surge of expression, not the end goal of publication. But the result was that Rukeyser gave the poems to her agent, and *Once: Poems* was published a few years later.

After graduating from college, Walker began a career of teaching and writing. She was among the first to teach university courses on the work of African American women writers, and she has since brought an understanding of their work to a wider audience. For example, Walker edited a collection of the writing of Zora Neale Hurston (page 750) called *I Love Myself When I Am Laughing . . .* (1979). In addition to poetry, short stories, and essays, Walker has written a number of well-received novels, including *Meridian* (1976), the Pulitzer Prize–winning *The Color Purple* (1982), *The Temple of My Familiar* (1989), and *Possessing the Secret of Joy* (1992).

According to the critic Donna Haisty Winchell, Walker "comes across in her writing from the 1980s and 1990s as a woman at peace with herself and with the universe. Some of the anger of her youth remains, but it is more tempered and more focused." This mellowing is evident in her 1983 collection of essays, *In Search of Our Mothers' Gardens*. In 1996, Walker published *The Same River Twice,* a memoir about the filming of her novel *The Color Purple*.

Before You Read

FROM IN SEARCH OF OUR MOTHERS' GARDENS

Make the Connection

Creativity Close to Home

The selection that follows is the second part of an essay about the creative spirit of African American women. In this section of her personal essay, Walker attempts to answer some questions she raised earlier: What did it mean for black women of previous generations to be artists? How were black women able to be creative despite limited opportunity and freedom? Walker explores these questions by examining her own mother's life.

Elements of Literature

Personal Essay

A **personal essay** (also called an **informal essay**) is a short work of nonfiction prose with a personal slant. Some of the best personal essays reveal a relationship between matters involving the writer personally and larger, more universal concerns. Such essays typically reveal deeply felt emotional involvement.

> **A** **personal** or **informal essay** is a short work of nonfiction prose with a personal slant.
>
> *For more on the Essay, see the Handbook of Literary Terms.*

Reading Skills and Strategies

Identifying the Main Idea: Outlining

Personal essays are often discursive—that is, they are not as tightly organized as formal essays are. Still, personal essays, like other essays, do contain main ideas. As a reader, it's up to you to identify those ideas and the details the writer uses to support them. As you read this essay, note each time Walker introduces a new topic. When you have finished your first reading, go back over the text and expand your notes into an outline. What are Walker's main ideas? What details (examples, anecdotes, and so on) does she use to support them? In your rereading, you should note any **key passages** that point to or support the main ideas.

from
In Search of Our Mothers' Gardens

Alice Walker

In the late 1920s my mother ran away from home to marry my father. Marriage, if not running away, was expected of seventeen-year-old girls. By the time she was twenty, she had two children and was pregnant with a third. Five children later, I was born. And this is how I came to know my mother: She seemed a large, soft, loving-eyed woman who was rarely impatient in our home. Her quick, violent temper was on view only a few times a year, when she battled with the white landlord who had the misfortune to suggest to her that her children did not need to go to school.

She made all the clothes we wore, even my brothers' overalls. She made all the towels and sheets we used. She spent the summers canning vegetables and fruits. She spent the winter evenings making quilts enough to cover all our beds.

During the "working" day, she labored beside—not behind—my father in the fields. Her day began before sunup, and did not end until late at night. There was never a moment for her to sit down, undisturbed, to unravel her own private thoughts; never a time free from interruption—by work or the noisy inquiries of her many children. And yet, it is to my mother—and all our mothers who were not famous—that I went in search of the secret of what has fed that muzzled and often mutilated, but vibrant, creative spirit that the black woman has inherited, and that pops out in wild and unlikely places to this day.

But when, you will ask, did my overworked mother have time to know or care about feeding the creative spirit?

The answer is so simple that many of us have spent years discovering it. We have constantly looked high, when we should have looked high—and low.

For example: In the Smithsonian Institution in Washington, D.C., there hangs a quilt unlike any other in the world. In fanciful, inspired, and yet simple and identifiable figures, it portrays the story of the Crucifixion. It is considered rare, beyond price. Though it follows no known pattern of quilt-making, and though it is made of bits and pieces of worthless rags, it is obviously the work of a person of powerful imagination and deep spiritual feeling. Below this quilt I saw a note that says it was made by "an anonymous Black woman in Alabama, a hundred years ago."

If we could locate this "anonymous" black woman from Alabama, she would turn out to be one of our grandmothers—an artist who left her mark in the

---

WORDS TO OWN

vibrant (vī′brənt) *adj.*: full of energy.

---

only materials she could afford, and in the only medium her position in society allowed her to use.

As Virginia Woolf[1] wrote further, in *A Room of One's Own:*

> Yet genius of a sort must have existed among women as it must have existed among the working class. [Change this to "slaves" and "the wives and daughters of sharecroppers."] Now and again an Emily Brontë[2] or a Robert Burns[3] [change this to "a Zora Hurston or a Richard Wright"] blazes out and proves its presence. But certainly it never got itself on to paper. When, however, one reads of a witch being ducked, of a woman possessed by devils [or "Sainthood"[4]], of a wise woman selling herbs [our root workers], or even a very remarkable man who had a mother, then I think we are on the track of a lost novelist, a suppressed poet, of some mute and inglorious Jane Austen. . . .[5] Indeed, I would venture to guess that Anon, who wrote so many poems without signing them, was often a woman. . . .

And so our mothers and grandmothers have, more often than not anonymously, handed on the creative spark, the seed of the flower they themselves never hoped to see: or like a sealed letter they could not plainly read.

And so it is, certainly, with my own mother. Unlike "Ma" Rainey's[6] songs, which retained their creator's name even while blasting forth from Bessie Smith's[7] mouth, no song or poem will bear my mother's name. Yet so many of the stories that I write, that we all write, are my mother's stories. Only recently did I fully realize this: that through years of listening to my mother's stories of her life, I have absorbed not only the stories themselves, but something of the manner in which she spoke, something of the urgency that involves the knowledge that her stories—like her life—must be recorded. It is probably for this reason that so much of what I have written is about characters whose counterparts in real life are so much older than I am.

But the telling of these stories, which came from my mother's lips as naturally as breathing, was not the only way my mother showed herself as an artist. For stories, too, were subject to being distracted, to dying without conclusion. Dinners must be started, and cotton must be gathered before the big rains. The artist that was and is my mother showed itself to me only after many years. This is what I finally noticed:

> Like Mem, a character in *The Third Life of Grange Copeland,*[8] my mother adorned with flowers whatever shabby house we were forced to live in. And not just your typical straggly country stand of zinnias, either. She planted ambitious gardens—and still does—with over fifty different varieties of plants that bloom profusely from early March until late November. Before she left home for the fields, she watered her flowers, chopped up the grass, and laid out new beds. When she returned from the fields she might divide clumps of bulbs, dig a cold pit,[9] uproot and replant roses, or prune branches from her taller bushes or trees—until night came and it was too dark to see.

1. **Virginia Woolf:** English novelist and critic. In *A Room of One's Own* (1929), Woolf says that, in order to write, a woman must have a room of her own (privacy) and the means to support herself (money).
2. **Emily Brontë:** English novelist and poet, best known for her novel *Wuthering Heights* (1847).
3. **Robert Burns:** eighteenth-century Scottish poet.
4. **"Sainthood":** In the early part of this essay, Walker talks about certain black women in the South called Saints. Intensely spiritual, these women were driven to madness by their creativity, for which they could find no release.
5. **Jane Austen:** English novelist, best known for *Pride and Prejudice* (1813).
6. **"Ma" Rainey:** nickname of Gertrude Malissa Nix Pridgett Rainey. She was the first great African American professional blues vocalist and is considered to be the mother of the blues.

7. **Bessie Smith:** One of the greatest of blues singers, Smith was helped to professional status by Ma Rainey. She became known in her lifetime as "Empress of the Blues."
8. ***The Third Life of Grange Copeland:*** Alice Walker's first novel, published in 1970.
9. **cold pit:** shallow pit, usually covered with glass, that is used for rooting plants or sheltering young plants from temperature variations in the spring.

WORDS TO OWN

medium (mē′dē·əm) *n.:* material for an artist.
profusely (prō·fyo͞os′lē) *adv.:* in great quantities.

Sunset and Moonrise with Maudell Sleet (1978) by Romare Bearden. From the *Profile/Part 1: The Twenties* series (Mecklenburg County). Collage on board (41″ × 29″).

Maudell Sleet's Magic Garden (1978) by Romare Bearden. From the *Profile/Part 1: The Twenties* series (Mecklenburg County). Collage on board (10⅛″ × 7″).

Whatever she planted grew as if by magic, and her fame as a grower of flowers spread over three counties. Because of her creativity with her flowers, even my memories of poverty are seen through a screen of blooms—sunflowers, petunias, roses, dahlias, forsythia, spirea, delphiniums, verbena . . . and on and on.

And I remember people coming to my mother's yard to be given cuttings from her flowers; I hear again the praise showered on her because whatever rocky soil she landed on, she turned into a garden. A garden so brilliant with colors, so original in its design, so magnificent with life and creativity, that to this day people drive by our house in Georgia—perfect strangers and imperfect strangers—and ask to stand or walk among my mother's art.

I notice that it is only when my mother is working in her flowers that she is radiant, almost to the point of being invisible—except as Creator: hand and eye. She is involved in work her soul must have. Ordering the universe in the image of her personal conception of Beauty.

Her face, as she prepares the Art that is her gift, is a legacy of respect she leaves to me, for all that illuminates and cherishes life. She has handed down respect for the possibilities—and the will to grasp them.

For her, so hindered and intruded upon in so many ways, being an artist has still been a daily part of her life. This ability to hold on, even in very simple ways, is work black women have done for a very long time.

This poem is not enough, but it is something, for the woman who literally covered the holes in our walls with sunflowers:

They were women then
My mama's generation
Husky of voice—Stout of
Step
With fists as well as
Hands
How they battered down
Doors
And ironed

Starched white
Shirts
How they led
Armies
Headragged Generals
Across mined
Fields
Booby-trapped
Kitchens
To discover books
Desks
A place for us
How they knew what we
Must know
Without knowing a page
Of it
Themselves.

Guided by my heritage of a love of beauty and a respect for strength—in search of my mother's garden, I found my own.

And perhaps in Africa over two hundred years ago, there was just such a mother; perhaps she painted vivid and daring decorations in oranges and yellows and greens on the walls of her hut; perhaps she sang—in a voice like Roberta Flack's[10]—*sweetly* over the compounds of her village; perhaps she wove the most stunning mats or told the most ingenious stories of all the village storytellers. Perhaps she was herself a poet—though only her daughter's name is signed to the poems that we know.

Perhaps Phillis Wheatley's mother was also an artist.

Perhaps in more than Phillis Wheatley's biological life is her mother's signature made clear.

10. **Roberta Flack's:** Roberta Flack is a popular African American singer-songwriter.

WORDS TO OWN

conception (kən·sep′shən) *n.*: mental formation of ideas.
ingenious (in·jēn′yəs) *adj.*: clever.

MAKING MEANINGS

First Thoughts

1. What do you find most admirable about Alice Walker's mother? Do you know anyone who also excels anonymously at something—like gardening or painting, singing or storytelling?

Shaping Interpretations

2. As a writer, how does Walker feel she has been enriched by her mother's storytelling?

3. On page 1104, in a key passage, Walker uses a **metaphor** and a **simile** to describe how African American women handed down this "creative spark" over the generations. What are these figures of speech? (Can you think of others that could be used?)

4. What do you think Walker the writer has learned from her mother the gardener?

5. In the last five lines of the poem Walker uses in the essay, she presents a **paradox,** or apparent contradiction. State the paradox in your own words, and tell what kinds of knowledge you think Walker is talking about.

6. What do you think Walker means when she says that she found her own "garden" in the process of searching for her mother's?

Challenging the Text

7. Walker describes her mother's life and feelings but never allows her mother to speak for herself. Would the essay be improved if it included quotations from Walker's mother? Explain.

Reading Check

a. Describe the kind of life Walker's mother led while Walker was growing up.

b. What secret does Walker hope to discover from examining her mother's life and the lives of other women like her mother?

c. In what two ways does Walker's mother express her creativity?

d. What happens to Walker's mother when she works in her garden?

CHOICES: Building Your Portfolio

Writer's Notebook
1. Collecting Ideas for an Evaluation

When you evaluate a **personal essay,** you might want to consider such criteria as interest of topic, clarity of theme, and emotional effect. Apply such criteria to Walker's essay, citing specific passages to support your evaluation. Save your notes for possible use in the workshop on page 1181.

Summarizing a Text
2. Creativity in Everyday Places

Refer to your reading notes and the outline you made of Walker's essay. Then, in three or four paragraphs, state the main ideas of the essay and summarize the details Walker uses to support and illuminate them. Conclude with your response to Walker's ideas.

Creative Writing / Art
3. Quiet Strengths

Write a **character sketch** of someone you admire who is not at all famous. Indicate exactly what you admire about this person. Try to include the person's occupation and a description of what he or she looks like. If you wish, include a picture or photograph.

Viewing and Representing
4. Bearden's Heroines

Pages 1105 and 1106 each feature a collage by American artist Romare Bearden (1914–1988). Look up *collage* in an encyclopedia or dictionary and try to figure out what bits of materials Bearden used in these works. Then, in a brief essay, analyze these collages and tell if you think they are appropriate for Walker's essay. Open your analysis by describing exactly what you *see* in each work.

Amy Tan

(1952–   )

Amy Tan had not planned to become a fiction writer. In fact, for years she worked as a freelance writer for high-technology companies, a career in which flights of imagination are not permitted. To ease the pressures of her job, she decided to take jazz piano lessons—and she began writing fiction. The result was the release of a dazzling new storyteller.

Tan's parents had fled Communist China and had come to the United States shortly before she was born in Oakland, California. Her mother, a nurse, was originally from Shanghai; her father, an engineer and a Baptist minister, came from Beijing.

After her father and young brother both died of brain tumors when Amy Tan was just fifteen, her mother took her away from the "diseased" house to Switzerland, where she finished high school. Her mother expected her talented daughter to become a neurosurgeon, as well as a pianist, in her spare time. When

they returned to the United States, Tan enrolled as a premed student at Linfield College, a Baptist school in Oregon, which had been selected by her mother. But she defied her mother by leaving Linfield to join her boyfriend at San Jose State University, where she changed her major from premed to English. Tan's mother took this defiance as a sort of death between them, and mother and daughter did not speak for six months.

Tan was well aware of her mother's narrative gift (she says her mother can talk for three hours straight), and perhaps it was this which eventually prompted her own desire to write. However, she was thirty-three before she wrote her first story. Called "Endgame" (retitled "Rules of the Game") and written for a Squaw Valley writers' conference, it was the first of many Tan stories that would explore the dynamic relationship between daughters and their mothers.

These stories were collected in 1989 in one volume, the now widely known best-seller *The Joy Luck Club* (also made into a popular movie). In it, stories about Chinese American daughters are interwoven with stories of their four Chinese mothers, who are members of a mahjongg club in San Francisco.

Tan's 1991 novel, *The Kitchen God's Wife,* was hailed by some critics as even more artistically successful than *The Joy Luck Club.* In this second book, a mother tells her grown daughter what life was like in China during World War II—and the daughter begins to see both her mother and herself with enlightened eyes. A third novel, *The Hundred Secret Senses* (1995), also explores a familial relationship— this time between two sisters whose lives are transformed during a visit to a small village in China.

Before You Read

FROM RULES OF THE GAME

Make the Connection

Parents and Children

At first, the following story appears to be about a Chinese American girl who stumbles into the forbidding world of championship chess and becomes an absolute whiz at it. But presently we come to understand that the story is about a matter far more familiar to us: the clash between a mother's authority over her children and her ambition for them, and a child's need to find his or her own way.

Quickwrite

Think about the rules of chess or another game you know. Then, write down some ways a game's rules might be similar to rules of human relations, especially between parents and children. What do you think the title of this story might mean? (Might it have more than one meaning?)

Elements of Literature

Motivation

Motivation refers to the reasons for a character's behavior. A writer can reveal motivation directly by telling us what makes a character tick. In many works, however, the writer shows us characters talking and acting but does not tell us the reasons for their behavior: We must sift through the details and then infer motivation. Tan's story fits into this second category. Pay particular attention to how the beat-up chess set arrives in the Jong family, how Waverly becomes interested in the game while her brothers play, and how her interest grows as theirs wanes. Then, ask yourself: What's really going on in that final match between Waverly and her true adversary and coach?

> **M**otivation refers to the underlying reasons for a character's behavior.
>
> *For more on Motivation, see the Handbook of Literary Terms.*

from Rules of the Game

from The Joy Luck Club

Amy Tan

My older brother Vincent was the one who actually got the chess set. We had gone to the annual Christmas party held at the First Chinese Baptist Church at the end of the alley. The missionary ladies had put together a Santa bag of gifts donated by members of another church. None of the gifts had names on them. There were separate sacks for boys and girls of different ages.

One of the Chinese parishioners had donned a Santa Claus costume and a stiff paper beard with cotton balls glued to it. I think the only children who thought he was the real thing were too young to know that Santa Claus was not Chinese. When my turn came up, the Santa man asked me how old I was. I thought it was a trick question; I was seven according to the American formula and eight by the Chinese calendar. I said I was born on March 17, 1951. That seemed to satisfy him. He then solemnly asked if I had been a very, very good girl this year and did I believe in Jesus Christ and obey my parents. I knew the only answer to that. I nodded back with equal solemnity.

Having watched the other children opening their gifts, I already knew that the big gifts were not necessarily the nicest ones. One girl my age got a large coloring book of biblical characters, while a less greedy girl who selected a smaller box received a glass vial of lavender toilet water.[1] The sound of the box was also important. A ten-year-old boy had chosen a box that jangled when he shook it. It was a tin globe of the world with a slit for inserting money. He must have thought it was full of dimes and nickels, because when he saw that it had just ten pennies, his face fell with such undisguised disappointment that his mother slapped the side of his head and led him out of the church hall, apologizing to the crowd for her son who had such bad manners he couldn't appreciate such a fine gift.

As I peered into the sack, I quickly fingered the remaining presents, testing their weight, imagining what they contained. I chose a heavy, compact one that was wrapped in shiny silver foil and a red satin ribbon. It was a twelve-pack of Life Savers and I spent the rest of the party arranging and rearranging the candy tubes in the order of my favorites. My brother Winston chose wisely as well. His present turned out to be a box of <u>intricate</u> plastic parts; the instructions on the box proclaimed that when they were properly assembled he would have an authentic miniature replica of a World War II submarine.

Vincent got the chess set, which would have been a very decent present to get at a church Christmas party, except it was obviously used and, as we discovered later, it was missing a black pawn and a white knight. My mother graciously thanked the unknown benefactor, saying, "Too good. Cost too much." At which point, an old lady with fine white, wispy hair nodded toward our family and said with a whistling whisper, "Merry, merry Christmas."

When we got home, my mother told Vincent to throw the chess set away. "She not want it. We

1. **toilet water:** perfumed after-bath skin freshener.

> A little knowledge withheld is a great advantage one should store for future use. That is the power of chess. It is a game of secrets in which one must show and never tell.

not want it," she said, tossing her head stiffly to the side with a tight, proud smile. My brothers had deaf ears. They were already lining up the chess pieces and reading from the dog-eared instruction book.

I watched Vincent and Winston play during Christmas week. The chess board seemed to hold elaborate secrets waiting to be untangled. The chessmen were more powerful than Old Li's magic herbs that cured <u>ancestral</u> curses. And my brothers wore such serious faces that I was sure something was at stake that was greater than avoiding the tradesmen's door to Hong Sing's.

"Let me! Let me!" I begged between games when one brother or the other would sit back with a deep sigh of relief and victory, the other annoyed, unable to let go of the outcome. Vincent at first refused to let me play, but when I offered my Life Savers as replacements for the buttons that filled in for the missing pieces, he relented. He chose the flavors: wild cherry for the black pawn and peppermint for the white knight. Winner could eat both.

As our mother sprinkled flour and rolled out small doughy circles for the steamed dumplings that would be our dinner that night, Vincent explained the rules, pointing to each piece. "You

---
WORDS TO OWN

intricate (in′tri·kit) *adj.:* complicated.
ancestral (an·ses′trəl) *adj.:* inherited.
---

have sixteen pieces and so do I. One king and queen, two bishops, two knights, two castles, and eight pawns. The pawns can only move forward one step, except on the first move. Then they can move two. But they can only take men by moving crossways like this, except in the beginning, when you can move ahead and take another pawn."

"Why?" I asked as I moved my pawn. "Why can't they move more steps?"

"Because they're pawns," he said.

"But why do they go crossways to take other men. Why aren't there any women and children?"

"Why is the sky blue? Why must you always ask stupid questions?" asked Vincent. "This is a game. These are the rules. I didn't make them up. See. Here. In the book." He jabbed a page with a pawn in his hand. "Pawn. P-A-W-N. Pawn. Read it yourself."

My mother patted the flour off her hands. "Let me see book," she said quietly. She scanned the pages quickly, not reading the foreign English symbols, seeming to search deliberately for nothing in particular.

"This American rules," she concluded at last. "Every time people come out from foreign country, must know rules. You not know, judge say, Too bad, go back. They not telling you why so you can use their way go forward. They say, Don't know why, you find out yourself. But they knowing all the time. Better you take it, find out why yourself." She tossed her head back with a satisfied smile.

I found out about all the whys later. I read the rules and looked up all the big words in a dictionary. I borrowed books from the Chinatown library. I studied each chess piece, trying to absorb the power each contained.

I learned about opening moves and why it's important to control the center early on; the shortest distance between two points is straight down the middle. I learned about the middle game and why tactics between two adversaries are like clashing ideas; the one who plays better has the clearest plans for both attacking and getting out of traps. I learned why it is essential in the endgame to have foresight, a mathematical understanding of all possible moves, and patience; all weaknesses and advantages become evident to a strong adversary and are <u>obscured</u> to a tiring opponent. I discovered that for the whole game one must

gather invisible strengths and see the endgame before the game begins.

I also found out why I should never reveal "why" to others. A little knowledge withheld is a great advantage one should store for future use. That is the power of chess. It is a game of secrets in which one must show and never tell.

I loved the secrets I found within the sixty-four black and white squares. I carefully drew a handmade chessboard and pinned it to the wall next to my bed, where at night I would stare for hours at imaginary battles. Soon I no longer lost any games or Life Savers, but I lost my adversaries. Winston and Vincent decided they were more interested in roaming the streets after school in their Hopalong Cassidy[2] cowboy hats.

On a cold spring afternoon, while walking home from school, I detoured through the playground at the end of our alley. I saw a group of old men, two seated across a folding table playing a game of chess, others smoking pipes, eating peanuts, and watching. I ran home and grabbed Vincent's chess set, which was bound in a cardboard box with rubber bands. I also carefully selected two prized rolls of Life Savers. I came back to the park and approached a man who was observing the game.

"Want to play?" I asked him. His face widened with surprise and he grinned as he looked at the box under my arm.

"Little sister, been a long time since I play with dolls," he said, smiling benevolently. I quickly put the box down next to him on the bench and displayed my <u>retort</u>.

Lau Po, as he allowed me to call him, turned out to be a much better player than my brothers. I lost many games and many Life Savers. But over the weeks, with each diminishing roll of candies, I added new secrets. Lau Po gave me the names. The Double Attack from the East and West Shores. Throwing Stones on the Drowning Man. The Sudden Meeting of the Clan. The Surprise from

---

2. **Hopalong Cassidy:** cowboy hero of movies and television from the 1930s through the early 1950s.

- -

WORDS TO OWN

obscured (əb·skyoord′) v.: concealed.
retort (ri·tôrt′) n.: quick answer.

- -

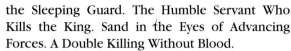

As I began to play, the boy disappeared, the color ran out of the room, and I saw only my white pieces and his black ones waiting on the other side. A light wind began blowing past my ears. It whispered secrets only I could hear.

the Sleeping Guard. The Humble Servant Who Kills the King. Sand in the Eyes of Advancing Forces. A Double Killing Without Blood.

There were also the fine points of chess etiquette. Keep captured men in neat rows, as well-tended prisoners. Never announce "Check" with vanity, lest someone with an unseen sword slit your throat. Never hurl pieces into the sandbox after you have lost a game, because then you must find them again, by yourself, after apologizing to all around you. By the end of the summer, Lau Po had taught me all he knew, and I had become a better chess player.

A small weekend crowd of Chinese people and tourists would gather as I played and defeated my opponents one by one. My mother would join the crowds during these outdoor exhibition games. She sat proudly on the bench, telling my admirers with proper Chinese humility, "Is luck."

A man who watched me play in the park suggested that my mother allow me to play in local chess tournaments. My mother smiled graciously, an answer that meant nothing. I desperately wanted to go, but I bit back my tongue. I knew she would not let me play among strangers. So as we walked home I said in a small voice that I didn't want to play in the local tournament. They would have American rules. If I lost, I would bring shame on my family.

"Is shame you fall down nobody push you," said my mother.

During my first tournament, my mother sat with me in the front row as I waited for my turn. I frequently bounced my legs to unstick them from the cold metal seat of the folding chair. When my name was called, I leapt up. My mother unwrapped something in her lap. It was her *chang,* a small tablet of red jade which held the sun's fire. "Is luck," she whispered, and tucked it into my dress pocket. I turned to my opponent, a fifteen-year-old boy from Oakland. He looked at me, wrinkling his nose.

As I began to play, the boy disappeared, the color ran out of the room, and I saw only my white pieces and his black ones waiting on the other side. A light wind began blowing past my ears. It whispered secrets only I could hear.

Scene from the movie *The Joy Luck Club.*
©Buena Vista Pictures Distribution, Inc.

"Blow from the South," it murmured. "The wind leaves no trail." I saw a clear path, the traps to avoid. The crowd rustled. "Shhh! Shhh!" said the corners of the room. The wind blew stronger. "Throw sand from the East to distract him." The knight came forward ready for the sacrifice. The wind hissed, louder and louder. "Blow, blow, blow. He cannot see. He is blind now. Make him lean away from the wind so he is easier to knock down."

"Check," I said, as the wind roared with laughter. The wind died down to little puffs, my own breath.

My mother placed my first trophy next to a new plastic chess set that the neighborhood Tao society had given to me. As she wiped each piece with a soft cloth, she said, "Next time win more, lose less."

"Ma, it's not how many pieces you lose," I said. "Sometimes you need to lose pieces to get ahead."

"Better to lose less, see if you really need."

At the next tournament, I won again, but it was my mother who wore the triumphant grin.

"Lost eight piece this time. Last time was eleven. What I tell you? Better off lose less!" I was annoyed, but I couldn't say anything.

I attended more tournaments, each one farther away from home. I won all games, in all divisions. The Chinese bakery downstairs from our flat displayed my growing collection of trophies in its window, amidst the dust-covered cakes that were never picked up. The day after I won an important regional tournament, the window encased a fresh sheet cake with whipped-cream frosting and red script saying, "Congratulations, Waverly Jong, Chinatown Chess Champion." Soon after that, a flower shop, headstone engraver, and funeral parlor offered to sponsor me in national tournaments. That's when my mother decided I no longer had to do the dishes. Winston and Vincent had to do my chores.

"Why does she get to play and we do all the work," complained Vincent.

"Is new American rules," said my mother. "Meimei[3] play, squeeze all her brains out for win chess. You play, worth squeeze towel."

By my ninth birthday, I was a national chess

3. **Meimei** (mā'mā'): Chinese for "little sister."

champion. I was still some 429 points away from grand-master status,[4] but I was touted as the Great American Hope, a child prodigy and a girl to boot. They ran a photo of me in *Life* magazine next to a quote in which Bobby Fischer said, "There will never be a woman grand master." "Your move, Bobby," said the caption.

The day they took the magazine picture I wore neatly plaited braids clipped with plastic barrettes trimmed with rhinestones. I was playing in a large high school auditorium that echoed with phlegmy coughs and the squeaky rubber knobs of chair legs sliding across freshly waxed wooden floors. Seated across from me was an American man, about the same age as Lau Po, maybe fifty. I remember that his sweaty brow seemed to weep at my every move. He wore a dark, malodorous suit. One of his pockets was stuffed with a great white kerchief on which he wiped his palm before sweeping his hand over the chosen chess piece with great flourish.

In my crisp pink-and-white dress with scratchy lace at the neck, one of two my mother had sewn for these special occasions, I would clasp my hands under my chin, the delicate points of my elbows poised lightly on the table in the manner my mother had shown me for posing for the press. I would swing my patent leather shoes back and forth like an impatient child riding on a school bus. Then I would pause, suck in my lips, twirl my chosen piece in midair as if undecided, and then firmly plant it in its new threatening place, with a triumphant smile thrown back at my opponent for good measure.

I no longer played in the alley of Waverly Place. I never visited the playground where the pigeons and old men gathered. I went to school, then directly home to learn new chess secrets, cleverly concealed advantages, more escape routes.

But I found it difficult to concentrate at home. My mother had a habit of standing over me while

4. **grand-master status:** top rank in international chess competition.

WORDS TO OWN

touted (tσut′id) *v.*: highly praised.
prodigy (präd′ə·jē) *n.*: extremely gifted person.
malodorous (mal′ō′dər·əs) *adj.*: bad-smelling.

I plotted out my games. I think she thought of herself as my protective ally. Her lips would be sealed tight, and after each move I made, a soft "Hmmmmph" would escape from her nose.

"Ma, I can't practice when you stand there like that," I said one day. She retreated to the kitchen and made loud noises with the pots and pans. When the crashing stopped, I could see out of the corner of my eye that she was standing in the doorway. "Hmmmph!" Only this one came out of her tight throat.

My parents made many concessions to allow me to practice. One time I complained that the bedroom I shared was so noisy that I couldn't think. Thereafter, my brothers slept in a bed in the living room facing the street. I said I couldn't finish my rice; my head didn't work right when my stomach was too full. I left the table with half-finished bowls and nobody complained. But there was one duty I couldn't avoid. I had to accompany my mother on Saturday market days when I had no tournament to play. My mother would proudly walk with me, visiting many shops, buying very little. "This my daughter Wave-ly Jong," she said to whoever looked her way.

One day, after we left a shop I said under my breath, "I wish you wouldn't do that, telling everybody I'm your daughter." My mother stopped walking. Crowds of people with heavy bags pushed past us on the sidewalk, bumping into first one shoulder, then another.

"Aiii-ya. So shame be with mother?" She grasped my hand even tighter as she glared at me.

I looked down. "It's not that, it's just so obvious. It's just so embarrassing."

"Embarrass you be my daughter?" Her voice was cracking with anger.

"That's not what I meant. That's not what I said."

"What you say?"

I knew it was a mistake to say anything more, but I heard my voice speaking. "Why do you have to use me to show off? If you want to show off, then why don't you learn to play chess."

My mother's eyes turned into dangerous black slits. She had no words for me, just sharp silence.

I felt the wind rushing around my hot ears. I jerked my hand out of my mother's tight grasp and spun around, knocking into an old woman. Her bag of groceries spilled to the ground.

"Aii-ya! Stupid girl!" my mother and the woman cried. Oranges and tin cans careened down the sidewalk. As my mother stooped to help the old woman pick up the escaping food, I took off.

I raced down the street, dashing between people, not looking back as my mother screamed shrilly, "Meimei! Meimei!" I fled down an alley, past dark curtained shops and merchants washing the grime off their windows. I sped into the sunlight, into a large street crowded with tourists examining trinkets and souvenirs. I ducked into another dark alley, down another street, up another alley. I ran until it hurt and I realized I had nowhere to go, that I was not running from anything. The alleys contained no escape routes.

My breath came out like angry smoke. It was cold. I sat down on an upturned plastic pail next to a stack of empty boxes, cupping my chin with my hands, thinking hard. I imagined my mother, first walking briskly down one street or another looking for me, then giving up and returning home to await my arrival. After two hours, I stood up on creaking legs and slowly walked home.

The alley was quiet and I could see the yellow lights shining from our flat like two tiger's eyes in the night. I climbed the sixteen steps to the door, advancing quietly up each so as not to make any warning sounds. I turned the knob; the door was locked. I heard a chair moving, quick steps, the locks turning—click! click! click!—and then the door opened.

"About time you got home," said Vincent. "Boy, are you in trouble."

He slid back to the dinner table. On a platter were the remains of a large fish, its fleshy head still connected to bones swimming upstream in vain escape. Standing there waiting for my punishment, I heard my mother speak in a dry voice.

"We are not concerning this girl. This girl not have concerning for us."

Nobody looked at me. Bone chopsticks clinked against the insides of bowls being emptied into hungry mouths.

I walked into my room, closed the door, and lay down on my bed. The room was dark, the ceiling

WORDS TO OWN

concessions (kən·sesh′ənz) *n. pl.*: acts of giving in.
careened (kə·rēnd′) *v.*: lurched sideways.

filled with shadows from the dinnertime lights of neighboring flats.

In my head, I saw a chessboard with sixty-four black and white squares. Opposite me was my opponent, two angry black slits. She wore a triumphant smile. "Strongest wind cannot be seen," she said.

Her black men advanced across the plane, slowly marching to each <u>successive</u> level as a single unit. My white pieces screamed as they scurried and fell off the board one by one. As her men drew closer to my edge, I felt myself growing light. I rose up into the air and flew out the window. Higher and higher, above the alley, over the tops of tiled roofs, where I was gathered up by the wind and pushed up toward the night sky until everything below me disappeared and I was alone.

I closed my eyes and pondered my next move.

SPRIMARY **Sources** AN INTERVIEW

An Interview with Amy Tan

In a magazine interview, Amy Tan answered questions about her stories of mothers and daughters in *The Joy Luck Club*. Here are some of her responses:

Q: Do you have advice to offer aspiring novelists?

A: You have to develop a discipline, and you have to learn that you can't always wait for inspiration. Also, I think young writers try to imitate the people they admire, and that's dangerous. No matter how well you imitate Tama Janowitz or Jay McInerney, it doesn't work. You have to find your own voice.

Q: How do Chinese Americans like your book?

A: My feelings were so personal; I didn't think anyone else felt that way. The surprise is how many Chinese people have said, "Your stories are so much like my family." They thought I had been eavesdropping in their living rooms.

Q: How does your mother feel about your success?

A: The day the book was number four on *The New York Times* Best Seller List, I showed the list to my mother. She looked at it, laid her finger across the line, and asked, "Who's number three? And two? And one?" She's very proud, but none of this impresses her too much, and she doesn't think that I should be impressed either. But she was also saying, "I think you should be number one."

Archive Photos.

—Joan Chatfield-Taylor, "Cosmo Talks to Amy Tan"

MAKING MEANINGS

First Thoughts

1. Did you find the relationship between mother and daughter believable? Why or why not?

Shaping Interpretations

2. What does Waverly's mother mean when she says, on page 1112, "She not want it. We not want it"? How do the boys' actions show cultural and generational **conflicts** between the mother and her children?

3. Review your Quickwrite notes. How does the "power of chess" relate to the relationship between Waverly and her mother?

4. What do you think is Mrs. Jong's **motivation** for showing off Waverly? Why does Waverly resent her mother's actions?

5. Near the end of the story, Waverly's imaginary opponent says, "Strongest wind cannot be seen." Where else in the story is that statement used? Explain what you think it means.

6. What do you think is the meaning of Waverly's fantasy at the story's end? What do you predict will be her "next move"?

7. Find passages in the story where rules of various sorts are talked about. What multiple meanings might the **title** have?

Reading Check

a. How did the Jongs get their first chess set?

b. Explain how young Waverly came to be allowed to play with her brothers.

c. Point out some of the ways in which Waverly's mother shows she is ambitious for her daughter and proud of her accomplishments.

d. As a result of Waverly's success at chess, what **conflicts** arise between her and her mother?

CHOICES: Building Your Portfolio

Writer's Notebook

1. Collecting Ideas for an Evaluation

In a review of *The Joy Luck Club,* the critic Susan Dooley wrote: "These women from China find trying to talk to their daughters like trying to plug a foreign appliance into an American outlet. The current won't work. Impulses collide and nothing flows through the wires except anger and exasperation." Write your thoughts on how well this critical evaluation applies to "Rules of the Game." Use specific examples from the story as well as your personal comments. Save your notes for possible use in the Writer's Workshop on page 1181.

Interpreting Characters

2. Visitors from Other Stories

In a brief essay, tell what you think would happen if Mrs. Jong and Cukita's mother (from Julia Alvarez's "Daughter of Invention" on page 1079) were to enter each other's story. If Mrs. Jong could be brought into Alvarez's story, whose side would she take—the mother's or the father's? If Cukita's mother could be introduced to Mrs. Jong, what advice would she give Mrs. Jong? Write one paragraph about each character. Be sure to explain *why* you think each character would behave in a particular way if she were inserted into another situation.

Speaking and Listening

3. Rules of the Games

Choose a sport or game familiar to you and other class members. Working in groups, prepare oral reports on the etiquette of the game—its unwritten rules, examples of gamesmanship, and the terms used to describe its special maneuvers or plays. Before you begin, review Tan's discussion of the essence of chess on page 1113.

Reading Skills and Strategies

VOCABULARY: BASE WORDS, ROOTS, AND WORD FAMILIES

Amy Tan opens "Rules of the Game" with a Christmas party at which the narrator receives a gift after satisfactorily answering a set of questions.

> He then *solemnly* asked if I had been a very, very good girl this year and did I believe in Jesus Christ and obey my parents. I knew the only answer to that. I nodded back with equal *solemnity*.

Notice the appropriateness of the narrator's answer. Tan uses a noun to describe the manner of the answer (*solemnity*) that is nearly identical to the adverb used to describe the tone of the question (*solemnly*). The two words, *solemnly* and *solemnity*, belong to the same word family.

In general, there are two broad categories of words in English: those that can be divided into smaller parts (*unkind, repackage*) and those that cannot (*proud, high*). Words that stand alone and are complete by themselves are called **base words:** *solemn, answer, equal.* Words that can be divided (*solemnity, equality*) are made up of two or more of these three word parts: **roots, prefixes, suffixes.** Roots are word parts that carry the core meaning of a word, but usually do not stand alone (the root *graph* is an exception). Most often, they are combined with a prefix and/or suffix to form a word. Words that share the same root or base word can be considered word families.

In the English language, many words are formed from Greek and Latin roots. To the right are some examples of common word roots.

Common Word Roots		
Root	Meaning	Examples
GREEK		
–anthrop–	human	anthropology
–chrom–	color	monochrome
–dem–	people	demagogue, democrat
–derm–	skin	dermatology
–log–, –logy–	study, word	logic, theology
–ortho–	straight	orthodox, orthography
–phil–	like, love	philanthropy
LATIN		
–audi–	hear	audio, auditorium
–ben–, –bene–	good	benign, beneficial
–cogn–	know	recognize
–duc–, –duct–	draw, lead	induce, deduct
–loc–	place	locality, locate
–magn–	large, grand	magnify, magnitude
–mor–, –mort–	death	moribund, mortal
–omni–	all	omniscient
–pon–, –pos–	place	impose, postpone
–prim–	early	primeval, primitive
–sacr–, –sanc–	sacred, holy	sacrilege, sanctify
–spir–	breath	expire, inspire
–uni–	one	unify, universe
–ver–	turn	reverse, aversion

Try It Out

At right are some other words from "Rules of the Game." Identify the word roots. Then, find at least two other words that belong to the same word family, using a dictionary if necessary. Do not include forms whose only difference is an **inflectional suffix**—a suffix that changes person, number, or tense (*–s, –ed, –ing*).

1. benefactor
2. auditorium
3. adversaries
4. opponent
5. sacrifice

word: *benefactor*	
root 1:	root 2:
other words:	other words:

Garrett Hongo

(1951–)

Charles Wright.

"For me, one voice among so many others, a voice I've tried to train as much out of a passion for English and American poetry as out of my loyalties to the Japanese American past of four generations and to the landscape of Hawaii, the place of my birth, it has been a *feeling* for language and its beauty that has brought me to poetry and kept me at it."

In this one long sentence, Garrett Hongo seems to unite all the most vital elements that characterize his work: a distinctive voice, a passion for poetry, loyalty to past generations, a sense of place, and a love of language itself.

Garrett Hongo was born in Volcano, Hawaii, and grew up on the North Shore of Oahu and in the Los Angeles area. He graduated from Pomona College in 1973 and earned a Master of Fine Arts degree from the University of California, Irvine, in 1980. His first poetry collection, *Yellow Light,* was published in 1982. But it was his second collection, *The River of Heaven* (1988), that made a strong impression on literary critics. The book was chosen as the Lamont Poetry Selection of the Academy of American Poets and was a finalist for a Pulitzer Prize. While writing, Hongo taught at the University of Missouri and the University of Houston before becoming professor of English at the University of Oregon. In 1995, he published a well-received prose work, *Volcano: A Memoir of Hawaii.*

Garrett Hongo's poems often center on the complexities facing Americans of Asian descent as they labor to establish a personal identity, interact with people of other backgrounds, and express themselves artistically. His poems also overflow with the common details of contemporary American popular culture, such as television shows and pop music, all delivered in a language and style that blends passion and delicacy.

Hongo says that he strives for "emotional nobility of some kind, the idea that poems might help produce and reveal our 'better nature.'" He reaches for "the *jen* of Confucianism

which was a notion of the innate moral and spiritual 'good' in people that impressed Ezra Pound as one of the highest poetic values; and the idea of *samadhi,* or sensate and sentient calm, that we get from Buddhism."

Hongo's wife, his friends, his fellow poets, all those who share his ideals—these are his audience, he tells us. Yet he adds with pride, "I think I must say that I write for my father, Albert Kazuyoshi Hongo, in a very personal way. I want to be his witness, to testify to his great and noble life, in struggle against anger, in struggle against his own loneliness and isolation for being a Hawaiian Japanese who emigrated to Los Angeles without much family or community. He was a great example to me of a man who refused to hate, or, being different himself, to be afraid of difference, who accepted the friendship of all the strange and underprivileged ostracized by the rest of 'normal' society— Vietnamese, Mexicans, Southern blacks, reservation Indians relocated to the city—and I want my poems to be equal to his heart." The following poem certainly is devoted to that goal.

Before You Read

WHAT FOR

Make the Connection

Language Matters

Sometimes we forget that language matters—it affects us in many important ways, whether it is spoken or written. The poem that follows zeroes in on spoken language—old Hawaiian chants, Buddhist mantras, the stories and songs of grandparents. We learn from language, the poem's speaker tells us, and we try to change the world with spoken words and syllables passed from generation to generation.

Reading Skills and Strategies

Identifying Specific Details

As you read the poem a second time, write down details that you feel are particularly vivid or interesting.

Elements of Literature

Refrain

A **refrain** is a word, phrase, line, or group of lines that is repeated several times in a poem. A poet may use a refrain to help establish rhythm, to emphasize a point, or to achieve some other effect. Short refrains typically appear at the ends of lines, but in the following poem they appear at the beginnings of lines.

What For

Garrett Hongo

At six I lived for spells:
how a few Hawaiian words could call
up the rain, could hymn like the sea
in the long swirl of chambers
5 curling in the nautilus of a shell,
how Amida's° ballads of the Buddhaland
in the drone of the priest's liturgy
could conjure money from the poor
and give them nothing but mantras,°
10 the strange syllables that healed desire.

I lived for stories about the war
my grandfather told over *hana* cards,°
slapping them down on the mats
with a sharp Japanese *kiai.*°

6. Amida's: *Amida* is Japanese for "Amitābha," Sanskrit for "infinite light." Amida is the great savior worshiped by members of the Pure Land sect, one of the most popular forms of Buddhism in eastern Asia.
9. mantras: hymns or other portions of sacred Hindu text, chanted or intoned as incantations or prayers.
12. *hana* cards: cards used in a Japanese game in which players attempt to match pairs of flower patterns. *Hana* is Japanese for "flower."
14. *kiai:* a Japanese onomatopoeic word for the sound made by slapping down *hana* cards.

15 I lived for songs my grandmother sang
   stirring curry into a thick stew,
   weaving a calligraphy of Kannon's° love
   into grass mats and straw sandals.

   I lived for the red volcano dirt
20 staining my toes, the salt residue
   of surf and sea wind in my hair,
   the arc of a flat stone skipping
   in the hollow trough of a wave.

   I lived a child's world, waited
25 for my father to drag himself home,
   dusted with blasts of sand, powdered rock,
   and the strange ash of raw cement,
   his deafness made worse by the clang
   of pneumatic drills, sore in his bones

17. Kannon's: In Japanese Buddhism, Kannon is the bodhisattva ("Buddha to be") of infinite compassion and mercy.

30 from the buckings of a jackhammer.
     He'd hand me a scarred lunchpail,
     let me unlace the hightop G.I. boots,
     call him the new name I'd invented
     that day in school, write it for him
35 on his newspaper. He'd rub my face
     with hands that felt like gravel roads,
     tell me to move, go play, and then he'd
     walk to the laundry sink to scrub,
     rinse the dirt of his long day
40 from a face brown and grained as koa° wood.

40. koa: Hawaiian mimosa tree valued for its wood and bark.

     I wanted to take away the pain
     in his legs, the swelling in his joints,
     give him back his hearing,
     clear and rare as crystal chimes,
45 the fins of glass that wrinkled
     and sparked the air with their sound.

     I wanted to heal the sores that work
     and war had sent to him,
     let him play catch in the backyard
50 with me, tossing a tennis ball
     past papaya trees without the shoulders
     of pain shrugging back his arms.

     I wanted to become a doctor of pure magic,
     to string a necklace of sweet words
55 fragrant as pine needles and plumeria,°
     fragrant as the bread my mother baked,
     place it like a lei of cowrie shells
     and *pikake*° flowers around my father's neck,
     and chant him a blessing, a sutra.°

55. plumeria: classification of fragrant, flowering, tropical American trees.
58. *pikake:* Hawaiian for "Arabian jasmine."
59. sutra: in general, one of the sacred scriptures of Buddhism.

A Different Story

In this excerpt from a personal essay, Garrett Hongo remembers his maternal grandfather, who was known by his last name, Kubota. During most of Hongo's childhood and adolescence, Kubota lived with the poet's family near Los Angeles, California. The grandfather is also remembered in "What For."

I was a teenager and, though I was bored listening to stories I'd heard often enough before at holiday dinners, I was dutiful. I took my spot on the couch next to Kubota and heard him out. Usually, he'd tell me about his schooling in Japan where he learned judo along with mathematics and literature. He'd learned the *soroban* there— the abacus, which was the original pocket calculator of the Far East—and that, along with his strong, judo-trained back, got him his first job in Hawaii. This was the moral. "Study *ha-ahd,*" he'd say with pidgin emphasis. "Learn read good. Learn speak da kine *good* English." The message is the familiar one taught to any children of immigrants: succeed through education. And imitation. But this time, Kubota reached down into his past and told me a different story. I was thirteen by then, and I suppose he thought me ready for it. He told me about Pearl Harbor, how the planes flew in wing after wing of formations over his old house in La'ie in Hawaii, and how, the next day, after Roosevelt had made his famous "Day of Infamy" speech about the treachery of the Japanese, the FBI agents had come to his door and taken him in, hauled him off to Honolulu for questioning, and held him without charge for several days. I thought he was lying. I thought he was making up a kind of horror story to shock me and give his moral that much more starch. But it was true. I asked around. I brought it up during history class in junior high school, and my teacher, after silencing me and stepping me off to the back of the room, told me that it was indeed so. I asked my mother and she said it was true. I asked my schoolmates, who laughed and ridiculed me

for being so ignorant. We lived in a Japanese-American community, and the parents of most of my classmates were the *nisei* who had been interned as teenagers all through the war. . . .

I was not made yet, and [Kubota] was determined that his stories be part of my making. He spoke quietly at first, mildly, but once into his narrative and after his drink was down, his voice would rise and quaver with resentment and he'd make his accusations. He gave his testimony to me and I held it at first cautiously in my conscience like it was an heirloom too delicate to expose to strangers and anyone outside of the world Kubota made with his words. "I give you story now," he once said, "and you learn speak good, eh?" It was my job, as the disciple of his preaching I had then become, Ananda to his Buddha, to reassure him with a promise. "You learn speak good like the Dillingham," he'd say another time, referring to the wealthy scion of the grower family who had once run, unsuccessfully, for one of Hawaii's first senatorial seats. Or he'd then invoke a magical name, the name of one of his heroes, a man he thought particularly exemplary and righteous. "Learn speak dah good Ing-rish like *Mistah Inouye,*" Kubota shouted. "He *lick* dah Dillingham even in debate. I saw on *terre-bision* myself." He was remembering the debates before the first senatorial election just before Hawaii was admitted to the Union as its fiftieth state. "You *tell* story," Kubota would end. And I had my injunction.

—Garrett Hongo
from "Kubota"

MAKING MEANINGS

First Thoughts

1. What **images** stood out for you as you read the poem? Why were they so effective?

Shaping Interpretations

2. What do you think the speaker means by saying "I wanted to become a doctor of pure magic" (line 53)?

3. What does the title of the poem mean?

4. Identify the two **refrains** of the poem. What effects do each of them have?

Extending the Text

5. In Primary Sources (page 1125), Garrett Hongo remembers holding his grandfather's "testimony" in his mind "like it was an heirloom." How do you think the testimony of previous generations comes down to us?

Left, A. K. Hongo (Garrett Hongo's father) on the docks of Honolulu Harbor, shipping out to Oakland, then boot camp, then Italy (1944).

Courtesy Garrett Hongo.

CHOICES:
Building Your Portfolio

Writer's Notebook

1. Collecting Ideas for an Evaluation

Establishing criteria for evaluating the emotional impact of a poem (or other work of art) is not easy. You might consider the power of the emotional effect, whether it appeals to sentiment or to more complex feelings, or whether it changes you in any way. Establish your own criteria for evaluating emotional impact, and then apply them to Hongo's "What For." Save your notes for possible use in the Writer's Workshop on page 1181.

Analyzing Technique

2. Details Add Up

Hongo includes much concrete detail in "What For." Review the notes you made while reading. Then, write a short essay in which you discuss the effect of supplying so much detail. Which details are especially powerful? Would the poem be as effective if it used only abstract generalizations?

Comparing Poems

3. Walt Whitman Redux?

Some critics say Garrett Hongo's style is similar to Walt Whitman's, partly because both poets repeat words, word order, and phrasing, include catalogs of concrete items, and show empathy for other people. Pick a poem or two by Whitman (pages 352–362), and in a brief essay, compare Whitman's style with Hongo's style in "What For."

Creative Writing

4. The Father's Poem

What might the father in Hongo's poem have thought of his son and his son's attitude toward him? Have the father tell us in a poem the structure and style of which resemble the final three stanzas of "What For."

Collection *21*

Lee
Baldwin
Plath
Borges
Dickey
Cisneros
Cofer
Dove

Autobiographia Literaria

**When I was a child
I played by myself in a
corner of the schoolyard
all alone.**

**I hated dolls and I
hated games, animals were
not friendly and birds
flew away.**

**If anyone was looking
for me I hid behind a
tree and cried out "I am
an orphan."**

**And here I am, the
center of all beauty!
writing these poems!
Imagine!**

—Frank O'Hara (1926–1966)

Andrea Lee

(1953–   )

© Jerry Bauer.

Andrea Lee grew up in Yeadon, a prosperous Philadelphia suburb favored by African American professionals. It was a place where grounds were well kept, children were sent off to good schools, and prejudice was something the residents knew only from books and television.

"Yeadon . . . was as solid a repository of American virtues and American flaws as any other close-knit suburban community," Lee wrote in the early 1980s. "It had, and still has, its own peculiar flavor—a lively mixture of materialism, idealism, and ironic humor that prevents the minds of its children from stagnating."

In 1978, Lee went to Russia with her husband, a graduate student in Russian history, for eight months' study at Moscow State University and for another two months in Leningrad (now St. Petersburg). The young Americans stood in lines and rode the subways with ordinary Russians. They absorbed, as Lee wrote, "a view of life in Moscow and Leningrad that was very different from that of the diplomats and journalists we knew." This yearlong trip resulted in a series of articles that were collected in her well-received book *Russian Journal,* nominated for a National Book Award in 1981.

Lee's novel *Sarah Phillips* was published in 1984. The title character shares with the author a prosperous upbringing and a Harvard education. Sarah is the daughter of an African American minister who combines old-fashioned Baptist charisma with a contemporary dedication to the civil rights movement. The reviewer Bruce Van Wyngarden praised *Sarah Phillips* as a "coming-of-age remembrance in which detail

and insight are delightfully, and sometimes poignantly, blended." The story that follows is an excerpt from that novel.

A longtime contributor to *The New Yorker,* Lee, who now lives in Italy, has proved herself as both a journalist and a novelist. Her style manifests the craft essential to both nonfiction and fiction. She combines the pinpoint accuracy of observation that we expect of nonfiction with the warmth that gives life to fictional characters. One critic called her writing "luminous," a word that suggests her appealing clarity and grace.

Before You Read

NEW AFRICAN

Make the Connection

Coming of Age

"New African" is about the love and conflicts in an African American family. The story is in particular about how a girl establishes a place for herself in the family and takes a huge step toward forging her own identity. Watch for the give-and-take as the narrator tries to come to terms with her father and her father's world.

Reading Skills and Strategies

Interpreting a Character

"New African" is in large part a character study of the narrator's father. As you read, write down details that give you insight into Reverend Phillips.

Elements of Literature

Internal Conflict

An **internal conflict** is a struggle between opposing forces within a person's mind. Much of the power and suspense of "New African" derives from several internal conflicts the narrator experiences as she struggles to make her own place in the world.

> **A**n **internal conflict** is a struggle between opposing forces within a person's mind.
>
> *For more on Conflict, see the Handbook of Literary Terms.*

Background

Before you read "New African," you might review the section on Puritan religious beliefs in the "Beginnings" introduction (see page 10). This story, set in Philadelphia in 1963, deals with a Baptist church whose members believe that baptism should be given only to those people who ask for it after receiving a special call from God.

ANDREA LEE 1129

New African

Andrea Lee

On a hot Sunday morning in the summer of 1963, I was sitting restlessly with my mother, my brother Matthew, and my aunts Lily, Emma, and May in a central pew of the New African Baptist Church. It was mid-August, and the hum of the big electric fans at the back of the church was almost enough to muffle my father's voice from the pulpit; behind me I could hear Mrs. Gordon, a stout, feeble old woman who always complained of dizziness, remark sharply to her daughter that at the rate the air-conditioning fund was growing, it might as well be for the next century. Facing the congregation, my father—who was Reverend Phillips to the rest of the world—seemed hot himself; he mopped his brow with a handkerchief and drank several glasses of ice water from the heavy pitcher on the table by the pulpit. I looked at him critically. He's still reading the text, I thought. Then he'll do the sermon, then the baptism, and it will be an hour, maybe two.

I rubbed my chin and then idly began to snap the elastic band that held my red straw hat in place. What I would really like to do, I decided, would be to go home, put on my shorts, and climb up into the treehouse I had set up the day before with Matthew. We'd nailed an old bushel basket up in the branches of the big maple that stretched above the sidewalk in front of the house; it made a sort of crow's nest where you could sit comfortably, except for a few splinters, and read, or peer through the dusty leaves at the cars that passed down the quiet suburban road. There was shade and wind and a feeling of high adventure up in the treetop, where the air seemed to vibrate with the dry rhythms of the cicadas; it was as different as possible from church, where the packed congregation sat in a near-visible miasma of emotion and cologne, and trolleys[1] passing in the city street outside set the stained-glass windows rattling.

I slouched between Mama and Aunt Lily and felt myself going limp with lassitude and boredom, as if the heat had melted my bones; the only thing about me with any character seemed to be my firmly starched eyelet dress. Below the scalloped hem, my legs were skinny and wiry,

---

1. **trolleys:** mass-transit vehicles that run along tracks set into the street.

the legs of a ten-year-old amazon,[2] scarred from violent adventures with bicycles and skates. A fingernail tapped my wrist; it was Aunt Emma, reaching across Aunt Lily to press a piece of butterscotch into my hand. When I slipped the candy into my mouth, it tasted faintly of Arpège;[3] my mother and her three sisters were monumental women, ample of bust and slim of ankle, with a weakness for elegant footwear and French perfume. As they leaned back and forth to exchange discreet tidbits of gossip, they fanned themselves and me with fans from the Byron J. Wiggins Funeral Parlor. The fans, which were fluttering throughout the church, bore a depiction of the Good Shepherd: a hollow-eyed blond Christ holding three fat pink-cheeked children. This Christ resembled the Christ who stood among apostles on the stained-glass windows of the church. Deacon Wiggins, a thoughtful man, had also provided New African with a few dozen fans bearing the picture of a black child praying, but I rarely saw those in use.

There was little that was new or very African about the New African Baptist Church. The original congregation had been formed in 1813 by three young men from Philadelphia's large community of free blacks, and before many generations had passed, it had become spiritual home to a collection of prosperous, conservative, generally light-skinned parishioners. The church was a gray Gothic structure, set on the corner of a rundown street in South Philadelphia a dozen blocks below Rittenhouse Square and a few blocks west of the spare, clannish Italian neighborhoods that produced Frankie Avalon[4] and Frank Rizzo.[5] At the turn of the century, the neighborhood had been a tidy collection of brick houses with scrubbed marble steps—the homes of a group of solid citizens whom Booker T. Washington,[6] in a centennial address to the church, described as "the ablest Negro businessmen of our generation." Here my father had grown up aspiring to preach

to the congregation of New African—an ambition encouraged by my grandmother Phillips, a formidable churchwoman. Here, too, my mother and her sisters had walked with linked arms to Sunday services, exchanging affected little catch phrases of French and Latin they had learned at Girls' High.

In the 1950s many of the parishioners, seized by the national urge toward the suburbs, moved to newly integrated towns outside the city, leaving the streets around New African to fill with bottles and papers and loungers. The big church stood suddenly isolated. It had not been abandoned— on Sundays the front steps overflowed with members who had driven in—but there was a tentative feeling in the atmosphere of those Sunday mornings, as if through the muddle of social change, the future of New African had become unclear. Matthew and I, suburban children, felt a mixture of pride and animosity toward the church. On the one hand, it was a marvelous private domain, a richly decorated and infinitely suggestive playground where we were petted by a congregation that adored our father; on the other hand, it seemed a bit like a dreadful old relative in the city, one who forced us into tedious visits and who linked us to a past that came to seem embarrassingly primitive as we grew older.

I slid down in my seat, let my head roll back, and looked up at the blue arches of the church ceiling. Lower than these, in back of the altar, was an enormous gilded cross. Still lower, in a semicircle near the pulpit, sat the choir, flanked by two tall golden files of organ pipes, and below the choir was a somber crescent of dark-suited deacons. In front, at the center of everything, his bald head gleaming under the lights, was Daddy. On summer Sundays he wore white robes, and when he raised his arms, the heavy material fell in curving folds like the ridged petals of an Easter lily. Usually when I came through the crowd to kiss him after the service, his cheek against my lips felt wet and gravelly with sweat and a new growth of beard sprouted since morning. Today, however, was a baptismal Sunday, and I wouldn't have a chance to kiss him until he was freshly shaven and

2. **amazon:** strong, athletic woman. The Amazons of Greek mythology were a race of female warriors.
3. **Arpège** (är·pezh'): brand of perfume.
4. **Frankie Avalon** (1940–   ): popular singer and film actor in the 1950s and 1960s.
5. **Frank Rizzo** (1920–1991): Philadelphia's mayor, 1972–1980.
6. **Booker T. Washington** (1856–1915): noted African American author and educator.

WORDS TO OWN

discreet (di·skrēt') *adj.*: wisely cautious.
affected (a·fekt'id) *v.* used as *adj.*: put on for show.

cool from the shower he took after the ceremony. The baptismal pool was in an alcove to the left of the altar; it had mirrored walls and red velvet curtains, and above it, swaying on a string, hung a stuffed white dove.

Daddy paused in the invocation and asked the congregation to pray. The choir began to sing softly:

> Blessed assurance,
> Jesus is mine!
> Oh what a foretaste
> Of glory divine!

In the middle of the hymn, I edged my head around my mother's cool, muscular arm (she swam every day of the summer) and peered at Matthew. He was sitting bolt upright holding a hymnal and a pencil, his long legs inside his navy-blue summer suit planted neatly in front of him, his freckled thirteen-year-old face that was so like my father's wearing not the demonic grin it bore when we played alone but a maddeningly composed, attentive expression. "Two hours!" I mouthed at him, and pulled back at a warning pressure from my mother. Then I joined in the singing, feeling disappointed: Matthew had returned me a glance of scorn. Just lately he had started acting very superior and tolerant about tedious Sunday mornings. A month before, he'd been baptized, marching up to the pool in a line of white-robed children as the congregation murmured happily about Reverend Phillips's son. Afterward Mrs. Pinkston, a tiny, yellow-skinned old woman with a blind left eye, had come up to me and given me a painful hug, whispering that she was praying night and day for the pastor's daughter to hear the call as well.

I bit my fingernails whenever I thought about baptism; the subject brought out a deep-rooted balkiness in me. Ever since I could remember, Matthew and I had made a game of dispelling the mysteries of worship with a gleeful secular eye: We knew how the bread and wine were prepared for Communion, and where Daddy bought his robes (Ekhardt Brothers, in North Philadelphia, makers also of robes for choirs, academicians, and judges). Yet there was an unassailable magic about an act as public and dramatic as baptism. I felt toward it the slightly exasperated awe a stagehand might feel on realizing that although he can identify with professional exactitude the minutest components of a show, there is still something indefinable in the power that makes it a cohesive whole. Though I could not have put it into words, I believed that the decision to make a frightening and embarrassing backward plunge into a pool of sanctified water meant that one had received a summons to Christianity as unmistakable as the blare of an automobile horn. I believed this with the same fervor with which, already, I believed in the power of romance, especially in the miraculous efficacy of a lover's first kiss. I had never been kissed by a lover, nor had I heard the call to baptism.

For a Baptist minister and his wife, my father and mother were unusually relaxed about religion; Matthew and I had never been required to read the Bible, and my father's sermons had been criticized by some older church members for omitting the word "sin." Mama and Daddy never tried to push me toward baptism, but a number of other people did. Often on holidays, when I had retreated from the noise of the family dinner table and sat trying to read in my favorite place (the window seat in Matthew's room, with the curtains drawn to form a tent), Aunt Lily would come and find me. Aunt Lily was the youngest of my mother's sisters, a kindergarten teacher with the fatally overdeveloped air of quaintness that is the infallible mark of an old maid. Aunt Lily hoped and hoped again with various suitors, but even I knew she would never find a husband. I respected her because she gave me wonderful books of fairy tales, inscribed in her neat, loopy hand; when she talked about religion, however, she assumed an anxious, flirtatious air that made me cringe. "Well, Miss Sarah, what are you scared of?" she would ask, tugging gently on one of my braids and bringing her plump face so close to mine that I could see her powder, which was, in accordance with the custom of fashionable colored ladies, several shades lighter than her olive skin. "God isn't anyone to be afraid of!" she'd continue as I looked at her with my best deadpan expression. "He's someone nice, just as nice as your daddy"—I had always suspected Aunt Lily of having a crush on my father—"and he loves you, in the same way your daddy does!"

"You would make us all so happy!" I was told at different times by Aunt Lily, Aunt Emma, and Aunt May. The only people who said nothing at all were Mama and Daddy, but I sensed in them a thoughtful, suppressed wistfulness that maddened me.

After the hymn, Daddy read aloud a few verses from the third chapter of Luke, verses I recognized in the almost instinctive way in which I was familiar with all of the well-traveled parts of the Old and New Testaments. "Prepare the way of the Lord, make his paths straight," read my father in a mild voice. "Every valley shall be filled, and every mountain and hill shall be brought low, and the crooked shall be made straight, and the rough paths made smooth, and all flesh shall see the salvation of God."

He had a habit of pausing to fix his gaze on part of the congregation as he read, and that Sunday he seemed to be talking to a small group of strangers who sat in the front row. These visitors were young white men and women, students from Philadelphia colleges, who for the past year had been coming to hear him talk. It was hard to tell them apart: All the men seemed to have beards, and the women wore their hair long and straight. Their informal clothes stood out in that elaborate assembly, and church members whispered angrily that the young women didn't wear hats. I found the students appealing and rather romantic, with their earnest eyes and timid air of being perpetually sorry about something. It was clear that they had good intentions, and I couldn't understand why so many of the adults in the congregation seemed to dislike them so much. After services, they would hover around Daddy. "Never a more beautiful civil rights sermon!" they would say in low, fervent voices. Sometimes they seemed to have tears in their eyes.

I wasn't impressed by their praise of my father; it was only what everyone said. People called him a champion of civil rights; he gave speeches on the radio, and occasionally he appeared on television. (The first time I'd seen him on Channel 5, I'd been gravely disappointed by the way he looked: The bright lights exaggerated the furrows that ran between his nose and mouth, and his narrow eyes gave him a sinister air; he looked like an Oriental villain in a Saturday afternoon thriller.) During the past year he had organized a boycott that integrated the staff of a huge frozen-food plant in Philadelphia, and he'd been away several times to attend marches and meetings in the South. I was privately embarrassed to have a parent who freely admitted going to jail in Alabama, but the students who visited New African seemed to think it almost miraculous. Their conversations with my father were peppered with references to places I had never seen, towns I imagined as being swathed in a mist of darkness visible: Selma, Macon, Birmingham, Biloxi.[7]

Matthew and I had long ago observed that what Daddy generally did in his sermons was to speak very softly and then surprise everyone with a shout. Of course, I knew that there was more to it than that; even in those days I recognized a genius of personality in my father. He loved crowds, handling them with the expert good humor of a man entirely in his element. At church banquets, at the vast annual picnic that was held beside a lake in New Jersey, or at any gathering in the backyards and living rooms of the town where we lived, the sound I heard most often was the booming of my father's voice followed by shouts of laughter from the people around him. He had a passion for oratory; at home, he infuriated Matthew and me by staging absurd debates at the dinner table, verbal melees[8] that he won quite selfishly, with a loud crow of delight at his own virtuosity. "Is a fruit a vegetable?" he would demand. "Is a zipper a machine?" Matthew and I would plead with him to be quiet as we strained to get our own points across, but it was no use. When the last word had resounded and we sat looking at him in irritated silence, he would clear his throat, settle his collar, and resume eating, his face still glowing with an irrepressible glee.

When he preached, he showed the same private delight. A look of rapt pleasure seemed to broaden and brighten the contours of his angular face until it actually appeared to give off light as

---

7. **Selma . . . Biloxi:** Selma, Alabama; Macon, Georgia; Birmingham, Alabama; and Biloxi, Mississippi: sites of significant civil rights protests during the 1960s.
8. **melees** (māʹlāzʹ): battles.

- -

WORDS TO OWN

wistfulness (wistʹfəl·nis) n.: vague longing.

- -

he spoke. He could preach in two very different ways. One was the delicate, sonorous idiom of formal oratory, with which he must have won the prizes he held from his seminary days. The second was a hectoring,[9] insinuating, incantatory tone, full of the rhythms of the South he had never lived in, linking him to generations of thun-

9. **hectoring:** bullying.

derous Baptist preachers. When he used this tone, as he was doing now, affectionate laughter rippled through the pews.

"I know," he said, looking out over the congregation and blinking his eyes rapidly, "that there are certain people in this room—oh, I don't have to name names or point a finger—who have ignored that small true voice, the voice that is the voice of Jesus calling out in the shadowy depths of the soul. And while you all are looking around and wondering just who those 'certain people' are, I want to tell you all a secret: They are you and me, and your brother-in-law, and every man, woman, and child in this room this morning. All of us listen to our bellies when they tell us it is time to eat, we pay attention to our eyes when they grow heavy from wanting sleep, but when it comes to the sacred knowledge our hearts can offer, we are deaf, dumb, blind, and senseless. Throw away that blindness, that deafness, that sulky indifference. When all the world lies to you, Jesus will tell you what is right. Listen to him. Call on him. In these times of confusion, when there are a dozen different ways to turn, and Mama and Papa can't help you, trust Jesus to set you straight. Listen to him. The Son of God has the answers. Call on him. Call on him. Call on him."

The sermon was punctuated with an occasional loud "Amen!" from Miss Middleton, an excitable old lady whose eyes flashed <u>defiantly</u> at the reproving faces of those around her. New African was not the kind of Baptist church where shouting was a normal part of the service; I occasionally heard my father mock the staid congregation by calling it Saint African. Whenever Miss Middleton loosed her tongue (sometimes she went off into fits of rapturous shrieks and had to be helped out of the service by the church nurse), my mother and aunts exchanged grimaces and shrugged, as if confronted by incomprehensibly barbarous behavior.

When Daddy had spoken the final words of the sermon, he drank a glass of water and vanished through a set of red velvet curtains to the right of the altar. At the same time, the choir began to sing what was described in the church bulletin as a "selection." These selections were always arenas for the running dispute between the choirmaster and the choir. Jordan Grimes, the choirmaster, was a Curtis[10] graduate who was partial to Handel,[11] but the choir preferred artistic spirituals performed in the lush, heroic style of Paul Robeson.[12] Grimes had triumphed that Sunday. As the

choir gave a spirited but unwilling rendition of Agnus Dei,[13] I watched old Deacon West smile in approval. A Spanish-American War veteran, he admitted to being ninety-four but was said to be older; his round yellowish face, otherwise unwrinkled, bore three deep, deliberate-looking horizontal creases on the brow, like carvings on a scarab.[14] "That old man is as flirtatious as a boy of twenty!" my mother often said, watching his stiff, courtly movements among the ladies of the church. Sometimes he gave me a dry kiss and a piece of peppermint candy after the service; I liked his crackling white collars and smell of bay rum.[15]

The selection ended; Jordan Grimes struck two deep chords on the organ, and the lights in the church went low. A subtle stir ran through the congregation, and I moved closer to my mother. This was the moment that fascinated and disturbed me more than anything else at church: the prelude to the ceremony of baptism. Deacon West rose and drew open the draperies that had been closed round the baptismal pool, and there stood my father in water to his waist. The choir began to sing:

> We're marching to Zion,
> Beautiful, beautiful Zion,
> We're marching upward to Zion,
> The beautiful city of God!

Down the aisle, guided by two church mothers, came a procession of eight children and adolescents. They wore white robes, the girls with white ribbons in their hair, and they all had solemn expressions of terror on their faces. I knew each one of them. There was Billy Price, a big, slow-moving boy of thirteen, the son of Deacon Price. There were the Duckery twins. There was Caroline Piggee, whom I hated because of her long, soft black curls, her dimpled pink face, and her lisp that ravished grown-ups. There was

13. **Agnus Dei** (äg′noos dä′ē′): Latin for "lamb of God," a very formal prayer for mercy and peace recited in the Catholic Mass.
14. **scarab** (skar′əb): beetle-shaped religious symbol of ancient Egypt.
15. **bay rum:** fragrant after-shave lotion.

10. **Curtis:** Curtis Institute of Music in Philadelphia.
11. **Handel:** George Frideric Handel (1685–1759), German-born composer of religious music, including the oratorio *Messiah*.
12. **Paul Robeson** (1898–1976): African American actor and singer, famous for his interpretations of black spirituals.

- -

WORDS TO OWN

defiantly (dē·fī′ənt·lē) *adv.*: strongly resisting.

- -

Georgie Battis and Sue Anne Ivory, and Wendell and Mabel Cullen.

My mother gave me a nudge. "Run up to the side of the pool!" she whispered. It was the custom for unbaptized children to watch the ceremony from the front of the church. They sat on the knees of the deacons and church mothers, and it was not unusual for a child to volunteer then and there for next month's baptism. I made my way quickly down the dark aisle, feeling the carpet slip under the smooth soles of my patent-leather shoes.

When I reached the side of the pool, I sat down in the bony lap of Bessie Gray, an old woman who often took care of Matthew and me when our parents were away; we called her Aunt Bessie. She was a fanatically devout Christian whose strict ideas on child rearing had evolved over decades of domestic service to a rich white family in Delaware. The link between us, a mixture of hostility and grudging affection, had been forged in hours of pitched battles over bedtimes and proper behavior. Her worshipful respect for my father, whom she called "the Rev," was exceeded only by her pride—the malice-tinged pride of an omnis-cient family servant—in her "white children," to whom she often unflatteringly compared Matthew and me. It was easy to see why my mother and her circle of fashionable matrons described Bessie Gray as "archaic"—one had only to look at her black straw hat attached with three enormous old-fashioned pins to her knot of frizzy white hair. Her lean, brown-skinned face was dominated by a hawk nose inherited from some Indian ancestor and punctuated by a big black mole; her eyes were small, shrewd, and baleful. She talked in ways that were already passing into history and parody, and she wore a thick orange face powder that smelled like dead leaves.

I leaned against her spare bosom and watched the other children clustered near the pool, their bonnets and hair ribbons and round heads outlined in the dim light. For a minute it was very still. Somewhere in the hot, darkened church a baby gave a fretful murmur; from outside came the sound of cars passing in the street. The candidates for baptism, looking stiff and self-conscious, stood lined up on the short stairway leading to the pool. Sue Anne Ivory fiddled with her sleeve and then put her fingers in her mouth.

Daddy spoke the opening phrases of the ceremony: "In the Baptist Church, we do not baptize infants, but believe that a person must choose salvation for himself."

I didn't listen to the words; what I noticed was the music of the whole—how the big voice darkened and lightened in tone, and how the grand architecture of the Biblical sentences ennobled the voice. The story, of course, was about Jesus and John the Baptist. One phrase struck me newly each time: "This is my beloved son, in whom I am well pleased!" Daddy sang out these words in a clear, triumphant tone, and the choir echoed him. Ever since I could understand it, this phrase had made me feel melancholy; it seemed to expose a hard knot of disobedience that had always lain inside me. When I heard it, I thought enviously of Matthew, for whom life seemed to be a sedate and ordered affair: He, not I, was a child in whom a father could be well pleased.

Daddy beckoned to Billy Price, the first baptismal candidate in line, and Billy, ungainly in his white robe, descended the steps into the pool. In soft, slow voices the choir began to sing:

> Wade in the water,
> Wade in the water, children,
> Wade in the water,
> God gonna trouble
> The water.

In spite of Jordan Grimes's efforts, the choir swayed like a gospel chorus as it sang this spiritual; the result was to add an eerie jazz beat to the minor chords. The music gave me goose flesh. Daddy had told me that this was the same song that the slaves had sung long ago in the South, when they gathered to be baptized in rivers and streams. Although I cared little about history, and found it hard to picture the slaves as being any ancestors of mine, I could clearly imagine them coming together beside a broad muddy river that wound away between trees drooping with strange vegetation. They walked silently in lines, their faces very black against their white clothes, leading their children. The whole scene was bathed in

WORDS TO OWN

omniscient (äm·nish′ənt) *adj.*: all-knowing.
sedate (si·dāt′) *adj.*: calm and composed.

ANDREA LEE 1137

the heavy golden light that meant age and solemnity, the same light that seemed to weigh down the Israelites in illustrated volumes of Bible stories, and that shone now from the baptismal pool, giving the ceremony the air of a spectacle staged in a dream.

All attention in the darkened auditorium was now focused on the pool, where between the red curtains my father stood holding Billy Price by the shoulders. Daddy stared into Billy's face, and the boy stared back, his lips set and trembling. "And now, by the power invested in me," said Daddy, "I baptize you in the name of the Father, the Son, and the Holy Ghost." As he pronounced these words, he conveyed a tenderness as efficient and impersonal as a physician's professional manner; beneath it, however, I could see a strong private gladness, the same delight that transformed his face when he preached a sermon. He paused to flick a drop of water off his forehead, and then, with a single smooth, powerful motion of his arms, he laid Billy Price back into the water as if he were putting an infant to bed. I caught my breath as the boy went backward. When he came up, sputtering, two church mothers helped him out of the pool and through a doorway into a room where he would be dried and dressed. Daddy shook the water from his hands and gave a slight smile as another child entered the pool.

One by one, the baptismal candidates descended the steps. Sue Anne Ivory began to cry and had to be comforted. Caroline Piggee blushed and looked up at my father with such a coquettish air that I jealously wondered how he could stand it. After a few baptisms my attention wandered, and I began to gnaw the edge of my thumb and to peer at the pale faces of the visiting college students. Then I thought about Matthew, who had punched me in the arm that morning and had shouted, "No punchbacks!" I thought as well about a collection of horse chestnuts I meant to assemble in the fall, and about two books, one whose subject was adults and divorces, and another, by E. Nesbit, that continued the adventures of the Bastable children.

After Wendell Cullen had left the water (glancing uneasily back at the wet robe trailing behind him), Daddy stood alone among the curtains and the mirrors. The moving reflections from the pool made the stuffed dove hanging over him seem to flutter on its string. "Dear Lord," said Daddy, as Jordan Grimes struck a chord, "bless these children who have chosen to be baptized in accordance with your teaching, and who have been reborn to carry out your work. In each of them, surely, you are well pleased." He paused, staring out into the darkened auditorium. "And if there is anyone out there—man, woman, child—who wishes to be baptized next month, let him come forward now." He glanced around eagerly. "Oh, do come forward and give Christ your heart and give me your hand!"

Just then Aunt Bessie gave me a little shake and whispered sharply, "Go on up and accept Jesus!"

I stiffened and dug my bitten fingernails into my palms. The last clash of wills I had had with Aunt Bessie had been when she, crazily set in her old southern attitudes, had tried to make me wear an enormous straw hat, as her "white children" did, when I played outside in the sun. The old woman had driven me to madness, and I had ended up spanked and sullen, crouching moodily under the dining-room table. But this was different, outrageous, none of her business, I thought. I shook my head violently and she took advantage of the darkness in the church to seize both of my shoulders and jounce me with considerable roughness, whispering, "Now, listen, young lady! Your daddy up there is calling you to Christ. Your big brother has already offered his soul to the Lord. Now Daddy wants his little girl to step forward."

"No, he doesn't." I glanced at the baptismal pool, where my father was clasping the hand of a strange man who had come up to him. I hoped that this would distract Aunt Bessie, but she was tireless.

"Your mama and your aunt Lily and your aunt May all want you to answer the call. You're hurting them when you say no to Jesus."

"No, I'm not!" I spoke out loud and I saw the people nearby turn to look at me. At the sound of my voice, Daddy, who was a few yards away, faltered for a minute in what he was saying and glanced over in my direction.

Aunt Bessie seemed to lose her head. She stood up abruptly, pulling me with her, and, while I was still frozen in a dreadful paralysis, tried to drag me down the aisle toward my father. The two of us began a brief struggle that could not have lasted for more than a few seconds but that seemed an endless mortal conflict—my slippery patent-leather shoes braced against the floor, my straw hat sliding cockeyed and lodging against one ear, my right arm twisting and twisting in the iron circle of the old woman's grip, my nostrils full of the dead-leaf smell of her powder and black skirts. In an instant I had wrenched my arm free and darted up the aisle toward Mama, my aunts, and Matthew. As I slipped past the pews in the darkness, I imagined that I could feel eyes fixed on me and hear whispers. "What'd you do, dummy?" whispered Matthew, tugging on my sash as I reached our pew, but I pushed past him without answering. Although it was hot in the church, my teeth were chattering: It was the first time I had won a battle with a grown-up, and the earth seemed to be about to cave in beneath me. I squeezed in between Mama and Aunt Lily just as the lights came back on in the church. In the baptismal pool, Daddy raised his arms for the last time. "The Lord bless you and keep you," came his big voice. "The Lord be gracious unto you, and give you peace."

What was curious was how uncannily subdued my parents were when they heard of my skirmish with Aunt Bessie. Normally they were swift to punish Matthew and me for misbehavior in church and for breaches in politeness toward adults; this episode combined the two, and smacked of sacrilege besides. Yet once I had made an unwilling apology to the old woman (as I kissed her she shot me such a vengeful glare that I realized that forever after it was to be war to the death between the two of us), I was permitted, once we had driven home, to climb up into the green shade of the big maple tree I had dreamed of throughout the service. In those days, more than now, I fell away into a remote dimension whenever I opened a book; that afternoon, as I sat with rings of sunlight and shadow moving over my arms and legs, and winged yellow seeds plopping down on the pages of *The Story of the Treasure Seekers,* I felt a vague uneasiness floating in the back of my mind—a sense of having misplaced something, of being myself misplaced. I was holding myself quite aloof from considering what had happened, as I did with most serious events, but through the adventures of the Bastables I kept remembering the way my father had looked when he'd heard what had happened. He hadn't looked severe or angry, but merely puzzled, and he had regarded me with the same puzzled expression, as if he'd just discovered that I existed and didn't know what to do with me. "What happened, Sairy?" he asked, using an old baby nickname, and I said, "I didn't want to go up there." I hadn't cried at all, and that was another curious thing.

After that Sunday, through some adjustment in the adult spheres beyond my perception, all pressure on me to accept baptism ceased. I turned twelve, fifteen, then eighteen without being baptized, a fact that scandalized some of the congregation; however, my parents, who openly discussed everything else, never said a word to me. The issue, and the episode that had illuminated it, was surrounded by a clear ring of silence that, for our garrulous[16] family, was something close to supernatural. I continued to go to New African—in fact, continued after Matthew, who dropped out abruptly during his freshman year in college; the ambiguousness in my relations with the old church gave me at times an inflated sense of privilege (I saw myself as a romantically isolated religious heroine, a sort of self-made Baptist martyr) and at other times a feeling of loss that I was too proud ever to acknowledge. I never went up to take my father's hand, and he never commented upon that fact to me. It was an odd pact, one that I could never consider in the light of day; I stored it in the subchambers of my heart and mind. It was only much later, after he died, and I left New African forever, that I began to examine the peculiar gift of freedom my father—whose entire soul was in the church, and in his exuberant, bewitching tongue—had granted me through his silence.

16. **garrulous** (gar′ə·ləs): talkative.

WORDS TO OWN
mortal (môr′təl) *adj.*: life-threatening; extreme.
sacrilege (sak′rə·lij) *n.*: violation of something sacred.
ambiguousness (am·big′yo͞o·əs·nis) *n.*: lack of clarity; uncertainty.

MAKING MEANINGS

First Thoughts

1. Do you find the narrator's attitudes and feelings believable? Why or why not?

Shaping Interpretations

2. In refusing to be baptized, what do you think Sarah is really objecting to? How would you explain the feeling of being misplaced that she experiences at the end of the story?

3. Refer- ring to the notes you made while reading, how would you **characterize** Sarah's father? What does Sarah mean in the tribute she pays to her father in the story's last sentence?

4. What **conflicts** between generations and cultures can you identify in the story?

5. The **title** of a work of art often is a key to its meaning. In what ways is the father a "new" African? In what ways is Sarah?

6. Is Lee's main purpose in this story to present a realistic record of a single experience in 1963, or is she presenting a broader **theme** about coming of age as an African American woman in the early 1960s? Support your answer with specific references to the story.

Reading Check

a. Describe the **setting** as it is presented in the opening of "New African." What details in the first three paragraphs help you feel the summer heat of the city?

b. In what ways does Sarah feel her brother growing away from her? What passages show that she regards him as more "acceptable" than she is?

c. What passages throughout the story reveal Sarah's **inner conflict** about her father's church?

d. Is there a **resolution** to Sarah's conflict by story's end? Explain.

CHOICES: Building Your Portfolio

Writer's Notebook

1. Collecting Ideas for an Evaluation

One characteristic of almost all good writing is the inclusion of interesting details. The details should be relevant to the work, not just tossed in for no apparent reason. "New African" contains many details about the setting and characters. Pick out at least three details, and write notes evaluating their contribution to the story's overall effect. Save your notes for possible use in the Writer's Workshop on page 1181.

Interpreting a Character

2. Breaking Free

In a brief essay, describe Sarah—her thoughts, her feelings, her relationships with others. Remember that **character** can be revealed by these methods: (a) describing physical appearance; (b) describing actions; (c) quoting spoken words; (d) showing people's responses to the character; (e) revealing private thoughts and feelings; and (f) direct comments by the author.

Creative Writing

3. A Face in the Crowd

Write a first-person narrative told from the **point of view** of a young person (any young person, including yourself) who is a member of a large audience attending a public function. Imitating Lee's style in the opening paragraphs of this story, have your narrator describe the setting and reveal what he or she sees, hears, and smells—and thinks about the setting and audience. Before you write, decide what tone your narrator will adopt in describing the situation. Then, read your narrative aloud for the class.

James Baldwin

(1924–1987)

James Baldwin felt compelled to write at length about being an African American "because it was the gate I had to unlock before I could hope to write about anything else." His essays flow from his conviction that a writer's duty is "to examine attitudes, to go beneath the surface, to tap the source."

One of the most controversial and stirring writers of the twentieth century, James Baldwin was born and raised in New York

Y. Coatsaliou/Sygma.

City's Harlem, where his stepfather was the minister of a small evangelical church. As a young man, Baldwin read voraciously and served as a junior minister for a few years at the Fireside Pentecostal Assembly. At the age of twenty-four, he used funds from a fellowship to move to Europe. While living in Paris, he completed his first—and some say best—novel, *Go Tell It on the Mountain* (1953). *Notes of a Native Son,* a collection of autobiographical essays published in 1955, established Baldwin as an American writer of the first rank. The critic Irving Howe said Baldwin was among "the two or three greatest essayists this country has ever produced."

Although he lived much of his life in France, Baldwin never relinquished his U.S. citizenship, and in later years he traveled back to his homeland so often that he considered himself a transatlantic commuter. While abroad, he wrote in a variety of forms, including novels, plays, essays, poetry, and book reviews. Two of Baldwin's plays, *The Amen Corner* (1955) and *Blues for Mister Charlie* (1964), were produced on Broadway.

In the 1950s, the decade that witnessed the early growth of the American civil rights

movement, Baldwin's audacious, searing scrutiny of racial injustice played a major role in forcing leaders, black and white, to come to terms with one of the nation's most anguishing problems—the treatment of African Americans. He saw himself as a "disturber of the peace," and some chided him for his unrelenting criticism. For instance, Benjamin DeMott wrote in the *Saturday Review,* "To function as a voice of outrage month after month for a decade and more strains heart and mind, and rhetoric as well; the consequence is a writing style ever on the edge of being winded by too many summonses to intensity."

In the early sixties, Baldwin's reputation grew with the publication of additional essays, *Nobody Knows My Name: More Notes of a Native Son* (1961) and *The Fire Next Time* (1963), a groundbreaking book on race relations that had wide influence. He later published several novels, participated in TV documentaries, and remained a prominent, humane advocate of racial justice in American life.

At the time of his death in France, Baldwin was working on a biography of the Reverend Martin Luther King, Jr. Soon after Baldwin died, two noted African American writers praised his lifework. Orde Coombs wrote, "Because he existed we felt that the racial miasma that swirled around us would not consume us, and it is not too much to say that this man saved our lives." Juan Williams of the *Washington Post* said, "America and the literary world are far richer for [Baldwin's] witness. The proof of a shared humanity across the divides of race, class, and more is the testament that the preacher's son, James Arthur Baldwin, has left us."

AUTOBIOGRAPHICAL NOTES

Make the Connection

Know Thyself

The ancient Greek philosopher Socrates believed that only an *examined* life is worth living. What exactly does it mean to live an examined life? At the least, it means stepping back from the whirl of daily activities and gaining some perspective on who you are, where you have been, and where you are heading. It means creating new angles of vision, asking questions, proposing answers. It means self-assessment as a part of self-creation. As you will see, James Baldwin certainly took Socrates' dictum to heart. The autobiographical notes that follow first appeared as a preface to Baldwin's acclaimed *Notes of a Native Son.*

Reading Skills and Strategies

Using Study Strategies: Outlining

As you read, begin an **outline** of Baldwin's essay by pausing to identify and write down the **main idea** of each paragraph. When you have finished reading the essay, go back over the text and add the most important **supporting details** for each main idea. If necessary, revise your paraphrases of Baldwin's main ideas so that they accurately reflect the text.

Autobiographical Notes

James Baldwin

I was born in Harlem thirty-one years ago. I began plotting novels at about the time I learned to read. The story of my childhood is the usual bleak fantasy, and we can dismiss it with the restrained observation that I certainly would not consider living it again. In those days my mother was given to the exasperating and mysterious habit of having babies. As they were born, I took them over with one hand and held a book with the other. The children probably suffered, though they have since been kind enough to deny it, and in this way I read *Uncle Tom's Cabin* and *A Tale of Two Cities* over and over and over again; in this way, in fact, I read just about everything I could get my hands on—except the Bible, probably because it was the only book I was encouraged to read. I must also confess that I wrote—a great deal—and my first professional triumph, in any case, the first effort of mine to be seen in print, occurred at the age of twelve or thereabouts, when a short story I had written about the Spanish revolution won some sort of a prize in an extremely short-lived church newspaper. I remember the story was censored by the lady editor, though I don't remember why, and I was outraged.

Also wrote plays, and songs, for one of which I received a letter of congratulations from Mayor La Guardia,[1] and poetry, about which the less said, the better. My mother was delighted by all these goings-on, but my father wasn't; he wanted me to be a preacher. When I was fourteen I became a preacher, and when I was seventeen I stopped. Very shortly thereafter I left home. For God knows how long I struggled with the world of commerce and industry—I guess they would say they struggled with *me*—and when I was about twenty-one I had enough done of a novel to get a Saxton Fellowship. When I was twenty-two the fellowship was over, the novel turned out to be unsalable, and I started waiting on tables in a Village[2] restaurant and writing book reviews—mostly, as it turned out, about the Negro problem, concerning which the color of my skin made me automatically an expert. Did another book, in company with photographer Theodore Pelatowski, about the store-front churches in Harlem. This book met exactly the same fate as my first—fellowship, but no sale. (It was a Rosenwald Fellowship.) By the time I was twenty-four I had decided to stop reviewing books about the Negro problem—which, by this time, was only slightly less horrible in print than it was in life—and I packed my bags and went to France, where I finished, God knows how, *Go Tell It on the Mountain.*

Any writer, I suppose, feels that the world into which he was born is nothing less than a conspiracy against the cultivation of his talent—which attitude certainly has a great deal to support it. On the other hand, it is only because the world looks on his talent with such a frightening indifference that the artist is compelled to make his talent important. So that any writer, looking back over even so short a span of time as I am here forced to assess, finds that the things which hurt him and the things which helped him cannot be divorced from each other; he could be helped in a certain way only because he was hurt in a certain way; and his help is simply to be enabled to move from one conundrum to the next—one is tempted to say that he moves from one disaster to the next. When one begins looking for influences one finds them by the score. I haven't thought much about my own, not enough anyway; I hazard that the King James Bible, the rhetoric of the store-

---

1. **Mayor La Guardia:** Fiorello La Guardia, mayor of New York City from 1934 to 1945.

2. **Village:** Greenwich Village, a section of Manhattan noted as a center for writers and other artists.

WORDS TO OWN

bleak (blēk) *adj.*: cheerless.
censored (sen′sərd) *v.*: cut or changed to remove material deemed objectionable.
assess (ə·ses′) *v.*: to evaluate; to judge the value of.
conundrum (kə·nun′drəm) *n.*: riddle.

---

front church, something ironic and violent and perpetually understated in Negro speech—and something of Dickens' love for bravura[3]—have something to do with me today; but I wouldn't stake my life on it. Likewise, innumerable people have helped me in many ways; but finally, I suppose, the most difficult (and most rewarding) thing in my life has been the fact that I was born a Negro and was forced, therefore, to effect some kind of truce with this reality. (Truce, by the way, is the best one can hope for.)

One of the difficulties about being a Negro writer (and this is not special pleading, since I don't mean to suggest that he has it worse than anybody else) is that the Negro problem is written about so widely. The bookshelves groan under the weight of information, and everyone therefore considers himself informed. And this information, furthermore, operates usually (generally, popularly) to reinforce traditional attitudes. Of traditional attitudes there are only two—For or Against—and I, personally, find it difficult to say which attitude has caused me the most pain. I am speaking as a writer; from a social point of view I am perfectly aware that the change from ill-will to good-will, however motivated, however imperfect, however expressed, is better than no change at all.

But it is part of the business of the writer—as I see it—to examine attitudes, to go beneath the surface, to tap the source. From this point of view the Negro problem is nearly inaccessible. It is not only written about so widely; it is written about so badly. It is quite possible to say that the price a Negro pays for becoming articulate is to find himself, at length, with nothing to be articulate about. ("You taught me language," says Caliban to Prospero,[4] "and my profit on't is I know how to curse.") Consider: the tremendous social activity that this problem generates imposes on whites and Negroes alike the necessity of looking forward, of working to bring about a better day. This is fine, it keeps the waters troubled; it is all, indeed, that has made possible the Negro's progress. Nevertheless, social affairs are not generally speaking

the writer's prime concern, whether they ought to be or not; it is absolutely necessary that he establish between himself and these affairs a distance which will allow, at least, for clarity, so that before he can look forward in any meaningful sense, he must first be allowed to take a long look back. In the context of the Negro problem neither whites nor blacks, for excellent reasons of their own, have the faintest desire to look back; but I think that the past is all that makes the present <u>coherent</u>, and further, that the past will remain horrible for exactly as long as we refuse to assess it honestly.

I know, in any case, that the most <u>crucial</u> time in my own development came when I was forced to recognize that I was a kind of bastard of the West; when I followed the line of my past I did not find myself in Europe but in Africa. And this meant that in some subtle way, in a really profound way, I brought to Shakespeare, Bach, Rembrandt, to the stones of Paris, to the cathedral at Chartres, and to the Empire State Building, a special attitude. These were not really my creations, they did not contain my history; I might search in them in vain forever for any reflection of myself. I was an <u>interloper</u>; this was not my heritage. At the same time I had no other heritage which I could possibly hope to use—I had certainly been unfitted for the jungle or the tribe. I would have to <u>appropriate</u> these white centuries, I would have to make them mine—I would have to accept my special attitude, my special place in this scheme—otherwise I would have no place in *any* scheme. What was the most difficult was the fact that I was forced to admit something I had always hidden from myself, which the American Negro has had to hide from himself as the price of his public progress; that I hated and feared white people. This did not mean that I loved black people; on the contrary, I despised them, possibly because they failed to produce Rembrandt. In effect, I hated and feared the world. And this meant, not only that I thus gave the world an altogether mur-

---

WORDS TO OWN
coherent (kō·hir′ənt) *adj.*: clear, logical, and consistent.
crucial (krōō′shəl) *adj.*: critical; decisive.
interloper (in′tər·lō′pər) *n.*: intruder; meddler.
appropriate (ə·prō′prē·āt) *v.*: to take over.

---

3. **bravura** (brə·vyoor′ə): florid, brilliant style.
4. **Caliban to Prospero:** Caliban, a rough creature, is Prospero's slave, whom Prospero tries to civilize in *The Tempest* by William Shakespeare. The quotation is from Act I, Scene 2.

derous power over me, but also that in such a self-destroying limbo[5] I could never hope to write.

One writes out of one thing only—one's own experience. Everything depends on how relentlessly one forces from this experience the last drop, sweet or bitter, it can possibly give. This is the only real concern of the artist, to recreate out of the disorder of life that order which is art. The difficulty then, for me, of being a Negro writer was the fact that I was, in effect, prohibited from examining my own experience too closely by the tremendous demands and the very real dangers of my social situation.

I don't think the dilemma outlined above is uncommon. I do think, since writers work in the disastrously explicit medium of language, that it goes a little way toward explaining why, out of the enormous resources of Negro speech and life, and despite the example of Negro music, prose written by Negroes has been generally speaking so pallid and so harsh. I have not written about being a Negro at such length because I expect that to be my only subject, but only because it was the gate I had to unlock before I could hope to write about anything else. I don't think that the Negro problem in America can be even discussed coherently without bearing in mind its context; its context being the history, traditions, customs, the moral assumptions and preoccupations of the country; in short, the general social fabric. Appearances to the contrary, no one in America escapes its effects and everyone in America bears some responsibility for it. I believe this the more firmly because it is the overwhelming tendency to speak of this problem as though it were a thing apart. But in the work of Faulkner, in the general attitude and certain specific passages in Robert Penn Warren, and, most significantly, in the advent of Ralph Ellison, one sees the beginnings—at least—of a more genuinely penetrating

> **THIS IS THE ONLY REAL CONCERN OF THE ARTIST, TO RECREATE OUT OF THE DISORDER OF LIFE THAT ORDER WHICH IS ART.**

search. Mr. Ellison, by the way, is the first Negro novelist I have ever read to utilize in language, and brilliantly, some of the ambiguity and irony of Negro life.

About my interests: I don't know if I have any, unless the morbid desire to own a sixteen millimeter camera and make experimental movies can be so classified. Otherwise, I love to eat and drink—it's my melancholy conviction that I've scarcely ever had enough to eat (this is because it's *impossible* to eat enough if you're worried about the next meal)—and I love to argue with people who do not disagree with me too profoundly, and I love to laugh. I do *not* like bohemia,[6] or bohemians, I do not like people whose principal aim is pleasure, and I do not like people who are *earnest* about anything. I don't like people who like me because I'm a Negro; neither do I like people who find in the same accident grounds for contempt. I love America more than any other country in the world, and, exactly for this reason, I insist on the right to criticize her perpetually. I think all theories are suspect, that the finest principles may have to be modified, or may even be pulverized by the demands of life, and that one must find, therefore, one's own moral center and move through the world hoping that this center will guide one aright. I consider that I have many responsibilities, but none greater than this: to last, as Hemingway says, and get my work done.

I want to be an honest man and a good writer.

6. **bohemia:** any nonconformist, unconventional community, often made up of writers and other artists.

5. **limbo:** borderland state of uncertainty and oblivion.

WORDS TO OWN

explicit (eks·plis'it) *adj.:* clear; definite.
pulverized (pul'vər·īzd') *v.:* crushed; destroyed.

• Toni Morrison (1931–   ) was awarded the Nobel Prize in literature in 1993 (see page 1174). She is noted for her novels *Song of Solomon* (1977) and *Beloved* (1987). She delivered this eulogy at Baldwin's memorial service at the Cathedral of St. John the Divine in New York City on December 8, 1987.

from On James Baldwin

Toni Morrison

Jimmy, there is too much to think about you, and too much to feel. The difficulty is your life refuses summation—it always did—and invites contemplation instead. Like many of us left here I thought I knew you. Now I discover that in your company it is myself I know. That is the astonishing gift of your art and your friendship: You gave us ourselves to think about, to cherish. We are like Hall Montana[1] watching "with new wonder" his brother saints, knowing the song he sang is us, "He is us."

I never heard a single command from you, yet the demands you made on me, the challenges you issued to me, were nevertheless unmistakable, even if unenforced: that I work and think at the top of my form, that I stand on moral ground but know that ground must be shored up by mercy, that "the world is before [me] and [I] need not take it or leave it as it was when [I] came in."

Well, the season was always Christmas with you there and, like one aspect of that scenario, you did not neglect to bring at least three gifts. You gave me a language to dwell in, a gift so perfect it seems my own invention. I have been thinking your spoken and written thoughts for so long I believed they were mine. I have been seeing the world through your eyes for so long, I believed that clear clear view was my own. Even now, even here, I need you to tell me what I am feeling and how to articulate it. So I have pored again through the 6,895 pages of your published work to acknowledge the debt and thank you for the credit. No one possessed or inhabited language for me the way you did. You made American English honest—genuinely international. . . .

The second gift was your courage, which you let us share: the courage of one who could go as a stranger in the village and transform the distances between people into intimacy with the whole world; courage to understand that experience in ways that made it a personal revelation for each of us. It was you who gave us the courage to appropriate an alien, hostile, all-white geography because you had discovered that "this world [meaning history] is white no longer and it will never be white again." Yours was the courage to live life in and from its belly as well as beyond its edges, to see and say what it was, to recognize and identify evil but never fear or stand in awe of it. It is a courage that came from a ruthless intelligence married to a pity so profound it could convince anyone who cared to know that those who despised us "need the moral authority of their former slaves, who are the only people in the world who know anything about them and who may be indeed, the only people in the world who really care anything about them.". . .

The third gift was hard to fathom and even harder to accept. It was your tenderness—a tenderness so delicate I thought it could not last, but last it did and envelop me it did. In the midst of anger it tapped me lightly like the child in Tish's[2] womb. . . .

You knew, didn't you, how I needed your language and the mind that formed it? How I relied on your fierce courage to tame wildernesses for me? How strengthened I was by the certainty that came from knowing you would never hurt me? You knew, didn't you, how I loved your love? You knew. This then is no calamity. No. This is jubilee. "Our crown," you said, "has already been bought and paid for. All we have to do," you said, "is wear it."

And we do, Jimmy. You crowned us.

---

1. Hall Montana: a character in Baldwin's novel *Just Above My Head.*
2. Tish's: Tish is a character in Baldwin's novel *If Beale Street Could Talk.*

MAKING MEANINGS

First Thoughts

1. What do you think were James Baldwin's main goals in writing "Autobiographical Notes"? Do you think he achieved his purpose? Explain.

Shaping Interpretations

2. Describe Baldwin's **tone** toward his subject matter. What specific words or details helped you to identify the tone? Do you share his attitude?

3. How do you think Baldwin feels about himself?

4. Baldwin says that Ralph Ellison was the first African American novelist "to utilize in language, and brilliantly, some of the ambiguity and irony of Negro life." What do you think he means?

5. Why does Baldwin say his "social situation" as an African American creates a dilemma for him as a writer?

6. Review your outline of Baldwin's essay. Then, in your own words, state the three most important **ideas** in the text. Explain why you chose them.

Challenging the Text

7. Do you agree with Baldwin's statement that "the world looks on [the artist's] talent with such a frightening indifference"? Back up your opinion with examples of contemporary writers, painters, musicians, or other artists.

Reading Check

a. According to the essay, what was the most crucial time in Baldwin's development? What did he learn about himself then?

b. How does Baldwin describe the business of the writer, and what does this have to do with what he calls "the Negro problem"?

c. According to Baldwin, how does a writer make use of his or her experiences?

d. What does Baldwin say is his greatest responsibility?

CHOICES: Building Your Portfolio

Writer's Notebook

1. Collecting Ideas for an Evaluation

When you evaluate nonfiction, you can focus on the writer's objectivity. That is, you can examine how balanced the writer is, how much evidence the writer uses to support his or her opinions and judgments. Examine Baldwin's essay to see if he offers examples, facts, and reasons for his views. Does he try to be objective in all his statements? Or are some statements purely subjective and emotional, not supported by hard evidence? Take notes on the ways Baldwin presents his views, and save your notes for the Writer's Workshop on page 1181.

Critical Writing

2. The Past Is Prologue

Baldwin believes that "the past is all that makes the present coherent." In a short essay, discuss the implications of this belief. You may want to consider the effects of the past on education, government, the arts, or an individual's intellectual or spiritual growth.

Critical Writing

3. Echoes of Emerson

Reread the excerpt from Ralph Waldo Emerson's "Self-Reliance" (page 224) closely. Then, in a few paragraphs, compare the **diction** and **tone** of Emerson's essay with those of Baldwin's "Autobiographical Notes."

Analyzing Diction

4. Handsome Again

In her eloquent eulogy (see **Connections** on page 1146), Toni Morrison praises Baldwin's use of language. Applying Morrison's criteria, such as honesty and clarity, analyze Baldwin's **diction** in "Autobiographical Notes." Be sure to support your analysis with examples from the text.

Sylvia Plath

(1932–1963)

Until her death in 1963, Sylvia Plath's life was, to most outward appearances, a model of achievement. This success, however, could not fully mask nor calm a fearsome inner turmoil. Plath was born in Boston and spent her early years in the nearby seaside town of Winthrop. Both her parents were immigrants—her father, a professor of biology, from Poland; her mother, a teacher of office skills, from Austria. Plath later seemed convinced that the reason for her emotional suffering as an adult was her father's death from diabetes when she was only eight.

© Rollie McKenna.

Plath started writing poems and stories in elementary school, and she first published a poem in a Boston newspaper around the time of her father's death. From an early age, she was persistent in finding a publisher for her work; for instance, she persevered through forty-five rejection slips from *Seventeen* magazine before landing a story there in 1950. Plath was awarded a scholarship to Smith College, where she flourished academically and continued to pursue creative writing. She won a much-coveted fiction prize from *Mademoiselle* magazine in her junior year and spent that summer as a guest editor in the magazine's New York office.

The first serious sign of dangerous turbulence in Plath's emotional life came at the end of that seemingly storybook summer, when she was overcome by depression and attempted suicide, an experience that became the basis for her novel, *The Bell Jar*. After psychiatric treatment and electroshock therapy—"the painful agony of slow rebirth and psychic regeneration," as she called it—she returned to college. But she was ill with manic depression, years before effective drug therapy was available.

After graduating from Smith, Plath attended Cambridge University in England on a Fulbright fellowship. At Cambridge, she met the noted English poet Ted Hughes, whom she married in 1956. They lived in Boston during most of the late 1950s and moved to London at the end of 1959. The following year, Plath's first book of poetry, *The Colossus,* was published, and their daughter Frieda was born; their son Nicholas was born in 1962.

In January 1963, Plath's famous autobiographical novel, *The Bell Jar,* was published. In the few weeks between its publication and her death, Plath wrote poetry at a furious pace—sometimes two or three poems a day. The subject matter and style of these poems, published posthumously in *Ariel* (1965), were different from her earlier work. Most poems in *The Colossus* were relatively restrained and formal, influenced by a number of poetic styles, from the classicism of John Crowe Ransom (page 577) to the exuberance of Theodore Roethke (page 1001). But the *Ariel* poems, especially the bitter poems about her father and her attempts at suicide, showed a violence and a frankness absent from her earlier work. Robert Lowell (page 948) wrote in the book's foreword, "These poems are playing Russian roulette with six cartridges in the cylinder, a game of 'chicken,' the wheels of both cars locked and unable to swerve." The poems were, he said, an "appalling and triumphant fulfillment" of her talents.

In 1963, Plath was separated from her husband and caring for their two young children in an unheated London flat. In February, during a very cold London winter, Plath's depression returned. She attempted suicide again. This time she succeeded.

In 1998, to mark what would have been Plath's sixty-fifth birthday, Hughes published *Birthday Letters*, a series of poems about Plath and their passionate but troubled relationship.

Before You Read

MIRROR

Make the Connection

Reflections

We all do it: We check our appearance in a mirror, partly to make sure we are appropriately groomed, partly in order to discover and polish our self-image. What might a mirror—"silver and exact"—think of the person peering into it?

Quickwrite

If a mirror could talk, what might it say about the concerns of the people passing before it? Write down a few observations that a "talking" mirror might make.

Elements of Literature

Personification

Personification is a figure of speech in which an object (such as a mirror) or an animal is given human qualities, such as feelings, thoughts, and attitudes. At its heart, personification is a type of metaphor in which two dissimilar things are compared. For instance, if you say "A mirror tells no lies," you are comparing a mirror to a person by giving it a human attribute.

Courtesy Marisa Del Re Gallery, New York.

Mirror IV (1976–1979) by George Tooker. Egg tempera on gesso panel (24″ × 20″).

Mirror

Sylvia Plath

I am silver and exact. I have no preconceptions.
Whatever I see I swallow immediately
Just as it is, unmisted by love or dislike.
I am not cruel, only truthful—
5 The eye of a little god, four-cornered.
Most of the time I meditate on the opposite wall.
It is pink, with speckles. I have looked at it so long
I think it is a part of my heart. But it flickers.
Faces and darkness separate us over and over.
10 Now I am a lake. A woman bends over me,
Searching my reaches for what she really is.
Then she turns to those liars, the candles or the moon.
I see her back, and reflect it faithfully.
She rewards me with tears and an agitation of hands.
15 I am important to her. She comes and goes.
Each morning it is her face that replaces the darkness.
In me she has drowned a young girl, and in me an old woman
Rises toward her day after day, like a terrible fish.

Before You Read
MUSHROOMS

Make the Connection

Amazing Nature

Have you ever thought about the power of nature—how flowers can appear out of nowhere after a rainstorm? how plants can slice through a sidewalk? how mushrooms can multiply silently overnight? What do such natural events make you think about? Could your reactions range from awe to horror?

Quickwrite

In a few sentences, describe some natural processes and tell how they make you feel.

Elements of Literature

Tone is the attitude a writer takes toward the subject of a work, the characters in it, or the audience. Tone, which results from the complex interplay of **diction** and **style,** can often be described in a word (for instance, playful, sarcastic, or tragic). As you read "Mushrooms" try to hear its tone.

Mushrooms
Sylvia Plath

Overnight, very
Whitely, discreetly,
Very quietly

Our toes, our noses
5   Take hold on the loam,
Acquire the air.

Nobody sees us,
Stops us, betrays us;
The small grains make room.

10   Soft fists insist on
Heaving the needles,
The leafy bedding,

Even the paving.
Our hammers, our rams,
15   Earless and eyeless,

Perfectly voiceless,
Widen the crannies,
Shoulder through holes. We

Diet on water,
20   On crumbs of shadow,
Bland-mannered, asking

Little or nothing.
So many of us!
So many of us!

25   We are shelves, we are
Tables, we are meek,
We are edible,

Nudgers and shovers
In spite of ourselves.
30   Our kind multiplies:

We shall by morning
Inherit the earth.
Our foot's in the door.

MAKING MEANINGS

Mirror

First Thoughts

1. What thoughts or feelings did "Mirror" evoke in you? Did you find the poem surprising? Explain. (Review your Quickwrite.)

Shaping Interpretations

2. Identify the **speaker** of the poem. In what ways does Plath **personify** the speaker?

3. Describe the qualities that the speaker claims to possess. What does the speaker imply by saying "the eye of a little god" (line 5)?

4. The last line of "Mirror" contains the striking **image** of "a terrible fish." How would you explain the significance of this image in the poem? What associations and emotional overtones does the image have for you?

Mushrooms

First Thoughts

1. What do you think this poem is really about?

Shaping Interpretations

2. Who is speaking in the poem?

3. What natural process do the speakers describe? What figures of speech help you to picture parts of that process?

4. "Blessed are the meek, for they shall inherit the earth" is a well known expression from the New Testament of the Bible. What **ironic** twist is given to this scripture at the end of the poem?

5. What **tone** do you hear in the poem? What specific words help create that tone?

6. Both "Mirror" and "Mushrooms" deal with realities that lurk beneath the surface of appearances. What would you say those realities are?

Extending the Text

7. What kind of people are like the mushrooms? Is the story told in the poem a sinister one or a comical one—or is it something else? Compare your interpretation with those of your classmates. How have life experiences affected your interpretations?

CHOICES:
Building Your Portfolio

Writer's Notebook
1. Collecting Ideas for an Evaluation

When you evaluate a work of literature, you must decide how much background information you'll need to supply—either on the writer or on the text. Draft the opening paragraph of an evaluation of Plath's "Mirror" or "Mushrooms," in which you present some biographical background information about the poet. (Your essay should be targeted at readers with no familiarity with Plath.) Save your draft for possible use in the Writer's Workshop on page 1181.

Contrasting Texts
2. Visions or Nightmares?

In a brief essay, compare and contrast Plath's attitude toward nature in "Mushrooms" with the attitude expressed toward nature in another text. Try Emerson's *Nature* (page 219), Thoreau's *Walden* (page 233), Dickinson's "Apparently with no surprise" (page 385), Frost's "Design" (page 560), or Bishop's "The Fish" (page 1035). Does each text see nature and the universe as benign or malevolent or indifferent? What does the text say about the relationship between human nature and the natural world? What is the tone of each text? What do you think of "Mushrooms" and the other text you've chosen?

Creative Writing
3. Nature Speaks

Imitate Plath's device in "Mushrooms" of having something in nature speak and describe its growing process. Before you start to write, decide what tone you will give your speaker or speakers. Will your speaker use prose or poetry? Be sure to refer to your Quickwrite notes.

Jorge Luis Borges
(1899–1986)

Jorge Luis Borges (hôr′hä loo·ēs′ bôr′hes) was born in Buenos Aires, Argentina. As a youth, Borges spent many hours reading in his father's large collection of Spanish and English books. He later wrote, "If I were asked to name the chief event in my life, I should say my father's library." Borges lived in Europe with his family from 1914 to 1921, attending school for four of those years in Geneva, Switzerland.

Returning to Buenos Aires, the highly educated Borges soon turned to writing and to editing literary journals. Beginning in the late 1930s, he earned a living mostly as a librarian and teacher, serving from 1955 to 1973 as director of Argentina's national library. Borges continued to write, and in the early 1960s he gained wide recognition as one of the world's great contemporary writers. He subsequently taught at leading universities (including Harvard) and was awarded high honors by numerous countries and educational institutions.

Borges's long list of publications (some translated into English) includes the remarkable stories in *Ficciones, 1935–1944* (1944); the

S. Bassouls/Sygma.

prose and poetry of *El hacedor* (1960); the poetry collection *Elogio de la sombra* (1969); and the subtle stories of *El libro de arena* (1975). Borges also translated into Spanish the writings of Herman Melville, Walt Whitman, Virginia Woolf, William Faulkner, Franz Kafka, and other noted authors. Translations into English of Borges's writing include *Selected Poems, 1923–1967* (1972) and *Borges: A Reader* (1981).

Borges began to lose his eyesight in his twenties, and as he grew into total blindness in his fifties, he took to dictating his works. Late in life, when Borges learned he was suffering from cancer, he returned to Switzerland. He married his longtime assistant and collaborator Maria Kodama just seven weeks before he died.

Before You Read
BORGES AND MYSELF

Background

Few writers create a body of literature so distinctive that its characteristics are immediately recognizable, widely imitated, and ultimately turned into an adjective—for example, *Dantean,* *Shakespearean, Emersonian, Whitmanesque, Kafkaesque.* In our time, *Borgesian* is an adjective frequently applied to writing that is mysterious, playful, ambiguous, and profoundly concerned with questions of identity, fate, time, and language.

Perhaps the writer who most fully exemplifies the experimental side of postmodern literature, Jorge Luis Borges has produced fictionlike essays, nonfictionlike stories, essaylike poems, and other hybrid, unclassifiable works. His characters are as

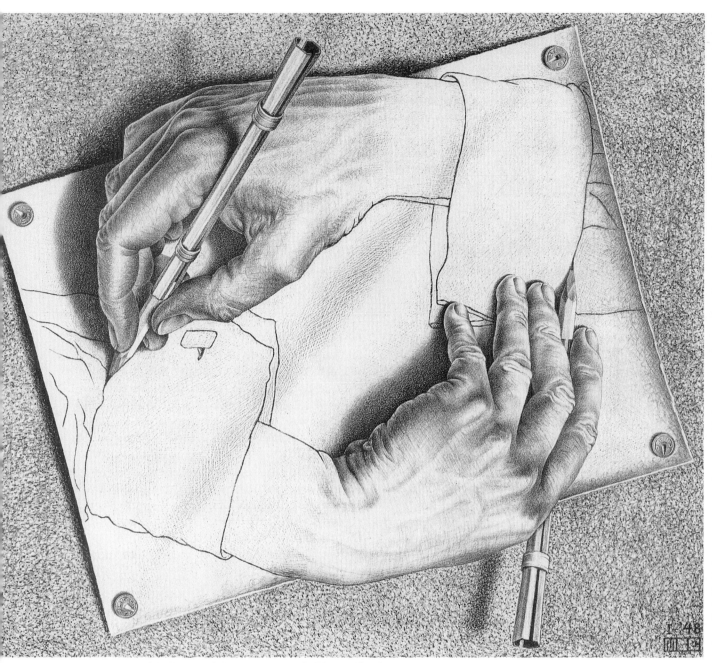

Drawing Hands (1948) by M. C. Escher. Lithograph (11⅛″ × 13⅛″).

hybrid as his forms. People meet their doubles and often don't know whether they are coming or going, literally, in the labyrinth of the universe. Borgesian time can be circular, events can be endlessly repeated, and the boundaries between dream and reality are often erased.

Influenced by Edgar Allan Poe's sense of fantasy and by Walt Whitman's vision of universality, Borges in his turn has had an enormous influence on contemporary literature. His stories-within-stories approach, his concern with personal identity, and his self-conscious literariness have become part of the common literary vocabulary of our age.

JORGE LUIS BORGES 1153

Borges and Myself

Jorge Luis Borges
translated by **Norman Thomas di Giovanni** *and* **Jorge Luis Borges**

It's to the other man, to Borges, that things happen. I walk along the streets of Buenos Aires, stopping now and then—perhaps out of habit—to look at the arch of an old entranceway or a grillwork gate; of Borges I get news through the mail and glimpse his name among a committee of professors or in a dictionary of biography. I have a taste for hourglasses, maps, eighteenth-century typography, the roots of words, the smell of coffee, and Stevenson's[1] prose; the other man shares these likes, but in a showy way that turns them into stagy mannerisms. It would be an exaggeration to say that we are on bad terms; I live, I let myself live, so that Borges can weave his tales and poems, and those tales and poems are my justification. It is not hard for me to admit that he has managed to write a few worthwhile pages, but these pages cannot save me, perhaps because what is good no longer belongs to anyone—not even the other man—but rather to speech or tradition. In any case, I am fated to become lost once and for all, and only some moment of myself will survive in the other man. Little by little, I have been surrendering everything to him, even though I have evidence of his stubborn habit of falsification and exaggerating. Spinoza[2] held that all things try to keep on being themselves; a stone wants to be a stone and the tiger, a tiger. I shall remain in Borges, not in myself (if it is so that I am someone), but I recognize myself less in his books than in those of others or than in the laborious tuning of a guitar. Years ago, I tried ridding myself of him and I went from myths of the outlying slums of the city to games with time and infinity, but those games are now part of Borges and I will have to turn to other things. And so, my life is a running away, and I lose everything and everything is left to oblivion or to the other man.

Which of us is writing this page I don't know.

---

1. Stevenson's: Robert Louis Stevenson (1850–1894), Scottish, author of *Treasure Island* and other adventure stories.

2. Spinoza (spi·nō′zə): Baruch Spinoza (1632–1677), Dutch philosopher.

James Dickey

(1923–1997)

"I came to poetry with no particular qualifications," James Dickey recalled in 1966. "I had begun to suspect, however, that there is a poet—or a kind of poet—buried in every human being . . . and that the people whom we are pleased to call poets are only those who have felt the need and contrived the means to release this spirit from its prison." Dickey's poetic spirit proved to be powerful and original.

Dickey, who was born in Atlanta, grew up with a greater interest in athletics than in academics, and published his first volume of poetry, *Into the Stone,* at the relatively late age of thirty-seven. He had led a life of action—as a high school football player, a soldier in wartime, and an enthusiastic hunter (sometimes with bow and arrow). Dickey had also been a successful advertising executive, handling major accounts ranging from potato chips to airlines. With the publication of *Into the Stone,* however, Dickey became a full-time poet. Like most poets, he also held teaching posts. For many years Dickey taught at the University of South Carolina.

At his best, Dickey was a poet of personal dilemmas gravely posed, of situations dramatized by moral alternatives or made urgent by haunting questions of guilt and regret. In exploring these situations, his poems often include multiple voices and perspectives—some human, some animal, some that represent mythological or supernatural beings. The result is a quality Dickey called "country surrealism," the often violent confrontation of primitive impulses and civilized values.

James Dickey.

The expansive range of Dickey's subject matter is matched by the vigor and skill of his "open" poetic techniques, which include such features as horizontal spacing within lines, inverted syntax, and a bold, often distinctly Southern tone. Paul Zweig, writing in *The New York Times Book Review,* observed that Dickey's poems are "like richly modulated hollers; a sort of rough, American-style bel canto advertising its freedom from the constraints of ordinary language. Dickey's style is so personal, his rhythms so willfully eccentric, that the poems seem to swell up and overflow like that oldest of American art forms, the boast."

One of the most popular and charismatic American poets of his generation, James Dickey not only won a National Book Award for his poetry and an appointment as Poetry Consultant to the Library of Congress, but also established himself as a skillful and entertaining reader of his own work.

Dickey produced fewer poems in his later years, but his visibility as a writer and public figure increased. In 1970, he published an immensely successful novel, *Deliverance,* about the brutal encounter of four suburban men with the Georgia wilderness. Two years later he appeared in a minor role in the very popular motion-picture adaptation of his novel. Dickey's turbulent life at the time is recalled in a poignant and somewhat bitter memoir by his son Christopher Dickey, *Summer of Deliverance* (1998).

The Lifeguard

James Dickey

In a stable of boats I lie still,
From all sleeping children hidden.
The leap of a fish from its shadow
Makes the whole lake instantly tremble.
5 With my foot on the water, I feel
The moon outside

Take on the utmost of its power.
I rise and go out through the boats.
I set my broad sole upon silver,
10 On the skin of the sky, on the moonlight,
Stepping outward from earth onto water
In quest of the miracle

This village of children believed
That I could perform as I dived
15 For one who had sunk from my sight.
I saw his cropped haircut go under.
I leapt, and my steep body flashed
Once, in the sun.

Dark drew all the light from my eyes.
20 Like a man who explores his death
By the pull of his slow-moving shoulders,
I hung head down in the cold,
Wide-eyed, contained, and alone
Among the weeds,

25 And my fingertips turned into stone
From clutching immovable blackness.
Time after time I leapt upward
Exploding in breath, and fell back
From the change in the children's faces
30 At my defeat.

Beneath them I swam to the boathouse
With only my life in my arms
To wait for the lake to shine back
At the risen moon with such power
35 That my steps on the light of the ripples
Might be sustained.

Beneath me is nothing but brightness
Like the ghost of a snowfield in summer.
As I move toward the center of the lake,
40 Which is also the center of the moon,
I am thinking of how I may be
The savior of one

Lake Superior, about 1948, by Lawren Stewart Harris. Oil on canvas (87 cm x 102.8 cm).

Hood Museum of Art, Dartmouth College, Hanover, NH. Gift of the artist, Lawren S. Harris, in memory of his uncle, William Kilborne Stewart, through the Friends of Dartmouth Library.

Who has already died in my care.
The dark trees fade from around me.
45 The moon's dust hovers together.
I call softly out, and the child's
Voice answers through blinding water.
Patiently, slowly,

He rises, dilating to break
50 The surface of stone with his forehead.
He is one I do not remember
Having ever seen in his life.
The ground I stand on is trembling
Upon his smile.

55 I wash the black mud from my hands.
On a light given off by the grave
I kneel in the quick of the moon
At the heart of a distant forest
And hold in my arms a child
60 Of water, water, water.

MAKING MEANINGS

First Thoughts

1. Write down one question you have about this poem.

Shaping Interpretations

2. Who is the speaker in "The Lifeguard"? Where is he, according to stanza 1? What are the children doing?

3. In stanza 2, what does the lifeguard do? What is he searching for?

4. According to the **flashback** in stanzas 3–6, what did the lifeguard do to try to save the boy that day? Why did he swim to the boathouse?

5. In stanza 7, we are back in the present. What is the lifeguard hoping to accomplish?

6. What does the lifeguard do in stanza 8? How do you interpret the events in lines 46–54?

7. One of the **themes** of the poem has to do with the miracle that the lifeguard hopes for: to save the boy. In developing that theme, Dickey makes **allusions** to two of Christ's miracles: walking on water and bringing a dead man to life. Which lines of the poem allude to these miracles?

CHOICES:
Building Your Portfolio

Writer's Notebook
1. Collecting Ideas for an Evaluation

Evaluate Dickey's poem in terms of how well it communicates its meaning. If there is any passage in the text that puzzles you, note it and describe the difficulty you have with it. Save your notes for possible use in the Writer's Workshop on page 1181.

Interpreting a Theme
2. Undoing What's Done

In an essay discuss the theme of the poem in light of Dickey's comment on page 1156. Could his **title** be interpreted on several levels? Refer to your Quickwrite notes.

Analyzing a Poem
3. Reality and Fantasy

"The Lifeguard" is written as an **interior monologue**—a narrative technique that records a character's internal flow of thoughts, memories, and fantasies. The poem mixes the speaker's actual experience with his thoughts and fantasies about that experience. In a short essay, describe these two aspects of the monologue. It may be difficult in some cases to differentiate between the real and the imagined, and you might discuss that aspect of the poem.

Speaking and Listening
4. A Verbal Vision

While Dickey avoids traditional patterns of meter and rhyme, he carefully controls **line length, spacing,** and **rhythm.** Rehearse and perform a reading of "The Lifeguard." Ask your listeners to evaluate your performance. Did you make the chronology clear? Did you successfully convey the speaker's emotional state?

Sandra Cisneros

(1954–   )

Sandra Cisneros remembers her Chicago childhood as solitary, even though, she says, her parents would be hard pressed to remember it that way. The nine members of her Mexican American family lived in cramped apartments where the only room with any privacy was the bathroom. But as the only female child in a family of six sons, Cisneros often felt as solitary as an only child.

To Cisneros, solitude proved important. If she had had a sister or a best friend, Cisneros thinks, she would not have buried herself in books. She read voraciously—lives of the saints, Horatio Alger's office-boy-makes-good stories, Doctor Doolittle books, Alice in Wonderland, and fairy tales. (She imagined herself as the lone sister in "Six Swans." Coincidentally, her family name is translated as "keepers of swans.")

Cisneros received a bachelor's degree from Loyola University, in Chicago, and then earned a master's at The Writers' Workshop at the University of Iowa. There she found her subject matter in her own life, and she began writing in earnest. Finding her own voice did not come easily or quickly for Cisneros; she did not realize for a long time that her best writer's voice was the voice of the home she grew up in, a voice that was a combination of her mother's South Side Chicago "tough" street English and her father's gentle, lulling Spanish. The result is a style that suggests a unique synthesis of the disparate languages of her childhood. Cisneros writes in English, but it is an English often heavily informed by Spanish diction and grammatical structure.

Cisneros's first book of poetry is called *Bad Boys* (1980); her first novel, *The House on Mango Street* (1983), won the American Book Award of the Before Columbus Foundation. The title of her second book of poetry, *My Wicked Wicked Ways* (1987), alludes to the title of the autobiography of Errol Flynn, a movie star of the 1930s and 1940s. In 1991, she published

© Rubén Guzmán.

another prose collection—*Woman Hollering Creek and Other Stories*. As the following selection tells you, Cisneros has lived in many places. In 1995, she was awarded a prestigious long-term fellowship by the John D. and Catherine T. MacArthur Foundation.

Growing up and attending college in Chicago, Cisneros led a circumscribed life and, like many young people (not just writers), desperately yearned to break away. She took comfort from thinking of Emily Dickinson (page 372), who seldom left her house, let alone her hometown, but still managed to create a magnificent legacy of creative work. Dickinson became Cisneros's source of inspiration, the image to which she hitched her dreams of becoming a professional writer. Only years later did Cisneros, all too aware of the struggles of working-class people (especially women), realize that Dickinson lived a uniquely privileged existence in circumstances any aspiring writer would envy: She had money, a fine education, her own room in her own house, and even household help to take care of time-consuming chores. Cisneros, growing up, had none of these advantages. Yet, like Dickinson, Cisneros has been able to take both the possibilities and the constraints of her unique situation and weave them into art.

Before You Read
STRAW INTO GOLD

Make the Connection

Transforming the Everyday
One of the oldest bits of advice to an aspiring author is simply to "write about what you know." Taking that advice, just about every good writer discovers that personal experience is what gives vitality and authenticity to literature. Some of the best writers have an uncanny ability to discover the essential that is hidden in the everyday, the universal that is hidden in the local. In the following autobiographical essay, Sandra Cisneros tells us about some of the raw material she has transformed into literature.

Reading Skills and Strategies

Identifying Main Ideas

In this essay, Cisneros voices a recurrent **theme** in American culture and literature: the possibility of transforming something very ordinary—even something considered a failure—into something successful, original, or beautiful. Make a cluster diagram and, as you read, fill in the large circles with Cisneros's main ideas and the small circles with her supporting details. Be sure to look for **key passages** (starting with the title) that point to her general theme.

Elements of Literature

Allusion

An **allusion** is a reference to someone or something that is known from history, literature, religion, politics, sports, science, or some other branch of culture. Cisneros builds an allusion into the title of this essay. To what old folk tale is she referring? What do you think she is suggesting through this allusion?

> **A**n **allusion** is a reference to someone or something from history, literature, the arts, politics, or some other branch of culture.
>
> *For more on Allusion, see the Handbook of Literary Terms.*

Straw into Gold:
The Metamorphosis of the Everyday

Sandra Cisneros

Diego Rivera.

When I was living in an artists' colony in the south of France, some fellow Latin-Americans who taught at the university in Aix-en-Provence invited me to share a home-cooked meal with them. I had been living abroad almost a year then on an NEA[1] grant, <u>subsisting</u> mainly on French bread and lentils so that my money could last longer. So when the invitation to dinner arrived, I accepted without hesitation. Especially since they had promised Mexican food.

What I didn't realize when they made this invitation was that I was supposed to be involved in preparing the meal. I guess they assumed I knew how to cook Mexican food because I am Mexican. They wanted specifically tortillas, though I'd never made a tortilla in my life.

It's true I had witnessed my mother rolling the little armies of dough into perfect circles, but my mother's family is from Guanajuato; they are *provincianos,* country folk. They only know how to make flour tortillas. My father's family, on the other hand, is *chilango*[2] from Mexico City. We ate corn tortillas but we didn't make them. Someone was sent to the corner tortilleria to buy some. I'd never seen anybody make corn tortillas. Ever.

Somehow my Latino hosts had gotten a hold of a packet of corn flour, and this is what they tossed my way with orders to produce tortillas. *Así como sea.* Any ol' way, they said and went back to their cooking.

1. NEA: National Endowment for the Arts, a federal agency that grants money to selected organizations and individuals so they may engage in creative pursuits.
2. chilango: variation of "*Shilango,*" name used by people of coastal Veracruz for those who live inland, especially the poor people of Mexico.

WORDS TO OWN

subsisting (səb·sist′iŋ) *v.* used as *adj.:* staying alive.

Woman Making Tortillas (1945) by Diego Rivera. Watercolor (12″ × 15¾″).

Courtesy of Mary-Anne Martin/Fine Art, New York. Reproducción autorizada por el Instituto Nacional de Bellas Artes y Literatura.

Why did I feel like the woman in the fairy tale who was locked in a room and ordered to spin straw into gold? I had the same sick feeling when I was required to write my critical essay for the MFA[3] exam—the only piece of noncreative writing necessary in order to get my graduate degree. How was I to start? There were rules involved here, unlike writing a poem or story, which I did intuitively. There was a step by step process needed and I had better know it. I felt as if making tortillas—or writing a critical paper, for that matter—were tasks so impossible I wanted to break down into tears.

Somehow though, I managed to make tortillas—crooked and burnt, but edible nonetheless. My hosts were absolutely ignorant when it came to Mexican food; they thought my tortillas were delicious. (I'm glad my mama wasn't there.) Thinking back and looking at an old photograph documenting the three of us consuming those lopsided circles I am amazed. Just as I am amazed I could finish my MFA exam.

I've managed to do a lot of things in my life I didn't think I was capable of and which many others didn't think I was capable of either. Especially because I am a woman, a Latina, an only daughter in a family of six men. My father would've liked to have seen me married long ago. In our culture men and women don't leave their father's house except by way of marriage. I crossed my father's threshold with nothing carrying me but my own two feet. A woman whom no one came for and no one chased away.

To make matters worse, I left before any of my six brothers had ventured away from home. I broke a terrible taboo. Somehow, looking back at photos of myself as a child, I wonder if I was aware of having begun already my own quiet war.

I like to think that somehow my family, my Mexicanness, my poverty, all had something to do with shaping me into a writer. I like to think my parents were preparing me all along for my life as an artist even though they didn't know it. From my father I inherited a love of wandering. He was born in Mexico City but as a young man he traveled into the U.S. vagabonding. He eventually was drafted and thus became a citizen. Some of the stories he has told about his first months in the

U.S. with little or no English surface in my stories in *The House on Mango Street* as well as others I have in mind to write in the future. From him I inherited a sappy heart. (He still cries when he watches Mexican soaps—especially if they deal with children who have forsaken their parents.)

My mother was born like me—in Chicago but of Mexican descent. It would be her tough streetwise voice that would haunt all my stories and poems. An amazing woman who loves to draw and read books and can sing an opera. A smart cookie.

When I was a little girl we traveled to Mexico City so much I thought my grandparents' house on La Fortuna, number 12, was home. It was the only constant in our nomadic ramblings from one Chicago flat to another. The house on Destiny Street, number 12, in the colonia Tepeyac would be perhaps the only home I knew, and that nostalgia for a home would be a theme that would obsess me.

My brothers also figured greatly in my art. Especially the older two; I grew up in their shadows. Henry, the second oldest and my favorite, appears often in poems I have written and in stories which at times only borrow his nickname, Kiki. He played a major role in my childhood. We were bunk-bed mates. We were co-conspirators. We were pals. Until my oldest brother came back from studying in Mexico and left me odd woman out for always.

What would my teachers say if they knew I was a writer now? Who would've guessed it? I wasn't a very bright student. I didn't much like school because we moved so much and I was always new and funny looking. In my fifth-grade report card I have nothing but an avalanche of C's and D's, but I don't remember being that stupid. I was good at art and I read plenty of library books and Kiki laughed at all my jokes. At home I was fine, but at

---

WORDS TO OWN

intuitively (in·tōō′i·tiv·lē) *adv.*: without conscious reasoning.
edible (ed′ə·bəl) *adj.*: capable of being eaten.
ventured (ven′chərd) *v.*: dared or risked going.
taboo (ta·bōō′) *n.*: something that is forbidden.
nomadic (nō·mad′ik) *adj.*: wandering.
nostalgia (näs·tal′jə) *n.*: longing.
obsess (əb·ses′) *v.*: take all of one's attention.

---

3. **MFA:** Master of Fine Arts.

La Llorona (*The Crying Woman*) by Carmen Lomas Garza. Gouache (18″ × 26″).

school I never opened my mouth except when the teacher called on me.

When I think of how I see myself it would have to be at age eleven. I know I'm thirty-two on the outside, but inside I'm eleven. I'm the girl in the picture with skinny arms and a crumpled skirt and crooked hair. I didn't like school because all they saw was the outside me. School was lots of rules and sitting with your hands folded and being very afraid all the time. I liked looking out the window and thinking. I liked staring at the girl across the way writing her name over and over again in red ink. I wondered why the boy with the dirty collar in front of me didn't have a mama who took better care of him.

I think my mama and papa did the best they could to keep us warm and clean and never hungry. We had birthday and graduation parties and things like that, but there was another hunger that had to be fed. There was a hunger I didn't even have a name for. Was this when I began writing?

In 1966 we moved into a house, a real one, our first real home. This meant we didn't have to change schools and be the new kids on the block every couple of years. We could make friends and not be afraid we'd have to say goodbye to them and start all over. My brothers and the flock of boys they brought home would become important characters eventually for my stories—Louie and his cousins, Meme Ortiz and his dog with two names, one in English and one in Spanish.

My mother <u>flourished</u> in her own home. She took books out of the library and taught herself to garden—to grow flowers so envied we had to put a lock on the gate to keep out the midnight flower thieves. My mother has never quit gardening.

This was the period in my life, that slippery age when you are both child and woman and neither, I was to record in *The House on Mango Street*. I was still shy. I was a girl who couldn't come out of her shell.

WORDS TO OWN

flourished (flʉr′ishd) *v.*: did well; blossomed.

How was I to know I would be recording and documenting the women who sat their sadness on an elbow and stared out a window? It would be the city streets of Chicago I would later record, as seen through a child's eyes.

I've done all kinds of things I didn't think I could do since then. I've gone to a <u>prestigious</u> university, studied with famous writers, and taken an MFA degree. I've taught poetry in schools in Illinois and Texas. I've gotten an NEA grant and run away with it as far as my courage would take me. I've seen the bleached and bitter mountains of the Peloponnesus.[4] I've lived on an island. I've been to Venice twice. I've lived in Yugoslavia. I've been to the famous Nice[5] flower market behind the opera house. I've lived in a village in the pre-Alps and witnessed the daily parade of promenaders.

I've moved since Europe to the strange and wonderful country of Texas, land of polaroid-blue skies and big bugs. I met a mayor with my last name. I met famous Chicana and Chicano artists and writers and *políticos*.

Texas is another chapter in my life. It brought with it the Dobie-Paisano Fellowship, a six-month residency on a 265-acre ranch. But most important, Texas brought Mexico back to me.

In the days when I would sit at my favorite people-watching spot, the snakey Woolworth's counter across the street from the Alamo (the Woolworth's which has since been torn down to make way for progress), I couldn't think of anything else I'd rather be than a writer. I've traveled and lectured from Cape Cod to San Francisco, to Spain, Yugoslavia, Greece, Mexico, France, Italy, and now today to Texas. Along the way there has been straw for the taking. With a little imagination, it can be spun into gold.

---

4. **Peloponnesus** (pel′ə·pə·nē′səs): large peninsula on the mainland of Greece.
5. **Nice** (nēs): port city in southern France.

WORDS TO OWN

prestigious (pres·tij′əs) *adj.*: impressive; having distinction.

J. Frank Dobie's Paisano Ranch.

MAKING MEANINGS

First Thoughts

1. What do you still want to know about Cisneros after reading this essay?

Shaping Interpretations

2. How would you interpret the essay's subtitle, "The Metamorphosis of the Everyday"?

3. It is characteristic of most American writers that they turn to their childhoods for subject matter. How do you explain Cisneros's interest in her childhood experiences?

4. Describe the **tone** of Cisneros's essay. Do you think it is appropriate for the subject matter?

5. Describe in your own words the kind of writer that Cisneros believes she has become. What qualities as a writer has she developed from the raw material of her personal experience?

6. What do you think Cisneros means when she says she found herself "documenting the women who sat their sadness on an elbow and stared out a window" (page 1164)?

7. Identify some fresh **images** and **figures of speech** in the essay that reveal Cisneros as an accomplished writer. How would you describe her style?

8. The title of the essay includes an **allusion** to the folk tale about Rumpelstiltskin. In the essay itself, how does Cisneros use that magical story as a metaphor for her writing? What do you think of the metaphor?

Reading Check

a. How do the writer's feelings about making the tortillas connect to her feelings about writing the MFA essay?

b. Describe Cisneros's experiences at school.

c. Exactly how did her family help shape Cisneros into a writer?

d. Why does Cisneros think nostalgia for a home is a **theme** that obsesses her?

CHOICES: Building Your Portfolio

Writer's Notebook

1. Collecting Ideas for an Evaluation

What qualities give life to the story of a life? In other words, what are your criteria for evaluating an autobiographical work? Think of autobiographies you have enjoyed, and make a list of their key characteristics. Among your criteria might be that an autobiography be honest, that it makes times and places come alive, that it reveals the writer's feelings. Save your notes for possible use in the Writer's Workshop on page 1181.

Analyzing Nonfiction

2. To What End?

Cisneros's essay is the revised version of a speech delivered at Texas Lutheran College. In a brief essay, discuss the following questions: What are the **key passages** in her essay? What are her **main ideas**? (Refer to your cluster diagram.) How would you state her general **theme**? If you had been a member of her audience, how would this speech have affected you?

Interpreting Contemporary Culture

3. Multicultural Celebrations

In essays and lectures, Cisneros has told of dual cultural influences on her writing. This mix of cultures is a common feature of the arts in a multicultural society like that of the United States. The writer Bernard Malamud (page 980), for example, often included Yiddish expressions in his English-language texts, thus combining two heritages. In a brief essay, identify and describe two or three specific examples of contemporary arts—writing, dance, music, painting, fashion, or another art form—that fuse elements of two or more cultural heritages. In what ways do such fusions of cultural influences enrich contemporary artistic expressions?

Judith Ortiz Cofer

(1952–   )

According to Judith Ortiz Cofer, "My family is one of the main topics of my poetry; the ones left behind on the island of Puerto Rico, and the ones who came to the United States. In tracing their lives, I discover more about mine." This impulse toward self-discovery and self-definition emerges in Cofer's stories, essays, and poems. By delving into her past, she clarifies her place in the present; by writing of those who shaped her life, she shapes her own life.

"We lived in Puerto Rico until my brother was born in 1954," Cofer has written. "Soon after, because of economic pressures on our growing family, my father joined the United States Navy. He was assigned to duty on a ship in Brooklyn [Navy] Yard . . . that was to be his home base in the States until his retirement more than twenty years later." Subsequently, Cofer's childhood was divided between a mainland American urban environment and Puerto Rico. She lived mostly in Paterson, New Jersey, but moved temporarily to Puerto Rico with her mother and brother when her father was at sea.

Cofer earned a master's degree in English from Florida Atlantic University in 1977 and then taught at the University of Miami and the University of Georgia, conducting poetry workshops on the side. Her first publication, *Latin Women Pray,* appeared in 1980. Since then she has published several additional volumes of poetry, including *Peregrina* (1986) and *Terms of Survival* (1987). Her semiautobiographical first novel, *The Line of the Sun* (1989), traces a family that moves from Puerto Rico to Paterson and is then caught between two cultural heritages. A reviewer of the novel describes Cofer as "a prose writer of evocatively lyrical authority." She has also published a volume of personal essays called *Silent Dancing: A Partial Remembrance of a Puerto Rican Childhood* (1990); *An Island Like You: Stories from the Barrio* (1995); and *The Year of Our Revolution: Selected and New Stories and Poems* (1998).

Some consider Cofer's *The Latin Deli* (1993), a collection of poetry and prose, her most powerful book. It is a mosaic of responses to cultural differences, an evocation of places past and present, and an engaging blend of poetry and lyrical prose. As Cofer has said, "The place of birth itself becomes a metaphor for the things we all must leave behind; the assimilation of a new culture is the coming into maturity by accepting the terms necessary for survival. My poetry is a study of this process of change, assimilation, and transformation."

Language, of course, plays a major role in such a transformation. In one interview, Cofer summed up what the dynamic force of language has meant to her: "The 'infinite variety' and power of language interest me. I never cease to experiment with it. As a native Puerto Rican, my first language was Spanish. It was a challenge, not only to learn English, but to master it enough to teach it and—the ultimate goal—to write poetry in it."

Arte Público Press/University of Houston.

Before You Read
THE LATIN DELI: AN ARS POETICA

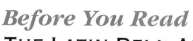

Make the Connection

Native Tongue

Language is our most common tool of self-expression. Hidden in the words we say, beneath the immediate practical meanings, are layers of personal associations, complex social implications, and even cultural histories. This is especially true of immigrants, who try to adjust to a new country but are still drawn to their former homelands. You may know recent immigrants who intermix words of their native language with English.

Quickwrite

On a sheet of paper, write some of the things an immigrant might remember with fondness about his or her native country. Be as precise as possible.

Elements of Literature

Concrete and Abstract Language

In literature, **concrete language** involves the use of well-chosen sensory details to evoke and describe a particular subject. In contrast, **abstract language** deals with a subject in general terms and emphasizes intangible concepts like qualities and values. In abstract language, there are few sensory words, and details do not play a large role. The following poem is a striking example of the effective use of concrete language. (*Ars poetica*, by the way, is Latin for "the art of poetry.")

The Latin Deli:
An Ars Poetica

Judith Ortiz Cofer

Presiding over a formica counter,
plastic Mother and Child magnetized
to the top of an ancient register,
the heady mix of smells from the open bins
5   of dried codfish, the green plantains°
hanging in stalks like votive offerings,°
she is the Patroness of Exiles,
a woman of no-age who was never pretty,
who spends her days selling canned memories
10 while listening to the Puerto Ricans complain
that it would be cheaper to fly to San Juan
than to buy a pound of Bustelo coffee here,
and to Cubans perfecting their speech
of a "glorious return" to Havana—where no one
15 has been allowed to die and nothing to change until then;
to Mexicans who pass through, talking lyrically
of *dólares* to be made in El Norte—

                          all wanting the comfort
of spoken Spanish, to gaze upon the family portrait
20 of her plain wide face, her ample bosom
resting on her plump arms, her look of maternal interest
as they speak to her and each other
of their dreams and their disillusions—
how she smiles understanding,
25 when they walk down the narrow aisles of her store
reading the labels of packages aloud, as if
they were the names of lost lovers: *Suspiros,*°
Merengues,° the stale candy of everyone's childhood.

                          She spends her days
30 slicing *jamón y queso*° and wrapping it in wax paper
tied with string: plain ham and cheese
that would cost less at the A&P, but it would not satisfy
the hunger of the fragile old man lost in the folds
of his winter coat, who brings her lists of items
35 that he reads to her like poetry, or the others,
whose needs she must divine, conjuring up products
from places that now exist only in their hearts—
closed ports she must trade with.

5. plantains: type of banana.
6. votive offerings: sacrifices made to fulfill a vow or offered in devotion.
27. *Suspiros* (sōōs·pē′rōs): type of small spongecake.
28. *Merengues* (mā·rān′gās): candy made of meringue (mixture of egg whites and sugar).
30. *jamón y queso* (khä·mōn′ ē kā′sō): Spanish for "ham and cheese."

MAKING MEANINGS

First Thoughts

1. What do you think of the woman who runs the deli? What does she do for her customers?

Shaping Interpretations

2. Describe in your own words the feelings of the customers in the deli.

3. Were you surprised that the proprietor of a deli and the things she sells could have so many important associations for the customers? Explain your answer.

4. The poem contains many sensory **images.** Identify at least one image each of sight, hearing, taste, smell, and touch.

5. What **concrete details** help make this poem very specific—and rooted in a particular time and place?

Extending the Text

6. Language is important to the deli's customers. Review your Quickwrite notes, and discuss the various ways immigrants to this country might have a perspective on language and culture that is different from the perspective of Americans who have lived their whole lives here.

Challenging the Text

7. In ancient Rome, the poet Horace (65–8 B.C.) wrote a treatise called *Ars Poetica,* or *The Art of Poetry,* setting forth his own rules for writing poetry. Since Horace's time, many poets have explored ideas about what makes a good poem. Why do you think Cofer subtitles her poem "An Ars Poetica"? In what sense might this poem reflect her ideas about what constitutes good poetry?

CHOICES:
Building Your Portfolio

Writer's Notebook
1. Collecting Ideas for an Evaluation

When you're evaluating a work of literature, it sometimes helps to **compare** it with a related work. Several poems in this book deal with the art of poetry. Poems by Marianne Moore (page 788), Archibald MacLeish (page 789), and Wallace Stevens (page 790) deal with the nature of poetry. Cofer's poem, on the other hand, does not contain explicit statements about poetry; we must infer from it her general beliefs about poetry. What do you think might be Cofer's definition of poetry? (Lines 16–17, 26–27, and 34–35 might give you some hints.) For each of the four poets, write a statement that sets forth the poet's definition of *ars poetica.* How are these poets' views of poetry alike and different? Save your notes for possible use in the Writer's Workshop on page 1181.

Analyzing a Poem's Sound / Music
2. The Music of Words

In a brief essay, analyze the musical qualities of Cofer's poem: its **rhythm, assonance, alliteration,** and other sound effects. If this poem were a piece of music, what musical qualities would it have? Describe the kind of music you associate with this poem, and, if possible, accompany your essay with a recording of vocal or instrumental music that "sounds" like the poem.

Art
3. Many Parts to the Whole

Cofer uses many **images** to craft this poem. Transfer her technique to the visual arts by making a collage or painting that unites numerous images in one work. You may want to follow Cofer's lead and use a deli as your subject; you could also assemble images of a restaurant, a ballgame, a city, or another subject.

Robert Severi/Gamma Liaison.

Rita Dove

(1952–   )

Rita Dove's best-known work, *Thomas and Beulah* (1986), is a sequence of poems (including the following selection) loosely based on the lives of her maternal grandparents. Dove described the poems in an interview:

I know that when I was writing the poems that went into *Thomas and Beulah* . . . I realized that what I was trying to tell, let's say, was not a narrative as we know narratives but actually the moments that matter most in our lives. I began to think, how do we remember our lives? How do we think of our lives or shape our lives in our own consciousnesses, and I realized that we don't actually think of our lives in very cohesive strands but we remember as beads on a necklace, moments that matter to us, come to us in flashes, and the connections are submerged.

This statement expresses the central concern of much of Dove's poetry: how memory shapes who we are—in other words, how we become ourselves.

In addition to *Thomas and Beulah,* Dove's books of poetry include *The Other Side of the House* (1988), *Grace Notes* (1989), *Selected Poems* (1993), and *Mother Love* (1995), a book largely inspired by the ancient Greek myths of Demeter and Persephone. The esteemed poetry critic Helen Vendler, writing in *The New Yorker,* has praised Dove's "laser glance" and "remarkable objectivity." Dove has also written short stories, a novel, and a verse play, but it is her poetry that has brought her renown. From 1993 to 1995, she served as poet laureate of the United States.

Born and raised in Akron, Ohio, Dove graduated *summa cum laude* from Miami University (in Ohio), studied literature at the University of Tübingen in Germany, and attended the noted Writers' Workshop at the University of Iowa, where she received a master's degree in 1977. After teaching at several universities, Dove became professor of English at the University of Virginia, Charlottesville, in 1989.

The joys and trials of raising a family play as large a part in Dove's life as they do in her writing. Dove says that after her daughter, Aviva, was born, she felt she was living "the story of many women who all have three full-time jobs: You teach, you do parenting, and you try to write, too. I just was tired all the time. I remember days when I came back home and fell asleep over dessert."

Besides writing on personal subjects, Dove interweaves historical themes, including race relations, into her verse. As she told the *Washington Post,* "Obviously, as a black woman, I am concerned with race. But certainly not every poem of mine mentions the fact of being black. They are poems about humanity, and sometimes humanity happens to be black. I cannot run from, I *won't* run from any kind of truth." This honesty, strength, and vision of universality are the very qualities that distinguish Dove's work.

go.hrw.com
LEO 11-21

THE SATISFACTION COAL COMPANY

Make the Connection

Moments That Matter

Rita Dove once said, "I think all of us have moments, particularly in our childhood, where we come alive, maybe for the first time. And we go back to those moments and think, 'This is when I became myself.'"

Reading Skills and Strategies

Responding to Aesthetic Elements

Aesthetic simply means "artistic" or "having to do with beauty and art." You can respond aesthetically to many things, including colors, forms, textures, words, and sounds. Before you read this poem, look at the way it is presented. Jot down your initial response to the visuals, including the black background. As you read, note your response to the poem's images and sound.

Background

In Dove's book *Thomas and Beulah,* "The Satisfaction Coal Company" appears as the second-to-last poem in the section on Thomas, a character who represents Rita Dove's maternal grandfather. Thomas found part-time work during the Great Depression of the 1930s as a cleaner at the offices of the Satisfaction Coal Company, in Akron, Ohio. Coal was still widely used to heat homes, which explains the importance of the coal scraps Thomas carries home. The poem that precedes "The Satisfaction Coal Company" in *Thomas and Beulah* tells of the stroke Thomas suffered; the section's next, and final, poem tells of Thomas's death in 1963.

***Aaron* by Thomas Hart Benton. Oil-tempera on canvas (30¼″ × 20¼″).**

The Pennsylvania Academy of Fine Arts, Philadelphia; Joseph E. Temple Fund. © T.H. Benton and R.P. Benton Testamentary Trusts/Licensed by VAGA, New York, NY.

The Satisfaction Coal Company

Rita Dove

1.

What to do with a day.
Leaf through *Jet.* Watch T.V.
Freezing on the porch
but he goes anyhow, snow too high
5 for a walk, the ice treacherous.
Inside, the gas heater takes care of itself;
he doesn't even notice being warm.

Everyone says he looks great.
Across the street a drunk stands smiling
10 at something carved in a tree.

The new neighbor with the floating hips
scoots out to get the mail
and waves once, brightly,
storm door clipping her heel on the way in.

2.

15 Twice a week he had taken the bus down Glendale hill
to the corner of Market. Slipped through
the alley by the canal and let himself in.
Started to sweep
with terrible care, like a woman
20 brushing shine into her hair,
same motion, same lullaby.
No curtains—the cop on the beat
stopped outside once in the hour
to swing his billy club and glare.

25 It was better on Saturdays
when the children came along:
he mopped while they emptied
ashtrays, clang of glass on metal
then a dry scutter. Next they counted
30 nailheads studding the leather cushions.
Thirty-four! they shouted,
that was the year and
they found it mighty amusing.

But during the week he noticed more—
35 lights when they gushed or dimmed
at the Portage Hotel, the 10:32
picking up speed past the B & O switchyard,°
floorboards trembling and the explosive
kachook kachook kachook kachook
40 and the oiled rails ticking underneath.

37. B & O switchyard: yard of
the Baltimore and Ohio Railroad
where train cars are switched
from one track to another to
make up trains.

3.

They were poor then but everyone had been poor.
He hadn't minded the sweeping,
just the thought of it—like now
when people ask him what he's thinking
45 and he says *I'm listening.*

Those nights walking home alone,
the bucket of coal scraps banging his knee,
he'd hear a roaring furnace
with its dry, familiar heat. Now the nights
50 take care of themselves—as for the days,

there is the canary's sweet curdled song,
the wino smiling through his dribble.
Past the hill, past the gorge
choked with wild sumac in summer,
55 the corner has been upgraded.
Still, he'd like to go down there someday
to stand for a while, and get warm.

"And the Winner Is . . .": Major Literary Awards

Music has the Grammy; Hollywood has the Oscar; television has the Emmy. Writers, too, have their own awards, although these are not the subject of lavish prime-time television specials. These awards are important for various reasons: They encourage promising young writers, reward established authors for lifetime achievement, and promote literary quality. Awards influence sales—a major award will double and sometimes triple sales of a book—but they are not given to reward commercial and popular success. The best-known literary awards are the Nobel, the Pulitzer (which Rita Dove won in 1987 for *Thomas and Beulah*), and the National Book Award.

- The Nobel Prize in literature is one of several international awards (others are given in the fields of physiology or medicine, physics, chemistry, economics, and for the promotion of world peace) established by Alfred Nobel, the Swedish chemist who invented dynamite. Perhaps to counter the negative aspects of his invention, Nobel wanted his profits to benefit those who have contributed to the "good of humanity." Recognizing that writing could be a powerful instrument for social reform and world peace, Nobel stipulated that the literature prize be given for "the most outstanding work of an idealistic tendency." Recent recipients include Isaac Bashevis Singer, Gabriel García Márquez, Derek Walcott, and Toni Morrison. Morrison, who received the confirmation call about her receipt of the award in the early hours of the morning, had trouble believing it. "I said, 'Why don't you send me a fax?' Somehow, I felt that if I saw a fax, I'd know it wasn't a dream or somebody's hallucination."

- Hungarian-born Joseph Pulitzer immigrated to America as a recruit for the Union army in the Civil War. After the war, he worked in St. Louis as a reporter for a German-language newspaper. In time, he became one of the leading newspaper magnates in the United States, and one of the most liberal. The Pulitzer Prizes are awarded annually in the fields of American journalism, literature, drama, and music. More than thirty of the authors in this book have won Pulitzer awards, including four-time winner Robert Frost.

- The National Book Awards were established in 1950 by several book-trade associations to recognize the most distinguished works of fiction, nonfiction, and poetry. The panel of judges includes authors, critics, creative writing instructors, and English professors. William Gaddis is one of the few people who have won the award twice, in 1976 and 1994. He remembers that he embarrassed his children during the first ceremony by holding up the envelope to make sure there was a check inside.

from An Interview with Rita Dove: Poet Laureate of the United States (1994)

We stood in a cool, dimly lit room in the Library of Congress with a nervousness to be expected when meeting the poet laureate of the United States. In our minds, we were reviewing possible questions and camera angles and hoping we would not seem immature or unprepared. When Rita Dove appeared, her energy and friendliness—together with her M & M multicolored fingernails—put us in a creative, relaxed frame of mind and led us to a fascinating interview with a remarkable writer.

Heritage: Why do you think it's important for the United States to have a poet laureate?

Rita Dove: Our country thrives on symbolism. Because it's so large and spread out, we get our energy when there are people to focus on. A poet laureate reminds us that the cultural life in this country is necessary. Practically speaking, it gives people someone to write to when they have questions. I can't tell you how many letters I get from people who simply say, "Here I am in Idaho, and I like to write poetry and I don't even know if there's anyone else around me who writes poetry." Then I am able to tell them how they can find someone: where they can go, what community centers there are, and how they can find out about poetry readings.

H: How do you see your appointment as poet laureate in terms of your career?

R. D.: It has given me incredible exposure and publicity that I did not count on at this point in my life. It has changed my life in the sense that I'm not going to have as much private time ever again, probably. But in terms of writing my poems, I'm trying very hard not to let it affect that. When I sit down to write, I don't think, "Well, there are all these people waiting. . . ."

I'm in my room; it's just me and a circle of light and the page. The main difference now is that it is harder to get to the room. Critics and reporters ask, "Won't it just give you pressure to do better on your next work?" I think that's not the point. The point is to write the poem, then let people think of it what they may.

H: Do you feel strongly about writing as an African American woman?

R. D.: It's extremely important for writers to write fully about their own experience and about whatever other experiences strike their fancy. It is important for all the stories to be told. I don't feel a particular obligation to write only about the African American experience or the experience of being a woman. I would not want to limit myself, and I don't think anyone should. But I also feel very, very lucky to be writing in a time when people are beginning to understand, to realize, that the experience of an African American woman could also have relevance to their life.

H: From where do you get your inspiration?

R. D.: I get it from everywhere: from other authors, from just walking down the street. Sometimes I think of myself as a giant sponge; I just keep soaking all this stuff up. I think that anything, *anything* that interests one is worthy of a poem. I don't cut things out by saying, "Well, this is math; there's nothing I can do with poetry and math." You never know.

—Moira Haney and Catherine Nicholas
Heritage, Spring 1994
James Madison High School
Vienna, Virginia

MAKING MEANINGS

First Thoughts

1. What do you think about the way this poem is presented and illustrated?

Shaping Interpretations

2. One of this poem's strengths is its **diction**—the poet's choice of words. For instance, Dove writes that lights "gushed" rather than "brightened." What other examples of unusual diction can you find in the poem? How did you respond to this poet's use of language?

3. Dove's poem teems with **images** and phrases related to time, like days of the week and seasons of the year. Identify some of these images and explain their significance in the poem.

4. How would you describe Thomas's response to the circumstances of his life? What do his reminiscences tell us about him? Support your interpretation with specific evidence from the poem.

5. State what you think is the central **theme** of Dove's poem. In what ways does part 3 develop this theme? Does the **title** suggest a clue?

Connecting with the Text

6. Dove has said that some individuals in her poems "are struggling to sing in their chains." How do you think this statement applies to Thomas, if at all? How does it describe his response to the circumstances of his life?

Reading Check

a. In the first and last stanzas of the poem, what seasons of the year are referred to?

b. What actions and events are described in part 2 of the poem? What things does Thomas notice during the week (lines 34–40)?

c. What things do we see other people, aside from Thomas, doing in the poem?

d. In part 3, what are Thomas's feelings about the sweeping? What does he want to do at the end of the poem?

CHOICES: Building Your Portfolio

Writer's Notebook

1. Collecting Ideas for an Evaluation

One way to make a judgment about a work you're reviewing is by evaluating how it supports—or does not support—a comment made by a critic or by the work's author. Reread the biography of Rita Dove on page 1170, as well as comments Dove made to the student interviewers in Student to Student (page 1175). Using a quotation from Dove as a starting point, make some notes on how well "The Satisfaction Coal Company" reflects or fails to reflect Dove's comments about "moments that matter" and other aspects of poetry. Save your notes for possible use in the Writer's Workshop on page 1181.

Interpreting a Poem

2. Moments of Discovery

One critic has written, "Dove's poems enter the mysterious by opening themselves to the moment of discovery. Usually that discovery is not rational, but emotional or physical." In a brief essay, explain how this statement applies to "The Satisfaction Coal Company."

Research / Speaking and Listening

3. Laurels for a Poet

Rita Dove once commented, "I'm hoping that by the end of my term people will think of a poet laureate as someone who's out there with her sleeves rolled up and working. . . ." With three or four other students, organize a panel discussion on the position of U.S. poet laureate. Panel members should report on (a) how the poet laureate is chosen; (b) the main functions of the post; (c) which poets have held the post in the past and who holds it now; and (d) how it compares with the similarly named post in Great Britain. After the panel discussion, field questions and comments from the class.

READ ON

Many works of contemporary literature use realistic language and graphic depictions of characters in crises and conflict. Be sure to check with your teacher and parent or guardian before reading any of the following books.

There's Always a Catch

"Orr was crazy and could be grounded. All he had to do was ask; and as soon as he did, he would no longer be crazy." Paradoxical military rules and the madness of war become a metaphor for life's absurdities in Joseph Heller's sharp satire *Catch-22* (Simon and Schuster). *Closing Time* (Simon and Schuster) is Heller's long-awaited sequel.

Yiddish Yarns

If you liked Bernard Malamud's "The Magic Barrel," then you'll probably enjoy Isaac Bashevis Singer's writing, largely rooted in the Polish-Jewish culture of his youth. Singer, whose work is mostly translated from the Yiddish, was awarded the Nobel Prize in literature in 1978 for his novels, memoirs, children's books, and, most notably, his dozens of short stories. *Collected Stories* (Farrar, Straus and Giroux) reveals the range and scope of this master storyteller.

Both Sides of the Story

Another consummate storyteller is Toni Morrison (see page 1146), winner of the 1993 Nobel Prize in literature. Morrison writes of the debilitating effects of oppression against African Americans on victim and perpetrator alike; she also explores the other side of the coin, writing about the richness of African American community and traditions. *Beloved* (Alfred A. Knopf) tells the story of a mother's desperate attempt to save her children from slavery.

Irrational Acts

Into the Wild and *Into Thin Air* (both Villard Books), both by journalist John Krakauer, are examples of nonfiction writing at its best. *Into the Wild* is the tragic story of a young man who, after graduation from college, set off to experience the wilderness, and on his way divested himself of every link to his past life. His adventure ended in an abandoned school bus in Denali National Park in Alaska. *Into Thin Air* is participatory journalism of the highest quality: Krakauer accompanied a guided ascent of Mt. Everest at the request of *Outside* magazine. Krakauer reached the summit but at a terrible cost. As it happened, an IMAX crew was on Everest; their film of the tragedy has been released.

A Nation of Poets

More people are writing poetry than ever before, and, happily, the audience for poetry is also growing—especially for coffeehouse readings. *Contemporary American Poetry,* edited by Donald Hall (Penguin), samples work published through the early 1970s. To explore the more recent work of poets such as Charles Olson, Denise Levertov, and Jimmy Santiago Baca, see *Postmodern American Poetry,* edited by Paul Hoover (Norton).

The American Language

High Tech's Influence

by Gary Q. Arpin

Before *high tech,* there was just plain *technology.* The nineteenth-century British author Richard Burton used the word *technology* in his book *Travels in Arabia and Africa* (1829) to refer to fairly simple practical arts, such as extracting dye from plants. In 1829, an American, Professor Jacob Bigelow, first used the word in its present meaning of "applied science" when he published *The Elements of Technology* (subtitled *On the Application of the Sciences to the Useful Arts*).

Training for New Vocabulary

The advanced technology of the early nineteenth century was chiefly steam, and the steam engine entered people's lives in the form of factories, steamboats, and train locomotives. The railroad's impact on American lives was speedy and unprecedented. In 1830, there were just 73 miles of railroad tracks in the United States. By 1850, the number had increased to some 8,900 miles, and by 1860, to about 30,600 miles. "The world has seen nothing like it before," Daniel Webster wrote. "The progress of the age has almost outstripped human belief."

The new application of steam technology required a host of new words. Where did these terms come from? The same processes of word formation applied to railroad terms as had applied to Americanisms in general. Some new words celebrated innovators; for instance, the *Pullman car,* a railroad car with berths for sleeping, was named after George Pullman, who invented it in 1865. Many other terms were formed by combining existing words, such as *redcap* and *whistle-stop.*

A substantial number of railroad terms were borrowed from earlier forms of transportation. Sailing ships and steamboats provided the railroad with terms like *berth*, *caboose, crew, gondola,* and *all aboard.* The stagecoach provided *car, coach, conductor,* and *station.* This process continues today, as each technology lends its words to its successors.

Most technological terms have a well-defined and specific job to do. Some terms find a broader popularity, usually through metaphor, and enter standard usage. To be *under pressure,* for example, is a phrase borrowed from the steam engine. Most of us use the term only in its metaphoric sense, without thinking about its origin. The train gave people a new way to speak of failure, when a project is *derailed*—and it also gave rise to a new social designation, *the wrong side of the tracks,* as well as such terms as *right of way* and *sidetrack.*

New Words from *Tele* and *Graph*

About the same time the railroad was crisscrossing the American continent, the telegraph was doing so, too. The word *telegraph* (coined from two Greek terms, *tele,* "afar," and *graphein,* "to write"), had been used in England since the eighteenth century to refer to various forms of semaphores (systems of signaling). However, it became popular only with the invention of the Morse telegraph in the mid–nineteenth century—another example of one technology lending its words to another.

Telegram is a true Americanism, coined in Albany, New York, in 1852. "A friend desires us to give notice," wrote an Albany *Evening Journal* reporter, "that he will ask leave . . . to introduce a new word. It is *telegram,* instead of *telegraphic dispatch*." The word, so politely brought into the world, encountered some vigorous opposition before being accepted. The reason? It was not a proper combination of Greek words. The proper word, purists argued, would be *telegrapheme.*

go.hrw.com

LE0 11-American Language

Tele and *graph* have been busy root words since the early nineteenth century. *Photograph* appeared in 1839 (*photo* is Greek for "light"). For a number of years, *photographist* fought it out with *photographer* before disappearing. Late in the nineteenth century came the *cinematograph* (*kinema* is Greek for "motion"). It was shortened to *cinema* in England, but changed to *moving picture* in the United States and later shortened to *movie*.

The *telephone* was invented in 1876 and the *phonograph* in 1877 (*phono* is Greek for "sound" or "voice"). The technology for wireless communication led to the *radiotelegraph* in 1903, which was shortened to *radio*.

Television first achieved commercial success in the late 1940s. The British shortened *television* to *telly*, while Americans abbreviated it to *TV*. (As we shall see, initials and acronyms became especially popular during this period in the United States.)

Acronyms: Convenient Abbreviations

One method of forming new words, now so popular that it almost threatens to overwhelm us, is the use of acronyms. The word *acronym* is probably an Americanism, although the practice is ancient. The term comes from the Greek words for "top" and "name," and refers to a word formed from the combination of the first letters of the words in a phrase. *Radar* was a technological acronym (from "*ra*dio *d*etecting *a*nd *r*anging"), and it quickly knocked out the British candidate, *radiolocator*. *Sonar* ("*so*und *n*avigation *a*nd *r*anging") followed, as did *laser* ("*l*ight *a*mplification by *s*timulated *e*mission of *r*adiation").

The acronym device was not the sole property of scientists and technologists. In the twentieth century, the military and other bureaucracies have bred many acronyms, from *AWOL* ("*a*bsent *w*ithout *l*eave"), coined in World War I, to *NATO* (*N*orth *A*tlantic *T*reaty *O*rganization) to *snafu* (*s*ituation *n*ormal, *a*ll *f*ouled *u*p). World War II saw the development of a great many acronyms, such as *WAVES* and *WAC* ("*W*omen *A*ppointed for *V*oluntary *E*mergency *S*ervice" and "*W*omen's *A*rmy *C*orps"), the women's branches of the U.S. Navy and Army.

Airplane Argot

The airplane had an effect on American culture in the twentieth century similar to the effect of the railroad in the nineteenth. When the Wright brothers patented their flying machine in 1906, the word *airplane* was already there, waiting for them. The new technology of *aeronautics* borrowed part of its name from sailing technology (*nautes* is Greek for "sailor"), and it borrowed a number of technical terms from sailing as well. *Cockpit, cabin, steward, rudder,* and many other terms were adapted from the ocean liners that the airplane would eventually make almost obsolete. New words and combinations, like *barnstorm, tailspin,* and *Mayday* (from the French *m'aidez,* "help me"), came into common usage as a result of the airplane.

Nautes, by the way, connects the ancient and the modern worlds in a strikingly direct way. In Greek mythology, the *Argonauts* sailed with Jason in a ship called the *Argo* in search of the Golden Fleece. The U.S. *astronauts* ("star sailors") sail to outer space in the twentieth century, as do the Russian *cosmonauts* ("universe sailors").

Terms like *countdown, blastoff, malfunction,* and *put on hold* are the legacy of jargon, or argot, from the space program. Airplane flyers had long had a number of colorful terms for unexplained malfunctions. The word *gremlin* was commonly used by pilots during World War II, but was later replaced by *bug,* which is still in use. The word today's astronauts probably use most often, though, is *glitch,* a term taken over by computer experts.

Computerspeak

Much of the language associated with computers is highly specific and may never be extended to a noncomputer field. Such computer terms include *RAM, ROM,* and *WYSIWYG,* acronyms for "*r*andom *a*ccess *m*emory," "*r*ead *o*nly *m*emory," and "*w*hat *you* *s*ee *i*s *w*hat *you* *g*et." People in

> One method of forming new words, now so popular that it almost threatens to overwhelm us, is the use of acronyms.

face • mail (fās′māl)
Technologically backward means of communication, clearly inferior to voice mail or E-mail. Involves actually walking to someone's office and speaking to him or her face to face. Considered highly inefficient and déclassé.

Definition from *The Microsoft Lexicon.*

the computer industry have adapted many standard English words to technical uses, though, and a number of these terms are edging back into the non-computer world with slightly different meanings. The most notable are nouns that have been changed to verbs. *Access, format, interface,* and *program* are being used as verbs with some frequency today. *Program* has already produced an offspring, *de-program,* referring to "reverse brainwashing."

Computer language is often lively and whimsical. If a programmer interferes with someone else's program, for example, he or she is said to *bomb the program* (not a nice thing to do). Programs that *stop* working unexpectedly *hang* or *crash,* sometimes as the result of a *spike,* or a surge in electricity. When we start a computer, we *boot* it. *Boot* is a shortening of *bootstrap,* which comes from the familiar expression "to pull yourself up by your bootstraps," meaning "to succeed on your own without the help of others," or, in computer jargon, "to be self-initiating."

Try It Out

1. **Researching technical terms.** The following terms, once associated only with trains, automobiles, or airplanes, have entered general usage. For each term, (1) identify the technology with which it was originally associated, and (2) give its meaning in general usage. You might want to refer to a dictionary.

   sidetrack
   stopover
   tune-up
   tank town
   tailspin
   nose dive

2. **Identifying acronyms.** Look at some newspapers or newsmagazines to find five acronyms related to technology that are in current usage. Remember that an acronym is an abbreviation that is pronounced like a word, not as separate letters.

3. **Computerspeak: Compiling a glossary.** Prepare a glossary of computer terms that includes definitions and origins of terms. Include pronunciations and illustrations, when visuals will help. You can be humorous. (The definition at the left of *face-mail* is from a lexicon of computer language used by Microsoft.)

"You've learned to respond to verbal commands. Now let's test your computer literacy."

Writer's Workshop

The history
of the written
word is rich a

Page 1

PERSUASIVE WRITING

EVALUATION

When you evaluate something, you present a well-considered judgment about its worth, offering reasons that support your stance and evidence that those reasons are valid. In English classes, you are often asked to evaluate works of literature; in life, you may need to evaluate anything from the color scheme of a room to a politician's voting record to your own job performance.

Prewriting

1. **Choose a literary work.** Of the stories and poems you have read in the Contemporary Literature collections, which moved you most strongly, either to delight or to distaste? Which seemed to be the most flawless—or most flawed—examples of their art forms? Which stayed in your mind the longest? Quickwrite a list of outstanding works from the Contemporary Literature collections. The ones that first spring to mind may be the ones that left the strongest impression; however, take a few moments to allow less obvious choices to emerge from the back of your mind. Circle two or three titles that seem promising. Then, skim over the circled works, and decide which to write about. If you completed and kept any of the Writer's Notebook activities from these collections, you may already have a head start on a topic for evaluation. Of course, you can always choose to evaluate a literary work you've encountered on your own, outside this textbook.

2. **Reacquaint yourself with the work.** Reread the work, the prereading and postreading materials, and your notes, immersing yourself in the work's content and your own response to it. Take new notes as you go along. You'll continue consulting the work as you move through the writing process.

3. **Explore the work in writing.** Put your thoughts and feelings about the work on paper in a quick paragraph or two. State your opinion of the work, and mention as many specific reasons for your stance as you can. Note passages, scenes, characters, or other literary elements that make strong impressions on you. Include both positive and negative responses to the work.

4. **Decide on your criteria.** To evaluate something, you must apply standards to it. These standards, or **criteria,** are objective rather than personal. Criteria are used to assess whether

Technology HELP

See Writer's Workshop 2 CD-ROM. *Assignment: Evaluation.*

ASSIGNMENT
  Write an essay evaluating a short story, essay, or poem.

AIM
  To inform; to explain; to persuade.

AUDIENCE
  Your classmates and teacher or a specialized audience interested in the subject of your evaluation.

Try It Out

In a small group, come up with as many valid criteria as you can for evaluating any of the following:

1. What are the qualities of a good elective course?
2. What makes a first-rate film?
3. What are the qualities of good conversation?
4. What qualities do you look for in a good teacher?
5. What are the qualities of an excellent radio station?

---

something is an excellent example of its type or kind. For example, if a car is what you wish to evaluate, you might use criteria like cost, gas mileage, repair record, and structural integrity. Similarly, the criteria you would apply to a literary work should agree, on the whole, with accepted critical standards of what makes a literary work successful or unsuccessful. It's important, of course, to develop criteria that are relevant to the unique characteristics of the subject you are evaluating. You might give a thumbs up to a popular science fiction novel because it is fast-paced, contains innovative ideas, and has interesting, larger-than-life characters. But the criteria you'd use to judge a more reflective, overtly "literary" novel would be quite different.

5. **Make a criterion-assessment-evidence chart.** Make a list of several criteria you think are important in the genre of literature you've chosen to evaluate. Then, make a three-column criteria-evaluation chart. In the left column, list your criteria. In the middle column, assess how you think the work either meets or does not meet each criterion, giving a brief reason for your judgment. In the right column, give text evidence for each assessment. To generate evidence for your chart, you might

- compare and/or contrast two works
- relate the work to your own experience
- cite the evaluations and judgments of experts

Model

"Rules of the Game"

Criterion	Assessment	Evidence
language fresh, vivid	very readable; suggests believable narrator's voice	many short, simple sentences; colloquial language; humor (second paragraph, p. 1111)
original treatment of theme	timeless: conflict between generations & cultures	Waverly & her mother have unpredictable responses to her chess victories
believable characterization	individuality of mother & daughter overcomes possible stereotypes	the mother's speeches in dialect are sometimes wise, sometimes not—she's complex (pp. 1113, 1117)
imaginative plot	a success story with a twist	the story is open-ended; ends with a question

Shoe by Jeff MacNelly, reprinted by permission: Tribune Media Services.

6. **Choose your final criteria.** You may not want to discuss every single one of your criteria when you draft your essay, and within a criterion you may not need to cite every aspect you evaluated or every piece of evidence. Mark or highlight the entries on your chart that seem strongest. Add new elements to your chart as you think of them.

Drafting

1. **Present your subject and judgment.** Think about how you can capture your reader's attention at the start of your essay—perhaps by opening with an anecdote, a description, a personal observation, or simply an arresting statement of your evaluation. Identify the work of literature you're evaluating, and express your basic judgment of it, if you haven't done so in your opening sentence. Your readers want to know from the start what you're discussing and what your thumbs-up or thumbs-down verdict is.

   Make your evaluation statement—your claim—specific and fresh. "'Rules of the Game' is one of the best stories I've ever read" does not give the reader any concrete idea of why you think Amy Tan's story is a good one. Indicate what you see in the literary work and why: "'Rules of the Game' is about a Chinese American girl who becomes a chess champion, but anyone who has ever been a teenager in conflict with a parent can identify with it."

2. **Clarify your criteria.** Your criteria should become apparent to the reader as you explore the reasons for your judgment. If your reasons for liking a story include its plot, characterization, and theme, for instance, readers who are familiar with literature will recognize those criteria. You might need to state your criteria explicitly, however, if you have omitted some that readers might have expected, if you have included unusual criteria, or if you give a different weight to certain criteria than your readers might.

3. **Develop your reasons coherently.** Most of your essay will be devoted to your reasons for your overall judgment of the literary work. Evidence to support your reasoning usually comes immediately after, or immediately before, each reason. Use your prewriting chart as a guide, and add details that a chart can't contain. Using transitional words and phrases (*in addition, moreover, likewise*) is one way to create a coherent flow from point to point. Even more important is the placement of your points. For instance, if you discuss plot first, then characterization, then theme, the reader should sense that you ordered those elements thoughtfully rather than just tossing them in the air and seeing which fell first. Their placement should reflect your understanding of the literary work. In evaluating Amy Tan's story, for example, you might show how characterization grows out of plot and how both elements lead to thematic insight.

Strategies for Elaboration

Use these strategies to find evidence from the text to support your literary evaluation:

- Keep rereading the work, and give yourself time to ponder what you've read.

- Go from a general question or issue to specific evidence. You may ask yourself, "Where can I find evidence for the characterization of Mrs. Jong?" and then search the story for any passages that contain her thoughts, spoken words, or vivid actions.

- Move from a specific point or question to an assessment or conclusion. You may wonder, "What does the last paragraph mean?" and then draw a conclusion about Waverly's possible future and her changing attitudes toward her mother and herself.

- Remember that in a strong work of literature, every word and action serves a purpose. Focus not only on the things you understand in the story or poem but also on the things you don't. Ask yourself, "Why did the author put that there?" When you find the answer, you'll have both a reason and the evidence for it.

Language Handbook HELP

See Ways to Achieve Clarity, pages 1235-1236.

Incorporating Supporting Evidence

In a literary evaluation, your main supporting evidence will be in the form of direct quotations and paraphrases from the work you're evaluating. Here are ways to smoothly incorporate supporting evidence into your evaluation:

1. If you're using a direct quotation, make it a seamless part of your sentence structure. A passage you're quoting directly should match the subject and tense of the sentence it's being woven into. Although you should try to avoid it, you may need to use brackets to indicate slight alterations you've made in the quotation to make it fit smoothly with the rest of your sentence.

2. Enclose a direct quotation in double quotation marks. If part of your quotation includes a character's dialogue, place that in single quotation marks. Be sure that you've copied the quote word-for-word as it appears in the work.

3. Use ellipsis points (. . .) to indicate the omission of any part of the quotation.

4. For both direct quotations and paraphrases, cite the page number from which the quotation is taken. For poetry, cite line numbers.

> **EXAMPLE**   Waverly, the story's narrator, "learn[s] why it is essential in the endgame to have foresight, a mathematical understanding of all possible moves, and patience . . ." (page 1113).

5. When you're quoting poetry, use a slash (/) with a space before and after it to indicate the end of a line.

---

4. **Avoid logical fallacies.**   To lend credibility to your essay, avoid:

- *hasty generalizations* (praising or condemning a work without weighing sufficient evidence)

- *overstatement* (giving the work an artificially high or low rating in order to make your evaluation seem dramatic)

- *either/or fallacy* (purporting that the work is all good or all bad)

- *straw-man arguments* (stacking the deck in favor of or against a work by comparing it to something that is clearly inferior or superior to it. A "straw man" is something that can be easily knocked down.)

5. **End decisively.**   You can conclude your essay by restating your judgment, summarizing your reasons, or doing both. Your conclusion should bring the essay to a definite close.

Evaluating and Revising

1. **Peer review.**   Exchange papers with one or more classmates. Address questions such as the following:

- What are the writer's criteria? Do they seem valid and well chosen?

- Are the reasons for the evaluation adequate and convincing?

- Are the reasons backed up by detailed, specific evidence?

- Does the essay help you understand the literary work better?

2. **Self-evaluation.**   Consider your peers' comments carefully. Act on those you agree with. Try reading the literary work one more time to see what new insights emerge. You'll be revising both for content (to strengthen your reasons and evidence) and for style (to make your essay more readable).

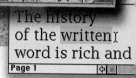
The history
of the written
word is rich and
Page 1

Language Workshop

WORDS TO THE WISE: USING EFFECTIVE DICTION

Consider the difference between these two sentences:

> He is almost sixteen, and though he doesn't have a beard yet, he has a man's mind in a boy's body.

> He is almost sixteen, **though beardless still,** a man's mind **indignantly captive** in **the frame of a child.**

In the second sentence (from John Updike's story "Son"), the boldface phrases are more imaginative, more rhythmical, and more precise than the phrases in the first sentence. The difference is in **diction,** or word choice. Diction may be plain or ornate, formal or informal, and so on. In this example, from Julia Alvarez's "Daughter of Invention," the informal, colloquial phrases are in boldface:

> She was **just fussing** with **little house things, don't mind her.**

To use effective diction in your writing, pay attention to the following:

1. Choose words that are appropriate to your subject. You would use technical words in a science report but informal, colloquial language in a personal essay.

2. Choose words that are appropriate to your audience. Your word choice when addressing third-grade students would differ from diction you would use with a group of high school students.

3. Choose words that are appropriate to your purpose. If you were writing a speech for your high school graduation, you would choose words that are different from those you'd use in writing a humorous letter to a friend.

4. Use precise, vivid words instead of vague ones. (Don't say "The weather was unfavorable." Say "For a week, the sun was hidden by fog.")

5. Use figures of speech when they are fresh and meaningful, but avoid **clichés.**

6. When choosing among synonyms, consider their different connotations.

Writer's Workshop Follow-Up: Revising

Reread the evaluation you wrote for the Writer's Workshop (page 1181). Examine it carefully for vague words and for phrases that don't quite say what you intended. Work to improve your diction, using a dictionary and a thesaurus to help you choose the most precise words.

Language Handbook HELP

See Glossary of Usage, pages 1252-1257.

Try It Out

For each sentence below, write a word or phrase describing the diction. Then state which words or phrases in the sentence led you to that conclusion.

1. For a small town, it was a pretty good show.
   —Tim O'Brien, *from "Speaking of Courage"*

2. It was in this tenement that the personality of my father first came fully into the orbit of my concern.
   —Richard Wright, *from Black Boy*

Reading for Life

Situation

You are a part-time employee at First XYZ Bank, working in its MIS (Management Information Systems) department. This department handles the bank's internal flow of information, which is vital to executives as they make decisions affecting the success of the bank. You receive a memorandum from the director of MIS discussing a purchase. The memo contains technical terms and abbreviations, some new to you. How do you comprehend a difficult memo?

Strategies

Isolate the memo's key information.

- First, read the heading of the memo carefully. You'll see at a glance who sent the memo and when, who is receiving it, and its subject.
- Next, skim over the memo to determine its purpose. Is it intended only to give you information? Does it ask for a reply? If so, determine the deadline for the reply.

Find supporting details.

- Third, read the memo closely. Highlight words or concepts that are unclear to you. Mark important passages. Write marginal notes.
- For anything unclear, first use context clues to determine meaning. If you remain uncertain, consult a colleague or a reference work.

Decide the appropriate response to the memo.

- Once you fully understand the memo, take appropriate action, if any is called for.

Using the Strategies

Read the sample memo on this page very closely.

1. Using context clues, determine what the abbreviations *NIC* and *specs* stand for.
2. Again using context clues, tell what the terms *server computers, client computers,* and *throughput* mean.
3. Explain the abbreviations *LAN* and *CPU* and the term *bits*. (If necessary, consult a person who knows computers or look up the abbreviations in a dictionary.)
4. Write the headings for a memo that replies to this memo. (What action does the phrase "copy Ed Smith" call for?)

Extending the Strategies

Write a short memo containing technical terms concerning computers, automobiles, filmmaking, or another field. The memo should be from a supervisor to an employee in a work situation. Context clues should explain some but not all of the technical terms.

Exchange memos with a classmate. After a half-hour or so, see whether each of you has understood the other's memo. If not, each might suggest ways (1) to write a clearer memo and (2) to get help when it is difficult to understand technical writing.

FIRST XYZ Bank

TO: All Staff in MIS Department
FROM: Dave Davison, Director of MIS
RE: Evaluating Network Interface Cards
DATE: June 19, 2000
CC: Edgar Smith, Director of Accounting

In order to improve the Bank's LAN, we are evaluating new NICs manufactured by several vendors. Specs are attached. The NIC we use plays a vital role in transmitting bits of data to and from our server computers and client computers. Please evaluate the NICs in terms of their throughput, CPU utilization, and cost. Please reply to me by 3 p.m. Friday (copy Ed Smith).

Attachments.

Learning for Life

State of the Arts: Celebrating Cultural Diversity

Problem

The vitality and diversity of contemporary American literature is shared by other contemporary American art forms, from the visual arts to theater. How can people be made more aware of the range and richness of the arts relating to the various cultures in their communities?

Project

Recommend ways that your school or community can promote awareness and appreciation of culturally diverse contemporary arts.

Preparation

1. Work with a partner or a small group to brainstorm a list of various art forms available in your community: dance, drama, poetry, story-telling, sculpture, opera, painting, and so on.
2. Formulate a list of *5W-How?* questions (*Who? What? When? Where? Why? How?*) about one or more of these art forms.

Procedure

1. Research local museums, galleries, performing-arts centers, playhouses, writers' groups, poetry readings, storytelling sessions, and other sources of art and culture in your community or city. Collect brochures, advertisements, mission statements, program notes, and the like from your sources.
2. Research local newspapers, magazines, newsletters, and other publications for write-ups or reviews of your local arts scene. Focus especially on arts from specific cultural groups: African American or Russian theater groups; galleries or museums of Latino art; local or visiting troupes who perform traditional Asian or Irish dance; community spaces for poetry readings celebrating ethnic diversity; and so on.
3. Arrange interviews with local museum directors, theater directors, gallery owners, arts reviewers, or any others who make their living from the arts (painters, writers, actors, and so on). Ask the people you interview about cultural diversity in their area, their predictions about where the arts are heading, local audience response to multi-cultural arts, and other questions relevant to your research.

Presentation

Present your findings in one of the following formats (or another that your teacher approves):

1. **Feature Article**
   Write a feature article on some aspect of culturally diverse art in your community, such as a Latino art gallery, a local American Indian craftsperson, or multicultural poetry readings. Submit your article to your school or local newspaper. Provide quotations from any interviews you've conducted.

2. **Multimedia Presentation**
   Working in a small group, create and present a multimedia exhibit showcasing examples of drama, music, visual art, dance, and other art forms available in your community. Demonstrate the variety of art forms available to the public, with an emphasis on cultural diversity.

3. **Advertising Campaign**
   With a small group, develop and present a "State of the Arts" advertising campaign for your school. Create posters, brochures, slogans, and other advertising tools. Emphasize cultural diversity in the arts, and highlight appropriate examples available in your community.

Processing

What did you learn about the importance of the arts to a community? How are multicultural trends in all the arts changing our cultural climate? In the years to come, what roles do you think the arts will fulfill in both celebrating diversity and uniting people of diverse backgrounds? Write a reflection for your portfolio.

HANDBOOK OF LITERARY TERMS 1189

COMMUNICATIONS HANDBOOK 1204

Active Reading Strategies 1204
Previewing and Setting a Purpose 1204
Reading Actively 1204
Dealing with Difficult Texts 1205
Making Sure You Understand a Text 1205

Study Skills 1205
Using a Dictionary 1205
Using a Thesaurus 1206
Using Study Guides 1206
Recognizing Logical Fallacies 1206

Research Strategies 1207
Using a Library or Media Center 1207
Using the Internet 1208

Evaluating and Citing Sources 1209
Taking Notes and
    Documenting Sources 1210
List of Sources Cited 1213

Writing for Life 1215
Writing Interoffice Memos 1215
Writing Effective Business Letters 1215
Writing a Personal Résumé 1217
College Admissions 1218
Proofreading 1218

Answering Essay Questions 1219

LANGUAGE HANDBOOK 1220

The Parts of Speech 1220

Agreement 1221

Using Verbs 1223

Using Pronouns 1225

Using Modifiers 1227

Phrases 1229

Clauses 1231

Sentence Structure 1232

Sentence Style 1235

Sentence Combining 1238

Capitalization 1238

Punctuation 1242, 1245

Spelling 1249

Glossary of Usage 1252

GLOSSARY 1258

HANDBOOK OF LITERARY TERMS

You will find more information about the terms in this Handbook on the pages given at the ends of the entries. To learn more about **Allusion,** for example, turn to pages 39, 186, 670, and 1159 in this book.

Cross-references at the ends of some entries refer to other entries in the Handbook containing related information. For instance, at the end of **Antagonist,** you are referred to **Protagonist.**

ALLEGORY   **A story or poem in which characters, settings, and events stand for other people or events or for abstract ideas or qualities.** An allegory can be read on one level for its literal meaning and on a second level for its symbolic, or allegorical, meaning. The most famous allegory in the English language is *The Pilgrim's Progress* (1678) by the English Puritan writer John Bunyan, in which Christian, on his journey to the Celestial City, meets such personages as Mr. Worldly Wiseman, Hopeful, and Giant Despair and travels to such places as the Slough of Despond, the Valley of Humiliation, and Doubting Castle. Puritans were trained to see their own lives as allegories of Biblical experiences. Nathaniel Hawthorne's and Edgar Allan Poe's fictions are often called allegorical.

See page 280.

ALLITERATION   **The repetition of the same or similar consonant sounds in words that are close together.** Alliteration is used to create musical effects and to establish mood. In the following line from "The Tide Rises, the Tide Falls" (page 177) by Henry Wadsworth Longfellow, the repetition of the *s* sound is an example of alliteration:

But the sea, the sea in the darkness calls

See pages 288, 355.
See also *Assonance, Onomatopoeia, Rhyme.*

ALLUSION   **A reference to someone or something that is known from history, literature, religion, politics, sports, science, or some other branch of culture.** T. S. Eliot drew on his knowledge of the Bible when he alluded to the raising of Lazarus from the dead in "The Love Song of J. Alfred Prufrock" (page 666). The title of Sandra Cisneros's essay "Straw into Gold" (page 1160) is an allusion to the folk tale about Rumpelstiltskin.

You won't understand the cartoon to the right unless you recognize the fairy tale it alludes to.

See pages 39, 186, 670, 1159.

AMBIGUITY   **A technique by which a writer deliberately suggests two or more different, and sometimes conflicting, meanings in a work.** Langston Hughes's poem "Harlem" (page 764) has an ambiguous ending; the title of Richard Wilbur's "The Beautiful Changes" (page 1006) is also deliberately ambiguous.

See page 493.

ANALOGY   **A comparison made between two things to show how they are alike.** In "The Crisis, No. 1" (page 108), Thomas Paine draws an analogy between a thief breaking into a house and the king of England interfering in the affairs of the American Colonies.

See pages 112, 890.

ANAPEST   **A metrical foot that has two unstressed syllables followed by one stressed syllable.** The word *coexist* (˘ ˘ ′) is an example of an anapest.

See also *Dactyl, Foot.*

ANECDOTE   **A very brief story, told to illustrate a point or serve as an example of something.** In Thomas Paine's "The Crisis, No. 1," the tale of the Tory tavern keeper and his child (page 108) is an anecdote.

See page 465.

ANTAGONIST   **The opponent who struggles against or blocks the hero, or protagonist, in a story.** In *The Narrative of the Life of Frederick Douglass,* Mr. Covey is Douglass's antagonist. In Herman Melville's *Moby-Dick,* the white whale is Ahab's antagonist.

See also *Protagonist.*

"They're offering a deal—you can pay court costs and damages, they drop charges of breaking and entering."
Drawing by Maslin. © 1988 The New Yorker Magazine, Inc.

ANTHROPOMORPHISM Attributing human characteristics to an animal or inanimate object. Writers often anthropomorphize animals or objects in order to achieve humorous or satirical effects.

See also *Personification.*

APHORISM A brief, cleverly worded statement that makes a wise observation about life. Benjamin Franklin's *Poor Richard's Almanack* is a book of aphorisms. Ralph Waldo Emerson's style is **aphoristic**—he incorporates many pithy sayings into his essays (which is why he is so quotable).

See pages 95, 222, 786, 1087.

APOSTROPHE A technique by which a writer addresses an inanimate object, an idea, or a person who is either dead or absent. Sor Juana Inés de la Cruz apostrophizes her critics in "World, in Hounding Me . . ." (page 76). Oliver Wendell Holmes apostrophizes a shell and his soul in "The Chambered Nautilus" (page 189).

See pages 188, 792, 795.

ARGUMENT A form of persuasion that appeals to reason, rather than emotion, to convince an audience to think or act in a certain way. The Declaration of Independence provides some famous examples of argument.

See page 112.
See also *Persuasion.*

ASSONANCE The repetition of similar vowel sounds followed by different consonant sounds, especially in words close together. Notice the repeated sound of *i* in these lines from "The Tide Rises, the Tide Falls" (page 177) by Henry Wadsworth Longfellow. Read the lines aloud to hear the verbal music created by assonance.

> The tide rises, the tide falls,
> The twilight darkens, the curlew calls

See page 355.
See also *Alliteration, Onomatopoeia, Rhyme.*

ATMOSPHERE The mood or feeling created in a piece of writing. A story's atmosphere might be peaceful, festive, menacing, melancholy, and so on. Edgar Allan Poe's "The Fall of the House of Usher," for example, conveys an atmosphere of gloom.

See page 262.
See also *Setting.*

AUTOBIOGRAPHY An account of the writer's own life. Benjamin Franklin's autobiography (page 86) is one of the most famous autobiographies in American literature. A selection from Richard Wright's autobiography, *Black Boy,* is on page 1015.

See pages 57, 97.

BALLAD A song or poem that tells a story. The typical ballad tells a tragic story in the form of a monologue or dialogue. Ballads usually have a simple, steady rhythm, a rhyme pattern, and a refrain, all of which make them easy to memorize. Ballads composed by unknown singers and passed on orally from one generation to the next are called **folk ballads. Literary ballads** are written to imitate the sounds and subjects of folk ballads. A strong tradition of folk ballads and of literary ballads exists in the United States. Country-and-western music, for example, frequently features songs written to imitate the older ballads. Here's the start of a favorite ballad, telling the story of Betsy and Ike:

> Oh don't you remember sweet Betsy from Pike,
> Who crossed the big mountains with her lover Ike,
> With two yoke of oxen, a big yellow dog,
> A tall Shanghai rooster, and one spotted hog?

> *Chorus:*
> Singing dang fol dee dido,
>   Singing dang fol dee day.

> One evening quite early they camped on the Platte.
> 'Twas near by the road on a green shady flat,
> Where Betsy, sore-footed, lay down to repose—
> With wonder Ike gazed on that Pike County rose.

BIOGRAPHY An account of someone's life written by another person. One of the most famous biographies in American literature is Carl Sandburg's multivolume life of Abraham Lincoln.

BLANK VERSE Poetry written in unrhymed iambic pentameter. Blank verse has a long history in English literature. It was used notably by such poets as Shakespeare and Milton in the sixteenth and seventeenth centuries and by Robert Frost in the twentieth.

See pages 569, 575.
See also *Iambic Pentameter.*

CADENCE The natural, rhythmic rise and fall of a language as it is normally spoken. Cadence is different from **meter,** in which the stressed and unstressed syllables of a poetic line are carefully counted to conform to a regular pattern. Walt Whitman was a master at imitating the cadences of spoken American English in his free verse.

See page 355.
See also *Free Verse, Meter, Rhythm*

CAESURA **A pause or break within a line of poetry.** Some pauses are indicated by punctuation; others are suggested by phrasing or meaning. In the lines below, the caesuras are marked by double vertical lines. These pauses are indicated by punctuation.

> Announced by all the trumpets of the sky,
> Arrives the snow, || and, || driving o'er the fields,
> Seems nowhere to alight: || the whited air
> Hides hills and woods . . .

> —Ralph Waldo Emerson,
> *from "The Snow-Storm"*

CATALOG **A list of things, people, or events.** Cataloging was a favorite device of Walt Whitman, who included long, descriptive lists throughout *Leaves of Grass.*

> See page 351.

CHARACTER **An individual in a story or play.** A character always has human traits, even if the character is an animal, as in Aesop's fables, or a god, as in the Greek and Roman myths.

The process by which the writer reveals the personality of a character is called **characterization.** A writer can reveal a character in the following ways:

- by telling us directly what the character is like: sneaky, generous, mean to pets, and so on

- by describing how the character looks and dresses

- by letting us hear the character speak

- by revealing the character's private thoughts and feelings

- by revealing the character's effect on other people—showing how other characters feel or behave toward the character

- by showing the character in action

The first method of revealing a character is called **direct characterization.** When a writer uses this method, we do not have to figure out what a character's personality is like—the writer tells us directly. The other five methods of revealing a character are known as **indirect characterization.** When a writer uses these methods, we have to exercise our own judgment, putting clues together to infer what a character is like—just as we do in real life when we are getting to know someone.

Characters are often classified as static or dynamic. A **static character** is one who does not change much in the course of a story. A **dynamic character,** on the other hand, changes in some important way as a result of the story's action. Characters can also be classified as flat or round. **Flat characters** have few personality traits. They can be summed up by a single phrase: the loyal sidekick, the buffoon, the nosy neighbor. In contrast, **round characters** have more dimensions to their personalities—they are complex, just as real people are.

> See pages 313, 981.
> See also *Motivation, Setting, Stereotype.*

CLICHÉ **A word or phrase, often a figure of speech, that has become lifeless because of overuse.** Some examples of clichés are "green with envy," "quiet as a mouse," and "pretty as a picture."

CLIMAX **That point in a plot that creates the greatest intensity, suspense, or interest.** The climax is usually the point at which the conflict in the story is resolved.

> See also *Plot.*

COMEDY **In general, a story that ends with a happy resolution of the conflicts faced by the main character or characters.** In many comedies, the conflict is provided when a young couple who wish to marry are blocked by adults. In many comedies, the main character at the end has moved into a world of greater freedom; this is the kind of comedy we see in Washington Irving's "Rip Van Winkle" (page 154). In literature, the word *comedy* is not synonymous with *humor.* Some comedies are humorous; some are not.

> See page 683.
> See also *Tragedy.*

CONCEIT **An elaborate metaphor or other figure of speech that compares two things that are startlingly different.** Often a conceit is also a very lengthy comparison. The conceit was a popular figure of speech in seventeenth-century English metaphysical poetry. In American literature, the poems of Edward Taylor (page 72) and Emily Dickinson (page 372) are known for their conceits. T. S. Eliot, in more recent literary history, also used conceits (page 661).

> See page 74.
> See also *Figure of Speech, Metaphor.*

CONCRETE POEM **A poem in which the words are arranged on a page to suggest a visual representation of the subject.** In English poetry in the seventeenth century, poets wrote concrete poems in the shapes of such things as crosses, altars, and wings; today, poets write concrete poems in every conceivable shape: waves, hearts, cats, flowers.

> See page 65.

CONFLICT **The struggle between opposing forces or characters in a story.** A conflict can be **internal,** involving opposing forces within a person's mind. In James Thurber's "The Secret Life of Walter Mitty" (page 625), for example, the title character has a comical internal conflict between his desire for heroism and his cowardice in the face of a formidable spouse. **External** conflicts can exist between two people, between a person and nature or a machine, or between a person and a whole society. In one segment of "Son" (page 1070), for example, John Updike shows the narrator in conflict with his son. Many stories have both internal and external conflict.

> See pages 607, 965, 1044, 1077, 1129.
> See also *Settings*.

CONNOTATION **The associations and emotional overtones that have become attached to a word or phrase, in addition to its strict dictionary definition.** The words *determined, firm, rigid, stubborn,* and *pigheaded* have similar dictionary definitions, but widely varying connotations, or overtones of meaning. *Determined* and *firm* both suggest an admirable kind of resoluteness; *rigid* suggests an inability to bend and a kind of mindless refusal to change. *Stubborn* and *pigheaded,* on the other hand, have even more negative connotations. *Stubborn* has associations with a mule, and *pigheaded* with the pig, which, wrongly or not, is an animal often associated with mindless willfulness. Here are some other words that are more or less synonymous but which have vastly different connotations: *fastidious* and *fussy; daydreamer* and *escapist; scent, odor, smell,* and *stink.* Words with strong connotations are often called **loaded words** or **suggestive words.**

> See pages 46, 281, 701, 726.

CONSONANCE **The repetition of the same or similar final consonant sounds on accented syllables or in important words.** The words *ticktock* and *singsong* contain examples of consonance. Some modern poets use consonance in place of rhyme.

COUPLET **Two consecutive rhyming lines of poetry.** If the two rhyming lines express a complete thought, they are called a **closed couplet.** The following lines are from a poem built on a series of closed couplets.

> If ever wife was happy in a man,
> Compare with me, ye women, if you can.
>
> —Anne Bradstreet, *from* "To My
> Dear and Loving Husband"

DACTYL **A metrical foot of three syllables in which the first syllable is stressed and the next two are unstressed.** The word *tendency* ($'$ $\smile$ $\smile$) is a dactyl.

> See also *Anapest, Foot.*

DENOUEMENT (dā′noo·mä*n*′) **The conclusion (or resolution) of a story.** In French, the word means "unraveling." At this point in a story, all the mysteries are unraveled, the conflicts are resolved, and all the questions raised by the plot are answered. Much modern fiction ends without a denouement, so that the story leaves us with a sense of incompleteness.

> See also *Plot, Resolution.*

DESCRIPTION **One of the four major forms of discourse, in which language is used to create a mood or emotion.** Description does this by the use of words that appeal to our senses: sight, hearing, touch, smell, taste. Walt Whitman gives a wonderful description of a Civil War battlefield in *Specimen Days* (page 363).

> See page 549.

DIALECT **A way of speaking that is characteristic of a certain social group or of the inhabitants of a certain geographical area.** Dialects may differ from one another in vocabulary, pronunciation, and grammar. One dialect has become dominant in America, and it is known as Standard English. This is the dialect used most often on national radio news and television news broadcasts. Many writers try to capture dialects to give their stories local color, humor, or an air of authenticity. Among the writers in this book who make skilled use of dialect are Mark Twain, Eudora Welty, Flannery O'Connor, William Faulkner, and Langston Hughes.

> See pages 512, 1055, 1066.
> See also *Vernacular.*

DICTION **A speaker or writer's choice of words.** Diction can be formal, informal, colloquial, full of slang, poetic, ornate, plain, abstract, concrete, and so on. Diction depends on the writer's subject, purpose, and audience. Some words, for example, are suited to informal conversations but are inappropriate in a formal speech. Diction has a powerful effect on the **tone** of a piece of writing.

> See pages 107, 1176.
> See also *Tone.*

DRAMATIC MONOLOGUE **A poem in which a character speaks to one or more listeners.** The reactions of the listener must be inferred by the reader. From the speaker's words, the reader learns about the setting, the situation, the identity of the other characters, and the personality of the speaker. The outstanding dramatic monologue in American literature is T. S. Eliot's "The Love Song of J. Alfred Prufrock." The poems in Edgar Lee Masters's *Spoon River Anthology* (page 693) are also dramatic monologues.

> See page 663.

ELEGY **A poem of mourning, usually about someone who has died.** Most elegies are written to mark a person's death, but some extend their subject to reflect on life, death, and the fleeting nature of beauty. The elegies in this book include William Cullen Bryant's "Thanatopsis" (page 171), John Crowe Ransom's "Bells for John Whiteside's Daughter" (page 578), and Theodore Roethke's "Elegy for Jane" (page 1002).

See pages 1004, 1100.

EPIC **A long narrative poem, written in heightened language, which recounts the deeds of a heroic character who embodies the values of a particular society.** Epics in English include *Beowulf* (c. 700) and John Milton's *Paradise Lost* (1667). Some critics view Walt Whitman's *Leaves of Grass* as an American epic in which the hero is the questing poet.

See pages 328, 350.

EPITHET **A descriptive word or phrase that is frequently used to characterize a person or thing.** The epithet "the father of his country" is often used to characterize George Washington. New York City's popular epithet, "the Big Apple," is frequently used by advertisers. Epics such as Homer's *Odyssey* and *Iliad* frequently use **stock epithets** over and over again to describe certain characters or places: "patient Penelope," "wily Odysseus," and "earthshaker" (for Poseidon).

See page 795.

ESSAY **A short piece of nonfiction prose in which the writer discusses some aspect of a subject.** The word *essay* comes from the French *essai*, meaning "to try," a derivation that suggests that the essay form is not an exhaustive treatment of a subject. Essays are sometimes classified as formal or informal, or as formal or personal (or familiar). The essay form has been especially popular in the twentieth century, particularly among American writers. Some famous American essayists of the past include Thomas Paine (page 106), Ralph Waldo Emerson (page 216), and Henry David Thoreau (page 230). More recent essayists include E. B. White, Alice Walker (page 1101), James Baldwin (page 1141), Annie Dillard, Joan Didion, Lewis Thomas, and Edward Abbey.

See page 1102.

EXPOSITION **One of the four major forms of discourse, in which something is explained or "set forth."** Exposition is most commonly used in nonfiction. The word *exposition* also refers to that part of a plot in which the reader is given important background information on the characters, their setting, and their problems. Such exposition is usually provided at the opening of a story or play. See Washington Irving's "Rip Van Winkle" for an example (page 155, starting second paragraph).

See page 815.
See also *Plot.*

FABLE **A very short story told in prose or poetry that teaches a practical lesson about how to succeed in life.** In many fables, the characters are animals that behave like people. The most ancient fabulist is the Greek Aesop; the most famous American fabulist is James Thurber (page 623), who produced two collections: *Fables for Our Time* and *Further Fables for Our Time.*

FARCE **A type of comedy in which ridiculous and often stereotyped characters are involved in silly, far-fetched situations.** The humor in a farce is often physical and slapstick, with characters being hit in the face with pies or running into closed doors. The American cinema has produced many farces, including those starring Laurel and Hardy, Abbott and Costello, and the Marx brothers.

FIGURE OF SPEECH **A word or phrase that describes one thing in terms of another and that is not meant to be taken literally.** Figures of speech always involve a comparison of two things that are basically very dissimilar. Hundreds of figures of speech have been identified by scholars; the most common ones are **simile, metaphor, personification,** and **symbol.** Figures of speech, also called, more generally, **figurative language,** are basic to everyday speech. Statements like "She is a tower of strength" and "He is a pain in the neck" are figures of speech.

See pages 78, 224, 228, 622, 1002.
See also *Conceit, Metaphor, Personification, Simile, Symbol.*

FLASHBACK **A scene that interrupts the normal chronological sequence of events in a story to depict something that happened at an earlier time.** Although the word was coined to describe a technique used by movie makers, the technique itself is at least as old as ancient Greek literature. Much of Homer's epic poem the *Odyssey* is a flashback. Willa Cather uses frequent flashbacks to reveal the past of Georgiana in "A Wagner Matinée" (page 540).

FOIL **A character who acts as a contrast to another character.** In Herman Melville's *Moby-Dick,* First Mate Starbuck is a foil to Captain Ahab.

FOOT **A metrical unit of poetry.** A foot always contains at least one stressed syllable and, usually, one or more unstressed syllables. An **iamb** is a common foot in English poetry: It consists of an unstressed syllable followed by a stressed syllable (˘ ′).

See also *Anapest, Dactyl, Iamb, Iambic Pentameter, Meter, Spondee, Trochee.*

FORESHADOWING **The use of hints and clues to suggest what will happen later in a plot.** A writer might use foreshadowing to create suspense or to prefigure later events. In "To Build a Fire" (page 496), for example, Jack London foreshadows the conclusion of his story by placing hints throughout the story.

See page 673.

FREE VERSE **Poetry that does not conform to a regular meter or rhyme scheme.** Poets who write in free verse try to reproduce the natural rhythms of the spoken language. Free verse uses the traditional poetic elements of **imagery, figures of speech, repetition, internal rhyme, alliteration, assonance,** and **onomatopoeia.** The first American practitioner of free verse was Walt Whitman (page 348). Some of Whitman's heirs are William Carlos Williams (page 778), Carl Sandburg (page 792), and Allen Ginsberg.

See pages 355, 742, 772.
See also *Cadence, Meter, Rhythm.*

HYPERBOLE **A figure of speech that uses an incredible exaggeration, or overstatement, for effect.** In *Life on the Mississippi* (page 453), Mark Twain uses hyperbole for comic effect. An example is Twain's response when Mr. Bixby tells him he must learn the shape of the Mississippi River throughout its course:

> Have I got to learn the shape of the river according to all these five hundred thousand different ways? If I tried to carry all that cargo in my head it would make me stoop-shouldered.
>
> —Mark Twain, *from Life on the Mississippi*

See pages 463, 622, 962.
See also *Understatement.*

IAMB **A metrical foot in poetry that has an unstressed syllable followed by a stressed syllable, as in the word *protect*.** The iamb (˘ ′) is a common foot in poetry written in English.

See page 176.
See also *Foot, Iambic Pentameter, Meter, Spondee, Trochee.*

IAMBIC PENTAMETER **A line of poetry that contains five iambic feet.** The iambic pentameter line is the most common in English and American poetry. Shakespeare and John Milton, among others, used iambic pentameter in their major works. So did such American poets as William Cullen Bryant, Ralph Waldo Emerson, Robert Frost, and Wallace Stevens. Here, for example, is the opening line of a poem by Emerson:

> ˘ ′ ˘ ′ ˘ ′ ˘ ′ ˘ ′
> In May, when sea-winds pierced our solitudes
>
> —Ralph Waldo Emerson,
> *from* "The Rhodora"

See page 180.
See also *Blank Verse, Foot, Iamb, Meter, Scanning.*

IDIOM **An expression that means something different from the literal definitions of its parts.** "Falling in love" is an idiom, as is "I lost my head."

See also *Figure of Speech.*

IMAGERY **The use of language to evoke a picture or a concrete sensation of a person, a thing, a place, or an experience.** Although most images appeal to the sense of sight, they also sometimes appeal to the senses of taste, smell, hearing, and touch as well.

See pages 218, 355, 701, 949, 1089.

IMAGISM **A twentieth-century movement in European and American poetry that advocated the creation of hard, clear images, concisely expressed in everyday speech.** The leading Imagist poets in America were Ezra Pound (page 773), Amy Lowell, H. D. [Hilda Doolittle], and William Carlos Williams (page 778).

See pages 533, 771.

IMPRESSIONISM **A nineteenth-century movement in literature and art that advocated a recording of the artist's personal impressions of the world, rather than a strict representation of reality.** Some famous American Impressionists in art are Mary Cassatt, Maurice Prendergast, and William Merritt Chase. In fiction, Stephen Crane pioneered a kind of literary impressionism in which he portrayed not objective reality but one character's impressions of reality. Crane's impressionistic technique is best seen in his novel *The Red Badge of Courage.*

See page 484.

INCONGRUITY **The deliberate joining of opposites or of elements that are not appropriate to each other.** T. S. Eliot's famous opening simile in "The Love Song of J. Alfred Prufrock" (page 663) joins two incongruous elements: a sunset and a patient knocked out by ether on an operating table. Incongruity can also be used for humor: We laugh at the sight of an elephant dressed in a pink tutu because the two elements are incongruous. Writers also use incongruity for dramatic effect. In Donald Barthelme's "Game" (page 956), the childish actions of the characters are in sharp contrast with the devastation they can cause by turning a key.

See page 962.

INTERIOR MONOLOGUE   A narrative technique that records a character's internal flow of thoughts, memories, and ideas. Parts of James Joyce's *Ulysses* and William Faulkner's *The Sound and the Fury* are written as interior monologues.

See page 1157.

INTERNAL RHYME   Rhyme that occurs within a line of poetry or within consecutive lines. The first line of the following couplet includes an internal rhyme.

> And so, all the night-*tide,* I lie down by the *side*
> Of my darling—my darling—my life and my bride

—Edgar Allan Poe, *from* "Annabel Lee"

See page 288.
See also *Rhyme.*

INVERSION   The reversal of the normal word order in a sentence or phrase. An English sentence normally is built on subject-verb-complement, in that order. An inverted sentence reverses one or more of those elements. In poetry written many years ago, writers often inverted word order as a matter of course, in order to have the words conform to the meter, or to create rhymes. The poetry of Anne Bradstreet (page 68) contains many inversions, as in the first line of the poem on the burning of her house:

> In silent night when rest I took

In prose, inversion is often used for emphasis, as when Patrick Henry, in his fiery speech to the Virginia Convention (page 102), said "Suffer not yourselves to be betrayed with a kiss" (instead of "Do not suffer [allow] yourselves," etc.).

See pages 69, 174.

IRONY   In general, a discrepancy between appearances and reality. There are three main types of irony:

1. **Verbal irony** occurs when someone says one thing but really means something else. Oliver Wendell Holmes uses irony when, in "Old Ironsides" (page 190), he urges that the warship be destroyed.

2. **Situational irony** takes place when there is a discrepancy between what is expected to happen, or what would be appropriate to happen, and what really does happen. A famous use of situational irony is in Stephen Crane's "A Mystery of Heroism" (page 487), in which a soldier risks his life to get water which is then spilled.

3. **Dramatic irony** is so called because it is often used on stage. In this kind of irony, a character in the play or story thinks one thing is true, but the audience or reader knows better. In Edwin Arlington Robinson's "Miniver Cheevy" (page 646). Miniver thinks he is too refined for his age, but in the reader's eyes, he seems foolish and somewhat pathetic.

See pages 422, 485, 683.

LYRIC POEM   A poem that does not tell a story but expresses the personal feelings or thoughts of a speaker. The many lyric poems in this textbook include the philosophic "Thanatopsis" by William Cullen Bryant (page 171) and the elegiac "Bells for John Whiteside's Daughter" by John Crowe Ransom (page 578).

See page 1008.

MAGIC REALISM   A genre developed in Latin America that juxtaposes the everyday with the marvelous or magical. Myths, folk tales, religious beliefs, and tall tales are the raw material for many magic realist writers. Gabriel García Márquez's work, particularly his novel *One Hundred Years of Solitude* (1970), established him as a master of the genre. Other prominent Latin American magic realists include Jorge Luis Borges, Julio Cortázar, and Isabel Allende. Among American writers, Donald Barthelme and Thomas Pynchon have been influenced by magic realism.

See page 996.

METAPHOR   A figure of speech that makes a comparison between two unlike things without the use of such specific words of comparison as *like, as, than, or resembles.* There are several kinds of metaphor:

1. A **directly stated metaphor** states the comparison explicitly: "Fame is a bee" (Emily Dickinson).

2. An **implied metaphor** does not state explicitly the two terms of the comparison: "I like to see it lap the Miles" (Emily Dickinson) is an implied metaphor in which the verb *lap* implies a comparison between "it" (which is a train) and some animal that "laps" up water.

3. An **extended metaphor** is a metaphor that is extended or developed over a number of lines or

with several examples. Dickinson's poem beginning "Fame is a bee" is an extended metaphor: The comparison of fame to a bee is extended for four lines:

> Fame is a bee.
>   It has a song—
> It has a sting—
>   Ah, too, it has a wing.

4. A **dead metaphor** is a metaphor that has been used so often that the comparison is no longer vivid: "The head of the house," "the seat of government," and "a knotty problem" are all dead metaphors.

5. A **mixed metaphor** is a metaphor that fails to make a logical comparison because its mixed terms are visually or imaginatively incompatible. If you say, "The President is a lame duck who is running out of gas," you've lost control of your metaphor and have produced a statement that is ridiculous (ducks do not run out of gas).

> See pages 74, 188, 246, 431, 452, 463, 622, 1002, 1066.
> See also *Conceit, Figure of Speech, Simile.*

METER **A pattern of stressed and unstressed syllables in poetry.** The meter of a poem is commonly indicated by using the symbol (´) for stressed syllables and the symbol (˘) for unstressed syllables. This is called **scanning** the poem.

Meter is described as **iambic, trochaic, dactylic,** or **anapestic.** These scanned lines from "Richard Cory" are iambic because they are built on iambs—an unstressed syllable followed by a stressed syllable.

> ˘ ´ ˘ ´ ˘ ´ ˘ ´
> And he was always quietly arrayed

> ˘ ´ ˘ ´ ˘ ´ ˘ ´ ˘ ´
> And he was always human when he talked

> See pages 69, 176, 396.
> See also *Cadence, Foot, Free Verse, Iamb, Iambic Pentameter, Rhythm, Scanning, Spondee, Trochee.*

METONYMY **A figure of speech in which a person, place, or thing is referred to by something closely associated with it.** Referring to a king or queen as "the crown" is an example of metonymy, as is calling a car "wheels."

> See also *Synecdoche.*

MODERNISM **A term for the bold new experimental styles and forms that swept the arts during the first third of the twentieth century.** Modernism called for changes in subject matter, in fic-

tional styles, in poetic forms, and in attitudes. T. S. Eliot (page 661) and Ezra Pound (page 773) are associated with the modernist movement in poetry. Their aim was to rid poetry of its nineteenth-century "prettiness" and sentimentality.

> See pages 525, 533.
> See also *Imagism, Symbolism.*

MOTIVATION **The reasons for a character's behavior.** In order for us to understand why characters act the way they do, their motivation has to be believable, at least in terms of the story. At times, a writer directly reveals motivation; in subtler fiction, we must use details from the story to infer motivation.

> See pages 586, 828, 1110.
> See also *Character.*

MYTH **An anonymous traditional story that is basically religious in nature and that usually serves to explain a belief, ritual, or mysterious natural phenomenon.** Most myths have grown out of religious rituals, and almost all of them involve the exploits of gods and humans. Works of magic realism often draw on myths or mythlike tales.

> See page 996.

NARRATIVE **The form of discourse that tells about a series of events.** Narration is used in all kinds of literature: fiction, nonfiction, and poetry. Usually a narrative is told in **chronological order**—in the order in which the events occurred. The other three major forms of discourse are **description, exposition,** and **persuasion.**

NATURALISM **A nineteenth-century literary movement that was an extension of realism and that claimed to portray life exactly as it was.** The naturalists relied heavily on the new fields of psychology and sociology, and they tended to dissect human behavior with complete objectivity, the way a scientist would dissect a specimen in the laboratory. The naturalists were also influenced by Darwinian theories of the survival of the fittest. Naturalists believed that human behavior is determined by heredity and environment; they felt that people have no recourse to supernatural forces and that human beings, like animals, are subject to laws of nature beyond their control. The outstanding naturalists among American writers are Theodore Dreiser, Stephen Crane (page 484), and Frank Norris. Some people consider John Steinbeck's *The Grapes of Wrath* a naturalistic novel, in which characters are the pawns of economic conditions.

> See pages 421, 484, 496.
> See also *Realism.*

OBJECTIVE CORRELATIVE **An object, a situation, or a chain of events that serves as the formula for a specific emotion.** The term was first used in an essay by T. S. Eliot.

See page 777.

OCTAVE **An eight-line poem, or the first eight lines of a Petrarchan, or Italian, sonnet.** In a Petrarchan sonnet, the octave states the subject of the sonnet, or poses a problem or question.

See page 180.
See also *Sestet, Sonnet.*

ODE **A lyric poem, usually long, on a serious subject and written in dignified language.** In ancient Greece and Rome, odes were written to be read in public at ceremonial occasions. In modern literature, odes tend to be more private, informal, and reflective. Robert Lowell's "For the Union Dead" (page 950) and Henry Timrod's "Ode on the Confederate Dead" (page 954) are examples of the personal, meditative ode.

ONOMATOPOEIA **The use of a word whose sound imitates or suggests its meaning.** The word *buzz* is onomatopoeic; it imitates the sound it names.

See pages 288, 355.

OXYMORON **A figure of speech that combines opposite or contradictory terms in a brief phrase.** "Sweet sorrow," "deafening silence," and "living death" are common oxymorons. (Some jokesters claim that phrases like "jumbo shrimp," "congressional leadership," and "limited nuclear war" are also oxymorons.)

See page 622.

PARABLE **A relatively short story that teaches a moral, or lesson, about how to lead a good life.** The most famous parables are those told by Jesus in the Gospels.

See pages 308, 567.

PARADOX **A statement that appears self-contradictory but that reveals a kind of truth.** Many writers like to use paradox because it allows them to express the complexity of life by showing how opposing ideas can be both contradictory and true. Emily Dickinson often used paradoxes, as in this line: "I taste a liquor never brewed" (page 382).

See pages 229, 248, 604, 1108.

PARALLEL STRUCTURE **(also called *parallelism*) The repetition of words or phrases that have similar grammatical structures.** Lincoln, in his Gettysburg Address (page 479), uses several memorable parallel structures, as when he refers to "government of the people, by the people, for the people."

See pages 115, 355.

PARODY **A work that makes fun of another work by imitating some aspect of the writer's style.** Parodies often achieve their effects by humorously exaggerating certain features in the original work.

See pages 289, 320, 624.

PERSONIFICATION **A figure of speech in which an object or animal is given human feelings, thoughts, or attitudes.** Personification is a type of metaphor in which two dissimilar things are compared. In "To the Fringed Gentian," William Cullen Bryant personifies a flower by giving it an eye and eyelashes:

> Then doth thy sweet and quiet eye
> Look through its fringes to the sky.

See pages 622, 737, 1002, 1035, 1042, 1151.
See also *Anthropomorphism, Apostrophe, Figure of speech.*

PERSUASION **One of the four forms of discourse, which uses reason and emotional appeals to convince a reader to think or act in a certain way.** Persuasion is used in the Declaration of Independence (page 116), in Patrick Henry's "Give me liberty, or give me death" speech (page 102), and in Thomas Paine's "The Crisis, No. 1" (page 108). Persuasion is almost exclusively used in nonfiction, particularly in essays and speeches.

See pages 101, 112.
See also *Argument.*

PLAIN STYLE **A way of writing that stresses simplicity and clarity of expression.** The plain style was favored by most Puritan writers, who avoided unnecessary ornamentation in all aspects of their lives, including church ritual. Simple sentences, everyday words from common speech, and clear and direct statements characterize the plain style. The plain style eliminates elaborate figures of speech and imagery. One of the chief exponents of the plain style in recent American literature was Ernest Hemingway (page 650).

See pages 12, 27, 35.
See also *Style.*

PLOT **The series of related events in a story or play, sometimes called the *story line*.** Most short-story plots contain the following elements: **exposition,** which tells us who the characters are and introduces their conflict; **complications,** which arise as the characters take steps to resolve their conflicts; the **climax,** that exciting or suspenseful moment when the outcome of the conflict is imminent; and a **resolution** or **denouement,** when the story's problems are all resolved and the story ends.

The plots of dramas and novels are somewhat more complex because of their length. A schematic representation of a typical dramatic plot follows. It is based on a "pyramid" developed by the nineteenth-century German critic Gustav Freitag. The **rising action** refers to all the actions that take place before the **turning point** (sometimes called the **crisis**). This is the point at which the hero experiences a reversal of fortune: In a comedy, things begin to work out well; in a tragedy, they get worse and worse. (In Shakespeare's plays, the turning point takes place in the third act. In *Romeo and Juliet,* for example, after he kills Tybalt in the third act, Romeo experiences one disaster after another.) All the action after the turning point is called **falling action** because it is leading to the final resolution (happy or unhappy) of the conflict. The major **climax** in most plays and novels takes place just before the ending; in Shakespeare's plays, it takes place in the fifth, or last, act. (In *Romeo and Juliet,* the major climax takes place when the two young people kill themselves.)

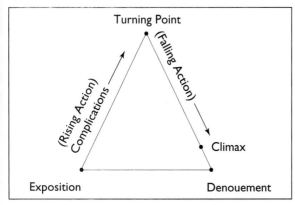

See also *Climax, Denouement, Exposition, Resolution.*

POINT OF VIEW The vantage point from which the writer tells a story. In broad terms, there are four main points of view: **first-person, third-person limited, omniscient,** and **objective.**

1. In the **first-person point of view,** one of the characters in the story tells the story, using first-person pronouns such as *I* and *we.* With this point of view, we can know only what the narrator knows. Mark Twain's novel *Adventures of Huckleberry Finn* is told from the first-person point of view, by the novel's main character, a boy named Huck Finn. One of the great pleasures of that novel, in fact, is that its point of view allows us to hear Huck's very distinct voice and dialect.

2. In the **third-person limited point of view,** an unknown narrator (usually thought of as the author) tells the story, but this narrator zooms in to focus on the thoughts and feelings of only one character. (This point of view gets its name because the narrator refers to all the characters as *he, she,* and *they;* this narrator does not use the first-person pronoun *I.*) Like the first-person point of view, however, this point of view also limits us to the perceptions of one character, but in this case the narrator can tell us many things about the character, things that the character himself (or herself) might be unaware of. For example, Eudora Welty tells "A Worn Path" (page 634) from the third-person limited point of view of her protagonist, an old woman named Phoenix Jackson. At one point, Welty's narrator tells us that Phoenix was "like an old woman begging a dignified forgiveness."

3. In the **omniscient point of view,** an omniscient, or "all-knowing," narrator tells the story, also using the third-person pronouns. However, this narrator, instead of focusing on one character only, often tells us everything about many characters: their motives, weaknesses, hopes, childhoods, and sometimes even their futures. This narrator can also comment directly on the character's actions. Washington Irving's "Rip Van Winkle" (page 154) is told from the omniscient point of view.

4. In the **objective point of view,** a narrator who is totally impersonal and objective tells the story, with no comment on any characters or events. The objective point of view is like the point of view of a movie camera; it is totally impersonal, and what we know is only what the camera might see. This narrator never gives any direct revelation of the characters' thoughts or motives. Ernest Hemingway (page 650) uses this objective point of view, which is why his stories often seem so puzzling to readers. "What happened?" we ask. The *reader* must infer what happens in Hemingway's stories, just as in real life we have to infer the motives, thoughts, and feelings of people we meet.

See pages 232, 467.

POSTMODERNISM A term for the dominant trend in the arts since 1945. Postmodern writing typically experiments with nontraditional forms and allows for multiple meanings. The lines between real and imaginary worlds are often blurred, as is the boundary between fiction and nonfiction. Other characteristics of postmodern literature are cultural diversity and an often playful self-consciousness; that is, an acknowledgment that literature is not a mirror that accurately reflects the world, but a created world unto itself.

See page 910.

PROTAGONIST **The central character in a story, the one who initiates or drives the action.** The protagonist might or might not be the story's hero; some protagonists are actually the villains in the story.

See page 814.
See also *Antagonist.*

PROVERB **A short, well-known statement that expresses a common truth or experience.** Many of Benjamin Franklin's sayings have become proverbs in American culture.

See page 465.

PUN **A "play on words" based on the multiple meanings of a single word or on words that sound alike but mean different things.** An example of the first type of pun is a singer explaining her claim that she was locked out of an audition because she couldn't find the right key. The second kind of pun can be found in the opening lines of Shakespeare's *Julius Caesar,* where a man who repairs shoes claims to be a mender of men's souls (soles). Puns are often used for humor, but some puns are a serious element in poetry.

See page 390.

QUATRAIN **A poem consisting of four lines, or four lines of a poem that can be considered as a unit.** The typical ballad stanza, for example, is a quatrain.

REALISM **A style of writing, developed in the nineteenth century, that attempts to depict life accurately without idealizing or romanticizing it.** Instead of writing about the long ago or far away, the realists concentrated on contemporary life and on middle- and lower-class lives in particular. Among the outstanding realistic novelists in America are Stephen Crane (page 484), Willa Cather (page 538), and John Steinbeck (page 606). European playwrights who wrote realistic dramas, including Henrik Ibsen, August Strindberg, and Anton Chekov, discarded artificial plots in favor of themes centering on contemporary society. They also rejected extravagant language in favor of simpler, everyday diction.

See pages 418, 820.
See also *Naturalism, Romanticism.*

REFRAIN **A word, phrase, line, or group of lines that is repeated, for effect, several times in a poem.** Refrains are often used in ballads and other narrative poems. "Nevermore" is a refrain in Poe's "The Raven" (page 282).

See pages 288, 1122.

REGIONALISM **Literature that emphasizes a specific geographic setting and that reproduces the speech, behavior, and attitudes of the people who live in that region.** Among the great regional writers of the twentieth century are Sinclair Lewis (Midwest); John Steinbeck (California); and William Faulkner, Flannery O'Connor, and Eudora Welty (the South).

See page 419.

RESOLUTION **The conclusion of a story, when all or most of the conflicts have been settled.** The resolution is also often called the *denouement.*

See also *Denouement, Plot.*

RHETORICAL QUESTION **A question asked for an effect, not actually requiring an answer.** In his speech to the Virginia Convention, Patrick Henry asks several rhetorical questions. Such questions presume the audience agrees with the speaker on the answers.

See page 105.

RHYME **The repetition of vowel sounds in accented syllables and all succeeding syllables.** *Listen* and *glisten* rhyme, as do *chime* and *sublime.* When words within the same line of poetry have repeated sounds, we have an example of **internal rhyme. End rhyme** refers to rhyming words at the ends of lines.

The pattern of rhymes in a poem is called a **rhyme scheme.** Rhyme scheme is commonly indicated with letters of the alphabet, each rhyming sound represented by a different letter of the alphabet. For example, the rhyme scheme of the following lines is *abab.*

Tell me not, in mournful numbers,	*a*
Life is but an empty dream!—	*b*
For the soul is dead that slumbers,	*a*
And things are not what they seem.	*b*

—Henry Wadsworth Longfellow,
from "A Psalm of Life"

Approximate rhymes (also called **off rhymes, half rhymes, imperfect rhymes,** or **slant rhymes**) are words that have some correspondence in sound but not an exact one. Examples of approximate rhymes are often found in Emily Dickinson's poems. *Flash* and *flesh* are approximate rhymes, as are *stream* and *storm,* and *early* and *barley.* Approximate rhyme has the effect of catching the reader off guard: Where you expect a perfect rhyme, you get only an approximation. The emotional effect is something like that of the sound of a sharp or flat note in music.

See pages 288, 380.
See also *Internal Rhyme, Rhythm, Slant Rhyme.*

RHYTHM **The alternation of stressed and unstressed syllables in language.** Rhythm occurs naturally in all forms of spoken and written language. The most obvious kind of rhythm is produced by **meter,** the regular pattern of stressed and unstressed syllables found in some poetry. Writers can also create less structured rhythms by using rhyme, repetition, pauses, and variations in line length and by balancing long and short words or phrases.

See pages 670, 761.
See also *Cadence, Free Verse, Meter, Rhyme.*

ROMANCE **In general, a story in which an idealized hero or heroine undertakes a quest and is successful.** In a romance, beauty, innocence, and goodness usually prevail over evil. Romances are traditionally set in the distant past and use a great deal of fantasy. The laws of nature are often suspended in a romance, so that the hero often has supernatural powers, as we see in the adventures of King Arthur and his knights. Stories set in the American West are in the romance mode, except that the supernatural elements are eliminated (though the sheriff-hero usually has a nearly magical skill with his gun). Today we also use the word *romance* to refer to a kind of popular escapist love story, which often takes place in an exotic setting.

See page 683.

ROMANTICISM **A revolt against rationalism that affected literature and the other arts, beginning in the late eighteenth century and remaining strong throughout most of the nineteenth century.** Romanticism is marked by these characteristics: (1) a conviction that intuition, imagination, and emotion are superior to reason; (2) a conviction that poetry is superior to science; (3) a belief that contemplation of the natural world is a means of discovering the truth that lies behind mere reality; (4) a distrust of industry and city life and an idealization of rural life and of the wilderness; (5) an interest in the more "natural" past and in the supernatural. Romanticism affected so many creative people that it was bound to take many different forms; the result is that it is difficult to define the word in a way that includes everyone who might be called a Romantic. In the nineteenth century, for example, Romantics were outspoken in their love of nature and contempt for technology. In this century, however, as nature has been taken over by developers and highways, some writers have taken a romantic view of machines, buildings, and other products of technology.

See pages 143, 144, 212, 770.
See also *Realism.*

SATIRE **A type of writing that ridicules the shortcomings of people or institutions in an attempt to bring about a change.** Satire can cover a wide range of tones, from gentle spoofing to savage mockery. In "Rip Van Winkle" (page 154), for example, Washington Irving pokes good-natured fun at the Van Winkles and the townspeople. In Donald Barthelme's "Game" (page 956), the satire is harsher, as it points out the absurdity and illogic of nuclear war games. Satire is always intensely moral in its purpose. Mark Twain, in *Adventures of Huckleberry Finn,* satirizes a whole spectrum of American life, but the thrust of the novel is moral: Twain is making us see things that should not be permitted to exist (slavery is one of them).

See pages 50, 962.

SCANNING **The analysis of a poem to determine its meter.** When you scan a poem, you describe the pattern of stressed and unstressed syllables in each line. Stresses or accents are indicated by the symbol (′) and unstressed syllables by the symbol (˘).

To him who in the love of Nature holds

Communion with her visible forms, she speaks

A various language: for his gayer hours

She has a voice of gladness, and a smile

—William Cullen Bryant,
from "Thanatopsis"

See also *Iambic Pentameter, Meter.*

SESTET **Six lines of poetry, especially the last six lines of a Petrarchan, or Italian, sonnet.** In the Petrarchan sonnet, the sestet offers a comment on the subject or problem presented in the first eight lines (the octave) of the poem.

See page 180.
See also *Octave, Sonnet.*

SETTING **The time and location in which a story takes place.** Setting can have several functions in fiction:

1. Setting is often used to create **conflict.** In the purest and often simplest form of story, a character is in conflict with some element of a setting: The narrator in Jack London's "To Build a Fire" (page 497) is in conflict with extreme cold (the cold wins).

2. Often the setting helps to create **atmosphere** or **mood,** as does Edgar Allan Poe's setting of a de-

caying mansion in "The Fall of the House of Usher" (page 263).

3. Setting can also create and delineate **character:** In William Faulkner's "A Rose for Emily" (page 716), Miss Emily Grierson's old-fashioned house with its musty rooms reflects her refusal to live in the present.

See pages 153, 539, 715, 1093.

SIMILE   **A figure of speech that makes an explicit comparison between two unlike things, using a word such as *like, as, than,* or *resembles.***

> Helen, thy beauty is to me
> Like those Nicéan barks of yore

—Edgar Allan Poe, *from* "To Helen"

See pages 622, 1002.
See also *Figure of Speech, Metaphor.*

SLANT RHYME   **A rhyming sound that is not exact.** *Follow/fellow* and *mystery/mastery* are examples of slant or approximate rhyme. Emily Dickinson frequently used the subtleties of slant rhyme.

See page 380.
See also *Rhyme.*

SOLILOQUY   **A long speech made by a character in a play while no other characters are on stage.** A soliloquy is different from a monologue in that the speaker appears to be thinking aloud, not addressing a listener.

SONNET   **A fourteen-line poem, usually written in iambic pentameter, that has one of two basic structures.** The **Petrarchan sonnet,** also called the **Italian sonnet,** is named after the fourteenth-century Italian poet Petrarch. Its first eight lines, called the **octave,** ask a question or pose a problem. These lines have a rhyme scheme of *abba, abba.* The last six lines, called the **sestet,** respond to the question or problem. These lines have a rhyme scheme of *cde, cde.*

The form used to such perfection by William Shakespeare is known as the **English, Elizabethan,** or **Shakespearean sonnet.** It has three four-line units, or **quatrains,** and it concludes with a **couplet.** The most common rhyme scheme for the Shakespearean sonnet is *abab, cdcd, efef, gg.*

Longfellow wrote many sonnets, such as "The Cross of Snow" (page 178), as did Edna St. Vincent Millay (page 697), Robert Frost (page 558), and E. E. Cummings (page 796).

See pages 180, 560.
See also *Octave, Sestet.*

SOUND EFFECTS   **The use of sounds to create specific literary effects.** Writers use devices such as **rhythm, rhyme, meter, alliteration, onomatopoeia, assonance, consonance,** and **repetition** to make the sounds of a work convey and enhance its meaning.

See pages 282, 288.

SPONDEE   **A metrical foot consisting of two syllables, both of which are stressed.** The words *true-blue* and *nineteen* are made of spondees. When Walt Whitman wrote "Beat! beat! drums," he used spondees. Spondaic feet are rarely used extensively because of their "thump-thump" sound. However, poets sometimes use spondees to provide a brief change from an iambic or trochaic beat or to provide emphasis.

See also *Foot, Meter, Trochee.*

STEREOTYPE   **A fixed idea or conception of a character or an idea that does not allow for any individuality, and is often based on religious, social, or racial prejudices.** Some common stereotypes are the unsophisticated farmer, the socially inept honor student, the dumb athlete, and the lazy teenager. Stereotypes, also called **stock characters,** are often deliberately used in comedies and in melodramas, where they receive instant recognition from the audience and make fully fleshed characterization unnecessary. Dame Van Winkle and Rip are stereotypes (page 154), as are Walter and Mrs. Mitty (page 625).

See pages 166, 631.
See also *Character.*

STREAM OF CONSCIOUSNESS   **A style of writing that portrays the inner (often chaotic) workings of a character's mind.** The stream-of-consciousness technique usually consists of a recording of the random flow of ideas, memories, associations, images, and emotions, as they arise spontaneously in a character's mind. William Faulkner, in his great novel *The Sound and the Fury,* used a stream-of-consciousness technique. Two of the other great writers that successfully used a stream-of-consciousness technique are the Irish writer James Joyce and the English writer Virginia Woolf.

See pages 530, 703.

STYLE   **The distinctive way in which a writer uses language.** Styles can be plain, ornate, metaphorical, spare, descriptive, and so on. Style is determined by such factors as sentence length and complexity, syntax, use of figurative language and imagery, and diction.

See pages 107, 1027.
See also *Plain Style, Stream of Consciousness, Tone.*

SURREALISM **A movement in art and literature that started in Europe during the 1920s. Surrealists wanted to replace conventional realism with the full expression of the unconscious mind, which they considered to be more real than the "real" world of appearances.** Surrealists, influenced by the psychoanalytic theories of Sigmund Freud, tried not to censor the images that came from their dreams or to impose logical connections on these images. This resulted in surprising combinations of "inner" and "outer" reality—a "suprareality." Surrealism affected writers as different as T. S. Eliot (page 661) and Donald Barthelme (page 955). Two famous Surrealist artists are Salvador Dali and Marc Chagall (see art on pages 982 and 989).

SUSPENSE **A feeling of uncertainty and curiosity about what will happen next in a story.** A key element in fiction and drama, suspense is one of the "hooks" a writer uses to keep the audience interested.

SYMBOL **A person, place, thing, or event that has meaning in itself and that also stands for something more than itself.** We can distinguish between **public** and **personal symbols**. The dove, for example, is a public symbol of peace—that is, it is widely accepted the world over as such a symbol. Uncle Sam is a public symbol that stands for the United States; a picture of a skull and crossbones is a public symbol of death; two snakes coiled around a staff is a widely accepted symbol of the medical profession.

Most symbols used in literature are personal symbols; even though a symbol may be widely used, a writer will usually adapt it in some imaginative, personal way so that it can suggest not just one, but a myriad of meanings. One of the most commonly used symbols in literature, for example, is the journey, which can stand for a search for truth, for redemption from evil, or for discovery of the self and freedom. The journey of Huck Finn and Jim down the Mississippi River has been interpreted to symbolize all of these concepts, and more.

The writers known as the Dark Romantics—Poe, Hawthorne, and Melville—used symbolism heavily in their works, owing to the allegorical nature of much of what they wrote. One of American literature's most famous symbols is Melville's white whale, Moby-Dick (page 313).

See pages 280, 298.
See also *Figure of Speech.*

SYMBOLISM **A literary movement that originated in late-nineteenth-century France, in which writers rearranged the world of appearances in order to reveal a more truthful version of reality.** The Symbolists believed that direct statements of feeling were inadequate; instead, they called for new and striking imaginative images to evoke complexities of meaning and mood. The French Symbolists were influenced by the poetry and critical writings of the American writer Edgar Allan Poe (page 260). The poetry of Ezra Pound (page 773), T. S. Eliot (page 661), and Wallace Stevens (page 783) is in the Symbolist tradition.

See pages 533, 770.

SYNECDOCHE **A figure of speech in which a part represents the whole.** The capital city of a nation, for example, is often spoken of as though it were the government: "Washington and Tehran are both claiming popular support for their positions." In "The Love Song of J. Alfred Prufrock" (page 663), T. S. Eliot writes, "And I have known the arms already. . . ." *Arms* stands for all the women he has known.

See also *Metonymy.*

SYNESTHESIA **The juxtaposition of one sensory image with another image that appeals to an unrelated sense.** In synesthesia, an image of sound might be conveyed in terms of an image of taste, as in "sweet laughter," or an image that appeals to the sense of touch might be combined with an image that appeals to the sense of sight, as in this example from Emily Dickinson: "golden touch."

See page 1091.

TALL TALE **An outrageously exaggerated, humorous story that is obviously unbelievable.** Tall tales are part of the folk literature of many countries, including America. Perhaps the most famous tall tale in American literature is Mark Twain's "The Celebrated Jumping Frog of Calaveras County."

THEME **The insight about human life that is revealed in a literary work.** Themes are rarely stated directly in literature. Most often, a reader has to infer the theme of a work after considerable thought. Theme is different from **subject**. A story's subject might be stated as "growing up," "love," "heroism," or "fear." The theme is the statement the writer wants to make about that subject: "For most young people, growing up is a process that involves the pain of achieving self-knowledge." Theme must be stated in at least one sentence; most themes are complex enough to require several sentences, or even an essay.

See page 634.

TONE **The attitude a writer takes toward the subject of a work, the characters in it, or the audience.** In speaking, we use voice inflections to show how we feel about what we are saying. Writers manipulate language in an attempt to achieve the same effect. For example, John Hersey takes an objective tone in telling about the nuclear explosion in *Hiroshima* (see "A Noiseless Flash," page 937). In contrast, the tone in Patrick Henry's speech to the Virginia Convention (page 102) is subjective, even impassioned. Tone is dependent on **diction** and **style,** and we cannot say we have understood any work of literature until we have sensed the writer's tone. Tone can be described in a single word: objective, solemn, playful, ironic, sarcastic, critical, reverent, irreverent, philosophical, cynical, and so on.

> See pages 577, 764.
> See also *Diction, Style.*

TRAGEDY   **In general, a story in which a heroic character either dies or comes to some other unhappy end.** In most tragedies, the main character is in an enviable, even exalted, position when the story begins (in classical tragedies and in Shakespeare, the tragic hero is of noble origin, often a king or queen, prince or princess). The character's downfall generally occurs because of some combination of fate, an error in judgment, or a personality failure known as a **tragic flaw** (Creon's stubbornness in *Antigone* or Hamlet's indecision, for example). The tragic character has usually gained wisdom at the end of the story, in spite of suffering defeat, or even death. Our feeling on reading or viewing a tragedy is usually exaltation—despite the unhappy ending—because we have witnessed the best that human beings are capable of.

> See page 683.
> See also *Comedy.*

TRANSCENDENTALISM   **A nineteenth-century movement in the Romantic tradition, which held that every individual can reach ultimate truths through spiritual intuition, which transcends reason and sensory experience.** The Tran-scendental movement was centered in Concord, Massachusetts, the home of its leading exponents, Ralph Waldo Emerson (page 216) and Henry David Thoreau (page 230). The basic tenets of the Transcendentalists were (1) a belief that God is present in every aspect of Nature, including every human being; (2) the conviction that everyone is capable of apprehending God through the use of intuition; (3) the belief that all of Nature is symbolic of the spirit. A corollary of these beliefs was an optimistic view of the world as good and evil as nonexistent.

> See pages 211, 212.

TROCHEE   **A metrical foot made up of an accented syllable followed by an unaccented syllable, as in the word *taxi*.** A trochee, the opposite of an iamb, is sometimes used to vary iambic rhythm.

> See also *Foot, Iamb, Meter, Spondee.*

UNDERSTATEMENT   **A statement that says less than what is meant.** Understatement, paradoxically, can make us recognize the truth of something by saying that just the opposite is true. If you are sitting down to enjoy a ten-course meal and say, "Ah! A little snack before bedtime," you are using an understatement to emphasize the tremendous amount of food you are about to eat. Understatement is often used to make an ironic point; it can also be used for humor.

> See pages 463, 1033.
> See also *Hyperbole.*

VERNACULAR   **The language spoken by the people who live in a particular locality.** Regionalist writers try to capture the vernacular of their area.

> See page 398.
> See also *Dialect.*

COMMUNICATIONS HANDBOOK

ACTIVE READING STRATEGIES

Use the following reading strategies to help you discover meaning in what you read and relate that meaning to your life.

PREVIEWING AND SETTING A PURPOSE

Previewing the Text Preview a reading assignment or a book to get an overview of its organization. Read the title and any information included about the author. Flip through the pages and look at the table of contents, the index, and any illustrations, charts, or diagrams. Note the genre of the text—poem, short story, play, essay—and the difficulty of the vocabulary. Finally, consider what you already know about the reading assignment or book and what you'd like to find out.

Setting a Purpose Before you begin to read, you should establish a clear purpose for reading. Purposes include (1) to be entertained, (2) to find out specific information, and (3) to learn about the craft of writing. You may have more than one purpose in mind as you read a particular text. Your purpose can dictate how closely you read and whether you take notes or use other study skills.

Activating Prior Knowledge As you read, you should recall your prior knowledge and experiences in order to look for connections with the text. For example, as you read from Emerson's essay "Self-Reliance" (page 224), you might recall that Benjamin Franklin's autobiography (page 86) also stresses self-reliance. In turn, you may consider the significance of this quality in American culture.

Constructing a KWL Chart To help you keep track of your prior knowledge and your new learning, make a three-column chart and use it before, as, and after you read a work. In the first column, write what you already know (K) about the work. In the middle column, write what you want (W) to know. In the last column, record what you learned (L) as a result of your reading.

K	W	L
What I **know**	What I **want** to know	What I **learned**

READING ACTIVELY

Making and Confirming Predictions For some texts, such as short stories and novels, you should occasionally think ahead to predict what will happen next. To start the process of making predictions, ask yourself questions like *Where will the plot lead to next? How will the character act when he begins to lose his struggle with nature?* Your answers will be predictions about what you are going to read. For example, in the first lines of Edgar Allan Poe's "The Fall of the House of Usher" (page 263), the narrator approaches a gloomy building. You predict that the Usher's house will not be a happy home and that the narrator will experience unsettling events there. As you read, adjust your predictions according to what you learn from the story.

Making Inferences An **inference** is an educated guess. Inferences about a literary work are based on clues in the text and on your own knowledge. For instance, the title of Edgar Allan Poe's "The Fall of the House of Usher" strongly suggests the inference that Roderick Usher and his house are headed for serious trouble. Jack London's title "To Build a Fire" (page 497) will almost automatically lead to the inference that fire will be an important subject of the story.

Conclusions and generalizations are types of inferences. A **conclusion** is a judgment based on evidence in a text. You will probably conclude from the speaker's words in Theodore Roethke's "Elegy for Jane" (page 1002) that he is deeply moved by the death of his student. A **generalization** is a broad statement based on specific examples. You might generalize from the stories by Ernest Hemingway (page 653) and Tim O'Brien (page 966) that soldiers have great difficulty readjusting to civilian life.

Noting Organization As you read, think about the way the writer presents ideas, people, and events. **Sequential,** or **chronological, order** arranges the events in a historical account or a story in the order in which they occur. You may find words such as *first, then, next, while,* and *finally.* Some great literary works, such as William Faulkner's "A Rose For Emily" (page 716), present events in **nonsequential order,** thereby "fragmenting" time. **Spatial order** tells you where one person or thing is in relation to another. Factual information is usually presented in **order of importance,** either from most to least important, or from least to most important.

Logical order, a type of sequential order, organizes ideas in terms of meaning, so that one idea leads directly to the next. In an essay, an argument is best made in logical order, rather than scattering ideas so that a point in paragraph six is explained in paragraph two.

DEALING WITH DIFFICULT TEXTS

When you're having difficulty understanding a text, try one or more of these strategies:

1. **Rereading.** Stop reading and go back to the last point at which you had a grasp on the text. Reread from there.
2. **Reading on.** Keep reading to see whether context clues and/or new information clarify the text.
3. **Pausing to reflect.** Stop and think about what you've read so far. Perhaps construct a graphic organizer.
4. **Asking questions.** Ask *who, what, where, when, why,* and *how* questions about the text.
5. **Using resources.** Use a dictionary or other reference works to clarify the meaning of a passage.

MAKING SURE YOU UNDERSTAND A TEXT

Paraphrasing, outlining, and summarizing are useful strategies to make sure you understand a text. When you **paraphrase,** you restate an entire work or passage in your own words. Paraphrasing helps you to clarify anything that may have been fuzzy as you read. Here is a paraphrase of the first verse of Edgar Allan Poe's "The Raven" (page 282):

One midnight, when I was tired and weak, glancing through / A lot of old albums and books, / As I was dozing off, I suddenly heard a tap, / As if a person were knocking at my door. / "There's a visitor knocking at my door," I thought. / "It's only a visitor."

A work of nonfiction, such as Thoreau's *Walden, or Life in the Woods* (page 233), can be **outlined** by showing its **main ideas** and **supporting details,** as below:

I. Main idea
 A. Supporting detail
  1. Supporting detail
  2. Supporting detail

A **summary** is a concise restatement of the principal ideas and details of a text (usually prose). You can do a summary in different ways—for example, in paragraph form or in a story map like the following:

Story Map

Basic situation
Setting
Main character
His or her problem
Main events or complications
Climax
Resolution

STUDY SKILLS

USING A DICTIONARY

Use a dictionary to find the precise meaning (**denotation**) and usage of words. The elements of a typical entry are explained below.

1. **Entry word.** The entry word shows how the word is spelled (capitalizing the first letter if required) and divided into syllables.
2. **Pronunciation.** Phonetic symbols, sometimes with diacritical marks above them, show how to pronounce the entry word. Accent marks indicate which syllables are stressed. A key to symbols usually appears on every other page.

3. **Part-of-speech label.** This label classifies the entry word as noun, adjective, adverb, and so forth. When a word can be used as more than one part of speech, definitions are grouped by part of speech. The sample entry shows four definitions for *derive* as a transitive verb (**vt.**) and one as an intransitive verb (**vi.**)
4. **Other forms.** Some dictionaries show the spellings of plural forms of nouns, principal parts of verbs (like **-rived'** and **-riv'ing** in the sample), and comparative and superlative forms of adjectives and adverbs.
5. **Word origin.** A word's **etymology** (et'ə·mäl'ə·jē) shows its linguistic history. According to the sample entry, the word *derive* comes from the Middle English word

deriven, which in turn comes from the Old French word *deriver,* which itself comes from the Latin word *derivare,* meaning "to divert." *Derivare* was created by adding the prefix *de-,* meaning "from," to the word *rivus,* meaning "stream." The sample entry shows that additional information on etymology appears in the entry for *rival.*

6. **Definitions.** If a word has more than one meaning, the meanings are numbered or lettered.
7. **Special-usage labels.** These labels identify special meanings or special uses of the word. Here, *Chem.* indicates that the fourth definition is a meaning of *derive* used in chemistry.
8. **Synonyms and antonyms. Synonyms** (words similar in meaning) and **antonyms** (words opposite in meaning) may appear at the end of an entry. Here, **—SYN.** RISE tells you that synonyms for *derive* are given in the entry for *rise.*
9. **Related word forms.** Different forms of the entry word are listed. Usually these are created by the addition of suffixes, such as in *derivable.*

Sample Dictionary Entry

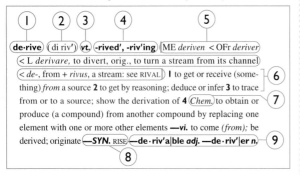

Webster's New World Dictionary of American English, Third College Edition.

USING A THESAURUS

A **thesaurus** is a collection of synonyms. You use a thesaurus to find a word with a specific meaning. There are two basic formats for a thesaurus. The first, developed by Peter Mark Roget (1779–1869), groups words in categories. To use Roget's format, follow these steps:

- In the index, look up the word that expresses the general meaning of the word you are looking for. You may be looking for a synonym of the verb *thin,* for example. Under *thin,* you find the words *dilute, rarefy,* and *weed.*
- Choose the subentry closest to the meaning you have in mind. In this case, suppose you choose *dilute.*
- Note the number that follows the subentry, and find it in the body of the text. There, you will find synonyms of *dilute.*

The second kind of thesaurus presents words in alphabetical order like a dictionary, as in the following example.

Sample Thesaurus Entry

commencement, *n.* **1.** [A beginning] —*Syn.* genesis, start, initiation; see **origin** 1. **2.** [Graduation ceremony] —*Syn.* convocation, graduation, commencement exercises, services; see **celebration** 1, 2, **ceremony** 2, **graduation.**

©1997 Webster's New World Thesaurus, Third Edition.

USING STUDY GUIDES

A **study guide** works as a reader's companion by providing help in understanding a text. It can clarify points and stimulate thinking. Study guides often include a biography of the author, critical reaction to the work, and analyses of characters, themes, and other literary elements. Many study guides also include suggestions for further reading and viewing.

A study guide usually examines a text in sections. A play by Eugene O'Neill, for instance, might be examined scene by scene or act by act. Besides giving a summary of the section, a study guide might include commentary, helpful information, and questions to consider.

RECOGNIZING LOGICAL FALLACIES

Writers should argue their points logically in order to convince readers. Sometimes, however, they use incorrect or fallacious reasoning. Be on the lookout for **fallacies.** They appear at first glance to be based on sound reasoning but in fact contain mistakes of logic. Here are six common fallacies; there are many more.

1. **Circular reasoning** or **"begging the question."** The writer restates a point just made as if it were a new conclusion. In the sentence *Alison is lazy because she doesn't like to work,* the clause after *because* just restates the opening clause and doesn't tell you why Alison is lazy. The sentence *Alison is lazy because she enjoys sitting around and daydreaming* gives you a reason for Alison's laziness.
2. **Arguing ad hominem ("to the person").** The writer attacks the person or people presenting the issue rather than dealing logically with the issue itself. In the sentence *People who oppose a lower speed limit don't care about children,* "people" who oppose lower speed limits are attacked—but reasons for lowering the speed limit are not given.
3. **Hasty generalization.** The writer draws a conclusion from insufficient evidence or from exceptional or biased evidence. In the sentence *Today's films are loaded with foul language,* the writer incorrectly categorizes all films, failing to account for the many films that have little or no foul language.

4. **Either-or fallacy** or **false dichotomy.** The writer presents only two alternatives when there are more than two. In the sentence *We have just two choices—either go to the ballgame or sit around the house,* the writer fails to mention additional choices like seeing a movie.

5. **False analogy.** The writer assumes that because two things are alike in some ways, they must be alike in other ways. Notice the false analogy in the sentence *Since player A and player B are the same height and are both fast runners, they must have similar batting averages.* The writer ignores other important reasons for a particular batting average.

6. **False cause.** This fallacy is also known as *post hoc, ergo propter hoc,* meaning "after this, therefore because of this." In this fallacy, the writer argues that because *A* preceded *B, A* caused *B.* For example, *Right after Jim joined the Cardinals as a bench warmer, the team began a ten-game winning streak.* The writer makes a false connection between a winning streak and a player who rarely plays.

(For more on fallacies, see page 1184).

RESEARCH STRATEGIES

When you're looking for information, where should you begin? You might first create a research plan that outlines the topics you want to explore or the questions you want to answer. Then you can begin your search for print and nonprint resources that might be relevant to your plan. When doing research, do not rely solely on one source; instead, consult as many reliable sources as possible. The following research strategies can help you find resources in a library or media center or on a computer linked to the Internet.

USING A LIBRARY OR MEDIA CENTER

Library Catalogs

A library's main resources usually are printed volumes stored on shelves. More and more often, however, libraries (or, as they are sometimes called, media centers) feature holdings stored in electronic form and accessed from a computer terminal or other electronic device. To find information in a library, start by looking in the catalog. Most libraries record their holdings in an **on-line,** or **computer, catalog.**

On-line catalogs vary from library to library. With some, you begin by searching for resources by **title, author,** or **subject.** With others, you simply enter **key words** related to the subject you're researching. With either system, when you enter the relevant information in response to on-screen prompts, a new screen will display a list of materials or subject headings related to your request. When you find an item you want to examine, write down the title, author, and **call number,** the code of numbers and letters that shows you where in the library the item is located.

Some libraries still use **card catalogs.** A card catalog is a collection of index cards containing key information about each library holding. The cards are arranged in alphabetical order by surname of author, by the first word of title (omitting initial articles), and—for works of nonfiction—by subject.

Other Library Resources

Every library has a **reference section** containing materials you can use only in the library. Reference works include encyclopedias; yearbooks; dictionaries; directories; almanacs; atlases; and **indices,** extensive alphabetical lists (often of books or periodicals). *Books in Print* is a useful index, as is *The Reader's Catalog.* Reference works can appear in electronic or print format. Because many reference books are updated periodically, look for the most recent edition.

Electronic Databases   These are large collections of information that you access at a computer terminal. Among the types of information stored on databases are statistics, biographical data, museum holdings, indices, and back issues of magazines.

There are two basic kinds of electronic databases. An **on-line database** is accessed at a computer terminal that is connected to a distant server computer that contains the database. Many computers can access the database at the same time. A **portable database** is available on magnetic tape, disk, CD-ROM, or other electronic medium not connected to a server computer. As a rule, only one person at a time can access the database.

A **CD-ROM** (compact disc–read-only memory) is a portable database stored on a disk that you access via a computer's CD-ROM drive. CD-ROMs can store not only text but also sound, images, and video clips. If you were to look up John Steinbeck in a CD-ROM encyclopedia, you might find a clip from a film version of one of his novels.

Periodicals   Most libraries hold a variety of periodicals as well as indices that help you locate information in them. To find up-to-date magazine or newspaper articles on a topic, look in an electronic index such as *InfoTrac, ProQuest,* or *EBSCO.* Some electronic indices provide summaries, or **abstracts,** of articles. Other databases allow you to access the entire text of articles, which you can read on screen or print out. The *Readers' Guide to Periodical Literature* is an excellent index to hundreds of periodicals. Back issues of periodicals may be stored in print form or on **microfilm** (a reel of film), **microfiche** (a sheet of film), CD-ROM, or other information storage-and-retrieval device.

Audiovisual Resources   Most libraries hold recordings of actors or authors reading books, videotapes of movies, and CDs and DVDs. These resources are useful when preparing a multimedia project.

USING THE INTERNET

The **Internet,** or **Net,** is a worldwide electronic network that connects millions of personal computers to other personal computers and to server computers containing vast amounts of data, words, and images. On the Net you can find information on almost any topic by accessing libraries, museums, electronic newspapers, government agencies, and many other sources. **E-zines** (often called **zines**) and **e-journals** are periodicals found only on-line. You gain access to the Net via Internet service providers (ISPs). The following are some ways in which the Internet can be used for research.

E-Mail

E-mail is an electronic message sent over a computer network. On the Internet you can use e-mail to contact institutions, businesses, and individuals. This is a quick and inexpensive method of consulting experts (located 1 mile or 10,000 miles away) on a topic you're researching. You can also use e-mail to exchange messages with students around the world.

Electronic Forums

Internet forums, or **newsgroups,** enable you to discuss and debate various subjects. You can post a question in a forum and receive responses from other knowledgeable people. Be careful, however: Responses may be incorrect.

The World Wide Web

The easiest way to conduct Internet research is on the World Wide Web (WWW). On the Web, information is provided on colorful, easy-to-access files

called **Web pages.** A Web page may include text, images, sounds, and even video clips.

Using a Web Browser   You can view Web pages with a **Web browser,** such as Netscape's *Navigator* or Microsoft's *Internet Explorer.* Every page on the Web has its own address, called a **URL,** or Uniform Resource Locator. If you know the URL of a Web page you want to access, enter it in the *location* field of your browser. See the accompanying illustration.

Web pages are connected by **hyperlinks,** which enable you to quickly reach relevant data by jumping from one page to another. These links are indicated by underlined or colored words or by images on your computer screen. When you click on hyperlink words or images, you are automatically transferred to another Web page.

Using a Web Directory and a Search Engine   With many millions of linked Web pages, how do you find the information you want? If you're looking for general information on a topic, go to a **Web directory** (such as Yahoo), a list of topics and subtopics created by experts to help you find an appropriate Web site. A directory is like a book's index. Begin with a broad category, such as Literature. Then, work your way down through the subtopics, from perhaps Native American: Literature to Native American: Authors until you find a Web page that looks promising, such as one on Joy Harjo.

Sample Web-Browser Screen (1998)

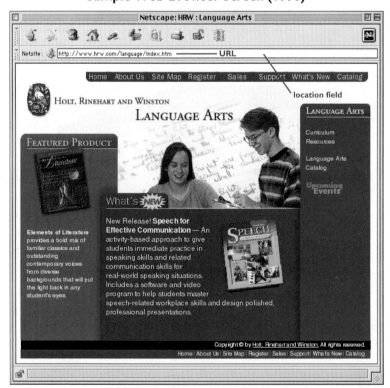

COMMON SEARCH OPERATORS AND WHAT THEY DO	
AND	Demands that both terms appear on the page; narrows search
+	Demands that both terms appear on the page; narrows search
OR	Yields pages that contain either term; widens search
NOT	Excludes a word from consideration; narrows search
–	Excludes a word from consideration; narrows search
NEAR	Demands that two words be in proximity; narrows search
ADJ	Demands that two words be in proximity; narrows search
" "	Demands the exact phrase; narrows search

If you are looking for more specific information, try using a **search engine,** an incredible software tool that indexes millions of Web sites. Some popular search engines are Lycos, AltaVista, and Excite. To use a search engine, enter a **search term,** which is one or more key words. The search engine will then list Web pages that contain your search term along with the first few lines of each page. A search term like the name *Crane* can produce thousands of results, or **hits,** including Web pages dealing with the bird or the heavy equipment. If you're looking for information on the writer Stephen Crane, most hits will be irrelevant. It's important, therefore, to refine, or tailor, your search.

Refining a Key-Word Search   Searches using more than one key word generally provide more focused results. Most search engines allow you to use **search operators** to create a string of key words. Common search operators include the capitalized terms AND, OR, NOT, ADJ (adjacent), and NEAR. Use these operators to focus your search. Here's how the operators work. Let's assume, for example, that you're looking for material on Stephen Crane and his novel *The Red Badge of Courage.* You might use this search term:

Stephen ADJ Crane AND Badge

This search term yields pages that contain the words *Stephen, Crane,* and *badge* but most likely nothing about birds or heavy equipment. Now suppose you want to learn more about Civil War fiction. If your first search turns up words about novels, you can expand your search by using OR:

novels OR stories

Doing a Phrase Search   Exact phrases often produce better results than single words or strings of key words. If you're looking for information on American poetry, for example, a search made with the unlinked key words *American* and *poetry* will yield thousands of pages about Americans and about poetry in general. On the other hand, a search using the exact phrase "American poetry"—signaled by quotation marks—will yield only pages containing that phrase.

Knowing Your Search Engine   Not all search engines operate in the same way. Some have rules about using uppercase and lowercase letters. Some require a plus sign or minus sign between key words, rather than the operator AND or NOT. Some require that you enter exact phrases within quotation marks. Some provide a list of options that enable you to search by exact phrases, individual words, and so on. Because the rules governing search engines differ, read the online Help information before you begin a search.

EVALUATING AND CITING SOURCES

Before you begin taking notes from any source—print or electronic or an interviewee—be sure your source provides information that is current, accurate, and free of strong bias. Evaluate both primary and secondary sources. **Primary** sources, or firsthand accounts, include letters, autobiographies, diaries, historical documents, and interviews. **Secondary sources,** which are derived from primary sources, include encyclopedias, documentary films, biographies, and historical books. To evaluate the usefulness of a source, use this 4R test.

1. **Relevant**   The source must have information *directly* related to your topic. To find out if a book is relevant, you can check its table of contents and index. For some books and for articles, skimming can help. *Book Review Digest* offers, for selected titles, useful summaries and review excerpts; videotapes and audiotapes sometimes provide written summaries of their content; and periodical indices may include summaries of articles.

2. **Reliable**   The source must be accurate. A periodical whose reputation depends on accuracy, such as *Smithsonian* or *National Geographic,* or a well-regarded authority, such as a scholar, generally can be counted on to fact-check rigorously before publication. If in doubt about the reliability of a source, consult an expert, such as a teacher or librarian.

3. **Recent**   For most topics, use sources that are as current as possible. Ongoing research findings can change perceptions, generalizations, and opinions. For example, the discovery of a poet's childhood illness can lead to a new interpretation of her or his poems about childhood. Often, long-ago political events are reinterpreted in light of newly discovered information.

4. **Representative**   If there are opposing viewpoints on your topic, you should consult sources that provide a variety of interpretations. If one interpretation is strongly favored, you should also consult another source with a different slant.

TAKING NOTES AND DOCUMENTING SOURCES

If you use another person's words or ideas without giving credit, you are **plagiarizing,** which is a serious offense. Avoid plagiarizing by acknowledging in your work the source of each quotation, paraphrase, statistic, figure, and idea that you found through research. Careful documentation starts with accurate source cards and notes.

Preparing Source Cards

As you gather information, you can save time and ensure accurate documentation by preparing source cards in the format needed for your report's **sources cited** list (see page 1213). Put each source on a 3-inch × 5-inch card, or record it in a computer file. Follow these guidelines:

1. **Assign each source a different number.**   When taking notes, it will save time to write the number rather than the author and title. Place the number at the top right of the card or computer entry.

2. **Record full publication data.** Data include subtitles, translators, and volume and edition numbers. Use a shortened form of the publisher's name, deleting initial articles and the type of business organization.

3. **Note the call number or location.** This information will help you reaccess the source quickly.

Sample Source Card

```
                                            3


  Williams, Tennessee. Memoirs.
  Garden City, New York:
  Doubleday, 1975.


       Central Performing Arts Library
```

Taking Notes

After evaluating your sources and preparing source cards, you are ready to read carefully and take notes. Use the following guidelines to prepare note cards that will be easy to use when writing your paper.

GUIDELINES FOR TAKING NOTES

1. Use a 4-inch × 6-inch note card, a half sheet of paper, or a separate computer file. Never put notes from more than one source on the same card or sheet of paper or in the same electronic file.
2. In the upper right, write the number you have assigned to the source.
3. In the upper left, use a word or phrase to identify the topic or main idea.
4. In the lower right, note the page numbers from which the information is taken.
5. Reread the note to be sure it is accurate.

Your notes may be direct quotations, summaries, or paraphrases. A **direct quotation** contains the author's exact words. When quoting directly, copy the statement word for word—including punctuation, capitalization, and spelling—and enclose the passage in quotation marks. A **summary** condenses the author's ideas and facts in your own words. A **paraphrase** restates information in your own words. To summarize or paraphrase, use lists and phrases instead of complete sentences.

Using Quotations

Relevant, interesting quotations add authority and punch to your research paper. The following chart describes several ways to use quotations effectively.

GUIDELINES FOR USING QUOTATIONS

- **Quote a whole sentence, introducing it in your own words.**

  EXAMPLE   Williams and Mead describe the author's year at the University of Iowa as very productive. "Tom's preoccupation at Iowa must have been work, and huge amounts of it" (69).

- **Quote part of a sentence within a sentence of your own.**

  EXAMPLE   According to his mother, Tennessee Williams changed his name because "Thomas Lanier Williams reminded him of bad poetry" (Williams and Mead 71).

- **Quote just one or a few words within a sentence of your own.**

  EXAMPLE   Williams gathered material for dialogue, collecting "colorful idioms of speech" at beaches and hotels (Williams and Mead 71).

- **Use an ellipsis (. . .) to indicate omissions from quotations.**   Sometimes you need only a part of a quotation to make your point. Insert an ellipsis where words have been deleted.

  EXAMPLE   According to Patricia C. Click, Williams used "glass as an important symbol of impermanence . . . to imply that nothing lasts" (43).

- **Set off longer quotations as extract blocks.**   If a quotation will be more than four typed lines, start a new line and indent the entire quotation ten spaces from the left. Double-space, and do not use quotation marks.

Formatting Electronic-Source Citations

Writing electronic-source citations for a list of sources cited can be difficult. On-line sources often change, and many do not provide all the information required. For instance, many Web pages don't identify an author. In such cases, include in your citation whatever relevant information is available.

The format for citing electronic sources depends on (1) whether the source is on-line or portable and (2) whether the source has an identical print version or stands alone.

Listed below are the elements required for the citation of various kinds of electronic sources—in the order in which they should appear. Most elements likely to be included are listed, but many actual citations will not include all possible elements. (Note: If a URL runs onto a second line, divide the address immediately *after* a slash mark or *before* a dot. Never use a hyphen to divide a URL.)

Source from a Computer Network, such as the World Wide Web, with an Identical Print Version

- author's last name, then first name
- title of poem, short story, essay, document, or similar short work, set off by quotation marks
- title of book or periodical, underlined
- name of editor of book, preceded by *Ed.*
- publication data for print version
- title of scholarly project, database, or professional or personal site, underlined; or, for a professional or personal site with no title, a description such as *Home page*
- volume or issue number
- number range, or total number, of any numbered pages or paragraphs
- date of electronic publication or latest revision
- name of any sponsoring institution
- date you accessed the information
- full URL, in angle brackets

EXAMPLE   Crane, Stephen. <u>The Red Badge of Courage</u>. New York: Appleton, 1895. <u>Hypertexts</u>. 1 Jan. 1998. U of Virginia. 27 Feb. 1998 <http://xroads.virginia.edu/~HYPER/CRANE/badge.html>.

Source from a Computer Network, such as the World Wide Web, with No Print Version

- author's last name, then first name
- title of poem, short story, essay, document, or similar short work, set off by quotation marks.
- title of scholarly project, database, periodical, or professional or personal site, underlined; or, for a professional or personal site with no title, a description such as *Home page*.
- name of editor of complete work or database, preceded by *Ed.*
- publication date or date of last revision
- number range or total number of any numbered sections
- name of any sponsoring organization
- volume, issue, or version number
- date you accessed the information
- the full URL, in angle brackets

EXAMPLE   "Arthur Miller." <u>The Kennedy Center Honors</u>. 1998. The Kennedy Center. 26 Apr. 1998 http://kennedy-center.org/honors/1984/miller.html>.

CD-ROM with a Print Version

- author's last name, then first name
- title of document or article, set off by quotation marks
- title of print version, underlined
- publication data for print version
- database title, underlined
- edition, release, or version number
- publication medium (CD-ROM)
- city of publication
- name of publisher of electronic version
- date of electronic publication

> EXAMPLE Miller, Arthur. <u>The Crucible.</u> New York:
> Bantam, 1959. <u>The Crucible.</u> CD-ROM.
> New York: Penguin, 1996.

CD-ROM with No Print Version

Omit the print information called for above.

> EXAMPLE "American Renaissance." <u>The History of
> American Literature.</u> CD-ROM. Chicago:
> CLEARVUE/eav, 1995.

Citing Sources

Parenthetical Citations   A short **parenthetical citation** gives source information in parentheses in the body of the text. It contains just enough information to lead a reader to the correct full entry in the sources cited list. Parenthetical citations include the author's last name and a page number, with these exceptions:

- a nonprint source such as an interview (Use name only.)
- a print source of only one page (Use name only.)
- a sentence that includes the author's name (Use page number only. See the first and fourth bulleted items in Guidelines for Using Quotations, page 1211.)
- an author with more than one entry on your list of sources cited (Add year of publication—for example: Roberts 1992, 65.)

For more information on specific kinds of parenthetical citations, see the chart below or the most recent edition of the Modern Language Association's *MLA Handbook for Writers of Research Papers.*

PARENTHETICAL CITATIONS
Works by One Author
Author's last name and page(s): (Click 43–44)
Works by More Than One Author
All authors' last names (or first author and *et al.* if more than three) and page(s): (Williams and Mead 71)
Multivolume Works
Author's last name, volume number, and page(s): (Morison 1:175)
Works with No Author Listed on Title Page
Full title (or a shortened version) and page(s): (<u>Merriam-Webster's Biographical Dictionary</u> 1061)
Literary Works Published in Several Editions
Full title and any information that would help readers find the quotation in any edition, such as chapter number or act, scene, and line numbers: (<u>The Crucible</u> 1)
Indirect Sources
Qtd. in ("quoted in") before the source and page(s): (qtd. in Click 43)
More Than One Source in the Same Citation
Relevant information for each source, separated by a semicolon: (Click 43; Williams and Mead 71)

Use the following guidelines for correctly placing parenthetical citations.

Placement of Citations

- Place the citation as close as possible to the material it documents. If possible, place it at the end of a sentence.
- Place a citation after closing quotation marks and before the end punctuation mark.
- For an extensive quotation, set as an extract block (see Guidelines for Using Quotations, page 1211), place the citation *two spaces after* the final punctuation mark.

LIST OF SOURCES CITED

The **sources cited** list, which you should include at the end of your report, contains all the sources, print and nonprint, that you credit in your paper. Other names for this list are *Bibliography* and *Works* or *Literature Cited,* but they are only appropriate if your sources are limited to books and articles.

Formatting   To prepare the sources cited list, center the words *Sources Cited* on a blank sheet of paper one inch from the top of the page. Double-space between "Sources Cited" and the first entry, and between all subsequent entries. Double-space within entries as well. Begin each entry on a new line, even with the left margin. If an entry runs more than one line, indent the subsequent line or lines in the entry five spaces.

As a general rule, alphabetize your sources by the author's last name. If there is no author (or editor), alphabetize by title, ignoring *A, An,* and *The* as the first word of the title. For example, *The Cambridge History of the Native Peoples of the Americas* would appear under *C* rather than *T*.

Publication Information   When providing publication information, use shortened forms of publishers' names, unless this would lead to confusion. Abbreviate U.S. state names and months of the year (except May, June, and July).

Page Numbers   You should include page numbers only for articles in periodicals or for other works that are part of a whole work, such as one essay in a book of essays. However, page and volume numbers aren't needed if entries are alphabetized, as in an encyclopedia.

SOURCES CITED: SAMPLE ENTRIES	
STANDARD REFERENCE WORKS	
Encyclopedia	"Miller, Arthur." Encyclopaedia Britannica: Micropaedia. 15th ed. 1997.
Biographical Reference	"Williams, Tennessee." Merriam-Webster's Biographical Dictionary. 1995 ed.
BOOKS	
Book with One Author	Miller, Arthur. Focus. New York: Reynal, 1945.
Book with Two or More Authors	Williams, Dakin, and Shepherd Mead. Tennessee Williams: An Intimate Biography. New York: Arbor, 1983.
Book with No Author Listed	American Statistics Index. Washington: Congressional Information Service, 1992.
Book with One Editor	Siebold, Thomas, ed. Readings on Arthur Miller. San Diego: Greenhaven, 1997.
Book with Two or More Editors	Block, Haskell, and Robert G. Shedd, eds. Masters of Modern Drama. New York: Random, 1962.
Translation	Williams, Tennessee. Pethe brau. Trans. Emyr Edwards. Llandysul, Wales: Gwasg, 1963. Trans. of The Glass Menagerie. New York: Random, 1945.

SELECTIONS FROM BOOKS	
Selection from Book of Works by One Author	Gould, Jean R. "Arthur Miller." Modern American Playwrights. New York: Dodd, 1966. 247–263.
Selection from Book of Works by Several Authors	Beaurline, Lester A. "The Director, the Script, and Author's Revisions: A Critical Problem." Papers in Dramatic Theory and Criticism. Ed. David M. Knauf. Iowa City: U of Iowa, 1969. 78–91.
Selection from Collection of Longer Works	Wilder, Thornton. Our Town. Three Plays. New York: Avon, 1957. 1–64.
ARTICLES FROM MAGAZINES, NEWSPAPERS, AND JOURNALS	
Weekly Magazine Article	Miller, Arthur. "Why I Wrote The Crucible." The New Yorker 21 Oct. 1996: 158–160.
Monthly or Quarterly Magazine Article	Berkvist, Robert. "The Big Daddy of Playwrights." After Dark Oct. 1981: 52–53.
Article with No Author Shown	"Tennessee Williams." Life Fall 1990: 78–79.
Daily Newspaper Article, with Byline	Kaufman, Sarah. "A Well-Forged Crucible." Washington Post 15 Nov. 1997: C3.
Daily Newspaper Article, No Byline	"Ever Earnest and Funny, Ever Relevant to Youth." The New York Times 7 Sept. 1997: B8.
Unsigned Daily Newspaper Editorial, No City in Title	"The Last Hurrah." Editorial. Star Ledger [Newark, NJ] 29 Aug. 1991: 30.
Scholarly Journal	Click, Patricia C. "The Uncertain Universe of The Glass Menagerie: The Influence of the New Physics on Tennessee Williams." Journal of American Culture 12 (1989): 41–45.
OTHER SOURCES	
Personal Interview	Wilson, August. Personal interview. 7 Jan. 1987.
Telephone Interview	Miller, Arthur. Telephone interview. 8 Oct. 1990.
Published Interview	Williams, Tennessee. Interview. More Memoirs of an Aesthete. Ed. Harold Acton. London: Methuen. 1970.
Radio or Television Interview	Halberstam, David. Interview. Book Notes. C-SPAN, Washington, DC. 1 July 1993.
Thesis or Dissertation	Fisher, Kerk. "The Front Porch in Modern American Drama: The Promise of Mobility in O'Neill, Williams, and Inge." Diss. U of Georgia, 1989.
Cartoon	Frascino, Edward. Cartoon. The New Yorker 2 Sept. 1991: 46.
Speech or Lecture	Browne, Sally. "Three American Playwrights: Wilder, Miller, and Hansberry." Bookbuilders. Lake Worth, FL. 26 Feb. 1998.
Recording	Robeson, Paul. "Going Home." Rec. 9 May 1958. Live at Carnegie Hall—1958. Vanguard, 1986.
Film or Filmstrip	A Streetcar Named Desire. Dir. John Erman. Perf. Ann-Margret, Treat Williams, Beverly D'Angelo, and Randy Quaid. Worldvision Enterprises, 1983.
Videotape	The Crucible. Dir. Raymond Rouleau. Perf. Simone Signoret, Yves Montand. 1957. Videocassette. Hen's Tooth Video, 1995.

WRITING FOR LIFE

The writing you do now prepares you for the writing you will do in college and in your career. Your ability to write clear and effective memos, business letters, and résumés will be a major factor in your success as a professional. As a student, you will write letters of application for admission to colleges and universities, and you will write résumés to apply for jobs at various companies and organizations. As an employee, you will write interoffice memoranda, or memos, and business letters communicating pertinent information.

When composing documents that others will read, follow the steps listed below. (Note: Computers and software programs make the writing process more efficient.)

- **Prewriting**   Make notes about the key points you want to include in your document, and how to present them.
- **Writing a Draft**   Compose a first draft, or version, of the document.
- **Evaluating and Revising**   Evaluate your draft closely, correcting any errors of spelling, grammar, and punctuation. Review the presentation of information and ideas for clarity and readability, and revise as necessary. Delete repetitive or irrelevant material.
- **Preparing the Final Version**   Fine-tune the revised draft as necessary to prepare a final version. Make sure you proofread the document.

WRITING INTEROFFICE MEMOS

In the business world, writing is structured and functional. One standard form of communication within a company or organization is the **memo** (or memorandum). Memos are concise messages that tell the reader *when, who, what, where, why,* and *how.* Memos contain guide words (*DATE, TO, FROM, SUBJECT*) that immediately identify the date, destination, origin, and purpose of a message. Memos generally cover only one of the following categories.

- **Meeting Notices**   Include the meeting date, time, place, purpose, and any other significant information that relates to the meeting, such as the agenda or the guests who will be attending.
- **Meeting Summaries**   Provide a brief, factual report of discussions and decisions. Include the names and titles of individuals involved.
- **Requests for Action or Information**   Open by making the request, and then follow with details. If you have several requests, list them, phrasing each one similarly. Include a deadline stating when you need a response.

WRITING EFFECTIVE BUSINESS LETTERS

Another essential form of business writing is the business letter. Whether you're writing to request information, make an offer, or register a complaint, your business letters can make a lasting impression on readers. If errors and inaccuracies or a sloppy appearance distract readers from the contents of a letter, you risk giving an impression of inefficiency or even incompetence. Keep these rules in mind:

1. Use formal, standard English.
2. Be clear.
3. Use the correct format.

Types of Business Letters

Request and Order Letters   You write a **request letter** to ask for information about a job, college, product, service, policy, or procedure. You write an **order letter** to order merchandise. When writing a request or order letter, include all important details relating to time, location, size, style, cost, and so on.

Complaint or Adjustment Letters   You write a **complaint** or **adjustment letter** when you are dissatisfied with a person, product, or service. Your letter should explain exactly what is wrong and should request a satisfactory resolution of the problem, such as a replacement of merchandise or a refund of your money. Keep the tone of your letter calm and courteous.

Letters of Application   A **letter of application** introduces you to a selection committee or a potential employer. The letter should provide the reader with enough information to determine whether you are a good candidate for a job, scholarship, college, or university. Keep the following points in mind when writing a letter of application.

1. Identify the job or situation for which you are applying, and mention how you heard about it.
2. Depending on the situation, include
   - your age, grade in school, and grade point average
   - your experience, activities, awards, and honors
   - the personal qualities that make you a good choice
   - the dates or times you are available
3. Provide references—names of two or three responsible adults, other than relatives, who agree to recommend you. Include their addresses and telephone numbers.

Sample Letter of Application, Block Style

Heading
Your address, including city, state, and ZIP code.
Your e-mail address
Date you write the letter

Inside Address
Name, title, and address of person you are writing to. Use a title (*Mr., Ms., Mrs., Dr., Esq.,* etc.) with the person's name, and put his or her business title after the name.

Salutation (greeting)
Use *Dear* followed by the person's title and last name and a colon. If the letter isn't addressed to a specific person, use a business title.

Body
Your message. If the body contains more than one paragraph, leave a blank line between paragraphs. Don't indent paragraph starts.

Closing
Use *Yours truly* or *Sincerely yours* followed by a comma.

Signature
Type or print your name, leaving space for your signature. Sign your name in ink.

Use "Enclosure" if you're including something with your letter.

1632 Garden View Drive
Anytown, PA 12345
mmanrique@ISP.com

September 23, 2000

Mr. John Lao
Director of Human Resources
XYZ Insurance Company
10 Central Avenue
Anytown, PA 12346

Dear Mr. Lao:

Are you looking for someone who carries out assignments efficiently and enjoys working with people? I have these qualities and other important business skills to bring to the position of administrative assistant you advertised in Sunday's Herald.

I am a 17-year-old junior at Jefferson High School and have completed courses in business English, word processing, and accounting. I can word-process at a rate of 50 words per minute while transcribing from recordings.

This past summer, as a receptionist at QRS Supply Company, I did filing and billing in addition to my regular duties. I feel at home in an office setting and enjoy taking on responsibility.

My résumé, which is enclosed, lists references who can tell you about my business skills and my personal strengths.

I believe that my background qualifies me for the position of administrative assistant. Please contact me by telephone at 555-1234 or by e-mail at mmanrique@ISP.com to set up an interview.

Yours truly,

Marisol Manrique

Marisol Manrique

Enclosure

WRITING A PERSONAL RÉSUMÉ

Your **résumé** (or **curriculum vitae** [CV]) summarizes who you are, what you have learned, and what you have accomplished. The information in your résumé should include skills and achievements that give a potential employer a positive overview of your qualifications. When you apply for a job, you usually include your résumé with your letter of application to potential employers.

The structure, organization, and overall appearance of your résumé will give the reader an impression of you and your abilities. Print out or type your résumé on white or ivory paper. Proofread it carefully, making sure there are no factual or typographical errors, erasures, correction fluid, or stray marks. Your goal is to get an interview. Try your best to make a good first impression.

The following **model résumé** is written in reverse chronological order; it lists the most recent work experience first.

MARISOL MANRIQUE

1632 Garden View Drive
Anytown, PA 12345
Telephone: (215) 555-1234
E-mail: mmanrique@ISP.com

EDUCATION:
Junior, Jefferson High School
Major studies: Business and foreign language courses
Grade point average: 3.0 (B)

WORK EXPERIENCE:

Summer 2000
Receptionist
QRS Supply Company
Anytown, PA

Summer 1998
Volunteer Office Worker
YWCA
Anytown, PA

SKILLS:

Word processing: 50 wpm

Business machines: Dictating, calculating, and copying machines; personal computers

Other languages: Spanish (fluent)

EXTRACURRICULAR ACTIVITIES:
Vice president, Future Business Leaders of America
Member, Spanish Club

REFERENCES:

Dr. Robert Robertson, Principal   (215) 555-6789
Jefferson High School
Anytown, PA

Ms. Mary Jackson, English Teacher   (215) 555-4567
Jefferson High School
Anytown, PA

Mr. Juan Ramos, Owner   (215) 555-3456
QRS Supply Company
Anytown, PA

COLLEGE ADMISSIONS

To apply to a college, you will have to complete an application. Most applications have two parts: the form and the essay.

Completing the College Application Form

Application forms usually ask for basic information about you: name, address, birth date, grade point average, extracurricular activities, and the educational background and occupations of your parents. Many colleges have adopted the Common Application form so that you need fill this form out only once and send it to all the schools you are applying to. The form can be downloaded from the Internet. It can also be sent by e-mail to many colleges. (Note: Some schools also require their own forms instead of or in addition to the Common Application form.)

Be sure to ask your high school to send a copy of your **transcript** to the colleges you apply to. A transcript lists all the courses you have taken in high school and the grades you earned.

Writing the Admission Essay

Most colleges and universities ask for an admission essay because it tells them things about you that can't be gleaned from bare facts. An essay reveals how you approach a question, how you think, what is important to you, and how well your education and experience have prepared you to express yourself verbally.

Consider these points as you prepare to write your admissions essay:

1. Read the question carefully. Be sure you are answering what is asked.
2. Be yourself. Admissions staff ask for the essay because they want to get to know you. The essay is an opportunity to introduce yourself to the admissions staff—to tell them what you think is really important about yourself, to express opinions about serious issues, to amuse them with your sense of humor, or, in some other way, to present yourself as a person and not a number. Write about something important to you. Your conviction will come across to the reader. Don't worry about what the reader might expect from you—say something you really want to say.
3. Be neat. Write as many drafts as necessary. Fine-tune until your essay is the best you can make it. Then, check the revised draft carefully for any errors in spelling, grammar, and usage before you produce the final version.

PROOFREADING

Proofreading refines the mechanics of your writing. A dictionary and a style book will serve as helpful reference tools when you proofread. As you review your writing, you might find this list of questions helpful: (1) Are all words spelled correctly? (2) Do subjects and verbs agree? (3) Do pronouns agree with their antecedents? (4) Are verb tenses consistent? (5) Are all proper nouns capitalized? (6) Are sentence fragments eliminated? (7) Are all punctuation marks appropriate?

As you proofread your work, use these standard proofreaders' marks:

PROOFREADERS' MARKS		
SYMBOL	**EXAMPLE**	**MEANING**
≡	Twenty-second street	Capitalize lowercase letter.
/	Sarah's Uncle	Lowercase capital letter.
∧	*of* the capital Maine	Insert.
℘	What's the the point?	Delete.
∩∪	a heavy back pack	Close up space.
∿	traegdy	Change order (of letters or words). Transpose.
¶	¶"Help," he yelled.	Begin new paragraph.
⊙	Stay calm⊙	Add period.
∧	Of course you may be wrong.	Add comma.

ANSWERING ESSAY QUESTIONS

Essay tests require you to think critically and to clearly express your understanding of a topic. Your answers to essay questions must be well-organized and include details to support your generalizations. A well-written answer must contain a complete response to a question.

Scan the questions on the test before you start writing. If you have a choice of questions, identify the ones you can answer best. Budget your time so you can give adequate attention to each question. These steps will help you better answer essay questions.

1. Read each essay question carefully, and notice whether a question has several parts.
2. Identify the important terms in the questions. Find the key verbs, and identify the tasks you must accomplish. Identify how much evidence is required for an adequate treatment.
3. Take a few minutes to prewrite. Make notes or a simple outline on scratch paper, organize your material logically, and write a thesis statement. Write one paragraph for each point you wish to make, and end with a paragraph that summarizes or restates your main points.
4. Evaluate and revise as you write. Watch for spelling and grammatical errors. You will not have time to redraft the entire essay, but you can edit to strengthen specific parts. Keep your paper neat.

Essay questions usually ask you to perform specific tasks expressed by the verb in the question. The following chart lists the task required by some key verbs.

ESSAY TEST QUESTIONS

KEY VERB	TASK	SAMPLE QUESTION
analyze	Take something apart to see how it creates meaning.	Analyze the plot of "The Magic Barrel."
argue	Take a stand on an issue, and give reasons supporting your opinion.	Argue whether your school should require students to wear a uniform.
compare/contrast	Discuss likenesses/differences.	Compare and contrast Hawkeye in Cooper's novel *The Last of the Mohicans* with Hawkeye in the 1992 movie of the same name.
define	Give specific details that make something unique.	Define the term *modernism* as it relates to literature.
demonstrate (also **illustrate, present, show**)	Provide examples to support a point.	Demonstrate T. S. Eliot's use of symbolism in his poetry.
discuss	Examine in detail.	Discuss the elements of realism in Tennessee Williams's *The Glass Menagerie*.
explain	Clarify, expound on, or give reasons for or a cause of something.	Explain why setting is important in "To Build a Fire."
interpret	Discuss or explain the meaning or significance of something.	Interpret the symbolism of wilderness in Wallace Stevens's "Anecdote of the Jar."
list (also **outline, trace**)	Give all steps (in order) or all details about a subject.	List the events that lead to the death of Willy Loman in *Death of a Salesman*.
summarize	Give a brief overview of the main points.	Summarize the plot of Amy Tan's *The Joy Luck Club*.

1 THE PARTS OF SPEECH

PART OF SPEECH	DEFINITION	EXAMPLES
NOUN	Names person, place, thing, or idea	poet, Sylvia Plath, city, Chicago, awards, Nobel Prize, *Of Mice and Men*, books, crew, herd, Harlem Renaissance, realism
PRONOUN	Takes place of one or more nouns or pronouns	
Personal	Refers to one(s) speaking (first person), spoken to (second person), spoken about (third person)	I, me, my, mine, we, us, our, ours you, your, yours he, him, his, she, her, hers, it, its, they, them, their, theirs
Reflexive	Refers to subject and directs action of verb back to subject	myself, ourselves, yourself, yourselves, himself, herself, itself, themselves
Intensive	Refers to and emphasizes noun or another pronoun	(same as examples for Reflexive)
Demonstrative	Refers to specific one(s) of group	this, that, these, those
Interrogative	Introduces question	what, which, who, whom, whose
Relative	Introduces subordinate clause	that, which, who, whom, whose
Indefinite	Refers to one(s) not specifically named	all, any, anyone, both, each, either, everybody, many, none, nothing, someone
ADJECTIVE	Modifies noun or pronoun by telling *what kind, which one, how many,* or *how much*	**a large black** box, **an able-bodied** worker, **that** one, **the five Iroquois** nations, **enough** time, **less** money, **many** choices
VERB	Shows action or state of being	
Action	Expresses physical or mental activity	write, receive, run, think, imagine, understand
Linking	Connects subject with word identifying or describing it	appear, be, seem, become, feel, look, smell, sound, taste
Helping (Auxiliary)	Assists another verb to express time, voice, or mood	be, have, may, can, shall, will, would
ADVERB	Modifies verb, adjective, or adverb by telling *how, when, where,* or *to what extent*	speaks **clearly, quite** interesting, **rather** calmly, arrived **there late**
PREPOSITION	Relates noun or pronoun to another word	about, at, by, for, of, in, on, through, according to, in front of, out of

(continued)

PART OF SPEECH	DEFINITION	EXAMPLES
CONJUNCTION	Joins words or word groups	
Coordinating	Joins words or word groups used in same way	and, but, for, nor, or, so, yet
Correlative	A pair of conjunctions that joins parallel words or word groups	both . . . and, not only . . . but (also), either . . . or, neither . . . nor
Subordinating	Begins subordinate clause and connects it to independent clause	although, as if, because, since, so that, unless, when, where, while
INTERJECTION	Expresses emotion	hey, oh, ouch, wow, well, hooray

2 AGREEMENT

AGREEMENT OF SUBJECT AND VERB

2a. A verb should agree in number with its subject. Singular subjects take singular verbs. Plural subjects take plural verbs.

SINGULAR The **character lives** on a farm in Yoknapatawpha County.

PLURAL **Both** of the stories **were written** by William Faulkner.

2b. The number of the subject is not changed by a phrase or a clause following the subject.

SINGULAR **Langston Hughes,** who wrote several books of poetry, **was** a major figure in the Harlem Renaissance.

PLURAL **The students,** as well as Ms. Ramos, **are** eager to use the new software.

2c. Indefinite pronouns may be singular, plural, or either.

(1) The following indefinite pronouns are singular: *anybody, anyone, anything, each, either, one, everybody, everyone, everything, neither, nobody, no one, nothing, somebody, someone,* and *something.*

EXAMPLE
Neither of the books **contains** that story.

(2) The following indefinite pronouns are plural: *both, few, many,* and *several.*

EXAMPLE
Both of the poems **were written** by Claude McKay.

(3) The indefinite pronouns *all, any, most, none,* and *some* are singular when they refer to singular words and are plural when they refer to plural words.

SINGULAR **Some** of her artwork **is** beautiful.
[*Some* refers to *artwork.*]

PLURAL **Some** of her paintings **are** beautiful.
[*Some* refers to *paintings.*]

2d. A *compound subject,* which is two or more subjects that have the same verb, may be singular or plural.

(1) Subjects joined by *and* usually take a plural verb.

EXAMPLE
Hemingway, Steinbeck, and Morrison are Nobel Prize winners.

A compound subject that names only one person or thing takes a singular verb.

EXAMPLE
Roderick Usher's **sister and** sole **companion is** Madeline.

(2) Singular subjects joined by *or* or *nor* take a singular verb.

EXAMPLES
Either Amy or Eric plans to report on William Byrd.
Neither the **rain nor** the **wind has stopped**.

(3) When a singular subject and a plural subject are joined by *or* or *nor,* the verb agrees with the subject nearer the verb.

EXAMPLE
Neither the **performers nor** the **director was** eager to rehearse.

Whenever possible, revise the sentence to avoid this awkward construction.

EXAMPLE

The **director was** not eager to rehearse the scene again, and neither **were** the **performers.**

2e. **The verb agrees with its subject even when the verb precedes the subject, such as in sentences beginning with** *here,* *there,* **or** *where.*

EXAMPLES

Here **is** [*or* here's] a **copy** of the Declaration of Independence.

Here **are** [*not* here's] two **copies** of the Declaration of Independence.

2f. **A** *collective noun* **(such as** *class, herd,* **or** *jury***) is singular in form but names a group of persons or things. A collective noun takes a singular verb when the noun refers to the group as a unit and takes a plural verb when the noun refers to the parts or members of the group.**

SINGULAR The **cast** of *A Raisin in the Sun* **is made** up entirely of juniors. [The cast as a unit is made up of juniors.]

PLURAL After the play, the **cast are joining** their families for a celebration. [The members of the cast are joining their families.]

2g. **An expression of an amount (a length of time, a statistic, or a fraction, for example) is singular when the amount is thought of as a unit or when it refers to a singular word. An amount is plural when it is thought of as many parts or when it refers to a plural word.**

SINGULAR **Twenty years was** a long time for Rip Van Winkle to sleep. [one unit]

PLURAL **Fifty percent** of the students **have** already **read** *Walden.* [The percentage refers to *students.*]

Expressions of measurement (length, weight, capacity, area) are usually singular.

EXAMPLES

Seventy-five degrees below zero was the air temperature in "To Build a Fire."

Four and a half miles was how far the man walked in an hour.

2h. **The title of a creative work (such as a book, song, film, or painting) or the**

name of an organization, a country, or a city (even if the name is plural in form) takes a singular verb.

EXAMPLES

"Birches" **was written** by Robert Frost.

The **United States calls** its flag Old Glory.

2i. **A verb agrees with its subject, not with its predicate nominative.**

SINGULAR One **symptom** of flu **is** sore muscles.

PLURAL Sore **muscles are** one symptom of flu.

AGREEMENT OF PRONOUN AND ANTECEDENT

A pronoun usually refers to a noun or another pronoun. The word to which a pronoun refers is called its *antecedent.*

2j. **A pronoun agrees with its antecedent in number and gender. Singular pronouns refer to singular antecedents. Plural pronouns refer to plural antecedents. A few singular pronouns indicate gender (neuter, feminine, masculine).**

EXAMPLES

Marianne Moore published **her** first book of poems in 1921. [singular, feminine]

Peyton Farquhar thinks **he** has escaped. [singular, masculine]

Benjamin Franklin wrote, "**Three** may keep a secret if two of **them** are dead." [plural]

2k. **Indefinite pronouns may be singular, plural, or either.**

(1) Singular pronouns are used to refer to the indefinite pronouns *anybody, anyone, anything, each, either, everybody, everyone, everything, neither, nobody, no one, nothing, one, somebody, someone,* and *something.* The gender of any of these pronouns is often determined by a word in a phrase following the pronoun.

EXAMPLES

Each of the **girls** has already memorized **her** part.

One of the **boys** gave **his** interpretation of "Nothing Gold Can Stay."

If the antecedent may be either masculine or feminine, use both the masculine and feminine pronouns to refer to it.

EXAMPLE

Anyone who is qualified for the job may submit **his** or **her** application.

NOTE Whenever possible, revise the sentence to avoid this awkward construction.

EXAMPLE

Anyone who is qualified for the job may submit an application.

(2) Plural pronouns are used to refer to the indefinite pronouns *both, few, many,* and *several.*

EXAMPLE

Both of the finalists played **their** best.

(3) Singular or plural pronouns may be used to refer to the indefinite pronouns *all, any, most, none,* and *some.* These indefinite pronouns are singular when they refer to singular words and are plural when they refer to plural words.

SINGULAR   **All** of our **planning** achieved **its** purpose.

PLURAL   **All** of your **suggestions** had **their** good points.

2l.   **A plural pronoun is used to refer to two or more singular antecedents joined by *and.***

EXAMPLE

Jerry and Francesca read the sonnets **they** wrote about Olaudah Equiano.

2m.   **A singular pronoun is used to refer to two or more singular antecedents joined by *or* or *nor.***

EXAMPLE

Neither **Cindy nor Carla** thinks **she** is ready to write the final draft.

2n.   **When a singular and a plural antecedent are joined by *or* or *nor,* the pronoun agrees with the nearer antecedent.**

EXAMPLE

Either **Jerry or** the **twins** will bring **their** stereo.

Revising Misleading Sentences

Sentences with antecedents joined by *or* or *nor* can be misleading when the antecedents are of different genders or numbers. Revise the sentences to avoid such constructions.

MISLEADING   Either Christopher or Tiffany will give her report on Transcendentalism. [The sentence suggests that Christopher may give Tiffany's report.]

REVISED   Either **Christopher** will give **his** report on Transcendentalism, or **Tiffany** will give **hers.**

2o.   **A collective noun (such as *audience, family,* or *team*) takes a singular pronoun when the noun refers to the group as a unit and takes a plural pronoun when the noun refers to the parts or members of the group.**

SINGULAR   The **debate club** elected **its** new officers.

PLURAL   The **debate club** will practice **their** speeches in this week's workshop.

2p.   **The title of a creative work (such as a book, song, film, or painting) or the name of an organization, a country, or a city (even if it is plural in form) takes a singular pronoun.**

EXAMPLES

The teacher read **"Mushrooms"** and then asked me to interpret **it.**

Anderson Outfitters advertises **itself** as "the first step in getting away from it all."

3 USING VERBS

REGULAR AND IRREGULAR VERBS

Every verb has four basic forms called the *principal parts:* the *base form,* the *present participle,* the *past,* and the *past participle.* A verb is classified as *regular* or *irregular* depending on the way it forms the past and past participle.

3a.   **A *regular verb* forms the past and past participle by adding *–d* or *–ed* to the base form. An *irregular verb* forms the past and the past participle in some other way.**

The following examples include *is* and *have* in parentheses to show that helping verbs are used with the present participle and past participle forms.

COMMON REGULAR AND IRREGULAR VERBS

BASE FORM	PRESENT PARTICIPLE	PAST	PAST PARTICIPLE
REGULAR			
ask	(is) asking	asked	(have) asked
attack	(is) attacking	attacked	(have) attacked
drown	(is) drowning	drowned	(have) drowned
plan	(is) planning	planned	(have) planned
try	(is) trying	tried	(have) tried
use	(is) using	used	(have) used
IRREGULAR			
be	(is) being	was, were	(have) been
begin	(is) beginning	began	(have) begun
catch	(is) catching	caught	(have) caught
drink	(is) drinking	drank	(have) drunk
drive	(is) driving	drove	(have) driven
go	(is) going	went	(have) gone
lend	(is) lending	lent	(have) lent
shake	(is) shaking	shook	(have) shaken
swim	(is) swimming	swam	(have) swum
tear	(is) tearing	tore	(have) torn
throw	(is) throwing	threw	(have) thrown

TIPS FOR SPELLING

Before adding the suffix *–ing* or *–ed* to form the present participle or the past or past participle of a verb, double the final consonant if the base form satisfies both of these conditions:

(1) It has only one syllable or has the accent on the last syllable.
(2) It ends in a single consonant preceded by a single vowel.

EXAMPLES
grin + -ing = gri**nn**ing
refer + -ed = refe**rr**ed

See page 1251 for exceptions.

NOTE   If you are not sure about the principal parts of a verb, look in a current dictionary. Entries for irregular verbs give the principal parts. If no principal parts are listed, the verb is a regular verb.

TENSES AND THEIR USES

3b. The *tense* of a verb indicates the time of the action or the state of being expressed by the verb.

(1) The *present tense* is used mainly to express an action or a state of being that is occurring now.

EXAMPLE
We **understand** now.

The present tense is also used

- to show a customary or habitual action or state of being
- to convey a general truth—something that is always true
- to make a historical event seem current (such use is called the **historical present**)
- to summarize the plot or subject matter of a literary work or to refer to an author's relationship to his or her work (such use is called the **literary present**)
- to express future time

EXAMPLES
For breakfast I **eat** cereal and **drink** orange juice. [customary action]

The earth **revolves** once around the sun each year. [general truth]
Several of the *Mayflower* passengers **die** before the ship **reaches** Plymouth. [historical present]
Moby-Dick **tells** the story of a man who **pursues** a white whale. [literary present]
The workshop **begins** tomorrow. [future time]

(2) The *past tense* is used to express an action or a state of being that occurred in the past but did not continue into the present.

EXAMPLES
Pepe **grabbed** his rifle and **crawled** into the brush.

(3) The *future tense* (*will* or *shall* + base form) is used to express an action or a state of being that will occur.

EXAMPLES
Elisa **will play** the part of Beneatha Younger.
I **will** [*or* shall] **serve** as her understudy.

(4) The *present perfect tense* (*have* or *has* + past participle) is used mainly to express an action or a state of being that occurred at some indefinite time in the past.

EXAMPLE
Have you **read** any stories by Sandra Cisneros?

The present perfect tense is also used to express an action or a state of being that began in the past and continues into the present.

EXAMPLE
My sister **has been** a Girl Scout for two years.

(5) The *past perfect tense* (*had* + past participle) is used to express an action or a state of being that was completed in the past before another action or state of being occurred.

EXAMPLE
Miss Emily returned the tax notice that she **had received.**

 NOTE Use the past perfect tense in "if" clauses that express the earlier of two past actions.

EXAMPLE
If he **had taken** [*not* would have taken *or* took] more time, he would have won.

(6) The *future perfect tense* (*will have* or *shall have* + past participle) is used to express an action or a state of being that will be completed in the future before some other future occurrence.

EXAMPLE
By the time Rip Van Winkle returns to his village, the Revolutionary War **will have occurred.**

3c. Avoid unnecessary shifts in tense.

INCONSISTENT	Shiftlet marries Lucynell and then abandoned her.
CONSISTENT	Shiftlet **marries** Lucynell and then **abandons** her.
CONSISTENT	Shiftlet **married** Lucynell and then **abandoned** her.

When describing events that occur at different times, use verbs in different tenses to show the order of events.

EXAMPLE
She now **works** for *The New York Times,* but she **worked** for *The Wall Street Journal* last year.

ACTIVE VOICE AND PASSIVE VOICE

3d. *Voice* is the form a verb takes to indicate whether the subject of the verb performs or receives the action.

A verb is in the *active voice* when its subject performs the action.

ACTIVE VOICE Julia Alvarez **wrote** "Daughter of Invention."

A verb is in the *passive voice* when its subject receives the action. A passive voice verb is always a verb phrase that includes a form of *be* and the past participle of an action verb.

PASSIVE VOICE "Daughter of Invention" **was written** by Julia Alvarez.

3e. Use the passive voice sparingly.

In general, the passive voice is less direct and less forceful than the active voice. In some cases, the passive voice may sound awkward.

AWKWARD PASSIVE A memorable speech was delivered by William Faulkner when the Nobel Prize was accepted by him in 1950.

ACTIVE William Faulkner delivered a memorable speech when he accepted the Nobel Prize in 1950.

The passive voice is useful
1. when you do not know the performer of the action
2. when you do not want to reveal the performer of the action
3. when you want to emphasize the receiver of the action

EXAMPLES
Hemingway **was** severely **wounded** during the war.
Many careless errors **were made** in some of the essays about Amy Tan.
Madeline Usher **had been buried** alive!

4 USING PRONOUNS

CASE

Case is the form that a noun or a pronoun takes to indicate its use in a sentence. In English, there are three cases: *nominative, objective,* and *possessive.*

The form of a noun is the same for both the nominative case and the objective case. A noun changes form only in the possessive case. Unlike nouns, most personal pronouns have one form for each case. The form a pronoun takes depends on its function in a sentence.

The Nominative Case

4a. A subject of a verb is in the nominative case.

EXAMPLES

They were happy that **he** was home from the war. [*They* is the subject of *were,* and *he* is the subject of *was.*]

4b. A predicate nominative is in the nominative case.

EXAMPLE

The one who jilts Granny Weatherall is **he.** [*He* follows *is* and identifies the subject *one.*]

The Objective Case

4c. An object of a verb is in the objective case.

EXAMPLES

My stepbrother and stepsister don't have driver's licenses yet, so I usually give **them** a ride to school. [*Them* is the direct object of the verb *give.*]

The Jazz Age collage earned **Donna and him** blue ribbons. [*Donna and him* is a compound indirect object of the verb *earned.*]

4d. An object of a preposition is in the objective case.

EXAMPLES

Did you send copies of *Blue Highways* to **her and him**? [*Her and him* is a compound object of the preposition *to.*]

The Possessive Case

4e. A noun or a pronoun preceding a gerund is in the possessive case.

EXAMPLE

Warren did not appreciate **Silas's** [*or* **his**] leaving during haying time. [*Silas's* (or *his*) modifies *leaving,* a gerund used as a direct object telling what Warren did not appreciate.]

SPECIAL PRONOUN PROBLEMS

4f. An appositive is in the same case as the noun or pronoun to which it refers.

EXAMPLES

The Ushers, **Madeline and he,** live in a gloomy mansion. [The appositive, *Madeline and he,* refers to the subject, *Ushers,* which is in the nominative case.]

Tom T. Shiftlet deceives both of them, **Mrs. Crater and her.** [The appositive, *Mrs. Crater and her,* refers to the object of the preposition, *them,* which is in the objective case.]

4g. The pronoun *who* (*whoever*) is in the nominative case. The pronoun *whom* (*whomever*) is in the objective case.

EXAMPLES

Who wrote *Dangling Man*? [*Who* is the subject of *wrote.*]

With **whom** did Moss Hart write the play? [*Whom* is the object of *with.*]

PERSONAL PRONOUNS

SINGULAR

	NOMINATIVE	OBJECTIVE	POSSESSIVE
FIRST PERSON	I	me	my, mine
SECOND PERSON	you	you	your, yours
THIRD PERSON	he, she, it	him, her, it	his, her, hers, its

PLURAL

	NOMINATIVE	OBJECTIVE	POSSESSIVE
FIRST PERSON	we	us	our, ours
SECOND PERSON	you	you	your, yours
THIRD PERSON	they	them	their, theirs

NOTE Notice in the chart that *you* and *it* have the same forms for the nominative and the objective cases. All other personal pronouns have different forms for each case. Notice also that only third-person singular pronouns indicate gender.

☞ For more information about possessive pronouns, see *its, it's* on page 1255, *their, there, they're* on page 1256, and *who's, whose* and *your, you're* on page 1257.

4h. **A pronoun ending in –*self* or –*selves* should not be used in place of a personal pronoun.**

EXAMPLE
Lupe and **I** [*not* myself] went to the ballet.

4i. **A pronoun following *than* or *as* in an elliptical construction is in the same case as it would be if the construction were completed.**

An ***elliptical construction*** is a clause from which words have been omitted. Notice how the meaning of each of the following sentences depends on the pronoun form in the elliptical construction.

NOMINATIVE CASE	I have known Leigh longer **than she.** [I have known Leigh longer than she has known Leigh.]
OBJECTIVE CASE	I have known Leigh longer **than her.** [I have known Leigh longer than I have known her.]

CLEAR PRONOUN REFERENCE

4j. **A pronoun should refer clearly to its antecedent. Avoid an ambiguous, a general, a weak, or an indefinite reference by (1) rephrasing the sentence, (2) replacing the pronoun with a noun, or (3) giving the pronoun a clear antecedent.**

AMBIGUOUS	Jody talked to Billy Buck while he was working. [*He* refers to either antecedent, *Jody* or *Billy Buck.*]
CLEAR	While Billy Buck was working, Jody talked to him.
CLEAR	While Jody was working, he talked to Billy Buck.
GENERAL	The wind rose, and dark clouds descended on the House of Usher. This seemed to bewilder Roderick. [*This* has no specific antecedent.]
CLEAR	The wind rose, and dark clouds descended on the House of Usher. These ominous conditions seemed to bewilder Roderick.
CLEAR	The rising wind and dark clouds that descended on the House of Usher seemed to bewilder Roderick.
WEAK	He was superstitious. One of these was that walking under a ladder brings bad luck. [The antecedent of *these* is not expressed.]
CLEAR	He was superstitious. One of his superstitions was that walking under a ladder brings bad luck.
CLEAR	He believed in many superstitions, one of which was that walking under a ladder brings bad luck.
INDEFINITE	In this history book, it refers to the American Civil War as the War Between the States. [*It* is unnecessary to the meaning of the sentence.]
CLEAR	This history book refers to the American Civil War as the War Between the States.

5 USING MODIFIERS

WHAT IS A MODIFIER?

A ***modifier*** is a word or group of words that limits the meaning of another word or group of words. The two kinds of modifiers are *adjectives* and *adverbs*.

COMPARISON OF MODIFIERS

5a. ***Comparison* refers to the change in the form of an adjective or an adverb to show increasing or decreasing degrees in the quality the modifier expresses.**

The three degrees of comparison are *positive, comparative,* and *superlative.*

(1) Most one-syllable modifiers form the comparative and superlative degrees by adding –*er* (*less*) and –*est* (*least*).

(2) Some two-syllable modifiers form the comparative and superlative degrees by adding –*er* and –*est*; others form the comparative and superlative degrees by using *more* and *most.* All two-syllable modifiers form decreasing comparisons by using *less* and *least.*

(3) Modifiers of more than two syllables form the comparative and superlative degrees by using *more* (*less*) and *most* (*least*).

POSITIVE	COMPARATIVE	SUPERLATIVE
neat	neater	neatest
simple	less simple	least simple
calmly	more calmly	most calmly
optimistic	less optimistic	least optimistic

(4) Some modifiers form the comparative and superlative degrees in other ways.

POSITIVE	COMPARATIVE	SUPERLATIVE
bad	worse	worst
far	farther (further)	farthest (furthest)
good (well)	better	best
little	less	least
many (much)	more	most

5b. Use the comparative degree when comparing two things. Use the superlative degree when comparing more than two.

COMPARATIVE   Although both puppies look cute, the **more active** one seems **healthier.**

SUPERLATIVE   Of the four plays that we saw, I think *Death of a Salesman* was the **most moving.**

5c. Avoid a double comparison or a double negative. A *double comparison* is the use of two comparative forms (usually –*er* and *more*) or two superlative forms (usually –*est* and *most*) to modify the same word. A *double negative* is the use of two negative words when one is enough.

EXAMPLES
Samuel Clemens is **better** [*not* more better] known as Mark Twain.
She did**n't** say **anything** [*not* nothing].

5d. Include the word *other* or *else* when comparing one member of a group with the rest of the group.

EXAMPLE
Esteban is taller than anyone **else** on the team.

5e. Avoid comparing items that cannot logically be compared.

ILLOGICAL   Hemingway's style is perhaps more imitated than any other American

writer. [illogical comparison between a style and a writer]

LOGICAL   Hemingway's style is perhaps more imitated than any other American writer's (style). [logical comparison of styles]

PLACEMENT OF MODIFIERS

5f. Avoid using a *misplaced modifier*—a modifying word, phrase, or clause that sounds awkward because it modifies the wrong word or group of words.

To correct a misplaced modifier, place the word, phrase, or clause as close as possible to the word or words you intend it to modify.

MISPLACED   Thoreau listened intently to the song of a distant robin looking at the glittering pond. [Was the robin or Thoreau looking at the pond?]

CLEAR   **Looking at the glittering pond,** Thoreau listened intently to the song of a distant robin.

☞ For information about phrases, see Part 6: Phrases. For more on clauses, see Part 7: Clauses.

5g. Avoid using a *dangling modifier*—a modifying word, phrase, or clause that does not sensibly modify any word or words in a sentence.

You may correct a dangling modifier by
- adding a word or words that the dangling word, phrase, or clause can sensibly refer to
- adding a word or words to the dangling word, phrase, or clause
- rewording the sentence

DANGLING   Alone, the mountain is virtually impossible to climb. [Who or what is alone?]

CLEAR   **For a person alone,** the mountain is virtually impossible to climb.

CLEAR   The mountain is virtually impossible **for a person** to climb **alone.**

DANGLING   After winning the Pulitzer Prize, the novel *Maud Martha* was written. [Who won the Pulitzer Prize?]

CLEAR   After winning the Pulitzer Prize, **Gwendolyn Brooks wrote** the novel *Maud Martha.*

CLEAR   After **Gwendolyn Brooks won** the Pulitzer Prize, **she wrote** the novel *Maud Martha.*

6 PHRASES

6a. A *phrase* is a group of related words that is used as a single part of speech and that does not contain a verb and its subject.

EXAMPLES

At two o'clock [adverb phrase], the event **of the year** [adjective phrase], the company picnic, **will commence** [verb phrase].

THE PREPOSITIONAL PHRASE

6b. A *prepositional phrase* begins with a preposition and ends with the *object of the preposition,* a word or word group that functions as a noun.

EXAMPLES

On the pillow was a strand **of gray hair.** [The noun *pillow* is the object of the preposition *on.* The noun *hair* is the object of the preposition *of.*]

Brian's Song is an inspiring story **about friendship and courage.** [Both *friendship* and *courage* are objects of the preposition *about.*]

(1) An *adjective phrase* is a prepositional phrase that modifies a noun or a pronoun. An adjective phrase usually follows the word it modifies. That word may be the object of another preposition.

EXAMPLES

Cassie Soldierwolf made a batch **of fry bread,** using a recipe very similar to that **of her ancestors.** [*Of fry bread* modifies the noun *batch. Of her ancestors* modifies the pronoun *that.*]

Sarah Kemble Knight kept a journal **of her trip to New York.** [*Of her trip* modifies the noun *journal. To New York* modifies *trip,* which serves as the object of the preposition *of.*]

More than one adjective phrase may modify the same word.

EXAMPLE

Sarah Kemble Knight's journey **on horseback from Boston to New York** was long and difficult. [*On horseback, from Boston,* and *to New York* modify the noun *journey.*]

(2) An *adverb phrase* is a prepositional phrase that modifies a verb, an adjective, or an adverb. An adverb phrase tells *how, when, where, why,* or *to what extent* (*how long* or *how far*).

More than one adverb phrase can modify the same word. Also, an adverb phrase can precede or follow the word it modifies.

EXAMPLES

During the Civil War, Louisa May Alcott worked **in a hospital as a nurse for six weeks.** [Each phrase modifies the verb *worked. During the Civil War* tells *when, in a hospital* tells *where, as a nurse* tells *how,* and *for six weeks* tells *how long.*]

VERBALS AND VERBAL PHRASES

A *verbal* is a form of a verb used as a noun, an adjective, or an adverb. A *verbal phrase* consists of a verbal and any of its modifiers or complements.

Participles and Participial Phrases

6c. A *participle* is a verb form that is used as an adjective. A *participial phrase* consists of a participle and all words related to the participle.

There are two kinds of participles—the *present participle* and the *past participle.*

(1) Present participles end in *–ing.*

EXAMPLES

The explorer could hear something **moving in the brush.** [The participial phrase modifies the pronoun *something. In the brush* is an adverb phrase modifying the present participle *moving.*]

A mountain lion stood there **watching him.** [The participial phrase modifies the noun *mountain lion.* The pronoun *him* is the direct object of the present participle *watching.*]

(2) Most **past participles** end in *–d* or *–ed.* Others are irregularly formed.

EXAMPLES

Obsessed with revenge, Captain Ahab pursued the white whale. [The participial phrase modifies the noun *Captain Ahab.* The adverb phrase *with revenge* modifies the past participle *obsessed.*]

Samuel Clemens, **better known as Mark Twain,** was born in Florida, Missouri, in 1835. [The participial phrase modifies the noun *Samuel Clemens.* The adverb *better* and the adverb phrase *as Mark Twain* modify the past participle *known.*]

Do not confuse a participle used as an adjective with a participle used as part of a verb phrase.

ADJECTIVE	The Vietnam Veterans Memorial, **designed** by Maya Ying Lin, is made of black granite.
VERB PHRASE	The Vietnam Veterans Memorial, which **was designed** by Maya Ying Lin, is made of black granite.

 For information about misplaced participial phrases, see page 1228.

Gerunds and Gerund Phrases

6d. **A *gerund* is a verb form ending in *–ing* that is used as a noun. A *gerund phrase* consists of a gerund and all words related to the gerund.**

EXAMPLES
Exercising regularly is important for maintaining good health. [The gerund phrase is the subject of the verb *is*. The adverb *regularly* modifies the gerund *exercising*.]

Dexter enjoyed **working at the golf club.** [The gerund phrase is the direct object of the verb *enjoyed*. The adverb phrase *at the golf club* modifies the gerund *working*.]

Walter Mitty daydreamed of **being a pilot.** [The gerund phrase is the object of the preposition *of*. The noun *pilot* is a predicate nominative completing the meaning of the gerund *being*.]

One way to build your vocabulary is **reading good literature.** [The gerund phrase is a predicate nominative explaining the subject *way*. *Literature* is the direct object of the gerund *reading*.]

Do not confuse a gerund with a present participle used as an adjective or as part of a verb phrase.

GERUND	I enjoy **reading** at night. [direct object of the verb *enjoy*]
PRESENT PARTICIPLE	I sometimes fall asleep **reading** at night. [adjective modifying the pronoun *I*]
PRESENT PARTICIPLE	Sometimes, I listen to classical music while I am **reading** at night. [part of the verb phrase *am reading*]

 NOTE A noun or pronoun directly before a gerund takes the possessive case.

EXAMPLES
Grandad's cooking tastes great.
The bandleader said that he was pleased with **our** marching.

Infinitives and Infinitive Phrases

6e. **An *infinitive* is a verb form that can be used as a noun, an adjective, or an adverb. An infinitive usually begins with *to*. An *infinitive phrase* consists of an infinitive and all words related to the infinitive.**

NOUNS
To find Moby-Dick was Ahab's burning ambition. [The infinitive phrase is the subject of *was*. *Moby-Dick* is the direct object of the infinitive *to find*.]

Ahab's burning ambition was **to find Moby-Dick.** [The infinitive phrase is a predicate nominative identifying the subject *ambition*.]

ADJECTIVES
Napoleon's plan **to conquer the world** failed. [The infinitive phrase modifies the noun *plan*. *World* is the direct object of the infinitive *to conquer*.]

The one **to ask** is your guidance counselor. [The infinitive modifies the pronoun *one*.]

ADVERBS
With his dog Wolf, Rip Van Winkle went into the woods **to hunt squirrels.** [The infinitive phrase modifies *went*. *Squirrels* is the direct object of the infinitive *to hunt*.]

Nearly everyone was reluctant **to speak to her.** [The infinitive phrase modifies *reluctant*. The adverb phrase *to her* modifies the infinitive *to speak*.]

The word *to*, the sign of the infinitive, is sometimes omitted.

EXAMPLE
Will you help [to] dry the dishes?

 NOTE Do not confuse an infinitive with a prepositional phrase that begins with *to*.

INFINITIVES	**To have** a friend, you need **to be** a friend.
PREPOSITIONAL PHRASES	Give one sample **to each** of the customers, and return the rest **to Rhonda.**

The Infinitive Clause

6f. **Unlike other verbals, an infinitive may have a subject. Such a construction is called an *infinitive clause*.**

EXAMPLE
Our teacher asked **us to read "Thanatopsis."** [*Us* is the subject of the infinitive *to read*. The entire infinitive clause is the direct object of *asked*.]

APPOSITIVES AND APPOSITIVE PHRASES

6g. An *appositive* is a noun or a pronoun placed beside (usually after) another noun or pronoun to identify or explain it. An *appositive phrase* consists of an appositive and its modifiers.

An appositive or appositive phrase usually follows the word it identifies or explains.

EXAMPLES

We went to the Navajo Gallery in Taos, New Mexico, to see R. C. Gorman's artwork *Freeform Lady.* [The appositive *Freeform Lady* identifies the noun *artwork.*]

Can you believe that I **myself** plan to become a writer? [The pronoun *myself* refers to the pronoun *I.*]

For emphasis, however, an appositive or appositive phrase may come at the beginning of a sentence.

EXAMPLE

A young painter, Jaune Quick-to-See Smith shows a deep awareness of her French, Shoshone, and Cree heritage.

Appositives are sometimes introduced by a colon or by the expressions *or, namely, such as, for example, i.e.,* or *e.g.*

EXAMPLES

The homeless shelter is accepting donations of the following items: canned **foods, blankets,** and winter **coats.**

Beneficial insects, **such as ladybugs** and **praying mantises,** can help control the population of harmful insects in a garden.

 For information on how to punctuate appositives, see pages 1243–1244.

---

7 CLAUSES

7a. A *clause* is a group of words that contains a verb and its subject and that is used as part of a sentence. There are two kinds of clauses: the *independent clause* and the *subordinate clause.*

THE INDEPENDENT CLAUSE

7b. An *independent* (or *main*) *clause* expresses a complete thought and can stand by itself as a sentence.

EXAMPLE

SUBJECT   VERB

Emily Dickinson wrote nearly eighteen hundred poems.

THE SUBORDINATE CLAUSE

7c. A *subordinate* (or *dependent*) *clause* does not express a complete thought and cannot stand alone as a sentence.

EXAMPLE

SUBJECT   VERB

that **we** **read**

The thought expressed by a subordinate clause becomes complete when the clause is combined with an independent clause.

EXAMPLE

The last book **that we read** was *Blue Highways.*

The Adjective Clause

7d. An *adjective clause* is a subordinate clause that modifies a noun or a pronoun.

An adjective clause follows the word or words that it modifies. Usually, an adjective clause begins with a relative pronoun, which (1) relates the adjective clause to the word or words the clause modifies and (2) performs a function within the adjective clause.

EXAMPLE

Li recommends every poem **that Denise Levertov has written.** [The relative pronoun *that* relates the adjective clause to the noun *poem* and serves as the direct object of the verb *has written.*]

An adjective clause may begin with a relative adverb, such as *when* or *where.*

EXAMPLE

From 1914 to 1931, Isak Dinesen lived in Kenya, **where she operated a coffee plantation.**

Sometimes the relative pronoun or relative adverb is not expressed.

EXAMPLE
The book [that] **I am reading** is a biography.

The Noun Clause

7e. A *noun clause* is a subordinate clause that may be used as a subject, a predicate nominative, a direct object, an indirect object, or an object of a preposition.

Words commonly used to introduce noun clauses include *how, that, what, whether, who,* and *why.*

EXAMPLES
A catchy slogan is **what we will need for this campaign.** [predicate nominative]
Emerson liked **what Whitman wrote.** [direct object]
The director will give **whoever does best in this audition** the lead role. [indirect object]

The word that introduces a noun clause may or may not have another function in the clause.

EXAMPLES
Do any of you know **who wrote *Spoon River Anthology*?** [The word *who* introduces the noun clause and serves as subject of the verb *wrote.*]
She told Walter **that he was driving too fast and should slow down.** [The word *that* introduces the noun clause but does not have any function within the noun clause.]

The word that introduces a noun clause is not always expressed.

EXAMPLE
I think [that] **I've read all of Langston Hughes's poetry.**

The Adverb Clause

7f. An *adverb clause* is a subordinate clause that modifies a verb, an adjective, or an adverb.

An adverb clause, which may come before or after the word or words it modifies, tells *how, when, where, why, to what extent,* or *under what condition.* An adverb clause is introduced by a **subordinating conjunction**—a word or word group that relates the adverb clause to the word or words the clause modifies.

EXAMPLES
William Cullen Bryant wrote the first version of "Thanatopsis" **when he was a teenager.** [The adverb clause modifies the verb *wrote,* telling *when* Bryant wrote the first version.]
Zoë can explain naturalism to you better **than I can.** [The adverb clause modifies the adverb *better,* telling *to what extent* Zoë can better explain naturalism.]

 NOTE An adverb clause that begins a sentence is always set off by a comma.

The Elliptical Clause

7g. Part of a clause may be left out when the meaning can be understood from the context of the sentence. Such a clause is called an *elliptical clause.*

EXAMPLES
Roger knew the rules better **than Elgin** [did].
While [he was] **living at Walden Pond,** Thoreau wrote his first book.

 For information about using pronouns in elliptical clauses, see page 1227.

8 SENTENCE STRUCTURE

SENTENCE OR FRAGMENT?

8a. A *sentence* is a group of words that has a subject and a verb and expresses a complete thought.

EXAMPLE
Benjamin Franklin lived in London and in Paris.

Only a sentence should begin with a capital letter and end with either a period, a question mark, or an exclamation point. A group of words that either does not contain a subject and a verb or does not express a complete thought is called a **sentence fragment.**

| FRAGMENT | Collapses during a storm. |
| SENTENCE | The House of Usher collapses during a storm. |

 For information about how to correct sentence fragments, see page 1236. For information about using end marks with sentences, see page 1242.

SUBJECT AND PREDICATE

8b. A sentence consists of two parts: a subject and a predicate. A *subject* tells *whom* or *what* the sentence is about. A *predicate* tells something about the subject.

In the following examples, all the words labeled *subject* make up the **complete subject,** and all the words labeled *predicate* make up the **complete predicate.**

SUBJECT	PREDICATE
Walt Whitman	wrote *Leaves of Grass.*

PREDICATE	SUBJECT	PREDICATE
Why did	Phoenix	walk to town?

The Simple Subject

8c. A *simple subject* is the main word or group of words that tells *whom* or *what* the sentence is about.

EXAMPLE
Harold Krebs, the protagonist of the story, returns home from the war. [The complete subject is *Harold Krebs, the protagonist of the story.*]

The Simple Predicate

8d. A *simple predicate* is a verb or verb phrase that tells something about the subject.

EXAMPLE
Did Judy **marry** Dexter? [The complete predicate is *did marry Dexter.*]

The Compound Subject and the Compound Verb

8e. A *compound subject* consists of two or more subjects that are joined by a conjunction—usually *and* or *or*—and that have the same verb.

EXAMPLE
Reuben and **I** are preparing a report on "A Wagner Matinée."

8f. A *compound verb* consists of two or more verbs that are joined by a conjunction—usually *and, but,* or *or*—and that have the same subject.

EXAMPLE
Kendra **recognized** the song but **had forgotten** its title.

How to Find the Subject of a Sentence

8g. To find the subject of a sentence, ask *Who?* or *What?* before the verb.

(1) The subject of a sentence is never within a prepositional phrase.

EXAMPLE
On the quarter-deck stood **Captain Ahab.** [Who stood? Captain Ahab stood. *Quarter-deck* is the object of the preposition *on.*]

(2) The subject of a sentence expressing a command or a request is always understood to be *you,* although *you* may not appear in the sentence.

COMMAND Identify two of the most striking characteristics of E. E. Cummings's poetry. [Who is being told to identify? *You* is understood.]

The subject of a command or a request is *you* even when a sentence contains a **noun of direct address—** a word naming the one or ones spoken to.

REQUEST Jordan, [**you**] please read aloud Jimmy Santiago Baca's "Fall."

(3) The subject of a sentence expressing a question usually follows the verb or a part of the verb phrase. Turning the question into a statement will often help you find the subject.

QUESTION Was Pearl Buck awarded the Nobel Prize in literature in 1938? [Who was awarded?]
STATEMENT **Pearl Buck** was awarded the Nobel Prize in literature in 1938.
QUESTION Where is the dog's leash? [Where is what?]
STATEMENT The dog's **leash** is where.

(4) The word *there* or *here* is never the subject of a sentence.

EXAMPLE
Here are your **gloves.** [What are here? Gloves are.]

COMPLEMENTS

8h. A *complement* is a word or a group of words that completes the meaning of a verb. There are four main kinds of complements: *direct object, indirect object, objective complement,* and *subject complement.*

The Direct Object and the Indirect Object

8i. A *direct object* is a noun, a pronoun, or a word group that functions as a noun and tells *who* or *what* receives the action of a transitive verb.

EXAMPLES

Kerry called **me** at noon. [called whom? me]

Captain Ahab sacrifices his **ship** and almost **all** of his crew. [sacrifices what? ship and all—compound direct object]

8j. An *indirect object* is a word or word group that comes between a transitive verb and a direct object. An indirect object, which may be a noun, a pronoun, or a word group that functions as a noun, tells *to whom* or *to what* or *for whom* or *for what* the action of the verb is done.

EXAMPLES

Emily Dickinson sent **Thomas Wentworth Higginson** four poems. [sent to whom? Thomas Wentworth Higginson]

Ms. Cruz showed **José** and **me** pictures of her trip to Walden Pond. [showed to whom? José and me—compound indirect object]

 NOTE A sentence that has an indirect object must always have a direct object as well.

 For more information about verbs, see Part 3: Using Verbs.

The Objective Complement

8k. An *objective complement* is a word or word group that helps complete the meaning of a transitive verb by identifying or modifying the direct object. An objective complement, which may be a noun, a pronoun, an adjective, or a word group that functions as a noun or adjective, almost always follows the direct object.

EXAMPLES

Everyone considered her **dependable.** [The adjective *dependable* modifies the direct object *her.*]

Many literary historians call Poe **the master of the macabre.** [The word group *the master of the macabre* modifies the direct object *Poe.*]

The Subject Complement

8l. A *subject complement* is a word or word group that completes the meaning of a linking verb and identifies or modifies the subject. There are two kinds of subject complements: the *predicate nominative* and the *predicate adjective.*

(1) A *predicate nominative* is the word or group of words that follows a linking verb and refers to the same person or thing as the subject of the verb.

A predicate nominative may be a noun, a pronoun, or a word group that functions as a noun.

EXAMPLES

Of the three applicants, Carlos is the most competent **one.** [The pronoun *one* refers to the subject *Carlos.*]

The main characters are **Aunt Georgiana** and **Clark.** [The nouns *Aunt Georgiana* and *Clark* refer to the subject *characters.*]

(2) A *predicate adjective* is an adjective that follows a linking verb and modifies the subject of the verb.

EXAMPLES

Eben Flood felt very **lonely.** [The adjective *lonely* modifies the subject *Eben Flood.*]

Shiftlet is **sly** and **scheming.** [The adjectives *sly* and *scheming* modify the subject *Shiftlet.*]

SENTENCES CLASSIFIED ACCORDING TO STRUCTURE

8m. According to structure, sentences are classified as *simple, compound, complex,* and *compound-complex.*

(1) A *simple sentence* has one independent clause and no subordinate clauses.

EXAMPLE

Thornton Wilder's *Our Town* is one of my favorite plays.

(2) A *compound sentence* has two or more independent clauses but no subordinate clauses.

EXAMPLE

Jack London was a prolific writer; he wrote nearly fifty books in less than twenty years. [two independent clauses joined by a semicolon]

 NOTE Do not confuse a simple sentence that has a compound subject or a compound verb with a compound sentence.

(3) A *complex sentence* has one independent clause and at least one subordinate clause.

EXAMPLE
Before we read *The Great Gatsby,* let's talk about the Jazz Age. [The independent clause is *let's talk about the Jazz Age.* The subordinate clause is *before we read* The Great Gatsby.]

(4) A *compound-complex* sentence has two or more independent clauses and at least one subordinate clause.

EXAMPLE
The two eyewitnesses told the police officer what they saw, but their accounts of the accident were quite different. [The two independent clauses are *the two eyewitnesses told the police officer* and *their accounts of the accident were quite different.* The subordinate clause is *what they saw.*]

SENTENCES CLASSIFIED ACCORDING TO PURPOSE

8n. Sentences may be classified according to purpose.

(1) A *declarative sentence* makes a statement. It is followed by a period.

EXAMPLE
Swimming fast toward the ship was the white whale.

(2) An *interrogative sentence* asks a question. It is followed by a question mark.

EXAMPLE
Have you ever read *Blue Highways*?

(3) An *imperative sentence* makes a request or gives a command. It is usually followed by a period. A strong command, however, is followed by an exclamation point.

EXAMPLES
Please give me the dates for the class meetings.
Read Act I of *A Raisin in the Sun* by tomorrow.
Help me!

(4) An *exclamatory sentence* expresses strong feeling or shows excitement. It is followed by an exclamation point.

EXAMPLE
What a noble leader he was!

9 SENTENCE STYLE

WAYS TO ACHIEVE CLARITY

Coordinating Ideas

9a. To *coordinate* two or more ideas, or to give them equal emphasis, link them with a connecting word, an appropriate mark of punctuation, or both.

EXAMPLE
Edgar Allan Poe wrote "The Raven"; Edgar Lee Masters wrote *Spoon River Anthology.*

Subordinating Ideas

9b. To *subordinate* an idea, or to show that one idea is related to but less important than another, use an adverb clause or an adjective clause.

An *adverb clause* begins with a subordinating conjunction, which shows how the adverb clause relates to the main clause. Usually, the relationship is *time, cause or reason, purpose or result,* or *condition.*

EXAMPLES
Whenever I think of Boston, I think of the Lowells. [time]
Janet got a lead role in *Our Town* **because she is one of the best actors in our school.** [cause]
Let's finish now **so that we won't have to come back tomorrow.** [purpose]

An *adjective clause* usually begins with *who, whom, whose, which, that,* or *where.*

EXAMPLE
Tamisha is the one **whose essay won first prize.**

☞ For more about adjective clauses and adverb clauses, see pages 1231–1232.

Using Parallel Structure

9c. Use the same grammatical form (*parallel structure*) to express ideas of equal weight.

1. Use parallel structure when you link coordinate ideas.

EXAMPLE

The company guaranteed **that salaries would be increased and that working days would be shortened.** [noun clause paired with noun clause]

2. Use parallel structure when you compare or contrast ideas.

EXAMPLE

Thinking logically is as important as **calculating** accurately. [gerund compared with gerund]

3. Use parallel structure when you link ideas with correlative conjunctions (such as *both . . . and, either . . . or, neither . . . nor,* and *not only . . . but also*).

EXAMPLE

With *Ship of Fools,* Katherine Anne Porter proved she was talented not only **as a short-story writer** but also **as a novelist.** [Note that the correlative conjunctions come directly before the parallel terms.]

When you revise for parallel structure, you may need to repeat an article, a preposition, or a pronoun before each of the parallel terms.

UNCLEAR	Through Kate Chopin's stories, we can learn almost as much about the author as the social condition of women in her era.
CLEAR	Through Kate Chopin's stories, we can learn almost as much **about** the author as **about** the social condition of women in her era.

OBSTACLES TO CLARITY

Sentence Fragments

9d. Avoid using a *sentence fragment*— a word or word group that either does not contain a subject and a verb or does not express a complete thought.

Attach the fragment to the sentence that comes before or after it, or add words to or delete words from the fragment to make it a complete sentence.

FRAGMENT	Nina Otero was one of the first Mexican American women. To hold a major public post in New Mexico.
SENTENCE	Nina Otero was one of the first Mexican American women **to hold a major public post in New Mexico.**

 For more information about sentence fragments, see page 1232.

Run-on Sentences

9e. Avoid using a *run-on sentence*—two or more complete thoughts that run together as if they were one complete thought.

There are two kinds of run-on sentences.

- A *fused sentence* has no punctuation at all between the complete thoughts.
- A *comma splice* has just a comma between the complete thoughts.

FUSED SENTENCE	Emerson praised Whitman's poetry most other poets sharply criticized it.
COMMA SPLICE	Emerson praised Whitman's poetry, most other poets sharply criticized it.

You may correct a run-on sentence in one of the following ways. Depending on the relationship you want to show between ideas, facts, and other information, one method will often prove to be more effective than another.

1. Make two sentences.

EXAMPLE

Emerson praised Whitman's poetry**.** **M**ost other poets sharply criticized it.

2. Use a comma and a coordinating conjunction.

EXAMPLE

Emerson praised Whitman's poetry**, but** most other poets sharply criticized it.

3. Change one of the independent clauses to a subordinate clause.

EXAMPLE

Emerson praised Whitman's poetry, **while most other poets sharply criticized it.**

4. Use a semicolon.

EXAMPLE

Emerson praised Whitman's poetry**;** most other poets sharply criticized it.

5. Use a semicolon and a conjunctive adverb followed by a comma.

EXAMPLE

Emerson praised Whitman's poetry**; however,** most other poets sharply criticized it.

Unnecessary Shifts in Sentences

9f. Avoid making unnecessary shifts in subject, in verb tense, and in voice.

AWKWARD	Athletes should be at the parking lot by 7:00 so that you can leave by 7:15. [shift in subject]
BETTER	**Athletes** should be at the parking lot by 7:00 so that **they** can leave by 7:15.
AWKWARD	She walked into the room, and she says, "The lights of the car outside are on." [shift in verb tense]
BETTER	She **walked** into the room, and she **said,** "The lights of the car outside are on."
AWKWARD	Russell Means starred as Chingachgook in *The Last of the Mohicans,* and an outstanding performance was delivered. [shift in voice]
BETTER	Russell Means **starred** as Chingachgook in *The Last of the Mohicans* and **delivered** an outstanding performance.

REVISING FOR VARIETY

9g. Use a variety of sentence beginnings.

The following examples show how a writer can revise sentences to avoid beginning with the subject every time.

SUBJECT FIRST	*Billy Budd* was published in 1924 and helped revive an interest in Melville's other works.
PARTICIPIAL PHRASE FIRST	**Published in 1924,** *Billy Budd* helped revive an interest in Melville's other works.
PREPOSITIONAL PHRASE FIRST	**In 1924,** *Billy Budd* was published and helped revive interest in Melville's other works.
ADVERB CLAUSE FIRST	**When** *Billy Budd* **was published in 1924,** it helped revive interest in Melville's other works.

Varying Sentence Structure

9h. Use a mix of simple, compound, complex, and compound-complex sentences in your writing.

The following paragraph shows a mix of sentence structures.

San Francisco is famous for its scenic views. [simple] Because the city sprawls over forty-two hills, driving through San Francisco is like riding a roller coaster. [complex] Atop one of San Francisco's hills is Chinatown; atop another is Coit Tower. [compound] The most popular place to visit is the San Francisco Bay area, where the Golden Gate Bridge and Fisherman's Wharf attract a steady stream of tourists. [complex]

 For information about the four types of sentence structure, see pages 1234–1235.

Revising to Reduce Wordiness

9i. Avoid using unnecessary words in your writing.

The following guidelines suggest some ways to revise wordy sentences.

1. Take out a whole group of unnecessary words.

WORDY	After climbing down to the edge of the river, we boarded a small houseboat that was floating there on the surface of the water.
BETTER	After climbing down to the edge of the river, we boarded a small houseboat.

2. Replace pretentious words and expressions with straightforward ones.

WORDY	The young woman, who was at some indeterminate point in her teenage years, sported through her hair a streak of pink dye that could be considered extremely garish.
BETTER	The **teenager** sported a streak of **shocking**-pink dye in her hair.

3. Reduce a clause to a phrase.

WORDY	Emily Dickinson fell in love with Charles Wadsworth, who was a Presbyterian minister.
BETTER	Emily Dickinson fell in love with Charles Wadsworth, **a Presbyterian minister.**

4. Reduce a phrase or a clause to one word.

WORDY	One of the writers from the South was William Faulkner.
BETTER	One of the **Southern** writers was William Faulkner.

10 SENTENCE COMBINING

Combining by Inserting Words and Phrases

10a. Combine related sentences by taking a key word (or using another form of the word) from one sentence and inserting it into another.

ORIGINAL   Jack London describes the man's attempt to build a fire. The description is vivid.

COMBINED   Jack London **vividly** describes the man's attempt to build a fire. [The adjective *vivid* becomes the adverb *vividly.*]

10b. Combine related sentences by taking (or creating) a phrase from one sentence and inserting it into another.

ORIGINAL   Our class is reading "Everyday Use." It is by Alice Walker.

COMBINED   Our class is reading "Everyday Use" **by Alice Walker.** [prepositional phrase]

Combining by Coordinating Ideas

10c. Combine related sentences whose ideas are equally important by using coordinating conjunctions (*and, but, or, nor, for, yet*) or correlative conjunctions (*both . . . and, either . . . or, neither . . . nor, not only . . . but also*).

The relationship of the ideas determines which connective will work best. When joined, the coordinate ideas form compound elements.

ORIGINAL   Robert Frost did not receive the Nobel Prize. Carl Sandburg never received it, either.

COMBINED   **Neither Robert Frost nor Carl Sandburg** received the Nobel Prize.

You can also form a compound sentence by linking independent clauses with a semicolon and a conjunctive adverb or with just a semicolon.

EXAMPLE
We planned to go swimming**; however,** the weather did not oblige.

Combining by Subordinating Ideas

10d. Combine related sentences whose ideas are not equally important by placing the less important idea in a subordinate clause.

ORIGINAL   The National Air and Space Museum is in Washington, D.C. It contains exhibits on the history of aeronautics.

COMBINED   The National Air and Space Museum, **which contains exhibits on the history of aeronautics,** is in Washington, D.C. [adjective clause]

ORIGINAL   Shiftlet married Lucynell. He wanted her mother's car.

COMBINED   Shiftlet married Lucynell **because he wanted her mother's car.** [adverb clause]

ORIGINAL   Judy Jones was married. Devlin told Dexter this.

COMBINED   Devlin told Dexter **that Judy Jones was married.** [noun clause]

11 CAPITALIZATION

11a. Capitalize the first word in every sentence.

EXAMPLES
The author Leslie Marmon Silko was born in Albuquerque, New Mexico.
Stop!

(1) Capitalize the first word of a sentence following a colon.

EXAMPLE
The police commissioner issued a surprising statement: **In** light of new evidence, the investigation of the Brooks burglary will be reopened.

(2) Capitalize the first word of a direct quotation that is a complete sentence.

EXAMPLE

When he finally surrendered in 1877, Chief Joseph declared, "**F**rom where the sun now stands I will fight no more forever."

When quoting from another writer's work, capitalize the first word of the quotation only if the writer has capitalized it in the original work.

EXAMPLE

When he finally surrendered in 1877, Chief Joseph declared that he would "**f**ight no more forever."

 For more information about using capital letters in quotations, see page 1246.

(3) Traditionally, the first word of a line of poetry is capitalized.

EXAMPLES

I placed a jar in Tennessee,
And round it was, upon a hill.
　　　—Wallace Stevens, from "Anecdote of the Jar"

NOTE Some writers, for reasons of style, do not follow this rule. When you quote from a writer's work, always use capital letters exactly as the writer uses them.

11b. Capitalize the first word in the salutation and the closing of a letter.

EXAMPLES

Dear Maria,　　　**D**ear Sir or Madam:　　　**S**incerely,

TYPE OF NAME	EXAMPLES	
Countries	**M**ozambique	**C**osta **R**ica
Continents	**N**orth **A**merica	**A**sia
Islands	**C**atalina **I**sland	**I**sle of **P**ines
Mountains	**B**lue **R**idge **M**ountains	**M**ount **M**c**K**inley
Other Land Forms and Features	**C**ape **C**od **M**ojave **D**esert	**I**sthmus of **P**anama **H**orse **C**ave
Bodies of Water	**G**reat **L**akes **A**mazon **R**iver	**S**trait of **H**ormuz **L**ake **H**uron
Parks	**M**ississippi **H**eadwaters **S**tate **F**orest **G**ates of the **A**rctic **N**ational **P**ark	
Roads, Highways, Streets	**R**oute 30 **I**nterstate 55 **P**ennsylvania **T**urnpike	**M**ichigan **A**venue **T**hirty-first **S**treet **M**orningside **D**rive

11c. Capitalize proper nouns and proper adjectives.

A **common noun** is a general name for a person, place, thing, or idea. A **proper noun** is the specific name of a particular person, place, thing, or idea. A **proper adjective** is formed from a proper noun. Common nouns are capitalized only if they begin a sentence (also, in most cases, a line of poetry) or a direct quotation or are part of a title.

COMMON NOUNS	PROPER NOUNS	PROPER ADJECTIVES
poet	**H**omer	**H**omeric epithet
country	**R**ussia	**R**ussian diplomat
state	**H**awaii	**H**awaiian climate

In most proper nouns made up of two or more words, do *not* capitalize articles (*a, an, the*), short prepositions (those with fewer than five letters, such as *at, of, for, to, with*), the mark of the infinitive (*to*), and coordinating conjunctions (*and, but, for, nor, or, so, yet*).

EXAMPLES

Army of the **P**otomac　　　"**W**riting to **P**ersuade"

(1) Capitalize the names of most persons and animals.

GIVEN NAMES	Julia	Richard
SURNAMES	Alvarez	Wright
ANIMALS	Moby-Dick	White Fang

(2) Capitalize geographical names.

NOTE The second word in a hyphenated number begins with a lowercase letter.

EXAMPLES

Forty-second Street
Eighty-ninth District

In addresses, abbreviations such as *St., Ave., Dr.,* and *Blvd.* are capitalized. For more about abbreviations, see pages 1242–1243.

(continued)

TYPE OF NAME	EXAMPLES	
Towns, Cities	Boston South Bend	Rio de Janeiro St. Petersburg
Counties, Townships, Provinces	Yoknapatawpha County	Lawrence Township
States and Territories	Wisconsin Yukon Territory	Nuevo León The Virgin Islands
Regions	New England the Sunbelt	the West Coast the Southwest

NOTE Words such as *north* and *western* are not capitalized when they indicate direction.

EXAMPLES
east of the river   driving southeast

☞ The abbreviations of names of states are always capitalized. For more about using and punctuating such abbreviations, see pages 1242–1243.

(3) Capitalize the names of organizations, teams, business firms, institutions, buildings and other structures, and government bodies.

TYPE OF NAME	EXAMPLES	
Organizations	National Science Foundation Guide Dog Foundation for the Blind	Future Farmers of America Disabled American Veterans
Teams	Detroit Pistons Harlem Globetrotters	Cedar Hill Bulldogs San Diego Padres
Business Firms	General Electric University Square Mall	Hip-Hop Music, Inc. La Fiesta Restaurant
Institutions	University of California, Los Angeles the Library of Congress	Mayo Clinic Habitat for Humanity
Buildings and Other Structures	Meadowlawn Junior High School the Pyramid of Khufu	the Golden Gate Bridge Rialto Theater
Government Bodies	Atomic Energy Commission Federal Bureau of Investigation	United States Marine Corps House of Representatives

(4) Capitalize the names of historical events and periods, special events, holidays and other calendar items, and time zones.

TYPE OF NAME	EXAMPLES	
Historical Events and Periods	Boston Tea Party Battle of Saratoga Middle Ages	Roaring Twenties French Revolution Mesozoic Era
Special Events	Olympics Earth Summit	Ohio State Fair Sunshine Festival
Holidays and Other Calendar Items	Wednesday September	Fourth of July Hispanic Heritage Month
Time Zones	Mountain Standard Time (MST) Eastern Daylight Time (EDT)	

NOTE Do not capitalize the name of a season unless the season is being personified or unless it is used as part of a proper noun.

EXAMPLES
The winter was unusually warm.
Overnight, Winter crept in, trailing her snowy veil.
We plan to attend the school's Winter Carnival.

(5) Capitalize the brand names of business products.

EXAMPLES

Borden milk   **C**olonial bread   **Z**enith television

Notice in these examples that the noun that follows a brand name is not capitalized. Also, over time, some brand names become common nouns. To find out if a name is a brand name, consult a current dictionary.

TYPE OF NAME	EXAMPLES	
Ships	*Cunard Princess*	**U.S.S.** *Forrestal*
Trains	*Orient Express*	*North Coast Limited*
Aircraft	*Spirit of St. Louis*	*Air Force One*
Spacecraft	*Atlantis*	*Apollo 11*
Monuments	**L**incoln **M**emorial	**S**tatue of **L**iberty
Awards	**A**cademy **A**ward	**P**ulitzer **P**rize
Planets, Stars, Constellations	**J**upiter **U**rsa **M**inor	**O**rion the **M**ilky **W**ay
Other Particular Things, Places, and Events	**U**nderground **R**ailroad **S**ilk **R**oute **H**urricane **A**ndrew	**T**reaty **O**ak **V**alkyries **M**arshall **P**lan

11d. Do not capitalize the names of school subjects, except for names of languages and course names followed by a number.

EXAMPLES

Spanish   chemistry   **C**hemistry II

11e. Capitalize titles.

(1) Capitalize a title belonging to a particular person when it comes before the person's name. Also capitalize abbreviations such as *Jr., M.D.,* and *Ph.D.* after a name.

EXAMPLES

General Davis   **M**s. Diaz   **P**resident Kennedy
Rev. Martin Luther King, **J**r.   **D**r. Kerry Jones, **M.D.**

In general, do not capitalize a title used alone or following a name. Some titles, however, are by tradition

TYPE OF NAME	EXAMPLES	
Religions and Followers	**I**slam	**R**oman **C**atholic
Holy Days and Celebrations	**E**piphany	**R**osh **H**ashanah
Holy Writings	**B**ible	**U**panishads
Specific Deities and Venerated Beings	**G**od the **P**rophet (**M**ohammed)	

(6) Capitalize the names of nationalities, races, and peoples.

EXAMPLES

Chinese   **J**ewish   **H**opi   **C**aucasian

(7) Capitalize the names of ships, trains, aircraft, spacecraft, monuments, awards, planets, and any other particular places, things, or events.

> **NOTE** Do not capitalize the words *sun* and *moon*. Do not capitalize the word *earth* unless it is used along with the names of other heavenly bodies that are capitalized.
>
> **EXAMPLES**
> This orchid grows wild in only one place on earth.
> Venus is closer to the sun than Earth is.

capitalized. If you are unsure of whether or not to capitalize a title, check in a dictionary.

EXAMPLE

Who is the **g**overnor of Kansas?

A title is usually capitalized when it is used alone in direct address.

EXAMPLE

Have you reached your decision, **G**overnor?

(2) Capitalize words showing family relationships except when preceded by a possessive.

EXAMPLES

Aunt Amy   my **a**unt   **M**other   Bill's **m**other

(3) Capitalize the names of religions and their followers, holy days and celebrations, holy writings, and specific deities and venerated beings.

> **NOTE** The words *god* and *goddess* are not capitalized when they refer to the deities of mythology. The names of specific mythological deities are capitalized, however.
>
> **EXAMPLES**
> The Greek **g**od of war was Ares.

(4) Capitalize the first and last words and all important words in titles of books, periodicals, poems, stories, essays, speeches, plays, historical documents, movies, radio and television programs, works of art, musical compositions, and cartoons.

Unimportant words in a title include articles (*a, an, the*), short prepositions (those with fewer than five letters, such as *of, to, in, for, from, with*), and coordinating conjunctions (*and, but, for, nor, or, so, yet*).

TYPE OF NAME	EXAMPLES
Books	*The Call of the Wild*
Periodicals	*Car and Driver*
Poems	"Once by the Pacific"
Stories	"The Fall of the House of Usher"
Essays and Speeches	"The Lost Worlds of Ancient America" "I Have a Dream"
Plays	*A Raisin in the Sun*
Historical Documents	Declaration of Independence
Movies	*Raiders of the Lost Ark*
Radio and TV Programs	*Star Trek: The Next Generation*
Works of Art	*Double Dutch on the Golden Gate Bridge*
Musical Compositions	"Lift Every Voice and Sing"
Cartoons	*Where I'm Coming From*

NOTE The article *the* before a title is not capitalized unless it is part of the official title. The official title of a book is found on the title page. The official title of a newspaper or periodical is found on the masthead (usually on the editorial page).

EXAMPLES
the *Odyssey*
the *Boston Herald*

The Wall Street Journal
The Man in the Iron Mask

For information about which titles should be italicized and which should be enclosed in quotation marks, see pages 1245 and 1247.

12 PUNCTUATION

END MARKS

 For information about how sentences are classified according to purpose, see page 1235.

12a. **A statement (or declarative sentence) is followed by a period.**

EXAMPLE
Felipe asked whether Edgar Allan Poe was primarily a poet, an essayist, or a short-story writer.

12b. **A question (or interrogative sentence) is followed by a question mark.**

EXAMPLE
Have you read any of Edgar Allan Poe's poetry?

12c. **A request or command (or imperative sentence) is followed by either a period or an exclamation point.**

EXAMPLES
Answer the phone, please.
Turn the music down now!

12d. **An exclamation (or exclamatory sentence) is followed by an exclamation point.**

EXAMPLE
What an imagination Edgar Allan Poe had!

 NOTE An exclamation point may be used after a single word (especially an interjection) as well as after a sentence.

EXAMPLE
Hey! Wait for me!

12e. **An abbreviation is usually followed by a period.**

(See the chart at the top of the next page for examples.)

Some common abbreviations, including many for units of measurement, are written without periods.

EXAMPLES
AM/FM, FBI, IOU, MTV, PC, ROTC, SOS, cc, db, ft, lb, kw, ml, psi, rpm [Use a period with the abbreviation *in.* (*inch*) to avoid confusion with the word *in*.]

TYPE OF ABBREVIATION	EXAMPLES
Personal Names	N. Scott Momaday E. A. Robinson
Organizations and Companies	Assn. Co. Corp. Ltd. Inc.
Titles Used with Names	Dr. Jr. Ms. Ph.D.
Times of Day	A.M. (*or* a.m.) P.M. (*or* p.m.)
Years	B.C. (*written after the date*) A.D. (*written before the date*)
Addresses	Ave. Blvd. Dr. St. P.O. Box
States	Ark. Fla. R.I. N. Mex.

> **NOTE** If an abbreviation has a period, do not place a period after it at the end of a sentence.

> **NOTE** Two-letter state abbreviations without periods are used only when the ZIP Code is included.
>
> **EXAMPLE**
> Springfield, **MA** 01101

COMMAS

12f. Use commas to separate items in a series.

EXAMPLE
The main characters are Huck, Tom, and Jim.

If all the items in a series are linked by *and, or,* or *nor,* do not use commas to separate them.

EXAMPLE
Saul Bellow **and** Isaac Bashevis Singer **and** Toni Morrison won Nobel Prizes.

12g. Use a comma to separate two or more adjectives preceding a noun.

EXAMPLE
Lincoln was a noble, compassionate, wise leader.

12h. Use a comma before *and, but, or, nor, for, so,* and *yet* when they join independent clauses.

EXAMPLE
I read an excerpt from Amy Tan's *The Joy Luck Club,* and now I want to read the entire book.

You may omit the comma before *and, but, or,* or *nor* if the clauses are very short and there is no chance of misunderstanding.

12i. Use commas to set off nonessential clauses and nonessential participial phrases.

A *nonessential* clause or phrase is one that can be left out without changing the meaning of the sentence.

NONESSENTIAL CLAUSE	Eudora Welty, **who was born in Mississippi,** uses her home state in many of her stories.
NONESSENTIAL PHRASE	Lee, **noticing my confusion,** rephrased her question.

An *essential* clause or phrase is one that can't be left out without changing the meaning of the sentence. Essential clauses and phrases are *not* set off by commas.

ESSENTIAL CLAUSE	Material **that is quoted verbatim** should be placed in quotation marks.
ESSENTIAL PHRASE	The only word **spoken by the raven** is *nevermore.*

12j. Use a comma after certain introductory elements.

(1) Use a comma after a one-word adverb such as *first, yes,* or *no* and after any mild exclamation such as *well* or *why* at the beginning of a sentence.

EXAMPLE
Yes, Hemingway is my favorite author.

(2) Use a comma after an introductory participial phrase or introductory adverb clause.

EXAMPLES
Standing on the quarter-deck, Captain Ahab spoke to his crew. [participial phrase]
After he had driven around the lake several times, he decided to go to the drive-in restaurant. [adverb clause]

(3) Use a comma after two or more introductory prepositional phrases.

EXAMPLE
At the end of the story, Walter Mitty imagines that he is facing a firing squad.

12k. Use commas to set off elements that interrupt a sentence.

(1) Appositives and appositive phrases are usually set off by commas.

EXAMPLE
My favorite book by Claude McKay, *Banjo,* was first published in 1929.

Sometimes an appositive is so closely related to the word or words it refers to that it should not be set off by commas.

EXAMPLE

The poet **Maya Angelou** read one of her poems on Inauguration Day.

(2) Words used in direct address are set off by commas.

EXAMPLE

Your essay, **Theo,** was well organized.

(3) Parenthetical expressions are set off by commas.

Parenthetical expressions are remarks that add incidental information or that relate ideas to each other.

EXAMPLE

Simón Bolívar liberated much of South America from Spanish rule; he went on, **moreover,** to become the most powerful person on the continent.

12l. Use a comma in certain conventional situations.

(1) Use a comma to separate items in dates and addresses.

EXAMPLES

On Friday, October 23, 1994, my niece Leslie was born.

Please address all further inquiries to 92 Keystone Crossings, Indianapolis, IN 46240. [Notice that a comma is not used between a state abbreviation and a ZIP Code.]

(2) Use a comma after the salutation of a friendly letter and after the closing of any letter.

EXAMPLES

Dear Rosa,   Sincerely yours,

(3) Use a comma to set off an abbreviation such as *Jr., Sr., RN, M.D., Ltd.,* or *Inc.*

EXAMPLE

Is Juan Fuentes, Jr., your cousin?

SEMICOLONS

12m. Use a semicolon between independent clauses that are closely related in thought and are not joined by *and, but, for, nor, or, so,* or *yet.*

EXAMPLE

"Tart words make no friends; a spoonful of honey will catch more flies than a gallon of vinegar."
—Benjamin Franklin, *Poor Richard's Almanack*

12n. Use a semicolon between independent clauses joined by a conjunctive adverb or a transitional expression.

A **conjunctive adverb** (such as *consequently, however,* or *therefore*) or a **transitional expression** (such as *as a result, for example,* or *in other words*) indicates the relationship of the independent clauses that it joins. Notice in the following example that a comma is placed after the conjunctive adverb.

EXAMPLE

Dexter knew that Judy was selfish and insensitive; **nevertheless,** he continued to adore her.

12o. Use a semicolon (rather than a comma) before a coordinating conjunction to join independent clauses that contain commas.

EXAMPLE

During the nineteenth century—the era of such distinguished poets as Longfellow, Whittier, and Holmes—most poetry was written in traditional metrical patterns; but one poet, Walt Whitman, rejected the conventional verse forms.

12p. Use a semicolon between items in a series if the items contain commas.

EXAMPLE

The summer reading list includes *Behind the Trail of Broken Treaties,* by Vine Deloria, Jr.; *House Made of Dawn,* by N. Scott Momaday; and *Blue Highways: A Journey into America,* by William Least Heat-Moon.

COLONS

12q. Use a colon to mean "note what follows."

(1) Use a colon before a list of items, especially after expressions such as *as follows* and *the following.*

EXAMPLE

The magazine article profiles the following famous American authors of the nineteenth century: Edgar Allan Poe, Nathaniel Hawthorne, and Herman Melville.

NOTE   Do not use a colon before a list that directly follows a verb or a preposition.

EXAMPLE

The anthology includes "The Raven," "Richard Cory," and "Thanatopsis." [The list directly follows the verb *includes.*]

(2) Use a colon before a quotation that lacks a speaker tag such as *he said* or *she remarked.*

EXAMPLE
Dad's orders were loud and clear: "Everybody up and at 'em."

(3) Use a colon before a long, formal statement or quotation.

EXAMPLE
Patrick Henry concluded his fiery speech before the Virginia House of Burgesses with these words: "Is life so dear, or peace so sweet, as to be purchased at the price of chains and slavery? Forbid it, Almighty God! I know not what course others may take; but as for me, give me liberty, or give me death!"

12r. Use a colon in certain conventional situations.

EXAMPLES
5:20 P.M. [between the hour and the minute]
Deuteronomy 5:6–21 [between chapter and verse in referring to passages from the Bible]
Dear Sir or Madam: [after the salutation of a business letter]
"Cold Kills: Hypothermia" [between a title and a subtitle]

13 PUNCTUATION

ITALICS

Italics are printed characters that slant to the right. To indicate italics in handwritten or typewritten work, use underlining.

PRINTED	Who wrote *Black Boy*?
HANDWRITTEN	*Who wrote* <u>*Black Boy*</u>?

13a. Use italics (underlining) for titles of books, plays, long poems, periodicals, newspapers, works of art, films, television series, long musical compositions, recordings, comic strips, computer software, court cases, trains, ships, aircraft, and spacecraft.

TYPE OF NAME	EXAMPLES	
Books	*The Scarlet Letter*	*Fifth Chinese Daughter*
Plays	*The Crucible*	*West Side Story*
Long Poems	*I Am Joaquín*	the *Epic of Gilgamesh*
Periodicals	*Reader's Digest*	*Newsweek*
Newspapers	*The Wall Street Journal*	the *Austin American-Statesman*
Works of Art	*The Kiss*	*The Starry Night*
Films	*Forrest Gump*	*Stand and Deliver*
TV Series	*Jeopardy!*	*Star Trek: The Next Generation*
Long Musical Compositions	*Liverpool Oratorio*	*Hiawatha's Wedding Feast*
Recordings	*Achtung Baby*	*Sketches of Spain*
Comic Strips	*Peanuts*	*Calvin and Hobbes*
Computer Software	*WordPerfect*	*Paintbrush*
Court Cases	*Plessy v. Ferguson*	*Bailey v. Alabama*
Trains, Ships	*Empire Builder*	*Queen Mary*
Aircraft, Spacecraft	*Solar Challenger*	*Apollo 11*

NOTE The article *the* before the title of a book, periodical, or newspaper is not italicized or capitalized unless it is part of the official title. The official title of a book appears on the title page. The official title of a periodical or newspaper is the name given on the masthead, which usually appears on the editorial page.

EXAMPLES
The article appeared in both the *Philadelphia Inquirer* and *The New York Times.*

☞ For examples of titles that are not italicized but that are enclosed in quotation marks, see page 1247.

13b. Use italics (underlining) for words, letters, numerals, and symbols referred to as such and for foreign words that have not been adopted into English.

EXAMPLES

Should the use of *their* for *there* be considered a spelling error or a usage error?

The teacher couldn't tell whether I had written a script *S*, the number *5*, or an *&*.

All U.S. coins are now stamped with the inscription *e pluribus unum*.

QUOTATION MARKS

13c. Use quotation marks to enclose a *direct quotation*—a person's exact words.

EXAMPLE

Chief Joseph said, "The earth is the mother of all people, and all people should have equal rights upon it."

Notice that a direct quotation begins with a capital letter. However, if the quotation is only part of a sentence, it does not begin with a capital letter.

EXAMPLE

Chief Joseph called the earth "the mother of all people."

(1) When the expression identifying the speaker divides a quoted sentence, the second part begins with a lowercase letter.

EXAMPLE

"I really have to leave now," said Gwen, "so that I will be on time." [Notice that each part of a divided quotation is enclosed in quotation marks.]

When the second part of a divided quotation is a new sentence, it begins with a capital letter.

EXAMPLE

"Teddy Roosevelt was the first U.S. president to express concern about the depletion of the nation's natural resources," explained Mr. Fuentes. "He established a conservation program that expanded the national park system."

(2) When used with quotation marks, other marks of punctuation are placed according to the following rules.

- Commas and periods are always placed inside the closing quotation marks.

EXAMPLES

"On the other hand," he said, "your decision may be correct."

- Semicolons and colons are always placed outside the closing quotation marks.

EXAMPLES

My neighbor said, "Sure, I'll buy a subscription"; it was lucky that I asked her on payday.

Edna St. Vincent Millay uses these devices in her poem "Spring": alliteration, slant rhyme, and personification.

- Question marks and exclamation points are placed inside the closing quotation marks if the quotation itself is a question or an exclamation. Otherwise, they are placed outside.

EXAMPLES

Was it you who wrote the poem "Upon Turning Seventeen"?

"What a tortured soul Reverend Dimmesdale is!" said Mr. Klein.

(3) When quoting a passage that consists of more than one paragraph, put quotation marks at the beginning of each paragraph and at the end of only the last paragraph.

EXAMPLE

"As he neared the house, each detail of the scene became vivid to him. He was aware of some bricks of the vanished chimney lying on the sod. There was a door which hung by one hinge.

"Rifle bullets called forth by the insistent skirmishers came from the far-off bank of foliage. They mingled with the shells and the pieces of shells until the air was torn in all directions by hootings, yells, howls. The sky was full of fiends who directed all their wild rage at his head."

　　　　　—Stephen Crane, "A Mystery of Heroism"

(4) Use single quotation marks to enclose a quotation within a quotation.

EXAMPLES

The teacher requested, "Jorge, please explain what Emerson meant when he said, 'To be great is to be misunderstood.'"

"Have you read 'Rip Van Winkle'?" Jill asked.

(5) When writing *dialogue* (a conversation), begin a new paragraph every time the speaker changes, and enclose the speaker's words in quotation marks.

EXAMPLE

"How far is it to the Owl Creek bridge?" Farquhar asked.

"About thirty miles."

"Is there no force on this side the creek?"

"Only a picket post half a mile out, on the railroad, and a single sentinel at this end of the bridge."

　　　　　—Ambrose Bierce, "An Occurrence at Owl Creek Bridge"

13d. Use quotation marks to enclose titles of short works, such as short stories, poems, essays, articles, songs, episodes of television series, and chapters and other parts of books.

TYPE OF NAME	EXAMPLES
Short Stories	"The Magic Barrel" "The Tell-Tale Heart"
Poems	"The Latin Deli" "Thanatopsis"
Essays	"On the Mall" "The Creative Process"
Articles	"Old Poetry and Modern Music"
Songs	"On Top of Old Smoky"
TV Episodes	"The Flight of the Condor"
Chapters and Parts of Books	"The World Was New" "The Colonies' Struggle for Freedom"

NOTE Neither italics nor quotation marks are used for titles of major religious works or titles of legal or historical documents.

EXAMPLES
Bible   Bill of Rights

For a list of titles that are italicized rather than placed in quotation marks, see page 1245.

ELLIPSIS POINTS

13e. Use three spaced periods called *ellipsis points* (. . .) to mark omissions from quoted material and pauses in a written passage.

ORIGINAL   The second half of the program consisted of four numbers from the *Ring,* and closed with Siegfried's funeral march. My aunt wept quietly, but almost continuously, as a shallow vessel overflows in a rainstorm. From time to time her dim eyes looked up at the lights which studded the ceiling, burning softly under their dull glass globes; doubtless they were stars in truth to her. I was still perplexed as to what measure of musical comprehension was left to her, she who had heard nothing but the singing of gospel hymns at Methodist services in the square frame schoolhouse on Section Thirteen for so many years. I was wholly unable to gauge how much of it had been dissolved in soapsuds, or worked into bread, or milked into the bottom of a pail.

—Willa Cather, "A Wagner Matinée"

(1) If the quoted material that comes before the ellipsis points is not a complete sentence, use three ellipsis points with a space before the first point.

EXAMPLE
The narrator notes, "The second half of the program . . . closed with Siegfried's funeral march."

(2) If the quoted material that comes before or after the ellipsis points is a complete sentence, use an end mark before the ellipsis points.

EXAMPLE
The narrator observes, "My aunt wept quietly. . . . "

(3) If one sentence or more is omitted, ellipsis points follow the end mark that precedes the omitted material.

EXAMPLE
Recalling the experience, the narrator says, "My aunt wept quietly, but almost continuously, as a shallow vessel overflows in a rainstorm. . . . I was still perplexed as to what measure of musical comprehension was left to her, she who had heard nothing but the singing of gospel hymns at Methodist services in the square frame schoolhouse on Section Thirteen for so many years."

(4) To show that a full line or more of poetry has been omitted, use an entire line of spaced periods.

ORIGINAL   If you were coming in the Fall,
I'd brush the Summer by
With half a smile, and half a spurn,
As Housewives do, a Fly.
—Emily Dickinson, "If you were coming in the Fall"

WITH OMISSION   If you were coming in the Fall,
I'd brush the Summer by
. . . .
As Housewives do, a Fly.

APOSTROPHES

13f. Use an apostrophe in forming the possessive of nouns and indefinite pronouns.

(1) To form the possessive of a singular noun, add an apostrophe and an *s*.

EXAMPLES
the minister's veil   Ross's opinion

NOTE When forming the possessive of a singular noun ending in an *s* sound, add only an apostrophe if the addition of *'s* will make the noun awkward to pronounce. Otherwise, add *'s*.

EXAMPLES
Douglass's autobiography   Texas' population

(2) To form the possessive of a plural noun ending in *s*, add only the apostrophe. If the plural noun does not end in *s*, add an apostrophe and an *s*.

EXAMPLES
the authors' styles   the Ushers' house
men's fashions   children's toys

(3) To form the possessive of an indefinite pronoun, add an apostrophe and an *s*.

EXAMPLES
each one's time   everybody's opinion

NOTE In such forms as *anyone else* and *somebody else*, the correct possessives are *anyone else's* and *somebody else's*.

(4) Form the possessive of only the last word in a compound word, in the name of an organization or business firm, or in a word group showing joint possession.

EXAMPLES
father-in-law's gloves   Roz and Denise's idea
Taylor, Sanders, and Weissman's law office

(5) Form the possessive of each noun in a word group showing individual possession of similar items.

EXAMPLE
Baldwin's and Ellison's writings

When a possessive pronoun is part of a word group showing joint possession, each noun in the word group is also possessive.

EXAMPLE
Walter Mitty's and **her** relationship

(6) When used in the possessive form, words that indicate time (such as *hour, week,* and *year*) and words that indicate amounts of money require apostrophes.

EXAMPLES
a week's vacation   five dollars' worth

13g. Use an apostrophe to show where letters, words, or numbers have been omitted in a contraction.

EXAMPLES
they had . . . **they'd**   Kerry is . . . **Kerry's**
let us . . . **let's**   of the clock . . . **o'clock**
where is . . . **where's**   1997 . . . **'97**

The word *not* can be shortened to *–n't* and added to a verb, usually without any change in the spelling of the verb.

EXAMPLES
is not . . . **isn't**   has not . . . **hasn't**

EXCEPTION
will not . . . **won't**

13h. Use an apostrophe and an *s* to form the plurals of all lowercase letters, some uppercase letters, numerals, and some words referred to as words.

EXAMPLES
There are two *r*'s and two *s*'s in *embarrassed.*
Soon after Tom and Lucynell said their *I do*'s, he abandoned her.

You may add only an *s* to form the plurals of such items—except lowercase letters—if the plural forms will not cause misreading.

EXAMPLES
Compact discs (**CDs**) were introduced in the **1980s.**
On her report card were three **A's** and three **C's.**

HYPHENS

13i. Use a hyphen to divide a word at the end of a line.

When dividing a word at the end of a line, remember the following rules:

(1) Do not divide a one-syllable word.

EXAMPLE
Peyton Farquhar was captured, and he was finally **hanged** from the bridge.

(2) Divide a word only between syllables.

EXAMPLE
Ernest Hemingway's *A Farewell to Arms* was **published** in 1929.

(3) Divide an already hyphenated word at the hyphen.

EXAMPLE
Stephen Crane died in Germany at the age of **twenty-eight.**

(4) Do not divide a word so that one letter stands alone.

EXAMPLE
One fine autumn day, Rip Van Winkle fell fast **asleep** in the mountains.

13j. Use a hyphen with compound numbers from twenty-one to ninety-nine and with fractions used as modifiers.

EXAMPLES
six hundred **twenty-five**
a **three-fourths** quorum [*but* **three fourths** of the audience]

DASHES

13k. Use dashes to set off abrupt breaks in thoughts.

EXAMPLE
The poor condition of this road—it really needs to be paved—makes this route unpopular.

13l. Use dashes to set off an appositive or a parenthetical expression that contains commas.

EXAMPLE
Several of the nineteenth-century American poets—Poe, Dickinson, and Whitman, for example—led remarkable lives.

PARENTHESES

13m. Use parentheses to enclose informative or explanatory material of minor importance.

EXAMPLES
Harriet Tubman **(**c. 1820–1913**)** is remembered for her work in the Underground Railroad.
On our vacation we visited Natchitoches **(**it's pronounced nak′ə·täsh′**)**, Louisiana.
Thoreau lived at Walden Pond for two years. **(**See the map on page 350.**)**

BRACKETS

13n. Use brackets to enclose an explanation within quoted or parenthetical material.

EXAMPLE
I think that Hilda Doolittle (more commonly known as H. D. **[**1886–1961**]**) is best remembered for her Imagist poetry.

14 SPELLING

UNDERSTANDING WORD STRUCTURE

Many English words are made up of roots and affixes (prefixes and suffixes).

Roots

14a. The *root* of a word is the part that carries the word's core meaning.

ROOTS	MEANINGS	EXAMPLES
–bio–	life	biology, symbiotic
–duc–, –duct–	lead	educate, conductor
–mit–, –miss–	send	remit, emissary
–port–	carry, bear	transport, portable

NOTE To find the meaning of a root or an affix, look in a dictionary. Most dictionaries have individual entries for word parts.

Prefixes

14b. A *prefix* is one or more letters or syllables added to the beginning of a word or word part to create a new word.

PREFIXES	MEANINGS	EXAMPLES
a–	lacking, without	amorphous, apolitical
dia–	through, across, apart	diagonal, diameter, diagnose
inter–	between, among	intercede, international
mis–	badly, wrongly	misfire, misspell

Suffixes

14c. A *suffix* is one or more letters or syllables added to the end of a word or word part to create a new word.

SUFFIXES	MEANINGS	EXAMPLES
–ation, –ition	action, result	repetition, starvation
–er	doer, native of	baker, westerner
–ible	able, likely, fit	edible, possible, divisible
–or	doer, office, action	director, juror, error

SPELLING RULES

ie and ei

14d. Write *ie* when the sound is long e, except after c.

EXAMPLES
believe   field   ceiling   receive
EXCEPTIONS
either   leisure   seize   protein

14e. Write *ei* when the sound is not long e.

EXAMPLES
eight   neighbor   weigh   foreign
EXCEPTIONS
ancient   view   friend   efficient

–cede, –ceed, and –sede

14f. The only English word ending in *–sede* is *supersede*. The only words ending in *–ceed* are *exceed*, *proceed*, and *succeed*. Most other words with this sound end in *–cede*.

EXAMPLES
accede   concede   intercede   recede

Adding Prefixes

14g. When adding a prefix, do not change the spelling of the root.

EXAMPLES
mis + spell = **mis**spell
inter + national = **inter**national

Adding Suffixes

14h. When adding the suffix *–ness* or *–ly,* do not change the spelling of the original word.

EXAMPLES
plain + ness = plain**ness**   casual + ly = casual**ly**
EXCEPTIONS
For most words ending in *y*, change the *y* to *i* before adding *-ness* or *-ly*.
empty + ness = empt**iness**   busy + ly = bus**ily**

 NOTE One-syllable adjectives ending in *y* generally follow rule 14h.

EXAMPLES
dry + ness = dry**ness**   shy + ly = shy**ly**

14i. Drop the final silent e before a suffix beginning with a vowel.

EXAMPLES
care + ing = car**ing**   dose + age = dos**age**
EXCEPTIONS
Keep the final silent e
- in a word ending in *ce* or *ge* before a suffix beginning with *a* or *o*: peac**eable**, courag**eous**
- in *dye* and in *singe* before *–ing*: dy**eing**, sing**eing**
- in *mile* before *–age*: mil**eage**

 NOTE When adding *–ing* to words that end in *ie*, drop the *e* and change the *i* to *y*.

EXAMPLES
die + ing = d**ying**   lie + ing = l**ying**

14j. Keep the final silent e before a suffix beginning with a consonant.

EXAMPLES
hope + ful = hop**eful**   love + ly = lov**ely**
EXCEPTIONS
awe + ful = aw**ful**   whole + ly = whol**ly**
nine + th = nin**th**   argue + ment = argu**ment**

14k. For words ending in y preceded by a consonant, change the y to i before any suffix that does not begin with i.

EXAMPLES
thirsty + est = thirst**iest**   plenty + ful = plent**iful**

14l. For words ending in y preceded by a vowel, keep the y when adding a suffix.

EXAMPLES
joy + ful = joy**ful**   obey + ing = obey**ing**
EXCEPTIONS
day—da**ily**   lay—la**id**   pay—pa**id**   say—sa**id**

14m. **Double the final consonant before a suffix that begins with a vowel if the word both**

(1) has only one syllable or has the accent on the last syllable

and

(2) ends in a single consonant preceded by a single vowel.

EXAMPLES
thin + est = thin**n**est   occur + ed = occu**rr**ed
EXCEPTIONS

- For words ending in *w* or *x*, do not double the final consonant.

    new + er = new**er** relax + ing = relax**ing**

- For words ending in *c*, add *k* before the suffix instead of doubling the *c*.

    picnic + k + ed = picnic**ked**

NOTE The final consonant of some words may or may not be doubled, such as *traveled / travelled*. If you are unsure about doubling a final consonant, consult a dictionary.

Forming the Plurals of Nouns

14n. **Remembering the following rules will help you spell the plural forms of nouns.**

(1) For most nouns, add –*s*.

EXAMPLES
players   islands   Jeffersons

(2) For nouns ending in *s, x, z, ch,* or *sh,* add –*es*.

EXAMPLES
classes   matches   taxes   Chávezes

(3) For nouns ending in *y* preceded by a vowel, add –*s*.

EXAMPLES
monkeys   alloys   McKays

In some names, diacritical marks (marks that show pronunciation) are as essential to correct spelling as the letters themselves. If you are not sure about the spelling of a name, check with the person whose name it is or consult a reference source.

EXAMPLES
Abolfat'h   Hélène   Bashō   Da 'Shawn

(4) For nouns ending in *y* preceded by a consonant, change the *y* to *i* and add –*es*.

EXAMPLES
fl**ies**   countr**ies**   troph**ies**
EXCEPTIONS
For proper nouns, add –*s*: Kennedys

(5) For some nouns ending in *f* or *fe,* add –*s*. For others, change the *f* or *fe* to *v* and add –*es*. For proper nouns, add –*s*.

EXAMPLES
gulfs   roofs   lea**ves**   kni**ves**   wol**ves**
Tallchiefs   Wolfes

(6) For nouns ending in *o* preceded by a vowel, add –*s*.

EXAMPLES
studio**s**   stereo**s**   Ignacio**s**

(7) For nouns ending in *o* preceded by a consonant, add –*es*.

EXAMPLES
tomato**es**   hero**es**   veto**es**

For some common nouns ending in *o* preceded by a consonant, especially those referring to music, and for proper nouns, add only an –*s*.

EXAMPLES
tacos   pianos   altos   Suros

NOTE For some nouns ending in *o* preceded by a consonant, either –*s* or –*es* may be added.

EXAMPLES
zeros *or* zeroes   mosquitos *or* mosquitoes

(8) The plurals of a few nouns are formed in irregular ways.

EXAMPLES
teeth   women   mice   geese

(9) For a few nouns, the singular and the plural forms are the same.

EXAMPLES
sheep   trout   aircraft   Japanese   Sioux

(10) For most compound nouns, form the plural of only the last word of the compound.

EXAMPLES
bookshel**ves**   baby sitter**s**   ten-year-old**s**

(11) For compound nouns in which one of the words is modified by the other word or words, form the plural of the noun modified.

EXAMPLES
sisters-in-law   runners-up   mountain goats

(12) For some nouns borrowed from other languages, the plural is formed as in the original languages.

EXAMPLES

alga—alg**ae**   hypothesis—hypothes**es**
ellipsis—ellips**es**   phenomenon—phenomen**a**

(13) To form the plurals of figures, most uppercase letters, signs, and words used as words, add an —s or both an apostrophe and an —s.

EXAMPLES

1990—1990**s** *or* 1990**'s**   *C*—*C*s *or* *C*'s
and—*and*s *or* *and*'s   *&*—*&*s *or* *&*'s

To prevent confusion, add both an apostrophe and an —s to form the plural of all lowercase letters, certain uppercase letters, and some words used as words.

EXAMPLES

The word *Mississippi* contains four *s*'s and four *i*'s. [Without an apostrophe, the plural of *i* could be confused with *is.*]

Because I mistakenly thought Flannery O'Connor was a man, I used *his*'s instead of *her*'s in my paragraph. [Without an apostrophe, the plural of *his* would look like the word *hiss,* and the plural of *her* would look like the pronoun *hers.*]

15 GLOSSARY OF USAGE

The **Glossary of Usage** is an alphabetical list of words and expressions with definitions, explanations, and examples. Some examples in this list are labeled *standard, nonstandard, formal,* or *informal.* The labels **standard** and **formal** identify usage that is appropriate in serious writing and speaking (such as in compositions and speeches). The label **informal** indicates standard English commonly used in conversation and in everyday writing such as personal letters. The label **nonstandard** identifies usage that does not follow the guidelines of standard English usage.

---

accept, except   *Accept* is a verb meaning "to receive." *Except* may be either a verb meaning "to leave out" or a preposition meaning "excluding."

EXAMPLES

I will **accept** another yearbook assignment. [verb]
Should the military services **except** women from combat duty? [verb]
I have read all of Willa Cather's novels **except** *My Ántonia.* [preposition]

affect, effect   *Affect* is a verb meaning "to influence." *Effect* may be either a verb meaning "to bring about or accomplish" or a noun meaning "the result [of an action]."

EXAMPLES

How did the House of Usher **affect** the narrator?
Renewed interest in *Moby-Dick* during the 1920s **effected** a change in Melville's reputation.
What **effect** did the war have on Paul Berlin?

all ready, already   *All ready* means "all prepared." *Already* means "previously."

EXAMPLES

Are you **all ready** to give your report?
We have **already** read that story.

all the farther, all the faster   Avoid using these expressions in formal situations. Use *as far as* or *as fast as.*

EXAMPLE

The first act was **as far as** [*not* all the farther] we had read in *A Raisin in the Sun.*

all together, altogether   *All together* means "everyone or everything in the same place." *Altogether* means "entirely."

EXAMPLES

My family will be **all together** for the holidays this year.
The president is **altogether** opposed to the bill.

allusion, illusion   An *allusion* is an indirect reference to something. An *illusion* is a mistaken idea or a misleading appearance.

EXAMPLES

In her stories, Flannery O'Connor makes numerous **allusions** to the Bible.
Illusions of success haunt Willy Loman.
Makeup can be used to create an **illusion.**

almost, most   Avoid using *most* for *almost* in all writing other than dialogue.

EXAMPLE

Almost [*not* most] everyone in class was surprised by the outcome in Ambrose Bierce's story "An Occurrence at Owl Creek Bridge."

a lot   Avoid this expression in formal situations by using *many* or *much.*

already   See **all ready, already.**

altogether   See **all together, altogether.**

among See **between, among.**

amount, number Use *amount* to refer to a singular word. Use *number* to refer to a plural word.

EXAMPLES

The library has a large **amount** of resource material about the Harlem Renaissance. [*Amount* refers to *material.*]

The library has a large **number** of books about the Harlem Renaissance. [*Number* refers to *books.*]

and, but In general, avoid beginning a sentence with *and* or *but* in formal writing.

and etc. *Etc.* stands for the Latin words *et cetera,* meaning "and others" or "and so forth." Always avoid using *and* before *etc.* In general, avoid using *etc.* in formal situations. Use an unabbreviated English expression instead.

EXAMPLE

We are studying twentieth-century American novelists: Ernest Hemingway, Margaret Walker, Jean Toomer, **and others** [*or* etc., *but not* and etc.].

and/or Avoid using this confusing construction. Decide which alternative, *and* or *or,* expresses what you mean, and use it alone.

any more, anymore The expression *any more* specifies a quantity. *Anymore* means "now; nowadays."

EXAMPLES

Do you know **any more** Caddo folk tales?
Kam doesn't work at the record store **anymore.**

any one, anyone The expression *any one* specifies one member of a group. *Anyone* is a pronoun meaning "one person, no matter which."

EXAMPLES

Any one of you can play the part.
Anyone can try out for the part.

anyways, anywheres Omit the final *s* from these words and others like them (*everywheres, nowheres, somewheres*).

EXAMPLE

I can't go **anywhere** [*not* anywheres] until I finish.

as See **like, as.**

as if See **like, as if.**

at Avoid using *at* after a construction beginning with *where.*

EXAMPLE

Where was Chief Joseph [*not* where was Chief Joseph at] when he delivered his surrender speech?

a while, awhile *A while* means "a period of time." *Awhile* means "for a short time."

EXAMPLES

Let's wait here **awhile**.
Let's sit here for **a while** and listen to the band.

bad, badly *Bad* is an adjective. *Badly* is an adverb. In standard English, *bad* should follow a sense verb, such as *feel, look, sound, taste,* or *smell,* or other linking verb.

NONSTANDARD	If the cole slaw smells badly, don't eat it.
STANDARD	If the cole slaw smells **bad**, don't eat it.

because In formal situations, do not use the construction *reason . . . because.* Instead, use *reason . . . that.*

EXAMPLE

The **reason** for the eclipse is **that** [*not* because] the moon has come between the Earth and the sun.

being as, being that Avoid using either of these expressions in place of *since* or *because.*

EXAMPLE

Because [*not* being as *or* being that] Ms. Ribas is a gemologist, she may know what these stones are.

beside, besides *Beside* is a preposition meaning "by the side of" or "next to." *Besides* may be either a preposition meaning "in addition to" or "other than" or an adverb meaning "moreover."

EXAMPLES

Rip Van Winkle laid his rifle **beside** him on the ground. [preposition]

No one **besides** Lurleen has read all of *Leaves of Grass.* [preposition]

I'm not in the mood to go shopping; **besides**, I have an English test tomorrow. [adverb]

between, among Use *between* to refer to only two items or to more than two when comparing each item individually to each of the others.

EXAMPLES

The money from the sale of the property was evenly divided **between** Sasha and Antonio.

Don't you know the difference **between** a simile, a metaphor, and an analogy? [Each figure of speech is compared individually to each of the others.]

Use *among* to refer to more than two items when you are not considering each item in relation to each other item individually.

EXAMPLE

The money from the sale of the property was evenly divided **among** the four relatives.

bring, take *Bring* means "to come carrying something." *Take* means "to go carrying something."

EXAMPLES

I'll **bring** my Wynton Marsalis tapes when I come over.

When he went hunting, Rip Van Winkle **took** his gun and dog.

but See **and, but.**

cannot (can't) help but Avoid using *but* followed by the infinitive form of a verb after the expression *cannot (can't) help.* Instead, use a gerund after the expression.

| NONSTANDARD | I can't help but tap my foot whenever I hear mariachi music. |
| STANDARD | I can't help **tapping** my foot whenever I hear mariachi music. |

compare, contrast Used with *to, compare* means "to look for similarities between." Used with *with, compare* means "to look for similarities and differences between." *Contrast* is always used to point out differences.

EXAMPLES

Write a simile **comparing** a manufactured product **to** something in nature.

How do the haiku of Taniguchi Buson **compare with** those of Matsuo Bashō?

The teacher **contrasted** the writing styles of Walt Whitman and Emily Dickinson.

could of See **of.**

double subject Do not use an unnecessary pronoun after the subject of a sentence.

EXAMPLE

Judy Jones [*not* Judy Jones she] fascinates Dexter Green.

due to Avoid using *due to* for "because of" or "owing to."

EXAMPLE

The game was postponed **because of** [*not* due to] rain.

each and every The expression *each and every* is redundant. Instead, use either *each* or *every* alone.

EXAMPLE

Every [*not* each and every] resident of Jefferson attended Miss Emily Grierson's funeral.

effect See **affect, effect.**

either, neither *Either* usually means "one or the other of two." *Neither* usually means "not one or the other of two." Avoid using *either* or *neither* when referring to more than two.

EXAMPLE

Consider writing about the Jazz Age, the Harlem Renaissance, or the Great Depression; **any one** [*not* either] of those topics would be interesting.

emigrate, immigrate *Emigrate* means "to leave a country or a region to settle elsewhere." *Immigrate* means "to come into a country or a region to settle there."

EXAMPLES

Claude McKay **emigrated** from Jamaica in 1912.

Claude McKay **immigrated** to the United States in 1912.

etc. See **and etc.**

every See **each and every.**

every day, everyday *Every day* means "each day." *Everyday* means "daily" or "usual."

EXAMPLES

Parson Hooper wore the black veil **every day.**

Walking the dog is one of my **everyday** chores.

every one, everyone *Every one* specifies every person or thing of those named. *Everyone* means "every person; everybody."

EXAMPLES

Every one of these poems was written by Anne Sexton.

Has **everyone** read "The Bells"?

except See **accept, except.**

farther, further Use *farther* to express physical distance. Use *further* to express abstract relationships of degree or quantity.

EXAMPLES

We swam **farther** than we usually do.

After discussing "The Road Not Taken" **further,** we agreed with Karl's interpretation of the poem.

fewer, less Use *fewer* to modify a plural noun and *less* to modify a singular noun.

EXAMPLES

Later in life, Emily Dickinson entertained even **fewer** guests.

Later in life, Emily Dickinson spent **less** time entertaining guests.

further See **farther, further.**

good, well Do not use the adjective *good* to modify a verb. Instead, use the adverb *well,* meaning "capably" or "satisfactorily." As an adjective, *well* means "in good health" or "satisfactory in appearance or condition."

EXAMPLES
The school orchestra played **well** [adverb].
He says that he feels quite **well** [adjective].
It's midnight, and all is **well** [adjective].

had of See **of.**

had ought, hadn't ought Do not use *had* or *hadn't* with *ought.*

EXAMPLE
His scores **ought** [*not* had ought] to be back by now.

half Avoid using an indefinite article (*a* or *an*) both before and after *half.*

EXAMPLE
We've waited for **half an hour** [*or* **a half hour**].

if, whether Avoid using *if* for *whether* in indirect questions and in expressions of doubt.

EXAMPLE
Dickinson wanted to know **whether** [*not* if] her poems were "alive."

illusion See **allusion, illusion.**

immigrate See **emigrate, immigrate.**

imply, infer *Imply* means "to suggest indirectly." *Infer* means "to interpret" or "to draw a conclusion."

EXAMPLES
The speaker of "Thanatopsis" **implies** that nature can allay one's fear of death.
I **infer** from the poem that nature can cure many ills.

in, into *In* generally shows location. *Into* generally shows direction.

EXAMPLES
Randall Jarrell was born **in** Nashville, Tennessee.
When Rip walked **into** the village, everybody stared.

irregardless, regardless *Irregardless* is nonstandard. Use *regardless* instead.

EXAMPLE
Regardless [*not* irregardless] of the children's pleas, their father said they had to go to bed.

its, it's *Its* is the possessive form of *it. It's* is the contraction of *it is* or *it has.*

EXAMPLES
The crew prepares for **its** fight with Moby-Dick.
It's [it is] Captain Ahab's obsession.
It's [it has] been many years since Ahab lost his leg.

kind of, sort of In formal situations, avoid using these terms for the adverb *somewhat* or *rather.*

| INFORMAL | Roderick became kind of agitated. |
| FORMAL | Roderick became **rather** agitated. |

kind of a(n), sort of a(n) In formal situations, omit the *a(n).*

| INFORMAL | What kind of an essay is Baldwin's "The Creative Process"? |
| FORMAL | What **kind of** essay is Baldwin's "The Creative Process"? |

kind(s), sort(s), type(s) With the singular form of each of these nouns, use *this* or *that.* With the plural form, use *these* or *those.*

EXAMPLE
This kind of gas is safe, but **those kinds** aren't.

lay, lie See **lie, lay.**

learn, teach *Learn* means "to gain knowledge." *Teach* means "to provide with knowledge."

EXAMPLE
The more you **teach** someone else, the more you **learn** yourself.

less See **fewer, less.**

lie, lay The verb *lie* means "to rest" or "to stay, to recline, or to remain in a certain state or position." Its principal parts are *lie, lying, lay,* and *lain. Lie* never takes an object. The verb *lay* means "to put [something] in a place." Its principal parts are *lay, laying, laid,* and *laid. Lay* usually takes an object.

EXAMPLES
Their land **lay** in the shadow of Rainy Mountain. [no object]
Eduardo **laid** the strips of grilled meat on the tortilla. [*Strips* is the object of *laid.*]

like, as In formal situations, do not use *like* for the conjunction *as* to introduce a subordinate clause.

| INFORMAL | Plácido Domingo sings like Caruso once did. |
| FORMAL | Plácido Domingo sings **as** Caruso once did. |

like, as if In formal situations, avoid using the preposition *like* for the conjunction *as if* or *as though* to introduce a subordinate clause.

| INFORMAL | The singers sounded like they had not rehearsed. |
| FORMAL | The singers sounded **as if** [*or* **as though**] they had not rehearsed. |

might of, must of   See **of.**

most   See **almost, most.**

neither   See **either, neither.**

nor   See **or, nor.**

number   See **amount, number.**

of   *Of* is a preposition. Do not use *of* in place of *have* after verbs such as *could, should, would, might, must,* and *ought* [*to*]. Also, do not use *had of* for *had.*

EXAMPLES
You ought to **have** [*not* of] studied harder.
If he **had** [*not* had of] remembered the name of the
   author of "Mending Wall," he **would have** [*not*
   would of] made a perfect score.

   Avoid using *of* after other prepositions such as
inside, off, and *outside.*

EXAMPLE
Chian-Chu dived **off** [*not* off of] the side of the pool
into the water.

on to, onto   In the expression *on to, on* is an adverb
and *to* is a preposition. *Onto* is a preposition.

EXAMPLES
Dexter held **on to** his winter dreams.
The cat leapt gracefully **onto** the windowsill.

or, nor   Use *or* with *either;* use *nor* with *neither.*

EXAMPLES
On Tuesdays the school cafeteria offers a choice of
   either a taco salad **or** a pizza.
I wonder why **neither** Ralph Ellison **nor** Robert
   Frost was given the Nobel Prize in literature.

ought   See **had ought, hadn't ought.**

ought to of   See **of.**

reason . . . because   See **because.**

regardless   See **irregardless, regardless.**

rise, raise   The verb *rise* means "to go up" or "to get
up." Its principal parts are *rise, rising, rose,* and *risen. Rise*
never takes an object. The verb *raise* means "to cause
[something] to rise" or "to lift up." Its principal parts
are *raise, raising, raised,* and *raised. Raise* usually takes an
object.

EXAMPLES
The queen **rose** from her throne. [no object]
The movers **raised** the boxes onto their shoulders.
   [*Boxes* is the object of *raised.*]

should of   See **of.**

sit, set   The verb *sit* means "to rest in an upright,
seated position." Its principal parts are *sit, sitting, sat,*
and *sat. Sit* seldom takes an object. The verb *set* means
"to put [something] in a place." Its principal parts are
set, setting, set, and *set. Set* usually takes an object.

EXAMPLES
The raven **sat** on the bust of Pallas above the door.
   [no object]
Eben **set** the jug down. [*Jug* is the object of *set.*]

some, somewhat   In formal situations, use *somewhat* instead of *some* to mean "to some extent."

EXAMPLE
My grades have improved **somewhat** [*not* some].

sort(s)   See **kind(s), sort(s), type(s)** and **kind of
a(n), sort of a(n).**

sort of   See **kind of, sort of.**

take   See **bring, take.**

teach   See **learn, teach.**

than, then   *Than* is a conjunction used in comparisons. *Then* is an adverb meaning "at that time" or
"next."

EXAMPLES
Tyrone is more studious **than** I am.
First, mix the wet ingredients; **then,** add the flour
   and other dry ingredients.

that   See **who, which, that.**

their, there, they're   *Their* is a possessive form of
they. As an adverb, *there* means "at that place." *There*
can also be used to begin a sentence. *They're* is the
contraction of *they are.*

EXAMPLES
The performers are studying **their** lines.
I will be **there** after rehearsal. [adverb]
There will be four acts in the play. [expletive]
They're performing a play by Lorraine Hansberry.

theirs, there's   *Theirs* is a possessive form of the
pronoun *they. There's* is the contraction for *there is*
or *there has.*

EXAMPLES
These posters are ours; **theirs** are the ones on the
   opposite wall.
There's [there is] a biography of W.E.B. DuBois
   in the library.
There's [there has] been a change in plans.

them Do not use *them* as an adjective. Use *those.*

EXAMPLE
Those [*not* them] lines illustrate Poe's use of internal rhyme.

then See **than, then.**

this here, that there Avoid using *here* or *there* after *this* or *that.*

EXAMPLE
This [*not* this here] magazine has an article about Andrea Lee.

try and, try to Use *try to,* not *try and.*

EXAMPLE
I will **try to** [*not* try and] finish my report on John Updike.

type, type of Avoid using the noun *type* as an adjective. Add *of* after *type.*

EXAMPLE
I prefer this **type of** [*not* type] shirt.

type(s) See **kind(s), sort(s), type(s).**

ways Use *way,* not *ways,* when referring to distance.

EXAMPLE
My home in Wichita is a long **way** [*not* ways] from Tokyo, where my pen pal lives.

well See **good, well.**

when, where Avoid using *when* or *where* to begin a definition.

NONSTANDARD	A predicament is where you are in an embarrassing situation.
STANDARD	A predicament is **an embarrassing situation.**

where Avoid using *where* for *that.*

EXAMPLE
I read **that** [*not* where] the Smithsonian Institution has preserved a great many of William H. Johnson's paintings.

where . . . at See **at.**

whether See **if, whether.**

who, which, that *Who* refers to persons only. *Which* refers to things only. *That* may refer to either persons or things.

EXAMPLES
Wasn't Beethoven the composer **who** [*or* that] continued to write music after he lost his hearing?
First editions of Poe's first book, **which** is titled *Tamerlane and Other Poems,* are worth thousands of dollars.
Is this the only essay **that** James Baldwin wrote?
I've never met or even seen the person **that** delivers our newspaper each morning.

who's, whose *Who's* is the contraction of *who is* or *who has.* *Whose* is the possessive form of *who.*

EXAMPLES
Who's [who is] going to portray the Navajo detective in the play?
Who's [who has] been using my computer?
Whose artwork is this?

would of See **of.**

your, you're *Your* is a possessive form of *you.* *You're* is the contraction of *you are.*

EXAMPLES
Is this **your** book?
I hope **you're** able to come to my graduation.

GLOSSARY

The glossary that follows is an alphabetical list of words found in the selections in this book. Use this glossary just as you use a dictionary—to find out the meanings of unfamiliar words. (Some technical, foreign, or more obscure words in this book are not listed here but are defined instead in the footnotes and sidenotes that accompany selections.) Many words in the English language have more than one meaning. This glossary gives the meanings that apply to the words as they are used in the selections in this book. Words closely related in form and meaning are usually listed together in one entry (*irk* and *irksome*); usually the definition is given for the first form only.

The following abbreviations are used:

adj.: adjective	*n.:* noun	*v.:* verb
adv.: adverb	*pl.:* plural form	

Unless a word is very simple to pronounce, its pronunciation is given in parentheses. A guide to the pronunciation symbols appears at the bottom of page 1259.

For more information about the words in this glossary, or about words not listed here, consult a dictionary.

abate (ə·bāt') *v.:* to lessen.

abdicate (ab'di·kāt') *v.:* to give up responsibility for.

abhor (ab·hôr') *v.:* to scorn; hate; disdain.

abominable (ə·bäm'ə·nə·bəl) *adj.:* disgusting; loathsome.

abrasion (ə·brā'zhən) *n.:* scrape.

abstinence (ab'stə·nəns) *n.:* staying away.

abyss (ə·bis') *n.:* gulf or void too deep for measurement.

acquiesce (ak'wē·es') *v.:* to agree or accept quietly.

acrid (ak'rid) *adj.:* bitter; irritating.

acrimonious (ak'ri·mō'nē·əs) *adj.:* bitter; harsh. —**acrimoniously** *adv.*

acute (ə·kyoot') *adj.:* keen; sharp.

admonish (ad·män'ish) *v.:* to warn mildly. —**admonishing** *v.* used as *adj.*

adversary (ad'vər·ser'ē) *n.:* opponent.

affected (a·fekt'id) *adj.:* put on for show.

affliction (ə·flik'shən) *n.:* pain; hardship.

affluent (af'loo·ənt) *adj.:* rich. —*adj.* used as *n.:* well-to-do people.

afford (ə·fôrd') *v.:* to give; provide. —**afforded** *v.* used as *adj.*

agitated (aj'i·tāt'id) *adj.:* anxious; frantic.

alacrity (ə·lak'rə·tē) *n.:* promptness in responding; eagerness.

allay (a·lā') *v.:* to lessen; relieve.

alleviate (ə·lē'vē·āt') *v.:* to relieve; reduce.

alliance (ə·lī'əns) *n.:* close association for a common objective.

ally (al'ī) *n.:* supporter; friend.

ambiguous (am·big'yoo·əs) *adj.:* unclear; not certain. —**ambiguousness** *n.*

amble (am'bəl) *n.:* leisurely pace.

amiable (ā'mē·ə·bəl) *adj.:* agreeable; likable.

anarchy (an'ər·kē) *n.:* complete disorder.

ancestral (an·ses'trəl) *adj.:* inherited.

anguish (aŋ'gwish) *n.:* pain and suffering; heartache.

anonymity (an'ə·nim'ə·tē) *n.:* the state of being unnamed or not identified.

antagonist (an·tag'ə·nist) *n.:* adversary; opponent.

antipathy (an·tip'ə·thē) *n.:* strong dislike.

apocryphal (ə·päk'rə·fəl) *adj.:* of questionable authority; false.

appalling (ə·pôl'iŋ) *adj.:* dismaying.

apparition (ap'ə·rish'ən) *n.:* unexpected sight or ghostlike figure that appears suddenly.

appease (ə·pēz') *v.:* to calm; satisfy.

appoint (ə·point') *v.:* to assign. —**appointed** *v.* used as *adj.*

appreciable (ə·prē'shə·bəl) *adj.:* measurable.

appropriate (ə·prō'prē·āt') *v.:* to take over.

arbitrary (är'bə·trer'ē) *adj.:* based on whims or individual preferences.

archaic (är·kā'ik) *adj.:* old-fashioned.

ardent (ärd''nt) *adj.:* intense; eager. —**ardently** *adv.*

arduous (är'joo·əs) *adj.:* difficult.

arrogant (ar'ə·gənt) *adj.:* proud and overly confident.

ascetic (ə·set'ik) *adj.:* severe; stern.

ascribe (ə·skrīb') *v.:* to attribute to a certain cause.

assailant (ə·sāl'ənt) *n.:* attacker.

assert (ə·surt') *v.:* to declare; claim.

assess (ə·ses') *v.:* to evaluate; to judge the value of.

atrocity (ə·träs'ə·tē) *n.:* cruelty; brutality.

attribute (ə·trib'yoot) *v.:* to believe to result from.

avarice (av'ə·ris) *n.:* greed.

aversion (ə·vur'zhən) *n.:* intense dislike.

avert (ə·vurt') *v.:* to prevent; turn away.

bedlam (bed'ləm) *n.:* place or condition of noise and confusion.

benefactor (ben'ə·fak'tər) *n.:* person who helps others.

benevolence (bə·nev'ə·ləns) *n.:* kindness.

bewitch (bē·wich') *v.:* to entice; fascinate. —**bewitching** *v.* used as *adj.*

blanch *v.:* to drain of color. —**blanched** *v.* used as *adj.*

bland *adj.:* mild. —**blandly** *adv.*

bleak (blēk) *adj.:* cheerless.

blithe (blīth) *adj.:* carefree.

brazen (brā'zən) *adj.:* bold. —**brazenness** *n.*

bustle (bus'əl) *v.:* to be busy or energetically active. —**bustling** *v.* used as *n.*

candid (kan'did) *adj.:* unbiased; fair.

cannonade (kan'ən·ād') *v.:* to fire artillery. —**cannonading** *v.* used as *n.*

caper (kā'pər) *n.:* foolish prank.

careen (kə·rēn') *v.:* to lurch sideways.

celestial (sə·les'chəl) *adj.:* divine; perfect.

censor (sen'sər) *v.:* to cut or change to remove objectionable material.

censure (sen'shər) *n.:* strong, disapproving criticism.

ceremonial (ser'ə·mō'nē·əl) *adj.:* formal.

chafe (chāf) *v.*: to become impatient.

chronological (krän′ō·läj′i·kəl) *adj.*: arranged in order of occurrence. —**chronologically** *adv.*

circumvent (sʉr′kəm·vent′) *v.*: to get the better of by craft or ingenuity.

clammy (klam′ē) *adj.*: cold and damp.

clamor (klam′ər) *n.*: loud noise; uproar.

cleft (kleft) *n.*: opening.

clientele (klī′ən·tel′) *n.*: customers; clients.

coherent (kō·hir′ənt) *adj.*: connected logically; clear; consistent.

coincide (kō′in·sīd′) *v.*: to occur at the same time.

commence (kə·mens′) *v.*: to start.

commodious (kə·mō′dē·əs) *adj.*: spacious.

communal (kə·myōōn′əl) *adj.*: belonging to an entire group or community.

complacency (kəm·plā′sən·sē) *n.*: self-satisfaction.

comply (kəm·plī′) *v.*: to obey a command; agree to a request.

comprise (kəm·prīz′) *v.*: to include.

conceive (kən·sēv′) *v.*: to think; imagine.

conception (kən·sep′shən) *n.*: idea; mental formation of ideas.

concession (kən·sesh′ən) *n.*: act of giving in.

confederate (kən·fed′ər·it) *n.*: ally; person who shares a common purpose with another.

confiscation (kän′fis·kā′shən) *n.*: seizure of property by authority.

conflagration (kän′flə·grā′shən) *n.*: huge fire.

conscientious (kän′shē·en′shəs) *adj.*: careful and honest; diligent; thorough. —**conscientiously** *adv.*

consequence (kän′si·kwens′) *n.*: result of an action.

consolation (kän′sə·lā′shən) *n.*: comfort.

console (kän′sōl′) *n.*: desklike control panel.

conspiracy (kən·spir′ə·sē) *n.*: secret plot with a harmful or illegal purpose.

constitution (kän′stə·tōō′shən) *n.*: physical condition.

constrain (kən·strān′) *v.*: to force.

consultation (kän′səl·tā′shən) *n.*: meeting to discuss or plan.

contemptuous (kən·temp′chōō·əs) *adj.*: scornful. —**contemptuously** *adv.*

contrivance (kən·trī′vəns) *n.*: scheme; plan.

conundrum (kə·nun′drəm) *n.*: riddle.

convene (kən·vēn′) *v.*: to assemble.

conviction (kən·vik′shən) *n.*: belief.

convivial (kən·viv′ē·əl) *adj.*: jovial; sociable.

copious (kō′pē·əs) *adj.*: great amounts of.

correspondence (kôr′ə·spän′dəns) *n.*: communication by letters.

countenance (koun′tə·nəns) *n.*: face.

craven (krā′vən) *adj.*: very fearful; cowardly.

crucial (krōō′shəl) *adj.*: difficult; decisive.

curry (kʉr′ē) *v.*: to groom.

debris (də·brē′) *n.*: rubble; broken pieces.

decrepit (dē·krep′it) *adj.*: run-down; worn out by age or use.

deference (def′ər·əns) *n.*: respect.

defiant (dē·fī′ənt) *adj.*: openly disobedient. —**defiantly** *adv.*: strongly resisting.

dejection (dē·jek′shən) *n.*: discouragement.

deluge (del′yōōj′) *n.*: rush; flood.

demeanor (di·mēn′ər) *n.*: behavior; conduct.

derision (di·rizh′ən) *n.*: ridicule; contempt.

discern (di·sʉrn′) *v.*: to notice; perceive. —**discernible** (di·sʉrn′ə·bəl) *adj.*

disclaimer (dis·klām′ər) *n.*: refusal of responsibility; giving up of a claim or connection.

disconsolate (dis·kän′sə·lit) *adj.*: unhappy. —**disconsolately** *adv.*

discourse (dis′kôrs′) *n.*: conversation.

discreet (di·skrēt′) *adj.*: wisely cautious.

disdain (dis·dān′) *v.*: to refuse; disapprove; scorn.

disembody (dis′im·bäd′ē) *v.*: to separate from the body. —**disembodied** *v.* used as *adj.*

disheveled (di·shev′əld) *adj.*: rumpled; messed up.

dispel (di·spel′) *v.*: to drive away. —**dispelling** *v.* used as *n.*

disperse (di·spʉrs′) *v.*: to scatter.

dispirit (di·spir′it) *v.*: to discourage. —**dispirited** *v.* used as *adj.*

dispute (di·spyōōt′) *v.*: to contest.

distraction (di·strak′shən) *n.*: mental disturbance or distress.

distraught (di·strôt′) *adj.*: troubled.

divergence (dī·vʉr′jəns) *n.*: variance; difference.

docile (däs′əl) *adj.*: passive.

doddering (däd′ər·iŋ) *adj.*: shaky; trembling from old age.

dominant (däm′ə·nənt) *adj.*: prevailing; principal.

dominion (də·min′yən) *n.*: rule.

dowry (dou′rē) *n.*: money or goods the bride brings with her in a marriage.

drily (drī′lē) *adv.*: matter-of-factly; without emotion.

drone (drōn) *n.*: monotonous hum.

dwindle (dwin′dəl) *v.*: to diminish.

edible (ed′ə·bəl) *adj.*: capable of being eaten.

effectual (e·fek′chōō·əl) *adj.*: productive; efficient.

effete (e·fēt′) *adj.*: sterile; unproductive.

elaborate (ē·lab′ə·rāt′) *v.*: to develop with great care. —**elaborately** *adv.*

elapse (ē·laps′) *v.*: to pass by; slip away.

elation (ē·lā′shən) *n.*: celebration.

eloquence (el′ə·kwəns) *n.*: well-articulated, persuasive speech.

elude (ē·lōōd′) *v.*: to escape. —**eluding** *v.* used as *adj.*

emaciate (ē·mā′shē·āt′) *v.*: to cause to be unusually thin. —**emaciated** *v.* used as *adj.*

---

fat, āpe, cär; ēven; is, bīte; gō, hôrn, look, tōōl; yōō, cure; yōō, use; oil, out; up, fʉr; get; joy; yet; chin; she; thin; then; zh, leisure; ŋ, ring; ə for *a* in *ago*, e in *agent*, i in *sanity*, o in *comply*, u in *focus*; ′ as in *battle* (bat′′l).

---

eminent (em'ə·nənt) *adj.*: well known for excellence; important; outstanding.

encumbrance (en·kum'brəns) *n.*: burden; hindrance.

engagement (en·gāj'mənt) *n.*: battle.

enmity (en'mə·tē) *n.*: hatred.

ensue (en·sōō') *v.*: to result.

enthrall (en·thrôl') *v.*: to fascinate.

entreat (en·trēt') *v.*: to ask sincerely; pray to.

epitaph (ep'ə·taf) *n.*: memorable or descriptive phrase written on a tombstone or in memory of the dead.

equivocal (ē·kwiv'ə·kəl) *adj.*: having more than one meaning.

eradicate (i·rad'i·kāt') *v.*: to eliminate.

erudite (er'yōō·dīt') *adj.*: scholarly; well informed.

ethereal (ē·thir'ē·əl) *adj.*: not earthly; spiritual.

eulogy (yōō'lə·jē) *n.*: public speech of praise.

evident (ev'ə·dənt) *adj.*: clear; obvious.

exaggeration (eg·zaj'ər·ā'·shən) *n.*: overstatement.

exalt (eg·zôlt') *v.*: to lift up.

excruciating (eks·krōō'shē·āt'iŋ) *adj.*: extreme; intense.

execration (ek'si·krā'shən) *n.*: angry word; curse.

exemplary (eg·zem'plə·rē) *adj.*: serving as a model.

expedient (ek·spē'dē·ənt) *n.*: convenience; means to an end.

expire (ek·spīr') *v.*: to die. —**expiring** *v.* used as *adj.*

explicit (eks·plis'it) *adj.*: clear; definite.

expunge (ek·spunj') *v.*: to erase; remove.

extremity (ek·strem'ə·tē) *n.*: limb of the body, especially a hand or foot. —**extremities** *n. pl.*

exuberant (eg·zōō'bər·ənt) *adj.*: intensely happy; visibly enthusiastic.

exult (eg·zult') *v.*: to rejoice greatly.

facilitate (fə·sil'ə·tāt') *v.*: to simplify.

fastidious (fas·tid'ē·əs) *adj.*: difficult to please; critical.

ferocity (fə·räs'ə·tē) *n.*: fierce cruelty.

fidelity (fə·del'ə·tē) *n.*: accuracy.

fitful (fit'fəl) *adj.*: restless. —**fitfully** *adv.*: irregularly; in stops and starts.

flippancy (flip'ən·sē) *n.*: impertinence; glibness.

florid (flôr'id) *adj.*: showy.

flourish (flur'ish) *v.*: to do well; blossom.

fraternal (frə·turn'əl) *adj.*: brotherly; friendly.

frenzy (fren'zē) *n.*: frantic behavior; wildness.

frippery (frip'ər·ē) *n.*: something showy, frivolous, or unnecessary.

frugal (frōō'gəl) *adj.*: thrifty; economical.

furrow (fur'ō) *n.*: groove in the land made by a plow.

furtive (fur'tiv) *adj.*: secret; stealthy. —**furtively** *adv.*

futile (fyōōt'l) *adj.*: useless; pointless.

gait (gāt) *n.*: way of walking; stride.

gall (gôl) *v.*: to irritate; anger.

garnish (gär'nish) *v.*: to top.

gaudy (gôd'ē) *adj.*: showy; lacking in good taste.

gaunt (gônt) *adj.*: very thin.

gesticulate (jes·tik'yōō·lāt') *v.*: to gesture, especially with the hands and arms, while speaking.

gregarious (grə·ger'ē·əs) *adj.*: sociable. —**gregariousness** *n.*

grope (grōp) *v.*: to search; fumble. —**groping** *v.* used as *adj.*

grotesque (grō·tesk') *adj.*: strange; absurd.

guffaw (gu·fô') *v.*: to burst out laughing. —**guffawing** *v.* used as *adj.*

guileless (gīl'lis) *adj.*: innocent or frank; without slyness.

gyration (jī·rā'shən) *n.*: circular movement; whirling.

habitual (hə·bich'ōō·əl) *adj.*: usual. —**habitually** *adv.* usually; by habit.

haggard (hag'ərd) *adj.*: wasted or worn in appearance.

hail *v.*: to greet.

haughty (hôt'ē) *adj.*: proud; disdainful of something or someone.

hedonism (hē'dən·iz'əm) *n.*: self-indulgent pursuit of pleasure. —**hedonistic** *adj.*

hierarchy (hī'ər·är'kē) *n.*: class system of social ranking.

hinder (hin'dər) *v.*: to thwart; impede.

humor (hyōō'mər) *v.*: to indulge.

hysteria (hi·ster'ē·ə) *n.*: uncontrolled excitement.

idealist (ī·dē'əl·ist) *n.*: one who believes in noble, though often impractical, goals; dreamer.

illumine (i·lōō'mən) *v.*: to light up.

immune (im·myōōn') *adj.*: protected.

impart (im·pärt') *v.*: to reveal.

imperative (im·per'ə·tiv) *adj.*: absolutely necessary; compulsory.

imperceptible (im'pər·sep'tə·bəl) *adj.*: not easily perceived.

impervious (im·pur'vē·əs) *adj.*: resistant; impenetrable.

impetuous (im·pech'ōō·əs) *adj.*: impulsive.

impious (im'pē·əs) *adj.*: irreverent.

implore (im·plôr') *v.*: to plead; entreat. —**imploring** *v.* used as *adj.*

imprecation (im'pri·kā'shən) *n.*: curse.

improvident (im·präv'ə·dənt) *adj.*: careless; not providing for the future.

inanimate (in·an'ə·mit) *adj.*: lifeless.

inarticulate (in'är·tik'yōō·lit) *adj.*: not understandable.

incapacitate (in'kə·pas'ə·tāt') *v.*: to disable. —**incapacitated** *v.* used as *adj.*

incendiary (in·sen'dē·er'ē) *adj.*: designed to cause fires.

incessant (in·ses'ənt) *adj.*: never stopping. —**incessantly** *adv.*

incised (in·sīzd') *adj.*: deeply marked.

inconceivable (in'kən·sēv'ə·bəl) *adj.*: unimaginable; beyond understanding.

indiscreet (in'di·skrēt') *adj.*: lack of care in speech or action.

indolent (in'də·lənt) *adj.*: lazy.

indubitable (in·dōō'bi·tə·bəl) *adj.*: that which cannot be doubted. —**indubitably** *adv.*

induce (in·dōōs') *v.*: to persuade; force; cause.

indulge (in·dulj') *v.*: to satisfy; please; humor.

inert (in·urt') *adj.*: inactive; dull.

inevitable (in·ev'i·tə·bəl) *adj.*: not avoidable.

infallible (in·fal'ə·bəl) *adj.*: sure; never wrong.

infirm (in·furm') *adj.*: physically weak.

ingenious (in·jēn′yəs) *adj.:* clever; original.

inherent (in·hir′ənt) *adj.:* inborn.

iniquity (i·nik′wi·tē) *n.:* wickedness.

inordinate (in·ôr′də·nit) *adj.:* excessive.

inscrutable (in·skrōōt′ə·bəl) *adj.:* mysterious.

insidious (in·sid′ē·əs) *adj.:* sly; sneaky.

insinuate (in·sin′yōō·āt′) *v.:* to suggest. —**insinuatingly** *adv.*

insipid (in·sip′id) *adj.:* bland; without flavor.

insolent (in′sə·lənt) *adj.:* arrogant.

insurrection (in′sə·rek′shən) *n.:* rebellion; revolt.

intangible (in·tan′jə·bəl) *adj.:* difficult to define; vague.

integrate (in′tə·grāt′) *v.:* to unify.

integrity (in·teg′rə·tē) *n.:* sound moral principles; honesty.

intent (in·tent′) *adj.:* purposeful.

interject (in′tər·jekt′) *v.:* to interrupt with; insert.

interloper (in′tər·lō′pər) *n.:* intruder; meddler.

interminable (in·tur′mi·nə·bəl) *adj.:* endless.

intermittent (in′tər·mit′nt) *adj.:* pausing occasionally.

interpose (in′tər·pōz′) *v.:* to put forth in order to intervene.

intersperse (in′tər·spurs′) *v.:* to place at intervals.

intimate (in′tə·māt′) *v.:* to state indirectly; hint.

intricate (in′tri·kit) *adj.:* complicated.

intrigue (in′trēg′) *n.:* scheming.

intuitive (in·tōō′i·tiv) *adj.:* known without conscious reasoning. —**intuitively** *adv.*

inviolate (in·vī′ə·lit) *adj.:* uncorrupted; safe.

irk (urk) *v.:* to annoy; irritate. —**irksome** *adj.* —**irked** *v.* used as *adj.*

itinerant (ī·tin′ər·ənt) *adj.:* traveling.

jaunty (jônt′ē) *adj.:* fashionable; confident; carefree.

jilt *v.:* to reject (as a lover).

jocular (jäk′yōō·lər) *adj.:* joking; comical.

judicious (jōō·dish′əs) *adj.:* cautious; wise.

laborious (lə·bôr′ē·əs) *adj.:* difficult; involving much hard work.

labyrinth (lab′ə·rinth′) *n.:* puzzling path.

lamentable (lam′ən·tə·bəl) *adj.:* regrettable; distressing.

languid (laŋ′gwid) *adj.:* weak, as from exhaustion.

legacy (leg′ə·sē) *n.:* inheritance.

list *v.:* to tilt.

loiter (loit′ər) *v.:* to spend time; hang around.

lore (lôr) *n.:* traditional knowledge or teachings.

lucidity (lōō·sid′i·tē) *n.:* clarity; rationality.

ludicrous (lōō′di·krəs) *adj.:* laughable; absurd.

lurk (lurk) *v.:* to hide unnoticed.

luxuriant (lug·zhoor′ē·ənt) *adj.:* rich; abundant.

machination (mak′ə·nā′shən) *n.:* plot; crafty scheme.

magnanimity (mag′nə·nim′ə·tē) *n.:* nobility of spirit.

malicious (mə·lish′əs) *adj.:* intentionally hurtful.

malign (mə·līn′) *adj.:* harmful; evil.

malleable (mal′ē·ə·bəl) *adj.:* capable of being shaped.

malodorous (mal·ō′dər·əs) *adj.:* bad smelling.

manifest (man′ə·fest′) *adj.:* plain; clear.

manifold (man′ə·fōld′) *adj.:* many and different.

margin (mär′jən) *n.:* extra amount.

marshal (mär′shəl) *v.:* to lead; guide. —**marshaling** *v.* used as *adj.*

martial (mär′shəl) *adj.:* warlike.

meager (mē′gər) *adj.:* poor; inadequate.

meditative (med′ə·tāt′iv) *adj.:* deeply thoughtful; reflective.

medium (mē′dē·əm) *n.:* means of expressing art.

melancholy (mel′ən·käl′ē) *adj.:* sad; sorrowful.

mesmerize (mez′mər·īz′) *v.:* to hypnotize. —**mesmerizing** *v.* used as *adj.*

mincing (mins′iŋ) *adj.:* affectedly dainty. —**mincingly** *adv.*

mirth (murth) *n.:* joyfulness.

misgiving (mis′giv′iŋ) *n.:* doubt; worry.

misnomer (mis·nō′mər) *n.:* wrong term or name.

moderate (mäd′ər·it) *adj.:* gentle.

monologue (män′ə·lôg′) *n.:* speech given by one person.

morbid (môr′bid) *adj.:* diseased; unhealthy.

morose (mə·rōs′) *adj.:* gloomy.

mortal (môr′təl) *adj.:* life-threatening; causing death.

mortar (môrt′ər) *n.:* cannon used to fire explosive shells.

municipal (myōō·nis′ə·pəl) *adj.:* belonging to a city or town.

mutual (myōō′chōō·əl) *adj.:* shared.

myriad (mir′ē·əd) *adj.:* countless.

nape (nāp) *n.:* back of the neck.

nauseate (nô′zhē·āt′) *v.:* to cause to feel sickness or discomfort in the stomach. —**nauseated** *v.* used as *adj.*

negotiate (ni·gō′shē·āt′) *v.:* to make a bargain; come to an agreement.

nether (neth′ər) *adj.:* lower.

nimbus (nim′bəs) *n.:* aura; halo.

nomadic (nō·mad′ik) *adj.:* wandering.

nominal (näm′ə·nəl) *adj.:* very small.

nostalgia (näs·tal′jə) *n.:* longing.

nuptial (nup′shəl) *adj.:* related to weddings or marriage.

oblique (ō·blēk′) *adj.:* slanted. —**obliquely** *adv.*

obliterate (ə·blit′ər·āt′) *v.:* to destroy.

obscure (əb·skyoor′) *v.:* to conceal. —**obscurity** *n.*

obsequious (əb·sē′kwē·əs) *adj.:* overly obedient; submissive.

obsess (əb·ses′) *v.:* to preoccupy; haunt. —**obsessed** *v.* used as *adj.*

obstinate (äb′stə·nət) *adj.:* stubborn.

obstruction (əb·struk′shən) *n.:* blockage; hindrance.

occult (ə·kult′) *adj.:* hidden.

ominous (äm′ə·nəs) *adj.:* sinister; dangerous; foreboding.

omnipotent (äm·nip′ə·tənt) *adj.:* all-powerful.

omniscient (äm·nish′ənt) *adj.:* all-knowing.

opaque (ō·pāk′) *adj.:* not transparent; not letting light pass through.

oppression (ə·presh′ən) *n.:* feeling of being tyrannized.

opulent (äp′yōō·lənt) *adj.:* abundant; plentiful.

oscillation (äs′ə·lā′shən) *n.:* regular back-and-forth movement.

ostentation (äs′tən·tā′shən) *n.:* conspicuous display. —**ostentatious** *adj.*

overcast (ō′vər·kast′) *adj.:* cloudy; gloomy.

overture (ō′vər·chər) *n.:* approach; offer.

pallid (pal′id) *adj.*: pale.

palpable (pal′pə·bəl) *adj.*: obvious; perceivable.

pandemonium (pan′də·mō′nē·əm) *n.*: wild confusion.

pauper (pô′pər) *n.*: extremely poor person.

pendulum (pen′dyōō·ləm) *n.*: freely swinging weight suspended from a fixed point to regulate a clock's movement.

penitent (pen′i·tənt) *adj.*: sorry for doing wrong.

pensive (pen′siv) *adj.*: thinking deeply or seriously. —**pensively** *adv.*

perennial (pər·en′ē·əl) *adj.*: recurring yearly.

perilous (per′ə·ləs) *adj.*: dangerous.

permeate (pʉr′mē·āt′) *v.*: to spread through and affect every part of.

perpetual (pər·pech′ōō·əl) *adj.*: constant; unchanging.

perpetuity (pʉr′pə·tōō′ə·tē) *n.*: eternity.

perseverance (pʉr′sə·vir′əns) *n.*: persistence.

persistent (pər·sist′ənt) *adj.*: continuing.

pertinent (pʉr′tə·nənt) *adj.*: to the point; applying to the situation.

perturbation (pʉr′tər·bā′shən) *n.*: feeling of alarm or agitation.

pervade (pər·vād′) *v.*: to spread throughout.

pervert (pər·vʉrt′) *v.*: to misdirect; corrupt.

petulance (pech′ə·ləns) *n.*: irritability; impatience.

philanthropies (fə·lan′thrə·pēz) *n. pl.*: charitable gifts.

pious (pī′əs) *adj.*: devoted to one's religion.

pivotal (piv′ə·təl) *adj.*: central; acting as a point around which other things turn.

placid (plas′id) *adj.*: calm; quiet.

plague (plāg) *v.*: to annoy.

plaintive (plān′tiv) *adj.*: expressing sadness.

plausibility (plô′zə·bil′i·tē) *n.*: believability.

plunder (plun′dər) *n.*: goods seized, especially during wartime.

poignant (poin′yənt) *adj.*: emotionally moving.

populous (päp′yōō·ləs) *adj.*: crowded with people.

portend (pôr·tend′) *v.*: to signify.

posterity (päs·ter′ə·tē) *n.*: generations to come.

potency (pōt′'n·sē) *n.*: strength; power.

precedence (pres′ə·dəns) *n.*: order.

précis (prā·sē′) *n.*: summary.

predominate (prē·däm′ə·nāt′) *v.*: to have influence over. —**predominating** *v.* used as *adj.*

preeminent (prē·em′ə·nənt) *adj.*: above all else. —**preeminently** *adv.*

preposterous (prē·päs′tər·əs) *adj.*: ridiculous.

prestigious (pres·tij′əs) *adj.*: impressive; having an excellent reputation.

pretense (prē·tens′) *n.*: false claim.

procure (prō·kyoor′) *v.*: to gain; obtain; acquire.

prodigal (präd′i·gəl) *adj.*: extremely abundant.

prodigious (prō·dij′əs) *adj.*: of great size and power.

prodigy (präd′ə·jē) *n.*: extremely gifted person.

profane (prō·fān′) *adj.*: irreverent.

profound (prō·found′) *adj.*: deep. —**profoundly** *adv.*

profundity (prō·fun′də·tē) *n.*: intellectual depth.

profuse (prō·fyōōs′) *adj.*: abundant. —**profusely** *adv.*: in great quantities.

propagate (präp′ə·gāt′) *v.*: to transmit; spread.

proportionate (prō·pôr′shən·it) *adj.*: having a correct relationship between parts; balanced.

prostrate (präs′trāt′) *adj.*: lying flat on the ground.

protrude (prō·trōōd′) *v.*: to stick out. —**protruding** *v.* used as *adj.*

provisional (prō·vizh′ə·nəl) *adj.*: temporary; for the time being.

provoke (prō·vōk′) *v.*: to enrage; anger.

prudent (prōōd′'nt) *adj.*: well thought out; cautious.

pulverize (pul′vər·īz′) *v.*: to crush; destroy.

radiation (rā′dē·ā′shən) *n.*: pattern; arrangement.

rakish (rāk′ish) *adj.*: dashing; jaunty. —**rakishly** *adv.*

rancor (raŋ′kər) *n.*: anger.

raucous (rô′kəs) *adj.*: loud; boisterous.

ravage (rav′ij) *n.*: act of violent destruction.

ravenous (rav′ə·nəs) *adj.*: very eager; hungry.

realm (relm) *n.*: kingdom.

recede (ri·sēd′) *v.*: to become more distant and indistinct.

recoil (ri·koil′) *v.*: to shrink away; draw back.

recollect (rek′ə·lekt′) *v.*: to remember.

reconcile (rek′ən·sīl′) *v.*: to make peace.

rectitude (rek′tə·tōōd′) *n.*: correctness.

reflective (ri·flek′tiv) *adj.*: thoughtful; contemplative.

reiterate (rē·it′ə·rāt′) *v.*: to repeat.

rejoinder (ri·join′dər) *n.*: answer.

relent (ri·lent′) *v.*: to soften; to diminish in intensity.

relinquish (ri·liŋ′kwish) *v.*: to give up.

rend *v.*: to rip apart violently. —**rending** *v.* used as *n.*

render (ren′dər) *v.*: to make.

rendezvous (rän′dā·vōō′) *n.*: meeting place. —*adj.*: meeting.

renounce (ri·nouns′) *v.*: to give up.

reprobate (rep′rə·bāt′) *n.*: person without any sense of duty or decency.

reprove (ri·prōōv′) *v.*: to reprimand.

reserve (ri·zʉrv′) *n.*: self-restraint.

resignation (rez′ig·nā′shən) *n.*: acquiescence; reluctant acceptance.

resolute (rez′ə·lōōt′) *adj.*: determined.

resolve (ri·zälv′) *v.*: to make a decision; determine.

retort (ri·tôrt′) *n.*: quick answer.

retraction (ri·trak′shən) *n.*: withdrawal.

revel (rev′əl) *v.*: to take pleasure.

revelation (rev′ə·lā′shən) *n.*: disclosure; something made known.

reverential (rev′ə·ren′shəl) *adj.*: deeply respectful.

reverie (rev′ər·ē) *n.*: daydream; fantasy; thought; musing.

rue (rōō) *v.*: to regret.

ruse (rōōz) *n.*: trick; deception.

sacrilege (sak′rə·lij) *n.*: violation of something sacred.

sagacious (sə·gā′shəs) *adj.*: wise; keenly perceptive.

sappy (sap′ē) *adj.*: foolish.

sarcastic (sär·kas′tik) *adj.*: scornful; mocking.

sate (sāt) *v.*: to satisfy.

saturated (sach′ə·rāt′id) *adj.*: completely soaked.

saucy (sô′sē) *adj.*: sassy; impertinent. —**saucily** *adv.*

savory (sā′vər·ē) *adj.*: appetizing; agreeable.

scour (skour) *v.*: to roam about searching.

scrupulous (skrōo′pyə·ləs) *adj.*: careful; painstaking.

scrutinize (skrōot′'n·īz′) *v.*: to carefully observe. —**scrutinizing** *v.* used as *adj.*

sedate (si·dāt′) *adj.*: calm and composed.

semblance (sem′bləns) *n.*: outward appearance; mere empty show; pretense.

seminary (sem′ə·ner′ē) *n.*: school for training ministers.

sensor (sen′sər) *n.*: detecting device.

sentinel (sen′ti·nəl) *n.*: guard; sentry.

serene (sə·rēn′) *adj.*: calm. —**serenely** *adv.*

sibling (sib′liŋ) *n.*: brother or sister.

similitude (sə·mil′ə·tōod′) *n.*: likeness.

simultaneous (sī′məl·tā′nē·əs) *adj.*: at the same time. —**simultaneously** *adv.*

singular (siŋ′gyə·lər) *adj.*: remarkable.

slough (sluf) *n.*: outer layer of snake's skin, shed periodically.

sobriety (sə·brī′ə·tē) *n.*: state or quality of being sober.

sojourn (sō′jurn) *n.*: short stay.

solace (säl′is) *v.*: to comfort.

solemn (säl′əm) *adj.*: serious. —**solemnity** *n.*

solidity (sə·lid′ə·tē) *n.*: firmness; solidness.

somber (säm′bər) *adj.*: gloomy; dark.

specious (spē′shəs) *adj.*: seemingly sound, but not really so.

spurn (spurn) *v.*: to reject with contempt.

squeamish (skwēm′ish) *adj.*: easily offended.

stolid (stäl′id) *adj.*: showing no emotion. —**stolidity** *n.*

striking (strī′kiŋ) *adj.*: impressive; attractive.

stupor (stōo′pər) *n.*: state of mental dullness; loss of the senses.

sublime (sə·blīm′) *adj.*: awe-inspiring.

subsequent (sub′si·kwənt) *adj.*: following.

subside (səb·sīd′) *v.*: to settle down.

subsist (səb·sist′) *v.*: to stay alive. —**subsisting** *v.* used as *adj.*

successive (sək·ses′iv) *adj.*: consecutive.

sultry (sul′trē) *adj.*: humid and still.

sundry (sun′drē) *adj.*: some.

superficial (sōo′pər·fish′əl) *adj.*: obvious; shallow.

superfluous (sə·pur′flōo·əs) *adj.*: unnecessary.

supplication (sup′lə·kā′shən) *n.*: earnest plea.

suppress (sə·pres′) *v.*: to restrain; hold back.

surmise (sər·mīz′) *n.*: guess.

sustain (sə·stān′) *v.*: to prolong. —**sustained** *v.* used as *adj.*

symmetrical (si·me′tri·kəl) *adj.*: equally balanced.

taboo (tə·bōo′) *n.*: something that is forbidden.

tacit (tas′it) *adj.*: implied but not expressed openly.

tactful (takt′fəl) *adj.*: skilled in saying the right thing.

tactile (tak′təl) *adj.*: able to be perceived by touch.

taut (tôt) *adj.*: tense; rigid.

tedious (tē′dē·əs) *adj.*: tiring; dreary.

temple (tem′pəl) *n.*: side of the forehead, just above and in front of each ear.

temporal (tem′pə·rəl) *adj.*: worldly.

tenuous (ten′yōo·əs) *adj.*: slight; insubstantial; not firm.

tepid (tep′id) *adj.*: lukewarm.

theologian (thē′ə·lō′jən) *n.*: scholar of religious doctrine.

torpor (tôr′pər) *n.*: inactive period.

tout (tout) *v.*: to praise highly.

traditional (trə·dish′ə·nel) *adj.*: established; customary.

tranquil (tran′kwil) *adj.*: calm; quiet.

transcendent (tran·sen′dənt) *adj.*: excelling; surpassing.

transcribe (tran·skrīb′) *v.*: to write down.

transient (tran′shənt) *adj.*: temporary; passing.

translucent (trans·lōo′sənt) *adj.*: allowing light to pass through.

tread (tred) *n.*: stepping.

trepidation (trep′ə·dā′shən) *n.*: anxious uncertainty.

tumultuous (tōo·mul′chōo·əs) *adj.*: stormy; turbulent.

turbulence (tur′byōo·ləns) *n.*: wild disorder.

tyranny (tir′ə·nē) *n.*: oppression.

ubiquitous (yōo·bik′wə·təs) *adj.*: everywhere at the same time.

ultimatum (ul′tə·māt′əm) *n.*: last offer; final proposition.

undulation (un′dyōo·lā′shən) *n.*: wavelike motion.

unobtrusive (un·əb·trōo′siv) *adj.*: inconspicuous; quiet. —**unobtrusively** *adv.*

unseemly (un·sēm′lē) *adj.*: improper.

upbraid (up·brād′) *v.*: to criticize severely.

valance (val′əns) *n.*: short decorative drapery.

valor (val′ər) *n.*: great courage.

vanity (van′ə·tē) *n.*: excessive pride.

vehement (vē′ə·mənt) *adj.*: emphatic. —**vehemently** *adv.*

venerable (ven′ər·ə·bəl) *adj.*: respected; esteemed for age or distinguished character.

vengeful (venj′fəl) *adj.*: intent on revenge.

venture (ven′chər) *v.*: to dare or risk going.

veritable (ver′i·tə·bəl) *adj.*: genuine; true.

vibrant (vī′brənt) *adj.*: full of energy.

vigilant (vij′ə·lənt) *adj.* used as *n.*: someone who is watchful.

vigor (vig′ər) *n.*: intense strength; vitality.

vindicate (vin′də·kāt′) *v.*: to prove correct. —**vindicated** *v.* used as *adj.*

virulent (vir′yōo·lənt) *adj.*: full of hate; venomous.

vista (vis′tə) *n.*: view.

vital (vīt′'l) *adj.*: filled with life.

vivacious (vī·vā′shəs) *adj.*: cheerful; lively.

void (void) *adj.*: empty.

volition (vō·lish′ən) *n.*: will.

volley (väl′ē) *n.*: firing of many shots at once.

vouch (vouch) *v.*: to guarantee.

vulnerability (vul′nər·ə·bil′ə·tē) *n.*: state of being open to attack.

wariness (wer′ē·nis) *n.*: caution; carefulness.

wearisome (wir′i·səm) *adj.*: fatiguing; exhausting.

wistfulness (wist′fəl·nis) *n.*: vague longing.

wither (with′ər) *v.*: to dry up; weaken.

wrought (rôt) *v.*: created; made.

ACKNOWLEDGMENTS

For permission to reprint copyrighted material, grateful acknowledgment is made to the following sources:

Agencia Literaria Carmen Balcells, S.A.: "Plenos Poderes" by Pablo Neruda. Copyright © 1958, 1959, 1961, 1962, 1964, 1967 by Pablo Neruda.

The American Scholar: From "An American Childhood in the Dominican Republic" by Julia Alvarez from *The American Scholar*, vol. 56, no. 1, Winter 1987. Copyright © 1986 by Julia Alvarez.

Andrews McMeel Universal: "Coyote Finishes His Work" from *Giving Birth to Thunder, Sleeping with His Daughter* by Barry Holstun Lopez. Copyright © 1977 by Barry Holstun Lopez. All rights reserved.

Arte Público Press: From *Silent Dancing* by Judith Ortiz Cofer. Copyright © 1990 by Judith Ortiz Cofer. Published by Arte Público Press—University of Houston, 1990. "The Latin Deli: An Ars Poetica" by Judith Ortiz Cofer from *The Americas Review*, vol. 19, no. 1. Copyright © 1991 by Judith Ortiz Cofer. Published by Arte Público Press—University of Houston, 1991. "Now and Then, America" from *Borders* by Pat Mora. Copyright © 1986 by Pat Mora. Published by Arte Público Press—University of Houston, 1986.

Ken Barnes: Definition of "facemail," compiled and edited by Ken Barnes from "The Microsoft Lexicon" from *Jeeem's Cinepad*. Available at http://www.cinepad.com/mslex.htm.

Elizabeth Barnett, Literary Executor: "Recuerdo" from *Collected Poems* by Edna St. Vincent Millay. Copyright © 1922, 1928, 1935, 1950 by Edna St. Vincent Millay and Norma Millay Ellis. Published by HarperCollins.

Beacon Press: "Autobiographical Notes" from *Notes of a Native Son* by James Baldwin. Copyright © 1955 and renewed © 1983 by James Baldwin.

Belles Lettres: Quote by Rita Dove from "Judith Pierce Rosenberg Interviews Our New Poet Laureate" from *Belles Lettres*, Winter 1993/94.

Susan Bergholz Literary Services, New York: "Daughter of Invention" from *How the Garcia Girls Lost Their Accents* by Julia Alvarez. Copyright © 1991 by Julia Alvarez. Published by Plume, a division of Penguin USA Inc. Originally published in hardcover by Algonquin Books of Chapel Hill. All rights reserved. "Straw into Gold" by Sandra Cisneros. Copyright © 1987 by Sandra Cisneros. First published in *The Texas Observer*, September 1987. All rights reserved.

Brandt & Brandt Literary Agents: From "Qualified Homage to Thoreau" by Wallace Stegner from *Heaven Is Under Our Feet*, edited by Don Henley and Dave Marsh. Copyright © 1991 by The Isis Fund.

Gwendolyn Brooks: "Exhaust the little moment," "The Explorer," and "of De Witt Williams on his way to Lincoln Cemetery" from *Blacks* by Gwendolyn Brooks. Copyright © 1991 by Gwendolyn Brooks. Published by Third World Press, Chicago, 60619, 1991.

Grace Cavalieri: From "Rita Dove: An Interview" by Grace Cavalieri from *American Poetry Review*, March/April 1995. Copyright © 1995 by Grace Cavalieri.

Joan Chatfield-Taylor: From "Cosmo Talks to Amy Tan" by Joan Chatfield-Taylor from *Cosmopolitan*, November 1989, pages 178–180. Copyright © 1989 by Joan Chatfield-Taylor.

Lucha Corpi and Catherine Rodríguez-Nieto: "Emily Dickinson" from *Palabras de Mediodía/Noon Words* by Lucha Corpi, translated by Catherine Rodríguez-Nieto. Copyright © 1980 by Lucha Corpi; translation copyright © 1980 by Catherine Rodríguez-Nieto. Published by El Fuego de Aztlán Publications, Berkeley, CA, 1980.

Curbstone Press: "Who Understands Me but Me" from *What's Happening* by Jimmy Santiago Baca. Copyright © 1982 by Jimmy Santiago Baca. Distributed by Consortium.

Delacorte Press/Seymour Lawrence, a division of Bantam Doubleday Dell Publishing Group, Inc.: From *Sextet: T. S. Eliot, Truman Capote and Others* by John Malcolm Brinnin. Copyright © 1981 by John Malcolm Brinnin.

Doubleday, a division of Random House, Inc.: From *The Power of Myth* by Joseph Campbell with Bill Moyers. Copyright © 1988 by Apostrophe S Productions, Inc., and Alfred van der Marck Editions. From "Drowning with Others" by James Dickey from *Self-Interviews*, recorded and edited by Barbara and James Reiss. Published by Doubleday, New York, 1970. From *The Theatre of the Absurd* by Martin Esslin. Copyright © 1961 by Martin Esslin. From "Preface" from *The Open Boat: Poems from Asian America*, edited and with an introduction by Garrett Hongo. Copyright © 1993 by Garrett Hongo. "Elegy for Jane," "Night Journey," and "Open House" from *The Collected Poems of Theodore Roethke* by Theodore Roethke. Copyright 1940, 1941, 1950 by Theodore Roethke.

Rita Dove: "The Satisfaction Coal Company" from *Selected Poems* by Rita Dove. Copyright © 1993 by Rita Dove. Quote by Rita Dove from *Washington Post*, April 17, 1987. Copyright © 1987 by Rita Dove.

Dutton Signet, a division of Penguin Books USA Inc.: "Borges and Myself" from *The Aleph and Other Stories* by Jorge Luis Borges, translated by Norman Thomas di Giovanni. Translation copyright © 1968, 1969, 1970 by Emece Editores, S.A., and Norman Thomas di Giovanni.

Faber and Faber Ltd.: From *The Criterion*, vol. IX, by T. S. Eliot. Copyright © 1967 by Faber and Faber Ltd.

Far Corner Books: "Trying to Name What Doesn't Change" from *Words Under the Words: Selected Poems* by Naomi Shihab Nye. Copyright © 1995 by Naomi Shihab Nye. Published by Far Corner Books, Portland, OR.

Farrar, Straus & Giroux, Inc.: "The Fish" (and excerpts) from *The Complete Poems 1927–1979* by Elizabeth Bishop. Copyright © 1979, 1983 by Alice Helen Methfessel. From "Introduction" and "The Death of the Ball Turret Gunner" from *The Complete Poems* by Randall Jarrell. Copyright © 1969 by Mrs. Randall Jarrell. "For the Union Dead" (and excerpts) from *For the Union Dead* by Robert Lowell. Copyright © 1959 by Robert Lowell; copyright renewed © 1987 by Caroline Lowell, Harriet Lowell, and Sheridan Lowell. From "Memories of West Street and Lepke" from *Life Studies* by Robert Lowell. Copyright © 1959 by Robert Lowell; copyright renewed © 1987 by Caroline Lowell, Sheridan Lowell, and Harriet Lowell. "The Magic Barrel" from *The Magic Barrel* by Bernard Malamud. Copyright © 1950, 1958 and renewed © 1977, 1986 by Bernard Malamud. From "The Murdered Albatross" from *Passions and Impressions* by Pablo Neruda, translated by Margaret Sayers Peden. Translation copyright © 1983 by Farrar, Straus, & Giroux, Inc. From "The Fiction Writer and His Country," from "Some Aspects of the Grotesque in Southern Fiction," and from "Writing Short Stories" from *Mystery and Manners* by Flannery O'Connor, edited by Sally and Robert Fitzgerald. Copyright © 1969 by the Estate of Mary Flannery O'Connor. From *The Habit of Being: Letters of Flannery O'Connor* by Flannery O'Connor, edited by Sally Fitzgerald. Copyright © 1979 by Regina O'Connor. From *The Nobel Lecture* by Isaac Bashevis Singer. Copyright © 1978 by The Nobel Foundation. Yiddish text copyright © 1978 by Isaac Bashevis Singer. "Sea Canes" from *Sea Grapes* by Derek Walcott. Copyright © 1976 by Derek Walcott.

Gerard Flynn: From *Sor Juana Inés de la Cruz* by Gerard Flynn. Copyright © 1971 by Twayne Publishers, Inc. Published in *Twayne's World Authors Series*, edited by John P. Dyson.

Fondo de Cultura Económica: "World, in hounding me, what do you gain?" by Sor Juana Inés de la Cruz from *Obras completas*, edited by Alfonso Méndez Plancarte. Copyright 1952 and © 1955 by Fondo de Cultura Económica.

The Estate of Robert Frost: Quote by Robert Frost from "Robert Frost Relieves His Mind," interviewed by Rose C. Feld, from *The New York Times Book Review*, October 21, 1923. Copyright 1923 by Robert Frost.

Fulcrum Publishing: "The Sky Tree" by

Joseph Bruchac from *Keepers of Life: Discovering Plants Through Native American Stories and Earth Activities for Children* by Michael J. Caduto and Joseph Bruchac. Copyright © 1994 by Fulcrum Publishing.

Gale Research, Inc.: Quote by Judith Ortiz Cofer from *Contemporary Authors, New Revision Series*, vol. 32, edited by James G. Lesniak. Copyright © 1991 by Gale Research, Inc.

Tess Gallagher: "Everything Stuck to Him" (also published as "Distance") from *Fires: Essays, Poems, Stories* by Raymond Carver. Copyright © 1975 by Raymond Carver; copyright © 1989 by Vintage Books; copyright renewed © 1991 by Tess Gallagher.

Paul Gitlin, Administrator of the Estate of Thomas Wolfe: "His Father's Earth" from *The Web and the Rock* by Thomas Wolfe. Copyright 1937, 1938, 1939 by Maxwell Perkins as Executor; copyright renewed © 1967 by Paul Gitlin, C.T.A., Administrator of the Estate of Thomas Wolfe.

Donald J. Greiner: Quote by Donald J. Greiner from *Dictionary of Literary Biography, Volume 143: American Novelists Since World War II, Third Series*, edited by James R. Giles and Wanda H. Giles. Published by Gale Research, Inc., 1994.

GRM Associates, Inc., Agents for the Estate of Ida M. Cullen: "Incident" and "Tableau" (and excerpts) from *Color* by Countee Cullen. Copyright © 1925 by Harper & Brothers; copyright renewed © 1953 by Ida M. Cullen.

Grosset & Dunlap, Inc., a division of Penguin Putnam Inc.: "Knoxville: Summer 1915" from *A Death in the Family* by James Agee. Copyright © 1957 by The James Agee Trust; copyright © renewed 1985 by Mia Agee.

Grove/Atlantic, Inc.: "Full Powers" from *A New Decade (Poems: 1958–1967)* by Pablo Neruda, translated by Alastair Reid. English translation copyright © 1969 by Alastair Reid. "The Journey" from *Dream Work* by Mary Oliver. Copyright © 1986 by Mary Oliver.

Harcourt Brace & Company: "The Life You Save May Be Your Own" from *A Good Man Is Hard to Find and Other Stories* by Flannery O'Connor. Copyright 1953 by Flannery O'Connor; copyright renewed © 1981 by Regina O'Connor. "The Jilting of Granny Weatherall" and excerpt from *Flowering Judas and Other Stories* by Katherine Anne Porter. Copyright 1930 and renewed © 1958 by Katherine Anne Porter. From "In Search of Our Mothers' Gardens" from *In Search of Our Mothers' Gardens: Womanist Prose* by Alice Walker. Copyright © 1974 by Alice Walker. "Women" (as it appears in "In Search of Our Mothers' Gardens") from *Revolutionary Petunias & Other Poems* by Alice Walker. Copyright © 1970 by Alice Walker. "A Worn Path" from *A Curtain of Green and Other Stories* by Eudora Welty. Copyright 1941 and renewed © 1969 by Eudora Welty. "The Beautiful Changes" from *The Beautiful Changes and Other Poems* by Richard Wilbur. Copyright 1947 and renewed © 1975 by Richard Wilbur. "Boy at the Window" from *Things of This World* by Richard Wilbur. Copyright 1952; renewed copyright © 1980 by Richard Wilbur.

Joy Harjo: From "Three Generations of Native American Women's Birth Experience" by Joy Harjo from *Ms.*, vol. II, no. 1, July/August 1991. Copyright © 1991 by Joy Harjo.

HarperCollins Publishers, Inc.: From *Dust Tracks on a Road* by Zora Neale Hurston. Copyright 1942 by Zora Neale Hurston; copyright renewed © 1970 by John C. Hurston. "The Handsomest Drowned Man in the World" from *Leaf Storm and Other Stories* by Gabriel García Márquez. Copyright © 1971 by Gabriel García Márquez. "Mirror" from *Crossing the Water* by Sylvia Plath. Copyright © 1963 by Ted Hughes. Originally appeared in *The New Yorker*. From *Black Boy* by Richard Wright. Copyright 1937, 1942, 1944, 1945 by Richard Wright; copyright renewed © 1973 by Ellen Wright.

Harvard University Press: "World, in hounding me, what do you gain?" #28 from *A Sor Juana Anthology*, translated by Alan S. Trueblood. Copyright © 1988 by the President and Fellows of Harvard College. Published by Harvard University Press, Cambridge, Mass. From *I: Six Nonlectures* by e. e. cummings. Copyright © 1953 by e. e. cummings. Published by Harvard University Press, Cambridge, Mass. From Chapter 10, "The Battle with Mr. Covey" and excerpts from *The Narrative of the Life of Frederick Douglass: An American Slave, Written by Himself*, edited by Benjamin Quarles. Copyright © 1960 by the President and Fellows of Harvard College. Published by Harvard University Press, Cambridge, Mass. From *Sor Juana: Or, The Traps of Faith* by Octavio Paz. Copyright © 1988 by the President and Fellows of Harvard College. Published by Harvard University Press, Cambridge, Mass.

Harvard University Press and the Trustees of Amherst College: "1624: Apparently with no surprise," "712: Because I could not stop for Death," "47: Heart! We will forget him!," "465: I heard a Fly buzz—when I died," "214: I taste a liquor never brewed," "1129: Tell all the Truth but tell it slant—," and from "288: I'm Nobody! Who are you?" from *The Poems of Emily Dickinson*, edited by Thomas H. Johnson. Copyright © 1951, 1955, 1979, 1983 by the President and Fellows of Harvard College. Published by The Belknap Press of Harvard University Press, Cambridge, Mass.

Heritage: "Imagination" by Shelby Pearl from *Heritage*, vol. 31, Spring 1991. Published by James Madison High School, Vienna, VA. From "An Interview with Rita Dove" by Moira Haney and Catherine Nicholas from *Heritage*, vol. 34, Spring 1994. Published by James Madison High School, Vienna, VA.

Hill and Wang, a division of Farrar, Straus & Giroux, Inc.: From "When the Negro Was in Vogue" from *The Big Sea* by Langston Hughes. Copyright © 1940 by Langston Hughes; copyright renewed © 1968 by Arna Bontemps and George Houston Bass. From *Night* by Elie Wiesel, translated by Stella Rodway. Copyright © 1960 by MacGibbon & Kee; copyright renewed © 1988 by The Collins Publishing Group.

Holocaust Museum & Library: Quote by Martin Niemöller from *Their Brothers' Keepers* by Philip Friedman. Copyright © by Holocaust Museum & Library.

Henry Holt and Company, Inc.: From *Interviews with Robert Frost*, edited by Edward Connery Lathem. Copyright © 1966 by Henry Holt and Company, Inc. "Design," "Neither Out Far Nor in Deep," "Nothing Gold Can Stay," and "Once by the Pacific" from *The Poetry of Robert Frost*, edited by Edward Connery Lathem. Copyright 1923, 1936, © 1956 by Robert Frost; copyright © 1964 by Lesley Frost Ballantine; copyright 1928, © 1969 by Henry Holt and Company, Inc.; copyright © 1997 by Edward Connery Lathem.

John Hopkins University Press: Quote by Tim O'Brien from "Two Interviews: Talks with Tim O'Brien and Robert Stone" by Eric James Schroeder from *Modern Fiction Studies*, 30 Spring 1984. Copyright © 1984 by Eric James Schroeder.

Houghton Mifflin Company: From *Let Us Now Praise Famous Men* by James Agee and Walker Evans. Copyright 1939, 1940 by James Agee; copyright 1941 by James Agee and Walker Evans; copyright renewed © 1969 by Mia Fritsch Agee and Walker Evans. All rights reserved. "Ars Poetica" from *Collected Poems 1917–1982*, by Archibald MacLeish. Copyright © 1985 by The Estate of Archibald MacLeish. All rights reserved. "The Bells" from *To Bedlam and Part Way Back* by Anne Sexton. Copyright © 1960 by Anne Sexton; copyright renewed © 1988 by Linda G. Sexton. All rights reserved. "Young" from *All My Pretty Ones* by Anne Sexton. Copyright © 1962 by Anne Sexton; copyright renewed © 1990 by Linda G. Sexton. All rights reserved.

International Creative Management, Inc.: From "Why I Wrote 'The Crucible'" by Arthur Miller from *The New Yorker*, October 21 & 28, 1996. Copyright © 1996 by Arthur Miller. Quote by Arthur Miller from *Critical Essays on Arthur Miller*, edited by James J. Martine. Copyright © 1960 by Arthur Miller. From "On James Baldwin" by Toni Morrison from *The New York Times Book Review*, December 20, 1987. Copyright © 1987 by Toni Morrison.

Jesse Jackson, Jr., on behalf of Jesse Jackson: From Reverend Jesse Jackson's speech to the Democratic Convention in 1988 from *Vital Speeches of the Day*, vol. LIV, no. 21, August 15, 1988. Copyright © 1988 by Jesse Jackson.

Estate of Kirkland C. Jones: Quotes by Kirkland C. Jones from *Dictionary of Literary Biography®, Volume One Hundred Twenty:*

American Poets Since World War II, Third Series, edited by R. S. Gwynn. Published by Gale Research, Inc., 1992.

The Heirs to the Estate of Martin Luther King, Jr., c/o Writers House, Inc., as agent for the proprietor: From "Letter from Birmingham City Jail" by Martin Luther King, Jr., from A Testament of Hope, edited by J. M. Washington. Copyright © 1963 by Martin Luther King, Jr., copyright © 1991 by Coretta Scott King. From "I Have a Dream" by Martin Luther King, Jr. Copyright © 1963 by Martin Luther King, Jr.; copyright renewed © 1991 by Coretta Scott King.

Alfred A. Knopf, Inc.: "A Noiseless Flash" from Hiroshima by John Hersey. Copyright 1946 and renewed © 1974 by John Hersey. "Kubota" from Volcano by Garrett Hongo. Copyright © 1995 by Garrett Hongo. "Dream Deferred," "Harlem," "I, Too," "The Weary Blues," and from "Let America Be America Again" from Collected Poems by Langston Hughes. Copyright © 1994 by the Estate of Langston Hughes. "The Girl Who Wouldn't Talk" from The Woman Warrior by Maxine Hong Kingston. Copyright © 1975, 1976 by Maxine Hong Kingston. "Autobiographia Literaria" from The Collected Poems of Frank O'Hara, edited by Donald Allen. Copyright © 1971 by Maureen Granville-Smith, Administratrix of the Estate of Frank O'Hara. "Mushrooms" from The Colossus and Other Poems by Sylvia Plath. Copyright © 1960 by Sylvia Plath. "Anecdote of the Jar," "Disillusionment of Ten O'Clock," and from "Of Modern Poetry" from Collected Poems by Wallace Stevens. Copyright 1923 and renewed 1951, 1954 by Wallace Stevens. "Of Modern Poetry" from The Palm at The End of the Mind by Wallace Stevens. Copyright © 1967, 1969, 1971 by Holly Stevens. Ten aphorisms from Opus Posthumous by Wallace Stevens. Copyright © 1957 by Elsie Stevens and Holly Stevens. "Son" from Problems and Other Stories by John Updike. Copyright © 1979 by John Updike.

Yusef Komunyakaa: Quote by Yusef Komunyakaa from "A Man of His Words" by Jeffrey Walker from Los Angeles Times, April 13, 1994. "Monsoon Season" from Toys in a Field by Yusef Komunyakaa. Copyright © 1986 by Yusef Komunyakaa.

Martin Levin: From "The Dogwood Tree: A Boyhood" from Five Boyhoods by John Updike, edited by Martin Levin. Copyright © 1962 and renewed © 1990 by Martin Levin.

Little, Brown and Company: From Blue Highways by William Least Heat-Moon. Copyright © 1982 by William Least Heat-Moon.

Liveright Publishing Corporation: "#225: somewhere i have never travelled, gladly beyond" and "what if a much of a which of a wind" (and excerpts) from Complete Poems: 1904–1962 by E. E. Cummings, edited by George J. Firmage. Copyright 1931, 1944, © 1959, 1972, 1991 by the Trustees for the E. E. Cummings Trust; copyright © 1979 by George James Firmage. From Introduction to New Poems (from Collected Poems: 1904–1962) by E. E. Cummings, edited by George J. Firmage. Copyright 1938, © 1966, 1991 by the Trustees for the E. E. Cummings Trust.

Macmillan Reference USA: From Webster's New World™ College Dictionary, Third Edition. Copyright © 1988, 1991, 1994, 1996, 1997 by Simon & Schuster, Inc.

Ellen C. Masters: From Across Spoon River by Edgar Lee Masters. Copyright 1936 by Edgar Lee Masters; copyright renewed © 1964 by Ellen Coyne Masters. Originally published by Farrar & Rinehart.

J. D. McClatchy: Quotes by Robert Lowell and James Dickey from Anne Sexton: The Artist and Her Critics, edited by J. D. McClatchy. Copyright © 1978 by J. D. McClatchy.

Merlyn's Pen, Inc.: "The Mirror Girl—stares back at me—" from "Walt and Emily Revisited" by Brigid Spackman from Merlyn's Pen, February/March 1993. Copyright © 1993 by Merlyn's Pen, Inc. First appeared in Merlyn's Pen: The National Magazines of Student Writing.

Merriam-Webster Inc.: Definition of "proud" from Webster's Third New International Dictionary, edited by Philip Babcock Grove, Ph.D. Copyright © 1993 by Merriam-Webster Inc.

William Morris Agency, Inc., on behalf of Edward Albee: From Conversations with Edward Albee, edited by Philip C. Kolin. Copyright © 1988 by Edward Albee.

New Directions Publishing Corporation: "Fall" from Black Mesa Poems by Jimmy Santiago Baca. Copyright © 1989 by Jimmy Santiago Baca. From "Early Success" from The Crack-up by F. Scott Fitzgerald. Copyright © 1945 by New Directions Publishing Corporation. "A Pact," "In a Station of the Metro," and "The River-Merchant's Wife: A Letter" from Personae: The Collected Poems of Ezra Pound. Copyright © 1926 by Ezra Pound. From "A Few Dont's by an Imagiste" from Literary Essays of Ezra Pound. Copyright © by Faber and Faber Ltd. From letter to Harriet Monroe from Selected Letters of Ezra Pound. Copyright © 1950 by Ezra Pound. "Pine Tree Tops" from Turtle Island by Gary Snyder. Copyright © 1974 by Gary Snyder. From The Autobiography of William Carlos Williams. Copyright © 1951 by William Carlos Williams. "The Great Figure," "The Red Wheelbarrow," and "Spring and All, section I" from Collected Poems: 1909–1939, vol. I, by William Carlos Williams. Copyright © 1938 by New Directions Publishing Corporation.

The New York Review of Books: Quote by Thomas R. Edwards from The New York Review of Books, November 24, 1983. Copyright © 1983 by NYREV, Inc. From "Fitzgerald Revisited" by Jay McInerney from The New York Review of Books, August 15, 1991. Copyright © 1991 by NYREV, Inc.

The New York Times Company: Quote by Carl Sandburg from The New York Times, Feb. 13, 1959. Copyright © 1959 by The New York Times Company. Quote by Sugar Ray Leonard from "Durán, Leonard Fit" from The New York Times, June 17, 1980. Copyright © 1980 by The New York Times Company. From "Malamud's Dark Fable" by Alan Lelchuk from The New York Times Book Review, August 29, 1982. Copyright © 1982 by The New York Times Company. From "Black and Well-to-Do" by Andrea Lee from The New York Times, 1984. Copyright © 1984 by the New York Times Company. From "Mississippi Honors a 'Native Son' Who Fled" by Edwin McDowell from The New York Times, November 23, 1985. Copyright © 1985 by The New York Times Company. From "Pictures of Malamud" by Philip Roth from The New York Times Book Review, April 20, 1986. Copyright © 1986 by The New York Times Company. From "The Promiscuous Cool of Postmodernism" by Denis Donoghue from The New York Times Book Review, June 22, 1986. Copyright © 1986 by The New York Times Company. Quote by Raymond Carver from "Grace Has Come into My Life" by Stewart Kellerman from The New York Times Book Review, May 15, 1988. Copyright © 1988 by The New York Times Company. Quote by Roberto Márquez from The New York Times Book Review, September 24, 1989. Copyright © 1989 by The New York Times Company. "A Poet's Safe Haven in Amherst" by Anne Bernays from The New York Times Magazine, Part 2: The Sophisticated Traveler, October 1, 1989. Copyright © 1989 by The New York Times Company. Quote by Tim O'Brien from "A Storyteller for the War That Won't End" by D.J.R. Bruckner from The New York Times, April 3, 1990. Copyright © 1990 by The New York Times Company. From a review of How the Garcia Girls Lost Their Accents by Julia Alvarez from The New York Times Book Review, October 6, 1991. Copyright © 1991 by The New York Times Company. Quote by Toni Morrison from "Toni Morrison Is '93 Winner of Nobel Prize in Literature" by William Grimes from The New York Times, October 8, 1993. Copyright © 1993 by The New York Times Company. "An American Story" by Anthony Lewis from The New York Times, November 26, 1993. Copyright © 1993 by The New York Times Company. "Poetry Emotion" by Anna Quindlen from The New York Times, April 16, 1994. Copyright © 1994 by The New York Times Company. Quote by Yusef Komunyakaa from "A Poet's Values: It's the Words over the Man" by Bruce Weber from The New York Times, May 2, 1994. Copyright © 1994 by The New York Times Company. From "The New Measure of Man" by Vaclav Havel from The New York Times, July 8, 1994. Copyright © 1994 by The New York Times Company. From Janet Maslin's review of The Crucible from The New York Times, November

27, 1996. Copyright © 1996 by The New York Times Company.

The New Yorker: From "James Thurber" from *E. B. White: Writings from "The New Yorker," 1927–1976.* Copyright © 1961, 1989 by E. B. White. Published by HarperCollins. Originally appeared in *The New Yorker.*

The Nobel Foundation: Acceptance speeches by William Faulkner, Ernest Hemingway, and John Steinbeck from *Nobel Lectures in Literature: 1901–1967,* edited by Horst Frenz. Copyright 1949, 1954, © 1962 by The Nobel Foundation.

Northern Illinois University Press: From *James Russell Lowell's The Biglow Papers: A Critical Edition* by Thomas Wortham. Copyright © 1977 by Northern Illinois University Press.

W. W. Norton & Company, Inc.: "Emily Dickinson" from *PM/AM: New and Selected Poems* by Linda Pastan. Copyright © 1971 by Linda Pastan. From "Still Just Writing" by Anne Tyler from *The Writer on Her Work,* vol. I, edited by Janet Sternburg. Copyright © 1980 by Janet Sternburg.

Harold Ober Associates Incorporated: From letter to George Freitag (August 27, 1938) from *Letters of Sherwood Anderson,* edited by H. M. Jones and Walter Rideout. Copyright 1953 by Eleanor Anderson. From the James Weldon Johnson Collection: Quotations from "Draft Ideas," December 3, 1964, by Langston Hughes, as they appear in *The Life of Langston Hughes, Volume II: 1941–1967—I Dream a World.* Copyright © 1986 by the Estate of Langston Hughes.

Tim O'Brien, c/o Janklow & Nesbit Associates: Slightly adapted from "Speaking of Courage" by Tim O'Brien from *The Massachusetts Review,* Summer 1976. Copyright © 1976 by Tim O'Brien.

Simon J. Ortiz: "Speaking" by Simon J. Ortiz. Copyright © 1989 by Simon J. Ortiz.

Pantheon Books, a division of Random House, Inc.: "House Taken Over" from *End of the Game and Other Stories* by Julio Cortázar, translated by Paul Blackburn. Copyright © 1967 by Random House, Inc.

The Paris Review: From "The Art of Fiction LXXXIII Julio Cortázar" from *The Paris Review,* vol. 26, no. 93, Fall 1984. Copyright © 1984 by The Paris Review, Inc.

Perspective: Quote by Andrew V. Ettin from *Perspective,* Spring 1967. Copyright © 1967 by Perspective.

Gerald W. Purcell Associates: "My Guilt" from *Just Give Me a Cool Drink of Water 'fore I Diiie* by Maya Angelou. Copyright © 1969 by Hirt Music, Inc.

G. P. Putnam's Sons: From "Rules of the Game" from *The Joy Luck Club* by Amy Tan. Copyright © 1989 by Amy Tan.

Random House, Inc.: "The Unknown Citizen" from *W. H. Auden: Collected Poems.* Copyright © 1940 and copyright renewed © 1968 by W. H. Auden. From *Death Comes for the Archbishop* by Willa Cather. Copyright 1927 by Willa Cather; copyright renewed © 1955 by the Executors of the Estate of Willa Cather. "A Rose for Emily" (and excerpts) from *A Rose for Emily* by William Faulkner. Copyright © 1930 and renewed © 1958 by William Faulkner. "New African" from *Sarah Phillips* by Andrea Lee. Copyright © 1984 by Andrea Lee. From Appendix from *Hugging the Shore* by John Updike. Copyright © 1983 by John Updike. "Is Phoenix Jackson's Grandson Really Dead?" from *The Eye of the Story* by Eudora Welty. Copyright © 1978 by Eudora Welty.

The Saturday Evening Post Society: From "I Saw Lee Surrender" by Seth M. Flint from *The Saturday Evening Post,* vol. 248, no. 5, July/August 1976. Copyright © 1976 The Saturday Evening Post.

Saturday Review: From "James Baldwin on the Sixties: Acts and Revelations" by Benjamin DeMott from *Saturday Review,* May 27, 1972, pp. 63–64. Copyright © 1972 by SR Publications, Ltd.

Scribner, a division of Simon & Schuster, Inc.: From *The Night Country* by Loren Eiseley. Copyright © 1971 by Loren Eiseley. From letter to Scottie Fitzgerald from *A Life in Letters,* edited by Matthew J. Bruccoli. Copyright © 1994 by The Trustees Under Agreement dated July 3, 1975. From "Absolution" from *The Short Stories of F. Scott Fitzgerald,* edited by Matthew J. Bruccoli. Copyright 1924 by American Mercury, Inc.; copyright renewed 1952 by Frances Scott Fitzgerald Lanahan. "Soldier's Home" from *The Short Stories of Ernest Hemingway.* Copyright 1925 by Charles Scribner's Sons; copyright renewed 1953 by Ernest Hemingway.

Shades Valley Resource Learning Center: "The Sea" by Elizabeth Enloe from *Counterpane,* vol. 18, 1993. Published by Shades Valley Resource Learning Center, Birmingham, AL.

Karl Shapiro, c/o Wieser & Wieser Inc., New York, NY: "Auto Wreck" from *Collected Poems 1940–1978* by Karl Shapiro. Copyright © 1978, 1987 by Karl Shapiro.

Sheaffer-O'Neill Collection, Connecticut College Library: Quote from letter by Eugene O'Neill as it appears in *Selected Letters of Eugene O'Neill,* edited by Travis Bogard and Jackson R. Bryer.

Simon & Schuster, Inc.: From *Catch-22* by Joseph Heller. Copyright © 1955, 1961 by Joseph Heller; copyright renewed © 1989 by Joseph Heller. "Poetry" (and excerpts) from *The Collected Poems of Marianne Moore.* Copyright 1935 by Marianne Moore; copyright renewed © 1963 by Marianne Moore and T. S. Eliot.

Estate of William Stafford: "At the Bomb Testing Site" from *West of Your City* by William Stafford. Copyright © 1960 by William Stafford. Published by Talisman Press.

St. James Press, an imprint of Gale Research, Inc.: Quote by Garrett Hongo and from "Rita Dove" by Julie Miller from *Contemporary Poets,* Fifth Edition, edited by Tracy Chevalier. Copyright © 1991 by St. James Press.

The Texas Folklore Society: Song lyrics from "Follow the Drinking Gourd" by H. B. Parks from *Follow de Drinkin' Gou'd,* Publications of the Texas Folklore Society, no. VII, edited by J. Frank Dobie. Copyright 1928 by the Texas Folklore Society.

Texas Rangers Baseball Club: Logo for Texas Rangers baseball team.

Thunder's Mouth Press: From "Anchorage," from "Motion," and "Remember" from *She Had Some Horses* by Joy Harjo. Copyright © 1983 by Joy Harjo.

Rosemary A. Thurber and the Barbara Hogenson Agency, Inc.: "A Biographical Sketch of James Thurber" from *Collecting Himself.* Copyright © 1989 by Rosemary A. Thurber. Originally published by HarperCollins Publishers. "The Secret Life of Walter Mitty" from *My World–and Welcome to It* by James Thurber. Copyright © 1942 by James Thurber; copyright renewed © 1970 by Helen Thurber and Rosemary Thurber. Originally published by Harcourt Brace & Co.

Time Inc.: From "Book of Changes" by Paul Gray from *Time,* December 6, 1976. Copyright © 1976 by Time Inc.

Times Mirror Magazines: From "Winning the Cold War" by Paul G. Gill, Jr., from *Outdoor Life,* vol. 191, February 1993. Copyright © 1993 by Times Mirror Magazines.

Emily Toth: From "Intimate and Untidy Stories" from *Kate Chopin* by Emily Toth. Copyright © 1990 by Emily Toth.

The University of New Mexico Press: From "Introduction" and from *The Way to Rainy Mountain* by N. Scott Momaday. Copyright © 1969 by The University of New Mexico Press. First published in *The Reporter,* January 26, 1967.

University of North Carolina Press: From *The Invasion of America* by Francis Jennings. Copyright © 1975 by the University of North Carolina Press.

University of Oklahoma Press: "For More Than a Hundred Winters Our Nation Was a Powerful, Happy and United People" by Black Hawk and "I Will Fight No More Forever" by Chief Joseph from *Indian Oratory: Famous Speeches by Noted Indian Chieftains,* compiled by W. C. Vanderwerth. Copyright © 1971 by the University of Oklahoma Press. Quote by Robert Frost from *Robert Frost: Life and Talks—Walking* by Louis Mertins. Copyright © 1965 by the University of Oklahoma Press.

University of Texas Press: "The Feather Pillow" from *The Decapitated Chicken and Other Stories* by Horacio Quiroga, translated by Margaret Sayers Peden. Copyright © 1976 by the University of Texas Press.

University Press of New England: "The Lifeguard" from *Poems 1957–1967* by James Dickey. Copyright © 1958, 1959, 1960, 1961, 1962, 1963, 1964, 1965, 1966, 1967 by James Dickey. "What For" from *Yellow Light* by Garrett Kaoru Hongo. Copyright © 1982 by Garrett Kaoru Hongo. Published by Wesleyan University Press. "We Never Knew" from *Dien Cai Dau* by Yusef Komunyakaa. Copyright © 1988 by Yusef Komunyakaa. "Changes; or, Reveries at a Window Overlooking a Country Road, with Two Women Talking Blues in the Kitchen" from *Neon Vernacular* by Yusef Komunyakaa. Copyright © 1993 by Yusef Komunyakaa. Published by Wesleyan University Press. "A Blessing" from *The Branch Will Not Break* by James Wright. Copyright © 1963 by James Wright. Published by Wesleyan University Press.

Pindar VanArman: "What About Glory" by Pindar VanArman from *Phoenix: The Gonzaga Fine Arts Magazine*, vol. XVI, no. 1, May 1992. Published by Gonzaga College High School, Washington, D.C.

Viking Penguin, a division of Penguin Putnam Inc.: From *Along This Way* by James Weldon Johnson. Copyright 1933 by James Weldon Johnson; copyright renewed © 1961 by Grace Nail Johnson. "Go Down Death—A Funeral Sermon" and "Preface" from *God's Trombones* by James Weldon Johnson. Copyright 1927 by The Viking Press, Inc.; copyright renewed © 1955 by Grace Nail Johnson. *The Crucible* by Arthur Miller. Copyright 1952, 1953, 1954, and renewed © 1980, 1981, 1982 by Arthur Miller. From "The State of the Theater" from *The Theater Essays of Arthur Miller* by Arthur Miller, edited by Robert A. Martin. Copyright © 1960 by Harper's Magazine. From "Raymond Carver" by Mona Simpson and Lewis Buzbee from *Writers at Work, Seventh Series*, edited by George A. Plimpton. Copyright © 1986 by The Paris Review. "The Leader of the People" from *The Red Pony* by John Steinbeck. Copyright 1938, and renewed © 1966 by John Steinbeck.

Villard Books, a division of Random House, Inc.: From *All I Really Need to Know I Learned in Kindergarten* by Robert L. Fulghum. Copyright © 1986, 1988 by Robert L. Fulghum.

Walden Woods Project, an Activity of The Isis Fund: From "Preface" by Don Henley from *Heaven Is Under Our Feet*, edited by Don Henley and Dave Marsh. Copyright © 1991 by The Isis Fund.

Washington Post Book World Service/Washington Post Writers Group: From William McPherson's review of Maxine Hong Kingston's *The Woman Warrior* from *Washington Post Book World*, October 10, 1976. Copyright © 1976 by Washington Post Book World Service/Washington Post Writers Group. From Jonathan Yardley's review of Raymond Carver's *Cathedral* from *Washington Post Book World*, September 20, 1983. Copyright © 1983 by Washington Post Book World Service/Washington Post Writers Group. From "Mah-Jongg and The Ladies of the Club" by Susan Dooley from *The Washington Post Book World*, March 5, 1989, p. 7. Copyright © 1989 by Washington Post Book World Service/Washington Post Writers Group.

Washington Post Writers Group: Quote by Juan Williams from *Washington Post*, December 2, 1987. Copyright © 1987 by The Washington Post.

Rhoda Weyr Agency, New York: "The One Who Was Different" from *The Lost World* by Randall Jarrell. Copyright © 1965 by Randall Jarrell. Reprinted in *The Complete Poems of Randall Jarrell*. Published by Farrar, Straus & Giroux, Inc., 1989.

Doretha Williams: "Africa" by Doretha Williams from *Calliope 1993*. Copyright © 1993 by Doretha Williams. Published by Topeka West High School, Topeka, KS.

The H. W. Wilson Company: From "Gabriel García Márquez" from *Spanish American Authors: The Twentieth Century* by Angel Flores. Copyright © 1992 by Angel Flores.

Donald Windham: From *Tennessee Williams' Letters to Donald Windham 1940–1965*, edited by Donald Windham. Copyright © 1976, 1977, 1980 by Donald Windham. Published in paperback by The University of Georgia Press, 1996.

The Wylie Agency, Inc.: "Game" from *Unspeakable Practices, Unnatural Acts* by Donald Barthelme. Copyright © 1968 by Donald Barthelme. From "Not-Knowing" by Donald Barthelme. Copyright © 1985 by Donald Barthelme.

Yale Collection of American Literature, Beinecke Rare Book and Manuscript Library, Yale University: From the James Weldon Johnson Collection: Quotations from "Draft Ideas," December 3, 1964, by Langston Hughes, as they appear in *The Life of Langston Hughes, Volume II: 1941–1967—I Dream a World*.

Yale University Press: From *Selected Letters of Eugene O'Neill*, edited by Travis Bogard and Jackson R. Bryer. Copyright © 1988 by Yale University.

David Young: From Introduction from *Magical Realist Fiction*, edited by David Young and Keith Hollaman. Copyright © 1984 by David Young.

SOURCES CITED

From "Revolutionary Charter" from *Inventing America: Jefferson's Declaration of Independence* by Garry Wills. Published by Doubleday, a division of Bantam Doubleday Dell Publishing Group, Inc., New York, 1978.

Quote by Diarmuid Russell from *Author and Agent: Eudora Welty and Diarmuid Russell* by Michael Kreyling. Published by Farrar, Straus & Giroux, Inc., New York, 1991.

From "Karl Shapiro" from *Contemporary Authors*, vol. 6, edited by Adele Sarkissian. Published by Gale Research Company, New York, 1988.

From "Karl Shapiro" from *American Poets, 1880–1945*, Second Series, edited by Peter Quartermain. Published by Gale Research Company, New York, 1986.

From "Washington Irving: 1783–1859" by William L. Hedges from *Major Writers of America*. Published by Harcourt Brace & Company, Orlando, FL, 1962.

From "The Rookers" from *Shiloh and Other Stories* by Bobbie Ann Mason. Published by HarperCollins Publishers, Inc., New York, 1982.

Quote by William Faulkner from "Preface" from *The Enigma of Thomas Wolfe*, edited by Richard Walser. Published by Harvard University Press, Cambridge, MA, 1953.

From "Interview with Anne Sexton" by Patricia Marx from *The Hudson Review*, vol. XVIII, no. 4, Winter 1965–66. Published by The Hudson Review, Inc., 1966.

From acceptance speech for the American Book Award for fiction, April 27, 1982, from *Hugging the Shore* by John Updike. Published by Alfred A. Knopf, Inc., New York, 1983.

Quote by Eugene O'Neill from *O'Neill: Son and Artist* by Louis Sheaffer. Published by Little, Brown and Company, Boston, MA, 1973.

Quote by Ezra Pound from *Remembering Poets* by Donald Hall. Published by New Directions Publishing Corporation, New York, 1977.

From *Selected Prose 1909–1965* by Ezra Pound, edited by William Cookson. Published by New Directions Publishing Corporation, New York, 1973.

From "The Phantom Dawn" from *The Spirit of Romance* by Ezra Pound. Published by New Directions Publishing Corporation, New York, 1968.

From "10. One True Sentence" from *Ernest Hemingway: A Life Story* by Carlos Baker. Published by Scribner, a division of Simon & Schuster, Inc., New York, 1969.

From "Notes Toward a Biography" by Lois Ames from *Tri-Quarterly*, no. 7, Fall 1966. Published by Tri-Quarterly Books, Northwestern University.

From "Some Self-Analysis" from *On the Poet and His Craft: Selected Prose of Theodore Roethke*, edited by Ralph J. Mills, Jr. Published by University of Washington Press, 1965.

From "Empty Bamboo" by Leslie Li from *American Identities: Contemporary Multicultural Voices*, edited by Robert Pack and Jay Parini. Published by University Press of New England, 1994.

PICTURE CREDITS

Page: 2 (left), Michael S. Yamashita/Woodfin Camp & Associates; 2–3, Kathleen Campbell/Tony Stone Images; 5 (center), Kirchoff/Wohlberg; 6–13 & 16–18 (background), Kirchoff/Wohlberg; 9 (top left), John Carter Brown Library/Brown University, Providence, Rhode Island, (right), Courtesy American Antiquarian Society; 14, Tom Bross/Stock Boston; 14–15 (background), Library of Congress; 15 (left), William Johnson/Stock Boston, (right), Richard Pasley/Stock Boston; 19 (background), Marion Stirrup/Alaska Stock Images; 20–21, Theo Westenberger; 27 (background), John Coletti/Stock Boston; 28–33 (background), Kirchoff/Wohlberg; 35, Haffenreffer Museum of Anthropology/Brown University, Providence, Rhode Island. Photo by Cathy Carver; 42–43 (background), Fred M. Dole—f/Stop Pictures; 48–49, Gene Ahrens/Bruce Coleman, Inc.; 52–53, Wendell Mentzen/Bruce Coleman, Inc; 54, Haffenreffer Museum of Anthropology/Brown University, Providence, Rhode Island; 56–57, 65 (background), Marc & Evelyne Bernheim/Woodfin Camp & Associates; 67, SuperStock; 68–70 (background), Reproduced by kind permission of the vicar and church wardens of St. Botolph's Church, Boston, England; 72–73 (background), 73, FPG International; 90–91 (top background), Telegraph Colour Library/FPG International; 96, B. Timmons/The Image Bank; 99 (upper left), Bruce Mathews/Image Quest, (lower right), Jim Madden/New England Stock Photo; 100–101 (center), John Henley/The Stock Market, (top background), Gene Moore/Phototake, (bottom background), Peter Cole/New England Stock Photo; 106–107 (background), 108 (background), 109 (inset left), 110 (inset top), 112 (background), North Wind Picture Archives; 109, 110, Joe Viesti/Viesti Associates; 120–121, Charlie Ott/Photo Researchers; 135, F. Cruz/SuperStock; 138–150 (background), Kirchoff/Wohlberg; 146, Charles Scribner's Sons, 1925; 151, Robert Maier/Animals, Animals; 154 (top), Neil Meyerhoff/Panoramic Images; 154 (bottom), 164, 165, Ronald F. Thomas/Bruce Coleman, Inc; 155, Courtesy Millport Conservancy, Lititz, Pennsylvania; 160, Robin Jane Solvang/Bruce Coleman, Inc.; 162, Gary Braasch/Tony Stone Images; 167, Photofest; 169–172, Kirchoff/Wohlberg; 173, Hitchcock-Chase Collection of Grass Drawings/Hunt Institute for Botanical Documentation/Carnegie Mellon University, Pittsburgh, Pennsylvania; 173, 182–185 (background), Kirchoff/Wohlberg; 187 (center), Courtesy *The Atlantic Monthly,* (bottom),

Massachusetts Historical Society, Massachusetts; 188, Scott Camazine/Photo Researchers; 189, The Library of the New York Botanical Garden (Bronx, New York); 190, 192, Culver Pictures; 203, F. Cruz/SuperStock; 206–214 (background), Branson Reynolds/Index Stock; 207 (left), Massachusetts Historical Society, Boston, (right), Cooper-Hewitt, National Design Museum, Smithsonian Institution/Art Resource, NY; 208 (right), 208–209 (bottom), 210–211 (bottom), North Wind Picture Archives; 212–213, Kirchoff/Wohlberg; 215, 218–221 (background), William D. Adams/Picture Perfect USA, Inc.; 215 (inset), David Julian/Phototake; 227, Kevin Alexander/Index Stock; 233, 234, 237, 243 © PhotoDisc, Inc. 1998; 249, 251, 254, Robert Essel/The Stock Market; 261, Kirchoff/Wohlberg; 279, Illustration by R. Hoffman; 282, 284–285, 286, Illustrations by Arvis Stewart for "The Raven"; 287, Reprinted by permission of Warner Books, Inc., New York, New York, USA. From *The Illustrated Edgar Allan Poe* by Wilfred Satty and Edgar Allan Poe. Copyright © 1976. All rights reserved; 291, 293–295 (background), Charles A. Mauzy/Tony Stone Images; 298–299, 304, 307, Tom Hopkins Studio; 314–315, Marion Stirrup/Alaska Stock Images; 321, Lon Lauber/Alaska Stock Images; 326, J. Coolidge/The Image Bank; 339, F. Cruz/SuperStock; 340–341, 359, Julie Habel/Woodfin Camp & Associates; 342–346 (background), Maria Stenzel/National Geographic Society Image Collection; 345 (top left), Courtesy of the Trustees of Amherst College/The Emily Dickinson Homestead; 345, Corbis-Bettmann; 345 (right), Courtesy of the Amherst History Museum at the Strong House, Amherst, Massachusetts; 347, University of Virginia Library, Charlottesville, Courtesy NGS; 351, Karen Kasmauski/Woodfin Camp & Associates; 353, From the David T. Vernon Collection of Native American Indian Art, Colter Bay Indian Arts Museum, Grand Teton National Park, Wyoming. Photo by J. Oldenkamp; 360–361 (background), W. Cody/Westlight; 367, AP/Wide World Photos; 368–370 (background), Eastcott & Momatiuk/Woodfin Camp & Associates; 371, Eastcott & Momatiuk/Woodfin Camp & Associates; 377 (background), Stephen P. Parker/Photo Researchers; 380, 384–385, Timothy Eagen/Woodfin Camp & Associates; 380 (bottom), Kirchoff/Wohlberg; 391, Brown Brothers; 405, F. Cruz/SuperStock; 424–425 (background), Lyle Leduc/Index Stock Photography; 425 (inset), 426 (background), Wallace Garrison/Index Stock Photography; 435–443 (background), Kirchoff/Wohlberg; 440 (bottom), Corbis-Bettmann; 448, University of Washington Libraries, Special Collections Division, Seattle, Washington; 449, Gene Ahrens/Bruce

Coleman, Inc.; 452, 454, 460, 461, Corbis-Bettmann; 467 (left), © Erika Klass; 468, Daniel Nichols/Gamma Liaison; 470, Allen Russell/Index Stock; 473, Brett Baunton/Tony Stone Images; 476–483 (background), Kirchoff/Wohlberg; 496–497, Don Pitcher/Alaska Stock Images; 500 (inset), Michael DeYoung/Alaska Stock Images, 500 (background), Alaska Stock Images; 503, Johnny Johnson/Alaska Stock Images; 503 (inset), 507, 508, Jeff Schultz/Alaska Stock Images; 509, Alaska Stock Images; 521, F. Cruz/SuperStock; 524–525 (top), Brown Brothers; 524–525 (bottom), UPI/Corbis-Bettmann; 526 (right), 527 (top right), Corbis-Bettmann, (top left), Archive Photos, (bottom left and bottom center), FPG International, (bottom right), Jeffrey D. Smith/Woodfin Camp & Associates; 528–529 (background), Kirchoff/Wohlberg; 532, Culver Pictures; 533, Courtesy Giraudon/Art Resource, New York; 534, Culver Pictures; 537, Ludovic Molin/Photonica; 539, Archive Photos; 540–541 (background), Kazuya Shimizu/Photonica; 540, Charles Shotwell/Panoramic Images; 545 (bottom), Color Box/FPG International; 559 (background), Royce Blair/The Stock Solution; 563 (inset), Rick Schafer/The Stock Market; 564, 565, © PhotoDisc, Inc. 1998; 566, Barry O'Rourke/The Stock Market; 567–568 (background), Ron Thomas/FPG International; 569–573, Don & Liysa King/The Image Bank; 583, Randy O'Rourke/The Stock Market; 584–587 (background), Kirchoff/Wohlberg; 586, 587, 594, 598–599, 600, 602, Liberty Collection/The Image Bank; 595, 606–607 (background), 616–617 (background), Culver Pictures; 616, Photofest; 624–625 (background), Kirchoff/Wohlberg; 634–635 (background), Marco Polo/Phototake; 643, Susan Stang/Photo Researchers; 652, Kirchoff/Wohlberg; 656–657 (background), Phototone; 688, Robert Brenner/PhotoEdit; 691, Nicholas Devore III/Photographers Aspen; 693, Frederic Stein/FPG International; 694 and 695, © PhotoDisc, Inc. 1998; 703–704 (top and bottom), 714–717, 722, 727, 729–731, Kirchoff/Wohlberg; 704 (left), FPG International; 732, R. A. Clevenger/Westlight; 733, Bonnot/The Image Bank; 734–735 (background), Phototone; 749, Stephen Marks/The Image Bank; 750, The Beinecke Rare Book and Manuscript Library, Yale University, New Haven, Connecticut. Estate of Carl Van Vechten, Joseph Solomon, Executor; 760, National Portrait Gallery, Smithsonian Institution/Art Resource, NY; 763 (top), Javier Romero Design/The Image Bank; 763 (bottom), Ayako Parks/Tony Stone Images; 770–772 (background), Picture Perfect, USA; 781, Index Stock; 788, Bridgeman Art Library, London/New York; 789 (background), Larry West/FPG International; 794, Telegraph Colour Library/FPG International; 798, Erich

INDEX OF SKILLS

LITERARY TERMS

The boldface page numbers indicate an extensive treatment of the topic.

Abstract language **1167**
Allegory 280, 281, **1189**
Alliteration 180, 282, **288**, 355, 365, 557, 563, 768, 1091, 1169, **1189**
Allusion 35, **39**, 46, 47, 83, 105, **186**, 262, 670, 1008, 1157, **1159**, 1165, **1189**
Ambiguity 493, 712, **1006**, 1008, 1147, **1189**
American dream **525, 529,** 585, 604, 622
Analogy
  literary 107, 112, 167, 384, **1189**
  word **890**
Anapest **1189**
Anecdote 107, 112, 333, 402, 465, **1189**
Antagonist 862, **1189**
Anthropomorphism **1190**
Antihero 660
Aphorism 71, 98, **222,** 229, 786, 1087, **1190**
Apostrophe 188, **792,** 795, **1190**
Archaic syntax and vocabulary 35
Archaism 35, **37,** 308
Argument 112, 332–333, **1190**
Assonance 355, 1169, **1190**
Atmosphere 180, **262,** 280, 281, 288, 308, 557, 605, 725, **921,** 931, 1093, **1190,** 1200
Attitude 996
Audience 742, 1140
Autobiography **57,** 66, 97, 751, 759, 1165, **1190**
Ballad **1190**
Biography 97, 557, **1190**
Blank verse 567, 569, **575, 1190**
Cadence 115, 344, 345, 355, 365, 742, **1190**
Caesura **1191**
Catalog **351,** 358, 365, 366, 405, 557, 795, **1191**
Character 97, 166, 289, 308, 320, 329, 430, 445, 509, 561, 569, 575, 586, 622, 631, 632, 642, 652, 669, 673, 696, 725, 805, 815, 828, 877, 900, 946, 973, 981, 994, 1025, 1027, 1033, 1038, 1044, 1053, 1066, 1075, 1077, 1108, 1110, 1129, 1140, **1191,** 1201
  dynamic/static 849, 877, **981,** 1191
  flat/round 1191
  stock 631
Characterization **313,** 430, 605, 683, 759, 961, 973, 994, 1044, 1053, 1140, **1191**
  direct/indirect **1191**
Cliché 1185, **1191**
Climax 888, 1087, **1191, 1198**
Closed couplet 1192
Coda 359
Colloquialisms 805, 1185, 1192
Comedy **683, 1191**
Comic relief 877
Complications 1197–1198
Conceding a point 333
Conceit 73, **74, 1191**
Concrete language **1167,** 1169
Concrete poem **1191**
Confessional school of poetry 916

Conflict 167, 374, 496, 510, 568, 576, **607,** 621, 660, 724, 814, 815, 828, 862, 888, 961, **965,** 973, 1033, 1038, **1044,** 1053, **1077,** 1087, 1119, **1129,** 1140, **1191–1192,** 1200
  external 510, **607,** 815, 862, **965, 1044,** 1053, **1077,** 1087, **1192**
  internal 510, **607,** 815, 862, **965,** 973, **1044,** 1053, **1077,** 1087, **1129,** 1140, **1191–1192**
Connotation 46, **281,** 308, 649, 683, 701, 726, 894, 956, 961, 1185, **1192**
Consonance **1192**
Context clues 37, 134, **168,** 228, 262, 308, 670, 947, 1186
Couplet 180, **1192,** 1201
Crisis 1198
Criteria 1181–1182
Dactyl **1192**
Definition 229
Deism 16, 561
Denotation 281, 334, 726
Denouement **1192,** 1198
Description **549,** 557, 642, 994, **1192**
Dialect **512–514, 1055,** 1066, **1192**
Dialogue 131, 132, 309, 405, 510, **569,** 575, 576, 671, 683, 900, 973, 994, **1013,** 1027
Diction 107, 113, 166, 366, 749, 805, 954, 1147, 1150, 1176, 1185, **1192,** 1203
Drama **813, 820, 823,** 901
  basic dramatic elements of 814, 815
  expressionist **823**
  realistic **820**
Dramatic monologue 649, **663,** 671, **1192**
Either/or fallacy 1184
Elegy 577, **1004,** 1100, **1193**
Elizabethan (Shakespearean) sonnet **180,** 1201
English sonnet. See Elizabethan (Shakespearean) sonnet.
Epic 328, 350, 351, **1193**
Epithet 795, **1193**
Essay 248, **1102, 1193**
Exaggeration 962
Exposition 815, **1193,** 1197
Extended definition 229
Fable 229, **1193**
Fact and opinion 1147
Falling action 1198
False cause fallacy 1207
Fantasy **962**
Farce **1193**
Fiction 683
Figure of speech (figurative language) 12, 35, 74, **78,** 83, 107, **224,** 228, 376, 396, 452, **622,** 670, 683, 742, 763, 786, 795, 799, 805, **1002,** 1004, 1038, 1042, 1066, 1100, 1108, 1149, 1151, 1165, 1185, **1193**
Flashback 131, 132, 547, 1093, 1157, **1193**
Foil **1193**
Folk ballad 1190
Folklore 162, 458, **732,** 758, 996
Folk tale 20, 162, 996, 1195
Foot 176–177, **1194**
Foreshadowing 132, 153, 320, 509, **673,** 683, 724, 931, **1194**
Form 745, 954, 1004, 1008
Frame story 1033

Free verse 344, 345, 350, **355,** 365, 366, 670, **742, 772,** 792, 796, **1194**
Generalizations 232, 246, 1204
Gothic 262, **274,** 280, 715, **728**
Haiku 772
Harlem Renaissance **534, 734,** 764, 766
Hasty generalizations 1184, 1206
Hero **147, 149,** 167, 366, 494, **531–532,** 607, 616, 622, 631, 642, 660, 663, 671, 673, 683, 934
Humor 452, 463, 464, 962
Hyperbole 463, **622,** 962, **1194**
Iamb 176–177, 180, **575,** 776, **1194,** 1196
Iambic pentameter 180, **575, 1194**
Idiom **1194**
Idyll 182
Imagery 66, 83, 107, 112, 125, 174, 178, 179, 186, 192, **218,** 228, 288, 289, 328, 355, 358, 362, 364, 365, 368, 370, 376, 385, 390, 431, 445, 493, 547, 557, 562, 576, 579, 669, 671, 701, 742, 745, 768, 774, 777, 779, 781, 782, 786, 792, 795, 799, 805, 946, **949,** 954, **975,** 978, 1004, 1011, 1013, 1025, 1038, 1053, 1066, 1075, **1089,** 1091, 1100, 1126, 1151, 1165, 1169, 1176, **1194**
Imagism 533, **771,** 773, **776,** 778, 779, 781, 787, 796, **1194**
Impressionism **484, 1194**
Incongruity 962, **1194–1195**
Induction 687
Inferences 153, 232, 280, 313, 862, 1169
Inflated diction 166
Informal essay. See Personal (informal) essay.
Inner story 1033
Interior monologue 1157, **1195**
Interpretive claim 805, 806
Inversion 69, 71, 113, 174, **1195**
Irony 192, 379, 391, 395, 463, **485,** 493, 494, 566, 621, 631, 642, 649, **683,** 684, 712, 749, 862, 888, 930, 934, 946, 962, 973, 1147, 1151, **1195**
  dramatic **1195**
  situational **485,** 493, **1195**
  verbal **1195**
Italian sonnet. See Petrarchan (Italian) sonnet.
Jargon 631, 801
Journal 222, 247
Key passages 1165
Legend 996
Literary ballad **1190**
Local color 419
Lyric poem 746, 1008, **1195**
Magic realism **996, 1195**
Main events 280, 328
Main idea (theme) 105, 112, 115, 125, 134, 166, 199, 218, 228, 262, 295, 298, 308, 352, 359, 364, 384, 404, 474, 547, 563, 604, 621, 622, 634, 642, 645, 660, 673, 683, 745, 786, 805, 961, 963, 1075, 1091, 1093, 1140, 1142, 1147, 1157, 1165, 1176, **1202**
Main point 931
Marxism **530**
Melodrama 818, 1201
Message 180, 193, 246, 361, 364, 390, 395, 563, 566, 568, 575, 649, 701, 742, 745, 749,

768, 799, 954, 1008, 1042

Metaphor 35, 71, 73, 74, 83, 105, 112, 178, 179, **188**, 192, 193, 228, 246, 320, 342, 379, 384, 385, 390, 391, 395, 396, 431, **452**, 463, 568, 576, 582, 622, 634, 642, 669, 670, 696, 701, 749, 784, 785, 803, 862, 931, 934, **1002**, 1008, 1035, 1038, 1066, 1091, 1100, 1108, 1149, 1165, 1178, 1193, **1195**
  comic 452, **463**
  dead **1196**
  extended 71, 73, 74, **188**, 192, 193, **452**, 463, 669, 934, **1195–1196**
  implied 582, 784, **1195**
  mixed **1196**
Meter 69, **176–177**, 179, 180, 345, 355, 365, 370, 379, 396, 575, 670, 701, 761, 786, 1157, **1196**, 1200
Metonymy **1196**
Metrical pattern 670, 772
Modernism **523**, 525, **533**, 657, 662, **914, 1196**
Monologue 329, 649, **663**, 671, 712, 1033, 1157
Mood 180, 186, 768, 777, 978, 1004, 1093, 1100, 1200
Moral 568, 649, 962
Motif 162
Motivation 36, 445, 493, **586**, 604, 605, **828**, 849, 862, 877, 888, **1110**, 1119, **1196**
Myth 617, 642, 663, 996, **1196**
Narrative 162, 1066, **1196**
Narrator 166, 547, 724, 759, 931, 961, 1044, 1053, 1066, 1075, 1087, 1129, 1154
Naturalism **421**, 467, **484**, **496**, 509, **1196**
Nonfiction **912**, 935, 1013, 1147
Novel 274, **417**, **422**, 935
Objective correlative **777**, **1197**
Objective reporting 931, **936**, 946, 947
Objectivism 778
Octave 180, **1197**, 1201
Ode **1197**
Omniscient narrator 547
Onomatopoeia 179, 180, **288**, 355, 557, 568, 768, **1197**
Ornate style 35, 1201
Overstatement 1184
Oxymoron **622**, **1197**
Parable 246, **308**, **567**, 568, **1197**
Paradox 229, **248**, 257, 384, **604**, 745, 782, 799, 994, 1108, **1197**
Parallelism (parallel structure) **115**, 125, 337, 355, 365, 402, 742, **1197**
Paraphrase 71, 193, 199, 218, 228, 229, 308, 395, 517, 670, 791, 799, 1210
Parody 289, 320, **624**, 631, **1197**
Personal (informal) essay **1102**, 1108
Personal symbol 1202
Personification 179, 281, 390, 395, 493, **622**, 649, **737**, 742, 745, **1002**, 1007, 1008, **1035**, 1038, 1042, 1100, **1149**, 1151, 1193, **1197**
Persuasion **101**, 105, 107, 112, 186, **1197**
Petrarchan (Italian) sonnet **180**, 1201
Plain style 12, **27**, **35**, **1197**
Plot **153**, 167, 496, 509, 605, 622, 725, 805, 900, 994, 1038, **1197–1198**
Plot sequence 725
Poetry **149**, 746, 791, **914**, 948, **977**, 1008, 1169, 1176

Point of view **232**, 247, 280, 309, 320, 329, 358, **467**, 474, 712, 713, 745, 805, 1140, **1198**
  first-person **232**, 247, 309, 358, 1140, **1198**
  objective **467**, **1198**
  omniscient 320, **467**, **1198**
  third-person limited **467**, **1198**
Postmodernism **910–911**, **913**, 918, 1152, **1198**
Protagonist 660, 663, 814, 815, 862, 994, **1199**
Proverb 465, 1066, **1199**
Psychoanalysis **530**, 657
Psychological novel **422**
Public symbol 1202
Pun 390, **1199**
Purpose 36, 55, 361, 742, 1140, 1147
Quatrain 180, **1199**
Quest 1066
Rationalism **13**, **18**, 143, 561
Realism **408**, 467, 820, 996, **1199**
Refrain 180, **288**, 289, 1042, **1122**, 1126, **1199**
Regionalism **419**, **1199**
Repetition 355, 365, 742, 768, 961
Resolution 576, 671, 961, 1087, 1140, 1198, **1199**
Reversal 684
Rhetorical question 105, 333, **1199**
Rhyme 69, 180, 282, **288**, 345, 355, 365, **380**, 395, 396, 563, 575, 670, 701, 776, 786, 791, 799, 1091, 1157, **1199**
  approximate **380**, 1091, **1199**
  end 575, 670, 791, **1199**
  exact **380**, 791
  half **380**, **1199**
  imperfect **1199**
  internal **288**, 670, **1195**, **1199**
  off **380**, **1199**
  slant 379, **380**, 395, 396, 563, 791, 799, **1199**, **1201**
Rhyme scheme 180, **288**, 289, 379, 561, 701, 799, **1199**
Rhythm 115, 282, 355, 563, 670, 701, 742, **761**, 768, 776, 782, 795, 1004, 1157, 1169, **1200**
Rising action 1198
Romance 673, **683**, 684, **1200**
Romantic hero 149
Romanticism **143**, **144**, 212, 247, 576, 746, **770**, **1200**
Romantic novel **417**
Satire **50**, 55, 166, 631, **962**, **1200**
Scanning poetry 176, 1196, **1200**
Sensory details 509, 557, 1011, 1025
Sensory language 131, 186, 262, 557, 1169
Sestet 180, **1200**, 1201
Setting **153**, 166, 289, 364, **539**, 547, 575, 622, 642, 669, 683, **715**, 724, 725, 727, 805, 961, 973, 1033, **1093**, 1100, 1140, **1200–1201**
Shakespearean sonnet. See Elizabethan (Shakespearean) sonnet.
Simile 35, 83, 379, 396, 561, 566, 568, 576, **622**, 669, 742, 768, **1002**, 1035, 1038, 1100, 1108, 1193, **1201**
Slang 398–400, 742, 795, **801–803**
Slant rhyme 379, **380**, 395, 396, 563, 791, 799, **1199**, **1201**
Soliloquy **1201**
Sonnet **180**, 560, **1201**

Sound effects (sound devices) 262, **282**, 288, 289, 365, 510, 563, 742, 786, 795, 1004, 1091, 1169, **1201**
Speaker 288, 289, 359, 384, 579, 582, 669, 670, 696, 742, 745, 749, 768, 785, 795, 978, 1004, 1008, 1011, 1038, 1042, 1151, 1156, 1157
Speaker's expectations 777
Spirituals **432**, 741
Spondee 177, **1201**
Stanza 772
Stereotype 166, 624, **1201**
Stock characters 1201
Stock epithets 1193
Straw-man arguments 1184
Stream of consciousness **530**, **703**, 712, 713, **1201**
Style 12, 27, **35**, 55, **107**, 112, 113, 166, 309, 361, 365, 366, 396, 660, 742, **1027**, 1033, 1038, 1066, 1126, 1150, **1201**, 1203
Subject 745, 786, 795
Subjective reporting 46, **936**, 946, 947
Subject matter 396
Surrealism **1202**
Suspense 132, 673, 947, 1129, **1202**
Symbol 193, **280**, 288, **298**, 308, 445, 563, 565, 566, 568, 724, 786, 931, 973, 978, 1038, 1100, 1193, **1202**
Symbolism 193, 214, 309, 320, 329, 533, 742, **770**, 796, 805, **1202**
Symbolists 661, **770**
Synecdoche **1202**
Synesthesia 799, **1010**, 1091, **1202**
Syntax 35, 133, 796, 799
Tableau vivant 747
Tall tale 463, 996, **1202**
Tense 361, 703
Theme. *See* Main idea (theme).
Thesis 806
Title 379, 381, 383, 384, 562, 566, 646, 670, 712, 724, 748, 749, 759, 782, 785, 786, 888, 954, 994, 1004, 1008, 1033, 1053, 1075, 1087, 1110, 1119, 1126, 1140, 1157, 1159, 1165, 1176
Tone 50, 55, 97, 131, 166, 174, 180, 288, 308, 355, 358, 364, 365, 366, 379, 382, 384, 391, 395, 396, 561, 563, 566, 576, **577**, 579, 605, 622, 649, 696, 701, 742, 745, **764**, 768, 774, 777, 786, 795, 797, 799, 900, 931, 954, 973, 1004, 1008, 1011, 1053, 1066, 1075, 1091, 1140, 1147, **1150**, 1151, 1165, **1202–1203**
Topic 749, 1066, 1108
Tragedy **683**, 888, **1203**
Tragic flaw 1203
Transcendentalism **210–212**, 226, 230, 296, 329, 365, 366, 381, 568, 649, 796, **1203**
Trochee **1203**
Turning point 777, 1198
Understatement **463**, 1033, **1203**
Urban folklore **732**
Vernacular **398–399**, 792, **1203**

READING AND CRITICAL THINKING

Active reading strategies 1204–1205. *See also* Dialogue with the Text.
Aesthetic elements, responding to 1171
Affixes, analyzing 475

Allusions, understanding **186, 670**
Analogies 107, 112, 167, 384, 890, 1189
  word, analyzing 890
Analysis questions (Shaping Interpretations)
  35, 46, 55, 66, 71, 74, 83, 97, 105, 112, 125,
  166, 174, 179, 186, 192, 228, 246, 257, 280,
  288, 308, 320, 328, 352, 355, 358, 361, 364,
  379, 384, 390, 395, 430, 445, 463, 474, 493,
  509, 547, 557, 561, 562, 566, 568, 575, 579,
  582, 604, 621, 631, 642, 649, 660, 669, 683,
  696, 701, 712, 724, 742, 745, 749, 759, 768,
  777, 782, 785, 791, 795, 799, 849, 862, 877,
  888, 930, 934, 946, 954, 961, 973, 978, 994,
  1004, 1008, 1011, 1025, 1033, 1038, 1042,
  1053, 1066, 1075, 1087, 1091, 1100, 1108,
  1119, 1126, 1140, 1147, 1151, 1157, 1165,
  1169, 1176
Anecdote 107, 112, 333, 402, 465, 1189
Appeal
  to credibility 71, 166, 288, 474, 496, 509,
    712, 994, 1119, 1140, 1151
  to emotion 74, 78, 83, 101, 105, 107, 112,
    179, 186, 281, 289, 308, 334, 355, 358, 364,
    374, 378, 379, 547, 774, 1053, 1126, 1147
  to logic 74, 101, 105, 107, 334, 374, 376,
    378, 379, 1147
Archaisms, understanding 308
Arguing *ad hominem* 1206
Associations 224, 228, 557, 663, 669, 742,
  761, 996, 1040, 1151, 1165
Author's purpose 36, 338, 361, 759, 1140,
  1147, 1183
Autobiography, analyzing 751, 759
Begging the question 1206
Blank verse, understanding 575
Brainstorming 203, 229, 258, 331, 339, 405,
  445, 515, 557, 582, 631, 632, 649, 686, 687,
  809, 896, 1187
Cause and effect 496, 509, 547, 557, 576,
  579, 582, 605, 622, 624, 632, 642, 649, 660,
  671, 684, **685–688**
Character
  drawing inferences about 313
  interpreting 660, 1129, 1140
  taking notes on 715
Character profile 652
Charts 21, 25, 37, 57, 66, 85, 105, 115, 133,
  153, 166, 167, 199, 310, 313, 329, 331, 332,
  366, 396, 401, 402, 422, 425, 431, 475, 557,
  576, 673, 689, 712, 726, 742, 745, 768, 795,
  803, 890, 896, 897, 994, 1066, 1087, 1182,
  1204
Chronological order, analyzing 39, 46, 280,
  725
Cluster diagrams 115, 671, 686, 725, 896,
  1075, 1159, 1165
Comic devices, identifying 463
Comparing themes across texts 359
Comparison and contrast 46, 47, 55, 76, 83,
  97, 105, 166, 174, 178, 179, 180, 192, 229,
  246, 290, 295, 365, 366, 370, 382, 390, 391,
  463, 509, 520, 521, 568, 622, 631, 649, 669,
  712, 725, 726, 732, 745, 749, 768, 777, 784,
  795, 889, 1004, 1038, 1066, 1087, 1151,
  1169
Comprehension questions (Reading Check)
  35, 46, 55, 66, 83, 97, 105, 112, 125, 166,
  192, 228, 246, 257, 280, 308, 320, 328, 430,
  445, 463, 474, 493, 509, 547, 557, 604, 621,

631, 642, 660, 683, 712, 724, 759, 849, 862,
  877, 888, 930, 946, 954, 961, 973, 994,
  1025, 1033, 1053, 1066, 1075, 1087, 1100,
  1108, 1119, 1140, 1147, 1165, 1176
Conclusions, drawing 105, 295, 687, 1204
Connotations, interpreting 956, 961
Context clues 37, 134, 168, 228, 262, 308,
  313, 670, 947, 1186
Craft, writer's. *See specific elements of literature
  in index of Literary Terms.*
Credibility, evaluating 338, 1209–1210
Details, interpreting 1013, 1025
Dialogue with the Text 425, 436, 728, 996
Difficult texts, dealing with 1205
Double-entry journal 73, 101, 105, 170, 174,
  232, 246, 313, 385, 804, 805, 896, 1154
Either/or reasoning 1207
Evaluation 696, 934, 947, 954, 963, 973, 978,
  994, 1004, 1008, 1011, 1025, 1033, 1038,
  1042, 1053, 1066, 1075, 1087, 1091, 1100,
  1108, 1119, 1126, 1140, 1147, 1151, 1157,
  1165, 1169, 1176
Evaluation questions (Challenging the Text)
  46, 66, 71, 83, 97, 166, 174, 179, 192, 246,
  257, 280, 288, 379, 384, 390, 395, 445, 463,
  474, 493, 509, 561, 568, 579, 604, 670, 724,
  759, 795, 888, 947, 961, 1033, 1108, 1147,
  1169
Evidence, gathering 97, 199, 280, 288, 295,
  332, 333, 356, 366, 474, 632, 687, 862, 889,
  897, 900, 1004, 1025, 1033, 1053, 1147,
  1176, 1182, 1184
Experience (personal), drawing on. *See Prior
  knowledge.*
Extended metaphor, analyzing an 73
False analogy 1207
Figures of speech, analyzing 78, 228, 622
Film review, analyzing a 900
Finding Common Ground 25, 76, 295, 370,
  732, 1000, 1154
Footnotes, checking 218, 262, 1258
Generalizations, making 232, 246, 1204
Glossary, using a 218, 262, 404, 1258
Graphic organizers, using 21, 25, 27, 37, 39,
  57, 66, 85, 105, 115, 130, 131, 133, 153,
  166, 167, 199, 200, 310, 313, 329, 331, 332,
  366, 396, 401, 402, 422, 425, 431, 475, 517,
  557, 576, 671, 673, 686, 689, 690, 712, 725,
  726, 742, 745, 768, 795, 803, 890, 894, 896,
  897, 899, 994, 1066, 1075, 1087, 1154,
  1182, 1204, 1205
Imagery, appreciating 701
Images, identifying 774, 777
Inferences, drawing 153, 166, 232, 246, 298,
  313, 328, 356, 569, 575, 586, 604, 1044,
  1053, 1077, 1087, 1169, 1204
Interpretation 46, 71, 295, 696, 701, 712,
  725, 742, 745, 749, 759, 768, 777, 782, 785,
  786, 791, 795, 799, 804, 828, 849, 862, 888,
  889, 934, 1033, 1053, 1087, 1151, 1154,
  1157, 1176. *See also* Analysis questions
  (Shaping Interpretations).
Interpreting texts 828, 849
Inversion, analyzing an 69
Key passages, identifying 1102, 1159, 1165
Knowledge questions (Reading Check) 35,
  46, 55, 66, 83, 97, 105, 112, 125, 166, 192,
  228, 246, 257, 280, 308, 320, 328, 430, 445,
  463, 474, 493, 509, 547, 557, 604, 621, 631,

642, 660, 683, 712, 724, 759, 849, 862, 877,
  888, 930, 946, 954, 961, 973, 994, 1025,
  1033, 1053, 1066, 1075, 1087, 1100, 1108,
  1119, 1140, 1147, 1165, 1176
KWL charts 21, 25, 57, 66, 422, 431, 1204
Literary language, analyzing 78
Loaded words, identifying 46, 281, 334–335,
  900
Logical fallacies, identifying 1184, 1206–1207
Main events, time line of 27, 35, 1069
Main idea (theme) 105, 112, 115, 125, 134,
  166, 199, 218, 228, 262, 295, 298, 308, 352,
  359, 364, 384, 404, 474, 547, 563, 604, 621,
  634, 642, 645, 660, 673, 683, 745, 786, 805,
  961, 963, 1075, 1091, 1093, 1140, 1142,
  1147, 1157, 1165, 1176, 1202
Main ideas, identifying 115, 663, 670, 1093,
  1100, 1102, 1108, 1142, 1147, 1159, 1165
Melodies of language, analyzing 180, 282, 288
Memoranda, reading 1186
Metaphors, analyzing 246, 670, 784, 1066
Modes of persuasion, recognizing 101, 105,
  107, 112, 186
Monitoring reading 134, 218, 281
Non-chronological order 1069
Nonsequential order 1204
Note-taking strategy 27
Noting organization 1204–1205
Observation 18, 50, 55, 186, 193, 353, 355,
  356, 566, 1066
Opinion 71, 83, 97, 125, 192, 193, 214, 228,
  246, 247, 248, 257, 280, 288, 308, 309, 352,
  355, 361, 365, 374, 379, 388, 390, 445, 464,
  474, 493, 509, 547, 561, 566, 568, 575, 579,
  604, 621, 631, 645, 649, 660, 670, 724, 744,
  759, 764, 768, 777, 784, 787, 791, 795, 799,
  828, 849, 862, 877, 888, 900, 931, 934, 946,
  947, 973, 978, 1004, 1008, 1011, 1033,
  1042, 1100, 1147, 1181
Oral interpretations, making 692
Outlining 896, 1142, 1205
Paradoxes, understanding 604
Paraphrasing 115, 166, 174, 193, 218, 228,
  390, 395, 575, 622, 670, 791, 799, 978,
  1091, 1205
Personal response (including First Thoughts
  and Connecting with the Text) 27, 35, 39,
  46, 50, 55, 57, 66, 69, 71, 73, 74, 78, 83, 85,
  97, 101, 105, 107, 112, 115, 125, 153, 166,
  170, 174, 176, 178, 179, 182, 186, 188, 190,
  192, 218, 224, 228, 232, 246, 248, 257, 262,
  280, 282, 288, 298, 308, 313, 320, 328, 351,
  352, 353, 355, 356, 358, 359, 361, 362, 364,
  374, 376, 378, 379, 381, 382, 383, 384, 385,
  386, 388, 390, 391, 392, 393, 395, 422, 425,
  430, 436, 445, 452, 463, 467, 474, 485, 493,
  496, 509, 539, 547, 549, 557, 560, 561, 562,
  564, 565, 566, 567, 568, 569, 575, 577, 579,
  580, 582, 586, 604, 607, 621, 624, 631, 634,
  642, 645, 646, 649, 652, 660, 663, 669, 670,
  673, 683, 692, 696, 698, 701, 703, 712, 715,
  724, 737, 742, 744, 745, 747, 748, 749, 751,
  759, 761, 764, 768, 774, 777, 779, 782, 784,
  785, 787, 791, 792, 795, 797, 799, 828, 849,
  862, 877, 888, 921, 930, 931, 932, 934, 936,
  946, 949, 954, 956, 961, 965, 973, 975, 978,
  981, 994, 1002, 1003, 1004, 1006, 1007,
  1008, 1010, 1011, 1013, 1025, 1027, 1033,
  1035, 1038, 1040, 1042, 1044, 1053, 1055,

1066, 1069, 1075, 1077, 1087, 1089, 1091, 1093, 1100, 1102, 1108, 1110, 1119, 1122, 1126, 1129, 1140, 1142, 1147, 1149, 1150, 1151, 1156, 1157, 1159, 1165, 1167, 1169, 1171, 1176, 1204

Poetry, responding to 76

Predicting and confirming 153, 166, 167, 192, 232, 262, 308, 320, 392, 425, 430, 436, 445, 509, 560, 561, 562, 565, 566, 634, 642, 673, 683, 728, 745, 748, 797, 799, 824, 973, 994, 1035, 1038, 1119, 1149, 1187, 1204

Prereading strategies 1204

Previewing texts 1204

Prior experience 47, 55, 66, 71, 74, 83, 97, 105, 112, 125, 170, 182, 382, 390, 452, 463, 464, 564, 607, 692, 698, 791, 792, 795, 804, 805, 921, 932, 954, 981, 1003, 1006, 1007, 1008, 1010, 1011, 1025, 1038, 1042, 1055, 1089, 1100, 1108, 1150, 1151, 1159, 1167, 1171, 1204

Prior knowledge 21, 112, 179, 190, 193, 248, 257, 328, 358, 359, 361, 376, 384, 393, 422, 515, 536, 561, 562, 580, 607, 660, 696, 742, 745, 759, 761, 805, 918, 934, 947, 954, 956, 1002, 1087, 1110, 1119, 1169, 1204

Problem solving 895

Pros and cons 332, 333

Purpose, setting a. See Setting a purpose for reading (Before You Read).

Purposes for reading 134

Question boxes 262, 264–279, 663–666

Reading actively 1204–1205

Reading closely for details 652, 703, 936

Reading for Life
  evaluating credibility of sources 338
  interpreting and constructing a graphic organizer 690
  monitoring your reading 134
  obtaining information from an Internet database 808
  reading a college guide 520
  reading a film review 900
  reading a textbook 404
  reading maps 202
  reading memoranda 1186

Reading poetry 567

Recognizing shared characteristics of cultures 368

Rereading 27, 69, 98, 115, 133, 134, 186, 199, 200, 201, 281, 337, 339, 361, 403, 431, 509, 516, 557, 622, 663, 696, 777, 782, 785, 795, 806, 807, 828, 899, 949, 1087, 1100, 1102, 1122, 1147, 1176, 1181, 1183, 1184, 1185, 1205

Resources, using 262

Responding to texts 125, 170, 467, 474, 549

Rhymes, understanding 670

Rhythm, understanding 670

Scanning data 808

Scanning poetry 176, 1196, 1200

Semantic features analysis 726

Sequential order 1204

Series-of-events chain 27, 687

Setting a purpose for reading (Before You Read) 27, 39, 50, 57, 69, 73, 76, 78, 85, 101, 107, 115, 153, 170, 176, 178, 182, 188, 190, 218, 224, 232, 248, 262, 282, 290, 298, 313, 351, 353, 356, 359, 362, 368, 374, 376, 378, 381, 382, 383, 385, 386, 388, 391, 392,

393, 422, 425, 436, 452, 467, 485, 496, 539, 549, 560, 562, 564, 565, 567, 569, 577, 580, 586, 607, 624, 634, 645, 646, 652, 663, 673, 692, 698, 703, 715, 728, 737, 744, 747, 748, 751, 761, 764, 774, 779, 784, 787, 792, 797, 828, 921, 932, 936, 949, 956, 965, 975, 981, 996, 1002, 1003, 1006, 1007, 1010, 1013, 1027, 1035, 1040, 1044, 1055, 1069, 1077, 1089, 1093, 1102, 1110, 1122, 1129, 1142, 1149, 1150, 1152, 1156, 1159, 1167, 1171, 1204

Skimming 166, 186, 404, 936, 1186

Sound effects, hearing 288

Sources
  evaluating the credibility of. See Credibility, evaluating.
  identifying 362

Spatial order 1204

Specific details 186, 280, 313, 1066, 1122, 1126, 1140
  identifying 1122, 1126

Stereotype 46, 166, 624, 1201

Story map 1205

Structure of poetry 799

Study skills 1205–1207

Study strategies, using 27, 1142

Summarizing 125, 246, 431, 474, 547, 568, 849, 994, 1011, 1100, 1108

Summarizing text 353, 355, 391

Supporting details 125, 167, 180, 247, 309, 696, 742, 805
  identifying 663, 670, 1093, 1100, 1102, 1108, 1142, 1186

Synthesis (including Extending the Text) 35, 55, 66, 97, 105, 112, 166, 174, 179, 192, 193, 246, 257, 288, 320, 328, 358, 361, 365, 384, 390, 430, 445, 474, 547, 557, 561, 563, 568, 575, 621, 631, 649, 660, 670, 696, 724, 742, 745, 749, 782, 795, 862, 877, 888, 931, 934, 947, 973, 978, 994, 1011, 1075, 1087, 1126, 1151, 1169

Text structures, analyzing 39, 46, 69, 73, 74, 496, 509, 624, 1069

Time line 27, 35, 828, 849, 1069, 1075

Tone, identifying 50, 55

Tracking responses 737

Translation 370

Understanding texts 1154

Venn diagrams 66, 745

Vocabulary, dictionary for 37

Word families, analyzing 1120

Word meanings, interpreting 956, 961

Word origins, tracing 310, 894

LANGUAGE (GRAMMAR, USAGE, AND MECHANICS)

Accept, except 1252

Adjective(s) 1220, 1227
  clauses 519, 1231, 1235
  phrases 1229
  proper 1239

Adverb(s) 1220, 1227
  clauses 519, 1232, 1235
  conjunctive 1244
  phrases 1229

Affect, effect 1252

Affixes 475

Agreement

  pronoun and antecedent 1222–1223
  subject and verb 1221–1222

All ready, already 1252

All the farther, all the faster 1252

All together, altogether 1252

Allusion, illusion 1252

Allusions 35, 39, 46, 47, 83, 105, 186, 262, 670, 1008, 1157, 1159, 1165, 1189

Almost, most 1252

A lot 1252

American English 127–129

Among, between 1253

Amount, number 1253

And, but 1253

And etc. 1253

And/or 1253

Anglo-Saxon influence 893–894

Any more, anymore 1253

Any one, anyone 1253

Anyways, anywheres 1253

Apostrophes
  with contractions 1248
  with plurals 1248
  with possessive case 1247–1248

Appositives 1226, 1231, 1243, 1249

As, like 1255

As if, like 1255

At 1253

A while, awhile 1253

Bad, badly 1253

Base sentence 201

Because 1253

Being as, being that 1253

Beside, besides 1253

Between, among 1253

Brackets 1249

Bring, take 1254

But, and 1253

Cannot (can't) help but 1254

Capitalization 1238–1242
  of titles 1242

Clauses 1231–1232
  independent 1231, 1244
  subordinate 1231, 1238
    adjective 519, 1231–1232, 1235
    adverb 519, 1232, 1235
    elliptical 1232
    nonrestrictive 519
    noun 1232
    restrictive 519

Colons 1244–1245
  in word analogies 890

Commas 1243–1244
  in compound sentences 1243
  in conventional situations 1244
  as interrupters 1243
  with introductory words, phrases, and clauses 1243
  with items in a series 1243
  with nonessential clauses and phrases 1243

Comma splice 1236

Compare, contrast 1254

Complements 1233–1234
  direct objects 1234
  indirect objects 1234
  objective complements 1234
  subject complements 1234
    predicate adjectives 1234
    predicate nominatives 1234

Conjunctions
  coordinating 133, 337, 1221, 1238
  correlative 337, 1221, 1238
  subordinating 519, 688, 689, 1221
Connotation 46, 281, 308, 649, 683, 701,
  726, 894, 956, 961, 1185, 1192
Contractions 1248
Dashes 384, 1249
Dialect 512–514, 1055, 1066, 1192
Diction 1185
Double comparison 1228
Double negative 1228
Double subject 1254
Due to 1254
Each and every 1254
Effect, affect 1252
Either, neither 1254
Ellipsis points 1184, 1247
Emigrate, immigrate 1254
End marks 1242–1243
Etc. 1253
Every day, everyday 1254
Every one, everyone 1254
Except, accept 1252
Farther, further 1254
Fewer, less 1254
Figures of speech 228, 622
Fragments 1232, 1236
Free verse 344, 345, 350, 355, 365, 366, 670,
  742, 772, 792, 796, 1194
Gerund 1230
Good, well 1255
Grammar 513, 514
Grammar books 195
Had ought, hadn't ought 1255
Half 1255
Humor 463
Hyphens 1248–1249
If, whether 1255
Illusion, allusion 1252
Imagery 701
Immigrate, emigrate 1254
Imply, infer 1255
In, into 1255
Inflated diction 166
Interjection 1221
Inversion 69, 71, 113, 174, 1195
Irregardless, regardless 1255
Italics (underlining) 1245–1246
Its, it's 1255
Japanese terms 947
Kind(s), sort(s), type(s) 1255
Kind of, sort of 1255
Language regulation 129
Language Workshop 133, 201, 337, 403, 519,
  689, 807, 899, 1185
Learn, teach 1255
Less, fewer 1254
Lie, lay 1255
Like, as 1255
Like, as if 1255
Metaphors 246, 431, 670, 1066
Modifiers 1227–1232
  adjective phrases 1229
  adjectives 1227
  adverb phrases 1229
  adverbs 1227
  comparative and superlative forms
    of 1227–1228

dangling 1228
  inserting 201
  misplaced 1228
  participial phrases 1229
  prepositional phrases 1229
Most, almost 1252
Neither, either 1254
Nor, or 1256
Noun(s) 1220
  case of 1225
  clauses 1232
  collective 1222, 1223
  common and proper 1239
  plural 1251
  possessive 1225, 1226, 1247–1248
Number, amount 1253
Of 1256
On to, onto 1256
Or, nor 1256
Paradox 229, 248, 257, 384, 604, 745, 782,
  799, 994, 1108, 1197
Parallel structure 337, 1235–1236
Parentheses 1249
Parenthetical expressions 1244, 1249
Parts of speech 1220–1221
Patterns of speech 195
Phrases 1229–1231
  adjective 1229
  adverb 1229
  appositive 1231
  gerund 1230
  infinitive 1230
  participial 1229
  prepositional 1229
  verbal 1229
Precise meanings 257
Prepositional phrases 1229
Prepositions 1220, 1226
Pronouns 1220, 1225–1227
  and agreement with antecedent 1222–1223
  case of 1225
    nominative 1226
    objective 1226
    possessive 1226
  demonstrative 1220
  and gender 1222
  indefinite 1220, 1221, 1222, 1223, 1247
  intensive 1220
  interrogative 1220
  personal 1220, 1227
  plural 1222–1223, 1226
  reference with 1227
  reflexive and intensive 1220
  relative 1220
  special problems with
    appositives 1226
    elliptical construction 1227
    -self or -selves 1227
    who and whom 1226
Punctuation 799, 1242–1249
  of dialogue 1246
  of titles 1245, 1247
Quotation marks 703, 1246–1247
Regardless, irregardless 1255
Rhyme 670
Rhythm 670
Rise, raise 1256
Run-on sentences 1236
Semicolons 1244

Sentences 1232–1238
  base 201
  classified by purpose 1235
  classified by structure 1234–1235
    complex 1235
    compound 1234
    compound-complex 1235
    simple 1234
  combining 133, 201, 519, 1238
  vs. fragments 1232, 1236
  kinds of 1234–1235
  run-on 1236
    comma splice 1236
    fused 1236
  structure of 749
  subject and predicate in 1233
    compound subjects 1221–1222, 1233
    compound verbs 1233
    finding the subject 1233
    simple predicates 1233
    simple subjects 1233
  varying the structure of 403, 1237
  wordy 1237
  writing clear 1236–1237
  writing effective 1235–1237
Sit, set 1256
Slang 398–400, 742, 795, 801–803
Slash (/) in quoting poetry 1184
Some, somewhat 1256
Sort of, kind of 1255
Spelling. See index of Vocabulary and Spelling.
Take, bring 1254
Than, then 1256
That, who, which 1257
Their, there, they're 1256
Theirs, there's 1256
Them 1257
This here, that there 1257
Transitional expressions 334, 518, 899, 1183,
  1244
Try and, try to 1257
Type, type of 1257
Usage 127–129, 195–197, 512–514, 801–803
Verbals and verbal phrases 1229–1230
  gerund 1230
  gerund phrase 1230
  infinitive 1230
  infinitive clause 1230
  infinitive phrase 1230
  participial phrase 1229–1230
  participle 1229–1230
Verbs 1223–1225
  action 1220
  active and passive voice of 1225
  agreement with subject of 1221–1222
  be, avoiding overuse of 1225
  helping (auxiliary) 1220
  irregular 1223–1224
  linking 1220
  principal parts of 1223
  regular 1223–1224
  special problems with
    lie and lay 1255
    rise and raise 1256
    sit and set 1256
  tense of 361, 703, 807, 1224–1225
    consistency of 807, 1225
    literary present 807
Vernacular 398–399, 792, 1203

Ways 1257
Well, good 1255
When, where 1257
Whether, if 1255
Who, which, that 1257
Who's, whose 1257
Wordiness 1237
Word meanings 257
Word order 174
Word parts 475, 1120, 1249–1250
Your, you're 1257

VOCABULARY AND SPELLING

Acronyms 1179, 1180
Affixes 475
Americanisms 127–129, 196, 399, 1178, 1179
Analogy 107, 112, 167, 384, 890, 1189
  word 890
Anglo-Saxon influence 893–894
Antonyms 1206
Archaisms 37, 308
Argot 801, 1179
Backwoods English 398
Base words 475, 1120
Borrowings 310, 802, 1178
Clipped forms of words 803
Coined words 399–400, 1179
Computer language 1179–1180, 1186
Context clues 37, 134, 168, 228, 262, 308, 313, 670, 947, 1186, 1218
Diacritical marks 1251
Dictionaries 37, 129, 134, 168, 310, 400, 561, 634, 726, 803, 890, 894, 1108, 1120, 1180, 1185, 1186, 1205–1206, 1258
  Webster's 195–197
Etymologies 129, 196, 197, 310, 1205–1206
  chart 310
Euphemisms 892–894
Jargon 631, 801
Latin influence 310, 893–894
Loaded words 46, 281, 334–335, 900
Loanwords 400, 802
Nonstandard spelling 197
OK 400
Prefixes 475, 1120, 1249
Pronunciation 127, 129, 196, 197, 512–514
Roots 475, 1120, 1249
Semantic features analysis 726
Specialized vocabulary 400
Spelling reform 195–197
Spelling rules 1250–1252
Suffixes 400, 475, 1120, 1224, 1250–1251
  derivational 475
  inflectional 475, 1120
Suggestive words 281
Synonyms 224, 726, 1185, 1206
Taboo words 892
Technology's influence 1178–1180, 1186
Thesaurus 726, 1185, 1206
Usage 127–129, 195–197, 512–514, 801–803
Verbs with *-cede, -ceed,* and *-sede* 1250
Word chart 37
Word families 1120
Word formation 475, 802, 1120, 1178–1180
Word map 168
Word parts 475, 1120, 1249–1250
Words with *ie* and *ei* 1250

WRITING

Admission essay (for college), writing an 1218
Advertisement, writing an 203, 339, 1187
Advice column, writing an 167
Agenda of topics, writing an 1000
Almanac, creating an 98
Analogy exercise, writing an 890
Analytical essay, writing an 786, 889
Analyzing
  causes and effects 496, 509, 547, 557, 576, 579, 582, 605, 622, 632, 642, 649, 660, 671, 684, 685–688, 889
  character 167, 329, 474, 605, 671, 696, 725, 889, 973, 994, 1025, 1053, 1119, 1140
  comedy 167
  conflict 167
  images 978, 1053, 1091
  literature 180, 186
  metaphors 934
  nonfiction 1147
  paradoxes 229
  poetry 71, 180, 186, 193, 289, 366, 380, 396, 576, 579, 582, 671, 696, 768, 777, 791, 799, 954, 963, 978, 1004, 1008, 1038, 1091, 1126, 1157, 1169, 1176
  prose 47, 55, 167, 198–200, 229, 247, 464, 510, 622, 642, 660, 684, 725, 732, 947, 973, 1108
  short stories 167, 510, 642, 660, 684, 725, 732, 973, 994, 1033, 1053, 1075, 1087, 1119, 1140
  suspense 947
  symbols 978
  theme 622, 963, 1075
  titles 1087
Aphorism, composing an 71
Apostrophe, writing an 795
Arguments, writing 332
Audience for writing, determining the 36, 130, 198, 331, 335, 401, 510, 515, 516, 685, 687, 804, 895, 897, 954, 1151, 1181
Autobiographical incident, writing an 36, 47, 55, 66, 71, 74, 83, 98, 105, 112, 125, 130–132
Autobiographical sketch, writing an 309
Background, writing about 1151
Block method. *See* Organizing a composition.
Booklet, writing a 98
Book of virtues, writing a 98
Brochure, writing a 203, 339, 405, 809, 1187
Bulletin, writing a 521
Bumper sticker, writing a 684, 745
Business letter, writing a 1215–1216
Business proposal, writing a 203
Causes and effects, analyzing 547, 557, 576, 579, 582, 605, 622, 632, 642, 649, 660, 671, 684, 685–688
Character sketch, writing a 1108
Choosing a subject 130, 198, 258, 289, 309, 329, 331–332, 401, 464, 515, 685–686, 779, 895, 1181
Chronological order. *See* Organizing a composition.
Cluster diagram, making a 115, 671, 686, 725, 896, 1075, 1159
College application form, writing on a 1218
Comic strip, creating a 98
Comparing and contrasting

poetry 76, 180, 365, 366, 396, 445, 557, 576, 579, 671, 696, 701, 742, 745, 749, 768, 777, 791, 795, 799, 954, 1004, 1038, 1042, 1126, 1151, 1169
  prose 36, 55, 66, 74, 83, 98, 105, 258, 329, 431, 445, 464, 517, 547, 605, 632, 759, 782, 931, 973, 1042, 1066, 1147
  values 229
Comparison-and-contrast essay, writing a 365, 396, 401–402
Conceit, devising a 74
Conclusion, writing the 132, 200, 335, 402, 518, 688, 806, 898, 994, 1038, 1184
Condensed story, writing a 309
Connotative language, using 281, 334–335, 897
Context, establishing the 131
Controlling idea, writing the 516
Controversial issue, writing about a 229, 247, 258, 281, 289, 309, 329, 331–336
Conversation, writing a 83, 749
Conveying tone 131, 518, 898
Counterarguments, writing 332
Cultural influences, writing about 1165
Descriptive writing 547, 777, 781, 782, 1100, 1151
Dialogue, writing 131, 132, 309, 405, 510, 576, 671, 973, 994
Dictionary definition, writing a 229
Double-column comparison–contrast chart, writing a 742
Drafting a composition 131–132, 200, 333–335, 402, 517–518, 688, 806, 897–898, 1151, 1183–1184, 1215
Dramatic techniques, writing about 132
Editorial, writing an 167
Elaboration strategies 131, 199, 332, 334, 402, 516, 687, 688, 805, 897, 1183
Emotional appeals, writing with 334
Encyclopedia entry, writing an 339
Epilogue, writing an 167
Epithet, writing an 795
Essay, writing a brief 36, 47, 55, 66, 71, 74, 83, 98, 125, 167, 180, 193, 229, 247, 258, 281, 309, 329, 366, 396, 431, 445, 464, 494, 510, 547, 557, 576, 579, 632, 649, 660, 671, 684, 696, 701, 725, 742, 759, 768, 786, 791, 799, 889, 931, 934, 947, 963, 973, 978, 994, 1004, 1008, 1011, 1025, 1033, 1038, 1042, 1066, 1075, 1091, 1100, 1108, 1119, 1126, 1140, 1147, 1151, 1157, 1165, 1169, 1176
Evaluation, making an 112, 132, 135, 200, 335–336, 402, 518, 688, 806, 898, 931, 934, 947, 954, 963, 973, 978, 994, 1004, 1008, 1011, 1025, 1033, 1038, 1042, 1053, 1066, 1075, 1087, 1091, 1100, 1108, 1119, 1126, 1140, 1147, 1151, 1157, 1165, 1169, 1176, 1181–1184, 1215
Evaluation forms, writing 901
Examples
  of a letter 1216
  of a résumé 1217
  from texts 1025
Expository writing 198–200, 401–402, 515–518, 685–688, 804–806
Feature article, writing a 1187
First-person point of view, writing from the 247, 309, 649, 1140
5W-How? questions

answering 405
writing 1187
Free-verse poem, writing a 365
Freewriting 83, 98, 125, 130–131, 150, 193,
288, 515, 632, 660, 698, 786, 1040
Generalizations, stating 687, 805, 806
Genre rewriting 281
Imagist poem, writing an 782
Interpretive essay, writing an 329, 696, 701,
712, 725, 742, 745, 749, 759, 768, 777, 782,
791, 795, 799, 804–806
Introduction, writing an 200, 333, 517, 688,
897, 1183
Journal entry, writing a 47, 55, 247, 431
Lead for essay, writing a 688
Letter, writing a 174, 431, 632, 791, 901,
1215–1216
Liner notes, writing 768
Literary analysis, writing a 167, 174, 180, 186,
193, 198–200
Loaded words, writing with 334
Loanword Lexicon, writing a 400
Logical appeals, writing with 334
Logical order. See Organizing a composition.
Magazine story, writing a 464, 684
Marginal notes, writing 1186
Meditation, writing a 193
Melody, writing a 799
Memoranda, writing 474, 1186, 1215
Monologue, writing a 329, 649, 671, 712, 1033
Multimedia script, writing a 135
Musical setting, writing a 180
Narrative, writing a 130–132
Narrowing focus of 198, 515
Nature personification, writing a 1151
Newspaper article, writing a 167, 281, 684,
768
Note from the artist, writing a 289
Order of importance. See Organizing a
composition.
Organizing a composition 200, 402,
1204–1025
with block comparison and contrast 517
with block method 401, 402, 806
in chronological order 131, 199, 200, 334,
516, 688, 806, 1038, 1204
in logical order 199, 200, 334, 516, 806,
1205
by order of importance 199, 200, 333–334,
517, 688, 806, 1204
with point-by-point comparison and
contrast 517
with point-by-point method 401, 402, 517,
806, 1183
Outlining 115, 199, 200, 404, 517, 686,
896–897
Overgeneralizations, avoiding 334
Paraphrasing 71, 115, 166, 193, 199, 218, 228,
229, 517, 670, 791, 799, 1210
Parody, writing a 289
Performance review, writing a 782
Persuasive letter, writing a 901
Persuasive writing 289, 331–336, 895–898,
1181–1184. See also Controversial issue.
Picture book, writing a 281
Picture poem, writing a 782
Place description, writing a 557
Play, writing a 135, 258
Poem, writing a 66, 112, 229, 281, 365, 396,

494, 576, 649, 701, 791, 934, 1038, 1042,
1126, 1151
Poetry, writing a definition of 791
Point-by-point method. See Organizing a
composition.
Point of view, writing from a 47, 55, 83, 247,
329, 431, 934, 1033, 1038, 1087, 1140,
1151
Portfolio building 36, 47, 55, 66, 71, 74, 83, 98,
105, 112, 125, 130–132, 167, 174, 180, 186,
193, 198–200, 229, 247, 258, 281, 289, 309,
329, 331–336, 365, 396, 401–402, 431, 445,
464, 474, 494, 510, 515–518, 547, 557, 576,
579, 582, 605, 622, 632, 642, 649, 660, 671,
684, 685–688, 696, 701, 712, 725, 742, 745,
749, 759, 768, 777, 782, 786, 791, 795, 799,
804–806, 889, 895–898, 931, 934, 947, 954,
963, 973, 978, 994, 1004, 1008, 1011, 1025,
1033, 1038, 1042, 1053, 1066, 1075, 1087,
1091, 1100, 1108, 1119, 1126, 1140, 1147,
1151, 1157, 1165, 1169, 1176, 1181–1184
Position statement, writing a 332
Prewriting 130–131, 198–199, 331–333, 401,
515–517, 685–687, 804–805, 895–897,
1181–1183, 1215
Problem-solution essay, writing a 889,
895–898
Product or business names, writing 197
Proofreaders' marks, table of 1218
Proofreading 1215, 1217, 1218
Proposal, writing a 98
Proposition, writing a 332
Publishing 339, 1187
Quickwrite 18, 21, 25, 57, 66, 85, 97, 150,
176, 178, 179, 182, 186, 188, 190, 192, 193,
214, 224, 248, 257, 346, 351, 352, 374, 376,
378, 381, 382, 383, 384, 385, 386, 388, 390,
392, 393, 395, 452, 464, 485, 493, 536, 539,
547, 560, 561, 562, 564, 565, 566, 580, 582,
607, 621, 622, 634, 645, 646, 649, 698, 701,
744, 745, 747, 748, 749, 761, 764, 768, 779,
781, 782, 786, 787, 791, 792, 797, 798, 799,
824, 828, 895, 896, 918, 921, 932, 965, 975,
978, 981, 994, 1002, 1003, 1004, 1006,
1007, 1008, 1010, 1011, 1035, 1038, 1040,
1042, 1055, 1066, 1089, 1110, 1119, 1149,
1150, 1151, 1156, 1157, 1167, 1169, 1181
Quotations, using 200, 516, 517, 791, 805,
1025, 1184, 1211
Rebuttal/response, writing a 112, 125, 229,
258, 494, 696, 791, 888, 978, 1004, 1011
Recording conclusions 295
Recording responses 25
Reflecting 135, 188, 203, 339, 405, 521, 809,
889, 901, 947, 1187
Report, writing a 98
Research paper, writing a 258, 445, 464, 474,
494, 510, 515–518, 1207–1214
Résumé, writing a 1217
Rewriting a text 35, 69, 132, 133, 174, 200,
201, 281, 335–336, 337, 390, 403, 474, 518,
519, 688, 689, 701, 806, 807, 898, 899,
1184, 1185, 1215
Rewriting literature 71, 309, 329, 632
Road map of life, drawing a 130
Scientific report, writing a 193
Screenplay, writing a 576, 684
Script for performance, writing a 83, 98, 135,
281, 396, 649, 660, 759

Sensory details, using 509, 557
Sentence style, improving 1235–1237
Setting, writing about 547, 576, 642, 725,
1100, 1140
Short-story adaptation, writing 474, 759
Short-story continuation, writing a 167, 445,
605, 622, 684, 712, 994
Short-story interpretation, writing a 309
Short-story writing 193, 339, 510, 642
for children 98
Simplified spelling passage, writing a 197
Song, writing a 112, 281
Specialized dictionary, compiling a 400
Specific details, using 186, 313, 1066, 1122,
1126, 1140
Stream of consciousness, writing in 712
Style, imitating a 557, 934
Summary, writing a 125, 198, 494, 517, 521,
582, 688, 725, 749, 806, 807, 1205, 1210
Supporting details, using 125, 167, 180, 247,
309, 696, 805
Survival manual, writing a 510
Thesis, writing the 516, 805
Thesis statement, writing a 198, 200, 247,
332, 366, 401, 516, 688, 805
Time line, creating a 27, 828, 849, 1069, 1075
Tone, conveying. See Conveying tone.
Topic list, writing a 331
Topic sentence. See Thesis statement, writing a.
Writer's Workshop 130–132, 198–200,
331–336, 401–402, 515–518, 685–688,
804–806, 895–898, 1181–1184
Writing for children 66, 193
Writing with computers 1215

SPEAKING, LISTENING, AND VIEWING

Ad campaign 203, 1187
Ad-lib 973
Art show 366
Audiotape 510
Chorus 365
Class discussion 684
Community planning 229
Costumes 135, 632, 696, 759
Creative enactment 258, 309, 396, 632, 660,
671, 759, 795, 934, 1025
Critical listening 510, 1169
Debate 129, 725
Dialogue, reading 1025
Discussion 25, 35, 36, 76, 125, 129, 132, 186,
229, 246, 295, 309, 370, 430, 732, 809, 901,
931, 1000, 1154, 1157
Displaying data 690
Dramatic monologue 649, 663, 671, 1192
Dramatization 135, 759
Evaluation team 901
Facial expressions 973
Film 616, 749
Finding Common Ground 25, 76, 295, 370,
732, 1000, 1154
Gestures 973
Graphic communication 809
Graphics exhibit 690
Humorous performance 289
Impersonation 247
Improvisation 605
Informational display 901

Interview 131, 135, 203, 339, 405, 521, 768, 809, 896, 1033, 1187
Inversions 71
Learning for Life
the changing world of work 405
environmental concerns 203
evaluating play choices 901
a model of self-reliance 339
monitoring the media 521
planning for the future 809
researching the immigrant experience 135
state of the arts: celebrating cultural diversity 1187
Mock interview 167, 405
Multimedia presentation 135, 576, 1187
Musical performance 768, 799
Musical setting 180
Oral evaluation 901
Oral interpretation 282, 1025, 1042
Oral presentation 193, 309
Oral report 98, 329, 782, 1119
Panel discussion 36, 83, 125, 329, 431, 521, 622, 1176
Partner work 25, 229, 309, 335, 396, 400, 403, 405, 464, 510, 515, 576, 605, 660, 671, 687, 688, 690, 785, 791, 804, 806, 890, 894, 896, 898, 934, 1008, 1184, 1186, 1187
Pauses in reading aloud 567
Peer review 132, 200, 335, 688, 806, 898, 1184
Performance 365, 696, 782
Photo-essay 809
Poetry reading 180
Props 135, 464, 632
Public reading 365
Public speaking 978
Questionnaire 494
Radio broadcast 405
Reading aloud
poetry 69, 177, 180, 186, 282, 288, 355, 358, 365, 380, 567, 576, 692, 782, 791, 792, 934, 975, 1042, 1091, 1157
prose 115, 247, 262, 339, 463, 464, 510, 732, 1087, 1140
Recording secretary 1154
Rehearsing 1157
Report 247
Responding visually 1091
Role-play 112, 510, 605, 1033
Self-evaluation 132, 200, 336, 688, 806, 898, 1184
Set design 759
Small-group work 25, 35, 36, 76, 83, 129, 132, 135, 229, 280, 281, 288, 295, 309, 329, 332, 370, 396, 400, 431, 510, 515, 521, 576, 622, 632, 686, 725, 732, 759, 782, 795, 799, 804, 806, 809, 896, 898, 901, 973, 1000, 1119, 1154, 1176, 1181, 1184, 1187
Solo reading 365
Speech. See Oral entries.
Speeches 1087
recasting 105
Staged performance 696
Statement, brief 36
Television interview 973
Telling a story 994
Video documentary 203, 809
Visual aids 1025
Visuals, evaluating 180, 464, 521
Voice control 247, 692, 1042, 1091

RESEARCH AND STUDY

Abstracts 1208
Almanacs 98
Audiovisual resources 1208
Bar graphs 690
Before-and-after charts 166
Catalogs
card 516, 1207
on-line 516, 1207
CD-ROM 1207
Citations 1211–1214
College guides, reading 520
Community resources 135, 474, 1187
Computer
databases 808, 1207
desktop publishing 405
fonts 396
Internet 1208–1209
Dictionaries 37, 129, 134, 168, 310, 400, 561, 634, 726, 803, 890, 894, 1108, 1120, 1180, 1185, 1186, 1205–1206, 1258
Webster's 195–197
Documentation 518, 1210–1214
Electronic sources 338
E-mail 1208
Encyclopedias 47, 134, 199, 339, 516, 1108
5W–How? questions 405, 1187
Gathering data 687
Glossaries 1258–1263
Glossary compilation 1180
Graphic organizers 21, 25, 27, 37, 39, 57, 66, 85, 105, 115, 130, 131, 133, 153, 166, 167, 199, 200, 310, 313, 329, 331, 332, 366, 396, 401, 402, 422, 425, 431, 475, 517, 557, 576, 671, 673, 686, 689, 690, 712, 725, 726, 742, 745, 768, 795, 803, 890, 894, 896, 897, 899, 994, 1066, 1075, 1087, 1182, 1204, 1205
Historical contexts 889
Historical maps 202
Internet 98, 134, 202, 247, 329, 338, 404, 405, 515, 520, 521, 690, 725, 808, 824, 889, 900, 1208–1209
Library 134, 135, 247, 338, 366, 404, 474, 515, 516, 605, 725, 901, 1207–1208
Library catalogs. See Catalogs.
Line graphs 690
Maps 202, 896, 1066
Map features 202
Mapping words 168
Microfilm or microfiche 1208
Newsgroups 1208
Note taking 69, 76, 78, 101, 115, 153, 313, 339, 365, 404, 445, 467, 474, 510, 516, 521, 549, 624, 642, 652, 703, 715, 737, 749, 785, 795, 936, 949, 1093, 1181, 1210–1213
On-line services 808
Outlines 115, 199, 200, 404, 517, 686, 896–897
Parenthetical citations 518, 806, 1212–1213
Periodicals 1207–1208
Pie graphs 690
Play choices, evaluating 901
Political maps 202
Primary sources 199, 516, 1209
Print sources 338, 405, 521, 690, 900
Readers' Guide to Periodical Literature 516
Research activities 25, 47, 66, 98, 105, 129, 134, 135, 193, 203, 247, 258, 329, 334, 339, 396, 402, 404, 405, 431, 445, 464, 510, 516, 521, 605, 725, 808, 809, 889, 896, 901, 934, 947, 1066, 1176, 1180, 1187
Research papers 258, 515–518, 1207–1214
Research strategies 1207–1209
Road maps 202
Search engines, Web 1208–1209
Secondary sources 199, 516, 1209–1210
Sidenotes 1258
Sources 199, 338, 402, 405, 474, 515, 516, 518, 687, 806, 808, 809, 1187, 1208–1209
Sources-cited list 518, 806, 1210–1214
Special-purpose map 202
Story maps 1205
Study guides 1206
Tables 686
Tests
analogy 890
essay 1219
Textbook reading 404
Thesauruses 726, 1185, 1206
Topographical maps 202
URLs (Uniform Resource Locators) 808
Video sources 338
Visiting locations 131
Visualizing 131
Web sites 808
Word origins 129, 310
World Wide Web (WWW) 1208–1209

CROSSING THE CURRICULUM

Activities
art
book design 366, 396
brochure 203, 339, 405, 809, 1187
bumper sticker 684, 745
calligraphy 98, 396
cartoon character 632
charts, graphs, maps 202, 229, 329, 809
collage 289, 576, 795, 1108, 1169
comic strip/cartoon 98, 281, 671
computer graphics 98
drawing/painting 66, 98, 174, 180, 193, 281, 290, 295, 405, 464, 782, 791, 795, 1004, 1091, 1108, 1169
engraving 464
informational display 809, 901
interpretation 464
multimedia presentation 135, 576, 1187
museum display 366
picture book 66
portrait 289
poster 203, 745, 1187
sketch 167
time line 135
visual images 339, 464
computer literacy 98, 405
culture 1165, 1187
drama 135, 396, 510, 632, 649, 660, 671, 759, 795, 973, 1025
geography 1066
history 366, 431, 889, 947
music 281, 365, 366, 396, 510, 576, 605, 696, 749, 759, 768, 795, 799, 1169
science 98, 247, 329, 510
social studies 229, 258
technical writing 193, 1186
video 203, 622, 632, 809

Art. See Activities, art.
Culture 1050, 1174. *See also* Activities, culture.
Features (Literature and . . .)
  culture 1050, 1174
  film 616
  folklore 162, 458
  health 142
  history 42, 440, 528, 908
  music 763
  photography 414
  politics 120
  popular culture 261, 274, 440, 528, 656, 732
  religion 10
  science 90
  social studies 210, 226, 1050
  technology 1084, 1178
Film 616, 749
Folklore 162, 458, 732, 758, 996
Health 142
History 42, 440, 528, 908. *See also* Activities, history.
Law 134

Media 179, 186, 331, 339, 464, 474, 510, 521, 631, 690, 809
Music 763. *See also* Activities, music.
News media 521
Photography 414
Politics 120
Popular culture 261, 274, 440, 528, 656, 732
Religion 10
Science 90. *See also* Activities, science.
Social studies 210, 226, 1050. *See also* Activities, social studies.
Technology 1084, 1178
Transcript 1218

CRITICAL COMMENTS

Absurd World ("Game") 961
Oddest Love Song, The ("The Love Song of J. Alfred Prufrock") 667
So Much Depends ("The Red Wheelbarrow") 779

Taking Dominion, Catching Tigers ("Anecdote of the Jar" and "Disillusionment of Ten O'Clock") 785
Tale of Self-Discovery, A ("The Magic Barrel") 993
Vision of Blacks and Whites United, A ("For the Union Dead") 953

CREATIVE PROBLEM SOLVING

Changing World of Work, The 405
Environmental Concerns 203
Evaluating Play Choices 901
Model of Self-Reliance, A 339
Monitoring the Media 521
Planning for the Future 809
Researching the Immigrant Experience 135
State of the Arts: Celebrating Cultural Diversity 1187

INDEX OF ART

FINE ART

Abbott, Elenore Plaisted, illustration for "The Minister's Black Veil" 298
Adventures of Huckleberry Finn, first edition cover 419
Albright, Ivan Le Lorraine, *That Which I Should Have Done I Did Not Do* 720
American Spelling Book, pages from *The* 128
Artist unknown, African American couple 481; American circus posters 549; *American Flag: A Mosaic of Faces* 916; American flag from Fort McHenry 140; American Indian baskets 46; American Indian string of wampum 46–47; American pewter button 108, 110; Apollo Theatre, Harlem 534; Armstrong, Louis 605; Baldwin, Sgt., of Company G 480; bandbox 207; Banneker, Benjamin 91; *Blood and Sand,* poster for 657; Boston Tea Party 5; *Brighton Beach Memoirs,* poster for 814; cannon 476; Chief Joseph 448; Chopin, Kate 435; Cooper, Gary, in *For Whom the Bell Tolls* 532; Cooper, James Fenimore 140; couple at outdoor party 602; couple at outdoor party (detail) 600; couples with red roadster 595; couples with blue roadster 598–599; cradle of Peregrine White 71; Crane, Stephen 484; dancing couple 587; dancing couple in profile 594; *Davy Crockett Almanac,* illustration from 398; *Death of a Salesman,* Playbill® from 822; Declaration of Independence 115; *Diary of Anne Frank,* Playbill® from *The* 813; Douglass, Frederick 424; *Down the Mississippi* 462; Dunbar, Paul Laurence 535; Einstein, Albert 526; *E Pluribus Unum* 18; ear of maize 29, 31, 32, 33; Eskimo comb 6; Fitzgerald, F. Scott 584, 604; Fitzgerald, F. Scott, with daughter Scottie 603; Freud,

Sigmund, looking at a manuscript 530; Frost, Robert 558; Frost, Robert, at John F. Kennedy's inauguration 574; Fuller, Margaret (after painting by Alonzo Chappel) 141; galley manned by slaves 61; General Lee's surrender 483; *Girls' Evening School* 206; *Grapes of Wrath,* poster for *The* 527; Great Seal of the United States, The 122–123; *Henry, Patrick* 100; hornbook 12–13; Howe, William 112; Iroquois wampum belt 44–45; Japanese netsuke in the shape of a frog 788; Jefferson, Thomas 117; ketubbah (marriage contract) (detail) 993; lady's shoe 440; Lindbergh, Charles, and the *Spirit of St. Louis* 526–527; London, Jack 495; *Lyceum Lecture by James Pollard Espy at Clinton Hall* 209; Massachusetts Bay Colony seal on meeting notice 9; *Meditation by the Sea* 176–177; map of Mississippi region and the Louisiana province 458–459; Ohio Hopewell coyote-effigy platform pipe 25; *Old Plantation, The* 434; Old State House, Boston 15; *Our Town,* poster for 814; painted sternboard from the ship *Mary and Susan* 323; Pearl Harbor attack 527; *Piano Lesson,* Playbill® for *The* 818; *Pilgrims Signing the Compact Aboard the Mayflower, November 11, 1620* 12; pilothouse of *The Great Republic* 457; *Plantation, The* 51; Poe, Edgar Allan 260; *Poor Richard's Illustrated,* engraving from 95; *Portrait of Ninigret II, Chief of the Niantic Indians* 39; Quapaw turtle-effigy vessel 23; Ransom, John Crowe 577; Revere, Paul, Boston house of 14; Revere, Paul, statue 15; Roosevelt, Franklin D. 527; Salem witches being arrested 4; *Scarlet Letter,* illustration (after painting by George F. Broughton) from *The* 208; Sioux moccasins 353; *Sir Isaac Newton, President of the*

Royal Society (after painting by Vanderbank) 13; sketch of a whale hunt on whalebone 208; slave ship lower deck 62–63; soldiers wounded in the Civil War 477; stamp from Stamp Act, 1765 5; Syng silver used at the signing of the Declaration of Independence 123; tenement-house alley gang 143; Thoreau, Henry David, in his traveling outfit 255; Thoreau's journal and a writing box 232; trade card of glove manufacturer 442; Union soldier 488; Victorian mirror 380; Vulcan making a new armor for Achilles 310; Wampanoag sash belonging to King Philip 40; warrant for the arrest of Ann Pudeator 10; *West Side Story,* Playbill® for 814; whaling logbook page 328; *Whaling Scene, A* 324–325; *Wheatley, Phillis,* from *Poems* 5, 113; Whitman, Walt 349; Wolfe, Thomas 548; woman golfer with scorekeeper 586; woman welding 527; wooden bowl 35
Audubon, John James, *Common Loon* 242; *Bobolink* 381

Badger, Joseph, *Reverend Jonathan Edwards* 77; *Mrs. Jonathan Edwards* 83
Bates, F. Russell, *First Muster of the Ancient and Honorable Artillery Company* 116
Bay Psalm Book, title page of 13
Bearden, Romare, *Maudell Sleet's Magic Garden* 1106; *Mecklenburg Evening* 758; *Out Chorus* 762; *Sunset and Moonrise with Maudell Sleet* 1105
Beasley, Phoebe, *Don't Buy* 913
Beaux, Cecilia, *New England Woman* 705
Bellows, George Wesley, *My Mother* 717
Benson, Frank, *Eleanor* 578; *Evening Light* 709
Benton, Thomas Hart, *Jacques Cartier's Discovery of the St. Lawrence River* 7; *Aaron* 1171

Bierstadt, Albert, *Emigrants Crossing the Plains* (detail) 138–139

Bingham, George Caleb, *Stump Speaker* from *Stump Speaking* 399

Birch, W., & Son, *Second Street, North from Market Street, with Christ Church, Philadelphia* 92

Birch, William, *Back of the State House in Philadelphia* 210

Bonnard, Pierre, *The Green Blouse* 711

Bradstreet family, embroidered chair seat cover 70

Brady, Mathew, Civil War photograph 408

Browere, Albertus Del Orient, *Rip Chased from Home by His Wife* (detail) 158; *Rip Van Winkle Asleep* (detail) 161

Burchfield, Charles, *Lilacs* 674; *Winter Twilight* 645

Burrow, E. I., Nautilus shell from *Elements of Conchology, according to the Linnaean system* (Plate XII) 188–189

Bustamente, Sergio, *Fish* 996; *Sun shape* 997; *Illuminated peacock with palm trees* 999

Cabrera, Miguel, *Sor Juana Inés de la Cruz* 75

Carte de viste photograph, Union army soldier with his wife 481

Cartiér-Bresson, Henri, photograph of Mohandas K. Gandhi 248

Cassatt, Mary, *The Cup of Tea* 436; *The Fitting* 439; *At the Opera* 545

Catlin, George, *Black Coat* 6; *Black Hawk and Five Other Saukie Prisoners* 447; *Black Hawk, Prominent Sauk Chief* (detail) 447

Chagall, Marc, *Birthday (L'Anniversaire)* 982; *The Rabbi* 989

Chandler, Winthrop, *The Battle of Bunker Hill* (detail) 17

Chapman, John Gadsby, *Evening Gun, Fort Sumter* (detail) 409

Chase, William M., *Memories* 375

Ch'ien Hsüan, Handscroll: *Wang Hsi-chih Watching Geese* (detail) 774–775

Clinedinst, Benjamin West, *Charge of VMI Cadets at New Market* 491

Cole, Thomas, *Expulsion from the Garden of Eden* (detail) 562

Cooke, George (attributed), *Patrick Henry Arguing the Parson's Cause* 102–103

Cordero, Helen, storyteller figurine 23

Corné, Michel Felice, *Landing of the Pilgrims at Plymouth* 28–29

Cranch, Christopher Pearce, caricature of Emerson from *Illustrations of the New Philosophy* 218

Cranch, John (attributed), *Sailors—Companion to the Tailors* 319

"Cross of Snow, The," manuscript page from 179

Cummings, E. E., *Self-Portrait* 796

Currier & Ives, *Champions of the Mississippi* 452-453

D'Arcangelo, Allan, *Highway US 1, Panel 3* 1060

Davis, Stuart, *Swing Landscape* 902–903

Davis, Varina, Quilt 408–409

Day of Doom, title page of The 8–9

Demuth, Charles Henry, *The Figure 5 in Gold* 780

Douglas, Aaron, *Go Down Death* 738

Dove, Arthur G., *Me and the Moon* 1090; *Sun* 1040–1041

Durand, Asher Brown, *Dover Plains, Dutchess County, New York* 219

Durrie, George Henry, *Winter in the Country: A Cold Morning* 184–185

Eakins, Thomas, *Edith Mahon* 541

Eaton, Joseph, *Herman Melville* 311

Elliott, John and William H. Cotton, *Julia Ward Howe* 410

Ellis, Charles, *Portrait of Edna St. Vincent Millay* 700

English School, *Portrait of a Negro Man (Olaudah Equiano)* 56

Escher, M. C., *Butterflies* 560; *Drawing Hands* 1153

Evans, Walker, photograph of Depression-era living room 1065

Evergood, Philip, *Her World* 751

Franklin, Benjamin, epitaph 85

Frothingham, James, *William Cullen Bryant* 169

Furness, William Henry, Jr., *Ralph Waldo Emerson* 216

Gardner, Alexander, *Abraham Lincoln* 141; *Abraham Lincoln* 410

Gaul, Gilbert, *Taps* 388

Goings, Ralph, *Pee Wee's Diner, Warnerville, N.Y.* 1056–1057

Grapes of Wrath, The, Poster 527

Greuze, Jean-Baptiste (after), *Benjamin Franklin* 84

Gropper, William, *Construction of the Dam* 352

Grylls, Harry, *Anne Bradstreet* 68

Hammond, Elisha (attributed), *Frederick Douglass* (detail) 432

Haring, Keith, *Untitled, 1980* 918

Harnett, William, *A Study Table* 222

Hart, Frederick, Vietnam Veterans Memorial (known as *The Three Fighting Men* or *The Three Servicemen*) (detail) 971

Harris, Lawren Stewart, *Lake Superior, about 1948* 1156

Heade, Martin Johnson, *Passion Flowers and Hummingbirds* 382

"Heart! We will forget him!," manuscript page of 374

Hicks, Thomas, *Oliver Wendell Holmes* 187

Hill, John W., *Fawn's Leap, Catskill, New York* (detail) 170

Homer, Winslow, *Leaping Trout* 1036–1037; *Prisoners from the Front* 411 (detail) 406–407; *The Veteran in a New Field* 570; *Young Soldier: Separate Study of a Soldier Giving Water to a Wounded Companion* 412

Hopper, Edward, *East Wind over Weehawken* 658; *Railroad Sunset* 1003; *Rooms by the Sea* 386–387

Hunt, William Morris, *Wounded Drummer Boy* 362

Hyde de Neuville, Baroness, *F Street, Washington, D.C.* 144

"I keep my pledge," manuscript page of 374

Inness, George, *Pastoral Scene* 376

Jackson, William Henry, *Mount of the Holy Cross–Colorado* 178

Jarvis, John Wesley, *Thomas Paine* 106; *Washington Irving* 152

Johns, Jasper, *Three Flags* 965

Johnson, Eastman, *A Ride for Liberty— The Fugitive Slaves* 357

Katz, Alex, *Eli* 1069

Keach, Benjamin, *The Progress of Sin* 78–81

Kensett, John Frederick, *Eaton's Neck, Long Island* 525

Kent, Rockwell, *Moby-Dick*, illustration from 313

Keppler, caricature of Mark Twain 465

Klimt, Gustav, *The Kiss (Der Kuss)* 798

Kneller, Sir Godfrey (studio of), *William Byrd* 49

Larson, Frank Edwin, *Mark Twain* 450

Lawrence, Jacob, *Frederick Douglass Series No. 9* 428; *No. 10* 427; *Harlem Street Scene* 765; *Harriet Tubman Series No. 9* 417, *No. 29* 480; *The Migration of the Negro, Panel No. 1* 735

Leaves of Grass, first edition cover of 366; first edition title page of 345

Lee-Smith, Hughie, *Boy with Tire* 1014–1015

Levine, David, *Benjamin Franklin* 18; *Benjamin Franklin* 86, 89, 91, 98; *Ralph Waldo Emerson* 212; *Stephen Crane* 493; *Walt Whitman* 343; *Washington Irving* 166

Lewis, Samella Sanders, *Prayer Meeting* 740

Lichtenstein, Roy, *Whaam!* 904–905

Ligon, Glenn, *Untitled (Ralph Ellison)* 911

Lindsay, Thomas Corwin, *The Hornet's Nest* 486–487

Live Oak Polka, illustration for The 141

Lomas Garza, Carmen, *La Llorona (The Crying Woman)* 1163

Lonewolf, Rosemary "Apple Blossom," *Coyote Crooner* 25

Lozowick, Louis, *Chicago* 793

Lundeberg, Helen, *Pioneers of the West* 614–615

Magritte, René, *The Empire of Light* 292; *The Lovers* 728

Marsh, Reginald, *The Normandie* 698–699

Martin, Donald, *Spring* 1007

Matteson, T. H., *The Trial for Witchcraft of George Jacobs, August 5, 1692* 10

Maxham, Benjamin D., *Henry David Thoreau* 230

McCollum, Rick, *Portrait of Edgar Allan Poe* 214

McLeary, Kindred, *Lower East Side* from *Scenes of New York* 744

Melchers, Julius Gari, *The Sermon* 302

Meynell, Lt. Francis, *Slave Deck of the Albanoz* 58

Miller, Alfred Jacob, *Lost on the Prairie* 354

Moby-Dick, title page of 208

Monet, Claude, *Woman with Parasol—Turned to Left* 378

Moran, Thomas, *Grand Canyon of the Yellowstone, The* 136–137; *Slave Hunt, Dismal Swamp, Virginia* 423

Motley, Archibald John, Jr., *Jockey Club* 766

Mount, William Sidney, *Long Island Farmer Husking Corn* 224

Nam June Paik, *Lucy* 910
Narragansett hemp basket 54
Narrative of the Captivity, Sufferings, and Removes of Mrs. Mary Rowlandson, A, title page of 38

Of Plimoth Plantation, manuscript page from 26, 37
O'Keeffe, Georgia, *The Radiator Building— Night, New York, 1927* 769
Olsen, Barbara, *Harriet Tubman and the Freedom Train* (detail) 433
Osgood, Charles, *Nathaniel Hawthorne* 296
Osgood, Samuel, *Mary Boykin Chesnut* 482
O'Sullivan, T. H., Artist sketching the battlefield of Gettysburg, July, 1863 415

Paradise, Phil, *Ranch Near San Luis Obispo, Evening Light* 608–609
Pardo, Oscar, *Madre e hija* 1078
Partington, J.H.E., *Ambrose Bierce* 466
Peale, Charles Willson, *Thomas Jefferson* 114
Peale, Rembrandt, *Thomas Jefferson* 16
Peckham, Robert, *John Greenleaf Whittier* 181
Pelham, Peter, *Cotton Mather* 15
Picasso, Pablo, *Guernica* 533
Pinney, Eunice, *The Cotters Saturday Night* (detail) 183
Pippin, Horace, *John Brown Going to His Hanging* 252–253
Poems, first printing cover of 380
Porter, Fairfield, *Laurence Typing* 1071

Red Badge of Courage, The, manuscript page of 484–485
Reindel, Edna, *Rosie the Riveter* 527
Reiss, Winold, *Countee Porter Cullen* 746; *James Weldon Johnson* 736; *Portrait of Langston Hughes* 760
Remington, Frederic, *Coming and Going of the Pony Express* 420
Riis, Jacob, Children in Mullen's Alley 418
Ritschel, William, *Rocks and Breakers, California* 564–565
Rivera, Diego, M., *Detroit Industry, West Wall* (detail) 528; *Woman Making Tortillas* 1160–1161
Rogers, W. A., Bicycling in Riverside Park, New York City 440–441
"Rose for Emily, A," manuscript page of 530–531
Rothermel, Peter F., *The Battle of Gettysburg: Pickett's Charge* 479

Saint-Gaudens, Augustus, Civil War monument 950; *The Puritan Deacon Samuel Chapin* 9

Satty, Wilfred, illustration from "The Fall of the House of Usher" 145; 287
Scarlet Letter, The, cover 297; title page of 297
Schohen Studio, Kate Chopin 435
Seal on meeting notice 9
Sebron, Hyppolite, *Broadway at Spring Street* 142
Segal, George, *Couple in Open Doorway* 1029
Shahn, Ben, *Concentration Camp* 927; *Village Speakeasy, Closed for Violations* (detail) 531
Sheets, Millard, *Old Mill, Big Sur* 581
Sloan, John, *Sixth Avenue Elevated at Third Street* 522–523
Solar, Alejandro Xul, *Uno* 1083
Southworth & Hawes, Unidentified women 477
Soyer, Moses, *Phyllis Seated* 981
Soyer, Raphael, *Passengers* 748
Starn, Mike & Doug, *L.* 1027
Steichen, Edward, *Willa Cather, 1926* 538
Stella, Joseph, *Night Fires* 771
Stillman, William James, *A Philosopher's Camp in the Adirondacks* 204–205
Swords and sabers of the Revolutionary War 109

Tartoue, P., photograph of blind Kiowa woman at Carnegie, Oklahoma, powwow 1094
Tenniel, Sir John (in the style of), illustration from Lewis Carroll's *Alice's Adventures in Wonderland* 962
Thoreau, Henry David, journal page 244
Thurber, James, drawings 624, 629, 631, 632
Tooker, George, *Mirror IV* 1149
Trumbull, John, *The Declaration of Independence, July 4, 1776* 119
Tsosie, Michael, sand painting 25

Uncle Tom's Cabin, advertisement for 421

Van Vechten, Carl, Zora Neale Hurston 750; Claude McKay 743; Richard Wright 1012
Vietnam Veterans Memorial (detail). See Hart, Frederick.
Vogue, cover of June 15, 1910, issue 443

Warrant for the arrest of Ann Pudeator 10–11
Welty, Eudora, A woman of the thirties, Hinds County 634, 640; Courthouse steps, Fayette 641; Courthouse town, Grenada 639; Fayette 640
West, Benjamin, *Benjamin Franklin Drawing Electricity from the Sky* 87
Weston, Edward, *Robinson Jeffers* 580
White, John, *Flamingo* 6; *Turtle* 6

Whitney's cotton gin 140
Wilson, Ellis, *Haitian Funeral Procession* 741
Wilson, John, *My Brother* 1019
Wood, Grant, *Death on Ridge Road* 681; *Fall Plowing* 553; *Spring Turning* 555; *Stone City, Iowa* 550; *The Sentimental Yearner* 647
Wust, Theodore, *Henry Wadsworth Longfellow* 141, 175
Wyeth, Andrew, *Quaker Ladies* 239; *Wind from the Sea* 392
Wyeth, N. C., *The Deerslayer,* title page of 146; *The Deerslayer* (detail) 147; *Rip Van Winkle,* illustration from 153; title page of 155

Yamagata, Yasuko, untitled scene following Hiroshima bombing in 1945 940
Young, William, headstone on Reverend Silas Bigelow's grave 72

Zeldis, Malcah, *Miss Liberty* 908

ILLUSTRATIONS

Nielsen, Cliff 262–263, 266, 273, 278
Photofest, decorative border for *The Crucible* in Collection 17
R. Hoffman 279
Stewart, Arvis 282, 284–285, 286

CARTOONS AND CARTOON STRIPS

Addams, Chas. 289
Barsotti, C. 669
Fisher/Punch/Rothco 512
Goldberg, Rube, *Peace Today* 909
Greg, *Luann* 802
Harbaugh/Rothco 803
MacNelly, Jeff, *Shoe* 1182
Maslin 1189
Rothco Cartoons 1180
Schulz, Charles, *Peanuts* 630
Schwadron/Rothco Cartoons 1180
Steiner, Peter 912
Thurber, James 624, 629, 631, 632
Watterson, Bill, *Calvin and Hobbes* 336, 561

MAPS

Central and South America xxvii
Hiroshima 945
Kiowas' Journey 1098
United States xxiv–xxv
United States Eastern Seaboard xxvi

INDEX OF AUTHORS AND TITLES ≡

Page numbers in italic type refer to the pages on which author biographies appear.

Absolution, from 583
Across Spoon River: An Autobiography, from 693
Adagia, from 786
Adams, Abigail 125
Agee, James 537, 1064
Aiken, Conrad 711
Albee, Edward 816, 817
All I Really Need to Know I Learned in Kindergarten, from 96
Alvarez, Julia *1076*, 1079
America 744
American Procession, An, from 211
American Scholar, The, from 206, 222
American Story, An 34
Anchorage, from 1039
Anderson, Sherwood 524, 536
Anecdote of the Jar 784
Angelou, Maya 423
Annabel Lee, from 1195
Apparently with no surprise 385
Ars Poetica 789
At the Bomb Testing Site 919
Auden, W. H. 963
Autobiographia Literaria 1127
Autobiographical Notes 1142
Autobiography, The, from (Franklin) 86
Autobiography, The, from (Jefferson) 116
Autobiography, The, from (Williams) 780
Auto Wreck 1010

Baca, Jimmy Santiago 360, 691
Baldwin, James *1141*, 1142
Ballou, Major Sullivan 477
Bambara, Toni Cade 514
Banneker, Benjamin 90
Barthelme, Donald *955*, 956
Battle-Pieces, from 415
Bay Psalm Book, The, from 11
Beautiful Changes, The 1006
Because I could not stop for Death 391
Bells, The 1089
Bells for John Whiteside's Daughter 578
Bernays, Anne 389
Bierce, Ambrose *466*, 468
Biglow Papers, The, from 513
Big Sea, The, from 766
Birches 567
Bishop, Elizabeth *1034*, 1035
Black Boy, from 1015, 1185
Black Hawk 446
Blessing, A 151
Blue and the Gray, The, from 476
Blue Highways, from 1057
Borges, Jorge Luis *1152*, 1154
Borges and Myself 1154
Boy at the Window 1007
Bradford, William 14, *26*, 28
Bradstreet, Anne *68*, 69, 1192
Brinnin, John Malcolm 668
Brooks, Gwendolyn 643, 741
Brooks, Van Wyck 828
Bruchac, Joseph *20*, 22

Bryant, William Cullen *169*, 171, 1197, 1200
"Butch" Weldy 694
Byrd, William *49*, 50

Cabeza de Vaca, Álvar Nuñez 8
Calvin & Hobbes (comic strip) 336, 561
Carver, Raymond *1026*, 1028, 1032
Catch-22, from 904
Cather, Willa 523, *538*, 540
Chambered Nautilus, The 189
Chesnut, Mary 482
Chicago 793
Chief Joseph 448
Chopin, Kate *435*, 437
Cisneros, Sandra *1158*, 1160
Cofer, Judith Ortiz *1166*, 1168
Commager, Henry Steele 476
Concord Hymn 99
Cooper, James Fenimore 148
Corpi, Lucha 345
Cortázar, Julio *290*, 291
Cosmo Talks to Amy Tan, from 1118
Coyote Finishes His Work 24
Crane, Stephen 408, *484*, 487, 494
Crèvecoeur, Michel-Guillaume Jean de *16*
Crisis, No. 1, The, from 108
Crockett, Davy 398
Cross of Snow, The 178
Crucible, The (Miller) 829
Crucible, The (Maslin) 900
Cullen, Countee *746*, 747, 748
Cummings, E. E. *796*, 797, 798

Daughter of Invention 1079
Death Comes for the Archbishop, from 523
Death in the Family, A, from 537
Death of a Salesman, from 822
Death of the Ball Turret Gunner, The 933
Death of the Hired Man, The 569
Declaration of Independence, The 116
Deerslayer, The, from 148
de la Cruz, Sor Juana Inés *75*, 76
DeLillo, Don 918
Description of New England, A, from 36
Design 560
Deutsch, Babette 579
Diary from Dixie, A, from 482
Dickey, James *1155*, 1156
Dickinson, Emily 342, *372*, 374, 376, 377, 378, 381, 382, 383, 385, 386, 388, 391, 392, 393, 394, 1196
Dickinson, Susan 346
Discordants, from 711
Disillusionment of Ten O'Clock 784
Donne, John 35
Donoghue, Denis 911
Douglass, Frederick *424*, 426, 432, 481
Dove, Rita *1170*, 1171, 1175
Deutsch, Babette 579
Dust Tracks on a Road, from 752, 758

Earth Only, The 23
Edwards, Jonathan 77, 79, 82
Eiseley, Loren 259
Elegy for Jane 1002

Eliot, T. S. *661*, 663
Ellison, Ralph 67
Emerson, Ralph Waldo 99, 206, 209, 213, *216*, 219, 222, 224, 349, 412, 1191, 1194
Emily Dickinson (Corpi) 345
Emily Dickinson (Pastan) 371
Emily Dickinson's Letters, from 394
En perseguirme, mundo... (World, in Hounding Me...) 76
Equiano, Olaudah *56*, 57
Esslin, Martin 823
Everything Stuck to Him 1028
Explorer, The 643

Fable for Critics, A, from 146
Fall 691
Fall of the House of Usher, The (Poe) 263
Fall of the House of Usher, The (Whittemore) 279
Fame is a bee, from 1196
Faulkner, William *713*, 716, 723, 724
Feather Pillow, The 729
Few Don'ts by an Imagiste, A, from 776
Fiddler Jones 694
First Fig 697
Fish, The 1035
Fitzgerald, F. Scott 525, 583, *584*, 587, 603
Flint, Seth M. 483
Follow the Drinking Gourd 434
For the Union Dead 950
Franklin, Benjamin *84*, 86, 95
Freud, Sigmund 530
Frost, Robert 534, *558*, 559, 560, 562, 564, 565, 567, 569, 574
Fulghum, Robert 96
Full Powers (Plenos Poderes) 369

Game 956
García Márquez, Gabriel *995*, 996, 997
Gettysburg Address, The 479
Gift from the Sea, from 215
Gill, Paul G., Jr. 508
Girl Who Wouldn't Talk, The 1045
Go Down, Death: A Funeral Sermon 737
Go Down, Moses 434
God's Trombones, from 740
Grapes of Wrath, The, from 513
Great Figure, The 780
Great Gatsby, The, from 525
Greiner, Donald J. 1075

Habit of Being, The, from 682
Handsomest Drowned Man in the World, The 997
Harjo, Joy *1039*, 1040
Harlem 764
Havel, Vaclav 917
Hawthorne, Nathaniel 223, 255, *296*, 298, 299
Hawthorne, Sophia Peabody 255
Hawthorne in Salem, from 828
Heart! We will forget him! 374
Heat-Moon, William Least *1054*, 1057
Heaven Is Under Our Feet, from 245
Heller, Joseph 904
Hemingway, Ernest 420, *650*, 653, 659

Henley, Don 245
Henry, Patrick *100*, 102
Here Follow Some Verses upon the Burning of Our House, July 10, 1666 69
Hersey, John *935*, 937
Higginson, Thomas Wentworth 394
Hiroshima, from 937
His Father's Earth 550
History of the Dividing Line, The, from 50
Holmes, Oliver Wendell *187*, 189, 190
Hongo, Garrett *1121*, 1122, 1125
House Made of Dawn, The, from 23
House Taken Over 291
How to Survive an Atomic Bomb, from 908
Hugging the Shore, from 905
Hughes, Langston 535, 733, 760, 761, 764, 766
Hunter, Alexander 478
Hurston, Zora Neale *750*, 752, 758
Huswifery 73

I died for Beauty—but was scarce 393
If you were coming in the Fall 376, 377
I Hear America Singing 352
I heard a Fly buzz—when I died 392
In a Station of the Metro 772
Incident 748
In Search of Our Mothers' Gardens, from 1102
Interesting Narrative of the Life of Olaudah Equiano, The, from 57
Invasion of America, The, from 7
Invisible Man, from 67
Irving, Washington 147, *152*, 154
I Saw Lee Surrender, from 483
I taste a liquor never brewed 382
I, Too 733

Jackson, Jesse 74
James, Henry 419
Jarrell, Randall 916, *932*, 933
Jeffers, Robinson *580*, 581
Jefferson, Thomas 17, *114*, 116, 124, 129
Jennings, Francis 7
Jilting of Granny Weatherall, The 704
Johnny Reb and Billy Yank, from 478
Johnson, Dorothy 616
Johnson, James Weldon 736, 737, 740, 742
Journals, from 222
Journey, The 19
Joy Luck Club, The, from 1110

Kate Chopin, from 443
Kazin, Alfred 211, 422
Keats, John 393
King, Martin Luther, Jr. 256
Kingston, Maxine Hong *1043*, 1045
Knoxville: Summer 1915, from 537
Komunyakaa, Yusef *974*, 975
Kubota, from 1125

Las Casas, Bartolomé de 8
Latin Deli: An Ars Poetica, The 1168
Lawrence, D. H. 214, 329
Leader of the People, The 609
Leaves of Grass, from 343, 344, 347, 399
Lee, Andrea *1128*, 1131
Letter from Birmingham City Jail, from 256
Letters from an American Farmer, from 16
Letters to Edith Brower, from 648

Let Us Now Praise Famous Men, from 1064
Lewis, Anthony 34
Life and Times of Frederick Douglass, The, from 481
Lifeguard, The 1156
Life on the Mississippi, from 453, 1194
Life You Save May Be Your Own, The 674
Lincoln, Abraham 416, 479
Lindbergh, Anne Morrow 215
London, Jack *495*, 497
Longfellow, Henry Wadsworth 150, *175*, 177, 178, 1199
Lopez, Barry 24
Love Song of J. Alfred Prufrock, The 663
Lowell, James Russell 143, 146, 513
Lowell, Robert 915, *948*, 950

MacLeish, Archibald 789
Magic Barrel, The 982
Malamud, Bernard *980*, 982
Man Who Shot Liberty Valance, The, from 616
Mann, Theodore 812
Maslin, Janet 900
Mason, Bobbie Ann 514
Masters, Edgar Lee 692, 693, 694, 695
McInerney, Jay 605
McKay, Claude *743*, 744
Melville, Herman 207, 208, 214, *311*, 313, 415, 449
Memories of West Street and Lepke, from 915
Mertins, Louis 559
Meyers, Jeffrey 529
Millay, Edna St. Vincent *697*, 699, 700
Miller, Arthur 814, 815, *821*, 822, 824, 825, 826, 827, 829
Minister's Black Veil, The 299
Miniver Cheevy 646
Mirror 1149
Moby-Dick, from 313, 321
Momaday, N. Scott *1092*, 1094
Monsoon Season 975
Moore, Marianne 787, 788
Mora, Pat 444
Morrison, Toni 1146
Motion, from 1039
Mr. Eliot, I Presume, from 668
Mrs. George Reece 695
Much Madness is divinest Sense 383
Mushrooms 1150
My Bondage and My Freedom, from 432
My Guilt 423
My Man Bovanne, from 514
My Sense of Divine Things 82
Mystery of Heroism, A 487

Narrative of the Captivity, A, from 40
Narrative of the Life of Frederick Douglass, The, from 426
Nature, from 219, 222
Neither Out Far Nor In Deep 565
Neruda, Pablo *367*, 369
New African 1131
New England Primer, The, from 10
New Poems, from 797
Niemöller, Martin 931
Night, from 921
Night Chant, The, from 23
Night Country, The, from 259

Night Journey 1003
Nobel Prize Acceptance Speeches:
  William Faulkner 723
  Ernest Hemingway 659
  John Steinbeck 620
Noiseless Flash, A 937
Notes on the State of Virginia, from 17
Nothing Gold Can Stay 562
Now and Then, America 444
Nye, Naomi Shihab 563

O'Brien, Tim 964, 966, 1185
O Captain! My Captain! 344
Occurrence at Owl Creek Bridge, An 468
O'Connor, Flannery 672, 674, 682
Ode on a Grecian Urn, from 393
Ode on the Confederate Dead 954
of De Witt Williams on his way to Lincoln Cemetery 741
Of Modern Poetry 790
Of Plymouth Plantation, from 28
O'Hara, Frank 1127
Old Ironsides 190
Old Manse, The, from 223
Oliver, Mary 19
Once by the Pacific 564
O'Neill, Eugene 818, 820
On James Baldwin, from 1146
Open House, from 1001
Ortiz, Simon J. 1067

Pact, A 346
Paine, Thomas *106*, 108
Pair of Silk Stockings, A 437
Parry, J. H. 6
Pastan, Linda 371
Peanuts (comic strip) 630
Perkins, David 138
Perrine, Laurence 561
Petit, the Poet 695
Pine Tree Tops 979
Plath, Sylvia *1148*, 1149, 1150
Plenos Poderes (Full Powers) 369
Poe, Edgar Allan 145, *260*, 263, 282, 287, 1195, 1201
Poetry 788
Poetry Emotion 977
Poet's Safe Haven in Amherst, A, from 389
Poor Richard's Almanack, from 95
Porter, Katherine Anne *702*, 704
Pound, Ezra 346, 533, 671, 769, 772, *773*, 774, 776
Psalm 137 47
Psalm of Life, A 150, 1199

Quindlen, Anna 977
Quiroga, Horacio 727, 729

Ransom, John Crowe *577*, 578
Raven, The 282
Recuerdo 699
Red Wheelbarrow, The 779
Remember 1040
Reminiscences of My Life in Camp, from 480
Resistance to Civil Government, from 249
Rhodora, The, from 1194
Richard Bone 693
Richard Cory 645
Rip Van Winkle 154

River-Merchant's Wife: A Letter, The 774
Robinson, Edwin Arlington *644*, 645, 646, 648
Roethke, Theodore *1001*, 1002, 1003
Rookers, The, from 514
Roosevelt, Franklin D. 524
Rose for Emily, A 716, 805
Rowlandson, Mary *38*, 40
Rules of the Game, from 1110

Sandburg, Carl *792*, 793
Sarah Pierrepont 82
Satisfaction Coal Company, The 1171
Schulz, Charles M. 630
Scott Fitzgerald: A Biography, from 529
Sea Canes 173
Secret Life of Walter Mitty, The 625
Self-Reliance, from 222, 224
Sextet, from 668
Sexton, Anne *1088*, 1089, 1090
Shapiro, Karl *1009*, 1010
Sherman, William Tecumseh 409
Shiloh 449
Shine, Perishing Republic 581
Sight in Camp in the Daybreak Gray and Dim, A 362
Sinners in the Hands of an Angry God, from 79
Sky Tree, The 22
Sloan, James Park 996
Smith, John 36
Smith, Sydney 206
Snow-Bound: A Winter Idyll, from 182
Snow-Storm, The, from 1191
Snyder, Gary 979
Soldier's Home 653
Some keep the Sabbath going to Church 381
somewhere i have never travelled,gladly beyond 798
Son 1070
Song of Myself, from 347, 353, 356, 359, 399
Soul selects her own Society, The 378
Speaking 1067
Speaking of Courage 966, 1185
Specimen Days, from 363, 477
Speech to the Virginia Convention 102

Spring and All 781
Stafford, William 919
Stein, Gertrude 531
Steinbeck, John 513, *606*, 609, 620
Stevens, Wallace *783*, 784, 786, 790
Still Just Writing, from 1074
Straw into Gold: The Metamorphosis of the Everyday 1160
Success is counted sweetest 388
Sullivan, Annie 419
Sun Still Rises in the Same Sky: Native American Literature, The 20

Tableau 747
Tan, Amy *1109*, 1110, 1118
Taylor, Edward *72*, 73
Taylor, Joan Chatfield 1118
Taylor, Susie King 480
Tell all the Truth but tell it slant 386
Thanatopsis 171, 1200
Thoreau, Henry David 213, *230*, 233, 249, 335
Thurber, James *623*, 625
Tide Rises, the Tide Falls, The 177
Timebends: A Life, from 825
Timrod, Henry 954
To Build a Fire 497
To Helen, from 1201
To My Dear and Loving Husband, from 1192
Toth, Emily 443
To the Right Honorable William, Earl of Dartmouth . . ., from 113
Truth, Sojourner 417
Trying to Name What Doesn't Change 563
Twain, Mark 97, *450*, 453, 465, 1194
Tyler, Anne 1074

Underworld, from 918
Unknown Citizen, The 963
Updike, John 905, *1068*, 1070
Upson, Theodore 476
Used-As-A-Shield (Teton Sioux) 23

Very Brief Account of the Destruction of the Indies, from 8

Wagner Matinée, A 540
Walcott, Derek 173
Walden, or Life in the Woods, from 233
Walker, Alice *1101*, 1102
War Is Kind 494
Way to Rainy Mountain, The, from 1094
Weary Blues, The 761
Webster, Noah 195
Welty, Eudora *633*, 634, 640
What For 1122
what if a much of a which of a wind 797
Wheatley, Phillis 113
When the Negro Was in Vogue, from 767
White, E. B. 629
Whitman, Walt 212, 342, 343, 344, 347, *348*, 352, 353, 356, 359, 362, 363, 399, 413, 477
Whittemore, Reed 279
Whittier, John Greenleaf *181*, 182
Who Understands Me but Me 360
Why I Wrote The Crucible: *An artist's answer to politics* 827
Wiesel, Elie *920*, 921
Wilbur, Richard *1005*, 1006, 1007
Williams, Tennessee 813, *822*
Williams, William Carlos *778*, 779, 780, 781
Winning the Cold War, from 508
Winter Dreams 587
Winthrop, John 2
Wolfe, Thomas *548*, 550
Woman Warrior, The, from 1045
World, in Hounding Me . . . (En perseguirme, mundo . . .) 76
Worn Path, A 634
Wright, James 151
Wright, Richard *1012*, 1015, 1185

Yamagata, Yasuko 942
Young 1090
Young, David 996
Young, Thomas Daniel 579

Zinsser, William 912